SPORT LAW

Now in its fourth edition, this text is still the only sport law textbook to introduce sport legal studies from a management perspective and integrate legal strategies to gain a competitive advantage in business. Acknowledging that students understand legal concepts better when they are tied to real sport management practice, the book is organized around the core management functions.

It provides concise explanations of key concepts, as well as current industry examples and legal cases, and gives the student all the legal knowledge they need to become confident and effective professionals in sport management, recreation, or sport education. This new edition includes additional contributions from leading sport law educators and practitioners, and has expanded coverage of important contemporary issues including:

- Sports injury and concussion litigation
- Impact of Covid-19 on events and leagues
- Gender discrimination, disability discrimination, sexual harassment, #metoo, and USWNT pay equity
- Intellectual property, licensing agreements, publicity rights, social media influencers, and digital privacy
- Student-athletes and marketing rights
- Sport gambling and state regulation
- Athlete activism, employee free speech, and collective bargaining
- Olympic and Paralympic restructuring
- NCAA Division 1 Coaches Contracts

The book contains useful features and ancillaries to help with teaching and learning, including managerial context tables, case opinions, focus cases, strategies for competitive advantage, discussion questions, and learning activities. It is an essential text for any course on sport law or recreation law, an invaluable supplement to any course on sport business and management, and an important reference for all sport management practitioners.

Online resources include a variety of exam questions for each chapter, featuring multiple choice, true or false, short answer exam questions and short essay questions, and a sample syllabus.

Editor

Anita M. Moorman is Professor of Sport Administration at the University of Louisville, USA. She teaches sport law and legal aspects of sport. Professor Moorman is licensed to practice law in the State of Oklahoma and was admitted to practice before the U.S. Supreme Court when she served as co-counsel for nine disability sport organizations on an amicus curiae brief in the landmark Americans with Disabilities Act case involving the professional golfer, Casey Martin (*Martin v. PGA Tour*, 2001). She served as an expert consultant for the SB206 California Community College Name, Image, and Likeness Working Group studying the impact of NIL policies and legislation on community college athletes. Her research interests include examining contractual and commercial relationships in sport and the unique impact that numerous Supreme Court decisions have had in the sport industry with a focus on participant rights in sport.

Non-Contributing Editors

Linda Sharp retired as Professor Emerita from the Sport Management program at the University of Northern Colorado, USA, where she taught courses in sport law, sport ethics, and issues in college sport. Her research focused on torts, contracts, and employment law in the context of a variety of sport organizations.

Cathryn Claussen retired as Professor Emerita from the Sport Management Program at Washington State University, USA, where she taught courses in sport law, sport ethics, and sport sociology. Her research focused on civil rights and civil liberties in the context of managing sport enterprises.

SPORT LAW

A Managerial Approach

4th Edition

Edited by Anita M. Moorman

Non-Contributing Editors:
Linda Sharp and Cathryn Claussen

NEW YORK AND LONDON

Fourth edition published 2021
by Routledge
2 Park Square, Milton Park, Abingdon, Oxon, OX14 4RN

and by Routledge
52 Vanderbilt Avenue, New York, NY 10017

Routledge is an imprint of the Taylor & Francis Group, an informa business

First edition published by Holcomb Hathaway 2007
Third edition published by Routledge 2014

British Library Cataloguing-in-Publication Data
A catalogue record for this book is available from the British Library

Library of Congress Cataloging-in-Publication Data
Names: Moorman, Anita M., editor. | Sharp, Linda A., editor. | Claussen, Cathryn L., editor.
Title: Sport law : a managerial approach / edited by Anita M. Moorman; non-contributing editors, Linda Sharp, Cathryn Claussen.
Description: Fourth edition. | Milton Park, Abingdon, Oxon ; New York, NY: Routledge, 2021. | Includes bibliographical references and index.
Identifiers: LCCN 2020033765 | ISBN 9780367338480 (hardback) | ISBN 9780367338503 (paperback) | ISBN 9780429322365 (ebook)
Subjects: LCSH: Sports--Law and legislation--United States. | Sports personnel--Legal status, laws, etc.--United States.
Classification: LCC KF3989 .S53 2021 | DDC 344.73/099--dc23
LC record available at https://lccn.loc.gov/2020033765

ISBN: 978-0-367-33848-0 (hbk)
ISBN: 978-0-367-33850-3 (pbk)
ISBN: 978-0-429-32236-5 (ebk)

Typeset in Joanna
by KnowledgeWorks Global Ltd.

Visit the eResources: www.routledge.com/9780367338503

To Dr. Betty van der Smissen who inspired a generation of legal educators and scholars. Since the second edition, we have recognized the impact she had on our field and continue to recognize her mentorship and the standards of rigorous scholarship she set for herself and us all.

To my mom who inspired me at an early age to be willing to confront injustice and to believe a woman can pursue any career she is passionate about.

CONTENTS

EXHIBITS

CONTRIBUTORS

Alicia Jessop is an Attorney and Associate Professor of Sport Administration at Pepperdine University, USA. Alicia is the founder of RulingSports.com. She has consulted for the National Basketball Players Association, Alliance of American Football and Women in Film.

Lisa Pike Masteralexis is Professor in the Mark H. McCormack Department of Sport Management and serves as Senior Associate Dean of the Isenberg School of Management at the University of Massachusetts-Amherst, USA. Her research focuses on sport law and labor relations in professional sport.

Lauren McCoy is Assistant Professor of Sport Management and the Program Director for the Sport and Fitness Administration graduate program at Winthrop University, USA. Her research interests include discrimination concerns in education and the workplace, social media privacy, and athlete's rights issues.

Kristi L. Schoepfer is Department Chair and Professor in the Department of Physical Education, Sport and Human Performance at Winthrop University, USA. Her research interests include risk management issues in sport.

Amanda M. Siegrist is Assistant Professor and Program Director of the undergraduate law program at Thomas More University, USA. Her research is focused in constitutional law, most notably around due process in interscholastic athletics.

Stephanie A. Tryce is Assistant Professor of Sports Marketing at Saint Joseph's University, USA. Her research interests are at the intersection of law, sports, and marketing, with a focus on social justice.

Erica J. Zonder is Associate Professor of Sport Management at Eastern Michigan University, USA. Her research focuses on Title IX and employment law issues in collegiate and professional sport.

PREFACE

The law is dynamic and rapidly evolving in numerous segments of the industry. Sport Law: A Managerial Approach, 4th Edition provides comprehensive discussion and analysis of legal issues in sport and recreation. The 4th Edition further captures recent and continuing developments including the problematic drafting of liquidated damages clauses in college coaches contracts during a period of frequent and escalating buyout amounts, the ongoing expansion of student-athlete commercial opportunities and changes to the NCAA regulatory approach toward commercial restraints on student-athletes, the impact of Covid-19 on the sport industry during an unprecedented moment in modern history; the imposition of liability across the sports landscape for sexual abuse of young athletes at the hands of coaches and medical personnel, and administrative failures in this regard; and a host of issues associated with venue operations, intellectual property, digital marketing and data privacy.

Rationale for a Text on Managerial Law for the Sport Enterprise

This text is driven by management functions, not legal topics. The main benefit of presenting sport/recreation law information in this way is that you, the reader, can use the information as a prospective sport/recreation manager, not as an aspiring attorney. It allows you to understand how the legal concepts relate to each management function, an integration that is not usually accomplished when the content is organized according to legal topics.

In implementing the managerial approach, we have adopted the framework used by Antoni Brack in his article entitled "The Paradigm of Managerial Law" (1997). Brack, a professor of business law at a Dutch university, wrote this article to suggest how to structure the primary legal course in a business school curriculum. Brack's suggestion was to structure courses as "managerial law," which links law to business functions, in an attempt to train prospective business managers to be legally informed and better professionals. By structuring courses in this way, we recognize that law courses in business schools should have a business orientation because business professionals need to be able to recognize and deal with legal difficulties, problems, risks, and costs in a pragmatic way. Thus, the traditional legal structure of a course should give way, according to Brack, to a structure based on business functions, which have more practical and operational meaning to prospective managers.

Organization of this Text

We have organized this text based on four commonly acknowledged business functions, with an orientation toward managerial law, as mentioned above. These functions are: (1) human resource management; (2) strategic management – governance; (3) operations management; and (4) marketing management. With the managerial law approach, legal topics are subsumed under the managerial components of each function. The legal topics have to fit the function to provide "optimal operational and strategic use" (Brack, 1997, p. 240).

Part I, "Introductory Legal Concepts," introduces readers to material that is necessary for an understanding of the legal system, legal resources, and managerial strategies to minimize liability. The remainder of the book is organized according to the previously mentioned four business functions common to all sport organizations.

Part II, "Human Resource Management," first looks at the legal issues surrounding managerial decisions in hiring, firing, disciplining, and evaluating employees, from the perspectives of contract law, tort law, and discrimination law. These chapters also cover liability for the acts of employees and statutory law pertaining to working conditions for employees. We include labor relations and collective bargaining matters within professional sport, and we address the role of the sport agent.

Part III, "Strategic Management: Governance," deals with governance issues in a variety of settings. We discuss the authority of professional and amateur athletic organizations and regulatory issues concerning athletes in professional sport, high school and college sport, and Olympic sport.

Part IV, "Operating Venues and Event Management," focuses on the legal issues pertinent to sport facilities and the development of events, including liability issues related to sport participants, participant violence, and the safety of spectators on our premises. We discuss a range of agreements central to the operation of facilities and events including lease agreements, promotional materials, game contracts, conduct codes, and exculpatory agreements as a component of this managerial function. Finally in this section we include planning and accessibility issues associated with financing, constructing, and operating sports facilities including a discussion of the Americans with Disabilities Act, and spectator searches and surveillance.

Part V, "Marketing Management," concerns the legal issues surrounding intellectual property matters such as trademarks, copyrights, patents, and publicity rights. In these chapters, we consider trade practices such as false advertising, social media influencers, and ambush marketing. We present contractual issues, including endorsement and sponsorship contracts. We discuss constitutional and civil rights issues pertinent to marketing and address sports information, media, and public relations concerns, such as broadcasting agreements, privacy rights, and defamation.

As you see, we have integrated the legal theories and concepts pertinent to each business function in such a way as to enable you to better use the law as you engage in decision making in your roles in sport and recreation organizations. In this way, we are suggesting that you use the legal theories in a pragmatic manner, to solve real-life problems found in sport enterprise.

Objectives of this Text

In conjunction with the managerial law approach discussed above, the specific objectives for this book include:

- Recognizing the role of legal knowledge in providing a competitive advantage.
- Recognizing the role of law and regulation in developing business strategies.
- Recognizing the role of preventive law in the management of sport and recreation organizations.

Special Features of the Text

In an effort to accomplish the foregoing objectives, the following text features are designed to facilitate the reader's understanding and application of the material.

Managerial Context Tables

Since one of our prime objectives is to have you understand the connections between legal theory and the practical uses of the law in your managerial functions, we have developed tables in each chapter to help with this. The introduction to each of these chapters includes a table identifying the managerial contexts, the major legal issues, the relevant law, and illustrative cases for that chapter. This table serves as an over-view of the chapter's content and reinforces the connections between your management responsibilities and the legal material presented.

Glossary of Legal Terms

Although legal terms will be defined when they are first presented, we also provide a glossary at the end of the book to refresh your understanding of legal concepts as you encounter them throughout the text.

Case Opinions

Most chapters contain one or more "Case Opinions" that have been chosen to illustrate particular legal points. For each case, we state the facts in our own language but use the actual language of the courts, in condensed versions, to give guidance on legal theory. Discussion questions follow each excerpted case. The specific cases have been selected because they represent landmark illustrations of important legal issues you need to understand as a sport or recreation manager.

Focus Cases

In Chapters 2–19 we present a number of "mini" case opinions, which we call "Focus Cases." These are very condensed (summarized) case opinions chosen to emphasize a key discussion point. You get the "flavor" of a court opinion without reading a lengthy discussion of the case and rationale.

Hypothetical Cases

In most chapters we also present a feature titled, "Considering …"; these are hypothetical "factual situa-tions" to be considered. Although sometimes these fact patterns are taken from actual cases, often they are created composites of fact patterns or legal theory. Each hypothetical situation is followed by questions which can be used as a learning tool comparing students answers to the "Analysis & Discussion" of the situation at the end of the chapter to check and hone student understanding of the material.

Competitive Advantage Strategies

To place particular emphasis upon the managerial law concept, we provide "Competitive Advantage Strate-gies" throughout each chapter. These strategies suggest practical methods to minimize or eliminate liabil-ity, based on the legal concepts discussed in that chapter.

Discussion Questions, Learning Activities, Case Studies, and Website Resources

The discussion questions, learning activities, and case studies found at the end of each chapter emphasize important concepts and will assist in the review of chapter material. Both the questions and the activities require an understanding of the legal principles presented in the chapter and are designed to encourage students to apply legal knowledge as an actual sport or recreation manager in a particular factual circum-stance. We also include one or more case studies at the end of each chapter providing more in depth analysis of a topic.

What's New in the Fourth Edition

For the fourth edition, we have retained all the Special Features discussed above and used in previous editions. We have also invited contributions from leading experts in the field in the areas of contract negotiations, employment discrimination, harassment, labor relations, risk management, marketing law and practice, and governance of professional sport organizations. Contributions from these experts have enriched the text with even more real world examples of legal issues confronting sport and recreation managers today. Lastly, we have included more than 25 new Case Opinions and Focus Cases throughout the text.

Further highlights of what's new in the fourth edition include:

Chapters 1, 2, and 3 have now been condensed into two chapters. Chapter 1 provides the foundation for the importance of integrating legal strategy with business strategy, and using the preventive law process to do that. Chapter 2 now contains a condensed discussion of legal research and the legal system to help students access and understand legal information using electronic sources.

Chapters 3–9 now cover the Human Relations Management function. Chapter 3 has been reorganized to facilitate an in-depth understanding of the complexities of college coaches' contracts with expanded discussion of unique clauses in Division 1 coaches contracts. Federal labor laws associated with minor league baseball players and interns has also been updated through 2020 federal statutory changes.

Strategic Management and Governance is now contained in Chapters 10–13. These chapters have been reorganized to provide a solid foundational discussion of Constitutional considerations and relevance to amateur athletic associations early in Chapter 11, so that progressing through high school, college, and Olympic sport, students can better identify when and where Constitution claims are significant considerations for sport managers.

Chapters 14–17 in Part IV now include an expanded foundation for general negligence liability and premise liability. We have also combined our discussion of safety of participants with participant violence so that all aspects of our relationships with participants are presented in a single chapter. Additionally, we have combined our contractual relationships into a single chapter so that students can fully understand the use of contractual agreements across the myriad of relationships existing in the venue and event operations context. And, we have combined planning and accessibility issues into a single chapter with a detailed discussion of the Americans with Disabilities Act.

Lastly, in Chapters 18 and 19 in Part V, Marketing Management, we have moved the discussion of publicity rights into Chapter 18, together with other forms of intellectual property such as trademarks, copyrights, and patents. This is a better placement for this discussion as publicity rights have become a recognized and important form of IP.

In summary, we take a unique approach in this sport law textbook. We hope that you will find this managerial law approach beneficial as you learn how to make legally sound decisions. Your knowledge of the law should help you make your organization more competitive and a better environment for participants and employees when you begin your career in sport and recreation business.

Anita M. Moorman, Editor

ACKNOWLEDGMENTS

This text was inspired by Linda Sharp in 2005 and resulted in an enriching collaboration between Linda, myself, and Cathy Claussen which has endured for more than 15 years. I am so grateful to Linda for including me in this project at its inception and for them both in trusting me to continue our legacy into the fourth edition.

I would like to thank the seven exceptional sport law colleagues who contributed their legal scholarship and expertise to this fourth edition. They all contributed their well-recognized expertise to this endeavor. They brought new voices and perspectives adding greatly to the quality of this text.

I have spent almost my entire academic career at the University of Louisville and have worked with, mentored, and been mentored by some of the most talented and generous colleagues in sport management. I may never know where other paths may have taken me, but am confident I have been blessed to have so many accomplished colleagues and intellectually curious students around me each and every day at UofL.

I want to thank my partner, Alison Miner, who has supported and encouraged me through four editions of this text. She has been a constant source of friendship and positivity even when Covid-19 turned our den into an office, writing room, library, and Zoom conference room.

Lastly a special thanks to my doctoral research assistant Nick Swim. He read, edited, researched, and provided a student perspective on each and every chapter in the text, and I could not have accomplished this without him.

GLOSSARY

Acceptance: An agreement to the terms of an offer as stated.

Act of God: Refers to a natural disaster that resulted in injury to the plaintiff; a defense to negligence. This defense will be upheld only if the Act of God is unforeseeable.

Actual authority: In agency law, the limits of an agent's authority, conveyed to the agent by the principal.

Actual cash value: The replacement value of property, minus depreciation.

Actual notice: Having been informed directly of something or having seen it occur; implies that the landowner knows of a danger through inspection by employees; also known as actual knowledge.

Aesthetic functionality: A doctrine that relates to whether a feature of a product is designed to make it visually appealing, but not source identifying which would preclude the product feature from securing trade dress protection from infringement.

Affirmative action: Preferential treatment to members of protected classes where their qualifications are essentially the same as those of members of a nonprotected class.

Affirmative defense: A defense used between private parties in civil litigation; it works to excuse a defendant's liability even if the plaintiff's claim is true, based on facts additional to those asserted by the plaintiff.

Agency: The relationship arising when one person (a "principal") manifests a desire to have another person (an "agent") act on the principal's behalf and remain subject to the principal's control, which the agent consents to do (Restatement [Third] of Agency § 1.01 Agency Defined).

Agency contract: An agreement in which a student-athlete or professional athlete authorizes a person to negotiate or solicit on behalf of the athlete a professional sports services contract or an endorsement contract.

Agency law: Defines how and when agency relationships are created, what rights and responsibilities exist between a principal and an agent, and what legal effect will be given to the acts of an agent in his or her dealings with third parties.

Agency relationship: A consensual relationship established for a lawful purpose by informal oral or formal written agreements; both parties (agent and principal) must have the legal capacity to enter into an agreement.

Agent: In agency law, the person acting on behalf of another party (the principal).

All risk policy: An insurance policy that seems to be all-encompassing, although some losses may not be covered because they are listed in the "exclusions" section of the policy.

Alternative dispute resolution: Methods other than trial for resolving legal conflict; the most common forms are arbitration and mediation.

Ambush marketing: An intentional effort to weaken or "ambush" a competitor's official association with a sports organization that had acquired its rights through payment of sponsorship fees.

Antitrust law: A body of law with the intent of preventing groups of competitors from reducing competition in the market. Prohibits predatory or exclusionary conduct designed to enable an organization to acquire or maintain monopoly power in a relevant market.

Apparent agency: A relationship that is created by the conduct of the principal that leads a third party to believe another individual serves as her agent.

Apparent authority: An instance when a principal has somehow conveyed to a third party that an agent has the authority to act, even though the agent does not have the actual authority.

Arbitrary mark: Trademark comprising words, names, or symbols that are in common linguistic use but that neither suggest nor describe any quality or characteristic of the good or service.

Arbitration: Submission of a dispute to a neutral decision maker for final and binding resolution.

Assault: An intentional tort involving some type of menacing or threatening behavior.

Assumption of risk: A defense asserting that a participant in an activity knows of the inherent risks (those risks that are obvious and necessary) of an activity; assumption of risk is frequently discussed as being either primary or secondary.

At will: Describes an employment arrangement under which the employer may fire the employee at any time, for any reason or for no reason; the employee also may quit at any time for any reason.

Athlete agent: An individual who enters into an agency contract with a student-athlete or professional athlete or, directly or indirectly, recruits or solicits a student-athlete or professional athlete to enter into an agency contract.

Attractive nuisance doctrine: A doctrine providing that there is an affirmative duty for landowners to use reasonable care to protect child trespassers who may be attracted to the property because of some manmade or artificial feature of the land that poses some serious danger to a child.

Back pay: A remedy for discrimination under Title VII of the Civil Rights Act of 1964; compensation for earnings for work missed due to an adverse employment action.

Bad faith cyber-squatting: Registering an Internet domain name that is similar to a trademark, with the purpose of reselling the name or diverting consumers from their desired website to the cyber-squatter's site.

Battery: The unwanted touching or striking of one person by another, with the intention of bringing about a harmful or offensive contact.

Binding precedent: The decisions of higher courts that establish the rule of law to be followed in similar cases in lower courts within the same jurisdiction.

Blurring: The effect of a use of a mark that is similar to a famous trademark, being used by a noncompetitor in a way that, over time, will diminish the famous trademark's value by detracting from its exclusiveness.

Bona fide occupational qualification (BFOQ) defense: A defense to a discrimination claim in which the employer must show that the criteria used that resulted in an adverse employment action were genuine qualifications for the job.

Breach of contract: An instance when one party fails to perform essential aspects of a contract.

Breach of duty: The second element in a negligence case; a failure to meet the required standard of care.

Building ordinance insurance: Insurance that covers the increased cost necessary to rebuild property to meet new building code standards that were not in effect when the building was originally constructed.

Burden of production: The defendant's responsibility to produce evidence supporting the defense without any accompanying burden to prove that the defense is true.

Burden of proof: The responsibility of proving the truth of a claim.

Business interruption insurance: Insurance that compensates for lost income if you have to close your business due to a covered occurrence on your property.

Business invitee: An individual who is on another person's premises with the assent of the landowner and who brings some economic benefit to the landowner.

Buy-out: A provision stating that if the exact amount of damages to be suffered when a party breaches the contract cannot be ascertained at the time the contract is signed, the parties may agree to an amount of damages that reasonably approximates the damages that would be sustained. Another term for liquidated damages.

Canons of interpretation: In contract law, a few basic principles for how courts interpret contracts.

Canons of statutory construction: Time-honored maxims that a court uses to guide and justify its interpretations of statutes.

Capacity: The principle that parties to a contract must be legally competent to enter into a contractual relationship.

Case brief: A succinct one- or two-page summary of a case that allows one to read it quickly and compare it with other cases.

Case law: *See* Common law.

Causation: The third element in a negligence case; the breach of the duty of care must result in damage to the plaintiff.

Caveat emptor: Let the buyer beware.

Certiorari: A request for an appeal to be heard by a higher court.

Choice of law clause: Clause in an agreement stating that the agreement will be governed by the laws of a particular state.

Civil causes of action: The legal grounds upon which to sue.

Civil courts: The location where cases that involve controversies of a noncriminal nature are heard.

Collective bargaining agreement (CBA): The contract that results from collective bargaining negotiations in which employees through their union and employers through a management negotiating team negotiate over mandatory subjects of bargaining.

Collective mark: A trademark that is used to indicate membership in an organization, such as a labor union.

Collective work: Content compiled from a number of contributions, created as separate and independent works, which are assembled into a collective whole for distribution and use; each separate contribution represents a distinct copyright from the work as a whole.

Commercial advantage: Commercial use of an individual's name, images, or other materials in advertising or the promotion and sale of a product or service.

Commercial speech: Speech that does no more than propose a commercial transaction, such as an advertisement.

Common law: The body of law created by courts when they render decisions interpreting existing laws as they apply to a particular case brought before the court.

Community of interests: Similarities in workers' jobs that will lead to common needs, desires, and goals being addressed through collective bargaining to make it more likely to create a labor settlement.

Comparative negligence: A system that allows a plaintiff to recover some portion of the damages caused by defendant's negligence, even if the plaintiff was also partially negligent and responsible for causing the injury.

Compensable injury: A physical injury or illness that a worker must suffer in order to receive workers' compensation.

Compensatory damages: Damages that an injured party can collect to compensate for a loss or injury suffered.

Complaint: A summary of allegations in a case.

Concerted action: Joint action between two or more parties.

Concurrent jurisdiction: The jurisdiction of two or more courts that are each authorized to deal with the same subject matter; for example, certain federal law claims may be heard by either a federal court or a state court.

Consent: The willingness that an act or invasion of an interest will take place.

Consideration: Something of value, such as money or personal services, given by one party to another in exchange for an act or promise.

Constitution: A foundational document that sets forth the basic operating principles of a government or organization, including limits on governmental power.

Constructive discharge: A reassignment of an employee in which the employee has not actually been fired but the impact of the reassignment has been essentially to take away the responsibilities for which he or she was hired.

Constructive notice: Presumed knowledge of dangers that a reasonable prudent facility owner would be aware of; also known as constructive knowledge.

Consumer: Any individual who purchases goods or services for personal or household consumption.

Contract: A promise or set of promises, for breach of which the law gives a remedy, or the performance of which the law in some way recognizes a duty.

Contract damages: Damages designed to put a nonbreaching party in the position it would have held if the contract had been performed as promised.

Contributory negligence: The principle by which a plaintiff who contributed in any way to his or her own injury may not recover any damages.

Counteroffer: An offer made in response to an initial offer.

Covenant not to compete: *See* Restrictive covenant.

Covenant of good faith and fair dealing: An expectation that both parties to a contract act fairly in their contractual dealings.

Criminal courts: The location where persons who are charged with a crime are prosecuted.

Damages: The final element in a negligence case; the loss caused by the defendant to the plaintiff or to his property.

Deceptive advertisement: An advertisement that contains a statement or an omission that is likely to mislead a reasonable consumer and that is important to the consumer's decision to buy or use a product.

Defamatory act: A false statement published to a third party, involving some degree of fault or negligence and causing actual damage.

Defensive lockout: A pre-emptive move by management to block an opportunistic strike by employees.

Denial of certiorari: A decision whereby either the U.S. Supreme Court or the highest state appellate court declines to hear a case and, having done so, allows the decision of the next lower court to stand.

Deposition: Oral testimony obtained under oath from a witness or a party to a case.

Descriptive mark: Trademark that describes the intended purpose, function, or use of the good.

Design defect: A product defect that exists when the very design of the product is flawed so as to render each item of that product unsafe.

Disabling impairment: An impairment that is permanent or long-term and that is not likely to be overcome with rest or treatment.

Disclosed principal: A classification of a principal in which a third party is aware of the identity of the principal and the fact that the agent is acting on behalf of the principal.

Disparate impact: A theory of liability used in deciding Title VII cases in which an employer's neutral employment practice has had a discriminatory effect on a protected class.

Disparate treatment: A theory of liability used in deciding Title VII cases in which an employer has intentionally discriminated against a member of a protected class.

Disparity of bargaining power: A situation in which one party gains an unfair bargaining position because it has much more power to make the contract terms in its favor.

Distraction doctrine: A doctrine providing that, in some cases, even though a condition appears to be open and obvious, the plaintiff may somehow be distracted from appreciating the danger.

Diversity of citizenship jurisdiction: The type of jurisdiction allowing a federal court to hear a case based on a state law claim when the parties to the lawsuit are residents of different states.

Dram shop acts: Statutes that provide for liability against those who commercially serve alcohol to minors or to persons who are visibly intoxicated when the inebriated individual subsequently injures a third party.

Due process: A constitutional provision that guarantees a person fair treatment in the process of a governmental decision to deprive the person of life, liberty, or property.

Duty: The first element in a negligence case; the defendant must have some obligation, imposed by law, to protect the plaintiff from unreasonable risk.

Duty of fair representation: A requirement that a union represent all employees in the bargaining unit fairly, even if the employees are not union members.

Eminent domain: The power of the state to appropriate private property for its own use without the owner's consent.

Employment practices liability (EPL) insurance: Insurance that covers injury to employees caused by wrongful employment practices such as sexual harassment; wrongful termination; defamation; invasion of privacy; breach of the employment contract; discrimination based on race, religion, age, gender, or disability; and so forth.

Enterprise coverage: Coverage that applies to employees who work for certain businesses or organizations that have at least two employees and that do at least $500,000 a year in business.

Equal Protection Clause: Found in the Fourteenth Amendment to the U.S. Constitution; it says that no state shall "deny to any person within its jurisdiction the equal protection of the laws."

Errors and omissions insurance: Insurance that covers the negligent or accidental acts of those who have professional knowledge or training.

Essential facility doctrine: A doctrine stating that refusing to share an essential facility that is economically unfeasible for a would-be competitor to duplicate (when that refusal would constitute a severe impediment to prospective market entrants) is an unreasonable restraint of trade.

Establishment Clause: Found in the First Amendment to the Constitution; it protects us from the government establishing a preferred religion; interpreted to mean that the government must be neutral with respect to religious matters.

Exculpatory agreement: Contract in which an individual or entity that is legally at fault tries to excuse itself from fault.

Exculpatory clause: A contractual provision that relieves an individual or entity from any liability resulting from a negligent act.

Express authority: A type of authority created when a principal and an agent make a written or oral agreement specifically defining the scope of the agent's authority.

Express warranty: A warranty that is explicitly made by a manufacturer or seller, either orally, in writing, or as a visual image; it makes an assertion of fact or a promise regarding the quality of the goods.

Fair use: Using a copyrighted work in a reasonable and limited way without the author's permission; fair use is a defense to a copyright infringement claim.

False advertising: A form of unfair and deceptive commerce involving misrepresentation.

Fanciful mark: The most distinctive trademarks; coined words that have been invented for the sole purpose of functioning as a trademark.

Fiduciary: A person who acts primarily for the benefit of another.

Fiduciary relationship: A relationship that is founded on trust or confidence, when one person has entrusted his or her interests to the integrity and fidelity of another.

First use: The first person to use a trademark in commerce has the superior rights to the mark, even if the mark has not been formally registered.

Fixation: A requirement that work being copyrighted be put into a tangible form, such as by being written down or recorded.

Force majeure clause: A contract clause that excuses or relieves a party from having to perform due to natural disasters or other "acts of God," war, or other situations beyond the control of either party.

Fraud: Intentional misrepresentations that are intended to induce action by another party, resulting in harm.

Fraudulent concealment: Occurs when a person knowingly withholds or conceals information from the plaintiff concerning the plaintiff's medical condition.

Free Exercise Clause: Found in the First Amendment to the Constitution; it protects our fundamental right to the free exercise of religious beliefs; interpreted to mean that the government may not target a particular religion for suppression.

Front pay: A remedy for discrimination under Title VII of the Civil Rights Act of 1964; compensation for future earnings that would have been received absent the discrimination.

Functional mark: A trademark that does not describe or distinguish the product or service but that is necessary for the product to exist.

Functionality: A concept used to prevent product designs or features that have a useful purpose from being monopolized under trademark law.

General duty: The duty of an employer to provide a place of employment that is free from hazards that cause or are likely to cause death or serious physical harm to employees.

Generic mark: The common descriptive name of a product or service; considered part of the public domain.

Good cause: A legally sufficient reason, such as unsatisfactory job performance or violation of workplace rules, that allows an employer to discipline or discharge an employee.

Good Samaritan statutes: State statutes providing that persons who act to help others in distress may not be sued for ordinary negligence based on their efforts to assist.

Goods: Tangible moveable objects, not including real estate or securities.

Goodwill: The favor that the management of a business wins from the public.

Guidance document: Interpretations by government agencies responsible for enforcing a variety of statutes such as Title XI, ADA, and Title VII. They can be in the form of letters, policy interpretations, or guidance documents made available to the public and normally entitled to deference by the courts when interpreting the relevant statutes or regulations.

Hazing: Any activity by which a person recklessly endangers the health or safety of an individual, or causes a risk of bodily injury, for purposes of initiation into, admission into, or affiliation with an organization or team.

Hold harmless clause: Contract clause in a lease stating that one party, usually the lessee, assumes the liability in the transaction in question. see also Indemnification clause.

Holding: The final ruling on a specific issue being decided.

Horizontal price fixing: A generally illegal arrangement among competitors to charge the same price for an item.

Horizontal restraints: Agreements between competitors that restrain free trade; for example, the player draft system spreads talent across teams in a league by preventing teams from vying economically for the best players.

Hostile environment harassment: A type of sexual harassment that occurs when an employee is subjected to repeated unwelcome behaviors that do not constitute sexual bribery but are sufficiently severe and pervasive that they create a work environment that interferes with the harassed employee's ability to perform his or her job.

Immunity: The ability to escape legal responsibilities; precludes a suit from being brought against a party.

Impasse: A stalemate in negotiations between a union and an employer, often leading to the use of an economic weapon by the union in the form of a strike or by management in the form of a lockout.

Implied authority: An agent's authority to act on behalf of a principal, implied by the conduct of the parties rather than set out in an oral or written agreement.

Implied warranty of fitness: A warranty that accompanies a sale in which the seller has reason to know the particular purpose of a purchase and the buyer relies on the seller's expertise in providing a product that is appropriate for that purpose.

Implied warranty of merchantability: An implied promise that a product is fit for its ordinary intended use and thus is merchantable.

Indemnification clause: Contract clause that provides for reimbursement to a party for a loss incurred by that party. see also Hold harmless clause.

Independent contractor: A person or business that provides goods or services to another entity under terms specified in a contract; an independent contractor is not an employee.

Individual coverage: Coverage for an employee when the organization that does not qualify as an enterprise and the employee regularly engages in activities involving interstate commerce or the production of goods for interstate commerce.

Individualized inquiry: Requirement under the Americans with Disabilities Act that a fact-specific inquiry relative to the stated purpose of a rule and a person's individual disability and circumstances must be undertaken to determine whether a requested modification of the rule is reasonable.

Injunctive relief: A remedy for discrimination under Title VII of the Civil Rights Act of 1964; orders the employer to cease unlawful practices or to engage in affirmative action.

Intent: The planning and desire to perform an act.

Intentional tort: A category of torts in which someone intentionally causes harm to person or property.

Interest arbitration: A method of settling disputes over the terms of a contract in which a neutral third-party arbitrator chosen by the parties renders a final and binding decision.

Intermediate scrutiny: A test to determine whether the Equal Protection Clause has been violated; assumes that rarely, but occasionally, the government may have an important reason to rely on a rule that contains a quasi-suspect classification (e.g., gender).

Interrogatory: Answers written under oath to a list of written questions.

Invitee: An individual who has a specific invitation to enter another person's property or is a member of the public in a public place.

Job Duties test: Part of a test for exemption from overtime pay; the employee's duties must be primarily involved in the executive, administrative, or professional aspects of the business.

Joint work: A collaboration between two or more authors, in which they are co-owners of the copyright of the work unless they have entered into an agreement to the contrary.

Jurisdiction: The authority to hear a case.

Just cause: Termination of a contract because the employee has engaged in behavior that violates the standards of job performance established by the employer.

Lease agreement: Contract giving rise to the relationship of lessor and lessee; contract for the exclusive possession of lands or premises for a determinate period of time.

Legal error: An erroneous interpretation of the law or application of legal procedure.

Legality: To be enforceable, the subject matter of a contract must not violate state or federal law.

Lessee: One who rents or leases property from another.

Lessor: One who rents or leases property to another.

Liability insurance: Insurance that covers bodily injury or property losses to a third party.

Libel: Written or published defamation of character. Libel has a broader definition than slander, because any number of tangible communications might fall under the heading of written communication.

License: Agreement that creates a privilege to go on the premises of another for a certain purpose but does not operate to confer on the licensee any title or interest in such property.

Licensee: An individual who is on the premises with the consent of the owner but who does not bring any economic benefit to the property owner.

Likelihood of confusion: The evidentiary burden that a trademark owner must meet to prove infringement of the trademark; consumers would be likely to associate the goods or services of one party with those of the other party as a result of the use of the marks at issue.

Limited duty rule: A rule used in baseball that provides a baseball facility has met its duty of care to spectators by providing seating that is protected from projectiles that leave the field of play.

Liquidated damages: A provision that sets up a reasonable approximation of damages required to satisfy a loss resulting from breach of contract. In employment contracts it may also be known as a buy-out clause.

Major life activity: A fundamental aspect of human living, such as walking, seeing, hearing, speaking, breathing, learning, working, and major bodily functions.

Mandatory subjects: Topics that management must bargain over in collective bargaining negotiations or risk being charged with an unfair labor practice; these topics include hours, wages, and terms and conditions of employment.

Manufacturing defect: A product defect that is the result of an error in the manufacturing and production process; one or more of the manufactured items are flawed, even though the design itself is a safe one.

Mediation: Submission of a dispute to an impartial decision maker who assists the parties in negotiating a settlement of their dispute.

Mens rea: The requisite intent to commit a crime; literally, "guilty mind."

Mitigation of damages: A principle that states that a nonbreaching party must act reasonably to lessen the consequences of a breach.

Modified comparative negligence: Generally, a plaintiff may not recover damages if the proportion of his or her negligence exceeds the proportion of the defendant's negligence.

Morals clause: A clause in a contract that provides for just-cause termination based on the employee's immorality, criminal behavior, or behavior that reflects poorly on the employer.

Named peril policy: An insurance policy that covers only the specific risks set forth in the policy.

National Letter of Intent (NLI): An agreement between a college or university and a prospective college student-athlete stating that the student will attend the institution for one year and will be provided with a financial aid award.

Negligence: Conduct that falls below the standard established by law for the protection of others against unreasonable risk of harm.

Negligence per se: Occurs when there is conclusive proof that a defendant has breached the standard of care when an injury is caused by the defendant's failure to meet a statutory requirement that was established for safety reasons.

Negligent hiring: The failure to properly screen employees, resulting in the hiring of someone who is not suitable for the position; the basic question is whether a manager acted reasonably in choosing a particular person to fill a position.

Negligent misrepresentation: A false statement given negligently to another party that the party reasonably relies upon, resulting in harm.

Negligent referral: The failure of an employer to disclose complete and factual information about a former or current employee to another employer when the failure to do so may result in harm to a third party.

Negligent retention: The retention of an employee after the employer became aware of the employee's unsuitability, thereby failing to act on that knowledge; the basic question is whether a manager acted reasonably in retaining an employee's services.

Negligent selection: The failure to properly screen independent contractors, resulting in the hiring of someone who is not suitable; similar to negligent hiring.

Negligent supervision: The failure to provide the necessary monitoring to ensure that employees perform their duties properly; the basic question is whether a manager acted reasonably in providing guidance and in overseeing an employee's actions.

Nonexempt employees: Workers who receive an hourly salary and who are entitled to overtime pay after working more than 40 hours in a five-day work week.

Offensive lockout: A move by management that usually occurs once an impasse is reached in negotiations, intended to pressure the union into accepting terms in an agreement favorable to management.

Offer: A conditional promise made to do or to refrain from doing something.

Open and obvious: A condition that an invitee knows of or that a reasonably careful person would have discovered upon careful inspection.

Originality: Requirement that a work be created by the author himself or herself and that it contain some minimal amount of creativity.

Partially disclosed principal: A classification of a principal in which a third party is aware that an agent is acting on behalf of another but does not know the identity of the principal.

Penalty provision: A damages provision that does not bear a reasonable relationship to the damages to be sustained and that are simply punishing a party for breaching a contract. Courts will not enforce penalty provisions.

Per se violations: Usually related to antitrust law, wrongdoings that are so obviously improper restraints on free trade that little other analysis is needed.

Permissive subjects: Topics that management is not obligated to negotiate over and the union cannot bargain to impasse over.

Perquisites (perks): Benefits that an employee may receive beyond a base salary and fringe benefits; for a coach these may include use of an automobile, payment for housing, or payment from endorsement contracts.

Persuasive precedent: Cases that a court may use but is not required to follow when deciding its cases.

Place of public accommodation: A place that accommodates the paying public; the place must affect interstate commerce and be principally engaged in selling food for consumption on the premises or exist for the purpose of exhibition or entertainment.

Preponderance of the evidence: The level of proof required to prevail in most civil cases; the winning party's evidence is more likely true than the losing party's evidence.

Preventive law: An approach that looks at all risks that could affect an institution's financial health; a broader view of risk management.

Prima facie case: A situation where the plaintiff's evidence is sufficient to prevail unless controverted by a defendant's evidence.

Primary assumption of risk: Occurs when a plaintiff understands and voluntarily agrees to accept the inherent risks of an activity.

Principal: In agency law, the person hiring or engaging an agent to act on behalf of the principal or to perform certain duties for the principal.

Prior similar incidents rule: A rule used to determine whether a certain incident was foreseeable by looking at what has occurred previously at that location; a sufficiently similar incident might make it foreseeable that another occurrence of that kind could happen.

Private right of action: Circumstance under which a court determines that a statute or provision that creates rights also supports a private plaintiff's remedy that can be achieved through a lawsuit, even though no such remedy is explicitly provided for in the statute.

Privity of contract: Occurs when a user and a provider have a direct contractual relationship.

Promissory estoppel: A quasicontractual remedy in which a party may have some recourse despite the fact that all the elements of a contract may not exist, based on reliance on a promise made.

Property right: Provision to the creator or owner of a copyright the exclusive economic and property interests to the work.

Protected classes: Classes of people designated as protected by a law; in the case of Title VII of the Civil Rights Act of 1964, these include race, color, religion, sex, and national origin.

Proximate cause: An act or failure to act, unbroken by any intervening act, that directly produces an event and without which the event would not have occurred.

Public figure: An individual who has, because of his or her activities, commanded sufficient continuing public interest.

Public invitee: An individual who is legally on public land.

Public official: A designation under the law of defamation determining what degree of fault must be proven before an individual can be held liable for false statements. Public officials must prove actual malice to recover for defamation.

Punitive damages: Payment in excess of actual damages that is awarded under certain circumstances, to punish the offender in the case of intentional torts.

Pure comparative negligence: Principle under which a plaintiff may recover damages even if the proportion of his or her negligence exceeds the defendant's negligence.

Qualified privilege: The privilege for employers, acting in good faith, to disclose information concerning an employee's work performance to those inside the current employer's operation or to prospective employers.

Quid pro quo harassment: A type of sexual harassment that occurs when an employer conditions a job-related benefit, such as a promotion or pay raise, on an employee's willingness to engage in sexual behavior; sexual bribery.

Ratification: Occurs when no actual agency exists, but a principal accepts or ratifies an agent's unauthorized acts after the fact.

Ratification/condonation principle: The principle that an act may be accepted or confirmed after the fact.

Rational basis review: The easiest test to determine whether the Equal Protection Clause has been violated; the government must simply have a rational basis for adopting the challenged rule, and it must be adopting the rule in order to accomplish a legitimate goal. This test is used for all group classifications other than suspect (e.g., race) or quasi-suspect (e.g., gender) classifications.

Rationale: The reasoning used by a court to justify its decision.

Reasonable accommodation: A modification in the work or academic environment that enables a qualified person with a disability to apply for a job, perform the essential functions of a job, or have equitable access to an educational program.

Reasonable factors other than age: A defense used when an employer has taken an adverse employment action that was motivated by an age-neutral factor.

Reasonable force: Lawful force that is reasonably necessary to accomplish a particular end, such as defense against attack or, in the case of a coach or teacher, to control, train, or educate a student.

Reasonable person: A reasonable person exercises judgment that meets societal expectations for prudence in decision making; an objective standard applied to judge behavior using a hypothetical individual; also known as reasonably prudent person.

Reasonably prudent person: *See* Reasonable person.

Reasonably prudent plaintiff: A hypothetical individual who is used as a standard to determine what a plaintiff should have done in a particular circumstance to protect his or her own safety.

Reassignment clause: A contract clause that gives an employer the right to transfer an employee to a different employment position in an organization.

Reckless misconduct: Occurs when an individual does an act or intentionally fails to do an act that it is his or her duty to do, knowing or having reason to know not only that the conduct creates an unreasonable risk of physical harm to another but also that such risk is substantially greater than that which is necessary to make the conduct negligent; also known as gross negligence or willful and wanton misconduct.

Recreational use statute: Statute providing some level of immunity for landowners who open their property to recreational use by the public with no fees charged.

Regulations: Rules created to operationalize statutes by providing more specific guidance.

Replacement value: An amount sufficient to replace property or equipment, subject only to the maximum amount set forth in the insurance policy.

Rescission: The right of a party to undo a contract and return the parties to the positions they had prior to the contract.

Reserve clause: A clause that has been used in professional sports contracts that functions to give teams a perpetual right to keep their players unless traded or released.

Respondeat superior: *See* Vicarious liability.

Restitution: An equitable remedy that involves returning the goods and/or property that were transferred under a contract.

Restrictive covenant: A clause in an employment contract that protects the interests of the employer by restricting the ability of the employee to take a comparable position in another organization.

Retaliation: Action taken in return for an injury or offense. Often refers to action by an employer against employees' efforts to obtain justice.

Revocable license: A license that may be revoked, withdrawn, or cancelled.

Right of attribution: A right that prevents others from claiming authorship or attributing authorship falsely to an individual.

Right of integrity: A right that prevents others from distorting, mutilating, or misrepresenting an author's work.

Right of publicity: The right of a famous individual to control the commercial value and use of his or her name, likeness, and image.

Rights arbitration: A method of settling disputes over the interpretation or application of a contract in which a neutral third-party arbitrator chosen by the parties renders a final and binding decision.

Rights to register: Rights that are created by both state and federal statutes and that provide certain benefits to a registrant.

Rights to use: Rights that are grounded in common law and that are created when a mark is used in commerce to identify a product or service.

Risk assessment: The process of determining the probability that particular risks will result in claims during a specific period, as well as determining the magnitude of the potential liability arising from such claims (Prairie & Garfield, 2004).

Risk evaluation: The process in which one assesses risks in conjunction with the mission of the organization and the importance of certain activities to that organization.

Risk management: The function or process by which an organization identifies and manages the risks of liability that rise from its activities (Prairie & Garfield, 2004).

Rollover clause: A clause that provides that, at the end of each year of a contract's term, the contract's term is automatically renewed for another year unless one party notifies the other of the intention not to roll over.

Rule of reason analysis: The requirement that a court balance the (economically) procompetitive effects of a rule against its anticompetitive effects.

Salary basis test: Part of a test for exemption from overtime pay, in which the employee must be paid a set and fixed salary that is not subject to variations because of quantity or quality of work.

Salary test: Part of a test for exemption from overtime pay, in which the amount of salary must meet a minimum level.

Sale: A contract by which title to goods is transferred from one party to another for a price.

Sales puffing: Expressions of opinion that are not made as factual representations about a product or service.

Scope of employment: The range of reasonable and foreseeable activities of an employee that further the business of the employer.

Secondary assumption of risk: Occurs when a plaintiff deliberately chooses to encounter a known risk and, in so doing, acts unreasonably.

Secondary meaning: Requirement that a trademark has become associated in the mind of the public with a particular source or origin; allows descriptive marks to obtain protection that they would otherwise not be entitled to receive.

Section 10(j) injunction: Refers to Section 10(j) of the National Labor Relations Act. It grants the National Labor Relations Board discretionary authority to seek a court order to prohibit an unfair labor practice.

Self-defense: Justified use of force when a person reasonably believes that it is necessary to defend himself or herself from attack.

Service mark: A trademark that relates to a service rather than a good or product.

Shared responsibility statute: A statute stating that participants in an activity assume the risks inherent in the activity; if the participant chooses to assume those risks, the activity provider does not owe a duty of care to the participant relative to those risks.

Slander: Spoken defamation of a person.

Sovereign immunity: A doctrine precluding the institution of a suit against the sovereign government without its consent; rooted in the inherent nature of power and the ability of those who hold power to shield themselves.

Specific hazard standard: A benchmark that must be met by an employer; it requires that employers adopt specific practices, means, methods, or processes that are reasonably necessary and appropriate to protect workers on the job.

Specific performance: A remedy provided by a court that orders a breaching party to perform the contract. May only be used when the subject of the contract is a unique good.

Standard of care: The degree of care a reasonable prudent person would take to prevent an injury to another.

Stare decisis: "Let the decision stand"; a refusal by a court to change a ruling on an issue that has already been decided.

State actor: A term used in constitutional law to describe an entity that is acting with the sufficient authority of the government and, therefore, is subject to regulation under the Fifth and Fourteenth Amendments, which prohibit the federal and state governments, respectively, from violating the rights laid out elsewhere in the Constitution.

Statute of frauds: A statute requiring that certain types of contracts be in writing.

Statute of limitations: A statute defining the time limits to undertaking a cause of action and providing a defense if the cause of action has not been filed in a timely fashion.

Statutes: Written laws created by legislatures, which are law-making bodies composed of elected representatives.

Strict scrutiny: The strictest test applied to determine whether the Equal Protection Clause has been violated; based on the premise that there is almost never a good reason for a law to differentiate on the basis of an immutable characteristic such as race.

Student-athlete: An individual who engages in, is eligible to engage in, or may be eligible in the future to engage in any intercollegiate sport.

Suggestive mark: A mark that subtly connotes something about the service or product but that does not actually describe any specific quality or characteristic of the good or service.

Suspect classification: A classification that is likely to be based on illegal discrimination; includes race, ethnicity, national origin, and alienage.

Tarnishment: The effect of a similar mark being used in such a way as to disparage or harm the reputation of a famous trademark; often used in connection with shoddy products or sexual, obscene, or socially unacceptable activities.

10(j) injunction: A court order to stop an employer from committing an unfair labor practice.

Territorial rights: Franchise relocation restrictions that prevent a competitor franchise from relocating into another team's market territory without league permission and adequate compensation for the potential loss of market share caused by the incursion.

Tort: A civil wrong other than a breach of contract; usually refers to the causing of damage or injury to property, a person, a person's reputation, or a person's commercial interests.

Trade dress: Distinctive packaging, including distinctive shape and appearance of a product or service.

Trade name: Any name used by a person to identify his or her business or vocation.

Trademark: A word, name, symbol, or device that has been adopted and used by a manufacturer or merchant to identify goods and to distinguish them from those manufactured or sold by others.

Trademark dilution: Damage to or weakening of a famous trademark, lessening its distinctiveness, even in the absence of any likelihood of confusion or competition.

Trademark infringement: The unauthorized use of another person's or business's trademark.

Trainee status: The status of a trainee, student, or intern who meets the eligibility criteria for exemption from the minimum wage and overtime pay requirements of the FLSA.

Trespasser: An individual who is on the premises without permission.

Trial on the merits: A trial that includes full arguments before a judge, who renders a final decision; if sufficient controversy remains after discovery is complete, then a trial on the merits will take place.

Undisclosed principal: A classification of a principal in which a third party is not aware that an agent is acting on behalf of another party.

Undue hardship: An accommodation that would impose an excessive cost or administrative burden on an organization; a court will not find an accommodation reasonable if it would impose an undue hardship on the organization.

Unfair dominance: Describes the situation where the party benefiting from a waiver has so much power in the transaction that it is not a fair deal; courts will not uphold the waiver when there is unfair dominance.

Unfair labor practice: According to the National Labor Relations Act, employers may not discriminate in regard to any term or condition of employment to encourage or discourage membership in any labor organization, nor interfere with employees in the exercise of their rights to associate with a labor union.

Unidentified principal: A category of principal in an agency relationship, where a third party is aware that an agent is acting on behalf of another but does not know the identity of the principal.

Unrelated business income tax (UBIT): A tax on income generated by a trade or business carried on by a tax-exempt organization that is not substantially related to the performance of its tax-exempt function.

Utilitarian functionality: A doctrine that relates to whether a product feature is essential to the product's purpose or use which would preclude obtaining trademark protection for that feature.

Vicarious liability: A doctrine that holds an employing organization (employer) responsible for certain acts of its employees, not because of any wrongdoing by the employer, but because the law has deemed it appropriate for the employer to be held accountable for the actions of its employees.

Volunteer: An individual who performs hours of service for a public agency for civic, charitable, or humanitarian reasons, without promise, expectation, or receipt of compensation for services rendered (29 C.F.R. § 553.101(a)).

Waiver: A type of contract in which one party gives up his or her right to sue the other party when that party has been negligent, thus altering the outcome that would transpire under the usual tort law principles.

Warranty: An assertion of fact or promise made by a manufacturer or seller that is relied upon as part of the consumer transaction.

Whistleblower statutes: Statutes that provide a system to protect, against discrimination and retaliation, those employees who report wrongful conduct by their employer to authorities.

White-collar exemption: Exemption from minimum wage and overtime pay received by a worker employed in a bona fide executive, administrative, or professional capacity; the worker is usually salaried and receives a higher rate of pay than an hourly worker.

Willful and wanton misconduct: See Reckless misconduct.

Work for hire: A work prepared by an employee within the scope of his or her employment, or contracted work that has been specially ordered or commissioned.

Work week: A period of 168 hours in seven consecutive days ($7 \times 24 = 168$); may begin on any given day and hour as determined by the employer.

Worst case scenario: In contract law, the worst that could happen; contracts are drafted on the basis of the worst case scenario in order to protect the client's interests.

Writ of certiorari: An order issued by the U.S. Supreme Court or a state's highest appellate court that directs a lower court to send up the case record for review.

Wrongful termination: A termination when the employee has been fired contrary to the terms of the contract or in violation of the law.

Part I

Introductory Concepts

To understand the legal theory in this text and to gain maximum benefit from this textbook, you will need to know some fundamental principles. The first two chapters of this text are intended to give you an overview of these principles. In Chapter 1, you will become familiar with why the study of law is essential for sport managers and how you can use legal theory in a management context to attain a competitive advantage for your sport/recreation organization. You will also learn how to use a proactive law mentality instead of a reactive law mentality as part of your decision-making process for your organization across a spectrum of business problems and challenges. You will learn about the concept of preventive law and how you may develop and implement a preventive law plan for your sport/recreation enterprise.

Chapter 2 provides information regarding the legal system in the United States, the anatomy of a lawsuit, and the way courts decide a variety of legal disputes. You will also learn about primary and secondary legal resources and about the process of conducting legal research. All of this information is necessary for you to be able to appreciate fully the legal theory and cases presented throughout the book. In addition, you will learn how to employee analytical tools based in legal reasoning concepts to improve your writing skills and problem-solving skills.

1 Introduction to Law and Management in Sport

Introduction

Learning legal issues through a management lens adds significant value for a course in the legal aspects of sport and recreation management. As sport and recreation programs become more sophisticated and students strive for sought-after positions in the sport and recreation fields, we need to approach legal material from the viewpoint of how you, as a prospective sport or recreation manager, might best learn and utilize the material. Thus, the term *manager*, as used in this book, refers to anyone, regardless of job title, who performs any of the managerial functions discussed throughout this text.

As you watch ESPN, listen to sports radio, or browse your newsfeed on social media, you will realize that much of the commentary does not deal with what is happening on the field or court. Many of these stories deal with legal issues pertaining to sport figures, sport organizations, and sport/recreational facilities (see Exhibit 1.1 for examples). Whether you become a coach, an athletic director at a high school or college, an administrator in a collegiate athletic conference, a supervisor in a park district, a manager of a fitness club, a social media director for a sport organization, or the commissioner of the National Women's Basketball Association (NWBA), you will find the content of this course, known conventionally as **sport law**, to be very useful to you. This is because managerial activities – such as hiring and overseeing personnel, supervising sport and recreation participants, providing sport and activity programming/instruction, administering sport and recreation facility operations, overseeing games or events, and implementing marketing initiatives – are functions routinely performed by a variety of persons working in sport, educational, and recreation organizations all of which carry with them significant legal implications.

The Need to Understand Legal Issues in Sport

One initial question arises as we begin to study legal issues in sport and recreation: *What is sport law?* Some commentators initially argued that there was no such legal theory as "sport law" (Cozzillio & Levinstein, 1997) and sport law simply referred to areas of the substantive law that relate to the context of sport. These commentators asserted that the legal theories, for example, tort law, contracts, labor relations, administrative law, or constitutional law, are the same regardless of whether the application is in the realm of sport and physical activity or pertains to other businesses or aspects of daily life. Others staked out a middle ground and agreed sport law was mostly traditional substantive law applied in a sport context, but also argued that certain applications make sport sufficiently different that it may be appropriate to characterize a resultant body of knowledge as sport law. These commentators recognized a growing "sport only" corpus of law in areas such as sport agents and Title IX (Gardiner, 1997; Shropshire, 1998). A more modern perspective has now evolved which acknowledges sport-related cases have resulted in the development of a body of sports law that is globally significant, particularly applicable in the sports context, and influential in the development of general legal principles (Lazaroff, 2001; Mitten, Davis, Duru, & Osborne, 2020;

Exhibit 1.1 Sample of legal issues pertaining to sport and recreation.

Situation	Legal Theory
A university football coach leaves to coach at another university.	Contract law
A professional sports team has an issue with the "salary cap" in signing a player.	Collective bargaining and contract law
A prosecutor charges an athlete with sexual assault.	Criminal law
A female basketball coach at a college asserts that she should be paid the same as the men's basketball coach.	Equal Pay Act and Title VII (federal statutes)
A youth sport organization is held liable for a coach who molested a team member.	Tort law – negligent hiring
A health club and equipment manufacturer are liable for injury when weight equipment malfunctions.	Tort law – negligence; products liability
Football players sue the NFL and the NCAA regarding the organizations' policies and procedures pertaining to concussions.	Negligence, fraudulent concealment
A sport business names its sports apparel with a name very similar to another product name.	Trademark law
A public high school requires the delivery of a prayer over the public address system before all home football games.	Constitutional law – First Amendment
A company terminates an endorsement contract with an athlete who was accused of criminal conduct.	Contract law
A whitewater rafting company uses a waiver to avoid liability for its own negligence.	Tort and contract law
A university eliminates the women's gymnastics team and the men's baseball team.	Title IX (a federal statute)
NCAA student-athletes sue the NCAA and videogame manufacturers based on their use of athletes' likenesses in games, and regulations prohibiting them from profiting from their name, image, or likeness.	Right of publicity & Anti-trust

Mitten & Opie, 2010). Regardless of which theoretical position you believe is correct, the reality is that the law is inextricably woven into the fabric of sport and recreation organizations and it is imperative that we recognize the pervasiveness of law as it affects sport and recreation.

For example, assume you have just been hired as the administrator of a local youth baseball league. As you begin your first week on the job, you are overwhelmed by how many of your responsibilities have legal implications. Your job requires you to answer questions such as: what provisions should be included in your lease agreement with the city parks department? How do you ensure that your coaches are competent and fit to work with young athletes? Are you permitted to hire seasonal employees and pay them fixed wages instead of minimum wage and overtime pay? What emergency medical care is available for participants? Do you need to have automated external defibrillators (AEDs) on site? What concussion protocols do you need to implement to protect participants? What policies and procedures should you implement to make sure that the crowd does not pose a danger to game officials or to other fans or players? How do you maintain equipment and the playing fields? What provisions should be included in your contracts with the vendors who will provide food and beverages at the games and your game officials? What levels of insurance are necessary? All of these questions have both managerial and legal implications.

In addition to proactively using our legal knowledge to make better management decisions, we must also understand the legal system in our country sometimes invites abuse of the system because of our "open door" philosophy of hearing disputes. Our legal system operates under the belief that we should allow citizens as much access to the formal legal adjudication of disputes as possible. This philosophy is fine when people use the system only to bring claims that are indeed meritorious. However, "Americans will sue each other at the slightest provocation" (Taylor & Thomas, 2003, p. 44). In other words, our country's judicial system allows lawsuits to be filed that may seem nonsensical at first glance, and we, as a very litigious nation, look for responsible parties to blame. So long as a claim has an underlying basis in law, the claim can be filed.

For example, fans often want to sue their own professional sport teams when they are displeased with the team's performance despite a long-standing policy of courts generally refusing to second guess sport leagues in enforcing their rules and regulations. Notwithstanding, New Orleans Saints fans filed three federal lawsuits against the National Football League (NFL) and game officials over the failure to call a blatant penalty during a playoff game in 2019 against the Los Angeles Rams. All three federal suits were dismissed in July of 2019, and one last state court case was finally dismissed by the Louisiana Supreme Court in September of 2019 (Associated Press, 2019; Triplett, 2019). In another example, a woman sued Jelly Belly after she accidentally consumed the company's Sport Beans product which contained more sugar than the company's traditional candy jelly beans. Sport Beans are an exercise supplement containing electrolytes and vitamins. She alleged she had been deceived about the sugar content because Jelly Belly's product label said "evaporated cane juice," which was just a substitute term for sugar. Jelly Belly contended that if she read the evaporated cane juice on the label then she should have also read the total sugar content information (McCleary, 2017). The district court eventually dismissed the case.

Both the *Saints* and the *Jelly Belly* cases highlight that, regardless whether the cases were frivolous or just unwinnable cases, companies must proactively prepare for defending a wide range of lawsuits on an ongoing basis and can also learn from these experiences to potentially prevent such claims (Tsai, 2020). We also need to look more closely at the law as a guide to creating better policies and procedures in our organizations. An understanding of the law certainly helps us to prevent litigation, but more importantly it enables us to make our organizations safer, and more hospitable and effective environments for our internal (employees) and external (clients, customers, athletes) constituencies. This perspective is central to the notion of using legal strategy and legal knowledge to gain a competitive advantage.

Knowledge of the Law as a Competitive Advantage

Although the legal environment surrounding sport and recreation business is just one facet of the managerial landscape, it is an important one to consider. In fact, since the first decade of the 21st century, legal scholars and business practitioners recognized that, "legal issues in general have emerged as the most important factor in the external environment in which business operates" (Siedel, 2002, p. 3). Historically, legal strategy was separate from business strategy and focused mainly on litigation responses and risk management. Instead of approaching legal issues from a negative or reactive perspective, we strive to present these issues in a manner that allows you to use your knowledge of the law to gain a competitive advantage over other organizations. In this way, legal "problems" may be transformed into opportunities for competitive advantage (Siedel, 2002).

As the words suggest, competitive advantage is something that gives an organization an advantage over competitors. This was Siedel's premise in his book *Using the Law for Competitive Advantage* (2002). Later, Siedel (2010) and Siedel and Haapio (2016) discussed the integral intersection of legal strategy and business strategy. Robert Bird (2011) concluded in his analysis of law, strategy, and competitive advantage that the law can be a source of sustainable competitive advantage because it can "confer significant value to firms through the protection of innovation, the enabling of free markets, and the efficient regulation of contracts" (p. 26). Finally, Bagley's book entitled *Winning Legally* (2005) emphasizes that knowledge of legal issues should enable managers to create value, marshal resources, and manage risk in their organizations. Bagley writes, "Managers must ensure that their legal strategy aligns with their business strategy" (p. 5). The legal strategy cannot simply be an afterthought but must be integrated with business strategy. Bagley reframes the relationship of law to business and encourages managers to look at the law not as a constraint but rather as a tool to generate more value for the business.

In keeping with the approach described above, this text emphasizes the competitive benefits of understanding and implementing the law properly within your sport organization. *Competitive advantage*, for our purposes, means not just an ability to make your business more profitable, but an opportunity to make your sport/recreation organization a superior one operationally. A superior operation translates into a safer and better-run organization, which, in turn, will be one that attracts more clients or participants.

A secondary benefit to recognizing the role of law is maximizing your ability to act assertively and competitively, allowing you to make better use of your legal counsel, whether they are in-house counsel or simply on retainer by your organization. The authors of this text, as attorneys, recognize the degree to which managers often view attorneys as "necessary evils." As you acknowledge the importance of using law as a competitive tool, you will be better able to use the legal counsel that is available to your organization. Instead of using your attorneys as "firefighters" to combat the conflagration of ongoing legal problems, you will learn how to use their talents proactively: to assist you in drafting policies, procedures, and contracts that will help you avoid or minimize liability from the outset. You will be able to integrate your legal decisions with your financial and operational strategies to better "manage" the law and your lawyers.

Using Preventive Law to Manage Risk

Prairie and Garfield (2010) suggest there is a distinct and important difference between risk management and preventive law. These authors define **risk management** as "the function and process by which [an organization] identifies and manages the risks of liability that arise from its activities" (p. 473). They note that the traditional view of risk management is often confined to risks resulting from lawsuits for personal injuries or property damage. While these are important risks for sport managers to consider, organizations would be better served by adopting a macro view of risk as it may impact the financial health or survival of the organization as a whole.

This perspective as identified by Prairie and Garfield is a "**preventive law**" focus. They explain, "The scope of preventive law provides the broader focus, to include environmental, political, economic, regulatory, institutional, and cultural risks" (p. 473) – essentially using the lens of preventive law to guide decision-making across the business. Preventive law's broader focus identifies risks that might not pose a direct monetary threat, but could threaten the success of the organization. For example, during the NCAA investigation into the academic fraud scandal at the University of North Carolina (UNC), a narrow risk management perspective may have only assessed the risk of direct monetary loses for the athletics program in the event the NCAA imposed a post-season or television ban on the men's basketball team, a common penalty used by the NCAA. However, a much greater risk was also present which could have threatened the accreditation of the university as a whole. Ultimately, UNC faced a one-year probation imposed by the Southern Association of Colleges and Schools Commission extending the scandal well beyond the athletics program and threatened the underlying integrity of the institution (New, 2015). Thus, a preventive law focus ensures that we consider all risks across the organization.

Siedel and Haapio (2016) also discuss the preventive law focus in the context of the "proactive law movement," which recommends embedding legal strategy with business strategy. The proactive view corresponds well to the preventive view that the risk management process is holistic and is relevant to every aspect of the organization. We will use these terms interchangeably, since both descriptions define a process of integrating legal strategy and risk management into an organization's overall business strategy to produce better outcomes for the business. Instead of narrowly looking at risk management as a necessary evil to ward off plaintiffs's lawyers, we will suggest ways in which the use of preventive or proactive legal strategies can add value to your organization. Even if there were no such phenomena as lawsuits or legal liability, any manager in a sport or recreation organization would be well-advised to adopt the strategies mentioned in this chapter, not simply to avoid or minimize liability, but to make the organization a better one for employees, participants, and spectators alike.

To begin, your risk management strategies should be congruent with your organizational culture. If you are committed to building a climate of value and responsiveness to the needs of your constituents, risk management is simply one more business tool to aid in accomplishing that goal (Bagley, 2005; Hanssen, 2005). The underlying culture of an organization and its core values drive an organization's views of risk management and safety concerns. For example, the NFL was characterized as a toxic workplace due to autocratic management, culture of fear, bullying, pervasive insecurity, profit at any price, low job security, and dangerous and life-threatening working conditions (Schwartz, 2014). When describing the NFL, business analysts remarked that "the sport is a total mess, and the league has never made more money" (para. 1), citing flattening ratings, increased competition from live streaming services, the mishandling of the political controversy surrounding Colin Kaepernick's protest against racial injustice, and denials of links between the sport and concussions (Boudway & Novy-Williams, 2018). In 2018, the NFL was tied for sixth place as one of the most polarizing brands, and they have been less than resolute in dealing with several controversies impacting the league and the brand. This example serves as a stark reminder that the cultural priorities of an organization drive all of its policies and practices. Risk management cannot be an afterthought. It cannot be viewed as a necessary evil. Managing risks is at the core of what your organization stands for and must be interwoven with every aspect of your business.

The vision of this book is to tie legal theory to managerial roles and functions to enable you to use the law to make better decisions for your organization. The essence of this vision as it pertains to risk management is to allow you to use these principles to fashion a better organization for all your constituents: employees, participants, and spectators. A better organization is a safer and more efficient one. Thus, this text presents legal issues with a broad focus across organizational functions to enable managers to adopt a **preventive law** posture, one that looks at all risks that could affect the organization's financial health. Next, we introduce the preventive law process.

The Preventive Law Process

Prairie and Garfield (2010) have identified five steps that make up the preventive law process. First, risk identification is undertaken, in which a legal audit is performed to identify all possible risks. Second, an assessment of the risks is undertaken. Third, the risks are evaluated. Fourth, a preventive law plan is designed. Fifth, the preventive law plan is implemented. Below we will elaborate on each of these steps.

Step One: Risk Identification – The Legal Audit

Before any sport or recreation organization can develop a plan to prevent injury or loss, the legal landscape of possible liability must be explored, this is called the *legal audit*. The legal audit is a snapshot of an organization's overall functions, activities, structures, and operations. The legal audit will include policies, procedures, and practices, while also addressing any patterns in lawsuits, claims, or complaints. This legal audit will enable sport managers to identify which practices, policies, or trends pose the most serious risks to the organization. The approach to the legal audit should be holistic. Of course, personal injury is a prime issue in sport/recreation organizations because of the nature of sport and physical activity; however, a review of the topics covered in this text and presented in Exhibit 1.2 will remind the reader that many prospective liabilities stem from issues other than personal injury. Exhibit 1.2 is based on the following hypothetical situation to illustrate the far-ranging nature of these liabilities:

> You are the newly hired general manager of Daily Fit, a health and fitness club. Your club has a gymnasium, a pool, and several exercise and weight rooms. You also have a sauna and offer child care services. You operate a juice bar and a cafe for members, and you serve wine and beer in the cafe. You have contracted with a number of personal trainers to give assistance to your members.
>
> You are a firm believer in preventive law, and you hire a consultant to perform a legal audit so you will have a better sense of what the landscape of liability may be. The consultant has prepared the list of possible concerns shown in Exhibit 1.2.

Exhibit 1.2 Possible risks for a health and fitness club.

Employment Issues	Premises Liability
Breach of employment contract	Slip and fall
Wrongful termination suit	**Pool safety & maintenance**
Defamation based on employment references	Security in club and parking lot
	Provision of emergency medical care, including use of
	automated external defibrillators
Discrimination based on race, gender, disability, age,	Routine maintenance and repair of equipment
religion, nationality	
Sexual harassment	Other types of emergencies, such as severe weather or a
Vicarious liability for actions of employees	bomb threat
Negligent hiring/retention/supervision claims	General cleaning and maintenance concerns
Contracts with independent contractors, such as	**Client/Participant Concerns**
personal trainers	
Working conditions – Occupational Safety & Health Act	Supervision
and Fair Labor Standards Act	Instruction
	Warnings
Workers' compensation	
Labor relations issues, if any employees are unionized	Equipment safety
	Child care
Employee theft	Food/drink preparation at juice bar
	Liability related to the service of alcohol
Facility Issues	Use of waivers/agreements to participate
	Invasion of privacy issues in locker room
Zoning issues	**Intellectual Property/Advertising**
Lease issues	Use of trademarks/copyrights
Disability access – Americans with Disabilities Act	False advertising
Contracts with service providers	Deceptive trade practices

The list in Exhibit 1.2 reflects a holistic approach to preventive law and, although not exhaustive, can serve as a checklist to help you consider where you might have exposure to loss or liability. You will note that the list of concerns covers a wide range of legal issues: tort law, contract law, employment law, administrative law, and intellectual property law concepts are all embedded in the legal audit.

Steps Two and Three: Risk Assessment and Risk Evaluation

The **risk assessment** component of the preventive law process is closely aligned with the **risk evaluation** component, so we will explore these two steps together. Using information developed from the legal audit, you are able to assess the risks in view of their frequency of occurrence and the magnitude of the risk. In this way, you can set priorities as to which risks must be addressed immediately and which can be handled in the normal course of maintenance and repair. **Risk assessment** is the process of "determining the probability that particular risks will result in claims during a specified period and the magnitude of the potential liability arising from such claims" (Prairie & Garfield, 2010, p. 480). This assessment may be done by looking at the history of prior claims at your sport/recreation organization, the types of litigation that have been brought against similar organizations, applicability of statutes and regulations, value of revenues or profits derived from the activity, and the cost to minimize or eliminate the risk. To address these risks, various sources of industry information for a risk assessment are available. For example, a trade association may compile statistics related to claims in your type of sport/recreation business. Many industry publications also discuss current legal issues and pending litigation. Chapter 2 references a number of legal resources for keeping abreast of current litigation in sport and recreation. Trade journals such as *SportsBusiness Journal*, *Athletic Business*, *Athletic Management*, and *Fitness Management* publish articles dealing with current cases and trends in litigation. You should also consult with your legal counsel and attend workshops to stay abreast of the trends in litigation related to your business. Many trade associations and other membership associations frequently host webinars and online groups on social media platforms providing rapid access to current events and trends. For example, during the Covid-19 pandemic an Event Professional Group was created on Facebook to connect event professionals around the world to share and monitor best practices for canceling, rescheduling, and operating events in the post-Covid-19 environment.

Next, **risk evaluation** directs us to evaluate the risks we have assessed in conjunction with the mission of our organization and the importance of the activities to our organization. In essence, during the risk evaluation stage, you are simply asking yourself is this risk something we want to eliminate, or something we should retain but try to minimize the potential for loss. For example, some activities may pose serious risks but are essential to your organization's mission or objectives, while others are outside the core services or products of your organization.

Let's consider the previous health and fitness club example. The club's cafe serves beer and wine and let's assume you have assessed that the sale of alcohol poses a significant risk in terms of: (1) potential liability for overconsumption and drunk driving; (2) potential liability for personal injury; (3) increased financial and administrative costs to secure appropriate licenses and permits; (4) increased employee costs to ensure cafe employees are legally permitted to serve alcohol; and (5) increased inventory costs for the cafe. Now you must evaluate these risks in light of the mission of the organization and the importance of alcohol sales to the overall success of the organization (see Exhibit 1.3). For a health and fitness club, the sale of alcohol is really peripheral to your core business. It is an amenity that you could probably eliminate without causing your clients great inconvenience and would likely be more reflective of the core values of your organization. Thus, in evaluating this risk, you may choose to eliminate the sale of alcohol. However, if you decided to include beer and wine in direct response to customer requests and your revenues from those sales have become an important revenue stream for the club, you may decide you need to evaluate how to continue to offer beer and wine while minimizing or eliminating the risks associated with those sales. The preventive law plan will identify specific strategies to address the risks revealed during the risk assessment and evaluation process.

This process should be used for all the risks identified during the legal audit. You can see from Exhibit 1.3 that it is holistic and uses a broad perspective to better inform our decisions whether to eliminate or retain the risk. As mentioned, even if profitable, you may decide to stop serving alcohol at the club. On the other hand, even though operating swimming pools often engenders much litigation, and if a drowning were to occur any litigation or settlement would be very costly, a swimming pool is at the core of your business activities. It would be inappropriate to shut down the pool operation because of the risk assessment; instead, you would need to develop preventive law strategies to manage those risks. Exhibit 1.4 represents the assessment and evaluation of the pool safety risks.

Exhibit 1.3 Assessment and evaluation of risks – Alcohol sales at health club.

Type of Risk	Frequency of Risk	Magnitude of Risk	Handling the Risk
Potential liability for a member over-consuming or drunk driving	Occasional	Severe – fatality could result	Implement strict purchase limits and review staff training
Potential liability for personal injury	Occasional	Moderate – serious injury could occur	Prohibit use of facility while under the influence; review and update membership agreement and usage policies
Increased costs to secure licenses and permits	Frequent	Slight	Determine cost breakeven point between sales and licensing costs
Increased labor costs	Frequent	Moderate	Determine options to use independent contractors to operate alcohol sales; limit sales to certain hours and use flexible staffing
Increased inventory costs	Occasional	Slight	Track beer and wine sales individually to calculate itemized profit projections

Exhibit 1.4 Assessment and evaluation of pool safety risks.

Type of Risk	Frequency of Risk	Magnitude of Risk	Handling the Risk
Pool does not meet statutory standards regarding drain covers	Occasional	Severe – fatality could result	Install drain covers in the next 24 hours
Bleachers missing some slats	Occasional	Moderate – slip or fall	Repair bleachers before the next event
Slight irregularity in locker room tile – patron could trip	Frequent	Slight – bruised toe	Repair tile during usual maintenance period, post signage
No emergency training for employees in getting outside assistance	Frequent	Fatality could result from delay	Begin training employees by the end of the week

The strategies to minimize or eliminate the risks from the alcohol sales and the pool safety examples are important parts of the preventive law process. Next, we explore how these strategies are developed as part of the preventive law plan.

Step Four: Development of the Preventive Law Plan

We can cope with risks according to four possible strategies: (1) risk elimination; (2) risk retention; (3) risk transfer; and (4) risk control (Prairie & Garfield, 2010).

Risk Elimination

Risk elimination should be used only if the exposure to risk greatly outweighs the benefits of retaining the activity or operation. Recall that the sale of alcohol may be peripheral to a fitness club operation and may be eliminated based on the prospect of huge losses. However, if you were the owner of a pro sport franchise, most likely you would not eliminate the sale of alcoholic beverages at games. In this context, the service of alcohol is a part of the fan experience, and it can be very lucrative. You would most likely adopt transfer and control strategies as discussed below. Risk elimination is not the preferred strategy to deal with most loss exposures. If you have incorporated activities within your business because they are congruent with your mission and core values, you will opt to keep those activities and find ways to control the risk, not eliminate the activities.

Risk Retention

Risk retention means that your organization chooses to bear the financial consequences of an activity. If your business is self-insured, you are retaining all the risk. Or, if you cannot obtain insurance for a particular risk, yet you have chosen to continue the activity, you are retaining the risk. For example, if you choose to run an event without event cancelation insurance (because it is too costly), and the event must be canceled because of extreme weather, your organization will bear the brunt of that financial loss. In this case, you are retaining the risk.

Risk Transfer

Risk transfer shifts the possible financial loss to another party. Organizations attempt risk transfer in a number of ways, including by procuring insurance, hiring independent contractors, and using contractual provisions. We will discuss these methods in more detail in other chapters. The most common risk transfer method is the procurement of insurance. Since any claim for a covered incident is paid by the insurance company, insurance is a risk transfer method. For example, Wimbledon was one of the few organizations to have the foresight to buy event cancelation insurance that included coverage for a pandemic, so when most event organizers were incurring significant losses during the Covid-19 pandemic, Wimbledon recovered around $141.7 million from its insurer (Turner, 2020).

Engaging an independent contractor, as we will discuss in Chapter 4, means that you shift the possible liability to that contractor. You will require the contractor to procure insurance for its own operations. For example, the vendor you hire to serve alcoholic beverages for a pro sport facility will be an independent contractor that must procure its own insurance. As you will learn in Chapter 4, a major benefit of using an independent contractor is that you avoid vicarious liability based on the actions of the independent contractor. Thus, this method transfers risk to the independent contractor.

Contractual provisions can also transfer risk. Using waivers with activity participants, as we will discuss in Chapter 16, essentially transfers the risk of financial loss to those participants, since they agree not to sue you if you have been negligent (see Chapter 14 for a discussion of negligence). You will also learn in Chapter 16 about the use of the indemnification clause, which essentially provides that Party A agrees to bear the liability of Party B's actions should a lawsuit result in a judgment against Party B. This type of risk transfer is common in commercial undertakings, such as venue lease agreements.

Risk Control

Risk control is the **key aspect of the preventive law plan**, since it involves the actual reduction of risk, not just methods to deal with the financial consequences of the risk. This strategy addresses the risks that you identify in your legal audit and involves developing plans to minimize the risks attendant to your operations. Since a sport or recreation organization, by its very nature, will always have inherent risks related to the activities that it provides, the focus here, relative to possible physical injury, is on reducing those risks that go beyond the inherent risks and arise from poor management, instruction, supervision, and so forth.

Consider our health and fitness club example again. Which preventive law strategies are incorporated into the preventive law analysis? Exhibit 1.5 aligns the suggestions for handling the risks produced by the risk assessment and evaluation with the most likely preventive law strategy. This alignment reveals that multiple strategies can be used together to address a single risk.

Step Five: Implementation of the Preventive Law Plan

A preventive law plan is only useful if it is properly and continuously implemented. As we have discussed, preventive law is simply one more management tool for attaining a competitive advantage in the sport/recreation marketplace. Although a risk management committee or legal counsel may be responsible for the actual development and implementation of the preventive law plan, *all* members of the organization

Exhibit 1.5 Aligning preventive law strategies with risks.

Type of Risk	Handling the Risk	Preventive Law Strategy
Potential liability for a member drunk driving	Implement strict purchase limits and review staff training; review insurance coverage	Risk Control; Possible Risk Elimination; Risk Transfer
Potential liability for personal injury	Prohibit use of facility while under the influence; review and update membership agreement and usage policies	Risk Control; Risk Transfer
Increased costs to secure licenses and permits	Determine cost breakeven point between sales and licensing costs	Risk Retention
Increased labor costs	Determine options to use independent contractors to operate alcohol sales; limit sales to certain hours and use flexible staffing	Risk Transfer; Risk Retention
Increased inventory costs	Track beer and wine sales individually to calculate itemized profit projections	Risk Retention

must understand the importance of preventive law and implement these strategies in their areas of expertise. Making the organization better for all constituencies is at the heart of preventive law, so the preventive law plan should become a cornerstone of the operation. As a simple example, if the media personnel in your business do not understand their contributions to preventive law, they will not view their role as vital to this agenda – and if they are not engaged, you will likely fail to see the results you want in terms of ensuring your public statements consistently reflect your organization's values, are accurate and timely, and help to persuade or inform your constituents about important organizational actions and positions. This lack of engagement could lead to a press release that may be tone deaf or contain inaccurate information, or a coach's post-game interview excluding important viewpoints or resulting in controversial statements, which could lead to damage the reputation of the organization, loss of fan support, or other financial losses.

A preventive law program may include a range of components, all dependent on the type of organization and the nature of industry in which it functions (Prairie & Garfield, 2010), but central to most preventive law programs are the following important components:

- Developing unambiguous policies and efficient procedures
- Adopting fair complaint procedures and conducting thorough and reliable investigations
- Drafting clear and workable contracts and administering them consistently
- Designing effective training programs
- Creating a positive institutional image and managing media/public relations

Developing Unambiguous and Efficient Policies and Procedures

Implementation of the preventive law plan begins with the promulgation of effective policies and procedures, such as the protocol to follow in a medical emergency or the protocol for hiring coaches to ensure that they are competent and suitable for your organization. Throughout this text, each chapter will include competitive advantage strategies, which will be helpful as you develop policies and procedures for the legal issues discussed throughout the book. Good policies and procedures not only provide evidence that you are acting reasonably, but they also communicate to all your constituents your commitment and concern. These policies are communication mechanisms for ensuring that all of your organization's personnel are in alignment regarding their obligations and performance standards.

Policies and procedures also ensure fairness and consistency in the workplace. They provide guidance for managers and employees alike in dealing with a variety of possible legal issues. Keep in mind that people may be less likely to bring a claim against your organization if they perceive that you are trying to "do the right thing" in terms of safety and fairness.

Adopting Fair Complaint Procedures and Conducting Thorough and Reliable Investigations

Many sport organizations function in an educational context in the United States and are subject to significant regulation at the state and federal levels. These state and federal regulations often require schools and universities to adopt complaint procedures for students, provide a system to notify and inform students of their rights, and resolve disputes involving students. They also mandate non-discrimination policies and practices across a broad spectrum of activities. Additionally, schools and universities are required to conduct investigations in response to reports of sexual harassment or sexual violence. Their failure to conduct proper investigations is often the basis of claims against schools and universities. In Chapters 11 and 12, we will examine the authority and operations of interscholastic and intercollegiate sport organizations in detail. These procedures may be quite different than requirements used in other business sectors or non-profit sectors dealing primarily with employees but maintaining fair, clear, and consistent complaint procedures can help to avoid numerous claims by employees and also help to comply with federal labor and non-discrimination laws.

Competitive Advantage Strategies

Implementing Preventive Law

- Use the preventive law process as another opportunity to become more competitive in the marketplace.
- Develop the preventive law plan as an extension of your organization's core values and to enhance the experience of all your constituents.
- Do not use the strategy of eliminating activities to reduce risks, unless the risks of an activity greatly outweigh its benefits.
- Use all available risk transfer strategies, including insurance, the use of independent contractors, and contractual means, such as waivers and indemnification clauses.
- Make sure all employees understand and are involved in the development of the preventive law program.
- Allocate sufficient time and resources to the development of the preventive law plan so that employees understand how important it is to your organization.

Drafting Clear and Workable Contracts and Administering Them Consistently

One of the advantages in contract law is that, generally, you have adequate opportunity to conduct negotiations and work through several drafts of a contract in order to produce a document that protects your organization's interests. See Chapter 3 for a discussion of this process in terms of drafting a contract with the "worst case" scenario in mind. The point here is that you have adequate time to assess a contract: you do not have to rush into a contractual undertaking. In this area in particular, you can truly take a preventive law approach.

Be careful to draft contracts that are congruent with your business practice and values. For example, if you are concerned about possible injuries related to alcohol consumption by spectators, your contract with the alcohol concessionaire should ensure that the concessionaire trains employees properly, follows proper protocol in the service of patrons, and offers incentives for drivers to remain sober. Although standard contracts for many transactions are readily available in books and online, they often will not reflect the nuances of your business or particular aspects of your state's laws, and hence may do more harm than good. For example, if you copy a waiver form from a book, but it does not use the language relating to negligence required by your state, the document will not protect you. You should always consult an attorney to develop an effective waiver form for your organization (see Chapter 16 for an in-depth discussion of waivers).

Design Effective Training Programs

The best policies and procedures are useless if they are not reflected in organizational practice. Therefore, effective training programs in such areas as employment practices, inspection and maintenance of facilities, proper supervision and instruction in your programs, and protection of your intellectual property are essential to the implementation of a preventive law program.

All employees, regardless of position, should become aware of the necessity of using preventive law strategies in all their work efforts. Everyone has a responsibility to foster a safe environment and to be cognizant of areas that could pose personal or financial risk. Since your preventive law plan is inextricably tied to your organization's core values, it is important to explain to employees just how the preventive law process enhances those values. As mentioned earlier, we must have fair complaint procedures, but we also must have employees properly trained to follow and implement those procedures.

The increase in employment litigation has particularly emphasized the need for employers to take preventive steps which includes quality training programs related to harassment and discrimination (Chapters 5 and 6 examine discrimination and harassment in employment in detail): "Structured properly, employee training not only mitigates potential liability and eliminates punitive damage awards, but also adds value to an organization and can eliminate problems of harassment and discrimination before they become litigation issues" (McLaughlin & Merchasin, 2001, para. 10). Employees are more likely to follow policies and procedures if they understand the value of those policies and procedures for the organization.

Creating a Positive Institutional Image and Managing Media/Public Relations

Sport and recreation is an essential and important aspect of society with a significant impact on the local and national economy, as well as attracting vast media attention. Sport and recreation combined is roughly valued above $600 billion globally (Business Wire, 2019). As such, how we manage our institutional brand or image in the media can impact whether consumers purchase our products, participate in our programs, watch our events, or hire our services. When consumers buy a product or service they are not just buying a product or service, they are also buying what the organization stands for – that is, its brand and image. Thus, a preventive law plan must include marketing and media plans that identify our management objectives covering our communications with a broad range of constituents, including students, athletes, ticket holders, media, donors, investors, and community organizations. The media plan should distinguish the varied types of media in the sport and recreation industries – broadcast media, print media, and social media; and how these media outlets function in a digital environment. The media plan must also be prepared to handle negative publicity or a crisis. Similarly, our marketing strategies may include advertising, sales promotions, or other marketing tactics, all of which are subject to a variety of consumer protection regulations prohibiting false advertising or deceptive trade practices.

Conclusion

One of the underlying themes of this book is to tie managerial functions to legal theory in an effort to help managers in sport and recreation organizations make their businesses more competitive in the marketplace. Competitive advantage stems, in part, from making your organization a better one for all your constituents. A better organization is one that enhances safety and minimizes loss to the organization. A preventive law program should be an extension of your core values and should be proactive and holistic in identifying all possible exposures for your type of organization. After you identify, assess, and evaluate your possible exposures to loss, you will design and implement a prevention plan. This plan will focus on risk control as you implement strategies to minimize the risks identified. You must have an organizational commitment to the preventive law process. It is not something that can be done once and then forgotten. The cycle of risk identification, assessment, evaluation, plan design, and plan implementation is continual.

Discussion Questions

1 What is the difference between the traditional concept of risk management and preventive law?
2 What are the five steps of the preventive law process? Discuss each.
3 Why is the concept of risk control at the heart of the preventive law process?
4 Discuss the aspects of designing a prevention plan.
5 Explain the necessity for an ongoing plan to address risk in an organization.

Learning Activities

Using the key words "risk management" or "preventive law," conduct an Internet search to find policies and procedures of various sport organizations. Have the organizations adopted a holistic approach to identifying risk? Are there gaps in the risks identified? Does it appear that each organization's philosophy is to incorporate risk management/preventive law into its core values?

Case Study

Assume that you have just been hired as the general manager of a minor league baseball team. Numerous lawsuits have been brought against the team in the past, ranging from personal injury claims to contract disputes, even a trademark infringement suit. You are convinced of the value of preventive law in any organization and feel that you need to begin the process with your franchise as soon as possible. In view of what you have learned in this chapter, discuss the measures you would take to institute the preventive law process in your franchise.

References

Associated Press. (2019, July 30). Judge rejects lawsuit tied to Rams-Saints playoff game. The Orange County Register. Retrieved from https://www.ocregister.com/2019/07/30/judge-rejects-lawsuit-tied-to-rams-saints-playoff-game/.

Bagley, C. E. (2005). *Winning legally*. Boston, MA: Harvard Business School Press.

Bird, R. C. (2011). Law, strategy, and competitive advantage. *Connecticut Law Review*, 44, 61–97.

Boudway, I., & Novy-Williams, E. (2018, September 13). The NFL's very profitable existential crisis. *Bloomberg Businessweek*. Retrieved from https://www.bloomberg.com/news/features/2018-09-13/nfl-makes-more-money-than-ever-and-things-have-never-been-worse.

Business Wire (2019, May 14). Sports – $614 billion global market opportunities & strategies to 2022. Retrieved from https://www.businesswire.com/news/home/20190514005472/en/Sports–614-Billion-Global-Market-Opportunities.

Cozzillio, J., & Levinstein, M. S. (1997). *Sports law*. Durham, NC: Carolina Academic Press.

Gardiner, S. (1997). *Sports law*. London, England: Cavendish Pub.

Hanssen, J. (2005, February–March). Corporate culture and operational risk management. *Bank Accounting & Finance*, 18, 35–38.

Lazaroff, D. E. (2001). The influence of sports law on American jurisprudence. *Virginia Sports & Entertainment Law Journal*, 1, 2.

McCleary, S. (2017). Sued over sugar in jelly beans, Jelly Belly's response: "This is nonsense." *Legal Newsline*. Retrieved from https://legalnewsline.com/stories/511116629-sued-over-sugar-in-jelly-beans-jelly-belly-s-response-this-is-nonsense.

McLaughlin, E., & Merchasin, C. (2001, January 29). Training becomes important step to avoid liability. *The National Law Journal*. Retrieved from https://www.seyfarth.com/dir_docs/publications/AttorneyPubs/McLaughlin.pdf.

Mitten, M. J., & Opie, H. (2010). Sports law: Implications for the development of international, comparative, and national law and dispute resolution. *Tulsa Law Review*, 85, 269.

Mitten, M. J., Davis, T., Duru, N. J., & Osborne, B. (2020). *Sports law and regulation*. New York, NY: Wolters Kluwer.

New, J. (2015, June 12). Accrediting body places UNC on probation. *Inside Higher Ed*. Retrieved from https://www.insidehighered.com/quicktakes/2015/06/12/accrediting-body-places-unc-probation.

Prairie, M., & Garfield, T. (2010). *College and school law*. Chicago, IL: ABA Publishing, American Bar Association.

Schwartz, T. (2014, October 17). The N.F.L. as a toxic workplace. *The New York Times*. Retrieved from https://dealbook.nytimes.com/2014/10/17/the-n-f-l-as-a-toxic-workplace/.

Shropshire, K. (1998). Introduction: Sports law? *American Business Law Journal*, 35(2), 181–184.

Siedel, G. J. (2002). *Using the law for competitive advantage*. San Francisco: Jossey-Bass.

Siedel, G. J. (2010). Using proactive law for competitive advantage. *American Business Law Journal*, 47, 641–686.

Siedel, G., & Haapio, H. (2016). *Proactive law for managers: A hidden source of competitive advantage*. London, England: Routledge.

Taylor, S., Jr., & Thomas, E. (2003, December 15). Civil wars. *Newsweek*, 142, 42–53.

Triplett, M. (2019, September 6). Court spikes Saints fan's lawsuit on NFC champ. *ESPN.com*. Retrieved from https:// www.espn.com/nfl/story/_/id/27554483/court-spikes-saints-fan-lawsuit-nfc-champ.

Tsai, V. (2020). Woman sues Jelly Belly because jelly beans contain sugar. *Kahanelaw.com*. Retrieved from https://kahanel- aw.com/this-weeks-wacky-wednesday-woman-sues-jelly-belly-because-jelly-beans-contain-sugar/.

Turner, H. (2020, April 10). Wimbledon's pandemic insurance coverage results in $141M payment. *PropertyCasualty360*. Retrieved from https://www.propertycasualty360.com/2020/04/10/wimbledons-pandemic-insurance-cover- age-results-in-141m-payout/?slreturn=20200506140058.

2 The U.S. Legal System and Using Legal Resources

Introduction

This chapter is intended to provide the reader with a basic understanding of the American legal system, as well as a rudimentary foundation for conducting legal research and accessing legal information. If you have a solid grasp of these fundamentals, you will be in a position to converse intelligently with legal counsel should it become necessary, and you will be capable of exploring the legal ramifications of an issue when it presents itself. Nevertheless, when you are faced with a legal problem, it is prudent to rely on an attorney's advice and use your own more limited research abilities only to develop an informative base upon which to interact with your lawyer.

The U.S. Legal System

The legal system of the United States is based on the balance of power created by having three branches of government – the legislature, the executive, and the judiciary. Each of these three branches is a source of law, and each fulfills a designated role in maintaining our system of government by rule of law (see Exhibit 2.1).

A **constitution** is the foundational document that sets forth the basic operating principles of a government, including limits on governmental power. Each of the 50 states has its own constitution, which usually mirrors the federal Constitution in many of the protections provided to its citizens. **Statutes** are written laws created by legislatures, which are law-making bodies comprised of elected representatives. **Regulations** are rules that are created to operationalize statutes by providing more specific guidance. As you can see in Exhibit 2.1, the legislative branch is not alone in creating new law. The executive branch also establishes law by virtue of its control over administrative agencies which then promulgate regulations to aid in the enforcement of statutes. As enacted by a legislature, statutes are often "bare bones" and require regulations to flesh them out so that people know how the laws are meant to apply to real-world situations. For example, Title IX is one paragraph long, but the U.S. Department of Education is responsible for implementing regulations based on Title IX that fill several pages.

The courts may also create law when they render decisions that interpret existing laws as they apply to a particular case. This type of law is collectively known as **common law**, or **case law**. Nevertheless, creation of new law is not the primary function of the courts, since they must operate within the framework of the laws that already exist, in contrast to the legislatures that are elected to represent the will of the people in creating new laws.

The laws created by these three governmental branches, along with state and federal constitutions, are considered primary legal sources. That is, they *are* law and carry authority as such, in contrast to secondary sources (discussed later in this chapter), which are merely commentary on the law and hold only explanatory or persuasive value.

Exhibit 2.1 Relationship of law to branches of government.

Branch of Government	Legislative Branch	Executive Branch	Judicial Branch
Source of Law	Congress and state legislatures	President or governor, administrative agencies	Federal and state courts
Type of Law	Statutes	Executive orders, agency regulations	Case law/common law
Role of Branch	Enact new laws, amend existing laws	Enforce existing laws	Interpret Constitution and other existing laws

Structure and Functioning of the Judicial System

The courts are the ultimate arbiters of the law, because in the end the courts are where disputes about the appropriate application of all types of laws to real problems are resolved. So let's focus now on understanding the structure and functioning of the judicial system.

Because the United States is a federal union of many states, we have both a federal court system and a state court system. See Exhibit 2.2 below, which depicts the hierarchical nature of the judicial system, and also shows how our judicial structure is split into the two systems. The court system of the state of Idaho is used as an example in this exhibit.

Courts have differing **jurisdiction** – authority to hear a case – depending on the location and subject matter of the case. As a general rule, the federal courts assert jurisdiction only over federal law claims – **federal question jurisdiction**. These are claims that are based on the U.S. Constitution, or federal statutes or regulations. In addition to jurisdiction involving federal laws, federal cases may also arise in the sport industry based on what is called **diversity jurisdiction**. In diversity jurisdiction cases, the case involves a dispute between parties who are citizens of different states where the amount in controversy exceeds $75,000. In these types of disputes, a party may file the lawsuit in federal court and typically the federal court will be applying state law to resolve the controversy. An example of diversity jurisdiction is illustrated in our Focus Case presented later in this chapter, *Pitino v. Adidas America, Inc.* (2018). Coach Pitino brought state tort claims against Adidas, but since the dispute involved alleged damages in excess of $75,000, and Pitino and Adidas were citizens of different states, the federal district court in the Western District of Kentucky had diversity jurisdiction to hear the dispute. For the most part, though, federal courts will hear only federal law claims.

State courts can hear both state law and federal law claims, which is referred to as, **concurrent jurisdiction**. Sometimes it becomes a strategic decision for the attorneys involved as to whether to bring a federal claim in federal court or in state court. For example, federal cases often move more quickly than a state court case, but a jury in a state court case may award more generous verdicts than a federal jury.

In both federal and state court systems, the trial court is the lowest-level court in the hierarchy, with the appellate court as the next level up, and the highest court is usually called the supreme court and is the court of last resort. (This is not always true: the highest court in New York is called the New York Court of Appeals.) An adverse decision by a lower court may be appealed to the next higher court, but the highest court in each jurisdiction may select which cases it does and does not wish to review.

The U.S. Supreme Court is very selective about the cases it chooses to hear. Those who wish to take an appeal to the Supreme Court must petition the Court by requesting **certiorari**. A **denial of certiorari** simply means that the Supreme Court declines to hear the case and, having done so, allows the decision of the lower court to stand. The same is true when a state supreme court refuses to hear an appeal. This does

Exhibit 2.2 Court hierarchies – federal and Idaho.

	Federal Courts	State Courts
Highest court	U.S. Supreme Court	Idaho Supreme Court
Appellate court	U.S. Circuit Court of Appeals	Idaho Court of Appeals
Trial court	U.S. District Court	Idaho District Court

not mean that the higher court agrees with or is giving any endorsement to the lower court's decision; it means only that the court is choosing to hear cases that seem more important or urgent at that point in time. Cases that resulted in a split of opinion in several lower appellate courts might be viewed as requiring immediate ultimate resolution.

A case may be appealed only on grounds of a **legal error** – that is, an erroneous interpretation of the law or application of legal procedure by the lower court. The trial court is entrusted with finding the facts – determining the credibility of the witnesses and the evidence. For example, if a professional athlete was put on trial for murdering his partner, the issue of whether the athlete owned a weapon similar to the weapon used in the murder is a factual question for the jury to consider at the trial court level. The jury's conclusion on that issue would not be appealable. However, whether or not the trial court properly admitted his ownership records into evidence would be an evidentiary legal issue that could serve as grounds for appeal, if that evidence should have been excluded as a matter of law. In deciding such issues, appellate courts review the trial court's record and the appellate briefs filed by the parties' attorneys, and they hear the attorneys' oral arguments. They do not hear witness testimony or similar evidence; instead, they simply accept the outcomes of the fact-finding performed by trial courts.

An appellate court may choose to *affirm* the decision of the lower court, to *reverse* the decision (thus transforming the loser into the winner), or to *remand* the case back to the lower court with instructions for it to re-examine the facts in light of the appellate court's interpretation of the legal principles to be applied.

Anatomy of a Lawsuit

The judiciary is composed of civil courts and criminal courts. **Criminal courts** are where persons charged with a crime against the state are prosecuted. **Civil courts** hear cases that involve controversies of a noncriminal nature. Examples of **civil causes of action** (i.e., legal grounds upon which to sue) include contract disputes, employment discrimination, and torts. A **tort** is a civil wrong other than a breach of contract, usually referring to the causing of damage or harm to property, a person, a person's reputation (e.g., slander or negligence), or a person's commercial interests.

In a criminal case, the defendant has the right to a trial before a jury of his or her peers. Civil suits differ in that some are tried before a jury and some are heard by a judge with no jury. Criminal and civil courts also differ in the burden of proof required. In a criminal case, the prosecution must prove *guilt beyond a reasonable doubt*, or the jury is supposed to vote to acquit the defendant. In contrast, in a civil trial, the burden of proof is much lower. The plaintiff has only to prove his or her case by a *preponderance of the evidence*; that is, that his or her case is more likely than not to be true. Here the scales of justice merely move off center, whereas in a criminal trial one side of the scales must drop all the way down with the weighty assurance of guilt. The composition of juries will also vary depending upon whether a case is in state court or federal court. Most state courts require 12 jurors but permit less than a unanimous verdict depending on whether it is a criminal or civil case, while in federal court the jury can have as few as six jurors but require that their verdict be unanimous.

Most sport law cases are brought in civil court, although occasionally a criminal case will arise that involves sports gambling, bribery, or excessive violence.

For a step by step description of the civil (and criminal) trial processes, as well as more details of the anatomy of a lawsuit, see the website of the Oklahoma federal district court system (the link to their website can be found in the Web Resources section). Further, Exhibit 2.3 below outlines the process followed in a civil trial.

Exhibit 2.3 The civil trial process.

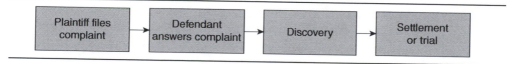

The following hypothetical example illustrates the civil trial process. Susan Spectator is injured in a 15-foot fall when the bridge she is crossing collapses as she and several other spectators follow their favorite professional golfer to the next hole. Susan then hires a tort lawyer with experience in negligence actions, who prepares a written **complaint** summarizing the allegations in Susan's case against the country club. This complaint includes a statement of the cause of action (negligence in this case), the remedy requested, and a brief summary of the facts supporting Susan's claim that the defendant is responsible for her injury.

Susan's complaint is filed with the court. The country club then files an answer to the complaint, admitting or denying each allegation. Alternatively, the country club's attorney can file a motion to dismiss the case, if it is clear that the plaintiff does not have a legitimate case. The judge assigned to the case then orders a period of discovery, during which the lawyers for both parties gather their evidence by such means as **depositions** (oral testimony obtained under oath from witnesses or the parties in the case) and **interrogatories** (answers written under oath to a list of written questions). For example, Susan's lawyer deposes the club's maintenance staff about the condition of the bridge and requests maintenance records to ascertain whether the club acted reasonably to keep the bridge in a safe state of repair.

Often, the results of discovery lead to an out-of-court settlement or to a successful motion for summary judgment (explained below), allowing all parties to avoid the time and expense of a full trial. If, however, a sufficient controversy remains after discovery is complete, then plaintiff Susan will pursue the matter through a full **trial on the merits**, which means that the issues will be fully argued and a final decision reached. If the country club is found to have been negligent in maintaining the bridge or in regulating the traffic flow based on the bridge's weight-bearing capacity, Susan will win her case and be awarded compensatory damages for her injury. **Compensatory damages** are monetary payments for actual injury or economic loss, and may include compensation for such things as medical expenses or property damage. If the country club is found grossly negligent, the court may award punitive damages. **Punitive damages** are payment of an amount beyond that required to compensate for a victim's injuries; the additional damages award is intended to punish the defendant for their grossly negligent or intentional misconduct.

Means of Concluding a Lawsuit

You will encounter three common ways of concluding a trial, other than a decision on the full merits of the case:

1 Rule 12(b)(6) motion to dismiss for failure to state a claim upon which relief can be granted.
2 Motion for summary judgment.
3 Petition for a preliminary injunction.

When a court grants any of these, the case to that point cannot carry any precedential value, because it has not received a full trial on the merits. For researchers, one value of such cases is their ability to shed light on how the courts might reason about the issue involved if the issue ever did reach a full trial. For example, recall the Saints lawsuit against the National Football League (NFL) from Chapter 1. That case was dismissed within just a few months of its filing, which could send a fairly strong signal to other fans, leagues, and teams that these lawsuits do not have much merit and we likely do not need to take immediate steps to modify our policies or practices to avoid future litigation, although the NFL did adopt new replay policies as part of its commitment to improve the replay system. However, had that case "survived" a motion to dismiss (see below) and instead been resolved on a motion for summary judgment it should serve as a greater warning and potential risk. The fact that the plaintiff was able to present a strong enough case to conduct discovery and prepare the case for trial suggests it was a viable claim and a claim that could potentially be raised against our organization if we were in a similar situation. It is useful as a sport manager to recognize the "stage" at which a case has been resolved to gain insight into how relevant the decision could be to her organization.

Motion to Dismiss for Failure to State a Claim

A motion to dismiss for failure to state a claim will be granted only when, even though all the plaintiff's factual allegations are accepted as true, the plaintiff fails to allege sufficiently a set of facts that would support a claim for relief based on the law invoked. For example, in *Pryor v. NCAA* (2002), the Third Circuit denied the motion of the National Collegiate Athletic Association (NCCA) to dismiss the plaintiff's Title VI claim because the plaintiff had alleged sufficient facts indicating that the NCAA might have engaged in intentional race discrimination in raising the initial eligibility standards when it adopted Proposition 16.

In contrast, in *Hispanic College Fund, Inc. v. NCAA* (2005), the Indiana Court of Appeals affirmed a trial court's granting of defendant NCAA's motion to dismiss. Plaintiff Hispanic College Fund (HCF) had filed a claim alleging that the NCAA acted arbitrarily and capriciously in creating a special rule that prohibited HCF from sponsoring an extra preseason college football game while allowing the Black Coaches Association to do so. Indiana law does not permit judicial review of the decisions of voluntary membership organizations absent fraud or other illegality. Because the HCF did not allege facts sufficient to show that its membership in the NCAA was not voluntary, nor any evidence of fraud or other illegality, the court affirmed the judgment of the lower court that no claim that the law recognizes as legitimate had been alleged in the complaint. Therefore, the lower court was correct in dismissing the case.

Motion for Summary Judgment

Summary judgment will be granted when there are no genuine issues of material fact, and thus the judge can decide the case without conducting a full trial by simply applying the law to the undisputed facts. For example, in *Mid-South Grizzlies v. National Football League* (1983), the facts were undisputed that the Grizzlies were a potentially successful football team in a rival league to the NFL, and that when they later sought to become a franchise in the NFL, but their request was denied. The court applied the law to those facts, finding that the NFL had not violated antitrust law in denying the Grizzlies' franchise request. Because the facts were not in dispute, the case did not have to go to a full trial for a determination as to which party's story was more credible. Instead, the court could grant the NFL's motion for summary judgment, because all it had to do was apply existing law to agreed-upon facts. (For more information, see the *Grizzlies* Focus Case in Chapter 10.)

Preliminary Injunction

A preliminary injunction will be granted when all of the following are true:

1 The plaintiff has a substantial likelihood of prevailing on the merits of the case.
2 The plaintiff will suffer irreparable injury if the preliminary injunction is not issued.
3 Issuing the injunction will not inflict a greater injury on the defendant than the one threatening the plaintiff.
4 The injunction will not have an adverse effect on the public interest.

For example, in *Johnson v. Florida High School Activities Association* (1995), the U.S. district court granted a preliminary injunction to order the Florida High School Activities Association (FHSAA) to allow a learning-disabled high school swimmer to compete during his senior year, even though he was 19 years old and in violation of the age limit rule. The reason included:

1 He was likely to prevail on his claim that denying him a waiver of the rule violated the Rehabilitation Act.
2 He would suffer irreparable injury if not allowed to compete during his final year of school.

3   Granting the waiver would not have significantly burdened the FHSAA.

4   Granting the waiver would have advanced the public interest in eliminating discrimination against individuals with disabilities.

Decision-Making Processes of the Courts

Courts must interpret statutes, regulations, constitutions, and common law (the law created by prior court decisions). In doing so, judges are supposed to act impartially. They attempt to follow certain guiding principles that restrain them from acting solely on the basis of personal philosophy, sympathy, or whim. It is important that you understand these principles so that you will be able to predict the outcome of cases related to your legal issues and so that you will be able to identify the pertinent facts that your lawyer will need.

Interpretation of Statutes

When construing a statute, a court will use certain time-honored maxims as tools of argument to guide and justify its interpretation. These are known as **canons of statutory construction**. Often, though, these canons contradict one another. In fact, two opposing canons are available for use in arguing most points of statutory interpretation. In an article now treated as a classic, one noted legal scholar compiled a selection of these competing canons and labeled them as "thrusts" and "parries" (Llewellyn, 1950).

An example is: "If the language is plain, it must be given effect." That is, it should be given a literal interpretation. A problem arises, though, when the statute is very old and a strict interpretation of the plain language would render an unjust result in light of contemporary circumstances. In this situation, another canon would be: "Do not give effect to the plain language if a literal interpretation would lead to an absurd result or thwart the obvious purpose of the statute."

For example, assume a federal statute passed in 1940 prohibits gambling activities conducted over the telephone wires. In more modern times, gambling activities might be conducted via wireless computer access. A literal interpretation of the statute might limit the legal prohibition to older technology, when in fact the probable intent of those who created that law was to prohibit easy access to gambling opportunities around the country – but they weren't aware at that time that future communications technology might not utilize telephone lines. A literal interpretation of the statute would lead to an absurd result (gambling using a wireless connection is legal, whereas it is prohibited if a telephone line is used) and would thwart the statute's obvious purpose.

Another type of problem arises when the statutory language is ambiguous and thus susceptible to differing reasonable interpretations. In such a case, a canon would indicate that the court must look to the original intent of the legislature to see what it had in mind when it enacted the statute. If the legislature thinks a court has misconstrued the legislative intent, it can pass a new statute amending the original law to assert its "true" intent. For example, Congress passed the Civil Rights Restoration Act of 1987 (CRRA) to correct the Supreme Court's misconstruction of the types of educational programs that Congress intended to count as recipients of federal funds under Title IX. The statutory language prohibited any educational "program or activity" that received federal funds from discriminating on the basis of sex. In *Grove City College v. Bell* (1984), the Supreme Court interpreted that language narrowly. The Court held that if a specific educational program did not receive federal funds, it need not comply with Title IX. In the CRRA, Congress said that the "program or activity" language was meant to be interpreted broadly, so that if any part of a university received federal funds, Title IX would apply to the entire educational program offered by that university.

Interpretation of Regulations

With regard to interpreting regulations issued by administrative agencies, the general rule is that courts will afford great deference to the interpretation made by the agency responsible for promulgating and enforcing those regulations. For example, courts have uniformly deferred to the U.S. Department of Education's Office for Civil Rights' policy interpretations when construing the athletics regulations that flesh out how Title IX should be applied to interscholastic and intercollegiate athletics. Sometimes, administrative agencies issue guidance documents, policy interpretations, and Dear Colleague Letters (such as the Dear Colleague Letters mentioned in Chapter 14 with regard to Title IX and athletics) that are intended as guidance for administrators and courts, and these may (or may not) be adopted by the courts and thus made "law" as part of case law decisions. The courts will tend to defer to these policy interpretations provided by the appropriate enforcing agencies.

Interpretation of Constitutions

The interpretation of a constitution, whether federal or state, is the particular responsibility of the courts – neither legislatures nor administrative agencies have any say about what a constitution might mean. Thus, court decisions interpreting constitutions are the final word on the subject. For example, the Establishment Clause in the First Amendment to the U.S. Constitution says that Congress shall pass no law respecting an establishment of religion. Based on the writings of the framers of the Constitution found in the Federalist Papers, we understand that they meant this clause to prohibit the establishment of a government-endorsed religion. However, the only interpretations of the Establishment Clause that have the authority of law – that is, that the courts will enforce – are the interpretations courts have handed down through the years as they decided cases in which that clause was implicated. Over time, the Supreme Court has interpreted that part of the First Amendment now means something close to the idea that the government should remain almost completely neutral with regard to religion.

Interpretation of Common Law

Common law is the body of case law that has developed over time as court decisions have been rendered and then relied upon in subsequent cases. Our common law legal system involves both a cumulative and an interpretive process.

Cumulative Process of the Common Law

The common law is cumulative in that it builds upon itself, adding layer after layer of case law to the edifice. Two guiding principles aid the cumulative process – *stare decisis* and binding precedent. *Stare decisis* means "let the decision stand." Under this principle, a court will usually refuse to change a ruling on an issue that has already been decided. This is common practice, as occasions when a court overrules a past decision are rare. For example, in 1972 the Supreme Court adhered to *stare decisis* in deciding not to overrule a 1922 Supreme Court decision, *Federal Baseball Club of Baltimore, Inc. v. National League of Professional Baseball Clubs*. The 1922 Court had ruled that professional baseball was not interstate commerce and hence not subject to antitrust laws. Although by 1972 pro baseball was obviously "big business" that crossed state lines, in *Flood v. Kuhn* (1972) the Court refused to violate *stare decisis* by overruling *Federal Baseball*, insisting that only Congress could eliminate the exemption from antitrust law for pro baseball that the earlier case had established.

The second guiding principle in the cumulative process of common law is the system of following binding precedent. There are actually two types of precedent – **binding precedent** and **persuasive precedent**. Within a given jurisdiction, the lower courts are bound by the precedent (or prior decisions) established by the courts above them. Decisions of the U.S. Supreme Court are binding precedent for all other courts in the land.

Competitive Advantage Strategies

The U.S. Legal System

- As you read or watch the news, pay attention to statements about the U.S. legal system and how it works. This is a good way to keep your memory fresh so you will feel comfortable when you apply your knowledge of the workings of the legal system to decision-making.
- If you face a legal problem and you are not certain you are interpreting it correctly, explain the facts to a trusted colleague and ask him or her to take a side and argue with you as if you both were lawyers making your best attempts to convince a judge of your position. This might assist you in clarifying some of the issues and determining whether you need to seek the counsel of an attorney.

To illustrate how this works, let's assume the Supreme Court of Washington state has decided that for Washington State University, dropping men's swimming is an appropriate way to correct gender imbalance in its athletics program under Title IX and does not constitute reverse discrimination against male athletes. All the lower courts in the state of Washington must now adhere to that ruling and cannot decide otherwise. If that same issue has not yet reached the Idaho Supreme Court, the Idaho Court of Appeals may choose to rely on the rationale of the Washington Supreme Court and adopt the same holding because it finds the Washington precedent *persuasive*. The Washington decision is not *binding* on the Idaho court because it was rendered in a different jurisdiction. The Washington decision may be persuasive, and indeed Idaho may adopt the same reasoning and reach the same conclusion as the Washington Supreme Court. But the Idaho Court of Appeals is only required to follow decisions rendered by the Idaho Supreme Court and the United States Supreme Court.

If the athletics director at the University of Idaho also then decides to drop men's swimming and is sued for reverse discrimination, she should be aware that, although the Idaho court may adopt the position and rationale of the Washington Supreme Court, this might not occur. Not being bound by law decided in another jurisdiction, the Idaho court might decide to find in favor of the male swimmers. The Idaho athletics director could have more confidence in persuasive precedent from other jurisdictions if a majority of those jurisdictions have decided the issue the same way. So, for example, if multiple states' Supreme Court rulings have made similar court rulings to that of Washington, the Idaho athletics director should feel safer with the legal ramifications of cutting the men's swimming program.

The combined effects of cumulative binding precedent and *stare decisis* lend uniformity, stability, and predictability to the law. The result is a society governed by the rule of law instead of the whimsy of whoever happens to be in power at a given moment in time. This system also enables individuals and businesses to make rational decisions about their actions with relative certainty about the legality of those actions, and it ensures that individuals residing in the same jurisdiction will receive similar and thus, fair treatment in the courts. However, the downside of a cumulative common law system is that the law changes slowly, and the changes that do occur depend on the happenstance of real-world problems occurring and finding their way into court. Legislatures can speed the process of change by enacting statutes purposively to address new issues. However, achieving legislative consensus on a complex or controversial issue can be difficult and time-consuming.

Interpretive Process of the Common Law

The saving grace of the common law system is that it is also an interpretive process. The law is made of words, and words are by nature subject to differing interpretations. The interpretive nature of judicial decision-making thus builds flexibility into case law. In fact, it is this interpretive space that lawyers manipulate when arguing a case on behalf of a client.

The lawyer uses two primary methods to persuade the court that her client's position should prevail. If past precedent is relevant and supportive of her case, the lawyer will *analogize*. That is, she will argue that the facts in her case are so similar to the facts in the prior cases that those earlier, supportive decisions should apply to her case, too. If, however, past cases are not supportive of her position, the lawyer will attempt to *distinguish* her case from those earlier cases by persuading the court of the significant factual and legal differences between them, thus justifying a different outcome in her case.

The result of this interpretive aspect of deciding case law is that a court can adapt existing law to situations that present a new twist on an issue. This flexibility is nevertheless constrained because the court must justify its decision based on the reasoned application of past cases. Thus, courts can adapt the law to social change, but they usually can only do so slowly. Again, this restrained flexibility contributes to legal and social stability.

Alternative Dispute Resolution

A lawsuit can be costly and time-consuming. It is not unusual for court costs and attorney's fees to add up to a significant amount of money, sometimes several hundred thousand dollars, especially if several preliminary motions are filed. The average civil lawsuit takes two years to conclude and may take as many as six to eight years to wind its way through the system if, for example, there are a full trial on the merits and one or two appeals or remands. The discovery phase alone can take several months to complete. In contrast, arbitrations generally are concluded in less than a year.

Alternative dispute resolution (ADR) methods for resolving legal conflicts may allow parties to avoid a trial. In choosing ADR, the parties opt for a private dispute resolution procedure instead of going to court. The most commonly used forms of ADR are arbitration and mediation. Other forms of ADR involve privately hiring ex-judges or ombudspersons (individuals appointed within organizations to settle disputes internally).

The American Arbitration Association (AAA) is a national not-for-profit educational organization dedicated to the resolution of disputes of all sorts through arbitration, mediation, and other forms of ADR. The AAA was formed in 1926, is headquartered in New York City, and has offices in cities throughout the United States. More information on arbitration and mediation can be found at the AAA website at www.adr.org. This site offers links to downloadable documents relevant to the arbitration of disputes arising in Olympic, collegiate, and professional sport. These documents are listed in the Web Resources section at the end of this chapter.

Arbitration vs. Mediation

It is important to distinguish between arbitration and mediation since, although both are forms of alternative dispute resolution, they work in very different ways. **Arbitration** involves submission of a dispute to a neutral decision-maker for *final and binding resolution*. Arbitrators affiliated with the AAA are trained to ensure that appropriate due process protections are observed throughout the arbitration process. Additionally, the arbitrator is granted the authority to award any relief that would have been available had the matter gone to court. **Mediation** is submission of a dispute to an impartial mediator, who assists the parties in *negotiating a settlement of the dispute*. The mediator facilitates joint discussions between disputing parties and may also hold separate meetings with each side and suggest possible grounds for settlement. However, the mediator does not have authority to force the parties to settle or to reach an agreement regarding the dispute. The mediator helps the parties to compromise and reach a mutually satisfactory settlement of the dispute. Therefore, parties that will have an ongoing relationship might prefer mediation over arbitration because they will be more likely to continue a positive working relationship after the dispute is resolved. If the mediation process is not working, the parties are free to abandon mediation at any time after the first meeting and pursue remedies in court. If a settlement is reached through mediation, it will be written up as an enforceable settlement contract.

Alternative Dispute Resolution in Sports

The past decade has seen an increased emphasis on using ADR to resolve sport disputes. For example, mediation is commonly used in federal court cases and was ordered in *Morgan v. U.S. Soccer Federation, Inc.* (2019) to attempt to resolve the lawsuit filed by several female national team players against the US Soccer Federation for alleged equal pay discrimination under the Equal Pay Act and intentional gender discrimination under Title VII. Mediation talks collapsed and the parties were unable to come to a resolution (Das, 2019). The players' case continued toward trial in the federal district court pursuant to their alleged claims. Ultimately, the federal district judge granted the federation's motion for summary judgment on the Equal Pay Act claim, but permitted the Title VII claim to continue to trial (Das, 2020). The players appealed the summary judgment in May 2020 and requested that the trial be postponed pending appeal (Hays, 2020). (Employment discrimination and harassment are discussed in Chapters 5 and 6.)

An agreement to arbitrate can appear in an individual contract with an athlete, in a collective bargaining agreement between a players association and an owners group, or in a particular sport organization's constitution and bylaws. Most professional players association rules now require that disputes between agents must be resolved through arbitration. In addition, challenges to league rules and salary disputes between professional athletes and their teams are also subject to arbitration under the league's collective-bargaining agreement. (Salary arbitration is discussed in detail in Chapter 7.) The U.S. Olympic and Paralympic Committee (USOPC) constitution and bylaws and the Ted Stevens Olympic and Amateur Sports Act require that arbitrations arising out of USOPC athletics grievances be administered in accordance with the Commercial Arbitration Rules of the AAA (AAA, "Commencing an arbitration"). (See also the AAA document "Athletes' Frequently Asked Questions for Olympic Movement Disputes Administered by the AAA" at www.adr.org.) The following **Focus Case** presents a challenge to an arbitration clause in a contract when a party also asserts claims based in tort.

Pitino v. Adidas America, Inc.

2018 U.S. Dist. LEXIS 137103 (*W.D. Ky.* 2018)	**FOCUS** CASE

FACTS

Former University of Louisville men's basketball coach Rick Pitino filed an action against Adidas America, Inc., asserting a single claim of outrage under Kentucky law. He alleged that Adidas knowingly or recklessly caused him emotional distress when its employees conspired to bribe University of Louisville basketball recruits, as detailed in a criminal complaint filed in the U.S. District Court for the Southern District of New York.

Adidas is the University of Louisville's athletic outfitter. In addition, the Endorsement Agreement between Pitino and Adidas provided that Pitino would endorse Adidas products and require the University's basketball coaching staff and players to wear only Adidas products during games, practices, and other team activities. In order to secure top basketball players for college programs with which it was associated, Adidas allegedly bribed recruits, including making arrangements for payments totaling $100,000 for one recruit to join the University of Louisville men's basketball team. Pitino asserted that he "now is publicly perceived as having participated or acquiesced in Adidas' actions" and has suffered "profound embarrassment, humiliation, and emotional injury" as a result of the company's "extreme and outrageous conduct." Adidas maintained that the Endorsement Agreement requires arbitration of Pitino's claim. It pointed to the Agreement's arbitration provision, which states:

> The parties agree that any dispute concerning the interpretation, construction or breach of this Agreement shall be submitted to a mediator agreed upon by the parties for nonbinding

confidential mediation at a mutually agreeable location…. If the parties fail to resolve their dispute through mediation, then the parties agree that the dispute shall be submitted to final and binding confidential arbitration before the American Arbitration Association in Portland, Oregon.

Adidas moved to dismiss the case. It argued that Pitino's claim is subject to mandatory arbitration under the parties' Endorsement Agreement.

HOLDING

Pitino's tort claims are arbitrable and subject to the arbitration clause in the Endorsement Agreement.

RATIONALE

Typically, the Court's inquiry when a party seeks to compel arbitration is whether the dispute is arbitrable meaning that (1) a valid agreement to arbitrate exists between the parties and (2) the specific dispute falls within the substantive scope of that agreement. Multiple courts, including the Eastern and Western Districts of Kentucky, have held that where the parties agree to arbitrate they provide a clear and unmistakable delegation of authority to the arbitrator to decide objections related to the scope or validity of the arbitration provision. To determine whether a particular claim or dispute falls within the scope of an arbitration agreement the court asks "if [the] action can be maintained without reference to the contract or relationship at issue" (NCR Corp., 512 F.3d at 814). If so, then the action is likely outside the scope of the arbitration agreement. But a party cannot avoid arbitration simply by renaming its claims so that they appear facially outside the scope of the arbitration agreement. In order to determine whether such renaming has occurred, a court must examine the underlying facts–when an otherwise arbitrable claim has simply been renamed or recast it will share the same factual basis as the arbitrable claim.

Here, the facts underlying Pitino's tort and contract claims are identical: both claims are based on Adidas's alleged bribing of a University of Louisville basketball recruit or his family. In the tort Complaint, Pitino alleges that "Adidas and its employees engaged in extreme and outrageous conduct by bribing a University of Louisville basketball recruit, or his family, to join the University of Louisville men's basketball team" and that Adidas breached its duties of good faith and fair dealing by conspiring with others to bribe the family of a University of Louisville basketball recruit.

Moreover, there is a "strong presumption in favor of arbitration," *Id.* at 813, and thus "any doubts concerning the scope of arbitrable issues should be resolved in favor of arbitration," particularly where–as here–the arbitration clause is broad. Given this standard and the shared factual basis between the claims, the Court finds that the claim asserted here is "at least *arguably* covered by" the Endorsement Agreement.

Pitino v. Adidas reinforces the strong policy favoring arbitration as a dispute resolution mechanism for contract disputes and claims closely associated with the performance of the contract. Other disputes involving professional sports, including disputes over partnership proceeds, termination of sports executives, the sale or relocation of a franchise, and payments under executive or partnership agreements, are also frequently resolved through ADR, primarily arbitration. Nevertheless, many issues are tried in the courts. A basic understanding of the fundamentals of legal resources and information can help sport and recreation management professionals work effectively with their legal counsel if litigation occurs.

Legal Resources

This section describes the many resources available to the public for conducting research on legal issues. Legal resources can be either primary or secondary resources.

Primary Legal Resources

As discussed earlier, primary resources in law consist of what actually is the law — that is, what may be relied upon in a lawsuit. These include constitutions, statutes, regulations, and case (common) law.

Constitutions, Statutes, Regulations

The U.S. Constitution provides the framework for the federal government and protects the fundamental rights of all citizens. Its protections of fundamental rights are applicable to the conduct of state governments by virtue of the 14th Amendment (cited as U.S. CONST. amend. XIV). Each of the 50 states has its own constitution, which provides citizens with protections similar to those in the U.S. Constitution (constitutions are cited in the following format: N.Y. CONST. art. X, § x.).

Federal statutes are codified in a series of volumes known as the U.S. Code (cited U.S.C. § x (year)). The U.S. Code Annotated (U.S.C.A.) is another series of volumes reporting federal statutes, but adding annotations regarding courts' interpretations of certain provisions, legislative history, and so forth.

The statutes of each state are similarly codified and published. An example is the Revised Code of Washington (cited as *Wash. Rev. Code* § x (year)). Many of the bound publications of these statutes contain annotations that identify court decisions construing the various sections or provisions of each statute. Recent amendments to the statutes are printed as pamphlets and placed in pockets at the back of the hardbound volumes until the volumes undergo a completely new printing. These pamphlets are known as "pocket parts."

Federal regulations are first proposed in the *Federal Register* and when finalized are codified in the *Code of Federal Regulations* (cited as volume XX C.F.R. § x (year)). For example, the gender equity in athletics regulations that implement Title IX are found in 34 C.F.R. § 106.41 (2013). Each state has regulations promulgated by various state agencies, as well.

Court Decisions

You may wish to read court decisions on a legal issue facing your sport or recreation organization so that you can determine whether the facts are analogous to your situation and gain an understanding of the courts' rationale for deciding the cases as they did. Court decisions are published in case reporters, which exist for both federal and state court decisions. Public law libraries and libraries at law schools carry hard copies of collections of case reporters and almost all case decisions are readily available from internet based sources. Additional digital resources are also discussed later in this section. Exhibit 2.4 summarizes the citation abbreviations for case reporters for the federal courts.

As Exhibit 2.4 shows, U.S. Supreme Court decisions are reported in three different case reporters, of which the official reporter is *United States Supreme Court Reports*. The most readily available and easiest to use version is the *Supreme Court Reporter*, and the third option is the *Lawyer's Edition*. In addition, full-text versions of the Supreme Court's decisions are available at www.supremecourt.gov (see Web Resources).

State court decisions are reported in state case reporters, such as the *California Reporter*. Most law libraries do not carry state case reporters, preferring to save space by carrying only regional reporters, which report court decisions for all the states in a region. Exhibit 2.5 summarizes the regional reporters and the states they include.

Exhibit 2.4 Case reporters for federal courts.

Court	Reporters	Abbreviations
U.S. District Courts U.S. Courts of Appeals U.S. Supreme Court	Federal Supplement (1st, 2nd, & 3rd Series) Federal Reporter (1st, 2nd, & 3rd Series) U.S. Supreme Court Reports Supreme Court Reporter Lawyer's Edition (1st and 2nd Series)	F. Supp.; F. Supp. 2d; F. Supp. 3d F., F. 2d, and F. 3d U.S. S. Ct. L. Ed. and L. Ed. 2d

Exhibit 2.5 Regional case reporters of state court decisions.

Regional Case Reporter	Abbreviations	States Included
Atlantic Reporter	A. and A.2d	CT, DE, ME, MD, NH, NJ, PA, RI, VT
North Eastern Reporter	N.E. and N.E.2d	IL, IN, MA, NY, OH
North Western Reporter	N.W. and N.W.2d	IA, MI, MN, ND, NE, SD, WI
Pacific Reporter	P., P.2d, and P.3d	AK, AZ, CA, CO, HI, ID, KS, MT, NM, NV, OK, OR, UT, WA, WY
South Eastern Reporter	S.E. and S.E.2d	GA, NC, SC, VA, WV
Southern Reporter	So. and So.2d	AL, FL, LA, MS
South Western Reporter	S.W., S.W.2d, and S.W.3d	AR, KY, MO, TN, TX

All case reporters are referenced in the same manner: first the volume number, then the name of the reporter, then the page number on which the first page of a particular case begins, and then the abbreviated name of the court and the year of the decision in parentheses. For example, *DeFrantz v. United States Olympic Committee* is reported at 492 F. Supp. 1181 (D.D.C. 1980), which means that you can find the case in volume number 492 of the *Federal Supplement* on page 1181, and that the case was decided in 1980 by the U.S. District Court of the District of Columbia. For Supreme Court cases, the name of the Court is not included in the parenthetical because the name of the reporter indicates that a Supreme Court case is being cited – only Supreme Court decisions are reported in the Supreme Court case reporters.

Secondary Legal Resources

Secondary resources are sources that are not in themselves law but that offer insight into or interpretation of the law. Secondary resources should never be relied upon as legal authority. They include the following:

Law Dictionaries

Black's Law Dictionary provides definitions of legal terms, including Latin terms and phrases commonly used in the law.

Legal Encyclopedias

Corpus Juris Secundum (C.J.S.) and *American Jurisprudence* (Am. Jur.) are legal encyclopedias that work like standard encyclopedias by providing a topical summary of a legal issue and referring the reader to other resources. These are a good place to begin your research if you know very little about your topic.

Case Summaries

American Law Reports (A.L.R.) covers both state and federal court decisions, providing case summaries as well as annotations with case commentaries and references to related cases. It is useful when you want to use a specific case as a starting point for your research.

Restatements

The restatements of the law (e.g., the *Restatement [Third] of Torts*) are written by legal experts who provide comprehensive summaries of the law on a broad topic such as torts. They contain exhaustive explanations and examples of application. These are most useful to someone who already has a working familiarity with the relevant area of the law. Often courts will rely on the restatements as a highly persuasive authority – although still not law – because they are written by the foremost legal analysts in their areas of expertise.

Treatises and Hornbooks

Treatises and hornbooks are scholarly books written by expert legal scholars that provide an in-depth treatment of a legal topic. For example, *Prosser and Keeton on Torts* is considered one of the most definitive treatments of tort law ever written (Keeton, Dobbs, Keeton, & Owen, 1984). You might use a treatise such as this one if you seek comprehensive background knowledge on your topic. A treatise will contain extensive legal analysis and substantial references to other resources on the topic.

Law Reviews and Business Publications

Law reviews are scholarly journals published by law schools that contain articles written by law professors, practicing attorneys, and advanced law students. Some law reviews focus exclusively on sport, for example, the *Marquette Sports Law Review*. Articles in law reviews offer extensive analyses of narrow legal topics (e.g., the constitutionality of mass searches of sports spectators). They are a good place to start your research if your topic is a newly developing area of the law or if you already have a working familiarity with the general context of your specific topic. Some other academic journals focus on sport law, the *Journal of Legal Aspects of Sport* and the *American Business Law Journal* feature a number of articles on sport. A number of business publications also feature law sections such as the *National Recreation and Park Association* monthly magazine includes a law review section.

Digital Legal Resources

The availability and efficiency of Internet-based legal research have grown dramatically as using the Internet has become ubiquitous in our society. Researchers can now perform a great deal of their research by means of a computer or by even using their smartphones or tablets. Both primary and secondary sources are often readily available through a variety of electronic databases and digital resources. Although Internet-based sources may never completely replace a trip to the law library on campus, it would be hard to imagine a sport management student not being able to write a comprehensive legal research paper using sources that are all available electronically. In fact, with the exception of perhaps a legal dissertation, a student should be able to develop a comprehensive understanding of a legal topic area using electronic legal resources exclusively. Nexis Uni is provided through most college and university libraries' electronic databases and is a valuable research tool. It allows you to search top news; general news; company, industry, and market news; legal news; company financial information; law reviews; federal case law; the U.S. Code; and state legal resources. Nexis Uni also includes a feature which will Shepardize a case. *Shepard's* is a citation system for updating your cases to ensure that you are not relying on out-of-date or overruled law – an essential component of doing legal research. However, it is complex and bewildering until you master it, so you should seek the help of a law librarian for your first attempt. *Shepard's* lists cases that have cited previous cases, as well as cases that have interpreted specific provisions of statutes. It codes cases according to whether they have been questioned, criticized, followed, reversed, or overruled.

Law Blogs

Today, law blogs serve an important function when conducting legal research, because a growing number of credible and reputable legal authorities are providing insightful opinions, commentary, and legal analysis via that medium. For example, the SCOTUS blog tracks developments by the Supreme Court. Some legal commentators and scholars now publish their opinions first on their own blogs, providing current analysis of ongoing litigation or discussing new case law developments. Popular law blogs focused exclusively on sport, such as the Sports Law Blog, are a useful legal resource for tracking current legal developments, reviewing credible commentary about legal issues, and linking to additional resources related to legal developments. If used cautiously and properly, legal blogs are quite effective research tools.

Websites

Websites give you access to many legal resources and are especially valuable in the event that you do not have access to any of the electronic databases. The following is a sampling of law-related websites:

- Cornell Law School's Legal Information Institute site is searchable for federal statutes (U.S. Code), state statutes, and Federal Rules of Civil Procedure, as well as federal and state court decisions (www. law.cornell.edu).
- Two sites, www.findlaw.com and www.law.com, allow registered users to receive daily or weekly email updates on recent developments in topical areas such as sport law. The FindLaw database is searchable for federal and state law.
- The Gender Equity in Sports Project (University of Iowa) site is searchable for historical information on gender equity in sports (http://bailiwick.lib. uiowa.edu/ge/).
- Law Crawler – Legal Search is a comprehensive site for legal research (http://lawcrawler.biz.findlaw. com).
- The Library of Congress "Thomas" website is a comprehensive site for U.S. legislative materials and treaties (http://thomas.loc.gov/home/thomas.php).
- The Marquette Law School site provides links to various sport law journals and newsletters, which can be accessed at www.law.marquette.edu by highlighting the Sports Law Institute link and clicking on *Publications & Research*.
- The National Archives site is a useful online source for historical materials (www.archives.gov).
- The National Center for State Courts provides a listing of court websites (www.ncsc.org).
- The Sport & Recreation Law Association (SRLA) website offers membership information, including participation in an annual conference. (www.srlawebsite.com).
- The United States Patent & Trademark Office (USPTO) website is searchable for registered trademarks and service marks (www.uspto.gov).

Analyzing Legal Information

As you realize by now, a myriad of legal resources are available for use in researching information related to legal problems and issues. For a comprehensive discussion of legal research in sport management; See, Moorman & Grady's (2020) *Legal Research*. In Andrew, D., Pederson, P., & McEvoy (Eds.). Research Methods and Design in Sport Management. Champaign, IL: Human Kinetics. Legal research can be a never-ending maze in which you can waste much time, unless you start with a good research plan. This next section will introduce you to the basics of legal research and organizing legal information.

Legal Research Basics

Managers are perfectly capable of conducting legal research and using legal research to aid their understanding of the legal issues they face. Generally, you will want your research to flow as follows:

1. Identify the specific issue to be research.
2. Find the relevant law.
3. Read and summarize the relevant law.
4. Organize the information you have collected.

As you review these four stages in your research process, remember that this is not a linear process. By that we mean legal research tends to be more iterative requiring the researcher to move back and forth through the stages as the information becomes better understood and more applicable to the specific problem or issue facing the manager. The plan outlined below should help keep you focused as you move through these four stages.

Stage 1: Identify Your Issue

When you identify your issue or problem, the more specific you can be, the better able you will be to narrow the parameters of your search for the relevant law. One strategy is to assess the facts of your problem by placing them in the following categories:

- Parties
- Objects
- Places

- Basic issue of the case
- Defenses
- Relief desired

This process of categorizing the facts will often suggest the specific legal issues that need to be researched. For example, let's categorize the following set of facts:

"Big Mucky Muck the Giant Duck," the team mascot for the Seattle Ducks, was up in the stands entertaining the spectators with his antics, when one of the spectators seated on the third base line was hit in the face by a batted foul ball that he did not see coming because he was watching the Duck's antics. His eye socket was shattered, resulting in $25,000 in medical expenses.

- What are the legal issues involved here?
- **Parties**: injured spectator; stadium management
- **Objects**: mascot entertainer; batted foul ball
- **Place**: spectator at baseball game seated on third base line; jurisdiction in the state of Washington
- **Basic issue**: Is management potentially liable to spectators for negligence?
- **Possible defenses**: contributory negligence; assumption of risk
- **Relief sought**: damages for injury

After categorizing the facts in this way, we can identify some of the specific legal issues involved:

- Does stadium management owe a duty of care to baseball game spectators to protect them from batted foul balls?
- If so, can management defend itself by arguing that spectators assume the risks inherent in being a baseball game spectator?
- If so, does employment of a mascot who entertains in the stands create an enhanced risk to spectators that they do not assume as an inherent risk?
- If so, can the injured spectator recover damages for injury? If so, in what amount?
- How does this jurisdiction determine the amount of blame, and thus the amount of damages, for which the defendant is responsible?

Once you have identified some specific legal issues, a law librarian, law professor, or other legal expert can help you identify any relevant legal issues you may be unaware of and help you determine keywords, phrases, and legal terms of art that will increase the efficiency of your search for relevant law.

Stage 2: Find the Relevant Law

Approaches to finding the law that is relevant to your issue will vary depending upon your level of familiarity with that area of the law and your proficiency in legal research. For example, if you are fairly familiar with negligence law in the context of sport, you might go directly to an electronic database such as NEXIS UNI and immediately begin searching for relevant cases.

If you are unfamiliar with the topic, however, you might wish to gain some background knowledge to develop a context for understanding the specific legal issues involved. A legal encyclopedia can be a good place to start, or, if the issue is relatively new, reading a few recent law review articles will provide you with different analyses of your topic. Treatises or hornbooks may also be useful at this stage. Once you have acquired some comfort with the overall context, you can use A.L.R. to find relevant cases or the annotations (if you have a statutory issue) in the U.S. Code Annotated to find cases interpreting relevant statutory provisions.

You can also use the plain language search function of a computerized database such as NEXIS UNI to begin to find cases. For example, you might click on the link for "Cases," and then the link for "State Cases," and enter a particular jurisdiction of interest, say California. Then, using a natural language search, type first-level keywords, for example, "inherent risk," into the *Keyword Search Terms* box. This broad of a search will produce more than 2,000 results. So you can either narrow your search by searching within results using narrowing keywords, for example, "baseball mascot" or you could try your initial search again this time using some combination of search terms such as "inherent risk" AND "baseball" AND "mascot". This search will produce fewer than 20 results and a much more manageable number of cases to review to find a case dealing with your precise issue: *Lowe v. California League of Professional Baseball*, 1997 Cal. App. LEXIS 532 (Cal. Ct. App. 1997).

Stage 3: Read and Summarize the Relevant Law

Once you have collected the cases and other primary resources in Stage 2, you must read them carefully and evaluate them for their relevance to your issue. Evaluation of the relevance of cases is made much easier by briefing each case. A **case brief** is a succinct one- or two-page summary of a case that enables you to assess and compare it quickly with other cases. See Exhibit 2.6 for the key elements of a case brief.

Exhibit 2.6 Elements of a case brief.

Facts

Briefly describe (in a few paragraphs) the facts (background) of the case. This is usually described at the beginning of the case. What happened that brought this case to court? You don't have to repeat all the Facts, just the really pertinent facts that are relevant to the court's decision.

Issue. What is the court deciding in this case? The issue is usually one or two sentences, found in the middle of the case. The case often includes language such as "the issue before the court is.... " The issue is often stated in the form of a question but may also be posed as a "whether" statement.

- Example: Is a high school athletic association a place of public accommodation under Title III of the Americans with Disabilities Act (ADA)?
- Example: The issue is whether a high school athletic association is a place of public accommodation under Title III of the Americans with Disabilities Act (ADA).

Holding

What did the court decide? This is also known as the ruling of the court. It is usually **only a sentence** (or even just a few words) long and is usually the last sentence in the case. Ideally, this is just a positive restatement of the issue – it answers the question the court is deciding.

- Example: "Yes, a high school athletic association is a place of public accommodation subject to Title III of the ADA."

Rationale

Why did the court decide the way it did? What were the reasons for the court's decision? The court will usually look at statutes, Constitutions, and prior court precedents in describing its rationale. The *rationale is the most important part of the brief* because it explains WHY the decision/outcome was reached which enables you to determine whether the same reasoning use by the court in this decision will apply in other similar situations that arise later on. Remember, a case goes to a full trial only for an issue that has not yet been squarely resolved in prior cases, and the *reasoning* in prior cases that have precedential value is what the courts will use as they apply the existing law to your new issue. Understanding the rationale of the courts in the cases you have collected allows you to guess how a court is likely to view your attempt either to analogize or to distinguish your case from past precedent. When organizing or trying to understand the court's rationale, it may be helpful to break the rationale down using the following approach: **Rule, Application, Conclusion**.

Many of the **Focus Cases** you will read throughout this text will follow a similar format as well. As you read, take notes on cases cited in the case you are reading, and read those cases, too. Repeat this process until you find that you are turning up no new information and the sources are becoming repetitious, referring to the same legal principles and sources for support. At this point, you can feel reasonably sure that you have "closed the loop" and will not turn up any more relevant information.

Don't forget to search the law of jurisdictions other than your own to find persuasive precedent that may bolster your position. At this point, it would be a good idea, now that you have a grasp of the relevant law, to review all the primary sources you have found, refine the issue(s) of interest, and read or reread some law review articles or other secondary sources for their analytical perspectives.

As you read the rationale of an opinion, look for language that identifies what the court identifies as the relevant law or legal standard applicable to the facts surrounding the legal issues. Also note how it makes the arguments justifying its conclusions on those issues. See Exhibit 2.7 for an example of a concise case brief.

Competitive Advantage Strategies

Putting Basic Legal Strategies to Work

- If you are in doubt as to whether you need to seek legal advice, conducting some preliminary legal research on your issue should aid you in making that determination.
- Be careful not to apply the fruits of your legal research to a situation not germane to that body of law. Sometimes nonlawyers will attempt to extend a legal principle to a problem governed by a completely different area of the law because doing so appears logical from an untrained perspective. When in doubt, consult a lawyer instead of relying on your own conclusions.
- Use a preventive law approach and consider retaining a lawyer to assist in drafting contracts and policies, as well as risk management planning, for your sport or recreation organization. Such an approach can contribute to management success and increased profitability by helping to create and foster a safe and thus appealing business environment, and by helping you avoid costly litigation.
- A preventive approach depends on effective communication between a knowledgeable client and a lawyer. Be sure you have a working understanding of the basic legal issues facing your organization or event. To facilitate clear communication with your attorney, know what information is relevant to enable him or her to provide the best legal advice.

Stage 4: Organize Your Information

You are now ready to put your information into a format that will enable you to resolve your legal problem or formulate your position on your legal issue. You will want to summarize the facts related to your problem, explain the legal issues identified, discuss what law and legal standards are applicable to resolve this problem, and analyze whether and how the law will apply to your situation or problem. It can be a daunting task to organize all the general information, cases, statutes, legal commentary, and legal or academic journal articles, but it is necessary to do so if you are going to effectively answer your research question.

Conclusion

You now have an understanding of the U.S. legal system and are acquainted with the basics of how to use and access legal information. If your organization is confronted with a decision to make or policy to formulate that has legal ramifications, doing some research on specific relevant legal topics will give you a

Exhibit 2.7 Sample case brief.

E.M. v. House of Boom Ky, LLC

575 S.W.3d 656 (Ky. 2019)

FACTS

House of Boom is a for-profit trampoline park in Louisville, Ky. The plaintiff purchased a ticket for her 11-year old daughter. She also signed a release of liability releasing all claims by herself and her minor child. Her daughter was injured when another girl landed on her after jumping off a 3-foot edge. The mother sued on behalf of her daughter for the injury. House of Boom moved for summary judgment relying on the release signed by the mother.

Issue: Whether a parent has the authority to sign a pre-injury exculpatory agreement or waiver on behalf of her daughter who was injured by another child while participating in the activities sponsored by a for-profit company.

HOLDING

No, a parent does not have the authority to sign a pre-injury waiver on behalf of a minor child terminating the child's right to compensation for injuries sustained while participating in activities sponsored by a for-profit company.

RATIONALE

Rule: Pre-injury waivers are not *per se* invalid in the Commonwealth but are generally disfavored and are strictly construed against the parties relying on them. The general common law in Kentucky is that parents have no right to compromise or settle their child's cause of action or no right to enter contracts on behalf of their child absent special circumstances or valid public policy justifications.

Application: This case does not present any special circumstances that would support a change in the common law related to protection for for-profit entities from liability based on pre-injury waivers signed by parents. Further, House of Boom's stated policy concerns about post-injury settlement agreements is not applicable to this situation since the pre-injury waiver is treated with much more suspicion than a post-injury release. A pre-injury waiver may remove an important incentive for an entity to act with reasonable care; these clauses are generally unilaterally imposed without genuine bargaining. House of Booms second public policy argument was that the waiver encourages affordable recreational activities. However, the public policy in that situation is applicable to non-commercial entities, not for-profit entities. The same public policy that deals with voluntarily opening private property or school district's property to allow community use does not apply to commercial entities. A commercial entity has the ability to purchase insurance and spread the cost among customers. It also has the ability to train it employees and inspect its premises to protect itself from negligence. A child does not have the ability to protect themselves from the negligence of others within the confines of a commercial establishment. Permitting these kinds of waivers would serve as a disincentive for commercial establishments to take reasonable steps to avoid injuries.

Conclusion: Under the common law of this Commonwealth, a parent has no authority to enter into contracts on a child's behalf, and we find no relevant policy justification to abrogate the common law to permit enforcement of an exculpatory agreement between a for-profit entity and a parent of a minor child.

good sense of what your options are. Again, it is critically important that you remember that, if you are not a trained lawyer, you should rely on your research only for informational purposes. Once you are familiar with the legal issues relevant to your topic, you should seek out competent legal advice to make important policy decisions. A working knowledge of the legal issues you face will help you to work successfully with your lawyer in organizational planning, policy-making, and risk management. It should also make your sport or recreation organization more attractive to your clientele and help you avoid financial loss due to litigation that might have been avoided.

Discussion Questions

1   When the higher court in a given jurisdiction declines to hear an appeal, how does that affect the decision rendered at the level below?

2   In your own words, explain the difference between a motion for summary judgment and a motion to dismiss for failure to state a claim. What precedential value do decisions on these motions have?

3   In your own words, explain the difference between binding precedent and persuasive precedent.

4   What are the pros and cons of a common law legal system founded on the principles of *stare decisis* and binding precedent?

5   What is the difference between mediation and binding arbitration? Why might parties in a dispute choose alternative dispute resolution instead of litigating in court?

6   What is the difference between primary and secondary legal resources?

7   How would a manager faced with a potential legal problem benefit from conducting some legal research and reading some relevant cases?

Learning Activities

1   Using NEXIS UNI or a similar online database, find a case on a sport law topic assigned by your professor and write a case brief summarizing it.

2   Consider the following sample statute:

NO VEHICLES ALLOWED IN CITY PARKS (Pullburg City Ordinance 1234.5(6)(a))

- What is the plain meaning of this statute?
- Does it apply to Tonka dump trucks? Bicycles? Baby strollers? Skateboards? Motorized scooters? Motorized wheelchairs? Emergency vehicles? Medi-vac helicopters?
- Is the statute more ambiguous than you initially thought?
- What might have been the legislative intent behind the law?

This exercise illustrates the interpretive nature of the law. It also makes clear why we need administrative agencies to issue regulations containing clear definitions of key terms and courts to render rulings interpreting how statutes should be applied.

3   On the website of the National Center for State Courts (www.ncsc.org), find information on the state court structure and hierarchy for the state in which you reside.

Case Study

1   Consider the following list of imaginary binding case precedents in your jurisdiction. Use it to analogize or distinguish the "cases" listed below.

2009 – Discrimination against reds is not allowed.

2014 – It is acceptable to exclude squares.

2020 – Discrimination against greens is not allowed.

Case A: You feel you have been discriminated against because you are purple. How would your lawyer argue your case? What would the opposing lawyer argue?

Case B: You feel you have been discriminated against because you are a purple square. How would your lawyer argue your case? What would the opposing lawyer argue?

Case C: You feel you have been discriminated against because you are a triangle. How would your lawyer argue your case? What would the opposing lawyer argue?

Case D: You feel you have been discriminated against because you are a translucent sphere. How would your lawyer argue your case? What would the opposing lawyer argue?

2   Repeat the steps above, but make the following substitutions:

Native Americans for reds

Men for triangles

Black people for purples

Women for squares

Hispanic or Latinos for greens

Israeli Jews for translucents

Transgender persons for spheres

References

Cases

DeFrantz v. USOC, 492 F. Supp. 1181 (D.D.C. 1980).

E.M. v. House of Boom Ky, LLC 575 S.W.3d 656 (Ky. 2019).

Federal Baseball Club of Baltimore, Inc. v. National League of Professional Baseball Clubs, 259 U.S. 200 (1922).

Flood v. Kuhn, 407 U.S. 258 (1972).

Grove City College v. Bell, 465 U.S. 555 (1984).

Hispanic College Fund, Inc. v. NCAA, 826 N.E.2d 652 (Ind. App. 2005).

Johnson v. Florida High Sch. Activities Association, 899 F. Supp. 579 (M.D. Fla. 1995).

Lowe v. California League of Professional Baseball, 1997 Cal. App. LEXIS 532 (Cal. Ct. App. 1997).

Mid-South Grizzlies v. NFL, 720 F.2d 772 (3d Cir. 1983).

Morgan v. United States Soccer Federation, Inc., Case No. 2:19-cv-01717 (C.D. Calif., March 8, 2019).

Pryor v. NCAA, 288 F.3d 548 (3d Cir. 2002).

Statutes

Civil Rights Restoration Act of 1987, 102 Stat. 28 (1988).

Other Sources

American Arbitration Association. (n.d.). *Commencing an arbitration for Olympic Movement and sport doping disputes.* Retrieved from www.adr.org/aaa/ShowPDF?doc=ADRSTG_004200.

Das, A. (2019, August 14). Mediation talks between U.S. women's team and U.S Soccer break down. *New York Times.* Retrieved from https://www.nytimes.com/2019/08/14/sports/uswnt-mediation-us-soccer.html.

Das, A. (2020, May 1). U.S. women's soccer team equal pay demands are dismissed by judge. *New York Times.* Retrieved from https://www.nytimes.com/2020/05/01/sports/soccer/uswnt-equal-pay.html.

Hays, G. (2020, May 8). USWNT players file appeal against ruling that quashed equal pay claims. *ESPN.com.* Retrieved from https://www.espn.com/soccer/united-states-usaw/story/4093248/uswnt-players-file-appeal-against-ruling-that-quashed-equal-pay-claims.

Keeton, W. P., Dobbs, D. B., Keeton, R. E., & Owen, D. G. (1984). *Prosser and Keeton on torts* (5th ed.). St. Paul, MN: West Group.

Llewellyn, K. N. (1950). Remarks on the theory of appellate decision and the rules or canons about how statutes are to be construed. *Vanderbilt Law Review,* 3, 395–406.

Web Resources

www.adr.org ■ This website for the American Arbitration Association provides links to downloadable documents relevant to sport managers. Select Education & Resources, then FAQs, and use the search term "athlete" to access "Athletes' Frequently Asked Questions for Olympic Movement Disputes Administered by the AAA." Also under Education & Resources, selecting the link to ADR Resources and using the search term "athlete" will yield a list of the following documents: "Sports Arbitration, Including Olympic Athlete Disputes," "Commencing an Arbitration for Olympic Movement Disputes," "Olympic Athlete Eligibility, NGB Determination, and Doping Disputes: An Overview," and "Using ADR to Resolve Collegiate Professional and Sport Business Disputes." A search of Rules & Procedures using the search term "Olympic" will give you access to the AAA's rules for the arbitration of Olympic doping disputes ("American Arbitration Association Supplementary Procedures for the Arbitration of Olympic Sport Doping Disputes," amended May 1, 2009, by "AAA Supplementary Procedures for the Arbitration of Anti-doping Rules Violations Summary of Changes." (For the amending document, use the link to Rules Updates.)

www.ncsc.org ■ The website of the National Center for State Courts provides information on state court structures and hierarchies.

https://www.oknd.uscourts.gov/summary-trial-process ■ This website contains a sample of the summary trial process in the Oklahoma court system.

www.supremecourt.gov ■ The official site of the Supreme Court contains the full text of the court's case opinions.

Part II

Human Resource Management

Introduction to Human Resource Management

Managing human resources effectively is an essential component of gaining a competitive advantage in the world of sport and recreation. Highly motivated employees who are treated with respect and concern are at the core of any successful enterprise. Therefore, it is critical that you understand the legal concerns pertinent to hiring, supervising, disciplining, evaluating, and terminating employees. You also need to understand the legal issues relevant to working conditions and the legal landscape surrounding your interactions with a very important "human resource" – the athletes who participate in your setting.

If you perform any of the diverse responsibilities related to the management of human resources, you will encounter a number of legal issues. You and your organization can be much more successful if you possess a fundamental understanding of some of the legal areas implicated in the human resources management function of a sport or recreation organization.

Legal Principles and Human Resources Management

Many legal areas are implicated in human resource management. In Chapter 3 you will learn about employment relations issues, after an overview of contract law principles is given. Chapter 3 focuses primarily on contract law issues in employment, including the drafting of an employment contract and employment-at-will principles, but it also addresses some tort theories as they pertain to employment. Chapter 4 focuses on the liability a sport/recreation organization may have for the acts of its employees, volunteers, or independent contractors. Chapter 5 has an extensive review of employment discrimination law, including aspects of race, gender, age, and disability discrimination. Chapter 6 continues to focus on employment discrimination, addressing sexual harassment and issues related to employee expression. Chapter 7 addresses legal aspects of federal minimum wage laws and working conditions, including the Fair Labor Standards Act, workplace safety, and workers' compensation law. Chapter 8 provides the fundamentals of labor relations law and collective bargaining. Chapter 9 focuses on agency relationships and the law related to athlete agents.

All of the human resource issues described in these chapters will require you to be knowledgeable in a variety of legal theories so that you can make effective decisions in the workplace. The following chapters explore each of these areas and their application in sport and recreation organizations.

3 The Employment Relationship

Creation and Termination of Employment

Introduction

Human resource management refers to the systems that relate to how people are employed, managed, and developed in organizations. The term human resources should not refer to the people employed within an organization, but rather represents the resources intrinsic to human beings which they can apply to various life and organizational tasks (Armstrong & Taylor, 2020). Managing human resources effectively is an essential component of gaining a competitive advantage in the sport marketplace. Managers from the largest multinational corporations to the smallest local businesses claim that managing people effectively is vital to being competitive in today's marketplace (Percy, 2019). Highly motivated employees who are valued and engaged are integral to the success of any enterprise. Therefore, we discuss the legal issues pertaining to establishing employment relationships with employees as well as concerns related to termination of employees in sport organizations. Understanding the legal issues will enhance your ability to make wise managerial decisions that are well-founded on legal principles.

This chapter discusses important contract principles related to employment relations. To help you understand those principles, it gives an overview of contract law as a foundation. The chapter discusses the principle of employment at will, contract employment, explores the issue of termination in that context, and also illustrates these in the context of a college coaches employment agreement. Finally, this chapter introduces possible tort causes of action that are particularly applicable when recruiting new employees. Chapter 4 will further explore tort issues arising in the employment context. Exhibit 3.1 provides an overview of this chapter's managerial contexts, major legal issues, relevant law, and illustrative cases.

Overview of Contract Law

As we discussed in Chapter 1 with regard to risk management and preventative law, contract law is an excellent vehicle for using the law to gain a competitive advantage. Most contracts of any complexity are negotiated over a lengthy period of time, and there are usually multiple drafts before the final contract is signed. This means that you have more than adequate opportunity to reflect upon the agreement and to consult with your attorney in order to arrive at a document that will best serve your interests and clearly sets forth the scope of your agreement.

Contract law is, essentially, concerned with clarifying and enforcing the will of the parties in determining agreements. Courts are concerned with trying to give effect to the parties' intent; courts do not try to rewrite contracts to make a better document for the parties or to make sure that each party has the best deal possible.

Exhibit 3.1 Management contexts in which employee relations issues may arise, with relevant laws and cases.

Management Context	Major Legal Issues	Relevant Law	Illustrative Cases
Contract law principles	What are elements of a contract?	Contract law	Jean
Authority to sign contract	When is organization bound by employee?	Actual vs. apparent authority	Huyett
Hiring employees	Employment contract	Reassignment clause	Monson
	Rights of competitors	Covenant not to compete	Northeastern Univ.
Termination of contracts	Breach of contract	Perquisites	Rodgers
		Just cause termination	O'Brien
		Liquidated damages	Kent State
Employment references	Liability for accuracy of information	Negligent misrepresentation/ fraud	Randi W. Williams
Recruiting employees	Liability for interfering with existing contract	Tortious interference with contractual relations	Bauer

Formation of a Contract

A **contract** is "a promise, or set of promises, for breach of which the law gives a remedy, or the performance of which the law in some way recognizes a duty" (Restatement [Second] of Contracts, 1981, § 1). The formation of a contract has four fundamental aspects: (1) agreement – offer and acceptance; (2) consideration; (3) capacity; and (4) legality.

Agreement – Offer and Acceptance

The formation of a contract begins with an **offer**, which is a conditional promise made to do or to refrain from doing something. The person making the offer is known as the **offeror**; and the person to whom the offer is being made is the **offeree**. For example, I may offer to sell you a certain piece of fitness equipment for $700. I have identified the terms of the offer; you know what piece of equipment we are discussing, and you know the price. I have communicated the offer to you. I am the offeror and you are the offeree.

If you agree to the terms as stated, you have given an **acceptance**, which is your unconditional assent or agreement to the terms of my offer. You have promised to pay me $700 for the fitness equipment. If you do not mirror the offer with your acceptance, you may become the offeror of a **counteroffer**. For example, if your response is that you want the equipment but will pay only $500, you are effectively rejecting my initial offer and making a counteroffer to me based on a price of $500. At this point, you have become the offeror and I am now the offeree. If I agree to the reduced price, I have accepted your counteroffer.

Consideration

Consideration involves the exchange of value. Both parties must be exchanging something of value for a valid agreement to be formed. One party gives up something of value in exchange for the other party's value. The exchange can be anything of value such as money for property or services; services for services, property for property, or a promise to provide money, property, or services.

If I promise to pay you $500 and ask for nothing in exchange, there is no contract. All we have is an unenforceable promise to make a gift to you of $500. However, if I agree to pay you $500 for a bicycle you own there is consideration (exchange of money for property). Generally, the courts do not inquire as to whether the value or consideration was too little or too much. Since, as discussed above, a basic premise of contract law is to allow private parties to engage in transactions of their own making, courts will not generally intervene to stop a bad deal from taking place. Let's assume that your bicycle was in very poor condition and I made a bad choice to pay $500 for it. However, I did so of my own volition and without any misrepresentations on your part about the condition of the bicycle. In this instance, the court would enforce the agreement even though I made a bad decision in purchasing the bicycle. Sometimes we may make good deals and other times we may make bad deals; it is not the prerogative of the courts to be intermediaries in the deals we make, only to ascertain that the law is followed.

Capacity

Capacity means the legal competence of the parties to the contract to enter into a contractual relationship. For example, minors are usually not bound by contracts, since the law makes a presumption that a minor lacks the legal competence (capacity) to enter into contracts. Thus, if a minor signs a contract, it is generally voidable at the option of the minor. That is, a minor can set aside a contract and the legal obligations stemming from that contract. We will elaborate upon this concept in conjunction with the discussions of waivers in Chapter 16. Other circumstances may also affect competence such as mental incompetence or intoxication which may also result in a lack of capacity. Lastly, when dealing with organizations and companies, the parties negotiating on behalf of the company or organization must have sufficient authority to bind the company to any resulting agreement.

Legality

Legality means that, to be enforceable, the subject matter of the contract must not violate state or federal law. A contract whose terms require the violation of law would be unenforceable. For example, since gambling is illegal in most places in the United States, a gambling contract in a location where gambling is illegal would not be enforceable. The Focus Case below illustrates the element of consideration and the element of capacity when entering into agreements with minors and agents.

Jean v. Francois

| *Case No. CACE19-002954*, Broward County, FL (2019) | **FOCUS** CASE |

FACTS

The plaintiff, Christophe Jean, entered into a contract with Leonard Francois on behalf of Mari Osaka and Naomi Osaka on March 21, 2012. Francois is the father of and agent for his daughters, who were pursuing professional tennis careers. On the date of the contract, the Osaka sisters were 14 and 15 years old, respectively. According to the terms of the contract, the "parties agree on a fixed fee of twenty percent (20%) on every tennis contract or monetary agreement on behalf of Marie (sic) Osaka and Naomi Osaka." The contract does not specify what, if any services, the plaintiff agreed to provide to the defendants. The contract further specified that the term of employment was indefinite and that either party could terminate with three months' notice in writing. The plaintiff alleges he performed services for five years under the contract and has not been compensated and has not received any income from the Osaka sisters' prize monies or endorsement deals. He sued the defendants for breach of contract. The defendants filed a motion to dismiss the complaint.

HOLDING

The Florida state district court granted the defendants' motion to dismiss.

RATIONALE

In order to succeed on a breach of contract claim there must be an enforceable contract. It is well-settled that contracts with minors are voidable and the minor has the right to disavow a contract because of minority. Mari and Naomi Osaka were 14 and 15 years old at the time of the alleged contract, and they have disavowed the contract. Even if the plaintiff has desired to validate the contract via court approval under Florida state law (Child Performer and Athlete Protection Act, § 743.08(3), Fla. Stat.) which permits court approval of artistic, creative, or professional sports contracts with minors, the law limits the terms of such contracts to three years. Here the term of the contract was indefinite and plaintiff never submitted the contract for court approval.

Additionally, under the law of Florida there are several basic requirements of a valid contract: offer, acceptance, consideration, and sufficient specification of essential terms. Consideration is the primary element moving the execution of the contract and absolutely necessary to the forming of a good contract. Put simply, absent consideration, there is no contract and never was. The subject contract reveals that it fails to set forth any consideration on behalf of the plaintiff. The contract is silent as to what, if any, obligation the plaintiff had under the contract.

Finally, any claim separately brought against the defendant, Francois, fails because he was acting in his capacity as an agent for his daughters. An agent signing in a representative capacity generally does not bind the signing party individually. Florida law imposes no personal liability on one signing in a representative capacity except in the rare circumstances where there is an express agreement to the contrary. Because no court ever approved the contract and Naomi and Mari Osaka, who were minors, have disavowed said contract, the court holds that the subject contract is not valid or enforceable.

Interpretation and Enforcement of Contracts

Canons of Interpretation

Because of this underlying philosophy of contract law, you should understand a few basic principles about how courts interpret contracts, called the **canons of interpretation** (see Exhibit 3.2). First, the courts try to interpret a contract as an integrated whole. This means that the courts always try to interpret a contract in a way that makes sense for the entire contract. The court reads sections of the contract together in an attempt to discover if there is cohesion throughout the document. Clauses of the document are tied together, sometimes in very complex ways, and the document should reflect agreement in all its parts.

Another canon of interpretation is that, in the event of ambiguity, a document will be interpreted most strictly against the party that drafted the document. What does this mean for you? It means that if you are the party that has the advantage of actually drafting the document, you need to make sure that the contract is very clear in its meaning. If there is ambiguity in the document you (or your attorney) have drafted, that ambiguity may lead to the court's favoring the other party when it tries to resolve the ambiguity.

Whenever you begin a negotiation or start to draft a document, you should always take the perspective of the **worst-case scenario**. Contracts are simply reflections of human understandings, and, as with all relationships, sometimes the relationship may deteriorate. Consider the hiring of a college coach, for example, when a coach is hired, generally everyone is excited about the prospect of new leadership in a program. The last thing that most people would think about is the dissolution of this partnership. However, the reality is that coaching contracts are breached frequently, either by a college that wants to move a program in a new direction or by a coach who seeks greener pastures. Therefore, the coaching contract must be written with the worst-case scenario in mind. The contract should be drafted to protect your organization's interests in the event the contract is terminated, either by you or by the other party.

Exhibit 3.2 Canons of interpretation of contract law.

1 The courts interpret a contract as an integrated whole.
2 The courts interpret a contract most strictly against the party that drafted the document, in the event of ambiguity.

Oral Contracts

If a contract has the elements of offer, acceptance, and consideration; the parties have capacity to enter into the agreement; and the subject matter is legal, must the contract be in writing to be enforceable? Generally speaking, oral contracts are enforceable, but the parties may have some difficulty establishing the terms of the contract, since there is nothing in writing. As good managerial practice, regardless of what the law permits, you should put every contract in writing.

Under certain circumstances, the courts will not enforce oral contracts. States have statutes known as the **statutes of frauds**, which require certain types of contracts to be in writing. For our purposes in sport or recreation settings, the following types of transactions must be in writing:

- Agreements for the sale of land or an interest in land.
- Contracts for the sale of goods priced at $500 or more.
- Contracts that cannot be performed within one year of the formation of the contract (Cross & Miller, 2018).

The sport and recreation industry has many common agreements that are required to be in writing in order to be enforceable. For example, a stadium lease agreement would fall under the first category of transaction. Purchasing team uniforms costing $500 or more exemplifies the second type. Finally, a game contract signed in 2021 for a game to be played in the year 2023 would be a contract that could not be performed within one year and thus must be in writing to be enforceable.

Disparity of Bargaining Power

In some situations, courts will find that a contract may violate notions of public policy and refuse to enforce the contract. See Chapter 16 for a discussion of public policy concerns and waivers. Another reason why some contracts are unenforceable is that an unconscionable **disparity of bargaining power** exists between the parties. The difference in power forces the signer to agree to the terms of the contract as dictated by the other party. There is no bargaining about the terms of the contract; the contract is written exclusively by one party, and the other party is forced to accept those terms in order to go forward with the transaction.

We have focused on the quasi-contractual remedy that may exist in certain situations in which a coach promises something to a prospective student-athlete that induces that athlete to attend the university. In most situations, however, student-athletes are confined to contract remedies based on the documents signed. One of these documents is the **National Letter of Intent** (NLI), which is an agreement between the institution and the prospect that the prospect will attend that institution full-time for one year and will be provided with a financial aid award ("About the National Letter of Intent," 2018). See the website www.nationalletter.org for more information about the program. Once the NLI is signed, the recruiting process stops, and no other schools are entitled to make contact with that recruit.

Some commentators have asserted, however, that the NLI exemplifies a disparity of bargaining power in collegiate athletics (Aragon & Miller, 2017). This is so, argue Aragon and Miller, because the prospective athlete cannot negotiate, in any way, to alter the content of the standardized NLI form, which does not incorporate any of the representations that a coach may have made during the recruiting process pertaining to playing time and other matters. Aragon and Miller contest that the NLI is not a contract itself, is not required for prospective student-athletes to compete at the intercollegiate level, and therefore advise young athletes not to sign them. The commentators believe that the most egregious issue pertains to the departure of a coach. The NLI is signed with an institution, not a coach. Therefore, if the coach leaves after a student has signed the NLI, that is not grounds for the student-athlete to void the agreement.

Aragon and Miller (2017) further argue that this is blatantly unfair, since the reality is that most athletes choose to attend an institution based on the coach, not on the institution itself. They suggest a reform of the NLI program, including revising the provision on coaching changes. They recommend that institutions and the National Collegiate Athletic Association (NCAA) should emphasize that the document is not a requirement and that the length of the one-year term of the NLI should be decreased.

Limitations on Authority to Contract

We introduced the concept of agents acting in a representative capacity earlier with regard to whether the essential element of contract formation, "capacity," was present. Organizations can act only through their representatives, who are often employees of the organization. For the purposes of agency law, the organization is characterized as the **principal** and the person acting on behalf of the principal is the **agent** (see Chapter 8). Related to the concept of capacity is the scope of authority of agents. For example, does the agent have authority to enter into agreements, and how much authority does the agent have to bind the principal.

The scope of authority of agents and types of agency agreements are more fully explored in Chapter 8, but we do want to briefly explore issues related to when agents have a scope of authority to bind the organization contractually. Agents have **actual authority** to engage in certain transactions. This means that the principal has conveyed to the agent what his limits of authority may be. The concept of **apparent authority** means that the principal has somehow conveyed to a third party that the agent has authority to act, even though the agent does not have actual authority. The hypothetical case below illustrates these principles.

Considering ... Apparent Authority

The manager (agent) at a sporting goods store (principal) has actual authority to make contracts up to a value of $15,000. This actual authority has been conveyed in writing to the manager. The manager, however, has entered into several transactions with vendors for amounts in excess of $15,000, and the store owners have taken no action against the manager for violating his actual authority.

The manager purchases equipment for $25,000 from a vendor with whom he has exceeded $15,000 before. The store owners now want to void the agreement.

Question

- How can the third-party vendor argue that the store owners should be bound by the agreement even though the manager violated his scope of actual authority?

Note how you would answer the question and then check your response using the Analysis & Discussion at the end of this chapter.

In the next case, an employee unsuccessfully argued that the state board of education should be bound by actions taken by the university president as an agent of the state board. Here, the court found that no actual or apparent authority existed.

Huyett v. Idaho State University

104 P.3d 946 (Idaho 2004)   **FOCUS** CASE

FACTS

Shirley Huyett was hired as the head women's basketball coach at Idaho State University (ISU) by the ISU President, Howard Gauthier, on June 29, 2001. It was a one-year contract. Huyett wanted a multiyear contract, and after Huyett began work at ISU, Gauthier made some vague references to the possibility of this.

During her one-year employment term, Huyett and ISU engaged in negotiations for a multiyear contract. ISU prepared a draft of a three-year employment contract but rescinded the draft before either party signed it. Huyett was placed on administrative leave, and she filed suit for breach of an express or implied contract for multiyear employment. The trial court entered summary judgment for the university, and Huyett appealed.

HOLDING

The Idaho Supreme Court affirmed, as it held that the state university did not have actual or apparent authority to enter into a multiyear employment contract with Huyett.

RATIONALE

In this case, the Idaho Board of Education is the principal and carries the authority to approve all employment contracts. The university and its employees are agents of the board. According to the policy and procedures of the board, no multiyear employment contracts are valid unless they have been approved by the board.

The ISU did not have actual or apparent authority to enter into a multiyear agreement with Huyett. University presidents are given authority only to negotiate contracts but not to bind the board. Apparent authority is based upon representations from a principal to a third party, and the board never indicated that the draft contract for multiple years was anything but a draft.

Contract Remedies for Breach of Contract

When one party fails to perform essential aspects of a contract, this is termed a **breach of contract**. Sometimes the breach may be remediable, but often the contract is terminated and the nonbreaching party is awarded the damages sustained as a result of the breach. In a contract case, the court is not attempting to punish the party that breached the contract; it is simply trying to compensate the innocent party for the loss of the bargain. Essentially, **contract damages** are designed to put nonbreaching parties in the position they would have held if the contract had been performed as promised (Restatement [Second] of Contracts, § 347, 1981).

Compensatory Damages

In most contract cases, the nonbreaching party can be compensated for the loss of the bargain through monetary or compensatory damages. These damages arise directly from the loss of the bargain.

For example, let's assume a sporting goods store agrees to sell X a football helmet for $125. X agrees to buy the helmet for that price, but the store now refuses to sell X the promised good. The store is in breach of the contract, and X still needs to obtain the helmet. X goes to the two other stores in the area that sell that model of helmet and finds that Store A is selling the helmet for $135 and Store B is selling the helmet for $150. What damages can X recover?

First, the general rule in a breach of a sales contract is that the buyer can recover the amount equal to the difference between the contract price and the market price. In this case, however, there are two market prices, $135 and $150, for the same item. So can X recover $25 ($150 market price from Store B minus $125 contract price), or can X recover only $10 ($135 market price from Store A minus $125 contract price)? Assuming that the item is identical, X's damages are limited to $10. According to the principle of **mitigation of damages**, a nonbreaching party must act reasonably to lessen the consequences of the breach. In this case, that would mean that X must choose to buy the item for the lesser price of $135 ($10 damages). This obligation to reduce the damages, if possible, is not absolute. X only has to act reasonably; it is not necessary to get bids on this helmet from every vendor in the United States, or to drive to another city where a vendor has a better price. X is only required to deal with the vendors X usually has dealt with for this type of equipment. The principle of mitigation of damages applies to all types of contracts, but it may be more difficult to implement than in the example just given. This principle in the context of college coaches' employment agreements will be discussed more fully in the next section.

Specific Performance

In certain rare circumstances, monetary damages will not suffice because the object of the contract is unique. If an item is unique, no matter what a breaching party pays, money damages will not compensate for the loss of the bargain, because the item cannot be purchased on the open market. For example, suppose you agree to sell me a Michael Jordan jersey worn during his final season game against the Washington Wizards. There is no other jersey worn by Michael Jordan on that date; it is unique. I agree to buy the jersey for $30,000. If you then breach the contract, money damages will not help me, because that item cannot be obtained elsewhere. **Specific performance**, that is, compelling a party to fulfill the terms of a contract, is the appropriate remedy, because that will force you to sell me the jersey for $30,000.

This remedy cannot be used with personal services contracts, however. If you owned the Los Angeles Lakers and LeBron James wanted to breach his employment contract with your franchise, you could not force LeBron to play for you by arguing that specific performance (playing) was necessary. Courts will not force people to compete or work against their will. Moreover, how would you ascertain that LeBron's performance was acceptable? He may be on the floor, but how could you enforce a quality performance?

Liquidated Damages and Penalty Provisions

Liquidated damages are an agreed upon amount of money to be paid in lieu of actual damages in the event of a breach of contract. Sometimes the proper amount of damages cannot be determined exactly. Although contract damages cannot be mere speculation, sometimes parties have to approximate the amount of damages that will be sustained. Employment contracts often have a **liquidated damages** provision because the parties would not be able to determine the amount of a breach exactly. The parties, therefore, agree to a liquidated damages provision that sets up the reasonable approximation of damages. These provisions are relatively common place in college coaches' contracts and later in this chapter you will study the case of *Kent State University v. Ford*, which illustrates this principle.

Care must be taken in drafting the liquidated damages provision, because courts do not uphold penalty provisions which appear to be simply punishing a party for breaching a contract. Courts will not uphold these provisions, nor will they award punitive damages, unless there is some fraudulent behavior. A case illustrating this concept was decided by a federal district court in Illinois when the court refused to enforce a health club's liquidated damages provision in its membership agreement (*Mau v. L.A. Fitness International*, 2010). In this situation, an agreement for personal training services was entered into, and the contract contained a termination clause providing that if the client cancelled, the client was still obligated to pay 50% of the remaining balance of the contract. The plaintiff canceled this contract due to poor performance by the club, but the client was still charged 50% of the remaining contract, in accordance with the termination clause. The court refused to uphold the damages clause as it held that:

> In fact, the fee set by the Termination Clause does not account in any way for the quality or lack of quality of Fitness' performance. It is precisely the same for an individual who received high quality personal training service at well-maintained facilities as for an individual who (like Mau) received deficient (or sometimes no) performance, or for someone who had been unable to access a Fitness workout facility at all as a result of Fitness' own deficient conduct.

The court's reasoning in Mau underscores the critical factor that differentiates the analysis required for Fitness' relationship with its customer group from that applicable to the classical one-to-one contractual relationship. In sum, such invariance to the gravity of the breach conclusively demonstrates that the Termination Clause is a penalty intended to secure performance (*Mau*, p. 850).

Rescission and Restitution

Rescission involves undoing the contract and returning the parties to the positions they had prior to the contract. It is often utilized when fraud, duress, mistake, or misrepresentation has taken place. **Restitution** involves returning the goods or property that was transferred under the contract. For example, if I pay you $1,000 for a tennis racquet because you misrepresent that it was used by Serena Williams in a tournament, I can rescind the contract and have the $1,000 restored to me if I ascertain that Serena Williams did not use this racquet.

Promissory Estoppel

Promissory estoppel is a quasicontractual remedy, meaning that a party may have some recourse despite the fact that some elements of the contract may have been left out. A court may substitute detrimental reliance (see item 3 in the list below) for the element of consideration (Restatement [Second] of Contracts § 90). Promissory estoppel is used when a party relies upon another party's promises and suffers an injustice. Promissory estoppel has three elements:

1 A promise is made that should reasonably be expected to induce reliance.
2 There is reliance upon that promise.
3 Some detriment occurs to the party that relied upon the promise.

Next, we explore promissory estoppel through a hypothetical situation in college athletics.

Considering ... Promissory Estoppel

Larry Lance, a former basketball player at Sports R Us University (SRU), received a grant-in-aid for three years, but his athletic scholarship was not renewed for his senior year. A notice of nonrenewal was given to Lance in a timely fashion. The NCAA allows universities the option of offering multi-year scholarships (NCAA, 2020a) and colleges in the Power Five conferences have implemented a rule preventing a multi-year scholarship from being canceled (New, 2015). However, SRU, like most universities has opted to not offer multiple-year scholarships and has no intention of offering anything but a one-year grant-in-aid, a fact that is well-known to all of SRU's coaches.

Lance acknowledges the foregoing facts of the situation, but he is concerned about the promises made to him when he was recruited to play at SRU. He decided to come to SRU only because the SRU basketball coach promised him that he would receive a scholarship for all four years at SRU, assuming Lance remained academically eligible, which he did. However, after three years on scholarship, the coach chose not to renew Lance's aid for his fourth and final senior year.

Question

- Does Lance have any recourse?

Note how you would answer the question and then check your response using the Analysis & Discussion at the end of this chapter.

In the case of *Giuliani v. Duke University* (2010), a federal district court addressed the issue of liability in a case in which a student-athlete relied upon oral representations made by a university golf coach. Duke golf coach Rod Myers recruited plaintiff to play golf at the university. Plaintiff asserted that his decision to enroll at Duke was strongly influenced by Myers's promises of "life-time access" to Duke's training facilities and the opportunity to compete in a highly competitive program. After Coach Myers unexpectedly passed away in 2007, Orin Daniel Vincent took over as head coach. On February 11, 2008,

Vincent immediately and indefinitely suspended plaintiff's eligibility to participate in Duke's athletic program. Plaintiff filed claims against Duke and Vincent asserting breach of contract, breach of the covenant of good faith and fair dealing, promissory estoppel, and tortious interference with the contract. The federal district court judge dismissed all of plaintiff's claims as he held that neither Myers's oral statements nor the provisions of the university's policy manuals were enforceable as binding contracts. There was no violation of the covenant of good faith and fair dealing since there was no enforceable contract. The promissory estoppel claim also failed under North Carolina law since state law did not allow the use of promissory estoppel to substitute for an otherwise nonexistent contract.

In a more recent case, Luke Hancock, together with four other former University of Louisville men's basketball players, sued the NCAA based on promissory estoppel. In *Hancock et al. v. NCAA* (2018), the players claim for promissory estoppel against the NCAA was based on the redaction of winnings, championships, and accolades from 2011 through 2014, while the plaintiffs were eligible student-athletes. These forfeits came as a part of the NCAA's sanctions against Louisville men's basketball that came in 2017–2018, following a lengthy scandal that included, at the time, both current and prospective players. The plaintiffs argue that they relied on the NCAA promises and the NCAA's failure to satisfy the promise has detrimentally impacted the plaintiffs. Here, the players contend that the NCAA "led [them] to believe that any and all wins, championships, awards, honors and achievements the plaintiffs earned as eligible student-athletes would be theirs, in perpetuity, absent a specific finding that they, individually, were ineligible" (McCann, 2018, para. 10). In other words, the players interpreted NCAA rules and assurances to mean that so long as they adhered to the letters and principles of amateurism, none of those players' accomplishments would be forfeited. The players' reliance is argued to be detrimental because the plaintiffs "worked innumerable hours and endured other, numerous sacrifices in order to maintain their eligible status" and have been wrongfully deprived of the value of their work, sacrifices, and achievements (McCann, 2018). The players settled the lawsuit in 2019 and the players' statistics and on-court achievements from the NCAA tournament were reinstated, and Luke Hancock will once again be recognized as the 2013 Final Four Most Outstanding Player (Zucker, 2019).

Employment Contracts

Employment relationships are generally of two types – employment-at will and contract employment. In many circumstances, employees do not have a contract designating their term of employment and in these situations the employment is termed **at will**. Employees who are considered contract employees will have either written or oral employment agreements that specify the term of their employment, job duties, compensation, and benefits. Contract employees have more protections than at will employees since generally an employer would need "cause" to terminate a contract employer prior to the expiration of the term of the agreement.

Employment at Will

The at will employment has no specified duration – it is "indefinite." The at will status means that the employer may fire the employee at any time, for any reason or for no reason. This rule also allows the employee to quit at any time for any reason. However, in practice the rule is usually more favorable to the employer's position than to the employee. It is not always clear whether one's employment is "at will." In the case of *Clark v. University of Bridgeport* (2011), the head volleyball/softball coach's employment was terminated by the university. The former employee sued the university for breach of the employment contract as she argued that she was not an employee at will because the letter she received in July 2008 provided for a term extending to June 30, 2013. The university argued that the language that it included in the letter identifying the position as "at will" should be conclusive on this point. The court held that an issue of fact existed on the question of whether the position was "at will" so summary judgment could not be granted for the university. This case illustrates the necessity for drafting agreements that are absolutely clear on whether the position is at will employment. There cannot be conflicting information or ambiguity on this issue.

Normally, at will employees serve at the pleasure of the employer and termination normally does not require "just cause." However, there are several public policy exceptions that may prohibit an employer from terminating an at will employee without just cause. These exceptions are discussed below.

Public Policy Exceptions

The most prevalent exception to the employment at will doctrine relates to public policy concerns. The majority of states have some sort of public policy exception, meaning that a dismissal is wrongful if an employer fires an employee for engaging in conduct that affects the employee and also affects some interest of the public at large (Riddle, 2015).

For example, both Congress and the states have passed anti-discrimination statutes prohibiting employment discrimination on the basis of race, ethnicity, gender, age, and so forth. Even if a person could not prevail on such a statutory claim – for example, if the employer does not have enough employees to be subject to statutory requirements (see Chapter 5 for a discussion of employment discrimination), it would still offend societal notions of fairness to allow an employer to fire an at will employee because of one of these protected characteristics. Other unacceptable reasons for discharge under the public policy exception are presented in Exhibit 3.3. The public policy exceptions are interpreted narrowly, however. The public policy must be well-established and well-defined in the jurisdiction in which the claim is filed.

Whistleblower Exceptions

In addition to the public policy exceptions, the federal government, and many states, have passed **whistleblower statutes** providing that employees who report illegal activities allegedly committed by their employer shall not be subject to discrimination or retaliation by the employer. Not all employee disclosure or whistleblowing is protected; however, most of the statutes protect employees who report violations or suspected violations of a state or federal statute (Pacella, 2018). A whistleblowing case arose from the California Whistleblower Protection Act (CWPA) when a strength and conditioning coach at a university filed an administrative complaint alleging that the head football coach had retaliated against him. The retaliation arose after the strength and conditioning coach reported improprieties relating to the misappropriation of athletic department property and possible violations of NCAA rules regarding the conduct of football practices to the university auditor (*Ohton v. Board of Trustees California State University*, 2007). This case has now been settled, San Diego State University paid Dave Ohton, a former strength coach, $2.7 million in February 2011 ("Former strength coach reaches settlement …," 2011). Another whistleblowing case arose from the University of North Carolina when former learning specialist, Mary Willingham, filed a suit against the school as a result of an alleged disruptive work environment. Willingham claimed that her whistleblowing actions regarding student-athletes' literacy rates resulted in her demotion, and workplace

Exhibit 3.3 Unacceptable reasons to discharge at will employees.

Employment discrimination on the basis of race, ethnicity, gender, age, etc.
Blowing the whistle about illegal conduct by the employer
Cooperating in the investigation of a charge against the company
Filing unfair labor practice charges with the National Labor Relations Board
Complaining or testifying about safety hazards in the workplace
Reporting OSHA violations

Source: Jackson, Schuler, & Werner, 2013.

Competitive Advantage Strategies

Employment at Will

- Personnel manuals should be developed with care and have language consistent with the underlying employment contracts or employment relationships (employment at will). The manual should include language disclaiming your intent to alter the employment contracts or relationships in any way.
- The exceptions to employment at will vary greatly from state to state. Consult an attorney when developing your employment policies related to employment at will.
- Be familiar with your state's whistleblower statutes.
- Carefully document misconduct and other determining factors applicable to the termination of an employee.
- Review state anti-discrimination laws paying close attention to local statutes in cities and counties that expand protections beyond those found in federal laws.

retaliation (Ganim, 2014). Her story on the "paper classes" at UNC, highlighted in part by CNN, launched arguably the most severe academic fraud case to plague the NCAA. The case has now been settled, the University of North Carolina paid Mary Willingham $335,000 (Ganim, 2015). As seen above, "at will" employment carries with it a host of exceptions, and employers must take careful stock of the purpose for terminating an employee and what laws or regulations apply.

Contract Employees and Employment Agreements

An employment agreement is a written or verbal agreement between the employer and the employee that outlines the basic details of the job such as start date, salary, and job duties. If you are a contract employee or are negotiating employment agreements on behalf of your employer, it is important to understand the common employment contract provisions and legal issues that arise in the context of the employment contract. For our purposes, we are going to illustrate these issues as they arise between a university and a coach. In addition, we will explore several clauses or provisions that are significant and individualized in current college coaches' contracts such as performance incentives, summer camps, and supplemental compensation. Head coaches' contracts, similar to executive employment agreements, are highly individualized. Typically, the higher the level of the coach or executive, the more intense the bargaining will be and the more individualized the contract terms will be. Greenberg (2019) has noted that in college athletics, "no two contracts are alike." Each university will approach the financial package differently and define the role of the coach within the philosophy of the individual educational institution. Greenberg further recommends that anyone representing coaches in negotiations continually monitor coaches' contracts for new and creative means of enhancing contracts to meet the competitiveness in the field and to meet the issues related to student-athlete welfare in today's college sports environment. Chapter 7 will explore professional athlete contracts in greater detail.

First, we will discuss provisions in coaches' contracts that would also be common to most employment agreements including: the term; duties and responsibilities; compensation; and termination. Next, we will discuss provisions which create unique challenges for coaches and universities in negotiating coaches' contracts, including: reassignment clauses; liquidated damages and buy-out provisions; restrictive covenants; morals clauses; and dispute resolution provisions. While other types of employment agreements may certainly include some of these unique provisions, the specific use of these provisions in college coaches' agreements has significantly impacted the college athletics landscape.

Standard Provisions Included in an Employment Agreement for Coaches

Term of the Contract

Generally, the term or duration of an employment agreement is stated as a number of years. For example, Dabo Swinney entered into a new employment agreement with Clemson in the summer of 2019 and the term of the contract "commences May 1, 2019 and ends December, 31, 2028." Swinney's employment term is for almost nine years and six months, which is an unusually long term for an employment agreement. Typically, coaching contracts specify a term of between four and seven years on average, depending upon the conference. In addition, some states have laws forbidding any state employee to have a term of employment that exceeds one year. These laws sometimes provide exclusions for very high-profile coaching contracts so that universities may hire coaches for multiyear agreements.

Another important aspect of the length of the contract relates to **rollover provisions**. For example, Coach Jones could have a five-year contract with a rollover provision. This clause provides that when an employee has a commitment for a specific number of years, at the end of each year, the contract's term is automatically renewed for another year unless one party notifies the other of the intention not to roll over. Thus, if neither party chooses to not extend the contract, the coach has a continuous five-year contract. In this example, the rollover provision is an *automatic rollover*, it occurs automatically unless a party expressly notifies the other of their desire not to extend the agreement. Rollover provisions can also be subject to *mutual consent* or the rollover can be contingent upon meeting certain *performance standards* such as wins or tournament/bowl appearances or championships.

Rollover clauses are often ambiguously drafted, with the result that the term of the contract is sometimes unclear. Also, to prevent the automatic rollover, an employer often has to give notice years in advance of its intention to let the contract expire. In the college athletics setting, this results in a "lame duck" coach who is likely to give less than complete effort, since he knows that he is unwanted by the university or who pursues new employment before the expiration of his present employment contract.

Duties and Responsibilities

The duties and responsibilities section of the employment contract sets out the duties and responsibilities that the employee is expected to perform. For example, a college coach has many responsibilities in addition to evaluating talent, preparing players for competition, and developing game day strategies. Coaches often have numerous programmatic responsibilities in the areas of budgeting, recruiting, scheduling contests, evaluating assistant coaches, public and media relations, and fundraising. These must all be set forth

---

Competitive Advantage Strategies

Contract Law

- Use the worst-case scenario in developing contracts for your organization. Contracts should serve your interests when the contractual relationship encounters difficulties, such as in cases of breach or termination.
- Even though oral contracts may be enforceable in many situations, it is good business practice to put all your contracts in writing to avoid disputes regarding their content.
- Avoid making promises that go beyond what a written agreement conveys. Under the theory of promissory estoppel, you may be liable for promises.
- Enforce the limits of actual authority that your organization has conveyed to employees. Remember that third parties may be able to use the concept of apparent authority to your organization's detriment.

in this section of the contract. This section should also provide that the coach will devote his/her primary efforts to fulfilling the responsibilities of the position. Duties of a head coach might be more generally described such as to "supervise and manage the football team and perform services consistent with the duties of a NCAA Division 1-A head football coach."

The contract should clearly state that the athletics program is only one aspect of the university's primary purpose of education. This should lead to a discussion of the coach's responsibility to make every effort possible to ensure that student-athletes meet their academic obligations. For example, the contract might require the coach to use his best efforts to ensure that he and every person under his supervision is engaging in safe and responsible treatment of student-athletes on the team.

Finally, there must be language identifying the coach's reporting and compliance obligations such as the coach's obligation to abide by all NCAA, conference, and university rules and regulations. In fact, the NCAA (Bylaw 11.2.1) mandates a stipulation in a coach's contract which provides that a coach found in violation of NCAA regulations shall be subject to disciplinary action as set forth in the NCAA enforcement procedures. There should also be language that reinforces the coach's responsibility to oversee the assistant coaches to make sure that all members of the coaching staff comply with all pertinent rules and regulations. Many coaches contracts now also include language requiring the coach to comply with all university requirements related to Title IX compliance, including reporting any information of sexual harassment or sexual violence.

Compensation

Compensation of the employee is a critical facet of any employment agreement. High-profile coaches with very competitive teams, for example, are often compensated very well, especially football coaches and the coaches of men's basketball teams. As of the 2018 season, there were four football head coaches making at least $7 million per year: Nick Saban of the University of Alabama ($8.3 million); Urban Meyer, then at The Ohio State University ($7.6 million); Jim Harbaugh of the University of Michigan ($7.5 million); Jimbo Fisher of Texas A&M University ($7.5 million) (USA Today, 2018). Additionally, in 2019, six Division I men's basketball coaches were to receive annual compensation exceeding $4 million (USA Today, 2019). Some commentators have found such excess of commercialism in coaches' contracts to be detrimental to the interests of the student-athletes (Greene, 2008).

A head coaching position in NCAA Division I has varied and complex financial engineering embedded in the compensation packages for these coaches. For example, in addition to base and supplemental salary, a range of compensation must be negotiated and defined, including: signing bonuses; retention or longevity bonuses; life insurance; deferred compensation; payoffs of previous employer buyouts; post coaching employment; interest-free or forgivable loans; retirement plans; annuities; expense accounts; relocation costs; disability payments; entrepreneurial sharing arrangements; use of publicity rights; and auxiliary earnings via radio, TV, and summer camps. In addition, as part of their nonguaranteed compensation, coaches at a number of universities have performance bonus clauses that award incentives related to athletic achievements and even academic goals. Although academic incentives are usually relatively small amounts compared to bonuses for athletic achievement, there is some concern that coaches are being given bonuses for accomplishments over which they have no direct control (Ridpath, 2017).

Even with employees who are less highly compensated than coaches, the language relating to compensation must be clearly stated. If an employee receives only a base salary and fringe benefits such as life insurance, health insurance, and a pension plan, this is a rather straightforward matter. Often, however, an employee may be compensated beyond these amounts with benefits that are known as **perquisites (perks)**. Unlike other areas of compensation such as salary or bonuses, the dollar value of perks may be difficult to ascertain or variable. In the case of a college coach, these perquisites may include such additional compensation as profits from radio and television shows; profits from summer sports camps held at the university; the use of an automobile and expenses for gas, insurance, and maintenance; payments for housing; payments for family travel; and membership in a variety of country clubs. Note that some of these perks may be paid directly by the employer, but others may accrue to the coach's benefit from outside sources. The point of contention with perquisites becomes apparent when an employer terminates an employee's contract without cause. In such a case, the employer is liable for damages, but the issue is whether it is liable for simply the amount due under the base salary, supplemental compensation, and fringe benefits aspects of compensation or whether the organization may be liable for the value of the perquisites, even if it does not actually pay out those benefits. This issue came to the fore in the following seminal case.

Rodgers v. Georgia Tech Athletic Association

303 S.E.2d 467 (Ga. Ct. App. 1983)   **FOCUS** CASE

FACTS

Pepper Rodgers was the football coach at the Georgia Institute of Technology in Atlanta in December 1979, when the university terminated Rodgers' employment without cause with two years remaining on his contract. After the university terminated Rodgers, it continued to pay him his normal monthly salary, pension, and insurance benefits, since the university had breached its contract with him. However, Rodgers asserted that the university owed him compensation for other items he lost when he was terminated. Twenty-nine "perquisite" items were mentioned in the suit, ten of which were not paid by the Georgia Tech Athletic Association, his employer. These 29 items included auto use and expenses, housing, season tickets to college and pro games, country club memberships, profits from radio and television shows, and profits from Rodgers's summer football camp. Rodgers sued, claiming that he should receive these lost revenues from the university in addition to the base salary and fringe benefits that the university was paying. The university claimed that it had met its legal responsibility to Rodgers by paying lost wages and fringe benefits. The trial court agreed with the university and dismissed the suit. Rodgers appealed.

HOLDING

The Georgia Court of Appeals reversed in part and affirmed in part as it held that Rodgers may recover perquisites over and above what the Georgia Tech Athletic Association paid directly.

RATIONALE

The appellate court first reviewed the pertinent provisions of Rodgers' contract. The contract stated that: "In addition to [regular compensation], as an employee of the Association, you will be entitled to various insurance and pension benefits *and perquisites* [emphasis added] as you become eligible therefor." This nebulous language regarding perquisites was sufficient, stated the court, to allow a jury to award some of the perquisites even though the employer did not pay them. Under contract damage principles, an employer may be responsible for some damages caused by its breach of contract even if a third party directly controlled the perquisite amounts.

The *Rodgers* case was a seminal decision regarding the recovery of perquisites by a coach if the university breaches its employment contract with the coach. To avoid the uncertainty associated with a termination without cause today, universities are very careful to identify exactly what amounts it may be responsible for in the event it breaches a contract. Generally, the practice is to identify, at the time the contract is negotiated, the exact damages that will be paid if a breach occurs. This practice is discussed below under the principle of liquidated damages.

Termination Provisions

In any contractual relationship, the parties must envision the time when the contract ends. Three critical issues arise when considering termination of the contract prematurely: (1) What is the justification for the termination? (2) Based upon that justification, what, if any, damages are owed? (3) What, if any, notice and process is required to terminate the contract? To examine these issues, we will discuss concepts of **just cause** termination which permits an employer to terminate an employee before the expiration of the contract based on the employee's failure to perform as specified in the contract. We will also explore termination **without cause** which is a common occurrence in collegiate athletics where both universities and coaches elect to terminate the contract prematurely for a variety of business or personal reasons. For example, the university may decide to "go a different direction" or just be unsatisfied with the coach's overall performance and the coach may pursue new more lucrative or prestigious employment opportunities. Both of these scenarios typically are not termination "for cause," thus, the party seeking to terminate prematurely will be liable for damages incurred by the other party. We will examine these challenges in greater detail next.

    Termination for just cause. Sometimes, the contract ends with the employer alleging that the employee breached the terms of the contract. When the employer ends the relationship in such a circumstance, it is taking the position that the termination is based on just cause. Thus, if an employer terminates an employee's contract for **just cause**, this means that the employer has not breached the employment contract; instead, the employee has breached the contract by engaging in behavior that violates the standards of job performance established by the employer. The expectations of job performance must be clearly stated in the employment contract and employee manuals. Most college coaches' contracts will have a section expressly identifying what actions or inactions will qualify as "cause" for purposes of termination. These clauses often include occurrences such as: (1) a material breach; (2) neglect of duty; (3) willful misconduct; and (4) acts of moral turpitude. However, the contracts also rarely specific what exact actions or inactions actually operate as a material breach or moral turpitude, leaving it open for interpretation and legal challenge when a university attempts to terminate for cause. This issue is illustrated in the following Focus Case which concerns Jim O'Brien, who was fired as the men's head basketball coach at The Ohio State University and sued the university, claiming that he was wrongfully terminated. The dispute centered on an interpretation of the language defining violation of NCAA or Big 10 rules as grounds for termination for cause.

O'Brien v. Ohio State University

2007 Ohio App. LEXIS 4316 (Sept. 20, 2007)	FOCUS CASE

FACTS

In 1997, plaintiff O'Brien was hired as the men's basketball coach at the defendant university. On May 14, 1998, Alex Radojevic, a talented basketball player from Yugoslavia, arrived on campus for an unofficial visit. At the time of the visit, Radojevic was enrolled at a community college in Kansas and was playing basketball for that community college. In the fall of 1998, O'Brien learned that Radojevic had played professional basketball for a Yugoslavian team. At trial, O'Brien testified that he believed Radojevic was not eligible to play college basketball since he had played professionally. However, O'Brien's staff continued to recruit Radojevic, and on November 11, 1998, Radojevic signed a National Letter of Intent with Ohio State and came for his official visit to the university in December 1998.

    Later, in December 1998, O'Brien was asked to provide some financial assistance to the Radojevic family, and O'Brien gave the family $6,000 from a drawer in his office desk. Plaintiff testified that he was certain that this "loan" did not violate NCAA rules since Radojevic was not able to be a college player.

In February 1999, however, when the defendant's athletic director, Andy Geiger, asked the plaintiff about Radojevic's status, O'Brien stated that he believed that Radojevic could regain his amateur status. Geiger had no knowledge of the loan to Radojevic. Radojevic never enrolled at Ohio State. He entered the National Basketball Association (NBA) draft and was drafted by the Toronto Raptors.

In March 1999, O'Brien completed a very successful season with the team, advancing to the Final Four in the NCAA Tournament. Based on this performance, Ohio State rewarded plaintiff with a new employment contract, with a substantial increase in compensation, effective September 12, 1999. On September 15, 1999, O'Brien signed an NCAA Certificate of Compliance certifying that during the 1998–1999 academic year he had "reported through the appropriate individuals any knowledge of violations of NCAA legislation involving [the] institution."

In April 2004, the plaintiff informed Geiger of the loan because the plaintiff knew that a lawsuit had been filed in which the loan would be revealed. After an internal investigation of this matter, the plaintiff was terminated in June 2004. The termination was a "for cause" termination, and the defendant alleged that the plaintiff had violated Section 4.1(d) of his employment contract, which required him to "know, recognize, and comply" with all applicable rules and regulations of the NCAA and to "immediately report to the Director [of Athletics] and to the Department of Athletics Compliance Office" if he had "reasonable cause to believe that any person had violated such laws, policies or regulations." The defendant university took the position that O'Brien's failure to report the loan made to Radojevic violated the above section and was a material breach of contract for which the university could terminate the contract for cause under Section 5.1(a), which stated that the university can terminate a contract if a material breach occurs. Section 5.1(b) was not mentioned as a reason for termination, but the language of that section referred to a rules violation committed by a coach that leads to a "major" infraction investigation by the NCAA or the Big 10 Conference. Defendant university received a notice from the NCAA that it was investigating the men's basketball program in May 2005. Three of the violations cited by the NCAA pertained to the Radojevic loan.

The plaintiff alleged that the university breached his employment contract in terminating him for cause. A trial was held in the Ohio Court of Claims, and the Court of Claims rendered judgment for O'Brien as it held that the university had breached the employment contract with plaintiff.

HOLDING

The Ohio Court of Appeals affirmed.

RATIONALE

The Court of Claims judge, who served as the fact finder, found that O'Brien made the loan for humanitarian reasons. He also found that Radojevic was ineligible to participate in athletics at the time that the loan was made, even though O'Brien had continued to recruit Radojevic after learning that he had played professional basketball in Yugoslavia.

The Court of Claims held that O'Brien's "single, isolated recruiting infraction" and O'Brien's failure to disclose that violation was not a material breach under the contract entitling Ohio State to terminate O'Brien for cause. Although O'Brien did breach his contract by making a loan under the circumstances given, this single failure of performance was not "so egregious as to frustrate the essential purpose of the contract." The appellate court agreed with the Court of Claims' finding that there was no material breach in this situation. First, the court noted that the extent to which Ohio State was deprived of the benefit it expected from the employment contract was not as significant as Ohio State asserted – the NCAA sanctions were minor and the damage to Ohio State's reputation was minor. Second, the breach of trust was reparable. Also, O'Brien forfeited substantial salary and benefits, and he had made a good faith effort to resolve the dispute.

The court also held that the wording of the contract favored the employee and, therefore, must be enforced absent unconscionability. Specifically, § 5.1(b) contemplates that the coach could retain employment during an investigation and remain employed unless serious sanctions were imposed. The court must honor the parties' agreement, which, in this case, greatly favored the coach. The Ohio State Supreme Court declined to hear the O'Brien appeal, so O'Brien was owed almost $3 million from Ohio State University. This case points out the consequences of a termination clause that was extremely unfavorable to the university.

As the O'Brien case illustrates, it is often not clear whether the coach's conduct is going to permit the university to terminate for cause. Coaches frequently challenge their termination as wrongful and seek significant damages in court or negotiate settlement or separation agreements. In several of the examples included in Exhibit 3.5, the university's purported justification for termination was abusive behavior toward athletes, however, most coach's contracts do not expressly identify this behavior as justifying termination for cause, thus, universities are left to assert their right to terminate based on the much vaguer language of moral turpitude or public disrepute clauses (Greenberg, 2013). Now universities are beginning to emphasize student-athlete welfare more prominently in the termination for cause provisions (Greenberg, 2019).

As mentioned in the previous Duties and Responsibilities section, contracts of university coaches will always include a provision requiring compliance with NCAA rules (or conference or university rules). However, as we saw in O'Brien, the termination for cause provisions would need to expressly include failure to fulfill these expectations among those actions to justify termination for cause. The more general language of "material breach" may or may not be sufficient to terminate for cause for NCAA rules violations. Usually, the types of rules violations that may lead to a just cause termination are intentional violations of major rules or repeated, willful violations of minor rules, and violations so severe as to subject the university to significant penalties by the NCAA. Settlement agreements with coaches should also include "clawback provisions," which require a coach to repay the settlement if the NCAA finds rule violations occurred in the coach's program during his direction of the program (Greenberg, 2010; Swerdlow, 2017).

Termination Without Cause

In other circumstances, the employer or employee may seek to end the contractual relationship without any acceptable reason to do so. This is known as a termination without just cause. (See Greenberg & Paul, 2013.)

Exhibit 3.4 Examples of settlements in potential termination for cause situations.

University	Coach	Sport	Settlement Amount	Date
Rutgers University	Mike Rice	Men's Basketball	$475,000	2013
University of Connecticut	Kevin Ollie	Men's Basketball	None yet, litigation pending for $11 million	2020
College of Charleston	Matt Heath	Baseball	$350,000	2019
University of Louisville	Rick Pitino	Men's Basketball	$0 (termination changed from firing to resignation)	2010
San Diego State University	Beth Burns	Women's Basketball	$3,356,250	2018
University of Hawaii	Gib Arnold	Men's Basketball	$1,098,000	2015
University of Central Arkansas	Russ Pennell	Men's Basketball	$7,000 per month thru March, 2021	2020
Colorado State University	Mike Bobo	Football	$1.8 million buyout instead of $5.5 million	2019
Grand Valley State	Morris Burger	Football	$90,000	2020

In this circumstance, an employer wishes to "fire" an employee who has not engaged in any behavior that would serve as "just cause" for termination. Also, an employee may wish to sever her relationship with an employer, usually to go on to another, better job. If there is no legitimate justification for terminating the contract before the term expires, this is known as termination without cause. That is, one party is breaching the contract by terminating it without legitimate justification for doing so under the contract provisions.

In the current climate of intercollegiate athletics, the ability to win games is often valued above all other considerations. Therefore, a coach's performance may be judged primarily by the standard of a win–loss record. The win–loss record is not generally included in the performance measures allowing a university to terminate a coach for just cause. However, many coaches are "fired" simply because of a failure to win enough games. This type of termination, assuming the coach's contract term has not expired, is a breach of contract by the university, because there is no just cause for terminating the coach. If the coach brings a cause of action against the university, the complaint alleges **wrongful termination**: the employee was terminated contrary to the terms of the contract. Similarly, if a coach fails to complete the term of his/her contract, the coach has breached the contract.

To anticipate an employee's or employer's breach of the employment contract, common practice is to include a **liquidated damages clause**, sometimes termed a **buy-out** provision. Liquated damages are used in a contract to identify actual damages that will occur but are difficult or impossible to prove. This amount is supposed to be the parties' best estimate at the time they execute the agreement of the damages that would be caused by a breach of either party. For a liquated damages provision to be enforceable it must meet three criteria:

1 Damages are difficult to estimate.
2 The amount specified represents a reasonable estimate of the anticipated damaged to the parties.
3 The provision does not operate as a penalty simply to coerce performance or punish the breach.

The following Case Opinion provides an example of a liquidated damages provision that was upheld against the coach who terminated his employment agreement.

Kent State University v. Ford

CASE OPINION   26 N.E.3d 868 (Ct. App. Ohio, 2015)

FACTS

In April of 2008, Ford and Kent State executed an employment contract, employing Ford as Kent State's head men's basketball coach for a period of four years. The contract included his salary, supplemental salary, and various incentives based on performance. It also contained the following provision:

> GENE A. FORD recognizes that his promise to work for the UNIVERSITY for the entire term of this four (4) year Contract is of the essence of this Contract with the UNIVERSITY. GENE A. FORD also recognizes that the UNIVERSITY is making a highly valuable investment in his continued employment by entering into this Contract and its investment would be lost were he to resign or otherwise terminate his employment with the UNIVERSITY prior to the expiration of this Contract. Accordingly, he will pay to the UNIVERSITY as liquidated damages an amount equal to his base and supplemental salary, multiplied by the number of years (or portion(s) thereof) remaining on the Contract.

In April 2010, Ford and Kent State renegotiated and executed a new employment contract, lasting for a term of five years, which increased his salary and supplemental salary by a total of $100,000, for a total salary of $300,000. This contract contained the same liquidated damages provision as above. During the first year of the new contract term, Joel Nielsen, the Kent State athletic director received a phone call from Ford's agent, requesting permission for Ford to speak to other schools regarding employment and granted such permission following the conclusion of the basketball season. At that time, Nielsen reminded Ford of the liquidated damages provision in the contract. Soon thereafter, Ford accepted the position at Bradley University, at an annual salary of $700,000.

On April 26, 2011, Kent State filed a complaint against Ford and Bradley University, asserting that Ford, the former head coach of the men's basketball team at Kent State, breached his contract by terminating his employment with Kent State four years before the contract's expiration and commencing employment with Bradley University. Kent State seeks to recover damages from Ford under the liquidated damages clause in Ford's employment contract.

In the trial court, Nielsen testified that the liquidated damages clause was included to protect the University by providing coaching continuity, which aids in recruiting players. Nielsen explained the cost associated with conducting a coaching search to replace Ford, including time and travel for interviews. He outlined as potential damages the "loss of investment" in Ford, including "equity" built up with fans and donors. Dr. Lester Lefton, president of Kent State University, testified that liquidated damages "make up some of the differences" from the loss in ticket sales, advertising, recruiting and "having to start all over again" when a coach leaves prematurely. He believed that such damages "deter" individuals from leaving early. Dr. Lefton explained that when a coach leaves prior to the expiration of the contract, "the program suffers, recruiting suffers, ticket sales suffer, alumni and fan support suffers, [and] donations suffer."

Ford filed a motion for summary judgment arguing that Kent State suffered no damages as a result of his departure. He asserted that the liquidated damages clause was defective, since its objective was "punitive deterrence of breach," and the amount was disproportionate to any anticipated or actual damages. The trial court concluded that Ford breached his employment contract and that the liquidated damages provision was enforceable and finding that, pursuant to the stipulation of the parties, $1.2 million was due to Kent State under the liquidated damages clause of the contract and awarded damages in that amount. Ford appealed.

HOLDING

Judgment of the trial court is affirmed and the liquidated damages clause is enforceable.

RATIONALE

The issues to be determined in this case are whether a contract with a liquidated damages clause is unenforceable when it requires a breaching university coach to pay his salary for each year remaining under the contract, when there is limited evidence of actual damages.

Liquidated damages are an agreed upon amount of money to be paid in lieu of actual damages in the event of a breach of contract. In *Samson Sales, Inc. v. Honeywell, Inc.* (1984), the Supreme Court of Ohio set forth the test for determining whether a liquidated damages provision should be upheld:

> Where the parties have agreed on the amount of damages, ascertained by estimation and adjustment, and have expressed this agreement in clear and unambiguous terms, the amount so fixed should be treated as liquidated damages and not as a penalty, if the damages would be (1) uncertain as to amount and difficult of proof, and if (2) the contract as a whole is not so manifestly unconscionable, unreasonable, and disproportionate in amount as to justify the conclusion that it does not express the true intention of the parties, and if (3) the contract is consistent with the conclusion that it was the intention of the parties that damages in the amount stated should follow the breach thereof.

The application of *Samson* to the facts of this case supports a conclusion that the liquidated damages provision was properly enforced by the lower court. The parties agreed on an amount of damages, stated in clear terms in Ford's second employment contract. Regarding the first factor, the difficulty of ascertaining the damages resulting from Ford's breach, it is apparent that such damages were difficult, if not impossible, to determine. Based on the testimony presented, the departure of a university's head basketball coach may result in a decrease in ticket sales, impact the ability to successfully recruit players and community support for the team, and require a search for both a new coach and additional coaching staff. Many of these damages cannot be easily measured or proven. This is especially true given the nature of how such factors may change over the course of different coaches' tenures with a sports program or team.

A similar conclusion regarding the difficulty of ascertaining damages from a university coach's breach was reached in *Vanderbilt Univ. v. DiNardo* (1999), one of the few cases related to liquidated damages in a university coaching scenario. The *DiNardo* Court found that damages from losing a head football coach are uncertain and "[i]t is impossible to estimate how the loss of a head football coach will affect alumni relations, public support, football ticket sales, contributions, etc. ... [T]o require a precise formula for calculating damages resulting from the breach of contract by a college head football coach would be tantamount to barring the parties from stipulating to liquidated damages evidence in advance" (*Id.* at 756). The court held that the university's head football coach was hired "for a unique and specialized position," with the parties understanding that damages could not be easily ascertained if a breach occurred, especially given that the provision was reciprocal and was the result of negotiations by both parties, which is the case in the present matter as well. (*Id.* at 757).

In this case, the contract stated that the liquidated damages clause was based on Kent State's "investment in [Ford's] continued employment." This is similar to DiNardo, where language was included regarding the importance of the "long-term commitment" and stability of the program (*Id.* at 756). The desire for Ford's continued employment, the renegotiation of his contract prior to its expiration, and Kennedy's statements to Ford that the contract would be renegotiated within a few years, made it clear that Kent State desired Ford to have long-term employment, which was necessary to establish the stability in the program that would benefit recruitment, retention of assistant coaching staff, and community participation and involvement. The breach of the contract impacted all of these areas.

Regarding the alleged unreasonableness of the damages, Ford takes issue with the fact that actual damages were not proven by Kent State. In cases involving a valid liquidated damages clause, however, "the party seeking such damages need not prove that actual damages resulted from a breach" (citation omitted). While some evidence of the value of the actual damages helps to determine the reasonableness of the liquidated damages, based on the record, we find that the damages were reasonable. Even if the damages to Kent State were based solely on hiring a replacement coach, finding a coach of a similar skill and experience level as Ford, which was gained based partially on the investment of Kent State in his development, would have an increased cost. Given all of the circumstances and facts in this case, and the consideration of the factors above, we cannot find that the liquidated damages clause was a penalty.

DISCUSSION QUESTIONS

1 What were some of the similarities between the liquidated damages provision in this case and the clause in *Dinardo*?
2 What were some of the reasons given by the court for concluding that damages for breach of contract by the coach are difficult to ascertain and what are some of the types of damages that are likely to be caused by a breach of contract?

Notice and Due Process Prior to Termination

For public employers, such as state universities, terminating employment may require notice and a hearing in order to meet the state's duty to provide due process under the U.S. Constitution. Constitutional issues in high school and collegiate athletics are explored in greater detail in Chapters 11 and 12. When a public employee asserts a protected property interest in his or her employment, the public employee must show that the protected property interest is derived from a source such as state law or contract, which requires a showing that the employee could have been fired only for good cause. As we know for contract employees, generally the employer must have cause in order to terminate the employment contract, therefore, most coaches and contract employees are entitled to some minimum due process prior to termination. While a contract employee with a protected property interest in continued employment is entitled to due process before termination, an at will employee, usually lacks the necessary property interest in his or her employment. (See *Kish v. Iowa Community College*, 2001.)

The standards pertaining to notice and any hearing process should be clearly set forth in the employment contract. Employee manuals can also provide for due process and incorporated by reference into the contract. The employment contract should always provide for some type of internal hearing to allow the employee to present evidence regarding why, in the employee's view, his behavior does not qualify as behavior allowing the organization to terminate the contract for just cause. This due process protection is intended to ensure that the termination is done in a fair manner.

Additional Unique Clauses and Issues in College Coaches' Contracts

Mitigation Clauses

As we know, termination and early firing of coaches is part of the coaching landscape. Universities are often obligated to pay millions of dollars to coaches even though those same coaches find new employment. For example, the University of Illinois at the end of the 2011–2012 football and basketball seasons terminated its football, and men's and women's basketball coaches which carried with it an obligation to pay $7.1 million in liquidated damages. Each of the coaches secured new employment in either broadcasting or coaching relatively quickly (Greenberg & Paul, 2013). If the university had included a mitigation clause in its contracts, some if not all of these damages could have been avoided.

We introduced the concept of mitigation of damages earlier in the chapter. This is a common issue that arises in situations when a coaches' contract is terminated early by the university and the university is obligated to pay significant liquidated damages to the coach. In an employment context, the duty to mitigate only requires reasonable efforts to obtain and maintain comparable employment (Greenberg & Paul, 2013). However, determining reasonableness can be complicated and terminated employees are not obligated to obtain any employment, but instead have the right to seek employment in their chosen field that is substantially equivalent to the prior employment. A better practice is for the employment agreement to expressly address the duty to mitigate in the event the university terminates the coach early. Coaches' contracts may include a specific clause that stipulates that the coach does not have a duty to mitigate damages. This would be the most beneficial for the coach and also the least susceptible to varying or inconsistent interpretations. However, with the continued escalation of buyout amounts in coaches contracts, it is becoming more common for the employment agreements to impose a duty to mitigate on the coach. Typically, these provisions will either allow the university to offset or reduce their liquidated damages payment by any amount the coach is earning in his new position, or in some instances, liquidated damages would cease all together once the coach has obtained new employment. At a minimum, these clauses should impose an affirmative duty to mitigate on the coach, define comparable employment, detail offset terms, and require notification of employment (Greenberg & Paul, 2013). Of course, a coach may oppose the inclusion of these provisions as well and prefer to accept less liquidated damages in exchange for no duty to mitigate.

Reassignment Clauses

Gives an employer the right to transfer an employee into a different employment position in the organization. For example, the university, as employer, may try to insert a reassignment clause into a coaching contract. This means that the university retains the right to transfer the coach to a different employment position in the university. The university could invoke this right of reassignment, for example, if it wants to make a coaching change but the coach has not breached the agreement. If the university were to terminate the coach, it would be subject to damages for breach. However, if a reassignment clause exists, the university may rightfully remove the coach from his current position and reassign him to other duties. If the coach refuses to accept the reassignment, that is a breach by the coach, and the university may terminate the contract for just cause (see below for a further discussion of the concept of just cause). However, if the university attempts to reassign a coach and it does not have the right to do so under the contract, the coach may argue that the university has breached the agreement by doing so. The coach would argue that this is a **constructive discharge**, which means that, although the coach has not been actually fired, the impact of the reassignment is essentially to take away the responsibilities for which he was hired.

The reassignment clause is usually highly detrimental to an employee's interest. If someone is hired to be a football coach, for example, that person, regardless of compensation, does not want to become the golf coach or the compliance coordinator. Compensation is not the issue; a coach wants to coach in his/her area of competence and to retain the status associated with the original position. In the following case, the validity of a reassignment clause was upheld against a coach.

Monson v. State of Oregon

901 P.2d 904 (Or. Ct. App. 1995)   FOCUS CASE

FACTS

Don Monson coached the men's basketball team at the University of Oregon from 1983 to 1992. After the 1991–92 season ended, the athletic director met with Monson and advised him that the basketball program was not "going in the direction he wanted" (p. 906) and that Monson was being reassigned to golf coach. Monson protested, saying that to accept this reassignment would be professional suicide. After Monson failed to accept the new assignment, the university considered him to have resigned and paid him no further compensation.

Monson sued the university for breach of contract, asserting that he had performed his obligations as basketball coach and that the term of his employment contract did not expire until June 30, 1994. Monson argued that the attempt to reassign him was a constructive discharge. The university responded that it had the right to reassign Monson under a clause in the contract that stated: "The position as offered is subject to all applicable provisions of State and Federal law, State administrative rules, and the regulations and policies of the State System of Higher Education and the University of Oregon" (p. 905). These regulations permitted the reassignment of any state employee.

A jury trial was held, and Monson was awarded $292,087.93. The university appealed.

HOLDING

The Oregon appellate court reversed the judgment of the trial court and held that reassignment was permitted.

RATIONALE

The primary issue upon appeal was whether the university had a right to reassign Monson.

The court reviewed the contract provisions that incorporated by reference all of the administrative rules and regulations governing all state employees, regardless of position. These rules and regulations did permit the reassignment of personnel. Therefore, the court reasoned that the university retained the right to reassign Monson and that, when it did so, it did not breach the employment contract with the coach.

Restrictive Covenants

Employment contracts often include **restrictive covenants**. The most common in a traditional employment relationship is the covenant not to compete. This covenant protects the interests of the employer and essentially restrict the ability of the employee either to terminate the contract early or to take a comparable job at another organization considered a competitor. For example, if a coach breaches his employment contract, the restrictive covenant may provide that he may not accept an employment opportunity that is in competition with the employer.

The enforceability of this type of clause is determined by state law. Generally, it is disfavored because it attempts to restrict an employee's ability to secure a new position. However, clauses that are drafted narrowly in terms of scope, geographic area, and time period usually are upheld. For example, if a university drafted a restrictive covenant attempting to prevent a football coach from ever coaching college football again anywhere in the United States, that clause would be overly restrictive and not enforced. However, if a football coach's contract with a Big 10 university had a clause preventing him from taking a head football coaching position at another Big 10 school in the next two years, that clause would most likely be upheld as a reasonable restrictive covenant.

The covenant not to compete clause is certainly relevant in other employment situations, as well. For example, in 2014 Nike sued three shoe designers. The three shoe designers were accused of planning to develop their own footwear design studio with the intention to consult with Adidas, one of Nike's prime competitors. Nike sued the trio for conspiring to share confidential design schemes and other trade secrets, arguing that the noncompete agreement they each signed as an employee of Nike prevented him from working for, consulting with, or otherwise being connected to any of Nike's competitors. The agreement also provided for a "Restriction Period" during which the noncompete agreement would be upheld for one year after employment at Nike ended (Rovell, 2014). The defendants filed a countersuit claiming invasion of privacy, and that their designs were independent of any of Nike's creative materials (Chung, 2015). Ultimately, the parties settled for an undisclosed amount (Kuehner-Hebert, 2015). A law review by Kerr (2018) discusses the noncompete clause issues associated with sport and entertainment agents under California law.

A contract dispute relating to a college football coach illustrates the covenant not to compete issue.

Northeastern University v. Brown

| 17 Mass. L. Rep. 443 (Mass. Super. Ct. 2004) | FOCUS CASE |

FACTS

Don Brown had been under contract with Northeastern University as its football coach since 2000. In July 2003, he signed a new contract with Northeastern, with a term through 2007–08. Article VII of his employment contract provided that he was not to negotiate or accept other employment during the term of his contract without first obtaining the written consent of the university president. A liquidated damages clause in the contract provided for a payment of $25,000 if Brown left Northeastern before the end of his contract.

In January 2004, Northeastern denied a request from the University of Massachusetts (UMass) to discuss employment with Brown. Nonetheless, Brown told his athletic director that UMass had offered him the position of football coach and he had declined. Brown submitted his resignation three days later in order to accept employment with UMass. Northeastern sued Brown, seeking a preliminary injunction to prevent Brown from coaching at UMass.

HOLDING

The Superior Court of Massachusetts granted the injunction against Brown.

RATIONALE

The issue before the court was whether Northeastern's only remedy was the liquidated damages provided for in the employment contract, or whether it could obtain an injunction preventing Brown from coaching at UMass. First, the court was very displeased with Brown's conduct, which it characterized as a "willful and intentional" breach of contract. In fact, the court said that Brown's "word was no good and his promises were lies." Further, Brown's breach was "obvious, brazen and defiant."

According to Massachusetts law, liquidated damages are not the exclusive remedy. An injunction may be granted to enforce a duty even if there is a provision for liquidated damages. In this case, there is strong evidence of irreparable harm to be suffered by Northeastern and its football program. The court noted that Brown knows all of Northeastern's plays and procedures, and he could use that knowledge against Northeastern. He also will try to recruit the same student-athletes, and the schools are rivals in the same conference. Therefore, the court issued an injunction forbidding Brown from working as an employee of UMass until further order of the court.

After the *Brown* ruling, Northeastern and UMass worked out a settlement. Brown was barred from coaching on the sidelines for three UMass games, and UMass paid Northeastern $150,000 ("Coach thieves beware," 2004). This lawsuit illustrates the type of remedy available against an employee who blatantly violates a covenant not to compete provision.

The case of *Marist College v. Brady* (2011) concerns a "non-recruit clause" inserted in a coach's contract as a type of restrictive covenant (Fitzgerald, 2010, 2012). In this case, Marist College first brought an action against James Madison University (JMU) as it alleged tortious interference with its contract with former head basketball coach Matt Brady. The contract between Marist and Brady contained a clause forbidding Brady to contact, without the consent of Marist, players he had previously recruited on behalf of Marist if Brady took a job with another institution. The contract also provided that Brady was precluded from discussing employment opportunities with another school without the written consent of Marist. Brady took the head coaching position at JMU, and the court found that, with the knowledge of JMU, Brady contacted former players he had recruited to attend Marist. These allegations were sufficient to support plaintiff's claim that JMU intentionally induced Brady to breach fiduciary duties arising from his contract with Marist. On June 30, 2010, a New York trial court granted a default judgment for the plaintiff in its lawsuit against the state of Virginia and James Madison University (Fitzgerald, 2010).

Thereafter, the lawsuit against Brady proceeded to trial in the New York court, and a jury verdict was rendered against Brady for breach of contract. However, the jury awarded no damages (Fitzgerald, 2012). Although Marist obtained a jury verdict, since no damages were awarded, it is hard to see a deterrent effect in terms of coaches "jumping ship." Assessing the viability of the "non-recruit" clause is also difficult, although some commentators have argued that this clause should be considered a violation of public policy, since it impedes the free choice of third parties (student-athletes who may wish to follow their coach and/or play for the person who recruited them initially) (Pauline & Wolohan, 2012).

Competitive Advantage Strategies

Employment Contracts

- Employment contracts should be developed with care and cover all the necessary aspects as indicated in this section.
- The termination clauses and liquidated damages provisions should be given particular attention.
- An employee cannot be terminated for just cause unless the prohibited behaviour is carefully delineated and understood.
- An employee should not be reassigned to another position in the organization unless the employement contract explicitly permits this.
- Morals clauses should be negotiated carefully with "provable" events for termination.
- Noncompete clauses should be drafted narrowly in terms of scope, geographic area, and time period.

Morals Clauses

A variety of behaviors are often included as grounds for a just cause termination as mentioned before including moral turpitude or public disrepute. These types of clauses are known as morals clauses. A **morals clause** provides for just cause termination based on immorality, criminal behavior, or behavior reflecting poorly upon the employer. Whereas the employee would naturally prefer a narrow definition of such behavior, the employer, of course, wants to broaden the language in this clause to retain the option of terminating the employee for conduct unfavorable to the employer but not necessarily criminal in nature. For example, a university will want language stating that any behavior by the coach that would tend to bring public ridicule upon the college or any failure to meet the ethical or moral standards of the community should be considered behavior that could result in termination. A case illustrative of this concept is *Spears v. Grambling State University* (2012), concerning a head football coach who was terminated for just cause. The Louisiana appellate court reversed a jury verdict finding that the coach had been terminated without just cause. In holding for the university, the court noted that the "coach was insubordinate to the university president, made public comments that impugned the reputation of the university and generated unfavorable publicity, and caused the university to be investigated by the NCAA" (*Spears*, p. 397).

Most endorsement contracts also contain morals clauses. These clauses are negotiated under the same competing considerations as discussed above. That is, the athlete endorser seeks to have the morals clause and thus termination of the endorsement contract limited to situations in which the athlete is convicted of a felony involving moral turpitude. The advertising company, however, wants to broaden the clause to cover behavior that has an adverse effect on either the athlete's reputation or the product brand's reputation, regardless of the illegality of the act.

An interesting situation regarding a moral's clause in an endorsement contract and the use of Twitter by a professional athlete arose in the case of *Mendenhall v. Hanesbrands, Inc.* (2012). In this case, Rashard Mendenhall, a running back for the Pittsburgh Steelers, signed an endorsement contract with Hanesbrands. In an extension of this contract, the morals clause was modified to include Section 17(a), which provided that "any situation or occurrence tending to bring Mendenhall into public disrepute, contempt, scandal, or ridicule, or tending to shock, insult, or offend the majority of the consuming public ..." would be grounds for immediate termination. Mendenhall used Twitter seemingly to support Osama bin Laden and Islam after bin Laden's death. Mendenhall received several negative comments opposed to his viewpoint, and Hanesbrands terminated the agreement based on its contention that a violation of Section 17(a) had occurred. Mendenhall then sued Hanesbrands alleging that the defendant unreasonably terminated the agreement because company officials simply disagreed with plaintiff's statements, not because

Section 17(a) was violated. The federal district court found that there was an issue of fact regarding the degree of the public's response to plaintiff's tweet that had to be resolved before the court could ascertain whether Section 17(a) was violated. In January of 2013, the lawsuit was settled (Edelman, 2013). This case illustrates the caution with which athletes should use social media as a forum for their own beliefs and also illustrates the need for endorsing companies to use clear language in setting the standards for termination. How would a company ever prove that "a majority of the consuming public" was "shock[ed], insult[ed], or offend[ed]" as stated in the morals clause of the Hanesbrands contract? High profile athlete activism and controversial behaviors making news headlines shed light on moral dilemmas faced by sponsors and endorsers. Pagar (2016) states that athlete actions can lead to business and legal difficulties for the sponsor. She further discusses how companies should use morals clauses to protect their brands, especially in light of Ryan Lochte's 2016 Rio Olympics suspension.

However, in an interesting turnabout, Vernon (2017) discusses the "reverse morals" clause. The premise of this article is that morals clauses are customarily installed for the benefit of the sponsor, while the endorser should be able to terminate the sponsorship or endorsement contract when the corporate sponsor or endorsing company has been tainted by scandal. The author claims that athletes have reputations to protect, much like the sponsoring brand, and that the reciprocal nature of a reverse morals clause would be able to provide that protection against the endorsee's unethical or criminal conduct, even financial bankruptcy (Vernon, 2017).

NCAA Requirements in Contracts with Athletics Staff

The NCAA Bylaw 11.2 specifically requires certain provisions in contractual agreements with athletics staff including the director of athletics, coaches, and any contracted or appointed athletics staff member (NCAA, 2020b). The first requirement relates to NCAA enforcement provisions and the second relates to reporting of athletically related income and benefits. Since 2013, the NCAA had enforced a policy allowing head coaches to be penalized for the NCAA rules violations of assistant coaches unless the head coach took preventive measures regarding this likelihood (Lens, 2018). For example, the NCAA suspended DePaul men's basketball head coach, Dave Leitao, for the opening three games of the 2019 for knowingly enabling a culture of silence while the former associate head coach, director of basketball operations, and former assistant director of basketball operations committed compliance infractions (Bauer-Wolf, 2019). The sanctions also included a team probation for three years (Bauer-Wolf, 2019). NCAA Bylaw 11.1.1.1 reinforces the importance of accountability and vicarious liability of head coaches for those reporting to them and Bylaw 11.2.1 requires the inclusion of a stipulation in all athletics staff' contracts that the staff member has an affirmative obligation to cooperate in the infractions process and that any individual found in violation of NCAA regulations shall be subject to disciplinary or corrective actions (NCAA, 2020c).

In addition, pursuant to NCAA Bylaw 11.2.2, coaching contracts and contracts with athletics staff must stipulate that the coach/staff member annually provide to the institution's president or chancellor a written, detailed account of athletically related income or benefits from sources outside the institution. In addition, the approval for the receipt of such income must be consistent with the institution's policy related to outside income for all employees. Sources of athletically related income include sport camps, country club memberships, payments for TV or radio shows, and endorsement contracts for athletic equipment.

Dispute Resolution Clauses and Separation Agreements

While almost all head coaches and now even many assistant coaches will have liquidated damages provisions in their contracts in the event of termination without cause, there still could be other types of disputes between the parties that could be resolved by submission to an impartial third party. As we learned in Chapter 2, arbitration and mediation could both be useful tools for coaches and universities to resolve

Exhibit 3.5 Dispute resolution clause — Football coach.

Football Head Coach Employment Agreement (University of Montana and Robert A. Stitt) dated December 16, 2014.

12 Dispute Resolution

   a If any dispute arises under this Agreement, the parties agree to attempt to resolve the dispute in good faith as follows:

      1 First, by informal negotiation.
      2 If informal negotiations fail to resolve the dispute, the parties agree to seek mediation using a mediator acceptable to both parties.
      3 If mediation fails to resolve the dispute within 30 days of initial mediation session, the parties agree to submit to binding arbitration under provisions of the Montana Uniform Arbitration Act ....The arbitration shall be conducted before a single arbitrator selected by the parties. If the parties have not selected an arbitrator within ten days of written demand for arbitration, the arbitrator shall be selected by the American Arbitration Association.

---

disputes rather than risk litigation. Despite how useful these provisions can be, they are still not commonly included in coaches' contracts. The employment agreement between Robert Stitt and the University of Montana is one of the few which included a provision for dispute resolution (see Exhibit 3.5). Typically, the dispute resolution clause sets forth the types of disputes that may be submitted for resolution and the method for dispute resolution. For example, the dispute resolution process between University of Montana and Coach Stitt envisions a progressive process beginning with informal negotiations and ending with binding arbitration (University of Montana, 2014). Any arbitration clause should state whether arbitration is compulsory and whether the arbitrator's decision is final and binding upon the parties. An article by Thomas and Van Horn (2016) is instructive on this issue with respect to college football coaches.

Separation agreements are also commonly used to resolve issues between the parties and prevent future litigation related to termination of the agreement. Greenberg and Park (2018) suggests that whether a termination is for cause or not for cause, the college and coach will enter into some form of an agreement such as a separation agreement, settlement, or release agreement. Greenberg further identifies a number of provisions to be included in a separation agreement including (a) acknowledgment of dismissal, that the dismissal was not for cause, and the exact severance date; (b) acknowledgment that the amount paid pursuant to the agreement are liquidated damages and that the amount paid is payment in full; (c) whether the payments continue to the estate of the coach in the event of his death; (d) whether the parties contemplate continued employment for some period of time prior to the termination date; (e) a full and complete release of all claims between the parties; (f) an agreement that neither party will sue the other; (g) that the amounts being paid are taxable income to the coach and that the coach has entered into the agreement voluntarily and under the advice of counsel; (h) release of any age discrimination claims; (i) no admission of liability by either party; (j) a nondisparagement and confidentiality agreement; (k) the return of any university property, continued cooperation related to any NCAA investigations; and agreement not to interfere with university athletics program operations.

The previous section explored the common and specialized provisions utilized in employment agreements and the legal issues associated with the negotiation and enforcement of our contractual agreements. In the next section, we explore the areas in which the execution and performance of contractual agreements may have legal implications in the area of tort law.

Tort Claims and Employment Agreements

Tort law is a broad area of the law that encompasses a variety of legal causes of action generally not arising from contract and Chapter 4 will delve more deeply into tort law and employment. However, there are a few areas in which contract law and tort law will overlap with one another especially as it relates to hiring and termination. You might recall we discussed earlier that coaches who are terminated without cause may sue for wrongful termination or other tort claims that relate to their contract termination. It is important to understand that our contractual agreements and performance of those agreements can implicate other issues under tort law instead of contract law. So, we turn our attention to some tort theories as they are applied specifically to our employment contractual relationships.

Defamation

Chapter 19 discusses the elements of the cause of action in defamation. In that chapter you will learn that defamation is a tort that protects one's reputation. In this chapter, we discuss how this tort has been claimed against employers most times in two types of situations. One related to providing references for employees; and the other related to comments made about the reasons for an employee's termination.

Many employers refuse to give references at all because of the threat of defamation liability. In some cases, employers make no statements regarding an employee's performance; they simply acknowledge that Employee X has been with the company for a certain number of years in a particular capacity. Obviously, a prospective employer's effort to select a good employee is severely hampered when little or no information is available from a current or past employer.

Truth is a complete defense to a defamation claim. Therefore, any information disclosed should be truthful and accurate, and documented in the employee's file. For example, if an employee was discharged for missing work, it should be documented in his employee file that he failed to report for work on a certain, verifiable, number of occasions. No comments relating to an employee's personality should be disclosed; nor should any secondhand information be discussed.

Most states also provide that an employer has a **qualified privilege** to disclose pertinent information. This means that an employer who acts in good faith may disclose information concerning an employee's work performance to individuals inside the current employer's operation or to prospective employers. The privilege is lost if the reference is given with actual malice – if it is intentionally or recklessly injurious to the employee. This privilege thus serves as a type of immunity against defamation claims, although the privilege does not prevent a lawsuit from being filed.

Negligent Misrepresentation/Fraud

Employers are not generally required to say anything about a current or former employee when a prospective employer inquires. Although the practice of withholding information may be detrimental to the prospective employer's ability to select wisely, there is no affirmative duty to disclose. However, if information is disclosed, then a duty arises to give accurate disclosure; an employment reference may not "distort" the information given. Giving inaccurate information may constitute negligent misrepresentation or fraud. Under Restatement (Second) of Torts, § 311, one who negligently gives false information to another, where the party reasonably relies upon that information resulting in harm to another, may be liable for **negligent misrepresentation**.

Providing false or inaccurate employee reference information is not the only employment situation in which negligent misrepresentation can occur. In the case of *Williams v. University of Minnesota* (2012), a jury rendered a verdict of approximately $1.25 million against the University of Minnesota (UM) after it found that head basketball coach Tubby Smith made negligent misrepresentations to Jimmy Williams about employment as an assistant coach. The jury found that Smith had offered an assistant coaching position to Williams, who was employed at Oklahoma State University (OSU). Williams immediately accepted the offer, resigned his position at OSU, and put his home on the market. However, the UM athletic director, Joel Maturi, refused to hire Williams because of recruiting violations with which he was involved when he was at UM in the 1970s and 1980s. After UM refused to hire Williams, he filed suit against Smith and UM.

The Minnesota appellate court affirmed the jury verdict. In 2012, the Minnesota Supreme Court reversed the jury verdict regarding negligent misrepresentation on the basis that no duty of care is owed to a prospective governmental employee; that is, a prospective employee is not entitled to protection against negligent misrepresentations by any representative of the government employer (*Williams v. Smith*, 2012). This holding is specific to Minnesota law regarding governmental employers. Regardless of the eventual outcome, the costs expended to defend this lawsuit were considerable. Therefore, policies should be instituted to prohibit head coaches from making employment offers to prospective assistant coaches or support staff. All offers should be made by the athletic director.

The following Focus Case addresses the concept of negligent misrepresentation.

Randi W. v. Muroc Joint Unified School District

929 P.2d 582 (Cal. 1997)   **FOCUS** CASE

FACTS

A school vice-principal, Robert Gadams, sexually molested a middle school student. The student sued Gadams and also sued the administrator's former employers who gave positive recommendations about Gadams to his current employer. Gadams had worked in three school districts prior to this incident. In each situation, Gadams had engaged in various types of inappropriate sexual behavior with students. However, none of these problems were disclosed in employment references that were relied upon by the current employer. In fact, some of the references referred to Gadams' "genuine concern" for students and described him as an "upbeat, enthusiastic administrator who related well to the students."

The plaintiff sued the former employers for negligent misrepresentation, alleging that the failure to disclose material information relating to Gadams' fitness for the job induced the current employer to hire Gadams, leading to the sexual assault upon the plaintiff.

The trial court upheld the defendants' motions to dismiss. The California Court of Appeals affirmed in part and reversed in part. The plaintiff appealed to the California Supreme Court.

HOLDING

The California Supreme Court affirmed in part, holding that the "misleading half-truths" supplied by former employers were actionable.

RATIONALE

The court held that the writer of a recommendation letter owes a duty not to misrepresent the facts and the character of a former employee, if making those misrepresentations would cause a foreseeable risk of physical injury to the prospective employer or to third persons (students, in this situation). It was not appropriate for defendants to make positive comments about the candidate without disclosing the rest of the information they possessed concerning his misconduct. The representations that Gadams was fit to interact appropriately and safely with female students were false and misleading, in view of the defendants' knowledge of Gadams' repeated sexual improprieties.

The *Randi W.* case was an important step in holding employers accountable for giving a complete picture of a job candidate. It stopped short, however, of forcing an employer to disclose. So, in this case, if one of the former school districts had said absolutely nothing about Gadams except that he worked for the district for a specified number of years in certain positions, there would have been no liability. Some commentators have argued that this is unacceptable, that employers should be forced to divulge information about an employee in a situation like this one where the health and wellbeing of a very vulnerable population is at stake (Swerdlow, 1991). The cause of action on this ground is known as **negligent referral**.

Tortious Interference with Contractual Relations

Tortious interference with contractual relations prohibits improper interference with existing contracts (Gleason, 2008). In considering whether a defendant's interference with a contract or a prospective contract is improper, a court will address a number of factors, including the motives and interests of the interfering party (Restatement [Second] of Torts § 767, 1977). The factors are often incorporated into individual state statutes which recognize inducement to breach a contract as a tort claim. For example, Tennessee statutes provide:

> It is unlawful for any person, by inducement, persuasion, misrepresentation, or other means, to induce or procure the breach or violation, refusal or failure to perform any lawful contract by any party thereto; and in every case where a breach or violation of such contract is so procured, the person so procuring or inducing the same shall be liable to in treble the amount of damages resulting from or incident to the breach of the contract. The party injured by such breach may bring suit for the breach and for such damages.

This statute was at the heart of a case brought by the Tennessee Titans against Lane Kiffin and the University of Southern California (USC) when Kiffin as head coach at USC contacted Kennedy Pola, the Titans running backs coach, and solicited his employment to become the USC Trojans's offensive coordinator and running backs coach (Puls, 2010). Pola accepted this job and left the Titans. In his contract with the Titans, Pola agreed that he would not solicit discussion or entertain employment with any other person or entity during the term of his agreement unless given written permission to do so by the Titans or the NFL Commissioner. Pola was not given any written consent to entertain Kiffin's offer. As you can see in this example, Pola has a restrictive covenant in his employment agreement with the Titans. The Titans allege that Kiffin was aware of Pola's contractual restrictions and intended to induce Pola to breach his contract with the Titans. The parties ultimately entered into a private settlement (Associated Press, 2011), and the Titans joined the ranks of organizations pursuing tortious interference claims when their employees are poached by their competitors.

According to Greenberg (2011), the claim of tortious interference with contract is essentially based upon the "notion that the possessor of a contract or other property right is entitled to pursue a claim against an intermeddler who adversely affects those property rights." In essence, then, the legal remedy recognizes that a business relationship is a property interest worthy of protection from unjustified interference or tampering. The following case deals with these principles.

Competitive Advantage Strategies

Tort Theories and Employment

- When giving employment references, do not discuss employees' personalities. Stick to the facts that you have documented in the employees' files.
- If you choose to disclose information about employees, give a balanced reference: provide information about the employee's strengths and weaknesses. Do not provide favorable information without also providing unfavorable – assuming that you have evidence to support anything you say about the employee.
- In recruiting an employee, do not attempt to induce that person to breach an existing employment contract.

Bauer v. Interpublic Group of Companies, Inc.

255 F. Supp. 2d 1086 (N.D. Cal. 2003)   **FOCUS** CASE

FACTS

The plaintiff, Francis Bauer, is a sports agent whose clients are professional football players. During the 2001 college football season, David Carr was quarterback for Fresno State University. Bauer met with Carr and his father in the summer of 2001 and was told that the father, Rodger, would handle all dealings with agents.

After Bauer held several conversations with Rodger and his wife, Sheryl, David Carr signed a representation agreement with Bauer on January 1, 2002. Soon thereafter, David Carr decided that he was uncomfortable being represented by Bauer, and he terminated the relationship within two weeks of the contract's execution.

Bauer believed that David Carr terminated the contract because he received information from the Interpublic Group of Companies, Inc., a competitor in the sport agent business and parent company of Octagon Football. In contrast, David Carr stated that he had initiated the contact with the defendant company (Octagon) and that the decision to terminate the agreement with Bauer had no relationship to any communications with Octagon. Bauer sued Interpublic for intentional interference with contract and unfair competition.

HOLDING

The court granted the defendant's motion for summary judgment.

RATIONALE

First the court noted the elements of a claim for intentional interference with contract. The elements are: (1) a valid contract between a plaintiff and a third party; (2) defendant's knowledge of this contract; (3) defendant's intentional acts designed to induce a breach or disruption of the contractual relationship; (4) actual breach or disruption of the contractual relationship; and (5) resulting damage.

The court then reviewed the evidence presented by plaintiff Bauer. If Carr did receive any information containing negative information about Bauer, there is no evidence that the defendant sent the information. There is no evidence that the defendant made any disparaging remarks about Bauer to Carr. Further, there is no evidence that the defendant had any input into Carr's decision to terminate the contract with Bauer. Carr was the party who initiated contact with the defendant after he decided to terminate his contract with Bauer.

In light of this evidence, Bauer could not show that the defendant induced Carr to terminate his contract with Bauer.

The *Bauer* case illustrates the type of situation that is often indicative of this tort. In the case of *Northeastern University v. Brown*, discussed earlier in the context of a coach violating the covenant not to compete, a case could also be made against UMass for tortious interference with contractual relations if evidence showed that UMass acted to induce a breach of Brown's coaching contract with Northeastern University.

Conclusion

Managing human resources effectively can help you gain a competitive advantage in the sport marketplace. To make good management decisions in this realm, you need a thorough understanding of contract law and employment law principles. This chapter provided an overview of contract law followed by a discussion of employment contracts. We also reviewed the legal principles pertaining to employment at will and wrongful termination. Finally, we addressed a number of tort causes of action that are applicable in employment matters. Understanding these legal principles should enable you to make sound decisions related to human resources and to assist in making your organization a better one for employees.

Discussion Questions

1 What are the benefits of using a worst-case scenario approach in drafting contracts?
2 Explain the concepts of agreement, consideration, capacity, and legality in the formation of contracts.
3 Are oral contracts generally enforceable? When are oral contracts not enforceable?
4 Give some examples from a sport setting to illustrate statute of frauds principles.
5 What are the remedies available in breach of contract actions? What is the usual remedy?
6 What are the limitations upon using specific performance?
7 What is the principle of mitigation of damages?
8 Contrast actual authority with apparent authority. When can a third party use apparent authority to bind an organization to a contract?

Learning Activities

1 As the current athletic director at a Division I university, you are in the process of negotiating an employment contract with Will Wynn, your new football coach. Answer the following questions in your role as athletic director in order to protect the university's interests in the contract.

   a. Discuss the purpose of the liquidated damages clause and whether it is in the university's best interest to have this in the contract with Wynn. What are your primary concerns with whether this clause will be enforceable, and how can you draft it in such a way to help alleviate those concerns?

   b. Discuss the covenant not to compete (restrictive covenant) and how you may use it to your benefit in the contract with Wynn. Discuss whether you would include a "conference wide restriction" as part of the restrictive covenant and what factors you should consider in imposing that restriction.

   c. Would the university prefer to have a stated term of years or a rollover clause? Explain.

   d. Discuss five other clauses that you would like to incorporate into the coaching contract to protect the university's interests.

2 Conduct an Internet search to find out how many college football coaches now have compensation "packages" that exceed $5 million per year. Try to ascertain how much of the compensation is base salary, how much is in the form of supplemental compensation and performance incentives.

Case Study

Review the *O'Brien* Focus Case and then answer the following questions related to that case.

1 The Court of Claims judge in this case interpreted the facts in favor of O'Brien when the judge characterized the loan as given for humanitarian reasons and not given to gain an improper recruiting advantage. What facts might support a more sinister interpretation of the coach's conduct?
2 Discuss how Ohio State could have strengthened its grounds for termination for cause.
3 Discuss the implications of this decision relative to other colleges that may wish to terminate coaches "for cause."
4 Consider the language of other termination provisions in coaches' contracts to determine how a termination clause may be written which favors the university. You may also consider the termination clauses in the coaches' contracts that may be found by using the coaches' contract databases included in the list of relevant websites below.

Considering … Analysis & Discussion

Promissory Estoppel

Lance cannot win on contract principles. This grant-in-aid (the contract between the student and SRU) clearly states that it was only for a one-year period (and he signed three of these throughout his career at SRU), and notice of nonrenewal was given timely. Under promissory estoppel principles, Lance does have a case. First, a promise was made by the coach that Lance would receive aid for all four years. This promise should reasonably be expected to induce reliance, since the coach is the person who makes decisions related to scholarships. Lance chose to attend SRU based upon the coach's promises, and Lance suffered a detriment since he received no aid in his senior year. The relationship between the coach and the prospect also contributes to the strength of Lance's case, since the disparity in bargaining power between coach and player makes reliance even more likely to occur. See a law review by Nomura (2009) that argues that promissory estoppel should be a viable remedy in situations like this.

Apparent Authority

The third-party vendor will argue that there was apparent authority to enter into the $25,000 contract. Since the store owners had taken no action before when the manager entered into contracts exceeding his actual authority, the third-party vendor reasonably believes that the agent has the authority to act. The principal will be bound to the agreement.

References

Cases

Bauer v. Interpublic Group of Cos., 255 F. Supp. 2d 1086 (N.D. Cal. 2003).
Clark v. University of Bridgeport, 2011 Conn. Super. LEXIS 1977 (July 29, 2011).
Giuliani v. Duke Univ., U.S. Dist. LEXIS 32691 (M.D.N.C. March 30, 2010).
Huyett v. Idaho State Univ., 104 P.3d 946 (Idaho 2004).
Kish v. Iowa Central Community College, 142 F. Supp. 2d 1084 (N.D. Iowa 2001).
Marist College v. Brady, 84 A.D.3d 1322 (2011).
Mau v. L.A. Fitness International, 749 F. Supp. 2d 845 (N.D. Ill. 2010).
Mendenhall v. Hanesbrands, Inc., 856 F. Supp. 2d 717 (M.D.N.C. 2012).
Monson v. State of Oregon, 901 P.2d 904 (Or. Ct. App. 1995).
Northeastern University v. Brown, 17 Mass. L. Rep. 443 (Mass. Super. Ct. 2004).
O'Brien v. Ohio State Univ., 2007 Ohio App. LEXIS 4316 (September 20, 2007).
Ohton v. Board of Trustees California State University, 56 Cal. Rptr. 3d 111 (Ct. App. 2007).
Randi W. v. Muroc Joint Unified School District, 929 P.2d 582 (Cal. 1997).
Rodgers v. Georgia Tech Athletic Association, 303 S.E.2d 467 (Ga. Ct. App. 1983).
Samson Sales, Inc. v. Honeywell, Inc., 465 N.E.2d 392 (1984).
Spears v. Grambling State University, 111 So.3d 392 (La.App. 1st Cir. 2012).
Vanderbilt University v. DiNardo, 174 F.3d 751 (6th Cir. 1999).
Williams v. Smith, 820 N.W.2d 807 (Minn. 2012).

Statutes

Child Performer and Athlete Protection Act, § 743.08(3) (Fla. Stat.).
Restatement (Second) of Contracts (1981).
Restatement (Second) of Torts (1977).

Other Sources

About the National Letter of Intent. (NLI). Retrieved from www.ncaa.org/wps/wcm/connect/nli/nli.

Aragon, L. W., & Miller, C. (2017). National letter of intent's basic penalty: Analysis and legal bases to end the practice. *Arizona State University Sports and Entertainment Law Journal, 7*(1), 7–92.

Armstrong, M., & Taylor, S. (2020). *Armstrong's handbook of human resource management practice* (15th ed.). New York, NY: Kogan-Page.

Associated Press. (2011, April 6). Titans, USC settle lawsuit of Pola hire. ESPN.com. Retrieved from https://www.espn.com/los-angeles/nfl/news/story?id=6301830.

Bauer-Wolf, J. (2019, July 24). DePaul basketball coach suspended by NCAA. *Inside Higher Ed.* Retrieved from https://www.insidehighered.com/news/2019/07/24/ncaa-suspends-depaul-head-mens-basketball-coach-three-games.

Chung, A. (2015, June 9). Nike settles with designers it accused of stealing secrets. *Reuters.* Retrieved from https://www.reuters.com/article/us-nike-adidas-settlement/nike-settles-with-designers-it-accused-of-stealing-secrets-idUSKBN0OP2GL20150609.

Coach thieves beware. (2004, November 27). *College Athletics Clips.* Retrieved from www.collegeathleticsclips.com/archives/000326.html.

Cross, F. B., & Miller, R.L. (2018). *The Legal Environment of Business* (10th ed.). Boston, MA: Cengage Learning.

Edelman, M. (2013, January 17). Settlement of lawsuit. *Forbes.* Retrieved from www.forbes.com/sites/marcedelman/2013/01/17/rashard-mendenhall-settle.

Fitzgerald, D. B. (2010, August). A beacon in Poughkeepsie: Marist claims victory over James Madison in coaching contract suit. *Sports Litigation Alert, 7*, 22–24.

Fitzgerald, D. B. (2012, June). Marist outfoxes ex-coach, but does not score damages. *Legal Issues in Collegiate Athletics*, 5–6.

Former strength coach reaches settlement with SDSU after protracted litigation. (2011, March). *Legal Issues in Collegiate Athletics, 12*, 2.

Ganim, S. (2014, July 1). Whistle-blower in University of North Carolina paper class case files lawsuit. CNN. Retrieved from https://www.cnn.com/2014/07/01/us/university-north-carolina-paper-class-lawsuit/index.html.

Ganim, S. (2015, March 17). UNC "fake classes" whistleblower to get $335K in settlement. CNN. Retrieved from https://www.cnn.com/2015/03/17/us/north-carolina-willingham-unc-settlement/index.html.

Gleason, J. P. (2008, May). Comment: From Russia with love: The legal repercussions of the recruitment and contracting of foreign players in the National Hockey League. *Buffalo Law Review, 56*, 599–654.

Greenberg, M. (2010). The use of clawback clauses in college coaches' contracts. *Marquette Sports Law.* Retrieved from https://law.marquette.edu/assets/sports-law/pdf/for-the-record/greenberg-v21no2.pdf.

Greenberg, M. J. (2011, January 4). Take my coach and I'll take you to court. *Marquette Sports Law.* Retrieved from https://law.marquette.edu/national-sports-law-institute/take-my-coach-and-ill-take-you-court-january-4-2011.

Greenberg, M. (2013, August 9). Mike Rice, Jr., for cause or not for cause. *Marquette Sports Law.* Retrieved from https://law.marquette.edu/assets/sports-law/pdf/rice.8613.pd.

Greenberg, M. J. (2019, July 1). Dabo Swinney: A new contract for a new coaching landscape. Marquette Sports Law. Retrieved from https://law.marquette.edu/assets/sports-law/DABO%20SWINNEY.pdf.

Greenberg, M. J., & Park, T. (2018, July 15). Separation agreements: When a university and a coach divorce. *Marquette Sports Law.* Retrieved from https://law.marquette.edu/national-sports-law-institute/greenbergs-coaching-corner.

Greenberg, M. J., & Paul, D. (2013). Coaches' contracts: Terminating a coach without cause and the obligation to mitigate damages. *Marquette Sports Law Review, 23*(2), 339–391.

Greene, L. S. (2008, Spring). UMKC sports law symposium: Emerging legal issues affecting amateur & professional sports: Football coach contracts: What does the student-athlete have to do with it? *UMKC Law Review, 76*, 665–696.

Kerr, N. R. (2018). Case comment: Independent Sports & Entertainment, LLC v. Fegan. *University of Denver Sports and Entertainment Law Journal, 21*, 1–6.

Kuehner-Hebert, K. (2015, June 10). Nike settles $10M suit against ex-designers. *CFO.com.* Retrieved from https://www.cfo.com/legal/2015/06/nike-settles-10m-suit-ex-designers/.

Lens, J. (2018). NCAA Head coach responsibilities legislation. *DePaul Journal of Sports Law, 14*(1), 33–66.

McCann, M. (2018, July 12). Should the NCAA be worried about the lawsuit it's facing from former Louisville players. *Sports Illustrated.* Retrieved from https://www.si.com/college/2018/07/12/louisville-ex-players-lawsuit-ncaa-luke-hancock.

NCAA. (2020a). Scholarships. NCAA.org. Retrieved from http://www.ncaa.org/student-athletes/future/scholarships.

NCAA. (2020b). Division I Manual By-law 11.2.1 and 11.2.2.

NCAA. (2020c). NCAA 2019–20 Division I Manual. Retrieved from https://web3.ncaa.org/lsdbi/reports/getReport/90008.

New, J. (2015, January 19). "Autonomy" arrives at the NCAA. *Inside Higher Ed.* Retrieved from https://www.insidehighered.com/news/2015/01/19/power-five-leagues-expand-athletic-scholarships-cover-full-cost-attendance.

Nomura, J. Y. (2009). Referring the recruiting game: Applying contract law to make the intercollegiate recruitment process fair. *Hawaii Law Review*, 32, 275–304.

Pacella, J. M. (2018). Silencing whistleblowers by contract. *American Business Law Journal*, 55(2), 261–313.

Pagar, C. B. (2016, September 24). Athletes, scandals and sponsorships: Why morals clauses are more important than ever [Web log post]. Retrieved from https://www.vlplawgroup.com/blog/athletes-scandals-sponsorships-morals-clauses-important-ever/.

Pauline, G. A., & Wolohan, J. T. (2012). An examination of the non-recruit clause in intercollegiate coaching contracts. *Journal of Legal Aspects of Sport*, 21, 219–238.

Percy, S. (2019, February 22). The five most important skills for managers to develop in 2019. *Forbes.com*. Retrieved from https://www.forbes.com/sites/sallypercy/2019/02/22/the-five-most-important-skills-for-managers-to-develop-in-2019/#2501fbd15e6d.

Puls, J. (2010, July 29). Tennessee Titans to sue Lane Kiffin. *Bleacher Report*. Retrieved from https://bleacherreport.com/articles/426548-tennessee-titans-to-sue-lane-kiffin.

Riddle, B. (2015, February 24). Employment at will comes with many exceptions in Kentucky. *The National Law Review*. Retrieved from https://www.natlawreview.com/article/employment-will-comes-many-exceptions-kentucky.

Ridpath, B. D. (2017, May 10). NCAA's APR release should be looked at with a very skeptical eye. *Forbes*. Retrieved from https://www.forbes.com/sites/bdavidridpath/2017/05/10/ncaas-apr-release-should-be-looked-at-with-a-very-skeptical-eye/#404115d061af.

Rovell, D. (2014, December 9). Nike sues former designers. *ABCNews.com*. Retrieved from https://abcnews.go.com/Sports/nike-sues-designers/story?id=27490031.

Swerdlow, J. (1991). Negligent referral: A potential theory for employer liability. *Southern California Law Review*, 64(2), 1645–1673.

Swerdlow, A. (2017, February 6). Modernizing termination clauses in NCAA coach contracts. *GeraldFoxLaw.com*. Retrieved from http://www.gerardfoxlaw.com/news/legal-perspectives/modernizing-termination-clauses-in-ncaa-coach-contracts/.

Thomas, R. S., & Van Horn, R. (2016). Are college presidents like football coaches? Evidence from their employment contracts. *Arizona Law Review*, 58(4), 901–958.

University of Montana. (2014, December). Football Head Coach Employment Agreement. Retrieved from https://hkm.com/football/wp-content/uploads/coach-contracts/robertstitt-mu-employment-contract.pdf.

USA Today. (2018). NCAA salaries: 2018 NCAAF coaches' salaries. *USA Today*. Retrieved from https://sports.usatoday.com/ncaa/salaries/.

USA Today. (2019). NCAA salaries: 2019 NCAAB coaches' pay. *USA Today*. Retrieved from https://sports.usatoday.com/ncaa/salaries/mens-basketball/coach.

Vernon, J. G. (2017, February 17). Is it time for athletes to demand reciprocal morals clauses in their endorsement deals? *Miller Canfield*. Retrieved from https://www.millercanfield.com.

Zucker, J. (2019, September 30). NCAA reaches settlement with Luke Hancock, Multiple ex-Louisville players. *Bleacher Report*. Retrieved from https://bleacherreport.com/articles/2856044-ncaa-reaches-settlement-with-luke-hancock-multiple-ex-louisville-players.

Web Resources

www.coacheshotseat.com/SalariesContracts.htm ■ This website deals with numerous issues related to college football coaches. The Salaries & Contracts aspect of the website has a list of coaches' compensation, and many of the actual contracts are appended.

www.loeb.com/sportslessonslearnedwebinar/ ■ A webinar provided by the law firm Loeb & Loeb in light of the Lance Armstrong scandal that provides information about how companies should use morals clauses to protect their brands.

www.usatoday.com/sports/college/salaries/ncaab/coach/ ■ This *USA Today* site sets forth contract provisions dealing with compensation for Division I men's basketball coaches in the year 2013. PDF files for many of the actual contracts are included.

www.usatoday.com/story/sports/ncaaf/2012/11/19/ncaa-college-football-head-coach-salary-database/1715543/ ■ This *USA Today* site sets forth contract provisions dealing with compensation for Football Bowl Subdivision coaches as of November 2012. PDF files for many of the actual contracts are included.

www.nationalletter.org ■ This site provides information about the National Letter of Intent Program, which is administered through the NCAA Eligibility Center office.

4 Employer Liability for Acts of Employees and Others

Introduction

This chapter discusses the circumstances in which employers will be held responsible for the actions of their employees. First, the concept of *respondeat superior* will be addressed in which employers are generally responsible for the actions of employees so long as the actions are taken within the scope of employment. Next, we discuss the legal theories of negligent hiring, supervision, and retention, followed by the issue of whether an employer may be liable for the actions of an independent contractor or volunteer. Last, we address the matter of whether a university may be vicariously liable for actions of its athletes.

This chapter continues to explore the notion of using legal strategies to gain a competitive advantage in the management of our human resources. In Chapter 3, we applied this notion in conjunction with effective legal strategies for creating employment relationships and defining the terms and conditions of those relationships through contracts. In this chapter, we explore ways in which you as a manager can minimize your organization's exposure to liability based on the actions of personnel, whether the personnel are employees, independent contractors, volunteers, or college athletes. See Exhibit 4.1 for an overview of this chapter's managerial contexts, major legal issues, relevant law, and illustrative cases.

Liability Related to Acts of Employees

This section provides an introduction to vicarious liability principles and discusses various forms of negligence that can occur in making employment-related decisions.

Vicarious Liability Principles

The doctrine of **vicarious liability** or *respondeat superior* (let the master respond) holds an employing organization (employer) responsible for certain acts of its employees, not because of any wrongdoing by the employer, but because the law has deemed it appropriate for the employer to be held accountable for the actions of its employees. Thus, the employer's liability is secondary or derivative in the sense that the employer itself is not a wrongdoer. As a policy matter, this doctrine is based on the belief that the employer generally receives the benefits of its employees' actions; therefore, when the employee does something that is not beneficial, the employer should also bear that responsibility. The doctrine is also predicated on the employer's ability to control employees and to procure insurance that covers the actions of employees. In short, an employer should bear employee liability as a cost of doing business.

Scope of Employment

The general rule of *respondeat superior* is that an employer will be responsible for the acts of an employee so long as the acts are done within the scope of employment to advance the business of the employer. Conduct is considered to be within the employee's **scope of employment** if "it is of the kind he is employed

Exhibit 4.1 Management contexts in which liability for actions of employees and others may arise, with relevant laws and cases.

Management Context	Major Legal Issues	Relevant Law	Illustrative Cases
Oversight of employees	Employer liability for actions of employees	Vicarious liability / *respondeat superior* Scope of employment	Smith
Hiring employees	Liability for hiring improperly	Negligent hiring	Anderson
Supervision of employees	Liability for supervising improperly	Negligent retention	
Retention of employees	Liability for retaining improperly	Negligent retention	
	Who is an independent contractor?	Criteria defining independent contractor	Zajaczkowski
Hiring independent contractors	Liability for actions of independent contractor	Negligent selection	
Choosing volunteers	Liability for actions of student-athlete	Vicarious liability	Lasseigne
Oversight of college athletes	Liability for actions of student-athlete	Vicarious liability	Kavanagh

to perform; it occurs substantially within the authorized time and space limits; and it is actuated, at least in part, by a purpose to serve the master" (Restatement [Second] of Agency § 228). For example, if a coach is driving the team van owned by the university and drives negligently, injuring a third party or the students aboard the van, that negligence of the employee/coach is imputed to the employer/university under the principle of *respondeat superior* so long as the accident occurred in the scope of employment, that is, while the employee was in the process of transporting the team.

Please note that an employee's job description as written in an employee handbook or an employee contract is usually not synonymous with the concept of scope of employment. Job descriptions do not generally encompass all of the duties actually performed by employees. As we saw in Chapter 3, often the employment contract includes a rather nebulous phrase to the effect that the employee is expected to do X, Y, Z, and "other duties as may be assigned." As in the previous example, if the coach drives negligently while transporting players to an away match, that negligence will certainly be within the coach's scope of employment, even if the duty of transporting players was not specifically delineated within the coach's contract.

The case of *Smith v. Gardner* deals with a college assistant baseball coach and whether his actions were within the scope of employment.

Smith v. Gardner

998 F. Supp. 708 (S.D. Miss. 1998)   **FOCUS** CASE

FACTS

The plaintiff was injured in a two-car automobile accident in the early morning hours of March 17, 1996. The plaintiff sued the driver of the other vehicle, Gardner, and Gardner's employer, San Jacinto College, based on Gardner's negligent driving. Gardner was employed as an assistant baseball coach with the college, and he was on a road trip with the team.

After the team was settled into a hotel on the night of March 16, Gardner left the hotel at midnight to buy some beer. He returned to the hotel and drank some of the beer. He then decided to go out again and purchase smokeless tobacco. He left again, driving the school van, and at 3:22 a.m. he was involved in the accident in question. He was driving while intoxicated.

The plaintiff asserted that the college should be vicariously liable for the actions of Gardner, arguing that Gardner's actions were within the scope of employment.

HOLDING

The federal district court granted the college's motion for summary judgment, as it held that Gardner's actions were not within the scope of employment.

RATIONALE

First, the court addressed the definition of "scope of employment," since an employer is not vicariously liable for the actions of an employee unless the actions are taken within the scope of employment. If an action is within the scope of employment, the employee is taking action in the course of and as the means to accomplish the purposes of employment and, therefore, in furtherance of the master's business. In contrast, if an employee abandons his employment and is engaged in some purpose of his own, this is not considered to be within the scope of employment.

In this case, Gardner, in driving around town after drinking enough beer to become intoxicated, was not in any sense about any conceivable business of the college, nor was he performing any act that could be considered incidental to his employment. Gardner was obviously a "frolicking employee engaged in affairs of his own."

Therefore, concluded the court, the college is not liable for Gardner's alleged negligence relating to the auto accident in question.

Competitive Advantage Strategies

Liability Related to Employees

- Develop protocols for hiring employees and ensure that they are followed in all circumstances, even if a candidate is "known" by the organization.
- Make sure that all protocols provide for reasonable investigation into applicants's backgrounds. What is reasonable investigation will vary depending upon the type of position and the person's involvement with vulnerable populations. For example, extra care should be taken when hiring employees who will work closely with children or with individuals who are disabled. Use criminal background checks to the extent permitted by state law.
- Require job applicants to sign a form authorizing you to obtain employment information from prior employers.
- Use a job application form that requires applicants to divulge whether they have been convicted of a felony and the details surrounding any conviction.
- Check the references provided and carefully document the responses.
- If you work in a youth sport organization, educate parents regarding issues of proper coaching relationships with young players and encourage parental involvement in observing coaching behaviors. Implement a reporting mechanism for parents to raise concerns with organization administrators.
- Train managers to supervise employees reasonably and to discipline employees in accordance with organizational policy.
- Develop a "no tolerance" policy regarding workplace violence. Violent or inappropriate behavior should never be overlooked or condoned by an organization, even if the person seems to be performing well in other aspects of the job.
- Train managers to deal with employees in stressful situations such as terminations, furloughs, and labor disputes.
- Train all employees to resolve workplace disputes through negotiation and respectful dialogue.
- Develop a threat assessment and response team to investigate any threats of violence and develop appropriate responses.

Exhibit 4.2 Types of workplace violence.

1   **Stranger violence** – committed by someone with no business relationship with the workplace.
2   **Customer/client violence** – committed by someone who receives services or buys products from the workplace.
3   **Employee violence** – committed by a current or former employee of the workplace.
4   **Domestic violence** – committed by family member or significant other of the employee.

Intentional Acts of Violence by Employees

Mielnicki (2014) identified four types of workplace violence (see Exhibit 4.2). Some of these types of violent acts will be explored in later chapters related to the Occupational Safety and Health Administration (OSHA)/workers' compensation (Chapter 9) or intentional torts (Chapter 14). For example, violence at the workplace can result in a fine by the OSHA or an injury to another employee prompting a workers' compensation claim. Intentional torts, which are deliberate actions, such as assault and battery, are usually undertaken to serve the employee's own interests, not to benefit the employer. Most acts of an intentional nature done by an employee are outside the scope of employment; therefore, vicarious liability would not apply to the employer. However, employee violence toward others does pose a risk for organizations and the potential for liability in the sport context needs to be further explored.

On occasion an intentional tort may be considered to be within the scope of employment. For example, in the case of *Nathans v. Offerman* (2013), a federal district court in Connecticut held that a battery by a minor league baseball player could be considered to be "within the scope of employment." In this case, the defendant employee, while at bat, was struck by a pitch. He charged the mound with his bat in hand, and during the melée hit the opposing team's catcher in the head with his bat. The defendant employer asserted that it should not be vicariously liable for the defendant employee's battery, since it was not in the scope of employment. However, the court noted that the Restatement (Second) of Agency § 245 provides exceptions in which an employee's intentional tort may be considered to be within the scope of employment. Two of these exceptions could apply here, that is, actions in excess of zeal in competition and fighting arising out of work for one's employer. Therefore, the court declined to grant summary judgment for the defendant employer as it held that whether this battery was in the scope of employment should be a determination made by the finder of fact (the jury).

While vicarious liability can be difficult to establish in cases dealing with intentional torts such as sexual assault, some scholars have criticized this limitation in cases involving sexual abuse or exploitation, instead calling for revising the doctrine of vicarious liability (Chamallas, 2013). Especially in light of the sexual abuse scandals at Penn State (Jerry Sandusky) and Michigan State University/USA Gymnastics (Larry Nassar), sport managers do need to recognize institutional liability for these actions can be sustained for negligence for a failure to protect in addition to the Title IX violations. Penn State ultimately settled for $109 million, one of the largest abuse settlements for a U.S. university in history, but was dwarfed by the MSU settlement of $500 million (Corrigan, 2018). Two additional examples to consider include a youth organization held vicariously liable for its representative's sexual assault of a child. In the case of *Southport Little League v. Vaughan* (2000), an appellate court in Indiana upheld a finding of vicarious liability against a Little League baseball club. The abuser was an equipment manager who molested several children in an equipment shed where he took them supposedly to distribute and check the fitting of baseball uniforms and equipment. One notable fact was that the abuser, through his roles as Little League official and equipment manager, had organizational authority to be alone with a participant in the equipment shed (Preston, 2006). Gibbons and Campbell (2003) warned of a trend where courts may reconsider holding organizations responsible for sexual assaults on children particularly if the organization placed their employees in a position of trust and authority. Consistent with Gibbons and Campbell's warning, several states have enacted or are considering passage of child victims' laws to extend the statute of limitations for child sexual abuse and to permit claims against employers and supervisors in charge of abusers (Baumann, 2019).

In addition to sexual abuse, it is increasingly common for schools and recreational organizations to face lawsuits involving the physical abuse of athletes and participants – particularly minors, the elderly and people with disabilities – by coaches, employees and volunteers. A good example of the problems faced by school and athletics administrators regarding the physical abuse of athletes by coaches is *Robinson v. Polk County School Board* (2013). Devarus Robinson was a football player on the Kathleen High School football team in Lakeland, Florida. While on the team, Robinson was constantly subjected to bullying and physical abuse by the school's head football coach, Irving Strickland. In particular, the court found that Strickland would twist Robinson's nipples – so much so that Robinson's nipples were permanently disfigured. Robinson reported the abuse to school administrators and Strickland acknowledged the abuse when he was questioned by school administrators. However, he was only given a written reprimand for his actions. It was clear from both medical records and the school board's reprimand of Strickland that there was a history of abuse and that school administrators and officials failed to protect Robinson from that abuse by removing Strickland as coach. As a result of the school board's negligence, the jury found against the Polk County School Board and awarded Robinson $125,000 (Wolohan & Gao, 2018).

Lastly, in some circumstances, an intentional tort may be considered to be within the scope of employment because the employer has engaged in some behavior that ratifies or condones the employee's propensity to engage in acts of that nature – this is the **ratification/condonation principle** (27 Am. Jur. 2d *Employment Relationship* § 381). In the case of *Tomjanovich v. Los Angeles Lakers*, Rudy Tomjanovich was severely injured by a punch thrown by Kermit Washington, a Lakers player, who was rewarded by the Lakers for his rough play. The Lakers, therefore, essentially condoned Washington's violent propensities, which led to this foreseeable attack upon Tomjanovich. This is an example of the ratification or condonation of behavior that would normally be outside the scope of employment. Ugolini (2007) provides an interesting law review discussing the National Football League's (NFL) responsibility for the behavior of its players.

In an example illustrating the concept of ratification or condonation, a lawsuit was filed against USA Swimming based on the actions of Rick Curl, founder of the Washington, D.C. area's most prominent swim club. Curl was banned for life in 2012 by USA Swimming after a revelation that Curl had a sexual relationship with a 13-year-old swimmer in the 1980s. In 1989, Kelly Currin and her parents signed an agreement with Curl in which the family agreed not to pursue criminal charges or disclose the abuse to law enforcement in exchange for $150,000, a decision she says she regrets to this day (Tenorio, 2012). Currin believed that USA Swimming had knowledge of Curl's actions and continued to allow him to serve as a swim coach nonetheless. Currin further stated that Berkoff [Vice-President, USA Swimming] knew by the early 1990s about sexual relationships between coaches and underage swimmers, including Curl and Currin, and USA Swimming had helped "create a culture that protects predator coaches and vilifies young victims" (Crouse, 2013, p. 13). USA Swimming as well as several other sport organizations face or have settled dozens of cases involving sexual abuse by coaches occurring over many years (Associated Press, 2020; Carp, 2018; Harris, 2020; Starr, 2020). This will be explored further in the negligent retention section later in this chapter. The hypothetical case presented in the negligent retention discussion later in the chapter also illustrates the ratification/condonation principle.

Negligence in Making Employment-Related Decisions

In contrast to the theory underlying *respondeat superior*, liability based on negligent hiring, supervision, or retention is predicated on the negligence of a managerial employee in making an employment-related decision. The basic tenets of negligence law apply (see Chapter 14's discussion of the elements of negligence). The standard of care imposed upon a manager who is making a hiring decision is to act as a reasonably prudent manager in the circumstance.

Negligent Hiring and Negligent Retention

The basic question underlying **negligent hiring** is whether a manager acted reasonably in choosing a particular person to fill a position. The underlying question in regard to **negligent retention** is whether a manager acted reasonably in retaining an employee's services after he knew or should have known of the employee's unfitness for the position. The primary difference between these two claims is timing. Negligent hiring occurs at the time of hiring, while negligent retention occurs during the course of employment (*Anderson v. Soap Lake School District*, 2018). We will explore both of these theories of liability.

Negligent Hiring

The tort of negligent hiring is concerned with the risk created by exposing members of the public to a potentially dangerous or unfit person. As the Restatement (Second) of Agency § 213 (1958) provides: "a person conducting an activity through servants or agents is subject to liability for harm resulting from his conduct if he is negligent or reckless … in the employment of improper persons." Negligent hiring occurs when an employer breaches its duty to hire safe and competent employees (Minuti, 1988). The manager must first ask, does that employee or candidate have the appropriate qualifications?

For example, there is considerable controversy regarding personal trainers and their qualifications (as discussed in Chapter 14). Since there is no overarching national standard, a manager must be diligent in choosing a personal trainer who has the necessary competence to deal safely and effectively with clients. In addition to qualifications, the manager must also ask, is the candidate suitable for the position in terms of personal characteristics and qualities? Is there something in the person's background that would affect the person's ability to do the job? If efforts to address these questions are neglected, and information should have been discovered by a manager who had acted with reasonable diligence in the hiring process, the manager may be liable for negligent hiring.

The following hypothetical case illustrates a rather prevalent scenario, the hiring of a coach for youth sport.

Considering … Negligent Hiring

You are the chief administrator of a local youth softball league in charge of hiring coaches for the upcoming season. The coaches are not well paid, and it is difficult to get enough coaches for your eight teams. The participants in the program are young girls, ages 8 to 14. The season is fast approaching, and you need to fill the last coaching position very quickly. Finally, a man applies who has just moved to your area. He seems very personable, and he tells you that he has coached softball for the last ten years in other youth organizations. You are very impressed with this person's knowledge of the sport and his outgoing personality, so you hire him, doing no reference checks whatsoever.

If you had done any investigation, you would have found out that his last coaching position ended with accusations against him of sexual abuse of his female players. A criminal background check would have revealed a prior conviction for a sexual offense with a minor.

One month after being hired, this coach sexually molests a girl on his team.

Question

- What liability can exist?

Note how you would answer the question and then check your response using the Analysis & Discussion at the end of this chapter.

Unfortunately, this type of scenario is frequently repeated across the United States. The nature of youth sport, with close ties between coaches and participants, increases the opportunity for child abuse to occur, as happened with Currin and Curl (USA Swimming), discussed previously. Abuse may include sexual, emotional, and physical abuse, as well as neglect (Brackenridge, Bringer, & Bishopp, 2005). Pedophiles often seek to serve as youth coaches because this role gives them easy access to a large number of potential victims (Montaldo, 2019). Organizations that work with children, such as youth leagues, the YMCA/YWCA, and Boys and Girls Clubs, must be very vigilant in their hiring practices because of the predatory nature of pedophiles and, of course, the very vulnerable populations that these organizations serve (Baumgaertner, 2019; Lytle, 2018).

Several initiatives have been taken to address the prevalence of sexual predators in youth sport. In Florida, the Lunsford Act was passed in 2005 requiring sports officials and other independent contractors to clear a fingerprinting and background check before being allowed on public school grounds when students are present (Ramirez, 2007). A number of other states have passed legislation requiring background checks, and governing bodies have also passed initiatives to require background checks for youth coaches and officials (Denver Basketball Officials, 2013). The U.S. Congress also passed the Safe Sport Authorization Act (SSAA) in February 2019 requiring all U.S. amateur sport national governing bodies to report known or a reasonable suspicion of child abuse within 24 hours to law enforcement not the governing bodies leadership (Stark, 2019). (The Safe Sport Act will be discussed in greater deal in Chapter 13 dealing with Olympic sport governance). Additionally, the National Alliance for Youth Sports has developed a volunteer screening process for youth sports volunteers (see Web Resources) and scholarly research has produced risk assessment instruments and screening procedures for organizations to identify candidates with a tendency toward abuse (Abel, Jordan, & Harlow, 2018; Baker & Byon, 2013; Turner, Rettenberger, & Yoon, 2014).

Negligent Retention

This issue may arise when a manager receives negative feedback about an employee or has direct knowledge of an employee's misdeeds yet does nothing to discipline or discharge that employee.

Rutgers University was involved in a situation that could have resulted in a suit based on negligent retention. Former men's basketball coach Mike Rice was captured on video abusing players by screaming at them, throwing basketballs at them, and using homophobic slurs; the video was compiled by fired athletics staff member Eric Murdock. Before submitting the video, in July 2012, Murdock had written to administrators, including then athletics director Tim Pernetti, about Rice's conduct. He obtained recorded material from the university to compile his video.

Administrators undertook an investigation. In December 2012, Pernetti showed the video to Mark Hershhorn, chair of the board of governors's intercollegiate athletics committee. At first, Hershhorn questioned its authenticity but said that, if it was authentic, Rice should be fired. However, Rice was only suspended that month. In March 2013, the video was aired by news media and Rice was fired in April (Grasgreen, 2013).

In July 2013, an independent inquiry commissioned by Rutgers University into the scandal that led to Rice's firing found school leadership exercised "insufficient oversight" over an insular and overly autonomous athletic department (Grasgreen, 2013). Rice should have been fired as soon as the video came to light in 2012; instead, because of poor communication by the president of the university and the board of trustees, Rice was allowed to keep his employment until April 2013. If a lawsuit had been brought against Rutgers by one of Rice's players who was "assaulted or battered" by Rice between July 2012 and April 2013, it probably would have been easy to make a case of negligent retention against various administrators in the Rutgers governance structure who failed to fire him when the allegations of abuse first came to light in 2012. The *Anderson v. Soap Lake School District* Focus Case below will be helpful as you are considering negligent hiring and negligent retention in the following hypothetical case.

Considering ... Negligent Retention

Bob Strong is the general manager of Fit and Well, a health and fitness club that is owned by Win Corporation. Strong is in charge of all employment-related matters, including hiring, firing, and disciplining employees.

Six months ago, Strong hired Adam Easton to be the club's director of fitness. Easton came highly recommended, with superb credentials. After one week on the job, Strong received a complaint from another employee, Tammy Riley, that Easton had screamed at her for making a scheduling mistake and had essentially backed her into a corner as he screamed, using his size and strength to intimidate her. Strong listened to Riley's story but did not investigate further and did not talk to Easton about this incident.

After one month on the job, Strong received another complaint about Easton's violent behavior from Jessica Barker, another club employee. On this occasion, Easton screamed obscenities at Barker and grabbed her arm to emphasize a point. Strong again listened to Barker's report but chose to do nothing, since Easton was doing a great job outside of these outbursts.

Over the course of the next five months, Strong received similar complaints from five other employees and one club patron about Easton's increasingly violent behavior. Strong once had a "chat" with Easton about the issue, but he never took any disciplinary action.

In the sixth month, Easton exploded and punched one of the club's patrons, sending her to the hospital with a broken jaw and a concussion. This patron is now going to sue Strong and Win Corporation based on Easton's intentional tort (battery). (Note that a criminal case could also be made against Easton.)

Question

- On what bases could the patron win her lawsuit?

Note how you would answer the question and then check your response using the Analysis & Discussion at the end of this chapter.

Anderson v. Soap Lake School District

423 P.3d 197 *(Wash. 2018)*	**FOCUS** CASE

FACTS

Michele Anderson suffered the tragic and heartbreaking loss of her daughter, Sheila Rosenberg, following the irresponsible actions of Rosenberg's high school basketball coach, Igor Lukashevich. Lukashevich invited Rosenberg to his home where he poured and drank shots of vodka with her. Shortly after leaving Lukashevich's home, Rosenberg was killed along with her boyfriend, Pavel Turchik, in a car accident. Lukashevich was hired by Soap Lake School District (SL) to coach the high school girls's varsity basketball team. He had no college degree, no certifications in teaching or education, and no child development or physical education training. His main qualifications were that he had played basketball for six years in middle school and high school and lived in the city of SL. He had also previously worked as assistant coach to the junior varsity boys' basketball team. At the time, Lukashevich was 22 years old and had completed a certificate program in cardiopulmonary resuscitation (CPR). With these modest credentials, he met the necessary qualifications for high school coaches listed in the Washington Interscholastic, which included a high school degree, 21 years of age, and holding a valid CPR certificate. SL required Lukashevich to list any criminal history, and he indicated that he had never been convicted of or charged with a crime.

SL also submitted his fingerprints for a background check and he passed both the Washington State Patrol's and Federal Bureau of Investigation's checks. Anderson filed suit against Lukashevich's employer, SL, for negligent hiring and negligent retention.

HOLDING

The court affirmed the dismissal of the plaintiff's claims.

RATIONALE

This court has not yet adopted a test for negligent hiring and/or retention of an employee. We now adopt the test used by the Courts of Appeals: to hold an employer liable for negligently hiring or retaining an employee who is incompetent or unfit, a plaintiff must show that the employer had knowledge of the employee's unfitness or failed to exercise reasonable care to discover unfitness before hiring or retaining the employee. *Scott v. Blanchet High Sch.* (1987); *Carlsen v. Wackenhut Corp.* (1994) ("To prove negligent hiring in Washington, the plaintiff must demonstrate that … the employer knew or, in the exercise of ordinary care, should have known, of its employee's unfitness at the time of hiring."). This holding parallels the rule in the Restatement (Second) of Torts § 307 (Am. Law Inst., 1965).

Negligent Hiring

Anderson first argues that SL was negligent when it hired Lukashevich to be the high school girls' basketball coach. An employer negligently hires an employee when it knew or should have known that the employee was unfit for the position. For example, in *Carlsen*, the Court of Appeals concluded that a company was potentially liable for negligent hiring when it failed to check the background and references of an employee who performed security functions. Despite the employee's providing incomplete and inconsistent information on his job applications, the employer failed to conduct a background check, which would have revealed the employee's criminal history. The employer also did not contact the employee's references to determine if he had a criminal history. Thus, the employer failed to learn of the employee's unfitness because it neglected to more thoroughly check the employee's background. Here, Anderson argues that SL negligently hired Lukashevich because he was unfit to coach without a college degree, teaching or education certifications, or child development training. SL knew that Lukashevich did not have a college degree or other teaching certifications. However, Lukashevich met the required qualifications of a high school coach promulgated by the WIAA: he had a high school degree, he was 22 years old, and he attended first aid and CPR training. Anderson fails to offer any evidence or theory on how or why Lukashevich's level of education and training constituted unfitness, especially when he met the minimum requirements of the WIAA, a nonprofit organization that governs school athletics in over 800 schools across Washington. Neither did Anderson present any evidence showing how or why the WIAA's qualifications for high school coaches are deficient. Thus, because Lukashevich met the official minimum requirements of the position and Anderson failed to identify additional training and certifications, there is no genuine issue of material fact that Lukashevich was a fit candidate to be hired as the SL high school girls' basketball coach based on his qualifications.

Negligent Retention

Negligent retention "consists of … retaining the employee with knowledge of his unfitness, or of failing to use reasonable care to discover it before … retaining him." (*Peck*, 827 P.2d 1108, quoting *Scott*, 747 P.2d 1124). Anderson argues that SL negligently retained Lukashevich because of his disregard for and violation of school policies regarding students and alcohol. However, there is no evidence that SL knew or should have known that Lukashevich was unfit in this respect. Anderson did not present any evidence that Lukashevich previously gave alcohol to minors during his tenure as assistant coach of the junior varsity boys' basketball team. Nor did she present any evidence that Lukashevich had a history of serving alcohol to minors. Instead, Anderson argues that SL failed to adequately check into Lukashevich's background because Kemp did not recall whether he had contacted Lukashevich's references. Even assuming that no one checked Lukashevich's references, Anderson presented no evidence showing that Lukashevich's references knew that Lukashevich gave alcohol to minors or that this was a fact that SL would have reasonably discovered had it contacted Lukashevich's references. It is not logical to infer that SL unreasonably failed to discover evidence of unfitness in these circumstances. None of the inquiries now suggested by Anderson would have revealed facts that would lead a reasonable person to conclude that Lukashevich was unfit to be a coach for a youth team.

Negligent Supervision

In **negligent supervision**, the basic question is whether a manager acted reasonably in guiding and overseeing an employee's actions. The degree and type of supervision considered reasonable is always related to the particular circumstance. This theory of liability is only applicable when the employee is acting outside the scope of his employment. If the employee is acting within the scope of employment, then the employer is vicariously liable as we discussed previously. Thus, consider the previous Focus Case, *Anderson v. Soap Lake School District*. In that case, Anderson had also asserted a negligent supervision claim against the school district. Her negligent supervision claim was permitted because the coach was acting outside the scope of his employment when he was serving alcohol to students at his home. According to *Anderson*, a duty of supervision extends to acts beyond the scope of employment when the employer knew or in the exercise of reasonable care should have known that the employee presented a risk of danger to other (*Anderson v. Soap Lake School District*, 2018). The knowledge element generally requires knowledge of dangerous tendencies of the particular employee. In *Anderson*, the Washington Supreme Court held there was no evidence that the school district knew or should have known the coach would service alcohol to student athletes.

However, it is important to point out that tort law is a matter of state law, so while the Washington state court required evidence of dangerous tendencies of the particular employee in question, some courts may apply broader knowledge requirement of general dangers that should be reasonably anticipated, such as sexual assault.

In addition to the acts of our employees, we also must exercise careful judgment in our selection and supervision of third parties such as independent contractors and volunteers. We will explore each of these relationships next.

Liability for Acts of Third Parties

Liability for Independent Contractors

One of the major benefits of engaging an **independent contractor**, a party doing work without the control of the hiring party except as to the ultimate result of the work, is that an employer avoids the prospect of vicarious liability based on the actions of the independent contractor. The rule is that one who hires an independent contractor is generally not liable for the negligent or intentional acts or omissions of the contractor.

Factors Determining Independent Contractor Status

The independent contractor is hired to produce a certain result but is not controlled as to the method in which he obtains that result; this is the prime factor that courts look at when ascertaining whether a party should be considered to be an independent contractor. When the courts attempt to determine the degree of control asserted, they look at a number of factors, as shown in Exhibit 4.3.

Exhibit 4.3 Factors used to determine independent contractor status.

---

1   Whether the alleged principal has the right to direct and control the work of the agent.
2   Whether the agent is engaged in a distinct occupation.
3   Whether the principal or the agent supplies the instrumentalities, tools, and the place of work.
4   The method of paying the agent.

Source: Zajaczkowski v. Connecticut State Soccer Association (2010).

In the following Focus Case, a state soccer association was sued on the basis that it should be vicariously liable for the actions of the referees of a soccer match.

Zajaczkowski v. Connecticut State Soccer Association

2010 Conn. Super. LEXIS 435 (2010)   **FOCUS** CASE

FACTS

The plaintiff was playing in an adult soccer game at West Beach Field in Stamford, Connecticut as a member of the Polonia Stamford soccer team. The plaintiff sustained personal injuries while in the act of scoring a goal when he collided with the goal keeper from the opposing team. Plaintiff sued the soccer association for negligence contending that the Connecticut State Soccer Association (CSSA) failed to properly supervise and train officials that they provided to referee the game. The CSSA moved for summary judgment arguing that they could not be vicariously liable for the referees, even if the referees were negligent, because they were independent contractors and not agents/employees of the association.

HOLDING

The motion for summary judgment was granted since the referees were not employees of the soccer association.

RATIONALE

As a general rule, an employer is not liable for the negligence of its independent contractors ... [T]he explanation for this rule most commonly given is that, since the employer has no power of control over the manner in which the work is to be done by the contractor, it is to be regarded as the contractor's own enterprise, and the contractor, rather than the employer, is the proper party to be charged with the responsibility of preventing the risk, and bearing and distributing it.

Accordingly, the court must determine whether the defendants have met their burden of establishing whether the referee was acting as their agent. Agency is defined as the fiduciary relationship which results from manifestation of consent by one person to another that the other shall act on his behalf and subject to his control, and consent by the other so to act ... Thus, the three elements required to show the existence of an agency relationship include: (1) a manifestation by the principal that the agent will act for him; (2) acceptance by the agent of the undertaking; and (3) an understanding between the parties that the principal will be in control of the undertaking. Several factors are used to assess whether such a relationship exists (see Exhibit 4.3). In addition, an essential ingredient of agency is that the agent is doing something at the behest and for the benefit of the principal ... Finally, the labels used by the parties in referring to their relationship are not determinative; rather, a court must look to the operative terms of their agreement or understanding.

In this case, the deposition of the licensed referee indicates that the referee was not an employee of the defendants and was not trained by the defendants. The referee attends clinics conducted by the United States Soccer Federation. The defendants do not train the referees. The referee stated that he is paid by the home team for the soccer match on a game by game basis. While the Amateur Soccer League of

Connecticut (ASLC) and the team managers can decide how many referees to assign to a soccer match, the CSSA designates the particular referee to be assigned working in conjunction with the Connecticut State Referees Program (CSRP). The CSRP is an organization separate and distinct from the two defendants that recruits referees who then are assigned to the CSSC and the ASLC matches. Any referee can choose to work a particular soccer match of their choosing or can decline to work a particular match. Once a referee is assigned to a match the defendants do not control the referee's conduct. The decision to play the game and to inspect the field, as well as the enforcement of the rules of the game are in the discretion of the individual referee. The defendants have satisfied their burden of demonstrating the absence of an agency relationship between either defendant and the referee for purposes of vicarious liability.

The factors listed in Exhibit 4.3 and used in the *Connecticut State Soccer Association* case are the ones that courts generally address in ascertaining whether a party is an independent contractor. The question of degree of control is critical. Control over *results* is consistent with a finding that a party is an independent contractor, but control as to the day-to-day *details* of how a party is to work reflects an employer–employee relationship. In the case of youth sport game officials, the trend is for courts to hold that they should be considered as independent contractors. At least 15 states have passed laws classifying sports officials as independent contractors for the purposes of workers' compensation analysis, an analysis that primarily addresses the degree-of-control factor discussed above (NASO, 2020). The D.C. Court of Appeals reached a similar conclusion to that in *Connecticut State Soccer Association* in holding that an amateur lacrosse official was an independent contractor in *Pennsylvania Interscholastic Athletic Association v. NLRB* (2019). The court of appeals also noted that almost every other jurisdiction has reached a similar conclusion (Green, 2019).

When you determine that you want an independent contractor relationship to exist, you should have a contract that clearly states that this is the case. However, you must treat the contractor, in all circumstances, in ways that are consistent with that relationship. For example, you wish to hire a personal trainer for your fitness club, and you want to avoid vicarious liability by having that person serve as an independent contractor. But since the person will not make a great deal of money and you need to add to your insurance enrollment to get better rates, you offer the person the opportunity to join the group health policy. This seemingly innocuous gesture may completely destroy the independent contractor relationship you attempted to set up. It is likely that a court would conclude you were treating the personal trainer as an employee, and you would likely have difficulty in establishing that your club should not be vicariously liable for the actions of that personal trainer. It is important that you set up the relationship properly and treat the person in ways that are consistent with that relationship. See Exhibit 4.4 for an example of language used in an independent contractor agreement.

Competitive Advantage Strategies

Liability for Acts of Independent Contractors

- If you wish to set up an independent contractor relationship, remember that you cannot control the details of the day-to-day operation if you wish to avoid vicarious liability. Your practice with the independent contractor must be consistent with your documentation.
- To avoid liability for negligent selection, develop a list of necessary credentials for the independent contractor and hire only contractors that meet those criteria.
- Require prospective independent contractors to provide you with a list of references. Check those references carefully.

Exhibit 4.4 Terms and conditions of an independent contractor agreement.

1   **Independent Contractor; Relationship of the Parties**. The parties aver that:

a   The Contractor is not subject to Company's control as to the means and methods of accomplishing the work to be performed hereunder, but the Company may specify and control the result to be accomplished including any specifications, standards, requirements, and deliverables.

b   The Contractor selects its own customers or clients and is free to contract with others during the term of this Contract.

c   The Contractor selects its own employees.

d   This Contract shall not be construed to create any partnership, joint venture, nor other agency relationship between the parties, who are independent of one another. It is expressly understood and agreed that the enforcement of the terms and conditions of this contract and all rights of action relating to such enforcement, shall be strictly reserved to the Company and the named Contractor. Nothing contained in this Contract shall give or allow any claim or right of action whatsoever by any other third person. It is the express intention of the parties that any such person or entity, other than the parties hereto, receiving services or benefits under this Agreement shall be deemed an incidental beneficiary only.

Negligent Selection of Independent Contractors

There is an exception to the general rule of nonliability for the actions of independent contractors. That exception is based on the theory of **negligent selection**, a concept closely analogous to negligent hiring. Restatement (Second) of Torts § 411 provides:

> An employer is subject to liability for physical harm to third persons caused by his failure to exercise reasonable care to employ a competent and careful contractor
>
> a.   to do work which will involve a risk of physical harm unless it is skillfully and carefully done, or
> b.   to perform any duty which the employer owes to third persons.

You have a duty to choose an independent contractor in a reasonable fashion; just as in negligent hiring, the employer has a duty to hire reasonably. The elements of negligence (see Chapter 14) apply here as they do to negligent hiring. The following hypothetical case illustrates the negligent selection legal principle that an organization can be held liable for the actions of an independent contractor if someone in the organization fails to use due care in the selection of the independent contractor. Although the organization will not be vicariously liable for the actions of the independent contractor, it can have liability based on negligent selection if it fails to use proper care in the choice of the independent contractor. The cost of a contract should not be the sole factor in hiring an independent contractor.

Considering … Negligent Selection

C. Lou Less, the athletic director at Clay City High School, is reviewing bids from bus companies. The high school needs to use an outside company to transport athletes to some of the away games. The contract with the chosen company will be set up as an independent contractor relationship. The Ace Bus Company has, by far, the lowest bid for the services, and Ms. Less decides to take that bid without doing any investigation of the company. Less also does not request any information from the bus company pertaining to its policies and procedures for driver certification. If an investigation had been undertaken, the record would have shown that several of Ace's drivers have been cited for reckless driving or driving while intoxicated.

En route to an away basketball game, one of the buses is involved in a serious vehicular accident. It was caused by an Ace driver who was driving while under the influence of alcohol. Several of the school's athletes are injured in the crash, and numerous lawsuits have been filed against the school district.

Ms. Less feels confident that there can be no liability for the school district in this case, because the contract with Ace Bus Company clearly designates it as an independent contractor, for which the school district has no vicarious liability.

Question

- Is Ms. Less correct in believing that there can be no school district liability here?

Note how you would answer the question and then check your response using the Analysis & Discussion at the end of this chapter.

Although we used a hypothetical case to illustrate this point, there has been concern that some Universities may be using charter bus companies that do not meet federal safety standards. ESPN disclosed that at least 85 Division I universities used charter bus companies during 2007 and 2008 that have had one or more deficient federal safety scores (Holtzman, 2009). This emphasizes the need to research bus companies and to choose those with proven safety records that meet federal safety standards; if proper research is not done and the incompetent bus company is at fault, the university may be liable for negligent selection.

Liability for the Acts of a Volunteer

A volunteer is someone who agrees to assist your organization in some capacity for no compensation. The question of whether an organization is liable for the acts of a volunteer is very closely aligned to the question of control discussed earlier in regard to independent contractors. The following Focus Case explores this issue.

Competitive Advantage Strategies

Liability for the Acts of a Volunteer

- Screen and select volunteers with the same care that you use for employees in the same capacities.
- Take particular care to screen volunteers who will be in positions of authority and trust with minors.

Lasseigne v. American Legion Nicholson Post #38

Lasseigne v. American Legion, Nicholson Post #38

543 So. 2d 1111 (La. Ct. App. 1989)   **FOCUS** CASE

FACTS

The plaintiff was injured while participating in a Little League baseball practice. He was hit in the head by a ball thrown by a teammate. The plaintiff alleged that the coaches were negligent in the way that they oversaw practice and in failing to advise the injured player's parents of his injury. The local post of the American Legion was also sued for vicarious liability based on the actions of the coaches.

The coaches were volunteers, and they were not selected by the local post. Each team was responsible for hiring its own coaches. The post simply oversaw the location of game sites, organized schedules, and provided umpires and team scorers.

The trial court granted the defendant post's motion for summary judgment.

HOLDING

The Louisiana Court of Appeal affirmed summary judgment for the post, as it held that there was no vicarious liability for the coaches' actions.

RATIONALE

The core issue was whether the local American Legion post could be vicariously liable for the actions of the coaches. The court noted that the coaches were not employees of the post. They were volunteers who were chosen by the private sponsors of the teams. The post had absolutely no control over the manner in which the coaches conducted practices. Absent any control over the way in which the coaches conducted their business, the post cannot be vicariously liable for the actions of the coaches.

As shown by the Focus Case, the fact that a person is a volunteer and is not paid for their work is not the essential point for determining the vicarious liability of an organization. The question is whether the organization exerted sufficient control over the actions of the volunteer in terms of the day-to-day execution of the volunteer's responsibilities. If that level of control exists, then vicarious liability may exist. The following hypothetical case illustrates this notion of control.

Considering ... Control over Volunteers

Joe Goodheart agreed to assist the coaches of the men's basketball team at Small Community College (SCC) by performing various tasks as directed by Coach Light. Coach Light asked Goodheart, who had a valid driver's license, to pick up a recruit at the airport and drive him to the hotel near campus. While on his way to the hotel, Goodheart drove negligently and the recruit was injured in the accident.

Question

- Can SCC be liable under vicarious liability, even though Goodheart was a volunteer?

Note how you would answer the question and then check your response using the Analysis & Discussion at the end of this chapter.

Because volunteers in most situations will not be considered employees, the risk of liability is low. However, the potential for personal injury claims still exists, and the reputational harm to an organization from lawsuits is potentially very high. The risk can be mitigated to a large extent by creating a volunteer handbook and/or volunteer orientation program that covers the essential elements of the volunteer activity and provides the volunteer with information on how to report any problem the volunteer may encounter while performing volunteer work.

Liability for the Acts of a Collegiate Athlete

Most courts have consistently held that the relationship between a university and its athletes is not one of employer–employee. (See Chapter 9 for a discussion of the workers' compensation cases dealing with this issue.) In the following Focus Case, a plaintiff attempted to argue that an athlete should be considered an agent of the university in order to impose vicarious liability upon the university.

Kavanagh v. Trustees of Boston University

795 N.E.2d 1170 (Mass. 2003)	FOCUS CASE

FACTS

The plaintiff, Kenneth Kavanagh, played basketball for the intercollegiate team at Manhattan College. The team was playing an away game at Boston University (BU) when Kavanagh was injured in a scuffle. Kavanagh attempted to break up a fight between the opponents and was punched on the nose by Levar Folk, a BU player. The blow broke Kavanagh's nose.

Kavanagh's claim against BU was based on vicarious liability, as he claimed that Folk was an agent of BU. This claim was dismissed by the trial court. Kavanagh appealed.

HOLDING

The Supreme Judicial Court of Massachusetts affirmed the dismissal of the action against Boston University.

RATIONALE

The court held that the relationship between a university and its athletes cannot be viewed as one of employment nor agency. A student is a buyer of education, not an agent of the school, and a student does not attend a university to do its bidding. The receipt of a scholarship by an athlete does not transform the relationship into an employment situation. Further, an athlete may be considered to be a "representative" of a school in some senses, but not in the legal sense.

The *Kavanagh* case reflects the current majority position: university athletes are not agents of their universities, nor are they employees. Therefore, imposing vicarious liability upon a university based on actions of its athletes is not warranted. Can there be liability against a college or high school based on the violent acts of intercollegiate or high school athletes? Since intercollegiate or high school athletes are not employees, there cannot be organizational liability for the violent acts of these athletes based on vicarious liability. However, a coach could be liable for negligent supervision, in which case the school district could be vicariously liable based on the actions of its employee coach. In *Brokaw v. Winfield-Mt. Union Community School District* (2010), a high school basketball player (McSorley) hit an opposing player (Brokaw), knocking Brokaw to the ground. The referee called a technical foul on McSorley and ejected him from the game. The Brokaw family sued McSorley for battery and also alleged that McSorley's coach (and the school district) should be liable for failing to control McSorley's conduct. The lower court, in a nonjury trial, found that McSorley had committed a battery and awarded $23,000 to Brokaw. The cause of action against the school district was dismissed. The Iowa Supreme Court analyzed the negligent supervision claim and found that there was no breach of duty in this case. Since contact is inevitable in a basketball game, it is always foreseeable, in a general sense, that an altercation might break out. However, the Iowa Supreme Court asserted that, in the facts of this case, the defendants did not know, nor in the exercise of reasonable care should they have known, that McSorley was likely to commit a battery in this contest. Therefore, in this situation, there was no negligent supervision.

Conclusion

The legal reality of *respondeat superior* means that sport organizations will have liability for the actions of employees while the employees are furthering the business of the employer (acting within the scope of employment). That is a cost of doing business.

However, it is entirely possible to avoid liability for negligent hiring, supervision, or retention if managers who are in charge of hiring, disciplining, and terminating employees are trained to act in a reasonably prudent manner. Organizations should adopt protocols to ensure that screening and selection of employees and volunteers are performed carefully.

If you desire to create an independent contractor relationship in order to avoid the prospect of vicarious liability, the document reflecting that relationship should clearly delineate that the organization retains control only as to the outcome of the work, not as to the details of how to accomplish it. The working relationship with the independent contractor should be consistent with that understanding.

Discussion Questions

1   What is the underlying rationale for *respondeat superior?* Explain why it is a derivative theory of liability as opposed to a direct theory of liability.
2   What is your understanding of the concept of scope of employment? Give examples from sport organizations of situations when an employee may be acting within the scope of employment, and give examples of situations when an employee may be acting on his or her own behalf.
3   When could a plaintiff use the argument that behavior was ratified or condoned by an employer? Give examples.
4   Explain the theory of negligent hiring and retention.
5   Explain why an organization may wish to set up an independent contractor relationship. What are the factors that courts look at in ascertaining whether a situation is an employment relationship or an independent contractor relationship?
6   Identify some of the most common working relationships in sport that may represent independent contractor relationships instead of employer/employee relationships.

Learning Activities

Many online sites deal with issues related to youth sport and the hiring of coaches and other personnel. Do an Internet search and find three different hiring or selection protocols followed by youth sport leagues or associations to ensure that those hired are suitable to work with children.

Case Study

The coach of Midwest University's men's basketball team, Bill Beam, has an excellent win–loss record, but he has a violent temper and often verbally abuses his players, both on and off the court. The athletic director has heard this abuse and has also seen the coach push and slap players on a number of occasions at practice. The athletic director, who is Beam's immediate superior, is intimidated by Beam and has never spoken to Beam about this behavior or in any way tried to discipline Beam. One day, after a humiliating loss to a rival university, Beam, in a fit of rage, grabs a player and slams him against a locker. The player suffers a concussion and a severe neck injury. If the player sues, what are the possible causes of action against Beam, the athletic director, and Midwest University?

Considering ... Analysis & Discussion

Negligent Hiring

Given the facts in the case, you acted negligently in hiring this coach, and the league will be liable under the usual *respondeat superior* principles for your negligent hiring, which occurred while you were in the scope of employment. The league may not be responsible under *respondeat superior* principles directly for the actions of the coach, since the sexual abuse may not within the coach's scope of employment. Also, there was no ratification or condonation of behavior, since the coach did not engage in any bad behavior at this job before he molested the player.

In this case, you have a duty to act reasonably in choosing coaches for the youth teams. No reasonable person would hire someone to coach children without investigating the applicant's credentials. No references were checked. An investigation would have ascertained that this coach was certainly an unfit choice to coach youth players, since a person with this background is likely to repeat this heinous behavior. Therefore, you breached your duty of care by hiring this person, which resulted in injury to a player.

Negligent Retention

First, there is negligent retention. Strong was put on notice that Easton had violent propensities and never took adequate action to discipline Easton or, if necessary, terminate Easton's employment. Strong had a duty of care to other employees and to patrons to act reasonably to facilitate a safe environment at the club. Strong's failure to do so resulted in a foreseeable event, the serious attack upon a patron. Since Strong acted negligently within the scope of his employment with Win Corporation, the employer is also liable under the general rule of *respondeat superior*.

This fact pattern also lends itself to an analysis under the ratification/condonation concept discussed earlier. Although Easton's behavior would not normally fall under *respondeat superior* since the battery was not within the scope of employment, it is arguable that Strong's failure to intervene over the months in which he had knowledge of Easton's violent behavior was a ratification or condonation of that behavior, thus essentially making it within the scope of employment.

Negligent Selection

Unfortunately, Ms. Less has overlooked the principle of negligent selection. In this case, the school district, through the negligence of Ms. Less, may be liable for choosing unwisely. There is a duty to use reasonable care in the selection of an independent contractor. That duty was breached in this case because no investigation concerning the competency of the drivers was done. If it had been done, it would have shown that Ace was not a wise choice because several of the drivers had poor driving records. This unreasonable choice of bus company led directly to the injuries. Under these facts, it would be easy to establish the negligence of Ms. Less, an employee of the school district, in choosing Ace Bus Company, and liability is a given.

Control Over Volunteers

In this case, the answer is yes, since Goodheart was negligent while he was performing a task directed by the coach. Goodheart was under the control of the coach when the incident occurred.

References

Cases

Anderson v. Soap Lake School District, 423 P.3d 197 (Wash. 2018).
Brokaw v. Winfield-Mt. Union Community Sch. Dist., 788 N.W.2d 386 (Iowa 2010).
Carlsen v. Wackenhut Corporation, 868 P.2d 882 (1994).
Kavanagh v. Trustees of Boston Univ., 795 N.E.2d 1170 (Mass. 2003).
Lang v. Silva, 715 N.E.2d 708 (Ill. App. Ct. 1999).
Lasseigne v. American Legion, Nicholson Post #38, 543 So.2d 1111 (La. Ct. App. 1989).
Nathans v. Offerman, 2013 U.S. Dist. LEXIS 15928 (D. Conn. February 5, 2013).
Pennsylvania Interscholastic Athletic Association v. NLRB, 926 F.3d 837 (D.C. Cir. 2019).
Robinson v. Polk County Sch. Bd., 2020 Fla. App. LEXIS 3017 (Fla. App. 2020).

Scott v. Blanchet High School, 747 P.2d 1124 (1987).

Smith v. Gardner, 998 F. Supp. 708 (S.D. Miss. 1998).

Southport Little League v. Vaughan, 734 N.E.2d 261 (Ind. Ct. App. 2000).

Tomjanovich v. Los Angeles Lakers, 1979 U.S. Dist. LEXIS 9282 (S.D. Tex. 1979).

Statutes

27 Am. Jur. 2d *Employment Relationship* § 381 (2005).

Restatement (Second) of Agency. (1958).

Restatement [Second] of Agency § 228.

Restatement (Second) of Agency § 245.

Restatement (Second) of Torts § 307.

Restatement (Second) of Torts § 411.

Other Sources

Abel, G. G., Jordan, A., & Harlow, N. (2018, August 16). Preventing child sexual abuse: Screening for hidden child molesters seeking jobs in organizations that care for children. *Sexual Abuse, 31,* 662–683.

Associated Press. (2020, February 15). How the Larry Nassar scandal has affected others. *WWMT.* Retrieved from https://wwmt.com/news/state/how-the-larry-nassar-scandal-has-affected-others-02-15-2020.

Baker, T. A., & Byon, K. K. (2013, December). Developing a scale of perception of sexual abuse in youth sports. *Measurement in Physical Education and Exercise Science, 18,* 31–52.

Baumann, B. (2019, May 22). New York and other states pass child victims laws – What are the implications for U.S. insurers? *GenRe.* Retrieved from https://www.genre.com/knowledge/blog/new-york-and-other-states-pass-child-victims-laws-en.html.

Baumgaertner, G. (2019, December 10). Youth sports create opportunities for sexual abuse. What can parents do? *The Guardian.* Retrieved from https://www.theguardian.com/sport/2019/dec/19/youth-sports-create-opportunities-for-sexual-abuse-what-can-parents-do.

Brackenridge, C. H., Bringer, J. D., & Bishopp, D. (2005). Managing cases of abuse in sport. *Child Abuse Review, 14*(4), 259–274.

Carp, S. (2018, December 6). USAG files for bankruptcy amid sexual abuse lawsuits. *SportsPro Media.* Retrieved from https://www.sportspromedia.com/news/usa-gymnastics-bankruptcy-usoc-larry-nassar-scandal.

Chamallas, M. (2013). Vicarious liability in torts: The sex exception. *Valparaiso University Law Review, 48,* 133–193.

Corrigan, M. (2018, May 17). Larry Nassar settlement breaks Penn State's record in the Sandusky case. *Daily Collegian.* Retrieved from https://www.collegian.psu.edu/news/crime_courts/article_cadf5a04-59fe-11e8-b14c-7f08d514c346.html.

Crouse, K. (2013, May 25). Abuse victim seeks ouster of swimming officials. *International Herald Tribune,* 13.

Denver Basketball Officials. (2013, June 14). New CHSAA background check policy for ALL sports officials. Retrieved from http://www.denverbasketballofficials.com/2013/06/14/new-chsaa-background-check-policy-for-all-sports-officials/.

Gibbons, M., & Campbell, D. (2003). Liability of recreation and competitive sport organizations for sexual assaults on children by administrators, coaches, and volunteers. *Journal of Legal Aspects of Sport, 13,* 185–229.

Grasgreen, A. (2013, July 23). More athletics undersight. *Inside Higher Ed.* Retrieved from www.insidehighered.com/news/2013/07/23/report-shows-how-rutgers-botched-handling-former-coach.

Green, L. (2019, June 14). Court rules sports officials are independent contractors. *NFHS.org.* Retrieved from https://www.nfhs.org/articles/court-rules-sports-officials-are-independent-contractors/.

Harris, B. (2020, June 10). Women sue USA Swimming over sexual abuse by coaches. *U.S. News.* Retrieved from https://www.usnews.com/news/sports/articles/2020-06-10/women-sue-usa-swimming-over-sexual-abuse-by-coaches.

Holtzman, B. (2009, March 31). Bus safety an issue for colleges. *ESPN.* Retrieved from http://sports.espn.go.com/espn/otl/news/story?id=3997988.

Lytle, K. (2018, May 3). Protection from sexual predators: How we keep youth sports athletes safe. *The Coloradoan.* Retrieved from https://www.coloradoan.com/story/sports/2018/05/03/youth-sports-athletes-safe-child-abuse-sexual-predators-andrew-vanderwal-fort-collins/548805002/.

Mielnicki, R. (2014, September 17). Risk management lessons from the NFL. *East Coast Risk Management.* Retrieved from https://eastcoastriskmanagement.com/risk-management-lessons-nfl/.

Minuti, M. (1988). Note: Employer liability under the doctrines of negligent hiring: Suggested methods for avoiding the hiring of dangerous employees. *Delaware Journal of Corporate Law, 13,* 501–534.

Montaldo, C. (2019, July 6). Profile and common characteristics of a pedophile. *ThoughtCo.* Retrieved from https://www.thoughtco.com/profile-of-pedophile-and-common-characteristics-973203.

National Association of Sport Officials. (2020). Legislation affecting sport officials. *NASO.org*. Retrieved from https://www.naso.org/resources/legislation/legislation-status.

Preston, M. B. (2006, October). Note: Sheldon Kennedy and a Canadian tragedy revisited: A comparative look at U.S. and Canadian jurisprudence on youth sports organizations' civil liability for child sexual exploitation. *Vanderbilt Journal of Transnational Law*, 39, 1333–1372.

Ramirez, E. (2007, March 14). Referees cry foul in Citrus County over school screening requirements. *St. Petersburg Times*, 10.

Stark, T. (2019, March 10). Federal law exists to protect children from sexual abuse in youth sports. *Indy Star*. Retrieved from https://www.indystar.com/story/opinion/2019/03/10/op-ed-federal-law-exists-protect-children-sexual-abuse-youth-sports/3107705002/.

Starr, A. (2020, March 11). USA Swimming to settle sex abuse lawsuit files by former Olympian. *NPR*. Retrieved from https://www.npr.org/2020/03/11/814377679/usa-swimming-to-settle-sex-abuse-lawsuit-filed-by-former-olympian.

Sushner, M. (2005, Spring). Are amateur sports officials' employees? *Sports Lawyers Journal*, 12, 123–154.

Tenorio, P. (2012, September 20). Swim coach Curl gets lifetime ban. *The Washington Post*, D04.

Turner, D., Rettenberger, M., & Yoon, D. (2014, December 18). Risk assessment in child sexual abusers working with children. *Sexual Abuse*, 28, 572–596.

Ugolini, J. M. (2007). Even a violent game has its limits: A look at the NFL's responsibility for the behavior of its players. *University of Toledo Law Review*, 39, 41–58.

Wolohan, J., & Gao, F. (2018, November). School board negligent in coach's abuse. *Athletic Business*. Retrieved from https://www.athleticbusiness.com/staffing/school-board-negligent-in-coach-s-abuse.html.

Web Resources

www.naso.org ■ This is the website of the National Association of Sports Officials. A special report on this site called "Officials & Independent Contractor Status" deals with the history of determining whether officials should be classified as independent contractors.

www.nays.org.cmscontent/File/Screening_UPDATE_2012.pdf ■ This section of the National Alliance for Youth Sports website allows access to the document entitled "Background Screening in Youth Sports," a 2012 document setting forth the screening process for any youth sports volunteer in any youth sports organization.

www.nrpa.org/uploadedFiles/nrpaorg/Membership/Endorsed_Business_Provider/NRPA%20recommended%20guidelines%20-%20Final.pdf ■ This section of the National Recreation and Park Association website accesses "Recommended Guidelines for Credentialing Volunteers." This program is important since 5% of all volunteers in parks and recreation "fall through the cracks," even though they have some criminal history.

www.sadlersports.com/riskmanagement/index.html ■ This website of a company specializing in insuring sports and recreation organizations provides a variety of reports on risk management issues, including one on types of background checks for volunteers in youth sport. This is a useful resource for employers or future employers concerned about minimizing liability.

5 Employment Discrimination, Part I: Terms and Conditions of Employment

Erica J. Zonder

Introduction

A critical aspect of human resource management is avoiding illegal employment discrimination. Employment discrimination may occur in many different forms and contexts. This chapter explores the legal issues involved in hiring, promotion, and termination decisions based illegally on race, sex, religion, age, or disability. Also covered here are compensation discrimination in salary arrangements and decisions regarding employee leave. Other forms of illegal employment discrimination, such as harassment and discriminatory treatment based on different forms of employee expression, are discussed in Chapter 6, and constitutional equal protection issues are covered in Chapter 12.

The federal statutes that apply to the types of employment discrimination covered herein are Title VII, Title IX, the Equal Pay Act (EPA), the Age Discrimination in Employment Act (ADEA), The Rehabilitation Act (Rehab Act), and the Americans with Disabilities Act (ADA). These federal statutes combine to provide comprehensive protection to employees against discriminatory employment practices. The U.S. Equal Employment Opportunity Commission (EEOC) is the federal agency primarily tasked with enforcing workplace discrimination claims. In 2018, the EEOC handled more than 76,000 new charges of workplace discrimination securing more than $500 million for victims (EEOC, 2019). Many states and cities have also enacted civil or human rights statutes and ordinances to provide relief for victims of illegal employment practices. However, the main focus of this chapter is on examining the applicable federal laws. For a summary of the issues, relevant laws, and primary cases discussed in this chapter, see Exhibit 5.1.

Hiring, Promotion, and Termination Decisions

This section discusses decisions to hire, promote, or terminate employees that involve intentional discrimination or the use of seemingly neutral employment policies that can disadvantage an entire group of people.

Discrimination on the Basis of Race or Sex

In sport, we still see obvious inequities in terms of race and gender, specifically in employment. For instance, head football coaches at both the college and professional level, are predominantly White, while the players are predominantly non-White. In 2016, among the National Football League (NFL) players, only 27.4 percent were White and similar numbers were expected in 2018 (Lapchick, 2017). In the 2019 season, 87.5 percent of NFL head coaches were White (Gasper, 2019) – there were only four minority head coaches among 32 teams despite the NFL's mandated "Rooney Rule," which requires including at least one minority applicant in the pool for in-person interviews for both head coach and general manager positions (Carroll, 2018). The NFL expanded the "Rooney Rule" in 2020 to require additional interviews of minority candidates for head coaching positions and at least one minority candidate for any

Exhibit 5.1 Management contexts in which employment discrimination may arise, with relevant laws and cases.

Management Context	Major Legal Issues	Relevant Law	Illustrative Cases
Hiring/promotion/termination	Race/sex discrimination	Title VII Title IX	Morris, Jackson Miller
	Age discrimination	ADEA	Austin
	Disability discrimination	§ 504, ADA	Lemire, Keith
Compensation determinations	Sex discrimination	Title VII, Title IX, Equal Pay Act, EEOC regulations	Stanley, Perdue
Employee leave decisions	Pregnancy	PDA	
	Family leave	FMLA	

coordinator, senior football operations, and general manager jobs. Teams and the league must also include female applicants for senior level executive positions (Patra, 2020). According to the 2017 College Sport Racial & Gender Report Card, 88 percent of National Collegiate Athletic Association (NCAA) Division I head football coaches were White, compared to only 41.5 percent of the Division I players (Lapchick, 2018a), and while not a Rooney Rule per se, presidents and chancellors of NCAA schools were asked to sign a diversity and inclusion pledge to affirm their commitment to diversity in the hiring process for athletics in 2016 (Johnson, 2017; NCAA, 2016). State legislatures are becoming increasingly interested in establishing this practice as state law, with Oregon being the first (in 2009) to enact a Rooney Rule-type law requiring its public universities to interview minority candidates as part of the process of hiring athletics directors and head coaches (ORS § 352.380(2)(b) (NCAA, 2012)).

In terms of gender, there are also equality issues in sport. In NCAA Division I, only 4.7 percent of head coaches of men's teams were women and, while that is not surprising, what is more surprising is that women held only 39.8 percent of head coaching positions for women's sports (Lapchick, 2018a). Women are also behind in terms of equality in collegiate administrative roles. In 1981, the NCAA member schools created the Senior Woman Administrator (SWA) position in order to "ensure women were involved in the male-dominated administration of college athletics" (NCAA, n.d., para. 2). The SWA is intended to be the designation for the highest-ranking female in a school's athletic department and allows for inclusion in decision-making, diverse points of contact for student-athletes and staff, and visibility of female role models among other outcomes. According to the NCAA, 99 percent of schools have an SWA (NCAA, n.d.). However, of 130 Football Bowl Subdivision (FBS) schools, only 9.2 percent of Athletic Directors are women (Lapchick, 2018b, p. 8). According to the Institute for Diversity and Ethics in Sports (TIDES), the grade for gender hiring at FBS schools overall is an "F" and "college sport remains behind professional sports regarding opportunities for women and people of color for the top jobs" (Lapchick, 2018b, p. 3). In the NFL, there has been slow progress in the last few years, as women have begun being hired for assistant coach and other positions. For example, in 2019, the Tampa Bay Buccaneers made history by becoming the first NFL team to have two full-time female coaches on their staff (Connley, 2019).

The continuing disparities in employment patterns and compensation have prompted a great deal of research exploring these gaps and potential explanations related to lifestyle choices, educational background, or lack of professional preparation or mentorship (Bower & Hums, 2013; Hancock & Hums, 2016; Hoffman, 2010). While some disparities may be explained by these factors, it is also likely that some are due to prejudicial stereotypes and attitudes manifesting themselves in discriminatory employment practices. This is particularly difficult to determine in the case of high-profile coaching and administrative positions because employment decisions are infused with a large amount of subjectivity on the part of the employer. Often, few objective criteria exist on which to compare applicants, and "organizational fit" is a major (and somewhat subjective) part of the hiring decision.

Also, standard institutional hiring procedures often are not followed when universities hire big-time coaches. For example, when hiring full-time faculty, universities typically require an approved position description/announcement, a national search, a minimum period of time for advertisement of the opening, documentation of efforts to recruit applicants from minority groups, documentation of how each

Exhibit 5.2 §703 of Title VII of the Civil Rights Act of 1964.

---

a It shall be an unlawful employment practice for an employer –

  1 to fail or refuse to hire or to discharge any individual, or otherwise to discriminate against any individual with respect to his compensation, terms, conditions, or privileges of employment, because of such individual's race, color, religion, sex, or national origin; or

  2 to limit, segregate, or classify his employees or applicants for employment in any way which would deprive or tend to deprive any individual of employment opportunities or otherwise adversely affect his status as an employee, because of such individual's race, color, religion, sex, or national origin.

---

candidate in the pool does or does not meet the listed minimum and preferred qualifications, and a post-hiring justification for why the hired candidate was chosen over the other finalists. These procedures are in place to enhance objectivity and fairness in the hiring process. However, when universities do not utilize these procedures in hiring high-level coaching staff, discrimination can be impossible to prove.

Title VII

A federal law that is in place to address discriminatory practices is Title VII of the Civil Rights Act of 1964, as amended by the Civil Rights Act of 1991. Title VII focuses on employment discrimination (see Exhibit 5.2). The phrasing "terms, conditions, or privileges of employment" applies to employment decisions related to such things as hiring, firing, layoffs, job training, discipline, job classifications, and provision of benefits.

Scope of Coverage

Title VII applies to employers that impact interstate commerce and that have 15 or more employees who work at least 20 calendar weeks in a given year. These employers may be governmental or in the private sector and may include educational institutions, labor unions, or players associations. Title VII does not apply to independent contractors. Additionally, **bona fide membership clubs** (such as exclusive country clubs that do not serve the general public) are exempt from Title VII, as are Native American tribes, and religious organizations hiring employees to perform religious functions. Covered employees include U.S. citizens employed by American employers outside the United States and non-U.S. citizens employed within the United States.

Protected Classes

The **protected classes** listed in the statute (race, color, religion, sex, and national origin) are the only ones covered by Title VII. The term "race" also refers to ethnicity, rather than being limited to the traditional anthropological definition of race, and thus protects identifiable ethnic groups, such as Hispanic or Jewish people. For example, a federal district judge recently reaffirmed that Jewish heritage is covered under Title VII's protections in a case involving Louisiana College's alleged refusal to hire an assistant football coach due to his "Jewish blood" (*Bonadona v. Louisiana College*, 2018; Whitford, 2018). Color-based discrimination refers to unlawful treatment on the basis of actual skin color, while national origin discrimination refers to an improper focus on place of ancestry. Place of ancestry is not the same as citizenship. The latter refers to where a person holds citizenship, not the nation in which a person or her ancestors were born. Because citizenship is not a protected class, an American ice hockey referee was unsuccessful in using Title VII to sue the National Hockey League for allegedly discriminating against U.S. citizens by hiring mostly Canadian citizens as referees (*Dowling v. United States*, 1979).

Title VII protects both women and men from sex discrimination. In *Medcalf v. University of Pennsylvania* (2001), a male was rejected for a job coaching a collegiate women's rowing team, and a female was hired instead. In denying the university's motion for summary judgment, the court found sufficient evidence of intentional sex discrimination in several statements made by the Senior Associate Athletics Director. In these statements, she indicated that the university preferred to hire a woman for the job in order to balance the mostly male coaching staff and to provide a female role model for the athletes. Conversely, in *Mollaghan v. Varnell* (2012), two male soccer coaches, John Mollaghan and John Vincent, filed suit against the Senior Woman Administrator and Athletic Director of University of Southern Mississippi (USM) asserting gender discrimination under Title VII, among other claims. Vincent was the Head Coach of the women's soccer team, while Mollaghan was an assistant coach. The Plaintiffs alleged that the administrators made it "clear" they preferred women to coach women's sports (para. 3), and they were "ultimately" replaced by a female. According to the Supreme Court of Mississippi, the evidence did not support that either coach was actually discharged, and further the evidence is "undisputed" that neither coach was replaced with a female – Vincent's one-year contract was not renewed and he was replaced as head coach with Mollaghan, and Mollaghan was replaced as interim coach (he actually accepted another position) by another male. It wasn't until four years later that the school hired a female coach (para. 33).

Sexual orientation was determined to fall under the "sex" protected class in a landmark Supreme Court case in 2020. Until 2020, the federal circuit courts were split on the issue, with the 2nd Circuit in *Zarda v. Altitude Express* (2018) ruling that the language prohibiting discrimination "because of … sex" includes sexual orientation. Zarda was a gay sky diving instructor who frequently led tandem jumps and who was fired after a complaint from a customer. The 6th Circuit similarly ruled that transgender discrimination was prohibited, whereas the 11th Circuit found that sexual orientation was not covered by Title VII, as an employee was fired for participating in a gay softball league. The Supreme Court consolidated the cases and ultimately ruled that LGBTQ discrimination is actionable under Title VII. According to the court "… It is impossible to discriminate against a person for being homosexual or transgender without discriminating against that individual based on sex" (*Bostock v. Clayton County*, 2020, p. 9). It also should be noted that as of June 2019, 24 states plus the District of Columbia had added sexual orientation and/or gender identity to the list of protected classes in their state employment discrimination laws (MAP, 2019), while 225 cities and counties offered such protections as of January 2018 (HRC, 2019). Additionally, Title IX and the Equal Protection Clause have been used successfully to challenge workplace harassment based on sexual orientation or gender identity. This is explained more fully in Chapters 6 and 12.

Finally, in addition to the long-established religions, Title VII protects people professing unorthodox beliefs that are sincerely held and not simply adopted as an ulterior means to some desired end (such as creating a religion to justify using unlawful hallucinogenic drugs).

Administration and Procedure

The federal agency that administers and helps enforce Title VII is the Equal Employment Opportunity Commission (EEOC). A Title VII claim is first filed with the EEOC, which then decides whether to investigate the claim. If the EEOC chooses not to investigate, it will issue a "right to sue" notice and the plaintiff can sue their employer directly. The EEOC issues regulations for implementing Title VII, which are generally enforced by the courts. Occasionally, the EEOC also issues guidelines for analyzing discrimination cases. Courts typically do not feel compelled to enforce mere guidelines but are free to use them if they find the reasoning behind them persuasive. An example of these guidelines that applies specifically to sport is the *Enforcement Guidelines on Sex Discrimination in the Compensation of Sports Coaches in Educational Institutions* (EEOC, 1997), discussed later in this chapter.

Remedies. The remedies available under § 706(g) of Title VII include:

- **back pay** for work missed due to the adverse employment action
- **front pay** for future earnings that would have been received absent the discrimination

- reinstatement of the employee to the position
- retroactive seniority
- **injunctive relief** ordering the employer to cease unlawful practices or to engage in affirmative action
- attorney's fees
- compensatory and punitive damages.

Types of loss that may be compensated include financial loss (past and future) and pain and suffering. The most typical relief granted is back pay for wages and benefits lost due to the illegal discrimination.

Theories of Liability and Defenses

Courts use two primary theories of liability in deciding Title VII cases – disparate treatment and disparate impact. **Disparate treatment** applies when an employer has *intentionally* discriminated against a member of a protected class. The **disparate impact** theory is used when an employer's *neutral* employment practice has had a discriminatory *effect* on a protected class of which the plaintiff is a member – so *unintentional* discrimination. Defenses include some legitimate nondiscriminatory reason for the adverse action, business necessity, and bona fide occupational qualification. The two theories of liability and the defenses are explained below.

Disparate treatment: Direct evidence. A disparate treatment claim requires a finding of intentional discrimination, which may be proved in two ways: with direct evidence of intent or by means of an inference from circumstantial evidence relating to the way the employer has treated others. An example of direct evidence of intentional discrimination is found in *Biver v. Saginaw Township Community Schools* (1986). In this case, the court found evidence of intentional discrimination in a school superintendent's statement that "hell would freeze over before he would hire a woman for a boys' coaching position." Such statements serve as direct evidence of intentional discrimination when they are directly related to the allegedly discriminatory action. In *EEOC v. NBC* (1990), Roth, the female plaintiff, had evidence that she had been the target of several sexist remarks during her attempts to be hired for the position of television sports director. But she was unable to provide evidence connecting those remarks to the hiring decision process, so the court found that her "direct evidence" of discrimination was inadequate.

Disparate treatment: Inference. In most instances, direct evidence of intent to discriminate is hard to come by. Thus, the more commonly used method of proving discriminatory intent is through inferential evidence using the *McDonnell Douglas* test established in *McDonnell Douglas Corp. v. Green* (1973). This is a burden-shifting test in which the plaintiff and defendant take turns shouldering evidentiary burdens (see Exhibit 5.3). Evidentiary burdens include the burden of production and the burden of proof. The **burden of production** is the responsibility to produce evidence without any burden to prove that the defense (in this case) is true. The **burden of proof** is the responsibility to prove the truth of an issue.

Under the *McDonnell Douglas* test, a plaintiff must first prove a **prima facie case** that discrimination has occurred (that is, provide initial support that the allegation is true). Establishing a prima facie case of discrimination is a critical first step in the *McDonnell Douglas* burden-shifting formula and

Exhibit 5.3 *McDonnell Douglas* burden-shifting analysis.

1 Plaintiff has burden of proof to establish a prima facie case of discrimination.
2 Defendant has burden of production to support LNDR (or affirmative defense such as bona fide occupational qualification (BFOQ)).
3 Plaintiff has burden of proof to establish that the defense is pretext.

Exhibit 5.4 *McDonnell Douglas* four-prong test for establishing a prima facie case of discrimination in hiring or job performance situations.

In a hiring situation, a prima facie case is shown by establishing that:

1　The applicant is a member of a protected class.
2　The applicant applied and was qualified for the job.
3　The applicant was rejected (not hired).
4　The employer hired a nonminority candidate or continued to search.

In a job performance situation, a prima facie case is shown by establishing that:

1　The employee is a member of a protected class.
2　The employee was performing the job satisfactorily.
3　The employee was discharged (fired) or subject to adverse treatment/change in working conditions.
4　The employee was treated less favorably than a similarly situated employee not in a protected class (nonminority) or the work was assigned to a nonminority employee.

typically involves a four-prong test as illustrated in Exhibit 5.4. Once the plaintiff has established by a **preponderance of the evidence** (i.e., the weight of the evidence tips in 'their' favor) that a prima facie case of discrimination exists, the burden of production, but not the full burden of proof, shifts to the defendant to provide evidence that the adverse action was taken for some *legitimate, nondiscriminatory reason* (the elements of this requirement are known by the acronym LNDR). If the defendant is successful in producing such evidence, the full burden of proof now rests upon the plaintiff to prove that the defendant's LNDR defense is pretext, that is, a sham or false reason disguising intentional discrimination. If the plaintiff is successful in proving pretext by a preponderance of the evidence, they win the lawsuit. In *Minnis v. Board of Supervisors of Louisiana State University* (2014), an African-American tennis coach alleged that he was fired due to race (as well as claims including disparate compensation, hostile work environment, and retaliation). The school had "elaborated" on its reasons for terminating Minnis to include a failure to meet established goals, his losing record, and morale issues, which went beyond the "poor performance" reason initially offered. Minnis argued that these shifting reasons showed evidence of pretext. The court found that an employer's reasons becoming more detailed as the dispute moves into adversarial proceedings is insufficient to create a jury question of pretext absent an actual inconsistency. Minnis failed to actually rebut the school's LNDRs. An example of a disparate treatment claim alleging both race and sex discrimination is found in the *Morris* case.

Morris v. Wallace Community College–Selma

125 F. Supp. 2d 1315 (S.D. Ala. 2001)　　　　　　　　　　　　**FOCUS** CASE

FACTS

The plaintiff Morris is a White female coach who had been employed full-time by a southern Black community college, Wallace Community College–Selma, since 1992. Although Morris expressed interest in being promoted to the position of athletics director in 1997, a Black male, Raji Gourdine, was chosen instead. The college said that it never accepted applications for the position of athletics director, but instead appointed someone in 1996 and also in 1997. The college also asserted that one of the criteria for the position was to hire an administrator, not a coach. However, the first person offered the position was a chemistry professor, not an administrator. The athletics director also claimed that Morris had been a troublemaker who had often spoken unfavorably about the administration, had failed to follow proper travel procedures, and had scheduled games without obtaining approval. However, all of her annual performance evaluations had been positive, and she had never received a written reprimand for any objectionable behavior. In fact, the college president appointed her to the position of assistant athletics director when Gourdine was appointed head athletics director.

As a coach, Morris was paid less than comparable Black male and female coaches, but she also had less work experience than they did when she was hired. She had no prior coaching experience, and her only experience related to physical education had been teaching three classes at the YMCA and aerobics at church. Morris was also offered a summer camp coaching job with less than a full load (and thus less compensation) than her Black colleagues, who received more lucrative summer employment.

Morris sued under Title VII, alleging race and sex discrimination for failure to promote, inequity in coaching compensation, and inequity in the awarding of summer employment contracts. The defendant moved for summary judgment on all these claims.

HOLDING

Morris produced evidence sufficient to create genuine issues of material fact sufficient to defeat the summary judgment motions on all the above claims.

RATIONALE

In this case, a court would apply the *McDonnell Douglas* test to decide the failure to promote claim.

Plaintiff's Burden of Proof to Establish a Prima Facie Claim. As a female, Morris obviously belongs to a protected class (prong 1; see Exhibit 5.4), since Title VII protects against sex discrimination. Her claim of race discrimination is covered under Title VII, even though she is White, because the statute prohibits race discrimination regardless of what race a person is. Here, we have a White person seeking a promotion in a historically Black institution, a place where she is in the minority. Therefore, the first prong of the *McDonnell Douglas* test is met. The "applied for the job" part of prong 2 (see Exhibit 5.4) of the test is satisfied because she expressed interest in being promoted to the position of athletics director when the job came open. An employer cannot avoid liability by appointing someone to an open position instead of accepting applications. If someone has learned of the job opening and expressed a desire to be considered for the position, the employer has a duty to consider that person along with the other potential appointees. The "qualified for the job" part of prong 2 is harder to determine, given these facts. However, the college's nonadherence to its hiring criterion of prior administrative experience, as evidenced by its first offering the athletics director job to a chemistry professor, casts doubt on the required qualifications for the job. Such inconsistency suggests that Morris could satisfy prong 2 by proving that she was at least minimally qualified. Her appointment as assistant athletics director shows that the administration must have thought she could perform the functions of an athletics director role sufficiently to assist the head director of athletics. This makes her appear to be at least as qualified as the chemistry professor, so the second prong is satisfied.

Prong 3 is obviously met as Morris was rejected for the position, and Prong 4 (see Exhibit 5.4) is met if that rejection was in favor of someone not in the protected class. In this case, a Black male was hired as director of athletics. Once again, Title VII protects against discrimination on the basis of race even if a plaintiff is White. Gourdine is in the majority ethnic group at the historically Black college, a fact that makes Morris' claim of race discrimination look a bit stronger. Being female also qualifies Morris as a member of a protected class in this situation.

Therefore, Morris has successfully made a prima facie claim of both race and sex discrimination.

Defendant's Burden of Production. It is now the college's turn to bring a LNDR defense. It must produce evidence that it had some legitimate nondiscriminatory reason for denying Morris the promotion. The college argued that she was not promoted because she was a troublemaker, and also because she was not an administrator and therefore did not meet one of the qualification criteria.

Plaintiff's Burden of Proof of Pretext. The burden now shifts back to Morris to prove that the two aspects of the LNDR defense are pretext. She showed that the promotion was not denied on the basis that she was a troublemaker by the fact that she had consistently received positive performance reviews and never received any written reprimands. She also succeeded in proving that the college did not really deny her the promotion because she lacked the required qualification of being an administrator by the fact that the college first offered the job to a chemistry teacher. Thus, Morris proved that the college's LNDR defense was bogus. Since the college could not articulate a legitimate reason for failing to promote her, the inference to be drawn is that the failure to promote must have been based on the fact that she is White and/or that she is female.

With regard to the claim that Morris suffered compensation discrimination, the college did not prove that she was paid equitably in comparison with similarly situated Black and/or male coaches. Finally, with regard to the alleged discrimination in summer employment contracts, there are no facts that indicate that the college had some legitimate nondiscriminatory reason for giving her less favorable summer contracts than the Black and/or male coaches. Thus, the college will be unable to satisfy its burden of producing evidence for a LNDR defense on this issue.

Disparate Treatment: Defenses. In a disparate treatment case alleging race discrimination, if the plaintiff successfully proves disparate treatment on the basis of race, no further defenses are available to the employer to avoid liability. However, in disparate treatment cases of alleged gender, national origin, or religious discrimination, an additional available defense (beyond a first defense – that the discrimination did not happen or the plaintiff cannot make a prima facie case) is known as the **bona fide occupational qualification (BFOQ) defense**. Here, the employer must show that the alleged discrimination was justified because members of the excluded protected class could not effectively perform the essential job functions. This defense is typically construed narrowly.

In *EEOC v. Sedita* (1993), the defendant health club, Women's Workout World, refused to hire men as fitness instructors or as management staff, asserting that its all-female clientele had a privacy interest in not being disturbed by the presence of males. Thus, they argued that being female was a BFOQ for filling those jobs. The court had previously ruled that a privacy-based BFOQ defense must satisfy a three-part test. The employer must establish: (1) there is a factual basis for believing that hiring any members of one sex would undermine the essence of the business; (2) the asserted privacy interest is entitled to protection under the law; and (3) no reasonable alternatives exist (*EEOC v. Sedita*, 1991). To satisfy (1), a showing that clients would not consent to service of the opposite sex satisfies the burden for a "factual basis": over 10,000 Club members signed a petition stating they would no longer patronize the club if males were hired. For (2), various courts had found that nudity and intimate touching implicates a protectable privacy interest – the Club maintains that a significant part of their business involves touching clients in sensitive areas for measurement and instruction. And lastly, (3) the reasonableness of alternatives – the Club disputed the economic feasibility of hiring men, maintaining they would have to restructure their facilities by putting in men's bathrooms, redesigning locker rooms, etc., as well as having an inability to reassign job duties to avoid intruding on privacy interests – the court decided that these questions were best left to be decided at trial. It is important to note here that the BFOQ defense is more easily used when comes to hiring employees as attendants in sex-segregated locker rooms. Also, customer preference often does not count as grounds for a BFOQ defense. In *Morris v. Bianchini* (1987), a health club management's desire to maintain a macho image for its customers by hiring only male athletics directors was determined to be unlawful reliance on customer preference. Such a policy would only perpetuate the entrenched gender stereotype that females are less capable of performing such jobs.

In a 2003 case dealing with a BFOQ, the Phoenix Suns settled a Title VII lawsuit brought by Kathryn Tomlinson, who had been employed by the Suns' "Zoo Crew" half-time entertainment troupe. After performing well in her job the first year, Tomlinson was not rehired because the next year the Suns restricted the hiring of Zoo Crew members to "males with athletic ability and talent." The Suns could not establish why being male was a BFOQ for working as a member of the Zoo Crew and agreed to a settlement payment of $82,500 in damages (Haner, 2003).

In contrast, religion can often succeed as a BFOQ in hiring decisions. A religious institution is allowed to hire a person of a particular religious persuasion if the job requires the performance of religion-related tasks. For example, a Catholic institution cannot be forced to hire a Baptist to teach religion classes. For nonsectarian activities, such as coaching the Catholic university's basketball team, it is less clear that religion would be a BFOQ, but nevertheless the courts have allowed it (*Corporation of Presiding Bishop of Church of Jesus Christ of Latter-day Saints v. Amos*, 1997). **A BFOQ defense is never available in cases based on race or color-discrimination**. A seniority system can also be used as an affirmative defense.

Disparate impact. As mentioned earlier, the disparate impact theory is used when, instead of evidence of discriminatory intent, a plaintiff has appropriate statistical evidence that a "neutral" employment practice has had a disparate impact or effect on members of a protected class in the relevant workforce pool. A burden-shifting test is used here as well, with the parties taking turns establishing evidentiary burdens in the same fashion as the *McDonnell Douglas* test: first the plaintiff's prima facie case, then the defendant's defense, and finally the plaintiff's chance to prove the defense is pretext for discrimination.

In disparate impact cases, the defense is slightly different from the LNDR defense used in disparate treatment cases, in that it is specifically tied to the employer's action being job-related. In these cases, once the prima facie case of disparate impact is established, the burden shifts to the employer to provide evidence that the neutral practice is job-related and a **business necessity**; that is, it is necessary as a means to achieving a legitimate business objective. If the defendant employer is successful in establishing business necessity, the burden shifts back to the plaintiff to prove that the ostensibly neutral employment practice is in fact pretext for discrimination. A way to prove pretext is to provide evidence that other methods are available for accomplishing the stated business goal that do not adversely impact the protected class.

Successful disparate impact claims are rare because of the difficulty in establishing that an appropriate workforce pool has been negatively impacted. An example of this difficulty is found in the following Case Opinion of *Jackson v. University of New Haven*.

Jackson v. University of New Haven

CASE OPINION   **228 F. Supp. 2d 156 (D. Conn. 2002)**

FACTS

In February, 1999 the head football coach at the University of New Haven (UNH) left to take a position with the Cleveland Browns of the NFL. This dispute arose out of the ensuing search for a new head coach at UNH. Beginning in early February of 1999, UNH posted the head coach position both internally and with the "NCAA market," an online professional publication for university and college athletics. The postings for the head coaching position listed the following requirements and duties:

- A bachelor's degree is required, master's degree preferred. Successful collegiate coaching experience required. Experience in recruiting, game coaching and knowledge of NCAA rules and regulations is essential.
- Implement and manage all aspects of a national caliber Division II football program in accordance with NCAA and university regulations. Areas of responsibility include, but are not limited to coaching, recruiting qualified student athletes, budget management, scheduling, hiring and supervising coaching staff, academically monitoring student-athletes, and promotions and fund-raising.

After receiving 36 applications, UNH's Search Committee, which had been established to select a new head coach, decided to interview six applicants-all of whom had college coaching experience and are Caucasian. Jackson, an African-American, was not among the six applicants interviewed. Jackson had no college experience, but had been a professional minor league football coach, earned several "coach of the year" honors as such a coach, and was inducted into the minor league football hall of fame. The defendants assert that they decided not to interview Jackson because he lacked the requisite collegiate coaching experience. From the six applicants interviewed, the Search Committee ultimately selected Darren Rizzi, who had been an assistant coach at UNH for four years, to fill the position of head coach. Jackson filed an action against the University and the Athletic Director alleging racial discrimination in violation of Title VII. Jackson appeared base his complaint on both the "disparate treatment" and "disparate impact" theories of recovery in that he alleges both that the challenged qualification had a discriminatory effect upon African Americans (disparate impact) and that the defendants intentionally discriminated against him based on his race (disparate treatment). The defendants moved for summary judgment on both claims.

HOLDING

The District Court granted the defendants' motion for summary judgment and dismissed Jackson's disparate impact claim, as well as his claim for disparate treatment based on race [the court's rationale for the disparate impact claim is detailed below].

RATIONALE

At the heart of this dispute lies the "collegiate coaching experience" requirement. The parties are in agreement that the posted job qualifications included that requirement and that all of the applicants selected for interviews possessed such experience. However, the parties differ markedly in their characterizations of that prior experience requirement. The defendants maintain that prior NCAA coaching experience was essential to ensure the selection of a candidate sufficiently well-versed in NCAA rules and regulations to both pass the NCAA's annual tests on such regulations and manage the UNH football team successfully. Jackson, however, asserts that the requirement of previous collegiate coaching experience was not necessary to ensure familiarity with NCAA rules and regulations and that it served to exclude otherwise qualified minority applicants, such as himself. Jackson asserts that the requirement that applicants have prior college coaching experience amounts to discrimination in violation of Title VII.

Unlike disparate treatment, in asserting a claim of disparate impact under Title VII a plaintiff need not allege that the discrimination was intentional. *Griggs v. Duke Power Co.*, 401 U.S. 424, 430–32, 91 S. Ct. 849, 28 L. Ed. 2d 158 (1971) ("[G]ood intent or absence of discriminatory intent does not redeem employment procedures or testing mechanisms that operate as 'built in head winds'"). It is enough that a facially neutral policy, such as the prior college coaching experience requirement at issue here, be shown to have an adverse impact on a protected group. *Id.* at 431, 91 S. Ct. 849 (noting that Title VII "proscribes not only overt discrimination but also practices that are fair in form, but discriminatory in operation"). Disparate impact cases, like disparate treatment cases, are governed by a "burden-shifting" framework. The Second Circuit reviewed the disparate impact burden-shifting framework in *NAACP, Inc. v. Town of East Haven*, 70 F.3d 219, 225 (2d Cir. 1995): "[A] plaintiff may establish a prima facie case of disparate impact by showing that use of the test causes the selection of applicants ... in a racial pattern that significantly differs from that of the pool of applicants" *Bridgeport Guardians, Inc. v. City of Bridgeport*, 933 F.2d 1140 (1991). Such a showing can be established through the use of statistical evidence which discloses a disparity so great that it cannot reasonably be attributed to chance. See *Hazelwood Sch. Dist. v. United States* (1977). To establish a prima facie case, the statistical disparity must be sufficiently substantial to raise an inference of causation. *Watson v. Fort Worth Bank and Trust* (1988). After a prima facie case is established, the employer has the burden of coming forward with evidence to show that the test has "a manifest relationship to the employment in question" *Albemarle Paper Co. v. Moody* (1975). If the employer can make such a showing, the plaintiff may nonetheless prevail if he can suggest alternative tests or selection methods that would meet the employer's legitimate needs while reducing the racially disparate impact of the employer's practices.

Here, as in the disparate treatment context, Jackson has failed to meet his burden of setting forth a prima facie case of disparate impact (sic). In making out a prima facie case for disparate impact under Title VII, the plaintiff bears the burden of demonstrating that a specific policy or practice of the defendant has had a disproportionately negative impact on the plaintiff's protected class. "To make this showing, a plaintiff must (1) identify a policy or practice, (2) demonstrate that a disparity exists, and (3) establish a causal relationship between the two." *Robinson*, 267 F.3d at 160 (citing 42 U.S.C. § 2000e-2(k) (1) (A) (I)). Here, Jackson alleges that the defendants' facially neutral hiring criteria (requiring prior college coaching experience), had a discriminatory impact on African-Americans. Specifically, Jackson asserts that because African-Americans have historically been under-represented in the ranks of NCAA coaches this requirement disproportionately excludes African-Americans from consideration. Statistics are often an important component of a disparate impact claim. See *Robinson*, 267 F.3d at 160 ("[S]tatistical proof almost always occupies center stage in a prima facie showing of a disparate impact claim"). The defendants here attack the sufficiency of the plaintiff's statistics. They argue that the plaintiff has not offered any statistical evidence to indicate a causal link between UNH's prior college coaching experience requirement and its negative impact on African-Americans. However, in its memorandum in opposition to the defendants' motion for summary judgment, Jackson does offer statistics suggesting a causal link between the prior experience requirement and its impact on African-Americans, by comparing the pool of applicants to those who were ultimately selected for interviews. Jackson notes that, of the 14 applicants whose race was identified, only 10 percent of the Caucasians (one out of ten) did not have college coaching experience, but 50 percent of the African-American candidates (two out of four) did not have college coaching experience. Further, Jackson noted that all six of the applicants selected for interviews were Caucasian. However, this statistical evidence fails to establish a sufficient causal link between the defendants' employment criterion and its impact on African-Americans.

The Second Circuit has recognized that exceedingly small sample sizes often result in statistically unreliable evidence. *Lowe v. Commack Union Free Sch. Dist.*, 886 F.2d 1364, 1371–72 (2d Cir. 1989) (holding that the fact that two out of three candidates under age 40 received favorable ratings while only 16 out of 34 candidates over age 40 received such ratings did not support a disparate impact claim in part because of "the unreliability of such a small statistical sample"). The Second Circuit has also indicated that a plaintiff's statistics must meet a certain threshold level of substantiality. See *Smith*, 196 F.3d at 365 ("Statistical data may be admitted to show a disparity in outcome between groups, but to make out a prima facie case the statistical disparity must be sufficiently substantial to raise an inference of causation."); *E.E.O.C. v. Joint Apprenticeship Comm. of the Joint Indus. Bd. of the Elec. Indus.*, (2d Cir. 1998) ("[A] plaintiff's statistical evidence must reflect a disparity so great it cannot be explained by chance."). Here, the relevant sample size is only 14 (of the 36 applicants, the race of only 14 has been identified), which is too small to yield a statistically significant result.

In *Smith*, the Second Circuit cautioned that in assessing whether a statistical disparity is "sufficiently substantial to establish a prima facie case of disparate impact, there is no one test that always answers that question." "Instead," the Court reasoned, "the substantiality of a disparity is judged on a case-by-case basis." *Id.* In this case, the plaintiff has failed to provide a sufficiently substantial disparity to survive summary judgment, because the sample is too small.

In addition to the statistics discussed above, the plaintiff has presented an article from the *Sports Business Journal*, which purportedly demonstrates the disparity of college football coaches that are African-American. However, this article – without more – does not present the type of substantial statistical evidence contemplated by the Second Circuit in *Smith*. It is only two pages long, and most of it is an opinion piece rather than a scientific statistical analysis. Even when the author does cite statistics, he does not disclose the basis for them or reveal their methodology.

Also, the article fails to set forth the type of statistics that are appropriate in a disparate impact analysis. The only statistics in the article concern the percentages of coaches in the various NCAA divisions that are African-American. However, the essence of a disparate impact analysis is a *comparison*. In *Carter v. Ball*, 33 F.3d 450 (4th Cir. 1994) the plaintiff brought a Title VII discrimination suit against the Secretary of the Navy. The plaintiff in that case attempted to offer statistical evidence "which purportedly demonstrate[d] a statistical imbalance in the Navy's promotional practices." 33 F.3d at 456. The Fourth Circuit upheld the district court's exclusion of the statistical evidence. In so holding, the court emphasized that: "[i]n a case of discrimination in hiring or promoting, the relevant comparison is between the percentage of minority employees and the percentage of potential minority applicants in the qualified labor pool. ... The mere absence of minority employees in upper-level positions does not suffice to prove a *prima facie* case of discrimination without a comparison to the relevant labor pool." *Id.* See *Wards Cove Packing Co. v. Atonio* (1989) ("the proper basis for the initial inquiry in a disparate-impact case" is "between the racial composition of the qualified persons in the labor market and the persons holding at issue jobs"). Here, the article offered by Jackson makes no such comparison. It simply recites the percentages of college coaches that are African-American. It does not offer statistics on the percentage of African-Americans that would be otherwise qualified for head coaching positions, but were not hired.

Finally, also in support of his disparate impact claim, the plaintiff asserts that the use of the prior college coaching experience requirement has yielded discriminatory results when applied to other athletic programs at UNH. The plaintiff contends that only one out of 23 coaches hired since 1993, when the plaintiff asserts the prior college coaching experience requirement was adopted for most head coaching positions at UNH, has been African-American. However, even if true, the Supreme Court held in *Wards Cove* that "[t]he percentage of nonwhite workers found in other positions in the employer's labor force is irrelevant to the question of a prima facie statistical case of disparate impact." 490 U.S. at 653. Thus, the plaintiff has failed to meet his burden of establishing a prima facie case of disparate impact, and this Court also grants summary judgment as to that claim.

QUESTIONS

1 How did the school's "neutral" hiring rule affect the likelihood of an African-American being hired as a head coach? Cite evidence brought by plaintiff Jackson in his attempt to prove a prima facie case of disparate impact race discrimination.

2 The court rejected Jackson's evidence of disparate impact. According to the court, what kind of evidence would have been acceptable instead? Could he have produced such evidence? Why or why not?

3 Should schools be given deference in terms of their hiring requirements/prior experience required for coaches? How subjective is this process?

Title IX

If an inappropriate employment action is taken by an employer that is an educational institution and a recipient of federal funds, the aggrieved employee may have, in addition to a Title VII claim, a cause of action under Title IX of the Education Amendments of 1972.

In *Cannon v. University of Chicago* (1979), the Supreme Court recognized that Title IX afforded a private right of action to plaintiffs, and in *North Haven Board of Education v. Bell* (1982), the Court established that

Title IX applies to claims of sex discrimination on the part of employees of educational institutions. Subpart E of the Title IX regulations specifically addresses employment discrimination in education institutions (34 C.F.R. § 106.51, (2013)). The courts are split, however, as to whether a Title IX employment discrimination claim is precluded by the availability of a Title VII claim in the same lawsuit. In the employment context, courts that *do* allow both claims usually analyze the Title IX claim similarly to a Title VII claim anyway, using the same *McDonnell Douglas* burden-shifting framework (see *Blalock v. Dale County Board of Education*, 1999). Title IX is enforced by the Department of Education's Office of Civil Rights (OCR) and unlike Title VII and the EEOC, it does not require that a Plaintiff file a complaint with the OCR before filing a lawsuit.

In 2005, the Supreme Court recognized the claim of "retaliation" under Title IX. Specifically, that:

> … Retaliation is discrimination "on the basis of sex" because it is an intentional response to the nature of the complaint: an allegation of sex discrimination. We conclude that when a funding recipient retaliates against a person *because* he complains of sex discrimination, this constitutes intentional "discrimination" "on the basis of sex," in violation of Title IX. (*Jackson v. Birmingham Board of Education*, 2005, para. 174)

The Court further explained the reporting incidents of discrimination is "integral to Title IX enforcement" and would be discouraged if retaliation were allowed – Title IX's enforcement "scheme would unravel" (para. 180). And, "teachers and coaches … are often in the best position" to identify discrimination (para. 181).

Acts of retaliation are an independent violation of Title IX. Thus, since 2005, a combination of state laws and Title IX, as well as Title VII, have been used more frequently by coaches who believe they were the subject of discrimination on the basis of sex, and in some cases, sexual orientation. These cases now often include retaliation claims in addition to the underlying discrimination claims. In 2015, University of Minnesota-Duluth women's hockey coach Shannon Miller filed suit against the University for Title IX Retaliation, along with a host of other claims, including sex discrimination under Title VII, violation of the EPA, and sexual orientation discrimination under the Minnesota Human Rights Act. As explained in *Jackson*, Title IX prohibits retaliation for good faith reporting or complaining about discriminatory practices. According to the complaint, Miller and her co-Plaintiffs engaged in protected activity that included "complaining to University administrators about discrimination against Plaintiffs on the basis of their sex and complaining to the University that its treatment of Plaintiffs, and of the women's hockey, softball, and basketball programs, may be in violation of Title IX" (*Miller v. Board of Regents of the University of Minnesota*, 2015, para. 181). And further that the University "deliberately and intentionally subjected Plaintiffs to adverse employment actions …for Plaintiff's advocacy of gender equity under Title IX" (para. 182). Ultimately a jury sided with Miller, awarding her $3.75 million which was later increased to nearly $4.2 million. The University filed a motion to overturn the verdict in 2019 (Olsen, 2019).

Also in 2019, the Head Golf Coach and Associate Athletic Director at Carroll College in Montana "became aware of inequities between women's sports and men's sports," including disparate scholarship spending, participation opportunities, treatment, benefits, funding, resources, and employment opportunities based on sex at the school and reported them to the Title IX Coordinator (*Macintyre v. Carroll College*, 2019, p. 20). Then, according to the plaintiff, he received his first negative employment review and was ultimately terminated from one position and had his salary cut in the other. The plaintiff also used a combination of state and federal law, filing one count of Title IX retaliation and one count of wrongful discharge-retaliation under Montana State law. This case is pending.

Other states, such as Iowa and Delaware, both of which have seen similar cases to Miller's, also have state laws that protect against sexual orientation discrimination. As of 2019, 26 states do not have any such protection (MAP, 2019), requiring a possible reliance only on Title IX and Title VII for sexual orientation discrimination. As stated earlier, the federal circuits are split on whether Title VII protects against sexual orientation discrimination. Under Title IX, there is also some ambiguity. In a 2001 "Dear Colleague" letter from the Department of Education, sexual orientation discrimination was not prohibited under Title IX (U.S. Dept. of Education, 2001). This stance was softened during the Obama administration and then reinstated in another "Dear Colleague" letter in 2017. As it stands in 2019, courts in the Second and Seventh Circuits have ruled Title VII protects against sexual orientation discrimination and would likely find that Title IX does as well, pending the aforementioned Supreme Court decision in 2020.

Discrimination on the Basis of Age

Discrimination based on the age of the employee may become a factor when businesses seek to cut costs. Older employees making higher salaries may be targeted for termination because a younger staff is generally a less expensive staff. In 1967, Congress enacted the Age Discrimination in Employment Act (ADEA) to protect older workers from employment discrimination. (See Exhibit 5.5.) The ADEA applies to employers with 20 or more employees and, unlike Title VII, it covers employees in Native American tribes, religious organizations, and private membership clubs, such as country clubs. However, in *Kimel v. Florida Board of Regents* (2000), the Supreme Court ruled that, unlike Title VII, the ADEA does not allow a private right of action against state government employers. The EEOC enforces the ADEA.

Employees 40 years of age and older are protected by the ADEA, and currently there is no upper age limit. That is, an employer must treat an 80-year-old employee the same as a 30 year old. Although research has shown that older workers are more reliable and committed to their jobs, are absent less often, and are harder working than younger employees, employers often have the opposite perception (Bennett-Alexander & Pincus, 1998). The ADEA was intended to protect older workers who may be limited by such stereotypical views about their ability or willingness to perform. Consequently, it does not protect young workers from discrimination based on the notion that they are too young (*General Dynamics Land Systems, Inc. v. Cline*, 2004). Examples of age discrimination that would be covered under the statute include:

- forcing retirement due to age;
- including age preferences in job advertisements;
- assigning older workers to jobs that do not allow them to be competitive for higher-level jobs within the organization;
- promoting a younger worker over an older one because the older worker may be planning to retire soon;
- hiring a younger worker over an older worker who is better qualified.

Because the language of the ADEA mirrors the language of Title VII, the courts usually analyze ADEA claims in the same manner as Title VII disparate treatment claims, using the *McDonnell Douglas* burden-shifting

---

Exhibit 5.5 The Age Discrimination In Employment Act of 1967, 20 U.S.C. § 623.

Section 4(a) It shall be unlawful for an employer –

1 to fail or refuse to hire or to discharge any individual or otherwise discriminate against any individual with respect to his compensation, terms, conditions, or privileges of employment, because of such individual's age;
2 to limit, segregate, or classify his employees in any way which would deprive or tend to deprive any individual of employment opportunities or otherwise adversely affect his status as an employee, because of such individual's age; or
3 to reduce the wage rate of any employee in order to comply with this chapter.

Exhibit 5.6 Prima facie case under ADEA.

For the ADEA, a prima facie case is shown by establishing that:

1   The plaintiff is a member of the protected class – in this case the 40 and over age group;
2   The plaintiff was qualified;
3   The plaintiff suffered an adverse employment action;
4   A person younger than the plaintiff was hired (need not be necessarily under 40).

---

analysis (discussed earlier) for claims resting largely on circumstantial evidence (see *Reeves v. Sanderson Plumbing, Products, Inc.*, 2000). That is, the plaintiff must prove a **prima facie** case of age discrimination, then the defendant must offer a LNDR defense, and then the plaintiff must disprove the proffered defense or show that it is pretext for discrimination. Exhibit 5.6 identifies how the prima facie case is proven for an ADEA plaintiff. The disparate impact theory of liability is rarely allowed under the ADEA, as according to the Supreme Court in *Smith v. City of Jackson* (2005), "the scope of disparate-impact liability under ADEA is narrower than under Title VII (para. 240)," primarily due to the "**reasonable factors other than age**" (RFOA) provision. Mixed-motives claims, in which a plaintiff alleges that the adverse action stems from both permissible and impermissible employer motives (*Gross v. FBL Financial Services, Inc.*, 2009) are not allowed under the ADEA. Instead, a viable age discrimination suit requires the plaintiff to sustain the burden of proving intentional discrimination based on age – a decision partially based on age, where other factors also led to an adverse employment action, will not give rise to liability under the ADEA. If an organization is liable for an ADEA violation, the law provides a number of remedies including reinstatement, back pay, injunctive relief, and attorney's fees. Reinstatement is often a preferred remedy, but may not be appropriate for some positions such as a coach. For example, Notre Dame was found to have violated ADEA when it fired Joseph Moore as the offensive line coach in 1996. Moore successfully sued Notre Dame under ADEA for his termination, but the court awarded damages rather than reinstatement, finding that Moore and the head coach would not be able to engage in a workable relationship due to likely hostility and under friction, and someone else was already hired into Moore's previous position (Wolohan, 2000).

In *Austin v. Cornell University* (1995), Plaintiffs Edward Austin and Henry McPeak had previously held seasonal positions as rangers at Cornell's golf course. They were not rehired before the start of the 1993 season. Austin was 73 years old and McPeak was 67 years old. The reason they were given is that the golf course was undergoing a reorganization (the course was implementing a new system of play with golfers teeing off both the first and tenth tees simultaneously). They were not told that their prior service was unsatisfactory. According to subsequent testimony, Cornell maintained that the men were not qualified to handle the increased responsibilities, both in that they would have to work "harder" and "did not want" increased hours (para. 744). Cornell eventually hired four new rangers, all of them younger than the Plaintiffs. The Plaintiffs established a prima facie case – because they worked as rangers the prior season and received no criticism, the court found them to be at least minimally qualified to perform the job. The Defendants' reasoning of a reorganization is an age-neutral reason for the adverse employment action (so a LNDR), leaving it to the Plaintiffs to establish pretext. The court found that comments made by Defendants that can reasonably relate to age-based stereotypes (McPeak was too "timid" and they could use some "fresh help"), the Plaintiffs being replaced by younger workers having no ranger experience, the lack of negative performance reviews, and finally that they never asked Plaintiffs if they would or could work more hours, they just assumed/perceived that they would not work 20 hours a week, could lead to a conclusion that age was more likely than not the basis of Cornell's decision. The *Austin* case is also important to remind us that the ADEA protects all employees, not just full-time employees.

The statute enumerates additional defenses that employers may use in responding to an ADEA claim, which include good cause, bona fide occupational qualification, reasonable factors other than age, and seniority. When employees' job performance is deemed unsatisfactory or they have violated workplace rules, an employer may discipline or discharge them, regardless of their age, under the **good cause** defense. If an age classification is a BFOQ that is reasonably necessary for satisfactory performance of the job, then the employer is justified in imposing an age restriction. In such a case, the employer would have to prove a factual basis for believing that older workers could not safely and effectively perform the essential job functions. This BFOQ defense is usually a difficult defense to prove, and in cases of jobs that impact public safety (e.g., firefighters and police officers) the ADEA already provides an exemption allowing the imposition of mandatory retirement.

The ADEA provides the **reasonable factors other than age (RFOA)** defense for use when, for example, an employer has taken adverse action against an employee because restructuring an organization required the elimination of a position or because the employee's work performance had deteriorated to the point of being unsatisfactory. In the latter case, the argument would be that the person was no longer doing acceptable work and was fired for that reason, not because of the person's age. The Supreme Court has interpreted this defense to mean that an adverse employment action motivated by an age-neutral factor that somehow correlates with age does not constitute disparate treatment of an older worker and thus does not violate the ADEA, such as setting a starting salary low to discourage older more experienced applicants or termination of employee to avoid paying pension benefits. (See *Hazen Paper Co. v. Biggins*, 1993.)

The following hypothetical case illustrates how this defense might be applied in the context of a sport-related employment action.

Considering … Reasonable Factors Other Than Age

Assume your local Parks and Recreation Department has a hiring policy that ties salary to years of experience; thus, the more years of experience, the higher the salary that must be paid to a new hire. Two people apply for the job of Physical Activities Director. One is Juanita Oldpro, who is 56 years old and has 25 years of experience in similar positions. The other is Justin Newby, who is 30 years old and has five years of relevant experience. The organization cannot afford to hire Oldpro because her years of experience require a salary that exceeds its budget by $10,000, so Newby is hired instead.

Questions

- If you were the hiring official at the Parks and Recreation Department, what would you tell Oldpro when you informed her that she did not get the job?
- If Oldpro threatened to sue you based on the fact that you hired a less qualified younger person, how would you respond to her?
- If Oldpro did in fact sue the Parks and Recreation Department for age discrimination, would your reason for not hiring her, if proven to be true, be considered acceptable under the ADEA?

Note how you would answer the questions and then check your responses using the Analysis & Discussion at the end of this chapter.

Discrimination on the Basis of Disability

Two federal statutes operate to protect persons with disabilities from workplace discrimination: Section 504 of the Rehabilitation Act of 1973 and the Americans with Disabilities Act of 1990 (see Exhibit 5.7). As of February 2018, people with disabilities constitute approximately 19.1 percent of the potential

Exhibit 5.7 Federal disability discrimination statutes in employment.

---

§504 of the Rehabilitation Act of 1973

No otherwise qualified individual with disabilities in the United States shall, solely by reason of his disability, be excluded from the participation in, be denied the benefits of, or be subjected to discrimination under any program or activity receiving federal financial assistance or under any program or activity conducted by any executive agency.

Title I of the Americans with Disabilities Act (ADA) (1990)

No covered entity shall discriminate against a qualified individual with a disability because of the disability of such individual in regard to job application procedures, the hiring, advancement, or discharge of employees, employee compensation, job training, and other terms, conditions, and privileges of employment.

---

workforce in America. The unemployment rate for people with disabilities is approximately 8 percent compared to 3.7 percent for persons with no disabilities (U.S. Dept. of Labor, 2020). Many employment decisions about applicants who are disabled are grounded in stereotypes, fear, or ignorance about the disability involved or the capabilities of individuals with disabilities.

Section 504 applies only to recipients of federal funds, so it was not until the passage of the ADA in 1990 that protection of the employment rights of persons who are disabled was extended to the private sector (more specifically, to employers with 15 or more employees). This extension of protection to the private sector is the primary difference between the two laws. In fact, the courts have used virtually the same analysis in deciding ADA cases as was developed for § 504 cases.

These laws prohibit discrimination against a qualified individual with a physical or mental impairment that substantially limits one or more major life activities, if the individual, with or without reasonable accommodation, can perform the essential duties of the job. There is no all-inclusive list of covered disabilities; instead, the courts are supposed to make their decisions on a case-by-case basis, paying attention to the particular facts in each case. If an accommodation is necessary to enable an employee to perform the essential job functions, it must be reasonable in scope and cost and not impose an undue hardship on the employer or constitute a fundamental alteration of the nature of the employer's program.

The Supreme Court has ruled that the ADA may not be used to sue a state government employer because Congress did not intend this statute to abrogate the Eleventh Amendment **sovereign immunity** (i.e., governmental immunity) from lawsuits enjoyed by the states (*University of Alabama v. Garrett*, 2001). With this ruling, legal recourse against public school and university employers was narrowed. Aggrieved state employees have to bring their disability claims under either § 504 or the Equal Protection Clause. Equal protection claims will be analyzed using rational basis review because disability is not considered a suspect classification (*City of Cleburne v. Cleburne Living Center, Inc.*, 1985).

The ADA was amended by the Americans with Disabilities Act Amendments Act of 2008 (ADAAA), which became effective in January 2009 and made some significant changes with regard to the interpretation and application of the ADA. The stated purpose of the ADAAA is to reinstate the availability of a broad scope of protection by rejecting certain requirements established in Supreme Court decisions and in EEOC regulations that are more restrictive than Congress intended (ADAAA, 2008). In particular, the ADAAA states that the terms "substantially limits" and "major life activity" must not be interpreted as significantly restrictive, and it instructs the EEOC to revise its regulations accordingly. As a result of this law, a significant amount of case law may now be of questionable reliability as precedent for deciding future cases brought under the ADA. A helpful resource for understanding the ADAAA is an official "Notice" (found on the EEOC's website at www.eeoc.gov/ada/amendments_notice.html) that provides a concise explanation of the changes made by this law (EEOC, 2009).

Elements of a Section 504 or ADA Employment Discrimination Claims

The elements necessary for a successful § 504/ADA claim include:

- Plaintiff has a *covered disability*.
- The disability *substantially limits a major life activity*.
- Plaintiff was discriminated against on the *basis of that disability*.
- No *reasonable accommodation* was made.

Covered Disabilities. Section 504/ADA provide several examples of covered disabilities including:

- *physical impairments* such as blindness, deafness, and cerebral palsy;
- *mental/psychological disorders* such as learning disabilities, schizophrenia, epilepsy, and dyslexia;
- *infectious/contagious diseases* such as tuberculosis and the human immunodeficiency virus (HIV).

The Court in *Toyota Motor Mfg. v. Williams* (2002) held that a disabling impairment is one that is permanent or long-term and that is not likely to be overcome with rest or treatment. This decision attempts to clarify the distinction between true disabilities, which are covered by the laws, and temporary injuries or conditions, which are not. Earlier, the Supreme Court had also ruled that impairment corrections, such as eyeglasses and high blood pressure medicine, should be mitigating factors in determining whether the treated condition substantially limited a major life activity (*Sutton v. United Airlines, Inc.*, 1999). Some of the standards enunciated in these two cases have been renounced by the ADAAA of 2008. For example, the only treatment measures allowed to be considered as mitigating factors on substantial limitation of a major life activity are ordinary eyeglasses and contact lenses. So, an employee with food allergies or diabetes would still be covered under ADA even though she successfully manages her condition with medication. Additionally, the statute specifies that a noncovered transitory impairment is one with a duration of six months or less (ADAAA, 2008).

In addition to people with current disabilities, the ADA covers people with past disabilities when the individual's record of having had an impairment might lead to discrimination. Examples include past drug addiction or alcoholism, where the individual is no longer engaged in substance abuse.

The ADA also covers situations where individuals are discriminated against because they are perceived as having a disability, when in fact they do not. Examples might include a person with severe facial scarring or a person who is a cancer survivor. Some employers believe that facial disfiguration might negatively impact the employee's ability to deal successfully with customers, or that cancer will recur, and thus they are unwilling to hire people with these characteristics, even though they are not truly disabled. However, plaintiff's asserting these claims must prove that the employer's perceptions about the conditions motivated the employment decision. The ADAAA makes clear that, now, a plaintiff using the "regarded as having" provision is *not* required to prove that the perceived disability substantially limits a major life activity. While at first glance this provision would seem to open the door to nearly any perceived disability being covered by the ADA, with no need to prove substantial limitation. However, there is another provision meant to limit abuse of this provision by excluding users of the "regarded as having" prong from being entitled to receive a reasonable accommodation. A "regarded as having" plaintiff could thus try to sue to get her job back, for example, but would not be able to get it back if she could not perform the essential job duties without reasonable accommodation. (See *Walker v. Venetian Casino Resort*, 2012.) If a "regarded as having" plaintiff who did not have a truly disabling condition succeeded in winning a lawsuit, then she could seek reinstatement to her job. According to one commentator, this last scenario illustrates the essence of an ADA claim – to prevent employment discrimination based on fears, myths, and stereotypes about disability (Long, 2008; see also, 29 C.F.R. pt. 1630, App. § 1630.2(l)).

Substantial Limit on a Major Life Activity. After determining that an applicant has a covered disability, the next step in the analysis is to assess whether that impairment substantially limits a **major life activity**. Major life activities include, but are not limited to, fundamental aspects of human living, such as "caring for oneself, performing manual tasks, seeing, hearing, eating, sleeping, walking, standing, lifting, bending, speaking, breathing, learning, reading, concentrating, and working" (ADAAA, 2008, § 3(2)(A)). A disability substantially limits working, for example, when the individual's ability to perform a broad range of jobs, not just one particular job or skill, is substantially limited (*Otis v. Canadian Valley-Reeves Meat Co.*, 1995). A disability substantially limits learning when it affects learning in a broad sense, instead of limiting learning only in one type of skill. The ADAAA added a nonexhaustive list of major bodily functions that also count as major life activities, such as immune, digestive, neurological, respiratory, circulatory, and reproductive functions (2008, § 3(2)(B)).

The *Lemire v. Silva* (2000) case illustrates how courts determine what counts as a covered disability and how they analyze whether that disability substantially limits a major life activity. The court's opinion also demonstrates the burden-shifting analysis used to determine liability in disability discrimination cases. As you read the *Lemire* case, you will see that the court ruled that being able to concentrate does not amount to a major life activity. As noted above, this view has been rendered obsolete by the ADAAA.

Lemire v. Silva

CASE OPINION   104 F. Supp. 2d 80 (D. Mass. 2000)

FACTS

The plaintiff Cassie Lemire was a field hockey coach at Sandwich High School from 1992 to 1996. She suffered from a panic disorder with agoraphobia, and her symptoms included anxiety attacks, fear of going to public places, and fear of being alone, among others. She was taking antidepressant medication during her coaching employment, but even with medication she would suffer occasionally from her symptoms. Lemire's psychiatrist reported that her disorder had inhibited her ability to travel far from home, her ability to interact with others outside her family, and her ability to work outside of her home.

In 1995, fliers were distributed at one of the field hockey games that contained a copy of one of Lemire's appointment cards for her psychological treatment, and that further read: "Do you think this person should be coaching your child? This is not a stable person." Some parents later complained to the principal and the athletics director about the suitability of Lemire as a coach, based on the idea that her panic disorder made her unstable. In 1997, the principal decided to institute a formal application process for the position of field hockey coach and told Lemire she would have to apply and be considered for re-hire by a search committee. Plaintiff claims she was the only incumbent coach ever to have to be screened by a search committee. The search committee recommended that Lemire be re-hired, and she was. Then a petition was circulated protesting her appointment, and the principal appointed an independent counselor to meet with the players and report back to him. The counselor's report indicated that the athletes respected Lemire's technical expertise but distrusted her because her behavior was unprofessional and demoralizing to them. Plaintiff then was discharged, and she brought suit under the Americans with Disabilities Act. Defendants moved for summary judgment.

HOLDING

The court denied defendants' motion for summary judgment on Lemire's ADA claim.

RATIONALE

The defendant has admitted, for purposes of summary judgment, that the plaintiff suffers from a mental impairment within the meaning of the ADA. The defendant argues, however, that plaintiff's impairment fails to limit substantially any of her major life activities. The plaintiff claims in response that her mental impairment has substantially limited major life activities: working and interacting with others... .

Working is undoubtedly a major life activity under the ADA. The EEOC has defined it as such in its implementing regulations. See 29 C.F.R. §1630.2(i) (1999).

The ability to interact with others, if defined broadly to include the most basic types of human interactions, is a major life activity. Human beings are fundamentally social beings. The ability to interact with others is an inherent part of what it means to be human... . The ability to interact is ... also essential to contemporary life... . The ability to travel is also a major life activity... . The ability to leave one's home and travel short distances is necessary in most cases to form and maintain social ties, earn a living, and purchase food and clothing. It is thus also at least as significant and as basic as learning and working. The ability to concentrate is not a major life activity. ... [L]imitations on the ability to concentrate can be more appropriately framed as limitations on the major life activities of working, learning, or speaking.

The evidence proffered by plaintiff demonstrates a genuine issue of material fact as to whether Mrs. Lemire was substantially limited in her ability to work [and] interact with others...

In determining whether the plaintiff is substantially limited in a major life activity, a court must consider three factors: (1) the nature and severity of the impairment; (2) the duration or expected duration of the impairment; and (3) the permanent or long term impact, or the expected permanent or long term impact of or resulting from the impairment. The court must take into account, also, the mitigating measures the plaintiff employs, such as medication.

In order to demonstrate that her ability to work is substantially limited, plaintiff must show that she is "significantly restricted in the ability to perform either a class of jobs or a broad range of jobs in various classes as compared to the average individual having comparable training, skills, and abilities. The inability to perform a single, particular job does not constitute a substantial limitation in the major life activity of working."

The plaintiff ... had to quit a security job in 1996 after four months of employment because she experienced several panic attacks while at work. ... Her treating psychiatrist, Dr. Julius Treibergs, has stated that her psychiatric disorder impairs her ability to work outside the home, to interact with people outside her family, and travel far away from home. A jury could infer from this evidence, if credited, that the plaintiff's mental impairment forecloses her from a sufficiently broad range of jobs to limit substantially her ability to work.

According to Ms. Lemire's treating psychiatrist ... her ability to interact with others in crowded places ... has and will continue to be impaired. A genuine dispute of material fact exists as to whether plaintiff's inability to interact with others in crowded places is a substantial limitation on her ability to interact with others.

An examination of an employee's "qualified" status requires consideration of whether the employee could perform the essential functions of the job and, if not, whether any reasonable accommodation by the employer would enable her to perform those functions... . The plaintiff has provided a sufficient explanation for a jury to find that ... she was able to perform the essential functions of her job at the time her employment was terminated.

The plaintiff has presented a prima facie case of discrimination. ... The burden thus shifts to the defendants to demonstrate a legitimate, non-discriminatory reason for firing plaintiff.

The defendants claim that they dismissed plaintiff because of Mrs. Warren's independent [counselor's] report. In those circumstances, the plaintiff needs to show that a reasonable jury could infer from the proffered evidence of record that defendants' stated reason is a mere pretext.

I conclude that the plaintiff has proffered sufficient evidence to warrant a reasonable jury in finding pretext. The testimony of Amy Orrico and Lee Reis is indirect evidence that the real reason for plaintiff's dismissal was her mental impairment. [Their testimony included evidence that a teammate's parent, Joseph Silva, told them plaintiff was an unsuitable coach because of her panic disorder; that he convinced the team to circulate the petition protesting Lemire's being rehired; that he met with the principal to urge him to fire Lemire; and that he had told them Lemire had been fired because she was seeing a psychiatrist.] The defendants' failure to inform plaintiff of the reason for her dismissal at the time is further indirect evidence that the real reason was discrimination. Finally, inconsistencies among defendants' contentions about when and on what basis Principal Norton decided to fire plaintiff are further indirect evidence of pretext.

QUESTIONS

1   How did the court reason that Lemire's panic disorder substantially limited her major life activities?
2   Could the defendants have done anything differently that might have given the court less reason to find that their LNDR defense might be pretext for discrimination?

Discrimination Based on the Disability. The alleged discriminatory treatment must be based on the plaintiff's disability rather than on other factors. For example, in the *Lemire* case, the plaintiff had to establish that she was fired not because the independent counselor determined that she had engaged in a pattern of unprofessional conduct but because she had a panic disorder.

No Reasonable Accommodation Provided. If the applicant or employee who is disabled can, with reasonable accommodation, perform the essential functions of the job, he must provide the requested accommodation. Failure to provide a reasonable accommodation may be employment discrimination. According to § 101 of the ADA, **reasonable accommodations** may include:

- rendering facilities and equipment readily accessible to and usable by those with disabilities.
- restructuring jobs by such means as modifying work schedules.
- reassigning an employee to a vacant position (only required when there is an existing reassignment policy available to all employees).
- modifying qualifying examinations or training materials, and providing interpreters or readers.

For example, consider the example of an employee with food allergies. Some suggestions for accommodation could include restricting areas where employees can consume allergenic foods, designating secure storage space for employee's lunch and serving utensils, providing additional time for lunch to allow an employee to travel home, and ensuring that non-allergenic options are available if meals are provided to employees. Another example could be an employee with epilepsy who could have seizures at work. Let's assume he is an assistant stadium manager and part of his job would require him to inspect the stadium on foot or while driving an ATV or golf cart, a reasonable accommodation could be provided so that he either does not have to drive the ATV or golf cart alone and is accompanied by other employees anytime they are conducting their inspections or otherwise moving between venues with an ATV or golf cart. The courts have approved accommodations costing up to $15,000 as reasonable, but what is considered reasonable rather than an **undue hardship** (excessive monetary cost or administrative burden) will depend in part upon the financial resources of the organization. Of employers surveyed between 2004 and 2019, 59 percent reported that accommodations they had made cost nothing; 36 percent reported a one-time cost of $500, 3 percent reported an annual, ongoing cost, and 1 percent said the accommodation required a combination of one-time and annual costs (Job Accommodation Network, 2019, p. 3).

Aside from the issue of expense, types of accommodations held to be unreasonable include:

- Tolerating employee misconduct stemming from a disability (*Maddox v. University of Tennessee*, 1995).
- Tolerating frequent absences from work (*Jackson v. Veterans' Administration*, 1994).
- Redesigning a job by eliminating many of the essential job functions that the employee could no longer perform (*Russell v. Southeastern Pennsylvania Transportation Authority*, 1993).

The Job Accommodation Network (http://askjan.org) offers practical advice for employers on how to provide reasonable accommodations for employees (Job Accommodation Network, 2018).

Direct Threat Exception

The Direct Threat Exception to an ADA claim originated from a standard articulated by the U.S. Supreme Court in a pre-ADA Section 504 case, *School Board of Nassau County v. Arline* (1987). The court assessed whether a teacher with tuberculosis posed a significant risk to her students. The analysis involves examining the severity of the risk and the likelihood of transmission occurring, as well as potential means of reducing the risk. If the risk is or can be made insignificant, the employee is protected by the law and must be allowed to continue performing the job. If, however, the risk does pose a direct threat to the safety and well-being of others, the employer is under no legal obligation to hire or maintain the employment of the affected individual. The bar for a direct threat defense to an ADA claim is relatively low, as the analysis considers

---

Competitive Advantage Strategies

Hiring, Promotion, and Termination

- Review all job application materials and interview questions to ensure that there are no inappropriate questions about information such as marital status and childcare, since these could be construed as evidence of sex discrimination.
- Advertise open positions and recruit applicants in such a way as to encourage a diverse pool of applicants.
- If you choose to implement an affirmative action plan, be sure to use a temporary method to move toward hiring goals. Do not state hiring goals (which are legitimate targets) in the form of strictly specified numerical requirements (which are unlawful quotas).
- Review workplace policies to ensure that hiring, training, scheduling, benefits, promotion, leave taking, and termination processes are provided or applied fairly to all employees.
- In case it becomes necessary to justify dismissal of an employee, keep records of performance appraisals that evaluate employees' performance as objectively as possible.
- Carefully define the essential functions of the jobs for which employees are hired, review all job announcements and position descriptions to ensure that only the duties essential to the job are presented.

(continued)

Competitive Advantage Strategies

Continued ...

- Make reasonable accommodations for employees with disabilities by ensuring that facilities are accessible and assistive equipment is available.
- Be aware that employers may not require a medical examination except *after an* offer of employment has been made. They then may withdraw the job offer based on the exam results *only* if the exam results show that the applicant cannot perform the job requirements after reasonable accommodation has been made.
- Seek external perspectives when trying to determine whether a proposed accommodation for a disability is reasonable or constitutes an undue hardship. The EEOC provides helpful information on its website at www.eeoc.gov/policy/docs/accommodation.html.
- Avoid asking interview questions with potentially discriminatory implications (see Exhibit 5.8). Interview questions for applicants with disabilities should center on what kinds of things applicants *can* do and what qualifications they *do* possess relative to the job, instead of what they cannot do or whether they have disabilities (see Exhibit 5.9).

whether the employer's belief about the direct threat is reasonable, not whether the threat actually exists (Blackburn-Koch, 2015).

In many sport-related disability cases, an issue arises as to whether an individual's disability poses a significant risk to others. The risk might be collision with an assistive device such as a metal brace or wheelchair, or contracting an infectious disease. For example, Magic Johnson, while an employee of the

Exhibit 5.8 Guide to appropriate pre-employment inquiries.

Topic	Acceptable	Unacceptable (Potentially discrimination)
Citizenship	Statement by employer that, if hired, applicant may be required to submit proof of authorization to work in the United States	"Are you a U.S. citizen?" Requirement that applicant produce naturalization papers or first papers
Age	"Are you over 18 years of age?" "If hired, can you furnish proof of age?"	"How old are you?" "What is your birth date?"
Marital/Family Status	"Do you have any responsibilities that would conflict with your ability to perform your job duties?"	"Are you married?" "Do you have any children?" "What are your childcare arrangements?"
Religion	None	"What is your religious denomination?" "What religious holidays do you observe?"
Race/Ethnicity	None	Questions about complexion or color of skin; other questions directly or indirectly indicating race or ethnicity
Arrests/ Convictions	"Have you ever been convicted of a crime?" (Clarify that a conviction will be considered only as it relates to ability to perform the indicated job.)	"Have you ever been arrested?"
Education	Applicant's academic, vocational, or professional education; schools attended	"What year did you graduate from high school (college)?"
Physical Condition	"Can you perform all of the duties outlined in the job description?"	"Do you have any physical disabilities?"

Exhibit 5.9 Interview guide for questions to avoid related to disabilities.

- Do you have a heart condition? Do you have asthma or any other difficulties breathing?
- Do you have a disability that would interfere with your ability to perform the job?
- How many days were you sick last year?
- Have you ever filed for workers' compensation? Have you ever been injured on the job?
- Have you ever been treated for mental health problems?
- What prescription drugs are you currently taking?

Source: EEOC, www.eeoc.gov/facts/jobapplicant.html.

Los Angeles Lakers basketball team, was diagnosed as HIV-positive. If he had been terminated due to his disease and had sued, the central issue would have been whether his HIV-positive status posed a direct threat (significant risk) of harm to the other participants.

In *Anderson v. Little League Baseball* (1992), a man confined to a wheelchair had served as first-base coach for three years without incident when the national Little League imposed a policy forbidding people in wheelchairs from coaching the bases. The policy was based on the idea that the wheelchair posed a significant risk to players who might be attempting to catch a foul ball. The court ruled that there was no evidence of significant risk, since the plaintiff had served as first-base coach safely for three years, and that the policy was based on stereotypes about the capabilities of people in wheelchairs.

Additional Defenses to Section 504/ADA Claims

To defend against a disability claim, an employer may show that the adverse employment action was not *solely* due to the plaintiff's disability but was job-related. For example, in *Maddox v. University of Tennessee* (1995), an assistant football coach alleged that he was fired because of his disability, which was alcoholism. The court found that the university terminated him not solely because of his alcoholism but because he embarrassed his employer by being arrested for drunk driving and being uncooperative with the arresting officer. Therefore, the court upheld his dismissal. In a more recent case, University of Southern California (USC) Head Football Coach Steve Sarkisian claimed he was fired for alcoholism without being given a chance to seek treatment. Sarkisian had shown up to work events while being under the influence. After the initial incident, USC had the coach sign an agreement which included required counseling sessions, which Sarkisian signed but denied he had a drinking problem. Ultimately, the parties agreed to arbitration, resulting in a decision for the school, based in part on Sarkisian's "having actively concealed" his disability (Polacek, 2018).

An employer could also show that the disabled person was fired or not hired because she could not perform the essential functions of the job. To succeed on this type of job-relatedness defense, the essential job functions must have been *objectively* defined by the employer such that they conform to business necessity and must not have been formulated with the purpose of excluding employees with disabilities. An employer may not require a medical examination of a prospective employee until after an employment offer has been made. If that exam shows that the applicant, with reasonable accommodation, would remain unable to perform the essential job duties, then the employer may retract the offer. The Rhode Island Commission for Human Rights awarded $20,000 in back wages to a man who was passed over for a high school softball coaching job partly because he refused to take a physical examination. The examination had been unlawfully requested by school district officials before an employment offer, after they found out about his prior medical history (Davis, 2006).

Moreover, even if all the elements for a successful disability claim are met, an employer may escape liability if the accommodation necessary to allow a person who is disabled to do the job would impose an undue burden on the employer or require a fundamental alteration in the nature of the employer's business. In *PGA Tour, Inc. v. Martin* (2001), the Supreme Court held that granting a waiver of the rule mandating that professional golfers walk the course to a golfer with a severe circulatory disorder in his legs would not constitute a fundamental alteration in the game of golf. Thus, the Tour was required to grant the waiver as a reasonable accommodation of Casey Martin's disability. This case, however, was decided under Title III of the ADA (discrimination in places of public accommodation) rather than as an employment discrimination case because individual sport professional athletes are not considered employees. Therefore, we discuss this case again in Chapter 12 (participation rights) and Chapter 17 (places of public accommodations and accessibility in sports venues).

In *Keith v. County of Oakland* (2013), a certified lifeguard alleged that he was not hired because he was deaf. The county had extended him an offer of employment at its wave pool, conditioned upon a pre-employment physical examination – a requirement that was stipulated in the job application. The doctor conducting the physical took a look at Keith's medical history and without real further inquiry expressed doubt as to whether any accommodations would be adequate to enable Keith to perform safely the duties of a lifeguard. After consulting an aquatics safety and risk management consulting firm, which also expressed concern about a deaf person's ability to work as a lifeguard, the county hiring official prepared a list of proposed accommodations for Keith and asked the consulting firm for feedback. After being told they still questioned Keith's ability to do the job safely, she and her supervisors revoked the offer of employment. In his lawsuit, Keith presented evidence that: with a hearing aid he could hear loud noises; the ability to hear is not essential to being an effective lifeguard because distressed swimmers exhibit visual signs of distress rather than calling for help; he could communicate effectively with swimmers and other lifeguards by blowing a whistle and using hand signals; and an interpreter would only be necessary during staff meetings and training sessions, not while on duty. Additionally, he provided convincing expert witness testimony about the successes of other deaf lifeguards. The Sixth Circuit court concluded that a reasonable jury could find that, with a few reasonable accommodations, such as the hand signal protocol and the interpreter, Keith was able to perform the essential functions of the job. The court reversed the district court's grant of summary judgment in favor of the county, and remanded the case back to the district court for further consideration.

Compensation and Benefits

During the 1990s the issue of gender equity in coaching salaries surfaced in the sport industry. Coaches of women's college teams, primarily in the sport of basketball, have filed lawsuits seeking salaries comparable to their counterparts coaching the men's teams at the same universities. These lawsuits claim that sex-based compensation discrimination occurred because the coaches of the women's teams were being paid less for doing the same job as the coaches of the men's teams. Since that time, we have also seen suits brought by athletes and front office employees questioning unequal pay (Goodman, 2019; Maise, 2019). These suits are typically brought under three laws: Title VII, Title IX, and the EPA of 1963.

The elements of sex discrimination claims under Title VII and Title IX were discussed earlier. The EPA (29 U.S.C. § 206(d)(1)), which is part of the Fair Labor Standards Act, requires that women be paid a similar wage to what men receive for doing similar work. That is, gender cannot be the basis for giving lower pay to an employee who does substantially equal work, which is defined as work requiring "equal skill, effort, and responsibility, and which [is] performed under similar working conditions." In the context of sport, coaching skills and effort required are not generally disputed. Instead, as we will see in the *Stanley* and *Perdue* cases, the central issue is usually differences in coaching responsibilities, such as revenue generation by filling stadiums or arenas with fans, public speaking, and fund-raising activities.

Under the EPA, pay differentials are permitted when they are based on seniority or merit, or for any reason other than gender. It is a comparison of the content of jobs, not a comparison of job titles, that determines whether the jobs will be considered similar. The jobs must be substantially equal in order for the court to find for the plaintiff.

Pay Discrimination in Coaching

The landmark case on this issue to date is *Stanley v. University of Southern California (Stanley II)* (1999), in which Marianne Stanley, then coach of the University of Southern California (USC) women's basketball team, refused during contract renegotiation to accept a salary less than that of George Raveling, then coach of the USC men's basketball team. USC refused to match his salary, and Stanley sued the university under the EPA.

In reviewing Stanley's request for a preliminary injunction to keep her job (*Stanley I*, 1994), the 9th Circuit Court initially held that coaching women's basketball was not substantially the same job as coaching men's basketball at the Division I level for three reasons: men's basketball coaches had greater responsibilities relative to public speaking and fund-raising than did coaches of women's basketball; the pressure on the men's coach to generate 90 times the revenue of the women's team was greater; and Coach Raveling had substantially better skills, qualifications, and experience than Stanley. Raveling had an educational background in marketing and nine years of experience in that field. He had 31 years of coaching experience, whereas Stanley had 17. Additionally, Raveling had experience as an author, actor, and television commentator. In comparison, Stanley had had several speaking engagements, had won four national championships (Raveling had won none), and had taken her team to three NCAA tournament playoffs while she was at USC.

In the eyes of the court, however, Stanley's qualifications did not match up to Raveling's. The court ultimately concluded that the question of substantial equality of the two coaching jobs need not be decided because the case could be decided on other grounds. The court based its final decision on the grounds that Stanley's lower pay was justified by a reason other than gender – that is, USC paid her less because she was less qualified as a coach than her counterpart (*Stanley II*, 1999).

In contrast to *Stanley* is *Perdue v. City University of New York* (1998). Molly Perdue, former women's basketball coach and women's sports administrator at Brooklyn College, successfully sued the college under the EPA for salary discrepancies between her coaching salary and that of the men's basketball coach, and her administrator's salary and that of the men's athletics administrator. Regarding her coaching responsibilities, Perdue established that she and the men's coach "coached 'basically' the same season, the same number of games, the same number of players, and the same number of practices. … Moreover, they both managed their team's budgets, scholarships, assistant coaches, scouting of opponents, game preparation, and ordering of equipment. … [T]hey both were responsible for the supervision, guidance, and counseling of athletes, and for team conduct … [and] were accountable to the same person" (*Perdue*, 1998, p. 334).

With respect to her duties as an athletics administrator, Perdue provided evidence that she and the men's program administrator "had the same eleven duties … [including responsibility] for the daily operations of sports, game scheduling, organizing team budgets, organizing student orientation, and administering the athletic program … [and] both reported to the same individual" (*Perdue*, 1998, p. 334). Thus, the court concluded that the jury had appropriately found that Perdue performed substantially equal work on jobs requiring equal skill, effort, and responsibility, under similar working conditions to that of her male counterparts, but for less pay. Therefore, the court awarded her $134,829 in back wages, $5,262 in unpaid retirement benefits, and $134,829 in liquidated damages, in addition to $85,000 in compensatory damages, for a total of $359,920, plus prejudgment interest on the back pay and compensatory damages in the sum of $83,264.94 through May 31, 1998, and $43.25 *per diem* to the date that judgment was entered. It also awarded Perdue attorney's fees in the amount of $339,399.60 and expenses in the amount of $16,982.19.

The major limitation of the application of Title VII and the EPA to the coaching salary equity issue is that the sex of the team and not the sex of the coach is the primary determinant of lower salaries for coaches of women's sports. These two laws, however, provide a remedy based on the sex of the employee. In *Jackson v. Armstrong School District* (1977), the women's basketball coaches in the school district were all earning the same salary regardless of their gender, whereas coaches of men's basketball were more highly paid. The court ruled that Title VII protects claimants on the basis of their sex and not the sex of the team they coach.

Over half of collegiate women's basketball teams are coached by men, and thus salary discrimination based on the sex of the team coached would negatively affect male coaches as well as females. So, if Geno Auriemma, coach of the University of Connecticut women's basketball team, were receiving a lower salary than the UConn men's basketball coach, he would have no remedy under Title VII or the EPA. The only recourse for him would be a Title IX claim. However, the 6th Circuit Court has suggested in dictum that a male coach of a women's team is not a member of a class protected by Title IX, even though he is affiliated with a protected class (the members of his team; *Arceneaux v. Vanderbilt University*, 2001). The courts have determined that Title IX employment discrimination claims should be analyzed in the same manner as Title VII claims, so most of the time, Title IX has been as ineffective as Title VII in resolving the coaching salary issue (but see *Tyler v. Howard University* (1993), where the women's basketball coach prevailed under Title IX and the EPA, and *Pitts v. Oklahoma* (1994), where the women's golf coach successfully sued under Title VII and Title IX).

In 1997, the EEOC issued its *Enforcement Guidelines on Sex Discrimination in the Compensation of Sports Coaches in Educational Institutions*. These guidelines, while not law, may be used by the courts as a persuasive indication of the intent behind the law when they decide future coaching salary cases. The existence of these guidelines, the success of some plaintiffs in the courts, and the desire to avoid the costs and negative publicity of litigation appear to have encouraged many university athletic departments with high-profile women's basketball teams to adjust the salaries of their women's team coaches to amounts comparable to their male counterparts (Claussen, 1995).

The EEOC guidelines run counter to some of the case law in several ways (see in particular *Stanley v. University of Southern California*, 1994 and 1999, discussed earlier). First, the courts have often, although not always, required that coaches of the same sport be used as the appropriate comparator for purposes of the EPA. The *Guidelines*, however, assert that coaching tasks and skills are common across many sports, so a female basketball coach is encouraged to use male coaches from sports besides basketball as comparators.

Second, the *Guidelines* state that "pay discrimination cannot be justified if the differences relied on for the proposition that the two jobs are not substantially equal are themselves based on discrimination in the terms and conditions of employment" (EEOC, 1997, p. 2). Thus, if a university has distributed marketing and promotional resources in a discriminatory fashion among men's and women's teams, revenue generation could not be used as a "factor other than sex" to justify salary disparity.

Third, the *Guidelines* say that the sex of the athlete coached is not acceptable as a "factor other than sex" that can justify salary disparity where the institution has limited females coaching only female athletes and they earn less than male coaches of male athletes. Such a situation would mean that the sex of the athletes coached was not a gender-neutral factor in the creation of the salary disparity. It remains to be seen whether courts that face this issue in the future will adopt these guidelines. If they do, the *Stanley* decision may become an aberration.

Pay Discrimination in Management and Administration

It is not just coaches who face equal pay issues in college sports, administrators have as well. In *EEOC v. George Washington University*, the Executive Assistant to the Athletic Director brought suit when a recently hired male who was performing allegedly similar duties was treated more favorably in terms of opportunities and salary. According to the complaint, Sara Williams was providing "high level administrative support" as well as "serving on the senior staff" of the athletic department when a male employee began working in the same department. She claimed he was given new opportunities while her opportunities were minimized, and then a new "Special Assistant" job was created with duties that were substantially similar to her own, at a much higher pay rate. Williams claims she was told that the job was off limits to her and created specifically for the male employee. The EEOC filed both EPA and Title VII claims on behalf of Williams in 2017. The case survived a motion to dismiss/motion to stay proceedings in 2019, as the court noted "one look at the job posting confirms that the Special Assistant duties therein are not only substantially equal, but nearly identical, to what Ms. Williams has alleged that she did in her role as Executive Assistant" so therefore the EEOC has "sufficiently pled a violation of the Equal Pay Act" (EEOC v. George Washington, 2019, para. 5). With regards to the Title VII claim, the court held that the EEOC had "plausibly pled a course of preferential treatment for [the male employee], to the detriment of Ms. Williams, that supports a reasonable inference of materially adverse effects on Ms. Williams career" and as such satisfies the low pleading threshold to allow the claim to continue. Williams is still employed at George Washington University, in a non-athletics capacity, while the Athletic Director and male employee no longer work for the school (Maise, 2019).

Pay Discrimination and Athletes

Equal Pay can also be an issue for the athlete. In 2019, the United States Women's National Soccer Team (USWNT) won their second straight World Cup, and fourth overall (1991, 1999, 2015, 2019). That same year, they filed suit against the United States Soccer Federation (USSF) alleging discrimination in violation of the EPA and disparate treatment under Title VII (some of the players had previously filed with the EEOC, which issued a "right to sue" letter). Specifically, the women's team members were paid significantly less than the men's team, and further experience less favorable conditions in other aspects of their employment such as training and travel conditions, playing matches on inferior surfaces, and allocating fewer resources to promote the women's team. According to the lawsuit, the USSF manages and controls both the women's and men's team, and has substantially similar requirements of all players in terms of competitive soccer skills, training, games (the women actually play more games than the men – 19 more games from 2015–2018), media responsibilities, national and international travel, adherence to Federation Internationale de Football Association (FIFA) rules, among others, the women's and men's teams are similarly situated for purposes of the Equal Pay Act (Morgan v. United States Soccer Federation, 2019). Using a scenario sketched out in the lawsuit, if both teams played 20 friendlies, a women's team player would earn only 38 percent of the compensation of a men's team player using the 2016 collective bargaining agreement, but potentially 89 percent under the new 2017 agreement (Kelly, 2019). The larger discrepancy is with World Cup compensation. The USSF would argue that FIFA sets the amount of compensation – total prize money for the 2019 Women's World Cup was $30 million, total prize money for the 2018 Men's World Cup was approximately $400 million (Schad, 2019; FIFA, 2018). The plaintiffs' attorney would argue that the "USSF has an obligation under US law to provide equal pay regardless of how FIFA discriminates" (Kelly, 2019, para. 27). The plaintiffs sought class certification for their action against USSF, and in November, 2019, the California federal district court granted the plaintiffs' motion for class certification (Morgan v. U.S. Soccer Federation, 2019). In granting the class certification, the district court also rejected one argument offered by USA Soccer that the USWNT had not suffered any injury in fact because each of the named plaintiffs had made significantly more money than the highest paid United States Men's National Soccer Team (USMNT) player, even though the women players were compensated less on a per-game basis. USSF was essentially arguing that the EPA cannot be violated if a female employee's total annual compensation exceeds that of a similarly situated male employee regardless whether the female employee receives a lower rate of pay than her male comparators. The district court rejected this argument and further stated that such an interpretation of the EPA would produce absurd results, clearly not intended by Congress. For example, if this logic was followed an employer could pay a woman $10 per hour and a man $20 per hour and not violate the EPA so long as the woman worked twice as many hours and earned as much as the man in total. The district court emphasizes that the EPA speaks in terms of "rate of pay," not total remuneration and total remuneration is not a proper point of comparison. However, in May 2020, the district court ruled for USSF dismissing the plaintiffs' EPA claims. The players filed an appeal which put the trial of the remaining claims on hold. If the parties do not settle the case, the outcome in court could have far reaching implications for female athletes across a broad spectrum of professional and Olympic sport organizations. Similar issues have arisen for the Women's National Basketball Association (WNBA), as while they get paid less than their National Basketball Association (NBA) counterparts (highest salary in the WNBA is $115,500, lowest in the NBA is $838,464), they also they receive less than 25 percent of their league's revenue, while the men get approximately 50 percent of theirs (Berri, 2018). It will bear watching as these labor disputes play out.

Employee Leave

Employment discrimination can encompass adverse employment actions other than improper hiring, firing, and promotion decisions or compensation discrimination. Sometimes employees are subjected to employment discrimination arising from their desire to take an extended leave of absence because they are pregnant or because they must contribute to the childcare needs of the family.

Pregnancy

In 1978, Title VII was amended by the addition of the Pregnancy Discrimination Act (PDA). This law was added in response to the growing numbers of women in the workforce who were being fired from their jobs because they became pregnant. This is an ongoing concern. A total of 2,790 claims were filed with the EEOC in 2018, resulting in monetary benefits of $16.6 million (EEOC, 2018). Often, employers believe that they should not have to accommodate the lengthy leaves that maternity may require (maternity leave provisions are not always a feature of employee leave policies). Another common attitude is that new mothers will become unreliable employees because of the demands of caring for a newborn child, given society's expectation that the mother be the primary caregiver. The PDA essentially requires employers to treat pregnancy like any other temporary inability to work and allow pregnant women to take leave time, and it forbids employers from using pregnancy as a factor in a decision to engage in an adverse employment action. In a coaching case, the Athletics Director at Centenary College of Louisiana terminated the women's basketball coach, Elizabeth Wamsley, after she gave birth to a child. Although she returned to work full-time ten days after giving birth, the athletics director stated his belief that Wamsley would not be able to commit fully to her coaching duties now that she was a mother. The EEOC brought suit on Wamsley's behalf, and Centenary College ultimately settled, agreeing to pay her $200,000 in damages (EEOC, 2008).

Although many female managers have confronted pregnancy discrimination, it has not been a high-visibility issue in sport so far. This topic has become increasingly relevant now that women play professional basketball. The 1999 collective bargaining agreement between the WNBA and the Women's National Basketball Players Association (WNBPA) included a section titled "Pregnancy Disability Benefit." This section provided that a player who could not perform her services as a result of her pregnancy would receive 50 percent of her base salary in accordance with the payment schedule in her standard player contract for the duration of the time she was unable to play due to pregnancy, or for the remaining term of her contract, whichever was shorter. It also provided that a player whose contract was terminated while she was pregnant would continue to receive medical benefits until the end of that playing season, or until the birth of her child, whichever was later in time (WNBPA, 1999).

These provisions of the Pregnancy Disability Benefit were continued in the 2008 collective bargaining agreement (in effect through September 30, 2013) with one change: a player terminated while pregnant is now eligible to receive medical benefits until the end of that playing season or three months after the birth of her child, whichever comes later (WNBA, 2008). The 2014 Collective Bargaining Agreement (CBA) again retained these provisions (WNBPA, 2014), while the 2020 CBA provides for a full salary while on maternity leave, an annual childcare stipend, and family planning benefits among other new elements (WNBA, 2020).

The collective bargaining agreements have not included any provision prohibiting the use of pregnancy as a factor in the decision whether to renew a player's contract. This omission might allow management to terminate pregnant players by simply not renewing their contracts.

Family Leave

For employees who have worked at least one year, the Family and Medical Leave Act (FMLA) of 1993 guarantees up to 12 weeks of unpaid leave per year that may be used for childbirth, adoption, or to care for sick primary family members. It also requires employers to provide the same job or its equivalent upon the employee's return. Because the FMLA is a highly detailed law, the application of which is not greatly influenced by the sport nature of the employment setting, we mention it here only to alert you to its existence and relevance for employers in the sport industry.

Conclusion

Employment discrimination can occur in the sport industry in several forms, including adverse employment actions based on a person's membership in a protected class, inequitable compensation on the basis of sex, and discriminatory application of employee leave policies. This chapter presented various grounds for pursuing employment discrimination claims that arise in the context of sport, as well as strategies to help managers avoid courses of action that could result in employment discrimination litigation. Familiarity with the application of various laws pertaining to illegal discrimination on the basis of race, sex, age, disability, and religion is an important aspect of human resource management. But it is even more important to put knowledge into practice by taking proactive steps to manage human resources in ways that accommodate differences that do not make a difference in job performance.

Discussion Questions

1 How does disparate impact analysis differ from disparate treatment analysis? Explain the different types of factual situations that would give rise to each theory of liability. Also, explain the different kinds of prima facie cases the plaintiff must prove for each. What are the implications for sport managers who are developing hiring criteria?

2 Would a professional baseball pitcher's shoulder injury that prevents him from pitching for one season be considered a covered disability under the Americans with Disabilities Act, as amended by the ADAAA? Why or why not?

3 What are the primary arguments that support the position that employers are justified in paying coaches of male college athletics teams more than coaches of female teams? What are the primary counterarguments?

Learning Activities

1   Assume you are the director of athletics at State University. Ben Winner, your longtime head football coach, was stricken with a degenerative disease two years ago and now can no longer walk. He must be carried on and off the field by his assistant coaches, but he continues to perform nearly all of the duties expected of the head coach. Some in the community are calling for you to replace Coach Winner because he presents such an appearance of weakness. Write a memo to the university president explaining why you have decided not to succumb to pressure to terminate Coach Winner's employment contract on the basis of his disability.

2   Assume you are the director of athletics at an NCAA Division I powerhouse in both men's and women's basketball. You must hire a new women's basketball coach. A press conference is scheduled for this evening at which sports reporters from the national media will be asking whether you plan to hire a woman or a man and whether you intend to pay the new coach a salary comparable to the whopping salary the men's team coach is being paid. How will you respond to those questions?

3   Assume you are the athletics director at a junior college, and you are about to hire a new head football coach. One of the hiring criteria the search committee wants to establish is that successful applicants must have at least two years of football playing experience at the college level. Do you have any reservations about including this criterion in the written position announcement? If so, write an email memo to the search committee members describing your concerns.

4   Visit the U.S. Department of Labor's website, www.dol.gov, and read more about the Family and Medical Leave Act, or visit the Equal Employment Opportunity Commission's site, www.eeoc.gov, and locate and read the entire document titled *Enforcement Guidelines on Sex Discrimination in the Compensation of Sports Coaches in Educational Institutions*. After reading the information, list the important points you think that sport managers ought to know.

Case Study

In 2013, San Diego State University's (SDSU) Head Women's Basketball Coach Beth Burns was "pressure(d)" to retire, or she would face termination. The University claimed that the "sole cause" for its decision was a video showing her striking a subordinate. Burns claimed that the physical contact shown in the video is incidental and in the heat of watching the game and coaching the team. Further, the previous and current presidents of the University had attended multiple games, sitting close to the bench, and had not only never criticized her bench behavior, but had written her commendation letters. Burns further claimed that she was being treated differently than her male colleagues, as a former football coach had slapped a student-athlete, in front of witnesses, but the school chose not to investigate and the coach was not disciplined. Burns also claimed that the real reason for the termination was her complaint regarding gender equity. She "repeatedly challenged" SDSU's disparate treatment of its women's basketball program, specifically the lack of equivalent benefits including equipment and facility time in the off-season, having to come out of pocket herself to purchase food and gear as well as pay for staff parking passes, the team having to move flooring, lack of a promotional plan for games, and no online ticket ordering. While Burns filed a lawsuit against SDSU in state court, she also possibly had federal law claims.

1   Can Burns successfully establish a prima facie case of sex discrimination under Title VII? On what grounds? Apply the four-prong test from McDonnell-Douglas.
2   Does Burns have a claim for Title IX retaliation? Why or why not?
3   How would Burns make the argument that SDSU's reasoning/defense is a pretext for discrimination?
4   In your estimation, who should win this case?

For further analysis, see Burns v. San Diego State University, Case no. 37-2014-00003408-CU-CO-CTL (2014).

Considering ... Analysis & Discussion

Reasonable Factors Other Than Age

You should tell Oldpro that, although she was well-qualified for the position, the organization could not afford to hire her based on the established pay scale. Her threat to sue should be met either with a polite refusal to comment or with a repeated statement of the reason she was not hired, coupled with a statement that this decision was completely unrelated to her age.

If Oldpro does in fact sue, your reason for not hiring her should be considered acceptable under the ADEA. If Oldpro makes out a prima facie case of age discrimination, your defense would be that linking salary to years of relevant work experience is an acceptable business practice and that she was not hired because of a reasonable factor other than age. That is, based on the organization's salary policy, Oldpro was not hired for budgetary reasons. (See EEOC v. Francis W. Parker School, 1994.)

References

Cases

Anderson v. Little League Baseball, 794 F. Supp. 342 (D. Ariz. 1992).

Arceneaux v. Vanderbilt Univ., 2001 U.S. App. LEXIS 27598 (6th Cir. 2001).

Austin v. Cornell Univ., 891 F. Supp. 740 (N.D.N.Y. 1995).

Biver v. Saginaw Township Cmty. Sch., 805 F.2d 1033 (6th Cir. 1986).

Blalock v. Dale County Bd. of Educ., 84 F. Supp. 2d 1291 (M.D. Ala. 1999).

Bonadona v. Louisiana College, et al. Case no. 1:18-cv-00224-DDD-MLH (2018).

Bostock v. Clayton County, 2020 WL 3146686, 590 U.S. __ (2020).

Burns v. San Diego State University, Case no. 37-2014-00003408-CU-CO-CTL (2014).

Cannon v. University of Chicago, 441 U.S. 677 (1979).

City of Cleburne v. Cleburne Living Ctr., Inc., 473 U.S. 432 (1985).

Corporation of Presiding Bishop of Church of Jesus Christ of Latter-day Saints v. Amos, 483 U.S. 327 (1987).

Dowling v. United States, 476 F. Supp. 1018 (D. Mass. 1979).

EEOC v. Francis W. Parker Sch., 1994 U.S. App. LEXIS 29366 (7th Cir. 1994), cert. denied, 115 S. Ct. 2577 (1995).

EEOC v. George Washington University, Case No. 17-1978 (D.D.C. 2019).

EEOC v. National Broadcasting Co., 753 F. Supp. 452 (S.D.N.Y. 1990).

EEOC v. Sedita, 755 F. Supp. 808 (N.D. Ill. 1991).

EEOC v. Sedita, 816 F. Supp. 1291 (N.D. Ill. 1993).

General Dynamics Land Systems, Inc. v. Cline, 124 S. Ct. 1236 (2004).

Gross v. FBL Financial Services, Inc., 2009 U.S. LEXIS 4535 (2009).

Hazen Paper Co. v. Biggins, 507 U.S. 604 (1993).

Jackson v. Armstrong Sch. Dist., 430 F. Supp. 1050 (W.D. Pa. 1977).

Jackson v. Birmingham Board of Education, 544 U.S. 167 (2005).

Jackson v. University of New Haven, 228 F. Supp. 2d 156 (D. Conn. 2002).

Jackson v. Veterans' Admin., 22 F.3d 277 (11th Cir. 1994).

Keith v. County of Oakland, 2013 U.S. App. LEXIS 595 (6th Cir. 2013).

Kimel v. Florida Bd. of Regents, 120 S. Ct. 631 (2000).

Korematsu v. United States, 323 U.S. 214 (1944).

Lemire v. Silva, 104 F. Supp. 2d 80 (D. Mass. 2000).

Ludtke v. Kuhn, 461 F. Supp. 86 (S.D.N.Y. 1978).

Maddox v. University of Tenn., 62 F.3d 843 (6th Cir. 1995).

McDonnell Douglas Corp. v. Green, 411 U.S. 792 (1973).

Macintyre v. Carroll College, Case 6:19-cv-00042-SEH (D. Mont. 2019).

Medcalf v. University of Pennsylvania, 2001 U.S. Dist. LEXIS 10155 (E.D. Pa. 2001).

Miller v. Board of Regents of the University of Minnesota, Case 0:15-cv-03740-RHK-LIB (D. Minn. 2015).

Minnis v. Board of Supervisors of Louisiana State University, 972 F. Supp. 2d 878 (2013).

Mollaghan v. Varnell, 105 So. 3d 291 (2012).

Morgan v. United States Soccer Federation, Case No. 2:19-CV-01717, Complaint (C.D. Cal. 2019).

Morgan v. United States Soccer Federation, Case No. 2:19-CV-01717, Order Re: Plaintiff's Motion for Class Certification (C.D. Cal. November 8, 2019).

Morris v. Bianchini, 1987 U.S. Dist. LEXIS 13888 (E.D. Va. 1987).

Morris v. Wallace Cmty. Coll.–Selma, 125 F. Supp. 2d 1315 (S.D. Ala. 2001).

North Haven Bd. of Educ. v. Bell, 456 U.S. 512 (1982).

Otis v. Canadian Valley-Reeves Meat Co., 52 F.3d 338 (10th Cir. 1995).

Perdue v. City Univ. of N.Y., 13 F. Supp. 2d 326 (E.D. N.Y. 1998).

PGA Tour, Inc. v. Martin, 532 U.S. 661 (2001).

Pitts v. Oklahoma, No. CIV-93-1341-A (W.D. Okla. 1994).

Reeves v. Sanderson Plumbing Products, Inc., 120 S. Ct. 2097 (2000).

Rickert v. Midland Lutheran College, 2009 U.S. Dist. LEXIS 78886 (D. Neb. 2009).

Rostker v. Goldberg, 453 U.S. 57 (1981).

Russell v. Southeastern Pa. Transp. Auth., 1993 U.S. Dist. LEXIS 12358 (E.D. Pa. 1993).

School Board of Nassau County v. Arline, 480 U.S. 273 (1987).

Smith v. City of Jackson, Mississippi, 544 U. S. 228 (2005).

Stanley v. University of S. Cal., 13 F.3d 1313 (9th Cir. 1994) [*Stanley I*]; 178 F.3d 1069 (9th Cir. 1999) [*Stanley II*]; cert. denied, 120 S. Ct. 533 (1999).

St. Augustine High School v. Louisiana High School Athletic Ass'n, 270 F. Supp. 767 (E.D. La. 1967), aff'd, 396 F.2d 224 (5th Cir. 1968).

Sutton v. United Airlines, Inc., 527 U.S. 471 (1999).

Toyota Motor Mfg. v. Williams, 122 S. Ct. 681 (2002).

Tyler v. Howard Univ., No. 91-CA11239 (D.C. Super. Ct. 1993).

University of Ala. v. Garrett, 531 U.S. 356 (2001).

Walker v. Venetian Casino Resort, LLC, 2012 U.S. Dist. LEXIS 145096 (D. Nev. 2012).

Zarda v. Altitude Express, No. 15-3775 (2d Cir. 2018).

Statutes and Regulations

29 C.F.R. pt. 1630, App. §1630.2(l) (2016).

Affirmative action plan; interview of qualified minority applicants. Oregon Revised Statutes (ORS) § 352. 380(2)(b) (2012).

Age Discrimination in Employment Act, 20 U.S.C. § 621 *et seq.*

Americans with Disabilities Act Amendments Act of 2008, Pub. L. No. 110–325, 122 Stat. 3553.

Americans with Disabilities Act of 1990, 42 U.S.C. § 12101 *et seq.*

Equal Pay Act of 1963, 29 U.S.C. § 206(d)(1).

Family and Medical Leave Act of 1993, 29 U.S.C. § 2611 *et seq.*

Pregnancy Discrimination Act, 42 U.S.C. § 2000e(k).

Rehabilitation Act of 1973, 29 U.S.C. § 701 *et seq.*

Title VII of the Civil Rights Act of 1964, as amended by the Civil Rights Act of 1991, 42 U.S.C. § 2000e *et seq.*

Title IX of the Education Amendments of 1972, 20 U.S.C. § 1681 *et seq.*

Title IX regulations, 34 C.F.R. § 106.51 (2013).

Other Sources

Bennett-Alexander, D. D., & Pincus, L. B. (1998). *Employment law for business* (2nd ed.). Boston: Irwin/McGraw-Hill.

Berri, D. (2018, September 4). WNBA Players Are Simply Asking for a Greater Share of WNBA Revenues. *Forbes*. Retrieved from https://www.forbes.com/sites/davidberri/2018/09/04/what-wnba-players-want/#36ae7d0e33eb.

Blackburn-Koch, B. (2015, April 22). ADA "Direct threat" defense just got a little easier. *The National Law Review*. Retrieved from https://www.natlawreview.com/article/ada-direct-threat-defense-just-got-little-easier.

Bower, G. G., & Hums, M. A. (2013). Career paths of women working in leadership positions within intercollegiate athletic administration. *Advancing Women in Leadership*, 33, 1–14.

Brown, G. (2011, April 20). Leaders push to diversify college football sidelines. *Latest News*. Retrieved from www.ncaa.org.

Carroll, C. (2018, December 31). What is the Rooney Rule? Explaining the NFL's diversity policy for hiring coaches. *Sports Illustrated*. Retrieved from https://www.si.com/nfl/2018/12/31/rooney-rule-explained-nfl-diversity-policy.

Claussen, C. L. (1995). Title IX and employment discrimination in coaching intercollegiate athletics. *University of Miami Entertainment & Sports Law Review*, 12(2), 149–168.

Connley, C. (2019, March 21). The Tampa Bay Buccaneers become the first NFL team to hire two full-time coaches. *CNBC*. Retrieved from https://www.cnbc.com/2019/03/21/tampa-bay-buccaneers-are-1st-nfl-team-to-hire-2-full-time-female-coaches.html.

Davis, P. (2006, October 5). Man denied coaching job could net $20,000 in back pay. *The Providence Journal*. Retrieved from www.projo.com.

Equal Employment Opportunity Commission. (1997, October). Enforcement guidelines on sex discrimination in the compensation of sports coaches in educational institutions. Retrieved from www.eeoc.gov/policy/docs/coaches.html.

Equal Employment Opportunity Commission. (2008, March 28). Centenary College to pay $200,000 to settle EEOC sex discrimination suit. Retrieved from www.eeoc.gov/eeoc/newsroom/release/3-28-08.cfm.

Equal Employment Opportunity Commission. (2009, March). Notice concerning the Americans with Disabilities Act (ADA) Amendments Act of 2008. Retrieved from https://www.eeoc.gov/statutes/notice-concerning-americans-disabilities-act-ada-amendments-act-2008.

Equal Employment Opportunity Commission (2018). Pregnancy discrimination charges. Retrieved from https://www.eeoc.gov/eeoc/statistics/enforcement/pregnancy_new.cfm.

Equal Employment Opportunity Commission. (2019, April 10). EEOC releases fiscal year 2018 enforcement and litigation data. Retrieved from https://www.eeoc.gov/eeoc/newsroom/release/4-10-19.cfm.

FIFA (2018). *Financial Report*. Retrieved from https://resources.fifa.com/image/upload/xzshsoe2ayttyquuxhq0.pdf.

Goodman, L. (2019, June 10). The best women's soccer team in the world fights for equal pay. *NYTimes.com*. Retrieved from https://www.nytimes.com/2019/06/10/magazine/womens-soccer-inequality-pay.html.

Gasper, C. L. (2019, March 2). Progress for minority NFL head coach and GM candidates has stalled. *Boston Globe*. Retrieved from https://www.bostonglobe.com/sports/patriots/2019/03/02/progress-for-minority-nfl-head-coach-and-candidates-has-stalled/9xhTEvyxKp5CVwmRNhMrFL/story.html.

Hancock, M. G., & Hums, M. A. (2016). A "leaky pipeline"?: Factors affecting the career development of senior-level female administrators in NCAA Division I athletic departments. *Sport Management Review*, 19(2), 198–210.

Haner, N. C. (2003). Suns, sports magic settle zoo crew suit. *Orlando Business Journal*. Retrieved from https://www.bizjournals.com/orlando/stories/2003/11/10/story5.html.

Hoffman, J. (2010). The Dilemma of the senior woman administrator role in intercollegiate athletics. *Journal of Issues in Intercollegiate Athletics*, 3, 53–75.

Human Rights Campaign (2019, June 7). State maps of laws & policies. Retrieved from https://www.hrc.org/state-maps/employment.

Job Accommodation Network. (2018, December 17). Five practical tips for providing and maintaining effective job accommodations. *Job Accommodation Network Accommodation and Compliance Series*. Retrieved from https://askjan.org/publications/Topic-Downloads.cfm?pubid=226472.

Job Accommodation Network. (2019, February 1). Workplace accommodations: Low cost, high impact. *Job Accommodation Network Accommodation and Compliance Series*. Retrieved from https://askjan.org/publications/Topic-Downloads.cfm?pubid=962628.

Kelly, M. (2019, July 8). Are U.S. Women's soccer players really earning less than the men? *The Washington Post*. Retrieved from https://www.washingtonpost.com/politics/2019/07/08/are-us-womens-soccer-players-really-earning-less-than-men/?noredirect=on&utm_term=.64de033494a7.

Lapchick, R. (2017). The 2017 racial and gender report card: National Football League. *Institute of Diversity and Ethics in Sport*. Retrieved from http://nebula.wsimg.com/63112e771048708d1b4213b554c6cd76?AccessKeyId=DAC3A56D8FB782449D2A&disposition=0&alloworigin=1.

Lapchick, R. (2018a). The 2017 college sport racial & gender report card. *Institute of Diversity and Ethics in Sport*. Retrieved from http://nebula.wsimg.com/5665825afd75728dc0c45b52ae6c412d?AccessKeyId=DAC3A56D8FB782449D2A&disposition=0&alloworigin=1.

Lapchick, R. (2018b). The 2018 racial and gender report card: D1 FBS leadership. *Institute of Diversity and Ethics in Sport*. Retrieved from https://docs.wixstatic.com/ugd/71e0e0_afa2563007e84b74b66aca9ea05418e2.pdf.

Long, A. B. (2008). Introducing the new and improved Americans with Disabilities Act: Assessing the ADA Amendments Act of 2008. *Northwestern University Law Review Colloquy*, 103, 217–229.

Maise, E. (2019, May 13). Federal judge rejects motion to dismiss pay discrimination lawsuit in athletic department. *The GW Hatchet*. Retrieved from https://www.gwhatchet.com/2019/05/13/federal-judge-rejects-motion-to-dismiss-pay-discrimination-lawsuit-in-athletic-department/.

McKindra, L. (2008, February 1). Minority panel asks for accountability in hiring. *The NCAA News*. Retrieved from www.ncaa.org.

Movement Advancement Project (2019, July 11). Non-discrimination laws. Retrieved from http://www.lgbtmap.org/equality-maps/non_discrimination_laws.

NCAA (n.d.). Senior Women Administrators. Retrieved from http://www.ncaa.org/about/resources/inclusion/senior-woman-administrators.

Olsen, T. (2019, March 13). UMD moves to overturn Miller verdict. *Duluth News Tribune*. Retrieved from https://www.duluthnewstribune.com/news/4584579-umd-moves-overturn-miller-verdict.

Patra, K. (2020, May 18). NFL instituting changes to Rooney Rule. *NFL: Around the NFL*. Retrieved from https://www.nfl.com/news/nfl-instituting-changes-to-rooney-rule.

Polacek, S. (2018, July 9). Judge rules USC doesn't owe Steve Sarkisian anything in $30 million lawsuit. *Bleacher Report*. Retrieved from https://bleacherreport.com/articles/2785252-judge-rules-usc-doesnt-owe-steve-sarkisian-anything-in-30-million-lawsuit.

Schad, T. (2019, July 10). Breaking it down: What exactly is the gap in pay between USWNT and USMNT players? *USA Today*. Retrieved from https://www.usatoday.com/story/sports/soccer/2019/07/10/breaking-down-pay-gap-between-uswnt-and-usmntplayers/1671361.

U.S. Department of Education (2001, January 19). OCR: revised sexual harassment guidance. Retrieved from https://www2.ed.gov/about/offices/list/ocr/docs/shguide.html.

U.S. Department of Labor (2020). Persons with a disability: Labor force characteristics summary. Retrieved from https://www.bls.gov/news.release/disabl.nr0.htm.

Whitford, E. (2018, July 18). Bias against Jews covered by Title VII, judge rules. *Inside Higher Ed*. Retrieved from https://www.insidehighered.com/news/2018/07/18/judge-denies-louisiana-colleges-motion-dismiss-discrimination-case.

Wolohan, J. (2000, March). Age discrimination illegal, potentially expensive for athletic departments. *Athleticbusiness.com*. Retrieved from https://www.athleticbusiness.com/civil-actions/adiscrimination-illegal-potentially-expensive-for-athletic-departments.html.

"WNBA and WNBPA Reach Tentative Agreement," (2020, January). Retrieved from https://www.wnba.com/news/wnba-and-wnbpa-reach-tentative-agreement-on-groundbreaking-eight-year-collective-bargaining-agreement/.

Women's National Basketball Association (2008). Women's National Basketball Association Collective Bargaining Agreement. Retrieved from www.wnbpa.org.

Women's National Basketball Association Collective Bargaining Agreement (2014). Retrieved from https://wnbpa.wpengine.com/wp-content/uploads/2017/07/WNBA-CBA-2014-2021Final.pdf.

Women's National Basketball Players Association. (1999). WNBA Collective Bargaining Agreement. Retrieved from www.wnbpa.org.

Web Resources

www.dol.gov ■ This is the U.S. Department of Labor's website. Among other things, it contains information about the Family and Medical Leave Act.

www.dol.gov/odep/ ■ This U.S. Department of Labor site provides research and resources on disabilities and the workplace, including disability employment statistics.

www.eeoc.gov ■ *This is the website of the Equal Employment Opportunity Commission. It contains much useful information on application of the federal employment discrimination laws.* Among the many linked documents is the EEOC's *Enforcement Guidelines on Sex Discrimination in the Compensation of Sports Coaches in Educational Institutions.*

www.eeoc.gov/ada/amendments_notice.html ■ This section of the EEOC site offers a helpful resource for understanding the Americans with Disabilities Act Amendments Act of 2008 (ADAAA). It provides a concise explanation of the changes made by the 2008 law.

www.eeoc.gov/policy/docs/accommodation.html ■ This document provides helpful information for those trying to determine whether a proposed accommodation for a disability is reasonable or constitutes an undue hardship.

www.eeoc.gov/policy/docs/preemp.html ■ The Equal Employment Opportunity Commission site offers resources for both employers and potential employees about the workplace and job application process. At this site, you will find the document *ADA Enforcement Guidance: Pre-employment Disability-Related Questions and Medical Examinations*, an explanation of the EEOC guidelines on hiring practices. It includes examples of questions related to disabilities that an employer should not ask on an application or during an interview.

www.askjan.org ■ The website for the Job Accommodation Network (a service provided by the U.S. Department of Labor's Office of Disability Employment Policy) provides information and resources on how employers can accommodate workers with disabilities. Those seeking to avoid discrimination in their hiring, promotion, or termination practices can visit the A to Z guide, grouped by disability or by topic, at www.askjan.org/links/atoz.htm.

www.tidesport.org ■ The Institute for Diversity and Ethics in Sport at the University of Central Florida "serves as a comprehensive resource for issues related to gender and race in amateur, collegiate and professional sports." It posts annual Racial and Gender Report Cards for organizations like the NBA, WNBA, MLB, and college sports, under the "Racial & Gender Report Card" link.

www.womenssportfoundation.org ■ The Women's Sports Foundation's website provides news and information about resources for addressing discrimination or harassment in sport based on gender, sexual orientation, and gender identity.

6 Employment Discrimination, Part II: Harassment and Employee Expression

Lauren McCoy

Introduction

As we saw in chapter 5, avoiding illegal employment discrimination is a critical aspect of human resource management. The previous chapter also discussed the legal issues involved in hiring, promotion, termination decisions, and in determinations regarding compensation and employee leave. Here in Chapter 6, we explore several other forms of illegal employment discrimination, such as harassment and discriminatory responses to different forms of employee expression. In particular, this chapter discusses sexual and racial harassment in the employment context and discriminatory treatment of employees for engaging in different forms of expressive activity. These may include seeking justice under antidiscrimination laws, whistleblowing, dress or grooming choices, engaging in speech while on the job, observance of religious practices, and unionizing activity.

As was true for the types of employment discrimination discussed in Chapter 5, the Constitution and several federal statutes apply to the types of employment discrimination we discuss in this chapter, as do civil or human rights statutes and ordinances enacted by most states and many cities. However, once again, the focus of this chapter is on examining the applicable *federal* laws governing harassment in the workplace. For a summary of the issues, relevant laws, and primary cases discussed in this chapter, see Exhibit 6.1. Harassment is included in this chapter rather than Chapter 12 where we discuss First Amendment and free speech issues. Many harassing behaviors may also involve some expressive activity – verbal, physical, or pictorial/symbolic statements. Because of this, people often believe that the First Amendment should protect their right to harass others. From the point of view of people in the workplace, harassment may appear to be a form of expressive activity by employees, so we have chosen to address it in that context. It should be kept firmly in mind, however, that in the eyes of the law, this type of behavior is harassing *conduct* rather than speech. Hence, the laws prohibiting harassment do not run afoul of the First Amendment.

Sexual and Racial Harassment

Discussions of harassing behaviors in the workplace typically focus on sex and race, but there may be other grounds that lead to similar harassment allegations. Sexual harassment is present when employment decisions are made contingent upon the performance of sexual favors. For example, a supervisor may threaten to deny an employee's promotion if the employee refuses to accede to a demand for sex. At other times, sexual or racial harassment can create an abusive work environment that makes it very difficult for an employee to perform his or her job. Situations like these are considered forms of sex or race discrimination prohibited under Title VII.

Exhibit 6.1 Management contexts in which employment discrimination may arise, with relevant laws and cases.

Management Context	Major Legal Issues	Relevant Law	Illustrative Cases
Workplace harassment	Sexual/racial/religious	Title VII (and Title IX with regard to sex)	Bowman, Cameli, Faragher
	Age and disability	ADEA and ADA	
	Sexual orientation	State & municipal laws	
Employer responses to employee expression	Employer retaliation	Title VII	Cox
		Title IX	Lowrey, Jackson
	Dress/grooming codes	First Amendment and Title VII	
	Injudicious speech/ whistleblowing	First Amendment	Dambrot, Williams
	Religious speech & team prayer	First Amendment and Title VII	Lumpkin, Kennedy, Johnson
	Religious practices	Title VII	Simmons

In 2018, 7,609 sexual harassment charges were filed, and 15.9 percent of those charges were filed by men (EEOC, 2018). The #MeToo movement, which began in 2007 by activist Tarana Burke and was popularized in 2017, has brought more attention to sexual harassment allegations through news reports along with lawsuits for many industries, including sport (Cooney, 2017). Often, sexual harassment claims are settled out of court to diminish negative publicity and save on litigation costs, but the settlement amounts can still be costly (Fenno, 2019). For example, former Carolina Panthers owner, Jerry Richardson sold the team after it was reported that substantial settlement payments were made to former employees following sexual and racial harassment allegations about Richardson's behavior (Wertheim & Bernstein, 2017). He was also fined $2.75 million by the National Football League (NFL) after an investigation into his conduct (Knoblauch, 2018).

Sexual Harassment

Based on the Equal Employment Opportunity Commission (EEOC) definition, courts have further defined two types of sexual harassment: quid pro quo and hostile environment. Exhibit 6.2 presents the EEOC's regulations defining sexual harassment.

Quid Pro Quo Harassment

When an employer conditions a job-related benefit, such as a promotion or pay raise, upon an employee's willingness to engage in sexual behavior this is considered **quid pro quo harassment**. An example of this might be a fitness club manager promising a promotion to the aerobics instructor if she will engage in a sexual relationship with him. This effectively constitutes sexual bribery, and an actionable claim of quid pro quo sexual harassment requires only one instance of such conduct.

Exhibit 6.2 EEOC sexual harassment regulations, 29 C.F.R. § 1604.11(a) (2013).

Sexual harassment is defined as unwelcome sexual advances, requests for sexual favors, and other verbal or physical conduct of a sexual nature where:

1   Submission to the conduct is made a term or condition of employment.
2   Submission to or rejection of such conduct is used as a basis for employment decisions.
3   The conduct has the purpose or effect of unreasonably interfering with an individual's work performance.
4   The conduct has the purpose or effect of creating an intimidating, hostile, or offensive working environment.

Hostile Environment Harassment

A second type of sexual harassment, known as **hostile environment harassment**, is much more difficult to define and consequently more difficult for courts to address because the standards have not been consistently applied (Keller & Tracy, 2008). Hostile environment sexual harassment occurs when an employee is subjected to repeated unwelcome behaviors that do not constitute sexual bribery but are sufficiently severe and pervasive that they create a work environment so hostile that it substantially interferes with the harassed employee's ability to perform his or her job. In *Harris v. Forklift Systems* (1993), the Supreme Court listed several factors that courts may consider in determining whether a sexually hostile environment exists, including:

- the frequency of the offensive conduct;
- the severity of the offensive conduct;
- whether the conduct is physically threatening or humiliating or merely an offensive utterance;
- whether the conduct unreasonably interferes with an employee's work performance.

It is necessary, therefore, to examine all the factual circumstances of a case to determine whether a hostile environment exists. Many types of behaviors fall into the gray area where courts must make a judgment call based on the specific facts of each case. These behaviors do not have to occur specifically in the workplace. Social media can highlight harassing behavior that is occurring in real-time or describe potential incidents. The #MeToo social media posts, as an example, described many charges of workplace harassment. Social media does not have to be monitored by the employer, but there should be encouragement to share these incidents with human resources as well (Brin, 2017). (See Exhibit 6.3 for examples.)

In *Harris*, the Supreme Court established that plaintiffs in hostile environment cases do not need to wait until they have proof of psychological injury before they can invoke the protection of the law. The Court also established that hostile environment claims are to be subjected to a two-pronged test, one prong being objective and the other subjective:

1 From an objective perspective, would a **reasonable person** in the same situation have perceived the resulting climate as hostile?
2 Did the plaintiff subjectively experience the conduct as sufficiently severe and pervasive that it created a hostile work environment for him or her, thereby making it difficult to perform his or her job?

(Courts use the concept of an abstract "reasonable person" as an "objective" standard to judge behavior in several areas of the law. A reasonable person would be a person exercising judgment that meets societal expectations for prudence in decision-making.)

Hostile environment sexual harassment claims may be brought in two types of cases:

1 where the offensive speech or conduct is sexual in nature;
2 where the offensive speech or conduct is harassment based on the victim's gender and is thus "based on sex" but not necessarily sexual in content.

Bowman v. Shawnee State University (2000) provides an example of a hostile environment sexual harassment case in which both types of offensive conduct are discussed.

Exhibit 6.3 Examples of conduct that may contribute to a sexually hostile work environment.

Unwelcome sexual touching, pinching, patting, or hugging.
Whistling or cat-calling.
Sexually suggestive or obscene notes, letters, or email.
Leering or sexually oriented gestures.
Obscene jokes or other vulgar language.
Display of sexually suggestive materials, including posters, calendars, or cartoons.

Bowman v. Shawnee State University

CASE OPINION   220 F.3d 456 (6th Cir. 2000)

FACTS

Plaintiff Thomas Bowman became a full-time instructor of physical education courses at Shawnee State University in 1988. Jessica Jahnke was hired in 1990 and soon became the dean of education. In 1991, Bowman was selected to serve as sports studies coordinator. Bowman claims that beginning in 1991 Jahnke sexually harassed him on multiple occasions, including one instance where she rubbed his shoulder for two seconds until he jerked away and said "no." Another incident occurred at a 1992 Christmas party, where Jahnke grabbed Bowman's buttocks when he was leaning against the stove in her house. Bowman told her that if someone did the same thing to her, she would have them fired. Jahnke responded that she "controlled [Bowman's] ass and she would do whatever she wanted with it" (p. 459). On two occasions, Jahnke suggested that Bowman share her whirlpool or swimming pool with her, without his girlfriend present. Bowman alleged numerous other instances of harassing behavior, but they were unrelated to sexual activity. In 1995, Jahnke wrote a memo to Bowman stating that she was angry at him for lying to her about teaching a class at Ohio University and was stripping him of his responsibilities as sports studies coordinator. This removal was short-lived, as the provost rescinded the removal within a few days, and Bowman's salary was never reduced. Nevertheless, Bowman brought a sexual harassment suit against the university and Jahnke. The district court dismissed the claim against Jahnke because individual liability does not attach under Title VII unless the individual defendant is the actual employer.

HOLDING

The circuit court affirmed the district court's decision that Bowman's sexual harassment claim failed because the harassment did not rise to the level necessary to have created a hostile work environment.

RATIONALE

To prevail [against an employer on a quid pro quo claim] under a sexual harassment claim without showing that the harassment was severe or pervasive, the employee must prove the following: (1) that the employee was a member of a protected class; (2) that the employee was subjected to unwelcomed sexual harassment in the form of sexual advances or requests for sexual favors; (3) that the harassment complained of was on the basis of sex; (4) that the employee's submission to the unwelcomed advances was an express or implied condition for receiving job benefits or that the employee's refusal to submit to the supervisor's sexual demands resulted in a tangible job detriment; and (5) the existence of respondeat superior liability.

* * *

Even if we assume that the loss of the Coordinator position constitutes a significant change in employment status, there is no tangible employment action in this case because the very temporary nature of the employment action in question makes it a non-materially adverse employment action. [Thus, the court concluded there was no quid pro quo sexual harassment.]

* * *

A plaintiff may [however] establish a violation of Title VII by proving that the sex discrimination created a hostile or abusive work environment without having to prove a tangible employment action. In order to establish a hostile work environment claim, an employee must show the following: (1) the employee is a member of a protected class; (2) the employee was subject to unwelcomed sexual harassment; (3) the harassment was based on the employee's sex; (4) the harassment created a hostile work environment; and (5) the employer failed to take reasonable care to prevent and correct any sexually harassing behavior.

* * *

Non-sexual conduct may be illegally sex-based and properly considered in a hostile environment analysis where it can be shown that but for the employee's sex, he would not have been the object of harassment. …

* * *

We agree with the district court that while Bowman recites a litany of perceived slights and abuses, many of the alleged harassing acts cannot be considered in the hostile environment analysis because Bowman has not shown that the alleged harassment was based upon his status as a male. … Bowman has not alleged that Jahnke made a single comment evincing an anti-male bias. …

* * *

The only incidents that may arguably be considered in the hostile work environment analysis are the 1991 shoulder rubbing incident, the 1992 Christmas party incident, the 1994 whirlpool incident, the 1994 swimming pool incident, and the 1995 meeting in Jahnke's office [in which she pushed him on the chest]. … [T]he incidents that may properly be considered are not severe or pervasive and, thus, do not meet the fourth element of the hostile environment analysis.

QUESTIONS

1   Why was this case treated as a hostile environment case rather than as a case of quid pro quo sexual harassment?
2   On what grounds did the court reject the idea that plaintiff Bowman had been subjected to a hostile working environment by his supervisor?
3   Do you think the decision in this case might have been different if it had been a male supervisor and a female victim instead of the other way around?

Bowman illustrates how a court deals with a hostile environment sexual harassment claim; however, hostile environment harassment claims may also be brought for harassment on the basis of one's race or religion under Title VII, one's age under the ADEA, or one's disability under the ADA. The courts deal with these additional types of hostile environment harassment claims by using the factors for analysis discussed earlier in connection with hostile environment sexual harassment claims (i.e., the factors articulated in *Harris v. Forklift Systems*). Additionally, sexual harassment that occurs in educational institutions that receive federal funds may be actionable under Title IX as well as Title VII.

Racial Harassment

Similar to sexual harassment, employers need to be focused on ensuring that they are not creating a hostile workplace. Fanatics, the sport merchandise company, paid $322,000 to a former employee, Vincent Perkins, who was subjected to racial discrimination. Perkins, who is Black, was repeatedly asked if he could read because "a lot of you guys can't read" and was called discriminatory names (Neal, 2019).

The following Focus Case, *Cameli v. O'Neal*, illustrates how a court dealt with a hostile environment racial harassment claim.

Cameli v. O'Neal

U.S. Dist. LEXIS 9034 (N.D. Ill. 1997)   **FOCUS** CASE

FACTS

Plaintiff Cameli, who is White, served as varsity basketball coach at predominantly Black Thornton High School from 1982 through 1994. In 1990, Richard Taylor, the superintendent of schools, forced Cameli to hire a Black assistant coach, Rocky Hill, to sit on the bench during varsity games. Cameli did not get along with Hill and thought he was a negative influence on the players. William O'Neal became principal of Thornton in 1993. O'Neal engaged in a series of decisions in which he forced Cameli not to cut players that Cameli wished to cut and reinstated players Cameli had cut from the team. Cameli alleged that he was also subjected to an atmosphere of repeated racial insults that rose to the level of a "hostile environment" for Title VII purposes. Particularly, he claims that Principal O'Neal told him on two separate occasions that Thornton would have a Black coach, that he had trouble relating to Black students, that it would look good to the Black community if he had another Black assistant on his bench, and that "no White coach was going to treat Black ball players that way." He also claims that O'Neal told the plaintiff's assistants that the plaintiff could not relate to Black students and that the athletic director and assistant principal also told the plaintiff that he would be Thornton's last White head coach.

Cameli sued under Title VII claiming he had been subjected to a racially hostile work environment. The defendant moved for summary judgment.

HOLDING

The court found that the conduct complained of by Cameli was not sufficiently severe or pervasive to create a hostile environment and granted defendant's summary judgment motion.

RATIONALE

Even though Cameli may have *subjectively* perceived his environment to be permeated with racial hostility, the *objective* test was not met here. Although several of the comments may have been racially insensitive and indeed unwarranted, Cameli was not subjected to vicious racial insults or ridicule, nor to physically threatening or humiliating actions that a reasonable person would conclude were severe enough or frequent enough over an extended period of time to create an abusive work environment. Moreover, Principal O'Neal's interference with Cameli's coaching decisions, although inappropriate and bothersome to the point of creating hostility, did not contribute substantially to a *racially* hostile atmosphere in Cameli's place of work.

Same-Sex/Same-Race Harassment

Increasingly, plaintiffs are bringing hostile environment claims when they have been harassed by someone of the same sex or same race. The Supreme Court held in *Bostock v. Clayton County, Georgia* (2020) that an employer firing an employee for being gay or transgender is in violation of Title VII. In the decision, the Court noted that Title VII prohibits employers from discrimination because of sex. For example, if an employee is harassed because he is attracted to men, this harassment is considered based on sex because this same behavior is tolerated by the employer when done by women.

This ruling extends the protections previously provided in *Oncale v. Sundowner Offshore Services, Inc.* (1998), which concluded that sexual harassment falls within the same category as sex discrimination. In *Oncale*, the Supreme Court ruled that same-sex sexual harassment may be a violation of Title VII where the harassment is not simply based on the harassee's sexual orientation but is harassment of a sexual nature perpetrated by a person of the same sex. For example, repeated derisive comments such as "everyone knows you're a faggot" and "everyone knows you take it up the ass" (as quoted from *Bibby*) are based on an employee's sexual orientation, and by themselves they would not trigger the protection of Title VII (*Bibby v. Philadelphia Coca-Cola Bottling Co.*, 2000). However, where sexually related taunts, forcible sexual acts and gestures, and physical assaults of a sexual nature are perpetrated by a same-sex harasser, Title VII is violated because the Supreme Court has interpreted such actions as being "based on sex" (*Oncale*, 1998). The Court further ruled that such conduct need not be motivated by sexual desire in order to be actionable. An Albuquerque car dealership, under an EEOC consent decree, agreed to pay $2 million after their former manager subjected over 50 men to sexual comments, propositioned them, and subjected them to regular touching over a ten-year period ("Pitre Car Dealership to Pay," 2014).

On the legislative front, the Employment Non-Discrimination Act (ENDA) is a bill that would prohibit employment discrimination based on gender identity and sexual orientation. An early version of the bill was introduced in Congress in 1994, and different versions have been reintroduced several times, most recently in 2013. While ENDA legislation has not been passed, President Obama signed an Executive Order in 2014 prohibiting federal contractors from discriminating based on sexual orientation or gender identity, amending an Executive Order previously signed by President Johnson (Hudson, 2014; O'Keefe, 2013). A directive from the Department of Labor in 2018 now allows for these same federal contractors to claim a religious exemption when fighting sexual orientation or gender identity discrimination charges (Department of Labor, 2018).

Relying on the recognition of same-sex sexual harassment by the Court in *Oncale*, the Eighth Circuit held that an African-American employee could bring a claim of same-race racial harassment against a supervisor who repeatedly called him "nigger" and "black boy" and referred to his Caucasian wife as "whitey" (*Ross v. Douglas County*, 2000).

Competitive Advantage Strategies

Sexual and Racial Harassment

- Adopt a harassment policy separate from a general antidiscrimination policy, and ensure that it is disseminated, explained, and enforced. Be sure that it covers racial and religious harassment in addition to sexual harassment. Ensure that the policy specifies alternatives to the immediate supervisor for receiving complaints.
- When creating policies that include definitions of prohibited behaviors (e.g., sexual harassment), make the definitions broader than what is actually defined by the law as illegal conduct so that enforcement of the policy cannot be construed as an admission of liability. An example would be: "Unwelcome conduct of a sexual nature is prohibited, regardless of whether it rises to the level of creating a hostile environment" (Neil, 2003).
- Do not assume that everyone understands what harassment is. It is a good idea to conduct employee training workshops that define harassment and describe procedures for handling harassment incidents.
- A clear and strong harassment policy should have, at a minimum, the components shown in Exhibit 6.4. For an example of an actual sexual harassment policy, see the policy appended to the court's opinion in *Robinson v. Jacksonville Shipyards, Inc.* (1991).

Exhibit 6.4 Essential elements of a harassment policy.

- A philosophy of zero tolerance for harassing behavior.
- A description of the legal definition of sexual, racial, and religious harassment, along with examples specific to your business.
- Reporting procedures for harassment complaints that make clear the following:
    - Steps to take if you are a target of harassment.
    - How to register a complaint and with whom (competence to handle such a complaint is an issue; also, employees should have an option to bypass their immediate supervisor in cases where the supervisor is the harassing party).
    - Retaliation against a complainant will not be tolerated.
- An investigation process that makes clear the following:
    - The confidentiality of the process.
    - Who will investigate the validity of the complaint.
    - Procedures for investigating the complaint.
- A description of applicable sanctions or disciplinary actions.
- An appeals process.

Employer Liability for Harassment

When a supervisor is guilty of harassing an employee, the supervisor's employer may be held strictly liable (vicarious liability; see Chapter 4) if the employer knew or should have known the harassment was occurring and an adverse employment action (such as discharge, demotion, or undesirable reassignment) was the tangible result (the typical quid pro quo case). The employer's only available defense is to disprove the claims of the plaintiff. Additionally, when the harassment is perpetrated by a non-supervisory employee or a non-employee such as a client or customer, the employer may be held strictly liable if the employer knew or should have known it was occurring and failed to take reasonable steps to prevent it. A harassment policy developed by employers can provide a defense to this employer liability because it provides an avenue for the plaintiff to report a problem and allows the employer to prevent the harassment. Exhibit 6.4 highlights essential elements to be included within a harassment policy. The lack of a consistent policy can lead to a larger problem that does not allow the employer to address harassment as it occurs. For example, current and former employees of the Dallas Mavericks described years of harassing behavior occurring at the organization as a "real life *Animal House*" with a lack of oversight and a failure by management to address concerns that left women feeling unsafe in the workplace. After an independent investigation, owner Mark Cuban implemented new protocols for investigating workplace misconduct, along with enhancing the reporting process and updating training for all staff to include domestic violence, sexual assault, and sexual harassment ("NBA statement," 2018; Wertheim & Luther, 2018).

A different situation is presented by hostile environment cases where adverse, tangible job consequences may have been threatened by a supervisor but did not occur. In *Burlington Industries, Inc. v. Ellerth* (1998), the Supreme Court ruled that in such cases the employer can still be held vicariously liable for the harassing actions of a supervisory employee. However, the employer may assert an **affirmative defense** (i.e., a defense that excuses rather than denies blame) by showing both of the following:

1   The employer exercised reasonable care to prevent and promptly correct any sexually harassing behavior.
2   The plaintiff employee unreasonably failed to take advantage of any preventive or corrective opportunities provided by the employer.

The *Ellerth* decision further noted that while having an anti-harassment policy with an explicit procedure for dealing with complaints is not always required to establish a successful affirmative defense, the existence of such a policy is a relevant factor for courts to consider under the first prong of the affirmative defense. Additionally, if an employer can demonstrate that the aggrieved employee unreasonably failed to use the established complaint procedure, this will normally suffice to meet the second prong of the affirmative defense.

To understand the rationale underlying employer liability for hostile environment sexual harassment, let's look at *Faragher v. City of Boca Raton* (1998).

Faragher v. City of Boca Raton

118 S. Ct. 2275 (1998)	**FOCUS** CASE

FACTS

Beth Ann Faragher brought an action against the City of Boca Raton and her supervisors after resigning from her employment as an ocean lifeguard, alleging that the supervisors had created a "sexually hostile atmosphere" at work by repeatedly subjecting her to "uninvited and offensive touching," by making lewd remarks, and by speaking of women in offensive terms. Faragher never complained to management about these incidents, although another female lifeguard had complained about harassment that she and other lifeguards, including Faragher, had endured. Although the city had a sexual harassment policy, it had not disseminated this policy to beach employees.

HOLDING

The Supreme Court held that an employer is vicariously liable for harassment caused by a supervisor, but that this liability is subject to an affirmative defense that addresses the reasonableness of the employer's conduct and the conduct of the plaintiff.

RATIONALE

The Supreme Court found that sexual harassment by a supervisor is not an act contemplated within the scope of his or her employment. However, the Court noted that an employer may be vicariously liable for such actions by employees under the Restatement (Second) of Torts § 219(2)(d), which provides that an employer "is not subject to liability for the torts of his servants acting outside the scope of their employment unless ... the servant purported to act or speak on behalf of the principal and there was reliance on apparent authority, or he was aided in accomplishing the tort by the existence of the agency relation." The Court agreed with Faragher's argument that the sexual harassment engaged in by her supervisors was made possible by the abuse of their supervisory authority, and it found that the aided-by-agency-relation principle was sufficient to hold an employer vicariously liable. The Court noted that the employment (agency) relationship allows the unwelcome contact between a supervisor and an employee and that the victim may be reluctant to complain about the actions of a supervisor. Also, when a supervisor discriminates against a subordinate, those acts depend on the supervisor's position of power over the employees who report to him or her.

The Court then noted that the city would have the opportunity to raise an affirmative defense but that this defense would likely be unsuccessful in this case because of the city's failure to disseminate its sexual harassment policy to the beach employees. Additionally, the city officials had made no attempt to keep a record of complaints or to monitor supervisors' conduct. Furthermore, the harassment policy did not contain a procedure for bypassing one's supervisor to register a complaint in situations where the harassing party was the supervisor.

Employee Expression

Employees sometimes provoke adverse employment actions by the way in which they choose to express themselves in the work environment. In this section we discuss legal issues of this nature that may arise in the sport or recreation context.

Retaliation for Seeking Justice/Whistleblowing under Title VII or Title IX

Title VII protects employees from employer **retaliation** for the employee's efforts to obtain justice under the statute. In *Cox v. National Football League* (1998), a plaintiff sued his employer under Title VII on the grounds that the employer had retaliated against him. Bryan Cox alleged he was fined one game day's pay ($87,500) in retaliation for his filing of a race discrimination lawsuit against the NFL for its failure to take measures to prevent racial harassment of players by fans. The court found that Cox had not demonstrated a causal link between the fine and the protected expression because over two years had passed between the two events and because there was ample evidence that the real basis for Cox's fine was his multiple instances of abusing fans and officials with profanity and obscene gestures. Should the Supreme Court rule that sexual orientation is a protected class under Title VII, cases like Jane Meyer's lawsuit against the University of Iowa would also qualify for protection from retaliation. Jane Meyer, a former employee of the University, filed a lawsuit under the Iowa Civil Rights Act claiming that she was paid less and demoted after filing a written complaint about discriminatory behavior toward homosexual women. A jury awarded Meyer $1.4 million in damages after finding that school officials discriminated against Meyer based on her gender and sexual orientation. The university settled later with Meyer and her partner, Tracey Griesbaum, who was the women's field hockey head coach, for $6.5 million (Emmert, 2017).

The courts have ruled that Title IX also prohibits retaliation, including retaliation for whistleblowing — that is, for criticizing the employing institution for gender inequities in athletics. In *Lowrey v. Texas A&M University System* (1998), Jan Lowrey was demoted from her position as women's athletics coordinator after she spoke out on Title IX issues with regard to Tarleton State University's athletic department. The court ruled that Title IX retaliation claims should be analyzed in the same way as Title VII retaliation claims, in that both should utilize the *McDonnell Douglas v. Green* (1973) burden-shifting framework. In the context of a retaliation claim, the plaintiff must prove a prima facie case by showing:

1 She engaged in activity protected by the statute.
2 The employer took adverse action against her.
3 A causal connection existed between the protected activity and the adverse employment action.

This framework applies even if the individuals accused of the initial harassment are not employees. Employers are responsible for their own negligence in failing to respond to harassment if that negligence does not protect the employee from retaliation. In *Summa v. Hofstra* (2013), Lauren Summa, a female graduate student employed as a part-time team manager for Hofstra University's football team, sued under Title VII after complaining about humiliating and sexually explicit comments about her made by some football players. The head coach moved to correct the harassment, but it continued and led to harassment training for the coaching and athletic department staff. The Second Circuit determined that the university avoided liability, not because the football players were non-employees, but because they had promptly responded to the harassment. However, because Summa was hired as a fall and spring team manager and was replaced after her complaints, it could be reasonably concluded that this action was in retaliation.

In *Jackson v. Birmingham Board of Education* (2005), Roderick Jackson, a male coach of a high school girls' basketball team, sued under Title IX claiming that he was fired in retaliation for complaining that his team was being treated inequitably. The Board of Education argued that Title IX does not provide a private right of action for a retaliation claim, but the Supreme Court disagreed, finding it important to protect those who report discrimination in order to enable the Title IX enforcement scheme to work as Congress envisioned. The Court held that there is indeed an implied private right of action for retaliation claims under Title IX. Subsequently, in 2007, Fresno State University agreed to pay $9 million to its former women's basketball coach and $5.2 million to its former volleyball coach after they each sued for sex discrimination and retaliation (Daysog, 2009; "Lesbian basketball coaches," 2008).

Dress/Grooming Codes

The federal courts are split on the issue of whether dress and grooming codes imposed by government actors violate the First Amendment right to freedom of expression. Most of these cases involve dress and grooming codes in schools, so they are discussed in greater detail in Chapter 13.

In the private sector, courts have generally ruled that employers may impose reasonable rules governing the appearance of their employees without running afoul of the sex discrimination provision of Title VII. For example, courts have upheld company policies stipulating appropriate hair length and appropriate clothing for the different sexes (see e.g., *Albertson's v. Washington Human Rights Comm'n*, 1976; *Fagan v. National Cash Register*, 1973; *Lockhart v. Louisiana-Pacific Corp.*, 1990; *Willingham v. Macon Telegraph Pub. Co.*, 1975). However, grooming or dress codes that differentiate on the basis of race or sex and that subject members of those groups to different conditions of employment as a result (e.g., requiring females, but not males, to wear skimpy, sexually suggestive clothing that results in the women being subjected to leers and lewd comments) would probably not be tolerated by the courts. These dress codes must also allow for reasonable accommodation of religious practices (see e.g., *Equal Employment Opportunity Commission v. Abercrombie & Fitch Stores, Inc.*, 2015; EEOC, n.d.).

A related issue is the use of training or employee manuals that direct employees to adjust their behavior on the basis of racist or sexist stereotypes. For example, Shawn Brooks, who was hired as an account executive by the Philadelphia Eagles Radio Network, was urged by his supervisor to use a best-selling book titled *Dress for Success* as a training manual for his job. One chapter, "When Blacks and Hispanics Sell to Whites (and Vice Versa)," included some advice that Brooks, who is Black, found offensive. One passage reads:

> Blacks selling to whites should not wear Afro hair styles or any clothing that is African in association. If you're selling to corporate America it is very important that you dress, not as well as the white salesmen, but better than them.

Another passage reads:

> If you are black selling to white Middle America, dress like a white.... This clothing conveys that you are a member of the establishment and that you are pushing no radical or other feared ideas.

When Brooks complained to an administrator, he was referred back to the offending supervisor. He resigned and filed a race discrimination and racial harassment claim with the Pennsylvania Human Rights Commission, which found in his favor (*Brooks v. CBS Radio*, 2009).

Considering … Employee Expression

NFL cheerleaders are expected to comply with specific requirements that highlight personal hygiene tips and clothing. Some of these requirements include controls on how cheerleaders conduct themselves outside of work. For example, New Orleans Saints cheerleaders have a team policy that banned nude, semi-nude, or lingerie pictures posted on a cheerleader's personal social media pages. The team also had a "no fraternization" policy that required cheerleaders to block all NFL players on social media and leave a restaurant or party if a player enters. In 2018, New Orleans Saints cheerleader, Bailey Davis, was fired after posting a photo of herself in a one-piece bathing suit on a private Instagram account. The Saints defended the firings as a culmination of violations of the anti-fraternization policy (Belson, 2018).

Questions

1   Do these conduct requirements discriminate based on sex? Are sex-specific dress and grooming codes in violation of Title VII?
2   What action should teams take to provide uniform conduct codes?

Note how you would answer the questions and then check your response using the Analysis & Discussion at the end of this chapter.

Injudicious Speech and Whistleblowing Under the First Amendment

The First Amendment to the U.S. Constitution protects the right of federal or state government workers to enjoy some freedom of speech when speaking as citizens on matters of public concern (Connick v. Myers, 1983; Pickering v. Board of Education, 1968; see Exhibit 6.5). According to the Supreme Court in Pickering, the interests of the employee as a citizen in commenting upon matters of public concern are to be balanced against the interests of the government employer in promoting efficiency of its services (the Pickering balancing test; see Exhibit 6.6). In Connick, the Court established that determining whether a specimen of speech refers to a matter of public concern (i.e., a matter that concerns important social or political ideas) depends on examining its content, form, and context. This issue of whether speech counted as speech about a public concern was central to the Dambrot v. Central Michigan University (1995) case.

In Dambrot, Keith Dambrot, the men's basketball coach at Central Michigan University (CMU) used racial slurs to refer to several of his players on multiple occasions. As a result, he was fired, and he sued claiming his freedom of speech had been violated. The court applied the Connick analysis of examining the content, form, and context of the speech to determine whether it touched on a matter of public concern. Finding that the coach's use of that word communicated no socially or politically important

Exhibit 6.5 Amendment I of the United States Constitution.

Congress shall pass no laws respecting an *establishment of religion*, or prohibiting the *free exercise* thereof; or abridging the freedom of speech, or of the press; or the right of the people peaceably to assemble, and to petition the government for a redress of grievances.

Exhibit 6.6 The Pickering balancing test.

In 2006 the Supreme Court decided the case of Garcetti v. Ceballos, which somewhat altered the application of the Pickering balancing test regarding the right to free speech of government employees. In this case, a deputy district attorney was denied a promotion for writing a memo recommending that the district attorney's office dismiss a case due to improper police behavior.

message to his players and that the form and context of the speech was intended to be motivational rather than to communicate important social and political ideas, the court ruled that Coach Dambrot's speech was not a matter of public concern. Instead, it was a racial slur that was of such low value as not to be the type of meaningful expression the First Amendment was designed to protect. Thus, the court did not have to proceed further to apply the *Pickering* balancing test in upholding the university's right to terminate the coach.

The *Pickering* analysis goes as follows:

1 Does the speech focus on a matter of public concern?
2 If not, there is no First Amendment protection.
3 If yes, then the *Pickering* balancing test will be applied.

In *Garcetti*, the Supreme Court held that the First Amendment does not prohibit managerial discipline of public employees for speech made pursuant to their official job duties. This ruling thus seems to add to the *Pickering* analysis a threshold inquiry into whether the speech was part of the employee's job. According to the dissent, however, a supervisor should be able to take disciplinary action when an employee's speech is inflammatory or misguided but not when it is legitimate yet unwelcome (e.g., whistleblowing).

The dissent also argued that it can be difficult to draw a clear line between a government employee speaking as a citizen and one speaking as an employee. This difficulty is exemplified in the *Lumpkin* case, discussed in the next section, on religious speech. As you read about that case, consider whether, when Reverend Lumpkin made his views known to the media, he was speaking as a citizen (albeit a minister) or as an employee of the San Francisco Human Rights Commission.

The Focus Case that follows illustrates how one court has applied the *Garcetti* decision to a controversy arising in the sport context.

Williams v. Dallas Indep. Sch. District

480 F.3d 689 (5th Cir. 2007)	**FOCUS** CASE FACTS

Williams was a high school athletic director and head football coach. During the 2003 school year, he had to ask the principal's office repeatedly for budget account information, and his requests were repeatedly ignored by the office manager. Two months later, he wrote a memorandum to the principal expressing his concerns about the handling of the school's athletic funds compared to standard operating procedures at other high schools in the school district. In the memo, Williams also implied that some corrupt practices were occurring in the management of athletics accounts.

Four days later, the principal removed Williams from his position as athletic director, and subsequently the school district declined to renew Williams's employment contract. Later that same month, the school district placed the principal and his office manager on administrative leave pending an investigation of their financial practices.

Williams sued, alleging that the retaliatory employment action violated his free speech rights. The district court granted summary judgment for the school district, holding that Williams's memo did not address a matter of public concern and thus did not warrant First Amendment protection.

HOLDING

The Fifth Circuit affirmed.

RATIONALE

The court stated that the *Garcetti* decision had added a threshold requirement to the *Pickering* analysis that requires shifting the focus from the content of the speech to the role the speaker occupied when the statements were made. The court acknowledged that the *Garcetti* opinion did not explicate the definition of speaking "pursuant to" one's "official duties," except to say that a formal job description is not dispositive on the issue. The court noted that the district court found Ceballos was acting pursuant to his official duties because he was performing a required task when he wrote his offending memo alleging police impropriety. And the court acknowledged that here, the athletic director was not required to write critical memos regarding athletics accounts to the high school principal. So the question the court engaged was the extent to which, under *Garcetti*, a public employee's speech is protected by the First Amendment if it is not made as part of a required job duty but is nevertheless related to expected duties.

The court distinguished Williams's memo from other cases: schoolteacher Pickering's protected speech in writing to a newspaper about the funding policies of his school board, and another schoolteacher's protected speech when she complained to her principal about the school's discriminatory hiring practices. In the eyes of the court, these were speech activities that could be engaged in by citizens who were not working for the government. In contrast, the statements Williams made in his memo were made in the course of performing his job as athletic director because he needed financial information to do his job effectively. It was part of his job to communicate with the principal's office about the athletics budget. Therefore, his statements were made pursuant to his official duties and, under *Garcetti*, were not protected by the First Amendment.

It is important to note that in *Garcetti* the Supreme Court expressly stated that it was not deciding whether the new threshold inquiry as to employee versus citizen status applied to the context of teaching or scholarship. Therefore, we may expect to see divergent applications of *Garcetti* by the circuit courts to issues arising in an educational context. (For a law review article addressing this issue, see Hutchens (2008).) Additionally, even though First Amendment protection may be limited in scope, various state and federal whistleblower laws may provide statutory protection to government employees who experience retaliation for whistleblowing activity.

Considering ... Political Speech

Sport has often been used as a platform to protest social issues on their teams and in the community. The "Syracuse 8" decided to sit out the 1970 season to bring racial equity to the program. In 2014, members of the St. Louis Rams jogged onto the field with their arms raised in a "don't shoot" gesture to protest the killing of an unarmed teenager by the police.

Following this tradition in 2016, Colin Kaepernick sat on the bench during the playing of the national anthem. He explained that his decision to sit was in protest of police brutality and oppression of people of color. His demonstration was later adjusted to a kneeling position in respect to the military. He was joined in these protests by other NFL players who demonstrated in various ways (sitting, kneeling, and raising a fist). After Kaepernick became a free agent in March 2017, he was unable to find a new team. He later filed a collusion grievance against the NFL, believing that his unemployment was in retaliation to his protests (Stites, 2017).

Questions

- If Kaepernick sued the NFL for a violation of his free speech under the First Amendment, how should the court decide the case?
- Can sport organizations set requirements to limit political demonstrations during the national anthems or during game play?

Religious Speech: First Amendment

In addition to freedom of speech, the First Amendment also protects our freedom of religion. There are two religion clauses in the First Amendment – the Free Exercise Clause and the Establishment Clause (see Exhibit 6.5). The **Free Exercise Clause** protects our fundamental right to the free exercise of our religious beliefs, unless these beliefs illegally cause harm to society (e.g., human sacrifice can be prohibited). The **Establishment Clause** was intended to prevent the establishment of a government-endorsed religion, but it has been broadly interpreted over the years to the point where now it is interpreted to mean that the government must be neutral with respect to religious matters.

Occasionally, an employee will express a religious viewpoint or take a political stance that is informed by a religious perspective. In such a case, the First Amendment may be implicated. For example, in *Lumpkin v. Jordan* (1997), Eugene Lumpkin, a Baptist minister who was a member of the San Francisco Human Rights Commission was fired after he made statements to the media denouncing homosexuality as a sinful abomination. One of the goals of the Human Rights Commission was to lead the community toward respect for homosexual citizens. When the plaintiff minister sued the city for religious discrimination, the court applied the *Pickering* balancing test (Exhibit 6.6) to rule in favor of the city. Finding that the plaintiff was fired because he made public statements at odds with his position of employment on the commission, the court held that he was not fired solely because of his religious beliefs. The court stated that because Reverend Lumpkin was a policymaker in the mayor's administration, his remarks would undermine the very policies the administration was striving to implement – a situation that the First Amendment principle of free speech would not protect.

Further, the court found that Lumpkin's removal did not violate the Free Exercise Clause because the mayor's interest in preventing disruption of his administration's goals outweighed Lumpkin's right to religious expression. Finally, Lumpkin's termination did not violate the Establishment Clause because the adverse employment action could not reasonably be construed as an endorsement of a particular religious view.

Team Prayer: First Amendment

Sometimes religious speech takes the form of prayer. We examine the issue of team prayer in the Focus Case below.

Kennedy v. Bremerton School District

869 F.3d 813 (9th Cir. 2017) **FOCUS** CASE

FACTS

Kennedy was a high school football coach from 2008 to 2015 at Bremerton High School. His contract expired at the end of each football season. The formal job requirements for the football coach reiterated this language by requiring Kennedy to "obey all Rules of Conduct before players and the public as expected."

Kennedy is a practicing Christian. His religious beliefs do not require him to lead any prayer before or after football games, but he is required to give thanks through prayer at the end of each game. After the game is over, Kennedy feels called to take a knee at midfield where the game was played and offer a quiet prayer. Since these prayers take place immediately after the game has ended, he wears a shirt or jacket that bears the school's logo. Initially, Kennedy performed these prayers alone; but after a few games, a group of players asked if they could join him. He directed the players to do whatever they chose, and they joined the prayer. Later, this prayer evolved into short motivational speeches at midfield after the game. Students, coaches, and other attendees were invited to participate. Kennedy's speeches included religious content and he concedes that they likely constituted prayers.

The Bremerton School District (School District) first learned of these prayers in September 2015 after being alerted to them by another employee. Superintendent Leavall sent a letter to Kennedy informing him that these speeches had to be free of religious material to "avoid alienation of any team member" (Kennedy, 2017, p. 8). Kennedy, in response, requested religious accommodation that would allow him to continue his midfield prayers. He believed these prayers occurred during non-instructional hours because his official coaching duties ended at the same time as the game. Since coaches had assigned duties both before and after games that lasted until the last student leaves the event, the School District denied his request and instead suggested that a private location could be made available to Kennedy for prayer.

Kennedy continued to pray at midfield after games until he was placed on paid administrative leave. Once the season ended, the School District conducted its annual evaluations and it was recommended that Kennedy not be rehired for failure to follow district policy. Kennedy sued, alleging this decision was in violation of his First Amendment and Title VII rights.

HOLDING

The Ninth Circuit affirmed the district court's denial of preliminary injunctive relief, concluding that the plaintiff spoke as a public employee when he kneeled and prayed on the football field immediately after games.

RATIONALE

The court used the Pickering/Garcetti analysis to determine whether the School District's decision to place Kennedy on paid administrative leave was in retaliation for exercising his First Amendment rights. First, there must be a factual determination as to the scope and content of the individual's job requirements. Next, the court will assess the constitutional significance of the speech and whether the employee's position impacted the speech or if he spoke as a non-employee citizen.

In applying these principles, the court concluded that Kennedy spoke as a public employee, not as a private citizen. Since his speech involved kneeling at the 50-yard line immediately after games in view of students and parents, it was not silent and alone. His job also required him to model good behavior while acting in an official capacity in front of students and spectators. By kneeling and praying on the 50-yard line, Kennedy sent a message about what he values as a coach, connecting the activity to his job functions. He did speak out against the superintendent's orders by continuing his prayers, but that is not enough to turn his employee speech into citizen speech. Therefore, his speech was not protected by the First Amendment.

Religious Speech: Title VII

Title VII may present an avenue for recourse in cases where employers take adverse action on the basis of religious speech, as demonstrated in the *Johnson Focus Case*.

Johnson v. National Football League

1999 U.S. Dist. LEXIS 15983 (S.D.N.Y. 1999)   **FOCUS** CASE

FACTS

Plaintiff J. Edwards Johnson V, also known as Yacub Abdul-Matin, who is African-American, converted to Islam while he was a football player at the University of Miami. Because of his religious involvement, he wrote two articles about race and religion that were published in the university newspaper and that he claims did not meet with the approval of his football coaches. He was also involved in a public controversy over his religion. Several professional football teams had expressed interest in Johnson, but all eventually changed their minds, allegedly due to the controversy he had been involved in while in college. Johnson filed suit, claiming that the NFL discriminated against him on the basis of his race and his religion by refusing to hire him as a professional football player. The NFL moved to have the suit dismissed for failure to state a claim upon which relief may be granted, claiming the complaint failed to allege any circumstances that could allow an inference that the NFL had engaged in discrimination.

HOLDING

The court denied the defendants' motion to dismiss.

RATIONALE

The court found that Johnson's claim alleged that he was profiled as a troublemaker because of the positions he took in college on religious issues and racial pride and the incidents that arose from his taking of these positions. His complaint further alleged that this profiling resulted in his name being withdrawn by the Atlanta Falcons after they had drafted him and that he was blackballed, causing other NFL teams to abandon interest in him. The court ruled that the complaint did in fact allege that Johnson was denied employment because of a combination of his race and his religion, and, therefore, it did state a claim upon which, if substantiated, relief could be granted under Title VII.

Religious Practices

Religious expression may arise in the employment context in situations where an employee refuses, for religious reasons, to adhere to an assigned work schedule that conflicts with the worker's observance of a Sabbath day or religious holiday or to an employer's policy regarding appropriate conduct, dress, or grooming. An employee who is terminated for such refusal may have a cause of action under Title VII, which, in addition to race, color, national origin, and sex, prohibits discrimination on the basis of religion. The worker's religion need not be an organized, widely recognized religion, as long as it involves sincerely held beliefs and takes the place of religion in the worker's life. Thus, even atheism has been construed as a religion under Title VII. Additionally, an employer's religious preferences may not be protected under Title VII if they are used to justify terminating an employee for discriminatory reasons. The Sixth Circuit in *Equal Employment Opportunity Commission v. R.G. & G.R. Harris Funeral Homes, Inc.* (2018) found that there is no freedom-of-religion exemption in Title VII and complying with the law does not create a substantial burden on the employer's religious practices.

Religion is treated differently from the other classes protected under Title VII, in that the employer is required to make a reasonable accommodation for the employee's religious practice unless doing so would cause undue hardship. For example, if an employee who adheres to modest dress requests permission to wear a long white skirt instead of white tennis shorts as a religious accommodation, this request should be granted because it does not impose an undue hardship on the employer (EEOC, n.d.). The courts consider several factors in determining whether a religious accommodation is reasonable or constitutes an undue hardship. These are listed in Exhibit 6.7.

Exhibit 6.7 Factors to consider in determining the reasonableness of religious accommodations.

- Size of the staff.
- Type of job employee does.
- Whether other employees were asked for their assistance in making the accommodation.
- The willingness of other employees to assist in making the accommodation.
- Cost of the accommodation.
- Administrative burdens of the accommodation.
- What has been done by similarly situated employers?

Some religious faiths prohibit the shaving of facial hair, and this might conflict with an organization's grooming code designed to ensure an appropriate public image for the organization. In such a case, a reasonable accommodation might be to reassign the employee to a position that does not involve dealing with the public, such as stocking shelves or handling paperwork.

The *Simmons* case shows how a court decides whether an organization has made a reasonable religious accommodation.

Simmons v. Sports Training Institute

1990 U.S. Dist. LEXIS 4877 (S.D.N.Y. 1990)   **FOCUS** CASE

FACTS

Plaintiff Bertrand Simmons was hired as a maintenance worker for the Sports Training Institute in July 1981. In August 1983, Simmons converted to the Seventh Day Adventist faith, which prohibits working on the Sabbath, which is considered to be from sundown Friday until sundown on Saturday. The plaintiff told his supervisor of his religious reason for no longer being able to work on Saturdays, and his work schedule was adjusted to accommodate his religious requirement. Simmons failed to tell his supervisor, however, that Friday afternoons were off-limits too.

Later, the plaintiff agreed to his supervisor's request to change his work schedule so that the plaintiff's brother, who was also employed there, could work during the day because he had been having difficulty staying awake at work. This change, however, meant that the plaintiff was once again scheduled to work on the Sabbath because his brother has been scheduled to work on Friday evening. Therefore, on the next Friday, the brothers traded shifts so that the plaintiff could observe his Sabbath. This upset the supervisor because it reinstated the plaintiff's brother to a double-shift situation in which he would again have "sleeping on the job" problems. When the plaintiff now made the supervisor aware of the Friday portion of the Sabbath, the supervisor accommodated Simmons's religious observance request again, which resulted in his being scheduled for the graveyard shift.

In September 1984, the plaintiff took a three-week vacation when his supervisor had granted him only two weeks. When he returned, plaintiff refused to give a satisfactory explanation for his delayed return, demanded to be returned to the morning shift, and refused to work graveyard. He was fired and subsequently sued the Sports Training Institute, alleging religious discrimination under Title VII.

HOLDING

The court dismissed the complaint.

RATIONALE

The court found that the plaintiff was terminated for insubordination based on his threat not to work the graveyard shift and the fact that he had taken an unauthorized week of vacation. Insubordination was a legitimate, non-discriminatory reason for plaintiff's dismissal, and the court found that this reason was not pretext for religious discrimination. Indeed, the supervisor had tried twice to accommodate Simmons's religious practice.

Conclusion

Employment discrimination can occur in the sport industry in several forms, including harassment perpetrated by employers or by fellow employees and unequal treatment of employees because of their

---

Competitive Advantage Strategies

Employee Expression

- Be sensitive to cultural differences that may relate to ethnicity, gender, age, or religion and that may affect the work environment. For example, such differences might impact celebrations of special events or clothing and grooming requirements.
- Respect the views of your employees, even if they are critical of your organization, as long as they are not expressed in such a way as to damage the effective functioning of the organization. Encourage your employees to offer criticism constructively, and remind them that even if the First Amendment does not protect employee speech that is an expected part of doing one's job, there are various whistleblower laws that might provide protection.

---

expressive activity. This chapter presented various grounds for pursuing these types of employment discrimination claims, as well as strategies to help managers avoid employment discrimination litigation.

Discussion Questions

1 How do hostile environment harassment claims (whether based on race or sex) differ from quid pro quo harassment claims?
2 What is the advantage to the employer of having the affirmative defense available in claims where there is no tangible adverse employment action?
3 For what two types of potentially discriminatory situations is an employer required to provide reasonable accommodation to an employee, unless doing so would cause undue hardship or cause a fundamental alteration of the business?
4 What kind of reasonable accommodation for religious practices could management offer to an employee in a situation where reassignment to a less visible work setting is impossible – for example, when the employee is a National Basketball Association (NBA) player?

Learning Activities

1 Assume you are an upper-level manager at the Entertainment and Sports Programming Network (ESPN) and have been given the responsibility of developing a sexual harassment policy for the entire company. Draft such a policy and then write a memo to your supervisor suggesting sound guidance for its dissemination, implementation, and enforcement.
2 Assume you are the President of U.S. Soccer. Your organization has a policy requiring athletes to stand respectfully during the playing of national anthems. Typically, players will stand with a hand over their heart and sing along. Megan Rapinoe complies with the rule to stand but does not stand with a hand over her heart or sing along. Write a memo providing guidelines for how individual teams or the related governing organization should handle future cases similar to this scenario. Be sure to include a statement explaining why these guidelines are important, as well as practical suggestions for reasonable accommodations.
3 Online, find a sport or recreation organization's harassment policy and critique it to see if it contains the critical components suggested in this chapter.

Case Study

Adam and Mark Larson are owners of Sport and Fitness Club, a health club chain based in Minnesota. The Larsons are "born again" Christians and their religious beliefs require them to act in accordance with the teaching of Jesus both in their personal and professional lives. As a result, their beliefs impact their hiring practices at Sport and Fitness Club. These practices include questioning prospective employees about their marital status and religious beliefs, terminating employees over a difference in beliefs; and refusing to promote those employees with differing religious beliefs. The Larsons also keep a bookshelf with Christian literature at the entrance of each health club.

Based on their interpretation of the Bible, Sport and Fitness club will not hire or will fire the following groups:

- Individuals living with but not married to a person of the opposite sex.
- A young, single woman working without her father's consent or a married woman working without her husband's consent.
- A person with a strong commitment to a non-Christian religion.
- Someone antagonistic to the Bible, including fornicators and homosexuals.

Despite these requirements, Sport and Fitness Club continues to hire and maintain the employment of individuals who fit into these groups. However, recently, several individuals who were not hired or not promoted in positions at Sport and Fitness Club believed that these qualifications were the reason for their adverse employment action. When challenged, the Commissioner of the Minnesota Department of Human Rights found that there was evidence of potential discrimination in these hiring practices. But the Commissioner also held that the owners' religious beliefs were sincerely held. It was stressed during the interview process and all associate membership directors were required to attend weekly Bible study sessions.

Susan is a former employee of Sport and Health Club. Susan is married to another woman. She did not disclose this relationship while working at Sport and Health Club. But when a patron who was an out lesbian spoke to her in the locker room, her colleagues began to question her sexuality. She even received a phone call at home from Adam Larson in which he told her that "homosexuality was against the word of God and associating with homosexuals was anti-Christian behavior." Shortly after this call, she was informed that her position was being terminated.

1 Assume you are a friend of Susan, and she knows you are taking a sport law class. She came to you seeking your informal (but hopefully well-informed) opinion (not to be construed as illegally practicing law without an attorney's license) on whether the phone call and questions she received constitutes sexual harassment. How would you respond and why?
2 Susan also wants your advice about whether her former employer, Sport and Fitness Club, would be legally allowed to make these decisions to protect their religious beliefs.
3 She also wants to know what you would advise about bringing a claim alleging employer retaliation under Title VII.

Considering ... Analysis & Discussion

Employee Expression

In this case, a court could likely find that the rules show different treatment between the sexes. Because the cheerleaders were held to a higher standard than the players, this subjects one group to a different condition of employment based solely on gender in violation of Title VII. To defend against this claim, the team would have to provide evidence that this difference is a necessary business function. It would be difficult to explain why these rules were one-sided if they are that important to business operations. An NFL spokesman stated in 2019 that the league office worked with clubs to revise these social media policies (Belson, 2019).

Political Speech

As we saw in the *Dambrot* case, public employees are entitled to First Amendment protection for expressing their views on matters of public concern, a category that definitely includes perspectives on social issues in America. Each NFL team is considered a private employer, meaning that their employees are not provided the same First Amendment protections. This does not mean that sport organizations are free to restrict speech as they choose. There are other federal and state laws, like the National Labor Relations Act (discussed in Chapter 7) that can protect employee speech in certain circumstances.

Many leagues do not have specific policies related to the national anthem. The NBA and WNBA require "players, coaches, and trainers to stand and line up in a dignified posture along the sidelines or on the foul line during the playing of the national anthem." NBA player Mahmoud Abdul-Rauf decided not to stand for the anthem during the 1994–1995 season. The NBA told him that he could remain in the locker room if he did not want to stand. He refused and was suspended one game. After he agreed to stand and pray during the national anthem. When WNBA players kneeled during the anthem in September 2016, they were not punished (Seifert, 2018).

References

Cases

Albertson's v. Washington Human Rights Comm'n, 544 P.2d 98 (Wash. Ct. App. Wa. 1976).

Bibby v. The Philadelphia Coca-Cola Bottling Co., 85 F. Supp. 2d 509 (E.D. Pa. 2000).

Bostock v. Clayton County, Georgia, 590 U.S. _____ (2020).

Bowman v. Shawnee State Univ., 220 F.3d 456 (6th Cir. 2000).

Brooks v. CBS Radio, Inc., 342 F.App'x 771 (3d Cir. 2009).

Burlington Indus., Inc. v. Ellerth, 118 S. Ct. 2257 (1998).

Cameli v. O'Neal, 1997 U.S. Dist. LEXIS 9034 (N.D. Ill. 1997).

Castleberry v. STI Group, 863 F.3d 259 (3d Cir. 2017).

Connick v. Myers, 103 S. Ct. 1684 (1983).

Cox v. NFL, 29 F. Supp. 2d 463 (N.D. Ill. 1998).

Dambrot v. Central Mich. Univ., 55 F.3d 1177 (6th Cir. 1995).

Equal Employment Opportunity Commission v. Abercrombie & Fitch Stores, Inc., 135 S. Ct. 2028 (2015).

Equal Employment Opportunity Commission v. R.G. & G.R. Harris Funeral Homes, Inc., 884 F.3d 560 (6th Cir. 2018).

Fagan v. National Cash Register, 481 F.2d 1115 (D.C. Cir. 1973).

Faragher v. City of Boca Raton, 118 S. Ct. 2275 (1998).

Garcetti v. Ceballos, 126 S. Ct. 1951 (2006).

Harris v. Forklift Systems, Inc., 510 U.S. 17 (1993).

Jackson v. Birmingham Bd. of Educ., 125 S. Ct. 1497 (2005).

Johnson v. NFL, 1999 U.S. Dist. LEXIS 15983 (S.D.N.Y. 1999).

Kennedy v. Bremerton School District, 869 F.3d 813 (9th Cir. 2017), cert. denied, (2019 U.S. LEXIS 804).

Lockhart v. Louisiana-Pacific Corp., 795 P.2d 602 (Or. Ct. App. 1990).

Lowrey v. Texas A & M Univ. Sys., 11 F. Supp. 2d 895 (S.D. Tex. 1998).

Lumpkin v. Jordan, 1994 U.S. Dist. LEXIS 17280 (N.D. Cal. 1994), aff'd, 109 F.3d 1498 (9th Cir. 1997).

McDonnell Douglas Corp. v. Green, 411 U.S. 792 (1973).

Oncale v. Sundowner Offshore Services, Inc., 523 U.S. 75 (1998).

Pickering v. Board of Educ., 88 S. Ct. 1731 (1968).

Robinson v. Jacksonville Shipyards, Inc. 760 F. Supp. 1486 (M.D. Fla. 1991).

Ross v. Douglas County, 234 F.3d 391 (8th Cir. 2000).

Simmons v. Sports Training Inst., 1990 U.S. Dist. LEXIS 4877 (S.D.N.Y. 1990).

State by McClure v. Sports Health Club, 370 N.W.2d 844 (Minn. 1985).

Summa v. Hofstra University, 708 F. 3d 115 (2d Cir. 2013).

Williams v. Dallas Indep. Sch. Dist., 480 F.3d 689 (5th Cir. 2007).

Willingham v. Macon Telegraph Pub. Co., 597 F.2d 1084 (5th Cir. 1975).

Constitution

U.S. Const. amend. I.

Statutes and Regulations

National Labor Relations Act, 29 U.S.C. § 158(a)(3).
Sexual Harassment Regulations, 29 C.F.R. § 1604.11(a) (2013).
Title VII of the Civil Rights Act of 1964, as amended by the Civil Rights Act of 1991, 42 U.S.C. § 2000e *et seq.*
Title IX of the Education Amendments of 1972, 20 U.S.C. § 1681 *et seq.*

Other Sources

Abramson, M. (2013, October 12). Knicks GM Steve Mills reiterates Isiah Thomas has no role with team. *New York Daily News*. Retrieved from https://www.nydailynews.com/sports/basketball/knicks/knicks-gm-mills-forget-isiah-article-1.1483383.

Belson, K. (2018, March 25). How an Instagram post led to a NFL cheerleader's discrimination case. *The New York Times*. Retrieved from https://www.nytimes.com/2018/03/25/sports/saints-cheerleader.html.

Belson, K. (2019, April 8). The cheerleader who blew the whistle on the NFL soldiers on. *The New York Times*. Retrieved from https://www.nytimes.com/2019/04/08/sports/cheerleader-bailey-davis-saints-nfl.html.

Brin, D. (2017, December 11). Social media is a major consideration in wave of sexual harassment allegations. *Society for Human Resource Management*. Retrieved from https://www.shrm.org/resourcesandtools/hr-topics/technology/pages/social-media-major-consideration-in-wave-of-sexual-harassment-allegations.aspx.

Cooney, S. (2017, October 19). Meet the woman who started #MeToo 10 years ago. *Time*. Retrieved from http://time.com/4988282/me-too-tarana-burke-interview/.

Daysog, R. (2009, April 14). Former Hawaii basketball coach sues UH over his dismissal. Retrieved from www.honoluluadvertiser.com.

Department of Labor (2018). Directive 2018-03. Retrieved from https://www.dol.gov/ofccp/regs/compliance/directives/dir2018_03.html.

Emmert, M. (2017, May 19). Iowa settles athletic discrimination cases for $6.5M. *Hawk Central*. Retrieved from https://www.hawkcentral.com/story/sports/college/iowa/2017/05/19/tracey-griesbaum-iowa-hawkeye-gary-barta-settlement/333218001/.

Equal Employment Opportunity Commission. (2018). Sexual harassment charges FY 2010-FY 2018. Retrieved from www.eeoc.gov/statistics/enforcement/sexual_harassment_new.cfm.

Equal Employment Opportunity Commission (n.d.). Religious garb and grooming in the workplace: Rights and responsibilities. Retrieved from https://www.eeoc.gov/eeoc/publications/qa_religious_garb_grooming.cfm.

Fenno, N. (2019, January 3). Cal State L.A. settles athletic department sex harassment lawsuit for $2.75 million. *Los Angeles Times*. Retrieved from https://www.latimes.com/sports/sportsnow/la-sp-sheila-hudson-lawsuit-20190103-story.html.

Hudson, D. (2014, July 21). President Obama signs a new executive order to protect LGBT workers. Retrieved from https://obamawhitehouse.archives.gov/blog/2014/07/21/president-obama-signs-new-executive-order-protect-lgbt-workers.

Hutchens, N. H. (2008). Silence at the schoolhouse gate: The diminishing First Amendment rights of public school employees. *Kentucky Law Journal*, 97, 37–77.

Keller, E. A., & Tracy, J. B. (2008). Hidden in plain sight: Achieving more just results in hostile work environment sexual harassment cases by re-examining Supreme Court precedent. *Duke Journal of Gender Law & Policy*, 15, 247.

Knoblauch, A. (2018, June 30). NFL fines Jerry Richardson $2.75M after investigation. NFL. Retrieved from http://www.nfl.com/news/story/0ap3000000938897/article/nfl-fines-jerry-richardson-275m-after-investigation.

Lesbian basketball coaches call foul. (2008, July 28). *Inside Higher Ed*. Retrieved from www.insidehighered.com.

Neal, D.J. (2019, April 25). Florida-based sports apparel giant pays $322,000 to settle racial discrimination suit. *Miami Herald*. Retrieved from https://www.miamiherald.com/news/business/article229408379.html.

Neil, M. (2003, September 26). When sexual harassment hits home. *ABA Journal Report*. Retrieved from www.abanet.org/journal.

O'Keefe, E. (2013, November 4). ENDA, explained. *The Washington Post*. Retrieved from https://www.washingtonpost.com/news/the-fix/wp/2013/11/04/what-is-the-employment-non-discrimination-act-enda/?noredirect=on&utm_term=.6839d07f63af.

Pitre car dealership to pay over $2 million to resolve EEOC same-sex sexual harassment suit. (2014, April 14). Retrieved from https://www1.eeoc.gov/eeoc/newsroom/release/4-1-14.cfm.

Seifert, K. (2018, May 24). How national anthem rules differ across sport leagues. *ESPN*. Retrieved from https://www.espn.com/nfl/story/_/id/20848575/rules-national-anthem-differ-sports-leagues.

Stites, A. (2017, October 19). Everything you need to know about NFL protests during the national anthem. *SB Nation*. Retrieved from https://www.sbnation.com/2017/9/29/16380080/donald-trump-nfl-colin-kaepernick-protests-national-anthem.

Wertheim, L. J., & Bernstein, V. (2017, December 17). Sources: Jerry Richardson, Panthers have made multiple confidential payouts for workplace misconduct, including sexual harassment and use of a racial slur. *Sports Illustrated*. Retrieved from https://www.si.com/jerry-richardson-carolina-panthers-settlements-workplace-misconduct-sexual-harassment-racial-slur.

Web Resources

www.eeoc.gov/laws/types/sexual_harassment.cfm ■ This U.S. Equal Employment Opportunity Commission website provides a definition of harassment, a statement of when an employer is liable for harassment, and statistics on the number of harassment charges the EEOC has received and resolved. It also provides links to a number of enforcement and guidance and policy documents, as well as links to Title VII of the Civil Rights Act of 1964, the Age Discrimination in Employment Act of 1967 (ADEA), and the Americans with Disabilities Act of 1990 (ADA) — violations of which can constitute harassment.

7 Labor Relations and Collective Bargaining in Sport

Lisa Pike Masteralexis

Introduction

Managers working in a unionized setting who understand and properly manage their workforce will put themselves and their organizations at a competitive advantage over those who do not invest the proper time managing labor relations. Labor peace keeps businesses moving forward in a position of strength, and if workers are satisfied, presumably, they are more productive. In fact, the National Labor Relations Act of 1935 (NLRA) was enacted by Congress to achieve industrial peace. Congress created labor laws to develop an environment that balanced the rights and interests of workers and employers.

Labor problems can be a distraction from running one's business and can have consequences for others not directly involved in the dispute. For instance, when there is a strike or lockout in professional sports, the labor stoppage affects not only the employers (teams who are representing management) and the employees (athletes who are bargaining unit members), but also those outside of the labor dispute. The longer the labor stoppage lasts, the more likely it is that team and league employees may lose jobs. Facility employees and concessionaires may go without work as long as the labor dispute lasts. Other related businesses, such as media corporations, suppliers of equipment and food, delivery companies, hotels, restaurants, and transportation in the area surrounding the venues that rely on business generated by games, also suffer lost revenue from the economic impact from games being canceled.

To understand and manage your labor force, it is crucial to have a working knowledge of labor laws and to make management decisions with those laws in mind. Protecting your management decisions and knowing when to work with a union is important. Making sure that all supervisors reporting to you are knowledgeable in labor laws is key to a successful relationship with your employees in a unionized setting.

Outside of professional team sports, sport managers will also likely encounter unionized workforces in a variety of settings, including facility management, interscholastic sports, and intercollegiate athletics at public institutions. Facility executives may manage employees from a variety of unions, such as laborers, carpenters, professional staff, and clerical unions, all with different **collective bargaining agreements (CBAs)**. In some cases, interscholastic coaches may be members of a teachers union. In collegiate athletics, staff members are often unionized, but coaches are not. One exception is the Pennsylvania State System of Higher Education, which has a union representing non-faculty athletic coaches and those parties began negotiating their sixth CBA in 2020 (APSCUF, 2015).

Exhibit 7.1 provides an overview of this chapter's managerial contexts, major legal issues, relevant law, and illustrative cases.

Labor Laws

Labor laws exist on both the state and federal levels. State labor laws apply to public entities, such as a state university's athletic department, and federal labor laws apply to private employers engaged in a business involving interstate commerce. Interstate commerce occurs when a business crosses state lines, so virtually

Exhibit 7.1 Management contexts in which labor problems may arise, with relevant laws and cases.

Management Context	Major Legal Issues	Relevant Law	Illustrative Cases
Union organizing and operating activities	Unfair labor practices: Interference/discrimination by employer against union members	National Labor Relations Act	NLRB v. AFL & AFLPOC
Unilateral implementation of change in working conditions	Unfair labor practices by union or management: Refusing to bargain in good faith Violating collective bargaining agreement	National Labor Relations Act	Morio v. NASL NFLPA v. NLRB & NFL Mang. Council
Workplace discrimination	Unfair labor practices: Employer discrimination or retaliation against union member Union discrimination or retaliation against nonmember	National Labor Relations Act	Nordstrom, d/b/a Seattle Seahawks & NFLPA; NFL Management Council and NFLPA
Duty of fair representation	Union unfair labor practice: Unfairly treating employee who is a union member or nonmember	National Labor Relations Act	Peterson v. Kennedy
Arbitration/dispute resolution	Arbitrator's authority Scope of review by court	Labor	Major League Baseball Players Association v. Garvey
Rights of retired employees	Contractual and fiduciary duties regarding marketing of retired players	Contract, agency	Parrish v. National Football League Players, Eller v. NFLPA

all private businesses are engaged in interstate commerce. The following examples illustrate the types of entities governed by state versus federal labor laws:

- The athletic director at the University of Massachusetts Amherst (UMass; a state agency), will have to engage with the public sector labor unions when working with clerical, custodial, professional, graduate assistant (student), and security staff who are either employed directly in the athletic department or by another unit on campus and serves the athletic program. UMass employees are members of the following units:

   - American Federation of State, County & Municipal Employees (AFSCME Local 1776): Covers non-exempt skilled trades, custodial, grounds, housing, food services, and security employees.
   - University Staff Association (USA/MTA): Covers non-exempt clerical, technical, and administrative employees.
   - Professional Staff Union/Massachusetts Teachers Association, (PSU/MTA): Covers mainly exempt administrative staff, and some non-exempt administrative staff.
   - Massachusetts Society of Professors (MSP): Covers all faculty and librarians.
   - Graduate Employee Organization (GEO): Covers teaching assistants and graduate assistants and graduate interns.
   - International Brotherhood of Police Officers (IBPO) Local A&B: Covers police officers.
   - Resident Assistant & Peer Mentors Union (RAPM) Local 2322.

   The activities of these bargaining units are governed by Massachusetts state labor laws

- The General Managers of the Boston Bruins, Boston Celtics, Boston Red Sox, New England Patriots, and New England Revolution hire athletes who are also union members working in Massachusetts. Professional athletes are members of national bargaining units (players associations) that negotiate with private multiemployer bargaining units (leagues). Therefore, the federal NLRA and the Labor Management Relations Act of 1947 (LMRA) govern the professional athletes' employment relationship in the private sector.

Labor Law History

Labor law is a body of law that evolved from federal statutes. Prior to the enactment of federal labor laws, there were only state court decisions involving common law that arose as a direct result of the labor movement. By and large, these decisions were not favorable to labor organizations. Although judges had discretion under common law, the ability of unions to act varied by state and by political climate, and, in most circumstances, pro-business doctrines dictated the legality of union conduct (Feldacker, 2000).

In the 19th century, state courts often considered concerted activities by workers such as strikes, work slowdowns, and picketing to be criminal conspiracies. In the first recorded American labor law case, *Commonwealth v. Pullis* (1806), a group of Philadelphia cordwainers (shoemakers) were convicted under the criminal conspiracy doctrine for attempting to impose a policy to force every shoemaker in the city to hire only their union members who charged uniform prices the group had set for their wage (Commons, et al., 1958). Today, that policy would be classified as a closed shop which is an organization with a rule requiring that only union members may be hired. One exception to this pro-business approach in early court cases was *Commonwealth v. Hunt* in 1842. In Hunt, the Boston Journeymen Bootmakers Society was charged with criminal conspiracy. The Society's constitution stated that its purpose was to engage in concerted activity to improve wages and working conditions. Its members had joined together to express their intent to encourage members to require certain wages from their employers and to pressure employers to hire members of the Society. The Massachusetts Supreme Judicial Court found those actions did not constitute criminal conspiracy but could have been had their goals been achieved through criminal means rather than through economic pressure (Hunt, 1842). In doing so, the Supreme Judicial Court paved the way for labor unions to be considered legal, provided the reason for their creation was not illegal, but its reason was deemed innocent, useful, and honorable in working to better their working conditions (*Commonwealth v. Hunt*, 1842). Prior to Hunt, the presumption in the courts was that labor unions were conspiracies meant to injure the economy. About 50 years later, employers soon began using the Sherman Act of 1890 as their legal maneuver to fight employee challenges. Section 1 of the Sherman Act of 1890 prohibits contracts, combinations, and conspiracies that restrain trade or commerce. The theory of **antitrust law** is to prevent groups of competitors from reducing competition in the market (see also Chapter 10). Employing the Sherman Act, employers argued that the actions of the employees engaged in concerted activity had the effect of reducing competition and injuring consumers.

The U.S. Supreme Court agreed that the Sherman Act applied to combinations of employees, upholding a treble-damage suit against a labor movement (*Loewe v. Lawlor*, 1908). Federal courts thereafter regularly issued injunctions against union activity, even if the Sherman Act was not ultimately applied to the labor activity. By issuing the injunctions, the courts assisted employers in thwarting concerted activities of employees. After *Loewe v. Lawlor*, concerted activity stopped by injunctions, coupled with the threat of the Sherman Act's treble-damage award, produced a chilling effect on union activities. Thus, Congress responded with the Clayton Act of 1914.

The Clayton Act created a statutory labor exemption from antitrust laws by limiting the use of antitrust laws against labor unions. Stating that the labor of a human being was not commerce, the Clayton Act's intent was to protect unions from being deemed illegal combinations or conspiracies when they were acting lawfully in their own self-interest. Courts interpreted this to mean that antitrust laws were unenforceable against unions engaged in legitimate objectives. However, courts continued to issue injunctions against labor when they determined a union's activities, such as a boycott of its employer's customers or a sympathy strike, were not legitimate objectives (*Duplex Printing Press, Co. v. Deering*, 1921). As a result, the U.S. Supreme Court continued to allow federal courts to grant injunctions against union activity that they deemed interfered with the free flow of goods in commerce (*Duplex Printing Press, Co. v. Deering*, 1921).

In response, Congress enacted the Norris-LaGuardia Act of 1932 to limit the powers of federal courts to grant injunctions in labor disputes, unless there is a threat of violence or provisions in the CBA allowed for an injunction to be granted. Norris-LaGuardia strengthened the Clayton Act's exemption of union activities from antitrust laws (see *United States v. Hutcheson*, 1940; and *Boys Markets, Inc. v. Retail Clerks' Union, Local 770*, 1970).

National Labor Relations Act

Enacted in 1935, the NLRA applies to private employers. Its preamble set forth the policy of the United States to

> eliminate ... or mitigate the causes of certain substantial obstructions to the free flow of commerce ... by encouraging collective bargaining and by protecting the exercise by workers of full freedom of association, self-organization, and designation of representatives of their own choosing, for the purpose of negotiating the terms and conditions of their employment or other mutual aid or protection. (NLRA, § 151, 2005)

With this language, the NLRA established employee rights, among them the right to negotiate with an employer over hours, wages, and terms and conditions of employment. The intent was to encourage workplace harmony between private employers and employees through collective bargaining. The NLRA also created a new federal agency, the National Labor Relations Board (NLRB), to administer labor laws in the United States. The two primary activities of the NLRB are as follows:

1 to conduct secret ballot union elections for certification and decertification.
2 to prevent and remedy unfair labor practices committed by management or union.

The NLRA applies to employees and employers in the private sector, drawing distinctions between employees for assignment to bargaining units such that employees in the same bargaining unit need not do the exact same job but must have common bargaining interests. It also established procedures for union certification and imposed obligations on management once a union is in place.

Taft-Hartley Act of 1947

Based on its focus on employee rights and unfair labor practices of employers, there was no doubt that the NLRA was pro-labor. A dozen years later, the Taft-Hartley Act amended the NLRA to balance the employee–employer relationship by stipulating

> the legitimate rights of both employees and employers in their relations affecting commerce, to provide orderly and peaceful procedures for preventing the interference by either with the legitimate rights of the other, to protect the rights of individual employees in their relations with labor organizations whose activities affect commerce, to define and proscribe practices on the part of labor and management which affect commerce .... (LMRA, § 141, 2005)

For example, NLRA § 7 gave employees the right to join or assist unions; the Taft-Hartley Act added the right of employees to choose not to join or assist unions. The NLRA grants employees the right to engage in concerted activity (strikes), and Taft-Hartley grants employers the right to engage in lockouts, allowing both sides to hold economic weapons. Further, NLRA § 8 prohibits management from discriminating against an employee on the basis of union membership; Taft-Hartley added a provision that prohibits the union from similar behavior against non-union members. NLRA § 9 was amended to include decertification among the NLRB's responsibilities. Once the Taft-Hartley Act amended the NLRA, the latter was renamed the LMRA. Often the names NLRA and LMRA are used interchangeably.

Labor Relations Applied to Professional Sport

Although the NLRA was enacted in 1935, the labor movement in professional sports did not start in earnest until the late 1960s and early 1970s. This was not for a lack of attempts, in 1885, John Montgomery Ward organized the first baseball players union. The Brotherhood of Professional Base Ball Players challenged the National League's salary cap, reserve clause, and sale of players with little success (Jennings, 1990). Numerous attempts to bargain collectively with owners occurred between 1885 and the National Basketball Players Association's signing of the first sports labor contract in 1967. Early collective action were attempts to engage owners in negotiations to solicit pension benefits, rather than attempts at full-blown unionization. Shrewd moves by owners fractured the solidarity in the players group, such as when the National Hockey League (NHL) Board of Governors crushed the 1958 formation of the National Hockey League Players Association (NHLPA; Cruise & Griffiths, 1991).

Often, professional sport labor movements were turned into company unions (Weiler, 2000). A company union occurs when the employer supports a union effort in its company, usually in order to thwart an independent union from representing its employees. A company union may be supported by management as a means of controlling its employees, since the union provides a voice for employees to negotiate with management. If management is controlling the union, that independent adversarial role is eliminated. Company unions are sometimes alleged when an independent union acts in a way that does not seem independent, such as when the union is too cordial with management. The early days of the Major League Baseball Players Association (MLBPA) operations (prior to arrival of union leader Marvin Miller) can best be described as a company union. Similarly, the tenure of former NHLPA executive director Alan Eagleson with his close relations with owners in the NHL, where the players union sought to appease management, the NHLPA acted more akin to a company union than a truly adversarial bargaining unit. A more recent example involves eSports athletes. The League of Legends Players Association (LOLPA) was created by Riot Games to "… provide centralized representation for players in tri-party negotiations (Riot-Owners-Players); they also provide access to vetted resources (e.g., legal/financial advice) to help players planning out their careers" (Stover, 2018, para. 30). Accusations that LOLPA was a company union followed. Riot Games has also unilaterally imposed team revenue sharing, minimum salaries ($75,000), and an academy league (minor league) in an attempt to adopt models from traditional sports (Stover, 2018). Thus, giving credence to the critique of a company union as no evidence exists that the players association negotiated over revenue sharing or minimum salaries. Considering that teams are tied to traditional leagues, it is not a stretch, real or perceived, to think that there was intent to create a company union. Even if well-intentioned, it is not appropriate for management to create the players association. Union movements must arise organically from the players themselves (Stover, 2018).

The decision that opened the door to unionization in baseball was a labor arbitration decision in 1969. In *The American League of Professional Baseball Clubs and the Association of National Baseball League Umpires,* Major League Baseball challenged the NLRB's jurisdiction over whether the umpires could unionize and argued that since MLB was exempt from antitrust laws based on *Federal Baseball* (1922), it should likewise be exempt from labor laws. The NLRB found MLB subject to labor laws because the idea that baseball was not engaged in interstate commerce could not be seriously accepted despite it being the basis of the *Federal Baseball* (1922) decision exempting baseball from antitrust (which continued due to *stare decisis*). MLB also argued that it had an internal system of self-regulation, so there was no need for NLRB involvement. The NLRB disagreed, arguing that the system that MLB was relying on would put the umpire before the Commissioner for a final resolution of disputes involving the Uniform Umpire's Contract, the Major League Agreement, and the Major League Rules. The NLRB recognized there was no evidence of a neutral third-party arbiter as the employers designed the system and that these employers were the same individuals who hired and managed the Commissioner. The NLRB noted that while this case involved umpires, professional baseball clubs employ a host of other employees, including professional athletes, clubhouse attendants, front office staff, scouts, groundskeepers, and maintenance staff, who would potentially seek assistance from the NLRB in the future.

Professional Sport Labor Unions

Today, virtually all North American major league teams and numerous international sports are unionized workplaces for professional athletes, but not for their coaches or front office staff. Reasons for this include the following:

- There are far fewer "white-collar" workers in unions.
- There is high turnover in front office and coaching positions.

- With intense competition for jobs, people might not be open to working together in a democratic union organizing movement.
- With intense competition for jobs, people may be fearful about leading organizing efforts.
- Organizing front office staff or coaches on a national, multiemployer level as the professional athletes have done is a challenging task.

The unionized workplaces that exist for professional athletes have been years in the making and differ from typical unionized settings. The dynamics of the professional sports labor relationship make every collective bargaining negotiation a battle. As a bargaining group, athletes are union members with short careers and, thus, a high turnover rate. Most professional athletes have little job security. As a result, most players want to achieve the best deal possible in their collective bargaining negotiations. With an average career length in professional sports hovering around three years, and most CBAs having terms of three or more years, players are motivated to negotiate for the best wages and working conditions possible. Comparing their bargaining goals with the average unionized hotel worker or teacher, who might be looking ahead to a 30-year career and five to ten collective bargaining negotiations during that time, one can see that there is less pressure in the short term on the hotel worker or teacher.

Many of the international sports unions act as collectives of the unions that are organized by country or region. For instance, in soccer (football), cricket, and rugby, the international players associations work to support the efforts at the national level. International players associations operate more like trade associations. Trade unions have the legal right to collectively bargain on behalf of their members and legal protection over striking, whereas the trade associations represent an industry. Trade associations may suggest wages or other benefits, but cannot force negotiations. The laws regulating unions vary by country or region and thus, international players associations may not have the standing to bargain on behalf of players internationally. That said, organizations such as FIFPro, which represents 65,000 male and female soccer/football players across the world, has considerable leverage and political muscle. See Exhibit 7.2 below for a list of many of the major national and international professional players associations.

There is great disparity in the level of talent among players and, thus, their need for the union is also varied. A player earning over $30 million a year, such as eight-time MLB All-Star and two-time American League Most Valuable Player, Mike Trout of the Los Angeles Angels, may not need the services of the union as much as a late-round draft pick or a player at the end of the roster. In fact, it seems that well-paid superstars like Trout, who to date has earned over $115 million and has a contract that guarantees close to $400 million more through the 2030 season, and the Phillies' Bryce Harper who is at the start of a 13-year, $330 million contract, or Manny Machado who is in the first year of a ten-year, $300 million contract, do not need a union. Their concerns in collective bargaining may be very different from those of a rank-and-file player or league journeyman. Players associations must represent star athletes making millions of dollars, as well as those earning league minimums. Exhibit 7.3 shows the disparities that exist between minimum-salaried players and the highest earners in their sports. When negotiating for the collective interests of the players, unions must struggle to keep the superstars and the players on the bench equally satisfied. Without the solidarity of all players, a players association loses its strength.

Players associations are typically national (vs. local) employee bargaining units that negotiate with a transnational, *multiemployer* bargaining unit. The high turnover rate for sports union members forces players associations to communicate their message constantly to new members. In spreading the message, players associations face logistical challenges of representing employees on different teams throughout the United States and Canada. Similarly, the multiemployer bargaining unit comes with challenges. It may also have vastly disparate bargaining priorities. For instance, compare the collective bargaining goals of the owners of the large-market New York Yankees or Los Angeles Dodgers to those of the owners of the small-market Kansas City Royals or Pittsburgh Pirates. Despite their differences in revenue and team payroll, in collective bargaining sessions the two must agree on their negotiating positions and strategies. The negotiations are pressure-packed league-level meetings that are highly publicized events followed as intently by the media as a pennant race.

Exhibit 7.2 Examples of national and international players associations.

- Arena Football League Players Union (AFLPU) – USA
- Canadian Football Players Association – Canada
- Fédération Internationale des Associations de Footballeurs Professionnels (FIFPRO) – Global
- Federation of International Cricketers' Associations (FICA) – Global
  - Australian Cricketers Association (ACA) – Australia
  - Cricketers Welfare Association of Bangladesh (CWAB) – Bangladesh
  - Irish Cricketers Association (ICA) – Ireland
  - New Zealand Cricket Players Association (NZCPA) – New Zealand
  - Scottish Cricketers Association (SCA) – Scotland
  - South Africa Cricketers Association (SACA) – South Africa
  - Sri Lankan Cricketers Association (SLCA) – Sri Lanka
  - West Indies Players Association (WIPA) – West Indies
- International Rugby Players (IRP) – Global
  - Irish Rugby Union Players Association (IRUPA) – Ireland
  - Japan Rugby Players Association (JRPA) – Japan
  - Giocarti D'Italia Rugby Association (GIRA) – Italy
  - New Zealand Rugby Players Association (NZRPA) – New Zealand
  - Pacific Islanders Players Association (PIPA) – Pacific Islands
  - Provale – France
  - Rugby Players Association (RPA) – England
  - Rugby Union Players Association (RUPA) – Australia
  - South African Rugby Players Association (SARPA) – South Africa
  - Welsh Rugby Players Association (WRPA) – Wales
- Major League Baseball Players Association (MLBPA) – North America
- Major League Soccer Players Union (MLSPU) – North America
- National Basketball Association Players Association (NBAPA) – North America
- National Football League Players Association (NFLPA) – USA
- National Hockey League Players Association (NHLPA) – North America
- Professional Hockey Players Association (PHPA) – North America
- Professional Lacrosse Players Association (PLPA) – USA
- Professional Women's Hockey Players Association (PWHPA) – North America
- United States Rugby Players Association (USRPA) – USA
- United States National Soccer Team Players Association (USNSTPA) – USA
- United States Women's National Soccer Team Players Association (USWNSTPA) – USA
- Women's National Basketball Players Association (WNBPA) – USA

The owners' propensity to "go to war" with their league's players association may seem ironic, because leagues favor unionized workforces. Professional sport leagues "need" unions to counter the many restrictive policies, such as the draft and free agency limitations. These provisions, on their own, would be subject to antitrust scrutiny, but if they are the product of collective bargaining, they are immune from

Exhibit 7.3 Disparities in pay among union members in North America.

League	Minimum Annual Salary	Highest-Paid Player (2018–2019)
Major League Baseball	$555,000	Stephen Strasburg (Washington Nationals) $38.3 million
Major League Soccer	$56,250	Zlatan Ibrahimović (LA Galaxy) $7.2 million
National Basketball Association	$582,180	Stephen Curry (Golden State Warriors) $37.5 million
National Football League	$495,000	Russell Wilson (Seattle Seahawks) $35 million
National Hockey League	$700,00	John Tavares (Toronto Maple Leafs) $15.9 million
Women's National Basketball Association	$57,000	Maximum player salary $215,000
National Women's Soccer League	$16,538	Maximum player salary $46,200
National Pro Fastpitch	$3,000	Maximum player salary around $20,000
National Women's Hockey League	$2,500	Maximum player salary $10,000

antitrust laws under the labor exemption (*Brown v. Pro Football, Inc.*, 1996). This doctrine will be discussed in greater detail later in the chapter.

Labor Law Rights in Practice

At the core of labor law are the rights granted to workers in § 7 of the NLRA. From this core, flows the employees' right to negotiate as a group with their employer, thereby "leveling the field" in their attempt to bargain for better benefits and working conditions. This "balancing" of power is accomplished through the protections guaranteed in § 7, the enforcement mechanisms of § 8, and the right to become an appropriate bargaining unit set forth in § 9. Our next section will examine the essential employee rights included in the NLRA, unfair labor practices that are deemed illegal under the NLRA, and remedies most commonly used in labor disputes.

Employee Rights

Section 7 of the NLRA sets forth three seminal employee rights:

1 the right to join or assist unions;
2 the right to engage in collective bargaining through a representative of one's own choosing;
3 the right to engage in concerted activity for one's own mutual aid and protection (29 U.S.C. § 157, 2005).

These rights guarantee that workers can choose to join unions and make the union the exclusive bargaining representative. Workers seeking to enforce these rights and collectively bargain with management can do so through two approaches. Employers may voluntarily recognize the employees in a union or they may force the employees to gain union status through an election. We will explore these three seminal employee rights in more detail below.

The Right to Join or Assist Unions

The first employee right is the right to join or assist unions. As mentioned above, if employers do not voluntarily recognize the employees in a union, the employees must gain union status through an election. Whether through voluntary recognition or an election, the goal is the **certification of an appropriate bargaining** unit for the employees. An election is required when 30 percent of the employees file authorization cards with the NLRB authorizing an election. Authorization cards are not used to authorize a union but rather to authorize an election.

Once the NLRB receives authorization cards, it evaluates whether the employees seeking an election are an appropriate unit for bargaining. Certifying workers in appropriate bargaining units brings stability to the collective bargaining process and facilitates agreement between the parties. If members of the unit were from disparate jobs, the needs and goals involved in the bargaining process would also be disparate. Creating division within the union negotiating group would likely lead to a breakdown in the process.

To certify a bargaining unit as appropriate, the NLRB examines the community of interests of proposed unit members to determine if they have enough in common to make bargaining successful. **Community of interests** includes such factors as:

- commonality of supervision;
- commonality of personnel policies and work rules;
- shared work areas and similarity of job duties and working conditions;
- similarity of methods for evaluation;
- similarities in pay and benefits;
- integration and interdependence of operations;
- history, if any, of collective bargaining between the parties (Feldacker, 2000; Gold, 1998).

In a case involving the North American Soccer League (NASL), the league challenged the NLRB's certification of all players into a national bargaining unit for purposes of collective bargaining (North American Soccer League v. NLRB, 1980). The NASL argued that local team units were the appropriate form of the bargaining unit. The NLRB disagreed, finding that where an employer has assumed sufficient control over the working conditions of the employees of its franchisees or member-employers, the NLRB may require employers to bargain jointly. Thus, the issues in the case were whether there was a joint employer relationship between the league and its member clubs and, if so, whether the designated bargaining unit of players was appropriate. The court agreed that labor relations were conducted on a league level, not delegated to individual teams, and, thus, the NLRB's designation was appropriate.

From the union's perspective, if the NASL had been successful in limiting bargaining to the local level, solidarity could easily have been threatened, since employers could conceivably trade away union supporters and undermine the local union's strength. Such a system could also undermine the union's strike threat. For instance, if a team in New York went on strike, the league could continue to play and just give any team playing New York a bye for that scheduled game. If the league could continue without that franchise, the power of the strike would be severely limited; games could continue, broadcasting would still occur, and only New York would lose revenue. With the shared revenue structures in place in most leagues, under such a circumstance the New York franchise would still receive a cut of revenues from the other games. Such a situation would severely disable the negotiating power of the players union.

When a union is designated as an appropriate bargaining unit, elections are held and if successful, the union is certified as the exclusive bargaining representative for employees. At this point, two important changes occur for employees. First, management is put on notice that it has a duty to bargain in good faith with the union. Second, the union has a duty of fair representation for its employee members. The **duty to bargain in good faith** requires management to bargain in good faith over hours, wages, and terms and conditions of employment. In fact, both sides have such a duty. Although employers can unilaterally impose permissive subjects and those that deal primarily with "management rights" that encompass managerial decisions that "lie at the core of entrepreneurial control" (Rabuano, 2002). Management need not negotiate these decisions with a union, but they may have to negotiate their impact on employment. The **duty of fair representation** requires that a union represent all employees in the bargaining unit fairly, even if the employees are not union members (Steele v. Louisville & Nashville Railroad Co., 1944).

Right to Collectively Bargain with Representative of One's Own Choosing

Once a union is in existence, management must engage in collective bargaining over mandatory subjects of bargaining or risk being charged with an unfair labor practice under § 8(a)(5) of the NLRA for failing to bargain in good faith (NLRB v. Katz, 1962). **Mandatory subjects** are hours, wages, and terms and conditions of employment. Mandatory subjects are items "plainly germane to the 'working environment' and not those 'managerial decisions which lie at the core of entrepreneurial control'" (Ford Motor Co. v. NLRB at 498, 1979). Good faith bargaining over mandatory subjects is required to achieve a CBA. Provisions in the CBA for wages include salaries; bonuses; severance and termination pay; and fringe benefits, such as life or disability insurance, health coverage, and practically anything else that has monetary value. The concept of hours includes any time spent at work; in professional sport this may include such provisions as training camp, practices, season, schedule, number of games, and so forth.

Terms and conditions of employment cover the majority of the remaining provisions in an employee's work life, including seniority, medical issues, grievance arbitration provisions, drug-testing provisions, safety concerns, and the like. In professional sports there are additional provisions that may affect more than one of these subjects. For instance, the draft provision affects wages. The position or slot into which someone is drafted affects the amount of money the athlete will earn in salary and bonuses. The draft also affects terms and conditions of employment, as it determines the team and geographic location where a player will work, as well as other factors, such as playing time (depending on the other players on that team or in the club's farm system), rosters, and coaches (*Mackey v. National Football League*, 1976). Mandatory subjects in sports are set forth later in the chapter in Exhibit 7.5.

In addition to mandatory subjects, there are also permissive subjects for bargaining. **Permissive subjects** are those that management is not obligated to negotiate over. An example of a permissive subject might be the NHLPA asking for its logo to appear on the NHL team uniforms or in NHL advertisements. There is no legal obligation for the NHL to negotiate with the NHLPA for such a provision, but the NHL can do so if it chooses. A union is not able to force bargaining over permissive subjects and therefore cannot bargain to impasse. An **impasse** is a stalemate in negotiations that often leads to an economic weapon being used by the union, in the form of a strike, or by management, in the form of a lockout.

Another example of a recent permissive subject applicable to the National Football League (NFL) is illustrated in benefits for retired players. Benefits for retired football players are not a mandatory subject of bargaining because retired players are not union members (*Eller v. NFLPA*, 2012). There is no obligation for the union to bargain collectively on the behalf of the retired players. In light of the discovery of concussion-related health issues that occur later in life for professional athletes, retirees have asked union and management to provide more on their behalf. Concussion-related dementia and other health issues create a host of financial needs and led to lawsuits in the NFL and NHL. These lawsuits have been settled with the leagues, but the settlements were made by a team of lawyers representing the retirees, not the union. (See also Chapter 15 for a discussion of the legal issues involved.)

Right to Engage in Concerted Activity

The last § 7 right, the right to engage in concerted activity, gives employees the right to strike or undertake similar activities (picketing, work slowdowns, etc.) to better their economic conditions (mutual aid) or address poor working conditions (protection). The right to engage in concerted activity provides protection for employees to work together to improve their working conditions. A strike, for example, is the employees' economic weapon to gain leverage over their employer. However, there is a limit as to the behavior that is protected. Any activity that interferes with the employer's ability to conduct business with customers (such as threatening customers or blocking entrances) or that leads to violence is not protected. In addition, the right to strike is recognized only over mandatory subjects, not permissive subjects for bargaining.

Management also has a right to engage in concerted activity in the form of a lockout. A lockout is a temporary work stoppage initiated by the employer to gain leverage over the union. The lockout is often viewed as management's equivalent to the strike. Lockouts are characterized as defensive or offensive. Management uses a *defensive lockout* as a preemptive move to block an opportunistic strike by employees. In sports, this might be used against the union if it was about to strike just before playoffs or finals.

Offensive lockouts are used to pressure the union into accepting terms in an agreement favorable to the employer. An offensive lockout usually occurs once an impasse is reached in negotiations. Leagues have increasingly used the offensive lockout as a management strategy in collective bargaining negotiations. Since 1990, leagues have imposed lockouts on employees nine times, in the following seasons:

- MLB: 1990
- NBA: 1995–1996; 1998–1999; 2011–2012
- NHL: 1994–1995; 2004–2005; 2012–2013
- NFL: 2011 (players) and 2012 (referees)

Four of the nine lockouts were imposed over a 14-month period (August 2011–October 2012) and were orchestrated as a strategy by the same outside counsel for the leagues to win their labor disputes. Because of the leverage they bring the leagues, it is safe to say that lockouts in professional sports are here to stay.

Unfair Labor Practices

Section 8 of the NLRA and the LMRA establishes employer and union unfair labor practices and provides enforcement mechanisms. We will explore a few examples of unfair labor practices recognized in professional sport, including union's failure to represent employees fairly, employer retaliation for engaging in union activity, and refusal to bargain in good faith. See Exhibit 7.4 for a complete list of unfair labor practices.

Union Failure to Represent Employees

If the union does not represent its employees fairly, it is an unfair labor practice under § 8(b)(1)(A), the section that prohibits interference with § 7 rights (*Miranda Fuel Co.*, 1962). Unions must represent employees without acting in an arbitrary, bad faith, or discriminatory manner (*Vaca v. Sipes*, 1967). For example, in *Vaca v. Sipes*, the plaintiff alleged that the union's decision to drop the pursuit of his grievance through the arbitration process was arbitrary and discriminatory. The U.S. Supreme Court held that a union's duty of fair representation "includes a statutory obligation to serve the interest of all members without hostility or discrimination toward any, to exercise its discretion with complete good faith and honesty, and to avoid arbitrary conduct" (*Vaca*, p. 177). Most breach of the duty of fair representation cases challenge a union's decision to pursue grievances on behalf of employees. In *Peterson v. Kennedy and NFLPA* (1985), the plaintiff, an NFL player, sued his union for failing to represent him fairly when it made an error in filing his grievance, thus causing the issue to be time-barred under the process set forth in collective bargaining. The court held that since the union's conduct amounted to no more than negligence, it did not meet the standard required for a duty of fair representation case. The court emphasized that unions are not liable for good faith, nondiscriminatory errors of judgment made in processing grievances. Thus, unions are not held liable for errors in judgment about whether to pursue a grievance, interpretations of CBAs, or representing an employee in the grievance arbitration process (*Vaca*, 1967).

Employer Retaliation for Union Activity

As noted in Exhibit 7.4, it is an unfair labor practice for an employer to interfere with, restrain, or coerce employees who are engaged in union activity (NLRA, § 8(a)(1)). It is also an unfair labor practice to discriminate against employees for such activity or for supporting the union (NLRA, § 8(a)(3)). In theory, this is straightforward, but in practice, it becomes difficult to apply, especially in a professional sport context. Decisions about discipline, retention, and termination often come from mixed motives, so for managers it is very important to keep a well-documented paper trail on union employees in the event that you must terminate a worker's employment.

Exhibit 7.4 Unfair labor practices of employers and unions as established by the National Labor Relations and Labor Management Relations Acts, 29 U.S.C. § 158 (2005).

Employer Unfair Labor Practice	Union Unfair Labor Practice
8(a)(1) – To interfere with, restrain, or coerce employees in the exercise of § 7 rights	8(b)(1) – To restrain or coerce employees in their exercise of § 7 rights
8(a)(2) – To dominate or interfere with a union or contribute financial or other support to it	8(b)(2) – To cause employer to discriminate against employee
8(a)(3) – By discrimination in regard to employment or any term or condition of employment to encourage or discourage membership in any labor organization	8(b)(3) – To refuse to bargain collectively with an employer
8(a)(4) – To discharge or discriminate against an employee because he has filed an unfair labor practices complaint or given testimony under NLRA	8(b)(5) – To require employees to pay excessive dues or discriminatory fees for membership under union security clause
8(a)(5) – To refuse to bargain collectively with employees' representative	8(b)(6) – To cause an employer to pay for services not performed

Mixed-motive cases often arise for professional athletes who are released from their jobs for a lack of skill, poor performance, or misconduct, but who are heavily involved in union activity. As club management compares two similarly talented players, if one is heavily engaged in union activities, it is easy to imagine how that factor might influence the decision as to which of the two to sign, release, or demote. By their contracts, athletes agree to be released at any time for lack of skill or ability. Determining whether a termination was related to a lack of skill or due to union involvement can be difficult. The analysis is compounded by the fact that union leaders are often league veterans whose performance may be in decline.

In *Nordstrom, d/b/a Seattle Seahawks and NFLPA* (1989), wide receiver Sam McCullum successfully challenged his release by the Seattle Seahawks as retaliation for his union activities. McCullum was a starting wide receiver for the Seattle Seahawks from 1976 to 1981. In 1981 he became his team's union player representative, giving him a prominent role in union activities. McCullum orchestrated a "solidarity" handshake with the opposing team at the start of a preseason game, which led to tension with his head coach. Despite that, McCullum started all preseason games. At the end of training camp, McCullum was released when the Seahawks traded for another wide receiver.

The test for determining whether an employer has violated § 8(a)(3) (discrimination on the basis of union activities) requires that an employee show that union activities were a motivating factor in the firing (*Wright Line, a Division of Wright Line, Inc.*, 1980). The burden then shifts to the employer to prove the employee would have been fired even if he had not engaged in union activities. McCullum was successful in showing that the acquisition of another wide receiver would not have occurred in the absence of management's animus against him for being an outspoken supporter of the union. McCullum also showed evidence of this animus by proving that the fines imposed on him for the solidarity handshake greatly exceeded those imposed on other NFL players. Having proved the unfair labor practice, McCullum was awarded back pay and damages (*Nordstrom*, 1991). Due to the speculative nature of professional sport playing careers and compensation, this was an exceptional feat.

Another case illustrating employer retaliation against players who exercised their § 7 right to strike is *NFL Management Council and NFLPA* (1992).

NFL Management Council v. National Football League Player Association

309 N.L.R.B. 78 (1992)   **FOCUS** CASE

FACTS

In the 1987 season, the NFL players went on strike as a result of reaching an impasse in collective bargaining negotiations. The NFL Management Council decided that if the NFLPA went on strike, it would use replacement players, many of whom were available, since a competitor league, the United States Football League, had recently folded. Most replacement players were those cut from prior training camps. After a one-week game cancelation, the NFL scheduled two weeks of games using replacement players. Fearing for their jobs, a number of striking players chose to cross the picket lines and returned to the playing field.

The NFLPA then called off the strike and sent players back to their clubs effective Thursday, October 15. The league, however, imposed a rule that striking veterans were not eligible to play the following weekend unless they had reported back to their clubs by 1:00 p.m. Wednesday. Despite this rule, the clubs used non-striker replacement players that weekend who had signed in as late as 4:00 p.m. on Saturday for Sunday's game and 4:00 p.m. Monday for the Monday night game, over the striking players who had returned by the designated deadline. The NFLPA filed an unfair labor practice charge against the league, stating that its rule violated § 8 of the National Labor Relations Act. The NFLPA claimed that the rule discriminated against striking players and deprived them of 1/16 of their annual salaries.

HOLDING

The NLRB upheld the complaint of an unfair labor practice against the NFL.

RATIONALE

In judging the NFL Management Council's conduct, the NLRB noted that the U.S. Supreme Court has recognized that some practices are inherently so prejudicial to union interests and so devoid of economic justification … that the employer's conduct carries an inference of unlawful intent so compelling that no one could believe the employer's protest of innocence. On the one hand, if the employer acts in this manner, the Court has given the NLRB free rein to find an unfair labor practice, even if management introduces evidence that the conduct was motivated by business considerations. On the other hand, if the employer shows evidence of legitimate and substantial business justifications for its conduct, and the NLRB determines that the impact on employee rights is comparatively slight, an anti-union motivation must be proved to sustain the unfair labor practice charge.

Applying the above principle, the NLRB found that the Wednesday deadline clearly constituted discriminatory conduct toward union members, because it applied a different standard to the strikers and also adversely affected worker rights, namely the right to strike. The NLRB and courts have recognized that the right to strike includes the right to an unconditional application to return to work. The teams argued that the Wednesday deadline was required for them to have sufficient time to prepare returning players and to take care of administrative changes. The NLRB found the NFL Management Council's justifications were weak, since the NFL had never before imposed such a deadline, not even when players held out and tried to renegotiate their contracts. Players in such a situation either returned to the club or were placed on an exempt list that still provided the players with compensation and service time. Further noting the late deadlines used for replacement players, the NLRB rejected the NFL justifications.

The following hypothetical case explores the process of forming a union and its likely impact on the employer, as well as the employees, in a sport facility.

Considering … Labor Law in Practice

Big City Arena (BCA) is owned and operated by Big City Sports and Entertainment (BCSE). BCSE operates its headquarters out of BCA. BCA is the only facility BCSE owns, but its facility management subsidiary operates numerous arenas throughout North America. BCSE also owns an NBA franchise, a Women's National Basketball Association (WNBA) franchise, and an NHL franchise, all of which play their home games at the BCA. A National Lacrosse League franchise is also a tenant, and the BCA attracts many major tours, from concerts to family events, as well as an occasional amateur sports championship. Needless to say, the arena is busy most nights of the year.

Bianca Colon is the general manager of the BCA. When she was promoted to the general manager position, the workers rejoiced. She had started at BCA as an usher while putting herself through college. Upon graduation, Bianca was hired as an event coordinator, and over ten years she worked her way to the top. She tries her best to accommodate employees' needs and create a positive work environment, but the reality is that BCSE is always under pressure to generate revenue through its arena operations to spend on its major league teams.

When BCSE acquired the teams, all budgets at the arena were cut. The BCA works on a skeletal staff compared to those at the other arenas that BCSE manages. Bianca feels tremendous pressure running the facility that is the home headquarters for the company. Having events virtually every night of the year is leading to morale problems for BCA staff. It is clear to the employees at the bottom of the organization that they do not and never will get the same perks as their BCSE colleagues on the professional teams.

In this environment, Bianca overhears BCA head usher Darryl Jones leading a group of employees in a conversation about their working conditions. Bianca hears them complaining about their low salaries; the long hours setting up before games and concerts and cleaning up after games, concerts, and other events; the lack of disciplinary protection as some employees have been fired when sickness prevents them from coming to work, and their lack of benefits (pension, healthcare coverage, and the like). The complaints become very frank and personal. At one point Darryl says, "Bianca has forgotten her roots. She no longer cares about the people who work for her. She is up with the big dogs now and only cares about moving up in the company." Bianca knows the employees are fed up and something must be done.

At the end of the discussion, Darryl Jones vows to do something about it, saying, "I'm going to call my friends at the Staples Center and find out the name of their union."

Questions

- If Darryl chooses to organize his workplace, what steps must he take?
- If Darryl starts an organizing campaign, what should Bianca do? Should she voluntarily recognize the union and then sit down with Darryl to negotiate for better working conditions? Should she try to stop Darryl's union organizing? Can she fire Darryl or others helping him to unionize BCA?
- If Darryl is successful in organizing and certifying a union at the BCA, what mandatory subjects would you imagine he and his team would ask for at the collective bargaining negotiations? What might Bianca and her team seek in those negotiations as they represent BCSE?

Note how you would answer the questions and then check your responses using the Analysis & Discussion at the end of this chapter.

Refusal to Bargain in Good Faith

As discussed previously, once the NLRB certifies a union, management has a duty to bargain in good faith over hours, wages, and terms and conditions of employment. In practice, management may unilaterally implement its last best offer and still fulfill the duty to bargain in good faith (*Brown v. Pro Football*, 1996). However, if management refuses to bargain in good faith on issues impacting hours, wages, or terms and conditions of employment, the union can assert that management is in violation of NLRA. These disputes often arise when the Commissioner of a professional sport league unilaterally imposes what it believes to fall within the scope of a permissive subject of bargaining related to management decisions rather than a mandatory subject covered by the NLRA.

Commissioners of professional sport leagues are granted power by their employers (the owners of the professional teams) to maintain the integrity of the game. Commissioners have power to approve player contracts to ensure the contracts do not circumvent rules. Commissioners make rules for conduct on and off the field, and they discipline players, clubs, owners, game officials, and other league and club employees. Commissioners resolve disputes between players and owners, teams, or the league, as well as disputes between owners the league. As a result, commissioners' decisions within their owner-granted powers may clash with the duty to bargain over mandatory subjects. It may be difficult for management to accept a requirement to bargain over rules and policies that historically have been unilaterally mandated by the league or commissioner. For instance, in NFLPA v. NLRB (1974), the NFLPA argued that imposition by the NFL Commissioner of a rule and corresponding fines without collective bargaining was a refusal to bargain in good faith.

National Football League Player Association v. National Labor Review Board

CASE OPINION   503 F.2d 12 (8th Cir. 1974)

FACTS

The National Football League Players Association petitioned the Eighth Circuit Court of Appeals to review an NLRB order dismissing a complaint against the NFL's Management Council (owners' collective bargaining representative). The complaint alleged that the NFL violated § 8(a)(5) and § 8(a)(1) of the NLRA by unilaterally establishing a rule that "any player leaving the bench area while a fight is in progress on the field will be fined $200." The court was not asked to judge the wisdom of the rule, but rather whether the NLRB erred in dismissing the complaint on the ground that the rule was adopted and promulgated by the NFL Commissioner rather than by the owners.

On January 22, 1971, the NLRB certified the NFLPA as the exclusive bargaining representative for NFL players and negotiations for a CBA began. The NFLPA, NFL, and each of the clubs signed the CBA on June 17, 1971. In early 1971, NFL Commissioner Pete Rozelle discussed with his staff the problem of injuries to players due to on-field violence. He directed a member of the NFL staff to discuss this problem with the owners' competition committee, which dealt with proposed changes in policy on the competitive aspects of football. The committee recommended a rule be established to fine players who left the bench during a fight on the field. At the March 25 meeting of the owners, the Commissioner explained the proposal to the clubs and they adopted the rule. Rozelle subsequently fined 106 players under the rule.

The NFLPA appealed the imposition of the fines on the grounds that the players had not been notified of the new rule and the rule violated the Collective Bargaining Agreement (CBA), which provided for good faith negotiations on any changes in employment conditions. Commissioner Rozelle responded that the clubs passed the rule and he had jurisdiction to impose the fines under the powers vested in him as Commissioner. On December 29, 1971, the NFLPA withdrew the matter from the Commissioner and requested the council begin negotiations on the rule. The council refused on the grounds that the Commissioner was acting within his powers and that the players only had the right to an appeal to him. The NFLPA filed an unfair labor practice charge with the NLRB on December 10, 1971, alleging the NFL's unilateral adoption of the rule was a refusal to bargain.

The NLRB found: (1) the union conceded that the commissioner had a right to adopt the bench-fine rule; (2) the bench-fine rule had in fact been promulgated by the commissioner, and the owners engaged in no meaningful or substantial conduct with respect to its adoption or promulgation; and (3) as a matter of law there is no substantive difference between the commissioner's imposing individual fines for conduct detrimental to the game after notice and hearing and promulgating the bench-fine rule. Thus, promulgation of the rule was within the Commissioner's authority. The NFLPA appealed.

HOLDING

The Eighth Circuit Court of Appeals reversed and remanded the case to the NLRB.

RATIONALE

The record does not support the NLRB's finding that the NFLPA conceded to the Commissioner the right to adopt and promulgate the bench-fine rule; to the contrary, the NFLPA denied he had such a right.

The NFLPA agreed only that the Commissioner had a right pursuant to the CBA to fine a player for conduct detrimental to the NFL *after notice and hearing*. The distinction was a meaningful one. If the Commissioner's power is limited in the manner the NFLPA suggests, each player who has been notified he is being charged with conduct detrimental to the game can at the hearing attempt to prove that the conduct in question is not, in fact, detrimental and to prove he did not engage in the proscribed conduct. If the Commissioner, *after notice and hearing*, decides that a player has been guilty of conduct detrimental to professional football, then the Commissioner shall have complete authority to fine or suspend.

The record also does not support the NLRB's finding that the Commissioner adopted the bench rule without meaningful or substantial conduct on the part of the Owners. The Commissioner discussed with his staff "his feeling that from now on if a player left the bench area during a fight, he felt he would have to fine him." But he was obviously concerned about the reaction of the Owners to such a course of action and instead of announcing his policy or simply imposing a fine, he asked a staff member to discuss the matter with the competition committee – a committee in which only management is represented. When that committee indicated its approval, he had the committee bring a recommended resolution to the Owners for their approval. It was only after Owners voted 24–2 in favor of the rule that the Commissioner sent out a press release that the bench-fine rule was in effect. At no time prior to the press release did the Commissioner discuss the problem of players leaving the bench during fights with the NFLPA. If, as the Employers contend, the Commissioner is the agent of both the NFL and the NFLPA, and promulgated the rule as their agent, one must assume a serious breach of ethics by the Commissioner if he talked to only one of his principals. And, no one suggests the Commissioner is an unethical man.

To summarize, every fact and inference supports the administrative law judge's conclusion that the rule was adopted and promulgated by the Owners. We hold the NFL, by unilaterally promulgating and implementing a rule providing for an automatic fine to be levied against any player leaving the bench area while an on field fight or an altercation is in progress, have engaged in unfair labor practices within the meaning of § 8(a)(5) and § 8(a)(1) of the Act.

QUESTIONS

1 Do you agree with the decision that Commissioner Rozelle did not promulgate the NFL bench-clearing rule? Why or why not?
2 If such a rule is, in fact, within the Commissioner's power, how might he have unilaterally imposed it without facing an unfair labor practice charge?

Remedies for Violations of Labor Laws and Unfair Labor Practices

When an unfair labor practice is alleged, the NLRB, through its attorneys, may seek a court order, called a **§ 10(j) injunction**, to stop the employer from committing the unfair labor practice. *Morio v. NASL* (1980), provides an example of a case where a §10(j) injunction was sought by Winifred Morio, regional director for the NLRB, against the NASL. *Morio v. NASL* established that collective bargaining in professional sport is best accomplished at the league level because labor issues are common across teams. Rules and policies are decided at the league level, individual contracts are uniform, and players may be traded from team to team. It would not make sense to have local units at the team level or the working conditions may vary by team across the league. Further, if collective bargaining units were certified at the local (team) level, there might be teams with employees who were unionized and then other units (teams) that would be nonunion. The practice of trading players could undermine labor relations as a player with a unionized team might later be traded to a nonunion team or vice versa.

Morio v. North American Soccer League (NASL)

CASE OPINION   501 F. Supp. 633 (S.D.N.Y. 1980)

FACTS

On August 16, 1977, the Union filed a petition for an election under Section 9(c) of the Act alleging that the League and each of its clubs constituted a single employer for purposes of collective bargaining. Hearings were held and briefs were submitted on the unique and complex issues of the appropriate bargaining unit in the professional soccer industry. Nine months later, the NLRB issued a decision directing an election among the soccer player employees of the clubs listed in the petition as well as other employers who had been granted franchises by the League and commenced operations of clubs during the intervening period.

The players participated in a secret ballot election supervised by the NLRB, wherein a majority of the votes were cast for the Union. On September 1, 1978, the Union was certified as the exclusive collective bargaining representative of the employees of the Clubs.

Subsequent to the certification, the League refused to bargain with the Union and contested the NLRB's determination of a single "League-wide unit" as being appropriate for collective bargaining. The Union filed an unfair labor practice charge on October 30, 1978. The General Counsel issued a complaint on November 24, 1978, against the Clubs which alleged, *inter alia*, that they had failed and refused to recognize and bargain with the Union in violation of Section 8(a) (1) and (5) of the Act.

NLRB Regional Director Morio seeks a temporary injunction pursuant to § 10(j) of the NLRA, pending the final disposition of matters before the NLRB. Respondents are the NASL and its 21 U.S.-based clubs. The NASL is a 24-team, nonprofit association, of which 21 are U.S.-based and three are based in Canada. Each of the member clubs is engaged primarily in the business of promoting and exhibiting professional soccer contests for the public. Collectively, these clubs annually gross revenue in excess of $500,000 and purchase and import interstate commerce goods and materials in excess of $50,000. The NLRB has found, and the Fifth Circuit affirmed, that the NASL and its member clubs are joint employers and that a collective bargaining unit composed of all NASL players on clubs based in the United States is appropriate.

All professional soccer players employed by NASL constitute a unit appropriate for collective bargaining within the meaning of § 9(b) of the act. This unit includes players on active, temporarily inactive, disabled, suspended, ineligible, and military eligibility lists. The unit does not include NASL officials, managerial/executive personnel of NASL or clubs, or players employed by the Canadian clubs. Since September 1, 1978, the union, by virtue of § 9(a) of the act, has been the exclusive representative of all employees for collective bargaining.

Morio alleges that she has reasonable cause to believe that NASL interfered with, restrained, and coerced employees in the exercise of rights guaranteed them under § 7 of the act by unilaterally changing the employment conditions (mandatory subjects) when:

1 On October 19, 1978, and thereafter, NASL required players to get permission from their clubs whenever they desired a particular brand of footwear, other than that selected by each NASL club.

2 On April 10, 1979, NASL initiated plans for a new winter indoor soccer season from November 1979 to March 1980.

3 On November 24, 1979, and continuing thereafter, NASL required players to participate in the winter indoor soccer season.

4 On October 16, 1979, NASL initiated and implemented plans to increase the 1980 regular summer outdoor soccer season schedule by two games and lengthen it by two weeks. It also reduced the maximum roster of all NASL clubs during the regular summer outdoor season from 30 to 26 players.

5 Commencing on October 19, 1978, through March 1979, and continuing thereafter, NASL bypassed the union and dealt directly with players in the unit. It solicited players to enter into individual employment contracts, and then negotiated and actually entered into individual employment
   contracts with them.

NASL conceded that it has done all of these actions and unilaterally changed the conditions of employment. The evidence introduced at the court hearing established that Morio had reasonable cause to believe
that the individual contracts NASL entered into with employees since September 1, 1978, constituted
96.8 percent of the existing individual contracts. The other 3.2 percent of the current individual player
contracts were entered into prior to the union's certification.

HOLDING

The district court for the Southern District of New York found reasonable cause to believe that NASL
engaged in unfair labor practices and that Morio was, therefore, entitled to injunctive relief, pending the
final determination of the charges before the NLRB.

RATIONALE

It is undisputed that NASL refused to bargain with the Union. However, NASL argued it had a right
to refuse to bargain with the Union while it pursued an appeal of the NLRB's determination of an
appropriate collective bargaining unit. NASL's duty to bargain with the Union arose when the Union
was certified as the exclusive bargaining representative. The fact that NASL was pursuing its right to
appeal did not, absent a stay of the NLRB's order, obviate their duty to bargain with the Union and
does not constitute a defense to an application for relief under § 10(j) of the Act where, as here, NASL
has apparently repeatedly refused to bargain with the Union and continuously bypassed the Union and
dealt directly with employees.

NASL's most vigorous opposition comes in response to Morio's application for an order requiring NASL to render voidable, at Union's option, all individual player contracts, whether entered
into before or after the Union's certification. NASL claims that such power in the hands of the Union
would result in chaos in the industry and subject NASL to severe economic loss and hardship since
these individual contracts are the only real property of NASL. The relief requested by Morio is not a
request to have all individual contracts declared null and void, nor that the "exclusive rights" provision
of the individual contracts, which bind the players to teams for a certain time, be rendered voidable.
Moreover, Morio seeks an order requiring NASL to maintain the present terms and conditions in effect
simply until NASL negotiates with the Union unless and until the agreement or a good faith impasse is
reached through collective bargaining. Morio does not, however, seek to rescind that unilateral provision which provided for the present summer schedule. The NLRB has consciously limited its request
for relief to prevent any unnecessary disruption of NASL business. The NLRB is seeking to render
voidable only those unilateral acts taken by the NASL that it admits have occurred. These unilateral
changes modify all existing individual contracts entered into before September 1, 1978, in deroga-
tion of the Union's right to act as the exclusive bargaining agent of all employees. The individual
contracts entered into since September 1, 1978, are apparently in violation of the duty of the NASL
to, in accordance with the Act, bargain collectively with the Union. The obligation is exclusive. This
duty to bargain with the exclusive representative carries with it the negative duty not to bargain with
individual employees.

Morio is entitled to an injunction enjoining NASL from giving effect to individual contracts entered
into prior to September 1, 1978, or any modification, continuation, extension or renewal thereof "to
forestall collective bargaining." *J. I. Case Co. v. NLRB*, 321 U.S. 332, 341 (1944). NASL refused to recognize
that only the Union has the right to waive its right to be the exclusive bargaining representative. In *National
Licorice Co. v. NLRB*, 309 U.S. 350 (1940), the Supreme Court held that the NLRB has the authority to order
an employer not to enforce individual contracts with its employees which were found to have been in

violation of the NLRA. Evidence discloses that Morio has reasonable cause to believe that NASL has used, and will continue to use, the individual contracts entered into prior to September 1, 1978, to forestall collective bargaining, and to continue to enforce them is to bypass and undermine support for the Union. With such contracts in place, NASL's determination not to bargain with the Union is well-fortified, so there simply is no incentive for NASL to bargain with the Union.

The NLRB is, therefore, entitled to the relief it seeks requiring NASL to render voidable certain provisions in the existing individual contracts that the Union requests, as set forth above. The Union has been permitted by the court to intervene in this action as a party petitioner. The court finds it is not the intent of Morio, as the NASL claims, to visit punitive actions on the NASL, and the requested relief with respect to the individual contracts has been carefully tailored to avoid chaos and economic hardship.

QUESTIONS

1. Why was it determined that local bargaining units were inappropriate for collective bargaining purposes?
2. Do you agree with the NASL's position that Morio's request to declare all contracts voidable (at the union's option) would result in chaos and subject NASL to severe economic loss and hardship, since these individual contracts are the only real property of NASL?
3. Clarify in lay terms what Morio is actually requesting of the court. Is it to "undo" all player contracts in the NASL? Do you believe this is a proper remedy under the circumstances?
4. Should a union have a right to determine whether a player's contract is voidable in this situation? What if the player decides that he does not want to void the contract? Should the union be able to overrule the players' wishes for the good of the other members of the union? How should collective versus individual bargaining be?

Collective Bargaining

When employees form a union and begin collective bargaining, their goal is to negotiate a contract with management that contains the mandatory subjects of their workplace. The process favors compromise between the two sides to further a peaceful and productive work environment. Collective bargaining in professional sports addresses negotiations over policies that are restrictive to employees, such as drafts, limits on free agency, salary caps, wage scales, and the like. Players have presented federal courts unique questions as to whether these restrictive provisions violate antitrust laws or are in fact protected from antitrust scrutiny when they are negotiated into a CBA. The following discussion elaborates on the law as it stands in this area.

Convergence of Labor and Antitrust Law

The restrictive policies and structures of professional sport leagues lend themselves to antitrust challenges. Restrictive practices are those that limit a player's ability to earn money or to move through a free market. They include such practices as age restrictions, the draft, the salary cap or luxury tax, and restrictions on free agency (*Denver Rockets v. All-Pro Management, Inc.*, 1971; *Linseman v. World Hockey Association*, 1977; *Mackey v. NFL*, 1976; *Smith v. Pro Football, Inc.*, 1978). Under labor laws, these practices, which might otherwise violate players' antitrust rights, may be shielded from antitrust liability, if negotiated into the CBA through the collective bargaining process (*Brown v. Pro Football*, 1996; *Clarett v. NFL*, 2004; *McCourt v. California Sports, Inc.*, 1979; *Wood v. NBA*, 1987). (See Chapter 10 for detailed discussion of regulation of professional sport and antitrust law.)

It is a competitive advantage for leagues to negotiate their restrictive practices through the collective bargaining process with a players union – so much so that in 2000, the NLRB filed a complaint against the Arena Football League and its member clubs. They sought to decertify the American Football League (AFL) Players Organizing Committee (AFLPOC) by claiming that owners coerced players into joining the union (Beard Group, 2000). Two players had complained to the NLRB that the AFL illegally recognized and supported the AFLPOC in order to form a union that would be sympathetic to management and to try to shield the owners from player antitrust suits. The complaint describes numerous instances in which the AFL and its teams, among other things, engaged in the following activities:

- "rendered unlawful assistance" to the AFLPOC;
- "solicited employee players" to sign union cards;
- "promised benefits to employee players if they formed or joined a union and engaged in collective bargaining";
- "threatened employee players" with reprisals and "threatened to discharge and release employee players" who refused to engage in collective bargaining;
- released players "to discourage employees" from refusing to form a union.

All of these activities are unfair labor practices. After two players filed complaints, the NLRB investigation found that the majority of AFL players never supported the AFLPOC. The NLRB discovered that the AFL owners illegally recognized AFLPOC, threatened AFL players, and illegally promised benefits to AFL players to coerce them to form a union (Beard Group, 2000).

Another example occurred in the NBA in 1996. At that time, star NBA players, such as Michael Jordan and Alonzo Mourning, sought to decertify the National Basketball Players Association (NBPA), while the NBA Commissioner publicly supported the players who favored keeping the players association. The attempts by NFL (2010–2011) and NHL (2012–2013) players to disclaim their union while in the midst of labor disputes stand as examples of the important role antitrust litigation threats actually play in players gaining leverage in collective bargaining.

All professional sport organizations except MLB are subject to antitrust laws. MLB is exempt because almost 100 years ago, the U.S. Supreme Court found that baseball was not engaged in interstate commerce and, thus, not subject to the Sherman Act (*Federal Baseball Club of Baltimore v. National League of Professional Baseball Clubs*, 1922). MLB's antitrust exemption survived two further Supreme Court challenges, and much of it remained intact through the enactment of the Curt Flood Act of 1998 (*Toolson v. New York Yankees*, 1953; *Flood v. Kuhn*, 1972).

The Curt Flood Act allows major league baseball players to sue their employers under the Sherman Act, but it does not remove baseball's immunity, since the exemption still applies to business areas as well as the league's employment relationship with minor league players. While at first blush it appears the Curt Flood Act opens MLB to increased antitrust litigation, it does not. Baseball, like all other unionized professional sports leagues, is shielded from antitrust liability by the labor exemption. It is well-established that during the term of a CBA, terms negotiated in that agreement are exempt from antitrust scrutiny (*Allen Bradley Co. v. Local No. 3, I.B.E.W.*, 1945; *Local No. 189, Amalgamated Meat Cutters & Butcher Workmen v. Jewel Tea Co.*, 1965; *United Mine Workers v. Pennington*, 1965). Provided that the defendant proves the plaintiff is, was, or will be a party to the CBA, that the subject being challenged on antitrust grounds is a mandatory subject for bargaining (hours, wages, and other terms and conditions of employment), and that the CBA was achieved through bona fide arm's-length bargaining (bargaining that occurs freely, without one party having excessive power or control over the other), the defendant's actions will be exempt from antitrust (*Brown v. Pro Football*, 1996; *Clarett v. NFL*, 2004; *Reynolds v. NFL*, 1978; *McCourt v. California Sports, Inc.*, 1979; *Wood v. NBA*, 1987). In *Wood v. NBA* (1987) and *Clarett v. NFL* (2004), the Second Circuit held that players outside of the process at the time a CBA is negotiated are still precluded from a successful antitrust challenge to a provision agreed to in collective bargaining. Further, Clarett extended this to anything that is a product of the collective bargaining process and the collective bargaining relationship, in *Clarett's* case specifically draft eligibility rules contained in the NFL constitution and by laws.

A number of cases raised the issue of whether the labor exemption continues to protect parties from antitrust scrutiny after a CBA has expired (*Bridgeman v. NBA*, 1987; *Brown v. Pro Football*, 1996; *NBA v. Williams*, 1995; *Powell v. NFL*, 1989). In *Brown v. Pro Football, Inc.*, which is discussed below, the U.S. Supreme Court noted that when a bargaining relationship exists between a league and a players association, labor policy favors limiting antitrust liability. Thus, if the league is engaged in lawful collective bargaining activities, the labor exemption will continue to insulate the employer from antitrust liability. The Court clarified, however, that it did not intend its holding to "insulate from antitrust liability every joint imposition of terms by employers, for an agreement amongst employers could be sufficiently distant in time and circumstances from the collective bargaining process that a rule permitting antitrust intervention would not significantly interfere with that process" (*Brown* at p. 250). Yet the Court did not give an example of such time and circumstance, as is shown in this Case Opinion.

Brown v. Pro Football, Inc.

CASE OPINION   518 U.S. 231 (1996)

FACTS

In 1987 the NFL–NFLPA CBA expired. The NFL and NFLPA began to negotiate a new contract, and in March 1989, during the negotiations, the NFL adopted Resolution G-2, a plan that would permit each club to establish a "developmental squad" of up to six rookies who, as free agents, had failed to secure a position on a roster. Squad members would practice and play in regular games as substitutes for injured players. Resolution G-2 provided that the club owners would pay all squad members the same weekly salary.

In April, the NFL presented the developmental squad plan to the NFLPA. The NFL proposed a fixed squad player salary of $1,000 per week. The NFLPA disagreed, insisting that the club owners give developmental squad players benefits and protections similar to those provided regular players and that they allow players to negotiate their salaries individually. Two months later, negotiations on the issue of developmental squad salaries reached an impasse. The NFL then unilaterally implemented the developmental squad program by distributing to the clubs a uniform contract that embodied the terms of Resolution G-2 and the $1,000 proposed weekly salary. The NFL advised club owners that paying developmental squad players more or less than $1,000 per week would result in disciplinary action, including the loss of draft choices.

In May 1990, 235 developmental squad players brought this suit against the NFL, claiming that their employers' agreement to pay them a fixed $1,000 weekly salary violated the Sherman Antitrust Act. The federal district court denied the employers' claim of exemption from the antitrust laws; it permitted the case to reach the jury, and it subsequently entered judgment on a jury treble-damages award that exceeded $30 million. The NFL and its member clubs appealed.

The court of appeals (by a split 2:1 vote) reversed. The majority interpreted the labor laws as waiving antitrust liability through the collective bargaining process, so long as such restraints operate primarily in a labor market characterized by collective bargaining. The court held, consequently, that the club owners were immune from antitrust liability. Brown appealed to the U.S. Supreme Court.

HOLDING

The U.S. Supreme Court upheld the Appeals Court decision that the development squad fixed wage was immune from antitrust liability due to the labor exemption.

RATIONALE

The immunity is what the U.S. Supreme Court has called the "nonstatutory" labor exemption from antitrust laws. The petitioners and their supporters concede, as they must, the legal existence of the exemption. They also concede that, where its application is necessary to make the statutorily authorized collective bargaining process work as Congress intended, the exemption must apply both to employers and employees. Consequently, the question in this case is one of determining the exemption's scope: Does it apply to an agreement among several employers bargaining together to implement after impasse the terms of their last best good-faith wage offer? Assuming that such conduct is unobjectionable as a matter of labor law and policy, we conclude that the exemption applies.

Labor law itself regulates directly, and considerably, the kind of behavior here at issue – the post-impasse imposition of a proposed employment term concerning a mandatory subject of bargaining. Both the NLRB and the courts have held that, after impasse, labor law permits employers unilaterally to implement changes in pre-existing conditions, but only insofar as the new terms meet carefully circumscribed conditions. For example, the new terms must be "reasonably comprehended" within the employer's pre-impasse proposals (typically the last rejected proposals), lest by imposing more or less favorable terms, the employer unfairly undermined the union's status. The collective bargaining proceeding itself must be free of any unfair labor practice, such as an employer's failure to have bargained in good faith. These regulations reflect the fact that impasse and an accompanying implementation of proposals constitute an integral part of the bargaining process. ...

Although the prior case law focuses upon bargaining by a single employer, no one here has argued that labor law does, or should, treat *multiemployer* bargaining differently in this respect. Indeed, the NLRB and court decisions suggest that the joint implementation of proposed terms after an impasse is a familiar practice in *multiemployer* bargaining.

* * *

In these circumstances, to subject the practice to antitrust law is to require antitrust courts to answer a host of important practical questions about how collective bargaining over wages, hours, and working conditions is to proceed – the very result that the implicit labor exemption seeks to avoid. And it is to place in jeopardy some of the potentially beneficial labor-related effects that multiemployer bargaining can achieve. That is because unlike labor law, which sometimes welcomes anticompetitive agreements conducive to industrial harmony, antitrust law forbids all agreements among competitors (such as competing employers) that unreasonably lessen competition among or between them in virtually any respect whatsoever. If the antitrust laws apply, what are employers to do once impasse is reached? If all impose terms similar to their last joint offer, they invite an antitrust action premised upon identical behavior (along with prior or accompanying conversations) as tending to show a common understanding or agreement. If any, or all, of them individually impose terms that differ significantly from that offer, they invite an unfair labor practice charge. Indeed, how can employers safely discuss their offers together even before a bargaining impasse occurs? A pre-impasse discussion about, say, the practical advantages or disadvantages of a particular proposal invites a later antitrust claim that they agreed to limit the kinds of action each would later take should an impasse occur. The same is true of post-impasse discussions aimed at renewed negotiations with the union. Nor would adherence to the terms of an expired CBA eliminate a potentially plausible antitrust claim charging that they had "conspired" or tacitly "agreed" to do so, particularly if maintaining the status quo were not in the immediate economic self-interest of some. All this is to say that to permit antitrust liability here threatens to introduce instability and uncertainty into the collective bargaining process, for antitrust law often forbids or discourages the kinds of joint discussions and behavior that the collective bargaining process invites or requires.

We do not see any obvious answer to this problem. We recognize, that, in principle, antitrust courts might themselves try to evaluate particular kinds of employer understandings, finding them "reasonable" (hence lawful) where justified by collective bargaining necessity. But any such evaluation means a web of detailed rules spun by many different non-expert antitrust judges and juries, not a set of labor rules enforced by a single expert administrative body, namely the NLRB. The labor laws give the NLRB, not antitrust courts, primary responsibility for policing the collective bargaining process. And one of their objectives was to take from antitrust courts the authority to determine, through application of the antitrust laws, what is socially or economically desirable collective bargaining policy.

Petitioners also say that irrespective of how the labor exemption applies elsewhere to multiemployer collective bargaining, professional sports is "special." We can understand how professional sports may be special in terms of, say, interest, excitement, or concern. But we do not understand how they are special in respect to labor law's antitrust exemption. We concede that the clubs that make up a professional sports league are not completely independent economic competitors, as they depend upon a degree of cooperation for economic survival. In the present context, however, that circumstance makes the league more like a single bargaining employer, which analogy seems irrelevant to the legal issue before us.

We also concede that football players often have special individual talents, and, unlike many unionized workers, they often negotiate their pay individually with their employers. But this characteristic seems simply a feature, like so many others, that might give employees (or employers) more (or less) bargaining power, that might lead some (or all) of them to favor a particular kind of bargaining, or that might lead to certain demands at the bargaining table. We do not see how it could make a critical legal difference in determining the underlying framework in which bargaining is to take place. Indeed, it would be odd to fashion an antitrust exemption that gave additional advantages to professional football players (by virtue of their superior bargaining power) that transport workers, coal miners, or meat packers would not enjoy. Ultimately, we cannot find a satisfactory basis for distinguishing football players from other organized workers. We therefore conclude that all must abide by the same legal rules. For these reasons, we hold that the labor exemption applies to the employer conduct at issue here. That conduct took place during and immediately after a collective bargaining negotiation. It grew out of, and was directly related to, the lawful operation of the bargaining process. It involved a matter that the parties were required to negotiate collectively. And it concerned only the parties to the collective bargaining relationship.

Our holding is not intended to insulate from antitrust review every joint imposition of terms by employers, for an agreement among employers could be sufficiently distant in time and in circumstances from the collective bargaining process that a rule permitting antitrust intervention would not significantly interfere with that process. We need not decide in this case whether, or where, within these extreme outer boundaries to draw that line. Nor would it be appropriate for us to do so without the detailed views of the NLRB, to whose specialized judgment Congress intended to leave many of the inevitable questions concerning multiemployer bargaining bound to arise in the future.

QUESTIONS

1 According to *Brown v. Pro Football*, when are actions involving labor relations in professional sport leagues no longer exempt from antitrust liability?

2 Is it fair to the union that the Court did not settle on a particular point in time at which the exemption from antitrust laws would end (i.e., expiration of the CBA, a strike or lockout, or impasse)?

As noted earlier in the chapter, in the past decade leagues have frequently pursued an offensive lockout strategy. In response, players have threatened to disclaim or decertify their players associations to gain leverage in collective bargaining negotiations. The disclaimer strategy has arisen in response to the *Powell v. NFL* (1989) decision, which held that the NFL was sheltered from antitrust liability by the labor exemption even after the CBA had expired and the parties had reached an impasse in negotiations. The message the players took from *Powell*, and later *McNeil v. NFL* (1992), was that in order to challenge restrictive practices in labor agreements, players must prevent the league from raising the labor exemption defense. By disclaiming the union, players are no longer parties to the CBA and the collective bargaining process. The players disclaim in the hope of filing a successful antitrust lawsuit. The players believe that gaining leverage, under the threat of treble damages, will enable them to negotiate a CBA more favorable toward their interests. In response, the owners have used lockouts fairly early in the negotiation process to economically challenge the players and gain leverage over them. Players' attempts at blocking such lockouts have failed (*Brady v. NFL*, 2011).

Federal labor policy favors collective bargaining between management and labor rather than employees resorting to the courts to gain leverage in the bargaining process. The next section will discuss collective bargaining negotiations and their product, CBAs.

Collective Bargaining Agreements

In collective bargaining negotiations, employees represented by their union and employers represented by a management team negotiate over mandatory subjects of bargaining, resulting in a contract called the CBA.

The CBA is a contract that is the product of collective bargaining negotiations. The collective bargaining relationship is an ongoing one. After the document is negotiated, it is drafted and ratified. During the term of the contract, there may be a need for changes. To change mandatory bargaining subjects (hours, wages, or terms and conditions of employment), union or management must initiate discussions and negotiations. Either side has the right to convince the other side to come back to the bargaining table to discuss or negotiate over a new or current term of employment. Managers who understand that unilateral changes in the workplace must be negotiated with the union before implementation will have a better relationship with employees and be less likely to face unfair labor practice charges. An exception to this rule occurs when the change qualifies as a management right, so-called "managerial decisions which lie at the core of entrepreneurial control" (*Ford Motor Co. v. NLRB* at 498, 1979).

Professional sports league CBAs have some key provisions that make up mandatory subjects for bargaining. These include the provisions shown below in Exhibit 7.5.

As you can see, some of the provisions do not fit neatly in the categories chosen for them, and some actually fit in more than one category. For instance, no strike–no lockout provisions do affect hours, because they give an expectation that players will work and will be allowed to work. They also, obviously, affect wages. The same can be said for the draft, free agency, and other player mobility provisions. In the next section, we explore in greater detail some of the critical aspects of collective bargaining.

Discipline

CBAs include at least one provision devoted to employee discipline. Discipline provisions are intertwined with grievance arbitration, which serves as the mechanism to challenge disciplinary action. The phrase "just cause" often appears in discipline provisions. This refers to a level of scrutiny used in evaluating whether an employee deserves the discipline rendered and, thus, sets limits on an employer's authority. It refers to cause (reason) for termination that is just, reasonable, honest, and fair.

Exhibit 7.5 Mandatory subjects for bargaining in professional sports CBAs.

Wage Provisions	Hour Provisions	Terms and Conditions of Employment
Salary caps/luxury taxes (team wide or based on players' service)	Training/spring training	Grievance arbitration: injury, medical, and labor grievance
Minimum salaries	Season schedule	Free agency
Fines	Postseason play	Draft
Salary arbitration	Travel	Discipline
Termination and severance pay	All-star game	Drug and/or human growth hormone testing
Licensing revenues	Exhibition games	Locker room and parking policies
Per diem pay	Charitable commitments	Player conduct
Fringe benefits (pensions, life and health insurance, etc.)	Winter or summer leagues	Health issues (medical care, access to records, right to second opinion)
Tickets	No strike–no lockout	Roster size (limits)
Charitable contributions	Public relations and promotional commitments	Anti-collusion policies

By negotiating discipline provisions, players have limited, or at the very least, better defined Commissioner powers. Grievance arbitration has also cut into the Commissioner's powers, since historically the Commissioner served as the arbitrator in disputes between players and the league or teams. By and large, this is still the case in on-field misconduct cases and one need only look to the Tom Brady deflategate case in the NFL to know that the Commissioner in the NFL retains the broadest power to not only assess a penalty, but to also serve as arbiter of the appeal (NFL Management Council v. NFLPA, 2016). Generally, outside of the NFL, the grievance process specifies that the player must first take his grievance to the Commissioner and then, based upon the outcome of that decision, may accept it or proceed to a neutral arbitration process. In the Brady case, the Second Circuit Court of Appeals found that Article 46 of the NFL–NFLPA CBA "empowers the Commissioner to take disciplinary action against a player he "reasonably judges" has engaged in conduct detrimental to the integrity or public confidence in the game of professional football" (NFLMC v. NFLPA, 2016). Article 46 allows the Commissioner to appoint a hearing officer to hear an appeal of his disciplinary action. Commissioner Goodell appointed himself and then confirmed the disciplinary action against Brady. Brady and the NFLPA appealed and the district court judge overturned Commissioner Goodell's decision on the grounds that Brady did not have sufficient notice that he could be suspended and not just fined for deflating footballs and because the NFL did not allow him to question certain NFL witnesses. On appeal, the court overturned the district court ruling in accordance with the federal labor policy of deferring to arbitration decisions as discussed in the MLBPA v. Garvey case below. Federal labor policy mandates judicial deference to arbitration when it is adopted through collective bargaining negotiation and deference to an arbitrator's decision unless it exceeds the scope of its authority or violates the CBA in any way. Since the union and Brady have agreed to give Commissioner Goodell the power to serve as arbitrator over his own decisions, the Second Circuit found that Brady must live with that decision. In coming to its conclusion, the court presumed that the NFLPA and Brady have equal bargaining power at the bargaining table and thus, should renegotiate a change in the Commissioner's powers through collective bargaining rather than challenge those powers in court. The NFLPA has ceded power to the NFL's Commissioner via Article 46 and thus, must abide by his decisions until Article 46 is renegotiated. Exhibit 7.6 presents excerpts on discipline from the North American league CBAs (the CBAs can be hundreds of pages long). This exhibit provides examples of disciplinary policies across leagues, as well as some specific aspects of the disciplinary policies common to the leagues, such as on-field vs. off-field misconduct, process for the gathering of evidence, right to hearings, processes for appeal, whether appeals are to the Commissioner or an impartial arbitrator, as well as fines and suspensions. As you review the discipline policies, pay close attention to the

Exhibit 7.6 Discipline.

	"One Penalty" Rule — A player cannot be disciplined by both the team and league for the same infraction	Fines	Advanced Notice of Disciplinary Action	Repeat Offenders
NFL-NFLPA Article 46: Commissioner Discipline NBA-NBPA Article VI: Player Conduct	"The Commissioner's disciplinary action will preclude or supersede disciplinary action by any Club for the same act or conduct." "The NBA's disciplinary action will preclude or supersede disciplinary action by any Team for the same act or conduct."	"A player may assert, … that any fine should be reduced because it is excessive when compared to the player's expected earnings for the season in question." "1/145th of the player's Base Compensation for each missed Exhibition, Regular Season or Playoff game for any suspension of less than twenty (20) games."	"The Commissioner will promptly send written notice of his action to the player, with a copy to the NFLPA." "The NBA shall provide the [NBPA] with such advance notice as is reasonable in the circumstances of any interview … by the NBA for alleged misconduct."	— "Repeat offenders will be subject to enhanced discipline."
NHL-NHLPA Article 18: Supplementary Discipline For On-Ice Conduct & Article 18-A: Commissioner Discipline For Off-Ice Conduct	—	"A fine may be in an amount up to 50% of the [Player's Salary] … but in no event shall it exceed $10,000 for the first fine and $15,000 for any subsequent fine imposed in any rolling twelve (12) month calendar period."	"The League agrees to notify the NHLPA immediately upon deciding to undertake an investigation that may result in Commissioner Discipline."	"Status as a "first" or "repeat" offender shall be re-determined every 18 months on a rolling basis."
MLB-MLBPA Article XII: Discipline	"A Club may only discipline a Player, or take other adverse action against him, when the Commissioner defers the disciplinary decision to the Club."	"A fine imposed by a Club … in excess of $10,000 may not be deducted from the Player's salary until such fine is finally upheld in the Grievance Procedure or the time in which to file a Grievance has expired."	"Written notice of discipline of a Player … imposed by the Commissioner of Baseball … or a Club … and the reason therefore shall in every case be given to the Player and the Association."	—
MLS-MLSPU Article 20: Discipline; Rules and Regulations	"In the event that both the Team and the League impose discipline for the same conduct, only the League-imposed discipline shall be effective."	"The maximum fine for tardiness for Players earning up to $400,000 in base salary for a second offense shall be $300."	"The Union will be provided with prompt notice of any Team discipline."	"Players will receive a warning for their first incident involving tardiness to a scheduled practice, medical appointment, appearance, Team meeting, or other Team function."
WNBA-WNBPA Article VI: Player Conduct	The WNBA's disciplinary action will preclude or supersede disciplinary action by any Team for the same act or conduct	"The WNBA and/or a Team may impose reasonable discipline on a player for any act or omission that fails to conform to the requirements set forth in Section 1 above. Such discipline may include reasonable fines and/or suspensions.	"The WNBA shall provide the [WNBPA] with such advance notice as is reasonable in the circumstances of any interview … by the WNBA for alleged misconduct."	"Repeat offenders will be subject to enhanced discipline."

differences in language and definitions, compare and contrast the processes, fines and suspensions, and who holds the power to levy discipline as well as whom decides appeals.

Dispute Resolution for Labor Disputes

When disputes arise in the labor relationship, they are often resolved through arbitration per the arbitration clause in the CBA. Arbitration is a process whereby the parties to a dispute choose to resolve it by jointly hiring a neutral third-party arbitrator to render a decision that is final and binding (see Chapter 2). It is a less costly, more efficient alternative to the court system or to a strike or a lockout as a means of resolving a disagreement. Arbitration clauses are common in labor agreements and are used by employees and employers to resolve disputes over interpretations of the CBA or to challenge disciplinary action. **Rights arbitration** is for disputes over the interpretation or application of a contract. **Interest arbitration** deals with disputes over the terms of contracts, such as salary arbitration (*Silverman v. MLBPRC*, 1995). First, we will explore examples of rights arbitration such as a player grievance alleging violations of the CBA and then interest arbitration in the form of a salary dispute.

Disputes will arise during the term of an agreement regardless of the quality of negotiating or the clarity of the language in the CBA. These disputes can be lodged through a grievance process, which should be negotiated into the CBA. The first step in the process takes place when one party files a grievance against the other. Unions generally file these on behalf of their employees. Grievance processes typically include the five steps shown in Exhibit 7.7. Often, the parties will seek an informal resolution before filing a grievance in an attempt to avert a grievance.

Player Grievances Alleging CBA Violations

For arbitration to work, both sides must agree that the arbitrator's decision is final and binding. Three U.S. Supreme Court cases in 1960, known collectively as the *Steelworkers* Trilogy, established federal policy that:

- courts should enforce arbitration clauses;
- they should do so without inquiring into the merits of a grievance;
- they should not intervene in an arbitrator's decision, provided that the arbitrator's award is based on the essence of the CBA.
  (See *U.S. Steelworkers v. American Mfg. Co.*, 1960; *U.S. Steelworkers v. Enterprise Corp.*, 1960; *U.S. Steelworkers v. Warrior Gulf Co.*, 1960.)

In other words, a court presumes that parties with a contract containing an arbitration clause should use it and a court should not substitute its decision for the arbitrator's decision. A court can overturn a decision only where the plaintiff can prove that the arbitrator abused his/her discretion or exceeded the scope of her authority, for example, by conflicting with express terms of the CBA, imposing disciplinary action, or crafting a resolution that is not expressly allowed in the contract.

Exhibit 7.7 Steps for resolving disputes leading to arbitration.

1   An employee discusses a grievance with the union rep or steward or reports it directly to a supervisor.
2   If the union representative and the employee agree the grievance has merit, they submit a formal written grievance.
3   The union representative and a management representative attempt to resolve the grievance.
4   The grievance may be heard before a committee to assist the two sides in resolving the dispute.
5   An arbitration hearing is held and an independent arbitrator or panel of arbitrators renders a decision.

The following Case Opinion illustrates how the Supreme Court strictly upholds the decision of an arbitrator, in line with the *Steelworkers* Trilogy discussed above.

Major League Baseball Players Association v. Garvey

CASE OPINION   532 U.S. 504 (2001)

FACTS

The MLBPA filed grievances against Major League Baseball clubs claiming they had colluded in the market for free-agent services after the 1985, 1986, and 1987 seasons, in violation of their CBA. A free agent is a player who may contract with any club, rather than one whose right to contract is restricted to a particular club. In a series of decisions, arbitrators found collusion by the clubs and damage to the players. The MLBPA and clubs entered into a Global Settlement Agreement, pursuant to which the clubs established a $280 million fund to be distributed to injured players. The MLBPA also designed a "Framework" to resolve individual players' claims, and, applying that Framework, recommended distribution plans for claims relating to a particular season or seasons. The Framework provided that players could seek an arbitrator's review of the distribution plan. The arbitrator would determine "only whether the approved Framework and the criteria set forth therein have been properly applied in the proposed distribution plan." The Framework set forth factors to be considered in evaluating players' claims, as well as specific requirements for lost contract-extension claims, where a player had a specific offer that was made and withdrawn due to collusion.

Steve Garvey, a retired, highly regarded first baseman, submitted a claim for damages of approximately $3 million. He alleged that his contract with the San Diego Padres was not extended to the 1988 and 1989 seasons due to collusion. The players association rejected Garvey's claim in February 1996, because he presented no evidence that the Padres actually offered to extend his contract. Garvey objected, and an arbitration hearing was held. He testified that the Padres offered to extend his contract for the 1988 and 1989 seasons and then withdrew the offer after they began colluding with other teams. He presented a June 1996 letter from Ballard Smith, the Padres' President and CEO from 1979 to 1987, stating that, before the end of the 1985 season, Smith offered to extend Garvey's contract through the 1989 season, but that the Padres refused to negotiate with Garvey thereafter due to collusion. The arbitrator denied Garvey's claim, after seeking additional documentation from the parties because he doubted Smith's credibility due to the "stark contradictions" between the 1996 letter and Smith's testimony in the earlier arbitration proceedings.

Garvey moved in federal district court to vacate the arbitrator's award, alleging that the arbitrator violated the Framework by denying his claim. The district court denied the motion. The court of appeals for the Ninth Circuit reversed by a divided vote. The court acknowledged that judicial review of an arbitrator's decision in a labor dispute is extremely limited, but it held that review of the merits of the arbitrator's award was warranted in this case, because the arbitrator "dispensed his own brand of industrial justice." The court recognized that Smith's prior testimony with respect to collusion conflicted with the statements in his 1996 letter. However, in the court's view, the arbitrator's refusal to credit Smith's letter was "inexplicable" and "border[ed] on the irrational," because a panel of arbitrators, chaired by the arbitrator involved here, had previously concluded that the owners' prior testimony was false. The court rejected the arbitrator's reliance on the absence of other corroborating evidence, attributing that fact to Smith and Garvey's direct negotiations. The court also found that the record provided "strong support" for the truthfulness of Smith's 1996 letter. The court of appeals reversed and remanded with directions to vacate the award.

The district court then remanded the case to the arbitration panel for further hearings, and Garvey appealed. The court of appeals reversed the district court and directed that it remand the case to the arbitration panel with instructions to enter an award for Garvey in the amount he claimed.

HOLDING

The Ninth Circuit Court of Appeals erred in reversing the order of the District Court denying the motion to vacate the arbitrator's award, and it erred further in directing that judgment be entered in Garvey's favor.

RATIONALE

Judicial review of a labor-arbitration decision pursuant to such an agreement is very limited. Courts are not authorized to review the arbitrator's decision on the merits despite allegations that the decision rests on factual errors or misinterprets the parties' agreement. It is only when the arbitrator strays from interpretation and application of the agreement and effectively "dispense[s] his own brand of industrial justice" that his decision may be unenforceable. When an arbitrator resolves disputes regarding the application of a contract, and no dishonesty is alleged, the arbitrator's "improvident, even silly, fact finding" does not provide a basis for a reviewing court to refuse to enforce the award.

To be sure, the Court of Appeals here recited these principles, but its application of them is nothing short of baffling. The substance of the court's discussion reveals that it overturned the arbitrator's decision because it disagreed with the arbitrator's factual findings, particularly those with respect to credibility. The Court of Appeals, it appears, would have credited Smith's 1996 letter, and found the arbitrator's refusal to do so at worst "irrational" and at best "bizarre." But even "serious error" on the arbitrator's part does not justify overturning his decision, where, as here, he is construing a contract and acting within the scope of his authority.

In *Garvey II*, the court clarified that *Garvey I* both rejected the arbitrator's findings and went further, resolving the merits of the parties' dispute based on the court's assessment of the record before the arbitrator. For that reason, the court found further arbitration proceedings inappropriate. But again, established law ordinarily precludes a court from resolving the merits of the parties' dispute on the basis of its own factual determinations, no matter how erroneous the arbitrator's decision. Even when the arbitrator's award may properly be vacated, the appropriate remedy is to remand the case for further arbitration proceedings. The Court of Appeals usurped the arbitrator's role by resolving the dispute and barring further proceedings, a result at odds with this governing law.

For the foregoing reasons, the Court of Appeals erred in reversing the order of the District Court denying the motion to vacate the arbitrator's award, and it erred further in directing that judgment be entered in Garvey's favor. The petition for a writ of certiorari is granted, the judgment of the Court of Appeals is reversed, and the case is remanded for further proceedings consistent with this opinion.

QUESTIONS

1   According to *MLBPA v. Garvey*, what is the standard for a court to use to vacate an arbitrator's award?

2   Supreme Court Justice Stevens strongly dissented with the majority decision in the *MLBPA v. Garvey* decision above. Stevens argued that, even in cases where the court sees clearly that the arbitrator's decision is irrational and the correct disposition of the matter is perfectly clear to the court, the only solution under *Garvey* would be to remand the decision for a new arbitration case, he found such a solution flawed. Do you agree or disagree with Stevens that courts should have some limited power to overturn arbitration decisions when it is obvious that the arbitrator erred?

Salary Disputes and Arbitration

As stated previously, arbitration clauses in CBAs specify that disputes over certain players' salaries be settled through arbitration. For example, through collective bargaining negotiations, both MLB and the NHL provide for disputes between an owner and an eligible player over the player's salary to proceed through arbitration processes. Both systems share the same goal of determining a player's worth for the upcoming season, but they are notably different. Baseball's system is "final offer," meaning the arbitrators must choose one side or the other's final offer. The arbitrators do this by choosing the midpoint between the two offers and determining whether the player is worth more or less than that midpoint. If more, the player's salary demand is met. If less, the club's salary offer becomes the salary for the upcoming season. In hockey, arbitrators have the ability to choose either an offer or an amount between the two offers. It is not a process for the faint of heart, as a player is forced to listen to the team argue as to why the player is not worth the value he seeks.

Player eligibility, the specific process, and the criteria for judging a player's worth also differ between baseball and hockey. Baseball players with at least three years but less than six years of major league service are eligible to file for salary arbitration. Those players considered "super twos" (the top 22 percent of major league service time for second-year players who have accumulated at least 86 days of service in the previous season) and those free agents whose clubs have elected salary arbitration are also eligible. Eligibility for the top 22 percent of players is determined annually. In 2018, the top 22 percent of players were those with at least two years and 134 games of service time and in 2017, it was two years and 123 games. NHL players are eligible for salary arbitration based upon a combination of their age at the time of their first contract and their seasons of service time. A season is considered ten or more games. Below are the qualifications for eligibility:

- Age 18–20 with four years of professional experience.
- Age 21 with three years of professional experience.
- Age 22–23 with two years of professional experience.
- Age 24 or older with one year of professional experience.

NHL clubs have the right to elect salary arbitration in lieu of making a qualifying offer. A qualifying offer is an offer that must be extended to a restricted free agent to retain negotiating rights to that player. Players making equal to or less than $660,000 must be offered 110 percent of the previous year's salary. Those earning from $660,000 to $1 million must be offered between 105 percent of $660,000 and $1 million, and those earning over $1 million must be offered 100 percent of $1 million NHL salary arbitration identifies two classes of players: Group I who earned more than $1.75 million in their previous season and Group II players eligible for salary arbitration who themselves choose not to go to salary arbitration. See Exhibit 7.8 comparing the baseball and hockey processes.

Additional Issues Involved in Professional Sport Collective Bargaining

While a significant amount of attention is focused on player grievances and salary disputes, the CBA covers a host of additional issues that the parties must negotiate in order to maintain labor peace and a well-managed league. Recently, issues of critical importance for the leagues include drug testing, salary caps, individual player contract provisions, and rights of retired players and college athletes. We will explore each of these next.

Drug Testing

The NLRB has held that drug and alcohol testing of employees is a mandatory subject for bargaining (*Johnson-Bateman Co. v. International Association of Machinists*, 1989). Although Congress has begun to press all

Exhibit 7.8 Salary arbitration comparison for MLB and NHL.

Salary Arbitration	Major League Baseball	National Hockey League
Eligibility	All players with at least three but less than six years of major league service time Super 2s – top 22 percent of players with at least two but less than three years of service time and at least 86 days of service in the immediately preceding season Free agents whose clubs opt for salary arbitration	Group II free agents (see footnote 5 for Group II definition) Club may opt for it if: Player is eligible for qualifying offer and is a Group II free agent with prior salary plus bonuses in excess of $1.75 million Player is a Group II free agent who has not accepted qualifying offer
Criteria	Contribution to club during past season Length and consistency of career contribution Past compensation Comparable baseball salaries (most weight to players within one year of player's service time) Physical or mental defects Recent club performance	Overall performance of player and Comparable players Number of games Length of service Overall contribution to club success Special leadership or public appeal Compensation of comparables
Inadmissible Evidence	Information on noncomparable players Financial condition of player and club (inability to pay) Testimonials, newspaper clippings, etc. Prior offers or negotiation history Cost to the parties of the arbitration process Salaries in other sports or professions	Information on noncomparable players Testimonials, newspaper clippings, etc. Reference to actual or potential walkaway rights Financial condition of club Prior offers or negotiation history Any prior award made to player
Arbitrator's Decision	No written decision or opinion, only chooses club offer or player demand Decision made within 24 hours of hearing	Written decision includes contract term, base salary, bonuses, inclusion of minor league salary, and statement of reasons for decision Decision made within 48 hours of close of hearing

sports for uniform drug testing, policies achieved through collective bargaining are more likely to be effective in protecting the rights and obligations of employees and employers, especially employee rights. Through a bargaining process, management and players will negotiate to develop fair provisions in regard to issues such as players' privacy rights; confidentiality surrounding the testing process and the results of tests; medical concerns that arise from the testing; the determination of which drugs to test for and what amounts of those drugs in one's system will subject a player to suspension; concerns over "what else" the organization might test for or might discover in testing; and the role of drug-testing results in international competition.

At the bargaining table the two sides may consider whether to include educational and rehabilitative components in the policies. The two sides can also negotiate testing policies and procedures in the context of other aspects of their employment relationship, such as disciplinary actions and arbitration provisions. Finally, the collective bargaining process is just that – a process. It is the negotiation of an agreement that will be interpreted and administered on a daily basis – an agreement that can be renewed, reviewed, and renegotiated when the parties find that conditions have evolved in such a way as to require the two sides to come back to the bargaining table to reopen the agreement.

Drug-testing provisions cover two categories of drugs: substances of abuse and performance enhancers. Substances of abuse are recreational drugs such as marijuana, cocaine, LSD, and the like. Performance enhancers are drugs such as anabolic steroids, amphetamines, and so forth. Drug-testing provisions may include penalties, opportunities for rehabilitation, and education on substances. See Exhibit 7.9 for penalties and discipline provisions of the performance-enhancing drug policies in the CBAs for MLB, the NBA, the NFL, and the NHL.

Exhibit 7.9 Disciplinary penalties of performance-enhancing drug policies in the CBAs for MLB, the NBA, the NFL, and the NHL.

	MLB	NBA	NFL	NHL
1st Offense	50-game suspension	5-game suspension and mandatory attendance in NBA antidoping program	4-game suspension	20-game suspension without pay
2nd Offense	100-game suspension	10-game suspension and counseling	8-game suspension without pay	60-game suspension without pay
3rd Offense	Lifetime ban	25-game suspension and counseling	One-year suspension without pay	Lifetime ban
4th offense		Minimum two-year suspension		

Competitive Advantage Strategies

Labor Relations and Collective Bargaining

- If you serve as a sport manager in a unionized workplace (or one that could become unionized), have a working knowledge of labor laws.
- If you are a manager in an organization employing unionized workers, strive to understand and abide by the processes, procedures, and rules set forth in the CBA. it is useful to ask legal counsel to guide you through collective bargaining and related employment decisions. For instance, if disciplining a union member, the manager must follow the protocol and procedures set forth in the CBA to avoid the possibility of facing a grievance or arbitration.
- Before implementing management decisions, consult the CBA or your human resources or legal counsel to ensure that your decisions are in line with your organization's labor agreement.

Salary Caps

Collective bargaining over compensation encompasses all of the wage and benefit provisions. With the exception of salary caps, luxury taxes, fines, tickets, and licensing revenues, the list of provisions tends to be the same regardless of the field that the labor agreement covers. The past three decades in professional sports have seen salaries rise at increasing rates as players have engaged in collective bargaining. Collective bargaining (and the use of agents) has allowed players to gain leverage and a greater portion of the pool of owners' revenues, which has grown exponentially through media and stadium growth. As a result, negotiations in professional sports have increasingly centered on salary caps and other wage restrictions, as well as on luxury tax systems designed to limit the percentage of revenue devoted to player salaries. Creative negotiators on each side have created hard caps, with none or minimum exceptions for exceeding the team cap limits, as well as soft caps, which allow for exceptions, such as room to sign veteran players or to replace injured or retired players. As a result of effective bargaining by the MLBPA, MLB is the only North American major league without an actual salary cap. MLB, however, in 1997 adopted a luxury tax. The current model adopted in 2003 is called the Competitive Balance Tax through which clubs are taxed on the portion of team salary that exceeds a set tax threshold for team salaries. In 2019, the tax threshold was $206 million, in 2020 it increases to $208 million, and in 2021 (the final year of the CBA), it will be $210 million. With labor negotiations beginning, it will be interesting to follow the players approach. Critics have noted the Competitive Balance Tax is in reality a soft salary cap due to its restrictive combination of the taxation of teams with the loss of draft picks for teams that exceed the threshold for a second year in a row. The tax threshold has only been exceeded eight times. In the time period of 2003–2018 MLB revenues have grown by 188 percent ($3.85 billion to $10.3 billion) while the tax threshold has grown by just 68 percent in that same time period ($117 million to $206 million). There are also allegations of collusion in the free agent market by owners, the effect of which is to drive salaries down (Normandin, 2019).

The salary cap was used in professional sports prior to its adoption in the NBA in 1984, but it has come to prominence through its use in the NBA and the NFL. Since it is a mandatory subject for bargaining, a salary cap cannot be unilaterally imposed but must be negotiated with the players. The salary caps are very complex collective bargaining provisions, which take up numerous pages in the CBA. A cottage industry has developed for experts with the labor and financial know-how to maneuver through these provisions; they are known as **capologists**. In addition to the team salary cap, there are also caps that single out particular groups of players, such as rookies.

Salary caps operate by calculating in the aggregate certain league revenues that are defined in the CBA. The players as a group receive a percentage of those defined revenues, and the number of clubs in the league divides that number. The resulting figure is the team salary cap. Lock (1998, pp. 322–323) explains that,

> from an accounting standpoint, the operation of the [NFL] salary cap is straightforward and inflexible: the cumulative cap dollars contained in a team's player contracts simply cannot exceed the salary cap. The calculation of cap dollars expended by a team in its player contracts for any particular year, however, does not necessarily equal the actual dollars in its player contracts or dollars actually paid to its players. Instead, the salary cap creates a theoretical ceiling on the amount of money teams can spend on players in any particular year, subject to the league's rules for calculating cap dollars. Under league rules, the ceiling can be exceeded from a cash flow standpoint, depending on a team's attitude toward risk and its willingness to push cap dollars into future contract years.

Salary caps are not exclusively North American. The salary cap in Australian Rules Football went into effect in 1987 and the Rugby CBA covering all men's and women's professional rugby in Australia also has a salary cap. The current cap of $5.5 million per team is derived by allocating 29 percent of defined gross revenues and that teams are required to spend a minimum of 90 percent of the cap figure on salaries (Fairbairn, 2018). To put this in perspective with North American salary caps, players in the NFL receive approximately 47 percent of defined revenues, in the NHL and NBA it is approximately 50 percent, in the new 2020 WNBA CBA agreement they will split 50 percent as well, but in the MLS players who in 2017 received just 28 percent of defined revenues, will receive approximately 40 percent of defined revenues under the new 2020–2024 CBA agreement (Lough, 2018; Pagels, 2014; WNBA Players Association, 2020; Young, 2019).

Individual Player Agreements and Collective Bargaining

Unique to labor relations in professional sports is the individual bargaining power of the employees. Employee-athletes have separate individual contracts that bind them to their employer-clubs, but they are also parties, through their players associations, to CBAs. The CBA takes precedence over the individual contract, but the two must work in concert. If not, the individual contract may violate provisions in the CBA. For example, assume the minimum salary in a league is $500,000. If a player is willing to play for $250,000, and his agent negotiated such a salary, it would undermine the union's work in negotiating for a higher minimum. As a result, the union has the right to "control" agents through the collective bargaining relationship. This is allowed under labor and antitrust laws so the union can protect its collective bargaining terms, because agents might otherwise "undercut" the terms that the union has negotiated on behalf of the players. Unions cannot act to restrict agents' activities in other aspects of the players' professional career and decision-making, such as marketing or financial advising. That said, the NFLPA does have a voluntary registration program for financial advisors due to a history of incompetent and fraudulent behavior by financial advisors toward football players. The key is that it is voluntary, not mandatory.

Unions and Rights of Retired Players

The National Football League Players Association and its marketing arm, Players, Inc., settled a lawsuit over their contractual and fiduciary duties to market retired players. The retired players, in *Parrish v. National Football League Players, Inc.* (2009), won a jury award of $28.1 million due to the NFLPA and Players, Inc.'s breach of their duty to market the retired players' names and likenesses. At issue was whether the defendants undertook a fiduciary duty to promote and to market all retired players who had signed Retired Player Group License Agreements (RPGLAs) but made no effort to do so and, further, whether the defendants' true commercial motive was to create an illusion of representation so that no one else would seek to sign up the retired players and to market them. The settlement of this case provided more than 2,000 former NFL players with $26.25 million, plus attorneys' fees and costs of an additional $6.53 million.

As noted earlier in the chapter, a question has arisen as to what responsibilities unions and leagues have to retired players who find in later years that they are subject to debilitating health as a result of injuries in their playing careers, particularly those due to CTE from concussions. Complicating the NFLPA cases is the fact that retired players have not felt the union has represented their interests. The challenge here, as in many unions, is that the current players are the ones who are union members, pay the dues, and vote on the union's leadership and direction. This situation results in union leaders focusing on current players, not previous union members (or future union members, for that matter). This creates a situation where the retirees are forced to seek relief through the courts, as we are seeing with concussion-related litigation, or through the benevolence of the two sides to allocate funds toward retiree benefits through collective bargaining or other means.

Unions and Rights of College Athletes

In 2014, a group of Northwestern University football players filed a petition with the NLRB's Regional Office in Chicago (Region 13) seeking an election to determine if College Athletes Players Association (CAPA) could become their exclusive bargaining representative. Northwestern University argued that scholarship athletes were not employees under Section 2(3) of the NLRA that defines employees. The Region 13 Director issued a decision finding that grant-in-aid scholarship football players at Northwestern were in fact employees (Northwestern and CAPA, 2014). The players were allowed to vote in an election, but the votes were impounded as Northwestern appealed the decision to the full National Labor Relations Board. The NLRB held that it did not have jurisdiction, rather than considering whether the grant-in-aid (scholarship) athletes were employees or not. Instead, the Board determined it would not promote stability in college athletics labor relations to assert jurisdiction due to the fact that the 125 NCAA Division 1 FBS football schools include a large number of public universities over which their state labor boards, rather than the NLRB will assert jurisdiction. Further, the nature of the NCAA is such that it exercises a high degree of control and supervision over FBS football through its rules and policies. The bottom line being that the NLRB indicated that asserting jurisdiction over a single football team in this case would impact all of those other NCAA member teams (Northwestern and CAPA, 2015). Interestingly, the NLRB did make clear that this was a unique circumstance and it did not preclude reconsideration of this issue in the future (NLRB, 2015).

As this text goes to print, there are four federal and 36 state bills proposed to grant college student-athletes the right to earn income from their name, image, and likeness, as well as some measures to address health and safety concerns. Three states, California, Colorado, and Florida have enacted state statutes (Masteralexis & Masteralexis, 2020). In late September 2019, California Governor Gavin Newsom signed the first bill into law, Senate Bill 206. Commonly called the Fair Play to Pay Act, it makes it illegal for California universities to revoke an athlete's scholarship or eligibility for taking money. Under the new law, schools will not pay athletes, but athletes can hire agents to seek compensation for marketing their name, image, and likeness (Benbow, 2019). California's law and Colorado's, which is modeled after California's, take effect on January 1, 2023. Florida's Governor signed its bill into law on June 12, 2020 and it takes effect on July 1, 2021. It is similar to California and Colorado's, but includes restrictions, such as stating payments to athletes must be market value in order to "preserve the integrity, quality, character, and amateur nature of intercollegiate sport," as well as not allowing colleges and universities to pay athletes directly (Murphy, 2020).

In response to the California law, NCAA President Mark Emmert predicted that the discussion of athletes as employees of the athletic department is looming. Moving on a parallel track to the California law, the NCAA has a working group of 19 high profile leaders in college athletics working on addressing athlete compensation issues because the law stands to conflict with NCAA amateurism and eligibility rules (Benbow, 2019). The NCAA has also requested that Congress look into creating a uniform statute rather than having different state laws throughout the nation. Beyond Congress, there may be a proposal from the Uniform Laws Commission (Murphy, 2020). All of these efforts are in lieu of unionization efforts by Division I athletes. So, while the athletes have not gained rights through collective bargaining, these statutes are changing the athletes' working conditions and if they are deemed employees by the NCAA, the NLRB could reasonably reconsider the issues raised in the Northwestern University case.

Emerging Issues: Women's Sport Negotiations

Labor relations in women's sports have evolved differently than in men's sports. For example, parental leave is often a topic of negotiation for women's leagues and is rarely mentioned in men's league collective bargaining negotiations. Additionally, women have taken a different approach to labor relations than have men, either by choice or based on circumstance, such as leverage or lack thereof. The MLS opened in 1996 and the players elected not to unionize, but instead sued the league the next year on the basis of antitrust, in an effort to challenge the structure and operation of player movement in the MLS which they argued worked to decrease player salaries (*Fraser v. MLS*, 1998). Around the same time (1996), the WNBA was created. In 1998, the WNBA players took a very different approach than the men in the MLS. The players chose to unionize, and cooperate with the upstart league in order to maintain labor peace and work with the league to grow the popularity of women's basketball, and women's sports in general. The result was a series of CBAs that rested much of the power in the hands of the WNBA, and drove even the most well-known players to compete in leagues overseas during the off-season in order to earn the type of desirable salary that was not being offered by the WNBA (Berri, 2018).

The patient approach to bargaining by the WNBPA has begun to yield positive results for the players, most notably with the new CBA that will last from 2020 through the 2027 season. The new deal provides players with increased financial opportunities as well as miscellaneous benefits that have been long sought-after by the union. With the signing of the new CBA, the WNBA agrees to a 50-50 share of league revenue with the players. The new revenue share agreement represents a significant increase in favor of the WNBPA, and closes the gap between the WNBA and the NBA, the latter of which has been employing a similar revenue sharing strategy for years (Antharaman, 2020).

In addition to increased financial incentives, the new CBA also includes other benefits for players and their families. Beginning with the 2020 season, all WNBA players will have solo hotel rooms and premium economy class air accommodations while traveling to away games. All players receive housing benefits, and players with children are entitled to a two-bedroom apartment, as well as maternity leave with full salaries. Parental leave is not mentioned in the CBA of the NBA financial incentives, the new CBA also includes a selection of other benefits for players and their families, such as a $5,000 childcare stipend, space for nursing mothers, and progressive family planning benefits of up to $60,000 in reimbursement costs (Antharaman, 2020; WNBA, 2020).

Another example of labor issues in women's sport is the ongoing story of the United States women's national soccer team, and their fight for equal pay compared to their male counterparts. Twenty-eight members of the US Women's National Team filed a gender discrimination suit in 2019 against the U.S. Soccer Federation. They raised the issue not only of pay inequality, but also of inferior working conditions such as healthcare, coaching, and travel accommodations compared to the men (Das, 2019). The women often play more games in a given year than the men, but are paid less annually. The complexity in assessing the situation is due to the fact that while both teams are paid and overseen by the U.S. Soccer Federation, they operate under separate CBAs. The U.S. Soccer Federation has responded that the differences are due to having two different CBAs, different revenue structures and different pay structures, but not due to sex (Associated Press, 2019). Members of the men's team are paid only if they make the team, while the women players receive a regular salary in addition to modest game bonuses. The resolution of the lawsuit is yet to be determined, as the world champion women's team continues to fight for equality, but the federation is trying to explain away the differences by hiding behind collective bargaining and a different structure for revenue and pay in women's soccer versus men's. Interestingly, the male players union has come out in support of the U.S. women's national team instructing the federation to stop its "false narrative" about the differences in collective bargaining and pay (Conley, 2020).

Emerging Issues: Unions and Rights of Minor League Athletes, eSports Athletes, and MMA Athletes

Collective bargaining provides opportunities for employees to negotiate with their employers over hours, wages, and terms and conditions of employment. While on the major league level in North America and in many international sports, collective bargaining between team sport athletes and their leagues is part of the working environment (see Exhibit 7.2), there are still many sports settings where collective bargaining is not the norm. Questions abound over athletes' rights in emerging sports such as eSports and mixed martial arts (MMA) organizations as well as NASCAR. The challenge these athletes face is whether individual athletes are independent contractors versus employees of organizations that have supervisory control over them. With emerging eSports teams and leagues, it is an issue that needs further evaluation. ESports has complexities that make it different from traditional sports, such as the worldwide nature of the leagues cause challenges as labor laws vary by country, the ages of the players, and the fact that the game companies own a license on the product. One commentator has suggested unions are needed and they might be best organized around games rather than leagues (Lavalli, 2019). Another group of potential union members are minor leaguers in baseball's multiple leagues and basketball's G-League. The G-League began voting on whether to unionize or not in April 2020 after receiving support from the NBPA (Zucker, 2020). In July 2021, the G-League players organized into a union that it named the Basketball Players Union (BPU). BPU has been recognized by the G-League as the players' exclusive bargaining agent for purposes of collective bargaining over mandatory subjects. The BPU will represent all G-League players, including those on the Select Team. Two-way players will continue to be represented by the NBPA (West, 2020). Two-way players are those with G-League and NBA contracts who move back and forth between the two leagues. The majority of their time is in the G-League with not more than 45 days in the NBA. Organizing the minor leagues will come with challenges, though, such as the constant movement of players, the vast geographic locations of teams hampering communication (although social media does help), the short-term careers, lower salaries, and disparities in bargaining power between stars and rank and file players.

Conclusion

Labor relations are a critical piece of the work environment in sports. Labor law has created a means for employees to bargain for safe and productive work environments. Labor laws, along with employment laws, delineate conduct that is acceptable in the work environment. The NLRA, in particular, sets forth the parameters of acceptable conduct by employers and employees in private-sector unionized workplaces. It sets forth a process of collective bargaining that allows employees and the employer to determine what issues must be resolved in their particular workplace to address through the negotiation process to develop a contract for their workplace. We find the most unionized workforces in the sport industry among professional athletes and in the facility management world. As a manager in the sport industry, it is critical that you make management decisions with an eye toward the CBA and its rules, policies, and procedures, lest you find yourself facing a grievance and arbitration process.

Discussion Questions

1 What factors make labor relations in professional sports unique, as opposed to labor relations in other industries?
2 What employee rights were gained through the National Labor Relations Act?
3 What do the NLRA and LMRA set forth as unfair labor practices?
4 Name five collective bargaining provisions for each mandatory subject of bargaining (hours, wages, and terms and condition of employment).
5 What is the role of arbitration in labor relations?
6 What is the labor exemption to antitrust? What is its relevance to professional sports labor relations?

Learning Activities

1 Conduct an Internet search for professional sport organization CBAs. Examine the provisions in the CBAs and assess whether the provisions relate to mandatory or permissive subjects for bargaining. Also, note how many niche or minor league sports are unionized. Good places to start are with Major League Soccer, the WNBA, the Pro Hockey Players Association (minor league hockey union) and internationally, Rugby Union or Football (soccer) leagues (Exhibit 7.2 in the chapter may provide some options). FIFPro is another place to look for international players associations as it serves as a trade association for the world's male and female football (soccer) players. As you evaluate the CBAs compare the complexities in those of established leagues versus those for whom collective bargaining is more recent. Examine professional sport league CBAs to compare and contrast the various provisions across leagues, such as those relating to drug testing, salary arbitration, grievance arbitration, salary caps, drafts, pensions, and other benefits. Also, discover whether there are provisions that are unique to each league.
2 Assume you are negotiating a new CBA in a league that has never been unionized, such as the NBA's G-League, minor league baseball, college athletics, or e sports. Another option is to use a league that has an expiring agreement. Research the key items for the negotiation and develop a strategy for CBA negotiations on the union or management side of the bargaining table.

Case Study

Assume the NBA's (Gatorade) G-League (G-League) players and front office staff joined forces and petitioned the NLRB for an election. The group voted to unionize and was certified. Within days of certification, G-LEAGUE owners voted to recognize the union only if bargaining occurred in local units in each city and only if they split off into two negotiating groups: players and front office staff. The owners also voted to adopt a more restrictive free agency system, add two new expansion teams, and set a date for an expansion draft. Further, G-LEAGUE owners enclosed a letter with the players' next contracts reminding them of the G-LEAGUE's loyalty to them when others deemed their careers over. The letter addressed the union movement by stating, "Opening the door to collective bargaining will only bring the G-LEAGUE the labor woes and financial disparities between large- and small-market teams faced by other leagues." The owners further argued that collective bargaining would drive them out of business financially and leave players unemployed.

The letter mobilized the player negotiating team. The lead negotiator was Trey Revelle. Revelle, a former NBA player who was banned two years ago for testing positive for marijuana and cocaine. Since then, Revelle underwent successful rehabilitation treatment and has been drug-free for two years. In fact, he spoke at the NBA–NBPA rookie training session on why players should avoid drugs. Revelle is currently playing in the G-LEAGUE to showcase his talents and get back on an NBA team.

Revelle left for a six-city tour to meet with G-LEAGUE players and held meetings in hotels far away from team facilities. During his meeting in Queens (NY), Revelle found himself face-to-face with the

G-LEAGUE Commissioner, who had been tipped off by one of the league's coaches. Their encounter ended in a shouting and shoving match. When Revelle reported to training camp the next month, he was the only player forced to submit to a G-LEAGUE-ordered drug test. The drug testing continued on a daily basis, leading many players to assume Revelle was back using drugs. Every test was negative. Revelle was also subjected to name-calling and criticism in the press by the coaching staff. This went on for three weeks, until Revelle cracked under the pressure and punched his coach. Later that evening, Revelle was notified that he was banned from the G-LEAGUE for violating the league' conduct policy.

1 Discuss whether Revelle has any rights under labor laws.
2 What other information would you need to gather to discover whether Revelle could challenge the Commissioner's decision?

Considering ... Analysis & Discussion

Labor Law in Practice

The first step for Darryl to take is to gather and bring to his nearest NLRB regional office signed authorization cards from at least 30 percent of the employees in an appropriate bargaining unit in his workplace. An appropriate bargaining unit is one in which the employees have common interests and will be seeking common goals in negotiation. The authorization cards are simply to authorize the NLRB to come in and run an election at the workplace, not to authorize a union. Once the cards are turned over to the NLRB and the unit is determined to be appropriate, the NLRB will come onsite to conduct an election. Often, workers in a union-organizing campaign will seek authorization cards from a majority of employees and then request that management voluntarily recognize the bargaining unit as the exclusive bargaining representative for the employees.

In terms of Darryl's organizing his co-workers, the NLRB has developed organizing rights for oral solicitation and literature distribution. In both cases, the solicitations must be made on the employee's free time. This could be free time within the constraints of the workday, such as during a break or during any time when employees are allowed to converse over non-work matters. The NLRB and courts have established the organizing rights and obligations of outside organizers and off-duty employees, but these issues are beyond the scope of this discussion.

In response to the question about what Bianca should do, she should not voluntarily recognize the union, in accordance with § 9 of the NLRA. Like most employers, BCSE probably does not want to lose control of business decisions regarding its employees. Under § 7 of the NLRA, once a union is in place, the employer must collectively bargain with employees over hours, wages, and terms and conditions of employment.

Further, what if the union led by Darryl Jones is not the only emerging union effort in the facility? If BCSE chooses Darryl's union over others, then further problems in the workplace may occur. Moreover, what if Darryl's complaints and actions are not representative of the rest of the employees at BCA? Then, by unilaterally and voluntarily recognizing Darryl's union, Bianca may have given a segment of her employees what they want, but she has not determined whether the whole workplace is interested in unionization. By going through the election and certification processes, BCSE will be assured that workers are properly placed in appropriate units for collective bargaining purposes. For instance, BCA's clerical staff might be best served in a different union group than its laborers or ushers and ticket takers.

If BCA does not want a unionized workplace, once management at BCSE is aware of a growing labor movement, it may decide to take active steps to stop the union from organizing. BCSE managers would have to move carefully in this effort so as not to violate the labor laws that protect employees who are organizing, joining, or assisting unions. It is important for Bianca to have a working knowledge of labor relations in her repertoire of skills.

> Bianca could present an anti-union speech to try to dissuade the employees from organizing. Bianca's speech can express her own or BCSE's opinions about the union, but it cannot include any threats to employees supporting the union, it cannot state that voting for the union is futile, it cannot appeal to racial prejudices, and it cannot promise benefits if the union is defeated. Under the "Peerless Plywood" rule, Bianca may speak against the union-organizing campaign on company time and may require her employees to attend a meeting and listen as a "captive audience." Bianca may not give an anti-union speech to a mass audience within 24 hours of the scheduled election, and she may not call employees into management areas that might intimidate them when she speaks to them about the union.
>
> Bianca must proceed carefully in dealing with Darryl Jones so as not to discriminate or retaliate. Doing so could make her vulnerable to an unfair labor practice charge for violating his NLRA § 7 rights to join or assist a union. Bianca should also seek out legal advice from BCSE attorneys before proceeding.

References

Cases

Allen Bradley Co. v. Local No. 3, I.B.E.W., 325 U.S. 797 (1945).

Boys Markets, Inc. v. Retail Clerks' Union, Local 770, 398 U.S. 235 (1970).

Brady v. NFL, 644 F. 3d 661 (8th Cir. 2011).

Bridgeman v. NBA, 838 F. Supp. 172 (D.N.J. 1987).

Brown v. Pro Football, Inc., 518 U.S. 231 (1996).

Clarett v. NFL, 369 F.3d 124 (2d Cir. 2004).

Commonwealth v. Hunt, 45 Mass. 111 (Mass S.J.C. 1842).

Commonwealth v. Pullis, Philadelphia Mayor's Court (1806).

Denver Rockets v. All-Pro Management, Inc., 325 F. Supp. 1049 (D.C. Cal. 1971).

Duplex Printing Press, Co. v. Deering, 254 U.S. 443 (1921).

Eller v. NFLPA, 872 F. Supp. 2d 823 (D. Minn. 2012).

Federal Baseball Club of Baltimore v. National League of Professional Baseball Clubs, 259 U.S. 200 (1922).

Flood v. Kuhn, 407 U.S. 258 (1972).

Ford Motor Co. v. NLRB, 441 U.S. 488, 498 (1979), quoting Fibreboard Corp. v. NLRB, 379 U.S. 203, 222–23 (1964) (Stewart, J. concurring).

Fraser v. Major League soccer, 7 F. Supp. 2d 73 (D. Mass. 1998).

Johnson-Bateman Co. v. International Ass'n of Machinists, 295 N.L.R.B. 180 (1989).

Linseman v. World Hockey Association, 439 F. Supp. 1315 (D.C. Conn. 1977).

Local No. 189, Amalgamated Meat Cutters & Butcher Workmen v. Jewel Tea Co., 381 U.S. 676 (1965).

Loewe v. Lawlor, 208 U.S. 274 (1908).

Mackey v. NFL, 543 F.2d 606 (8th Cir. 1976).

Major League Baseball Players Assn. v. Garvey, 532 U.S. 504 (2001).

McCourt v. California Sports, Inc., 600 F.2d 1193 (6th Cir. 1979).

McNeil v. NFL, 790 F. Supp. 871 (D. Minn. 1992).

Miranda Fuel Co., 140 N.L.R.B. 181 (1962).

Morio v. NASL, 501 F. Supp. 633 (S.D.N.Y. 1980) aff'd, 632 F.2d 217 (2d Cir. 1980).

NASL v. NLRB, 613 F.2d 1379 (5th Cir. 1980).

NBA v. Williams, 45 F.3d 684 (2d Cir. 1995).

NFL Management Council and NFLPA, 309 N.L.R.B. 78 (1992).

NFL Management Council v. NFLPA, 820 F. 3d 527 (2d Cir. 2016).

NFLPA v. NLRB, 503 F.2d 12 (8th Cir. 1974).

NLRB v. AFL and AFLPOC (unpublished case; see Beard Group, 2000, in below References for information)

NLRB v. Katz, 369 U.S. 736 (1962).

Nordstrom, d/b/a Seattle Seahawks and NFLPA, 292 N.L.R.B. 899 (1989).

Nordstrom, d/b/a Seattle Seahawks and NFLPA, 304 N.L.R.B. 78 (1991).

Northwestern University and College Athletes Players Association, 362 NLRB N. 167 (2015).

Northwestern University and College Athletes Players Association, Case No. 13-RC-121359 (2014).

Parrish v. National Football League Players, Inc., No. C07-00943 WHA (N.D. Calif. 2009).

Peerless Plywood Co., 107 N.L.R.B. 427 (1953).

Peterson v. Kennedy and NFLPA, 771 F.2d 1244 (9th Cir. 1985).

Powell v. NFL, 930 F.2d 1293 (8th Cir. 1989).

Reynolds v. NFL, 584 F.2d 280 (8th Cir. 1978).

Silverman v. MLB Player Relations Comm., 880 F. Supp. 246 (S.D.N.Y. 1995).

Smith v. Pro Football, Inc., 593 F.2d 1173 (D.C. Cir. 1978).

Steele v. Louisville & Nashville R.R. Co., 323 U.S. 192 (1944).

The American League of Professional Baseball Clubs and the Association of National Baseball League Umpires, 180 N.L.R.B. 190 (1969).

Toolson v. New York Yankees, 346 U.S. 917 (1953).

United Mine Workers v. Pennington, 381 U.S. 657 (1965).

United States v. Hutcheson, 32 F. Supp. 600 (E.D. Mo. 1940).

U.S. Steelworkers v. American Mfg. Co., 363 U.S. 564 (1960).

U.S. Steelworkers v. Enterprise Corp., 363 U.S. 593 (1960).

U.S. Steelworkers v. Warrior Gulf Co., 363 U.S. 574 (1960).

Vaca v. Sipes, 386 U.S. 171 (1967).

Wood v. NBA, 809 F.2d 954 (2d Cir. 1987).

Wright Line, a Division of Wright Line, Inc., 251 N.L.R.B. 1083 (1980), *enforced*, 662 F.2d 899 (1st Cir. 1981), *cert. denied*, 455 U.S. 989 (1982).

Statutes

Clayton Act of 1914, 15 USCS § 17 (2006).

Labor Management Relations Act (Taft-Hartley Act of 1947), 29 USCS § 141, *et seq.* (2005).

National Labor Relations Act, 29 USCS § 151, *et seq.* (2005).

Norris-LaGuardia Act of 1932, 29 USCS §§ 101–115 (2006).

Sherman Antitrust Act of 1890, 15 USCS § 1, *et seq.* (2006).

Other Sources

Antharaman, M. (2020, January 21). WNBA Players' New Contract Is a Good Step – but It's not Enough. *Slate.com*. Retrieved from https://slate.com/culture/2020/01/wnba-cba-contract-critique-progressive-inadequate.html.

APSCUF (2015). Collective bargaining agreement between the Association of Pennsylvania State Colleges and University Faculties and the Pennsylvania State System of Higher Education for the Non-Faculty Athletic coaches. (July 1, 2015–June 30, 2019). Retrieved from https://www.apscuf.org/contracts/APSCUFcoachesCBA2015-19.pdf.

Associated Press (2019, May 7). U.S. Soccer formally denies claims of gender discrimination in response to USWNT. *Sports Illustrated*. Retrieved from https://www.si.com/soccer/2019/05/07/us-soccer-uswnt-lawsuit-gender-discrimination-equal-pay-response.

Beard Group, Inc. (2000, September 19). Class action reporter. *Bankrupt.com*. Retrieved from http://bankrupt.com/CAR_Public/000919.MBX.

Benbow, D. H. (2019, October 3). NCAA president Mark Emmert says Fair Play to Pay Act turns student-athletes into employees. *Indianapolis Star*. Retrieved from https://www.indystar.com/story/sports/college/2019/10/03/ncaa-president-mark-emmert-responds-california-fair-play-pay-act/3850522002/.

Berri, D. (2018, September 4). WNBA players are simply asking for a greater share of WNBA revenues. *Forbes*. Retrieved from https://www.forbes.com/sites/davidberri/2018/09/04/what-wnba-players-want/#5727c7da33eb.

Commons, J. R., Phillips, U. B., Gilmore, E. A., Sumner, H. L., & Andrews, J. B. (1958). *A documentary history of American industrial society* (Vol. III). Cleveland, OH: The Arthur H. Clark Company.

Conley, J. (2020, February 3). In show of solidarity, U.S. Men's Soccer team slams officials for "Systematic" pay discrimination against USWNT. *Common Dreams*. Retrieved from https://www.theguardian.com/football/2019/jul/29/us-soccer-equal-pay-womens-players-mens-players-uswnt.

Cruise, D., & Griffiths, A. (1991). *Networth: Exploding the myth of pro hockey*. Toronto: Penguin.

Das, A. (2019, March 8). U.S. Women's Soccer team sues U.S. Soccer for gender discrimination. *New York Times*. Retrieved from https://www.nytimes.com/2019/03/08/sports/womens-soccer-team-lawsuit-gender-discrimination.html.

Fairbairn, P. (2018, September 1). Rugby welcomes new collective bargaining agreement. Retrieved from http://rupa.rugby/rupa-news/story/rugby-welcomes-new-collective-bargaining-agreement.

Feldacker, B. (2000). *Labor guide to labor law* (4th ed.). Upper saddle river, NJ: Prentice Hall.

Gold, M. E. (1998). *An introduction to labor law* (2nd ed.). Ithaca, NY: ILR Press/Cornell University Press.

Jennings, K. M. (1990). *Balls and strikes: The money game in professional baseball*. New York, NY: Praeger Publishers.

Lavalli, T. (2019, July 9). Has the time come for esports athletes to form a players union? *Online Gambling.com*. Retrieved from https://www.onlinegambling.com/news/2019/07/has-the-time-come-for-esports-athletes-to-form-a-players-union/.

Lock, E. (1998). The regulatory scheme for player representatives in the National Football League: The real power of Jerry Maguire. *American Business Law Journal*, 35(2), 319–347.

Lough, N. (2018, August 9). The case for boosting WNBA player salaries. *The Connection*. Retrieved from http://theconversation.com/the-case-for-boosting-wnba-player-salaries-100805.

Major League Soccer Players Association (2020). 2020–2024 Collective Bargaining Agreement. Retrieved from http://mlsplayers.org/2020-cba.

Masteralexis, L., & Masteralexis, J. (2020, March 5). *They finally killed the golden goose: An analysis of the recent legislative responses nationwide to income inequality in the NCAA*. Presentation at the Sport and Recreation Law Conference, Louisville, KY.

Murphy, D. (2020, June 13), Florida name, image, likeness bill now a law; state athletes can profit from endorsements next summer. *ESPN.com*. Retrieved from https://www.espn.com/college-sports/story/_/id/29302748/florida-name-image-likeness-bill-now-law-meaning-state-athletes-profit-endorsements-next-summer.

National Labor Relations Board (2015, August 17). Board unanimously decides to decline jurisdiction in the Northwestern Case. Retrieved from https://www.nlrb.gov/news-outreach/news-story/board-unanimously-decides-decline-jurisdiction-northwestern-case.

Normandin, M. (2019, January 31). MLB's luxury tax became a salary cap because of decades of failures. *Deadspin*. Retrieved from https://deadspin.com/mlbs-luxury-tax-became-a-salary-cap-because-of-decades-1832200596.

Pagels, J. (2014, August 19). Are salary caps for professional athletes fair? *Priceonomics*. Retrieved from https://priceonomics.com/are-salary-caps-for-professional-athletes-fair/.

Rabuano, M. M. (2002). Comment: An examination of drug testing as a mandatory subject of collective bargaining in Major League Baseball. *University of Pennsylvania Journal of Labor and Employment Law*, 4, 439.

Stover, T. (2018, February 12). The rise of esports: League of Legends takes on traditional sports (with their help). *Mindfray*. Retrieved from https://mindfray.com/debate/rise-esports-league-legends-traditional-sports/.

Weiler, P. C. (2000). *Leveling the playing field*. Cambridge, MA: Harvard University Press.

West, J. (2020, July 21). G League players for union with assistance from NBPA. *Sports Illustrated*. Retrieved from https://www.si.com/nba/2020/07/21/g-league-players-form-union/.

WNBA. (2020, January 14). WNBA and WNBPA reach tentative agreement on ground breaking eight-year collective bargaining agreement. *WNBA.com*. Retrieved from https://www.wnba.com/news/wnba-and-wnbpa-reach-tentative-agreement-on-groundbreaking-eight-year-collective-bargaining-agreement/.

Young, J. (2019, April 29). CBA talk: Comparing MLS player salaries to leagues around the world. *American Soccer Analysis*. Retrieved from https://www.americansocceranalysis.com/home/2019/4/22/cba-talk-comparing-mls-player-salaries-to-leagues-around-the-world.

Zucker, J. (2020, April 24). Report: NBA's G-League players begin voting Saturday on creation of union. *Bleacher Report*. Retrieved from https://bleacherreport.com/articles/2888519-report-nbas-g-league-players-to-begin-voting-saturday-on-creation-of-union.

Web Resources

https://www.dol.gov/OLMS/regs/compliance/cba/2019/private/30MajorClubs_K9831_060122.pdf ■ This site features Major League Baseball's collective bargaining agreement.

https://mlsplayers.org/resources/cba ■ This site features Major League Soccer's collective bargaining agreement. It is available in English, French, Portuguese, and Spanish.

https://www.nbpa.com/cba ■ This site features the National Basketball Association's collective bargaining agreement. https://nflpaweb.blob.core.windows.net/media/Default/PDFs/Active%20Players/2011%20CBA%20Updated%20with%20Side%20Letters%20thru%201-5-15.pdf ■ This site features the National Football League's collective bargaining agreement.

https://www.nhlpa.com/the-pa/cba ■ This site features the National Hockey League's collective bargaining agreement.

https://wnbpa.com/cba/ ■ This site features the Women's National Basketball Association's collective bargaining agreement.

https://fifpro.org/en/ ■ This site represents the worldwide association for all 60,000 professional footballers, male and female across the globe. It has great information about the World Players Union that currently has 65 national players associations as their members.

8 The Law of Agency and Athlete Agents

Lisa Pike Masteralexis

Introduction

Athlete representation, also known as the athlete agent or sport agent business, is a visible and highly publicized element of the sport industry. This segment of the sport industry presents many unique challenges for sport managers. This chapter introduces basic notions of agency law and how those principles apply in a sport management context. It explores in detail the specific laws applicable to athlete agents and the unique legal issues related to athlete representation. The first section discusses the creation of an agency relationship, the scope of authority of agents, and the duties between principals and agents. The second section focuses on specific issues and disputes that may arise between athletes and agents. The last section concentrates on the regulation of athlete agents in their dealings with student-athletes who still possess amateur eligibility, as well as the role of professional players associations in promoting the interests of professional athletes. Exhibit 8.1 presents the management contexts and applicable laws discussed in the chapter.

The Law of Agency

Agency is the relationship that arises when one party (or person), "the principal" manifests assent to another party, "the agent," that the agent shall act on the principal's behalf and subject to the principal's control, and the agent manifests assent or otherwise consents to do so (Restatement [Third] of Agency § 1.01 Agency Defined, 2006). Simply put, the term "agency" describes a relationship between two parties in which one party (the agent) agrees to act as a representative of the other party (the principal). The principal is the person hiring or engaging the agent to act on behalf of the principal or to perform certain duties for the principal. One important aspect of this relationship is that the agent has a **fiduciary duty** to act loyally for the principal's benefit in all matters connected with the agency relationship (Restatement [Third] of Agency § 8.01 General Fiduciary Principle, 2006). Fiduciary duty will be explored more fully later in this chapter.

Almost every business enterprise requires the efforts of more than one person – engaging those persons to assist the enterprise is the essence of the agency relationship. **Agency law** defines how and when agency relationships are created, what rights and responsibilities exist between a principal and an agent, and what legal effect will be given to the acts of an agent in dealings with third parties. Agency law governs relationships when one person hires or employs another to do his or her work, sell his or her goods, and/or acquire property on his or her behalf. The resulting transaction is as valid as if the employer/principal were present and acting in person. A person can be hired to do work for another in a variety of ways.

The typical athlete representation relationship involves the athlete agent (agent) being hired by an athlete (principal) to negotiate contracts with a professional sport team where this team is agreeing to pay for athletic services. The principal (athlete) has an objective to obtain a favorable contract with

Exhibit 8.1 Management contexts pertaining to agency, with relevant laws and cases.

Management Context	Major Legal Issues	Relevant Law	Illustrative Cases
Negotiation of business transactions	Creation of agency relationships	Agency law	*Clark Advertising Agency*
		Contract law	
Employer/principal liability for employee/agent acts	Authority of agents to act	Agency law, contract law, tort law	*Jones*
	Duties and responsibilities of agents/principals		*Sims v. Argovitz*
Student-athletes' amateur status	NCAA eligibility Dealings with agents	Agency law UAAA SPARTA	*U.S. v. Piggie*
Player representation	Regulation of athlete agents	UAAA SPARTA	*Alabama v. Goggins*
		Professional player association rules	*Hilliard v. Black*

the professional team and the athlete agent (agent) is the one employed to act on the athlete's behalf to achieve that objective. Another example of the athlete representation relationship occurs when the athlete agent is hired to negotiate endorsement contracts for professional or Olympic athletes with companies for products the athlete will endorse and/or lend his/her name and likeness to in advertising. In addition to the athlete representation relationship, agency relationships exist in a multitude of situations, many of which we experience on a daily basis. Even the simplest transaction at a retail store involves an agent (sales clerk) and a principal (store employer). Thus, most members of a given population have experienced interacting with an agent. As another example, if you worked in a college stadium ticket office, such as Cardinal Stadium at the University of Louisville, you would be an agent for the University of Louisville Athletic Association (ULAA), and the ULAA would be your principal. Virtually anyone who has had a job has served in a representative capacity for an employer and has been affected by agency law. Three basic types of agency relationships exist:

1 Employee and employer relationship (this relationship results when an employer hires an employee to perform some form of service).
2 Principal and agent relationship (this relationship results when a principal hires an agent and gives that agent authority to act and enter into contracts on the principal's behalf).
3 Principal and independent contractor relationship (this relationship results when a person or business, that is not an employee, is employed by a principal to perform a certain task on the principal's behalf). Critical factors in determining independent contractor status were presented in Chapter 4.

Most agency relationships occur as part of an employment relationship, as discussed in detail in Chapter 4. However, two other types of agency relationships are also visible in the sport industry. An example of the second type of agency relationship, the classic principal and agent relationship, is the athlete agent and professional athlete. The third agency relationship, the independent contractor relationship, is often illustrated through a new stadium construction project in which a university engages an independent general contractor. All contractual relationships involve the realization of a benefit to one party through the performance of another party. However, the second type of agency relationship – principal and agent relationship – is the only one that carries with it the fiduciary duty general principle. This is an important distinction, since an agent's fiduciary duty is the essence of the agency relationship.

A **fiduciary** is defined as a person who acts primarily for the benefit of another. The nature of the **fiduciary relationship** is that one person entrusts his or her interests to another and that the agent must act loyally for the principal's benefit in all matters connected with the agency relationship. The traditional employee-employer relationship does not normally create a fiduciary relationship. Thus, an assistant athletic director for development at a university would likely not be in a fiduciary relationship with the employer. This individual would of course be required to perform tasks that benefit the employer and comply with various company policies, but the heightened duties associated with a fiduciary relationship would not exist in this relationship. Several former student-athletes from the University of North Carolina sued the National Collegiate Athletic Association (NCAA) following the 2011 UNC academic fraud scandal involving steering UNC athletes toward academically unsound or easy classes in order to maintain athletic eligibility (*McCants v. NCAA*, 2016; Wainstein, Jay, & Kukowski, 2014). These student-athletes asserted claims of negligence and breach of fiduciary duty against the NCAA. They alleged that the NCAA had voluntarily assumed a fiduciary duty to protect the education and educational opportunities of student-athletes. The federal district court dismissed that claims finding that a fiduciary duty requires more than a mere voluntary undertaking. The court held under North Carolina law,

> there must be a fiduciary relationship where there has been a special confidence reposed in one who in equity and good conscience is bound to act in good faith and with due regard to the interests of the one reposing confidence. (p. 747)

The existence or the nonexistence of a fiduciary relationship depends on the circumstances in each case. Historically, these relationships are easily present between spouses; attorney and client; trustee and beneficiary; and partners to a partnership. However, most courts refuse to recognize a fiduciary relationship between employee and employer, corporations and shareholders, and in the academic setting between university and its students. The *McCants* court determined that the same reasons for not extending a fiduciary relationship in an academic setting were equally applicable to the relationship between student-athletes and the NCAA.

Perhaps, the easiest way to distinguish fiduciary relationships from other types of contractual agency relationships is to ask whether a high degree of trust or confidence is vested by the principal in the agent. So while the relationship between the NCAA and a student-athlete is not a fiduciary relationship, both student-athletes and professional athletes will enter into agency agreements that are fiduciary relationships throughout their careers. Fiduciary duties and other unique issues involving agency relationships are covered in this chapter.

Creation of the Agency Relationship

Agency relationships can only be created by the mutual consent of the parties. Thus, the creation of the agency relationship essentially involves two steps: (1) manifestation by the principal and (2) consent by the agent (Kleinberger, 2017). An agency relationship can be established by informal oral agreements or by more formal written agreements. Consider the following example of when an agency relationship has been created. Alison is disappointed to learn that her favorite hiking guide, Adam, will be unavailable during her upcoming trip to the Grand Canyon, and she sends the following email to Adam: "So sorry you are not available, could you locate and hire me another guide of your quality and price range for the dates I sent you." Adam hits the "reply" button and types, "Sure, no problem." He promptly receives an automated "out of the office" reply from Alison indicating that she is gone for two weeks. A principal–agent relationship has been created. Alison has manifested her intent to engage Adam as her agent, and Adam has consented to serve in that capacity. It is irrelevant that the principal, Alison, may yet be unaware of the agent's consent. (See Kleinberger, 2017, for more examples of agency relationships.)

An agency agreement is a contract; thus, as discussed in Chapter 3, basic contract principles will apply. For example, the underlying objective of the agency relationship must relate to a lawful purpose, and both parties (agent and principal) must have the legal capacity to enter into the agency agreement. (See Chapter 3 regarding the essential elements of a contract and legal capacity.) Assuming the objective of the principal

Exhibit 8.2 Creation of agency relationships.

Actual authority: Express	Formal written or oral agreement is made between the parties.
Actual authority: Implied	Agency relationship is implied from the conduct of the parties.
Apparent authority	Third party relies on conduct of the principal suggesting that agent has authority, so principal is estopped from denying agency relationship.
Ratification	No actual agency exists, but the principal accepts or ratifies the unauthorized acts of the agent.

is lawful and both parties have the legal capacity to enter into the agreement, an agency relationship is created, and the agent has the authority to act on behalf of the principal. The agent's authority to act is either (1) actual, (2) apparent, or (3) arising as a result of the principal's ratification of the agent's acts. Actual authority can be express or implied (see Exhibit 8.2).

Actual Authority

Express authority is created when the parties make a written or oral agreement specifically defining the scope of the agent's authority. An example of an express authority would be contained in the Standard Representation Agreement. This agreement is required by professional players association regulations and must be used between sport agents and their professional athlete clients (principals). Although an express agency can be an oral agreement, written agreements are more common, a better business practice, and required by most professional sport players associations. Players associations require standard representation agreements to protect players from incompetent or fraudulent behavior by their agents. Players associations also require these agreements because they are delegating some of their exclusive representation to the agents who engage in individual negotiations on behalf of the players. Through these agreements and their regulations, players associations protect their collectively bargained provisions and set minimum standards for the activities carried out by agents on behalf of their players (principals). Such an agreement might begin with declarations as follows:

> WHEREAS, Johnny Newby (hereinafter referred to as "Player") and Samantha Smart (hereinafter referred to as "Agent") have agreed upon the terms of Agent's representation of Player pursuant to the National Roundball League Players Association Standard Representation Agreement (the "Agreement");

> WHEREAS, Player desires to engage Agent's services for the enhancement of Player's athletic, professional, and community profile; and

> WHEREAS, Player and Agent desire to memorialize their agreement related to Player's full range of compensable activities, the parties agree as follows …

Once an agent and a professional athlete have entered into a Standard Representation Agreement, this agreement empowers the agent to negotiate the player's compensation with the team. In the agreement, compensation is specifically defined as salaries, signing bonuses, reporting bonuses, roster bonuses, and any performance incentives earned by the player during the term of the contract. This agency agreement, however, would not authorize the agent to negotiate for endorsements on behalf of the athlete or perform financial or investment services for the athlete. Thus, if the agent presented to Nike as possessing the authority to act on behalf of the athlete and committed the athlete by executing an endorsement agreement, that contract would not be enforceable against the athlete. Nike, however, would have a claim for breach of contract against the agent.

You may want to review a sample Standard Representation Agreement for one of the professional players associations. For example, the National Football League Players Association's (NFLPA) Standard Representation Agreement may be found online (see Web Resources at the end of this chapter). Exhibit 8.3 below sets forth a sample clause defining the work that the player has engaged his agent to perform on his behalf.

Exhibit 8.3 Sample contract services clause in player/agent agreement.

> 1 Contract Services Player hereby retains Contract Advisor to represent, advise, counsel, and assist Player in the negotiation, execution, and enforcement of his playing contract(s) in the National Football League (NFL). In performing these services, Contract Advisor acknowledges that he/she is acting in a fiduciary capacity on behalf of Player and agrees to act in such manner as to protect the best interests of Player and assure effective representation of Player in individual contract negotiations with NFL Clubs. Contract Advisor shall be the exclusive representative for the purpose of negotiating player contracts for Player. However, Contract Advisor shall not have the authority to bind or commit Player to enter into any contract without actual execution thereof by Player. Once Player agrees to and executes his player contract, Contract Advisor agrees to also sign the player contract and send a copy (by email, facsimile, or overnight mail) to the NFLPA and the NFL Club within 48 hours of execution by Player.
>
> Player and Contract Advisor (check one): [ ] have [ ] have not entered into agreements or contracts relating to services other than the individual negotiating services described in this Paragraph (e.g., financial advice, tax preparation). If the parties have, complete 3(A) and 3(B) below.
>
> A Describe the nature of the other services covered by the separate agreements: [space provided]
> B Contract Advisor and Player hereby acknowledge that Player was given the opportunity to enter into any of the agreements described in Paragraph 3(A) above and this Standard Representation Agreement, without the signing of one agreement being conditioned upon the signing of any of the other agreements in violation of Section 3(B)(22) of the NFLPA Regulations Governing Contract Advisors (Initial below). (NFLPA Standard Representation Agreement, 2016).

Implied authority is not expressly provided for in any written or oral agreement, but rather is implied by the conduct of the parties. The implied authority extends to those areas that are necessary for the agent to complete the objectives of the principal. The agent must have a justifiable belief in the authority to act, based on something the principal has said or done. For example, Eric is the head golf pro and sales manager at a private country club. Eric probably does not have a written or oral agreement detailing every duty he has with the club, but he will have the implied authority to make agreements and engage in transactions that are attendant with his operation of the course and pro shop. Thus, when Eric orders new sets of clubs and merchandise for the pro shop from a supplier, the supplier will naturally invoice the country club for the order. The club would not be able to avoid paying the charges simply because Eric's employment agreement did not expressly authorize him to order clubs and merchandise for the pro shop. Eric's authority on behalf of the country club is implied, because compiling inventory for sale is a customary act of a sales manager, and Eric was justified in his belief that, when he was hired by the principal as the head golf pro, he would be responsible for these types of acts.

Apparent Authority

Apparent authority is created by the conduct of the principal that leads a third party to believe another individual serves as the principal's agent (Restatement [Third] of Agency § 2.03 Apparent Authority, 2006). If the third party relies on the principal's conduct, the principal will not be permitted to deny the existence of an agency relationship simply because there is no formal agreement. Apparent authority cannot be based on the actions of the agent alone. The principal is the source of the third party's reliance, and the apparent authority must be based upon the justifiable belief of the third party in the principal's conduct (Restatement [Third] of Agency § 3.03 Creation of Apparent Authority, 2006). Apparent authority is presented in the Focus Case below *Clark Advertising Agency v. Tice* (1974).

Ratification of Agency

An agency relationship can also be created through **ratification**, which occurs when the agent did not in fact have authority to act on behalf of the principal, but the principal accepts or ratifies the agent's act after the act was done. For example, Blake, a professional athlete, has hired Megan as a financial advisor with specific instructions that all investments must be pre-approved by him. Blake deposits $100,000 with Megan's company to facilitate transactions. Megan discovers a great new business start-up and invests $10,000 of Blake's money. She does not seek Blake's prior approval for the investment. Blake receives his monthly accounting statement, notices a new investment account on his statement, and calls Megan to question the investment. Megan apologizes and explains that the investment is already producing income for him. Blake asks Megan to monitor the investment closely and to deposit all income into his personal investment account. Blake's conduct in accepting the earnings on the investment would act as a ratification of Megan's authority for that transaction.

Understanding the scope of the agent's authority is necessary to determine whether the principal will be responsible for the acts of the agent. The principal is not liable if the agent does not have the authority to act on his or her behalf. If an agent has no authority to act on behalf of the principal or exceeds the designated authority, then the agent cannot bind the principal to a contract. If an agent enters into an unauthorized agreement with a third party, the agent will be liable to the third party. Also, if an agent knowingly misrepresents his or her alleged authority, then the agent may be liable to the third party both on the contract and in tort (see Chapter 4 regarding tort liability of agents and employees).

The following Focus Case demonstrates the concept and scope of apparent authority.

Clark Advertising Agency v. Tice

490 F.2d 834 (5th Cir. 1974)   **FOCUS** CASE

FACTS

Clark Advertising Agency (Clark) sued the American Hot Rod Association (AHRA) and its president, James Tice, for payment under a contract for advertising and promotional services. The parties had a previous written contract for advertising services for the Winter Nationals Race in Phoenix, Arizona, but proceeded under an oral contract for the race in question in West Palm Beach, Florida. Clark and Tice held initial talks regarding expenditures and fees, and such fees were to approximate those under the prior agreement for Phoenix. However, further discussions regarding an increase in fees and costs were held between Clark and two other AHRA officers, the vice president (Ballah) and the comptroller (Harkins). When Clark presented a total bill under the oral contract seeking the increased fees and costs discussed with Ballah and Harkins, AHRA refused payment, and Clark sued. AHRA contended that Ballah and Harkins did not have authority to bind AHRA during negotiations with Clark.

HOLDING

The court decided in favor of Clark.

RATIONALE

Whether or not either of these officers actually had express or implied authority to bind AHRA, the court held that there is ample evidence to find that they had apparent authority. The court stated that apparent authority exists whenever a principal manifests to a third person that an officer or agent may act on its behalf, and the third person believes in good faith that the authority exists. When that third person reasonably relies upon that apparent authority to his detriment, the principal is estopped to deny the authority (Restatement [Second] of Agency § 8, 1958; Henn, *Law of Corporations*, § 226, 2d ed., 1970). Tice testified that he did not know all the terms of the "loose verbal agreement," since he ceased to be personally involved and left the negotiations to Ballah and Harkins. Similarly, after the race Tice left it to Harkins to negotiate with Clark for a settlement of his services in Florida. By leaving the detailed negotiation work to Ballah and Harkins, Tice created the appearance that they had authority to conduct those negotiations.

Exhibit 8.4 Summary of duties in an agency relationship.

Duties of the Principle to the Agent	Duties of the Agent to the Principal
Duty of compensation and reimbursement Duty to provide safe working conditions Duty of performance (reasonable care and skill)	Duty of cooperation Duty of loyalty (good faith) Duty of accounting (for funds and property) Duty of obedience (to follow instructions)

Duties Involved in the Agency Relationship

As mentioned previously, the principal–agent relationship is considered a fiduciary relationship that carries with it a number of duties between the agent and the principal. The nature of the fiduciary relationship is that one person entrusts his or her interests to another and that this agent must act loyally for the principal's benefit in all matters connected with the agency relationship. These interests could include money, property, or other legal rights and responsibilities. Thus, the essence of an agency relationship requires that the agent owes the principal the utmost loyalty and good faith to act in the best interest of the principal, to follow the instructions of the principal, and to exercise reasonable care, competence, and diligence. In serving the interests of the principal, the agent may not engage in self-dealing and must avoid conflicts of interest and competing interests. The agent must also account to the principal for any funds or property coming into the agent's possession (Restatement [Third] of Agency § 8.02–8.12, 2006).

Similarly, the principal owes duties to the agent. The principal must compensate the agent for his or her services, as well as reimburse the agent for customary expenditures incurred while acting on behalf of the principal, such as travel expenses or telephone charges. The principal has a duty to provide safe working conditions for the agent (see Chapter 9). The principal must also cooperate with the agent so the agent is able to perform his or her duties (Restatement [Third] of Agency § 8.14–15, 2006). Thus, if Mary hired Evan to sell her baseball card collection on eBay, Mary must grant Evan reasonable access to the collection to photograph and inventory it, allowing him to fulfill his obligations as Mary's agent (see Exhibit 8.4 for a summary of the duties involved in an agency relationship).

Another example of the duties involved in an agency relationship is offered in the case of *Billy Sims v. Jerry Argovitz* (1985). In that case, an agent breached his fiduciary duty, and, as a result, the court rescinded (canceled) the contract that had been executed between Billy Sims and the Houston Gamblers. The district court found that the Houston contract resulted from an unconscionable breach of a fiduciary duty. This case illustrates how an agent, in this case Argovitz, breached the duty of loyalty and good faith that lies at the heart of a fiduciary relationship.

The Detroit Lions and Billy Sims v. Jerry Argovitz

CASE OPINION   580 F. Supp. 542 (E.D. Mich. 1984)

FACTS

In 1980, the Detroit Lions, a National Football League franchise, drafted Sims and signed him to a four-year contract that expired on February 1, 1984. Jerry Argovitz entered into an agency agreement with Sims early in 1980 and counseled him on numerous matters. Sims and Argovitz developed a confidential relationship in which, as Argovitz testified, Sims looked up to him like a father. Sims sought Argovitz's advice on significant professional, financial, and personal matters.

From April 1982 through June 1983, Argovitz negotiated with the Lions for a renewed contract with for Sims. On May 5, 1983, Argovitz announced at a press conference that his application for a franchise in the new United States Football League (USFL) had been approved for the Houston Gamblers. Sims was present at the press conference. While his application for a USFL franchise in Houston was pending, Argovitz continued negotiations with the Lions on behalf of Sims. On April 5, 1983, Argovitz offered Sims's services to the Lions for $6 million over a four-year period. The offer included a demand for a $1 million interest-free loan to be repaid over ten years, and for skill and injury guarantees for three years. The Lions quickly responded with a counter offer on April 7, 1983, in the amount of $1.5 million over a five-year period with additional incentives. The negotiating process was working. During May or June 1983, Argovitz decided to seek a contract for Sims with the Gamblers. On May 3, 1983, with his Gamblers franchise assured, Argovitz significantly reduced his offer to the Lions. He now offered Sims to the Lions for $3 million over a four-year period. The negotiations between the Lions and Argovitz were progressing normally, not laterally as Argovitz represented to Sims. The Lions were not "dragging their feet." Throughout the entire month of June 1983, Mr. Frederick Nash, the Lions's negotiator, was involved in investigating the possibility of providing an attractive annuity for Sims and at the same time doing his best to avoid the granting of either skill or injury guarantees. The evidence establishes that on June 22, 1983, the Lions and Argovitz were very close to reaching an agreement on the value of Sims's services.

On June 29, 1983, Sims arrived in Houston, believing that the Lions were not negotiating in good faith and were not really interested in his services. On June 30, 1983, the Gamblers offered Sims a $3.5 million, five-year contract that included nonmonetary fringe benefits Sims valued greatly. Argovitz told Sims that he thought the Lions would match the Gamblers' financial package and offered to telephone them. But, it is clear from the evidence that neither Sims nor Burrough believed that the Lions would match the offer. Sims told Argovitz not to call the Lions for purely emotional reasons according to the district court. On the afternoon of June 30, while negotiations were proceeding, the Lions's attorney called Argovitz. Argovitz was present at his office but declined to accept the call. Argovitz attempted to return the call only after 5:00 p.m., when the Lions's attorney had left for the July fourth weekend. The district court found these actions further breached Argovitz's fiduciary duty toward Sims. Argovitz then left for the holiday weekend. The next day, July 1, 1983, Sims signed an exclusive contract with the Gamblers.

In July 1983, having not been informed of these events, the Lions sent Sims a further offer through Argovitz. On November 12, 1983, at Argovitz's instigation, Sims met with him and re-executed the Gamblers contract. Sims also signed a waiver of any claim he might have against Argovitz. Although at this time Argovitz had sold his agency business and no longer represented Sims, Argovitz did not inform Sims' new agent of his intention to have Sims sign a waiver, nor did Argovitz, despite his fiduciary relationship with Sims, advise Sims to seek independent advice before signing the waiver. On December 16, 1983, Sims executed a second exclusive contract with the Lions for $1 million more than his Gamblers contract.

On December 18, 1983, the Lions and Sims brought this suit against Argovitz and the Gamblers seeking rescission of the Gamblers contract with Sims.

HOLDING

The district court rescinded (voided) the contract between Billy Sims and the Houston Gamblers.

RATIONALE

The relationship between a principal and agent is fiduciary in nature, and as such imposes a duty of loyalty, good faith, and fair and honest dealing on the agent. The court stated "We are dismayed by **Argovitz's** egregious conduct. The careless fashion in which **Argovitz** went about ascertaining the highest price for Sims' service convinces us of the wisdom of the maxim: no man can faithfully serve two masters whose interests are in conflict." It is uncontested that Argovitz had a personal interest in Sims's contracting with the Gamblers, who as a new team in a new football league, the Gamblers would have greatly benefited from the star attraction of a player of Sims's caliber. Argovitz's self-dealing arose from this conflict with his fiduciary duty to advance Sims's best interests.

Under Texas law, the district court found that where an agent has an interest adverse to that of his principal, in a transaction in which he purports to act on behalf of his principal, the transaction is voidable by the principal unless the agent disclosed *all material facts* within his knowledge that might affect the principal's judgment. … This remains true even if the contract is fair. The district court found as a matter of fact that "[a]t no time prior to December 1, 1983, was Sims aware" of all material facts regarding Argovitz's involvement with the Gamblers and Argovitz's failure to pursue Sims' interests in negotiations with the Lions. The district court found that Argovitz manipulated Sims' contract negotiations with the Lions during the spring of 1983 in light of Argovitz's own interest in the Gamblers. The court also found that Argovitz misrepresented the negotiations with the Lions as not progressing when in fact they were progressing normally. Argovitz maintained that he satisfied his duty of disclosure simply by telling Sims that he was partial owner of the Gamblers and by telling Sims that the Lions would match the financial elements of the Gamblers's offer. A review of the facts, as found by the district court, reveals that these are but a few of the material disclosures that Argovitz should have made. The court found that Argovitz had failed to show that he informed Sims of the following facts including: (a) The relative values of the Gamblers's contract and the Lions's offer that Argovitz knew could be obtained; (b) that there was significant financial differences between the USFL and the NFL not only in terms of the relative financial stability of the Leagues, but also in terms of the fringe benefits available to Sims; (c) Argovitz's 29 percent ownership in the Gamblers, Argovitz's $275,000 annual salary with the Gamblers, and Argovitz's five percent interest in the cash flow of the Gamblers; (d) that both Argovitz and Burrough failed to even attempt to obtain for Sims valuable contract clauses which they had given to Kelly on behalf of the Gamblers; and (e) that Sims had great leverage and Argovitz was not encouraging a bidding war that could have advantageous results for Sims. Thus, the district court granted rescission of the contract between the Gamblers and Sims because it found that under Texas law Argovitz had breached his fiduciary duty as Sims's agent and confidant.

QUESTIONS

1 What duties does the court identify in the fiduciary relationship between a principal and an agent?
2 According to the court, if an agent has a conflict of interest with the interests of the principal, what must the agent disclose to the principal before entering into a transaction?
3 What information should Argovitz have provided to Sims to avoid breaching his fiduciary duty?

Contractual Liability of the Principal and the Agent

Our discussion of how agency relationships are created, the scope of the agent's authority, and the duties owed between the principal and the agent is particularly important in the understanding of how agency law affects business transactions. Agents have the ability to bind both themselves and their principals in contract (see Chapter 3) and in tort. With regard to contractual obligations, agency law defines the rights of third parties who enter into agreements with agents and the corresponding liability of the agents or the principals for those agreements.

Classifications of Principals

Contractual liability will depend on how the principal is classified and the scope of authority of the agent. A principal can be *disclosed*, *unidentified*, or *undisclosed* (Restatement [Third] of Agency § 1.04, 2006). If the principal is **disclosed**, this simply means the third party is aware of the identity of the principal and that the agent is acting on behalf of the principal, such as in a registered athlete agent's contract negotiation on behalf of a professional athlete. A principal is **unidentified** if the third party is aware that the agent is

Exhibit 8.5 Classifications of the principal and the liability
of the principal and agent.

Classification	Principal	Agent
Disclosed	Liable	Not liable
Unidentified	Liable	Possibly liable
Undisclosed	Liable	Liable

acting on behalf of another but does not know the identity of the principal. For example, a sport marketing consulting company may be attempting to match a number of its clients with sponsorship opportunities with a sport organization. The sport organization may be unaware which clients the consulting company wants to secure a sponsorship for, but it is aware that the consulting company is acting on behalf of another. An **undisclosed** principal exists if the third party is not aware that the agent is acting on behalf of another, such as when a buyer on eBay bids on an item during a sport memorabilia auction. The seller of the item has no way of knowing whether the buyer is purchasing the item for his or her own use, for resale to a third party, or on behalf of a specific third party; thus, if the purchase is on behalf of another, the principal is undisclosed.

The classification of the principal is important for determining the liability of the principal and of the agent. If an agency relationship is disclosed, the principal is bound by the contracts entered into by the agent and is liable to the third party and to those contracts. However, the agent is not liable to the third party, as the third party knew to be dealing with an agent as a representative for the principal. Thus, if a professional athlete (a disclosed principal) breaches his or her agreement with a professional sport franchise, the professional sport franchise cannot sue the agent for the breach of contract; its only recourse is against the athlete (principal). As Exhibit 8.5 indicates, the principal is always liable for the authorized acts of an agent; however, the agent's liability varies depending upon whether the existence of the principal is disclosed to the third party with whom the agent is dealing.

The following Focus Case illustrates the notion that if an agency relationship is disclosed to a third party who enters into a contract negotiated by an agent, only the principal is liable for a breach of that agreement.

Jones v. Archibald

360 N.Y.S 2d 119 (App. Div. 1974)   **FOCUS** CASE

FACTS

All-Pro represented Nate Archibald, a professional athlete, in contract negotiations and financial management. The plaintiff, Jones, contacted Nate Archibald to make a one-day appearance at Jones' boys' camp and was told by Archibald to contact his agent, All-Pro. All-Pro informed plaintiff that Archibald would appear at the camp on August 15. Jones paid the agreed amount for Archibald's appearance. On August 9, All-Pro was notified by Archibald that circumstances would prevent him from making the appearance. All-Pro sent this information by mail to Jones on August 10 (five days before the scheduled appearance), along with a refund of the money previously paid by Jones. Jones received this letter on August 14. Jones sued Archibald, as principal, and All-Pro, as agent, alleging that All-Pro was Archibald's authorized agent in the transaction, that Archibald willfully breached the contract, that All-Pro knew or should have known that Archibald would not appear, that All-Pro knew or should have known that its method of communicating to plaintiff would not allow sufficient time to secure a replacement, and that as a result Jones was damaged in the amount of $200,000.

HOLDING

The court held that the agent, All-Pro, could not be held liable for any breach of the appearance agreement.

RATIONALE

The court first observed that where there is a disclosed principal–agency relationship, as in this case, the agent is not personally bound unless there is clear and explicit evidence of the agent's intention to substitute or add his personal liability for, or to, that of his principal. A disclosed agent who acts for another in negotiating a contract in the business interests of his principal will not be deemed to have intended to bind himself personally unless the intent to do so is manifested with reasonable clarity. All of the contracts between plaintiff and All-Pro were by correspondence. Nothing contained in the record indicates any intention on All-Pro's part to assume or undertake any individual, independent responsibility or obligation. As such, All-Pro could not be held liable for any breach of the appearance agreement. However, the court did state that Jones still had his cause of action against the principal, Nate Archibald.

If the principal is unidentified, both the agent and the principal are considered parties to the contract, and each may be liable for the contract.

Consider the following example: many auction houses, such as Goldin Auctions, conduct dozens of auctions and private sales each year of fine art, antiques, jewelry, and other expensive collectibles, including sports memorabilia. Many of the bidders at these auctions are agents attempting to secure items for their principals. Usually, the identity of the principal is not disclosed. Goldin, as well as the other bidders, certainly knows that a bidder may be acting in a representative capacity but usually has no idea who the agent represents or who is the ultimate purchaser of the item. In such cases, both the agent and the principal may be liable for the contract. If the agent fails to pay the sale price as agreed, the agent will likely be liable to Goldin directly. However, assuming the agent is less able to pay than his wealthy principal, Goldin may also be able to seek payment from the principal, if Goldin can prove the identity of the principal and can prove the agent acted with actual authority (Kleinberger, 2017).

If the principal is undisclosed, both the agent and the principal may be liable on the contract, but the third party may have to sue them alternatively. Suing alternatively means that if either the agent or principal denies liability, the third party must choose which one it will seek to hold accountable on the contract, and once the third party makes this choice, he/she is precluded from suing the one not chosen.

Athletes and Athlete Agents

In addition to breach of fiduciary duty as discussed in the *Sims v. Argovitz* case, the relationship between athlete agents and both student-athletes and professional athletes can raise a number of complex legal issues. Legal issues affecting athletes and agents primarily arise in three areas: (1) the relationship between the athlete agent and the athlete once an agency relationship is created; (2) the interactions of athlete agents with student-athletes in an attempt to secure an agency relationship; and (3) relationships between agents and agencies when competing for athlete clients or when agents leave one agency for another.

The first area involves the conduct of the agency relationship itself, such as whether an agent has acted in the best interests of the principal, whether the agent has performed competently, or whether the principal has interfered with the agent's ability to perform. These legal issues usually involve an athlete agent and either a professional athlete or a student-athlete who is actively pursuing a career as a professional athlete. The primary focus is on the adequacy of the performance of the agency agreement, either by the athlete (principal) or by the athlete agent/representative (agent). For example, Detroit Pistons guard Ben Gordon sued his former financial advisors over a $1.3 million disputed real estate investment (Associated Press, 2010). Gordon also alleged a breach of fiduciary duty, but the court determined that the advisors' switching from a flat fee to a percentage fee was not a breach of fiduciary duty, since Gordon received statements reflecting the new fees and paid them.

The second area involves the interaction of athlete agents with student-athletes who may have amateur eligibility remaining. In this area, the legal issues that arise relate to whether the athlete agent has complied with existing athlete agent laws and acted properly and truthfully with the student-athlete so that, if the student-athlete chooses to engage the agent's services, it is with full knowledge of the effect it may have on amateur status and eligibility. In this area, additional legal issues arise related to protecting the interests of colleges and universities that may be subject to NCAA penalties and may incur significant financial losses if an ineligible student-athlete participates in the institution's intercollegiate athletic program after engaging an agent.

One of the first such examples of this occurred in 1996 when the University of Massachusetts and the University of Connecticut were both stripped of their victories in the 1996 NCAA men's basketball tournament and suffered financial penalties for the illegal acceptance of gifts from an agent by players Marcus Camby of UMass and Kirk King and Ricky Moore of UConn (Taylor, 1997). Since that time, agent interactions with student-athletes continues to be a serious problem in college athletics. One recent example of this was when the NCAA levied penalties against the University of Louisville's Athletic Department after basketball player Brian Bowen II accepted gifts from Adidas and an agent working for ASM Sports (Norlander, 2018). Later, that same agent made bribe payments to an assistant coach at the University of South Carolina to arrange meetings with star guard P. J. Dozier (Taylor, 2020). These specific cases make up only part of a larger FBI investigation into fraud and other illegal activity around NCAA Division I men's basketball (Estes, 2018).

The third area of legal issues concerning athletes and agents involves an increasing number of disputes between agents and agencies. These disputes currently relate primarily to noncompete clauses (see Chapter 3) in agent employment agreements that impair the agent's ability to either start his or her own agency or leave one agency to work for another agency. Thus, several agents have proactively filed lawsuits seeking declaratory judgments on the enforceability of the noncompete clauses in their contracts. Basketball agent Aaron Mintz left his employer, Priority Sports & Entertainment, to join Creative Artists Agency. Mintz sued to have the noncompetition clause in his contract with Priority Sports determined to be invalid. The court dismissed the claim, since there was no evidence Priority Sports intended to enforce the clause. Mintz was ultimately awarded $85,000 in damages for emotional distress for invasion of privacy resulting from Priority Sports hacking into Mintz's email account (Heitner, 2012). Then, in 2013, Sean Howard sued the agency Octagon for similar relief when he left Octagon and founded his own agency, PRIME Athletes (Heitner, 2013).

The next sections of this chapter will examine a number of the legal issues that arise in the dealings of student-athletes and professional athletes with athlete agents.

Student-Athletes and Agents

Especially relevant for sport managers today is the ever-increasing amount of state and federal regulation of athlete agents. Legal issues relating to athlete agents' dealings with student-athletes are currently subject to a patchwork of both state and federal regulations. The regulatory law for sport agents may indeed be one of the most confusing and complex areas in the sport industry. One reason is that prior to the Uniform Athlete Agent Act being enacted, states would react to scandals by drafting a regulation based on that ethical dilemma. As a result, many of early laws were reactionary and focused on keeping student-athletes eligible, rather than addressing the root cause of the unethical behavior and challenges it created for the citizens of the state. Athlete agents, university compliance officers, student-athletes, professional athletes, employees of the NCAA enforcement staff, and contract negotiators for a professional sports team – all should understand the legal issues and laws affecting athlete agents.

Athlete Agent Regulation

Fierce competition among athlete agents and fears of unscrupulous athlete agent practices, as discussed earlier, continue to challenge the intercollegiate/interscholastic industry segments. Consider the following statement from the National Conference of Commissioners of Uniform State Laws (NCCUSL) now known as the Uniform Law Commission, as it initially began to draft a uniform law for regulating athlete agents (University of Pennsylvania Law School, n.d.):

> With the proliferation of professional sport franchises in the United States, and the immense sums now paid to athletes for commercial endorsement contracts, it is no surprise that the commercial marketplace in which athlete agents operate has become very competitive. And while maximizing the income of one's clients is certainly the "American way" (as well as good business practice), the recruitment of a student-athlete while he or she is still enrolled in an educational institution may cause substantial eligibility or other problems for both the student and the school, especially where the athlete is not aware of the implications of signing the agency agreement or where agency is established without notice to the athletic director of the school. The problem becomes even more acute where an unscrupulous agent misleads a student. While several states have enacted legislation to address these issues, agent registration and disclosure requirements vary greatly from state to state, causing confusion among student-athletes, athletic departments, educational institutions, and the agents themselves.

The NCCUSL completed in the Uniform Athlete Agents Act (UAAA) in 2000. It was later revised in 2015 and an additional amendment was added in 2019. Some commentators have questioned whether the UAAA really achieves its goal of protecting student-athletes (Edelman, 2013). In Addition to the 44 states that have adopted the UAAA two states, Michigan and Ohio have enacted their own versions of athlete agent legislation. Six states and one U.S. territory have no existing laws regulating athlete agents. Arizona enacted the UAAA, but has since repealed certain sections. Exhibit 8.6 summarizes U.S.

Exhibit 8.6   Uniform Athlete Agents Act.

States and others that have adopted the Uniform Athlete Agents Act:
Alabama, Arizona, Arkansas, California, Colorado, Connecticut, Delaware, District of Columbia, Florida, Georgia, Hawaii, Idaho, Illinois, Indiana, Iowa, Kansas, Kentucky, Louisiana, Maryland, Minnesota, Mississippi, Missouri, Nebraska, Nevada, New Hampshire, New Mexico, New York, North Carolina, North Dakota, Oklahoma, Oregon, Pennsylvania, Rhode Island, South Carolina, South Dakota, Tennessee, Texas, U.S. Virgin Islands, Utah, Virginia, Virgin Islands, Washington, Washington, D.C., West Virginia, Wisconsin, and Wyoming

States where adoption of the Uniform Athlete Agents Act is currently under consideration:
New Jersey (as of 2019)

States with their own versions of athlete agent legislation:
Michigan, Ohio

States and territories with no existing laws regulating athlete agents:
Alaska, Maine, Massachusetts, Montana, New Jersey, Puerto Rico, and Vermont

Current and updated information regarding enactment of the UAAA (Revised) is available in the Web Resources at the end of the chapter.

state and territory regulation of athlete agent activities. However, as states without specific athlete agent legislation, such as Massachusetts, are filing bills for college athletes to benefit from their NIL (name, image, and likeness), they are incorporating UAAA and the Sports Agent Responsibility and Trust Act (SPARTA) by reference.

Athlete agents are also regulated under federal law. In September 2004, the U.S. Congress passed the SPARTA to supplement the requirements of the UAAA and to provide some protection for student-athletes located in those states with no current form of athlete agent regulation. Add to this the penalties potentially imposed by the NCAA on its members (universities) if a student-athlete has had dealings with an agent and continues to compete as an amateur, and the landscape of athlete agency has become complex and challenging for sport managers. Thus, a basic understanding of the state and federal regulation of athlete agents is needed. This section will introduce the common elements in both the state and federal laws, as well as some unique features and limitations of the current legislative acts.

The Uniform Athlete Agents Act

Prior to the availability of the Uniform Athlete Agents Act, at least 28 states had adopted some form of athlete agent regulation. However, those state statutes varied considerably from state to state, and compliance with an athlete agent act in one state was effective only in that state. Thus, an athlete agent seeking to do business in each state was required to comply with 28 different sets of requirements and 28 different regulatory schemes. Thus, the NCCUSL, designed the UAAA to eliminate some of the inconsistency among the various state statutes. The NCCUSL (n.d.) identified seven essential provisions of a uniform act:

- **Registration**. One must obtain a certificate of registration from a state in order to act as an athlete agent.
- **Reciprocity of registration**. An athlete agent who has a valid certificate of registration in one state may cross-file that application (or its renewal) in all other states that have adopted the act.
- **Notice to the educational institution**. To help protect the student-athlete's eligibility, notice of an agency contract must be given to the educational institution.
- **Voidable agency contract**. In a further effort to protect the student-athlete's eligibility, the student-athlete has the right to cancel an agency contract without penalty within 14 days after the contract is signed.
- **Notice required in agency contract**. An agency contract must contain a conspicuous notice informing the student-athlete of the possibility of losing his or her eligibility, the requirement to give notice of the contract to the educational institution, and the student-athlete's right to cancel the contract.
- **Regulations on athlete agent's conduct**. The act regulates an athlete agent's conduct, including prohibiting the agent from initiating contact with a student-athlete or pre-dating or post-dating a contract.
- **Penalties and remedies**. The act establishes civil and criminal penalties for violations of the act. In addition, an educational institution has a civil remedy when it is damaged by prohibited conduct of an athlete agent or student-athlete.

U.S. state and territory regulation of athlete agent activities (Uniform Law Commission, 2015, 2019).

UAAA Definitions. Section 2 of the UAAA contains the relevant definitions of persons and contracts covered by and subject to the act. The key definitions are for an **athlete agent**, a **student-athlete**, and an **agency contract**. These are set out in Exhibit 8.7.

The definition of an athlete agent is very broad and includes those individuals who recruit and solicit potential student-athletes, as well as those who actually enter into an agency agreement with a student-athlete. Thus, the definition includes "runners" working for an agent to recruit or solicit student-athletes

Exhibit 8.7 UAAA key definitions.

Sections 2(1), (2), and (19) of the Revised UAAA (2015, 2019) definitions of agency contract, athlete agent, and student-athlete.

(1) "Agency contract" means an agreement in which a student-athlete authorizes a person to negotiate or solicit on behalf of the student-athlete a professional-sports-services contract or an endorsement contract.

(2) "Athlete agent":

A means an individual, whether or not registered under this [act], who: (i) directly or indirectly recruits or solicits a student-athlete to enter into an agency contract or, for compensation, procures employment or offers, promises, attempts, or negotiates to obtain employment for a student-athlete as a professional athlete or member of a professional sports team or organization; (ii) for compensation or in anticipation of compensation related to a student-athlete's participation in athletics: (I) serves the athlete in an advisory capacity on a matter related to finances, business pursuits, or career management decisions, unless the individual is an employee of an educational institution acting exclusively as an employee of the institution for the benefit of the institution; or (II) manages the business affairs of the athlete by providing assistance with bills, payments, contracts, or taxes; or (iii) in anticipation of representing a student-athlete for a purpose related to the athlete's participation in athletics: (I) gives consideration to the student-athlete or another person; (II) serves the athlete in an advisory capacity on a matter related to finances, business pursuits, or career management decisions; or (III) manages the business affairs of the athlete by providing assistance with bills, payments, contracts, or taxes; but

B does not include an individual who: (i) acts solely on behalf of a professional sports team or organization; or (ii) is a licensed, registered, or certified professional and offers or provides services to a student-athlete customarily provided by members of the profession, unless the individual: (I) also recruits or solicits the athlete to enter into an agency contract; (II) also, for compensation, procures employment or offers, promises, attempts, or negotiates to obtain employment for the athlete as a professional athlete or member of a professional sports team or organization; or (III) receives consideration for providing the services calculated using a different method than for an individual who is not a student-athlete.

(19) "Student-athlete" means an individual who engages in, is eligible to engage in, or maybe eligible in the future to engage in, any intercollegiate sport. If an individual is permanently incligible to participate in a particular intercollegiate sport, the individual is not a student-athlete for purposes of that sport (UAAA, 2019).

to enter into an agency contract. Only individuals are within the definition of athlete agent and, therefore, subject to the act. Corporations and other business entities do not come within the definition of athlete agent and, therefore, are not covered by the act. Individuals employed as athlete agents by a corporation or other business entity, such as Endeavor (WME/IMG), CAA Sports, Octagon, or Athletes First, are required to register in their individual capacity. Representatives of "professional sports teams or professional sports organizations," such as football or hockey teams, are excluded from the definition of athlete agent as long as they are acting on behalf of their teams or organizations. For example, a professional athlete who gives a student-athlete information about the qualifications of an athlete agent is not required to register under the UAAA unless the professional athlete also attempts to recruit or solicit the student-athlete to sign an agency contract. In addition to the registration requirements outlined in the UAAA, many institutions require agents to register prior to contacting student-athletes at the institution, plus the NCAA has now started a very limited certification for agents in basketball to assist a select group of men's basketball players to assess their potential for the National Basketball Association (NBA) draft. The University of Louisville, for example, requires agents to register with the university and with the Commonwealth of Kentucky. The school also conducts regular NCAA rules education sessions with student-athletes and coaches regarding contact with agents. After multiple scandals have rocked college basketball, with one of the most highly publicized resulting in federal convictions of three sports agents, college coaches, and athletic product company employees on the grounds of bribery and wire-fraud, the Uniform Law Commission revised and amended UAAA. The revisions address some of the issues that arose in that scandal involving agents who were business managers and financial advisors who bribed college basketball coaches to pressure and direct families to the agents. In a related scheme, the agents worked with a senior executive at a sport product company to funnel bribes to high school players and their families to direct those athletes to coaches and schools who were sponsored by that product company (U.S. Attorney's Office, 2017). (Some states have adopted the revised version, while others are still acting under the original UAAA.)

The definition of student-athlete is also particularly important, since the UAAA expressly excludes, for purposes of a particular intercollegiate sport, any individual who is permanently ineligible to participate in that sport. Thus, the UAAA does not apply to or affect the activities of athlete agents working with athletes who are already professional athletes or who do not have any amateur eligibility remaining. However, the definition of student-athlete does apply to a two-sport athlete who has eligibility remaining in one sport. For example, an individual who is a student-athlete in football who has signed a contract to play professional baseball is not a student-athlete in baseball but is in football. Thus, any individual dealing with that student-athlete regarding professional services or endorsement contracts in professional football would be covered by the UAAA. The definition of student-athlete also includes individuals who are not yet in college, such as high school students, high school dropouts, and high school graduates who may have future eligibility for intercollegiate sports.

UAAA Requirements. The basic requirements of the Uniform Athlete Agents Act mandate *registration, disclosure, notification,* and *penalties/remedies*. In particular, the UAAA provides for the uniform *registration,* certification, and background checking of athlete agents who seek to represent student-athletes. The UAAA requires that specific warnings and *disclosures* be provided to student-athletes in the agency agreement and further requires *notification* be provided to educational institutions when an agent and a student-athlete enter into an agency agreement. The UAAA also permits an educational institution to bring a civil cause of action for damages resulting from a breach of the UAAA duties.

Agent registration. Sections 4 and 5 of the UAAA require agents to register and disclose their training, experience, and education. Registration requirements are stated in Section 4 (see Exhibit 8.8).

Agents must register in each state in which they have established sufficient minimum contact that would normally make them subject to the jurisdiction of the state courts. For example, if an individual whose principal place of business is in State A contacts a student-athlete in State B, the agent is acting as an athlete agent in both states and is, therefore, required to register in both states. However, subsection (b) of § 4 provides a safe harbor for an unregistered individual with whom a student-athlete *initiates* communications. If a student-athlete in the State of Oklahoma (where the UAAA was adopted) contacts an athlete agent with an athlete representation firm in Massachusetts (with no UAAA yet), the Massachusetts athlete agent has not violated the Oklahoma UAAA by attempting to enter into an agency agreement, so long as registration is completed in Oklahoma within seven days of the initial contact by the student-athlete. The agent must apply for registration within seven days from the *beginning* of any effort to recruit or solicit the student-athlete to enter into an agency contract. If the agent does not attempt to recruit or solicit the student-athlete to sign an agency contract, registration is not required. Agents who are issued

Exhibit 8.8 Agent registration requirements.

Section 4 of the UAAA.

a   Except as otherwise provided in subsection (b), an individual may not act as an athlete agent in this state without holding a certificate of registration under this [act].

b   Before being issued a certificate of registration under this [act] an individual may act as an athlete agent in this state for all purposes except signing an agency contract, if:

   1   a student-athlete or another person acting on behalf of the athlete initiates communication with the individual; and

   2   *not later than seven days* after an initial act that requires the individual to register as an athlete agent, the individual submits an application for registration as an athlete agent in this state;

   3   an agency contract resulting from conduct in violation of this section is void, and the athlete agent shall return any consideration received under the contract (UAAA, 2019).

Exhibit 8.9   UAAA warning requirement for student-athlete agency contracts.

WARNING TO STUDENT-ATHLETE

IF YOU SIGN THIS CONTRACT:

1   YOU MAY LOSE YOUR ELIGIBILITY TO COMPETE AS A STUDENT-ATHLETE IN YOUR SPORT;
2   IF YOU HAVE AN ATHLETIC DIRECTOR, WITHIN 72 HOURS AFTER ENTERING INTO THIS CONTRACT, BOTH YOU AND YOUR ATHLETE AGENT MUST NOTIFY YOUR ATHLETIC DIRECTOR; AND

YOU MAY CANCEL THIS CONTRACT WITHIN 14 DAYS AFTER SIGNING IT. CANCELATION OF THIS CONTRACT MAY NOT REINSTATE YOUR ELIGIBILITY (UAAA, 2019).

---

a valid certification of registration in one state may cross-file that application in all other states that have adopted the UAAA. This aspect of the act simplifies regulatory compliance for athlete agents and enables all jurisdictions to obtain dependable, uniform information on an agent's professional conduct in other states.

Disclosure. The loss of intercollegiate eligibility can have serious consequences for both the student-athlete and the university. Student-athletes may be unaware that their eligibility may be at risk when they enter into an agency agreement. The UAAA requires all agency contracts to be in a recorded form and signed by the student-athletes.

Section 10 of the UAAA requires the agency contract to state that the agent is registered and list all states in which (s)he is registered. It must include the fees to be charged for services, the reimbursements to be charged, and anyone else who will be paid by the athlete for services in accordance with the contract. It must contain the warning shown in Exhibit 8.9 in all capital letters in close proximity to the signature of the student-athlete. This warning is intended to make sure the student-athlete is aware that amateur eligibility may be lost by entering into an agency agreement and must also include a separate record to be signed by the athlete (or the parent or guardian, if the athlete is a minor) to acknowledge that by signing the contract (s)he will lose eligibility to participate in the athlete's sport. Student-athletes also have a statutory right to cancel an agency contract within 14 days after the contract is signed, without penalty. A student-athlete who opts to void an agency contract under this section is required to return any consideration received as an inducement to the signing of the agency contract, because such inducement is prohibited (Uniform Law Commission, 2019).

It is important to note that even if a student-athlete exercises the right to cancel the contract this may not restore his eligibility. For example, under the NCAA By Laws, a student-athlete loses his eligibility if he does any of the following:

a   enters into an agreement with an agent (NCAA Division I Manual, By law 12.1.2(g));
b   retains an agent (By law 12.2.4.3);
c   the student-athlete or their family accepts transportation or other benefits from an agent (By law 12.3.1.2);
d   ever has agreed (orally or in writing) to be represented by an agent for the purpose of marketing his or her athletics ability or reputation in that sport (By law 12.3.1).

The NCAA is not required to reinstate a student-athlete's eligibility just because the student-athlete legally cancels the agency agreement (NCAA, n.d.a, n.d.b). Student-athletes are allowed, however, in accordance with by law 12.3.2, to hire a lawyer to secure advice about entering into a professional sports contract, provided that the lawyer is paid for their services and that lawyer is not intended to be their agent. The same can apply to a financial advisor from whom the athlete seeks advice, pays, and that financial advisor is not intending to serve as an agent in the future (NCAA, n.d.b.).

Notification. The potential loss of a student-athlete's eligibility is a serious concern for athletic programs at educational institutions. Section 11 of the UAAA requires both the agent and the student-athlete to notify the athletic director that an agency agreement has been entered into within 72 hours of signing the agreement or before the athlete's next scheduled athletic event, whichever occurs first. The purpose of notification is to protect an educational institution from sanctions or other penalties that could result from allowing an ineligible player to participate. The penalties imposed by the NCAA can be severe, such as loss of scholarships, prohibition from championship events, probation, negative publicity, and forfeiture of tournament winnings or other revenue. The monetary penalties can be very substantial when revenues are lost from participation in a football bowl game or a postseason basketball tournament. Courts have recognized the adverse impact, both financial and operational, that NCAA penalties can have on educational institutions. For example, in *United States v. Piggie* (2002), Myron Piggie had created a secret scheme to pay talented high school athletes to play for his "amateur" summer team. The scheme produced multiple violations of NCAA rules, since many of these athletes later signed letters of intent to play collegiate basketball. The ultimate ineligibility of these athletes resulted in NCAA violations and lost scholarships for several universities, including UCLA, Duke, the University of Missouri, and Oklahoma State University. Total costs for those universities neared $250,000.

Prohibited Conduct. Section 14 of the UAAA describes the athlete agent conduct prohibited under the act that will give rise to both civil and criminal penalties (see Exhibit 8.10). In 2019, an amendment was made to the UAAA in reaction to a significant 2018 rule change by the NCAA. The new NCAA rule allows student-athletes, specifically basketball players to receive certain benefits from NCAA certified agents during, but only during the process of selecting an agent. The rule was designed to give these athletes a chance to seek advice before forgoing their eligibility and entering the NBA draft. If, before the beginning of the following season, they do not sign a professional contract and terminate the agency contract, they are allowed to retain eligibility.

Exhibit 8.10 **Section 14** of the UAAA: Prohibited conduct for athlete agents.

An athlete agent, with the intent to induce a student-athlete to enter into an agency contract, may not:

1. give any materially false or misleading information or make a materially false promise or representation;
2. furnish anything of value to the athlete a student-athlete or another individual, if to do so may result in loss of the athlete's eligibility to participate in the athlete's sport, unless:
   a. the agent notifies the athletic director of the educational institution at which the athlete is enrolled or at which the agent has reasonable grounds to believe the athlete intends to enroll, not later than 72 hours after giving the thing of value; and
   b. the athlete or, if the athlete is a minor, a parent or [guardian] of the athlete acknowledges to the agent in a record that receipt of the thing of value may result in loss of the athlete's eligibility to participate in the athlete's sport;
3. initiate contact, directly or indirectly, with a student-athlete or, if the athlete is a minor, a parent or [guardian] of the athlete, to recruit or solicit the athlete, parent, or [guardian] to enter an agency contract unless registered under this [act];
4. fail to create, retain, or permit inspection of the records required by Section 13;
5. fail to register when required by Section 4;
6. provide materially false or misleading information in an application for registration or renewal of registration;
7. predate or postdate an agency contract;
8. fail to notify a student-athlete or, if the athlete is a minor, a parent or [guardian] of the athlete, before the athlete, parent, or [guardian] signs an agency contract for a particular sport that the signing may result in loss of the athlete's eligibility to participate in the athlete's sport;
9. encourage another individual to do any of the acts described in paragraphs (1) through (8) on behalf of the agent; or
10. encourage another individual to assist any other individual in doing any of the acts described in paragraphs (1) through (8) on behalf of the agent.
11. fail to notify a student-athlete before the student-athlete signs or otherwise authenticates an agency contract for a particular sport that the signing or authentication may make the student-athlete ineligible to participate as a student-athlete in that sport.

The UAAA amendment applies to Section 14 above, Prohibited Conduct, and adds two exceptions to the previous rule prohibiting an agent from furnishing a thing of value to a student-athlete (uniformlaws. org). These exceptions include:

a the agent notifies the athletic director of the educational institution at which the athlete is enrolled or at which the agent has reasonable grounds to believe the athlete intends to enroll, not later than 72 hours after giving the thing of value; and

b the athlete or, if the athlete is a minor, a parent or [guardian] of the athlete acknowledges to the agent in a record that receipt of the thing of value may result in loss of the athlete's eligibility to participate in the athlete's sport (Uniform Law Commission, 2019).

The amendment makes no mention of basketball or the specific type of expense allowed with these exceptions, such that a future amendment may not be needed if the NCAA were once again to update its rules (Uniform Law Commission, 2019).

The UAAA stands at the center of recent lawsuits involving Zion Williamson, the NBA's 2019 first-round draft pick of the New Orleans Pelicans. Williamson, a power forward who played one year at Duke University, hired marketing agency, Prime Sports, in late April 2019. Then, on May 31, 2019 he fired Prime Sports and its President, Gina Ford as he had just signed with competitor, CAA Sports the day before. Ford sought mediation or threatened to sue as she had a five-year agreement with Williamson (Al-Khateeb, 2020). Williamson responded with a lawsuit alleging that Ford had violated the UAAA, which is the law in North Carolina. Williamson alleged that the agreement was unlawful "because Prime Sports is not certified by the National Basketball Players Association or a registered athlete agent in North Carolina or Florida. Additionally, the agreement failed to contain, as required under the UAAA, a conspicuous notice in boldface type in capital letters informing the athlete that by signing the agreement he was losing his eligibility to compete as a student-athlete." (Wojnarowski, 2019). For her part, Ford responded with a lawsuit in Florida, her principal place of business, that alleged Williamson breached his contract and that the UAAA did not void their contract because Williamson had already declared for the draft with no intention of going back to Duke (Al-Khateeb, 2020). As this text goes to print, the Florida lawsuit is stalled awaiting the trial in the North Carolina case and is getting ugly as Ford has submitted interrogatories seeking a yes or no declaration from Williamson as to whether he or his family received financial benefits from Duke or others that would potentially have ruined his eligibility at Duke (Kolin, 2020).

Penalties. Sections 15 and 16 of the UAAA establish the civil and criminal penalties available for violations of the act. It was debated whether athlete agents should be subjected to criminal sanctions, but eventually the conclusion was drawn that, due to the degree of financial motivation in professional sport athlete representation, some potential criminal penalty was necessary to discourage those individuals who are willing to engage in improper or illegal conduct. Each state adopting the UAAA determines whether the criminal penalty will be a misdemeanor or a felony. Additionally, due to the wide variation in criminal penalties provided for by already existing acts, the type of criminal penalties to be imposed was also left to the states.

Section 15 gives each state the flexibility to adopt penalties it believes best serve the interests of its citizens. As many states have included both civil and criminal penalties in athlete agent regulations, it behooves someone interested in this sector of the sport industry to become familiar with the relevant body of law. Alabama and North Carolina are examples of states taking a firm stance toward athlete agent misconduct by including criminal penalties for violations. In Alabama, two sports agents were arrested and charged with a felony for failing to register as an agent and a misdemeanor for initiating contact with a student-athlete (Dujardin, 2008). After a few nights in jail, the supervisory agent pleaded guilty to a lesser charge and blamed his underling for the mistake (Dujardin, 2011). In North Carolina, former NFL agent Terry Watson pleaded guilty to violating North Carolina's sports agent law by providing thousands of dollars in improper benefits to three former Tar Heels football players to entice them into signing contracts with him. Watson received 30 months of probation and a $5,000 fine, while Judge Graham Shirley issued a suspended jail sentence of six to eight months. Watson pleaded guilty to the 13 counts of athlete agent inducement for providing roughly $24,000 in cash and travel accommodations to eventual NFL players Robert Quinn, Marvin Austin and Greg Little in 2010 (Associated Press, 2017a). However, generally, these criminal penalties are low level felonies or misdemeanors and often are not a priority for law enforcement to investigate. More often than not, those violating the state statutes instead will pay a fine for the violation (Associated Press, 2017b).

Section 16 creates a civil remedy specifically for educational institutions. It permits a college or university to sue either the athlete agent or former student-athlete for damages, including losses and expenses incurred as a result of the educational institution's being penalized, disqualified, or suspended from participation. Section 16 also allows the educational institution to recover its costs and reasonable attorneys' fees. Educational institutions are typically reluctant to bring an action against a former student-athlete, since suing a former student-athlete could create negative publicity for the university and hinder future recruiting of athletes. However, there are certain situations, such as the 1996 one involving the University of Massachusetts and its basketball player Marcus Camby. In that instance, highly improper conduct by a student-athlete who ultimately received a lucrative professional contract, even though his conduct caused serious financial losses to his educational institution via penalties due to NCAA violations. Camby did eventually pay back the institution through donations to the University Health Services and the School of Education (Associated Press, 1997). Interestingly, the losses from his misconduct were suffered by the athletic department, yet it was not a beneficiary of his gift.

The following hypothetical case will let us explore how the UAAA provisions might be interpreted and applied. The UAAA is available in the Web Resources. Please consult the UAAA to answer the questions and then check your responses using the Analysis and Discussion at the end of this chapter.

Considering … Athlete Agent Behavior

Josh is a "runner" for Steve Shady, a prominent sports agent. While on campus at Big State University (BSU) in the State of Missolina, Josh, without informing the administration of his presence on campus, meets with Marcus Goode, BSU's star running back. Goode is a sophomore and has two years of eligibility remaining in the NCAA. BSU competes in NCAA FBS Division I. The State of Missolina adopted the UAAA in 2019. Josh represents that Shady is prepared to provide the following to Goode should he agree to be represented by Shady:

1 the keys to a Mercedes-Benz S-500 parked right outside Goode's apartment;
2 $5,000 cash;
3 training at Shady's posh Miami, FL, workout facility in preparation for the NFL draft camp next spring.

Questions

- Is the meeting between Goode and Josh subject to the provisions of the UAAA?
- Assume Goode agrees to be represented by Shady at this meeting. Has the UAAA been violated, and, if so, what are the potential penalties?
- Assume further that Goode later signs a representation agreement. Would either the meeting or the signing of the representation agreement adversely affect his amateur eligibility with the NCAA?

Assume that 13 days after signing the representation agreement, Goode has a change of heart and notifies Shady that he wants to cancel the contract. May he do so? What, if any, impact will the cancelation have on Goode's amateur eligibility?

Section 16 of the original UAAA allowed for the possibility of a civil action against its student-athletes, but educational institutions must carefully consider whether to exercise that right. The revised version of the UAAA was amended based on Section 18897.8 of the California Business and Professions Code, removes the cause of action against a student-athlete and gives the student-athlete a cause of action against the agent. The student-athlete may also bring an action against an athlete agent under existing agency law (as discussed in the first section of this chapter) for breach of contract, or breach of fiduciary duty (Uniform Law Commission, 2019).

Sports Agent Responsibility and Trust Act

As mentioned earlier, even though 43 states and U.S. territories have adopted the UAAA as of July 2013, several states still have no laws regulating athlete agents. Thus, in those states, student-athletes and educational institutions have had little, if any, protection from unscrupulous athlete agents. To address this gap in state regulation, Congress passed the *Sports Agent Responsibility and Trust Act (SPARTA)* in September 2004 as a supplement to the requirements of the UAAA and to provide some protection for student-athletes located in those states (*Sports Agent*, 2003).

SPARTA provides some of the protections of the UAAA but is not as comprehensive. Like the UAAA, SPARTA seeks to prevent agents from luring student-athletes into signing agency contracts by offering valuable gifts and providing false or misleading information. SPARTA designates certain conduct by athlete agents regarding their contractual dealings with student-athletes as unfair and deceptive trade practices subject to the regulatory authority of the Federal Trade Commission. SPARTA specifically prohibits an athlete agent from providing false or misleading information; making false or misleading promises; and providing anything of value, such as gifts, cash, or loans, to student-athletes.

SPARTA also requires that agents provide student-athletes with disclosures and warnings, similar to those required in the UAAA, regarding the effect entering into an agency contract has on eligibility. Failure to make the required disclosures is a violation of the act. Violating any portion of the act exposes the athlete agent to civil fines of up to $11,000 per day, per offense. In addition, SPARTA extends enforcement authority to the individual states' Attorney General offices, so that each state can impose fines on athlete agents who violate the act. SPARTA lacks the UAAA's extensive registration requirement, and in § 8 of SPARTA Congress specifically states that it "serves as a vital federal backstop in all states that have yet to adopt the UAAA and contains a 'Sense of Congress' section which urges states to enact the UAAA and its important athlete agent registration requirements" (NCAA, n.d.c).

Professional Athletes and Agents

When you think of a sport agent or athlete agent, you might envision Scott Boras, one of the leading sport agents, who represents more than 100 MLB players, or Tom Condon of Creative Artists Agency, representing billions of dollars in current player contracts in the NFL (Belzer, 2013). However, most professional athlete contract negotiations do not involve hundreds of millions of dollars and superstar agents like Scott Boras. The life of a sport agent is grueling and demanding. In its most basic form, whether you are a successful sport agent or a determined aspiring agent, the main job of a sport agent is still contract negotiation. Thus, it is important that athlete agents possess the necessary training, skills, and expertise to be effective negotiators. The agency relationship is an express agency at the major league level, since major league professional sports require the athlete representatives to be certified by the players association and to use a Standard Representation Agreement for agents and athletes.

However, athlete representation where the agent serves as marketing and branding, public relations, or financial consultant, which are becoming more common, could involve any of the various types of agency relationships described earlier and thereby raise additional issues involving the agent's mishandling of an athlete's funds. These types of disputes involve tort law principles, such as fraud and misrepresentation, in addition to contract issues. Many of these issues were present in the highly publicized case involving sport agent Tank Black, chairman and CEO of the athlete representation firm Professional Management, Inc.

(PMI). Black involved several NFL players in a pyramid and money laundering scheme in coordination with two different companies Black operated. While Black was president of Black Americans of Achievement, Inc. (BAOA), this organization produced a board game celebrating the accomplishments of African Americans. Black arranged for his PMI clients to promote BAOA's board game in exchange for free, restricted BAOA stock. However, the clients (athletes) were never informed of these arrangements and never agreed to endorse the BAOA board game. BAOA issued two million shares of free stock in the names of 15 PMI clients, and BAOA sent stock certificates to PMI. Black, in turn, sold the BAOA stock to his clients at PMI for prices that were above current market prices at the time. Black sold the BAOA stock to Ike Hilliard and other PMI clients for $1,240,000. Black then directed PMI clients to pay for BAOA stock with checks made payable to PE Communications, Inc. (PE), a shell company also created by Black. Black also directed that over $1 million in funds be transferred from the PE account to his personal bank accounts. Ultimately Black was decertified as an NFLPA player agent, and on May 7, 2002, he was sentenced to serve 60 months in prison and ordered to pay $12 million in restitution stemming from charges that he defrauded his athlete clients in multiple investment schemes over a three-year period (Hilliard v. Black, 2000).

As described in the previous section, a number of states have enacted protection for student-athletes who are victimized by unscrupulous athlete agents. The UAAA and SPARTA both focus on protecting student-athletes and educational institutions. Thus, for those athletes who are no longer student-athletes but instead are active professional athletes, only traditional contract, tort, and agency law is available to protect them from a breach of an agency agreement, breach of fiduciary duty, or fraud. As a result, most professional players associations (labor unions for professional athletes; see Chapter 7) have developed registration and certification procedures for agents and impose limitations on fees as a means of minimizing the potential for athlete agents to exploit athletes.

Players Association Regulations

Players associations have been instrumental in growing athletes' incomes through collective bargaining agreements and their efforts to open the market to athletes through free agency. Athletes have relied on sports agents to represent them individually. The players associations are then dependent on player agents to work in concert with them, but also find themselves in the unenviable position of policing agents. Due to the scarcity of clients and the nature of the athlete representation business is fraught with problems discussed previously (incompetence, fraud, overly aggressive client recruitment, bribery, and the like). In response, players associations have taken steps to regulate the business, as have some professional leagues.

The players unions are legally able to certify agents in order to protect their members (athletes) from unscrupulous behavior and to protect their collectively bargained provisions in the CBA (Collins v. NBPA, 1991). For instance, if a minimum salary in a league is set at $600,000 and an agent agrees to sign a player to a team for $400,000, it would undermine the union's work in collective bargaining. Even if the player wanted to sign for $400,000, he could not do so. The union can take steps to require agents to be certified and even test their knowledge before allowing them to represent the players. The union can keep agents from entering the profession, by refusing to certify them. This right does not extend to agents who are solely financial or marketing advisors. The union can, however, seek voluntary registration or certification for agents doing that work. A good example is the NFLPA's voluntary registration program financial advisors. The NFLPA Financial Advisor's program was the idea of the players themselves. Between 1992 and 2002, the NFLPA estimated that 78 players lost a total of $42 million from unscrupulous financial advisors and agents (Bergeron, 2011). It was created to provide players with a list of qualified financial advisors (NFLPA, 2020). Financial advisor registration is voluntary whereas agent certification is mandatory, meaning the NFLPA can ban uncertified agents from working with NFL players. It cannot do so for the financial advisors. However, a player agent who is also providing financial advice, must also be registered with this program (NFLPA, 2020). It is worth noting that if the NFLPA were to adopt a stricter vetting process, let's say required certification rather than voluntary registration, it may face a potential antitrust action by a financial advisor rejected from certification. Regulating financial advisors is outside of the union's labor exemption to antitrust which protects them from such a suit when the union is acting in its own self-interest to protect its labor activities and collective bargaining. Regulating agents engaged in individual negotiations of standard player contracts which are incorporated into the CBAs by reference is within the protected powers of the union, while regulating financial advisors is not.

Exhibit 8.11 below is a sampling of the players association regulations governing player agents in the United States.

Exhibit 8.11 Players associations' regulations.

	Application Fee/Annual Fee	Qualifications	Grounds for Denial of Certification/Violations	Enforcement and Appeals
NFL NFLPA	$2,500/$1,500 if you represent 0–10 players, $2,000 for 10+ players	• Undergraduate AND postgraduate degrees • Attend at a two-day seminar • Score of 70 or better on a multiple-choice exam • Obtain liability insurance • Authorize background check	• Making false or misleading statements in the application. • Misappropriating funds, embezzlement, theft, or fraud. • Making payments to a player to encourage utilizing the agent's services.	• Disciplinary action handled by a three–five person • Committee on Agent Regulation and Discipline (CARD). • Appeals and other disputes handled through arbitrations.
NBA NBPA	$250 (plus pro-rated annual fee for rest of season)/0–9 players: $2,500, 10–19 players: $5,000, 20+ players: $7,500	• Pass multiple choice exam • Negotiate at least one player contract within five years • Attend an NBPA seminar for each of first three years • Authorize background check	• Making false or misleading statements in the application. • Misappropriating funds, embezzlement, theft, or fraud. • Making payments to a player to encourage utilizing the agent's services. • Engaging in conduct which violates any NCAA regulations. • Soliciting or accepting money from any NBA team which would create a conflict of interest. • Gambling on any NBA game.	• All disputes handled through arbitration. • Arbitrator will hold hearings in New York city, which can be also moved to either Los Angeles or Chicago.
MLB **MLBPA**	$2,000/$1,500	• Pass written examination • Be designated as Agent by current MLB player • Authorize and complete background check	• Failure to cooperate with the MLBPA in the processing of application. • Making false or misleading statements in the application. • Failure to comply with fee disclosures and limitations. • Failure to adequately supervise those working on behalf of the agent.	• If legal questions affect the certification decision, the application is referred to the Assistant General Counsel for Agent Regulation • Other disputes handled through arbitration.

(Continued)

Exhibit 8.11 (Continued)

	Application Fee/Annual Fee	Qualifications	Grounds for Denial of Certification/Violations	Enforcement and Appeals
MLS MLSPA* USSF	$400/$50	• No financial or violent crimes convictions on record	• Must not charge client more than 3% basic gross income. • Financial or violent crimes on record.	• Violations of the FIFA Disciplinary Code are handled by the FIFA Disciplinary Committee.
NHL NHLPA	$2,100	• *Immediate Certified Status:* Represents a current player • *Interim Certified Status:* May negotiate for client while application is reviewed • *Pending Certified Status:* Represents an unsigned draft pick • Authorize background check	• False or misleading statements in the application. • Misappropriating funds, embezzlement, theft, or fraud. • Agent has been previously suspended by another government agency or players association.	• The NHLPA will assign a panel of three arbitrators with one-year terms. • These panel members will hear disputes on a rotating basis. • Hearings will be held in Toronto or an otherwise agreed upon city.

* MLSPA doesn't yet have a certification program. All above rules set by United States Soccer Federation (USSF) and Federation Internationale de Football Association (FIFA).

Competitive Advantage Strategies

The Law of Agency and Athlete Agents

- When establishing an agency relationship, follow basic contract principles, such as clearly identifying the parties, desired outcomes or objectives of the agency agreement, the duration of the agency, and the scope of authority of the agent.
- Even though oral agency agreements are enforceable, a better practice is to put agency agreements in writing.
- Athlete agents must educate themselves regarding the requirements of state laws such as UAAA and federal laws such as SPARTA before contacting prospective clients or embarking on a sport agency enterprise.
- Athlete agents must educate themselves on the players association or league regulations in the particular sports that they are working. They must see to it that they are certified or registered with the appropriate players association per their regulations.
- Prospective athlete agents should seriously evaluate the economic potential in the highly competitive field of athlete representation. The prospective agents should consider that the players associations in professional sports limit the agent's earnings to a single digit percentage of the athletes' salary. It varies by league, but all fall under 5 percent. There are not the same limits on income earned through marketing and sponsorship opportunities. There are also no limits, other than what is set by the market, on fees charged to athletes in individual sports or Olympic sports. Approximately half of all athlete agents do not have a single active player and those representing minor leaguers will not see a pay day for their efforts until the player gets to the major leagues. And even then, the fees may not come from the athlete's full salary, but only that differential in salary which exceeds the collectively bargained minimum salary in accordance with players association guidance.

- Those working in college athletics at any level should be familiar with the legal restrictions on athlete agents, as well as those imposed by the NCAA and other amateur athletic associations to protect the interests of the university in the event a student-athlete's eligibility becomes an issue. The NCAA has its own form of certification for a select group of agents to allow some student-athletes in Men's Basketball to hire agents to give those athletes a meaningful assessment of the professional prospects and whether it was in their interest to declare for the NBA draft. It will be interesting to see how the NCAA will expand on this select certification (NCAA, 2019). A university compliance officer may want to create informational brochures and conduct informational and educational seminars for student-athletes to aid them in understanding what contact is permissible with agents, and to proactively notify agents of their obligation to register with the state before contacting any student-athletes. The NCAA also offers materials on its website.

Conclusion

Typically, legal issues affecting athletes and agents arise in two main areas: agency for professional athletes and agency for student-athletes. This chapter introduced basic notions of agency law, including how agency relationships are created, the scope of an agent's authority, and the duties existing between agents and principals. This chapter also identified the numerous ways in which athlete agents are regulated in their dealings with student-athletes, including state regulations, the Uniform Athlete Agents Act (Revised and Amended), and the federal statute SPARTA. Last, this chapter summarized other, private restrictions imposed on athlete agents by professional players associations and sport governing bodies. A solid understanding of basic agency law is important to enable any sport manager to function effectively as a representative (employee) of a sport organization. In addition, a thorough understanding of how agency laws have been applied to athlete agents and the regulations in this area will be very useful for sport managers who negotiate player contracts, evaluate athletic eligibility for a university or the NCAA, or pursue a career as an athlete agent.

Discussion Questions

1 What are the different ways in which an agency relationship may be created?
2 Identify and explain each of the duties owed by the principal to the agent and by the agent to the principal.
3 How is apparent agency different from express agency?
4 Explain the different classifications of principals and how the classification affects the liability of the principal for the actions of an agent.
5 What are the seven essential provisions of the UAAA? Explain and demonstrate your understanding of each of the provisions.
6 What is the primary purpose of SPARTA? What are its limitations?
7 What requirements do professional sport leagues use to try to ensure athlete representatives are competent and professional in their representation of athletes?

Learning Activities

Find out what information is available online from the NCAA for student-athletes regarding athlete agents. From that information, can you determine the difference between an advisor and an agent? What is the significance of that difference? Go to www.ncaa.org and search for "agent information."

Case Study

Len Bias played basketball at the University of Maryland in the mid-1980s. He was an outstanding player and was projected to be a top NBA draft selection. On June 17, 1986, the Boston Celtics drafted him into the NBA. Two days later, he was found dead in his dorm room from a cocaine overdose. Prior to his death, he had instructed his agent, Advantage International, Inc., to take out a $1 million life insurance policy. The policy was not issued prior to his death. Bias' estate sued Advantage for failing to take out the policy.

1   What duties has Advantage allegedly breached, if any?
2   What do you think the court's decision was? (See *Bias v. Advantage International, Inc.*)

Considering ... Analysis & Discussion

Athlete Agent Behavior

Shady would clearly fall within the definition of an athlete agent under the UAAA, because he represents himself to the public as an athlete agent. Josh would also come under the athlete agent definition, because it applies to anyone who directly or indirectly recruits or solicits a student-athlete to enter into an agency agreement. Goode meets the definition of a student-athlete since he still has amateur eligibility remaining. As such, all the parties involved are subject to the acts. Josh and Shady must be registered under the act; thus, if Josh is not registered, his meeting would constitute a violation, since he initiated the contact. Had Goode initiated the contact, Shady or Josh could have met with Goode and registered later. Assuming that Josh is registered, the meeting itself does not violate any of the restrictions imposed by the UAAA.

Neither Shady nor Josh may offer Goode anything of value unless and until Goode executes an agency agreement. Thus, the verbal promises made by Josh violate the act, even though the promises were only offers to give Goode money or items of value if he signed with Shady. The inducement to sign is prohibited. If, during the course of the meeting, the proper disclosures are made and Goode executes the agency agreement, Shady or Josh may offer money or items of value to Goode. Remember, the primary purpose of the UAAA is to provide the student-athlete with adequate notice of the type of relationship he is entering into and the ramifications of that decision.

Once Goode agrees to be represented by Shady, whether in a formal agency agreement or just verbally, his amateur eligibility will likely be lost, based upon the NCAA restrictions on student-athletes and agents. If Goode decides he would like to cancel the contract, the UAAA gives him 14 days to so. He could cancel it, return anything of value provided to him by Shady, and no longer be bound to the agency agreement. However, even if he legally cancels the agreement and returns any items of value or money received, the NCAA is not obligated to reinstate his amateur eligibility.

References

Cases

Bias v. Advantage Int'l, Inc., 905 F.2d 1558 (D.C. Cir. 1990).
Clark Adver. Agency v. Tice, 490 F.2d 834 (5th Cir. 1974).
Collins v. NBPA, 850 F. Supp. 1468 (1991), *aff'd per curium*, 976 F.2d 740 (10th Cir. 1992).
Detroit Lions, Inc. and Billy Sims v. Argovitz, 767 F.2d 919 (6th Cir. 1985).
Hilliard v. Black, 125 F. Supp. 2d 1071 (N.D. Fla. 2000).

McCants v. NCAA, 201 F. Supp. 3d 732 (M.D.N.C. 2016).
Jones v. Archibald, 360 N.Y.S.2d 119 (App. Div. 1974).
United States v. Piggie, 303 F.3d 923 (8th Cir. 2002).

Statutes

Restatement (Third) of Agency § 1.01 Agency defined (2006).
Restatement (Third) of Agency § 1.04 Terminology (2006).
Restatement (Third) of Agency § 2.03 Apparent authority (2006).
Restatement (Third) of Agency § 3.03 Creation of apparent authority (2006).
Restatement (Third) of Agency § 8.01 General fiduciary principle (2006).
Restatement (Third) of Agency § 8.02 No self-dealing (2006).
Restatement (Third) of Agency § 8.03 No conflict of interest (2006).
Restatement (Third) of Agency § 8.04 Avoid competition or competing interests (2006).
Restatement (Third) of Agency § 8.05 No misuse property of funds of principal; avoid disclosure of confidential information (2006).
Restatement (Third) of Agency § 8.08 Duty of care, competence, and diligence (2006).
Restatement (Third) of Agency § 8.09 Duty to act within scope of authority and comply with lawful instructions (2006).
Restatement (Third) of Agency § 8.10 Duty of good conduct – refrain from actions that may damage principal's enterprise (2006).
Restatement (Third) of Agency § 8.11 Duty to provide information to principal (2006).
Restatement (Third) of Agency § 8.12 Duty of accounting (2006).
Restatement (Third) of Agency § 8.14 Duty to indemnify (2006).
Restatement (Third) of Agency § 8.15 Deal fairly and in good faith, such as information about risks of physical harm or pecuniary loss (2006).
Sports Agent Responsibility and Trust Act, 15 U.S.C. § 7801, *et seq.* (2009).
Sports agent responsibility and trust act: Hearing before the Subcommittee on Commercial and Administrative Law of the Committee on the Judiciary, House of Representatives, 108th Cong., 1. (2003).
Uniform Law Commission (2019). Revised Uniform Athlete Agents Act of 2015 (Last Amended 2019). Retrieved from https://www.uniformlaws.org/HigherLogic/System/downloadDocumentFile.ashx?DocumentFileKey=65a7fcb8-177e-80c1-5468-64301f80b4c&forceDialog.
Uniform Law Commission (2015). Why your state should adopt the revised uniform athlete agents act. Retrieved from https://www.uniformlaws.org/HigherLogic/System/Download DocumentFile.ashx?DocumentFileKey=4c450e99-06a8-21ba-2cff-883b8a80e38c&force Dialog=0.

Other Sources

Al-Khateeb, Z. (2020, May 13). Zion Williamson lawsuit explained: What to know about allegations of impermissible benefits at Duke. *The Sporting News*. Retrieved from https://www.sportingnews.com/us/ncaa-basketball/news/zion-williamson-lawsuit-agent-duke-explained/15av17fnk80a5178k7elcunsqr.
Associated Press. (1997, July 21). Camby repays tourney money. *The New York Times*, p. 1(28) (Late Edition).
Associated Press. (2010, January 28). Financial advisors to pay out $1.3 million. *ESPN.com* .Retrieved from http://sports.espn.go.com/nba/news/story?id=4867453.
Associated Press. (2017a, April 17). Ex-NFL agent Terry Watson pleads guilty to giving cash to 3 former UNC players. *ESPN.com*. Retrieved from https://www.espn.com/college-football/story/_/id/19180813/ex-nfl-agent-pleads-guilty-multi-year-north-carolina-tar-heels-sports-agent-probe.
Associated Press. (2017b, November 1). Violation of sport agent laws tough for states to prosecute. *USA Today*. Retrieved from https://www.usatoday.com/story/sports/ncaab/2017/11/01/violation-of-sports-agent-laws-tough-for-states-to-prosecute/107223304/.
Bergeron, E. (2011, August 25). Zero-sum game. *ESPN The Magazine*. Retrieved from http://espn.go.com/nfl/story/_/id/6895017/nfl-michael-vick-typifies-howeasily-nfl-players-go-bankrupt-espn-magazine.
Cavanaugh, J. (1997, May 9). UMass and UConn lose '96 honors. *The New York Times*, p. B21 (Late Edition).
Dujardin, P. (2008, October 7). Sports agent arrested for violating Alabama law. *Daily Press*. Retrieved from https://www.dailypress.com/news/dp-xpm-20081007-2008-10-07-0810060150-story.html.
Dujardin, P. (2011, February 25). Sports agent predicts full comeback. *Daily Press*. Retrieved from http://articles.dailypress.com/2011-02-25/news/dp-nws-sports-agent-20110225_1_raymond-l-savage-alabama-football-startyrone-prothro.

Edelman, M. (2013, June 4). Will the new Uniform Athlete Agents Act continue to pander to the NCAA? *Forbes.com*. Retrieved from https://www.forbes.com/sites/marcedelman/2013/06/04/will-the-new-uniform-athlete-agents-act-continue-to-pander-to-the-ncaa#2eb8fb032.

Estes, G. (2018, February 23). How did an upstart agent disrupt college hoops? *Louisville Courier Journal*. Retrieved from https://www.courier-journal.com/story/sports/college/kentucky/2018/02/23/christian-dawkins-nba-agent-andy-miller-college-basketball-recruiting/366449002/.

Heitner, D. (2012, November 19). Basketball agent Aaron Mintz awarded $85,000 for emotional distress caused by Priority Sports. *SportsAgentBlog.com*. Retrieved from http://sportsagentblog.com/2012/11/19/mintz/.

Heitner, D. (2013, May 12). Football agent's lawsuit against former agency asks court to void parts of employment agreement. *Forbes.com*. Retrieved from http://www.forbes.com/sites/darrenheitner/2013/05/12/football-agents-lawsuit-against-former-agency-asks-court-to-void-parts-of-employment-agreement/.

Kleinberger, D. S. (2017). *Agency, partnerships, and LLCs* (5th ed.). New York, NY: Wolters Kluwer.

Kolin, E. (2020, June 12). Breaking down the lawsuits of former Duke men's basketball star Zion Williamson. *The Chronicle*. Retrieved from https://www.dukechronicle.com/article/2020/06/duke-basketball-zion-williamson-allegations-lawsuits-prime-sports-gina-ford-pay-to-play-daniel-wallach.

National Collegiate Athletic Association (NCAA). (n.d.a). *Applicable agent legislation*. Retrieved from http://fs.ncaa.org/Docs/ENF/UAAA/map/index.html.

National Collegiate Athletic Association (NCAA). (n.d.b). Overview of NCAA legislation for NFLPA financial advisors. Retrieved from https://www.ncaa.org/sites/default/files/20160419Overview%20of%20NCAA%20Legislation%20for%20NFLPA%20Financial20Advisors.pdf.

National Collegiate Athletic Association (NCAA). (n.d.c). Agent information. Retrieved from http://www.ncaa.org/enforcement/agents-and-amateurism.

NFLPA (2020). Financial Advisors: Frequently asked questions. Retrieved from https://www.nflpa.com/financial-advisors/faq.

Norlander, M. (2018, November 9). Former Louisville recruit Brian Bowen sues Adidas and wants it to stop sponsoring college basketball. *CBSsports.com*. Retrieved from https://www.cbssports.com/college-basketball/news/former-louisville-recruit-brian-bowen-sues-adidas-and-wants-it-to-stop-sponsoring-college-basketball/.

Taylor, C. (2020, February 4). Carolina basketball: Tanner addresses notice of allegations. *The Times and Democrat*. Retrieved from https://thetandd.com/sports/local/carolina-basketball-tanner-addresses-notice-of-allegations/article_5405cc58-0929-5fdd-a517-efcc4465ba48.html.

Taylor, P. (1997, September 15). Tangled web Marcus Camby was both victim and villain in his illicit dealings with agents while at UMass. *Sports Illustrated*. Retrieved from https://vault.si.com/vault/1997/09/15/tangled-web-marcus-camby-was-both-victim-and-villain-in-his-illicit-dealings-with-agents-while-at-umass.

University of Pennsylvania Law School. (n.d.). Uniform athlete agents act: Policy statement. Retrieved from www.law.upenn.edu/bll/ulc/uaaa/aaps0615.htm.

U.S. Attorney's Office (2017, Sept. 26). U.S. Attorney (S.D.N.Y.) announces the arrest of 10 individuals, including four Division I coaches, for college basketball fraud and corruption schemes. Retrieved from https://www.justice.gov/usao-sdny/pr/usattorney-announces-arrest-10-individuals-including-four-division-i-coaches-college.

Wainstein, K. L., Jay III, J. A., & Kukowski, C. D. (2014, October 16). Investigation of irregular classes in the department of African and Afro-American Studies at the University of North Carolina at Chapel Hill. *Cadwalader*. Retrieved from https://carolinacommitment.unc.edu/files/2014/10/UNC-FINAL-REPORT.pdf.

Wojnarowski, A. (2019, June 13). Zion sues to end arrangement with marketing firm. *ESPN.com*. Retrieved from https://www.espn.com/nba/story/_/id/26966863/zion-sues-end-agreement-marketing-firm.

Web Resources

http://reg.mlbpaagent.org/Documents/AgentForms/Agent%20Regulations.pdf ■ This document provides the regulations governing MLBPA agents.

https://nbpa.com/agents/becoming-an-agent ■This site provides the information on becoming a registered NBPA sports agent representing basketball players.

https://www.ncaa.org/enforcement/agents-and-amateurism ■ This site provides information about the NCAA's regulations regarding student-athletes and amateurism.

https://nflpaweb.blob.core.windows.net/media/Default/PDFs/Agents/RegulationsAmendedAugust2016.pdf ■ The document at this site contains the NFLPA's Standard Representation Agreement, in Appendix D.

https://www.nflpa.com/ ■ The NFL Players Association site provides several useful links to help understand the services it provides to NFL players. You can also access the entire Collective Bargaining Agreement for the NFL from this site.

https://www.nflpa.com/about/rules-and-regulations ■ This site provides links to NFL rules and regulations that apply to agents, financial advisors, and player conduct policies.

www.sportsagentblog.com ■ This blog, focusing on athlete agents, provides useful tools for students conducting research about athlete agents and related issues in professional sport.

https://www.uniformlaws.org/committees/community-home?CommunityKey=cef8ae71-2f7b-4404-9af5-309bb70e861e ■ This site provides the most recently updated Uniform Athlete Agents Act from 2019.

https://www.uniformlaws.org/viewdocument/final-act-with-comments-134?CommunityKeycef8ae71-2f7b-4404-9af5-309bb70e861e&tab=librarydocuments ■ This site presents current and updated information regarding revisions of and amendments to the UAAA.

https://www.ussoccer.com/federation-services/intermediaries ■ This site provides the FIFA regulations for intermediaries working in soccer (football) as well as the list of registered intermediaries.

9   Wage and Workplace Regulations

Introduction

This chapter explores legal issues in the workplace related to employee compensation, workplace safety and health standards, and workers' compensation for work-related injuries. How effectively we manage these issues in the workplace can significantly impact worker productivity and organizational success. The Department of Labor (DOL) administers and enforces more than 180 federal laws related to workplace activities (DOL, n.d.a). These regulations cover workplace activities for about 10 million employers and 143 million workers. Obviously, we cannot examine each of these laws. Instead, we introduce some legal requirements that regularly impact workers in sport and recreation organizations. As we learned in Chapter 3, the employment relationship is a contractual relationship between an employer and an employee. In addition to restraints or limitations arising from the employment contract, federal and state laws also provide a number of regulations affecting employers and employees.

First, this chapter covers laws affecting minimum wage and overtime pay under the Fair Labor Standards Act (FLSA). Next, the chapter focuses on workplace safety and health standards provided for in the Occupational Safety and Health Act (OSHA). Both of these laws are federal laws applicable to worksites in the United States. Last, the chapter examines state workers' compensation laws. Each state has its own system for administering workers' compensation laws.

See Exhibit 9.1 for an overview of this chapter's managerial contexts, major legal issues, relevant law, and illustrative cases.

Fair Labor Standards Act

The law with the greatest impact on working conditions in terms of wages and hours is the Fair Labor Standards Act (FLSA). The FLSA was passed by Congress on June 25, 1938, and it is administered by the U.S. Department of Labor's Wage and Hour Division (DOL). The main objective of the FLSA is to eliminate "labor conditions detrimental to the maintenance of the minimum standards of living necessary for health, efficiency, and general well-being of workers" (FLSA, 2020, § 202). The FLSA establishes standards for minimum wages, overtime pay, recordkeeping, and child labor. These standards protect more than 143 million workers, both full-time and part-time, in the private and public sectors (DOL, 2009a). However, FLSA does not regulate or require: (1) vacation, holiday, severance, or sick pay; (2) meal or rest periods, holidays off, or vacations; (3) premium pay for weekend or holiday work; (4) pay raises or fringe benefits; or (5) a discharge notice, reason for discharge, or immediate payment of final wages to terminated employees.

Overview of Coverage and Penalties

The FLSA can apply to workers in one of two ways. First, the FLSA provides what is known as **enterprise coverage**, which applies to employees who work for certain businesses or organizations that have at least two employees and do at least $500,000 a year in business (DOL, 2009a). Enterprise coverage also

Exhibit 9.1 Management contexts and legal issues pertaining to working conditions, with relevant laws and cases.

Management Context	Major Legal Issues	Relevant Law	Illustrative Cases
Determining employee compensation and job duties	Overtime pay	FLSA	
	Minimum wages		
	Exemptions for administrative employees and amusement businesses		*Adams, Bridewell, Jeffery, Liger, Perez*
Use of interns and trainees	Exemptions for interns and volunteers	FLSA	*Hill, Shkuratova, Glatt, Chen*
Minor League baseball players Creating a safe workplace	Exceptions to overtime pay On-the-job injuries Employees handling dangerous substances or being exposed to blood or dangerous pathogens	FLSA/SAPA OSHA	*Seene*
Employer liability for injuries to employees	Workers' compensation for on-the-job injuries	State workers' compensation regulations and programs	*Dozier, Savage, Elmhurst Park, James*
	Professional and college athletes as employees		*Uhlenhake, Rowe, Palmer, Matthews, Tupa, Rensing, Dawson*

includes hospitals, businesses providing medical or nursing care for residents, schools and preschools, and government agencies. Second, the FLSA provides for **individual coverage** in cases where an organization does not qualify as an enterprise but an employee regularly engages in activities involving interstate commerce or the production of goods for interstate commerce. Regularly sending and receiving postal mail; making and receiving long-distance telephone calls or receiving electronic orders from out-of-state customers; shipping goods to another state or receiving goods from other states; accepting credit cards from out-of-state banks; and keeping records of those goods all qualify as engaging in interstate commerce. Thus, it is highly unlikely that a business would not be subject to the FLSA in today's global economy.

The Department of Labor has a clear policy of investigating alleged violations of the FLSA. In 2019, the DOL initiated more than 20,000 compliance actions, resulting in $226 million in payments of back wages to employees (DOL, 2019a). Employers that willfully or repeatedly violate the minimum wage or overtime pay requirements are subject to a civil monetary penalty of up to $1,100 for each such violation. A second conviction may result in imprisonment. The DOL may also bring suit for back pay and an equal amount in liquidated damages, and it may obtain injunctions to restrain persons from violating the act. It is also a violation to fire or in any other manner discriminate against an employee for filing a complaint or for participating in a legal proceeding under FLSA.

Minimum Wage and Overtime Requirements

The FLSA originally established maximum working hours of 44 hours per week for the first year after its passage, 42 for the second, and 40 thereafter. Minimum wages of 25 cents per hour were established for the first year and 30 cents for the second, rising to 40 cents over the next six years. Of course, that was in the late 1930s and early 1940s. Since that time, the maximum working hours per workweek remains at 40. In 2007, a minimum wage increase established an incremental increase of the minimum wage to $5.85 in 2007 and then $7.25 beginning July 2009. Despite increased cost of living across the country, the federal minimum wage as of January 1, 2020 is still set at $7.25 per hour. However, beginning January 1, 2020, the minimum wage for federal contractors was increased to $10.80 per hour (DOL, 2020a).

In addition, individual states may also establish a minimum wage above the federal minimum wage for employers operating within that state. As of January 1, 2020, 31 states and the District of Columbia have minimum wages above the federal minimum wage (NCSL, 2020).

The FLSA is intended to provide broad protection to employees; thus, all employees are covered unless an employer can qualify for one of a limited number of exceptions which will be discussed later in this Chapter. Covered (**nonexempt employees)** therefore naturally include any employee who does not meet a specific exception provided for in the FLSA. Non-exempt employees cannot waive their right to overtime pay, nor can an employee agree to work more than 40 hours at regular pay. Hourly employees who work in excess of 40 hours per week are entitled to the established overtime rate of at least one and one-half times the employee's regular hourly wage for all hours worked in excess of 40 hours. Overtime requirements apply to a **workweek** which is a period of 168 hours in seven consecutive days ($7 \times 24 = 168$). Hence, overtime pay is not required just because an employee works more than eight hours in a day; rather, the critical time period is the workweek. A workweek may begin on any given day and hour, as determined by the employer. Each workweek stands alone, so that the time an employee works cannot be averaged over, for example, a month. In addition, to qualify for overtime pay, an employee must have actually worked 40 hours. Thus, if an employee works 40 hours during one workweek and also is paid for an eight-hour holiday day, bringing the total hours paid to 48, the employee is not entitled to overtime pay for the eight hours above 40, since she did not actually work more than 40 hours in a given workweek. Employers are not required to pay extra to an employee who works on a holiday, although this is a fairly common practice.

Under FLSA, calculating overtime pay is straightforward. For example, Deion is a customer service representative (salesperson) for Planet Fitness with a regular hourly wage of $12 per hour. If Deion works 45 hours in a week, for the five hours over 40 hours, Deion must be paid time-and-a-half. In this case, it would be $1.5 \times \$12 = \$18 \times$ five overtime hours = $90. Deion's total wage for that week would be $\$12 \times$ 40 hours = $480 + $90 (overtime pay) = $570.

Exemptions and Exclusions Under the FLSA

As previously mentioned, the FLSA contains a limited number of exceptions from the mandatory minimum wage and overtime provisions for certain employee groups. Some employees may be covered under an express exemption in FLSA and other worker groups are not considered "employees" under the act and are therefore excluded from its coverage. Several of these exceptions occur frequently in the sport and recreation industries. Two exemptions are frequently encountered in the sport industry: (1) executive, administrative exemption, and learned professional; and (2) the seasonal amusement and recreational establishments exemption. In addition, interns and students may not be considered employees, thus, are excluded from FLSA coverage. And lastly, Congress enacted the Save America's Pastime Act in 2018 limiting minor league baseball players' protections under FLSA. The legal requirements for these exceptions and how these exceptions impact sport industry employers and employees are discussed below.

Executive, Administrative, and Learned Professional Exemptions

Section 13(a)(1) of the FLSA, codified at 29 U.S.C. § 213(a)(1), exempts from both minimum wage and overtime pay any employee employed in a bona fide executive, administrative, creative, computer, or professional capacity or in the capacity of outside salesperson (these are often referred to as the **white-collar exemptions**). The DOL routinely publishes and updates "Fact Sheets" which summarize these requirements and regulations and are a highly useful resource for sport managers to review as they are classifying employees (DOL, 2020b).

Generally, exempt employees are salaried and receive higher rates of pay than hourly workers. The rationale behind the exemption is that these employees enjoy a professional position at a set salary and, therefore, should not receive an additional benefit for working more than 40 hours per week. The exemptions were premised on the belief that the exempted workers typically earn salaries well above the minimum wage. These workers were presumed to enjoy other compensatory privileges, compared to the workers entitled to overtime pay, such as above-average fringe benefits, greater job security, and better opportunities for advancement (29 C.F.R. Part 541, 2014). Further, the type of work that exempt workers perform is difficult to standardize to any time frame and cannot be easily extended to other workers, making enforcement of the overtime provisions difficult.

In the sport and recreation industries, the exemptions used most frequently by employers are the administrative, learned professional, executive, and outside sales exemptions. Each exemption requires the employer to demonstrate that an employee is exempt from the overtime provisions of FLSA and meets the requirements of the exemption. To qualify for one of the white-collar exemptions, the employer cannot simply classify an employee as an outside salesperson or an administrative employee. The employee's title or job description does not determine whether his position qualifies for an exemption.

For the administrative, learned professional, and executive exemptions, the employer must evaluate both the **salary level** and the **employee's job duties** to determine whether overtime pay is due. The DOL regulations provide a three-part test for the white-collar exemptions. An organization that believes it qualifies for one of the white-collar exemptions but is unable to satisfy one of the exemption tests faces considerable risk. A business could be liable for thousands or even millions of dollars in penalties, back wages, and legal costs if it incorrectly categorizes an employee as an exempt employee and fails to pay overtime or minimum wages. For example, Dick's Sporting Goods was sued in 2020 in a suit seeking millions of dollars in overtime pay restitution alleging that Dick's misclassified their assistant managers as exempt employees and required them to work long uncompensated overtime hours (*Juric v. Dick's Sporting Goods, Inc.*, 2020). Dick's settled similar cases in 2011 and 2015 for $15 million and $10 million, respectively (Chochrek, 2020). Next, we discuss each part of the three-part test. The employer must be able to satisfy each of these tests in order to be exempt from the minimum wage and overtime requirements:

1 **Salary basis test**: The employee must be paid a predetermined and fixed salary that is not subject to variations because of quantity or quality of work.
2 **Salary test**: The amount of the salary must be paid at or above a minimum level.
3 **Duties test**: The employee's duties must be primarily involved in the executive, administrative, learned professional functions of the business (a separate "duties" test applies for each of the white-collar exemptions).

Salary Basis Test

To meet the salary basis test for exemption from overtime, the employee must be paid a predetermined sum of money for each work week regardless of the number of hours actually worked. An employee must be paid for this time period regardless of quantity or quality of work and must be paid if the employee works any period of time within a particular work week. The employer also cannot deduct pay from the employee's salary for work stoppages controlled by the employer. Thus, salaried employees of the NHL were still required to be paid by their individual team employers, even though a work stoppage occurred when the owners and players reached an impasse in their labor negotiations in 2004. The employers would have had to terminate the employees in order to avoid paying their salaries. Employers also cannot unilaterally require the salaried employees to accept less pay for working fewer hours. If an employee is ready, willing, and able to work during a specific pay period, he or she must be paid for that period to meet the salary basis test and to qualify for the exemption from minimum wage and overtime pay. It is not uncommon to pay nonexempt employees on a salary basis. For example, a ticket office employee in a collegiate athletic department might be paid a monthly salary of $1,250, which would be above the minimum hourly wage if he only worked 40 hours per week, but since he is nonexempt, if he works more than 40 hours per week he would have to be paid overtime wages.

Salary Test

The salary test has been the subject of considerable scrutiny since 2016 due to increasing pressure to increase the minimum annual salary required for the exemption. Beginning on January 1, 2020, a new salary test took effect raising the minimum salary level from $455 to $684 per week (the equivalent of $35,568 per year). Under the new salary test, an exempt employee's weekly salary must be at least $684 per week or $35,568 annually. Simply stated, any employee paid less than $35,568 per year or $684 per week will be nonexempt and covered by FLSA protections and will be entitled to overtime pay regardless of the job duties (DOL, 2020c).

Job Duties Test

Under the new job duties test, the employee's job duties must fit into one of the following categories in order to qualify for an exemption: executive, administrative, learned professional, creative professional, computer employee, or outside sales employee. For example, the executive exemption requires that the employee's primary duty must be *managing the enterprise*, or managing a customarily recognized department or sub-division of the enterprise. Management is generally described to include a long list of activities such as interviewing, selecting, and training of employees; setting and adjusting their rates of pay and hours of work; directing the work of employees; maintaining production or sales records for use in supervision or control; appraising employees' productivity and efficiency for the purpose of recommending promotions or other changes in status; handling employee complaints and grievances; disciplining employees; planning the work; determining the techniques to be used; apportioning the work among the employees; determining the type of materials, supplies, machinery, equipment or tools to be used or merchandise to be bought, stocked and sold; controlling the flow and distribution of materials or merchandise and supplies; providing for the safety and security of the employees or the property; planning and controlling the budget; and monitoring or implementing legal compliance measures. (See Exhibit 9.2 listing the specific duties for each of the white-collar exemptions.)

In applying these tests, consider the following example, a minor league baseball team may hire Tamika as an assistant sales manager and offer her a small starting salary of $23,000 (approximately $442 per week or $11.05 per hour – clearly above the minimum wage), expecting Tamika to work her normal 40-hour week in the office, as well as work dozens of game nights during evenings and on weekends. It is entirely likely that Tamika could work in excess of 70 hours per week, which would reduce her hourly wage to $6.31 per hour (clearly below the minimum wage). Thus, the reasoning behind the exemption rules is that simply giving an employee, such as Tamika, a manager's title and a small salary and then demanding well over a 40-hour work week is unacceptable and not permitted under the FLSA.

Thus, to qualify for the exemption the team must also demonstrate, under the *duties test*, Tamika's job duties fall within one of the exempt categories. If claiming the administrative exemption, for example, Tamika must perform duties described for the administrative exemption. Under the *salary basis test*, Tamika must be paid her salary when the team is traveling or during the off-season, even though she may work fewer than 40 hours during a given week. And under the *salary test*, she must be paid a minimum of $35,568 annually or $684 weekly. If the team fails to meet any of these tests, Tamika is not an exempt employee, and the team must pay overtime wages under FLSA.

Two common positions in sport that are particularly susceptible to possible misclassification are assistant coaching and athletic training positions. Head coaches and head athletic trainers are likely to be exempt as executives or learned professionals, but assistant coaches and assistant athletic trainers are probably not exempt. Coaches and trainers who work significantly more than 40 hours per week, are paid a relatively low salary, and do not supervise other employees and exercise direct and independent judgment will have to be paid at least $35,568 per year to comply with the FLSA (see, Joint Statement by CUPA and NCAA (2016) regarding the exempt status of coaches and trainers). However, the DOL has issued an

Exhibit 9.2 Exempt employee categories under the FLSA.

Job Duty Exemption Category	Job Duties	Example Representative Positions
Executive	Primarily, duty requires managing an enterprise, subdivision, or customarily recognized department. Regularly directs the work of at least two other full-time employees; is authorized to hire or fire, or influences decisions to hire, fire, or promote other employees. Minimum salary = $684 per week paid on a salary basis	Associate athletic director for marketing in a college athletic department
Administrative	Primarily, performs office or non manual work directly related to general business operations. Must exercise discretion and independent judgment with respect to matters of significance ("discretion and independent judgment" means making independent choices free from immediate direction and supervision). Minimum salary = $684 per week paid on a salary basis	Ticket sales manager with a professional sports team
Learned professional	Primarily, performs work requiring advanced knowledge in a field of science or learning, defined as work predominantly intellectual in character and requiring consistent exercise of discretion and judgment. Employee acquired advanced knowledge through a prolonged course of specialized intellectual instruction. Minimum salary = $684 per week paid on a salary basis	College faculty or Coach
Creative professional	Primarily performs work requiring invention, imagination, originality, or talent in a recognized field of artistic or creative endeavor. Minimum salary = $684 per week paid on a salary basis	Professional photographer
Computer employee	Computer systems analyst, computer programmer, software engineer, or other similarly skilled worker in the computer field. Primarily, applies systems analysis techniques and procedures. Is compensated either on a salary basis at not less than $684 per week OR $27.63 per hour if on an hourly basis	Computer systems manager for a collegiate athletic department
Outside sales employee	Primarily, makes sales or obtains orders or contracts for services or use of facilities. Is customarily and regularly engaged away from the employer's place of business. No minimum salary	Sales representative for a sport medicine supply company

opinion letter that some coaches may also qualify as teachers (who are exempt employees under FLSA) if their primary duties involve teaching, tutoring, instructing, or lecturing in the activity of imparting knowledge (Green, 2018).

Many entry-level positions within sport organizations would likely not meet the administrative exemption listed below, but even if they do satisfy the duties test in the administrative exemption, the minimum salary still must be $35,568 per year or $684 per week. The weekly pay structure does provide employers some flexibility, in that they could decide to budget only $25,000 for an entry-level position and establish the position for less than nine months. Thus, the salary test would be met,

Exhibit 9.3 Administrative exemption – primary duty analysis.

Primary duty includes exercise of discretion and independent judgment with respect to matters of significance and implies that the employee has authority to make an independent choice, free from immediate direction or supervision. This involves the comparison and evaluation of possible courses of conduct, and acting or making a decision after the various possibilities have been considered. To meet this criterion, two or three of the following must apply:

- The employee has authority to formulate, affect, interpret, or implement management policies or operating practices.
- The employee carries out major assignments in conducting the operations of the business.
- The employee performs work that affects business operations to a substantial degree.
- The employee has authority to commit the employer in matters that have significant financial impact.
- The employee has authority to waive or deviate from established policies and procedures without prior approval, and other factors set forth in the regulation.
- The employee has authority to negotiate and bind the company on significant matters.
- The employee provides consultation or expert advice to management.
- The employee is involved in planning long- or short-term business objectives.
- The employee investigates and resolves matters of significance on behalf of management.
- The employee represents the company in handling complaints, arbitrating disputes, or resolving grievances.

---

since the employee would be paid more than $684 per week over the 36-week period. Of course, if the duties test is not met, the employee would have to be paid at least minimum wage and would be entitled to receive overtime pay.

Since most entry-level and middle management positions in the sport industry would only potentially meet the administrative exemption, it is an important exemption to understand for sport managers and executives. Exhibit 9.3 provides additional details on the administrative exemption.

Seasonal Amusement or Recreational Establishment Exemption

A second exemption common in sport or recreation industries is an exemption for businesses in the amusement and recreational sectors that operate seasonally or earn most of their profits during a compressed period of time. Section 213 of the FLSA provides as follows:

Exemptions

a. Minimum wage and maximum hour requirements. The provisions … shall not apply with respect to – (3) any employee employed by an establishment which is an amusement or recreational establishment, [or] organized camp, … if

  A. it does not operate for more than seven months in any calendar year, or
  B. during the preceding calendar year, its average receipts for any six months of such year were not more than 33.333 per centum of its average receipts for the other six months of such year. …

To qualify for the seasonal amusement or recreational exemption, the employer must demonstrate that it has satisfied one of the two tests set forth in the exemption. These two tests are (1) the *seven months operations test* and (2) the *average receipts test*. The seven months operations test commonly applies to seasonal or recreational establishments (e.g., an amusement park, a swimming pool, or a summer camp) that operate for fewer than seven months each year and then close down completely. But for those enterprises operating for more than seven months, the only available exemption is the average receipts test. For example, an indoor baseball training facility may be open year round but earn the majority of its revenue during the winter months. The exemption would apply as follows: the facility operated for twelve months in the preceding calendar year. The total receipts for September, October, November, December, January, and February (the six months in which the receipts were largest) totaled $260,000, a monthly average of $43,333; the total receipts for the other six months totaled $75,000, a monthly average of $12,500. Because the average receipts of the latter six months were not more than 33.333 percent of the average receipts for the other six months of the year, the exemption would apply (DOL, 2008).

Typically, whether the employer can qualify for this exemption will initially require the employer to demonstrate that the employer's business is a seasonal amusement or recreational establishment and is eligible to seek the exemption. Next, the employer would have to demonstrate that its business operations can meet one of the two required tests in subsection (A) and (B) in order to use the exemption. We are going to explore each of these requirements.

Seasonal Amusement and Recreational Establishments Defined

The FLSA does not define amusement or recreational establishment, although certain businesses have been consistently understood to be covered such as amusement parks, golf clubs, summer sports camps, and beaches. The Department of Labor regulations have offered interpretations defining amusement or recreational establishments as those frequented by the public for its amusement or recreation. This definition suggests that the employer seeking the exemption must be in the amusement or recreation business. However, a recurring question relates to whether businesses operating in conjunction with an amusement or recreational establishment are eligible to seek the exemption, such as concessionaires.

The federal law on this question is in flux. Some jurisdictions apply "the single establishment test" which would limit the exemption to businesses directly providing the amusement or recreational services and those enterprises that sells goods in conjunction with an amusement or recreation activity such as pro shops or dry goods stores in national parks that are part of a single establishment. However, the Second Circuit Court of Appeals found that "concessionaires that sell food, drink, and merchandise at amusement or recreational sites have the requisite amusement or recreational nature to qualify for the exemption" (*Hill v. Del. N. Cos. Sportservice, Inc.*, 2016, p. 289–290). William Hill and Tanica Brown worked as retail supervisors for Maryland Sportservice's concessions at the Orioles Team Store in Oriole Park, Baltimore, Maryland. The court of appeals in *Hill* adopted a definition of concessionaires as "establishments whose purpose is to sell goods and services on the premises of an amusement or recreational host facility to the host's customers for their use or consumption on the host's premises as they participate in the host' amusement or recreational activities" (p. 292).

Prior to *Hill*, most jurisdictions followed the single establishment test. Under the single establishment test, only if the operations of the concessionaires and the host establishment were part of a single establishment, could both the concessionaire and the host establishment meet the requirements for the exemption. For example, DOL determined in 2009 that a concessionaire at a privately owned recreational establishment with an exclusive contract to provide catering services is not itself an amusement or recreational establishment, but instead was legal entity separate from the recreational establishment. Therefore, the concessionaire was not eligible for the exemption (DOL, 2009b). The decision in *Hill* may have resolved some ambiguity, at least in the Second Circuit, but sport managers in the concessions or contract services for venues and events should exercise caution in asserting this exemption and host venues and events should be aware of the potential for exploitation with influxes of atypical labor during major sporting events. (See McLeod, Holden, Hawzen, & Chahardovali, 2019.)

The courts have also refused to recognize the seasonal enterprise exemption when a single ownership group controlled two different entities and the ownership group clearly operated year-round. The Sanford-Orlando Kennel Club (SOKC) owned CCC Racing and SOKC, which were operating a greyhound racing spring meet as one entity for six months and then operating a fall meet as the other entity for six months. The Florida district court considered whether the two companies should be treated as separate seasonal establishments or as a single establishment that operates year-round. The crucial factor in determining whether two businesses constitute a single establishment or separate establishments under the FLSA is the integrity of the economic, physical, and functional separation between the business units. The court concluded that although CCC Racing and SOKC operate during different times of the year, this fact alone does not suffice to establish that the two companies are truly seasonal businesses. Rather, the possibility remains that CCC Racing and SOKC were founded or maintained on a separate basis for spurious or sham reasons (*Perez v. Sanford-Orlando Kennel Club*, 2006, p. 1091).

The court denied the tracks' motion for summary judgment, and the kennel clubs were later found liable for willful violations of FLSA at a jury trial. The *Perez* holding could be in conflict with the *Hill* rationale, thus reminding us that this area of law is still evolving.

Application of the Seasonal Operations and Receipts Tests

Once an employer is deemed to be eligible to seek the exemption, next, it must demonstrate that it meets either the *seasonal operation test* in subpart A or the *receipts test* in subpart B of § 213(a)(3) to use the exemption. Our first Focus Case applies the receipts test in the context of a golf club which we know qualifies as an amusement or recreational establishment.

Shkuratova v. Farm Neck Association

| 2018 U.S. Dist. LEXIS 157712 (D. Mass. 2018) | **FOCUS** CASE |

FACTS

The Links at Martha's Vineyard, Inc. ("The Links") is a Massachusetts corporation and the plaintiff's former employer. It does business as Farm Neck Golf Club ("Golf Club"). Anna Shkuratova was hired as a line cook at the Golf Club in May 2016. She started on May 9, 2016, at $15.00 per hour. Her hourly rate increased to $16.00 beginning June 27, 2016. On several occasions, she worked over 40 hours in one week and was not compensated at a rate higher than her regular hourly rate. The Golf Club has several operating departments, including golf, tennis, maintenance, a restaurant, and administration. It is a membership club but its facilities are also open to the public for a fee. It operates on a seasonal basis with slight differences among activities. Tennis usually opens at the beginning of May and closes on November 1, golf operates from mid-April through December 24, and the restaurant operates from mid-April through late November. Shkuratova sued, alleging violations of FLSA because the defendants failed to pay overtime for hours she worked in excess of 40 per week. The defendants moved for summary judgment, contending that the plaintiff's employer is a seasonal amusement or recreational establishment exempt from the FLSA's overtime requirements. (See 29 U.S.C. § 213(a)(3).)

HOLDING

Motion for summary judgment was granted since the Golf Club satisfied the FLSA exemption.

RATIONALE

The FLSA generally requires that employees be compensated for hours worked in excess of 40 in a single workweek at a rate of pay of not less than one and one-half times the employee's regular rate. 29 U.S.C. § 207(a)(1); *Cash v. Cycle Craft Co.*, 508 F.3d 680, 682-83 (1st Cir. 2007). It also establishes various exemptions from this general rule, including an exemption from the overtime requirement for seasonal amusement or recreational establishments. The employer shoulders the burden of establishing that it is entitled to an exemption. There does not appear to be any dispute that the Golf Club qualifies as "an amusement or recreational establishment." See 29 C.F.R. § 779.385 (defining "amusement or recreational establishments"); *Hays v. City of Pauls Valley* (public golf course); *Brock v. Louvers & Dampers, Inc.* (private, for-profit golf club). The critical issue then is whether the Golf Club qualifies for the exemption under either the seasonal operation test in subpart A or the receipts test in subpart B. The Golf Club as a whole, and the restaurant in particular, operate for more than seven months in the calendar year, and therefore the club does not qualify under the seasonal operation test. The Golf Club, however, has demonstrated that it satisfies the receipts test. (See *Hill v. Del. N. Cos. Sportservice, Inc.*, 2016.) According to financial data presented in the record, during the calendar year preceding the plaintiff's employment, 2015, the months with the highest receipts for the Golf Club's operations were April, May, June, July, August, and September. The total receipts for those months were $5,979,081.31 with a monthly average of $996,513.55. The lowest six months were January, February, March, October, November, and December. The total receipts for those months were $456,753.59, with a monthly average of $76,125.60. The lowest six months were therefore only 7.6 percent of the highest six months, well below the statute's 33.333 percent threshold. The Golf Club qualifies for the statutory exemption because it is a recreational or amusement establishment as defined in the statute and its average receipts for the six lowest months in 2015 were not more than 33 percent of the average receipts for the six highest months.

Both major league and minor league sports teams have often asserted the amusement and recreational exemption. The operations of minor league and major leagues also typically would have no problem qualifying as amusement or recreational activities, however, both the seasonal operations test and the receipts test have been met with mixed results. These next few cases examine both the seasonal operations tests and the receipts tests as applied in minor league and major league sports.

First, in *Adams v. Detroit Tigers, Inc.* (1997), the Detroit Tigers were sued by a number of batboys who claimed that they were not paid overtime compensation and minimum wages for their work, in violation of state and federal law. The baseball team argued that it was exempt. Specifically, the baseball team contended that it was an amusement or recreational establishment that either operated for not more than seven months in a calendar year or had average receipts for any six months of a calendar year that were less than 33.333 percent of average receipts for the remaining months of that year. Both parties agreed that the baseball team as a whole was a recreation or amusement establishment. The court further found that the batboys were an intricate part of this establishment and were not independent of the baseball team. However, the court granted the Tigers' motion for summary judgment, because the Tigers had shown that the baseball team met the wage-hour exemptions, since the batboys were employed for only seven months of the year and the off-season receipts were less than 33.333 percent of the average of in-season receipts for the remainder of the year. The court dismissed the batboys' wage-hour cause of action.

In *Bridewell v. The Cincinnati Reds* (1995), maintenance employees for the Cincinnati Reds sued for overtime wages. The Ohio federal district court granted summary judgment in favor of the Reds and found that the team was not liable for plaintiffs' overtime wage claims, because it was entitled to the exemption under the FLSA for recreational and amusement establishments that operate less than eight months per year. However, the court of appeals reversed, concluding that the Reds held regular-season home games at Cincinnati's Riverfront Stadium and that the Reds had the exclusive right to sell advertising on signs at the stadium throughout the year, to operate the scoreboard during baseball and football games, and to contract with a concessionaire to operate at baseball and football games. The court of appeals also noted that the Reds employed 120 employees year-round and as many as 700 employees at peak periods. The court of appeals held the team was not entitled to the exemption under the FLSA for recreational and amusement establishments, because the facts established that the defendant, in fact, operated year-round in various capacities.

Finally, in *Jeffery v. Sarasota White Sox, Inc.* (1995), the plaintiff was a grounds-keeper employed by the Sarasota White Sox to maintain a baseball complex leased by the White Sox during spring training. The city owned the complex, which was open year-round but used by the defendant only on a seasonal basis. The plaintiff sued the defendant seeking damages for unpaid overtime wages pursuant to the FLSA. On appeal, the court affirmed the trial court's grant of summary judgment for the defendant, since the defendant was an amusement or recreational establishment exempt from the mandatory overtime provisions of the FLSA. An establishment is seasonal if it satisfies the six-month receipts test, even if the establishment is open for more than seven months a year.

The following Case Opinion is useful to examine how a court has compared the holdings in *Bridewell* and *Jeffery* and further explores whether a major league sports team (then known as the New Orleans Hornets, now the New Orleans Pelicans) could successfully assert the amusement and recreational exemption as compared to a minor league sports team.

Liger v. New Orleans Hornets NBA Ltd. Partnership

CASE OPINION   566 F. Supp. 2d 680 (E.D. La. 2008)

FACTS

The plaintiffs filed this action on May 27, 2005. The plaintiffs are former employees of the Hornets and are seeking compensation for allegedly unpaid overtime wages. The plaintiffs worked in the "business enterprise" of the organization, specifically in sales and fan relations. Under the FLSA, the maximum work week for an employee of an enterprise engaged in commerce is 40 hours (29 U.S.C. § 207(a)(1) (2006)). If an employee works longer, he must receive overtime compensation at a rate of at least one and one-half times his regular rate of pay. The Hornets argued that they were an amusement or recreational establishment, which is exempt from the overtime and minimum wage compensation requirement.

HOLDING

The court held the Hornets were a year-round operation, and thus could not qualify for the amusement and recreation exemption.

RATIONALE

The Hornets are an organization that is involved in the amusement or recreation of professional basketball games. The Hornets argued that it was not liable to the sales employees because it was exempt under the seasonal amusement and recreation exemption of the FLSA.

The sales employees relied on the decision in *Bridewell v. The Cincinnati Reds*, which held that the Cincinnati Reds were a year-round operation. The Hornets relied on *Jeffery v. Sarasota White Sox, Inc.*, to argue that it only operated for seven months of the year. The court held that reliance upon *Jeffery*, however, was insufficient to find in favor of the Hornets. In *Jeffery*, the Eleventh Circuit found that a minor league baseball team did not operate for seven months out of the year, although some employees were employed year-round. In that case there was no dispute regarding the length of the operating season. The court was not convinced that the operative scale of a minor league baseball team was analogous to that of an NBA franchise.

The sales employees' reliance on *Bridewell* was more appropriate. In *Bridewell*, the Sixth Circuit found that a major league baseball team was a year-round operation, despite the fact that they did not provide "amusement and recreation" year-round. Additionally, the court observed that "the fact that the Reds employ 120 year-round workers compels the conclusion that they 'operate' year-round," stating that: "[w]hile a truly seasonal business that employs an insignificant number of workers year-round could conceivably qualify for the exemption, the fact that the Reds employ 120 year-round workers compels the conclusion that they 'operate' year-round." The Hornets admit that it employs over 100 personnel in year-round positions. In addition, the NBA regular season typically begins in October and ends in April; in combination with preseason and post-season games, the Hornets have the opportunity to participate in games for nine months each year. Finally, the NBA draft occurs each June; thus, the Hornets operate in the summer even when they do not make the playoffs. Therefore, the court found the reasoning and holding of *Bridewell* to be more analogous to Liger's situation than *Jeffery*. Consequently, the court found that the Hornets were a year-round operation, and thus, could not qualify for the exemption under FLSA, 29 U.S.C. § 213 (a)(3)(A).

QUESTIONS

- Why did the court determine that the operations of a National Basketball Association team were more analogous to the operations of a Major League Baseball team than to a minor league baseball team?
- What were the key characteristics of the Hornets' operations that led the court to conclude it was a year-round operation?

Several minor league teams have been successful is utilizing the seasonal amusement or recreation exemption with regard to employees who only work seasonally or where year-round operations were minimal (groundskeepers and ball boys) but if employees are contributing to year-round revenue activities (sales) or the employer is operating year-round, the exemption may not be available for those employees. Additionally, even though we know concessionaires may be eligible for the exemption separate from the host organization, the Wisconsin state court of appeals denied an exemption for the concessionaire at Lambeau Field, home of the Green Bay Packers. Green Bay Sportservice (GBS) operated Curly's Pub, a bar and restaurant open year round to the public as part of its contract with Lambeau Field. Two employees sued for GBS's failure to pay overtime wages. The court of appeals said GBS may be able to qualify as a concessionaire under the definition offered in *Hill* but only so long as the employer engages in *de minimis* level of non-concessionaire activities. *Hill* had identified several outside operations at Oriole Park such as operating the team store, restaurant, and rental of lounges at Oriole Park. In *Hill*, those activities were viewed as *de minimis* to the primary concessionaire activities, therefore, the exemption was available. But GBS, was unable to prove its non-game day revenues and operations were *de minimis*. Furthermore, GBS did not offer credible evidence of their average receipts from Curly's Pub or other activities. Thus, the court of appeals held GBS did not qualify for the exemption (*Green Bay Sportservice, Inc. v. Wisconsin Department of Workforce Development*, 2018). Major league teams are typically not going to be able to meet either the seasonal operations test or the receipts test, since they routinely have regular, year-round operations and their sales, sponsorships, and broadcasting revenues are not likely to be limited to a short period of time. We will discuss minor league baseball players in a later section in this Chapter.

Internship Programs

It may not be necessary to pay an intern minimum wage or overtime wages if the employer's internship program is structured in such a way that the students or interns are not considered employees under FLSA (29 U.S.C. §§ 203(e)(1)). The value of experiential learning has been well-documented in business and academic journals (Binder, Baguley, Crook, & Miller, 2015; Briggs, 2000; Cates-McIver, 1998; Crumbley & Sumners, 1998; Haghighi, 1998; Kelsey, 2002; Rothman & Sisman, 2016; Silva, Lopes, & Costa, 2016; Singer, 2000; Whalen & Barnes, 2001). Sport management students are encouraged to volunteer and seek internships to improve their employment opportunities (Lee, Kane, Gregg, & Cavanaugh, 2016). It could easily be argued that no single step in a sport management career path is as important and valuable as the internship. However, sport industry internships have been criticized based on their compensation structures (Genzale, 2005; Moorman, 2004; Schoepfer & Dodds, 2011; Shellenbarger, 2009; Stier, 2002).

The Supreme Court has held that the words "to suffer or permit to work," as used in the FLSA to define the term "employ," do not make all persons employees who work for their own advantage on the premises of another without any agreement for compensation. The DOL originally issued guidance in 2010 as to whether interns were employees under the FLSA. According to the 2010 DOL's six-factor test, an intern was an employee unless all of the following factors were met: (1) the internship, even though it included actual operation of the facilities of the employer, was similar to training which would be given in an educational environment; (2) the internship experience was for the benefit of the intern; (3) the intern did not displace regular employees, but worked under close supervision of existing staff; (4) the employer that provided the training derived no immediate advantage from the activities of the intern, and on occasion its operations may actually have been impeded; (5) the intern was not necessarily entitled to a job at the conclusion of the internship; and (6) the employer and the intern understood that the intern was not entitled to wages for the time spent in the internship.

The DOL's 2010 six-part test was viewed by many employers as too rigorous. Employers argued that it was simply too difficult to satisfy each of the six requirements. Additionally, four federal appellate courts had rejected the DOL's six-part test and instead adopted a "primary beneficiary" test to determine whether an intern is an employee under the FLSA. The primary beneficiary test used a more flexible seven-factor test where all factors were weighed and balanced to determine if the overall nature of the internship qualified. As a result, on January 5, 2018, DOL adopted a new guidance for internship programs to resolve conflicts resulting from these court decisions applying the DOL's previous 2010 guidance (Wilkinson & Smith, 2018). The 2018 Fact Sheet #71 adopted the primary beneficiary test for evaluating internship programs and determining whether students and interns were employees for purposes of FLSA. The new Fact Sheet lists seven factors to consider for evaluating whether an intern is an employee. See Exhibit 9.4 for the DOL primary beneficiary test factors (DOL, 2018). If the factors listed in Exhibit 9.4 are met as a whole, an employment relationship does not exist under the FLSA, and the Act's minimum wage and overtime provisions do not apply to the intern. However, the DOL cautions that the exclusion from the definition of employment is necessarily narrow because the FLSA's definition of "employ" is very broad. Whether interns are employees under the FLSA will depend upon all of the circumstances surrounding their activities on the premises of the employer.

Exhibit 9.4 DOL criteria for an internship programs under FLSA – The primary beneficiary test (DOL, 2018).

1   The extent to which the intern and the employer clearly understand that there is no expectation of compensation. Any promise of compensation, express or implied, suggests that the intern is an employee – and vice versa.

2   The extent to which the internship provides training that would be similar to that which would be given in an educational environment, including the clinical and other hands-on training provided by educational institutions.

3   The extent to which the internship is tied to the intern's formal education program by integrated coursework or the receipt of academic credit.

4   The extent to which the internship accommodates the intern's academic commitments by corresponding to the academic calendar.

5   The extent to which the internship's duration is limited to the period in which the internship provides the intern with beneficial learning.

6   The extent to which the intern's work complements, rather than displaces, the work of paid employees while providing significant educational benefits to the intern.

7   The extent to which the intern and the employer understand that the internship is conducted without entitlement to a paid job at the conclusion of the internship.

The following Focus Case from the film production industry contributed to the DOL's decision to adopt the primary beneficiary test.

Glatt v. Fox Searchlight Pictures

811 F.3d 528 (2d Cir. 2015)   **FOCUS** CASE

FACTS

Glatt and Footman were unpaid interns who worked on production of the film *Black Swan* in New York. After production ended, Glatt took a second unpaid internship relating to *Black Swan's* post-production. Glatt and Footman did not receive any formal training, performed routine tasks such making photocopies and coffee, traveled to secure signatures on paperwork, and assisted with tracking and reconciling purchase orders. Glatt and Footman sued Fox Searchlight (the production company) for violations of FLSA. Glatt and Footman moved for summary judgment holding they were "employees" covered by the FLSA and do not fall under the "trainee" exception established by *Walling v. Portland Terminal Co.*, 330 U.S. 148 (1947). The district court applied the DOL six-factor intern test and concluded that plaintiffs had been improperly classified as unpaid interns rather than employees and granted their partial motion for summary judgment. Fox appealed to the court of appeals.

HOLDING

The district court did not apply the correct standard in evaluating whether Glatt and Footman were employees; therefore, the summary judgment is vacated.

RATIONALE

The strictures of the FLSA apply only to employees. The FLSA unhelpfully defines "employee" as an "individual employed by an employer" (§203(e)(1)). The Supreme Court has yet to address the difference between unpaid interns and paid employees under FLSA. When properly designed, unpaid internship programs can greatly benefit interns. For this reason, internships are widely supported by educators and by employers looking to hire well-trained recent graduates. However, employers can also exploit unpaid interns by using their free labor without providing them with an appreciable benefit in education or experience. Recognizing this concern, all parties agree that there are circumstances in which someone who is labeled an unpaid intern is actually an employee entitled to compensation under the FLSA but do not agree on what circumstances or standards should be used to identify employees.

The plaintiffs urge us to adopt a test whereby interns will be considered employees whenever the employer receives an immediate advantage from the interns' work. The plaintiffs argue that focusing on any immediate advantage that accrues to the employer is appropriate and that we should defer to the DOL Intern Fact Sheet. The defendants urge us to adopt a more nuanced primary beneficiary test. Under this standard, an employment relationship is created when the tangible and intangible benefits provided to the intern are greater than the intern's contribution to the employer's operation. They argue that the primary beneficiary test best reflects the economic realities of the relationship between intern and employer. We agree with defendants that the proper question is whether the intern or the employer is the primary beneficiary of the relationship.

The primary beneficiary test has three salient features. First, it would focus on what the intern received in exchange for his work. Second, it would accord courts the flexibility to examine the economic reality as it existed between the intern and the employer. Third, it acknowledged that the intern-employer relationship should not be analyzed in the same manner as the standard employer-employee relationship because the intern entered into the relationship with the expectation of receiving educational or vocational benefits that were not necessarily expected with all forms of employment. Moreover, a non-exhaustive set of considerations to aid courts in determining whether an unpaid intern was an employee for purposes of the FLSA should be used (see Exhibit 9.4). Applying these considerations requires weighing and balancing all of the circumstances. No one factor is dispositive and every factor need not point in the same direction for the court to conclude that the intern is not an employee entitled to the minimum wage. In addition, the factors we specify are non-exhaustive – courts may consider relevant evidence beyond the specified factors in appropriate cases.

There are several cases similar to *Glatt*, one of which involves interns for Madison Square Garden (MSG) in which interns were allegedly asked to work as many as five days a week, helping with ticket and sponsorship sales, administrative projects, and logistics pertaining to the organization of sport and entertainment events at the arena. The suit sought damages to cover unpaid wages for misclassified workers stemming back to 2007 and could have involved as many as 1,000 former interns (Belzer, 2013). The case was settled out of court and the managing partners of MSG agreed to pay the former interns $795,000, giving each intern between $209–$677. Additionally, Los Angeles Clippers faced a wage class action lawsuit by interns. The argument from the interns is that they completed tasks that were associated with little learning experience and added value to the organization. Cooper, the intern filing suit was involved with contacting season ticket holders and setting up team youth basketball camps (Vehling, 2014). Under FLSA, the burden is on the employer to demonstrate that the criteria are satisfied. Essentially, if a company is using interns as a low-cost or no-cost replacement for regular employees or if the internship does not include substantive educational components, the company may have difficulty meeting the criteria. The DOL's decision to adopt the "primary beneficiary" test was welcome news for employers with internship programs. The test focuses on what the intern receives in exchange for her work, allows for flexibility in examining the economic reality between the intern and the employer, and acknowledges the distinction between intern-employer and employee-employer relationships. Nonetheless, employers should continue to ensure that internship programs are designed to primarily benefit interns.

The following hypothetical case explores the intern exemption in the context of the sport industry. As you structure your internship program, you should review the DOL guidance Fact Sheet #71 (DOL, 2018), any relevant state guidance, and the previous Case Opinion so that you have a thorough understanding of the legal issues.

Considering … Interns Under the FLSA

Assume you have recently been hired as the marketing and promotions director for a minor league professional sports team. You have two full-time salespeople who also help with game day promotions and operations, but you want to partner with the local university's sport management program to provide opportunities for the students to learn about the professional sports industry and also to get some help for your game day promotions and operations. You have a limited budget and will not be able to pay the students for their help.

Questions

- What options do you have to use these students without paying for their services?

- How would you structure your internship program to make sure it is compliant with the FLSA?

Note how you would answer the questions and then check your responses using the Analysis & Discussion at the end of this chapter.

Minor Leagues Baseball Players' Exemption

One new exclusion under FLSA highlights the plight of minor league baseball players. As we saw in Chapter 7, most professional athletes are represented by a player's union and engage in collective bargaining with their respective leagues regarding wages, however, one exception is minor league baseball players. Minor league baseball players are not represented by a union, so are unable to collectively negotiate higher wages or improved working conditions. Thus, they have attempted to use the FLSA to address low wages. For many years, minor league baseball players alleged that they were not being paid minimum wage or overtime, even though they work far more than 40 hours when you consider travel time, time spent at the ballpark pre-game and post-game, and other workouts. In 2014, a group of former minor leagues players sued MLB, Commissioner Selig, and three MLB teams asserting claims under FLSA. The case also importantly sought class action status potentially expanding the case from the 50+ original plaintiffs to potentially all players who played in the minor leagues between 2011 and 2015 (Grow, 2019; *Seene v. Office of the Commissioner of Baseball*, 2014).

In response to *Seene*, MLB successfully lobbied Congress to enact the Save America's Pastime Act (SAPA) in 2018 intended to protect MLB and MiLB from these federal claims going forward. SAPA established a new exemption MiLB players as exempt employees, shielding the leagues from paying minimum wages and overtime pay. SAPA amended Section 213 of FLSA and added a new exemption as follows:

> (19) any employee employed to play baseball who is compensated pursuant to a contract that provides for a weekly salary for services performed during the league's championship season (but not spring training or the off season) at a rate that is not less than a weekly salary equal to the minimum wage under section 206(a) of this title for a workweek of 40 hours, irrespective of the number of hours the employee devotes to baseball related activities. (29 U.S.C. § 213(a)(1)(19), 2018)

To qualify for the exemption, teams must pay players in the minor league system at least $290 per week (federal minimum wage of $7.25 per hour based on a 40-hour workweek) and would not be eligible for overtime compensation when they worked over 40 hours. While this is an increase in salary for some minor league players, the bill also states that players are not entitled to payment during the off-season and spring training. The payment during spring training has been of some discussion as of late, baseball spring training lasts over a month and for some minor league players, much longer. Nevertheless, the SAPA has addressed this issue on the federal level, keeping MLB and MiLB safe from any litigation on the matter at the federal level (Grow, 2019).

SAPA only applies prospectively, thus, although current minor league players are subject to SAPA, the *Senne* case is still pending and MLB still faces potential liability for its past underpayment of minor league players. The Ninth Circuit handed the *Senne* plaintiffs a victory in November, 2019 by ruling that the players could proceed as a class action lawsuit on their FLSA claims (*Senne v. Kansas City Royals Baseball Corp.*, 2019). Although SAPA provides significant protection to MLB, the league has been heavily criticized by media and legal commentators and the exact scope of SAPA's protection will likely be determined in future legal challenges (Grow, 2019).

Volunteers Under the FLSA

Volunteerism is a significant element of the sport and recreation industry. Not only is volunteerism an important way for students to gain meaningful experience, but many sport organizations rely heavily on volunteers to aid in event management. For example, during the 2019 Boston Marathon, 9,700 volunteers were utilized to help run the event (Dwyer, 2019).

And the Olympic Organizing Committee for London 2012 utilized more than 70,000 local volunteers and the Tokyo 2020 Games received more than 200,000 volunteer applications (Olympic.org, 2012; Olympic.org, 2019). Even a small local event may have operational difficulties without the aid of volunteers.

The FLSA defines employment very broadly; however, individuals who volunteer or donate their services, usually on a part-time basis, for *public service, religious, or humanitarian objectives*, not as employees and without contemplation of pay, are not considered employees of the religious, charitable, or similar non-profit organizations that receive their service (DOL, n.d.b). The FLSA defines a **volunteer** as "an individual who performs hours of service for a public agency for civic, charitable, or humanitarian reasons, without promise, expectation or receipt of compensation for services rendered" (29 C.F.R. § 553.101(a)). For example, members of civic organizations may volunteer to drive a school bus to carry a football team or school band on a trip. Similarly, an individual may volunteer to help in a youth program as a camp counselor or scoutmaster, to solicit contributions or participate in a benefit program for a university athletic team, or to volunteer other services required by charitable, educational, or religious programs. Volunteer services requests from the employer must be offered freely and without pressure or coercion, direct or implied (see 29 C.F.R. § 101.553.101(c)). The individual cannot be a volunteer if otherwise employed by the same public agency to perform the same type of services as those which the individual performs as a volunteer (see 29 C.F.R. §§ 553.101(d); 553.102(a)). For example, an employee in the university gift shop may volunteer to distribute educational materials during a health promotion fair but not to work more hours in the gift shop. Volunteers are not employees for purposes of minimum wage and overtime pay requirements under FLSA.

However, under the FLSA, employees may not volunteer services to *for-profit* private-sector employers. When Congress amended the FLSA in 1985, it made clear that people are allowed to volunteer their services to public agencies and their community, but in most circumstances for-profit employers may not allow their employees to volunteer for work connected to their organization without compensation. There are a few circumstances, however, when a private-sector employer may legitimately ask an employee to "volunteer," if the activity can reasonably be regarded as charitable or civic in nature. For example, some companies may regularly host charitable events such as 5K runs or golf scrambles. Under these circumstances, the company should be able safely to invite employees to help or give their time to such an event, so long as all of the following are true:

1 The activities occur outside of the employees' normal working hours.
2 There is no obligation to participate or ramifications for choosing not to participate.
3 The employees have no expectation of compensation for their time helping with the event.
4 The activities performed are different from the normal duties performed by the employees (Newcomb, 2019).

As to volunteering outside of the organization, many large employers actually offer additional benefits to employees who choose to volunteer in the community as a "representative" of their employer. A 2019 DOL Opinion Letter reaffirmed that an employer may use an employee's time spent volunteering during a company sponsored community service program as a factor in calculating whether to pay the employee a bonus so long as the program is charitable and voluntary (DOL, 2019b).

A different twist on the use of volunteers by for-profit companies involves using members of the public as volunteers at sport or special events organized by for-profit sport organizations. The FLSA does not contemplate for-profit enterprises using unpaid volunteers to support their business operations. Although there is very little court precedent on the use of volunteers by for-profit businesses, in *Chen v. Major League Baseball*, MLB was sued in 2013 by a volunteer alleging violations of the FLSA and New York state labor laws for using thousands of unpaid volunteers at for-profit events such as the All-Star FanFest (Minniti, 2013). Being keenly aware of this pending litigation, the NFL opted to hire temporary paid workers to assist with the 2014 Super Bowl in New Jersey and to require unpaid volunteers to sign a waiver that they would not join the class action lawsuit (Pedulla, 2014). Although Chen's case was ultimately dismissed (Chen v. MLB, 2014, 2015), this is an issue sport managers in for-profit organizations should give careful consideration before using the services of volunteers to assist in their event operations.

Competitive Advantage Strategies

Complying with the Fair Labor Standards Act

- Regularly review and prepare employee position descriptions and duties lists for existing employees based upon operational needs.
- Create complete employee position descriptions and duties lists for all new hires based upon operational needs.
- After reviewing the FLSA exemption requirements, determine which employees are nonexempt, and pay overtime when appropriate.
- Evaluate status of seasonal employees to determine whether the amusement and recreation exemption applies.
- Evaluate employee work habits to determine whether employees are "suffered or permitted" to work extra hours in the day, such as working during lunch or prior to or after regular work hours.
- Maintain employee work records for at least three years.
- Evaluate part-time employees to determine whether minimum wage and overtime practices are compliant.
- Review agreements with independent contractors. If a person has more characteristics of an employee than an independent contractor (see Chapter 4), wage and hour requirements may apply.
- Review how interns are used and determine whether such use meets the internship program exception from paying minimum wage and overtime.
- Use a written internship agreement addressing the primary benefits criteria, and include mention that your organization and the intern understand that the intern is not entitled to wages nor entitled to a job at the completion of the internship.

State and Federal Workplace Regulations

Workers' compensation programs are administered at the state level and assist employees injured in work-related accidents to obtain medical care and lost earnings while recovering from their injuries. OSHA works cooperatively with state based workers compensation programs to define workplace safety standards. We will first explore OSHA's regulation of the workplace and then examine how workers' compensation programs operate generally, and also how those programs impact professional and college athletes, specifically.

OSHA and Workplace Safety

The Occupational Safety and Health Act of 1970 is administered by the Occupational Safety and Health Administration and covers most private sector employers and their employees in the 50 states, the District of Columbia, Puerto Rico, and other U.S. territories. OSHA also covers some public sector employers and employees (DOL, 2013). Employers have a general duty to provide their employees with a safe and healthful work environment free from serious hazards. Safety and health conditions in most private industries are regulated by OSHA or OSHA-approved state programs.

Employers covered by the act must comply with the regulations and the safety and health standards promulgated by OSHA. OSHA enforces the act through workplace inspections and investigations. The act defines an employer as any "person engaged in a business affecting commerce who has employees," but does not include the United States or any State or political subdivision of a State (DOL, 2013). Therefore, the act applies to employers and employees in such varied fields as manufacturing, construction, retail, agriculture, law, and medicine, and it includes nonprofits, organized labor, and private educational institutions. The act establishes a separate program for federal government employees and extends coverage to state and local government employees only through each state's OSHA-approved plans. Sport organizations can be affected in a number of ways, ranging from safety standards applicable to a new sports stadium construction project to the ergonomic design of a computer station in a ticket office. OSHA has two primary regulatory functions:

1 setting standards.
2 conducting inspections to ensure that employers are providing safe and healthful workplaces.

OSHA also encourages states to develop and operate their own job safety and health programs. OSHA approves and monitors these "state plans," which operate under the authority of state law. Currently 22 states and jurisdictions operate complete state plans (covering both the private sector and state and local government employees), and five states and one U.S. territory five (Connecticut, Illinois, New Jersey, New York, Maine, and the Virgin Islands) have plans that cover state and local government employees only (DOL, n.d.b). States with OSHA-approved job safety and health plans must set standards that are at least as effective as the federal standards. Most but not all of the state-plan states have adopted standards identical to the federal standards.

The act also provides protection for employees who report safety or health concerns. Thus, employers may not discriminate or retaliate against an employee who raises or reports safety or health concerns. The provisions in most public safety laws and many environmental laws protect employees who complain about violations of the law by their employers. These provisions are known as whistleblower protections (see Chapter 3). If an employer discriminates or retaliates, the employee can file a complaint with OSHA. OSHA enforces the whistleblower protections in most laws. Remedies can include job reinstatement and payment of back wages.

Safety Standards

OSHA may set a **specific hazard standard** that must be met by an employer and may require that employers adopt specific practices, means, methods, or processes reasonably necessary and appropriate to protect workers on the job. Regardless whether OSHA has set forth a standard addressing a specific hazard, employers also must comply with the **general duty** clause in the act. The general duty clause (Section 5(a)(1)) states that each employer "shall furnish … a place of employment which is free from recognized hazards that are causing or are likely to cause death or serious physical harm to his employees" (29 U.S.C. § 654, 2004).

Employers must become familiar with the specific standards applicable to their establishments and eliminate those specific hazards, as well as general hazards that are likely to cause death or serious injury to employees. Compliance with standards may include ensuring that employees have been provided with, have been effectively trained on, and use personal protective equipment when required for safety or health. Employees must comply with all rules and regulations that apply to their own actions and conduct. In addition to enforcing the standards, OSHA provides guidance documents for employers so that they understand how to make their workplaces safer. For example, following the 2020 pandemic, OSHA developed a *Guidance on Preparing Workplaces for COVID-19*. A guidance such as this is not a new law or regulation, but instead advisory to aid employers and reduce the impact of COVID-19 on businesses, workers, customers, and the public (DOL, 2020d).

One notable segment of the sport industry affected by OSHA involves athletic trainers and medical personnel. Knowledge of OSHA guidelines for preventing disease transmission is essential for these individuals. OSHA's regulations regarding the prevention of transmission of bloodborne pathogens detail a number of requirements that affect athletic training and medical staff members. Of particular importance is the requirement that employers establish an exposure control plan to eliminate or minimize employee exposures. Employers must also provide personal protective equipment, such as gloves, gowns, and masks, while also providing information and training to employees covering the dangers of bloodborne pathogens, preventive practices, and post-exposure procedures.

For a simple example of how these requirements should be implemented, consider an athletic trainer who is working at a men's basketball game when a member of the team is struck in the head, resulting in a bloody nose. As we watch on television or at the game, we may see the trainer grab a bandage or gauze pad and place it on the injury to stop the bleeding. In fact, it was not at all uncommon a few years ago for the trainer not to wear protective gloves when treating this type of injury. However, under the OSHA guidelines on bloodborne pathogens, an exposure control plan should require all employees to have protective gloves immediately available and mandate that all employees must use these gloves when treating any injury where bleeding is present.

Many specific OSHA standards relate to the manufacturing, construction, and transportation industries. For example, during Louisville's construction of its downtown arena, the construction company entered into a site-based construction partnership agreement with the Kentucky Department of Labor OSHA as part of a Construction Partnership Program run by OSHA's Division of Education and Training. A Construction Partnership Program agreement is a voluntary agreement that allows OSHA to make quarterly consultations and site visits to conduct safety and health surveys and requires construction company employees to complete extensive safety training programs (Louisville Arena Authority, 2008). The training programs include a variety of topics, including rigging safety, fall protection, forklift safety, accident analysis, hazard communication, bloodborne pathogens, first aid/CPR defibrillator, top driver safety, fire protection safety, respirator training, and scaffolding safety. Such a program is a proactive approach to OSHA compliance and avoiding OSHA claims. Entering into a program such as this can also serve to improve financing and bonding opportunities for new facilities.

Investigations

During the construction of U.S. Bank Stadium, the home of the Minnesota Vikings, they had two accidents occur in a three-month span over the summer of 2015. First, in May, a worker fell from the scaffolding, but was released from the hospital a week later. However, in August, a worker also fell from the north side of the stadium roof and later died from his injuries. This led to OSHA coming down with harsh financial fines to the construction companies employed by the Vikings (Johnson, 2016). Additionally, on June 5, 2020 construction was halted on SoFi Stadium in Los Angeles after a construction iron worker fell to his death at the construction site and California's state OSHA office (CAL-OSHA) began an investigation into the death (Navarro, 2020). If a state OSHA, such as Cal/OSHA in this case, determines that a condition or practice creates an imminent hazard, it can issue an Order Prohibiting Use, which would halt construction and possibly delay timely completion of a construction project that is noncompliant and/or hazardous. Organizations should retain all documents pertaining to construction in the event of an accident and resulting OSHA investigation. Sport managers who are involved in the construction of a new sport facility must be proactive in meeting their obligations under OSHA, as well as other building code requirements. The Department of Labor offers numerous resources for facility managers and operators during construction projects.

OSHA's relevance for construction projects is highly visible; however, many other sport organization operations are also subject to OSHA standards, even if not quite as visibly. Most sport organizations will be covered primarily by the general duty clause; that is, they need to ensure that their place of employment is free from hazards. For example, an employee of a minor league hockey team is responsible for placing signage around the ice rink prior to each game. One day, as the employee is hanging the signage behind the hockey goal, a player who is practicing on the ice hits the employee in the back of the head with the puck and knocks him unconscious. The employee does not have any permanent injuries, but any

---

Competitive Advantage Strategies

Workplace Safety and Health

- Be sure all required OSHA information and posters are displayed for employees.
- Determine which OSHA standards and regulations apply to your organization.
- Conduct safety compliance audits of your company to identify and correct any violations.
- Establish a team to deal with catastrophic occurrences, fatalities, and OSHA-related public relations issues.
- Determine who will be responsible for over-seeing safety and health concerns in your organization, and designate that person as your OSHA contact.
- Regularly review your safety records to ensure that your organization is in compliance with recordkeeping and reporting requirements.
- Make sure all training manuals, safety manuals, and other written employee training programs are up to date and easily accessible.
- Incorporate safety discussion at all stages of the value chain, including procurement, design, manufacturing, service, and end of life. It is cheaper to design safety at the outset rather than to have to retrofit for safety in response to an injury. Contractors with proven safety records should be selected.

---

injury requiring more than minor first aid must be reported to OSHA. This is the type of injury that OSHA would expect the employer to have provided standards and training to avoid. It is likely that permitting the hockey players to practice on the ice at the same time that employees are setting up the event creates an unsafe working condition. This condition could easily be remedied by implementing safety procedures to monitor access and usage of the ice rink when employees are present and by properly training employees as to these safety procedures.

Overview of Workers' Compensation Law

Each of the 50 states has enacted workers' compensation statutes. These statutes, many of which were enacted in the early part of the twentieth century, were put into effect because workers were not able to recover against their employers, under common law principles, for injuries on the job. Thus, many workers were left without a remedy for injuries that occurred at their place of employment. To remedy this injustice, state implemented workers' compensation systems requiring the employer to pay compensation for work-related injuries and illnesses. These systems are designed to serve as a compromise between the employee's interest in compensation for work related disabilities and injuries, and the employer's interest in avoiding costly litigation. These laws provide benefits for dependents of workers whose work-related accidents or illnesses resulted in their death. These laws also protect employers and fellow workers by limiting the amount an injured employee can recover from an employer and by eliminating the liability of co-workers in most accidents. Although each state has its own workers' compensation system, these systems tend to share common characteristics about the types of claims and compensation; types and scope of insurance coverage; and administrative procedures. However, as we will discuss later in this section, coverage varies for professional athletes under these systems (Friede, 2015).

When a claim falls within the coverage of the workers' compensation statute, that claim is exclusive, meaning that the worker's only remedy is under workers' compensation. The employee's compensation is determined by a schedule of compensation under the statute. For example, under the Massachusetts

Exhibit 9.5 Essential elements entitling an injured worker to workers' compensation.

1 A compensable injury must have occurred.
2 The injury must be accidental, occupational disease, or cumulative trauma.
3 The injury must arise out of employment.

workers' compensation schedule, an employee who suffers the total loss of use of one eye would receive a sum equal to the average weekly wage in the commonwealth at the date of the injury multiplied by 39 (A.L.M., 2009). The use of the multiplier 39 is simply the formula adopted by the Commonwealth of Massachusetts to set a value for the injury. Clearly, it is difficult to place a dollar value on the loss of an eye, but one purpose of the workers' compensation formula is to provide specific recovery amounts for a broad range of injury types. A different state may use a different multiplier. An employee is limited to recovering the predetermined amount based on the worker's level of impairment, payments for medical expenses, and degree of disability, as determined by the state's workers' compensation scheme and formulas. As we will discuss later, an employee may seek to show that workers' compensation is not applicable to his or her injury, because the benefits are limited.

Scope of Coverage

Although the specific language of the statutes varies from state to state, three essential elements must be met for an injured employee to be entitled to workers' compensation (see Exhibit 9.5). Each of these elements is described more fully below.

Compensable Injuries

Generally, to have a **compensable injury**, a worker must suffer a physical injury or illness. Psychological or emotional injuries are often excluded from the coverage of the act. In addition, laws may exclude compensation for injuries that are intentional or self-inflicted; result from the employee's horseplay or voluntary intoxication (either alcohol or drug-induced); arise from voluntary participation in off-duty recreational, social, or sporting events; result from "acts of God" (unless a person's job exposes him to a greater risk of injury from such acts); or are inflicted by someone else for personal reasons unrelated to employment.

Types of Injuries

Injuries that result from intentional acts are not considered accidental injuries for purposes of workers' compensation. For example, if a worker punches a co-worker on the job, this is not an accidental injury and is not compensable. Sexual harassment at the workplace may be considered intentional conduct and may be excluded under the statute. However, even in cases where the employee's own negligence may have contributed to his injury, he is still entitled to workers' compensation. For example, Bradley, a special events coordinator for a local nonprofit organization, has transported several boxes of promotional items to be given away at the annual celebrity golf scramble. Bradley arrives at the golf course pro shop and loads the materials into a golf cart to distribute on the course. While driving to a location on the course, Bradley drives at an excessive speed, causing the golf cart to flip over, and is injured. While certainly Bradley's own negligence has contributed to his injuries, he is still entitled to recover workers' compensation for his injuries, since the injuries were the result of an accident. Occupational disease claims are also covered which may include diseases resulting from exposure to toxins over a period of time. While, cumulative trauma claims that resulted from sustained exposure to trauma over a period of time, also require coverage. These injuries are caused by repeated shocks or slight injuries to the body that by themselves may not be disabling, but their cumulative effect results in a recognizable injury. A good example of cumulative trauma claims is CTE experienced by many former NFL and NHL players due to repetitive exposure to concussions and head trauma.

Injuries Arising Out of Employment

The third element for entitlement to workers' compensation is whether the injury "arose out of employment." This is often a difficult issue to resolve. Courts look at whether the injury is tied to some condition, activity, or requirement of employment. Although each state may use different language to decide whether the injury "arose out of employment," and no single factor is determinative, courts often consider the following factors (van der Smissen, 1990):

1 whether the injury occurred during working hours;
2 whether the injury occurred on the employer's premises;
3 whether the injury occurred during an activity initiated by the employer;
4 whether the employer exercised any degree of control or direction over the employee's activity;
5 whether the employer benefited or stood to benefit from the employee's activity.

An injury does not have to occur at the employer's worksite or while the employee is actually working. Injuries to employees who are making deliveries or walking through a parking lot may fall within the reach of workers' compensation. If an employer urges employees to participate in employer-sponsored activities, such as a fitness event or a company softball game or other recreational activity, there may be liability under workers' compensation. An activity is considered employer-sponsored if: (a) they employer paid for/organized the activity; (b) the activity was on the employer's premises; (c) the employer supervised the activity; (d) the employer paid the entry fee; (e) the employer purchased uniforms or equipment; (f) only employees participated in the activity; or (g) the employer received economic or intangible benefits from the employees' participation.

In a case that involved a school district, a teacher/coach tore his Achilles tendon while playing basketball in an evening fundraising game, which was held to benefit the school's basketball program (*Dozier v. Mid-Del Sch. System*, 1998). A team of teachers, coaches, and former school athletes had been playing against employees of a radio station. The teacher/coach's claim for workers' compensation benefits was initially denied on the basis that the injury occurred during a voluntary recreational activity, but an appellate court reversed, holding that the injury "arose out of employment." The court noted that the teacher/coach was encouraged to participate in the fundraiser to help the athletic programs survive. Under the language of the statute, the employer "derived a substantial direct benefit from the activity," and the injury was compensable under the workers' compensation law. In another case, a teacher who was injured during a basketball game between students and teachers was able to recover workers' compensation (*Highlands County Sch. Bd. v. Savage*, 1992). This case was easier to resolve, because the game was held during regular school hours and teachers were required to participate or at least attend the game as spectators.

In another case, a fitness instructor, Murphy, injured his leg while playing wallyball during his work shift at the Elmhurst Park fitness facility. Murphy was found to be entitled to workers' compensation, even though the park district had argued the game was a voluntary recreational activity. The Illinois court of appeals agreed with the findings of the workers' compensation commission that the instructor's participation clearly benefited the park's business, that recreation was inherent in Murphy's job, and that his reason for participating was not for his own diversion but for his employer's benefit (*Elmhurst Park District v. Illinois Workers' Compensation Commission*, 2009). However, recently the Delaware Supreme Court held that an employee of a law firm was not injured in the scope of employment when he tore his Achilles tendon during a firm softball game. The law firm sponsored a team in the Wilmington Lawyer's Softball League and referred to the league frequently during recruitment of employees, but the court held softball was outside the "orbit of employment" and the law firm derived no business benefit from its participation (*James v. Weller*, 2018).

Considering ... Injuries Arising out of Employment

Jackson owns a sport marketing firm with about a dozen employees. To build goodwill and team-work, he sponsors a company softball team and strongly encourages all of the employees to play. In fact, Jackson gives special benefits to those who play on the team. During a league game after work hours at a public softball field, the team's shortstop, Gin, sprains her ankle while running the bases.

Questions

- Can Jackson's company be held responsible for paying Gin's workers' compensation claim?

- What factors would a court look at when deciding whether this injury arose out of employment? And was employer-sponsored?

Note how you would answer the questions and then check your responses using the Analysis & Discussion at the end of this chapter.

Workers' Compensation and the Professional Athlete

In professional sports, the accidental nature of the injury is a critical issue, since many injuries are possible in sport due to the physical and possibly violent nature of the game. Most states have specifically included professional athletes in their workers' compensation programs. The following Focus Case examines whether a professional athlete's injury qualified for workers' compensation benefits.

Pro-Football, Inc. v. Uhlenhake

558 S.E.2d 571 (Va. Ct. App. 2002)   **FOCUS** CASE

FACTS

The Workers' Compensation Commission (WCC) entered an award of permanent partial disability benefits in favor of Jeffrey A. Uhlenhake, a professional football player, for injury to his left foot. Pro-Football, Inc. (Washington Redskins) contends injuries to a professional football player are not covered by the Workers' Compensation Act. Beginning in 1996, Uhlenhake was employed by Pro-Football as an offensive lineman for the Redskins football team. During his career, Uhlenhake experienced a number of physical injuries in training, practices, and games. Specifically, Uhlenhake injured his left foot, left ankle, and left knee. An orthopaedic surgeon examined Uhlenhake in 1999 and determined that he had a permanent impairment of his left ankle due to arthritis and of his left knee due to an ACL injury. Uhlenhake filed a claim for permanent partial disability workers' compensation benefits based upon injuries to his left ankle, foot, and knee. Following an evidentiary hearing, the WCC ruled that injuries sustained in employment by professional athletes are covered by the Workers' Compensation Act and that Uhlenhake was entitled to permanent partial disability benefits for 5 percent loss of the use of his left foot and 14 percent loss of use of his left leg and for medical benefits. Pro-Football appealed.

HOLDING

The WCC correctly ruled that professional football players are covered under the Workers' Compensation Act when they suffer injuries in the game they are employed to perform.

RATIONALE

Pro-Football contended that injuries resulting from voluntary participation in activities where injuries are customary, foreseeable, and expected are not accidental within the meaning of the workers' compensation laws. The Virginia Workers' Compensation Act provides that "'injury' means only injury by accident arising out of and in the course of employment." The Act does not ... specifically define the term "injury by accident." To establish an "injury by accident," a claimant must prove (1) that the injury appeared suddenly at a particular time and place and upon a particular occasion, (2) that it was caused by an identifiable incident or sudden precipitating event, and (3) that it resulted in an obvious mechanical or structural change in the human body.

The principle is well-established that "to constitute injury by accident it is not necessary for the Plaintiff to prove that there must be a ... 'fortuitous circumstance' ... [or] that there should be an extraordinary occurrence in or about the work engaged in." The evidence proved that Uhlenhake was engaged in an activity required by his employment. He was employed by Pro-Football to train, practice, and play in football games, which is the business of Pro-Football. This is not a case of an injury "resulting from an employee's voluntary participation in employer-sponsored off-duty recreational activities which are not part of the employee's duties." Likewise, this is not a case in which the "injury was the direct result of [an employee] taking a risk of his own choosing, independent of any employment requirements, and one that was not an accepted and normal activity at the place of employment." Uhlenhake was at all relevant times engaged in an activity within the scope of his employment contract.

In addition to explaining when an injury is a result of an accident that would permit workers' compensation benefits to be paid, the *Uhlenhake* case also addresses the nature of football as a dangerous sport and the matter of whether players should expect to be injured. Pro-Football had argued that by engaging in conduct that is physically dangerous and that has a high likelihood of injury, players must "automatically" expect to be injured. In support of its contentions, Pro-Football cited two appellate court decisions in other jurisdictions, *Rowe v. Baltimore Colts* (1983) and *Palmer v. Kansas City Chiefs Football Club* (1981).

However, the appellate court stated that "the *Rowe* and *Palmer* decisions are contrary to the decisions in the great majority of jurisdictions. Injuries in [professional] sports are so routinely treated as compensable in the great majority of jurisdictions that they seldom appear in reported appellate decisions" (Friede, 2015; Larson, 2001). Both Larson and Friede note that *Palmer* is the only surviving appellate decision denying compensation for injury in a professional team sport as a non-compensable injury. In *Pro-Football, Inc. v. Tupa* (2012) the Maryland court of appeals rejected Pro-Football's argument that an athlete's injuries were not accidental within the meaning of the Maryland workers' compensation act. The court of appeals held that *Rowe* was inconsistent with current statutory and case law and agreed with overruling *Rowe* (*Pro-Football v. Tupa*, 2012). Therefore, despite a few decisions to the contrary, it is clear that professional football players are covered workers when they suffer injuries in the game they are employed to perform. A few states do expressly exclude professional athletes from the statutory definition of "employee" or establish different scales for professional athletes wages for purposes of compensation. States that exclude them entirely generally require that professional teams retain private insurance in lieu of workers' compensation (Friede, 2015).

A continuing issue relates to professional athletes' seeking workers' compensation benefits in multiple states. Despite the NFL's settlement agreement with over 5,000 former NFL players experiencing concussion related trauma, California experienced a dramatic increase in workers' compensation claims from former professional athletes (Ezell, 2013). Over the past 20 years, thousands of retired professional athletes have sought workers' compensation benefits in California for work-related injuries sustained during the course of their careers. The attractiveness of California's workers' compensation benefits is that it permits recovery for cumulative injury that occurred over time and that a player may not be aware of until after retirement (Israel, 2013). Retired players could have received significant payouts, up to $250,000, simply because they played a handful of games in California during the course of their career while employed by a team in another state or states (Israel, 2013). Several federal court case, however, appear to have curtailed this practice and upheld NFL arbitration decisions holding that a player's filing of a workers' compensation claim in California is a breach of the choice of law provisions in their player contract (*Cincinnati Bengals v. Abdullah*, 2013; *Matthews v. NFL Mgt. Council*, 2012). You may recall from Chapter 3 that a common provision in a contract is a choice of law clause, in which the parties agree that any disputes will be resolved in a certain state according to that state's law. Most player contracts contain a provision similar to that found in Matthews' contract with the Titans, which provided that "jurisdiction of all workers compensation claims and all other matters related to workers compensation benefits, shall be exclusively determined by and exclusively decided in accordance with the laws of the State of Tennessee" (Grotzinger, Hooper, & Israel, 2012, para. 3). The NFL arbitrator determined that both Matthews' and Abdullah's choice of law provisions were enforceable and that the players should cease and desist from pursuing workers' compensation benefits in California.

Workers' Compensation and the Collegiate Athlete

In the course of playing a sport for an educational institution, a student-athlete may suffer an injury. Some players have argued that they should receive workers' compensation for such injuries. Although a few players were able to convince courts in early cases (*University of Denver v. Nemeth*, 1953; *Van Horn v. Industrial Accident Comm'n*, 1963) that they should be considered "employees" of the university, most courts today are in agreement that student-athletes at universities should not be considered employees. In addition, many states expressly exclude student-athletes as employees in their worker compensation statutes. The student-athlete's claim for workers' compensation is based on the argument that the receipt of an athletic scholarship constitutes an employment contract in which the athlete exchanges the work of athletic performance for the pay of scholarship monies. More recent cases have consistently held that student-athletes were not covered employees under state worker compensation statutes in cases where student-athletes sued their respective universities (see *Rensing v. Indiana State University Board of Trustees*, 1983; *Townsend v. State of California*, 1984). Further, courts in other jurisdictions have generally found that such individuals as student-athletes, student leaders in student government associations, and student resident hall assistants are not "employees" for purposes of workers' compensation laws unless they are also employed in a university job in addition to receiving scholarship benefits.

Competitive Advantage Strategies

Workers' Compensation

- When sponsoring teams or events, do not mandate participation or reward employees who participate in these activities.
- Communicate with employees regarding the events and make sure that they understand that participation is truly voluntary.
- Do not hold sport or fitness events on company premises.
- Do not attempt to control these events; confine your support to providing economic support.
- Workers' compensation insurance is expensive. Do your homework and get lower-risk classifications for your business and employees, where possible.

The non-employee status of student-athletes is a topic of continuing criticism and concern. For example when Kevin Ware, basketball player for the University of Louisville, suffered a horrific injury during the 2013 NCAA Men's Basketball Championship, several commentators raised the question of who would pay for Ware's medical expenses and what compensation would he receive, if any, for his injuries (Diamond, 2013; Pennington, 2013). Ware's medical bills would be covered by his personal health insurance (which all NCAA athletes are required to have), any University supplemental insurance policy (which is optional), and the NCAA's supplemental insurance policy applicable to NCAA championships (Moore, 2013). Of course, Ware was not an employee of the University of Louisville and was not injured in the scope of his employment, so he would not be entitled to workers' compensation benefits.

Although not a workers' compensation case, in a recent decision of the Ninth Circuit Court of Appeals, USC football player Lamar Dawson sued the PAC-12 and the NCAA alleging that the NCAA and PAC-12 acted as employers. The appellate court concluded that there was no employment relationship between Dawson and the NCAA/PAC12, it also stated "we need not address whether Dawson's scholarship engendered an expectation of compensation or whether his scholarship amounted to compensation" leaving that question open for future decisions (*Dawson v. NCAA*, 2019, p. 909). As student-athletes continue to raise challenges to university and NCAA restraints on their compensation (see Chapter 7) and challenge their status as student-athletes rather than employees, court decisions in other areas of labor law may potentially influence their legal rights areas such as workers' compensation (Baker, 2019; Bivens, 2017).

Premiums for Workers' Compensation Insurance

Since employers have no choice but to provide workers' compensation to employees, employers must secure insurance to cover these claims. There are two important points to consider regarding the cost of this insurance. First, the cost of premiums declines as the number of workplace injuries declines. Therefore, it is in an employer's interest to have safety and risk management programs in place. Second, employers must understand the classification systems for types of workers and ensure that workers are not placed in a "high risk" category, for which the premiums are higher. For example, all employees in a fitness club do not have the same physical demands, yet some employers allow their clerical employees to be classified with their fitness instructors, which results in a higher premium than necessary for those employees who are in "harmless" desk jobs. Also, care must be taken that the entire operation is not lumped together with high-risk endeavors, which also have high premiums. For example, some states classify as an "amusement" business anything ranging from the health, fitness, or tennis club to the traveling carnival. Obviously, the carnival operation can be expected to have a much higher rate of injury than the health club. The health club owner will be greatly disadvantaged if she does not see that the club receives the proper classification.

Conclusion

This chapter explored legal issues in the workplace related to employee compensation, workplace safety and health standards, and workers' compensation for work-related injuries. We identified and discussed laws affecting wages as provided in the FLSA and issues arising in the sport industry, including the use of interns and volunteers, numerous exemptions to FLSA. We explained workplace safety and health standards required under the Occupational Safety and Health Act, and we examined state workers' compensation laws and the treatment of professional athletes and student-athletes as workers for purposes of workers' compensation. How well a manager knows and understands these legal issues can provide her with a competitive advantage in the workplace and lead to increased employee productivity and effectiveness.

Discussion Questions

1 Identify and explain the rights that employees are given under the FLSA.
2 Explain the two tests used to determine whether an employee is exempt from overtime requirements under the seasonal amusement and recreational establishment exemptions in the FLSA.
3 Explain how minor league baseball players must be compensated under the SAPA?
4 Identify the five factors used in determining whether a person is working within the scope of employment under workers' compensation principles.
5 What are the two primary functions of OSHA regulations?

Learning Activities

1 As you know, many organizations, including sport organizations, experienced financial difficulty during the Covid-19 pandemic that began in early 2020. As a result, many companies had to make difficult choices about whether or not they should furlough or terminate employees during shutdown periods in order to reduce costs. Visit the Department of Labor website located at the following link: www.dol.gov/whd/flsa/index.htm. From this page, locate information or guidance on the legal issues that arise from an organization's decision to furlough any or all of its employees. Specifically, see if you can find an answer to whether a salaried exempt employee can voluntarily take time off work due to lack of work.

Case Study

You obtained an internship with a professional baseball team, and you were injured when several boxes of dashboard promotional toys fell on you in the supply and copy room at the team offices. You receive a meal voucher and free parking for each game for helping with promotions at the 50 home games required under your internship agreement. Are you entitled to workers' compensation? Review *Hallal v. RDV Sports*, 682 So.2d 1235 (Fla. Dist. Ct. App. 1996), where an appellate court held that workers' compensation was the exclusive remedy in a similar situation. How might the decision in *Glatt* impact your workers' compensation claims?

Considering ... Analysis & Discussion

Interns Under the FLSA

In order to use these students as interns without paying for their services, you have to demonstrate that you are in compliance with the DOL guidance on Internship Programs. It would be a good idea to develop a formal intern/student trainee handbook outlining the relationship. This handbook could specifically address the factors in the DOL Fact Sheet #71. When using students as interns, consider these guidelines:

1 Make sure the students are not displacing regular employees. Since you will retain your two salespersons, this element should be satisfied.
2 Complete a written agreement with the trainees stating there is no expectation or guarantee of employment upon completion of the internship and no expectation of wages during the internship.
3 You must provide close supervision and a hands-on educational experience. This may mean that you have to limit the number of student interns you have, in order to provide the level of supervision and experience needed. You may also want to conduct regular training sessions or meetings with interns to present specific professional development training or information for their benefit.

4 The primary benefits of the internship should be the students rather than the organization so it may be a good idea to limit internships to only those students who are receiving academic credit for the experience. As mentioned above, you should permit the interns to engage in activities that would not normally be available to them as a regular paid employee, such as sitting in on planning or strategy sessions with senior staff or participating in webinars. Typically, in these higher-level meetings the organization is being benefited very little by the involvement of the intern, but the experience is very helpful for the student.

Injuries Arising Out of Employment

Jackson can be held liable for Mary's injury if it is determined that the injury arose out of Mary's employment. Thus, we must apply the five factors and consider results from similar cases to reach a conclusion. Of the five factors, the first two do not help Mary's case, since the event was not during normal working hours and was not held on company premises. However, the remaining three factors must be considered. Jackson sponsors the event, strongly encourages employees to participate, and even provides employees special benefits if they participate. It is likely that these facts alone would demonstrate that the employer initiated and controlled the activity sufficiently for a court to find that Mary's injury arose from her employment. With regard to whether the employer stood to benefit, while it is not as clear a case as *Dozier* or *Savage*, where the employer's fundraising event benefited from the employee's participation, one could still certainly argue that the company's desire to build goodwill and teamwork were sufficient benefits to conclude that the injury arose from Mary's employment, similar to the *Elmhurst Park* case.

References

Cases

Adams v. Detroit Tigers, Inc., 961 F. Supp. 176 (E.D. Mich. 1997).

Bridewell v. The Cincinnati Reds, 68 F.3d 136 (6th Cir. 1995).

Brock v. Louvers & Dampers, Inc., 817 F.2d 1255, 1259 (6th Cir. 1987)

Chen v. Major League Baseball, Case No. 13 CV 5494 [Class Action Complaint] (S.D.N.Y. 2013) (U.S. District Court).

Chen v. Major League Baseball, Case No. 13 Civ. 5494 (JGK) [Opinion and Order] (S.D.N.Y. 2014) (U.S. District Court).

Chen v. Major League Baseball Properties, 798 F.3d 72 (2d Cir. 2015).

Cincinnati Bengals v. Abdullah, 2013 U.S. Dist. LEXIS 5910 (S.D. Ohio 2013).

Dawson v. NCAA, 932 F.3d 905 (9th Cir. 2019).

Dozier v. Mid-Delaware School System, 959 P.2d 604 (Okla. Ct. App. 1998).

Elmhurst Park District v. Illinois Workers' Compensation Commission, 917 N.E.2d 1052 (Ill. App. 2009).

Glatt v. Fox Searchlight, 811 F.3d 528 (2d Cir. 2015).

Green Bay Sportservice, Inc. v. Wisconsin Dept. of Workforce Development, 912 N.W.2d 518 (Wis. Ct. App. 2018).

Hays v. City of Pauls Valley, 74 F.3d 1002, 1006 (10th Cir. 1996).

Highlands County Sch. Bd. v. Savage, 609 So.2d 133 (Fla. Dist. Ct. App. 1992).

Hill v. Delaware North Companies Sportservice, Inc., 838 F.3d 281 (2d Cir. 2016).

James v. Weller, Del. Super. LEXIS 150 (2018, March 29), aff'd, 196 A.3d 1252 (Del. 2018).

Jeffery v. Sarasota White Sox, Inc., 64 F.3d 590 (11th Cir. 1995).

Juric v. Dick's Sporting Goods, Inc., Case No. 2:20-cv-651 [Class and Collective Action Complaint] (W.D. Pa., May 4, 2020).

Liger v. New Orleans Hornets NBA Ltd. Pshp, 565 F. Supp. 2d 680 (E.D. La. 2008).

Matthews v. NFL Mgt. Council, 688 F.3d 1107 (9th Cir. 2012).

Palmer v. Kansas City Chiefs Football Club, 621 S.W.2d 350 (Mo. App. 1981).

Perez v. Sanford-Orlando Kennel Club, 469 F. Supp. 2d 1086 (M.D. Fla. 2006), aff'd, 515 F.3d 1150 (11th Cir. 2008).

Pro-Football v. Tupa, 51 A3d 544 (Md. Ct. App. 2012).

Pro-Football, Inc. v. Uhlenhake, 558 S.E.2d 571 (Va. Ct. App. 2002).

Rensing v. Indiana State Univ., 444 N.E.2d 1170 (Ind. 1983).

Rowe v. Baltimore Colts, 53 Md. App. 526, 454 A.2d 872 (Md. App. 1983).

Senne v. Office of the Commissioner of Baseball, Case No. 14-cv-00608 (N.D. Cal. February 7, 2014).

Senne v. Kansas City Royals Baseball Corp., 934 F.3d 918 (9th Cir. 2019).

University of Denver v. Nemeth, 257 P.2d 423 (Colo. 1953).

Van Horn v. Industrial Accident Comm'n, 33 Cal. Rptr. 169 (Cal. Ct. App. 1963).

Statutes

1. 29 C.F.R. § 779.385 (2020).

2. 29 U.S.C. § 213(a)(1)(19) (2018).

3. 29 U.S.C. § 213(a)(3) (2018).

Annotated Law of Massachusetts, GL, ch. 152, § 36 Payment for Certain Specific Injuries (2009).

Fair Labor Standards Act (FSLA) of 1938, 29 U.S.C. §§ 201, *et seq.* (2013).

Occupational Safety and Health Act of 1970, 29 U.S.C. §§ 651, *et seq.* (2004).

Save America's Pastime Act, 29 U.S.C. § 213(a)(1)(19) (2018).

Other Sources

Baker, T. (2019, August 15). Narrow decision favoring NCAA and PAC-12 fails to resolve whether college athletes are employees. Forbes.com. Retrieved from https://www.forbes.com/sites/thomasbaker/2019/08/15/narrow-ninth-circuit-decision-favoring-the-ncaa-and-pac-12-fails-to-resolve.

Belzer, J. (2013, September 18). Madison Square Garden intern lawsuit could create disastrous precedent for sports industry. *Forbes.com.* Retrieved from http://www.forbes.com/sites/jasonbelzer/2013/09/18/madison-square-garden-intern-lawsuit-could-create-disastrous-precedent-for-sports-industry/.

Binder, J. F., Baguley, T., Crook, C., & Miller, F. (2015, April). The academic value of internships: Benefits across disciplines and student backgrounds. *Contemporary Educational Psychology*, 41, 73–82.

Bivens, G. J. (2017). NCAA student athlete unionization: NLRB punts on Northwestern University football team. *Penn State Law Review*, 121(3), 949–978.

Briggs, T. W. (2000, February 21). Stint on copy desk helps an intern correct his course. *USA Today*, p. 6D.

Cates-McIver, L. (1998, October). The value of internships and co-op opportunities for college students. *Black Collegian*, 29(1), 72–74.

Chochrek, E. (2020, May 6). Dick's Sporting Goods assistant managers claims they weren't paid for overtime. *Footwear News*. Retrieved from https://footwearnews.com/2020/business/legal-news/dicks-sporting-goods-assistant-managers-overtime-pay-1202980283/.

Crumbley, D. L., & Sumners, G. E. (1998, October). How businesses profit from internships. *The Internal Auditor*, 55(5), 54–58.

CUPA & NCAA. (2016). Payment of coaches and athletic trainers under federal law. Retrieved from https://www.ncaa.org/sites/default/files/AWFIN_White-Paper-Exempt-Status-of-Coaches-and-Trainers_20160520.pdf.

Diamond, D. (2013, March 31). What does the NCAA owe Kevin Ware. *Forbes.com.* Retrieved from http://www.forbes.com/sites/dandiamond/2013/03/31/what-does-the-ncaa-owe-kevin-ware/.

Dwyer, D. (2019, April 9). It started because of the jackets. But more than 30 years later, he is still volunteering for the Boston Marathon. *Boston.com.* Retrieved from https://www.boston.com/sports/boston-marathon/2019/04/09/volunteer-boston-marathon.

Ezell, L. (2013, October 8). Timeline: The NFL's concussion crisis. *PBS: Frontline.* Retrieved from https://www.pbs.org/wgbh/pages/frontline/sports/league-of-denial/timeline-the-nfls-concussion-crisis/#2002.

Friede, M. (2015). Comment: Professional athletes are "seeing starts": How athletes are "knocked-out" of states' workers' compensation systems. *Hamline Law Review*, 38, 519–555.

Genzale, J. (2005, July 11). Use interns, get more than you pay for. *Street & Smith's SportsBusiness Journal*, 8(11), 26.

Green, L. (2018, April 9). Fair Labor Standards Act opinion letter on coaches. *National Federation of State High School Associations.* Retrieved from https://www.nfhs.org/articles/fair-labor-standards-act-opinion-letter-on-coaches/.

Grotzinger J., Hooper, D., & Israel, J. (2012, August 21). Ninth Circuit issues key decision concerning professional athletes and the California Workers' Compensation System. *Martindale.com.* Retrieved from http://www.martindale.com/litigation-law/article_Greenberg-Traurig-LLP_1572892.htm.

Grow, N. (2019). The Save America's pastime Act: Special-interest legislation epitomized. *University of Colorado Law Review*, 90, 1013–1049.

Haghighi, H. (1998, December 20). The right tools. *The New York Times*, 30.

Israel, J. L. (2013, March 22). Has the legal tide turned against retired professional athletes seeking California workers' compensation benefits? *Sports Litigation Alerts*, 10(5).

Johnson, B. (2016, December 8). "Inadequate" fall protection cited in stadium fatality. *Finance & Commerce.* Retrieved from https://finance-commerce.com/2016/12/inadequate-fall-protection-cited-in-stadium-fatality/.

Kelsey, J. M. (2002). Fighting fires with interns: Building a program that keeps YOU on track. *Public Relations Quarterly*, 47(3), 43–45.

Larson, L. K. (2001). *Larson's workers' compensation law* § 22.04[1][b]. Dayton, OH: Matthew Bender.

Lee, J. W., Kane, J. J., Gregg, E. A., & Cavanaugh, T. (2016). Think globally, engage pedagogically: Procuring and supervising international field experiences. *Journal of Hospitality, Leisure, Sport & Tourism Education*, 19, 115–120.

Louisville Arena Authority. (2008, November 20). Press Release: Arena construction company to sign unprecedented agreement with OSHA regarding oversight. Retrieved from www.arenaauthority.com/news.aspx.

McLeod, C. M., Holden, J. T., Hawzen, M. G., & Chahardovali, T. (2019). Do influxes of atypical labor make sport event workers prone to exploitation. *Sport Management Review*, 22, 527–539.

Minniti, C. S. (2013, September 13). Don't "volunteer" to pay your "volunteers"! *Forbes.com*. Retrieved from http://www.forbes.com/sites/theemploymentbeat/2013/09/13/dont-volunteer-to-pay-your-volunteers%E2%80%BC/.

Moore, D. L. (2013, April 2). Louisville says Kevin Ware will have no medical bills. *USA Today*. Retrieved from http://www.usatoday.com/story/sports/ncaab/2013/04/01/kevin-ware-louisville-cardinals-medical-bills/2044871/.

Moorman, A. M. (2004). Legal issues and supervised internship relationship: Who is responsible for what? *Journal of Physical Education, Recreation, and Dance*, 75(2), 19–35.

National Conference of State Legislatures (NCSL). (2019). State minimum wages: 2019 minimum wage by state. Retrieved from http://www.ncsl.org/research/labor-and-employment/state-minimum-wage-chart.aspx#Table.

Navarro, H. (2020, June 5). Construction halted on SoFi Stadium in Inglewood after worker dies. *NBC Los Angeles*. Retrieved from https://www.nbclosangeles.com/news/local/construction-worker-dies-while-working-on-sofi-stadium-in-inglewood/2375587/.

Newcomb, S. (2019, April 30). Do I have to pay employees to attend company-sponsored volunteer events? *JDSupra.com*. Retrieved from https://www.jdsupra.com/legalnews/do-i-have-to-pay-employees-to-attend-36121/.

Olympic.org. (2012, July 21). London 2012 News: Volunteers: Helping to make the games happen. Retrieved from http://www.olympic.org/news/volunteers-helping-to-make-the-games-happen/168630.

Olympic.org. (2019). More than 200,000 applications received for Tokyo 2020 volunteer programme. IOC. Retrieved from https://www.olympic.org/news/more-than-200-000-applications-received-for-tokyo-2020-volunteer-programme

Pedulla, T. (2014, January 29). The price for the Super Bowl volunteers. *The New York Times*, p. B10.

Pennington, B. (2013, April 5). In a moment it all can be gone. *The New York Times*, p. B11. Retrieved from http://www.nytimes.com/2013/04/05/sports/ncaabasketball/broken-leg-renews-focus-on-college-athletes-health-insurance.html?pagewanted=all&_r=1&.

Rothman, M., & Sisman, R. (2016). Internship impact on career consideration among business students. *Education & Training*, 58, 1003–1013.

Schoepfer, K.L., & Dodds, M. (2011). Internships in sport management curriculum: Should legal implications of experiential learning result in the elimination of the sport management internship? *Marquette Sports Law Review*, 21, 183–201.

Shellenbarger, S. (2009, January 28). Do you want an internship? It'll cost you. *The Wall Street Journal*, p. D1.

Silva, P., Lopes, B., & Costa, M. (2016). Stairway to employment? *Internships in higher education. Higher Education*, 72, 703–721.

Singer, J. M. (2000, February 21). Students leap into internships and land jobs after college. *USA Today*, p. 6D.

Stier, W. F., Jr. (2002). Sport management internships: From theory to practice. *Strategies – A Journal for Physical and Sport Educators*, 15(4), 7–9.

U.S. Department of Labor (DOL). (n.d.a). *Exemptions*. Retrieved from www.dol.gov/elaws/esa/flsa/screen75.asp.

U.S. Department of Labor (DOL). (n.d.b). *State occupational health and safety plans*. Retrieved from http://www.osha.gov/dcsp/osp/.

U.S. Department of Labor (DOL). (2008a, July). Fact sheet #17A: Exemption for executive, administrative, professional, computer & outside sales employees under the Fair Labor Standards Act (FLSA). Retrieved from http://www.dol.gov/whd/regs/compliance/fairpay/fs17a_overview.htm.

U.S. Department of Labor (DOL). (2008b, July). Fact sheet #18: Section 13(a)(3) exemption for seasonal amusement or recreational establishments under the Fair Labor Standards Act (FLSA). Retrieved from www.dol.gov/esa/regs/compliance/whd/whdfs18.htm.

U.S. Department of Labor (DOL). (2008c, December). 2008 statistics fact sheet. Retrieved from http://www.dol.gov/whd/statistics/2008FiscalYear.htm.

U.S. Department of Labor (DOL). (2009a, July). Fact sheet #14: Coverage under the Fair Labor Standards Act (FLSA). Retrieved from http://www.dol.gov/whd/regs/compliance/whdfs14.htm.

U.S. Dept. of Labor (DOL). (2009b, January 15). DOL opinion letter. Retrieved from https://www.dol.gov/sites/dolgov/files/WHD/legacy/files/2009_01_15_11_FLSA.pdf.

U.S. Department of Labor (DOL). (2010, April). Fact Sheet #71: Internship Programs under the Fair Labor Standards Act (FSLA). Retrieved from http://www.dol.gov/whd/regs/compliance/whdfs71.htm.

U.S. Department of Labor (DOL). (2013). *All About OSHA*. Retrieved from https://www.osha.gov/Publications/all_about_OSHA.pdf.

U.S. Dept. of Labor (DOL). (2018, January). Fact sheet #71: Internship programs under the Fair Labor Standards Act (FSLA). Retrieved from https://www.dol.gov/agencies/whd/fact-sheets/71-flsa-internships.

U.S. Dept. of Labor (DOL). (2019a). Fiscal year data for WHD. *U.S. Department of Labor*. Retrieved from https://www.dol.gov/agencies/whd/data/charts/fair-labor-standards-act.

U.S. Dept. of Labor (DOL). (2019b, March 14). Opinion Letter. FLSA2019-2.

U.S. Dept. of Labor (DOL). (2020a). Executive order 13658, establish a minimum wage for contractors: Annual update. *U.S. Department of Labor*. Retrieved from https://www.dol.gov/whd/flsa/eo13658/.

U.S. Dept. of Labor (DOL). (2020b). Fact sheet: Final rule to update the regulations defining and delimiting the exemptions for executive, administrative, and professional employees. Retrieved from https://www.dol.gov/sites/dolgov/files/WHD/legacy/files/overtime_FS.pdf.

U.S. Dept. of Labor (DOL). (2020c). Fact sheet #17D: Exemption for professional employees under the Fair Labor Standards Act (FLSA). Retrieved from https://www.dol.gov/sites/dolgov/files/WHD/legacy/files/fs17d_professional.pdf.

U.S. Dept. of Labor (DOL). (2020d). Guidance on preparing workplaces for COVID-19. *U.S. Department of Labor*. Retrieved from https://www.osha.gov/Publications/OSHA3990.pdf.

van der Smissen, B. (1990). *Legal liability and risk management for public and private entities*, § 25.342. Cincinnati, OH: Anderson.

Vehling, A. (2014, June 11). Los Angeles Clippers face wage class action by interns. *Law 360*. Retrieved from https://www.law360.com/articles/546613/los-angeles-clippers-face-wage-class-action-by-interns.

Whalen, E., & Barnes, A. (2001, July–August). Internship payoffs … and trade-offs. *The Quill*, 89(6), 18–19.

Wilkinson, C., & Smith, D. B. (2018, January 10). Are interns actually employees? DOL adopts new guidance for assessing whether interns qualify as employees. *Orrick Employment Law and Litigation*. Retrieved from https://blogs.orrick.com/employment/2018/01/10/are-interns-actually-employees-dol-adopts-new-guidance-for-assessing-whether-interns-qualify-as-employees/.

Web Resources

www.dol.gov/elaws/esa/flsa/screen75.asp ■ The U.S. Department of Labor developed this E-Law Advisor to help employees and employers understand the exemptions to the overtime pay provisions of the Fair Labor Standards Act (FSLA).

www.dol.gov/whd/regs/compliance/fairpay/fs17c_administrative.pdf ■ This fact sheet provides general information on the exemption from minimum wage and overtime pay provided by Section 13(a)(1) of the FLSA.

www.dol.gov/whd/regs/compliance/whdfs18.pdf ■ This fact sheet provides information about the Section 13(a)(3) exemption from minimum wage and overtime pay to seasonal and recreational employee under the FLSA.

www.dol.gov/whd/regs/compliance/posters/minwagebwp.pdf ■ The Wage and Hour Division of the DOL has created this poster, which summarizes the Fair Labor Standards Act's minimum wage provisions.

www.dol.gov/elaws/esa/flsa/docs/volunteers.asp ■ This fact sheet explains the FLSA definition of volunteers.

www.dol.gov/elaws/esa/flsa/docs/trainees.asp ■ This fact sheet explains the criteria for determining whether trainees or students are employees of an employer under the FLSA.

www.dol.gov/whd/regs/compliance/whdfs71.htm ■ This fact sheet (#71) provides guidance for internship programs under the Fair Labor Standards Act (FSLA).

Part III

Strategic Management/Governance of Sport Organizations

Legal Issues Arising in Governance Contexts

In both amateur and professional sport, governing bodies generate, implement, and enforce rules and policies defining the manner in which their particular sports operate. Examples of such governing bodies include the United States Olympic & Paralympic Committee (USOPC), the NCAA, and the NBA. A sport organization must define and regulate its own structure and functioning, the relationship between it and the entities it governs, and the conduct of those entities. These governing relationships can be complex and have multiple layers. For example, Major League Baseball governs the 30 major league professional baseball teams in two leagues (American League and National League) as well as the 256 teams affiliated through the Minor League system. The NCAA governs the 1115 member institutions' (universities and colleges) respective athletics programs divided across three divisions impacting approximately 460,000 student athletes (NCAA, 2019a, 2019b). And the USOPC governs 45 national governing bodies such as USA Track & Field and a host of other recognized and community based amateur sport organizations (USOPC, 2019). Governed entities may also include coaches, officials, and administrators, as well as athletes, who are subject to the rules and regulations of the governing bodies of their particular sport.

In governing their sport, a sport governing body may find its regulatory activities and strategic management decisions subject to legal challenge. Examples might include decisions regarding how to regulate league expansion, contraction, and franchise location; allocation of league resources; athlete eligibility and disciplinary actions; and dispute resolution procedures. Strategic decision-making in these areas involves issues of fairness to individuals and organizations, as well as fair competition in the marketplace.

Legal Principles and Strategic Management

Several legal principles are relevant to strategic decision-making by sport governing bodies, including procedural fairness under the law of private associations, the Constitutional right to due process, and freedom from unfair discrimination in the provision of services. Additionally, due to the entertainment business aspects of professional, collegiate, and Olympic sport, one of the most frequently invoked legal principles is fair competition under antitrust law. Chapter 10 discusses the legal principles relevant to the governance of professional sport with an emphasis on the impact of federal anti-trust laws. Chapter 11 covers governance issues in Olympic and Paralympic sport and deals with a variety of legal principles, including application of the Ted Stevens Olympic and Amateur Sports Act (OASA), antidiscrimination laws, and procedural fairness. Chapter 12 discusses the legal principles involved in the structure and governance of high school and college athletics organizations generally and then Chapter 13 focuses more closely on the rights of athletes and participants in high school and collegiate athletics environments.

The purpose of Part III is to provide information about the legal issues and principles pertaining to sport governance, because when management makes a poor governance decision, it may have costly legal consequences.

10 Governance Issues in Professional Sport

Alicia Jessop

Introduction

The governance of professional sport features a myriad of legal issues, namely: contract law, labor law, the law of private associations, and federal antitrust law. This chapter will examine these bodies of law through the lens of the governance of professional sport. Governance of professional sport may be roughly divided into governance of team sports by professional sports leagues and governance of individual sports by entities operating professional tours, which includes tour players associations. This chapter first discusses the power of the commissioner of professional sports leagues in light of labor law, as well as the law underlying judicial review of commissioners' decisions by examining recent legal challenges to the commissioner's authority. An overview of antitrust law is provided next as a foundation to understanding the remaining governance issues pertinent to the authority of professional sports leagues, including the legal structure of leagues, applications for sport franchises, team ownership, franchise relocation, rival leagues, and equipment regulation. The chapter then examines governance issues related to individual professional sports, including the organizational structure of tour players associations, control of events, equipment regulation, and disciplinary authority. Exhibit 10.1 depicts the management contexts and applicable law discussed in this chapter.

Professional Team Sports and the Power of the Commissioner

Generally, the structure of American professional team sports leagues is organized under three units: the commissioner, a league board of governors or owners committee, and a centralized league office. This section defines the source and role of the commissioner and examines the extent of the commissioner's power to govern.

The role of the commissioner is unique to professional team sports. First created in 1921 following MLB's "Black Sox" scandal during the 1919 World Series, the position of commissioner was invented by team owners as a mechanism to ensure integrity in the governance of a league's affairs. Team owners adopted and defined the duties, powers, and limitations of the position in their individual league governing documents, called constitutions and bylaws. League constitutions and bylaws grant commissioners authority to govern over league, team, and player affairs. The commissioner's authority affords he or she broad power to act in the "best interests of the game." This "best interests of the game" power envisioned a commissioner who can act unilaterally against clubs, players, and even owners if he believes they have done something that could threaten the integrity of the game or the public trust in it. The power is perceived as being unfettered, because in granting the power, league constitutions and bylaws give commissioners wide authority in these areas to exercise it in any manner, so long as from the commissioner's perspective, doing so preserves and promotes the best

Exhibit 10.1 Management contexts in which governance issues may arise, with relevant laws and cases.

Management Context	Major Legal Issues	Relevant Laws	Illustrative Cases
Sport league governance	Commissioner power	Private associations; labor law; tortious interference with contract	*Finley, Chicago National League, Brady I, Brady II, FanExpo LLC v. NFL*
	League structures	Sherman Act	*Fraser, Brown, American Needle*
	Franchise applications	Sherman Act	*Mid-South Grizzlies*
	Cross-ownership	Sherman Act	*NASL v. NFL*
	Ownership transfer	Sherman Act	*Piazza*
	Franchise relocation	Sherman Act	*Raiders I, City of San Jose v. Office of the Commissioner of Baseball, City of Oakland v. The Oakland Raiders*
	Rival leagues	Sherman Act	*NASL v. NFL, Philadelphia World Hockey, USFL v. NFL, AFL v. NFL, Hecht*
	Equipment regulation	Sherman Act; negligence	*Schutt, In Re National Football Players' Concussion Injury Litigation*
Individual sport tour governance	Event control	Sherman Act	*Volvo, JamSports, PGA Tour v. Martin*
	Equipment regulation	Sherman Act	*Gunter Harz, Weight-Rite, Gilder*
	Disciplinary authority	Sherman Act	*Blalock, Hipperdinger*

interests of the league. Examples of areas in which league constitutions and bylaws generally allow the commissioner to engage include:

- Approval of player contracts.
- Rule-making.
- Dispute resolution between player and club, between clubs, or between player or club and the league.
- Disciplinary matters involving players, clubs, front office personnel, owners, and others involved with the league.

Additionally, the commissioner's role can also include restraining excessive exercise of owners' powers that would be detrimental to fans or the sport; serving as lead negotiator for league-wide contracts, such as television deals; and serving as a negotiator for owners in labor disputes with players associations. (For analyses of the role of commissioners, see Lentze, 1995; Daniels & Brooks, 2009). Despite the broad scope of authority held by the Commissioner, it is not truly limitless. Next we will explore a few avenues for limiting or challenging the decisions or acts of the commissioner.

First, the commissioner is selected and hired by the team owners, and therefore could be fired or replaced by those same team owners. The conditions under and manner in which the commissioner could be terminated or replaced would be stipulated in their employment agreement and also addressed in the constitution and bylaws of the league. However, the commissioner can wield the best interests of the game power unilaterally over team owners, a unique aspect of the professional team sports governance model. To demonstrate this uniqueness, consider the typical corporate governance model, where an organization is led by a chief executive officer (CEO), who is hired by and acts under the authority of a board of directors. In the professional team sports governance model, team owners could be imagined as similar to a corporate board of directors. Similar to how a board of directors selects and hires a CEO, team owners select and hire the commissioner. However, unlike a board of directors, team owners do not oversee the decision-making of a commissioner. Thus, the best interests of the game power granted to the commissioner authorizes the commissioner to make decisions that may be unfavorable to team owners and may even include imposing restrictions or penalties on team owners so long as those decisions are shown to be in the best interests of the game or league as a whole.

An example of commissioner decision-making that went against the interest of one team owner arose in 2014 when TMZ.com published a recording of then Los Angeles Clippers owner, Donald Sterling, making racist comments. The racist comments, which attacked the African-American community, including former NBA player Magic Johnson, were quickly denounced by NBA players and fans, with a number of sponsors suspending their partnerships with the team. A mere four days after the recording was released, NBA commissioner Adam Silver – who had been hired to the position less than three months earlier – utilized his best interests of the game power to issue a lifetime NBA ban for Sterling and fined him $2.5 million (Berman, 2014).

Adam Silver's handling of the Donald Sterling case demonstrates that while commissioners possess wide discretion, their power is limited by the terms of their respective league's governing documents. Generally, at the league governance level, these documents are the constitution and bylaws. Regarding the Sterling case, the fine Silver could issue was limited by the NBA's charter. Similarly, the fines commissioners levy against players are limited by league constitutions, bylaws, and collective bargaining agreements. Further, while Silver utilized his best interests of the game power to ban Sterling from the NBA for life, he did not have the power to force Sterling to sell the Clippers. This is because the NBA's constitution and bylaws specified that a vote of three-fourths of league owners was necessary to force the sale. While a vote of NBA owners was scheduled, it ultimately did not take place as Sterling's wife, Shelly, facilitated bids for the team and ultimately, NBA owners approved the sale of the team to former Microsoft CEO, Steve Ballmer.

Second, along with the possibility of being fired by team owners, another limitation commissioners face to their power is the dispute resolution rights contained in the governing documents and collective bargaining agreements governing relations with the owners and employees. Challenges in the form of an appeal or arbitration or some combination of these mechanisms have been brought by team owners, front office executives, and players alike. Further, some have questioned whether these powers make a commissioner a neutral party, or whether the commissioner remains primarily an agent of team owners (see *National Football League Players Association v. National Labor Relations Board*, 1974). The players believe that the commissioner is "on the side" of the employers or owners as a group; however, in certain situations owners also find themselves desiring to limit the power of the commissioner. Commissioners have faced various appeals alleging that their actions extended beyond the power granted to them under leagues' constitutions, bylaws or collective bargaining agreements.

One such example arose in 2010 when a group of New Orleans Saints players and coaches allegedly offered bounties for team members to knock opposing teams' players out of games or cause them injuries. The NFL began investigating allegations in early 2010, and several Saints assistant coaches allegedly encouraged the destruction of documents and instructed players to lie to NFL investigators. Sanctions did not emerge from the initial investigation. However, the NFL reopened the case in early 2012 based on new expansive authority given under the 2011 collective bargaining agreement to NFL Commissioner, Roger Goodell. This authority allowed the NFL commissioner to discipline players and hear and decide appeals of discipline issued related to protecting the integrity of the game. The NFL reported its investigation unveiled a bounty program created by a Saints assistant coach, which spanned two-years and involved up to 27 Saints players. The Saints assistant coach, along with the team's then head coach and owner took responsibility for the program, while accused players largely denied knowledge of or involvement in the program. With no precedent guiding him, in March 2012, commissioner Goodell utilized the best interests of the game power to suspend the Saints' head coach for one-year; two assistant coaches for six and eight games, respectively; and another assistant coach indefinitely. The team was also stripped of its second-round NFL Draft picks in 2012 and 2013 and fined $500,000 (Terrell, 2012).

Despite previously taking responsibility for the alleged bounty program, the Saints' head coach, two of the assistant coaches and the team appealed their sanctions. The appeals were initially heard and decided by the NFL commissioner, who upheld the penalties. Following the appeals, Goodell disciplined four

Saints players for their alleged involvement in the bounty scheme. The suspensions ranged in length from three games to a full season. The players appealed their suspensions, and in accordance with the collective bargaining agreement, an appeals panel was formed, which ordered Goodell to reconsider the penalties. Goodell recused his authority and appointed former NFL commissioner, Paul Tagliabue, to hear and decide the players' appeals. Ultimately, Tagliabue overturned the players' suspensions, finding that the team's coaches engaged in serious misconduct (Terrell, 2012).

While players in the Saints bounty case invoked the right granted to them under the collective bargaining agreement to have an appeals panel review their case, other collective bargaining agreements have also subjected commissioner disciplinary actions to review through arbitration. Following then NBA commissioner David Stern's decision to suspend the former Ron Artest (Metta World Peace), Jermaine O'Neal, and two other Indiana Pacers players who participated in a 2004 physical altercation with fans in the stands, the National Basketball Players Association (NBPA) filed an appeal to an arbitrator under the league's collective bargaining agreement. The arbitrator upheld the commissioner's decision to suspend the players, but reduced the length of O'Neal's suspension from 25 to 15 games, due to his not entering the stands. The NBA challenged the authority of the arbitrator to review Stern's decision. The district court ruled that the provisions of the collective bargaining agreement made clear that while the commissioner's authority to impose discipline for on-court misbehavior was not arbitrable, the arbitrator had authority to review the commissioner's disciplinary actions for off-court misconduct, therefore making arbitration warranted in the case (*NBA v. Artest*, 2004).

Similar challenges have been made in MLB. For example, consider MLB Commissioner Bud Selig's 211-game suspension of Alex Rodriguez for alleged use of performance-enhancing drugs (PEDs). After MLB sued Biogenesis, the alleged supplier of PEDs to players, for allegedly inducing players to violate their baseball contracts, the clinic settled out of court in exchange for providing MLB with client information. That information led to the Rodriguez suspension – the longest non-lifetime suspension in the history of MLB. Rodriguez appealed Selig's decision to an independent arbitrator, arguing he never failed a drug test, the evidence was only accusatory in nature, and the penalty was excessive compared to the penalty structure established in the league's collective bargaining agreement and Joint Drug Agreement. Ultimately, the arbitrator reduced the suspension to 162 games – a full MLB season – but found Rodriguez violated terms of MLB's collective bargaining agreement and Joint Drug Agreement. In upholding a large majority of the initial suspension, the arbitrator argued Rodriguez engaged in continuous and prolonged use or possession of multiple substances, allowing the commissioner to stray from the prescribed penalty for a single positive test under the Joint Drug Agreement (McCann, 2013; Jaffe, 2014).

Lastly, in very limited circumstances an owner or player may seek judicial review through litigation of a commissioner's actions. In litigation, courts typically accord substantial deference to the commissioner's judgment on issues within the scope of the commissioner's authority. As such, penalties levied by commissioners are typically upheld by the judicial system. However, courts are willing to invoke the law of private associations to assert judicial review of a sport organization's actions. The law of private associations (also known as the law of voluntary associations or contractual due process) refers to a common law principle enabling a court to review the actions of a private association. Under the law of private associations, members of associations are in a contractual relationship with the association, which requires the organization to provide members with reasonable due process. Thus, a court may review the actions of such an association when it has allegedly violated its own rules or implemented arbitrary and capricious decisions that violate procedural fairness. In so doing, a court requires that a commissioner's actions:

- are within the scope of defined authority;
- are made in good faith;
- comport with basic tenets of procedural fairness;
- are not made in violation of state or federal law.

One such case arose during the 2015 AFC Championship Game, when the New England Patriots were accused of deflating footballs used in the game. The NFL launched an investigation led by league and external counterparts. The investigative report found it "more probable than not" that footballs were intentionally deflated during the game and quarterback Tom Brady was likely aware that a rules violation was taking place. During the investigation, Brady declined to provide the investigative team with emails, text messages, and other communicative records made during the relevant period. Subsequently, NFL commissioner Goodell delegated his authority to penalize players for conduct detrimental to the integrity of the league to then senior vice president of NFL player engagement, Troy Vincent. Upon conclusion of the investigation, Vincent issued a four game suspension against Brady. Brady appealed the suspension, which under the terms of the then collective bargaining agreement, allowed Goodell the power to hear and decide the appeal. The NFLPA asked Goodell to recuse himself from the appeal and appoint a neutral arbitrator, which Goodell rejected, citing the power granted to him under the 2011 NFL-NFLPA collective bargaining agreement. Following the hearing, Goodell upheld the original suspension (Flynn & Maiman, 2016). While on its face the Brady investigation was a case about the amount of air pressure inside of a football, the real battle between Brady and the NFLPA against Goodell and the NFL was challenging the breadth of the commissioner's power under the 2011 collective bargaining agreement. Subsequent to the appeal, both sides turned to litigation. The following Focus Case highlights how the federal district court considered the challenge to the NFL Commissioner's authority asserted by Brady.

NFL Management Council v. NFL Players Association

820 F.3d 527 (2d Cir. 2016)   **FOCUS CASE**

FACTS

The NFL filed a motion in New York federal court to confirm the arbitration decision to uphold Brady's suspension. The following day, the NFLPA filed a lawsuit in Minnesota federal court to vacate Brady's suspension. In its case, the NFLPA asserted that the evidence did not justify the penalty, the collective bargaining agreement was violated by Goodell delegating his disciplinary authority and issuing a penalty not prescribed under the CBA, and the appeal hearing was unfair (Bieler, 2015; NFLPA, 2015). In September 2015, a district court judge held for the NFLPA in a case known as *Brady I*, vacating Brady's suspension. In vacating the suspension, the district court judge found that the four-game suspension for general awareness of footballs being under-deflated violated the collective bargaining agreement, because it was not prescribed in the CBA as a potential penalty. As such Brady was absent notice that he could face said penalty. Further, the judge found Goodell too broadly imposed his ability to discipline players under the CBA's "conduct detrimental" to the integrity of the game policy, arguing player policies related to equipment violations should have guided the breadth of the penalty. Moreover, the judge found that Brady was denied due process as he was not allowed to question a co-investigator during the arbitration appeal hearing nor granted access to relevant files during the process (NFL *Mgmt. Council v. NFL Players Ass'n*, 2015). While the district court's ruling meant Brady could play during Week 1 of the 2015 NFL season, the NFL quickly appealed the decision.

HOLDING

The Court of Appeals reversed the district court's decision and reinstated Brady's suspension finding the commissioner properly exercised broad discretion provided under the CBA.

RATIONALE

In *Brady II*, the U.S. Second Circuit Court of Appeals reversed the district court's ruling and reinstated Brady's four-game suspension. The Second Circuit found, "… that the commissioner properly exercised his broad discretion under the collective bargaining agreement and that his procedural rulings were properly grounded in that agreement and did not deprive Brady of fundamental fairness." It found that the three bases the district court identified for overturning Brady's suspension were insufficient. With respect to the first basis, lack of adequate notice of the suspension, the Second Circuit found that the "punishments listed for equipment violations" under the League Policies for Players "are minimum ones that do not foreclose suspension." Related to the second basis that exclusion of testimony from the NFL's general counsel, Jeff Pash, precluded Brady's suspension, the court found that it is in the arbitrator's discretion as to which witnesses are heard during arbitration. Finding no misconduct, the Second Circuit argued that Goodell denying the NFLPA's motion to call the NFL's general counsel to testify did not violate fundamental fairness. Finally, related to the third basis that precluding Brady from accessing interview notes and memoranda generated by the NFL's investigative team amounted to fundamental unfairness, the Second Circuit found that the collective bargaining agreement did not require exchange of such notes and as such, Brady did not incur fundamental unfairness.

The Second Circuit's decision in *Brady II* demonstrates that courts are likely to side with a league so long as a league is following the terms and standards adopted in its respective governing documents and not engaging in fundamental unfairness.

After the Second Circuit's decision, Brady announced that he would end his legal challenge and serve his four-game suspension at the beginning of the 2016 season. While Patriots fans may have lost Brady's services for four-games, NFL players lost much more in the case, as the power differential between them and the commissioner in disciplinary proceedings under the 2011 NFL-NFLPA CBA only widened (Flynn & Maiman, 2016). The application of the law of private associations as it relates to judicial review of decisions made by a commissioner is discussed more fully in the *Finley* case.

Charles O. Finley & Co. v. Kuhn

CASE OPINION   569 F.2d 527 (7th Cir. 1978) cert. denied, 439 U.S. 876 (1978)

FACTS

Plaintiff Finley & Co., then owner of the Oakland Athletics baseball club, sold their contract rights to three star players just before the trading deadline. They sold the rights to Joe Rudi and Rollie Fingers to the Boston Red Sox for $2 million and the rights to Vida Blue to the New York Yankees for $1.5 million. Three days later, baseball Commissioner Bowie Kuhn disapproved these contract assignments on the basis that they were contrary to the best interests of baseball. He was particularly concerned that the arrangements would debilitate the Oakland A's, disrupt the competitive balance among teams in the American League by allowing the more affluent clubs to buy up the best talent, and exacerbate the then unsettled status of the reserve system. The owner of the A's then brought this suit, alleging that the Commissioner had exceeded the scope of his authority, and that he breached his contract with the baseball clubs because his disapproval of the sales was arbitrary and capricious. Also, at issue in a subsequent request for declaratory judgment was whether the covenant not to sue (waiver of recourse to the courts) found in the Major League Agreement was valid and enforceable. The lower court ruled in favor of the Commissioner on all of the above claims, and the owner of the Oakland A's brought this appeal.

HOLDING

The 7th Circuit affirmed the rulings of the district court.

RATIONALE

Basic to the underlying suit brought by Oakland and to this appeal is whether the Commissioner of baseball is vested by contract with the authority to disapprove player assignments which he finds to be "not in the best interests of baseball."

November, 1920, the major league club owners … all signed what they called the Major League Agreement, and Judge Landis assumed the position of Commissioner … . The agreement, a contract between the constituent clubs of the National and American Leagues, is the basic charter under which Major League Baseball operates. The Major League Agreement provides that "the functions of the Commissioner shall be … to investigate … any act, transaction or practice … not in the best interests of the national game of Baseball" and "to determine … what preventive, remedial or punitive action is appropriate in the premises, and to take such action … ." Art. I, Sec. 2(a) and (b).

He has also been given the express power to approve or disapprove the assignments of players. In regard to nonparties to the agreement, he may take such other steps as he deems necessary and proper in the interests of the morale of the players and the honor of the game. The Major League Agreement also provides that "in the case of conduct by Major Leagues, Major League Clubs, officers, employees, or players which is deemed by the Commissioner not to be in the best interests of Baseball, action by the Commissioner for each offense *may include*" a reprimand, deprivation of a club of representation at joint meetings, suspension or removal of non-players, temporary or permanent ineligibility of players, and a fine not to exceed $5,000 in the case of a league or club and not to exceed $500 in the case of an individual. Art. I, Sec. 3.

The district court considered the plaintiff's argument that the enumeration in Article I, Section 3 of the sanctions, which the Commissioner may impose, places a limit on his authority inasmuch as the power to disapprove assignments of players is not included. The court concluded that the enumeration does not purport to be exclusive and provides that the Commissioner may act in one of the listed ways without expressly limiting him to those ways.

Oakland was contending that the Commissioner could set aside assignments only if the assignments involved a Rules violation or moral turpitude. In its briefs on appeal, Oakland summarized this branch of its argument by stating that the Commissioner's "disapproval of the assignments … exceeded [his] authority under the Major League Agreement and Rules; was irrational and unreasonable; and was procedurally unfair."

The plaintiff has argued that it is a fundamental rule of law that the decisions of the head of a private association must be procedurally fair. Plaintiff then argued that it was "procedurally unfair" for the Commissioner to fail to warn the plaintiff that he would "disapprove large cash assignments of star players even if they complied with the Major League Rules."

We conclude that the evidence fully supports, and we agree with, the district court's finding that

the history of the adoption of the Major League Agreement in 1921 and the operation of baseball for more than 50 years under it, including: the circumstances preceding and precipitating the adoption of the Agreement; the numerous exercises of broad authority under the best interests clause by Judge Landis and … Commissioner Kuhn; the amendments to the Agreement in 1964 restoring and broadening the authority of the Commissioner; … and most important the express language of the Agreement itself — are all to the effect that the Commissioner has the authority to determine whether *any* act, transaction or practice is 'not in the best interests of baseball,' and upon such determination, to take whatever preventive or remedial action he deems appropriate, whether or not the act, transaction or practice complies with the Major League Rules or involves moral turpitude.

Any other conclusion would involve the courts in not only interpreting often complex rules of baseball to determine if they were violated but also, as noted in the *Landis* case, the "intent of the [baseball] code," an even more complicated and subjective task.

The Rudi–Fingers–Blue transactions had been negotiated on June 14 and 15, 1976. On June 16, the Commissioner sent a teletype to the Oakland, Boston and New York clubs and to the Players' Association expressing his "concern for possible consequences to the integrity of baseball and public confidence in the game" and setting a hearing for June 17. Present at the hearing were 17 persons representing those notified. At the outset of the hearing the Commissioner stated that he was concerned that the assignments would be harmful to the competitive capacity of Oakland; that they reflected an effort by Boston and New York to purchase star players and "bypass the usual methods of player development and acquisition which have been traditionally used in professional baseball"; and that the question to be resolved was whether the transactions "are consistent with the best interests of baseball's integrity and maintenance of public confidence in the game." He warned that it was possible that he might determine that the assignments should not be approved. Mr. Finley and representatives of the Red Sox and Yankees made statements on the record. No one at the hearing, including Mr. Finley, claimed that the Commissioner lacked the authority to disapprove the assignments, or objected to the holding of the hearing, or to any of the procedures followed at the hearing.

On June 18, the Commissioner concluded that the attempted assignments should be disapproved as not in the best interests of baseball. In his written decision, the Commissioner stated his reasons which we have summarized … . The decision was sent to all parties by teletype. The Commissioner recognized "that there have been cash sales of player contracts in the past," but concluded that "these transactions were unparalleled in the history of the game" because there was "never anything on this scale or falling at this time of the year, or which threatened so seriously to unbalance the competitive balance of baseball." The district court concluded that the attempted assignments of Rudi, Fingers and Blue "were at a time and under circumstances making them unique in the history of baseball." We conclude that the evidence fully supports, and we agree with, the district court's finding and conclusion that the Commissioner "acted in good faith, after investigation, consultation and deliberation, in a manner which he determined to be in the best interests of baseball" and that "whether he was right or wrong is beyond the competence and the jurisdiction of this court to decide."

We must then conclude that anyone becoming a signatory to the Major League Agreement was put on ample notice that the action ultimately taken by the Commissioner was not only possible but probable. The action was neither an "abrupt departure" nor a "change of policy" in view of the contemporaneous developments taking place in the reserve system, over which the Commissioner had little or no control, and in any event the broad authority given to the Commissioner by the Major League Agreement placed any party to it on notice that such authority could be used.

QUESTIONS

1 How broad is the scope of the commissioner's power, according to the *Finley* court?
2 Is the commissioner's discretionary power to act unilaterally in the best interests of the game limited to certain topics, such as player misconduct? If not, to what areas of "baseball life" does the commissioner's "best interests" power extend?
3 How did the court apply the law of private associations in deciding this case? What are the implications for limits on the decision-making power of the commissioner?

The *Finley* case stands for the proposition that courts will not interfere with the authority of the commissioner to act in the best interests of the game, as long as the action is allowed by the league's constitution, bylaws and/or collective bargaining agreement and is not arbitrary, capricious or violative of traditional notions of due process.

Compare this decision with the ruling in *Chicago National League Ball Club v. Vincent* (1992). In this case, the court asserted its right to review baseball commissioner Vincent's decision to restructure the divisions of the National League. The court ruled that the commissioner exceeded his authority when he ordered the transfer of the Chicago Cubs to the Western Division of the National League over the team's objection. A team's right to veto a transfer decision is provided in MLB's constitution, and the court found that the best interests of baseball clause did not supersede enumerated rights in the league's constitution.

After *Finley*, league commissioners and executives must carefully evaluate not only the commissioners' best interests of the game power, but their respective bylaws and constitutions, to ensure policies are in place to effectively ensure continued fan support and belief in their games.

Overview of Antitrust Law

As it relates to professional sport, many governance issues involve antitrust law causes of action. Thus, it is important to have a foundational understanding of how federal antitrust law operates. Antitrust laws generally prohibit unlawful mergers and business practices that interfere with a free and open marketplace. The law was enacted to promote and protect the operation of free market capitalism, with the resulting benefits to consumers being a wider range of product options at lower prices. In the United States, federal antitrust law is codified under the Sherman Antitrust Act of 1890 (the "Sherman Act"), a law passed by Congress in the face of the power of the country's growing industrial economy being held by a few companies, and thus, stimmying competition and consumer choice. Related to sport, two sections of the Sherman Act guide the interstate commerce dealings of many leagues: Sections 1 and 2.

Section 1 of the Sherman Act (15 U.S.C. § 1) prohibits unreasonable restraints on trade or commerce. Examples of restraints on trade include: price fixing, bid rigging, allocation of customers and limitations on output (Department of Justice, 2017). To successfully allege a violation of Section 1 of the Sherman Act, a plaintiff must allege (1) a **concerted action** (i.e., joint action between two or more parties); (2) that unreasonably restrains trade in a relevant market (i.e., price fixing, bid rigging, allocation of customers, and/or limitations on output); and (3) involves interstate commerce (i.e., business flowing across two or more state lines). *Relevant market* refers to the economic market in which the defendant's business operates. For example, imagine that the Stars and Stripes are two teams in one league (a relevant market), but located in different states (interstate commerce). The Stars and Stripes play each other twice a year, with one game being played at each team's home stadium. Wanting to generate the most revenue from the game, the Stars' vice president of ticket operations calls the Stripes' vice president of ticket operations and asks if the team would consider artificially inflating the price of tickets above what the market price (price fixing). The Stripes' vice president of ticket operations agrees to engage in this behavior (concerted action). This would be a violation of § 1 of the Sherman Act.

Section 2 of the Sherman Act prohibits monopolies, attempts to monopolize or conspiracies to monopolize any part of trade or commerce. Notably, like Section 1 of the Sherman Act, the alleged monopolistic action must involve interstate commerce (15 U.S.C. § 2). Section 2 does not prohibit monopolies that have occurred naturally as the result of one competitor having a superior product or exercising better business sense, or by historic accident. Rather, it forbids *predatory behavior* by which a competitor attempts to establish or maintain a monopoly. As an example, if Wham-O Frisbee Company invents Frisbees and turns out to be the only manufacturer that produces flying disks that fly well, it will quickly establish a natural monopoly, which is not illegal. However, if Wham-O seeks to protect its monopoly by buying up all potential competitors, it would be guilty of willful monopolization in violation of § 2 of the Sherman Act.

Professional sports (particularly those with teams in a league structure) present a unique challenge to the traditional application of antitrust law to businesses. Conventional businesses, such as Reebok, Adidas, and Nike are direct competitors, compete for the same consumers, and have an economic interest in putting each other out of business or attracting consumers away from their competitors. Professional sports teams within a single league, on the other hand, have an interest in not competing too strongly economically with rival teams. This is because to attract and retain consumers by maximizing entertainment value, leagues must maintain competitive balance across teams so game outcomes are truly contested and uncertain. Another way of thinking about this, is to consider that if one team put all other teams out of business, it would have no teams to compete against, and thus, no product to sell. Beyond that, if one team in a league was able to dominate over all others, by for example, being able to significantly outspend others on free agents, it could negatively impact the overall success of and interest in the league. Thus, despite being competitors, teams must engage collectively to make decisions to promote economic competitiveness. It is important to distinguish between playing competitiveness and economic competitiveness when exploring the application of antitrust law to sport governance. Concerted action to ensure playing competitiveness does not trigger Sherman Act analysis. Rather, it is maintaining *economic* competitiveness that is the focus of antitrust law.

When hearing and deciding Sherman Act cases, courts apply one of two legal standards: the per se rule or the Rule of Reason.

Courts apply the **per se rule** when the facts alleged involve business practices that are obviously anticompetitive restraints on free trade (eliminating competition). If the practice is considered a per se violation, no further evidence of economic effects are needed. Section 1 of the Sherman Act defines certain behaviors as amounting to per se violations of the Sherman Act: collusive bidding, tying arrangements, and horizontal group boycotts. Examples of fact patterns involving per se violations of the Sherman Act include agreements between business competitors to fix prices so one company does not undersell another and two business competitors dividing the geographic market into exclusive business territories.

As noted above, the interdependence of teams within a professional sports league in producing an entertaining product attractive to fans requires collective agreements, such as market divisions and eligibility requirements, that would normally appear to be per se violations of § 1 of the Sherman Act if engaged in by conventional businesses. However, all recent court cases considering antitrust challenges involving professional sport leagues declined to apply the per se rule based on the unique needs of sport organizations to enter into some agreements and adopt rules necessary for the teams to compete. Thus, in most cases involving professional sports leagues, courts apply the second standard of analysis, the **Rule of Reason**, which accommodates the economic competitive balance needed to provide a successful professional sport entertainment product with the intent of antitrust law to prohibit unlawful or unfair business practices. (See Exhibit 10.2.)

The Rule of Reason analysis is a balancing test where the court must examine the facts of each case where the plaintiff typically argues that the restraints are anti-competitive and harmful to consumers and the defendant responds with assertions that the pro-competitive effects outweigh any potential anticompetitive effects. The **Rule of Reason analysis** requires a court to balance the alleged pro-competitive effects of the business practice against the asserted anticompetitive effects of the business practice in a burden shifting balancing test. Under the Rule of Reason test, courts apply a totality of the circumstances test and also consider the intent and motive of the defendants in balancing the elements. Since the Rule of Reason is a balancing test, if the anticompetitive effects of a practice outweigh its pro-competitive effects, a violation of the Sherman Act will be found.

Exhibit 10.2 Rule of reason analysis applied to sport organizations.

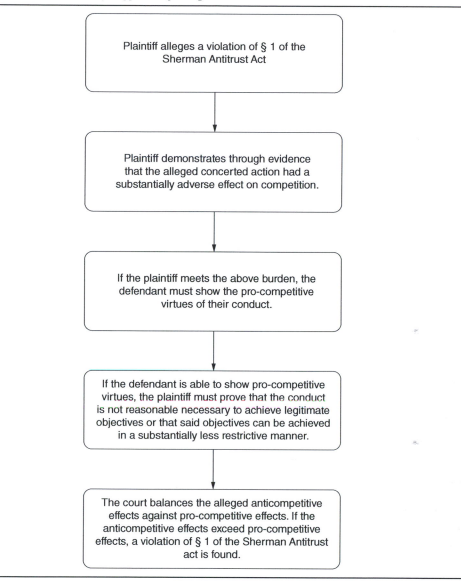

Plaintiff alleges a violation of § 1 of the
Sherman Antitrust Act

Plaintiff demonstrates through evidence
that the alleged concerted action had a
substantially adverse effect on competition.

If the plaintiff meets the above burden, the
defendant must show the pro-competitive
virtues of their conduct.

If the defendant is able to show pro-competitive
virtues, the plaintiff must prove that the conduct
is not reasonable necessary to achieve legitimate
objectives or that said objectives can be achieved
in a substantially less restrictive manner.

The court balances the alleged anticompetitive
effects against pro-competitive effects. If the
anticompetitive effects exceed pro-competitive
effects, a violation of § 1 of the Sherman Antitrust
act is found.

In *Law v. National Collegiate Athletic Association* (1998, p. 1019), the Tenth Circuit Court summarized the application of the rule of reason analysis to sport league restraints as follows:

> [T]he plaintiff bears the initial burden of showing that an agreement had a substantially adverse effect on competition … . If the plaintiff meets this burden, the burden shifts to the defendant to come forward with evidence of the pro-competitive virtues of the alleged wrongful conduct … . If the defendant is able to demonstrate pro-competitive effects, the plaintiff then must prove that the challenged conduct is not reasonably necessary to achieve the legitimate objectives or that those objectives can be achieved in a substantially less restrictive manner. … Ultimately … the harms and benefits must be weighed against each other in order to judge whether the challenged behavior is, on balance, reasonable.

Defining the relevant geographic and product markets is an important part of the analysis for determining whether a violation of § 1 or § 2 has occurred. The more broadly a geographic market is defined, the smaller the alleged monopolist's market share will be, and thus the less likely it is to be found guilty of a Sherman Act violation. Similarly, the more interchangeable the alleged monopolist's product is with the products of competitors, the less the market dominance of the alleged monopolist. A 70 percent share of the relevant market is generally considered the threshold for a finding of monopoly power (Department of Justice, 2015).

Although teams within a given league compete with each other for fan dollars, this intrabrand competition must be limited by agreements or rules designed to maintain the economic health of all teams in the league. In the labor relations context, such agreements include efforts to spread athletic talent across teams, such as the draft system, limits on free agency, and salary caps which were discussed in Chapter 8. In the organizational governance context, such agreements include rules establishing restrictions on league structure and restrictions on franchise or event ownership, location, and equipment.

Antitrust Issues and the Structure and Governance of Pro Sport Leagues

Legal Structures of Pro Sports Leagues

Professional sports leagues have experimented with different types of organizational structures, in part to attempt to reduce their exposure to antitrust liability. This section explores the legal ramifications of different league structures.

Traditional Structure

Professional sports leagues have traditionally been structured as nonprofit incorporated or unincorporated associations of clubs, where each member club has separate and independent ownership. It is worth noting that in recent years, several professional leagues, including the NFL and MLB, have given up their league tax-exempt status granted under § 501(c)(6) of the Federal Income Tax Code, facing pressure from Congress and fans (Harwell & Hobson, 2015). Different sports have specific rules regarding club ownership, as discussed later in the chapter. Exhibit 10.3 reflects how responsibilities are divided in a traditionally structured professional sports league.

The primary advantage of the traditional structure is its capacity of profit-making potential for individuals wanting to make an ownership investment, and thus the incentive it provides for those owners to maximize the value of each team. Sharing league-wide revenues also links the individual owners' interests to the general welfare of the league, further building the case that the traditional structure falls under the Sherman Act.

The primary disadvantage of the traditional model is that the necessary agreements among owners "for the good of the league as a whole" subject the league to potential liability under the Sherman Act for entering into agreements that unreasonably restrain free trade under § 1.

Single Entity Structure

In several lawsuits, traditional professional sports leagues argued they were operating as a single entity offering a league-generated entertainment product rather than a collection of individual entities (e.g., teams) in economic competition with one another. In doing so, team owners argued that owner agreements restraining trade are "agreements" between internal parts of one entity and do not restrain trade between competing entities; hence, they do not violate antitrust law. This "single entity defense" has been largely rejected by courts, which find that leagues are associations of individually owned teams that

Exhibit 10.3 Traditional professional sports league structure and division of responsibilities.

League office conducts centralized league operations such as:

- Scheduling games
- Hiring and training officials
- Disciplining players
- Marketing and licensing logoed merchandise
- Negotiating broadcasting contracts/Commercial marketing contracts

---

League board of directors or owners committee oversees policy making on issues such as:

- Franchise relocation
- League expansion or contraction
- Playing facility issues
- Collective bargaining
- Rules of play
- Revenue sharing of non-locally generated revenue

Individual teams have responsibility for matters such as:

- Facility acquisition, leasing, and operations
- Team marketing
- Ticket sales and luxury seating
- Arrangements for local broadcasting contracts
- Player and employment relations

---

compete with each other economically (see, e.g., *North American Soccer League v. National Football League*, 1982; *Los Angeles Memorial Coliseum v. National Football League (Raiders I)*, 1984; *Sullivan v. National Football League*, 1994; but contrast *San Francisco Seals, Ltd. v. National Hockey League*, 1974). To demonstrate how teams compete with each other economically, consider how leagues' constitutions and bylaws specify which media markets respective teams can broadcast and advertise in. Such rules, which preclude teams from broadcasting and advertising in every geographic region that may be desirable to them, can be seen as anticompetitive restraints on trade. Such rules are subject to antitrust scrutiny, and courts will apply Rule of Reason analysis to determine potential violations of the Sherman Act, unless an allegation falls under the realm of the per se rule.

Several leagues have attempted structuring themselves explicitly as single entities to avoid antitrust exposure. Under the structure of these leagues, all investors own undivided interests in the whole league and share all expenses and revenues based on the percentage of their respective ownership interests. Leagues that have attempted to achieve deliberate single entity status include, but are not limited to: Major League Soccer (MLS), the Women's United Soccer Association (WUSA), the Women's National Basketball Association (WNBA), and the Arena Football League (AFL). In *Fraser v. Major League Soccer* (2002), several MLS players sued the league under the Sherman Act, claiming the single entity structure was an attempt to unreasonably restrain trade by limiting economic competition among teams and depressing player salaries. The First Circuit court of appeals upheld the validity of the single entity structure and ruled against the players. However, it also found that the structure of MLS was in actuality a hybrid model combining some elements of a single entity structure with elements of a traditional league. Ultimately, even though the legal structure might be legally viable, the WUSA abandoned the single entity structure in its last-gasp effort to attract new investors before it folded in 2003. And the WNBA has likewise returned to the traditional model of individual ownership in an apparent effort to create stability independent of the NBA's support structure.

The Supreme Court has only touched on the legal structure issue in *Brown v. Pro-Football, Inc.* (1996), confirming that professional sports clubs must cooperate for their economic survival and as such, are not completely independent competitors. The Court did not rule on the issue of whether a league is a group of cooperating separate entities subject to the Sherman Act or an integrated single entity that does not compete with itself and thus, not subject to the Sherman Act. However, in *American Needle, Inc. v. National Football League* (2010), the Supreme Court indicated that each NFL football team is a potential competitor with the others, and thus actions of National Football League Properties (NFLP) were not insulated from § 1 of the Sherman Act simply because the league formed a joint venture entity to market its intellectual property. Instead of a structural analysis focused on whether the NFLP is a single entity, the Court endorsed a functional analysis approach, analyzing the identity and decision-making actions of the actors involved (i.e., the teams). The Court concluded that the NFLP's grant of an exclusive headwear license to Reebok resulting in the loss of American Needle's license was potentially a concerted action by the teams in violation of the Sherman Act. The Court further determined NFLP's exclusive headwear license to Reebok deprived the market of independent centers of economic decision making. The Court reversed and remanded the case for further consideration. For a thorough (pre-*American Needle*) discussion of single entity structure, see McKeown (2009).

Despite the commissioner's broad "best interest" authority and attempts to use different legal structures, many league business decisions will trigger antitrust scrutiny and continue to test the boundaries of the commissioner's authority. Next we explore several common areas in which the league or the commissioner's business decisions have been challenged, including the awarding or relocation of sport franchises, negotiating of league contracts, restraints on team ownership, interference with rival leagues, and regulation of equipment.

Applications for Sport Franchises

Professional sports leagues have rules governing a prospective team's application for a franchise within the league. Prospective owners have argued such rules constitute concerted action unreasonably restraining trade in violation of § 1 of the Sherman Act. The *Mid-South Grizzlies* case provides an example in which a court decided this issue.

Mid-South Grizzlies v. National Football League

720 F.2d 772 (3rd Cir. 1983)	FOCUS CASE

FACTS

In 1974 and 1975, the Grizzlies, with their hometown in Memphis, Tennessee, were part of the World Football League. After the league disbanded in midseason in 1975, the Grizzlies applied to the NFL for a franchise in that league. The NFL had no franchise in Memphis, and placing a team there would not have infringed on the home territory of any existing NFL franchise. The Grizzlies provided evidence that they were an established enterprise with a reasonable chance of business success in a desirable market location. Nevertheless, the NFL rejected the Grizzlies' application for a franchise, and the Grizzlies sued under antitrust law, alleging that the rejection was made in bad faith out of ill will because the team had played in a rival league to the NFL. Essentially, the Grizzlies claimed that the NFL's negative vote on their franchise application constituted an antitrust violation because it unreasonably restrained trade by preventing them from competing within the NFL. The lower court granted summary judgment for the NFL, and the Grizzlies appealed.

HOLDING

The Third Circuit affirmed the decision of the District Court, holding that the NFL's rejection of the Grizzlies' franchise application did not violate the Sherman Act.

RATIONALE

The court applied the Rule of Reason analysis typically used to analyze the competitive effects of concerted action by league members under § 1 of the Sherman Act. (Refer back to Exhibit 10.2.) Here, the court found that the Grizzlies failed to satisfy their initial burden of showing any actual or potential injury to economic competition resulting from the denial of their franchise application. The nearest NFL franchise to Memphis was over 280 miles away in St. Louis, and thus there was no evidence that a Memphis team and a St. Louis team would compete for the same spectators, local broadcasters, merchandise customers, and so forth. Therefore, in the eyes of the court, there was no potential intraleague competition in the relevant product market that the NFL could be harming with its denial of a franchise to the Grizzlies. Moreover, the court believed that the NFL could show procompetitive interleague effects because the rejection left Memphis available as a future site for a franchise in a competing league, as well as leaving the Grizzlies club as a potential competitor in a future rival league. Therefore, the court concluded that the Grizzlies failed to make the necessary showing of injury to competition necessary to succeed on their antitrust claim.

Negotiating League Wide Business Contracts

Examining a case involving former NFL quarterback, Tony Romo, demonstrates how sometimes league rules enforced against players compete against leagues' sponsorship revenue generating endeavors. In 2015, a company founded by Romo, The Fan Expo, LLC, sued the NFL for tortious interference with an existing contract. The lawsuit arose after a number of active NFL players scheduled to attend the National Fantasy Football Convention in Las Vegas, which was organized and operated by The Fan Expo, LLC, backed out after the NFL commissioner sent the players a message that "attendance at the event would violate the NFL's gambling policy and that the players could be subject to discipline." Thereafter, The Fan Expo, LLC canceled the 2015 event, but worked toward holding a similar event in 2016. The Fan Expo, LLC signed a sponsorship agreement with Electronic Arts, Inc. (EA) for the 2016 convention, which would feature an EA Sports Madden NFL 17 competition between NFL players and fans. As part of the sponsorship, EA sent The Fan Expo, LLC the video game logo, which included the NFL's logo and was subsequently uploaded onto The Fan Expo, LLC's website. The NFL did not approve of the publication of the EA Sports Madden NFL 17 logo on The Fan Expo, LLC's website and upon seeing it published on the website, NFL attorneys called EA to inform the company the league was involved in a lawsuit with The Fan Expo, LLC. Shortly thereafter, EA informed The Fan Expo, LLC that it would not participate in the 2016 convention.

During subsequent communications with The Fan Expo, LLC, the NFL clarified that it did not object to EA participating in the convention, but did not approve of the use of the NFL logo in promotional materials for the event. Ultimately, the 2016 convention was canceled by The Fan Expo, LLC, which thereafter filed suit in Texas state court. Ultimately, a Texas appeals court granted summary judgement for the NFL, finding that the league did not direct EA to end its sponsorship with The Fan Expo, LLC, but rather, merely demanded that its logo be removed from all convention advertising. (*Fan Expo, LLC v. NFL*, 2019).

The proliferation of daily fantasy sports advertising and subsequent signing of league- and team-wide sponsorships with daily fantasy sports companies beginning in 2015 may cause some surprise over how the NFL handled the *Fan Expo, LLC* case. The 2015 NFL season saw daily fantasy sports companies, FanDuel and DraftKings, spending tens of millions of dollars on advertising in an attempt to gain control of the burgeoning daily fantasy sports marketplace. The companies' marketing efforts were punctuated by their signing of multi-year partnership deals with individual leagues. In 2015, DraftKings signed partnerships with MLB and the NHL and FanDuel signed an agreement with the NBA.

Notably, while individual NFL teams signed partnerships with daily fantasy sports operators, the league itself avoided the space until 2019, when it signed an official partnership with Caesars Entertainment (Jessop, 2018; Mashayekhi, 2019).

The growing number of states legalizing sport gambling following the Supreme Court's decision in *Murphy v. NCAA* ("*Christie II*") (2018) provides another example of how league commissioners' best interests of the game power intersects with leagues' bylaws and constitutions. The Supreme Court overturned the Professional and Amateur Sports Protection Act ("PASPA") on 10th Amendment grounds and subsequently allowed individual states to choose to legalize sports gambling within their own borders. This has led to increased partnerships between leagues and teams in the sports gambling space. Following the *Christie II* decision, numerous teams have signed partnerships with daily fantasy sports operators, international gaming companies and local casinos (Legal Sports Report, 2019). The impact sports gambling will have on teams' revenues will be determined over time. In the infancy of all 50 states being able to legalize sports betting within their borders, unique revenue generating strategies have been proposed, such as the Chicago White Sox and Chicago Cubs evaluating whether to open sportsbooks inside of their ballparks. Given that it was the White Sox's sports gambling scandal during the 1919 World Series that led MLB to be the first American league to adopt the role of the commissioner and grant the commissioner widespread authority through the best interests of the game power, sports gambling presents league leaders a challenge in balancing potential revenue generation with protecting the integrity of their games. (Gleeson, 2019). As such, league commissioners and executives must carefully evaluate not only the commissioners' best interests of the game power, but their respective bylaws and constitutions, to ensure policies are in place to effectively ensure continued fan support and belief in their games.

Team Ownership

Leagues typically have ownership rules setting eligibility criteria for acceptable types of owners, and these rules have also been challenged under antitrust law. Major League Baseball has no formal ownership criteria, but considers such things as commitment to the local franchise area, amount of financial capital, and an ownership structure that poses no conflicts with the interests of the league (Friedman & Much, 1997). In contrast, the NFL has fairly restrictive ownership requirements that prohibit public ownership of a franchise (with the exception of the Green Bay Packers, who were publicly owned before the NFL created this rule and were grandfathered in). The NFL also prohibits corporate ownership of a franchise (again with one exception: in the mid-1980s Eddie DeBartolo transferred ownership of the San Francisco 49ers to a property development corporation he owned, and the NFL fined him but let the new ownership arrangement stand (Lite, 1999)).

Cross-Ownership

Cross-ownership refers to ownership of more than one sport franchise. The NFL completely prohibited cross-ownership until 1997 when it revised its ownership rules and none of the other American "Big 4" men's professional sports leagues (MLB, NBA, and NHL) expressly forbid cross-ownership. The NFL's relaxation of cross-ownership rules began in 1982, when the former North American Soccer League (NASL) sued the NFL, alleging that the football league's rule banning cross-ownership of teams in competing leagues violated § 1 of the Sherman Act (*North American Soccer League v. National Football League*, 1982). The court found that the market supply of investors with sufficient capital and skill to purchase expensive sports franchises was quite limited, and the NFL's ban on cross-ownership served to significantly restrict that supply, thereby creating a substantial restraint on free trade harming the capital-poor NASL.

The Second Circuit struck down the NFL's cross-ownership ban, but only as applied in the Second Circuit. In 2018, the NFL eliminated its strict ban on cross-ownership, allowing NFL team owners to own other sports franchises in the same geographic market. Prior to the amendment, owners were required to divest their interests in non-NFL professional teams. For instance, when Stan Kroenke purchased the Los Angeles Rams, he was required to transfer ownership of the Colorado Avalanche and Denver Nuggets to his children. As a result of the rule change, Kroenke could regain ownership of all three teams (Florio, 2018).

Transfer of Ownership

League restrictions on transferring team ownership can also run afoul of antitrust law. In *Piazza v. Major League Baseball* (1993), the plaintiffs sought to buy the San Francisco Giants and relocate them to Florida. MLB precluded the plaintiffs from purchasing the team after a background check completed by the league allegedly raised some concerns. The plaintiffs sued, alleging a conspiracy among MLB owners to interfere with their efforts to buy the team. Eventually, the team sold for $15 million less than the plaintiffs offered, which evidenced that the owners' action reduced competition among bidders for the team. The court allowed the plaintiffs' antitrust claim to proceed, and the case was eventually settled out of court, with Major League Baseball agreeing to apologize and pay the plaintiffs $6 million (Sanchez, 1994). Other courts have rejected the *Piazza* analysis, reasoning that the point of antitrust law is not to protect sport entertainment producers (e.g., team owners or potential owners) from each other, but to protect against consumer harm by preventing anticompetitive conduct by those producers (*Baseball at Trotwood, L.L.C. v. Dayton Professional Baseball Club, L.L.C.*, 1999).

Courts tend to allow leagues to reject ownership transfers to prospective owners when the rejection is based on sufficient evidence of a lack of adequate financial capital, a lack of character, or insufficient business skills. According to the courts, these kinds of rejections serve to enhance intrabrand competition (e.g., the ability of MLB to compete with other types of sports entertainment offerings) by preserving the quality of the league's product. (See, *National Basketball Association v. Minnesota Professional Basketball, L.P.*, 1995.)

Franchise Relocation

The franchise rights of team owners include **territorial rights**, which prevent a franchise from relocating into a competitor team's market territory without league permission and adequate compensation for the potential loss of market share caused by the incursion. Franchise relocation restrictions can include a requirement that the move be approved by a three-fourths vote of the owners or a majority vote of the board of governors, for example. Typical justifications for restrictions on franchise relocation include ensuring that:

- Relocation sites have sufficient demographic and other characteristics to maintain league stability.
- Relocation does not negatively affect team travel and scheduling of games.
- The new territory does not encroach on existing team territorial rights.
- Relocation does not reduce the geographic diversity required for successful league-wide marketing.
- Relocation honors contractual and ethical duties (including loyalty) to cities.

These restrictions, however, have also been challenged under antitrust law. The *Raiders I* case demonstrates how a court analyzed a franchise relocation in the NFL.

Los Angeles Memorial Coliseum v. National Football League (Raiders I)

726 F.2d 1381 (1984), cert. denied, 469 U.S. 990 (1984)   **FOCUS** CASE

FACTS

In 1978, the Los Angeles Rams moved their operation from the Los Angeles Coliseum to Anaheim Stadium, leaving the Coliseum without a major tenant. After their lease with the Oakland Coliseum expired that same year, the Oakland Raiders participated in negotiations for a move to the L.A. Coliseum and, in 1980, entered into an agreement to do so. Subsequently, the NFL owners voted 22–0, with five abstentions, against the move, under Rule 4.3 of the NFL Constitution. Rule 4.3 required the approval of three-fourths of the owners for a franchise relocation to a different city, regardless of whether the move was within or outside the team's original home territory. The Raiders then sued the NFL, claiming that Rule 4.3 violated § 1 of the Sherman Act, which prohibits concerted actions resulting in unreasonable restraints on trade. The District Court ruled in favor of the Raiders, and the NFL appealed.

HOLDING

The Ninth Circuit affirmed the decision of the district court and enjoined the NFL from preventing the Raiders' relocation to Los Angeles.

RATIONALE

The court found that Rule 4.3 divides up the market among the 28 teams of the NFL, which, in a non-sport situation, would violate § 1 of the Sherman Act. However, it also found that in order to produce the sports entertainment product, a professional league needs to be able to divide the market with territorial restrictions. Therefore, the court did not find a per se violation of antitrust law. Instead, it applied the Rule of Reason analysis, comparing the procompetitive effects of the rule to its anticompetitive effects.

Among the procompetitive effects identified by the court were:

- Exclusive territories aid new teams in achieving financial stability.
- Stability helps to maintain competitive performance balance among teams.
- Territories foster fan loyalty and team rivalries, which contribute to greater spectatorship, both live and televised.
- Preventing relocations from taking place before local governments can recover their investment maintains public confidence and interest in the NFL.
- Geographic diversity aids in collective negotiation of television rights with the networks.

The court balanced these against the anticompetitive effect of insulating teams from intraleague economic competition with each other, which allows them to set monopoly prices that harm consumers.

According to the court, there were less restrictive means to accomplish the same procompetitive goals. For example, the NFL could adopt a set of objective guidelines to follow in making franchise relocation decisions, thus eliminating the subjectivity (and hence possible bias) of a vote by the owners. Objective factors might include such things as population base, fan loyalty, economic impact projections, location continuity, facilities, and regional balance of teams. Here, the NFL made no evidentiary showing that the Los Angeles market could not sustain two pro football teams or that the relocation would harm the league's regional balance or have a negative effect on the league itself. Finally, the NFL failed to prove that the rule's effect of promoting intrabrand competition (providing a strong league-wide product that could compete successfully against other professional sports and entertainment options) was greater than the negative effect on intrabrand (intraleague) competition.

Three years after it decided *Raiders I*, in *National Basketball Association v. SDC Basketball Club, Inc.* (1987) the Ninth Circuit stated that, although leagues could use the objective factors identified in *Raiders I* to justify a relocation restriction rule, reliance on such objective factors was not a *necessary* condition for establishing the rule's legality. Therefore, at least for franchise relocations in the states located in the Ninth Circuit's jurisdiction, a professional sports league may not have to justify a restrictive relocation rule with an objective analysis, as long as it can identify sufficient procompetitive effects to counterbalance the negative effects of the rule.

The City of San Jose experienced an outcome different from the Raiders' in a lawsuit filed against the Office of the Commissioner of Baseball, which demonstrates how MLB's antitrust exemption impacts its teams' relocations. Competing in the dilapidated Oakland Coliseum – the only venue then shared by a MLB and NFL team – and experiencing declining attendance and revenue, the Oakland A's were recruited by San Jose lawmakers to relocate. The city promised to build the team a modern stadium, featuring a naming rights partner and the location would put the A's closer to the bourgeoning Silicon Valley. The issue with San Jose's recruitment, though, is the city lies in the San Francisco Giants' territory, as outlined by the MLB Constitution. While the Giants showed no interest in relocating to San Jose, thanks to the relatively recent building of their San Francisco waterfront ballpark, the team did not want to relinquish its territory rights to the valuable San Jose area (Mathai, Sanchez, & Preuitt, 2013).

While the Giants were unwilling to voluntarily relinquish their territory rights, MLB's Constitution provides that a vote in favor of allowing a team to relocate to another team's territory can be approved by three-quarters of MLB teams. However, four-years after the A's announced plans to relocate, the vote still hadn't taken place, prompting the City of San Jose to sue MLB on antitrust grounds in 2013. In deciding the case, the 9th Circuit held that MLB's antitrust exemption for franchise relocation was maintained by the Curt Flood Act and dismissed the City of San Jose's case under the Sherman and Clayton Acts (*City of San Jose v. Office of the Commissioner of Baseball*, 2015).

Although antitrust challenges are some of the most common legal issues associated with franchise decisions, host cities and communities in which professional sports teams are located have additional legal remedies available to them when interacting with professional sport teams and leagues. For example, a soon-to-be-abandoned host city will often try to retain its team. The City of Oakland attempted to use its power of **eminent domain** – the power of the government to appropriate private property for public use without the owner's consent – to take ownership of the Raiders and thus prevent them from moving to Los Angeles. However, a California appellate court ruled that such a taking would be unconstitutional, because of the inhibitory negative effect it could have on interstate commerce by enabling the city to prevent the team's relocation out of Oakland indefinitely (*City of Oakland v. Oakland Raiders*, 1985).

Competitive Advantage Strategies

Working in Antitrust Law

- If you are considering adopting league-wide rules regarding team ownership or franchise location, be sure to ask an attorney familiar with antitrust law to help you determine how to define the relevant market.
- Also seek help weighing the projected anticompetitive effects of your new rule versus the projected procompetitive effects on economic competition within that market.
- Ask your attorney to determine the most recent precedent in the appropriate jurisdiction.
- With all this information, you and your lawyer can attempt to predict how a court would decide your case if your rule were challenged under the antitrust laws.
- This will give you guidance as to whether to adopt your proposed rule, alter it, or abandon the idea.

Another effective way for a city to protect its investment in a professional sport franchise and encourage a team to stay put is to include a liquidated damages clause in the facility lease contract. Liquidated damages clauses in contracts specify the amount each party agrees to compensate the other if it breaches the contract. The amounts written into liquidated damages clauses must be reasonable estimates of the damages the parties will face if a breach occurs. Liquidated damages cannot be excessive in amount or serve to hold either side hostage to the terms of the contract. However, knowing that the team will have to pay a pre-negotiated liquidated damages amount could serve to make a team rethink its decision to relocate.

While cities have successfully utilized liquidated damages clauses to prevent teams from relocating, not every city has taken this approach. For instance, in its lawsuit against the NFL, its teams and owners resulting from the Rams' relocation from St. Louis to Los Angeles, the City of St. Louis alleged a cause of action for breach of contract, among other claims. However, in the lawsuit the City of St. Louis did not seek liquidated damages, but rather, damages determined at trial (St. Louis Post-Dispatch, 2017). Similarly, in late 2018, the City of Oakland sued the Raiders and NFL alleging causes of action for antitrust law and breach of contract resulting from the team's relocation. The breach of contract claim centered on allegations that the City of Oakland was beneficiary to the NFL's Constitution and Relocation Policies and said contracts were breached with the approval of the Raiders' relocation. Given that the City of Oakland's breach of contract claim arose from allegations centered on NFL contracts – and not the city's lease agreement with the Raiders – the city did not seek to enforce a liquidated damages clause in its prayer for relief (*City of Oakland v. The Oakland Raiders*, 2018).

Cities that have brought breach of contract lawsuits based on a facility lease have also succeeded in persuading courts to enjoin teams from playing home games elsewhere until the expiration of the lease (see, e.g., *City of New York v. New York Jets Football Club, Inc.*, 1977; *City of New York v. New York Yankees*, 1983; *Metropolitan Sports Facilities Commission v. Minnesota Twins Partnership*, 2002).

Rival Leagues

American professional team sports tend not to sustain more than one professional league per sport for very long. When new leagues threaten existing leagues, the existing leagues have occasionally taken steps to preserve their market position that risk violating antitrust law. In the past, leagues have attempted to thwart rivals in several ways, including: (1) using cross-ownership rules to limit initial investment capital; (2) restricting the supply of players through the use of a reserve clause; (3) tying up television contracts to limit media exposure; and (4) limiting the availability of sites for rival teams by adding expansion teams or controlling playing facilities.

Using Cross-Ownership Rules to Limit Initial Investment Capital

In *North American Soccer League v. National Football League* (1982), the fledgling NASL claimed that the NFL's ban on cross-ownership violated § 1 of the Sherman Act, because it prevented NASL clubs access to a substantial segment of the market supply of investors with sufficient sport management skill and capital to become owners of a professional sport team. The court agreed that the cross-ownership ban was anticompetitive, because it would have kept at least some NASL teams from competing effectively with the NFL for spectators and television revenue. Therefore, the Second Circuit remanded the case with instructions for the lower court to enter a permanent injunction prohibiting the NFL's ban.

Restricting the Supply of Players

One way the supply of players has been limited is through the use of a **reserve clause** in player contracts. The reserve clause gives teams a perpetual right to keep reserve clause players unless the players are traded or released by the team. The NHL's use of a reserve clause in the standard contract was challenged by the rival upstart World Hockey League as an illegal monopolization effort, because it restricted the available pool of capable professional hockey players (*Philadelphia World Hockey Club, Inc. v. Philadelphia Hockey Club, Inc.*, 1972). The court agreed, finding that the NHL's intent was to maintain its monopoly over the supply of major league hockey players and thus, its position as the only major professional hockey league. The court issued a preliminary injunction against the enforcement of the NHL's reserve clause.

Restricting Television Exposure

Another suit by an upstart league against the NFL was brought by the United States Football League (USFL), alleging that the NFL exercised illegal monopoly power by entering into television contracts with all three major networks (thus tying them up) and pressuring them to refuse to broadcast USFL games (*United States Football League v. National Football League*, 1988). According to the USFL, acquiring a network contract was essential to its survival as a league, and the NFL's actions prevented them from doing so. The court found that the NFL's television contracts were not exclusive and that there was plenty of prime-time space left in which the networks could have broadcast USFL games. It further found that the USFL moved several teams out of desirable television markets into smaller cities and changed from a spring to fall playing season, putting it into direct competition with the NFL, and that these changes reduced the USFL's attractiveness to investors and the television networks. The court concluded that these management decisions were the real reason that the USFL lacked a network television contract and affirmed the jury's verdict in favor of the NFL.

Restricting Playing Sites

In another suit against the NFL, the upstart American Football League (AFL) claimed that the NFL's expansion by adding new teams in Dallas and Minneapolis was an unlawful effort to monopolize professional football. Section 2 of the Sherman Act prohibits predatory or anticompetitive conduct designed to enable the willful acquisition or maintenance of monopoly power in a relevant market. In this case, the NFL already had 12 teams in 11 other cities at the time of the expansion, and the AFL had eight teams in eight cities. The court found that 31 American cities had a sufficient population base to make them desirable sites for franchises and that the NFL occupied 11 of those, so the AFL could compete for the other 20.

Moreover, in the court's view, the relevant geographic market in which franchises could be established was not limited to those 31 cities, but nationwide. It further found that when in direct competition for the same site, each league had won once. Also, the fact that the NFL already occupied the most desirable cities could not be held against it, simply because it happened to be first on the "scene." Under the law, an entity that has natural monopoly power because of the success of its business is allowed to enjoy and build on that power unless it misuses that power to further its monopoly. In the court's words, "[w]hen one has acquired a natural monopoly by means which are neither exclusionary, unfair, nor predatory, [it] is not disempowered to defend [its] position fairly" (*American Football League v. National Football League*, 1963, p. 131). The court concluded that the NFL did not monopolize the market for professional football.

Exclusive facility leases are another means of restricting playing sites. In *Hecht v. Pro-Football, Inc.* (1977), the D.C. Circuit Court found that the Washington Redskins' 30-year exclusive-use lease of Robert F. Kennedy ("RFK") Stadium was a restrictive covenant that could violate the **essential facility doctrine**. This doctrine holds that refusing to share an essential facility that would be economically unfeasible for a would-be competitor to duplicate, when that refusal would constitute a severe impediment to prospective market entrants, is an unreasonable restraint of trade. The court found that the plaintiff presented sufficient evidence that in 1965 RFK Stadium was indeed the only stadium in the area suitable for professional football and that for the Redskins to share the stadium with an AFL franchise was practical as long as proper agreements were made regarding scheduling, use of locker rooms, and so forth. The case was remanded for a new trial in light of these findings.

Regulation of Equipment

One notable example of league responsibilities related to equipment regulation is seen in the litigation alleging the NFL and NHL did not warn players of the dangers of exposure to concussions and repeated head trauma and helmet makers' products did not provide adequate protection against these dangers.

In 2011, former NFL player, Ray Easterling, sued the NFL and helmet maker, Riddell, alleging that the parties were involved in a "concerted effort of deception and denial" in addressing and protecting against player concussions. In total, 4,500 other former NFL players would file or join the lawsuit, which was consolidated and brought in U.S. District Court in Pennsylvania. The plaintiffs suffered concussions during their playing careers, with many diagnosed with dementia, Parkinson's disease and others suffering from the effects of Chronic Traumatic Encephalopathy (CTE), a neurodegenerative disease only diagnosable after death. The complaint alleged claims of wrongful death, fraud, negligence, design and manufacturing defect, among others (*In Re National Football Players' Concussion Injury Litigation*, 2012).

At the time of the lawsuit, Riddell was the official helmet partner of the NFL, a partnership beginning in 1989 (Sports Business Daily, 2013). Following the 2012 suicide deaths of Easterling and former NFL star, Junior Seau, who were both diagnosed with CTE posthumously, the NFL settled the concussion litigation in 2013. In the settlement, the NFL agreed to pay $765 million to players, but did not admit wrongdoing (Ezell, 2013).

The litigation has led to changing equipment standards for the respective leagues. Following the settlement, the NFL terminated its official partnership with Riddell in 2014, allowing players to wear helmets of their choosing conforming to the league's standards (Sports Business Daily, 2013). Along with rules changes related to allowable helmets and disallowing players from using their heads to hit, the NFL and NFLPA have engaged in studies led by biomechanical experts on the safety and efficacy of helmets, leading to the banning of some designs (NFL, n.d.). The NFL and NFLPA now rank the efficacy of various helmet models in withstanding impacts, with helmets being rated as green, yellow, and red. Helmets falling under the red category were banned beginning in the 2019 NFL season. Teams whose players wear banned helmets face NFL discipline (Maske, 2019). The new helmet rules were challenged in 2019 when NFL player, Antonio Brown, sought to compete wearing a banned helmet. When Brown was informed that the helmet he had competed in his entire career was banned, he filed a grievance seeking an exception allowing him to continue wearing it. An arbitrator heard his grievance and denied his request (Gordon, 2019). Thereafter, Brown filed a second grievance arguing that the NFL's helmet rule was being arbitrarily applied to him, since other players received a one-year deferral period to replace helmets on the banned list. Brown's second grievance was also denied, meaning he was not allowed to compete in the banned helmet and required to adopt an approved helmet to continue playing in the NFL (Patra, 2019).

Additionally, professional sports teams often sign exclusive contracts with equipment suppliers. Whether exclusive contracts constitute illegal use of monopoly power has also been addressed in the courts. In *Schutt Athletic Sales Co. v. Riddell, Inc.* (1989), the NFL granted an exclusive right to Riddell to place its logo on its football helmets used during NFL games. Under the terms of the contract, players who wore helmets manufactured by other companies were not allowed to display those companies' logos on their helmets. The plaintiff alleged that high school and college consumers would make helmet purchase decisions based on what they saw professional football players using. The court ruled that the plaintiff did not provide sufficient evidence that this exclusive contract would adversely affect competition in such a broad market and upheld the contract.

Governance of Professional Individual Sports

Professional individual sports have very different organizational structures than professional team sports. Differences in organizational structure mean that governance of individual sports also differs from governance of professional team sports. For example, because individual sport athletes are not employees, employment discrimination and labor laws are not applicable to them, nor is the labor exemption from antitrust law (see Chapter 7). However, following the Supreme Court's decision in *PGA Tour, Inc. v. Martin* (2001; see Chapter 17), touring professionals are likely to be considered contestants with the right to be protected from discrimination in access to tournament play under the place of public accommodations provisions in several civil rights statutes.

Organizational Structure

Professional individual sports are generally organized around events or combinations of events into tours and governed by players associations composed of active players and other stakeholders, such as tournament directors. These athletes are not signed by a team and are not salaried employees, but generate income by winning prize money and garnering appearance fees. For example, the Women's Tennis Association (WTA) Tour, governed by a seven-person board of directors, is the major professional tennis tour for women. In 2018, more than 2,500 players from 100 nations competed for more than $164 million in prize money at 55 tour events and four grand slams held in 29 countries (WTA, 2019b). The Ladies Professional Golf Association (LPGA), the major professional golf tour for women, has been operational since 1950. It is a nonprofit organization governed by a commissioner and a board of six independent directors, six LPGA Player Directors (the LPGA's player executive committee) and the president of the LPGA Teaching and Club Professionals (LPGA, 2019a). In 2019, the LPGA Tour included 33 events in 11 countries and awarded prize money totaling nearly $68 million (LPGA, 2019b). The men's Professional Golfers' Association Tour (PGA Tour) is also a nonprofit organization operating with a commissioner (PGA Tour, 2019a). In 2018–2019, the PGA Tour offered 50 official tournaments with over $333 million in prize money (PGA Tour, 2019b).

Control of Events & Competition

The person or entity in charge of an individual sport event is typically known as the owner, producer, or promoter of the event and is entitled to all the revenue unless there has been an agreement to share it with other entities. For example, a contractual arrangement may be made so that concessions revenues are shared with the facility owner or parking revenues are shared with the host city.

When a players association or organized tour is involved, the producer of an individual event will generally have to agree to players association or tour rules about how the event is operated. Players associations often "sanction" or officially recognize certain events as counting toward player rankings, and they may require event producers to pay a fee for the privilege of being a sanctioned event. The event producer usually also has to yield some control over an event to the players association or tour. For example, the producer may give up the authority to select officials, schedule the event independent of the tour schedule, or control who is eligible to participate. Finally, the event producer may have to agree to surrender certain revenue-generating processes to the tour, such as the sale of exclusive sponsorship signage and advertising rights, or the negotiation of television contracts. Nevertheless, the event producer often retains significant responsibilities for staging the event, such as procuring equipment, arranging for parking and transportation to the venue(s), providing security systems and personnel, arranging for concessions services, and handling operations during the event. The complexity of the relationships among the event producer, players association, and tour organization often makes it difficult to say who is actually "producing" the event.

The following *Volvo* case is one which highlights the complex relationships discussed, further causing the district court judge to believe that antitrust law did not apply to the dispute. The circuit court reinstated the claims dismissed by the district court, finding sufficient evidence to support the pleadings. After the case was remanded to the district court, the parties settled out of court, so a trial on the merits did not take place. Nevertheless, the case illustrates the challenges of applying antitrust law to sports tours, where it may be difficult to identify who controls events – and thus also difficult to identify the procompetitive and anticompetitive effects of the parties' actions.

Volvo North America Corp. v. Men's Int. Professional Tennis Council

857 F.2d 55 (2nd Cir. 1988)   **FOCUS** CASE

FACTS

The plaintiffs, Volvo, IMG, and ProServ, were owners and producers of certain men's professional tennis events. The Men's International Professional Tennis Council (MIPTC), the precursor to the Association of Tennis Professionals (ATP), along with the International Tennis Federation (ITF), sanctions and schedules professional tennis events, including the Davis Cup events, the Grand Prix events, and the four Grand Slam tournaments. At the time this lawsuit was filed, Volvo owned, produced, and sponsored only sanctioned tournaments, but IMG and ProServ owned and produced both sanctioned events and non-sanctioned special events. A rival tour, World Championship Tennis (WCT), owned eight Grand Prix events before being integrated into the Grand Prix as the result of an earlier antitrust lawsuit. Volvo was the overall sponsor of the Grand Prix tournament series for several years but was passed over by the MIPTC in 1984 in favor of another sponsor. In 1985, Volvo assigned its contract rights with Madison Square Garden and NBC to the MIPTC. In exchange, the MIPTC agreed to sanction one of Volvo's tennis events on the condition that Volvo agree not to sponsor any special events in the United States during other Grand Prix tournaments or in any Grand Prix host city. After that agreement was reached, a senior administrator of the MIPTC allegedly attempted to intimidate tournament owners and producers into avoiding any association with Volvo in future Grand Prix events. Volvo, IMG, and ProServ sued the MIPTC under antitrust laws, claiming that several MIPTC rules limited their ability to compete with events sanctioned by the MIPTC and owned and produced by the WCT. One such rule required tennis players who wanted to compete in any Grand Prix event to sign a Commitment Agreement that required them to participate in an expanded minimum number of Grand Prix tournaments and to limit their participation in non-sanctioned events. Another required owners and producers of sanctioned events to agree to contribute to a bonus pool of money used to reward players who performed well at sanctioned events. The district court found no claim upon which relief could be granted, seeing no evidence of an antitrust violation, and dismissed the case after the pleadings stage.

HOLDING

On appeal, the Second Circuit reversed and remanded the case back to the district court, finding that sufficient evidence existed to support a complaint for violations of antitrust law.

RATIONALE

The court found that the complaint adequately alleged that the MIPTC engaged in price fixing, horizontal market division, and group boycott behavior under § 1 of the Sherman Act, as well as monopolization, attempted monopolization, and conspiracy to monopolize under § 2. The plaintiffs alleged that event producers had to agree to ceilings on player compensation in order to get their event sanctioned, and the court said that, if true, this was price fixing. The court also found that the MIPTC's agreement with the WCT when it was integrated into the Grand Prix divided the market between the two formerly competing tennis circuits through their arrangement to schedule their respective events in different cities and during different weeks, thus giving the WCT preferential treatment over other event producers such as Volvo. The court further found evidence of a group boycott in the players' Commitment Agreements, which prevented participation by any player who did not accept the conditions imposed in that agreement. Moreover, the extraction of Commitment Agreements from players, the earlier merger with the WCT, and the required contributions to the bonus pool all served to support the plaintiff's § 2 monopolization claims. Thus, the circuit court reinstated Volvo's case and remanded it back to the district court to allow it to go forward. It was later settled out of court.

The *Volvo* case serves to illustrate the fact that antitrust law may present limits on a professional tour's ability to control the events in its sport. In addition to the *Volvo* case, a 2018 antitrust lawsuit filed by three Olympic swimmers in the U.S. District Court for the Northern District of California seeks to use antitrust law to limit the role of governing bodies in determining which events athletes can compete in. The three swimmers sued FINA, the international federation for swimming, after FINA allegedly threatened to ban swimmers who participated in an event sanctioned by a competing swim competition organizer. According to the swimmers and the competing swim competition organizer, which filed a separate lawsuit against FINA, FINA's action was anticompetitive as it precluded the swimmers from earning a higher wage than it offered (Associated Press, 2018). As of the date of publication, the lawsuit had not been settled nor decided, yet, the legal arguments raised in it are important for sport managers to be cognizant of as they relate to managing athletes' participation in competing governing bodies' events.

In addition to antitrust challenges, sport managers also need to be aware of additional legal challenges that may arise from their interactions with rival tour operators. For example, In *JamSports v. Paradama Productions, Inc.* (2005), the event control issue was whether Clear Channel Communications, Inc. violated the law in taking action to prevent JamSports from competing as a new entrant in the professional motocross tour market. JamSports brought claims under antitrust law, but also asserted claims of tortious interference with contract.

In the case, JamSports entered into a 90-day exclusive negotiating period with the American Motorcyclist Association (AMA) regarding a contract to be the exclusive promoter for AMA Pro Racing's supercross dirt bike events. Clear Channel, the previous promoter, attempted to derail the deal during that 90 day period by such means as: approaching AMA Pro to attempt to get the contract for itself, even though aware of the agreement for an exclusive negotiating period; attempting to lock up several supercross stadiums (so JamSports would be unable to promote its tour at those venues) by "arm-twisting" the facility managers; using leverage from the other motorsports events and concert business arms of Clear Channel; and attempting to close a deal with the international federation for motorcycle sports to start a rival supercross tour, which would subject AMA Pro to risk of expulsion from the international federation if it contracted with JamSports.

The court granted summary judgment in favor of Clear Channel on JamSports' claim that Clear Channel violated the essential facilities doctrine, finding instead that there were several adequate stadiums from which JamSports had not been blocked. However, it found that a reasonable jury could conclude that had Clear Channel not prevented JamSports from promoting AMA Pro's tour, both companies would have promoted competing series, resulting in increased fan consumption opportunities and potentially lower ticket prices – procompetitive effects. The court therefore denied Clear Channel's motion for summary judgment that was based on the idea that JamSports could not show antitrust-type injury. Moreover, based on the strong-arm tactics Clear Channel used to try to lock up key stadiums, the court found sufficient evidence of conduct intended to hinder competition to allow JamSports' § 2 monopolization claim to survive a motion for summary judgment (*JamSports*, 2005).

When the case was finally tried, the jury found Clear Channel knowingly interfered with JamSports' prospective contract for its own competitive advantage, but then the jury inexplicably rejected JamSports' antitrust claims. The jury assessed compensatory damages of over $17 million and punitive damages of $73 million against Clear Channel for tortious interference of contract and for doing the same to gain a prospective competitive advantage. It also assessed compensatory damages of $169,000 against AMA Pro for breaching its prospective contract with JamSports. In a later appeal, the district court expressed its view that the jury rejected the antitrust claims because it was confused by the complexity of the issues. To address the confusion and render a coherent ruling, the court reversed the judgment on the interference with prospective competitive advantage claim and ordered a new trial on the issue of damages with respect to the regular tortious interference with contract claim (*JamSports*, 2005).

As evident in the *JamSports* case, courts are willing to review the authority of professional sports tours to control their events in legal contexts other than antitrust challenges.

Regulation of Equipment & Dress Codes

Most governing bodies for individual professional sports have rules specifying what counts as acceptable equipment and what is considered illegal equipment. In addition, governing associations will establish guidelines for appropriate apparel to be worn during competition.

Equipment

Equipment that would confer an unfair advantage, present safety concerns, or fundamentally alter the nature of the sport is likely to be prohibited. Occasionally, the justification for an equipment restriction is less clear, and the equipment manufacturer will bring suit alleging that the rule prohibiting its equipment is an unreasonable restraint of trade. The *Gunter Harz* case provides an example of the arguments that may be made by both sides in a dispute about the appropriateness of a new development. Here, the development pertains to tennis racquet stringing.

Gunter Harz Sports, Inc. v. United States Tennis Association, Inc.

511 F. Supp. 1103 (D. Neb. 1981)	FOCUS CASE

FACTS

The United States Tennis Association is the recognized sanctioning organization for amateur and professional tournament tennis in America. It is a member of the International Tennis Federation (ITF), which is the organization recognized by the International Olympic Committee as the international governing body for the sport of tennis. The ITF is responsible for upholding the uniform international rules of tennis that it promulgates. Changes to the rules of tennis can be made only upon a two-thirds majority vote of the ITF's Committee of Management. The USTA is bound to adhere to ITF rules in order to ensure its athletes' eligibility for international competition.

During the early 1970s, a new method of stringing a tennis racquet, called "double stringing," was developed that imparted significantly greater spin on the ball and hence greater control. After conducting an inquiry into the effects of double stringing, as well as taking notice of player threats to boycott the French Open Championship to protest its use, the ITF's Committee of Management voted to issue a temporary ban on the use of double-strung racquets to give the ITF more time to conduct research on its effects on match play. Two weeks later, the USTA announced that it would honor the ITF's temporary ban.

Approximately seven months later, the ITF announced it would introduce a new rule on acceptable tennis racquet specifications. This rule would include a provision requiring stringing patterns conform to specification outlawing double stringing. According to the ITF, the purpose of this rule was to prevent undue spin on the ball that could result in a fundamental change in the character of the game of tennis. The vote passed by the two-thirds majority needed, and therefore all national associations belonging to the ITF, including the USTA, were expected to adopt the new rule.

Meanwhile, the manufacturer of a double-strung racquet begun marketing its racquet and stringing kits. After the new rule was adopted, the manufacturer sued under § 1 of the Sherman Act, claiming that the rule was the result of a group boycott by the tennis governing bodies intended to restrain trade in the manufacture and distribution of this new racquet and stringing kit.

HOLDING

The court held that the USTA's endorsement of the temporary ban and ultimate adoption of the new rule were rationally related to legitimate goals and did not constitute an unreasonable restraint of trade under § 1.

RATIONALE

As a preliminary matter, the court dismissed the idea that the USTA was "forced" to adopt the ITF's rule as a condition of membership, saying that acquiescence in an illegal scheme is just as illegal as creating it. It then went on to apply rule of reason analysis, which entailed deciding four issues:

1 Whether the concerted action by the governing bodies was intended to accomplish an end consistent with the policy.
2 Whether the action was reasonably related to that goal.
3 Whether the action was narrowly tailored to achieving that goal.
4 Whether procedural safeguards were in place to prevent arbitrariness and allow for judicial review.

First, it found that the collective action in adopting the ban and ultimately the new rule was intended to accomplish the legitimate goals of preserving the essential character and integrity of the game of tennis and of preserving competition by attempting to govern the game in an orderly manner with uniform rules. Second, the court found that the actions of the ITF and USTA were reasonably related and indeed necessary to preserving the character of the game by preventing exaggerated spin on the ball. Third, it determined that the temporary ban was narrowly tailored to ensuring that the game was conducted in an orderly manner, and that an appeals procedure was built into the rule so that a case-by-case determination could be made as to whether an individual racquet met the acceptable standard. Finally, the court found that the actions of the USTA were procedurally adequate with regard to the plaintiff because they provided a reasonable response to him in a letter when he finally requested an appearance to promote his product. Thus, the court held that the USTA had not violated the Sherman Act.

Most of the time, as in *Gunter Harz*, courts grant substantial deference to sport organizations' decisions that regulate equipment. For example, in *Weight-Rite Golf Corp. v. United States Golf Association* (1991), a ban on a wedged shoe designed to improve weight distribution during the golf swing was upheld. However, occasionally a court interferes with such decisions. In *Gilder v. PGA Tour* (1991), the court affirmed a preliminary injunction striking down a ban on clubs with U-shaped grooves on the face, instead of the usual V-shaped grooves. In *Gilder*, there was conflicting evidence as to the degree to which the new design improved players' scores by enabling them to impart more spin on the ball. Several players testified that the clubs with the U-shaped grooves imparted more control, thus decreasing the level of skill required to keep golf shots in the fairways and taking away the advantage previously possessed by those with more skill. In fact, 60 percent of the tour players polled supported the ban on these clubs. However, conflicting testimony came from other players who felt the shape of the grooves was irrelevant. The appellate court held that the lower court did not abuse its discretion in issuing a preliminary injunction until a full trial on the merits could be completed.

It is difficult to distinguish the *Gilder* court's reasons for overturning the PGA Tour's ban from the courts' affirmations of similar bans in the *Gunter Harz* and *Weight-Rite* cases. *Gilder* may stand for the proposition that sport governing bodies may be subject to challenge if they attempt to ban equipment that does not have significant game-altering potential. The lesson for managers is probably that it is important to marshal evidence justifying equipment regulations in case you are sued and the court questions your decision.

Gilder notwithstanding, rules specifying acceptable equipment standards are rarely challenged in court. For example, the USGA continues regulating golf club design. In fact, in November 2012 the USGA and the Royal & Ancient Golf Club of St. Andrews announced that, because some tour players believe it makes putting easier, using a long putter braced against one's chest (known commonly as a "belly putter") would become illegal effective January 1, 2016 (Rubenstein, 2013). The question left is this: what constitutes an acceptable technological development versus what constitutes a technological development that changes the game significantly enough in an undesirable way that a ban is justified?

Examine a hypothetical case in which a technological development does not alter the game of golf significantly.

Considering … Equipment Standards

Shalloway, Inc. designs, manufactures, and sells a golf club called the Longshot. The shaft of the Longshot is made with new technology enabling a golfer to consistently drive the ball 10 yards farther than with a traditional driver. The USGA governs the game of golf in the United States, Canada, and Mexico; it is the source of the Official Rules of Golf adhered to in those countries. The Royal & Ancient Golf Club of St. Andrews (R & A) plays the same role in Europe.

The USGA bans the Longshot as a nonconforming club – that is, the club does not conform to USGA's rules regulating acceptable equipment. The R & A, however, finds the club acceptable. As a result of the USGA's ban, pro shops at golf courses throughout the United States are unwilling to stock many of the Longshot clubs, which will harm Shalloway's business prospects.

Questions

- If Shalloway sues the USGA claiming the ban constitutes an unreasonable restraint of trade under § 1 of the Sherman Act, how is the court likely to rule?
- How would it affect your analysis if the USGA and the R & A entered into an agreement, in the interest of international parity, to jointly ban the Longshot?

Note how you would answer the questions and then check your responses using the Analysis & Discussion at the end of this chapter.

Dress Codes

Similar to equipment standards, many individual sport governing bodies have developed dress codes that athletes participating in the sport must abide by. For instance, in 2017 the LPGA adopted a new dress code, which banned "plunging" necklines; leggings, unless under a skort or shorts; workout gear and jeans; joggers; and racerback tops without a collar for tournaments. Additionally, the LPGA specified that golfers' skirts, skorts or shorts "… MUST be long enough to not see [their] bottom area…" (Mayo, 2017). Like the LPGA, the WTA also has rules specifying what tennis players under its governance may wear to compete. The WTA's dress code is broadly written, specifying that "[f]or Tournament matches all players will be expected to dress and present themselves in a professional manner." While sweatshirts, sweat pants, t-shirts, jeans, and cut-offs are banned for matches, in 2019 the WTA revised its dress code to allow players to wear leggings and compression shorts both under and without a skirt, dress or shorts, so long as certain requirements are met (WTA, 2019a). The change by the WTA allowing players to wear leggings and compression shorts came after the French Tennis Federation indicated it would ban players from wearing compression suits, after Serena Williams competed in the French Open wearing one (Aziz, 2019).

The French Open's amendment to its dress code following Williams' donning a compression suit in the tournament calls into question whether dress codes are applied evenly to both genders. According to Williams, she wore the compression suit to promote blood circulation while playing, after suffering blood clots during pregnancy. In response to news that the French Open would subsequently ban players from wearing compression suits, some questioned whether similar bans would be implemented against male athletes making apparel choices for health reasons (McLaughlin, 2018). Similar questions were raised in 2018 when tennis player, Alizé Cornet, was penalized after her sports bra briefly showed while she was turning her top around after recognizing it had been put on the wrong way. Cornet was penalized under a rule prohibiting female tennis players from removing their shirts on the court. Notably, male players do not play under the same rule (Kelner & Lutz, 2018). Questions over the fairness and arbitrariness of dress codes as applied to women present an opportunity for sport managers to develop policies promoting equity.

Disciplinary Authority

Disciplinary authority in individual sports presents an interesting dilemma: active players may be in a position to make disciplinary decisions affecting their fellow competitors. This was the case in *Blalock v. Ladies Professional Golf Association* (1973). Professional golfer, Jane Blalock, was observed by monitors illegally moving her ball during tournament play. Blalock's penalty for cheating was decided by the LPGA's Executive Board, which was composed of five active fellow golfers. Initially, the board recommended Blalock be fined $500 and put on probation for the remainder of the season. A few days later, members of the board changed their minds and imposed a one-year suspension. Blalock sued the LPGA, claiming her suspension was a group boycott that was a per se restraint of trade. Under LPGA rules, a member could not compete for prize money in non-LPGA sanctioned tournaments, so Blalock's suspension completely restrained her ability to earn a living as a player for one year.

The court held that the suspension was indeed a per se restraint of trade not requiring application of Rule of Reason analysis. Central to the court's holding was the fact that Blalock's penalty was determined by her competitors in a completely subjective manner, which could have been motivated by self-interest in eliminating her as a competitor. The defendants argued two prior cases established precedent for the idea that disciplinary action in a self-regulated sport did not violate antitrust law (*Molinas v. National Basketball Association*, 1961; *Deesen v. Professional Golfers' Association of America*, 1966). However, the court distinguished those two cases on the basis that active competitors did not compose a majority of the decision making authority.

Due to professional individual sport athletes serving on the executive boards of their players associations, they have influential voices in shaping governance policies, including provisions establishing disciplinary procedures. For instance, although professional tennis is not known for having a large drug abuse problem, the men's players association – the Association of Tennis Professionals (ATP) – voluntarily implemented a drug-testing program in the late 1980s focused on recreational drugs. In 1990, testing was extended to performance-enhancing drugs (International Tennis Federation, 2013). The International Tennis Federation has administered and enforced the tennis antidoping program at all ATP-sanctioned events since 2006 and at WTA events since 2007. This is done in full compliance with the World Anti-Doping Agency (WADA) Code (International Tennis Federation, 2013). (See Chapter 11 on governance of Olympic sport for more details on WADA.) Appeals are brought to the International Court of Arbitration for Sport (CAS) rather than in American legal system (see Chapter 11).

The sport of tennis seems to be serious about its drug policy. In 2004, the ATP issued the maximum two-year suspension to then #491 ranked player Diego Hipperdinger for testing positive for cocaine, in addition to requiring him to forfeit all ranking points and prize money earned since the date of his positive test (Association of Tennis Professionals, 2004). Hipperdinger appealed his case to the Court of Arbitration for Sport. The panel upheld the two-year suspension as reasonable and stated Hipperdinger should have known better than chew unknown leaves for several days in Chile without inquiring as to what they were. Since he had an otherwise clean drug history and there was some question as to the accidental nature of his cocaine consumption, the CAS allowed his two-year suspension to start from the date of the urine sample collection instead of from the date of the decision by the original antidoping tribunal. Thus, his suspension was cut short by approximately five months (*Hipperdinger v. ATP Tour, Inc.*, 2005).

In March 2013, the ITF, ATP, and WTA announced their joint intention to implement an Athlete Biological Passport Programme, beginning in 2013. This program requires an increased number of blood tests per year, and develops an electronic file for each athlete "in which profiles of biological markers of doping and results of doping tests are collated over a period of time that can be used to detect variances from an athlete's established levels that might indicate doping" (International Tennis Federation, 2013b).

Competitive Advantage Strategies

Governance of Professional Individual Sports

- In *PGA Tour, Inc. v. Martin*, the Supreme Court overrode the PGA Tour's authority as the governing body of professional golf in the United States to define the rules of its sport. Taken together, the *Volvo*, *JamSports*, and *Martin* cases show that event producers and tour operators must be careful to consider a variety of potential legal challenges when making decisions about rules controlling their event(s). Event producers and tour operators must be familiarized with the implications of antitrust, contract, tort, and other laws for decisions about event control to exercise foresight in decision making and avoid costly litigation and negative publicity.
- Managers in an individual sport that has not yet regulated equipment but is moving in that direction must identify strong, legitimate policy reasons to support regulations, and ensure regulations are not overbroad, but go no further than necessary to accomplish policy goals.
- Those in the management level of an individual professional sport should invite their lawyer to meet with the executive board to share perspective on how antitrust law might apply to activities and use this information when creating or changing rules and policies.
- When designing, modifying, and implementing disciplinary procedures, find a way to avoid the "Blalock" problem of active athletes subjectively imposing sanctions on fellow competitors.

In 2008, both the LPGA and the PGA Tours implemented their own drug testing programs (Sirak, 2008). Both organizations also joined with other golf governing bodies worldwide to adopt a model antidoping policy effective in 2008 (LPGA, n.d.).

Related to players' roles in disciplinary authority, thanks to their stature on players associations, players also have the power to modify rules unfairly punishing them. For instance, WTA's reversal on banning compression suits, discussed above, was led by calls from the WTA Players' Council. Similarly, in 2018 the WTA adopted a rule creating a special ranking for players returning from injury, illness or pregnancy, after top-ranked players, Williams and Victoria Azarenka, were left unranked upon returning to competition from pregnancy. The special ranking rule change was similarly largely driven by the WTA Players' Council (Martin, 2018).

Conclusion

Many aspects of professional sport governance can raise legal issues, particularly in the area of antitrust law. Although many of the governance issues facing professional team sport managers differ from those confronted by a manager of professional individual sport tours, the underlying legal principles are similar. Governance activity relative to professional sports organizations is fraught with risks running afoul of the Sherman Act, because governing body decision making often has economic consequences. Often, these economic consequences are intentionally driven, since the purpose of professional sport is to make a profit by providing an entertainment product. The more managers of professional sport organizations know about the potential legal ramifications of their policies and rule-making, the better able they will be to compete successfully in the sport industry.

Discussion Questions

1 It is arguable that the court in *Mid-South Grizzlies v. NFL* (1983) ignored the anticompetitive effect of the NFL's franchise rejection on football fans. Refusing to expand the league to accommodate fan demand for additional franchises would have a negative effect on competition by denying those

fans consumption opportunities. Adding a franchise ought to increase intrabrand (within-league) economic competition among NFL clubs; at the very least, it wouldn't reduce such competition. Was this case decided correctly?

2 Would reducing intrabrand competition by limiting the number of franchises in a league actually have a procompetitive effect by increasing the potential for inter-brand competition of the league with leagues in other sports that may have, for example, an overlapping season?

3 Would a league's unilateral decision to eliminate one or more economically inviable teams violate the antitrust laws by reducing intrabrand competition?

4 How would you distinguish between newer composite materials for tennis racquet frames that have changed the game by adding more power and "double stringing" that would have changed the game by adding more control? Is there a real difference? According to tennis champion Martina Navratilova, the newer frames have significantly changed the game because the much-improved groundstrokes make it very difficult for serve-and-volley players to succeed (Tennis, 2006). If not, can you speculate as to why technology changes in frames have not been challenged but double-strung racquets were banned?

5 In the *Blalock* case, the court found a per se violation of § 1 of the Sherman Act. If the court applied the Rule of Reason balancing of the procompetitive and anticompetitive effects of the suspension, would Blalock still have come out the winner? Why? Was *Blalock* wrongly decided?

Learning Activities

1 Assume you have been named the commissioner of a new league for professional women's rugby, the National Women's Rugby League (NWRL). You are considering structuring the NWRL as a single entity rather than as a traditional league. Examine the *Fraser v. Major League Soccer* (2002) and *Brown v. Pro-Football, Inc.* (1996) cases for clues as to what factors courts deem important in finding the existence of a legitimate single entity structure. Then take a close look at the Supreme Court's 2010 ruling in *American Needle*. Write a two-column outline comparing the pros and cons of the two league structures. Finally, write a two- to three-page memo to your prospective investors/team owners selling them on the virtues of your preferred structure. Be sure to read the McKeown (2009) law review article for additional information.

2 Legendary baseball player Pete Rose was banned for life from involvement with professional baseball for allegedly gambling on his sport. Using the Internet, find information about this. Was his punishment reviewed by an arbitrator? Did it get judicial review? Find information about the suspensions of John Rocker (Atlanta Braves) and Ron Artest (Metta World Peace) and Jermaine O'Neal (Indiana Pacers), and compare their situations with that of Rose. What justifies the huge disparity in their penalties? Given the Supreme Court's decision in *Murphy v. NCAA*, allowing individual states to legalize sport gambling within their borders and the growing number of partnerships between gambling companies and professional sport leagues, should Rose's lifetime ban from MLB be revisited?

3 In 2013, the NHL and NHLPA adopted a rule that players who have played less than 26 games in the league would have to wear a protective visor shield on their helmet during competition. If the NHL wanted to adopt a rule that players must wear full face coverage, such as a cage across their helmets, could the league be liable under the antitrust laws for imposing an unreasonable restraint on trade if it handed down significant suspensions for players who broke the rule? If, on the other hand, the NHL does not adopt such a rule, is it potentially liable under other laws for failing to insist on proper safety equipment? The commissioner of the NHL has asked you to develop a policy that he can implement to address these issues. Draft that policy.

Case Study

This case study is based on the trial proceedings for *Bryan v. ATP Tour, Inc.*, 2005 WL 2576512 (S.D. Tex. 2005).

The Executive Board of the Men's Professional Tennis Tour (MPTT) has announced changes to its rules pertaining to doubles play for the upcoming tour season. The Executive Board consists of three player representatives and three tournament directors. The MPTT "Doubles Enhancement" rules changes, listed below, apply to all MPTT Tour events except the four grand slam tournaments, which are not controlled by the MPTT. (However, grand slam seeding is determined by points accumulated during the previous 12 months of MPTT Tour competition.)

1 Sets will be first to five games instead of six.
2 Tie-breakers will be played at 4–4 instead of 6–6.
3 Instead of regular scoring, games will use no-ad scoring, meaning that at deuce, the receiving team will choose whether the serve will go to the deuce or ad court, and whoever wins the next point will win the game.
4 At one set all, a match tiebreaker will be played that is first to 10 points, win by two.
5 Players are prohibited from entering a doubles draw unless they also enter the singles draw, instead of being able to enter one or the other or both.
6 Doubles draws shall be seeded according to the players' combined singles and doubles rankings, instead of based on the players' best ranking in either singles or doubles.

The MPTT's stated goal in implementing these rule changes is to make doubles a more attractive and vital part of the men's pro tennis circuit, by making doubles matches shorter and of a more predictable length for ease in scheduling and more showcasing on feature courts; offering entertainment that will be more marketable to fans, sponsors, and television broadcasters; and making doubles matches less demanding in an attempt to attract more recognized players from the singles draw. The MPTT has included in press releases about the rules changes the following quote from the 2005 Master's Cup doubles champion: "It's better to play shorter doubles matches to encourage singles players to play more doubles. If the rules changes result in more singles players playing doubles, it will be better for the game, better for doubles, better for the tournament and the fans."

Not everyone feels the same way. As professional tennis has evolved, specialization has occurred, and high-level doubles play requires a very different set of skills from high-level singles play. Several of the world's top doubles players are doubles specialists who do not have very high singles rankings. In fact, very few highly ranked singles players play doubles, and many doubles specialists do not play singles at all. Many top-ranked singles players have stated that they would not be induced by the new rules to participate in doubles, because they prefer to concentrate their energy on their singles play.

Forty-five doubles specialists, led by Joe Dublin, have joined as plaintiffs to sue the MPTT. The plaintiffs have defined men's professional tennis as the relevant product market, with submarkets of singles and doubles. They contend that the new rules "will upset tradition and unfairly change the system to exclude doubles specialists in favor of singles players." The plaintiffs assert that not only will the new seeding system exclude doubles players in regular Tour events, it will also exclude most doubles players from the doubles draw at the grand slam events because those draws are seeded according to Tour rankings based on play during the preceding year.

Rules that have the effect of replacing doubles specialists with singles players in the doubles draw will increase the profits of tournament directors by reducing the costs of providing housing for a separate group of doubles players, reducing the costs of marketing and promoting doubles, and reducing the costs of offering lucrative prize money to compete with other tournaments for the best doubles entrants. The plaintiffs contend, therefore, that the tournament directors, who are business competitors, have joined in an agreement that unreasonably restrains trade under § 1 of the Sherman Act. They also claim that the new rules constitute a group boycott in violation of § 1 because they force out doubles specialists.

For their § 2 claim, the plaintiffs will have to prove that the MPTT is engaging in a willful attempt to assert or maintain monopoly power in the product market of men's professional tennis. Plaintiffs argue that the MPTT Tour enjoys monopoly power over men's professional tennis, including its submarkets of singles and doubles. They further argue that the new rules were enacted with a specific intent to ensure that the singles submarket enjoys monopoly power by destroying competition in the doubles submarket (tournaments will no longer have to compete for the best doubles players). This will harm consumers by turning doubles into a sideshow of singles players, providing a less skilled and therefore less attractive entertainment product. Effectively, doubles will be reduced from being its own legitimate sport to being a marketing tool – an opening act – for the singles tournaments.

The plaintiffs seek a permanent injunction against implementation of the new rules, as well as court costs, attorney's, fees, and any further relief the court deems proper.

1   Are the plaintiffs likely to succeed on their § 1 claim?
2   Are the plaintiffs likely to succeed on their § 2 claim?
3   Should the MPTT's Executive Board reconsider the rule changes in light of the lawsuit?
4   If so, what new changes to the "Doubles Enhancements" would enable the MPTT to turn this situation into a public and player relations success story?

Considering ... Analysis & Discussion

Equipment Standards

A § 1 violation requires concerted (joint) action in restraint of trade. Here, the USGA is acting alone, so the court would probably reject this claim. If, however, the USGA and the R & A agree to ban the Longshot, there is concerted action. The next question is whether that agreement unreasonably restrains trade. Following the rule of reason analysis used by the majority of courts and exemplified in the *Gunter Harz* case, the court would probably find the ban reasonable. First, the ban is intended to achieve international parity in equipment standards, thus ensuring a level playing field for golfers. Second, the ban seems reasonably related to that goal. Third, the ban seems narrowly tailored to accomplishing the stated goal, since there is no other way to protect against the advantage the club confers on those who use it. Fourth, there is no evidence of procedural unfairness to Shalloway, which successfully sells several other models of golf clubs. Thus, competition in the market for golf drivers is not unreasonably restrained by the ban on this one club. Therefore, the court would probably uphold the ban. However, if the court felt that the advantage conferred by the Longshot (a mere 10 yards) was not likely to alter the nature of the game significantly, following *Gilder* there is a possibility that it might find the ban unreasonable in relation to the golf organizations' stated goal and thus a violation of § 1.

References

Cases

AFL v. NFL, 323 F.2d 124 (4th Cir. 1963).
American Needle, Inc. v. NFL, 538 F.3d 736 (7th Cir. 2008), rev'd & remanded, 130 S. Ct. 2201 (2010).
Baseball at Trotwood, L.L.C. v. Dayton Prof'l Baseball Club, L.L.C., Case No. C-3-98-260 (S.D. Ohio 1999) (unpublished opinion).
Blalock v. LPGA, 359 F. Supp. 1260 (N.D. Ga. 1973).
Brown v. Pro-Football, Inc., 518 U.S. 231 (1996).
Bryan v. ATP Tour, Inc., 2005 WL 2576512 (S.D. Tex. 2005) (trial pleadings).
Charles O. Finley & Co. v. Kuhn, 569 F.2d 527 (7th Cir. 1978), *cert. denied*, 439 U.S. 876 (1978).

Chicago National League Ball Club, Inc. v. Vincent, U.S. Dist. LEXIS 14948 (N.D. Ill. 1992).

City of NY v. New York Jets Football Club, Inc., 394 N.Y.S.2d 799 (N.Y. Sup. Ct. 1977).

City of NY v. New York Yankees, 458 N.Y.S.2d 486 (N.Y. Sup. Ct. 1983).

City of Oakland v. Oakland Raiders, 1985 Cal. App. LEXIS 2751 (Cal. Ct. App. 1985).

City of Oakland v. The Oakland Raiders et al., 3:18cv7444 (N.D. Cal. 2018) (trial pleadings).

City of San Jose v. Office of the Comm'r of Baseball, 776 F.3d 686 (9th Cir. 2015), *cert. denied*, 136 S. Ct. 36 (2015).

Deesen v. PGA, 358 F.2d 165 (9th Cir. 1966).

Fan Expo, LLC v. NFL, 2019 Tex. App. Lexis 4201 (Tex. App. 2019).

Fraser v. MLS, L.L.C., 284 F.3d 47 (1st Cir. 2002).

Gilder v. PGA Tour, Inc., 936 F.2d 417 (9th Cir. 1991).

Gunter Harz Sports, Inc. v. USTA, 511 F. Supp. 1103 (D. Neb. 1981), *aff'd*, 665 F.2d 222 (8th Cir. 1981).

Hecht v. Pro-Football, Inc., 570 F.2d 982 (D.C. Cir. 1977), *cert. denied*, 436 U.S. 956 (1978).

Hipperdinger v. ATP Tour, Inc., Arbitration CAS 2004/A/690 (2005).

In Re National Football Players' Concussion Injury Litigation, No. 2:12-md-02323-AB (E.D. Pa. 2012).

JamSports v. Paradama Prods, Inc., 336 F. Supp. 2d 824 (N.D. Ill. 2004) (Motions for Summary Judgment); 382 F. Supp. 2d 1056 (N.D. Ill. 2005).

Law v. NCAA, 134 F.3d 1010 (10th Cir. 1998).

Los Angeles Mem'l Coliseum v. NFL (Raiders I), 726 F.2d 1381 (9th Cir. 1984), *cert. denied*, 469 U.S. 990 (1984).

Metropolitan Sports Facilities Comm'n v. Minnesota Twins P'ship, 638 N.W.2d 214 (Minn. Ct. App. 2002).

Mid-South Grizzlies v. NFL, 720 F.2d 772 (3rd Cir. 1983).

Molinas v. NBA, 190 F. Supp. 241 (S.D.N.Y. 1961).

Murphy v. NCAA (Christie II), 138 S. Ct. 1461 (2018).

NASL v. NFL, 670 F.2d 1249 (2nd Cir. 1982), *cert. denied*, 459 U.S. 1074 (1982).

National Football League Players Ass'n v. National Labor Relations Bd, 503 F.2d 12 (8th Cir. 1974).

NBA v. Artest, 2004 U.S. Dist. LEXIS 26249 (S.D.N.Y. 2004).

NBA v. Minnesota Prof'l Basketball, L.P., 56 F.3d 866 (8th Cir. 1995).

NBA v. SDC Basketball Club, Inc., 815 F.2d 562 (9th Cir. 1987).

NFL Mgmt. Council v. NFL Players Ass'n, 125 F. Supp. 3d 449 (S.D.N.Y. 2015).

NFL Mgmt. Council v. NFL Players Ass'n, 820 F.3d 527 (2nd Cir. 2016).

PGA Tour, Inc. v. Martin, 532 U.S. 661 (2001).

Philadelphia World Hockey Club, Inc. v. Philadelphia Hockey Club, Inc., 351 F. Supp. 462 (E.D. Pa. 1972).

Piazza v. MLB, 831 F. Supp. 420 (E.D. Pa. 1993).

San Francisco Seals, Ltd. v. NHL, 379 F. Supp. 966 (C.D. Cal. 1974).

Schutt Athletic Sales Co. v. Riddell, Inc., 727 F. Supp. 1220 (N.D. Ill. 1989).

Sullivan v. NFL, 34 F.3d 1091 (1st Cir. 1994).

USFL v. NFL, 842 F.2d 1335 (2nd Cir. 1988).

Volvo N. Am. Corp. v. Men's Int'l Prof'l Tennis Council, 857 F.2d 55 (2nd Cir. 1988).

Weight-Rite Golf Corp. v. USGA, 766 F. Supp. 1104 (M.D. Fla. 1991).

Statutes

Sherman Act, 15 U.S.C. §§ 1–2.

Other Sources

Associated Press. (2018, December 8). Suit filed against FINA after governing body nixes independent meet. *APNews.com*. Retrieved from https://www.apnews.com/d7f104cdbf5e4e5e936abe3d3fc08.

Association of Tennis Professionals. (2004, July 23). Player suspended two years for doping offense. Retrieved from www.atptennis.com

Aziz, S. (2019, February 20). After catsuit controversy, women's tennis "modernizes" dress code. *Aljazeera*. Retrieved from https://www.aljazeera.com/indepth/features/catsuit-controversy-women-tennis-modernises-dress-code-190219190220706.html.

Berman, M. (2014, April 29). Donald Sterling banned for life from the NBA, fined $2.5 million. *The Washington Post*. Retrieved from https://www.washingtonpost.com/news/post-nation/wp/2014/04/29/donald-sterling-banned-for-life-from-the-nba-fined-2-5-million-dollars/.

Bieler, D. (2015, July 29). NFL union files court petition seeking to have Tom Brady's suspension overturned. *The Washington Post*. Retrieved from https://www.washingtonpost.com/news/early-lead/wp/2015/07/29/nfl-union-files-court-petition-seeking-to-have-tom-bradys-suspension-overturned/?utm_term=.5f131f7e90a2.

Daniels, C. J., & Brooks, A. (2009). From the Black Sox to the skybox: The evolution and mechanics of commissioner authority. *Texas Review of Entertainment & Sports Law, 10*, 23–55.

Department of Justice (2015). Competition and monopoly: Single-firm conduct under Section 2 of the Sherman Act: Chapter 2. *The United States Department of Justice.* Retrieved from https://www.justice.gov/atr/competition-and-monopoly-single-firm-conduct-under-section-2-sherman-act-chapter-2.

Department of Justice (2017, January 5). Antitrust laws and you. *The United States Department of Justice.* Retrieved from https://www.justice.gov/atr/antitrust-laws-and-you.

Ezell, L. (2013, October 8). Timeline: The NFL's concussion crisis. *PBS.* Retrieved from https://www.pbs.org/wgbh/pages/frontline/sports/league-of-denial/timeline-the-nfls-concussion-crisis/.

Florio, M. (2018, October 17). NFL finally ditches cross-ownership policy. *NBC Sports.* Retrieved from https://profootballtalk.nbcsports.com/2018/10/17/nfl-finally-ditches-cross-ownership-policy/.

Flynn, E., & Maiman, B. (2016, January 15). A timeline of the Deflategate controversy. *SI.com.* Retrieved from https://www.si.com/nfl/new-england-patriots-tom-brady-deflategate-anniversary-timeline.

Friedman, A., & Much, P. J. (1997). *1997: Inside the ownership of professional sports teams.* Chicago: Team Marketing Report.

Gleeson, S. (2019, June 17). With new Illinois gambling bill, Cubs consider opening sportsbook at Wrigley Field. *USA Today.* Retrieved from https://www.usatoday.com/story/sports/mlb/cubs/201 9/06/17/illinois-cubs-consider-opening-sportsbook-wrigley-field/1478044001/.

Gordon, G. (2019, August 12). Arbitrator denies Antonio Brown helmet grievance. *NFL.com.* Retrieved from http://www.nfl.com/news/story/0ap3000001040984/article/arbitrator-denies-antonio-brown-helmet-grievance.

Harwell, D., & Hobson, W. (2015, April 28). The NFL is dropping its tax-exempt status. Why that ends up helping them out. *The Washington Post.* Retrieved from https://www.washingtonpost.com/news/business/wp/2015/04/28/the-nfl-is-dropping-its-tax-exempt-status-why-that-ends-up-helping-them-out/.

International Tennis Federation. (2013, March 7). Anti-Doping Programme to introduce biological passport. Retrieved from www.itftennis.com/antidoping/news/articles/anti-doping-programme-to-introduce-biological-passport.aspx.

Jaffe, J. (2014). Breaking down Frederic Horowitz's decision in Alex Rodriguez case. *SI.com.* Retrieved from https://www.si.com/mlb/strike-zone/2014/01/14/alex-rodriguez-frederic-horowitz-appeal-suspension.

Jessop, A. (2018). 21st century stock market: A regulatory model for daily fantasy sports. *Journal of Legal Aspects of Sport, 28*, 39–62.

Kelner, M., & Lutz, T. (2018, August 29). U.S. Open apologizes after Alizé Cornet penalised for briefly removing shirt. *The Guardian.* Retrieved from https://www.theguardian.com/sport/2018/aug/29/alize-cornet-penalty-shirt-removal-us-open-tennis-heat.

Legal Sports Report (2019, March 28). US sportsbook and casino team sponsorship tracker. *Legal Sports Report.* Retrieved from https://www.legalsportsreport.com/sports-betting-deals/.

Lentze, G. (1995). The legal concept of professional sports leagues: The commissioner and an alternative approach from a corporate perspective. *Marquette Sports Law Journal, 6*, 65–94.

Lite, J. (1999, May 13). DeBartolo, in complaint, demands rescission of 49ers sale to corporation. *Associated Press State & Local Wire, Sports News.* Retrieved January 8, 2006, from LEXIS-NEXIS.

LPGA (2019a). About the LPGA. Retrieved from https://www.lpga.com/about-lpga.

LPGA (2019b). 2019 LPGA tour schedule. Retrieved from https://www.lpga.com/tournaments.

LPGA (n.d.). Leading golf organizations come together for anti-doping. Retrieved from www.lpga.com/content_1.aspx?pid=12761&mid=4.

Martin, J. (2018, December 21). Following Serena Williams' return, WTA changes rules on ranking after pregnancy and dress code. *CNN.com.* Retrieved from https://www.cnn.com/2018/12/18/tennis/wta-rule-changes-ranking-after-pregnancy-dress-code-trnd/index.html.

Mashayekhi, R. (2019, April 10). Inside the battle for the future of sports betting. *Fortune.* Retrieved from http://fortune.com/longform/sports-betting-battle/.

Maske, M. (2019, April 12). NFL players, including Tom Brady, will have to be in approved helmets this season. *The Washington Post.* Retrieved from https://www.washingtonpost.com/sports/2019/04/12/nfl-players-including-tom-brady-will-have-be-approved-helmets-this-season/?utm_term= .bc3f6e4f58ed.

Mathai, R., Sanchez, K., & Preuitt, L. (2013, June 18). San Jose. Sues MLB over A's move. *NBC Bay Area.* Retrieved from https://www.nbcbayarea.com/news/local/San-Jose-Sues-MLB-Over-As-Move-212011811.html.

Mayo, A. (2017, July 14). LPGA alerts players that a stricter dress code is coming. *Golf Digest.* Retrieved from https://www.golfdigest.com/story/lpga-alerts-players-that-a-stricter-dress-code-is-coming.

McCann, M. (2013, December 31). Hernandez trial, O'Bannon case, Top 10 moments for sports law in '13. Sports Illustrated. Retrieved from http://sportsillustrated.cnn.com/more/news/ 20131231/.

McKeown, J. T. (2009). 2008 Antitrust developments in professional sports: To the single entity and beyond. *Marquette Sports Law Review, 19*, 363–393.

McLaughlin, E. C. (2018, August 27). Why Serena Williams' catsuit ban matters, and what it says about us. *CNN.com.* Retrieved from https://www.cnn.com/2018/08/27/tennis/serena-williams-catsuit-ban-racism-misogyny/index.html.

NCAA (2019a). NCAA Member Schools. Retrieved from http://www.ncaa.org/about/resources/researc h/ncaa-member-schools.

NCAA (2019b). Student-athletes. Retrieved from http://www.ncaa.org/student-athletes.

NFL (n.d.). Health and safety. *NFL.com*. Retrieved from https://operations.nfl.com/football-ops/nfl-ops-honoring-the-game/health-safety/.

NFLPA (2015, July 29). NFLPA files petition on behalf of Tom Brady in Minnesota District Court. *NFLPA.com*. Retrieved from https://www.nflpa.com/news/all-news/nflpa-files-petition-on-behalf-of-tom-brady-in-minnesota-district-court.

Patra, K. (2019, August 23). Second Antonio Brown helmet grievance concludes. *NFL.com*. Retrieved from http://www.nfl.com/news/story/0ap3000001043733/article/second-antonio-brown-helmet-grievance-concludes.

PGA Tour (2019a). About PGA Tour. Retrieved from https://www.pgatour.com/company/aboutus.html.

PGA Tour (2019b). Tournament schedule. Retrieved from https://www.pgatour.com/tournaments/schedule.2019.html.

Rubenstein, L. (2013, February 20). Is anchoring a stroke of golf? *The Globe and Mail*. Retrieved from https://www.theglobeandmail.com/sports/golf/golf-news/rubenstein-is-anchoring-a-stroke-of-golf/article8879132/.

Sanchez, R. J. (1994, September 30). MLB owes investors apologies, $6 million. *USA Today*, p. 11C.

Sirak, R. (2008, January 11). The truth about testing. *Golf World*. Retrieved from www.golfdigest.com/golfworld.

Sports Business Daily (2013, October 25). NFL announces end of Riddell deal as official helmet following '13 season. *Sports Business Daily*. Retrieved from https://www.sportsbusinessdaily.com/Daily/Issues/2013/10/25/Marketing-and-Sponsorship/Riddell.aspx.

St. Louis Post-Dispatch (2017, April 12). PDF: St. Louis, St. Louis County lawsuit filed against NFL. *St. Louis Post-Dispatch*. Retrieved from https://www.stltoday.com/sports/football/professional/pdf-st-louis-st-louis-county-lawsuit-filed-against-nfl/pdf_b18dd730-f51b-5870-9bb4-09b80c74862c.html.

Tennis (2006, January). The world according to Martina Navratilova, p. 18.

Terrell, K. (2012, December 11). New Orleans Saints bounty scandal timeline. *NOLA.com*. Retrieved from https://www.nola.com/saints/2012/12/bounty_scandal_timeline.html.

USOPC (2019). Member organizations. Retrieved from https://www.teamusa.org/About-the-USOPC/Structure/Member-Organizations.

WTA (2019a). 2019 WTA Official Rulebook. *WTA*. Retrieved from http://wtafiles.wtatennis.com/pdf/publications/2019WTARulebook.pdf.

WTA (2019b). About the WTA. Retrieved from https://www.wtatennis.com/about-wta%20.

Web Resources

www.itftennis.com/antidoping/home.aspx ■ Antidoping policies, regulation of tours, and discipline of players have all made their way into the sports spotlight. The antidoping page on the International Tennis Federation's website lays out its policies, provides statistics and a list of prohibited substances, and gives updates on cases that involve member players.

www.lpga.com/corporate/ladies-golf/anti-doping-information.aspx ■ Organizations like the PGA and LPGA have the authority to regulate the rules of their sport and determine who can participate in it. This has included the power to implement drug testing as part of antidoping measures. The LPGA website offers a set of links related to its antidoping efforts and information on its drug-testing program.

11 Governance Issues in High School and College Athletics

Amanda M. Siegrist

Introduction

When athletics programs were first introduced in high school and college campuses in the late 1800s, they were student-directed activities. Quickly, however, concerns about injury rates, recruiting abuses, professionalization, and commercialization provided the impetus for creating governing bodies to establish rules and enforcement mechanisms to address these issues. The National Collegiate Athletic Association (NCAA) was established in 1906 to govern college athletics, and now represents more than 1,000-member institutions. The National Association of Intercollegiate Athletics (NAIA), originated in 1937, is the governing body for nearly 300 smaller institutions. Other governing bodies in college sport include the National Christian College Athletic Association (NCCAA), the United States Collegiate Athletic Association (USCAA; an organization that governs athletics for approximately 50 very small colleges), and the National Junior College Athletic Association (NJCAA).

At the high school level, all but three states had their own state high school athletic associations by 1923, and in that year the entity that evolved into the National Federation of State High School Associations (NFHS) was formed (NFHS, 2019). The NFHS now oversees interscholastic athletics in the U.S. with an all-time record high of 7,980,886 participants (NFHS, 2019).

In this chapter, we first explore governance and regulatory authority in high school athletics and then do the same for college athletics. Important governance issues discussed include the concept of due process, equal protection under the law, the relationship of governing bodies with their member institutions in terms of governance structure and functions, and the scope of regulatory authority of governing bodies. Exhibit 11.1 lists the management contexts, legal issues, and relevant law discussed in this chapter.

Governance and Scope of Regulatory Authority in High School Athletics

This section briefly describes the areas in which high school athletic associations typically assert regulatory authority, including areas such as eligibility to participate for athletes and membership requirements for schools to join the association. We will also examine the basic governance structure of these associations. However, our primary focus is the scope of a voluntary athletic association's authority over those subject to their rules and regulations and the limits on that authority that may be derived from their governing documents themselves or imposed through judicial review. Administrators working in interscholastic athletics will be at a competitive disadvantage if they do not understand the limits on their regulatory authority. By understanding these limits, they will reap the twin benefits of being better able to administer their programs in a fair and equitable manner, thus providing a positive experience for all stakeholders while avoiding costly and time-consuming litigation.

Authority to govern interscholastic athletics within a state is granted to the state association by the state legislature or by judicial decision. Each state's high school athletic association is responsible for implementing and enforcing regulations governing interscholastic athletics participation of the member

Exhibit 11.1 Management contexts and legal issues pertaining to interscholastic and intercollegiate athletics governance, with relevant laws and cases.

Management Context	Major Legal Issues	Relevant Law	Illustrative Cases
High school governance	Home/charter schools	State association rules	McNatt, Davis
	State actor status and due process	Case law and Due Process Clause	Goss Brentwood Academy Taylor
	Judicial deference to policy and equal protection	Equal Protection Clause Law of voluntary associations	Letendre
College governance	State actor status and due process and equal protection	Case law and Due Process Clause Equal Protection Clause	Tarkanian, Cohane
	NCAA rules infractions	NCAA rules	Oliver
	Athlete eligibility	Law of voluntary associations; Antidiscrimination laws; Antitrust laws; and ADA	Bloom, Pryor, Smith, Bowers
	Coaching compensation	Antitrust laws	Law v. NCAA
	Restrictions on athletics-based aid	Antitrust laws	White v. NCAA
	Restricted postseason play	Antitrust laws	NIT v. NCAA
	Business of other organizations	Antitrust laws	NCAA v. Board of Regents, Adidas, Warrior Sports
	NCAA certification	NCAA rules	
	Athletics reform	Equity in Athletics Disclosure Act	
	Athletic conference contracts	Contract law	Trustees of Boston College

high schools. Most have adopted the NFHS playing rules for the various sports. Member high schools are typically permitted to determine their own general participation policies, as long as they also abide by the state association's rules, which are designed to create a level playing field for all member schools within that state. Issues covered to ensure fair competition amongst all member schools within that state range from amateurism to health and safety regulations to eligibility requirements. These rules are approved and enacted by the voting representatives from the member institutions. The vast majority of member schools in a typical high school athletic association are public schools. Those same public schools will also have significant representation on the governing board (Board of Directors or Board of Trustees), which is responsible for implementing and enforcing the rules of the association. Charter schools and private schools will also have representation on the governing board but usually a much smaller proportion of representation than the public schools.

High School Athletic Association Regulatory Authority

The following sections discuss the areas that high school athletic associations typically regulate, as well as the limits of their authority to regulate.

Typically Regulated Areas of Interscholastic Athletics

High school athletic associations are commonly recognized for regulating students' eligibility to participate in high school sports, which includes such issues as academic eligibility, transfer between schools, age limits, athlete conduct and discipline, and dress/grooming. In addition to regulations impacting student eligibility and participatory rights, high school athletic association regulations encompass a broad range of activities. For example, the Utah High School Activities Association (UHSAA) 2019–2020 Handbook is 160 pages in length containing the Constitution and Bylaws for the UHSAA

Exhibit 11.2 Areas of interscholastic athletics commonly regulated by the UHSAA.

Eligibility to participate
    Academic eligibility   Transfer between schools   Age limits
    Athlete conduct and discipline   Charter school students   Homeschoolers
    Dress/grooming   Transgender participation   Pay-to-Play Programs
Recruiting practices & undue influence
Drug testing of athletes
Health and safety requirements
Activity seasons and participation Limits
Coaches, Athletic Director, and Officials' certification
Membership criteria
Sanctioning of sports
Sportsmanship or fan conduct

---

and all the rules and regulations applicable to high school athletics and performing arts activities in the State of Utah (UHSAA, 2019). It is comprehensive and detailed, impacting students, parents, coaches, administrators, member schools, officials, advertisers, and spectators. Exhibit 11.2 provides a brief summary of the areas subject to UHSAA regulation and oversight, which is representative of the typical high school athletic association today.

Clearly, with such far-reaching regulatory authority in a complex environment such as education, high school athletic associations must continually evaluate the needs of their members and identify future trends or challenges impacting athletics within the context of education. One such example is presented in creating rules and regulations to address charter schools and home-schooled students.

Charter Schools and Home-Schooled Students

Access to extracurricular and athletic opportunities for home-schooled students created challenges for high school athletic associations beginning in the 1980s and 1990s, and today's growth of charter schools has created similar challenges for determining whether students at charter schools are permitted to participate in extracurricular athletic activities. Some of the major concerns voiced by opponents of allowing such participation are that it would: (1) dilute already limited resources available for enrolled students; (2) allow homeschoolers to play without having to comply with all of the school rules; (3) dilute school spirit; and (4) encourage recruiting of star athletes. The following states currently allow homeschool students to participate in public school sports: Alabama, Arizona, Colorado, Florida, Massachusetts, Minnesota, Nevada, New Hampshire, New Mexico, North Dakota, Ohio, Oregon, Pennsylvania, Rhode Island, South Carolina, Utah, Vermont, Washington, Wisconsin, and Wyoming (Farris & Smith, 2019). States with certain allowances and specific requirements in order to be eligible are: Alaska, Arkansas, Georgia, Hawaii, Idaho, Illinois, Indiana, Iowa, Kansas, Kentucky, Louisiana, Maine, Michigan, Missouri, Nebraska, New Jersey, North Carolina, South Dakota, Tennessee, Texas, and Virginia (Farris & Smith, 2019). In total, there are only nine states who disallow homeschool students to participate in their public-school sports. Those nine states are: California, Connecticut, Delaware, Maryland, Mississippi, Montana, New York, Oklahoma, and West Virginia (Farris & Smith, 2019). This is rapid expansion from 2013 when only 25 states allowed this eligibility ("Should home schoolers," 2013).

For a public charter school, regulations are still in an early stage of development. Some states will explicitly provide for charter school students to have the same opportunities as noncharter school students. Others may prohibit charter school students from participating, and still, others are silent. For example, in the Commonwealth of Kentucky, public charter schools have no obligation to provide interscholastic sport, but they may choose to provide sports and other extracurricular activities so long as they follow the Kentucky High School Athletic Association rules. A common question is whether a charter

Competitive Advantage Strategies

Governance and Regulatory Authority in High School Athletics

- If you work in high school athletics administration, become familiar with the home school and charter school movements. If your state or school district has not yet formulated policies to address the issue of athletics participation for students in these situations, be proactive. Find out what other school districts or states have done and try to determine what the best policy would be for your state or school district. Then work on formulating and implementing that policy.

- If you are an administrator of interscholastic athletics, be sure that your waiver and enforcement processes are followed in a fair and rational manner, so that a court cannot find that you acted in an arbitrary and capricious manner and thereby overturn your decisions. Careful and judicious decision-making in these areas can prevent much ill will, negative publicity, and costly litigation.

- Ensure policies and disciplinary action are consistent across sport, gender, season and scope; avoid too much freedom to individual coaches to make his or her own determinations and rules, as this may lead to some arbitrary and capricious results as well.

school student can participate on a sports team at a traditional public school while attending a charter school. Usually, if the charter school offers the sport, the student would have to play on the charter school team. However, if the charter school does not offer the sport the student may want to participate on the traditional public school team in her district. Each state may answer this question differently. Kentucky would not allow the student to participate at another school because its charter school laws want to discourage "basketball academy charter schools" and to encourage schools to offer a wide range of options if they are going to include sports at the school (Spears, 2017). Utah, mentioned previously, has a Utah Charter and Small Schools Athletic League (UCSSAL), which administers and supervises interscholastic athletics among its member schools. But some charter schools in Utah could also choose to join the UHSAA instead of the UCSSAL.

The majority of the states will have restrictions and limitations on allowing the participation for charter schools and home-schooled students, and as such, the role of the legislatures is vital for those who want to expand their base of support. The courts have been fairly consistent in rejecting home-schoolers' claims of a constitutional right to participate in athletics in the public schools (Batista & Hatfield, 2005) (see, e.g., *McNatt v. Frazier School District*, 1995 – denial of participation did not violate Equal Protection Clause; but see, e.g., *Davis v. Massachusetts Interscholastic Athletic Association*, 1995 – under Equal Protection Clause, distinguishing in-school-building students from out-of-school-building students was not rationally related to state high school athletic association's legitimate goal of prohibiting total nonattenders from participating in extracurricular activities). Next we explore how the U.S. Constitution impacts the regulatory activities of state high school athletic associations and public schools.

High School Athletic Associations as State Actors

At its most basic level, the U.S. Constitution provides a framework for our government, and defines and limits the authority of each branch of government. The first ten amendments to the Constitution, known as the Bill of Rights, also guarantees certain basic rights for its citizens. Today the U.S. Constitution has 27 amendments. Essentially, the U.S. Constitution restrains the power of government and ensures the rights of citizens. Consequently, actions and decisions by governmental entities are subject to what is known as "constitutional scrutiny" because those actions or decisions must be both consistent with the authority of the governmental entity (state or federal), and also not impermissibly intrude upon the protected rights of the citizens. Most governmental entities are easy to recognize – public high schools, metro parks, state universities, local fire district, county court house, and county clerk's offices are easy to identify as governmental entities or agencies. However, states also delegate or partner with private organizations to provide services to the public and it is not always as clear whether those private organizations, such as a high school athletic association, who act in the capacity of a government entity or what is referred to as a "**State Actor**."

Thus, a threshold question arises when dealing with high school athletic associations as to whether they are considered a "State Actor." This is a critical inquiry, because if the private organization is deemed a State Actor, then the rules, regulations, and decisions of the organization are subject to constitutional scrutiny and those rules and regulations could be challenged as a violation of the basic rights guaranteed in the U.S. Constitution such as due process, equal protection, or free speech. As mentioned earlier, high school athletic associations, although they are private voluntary membership associations or private corporations, are granted their authority to regulate interscholastic athletics by the state. Additionally, public officials typically serve as staff or officers in the state high school athletic associations. The courts have traditionally viewed these private organizations as state actors for purposes of constitutional issues. The traditional view that state high school athletic associations are state actors was affirmed by the Supreme Court in *Brentwood Academy v. Tennessee Secondary School Athletic Association* (2001). In that case, the Court held that the Tennessee Secondary School Athletic Association (TSSAA) was a state actor due to "the pervasive entwinement of public institutions and officials in [the] composition and workings" of the association (p. 298). Let's take a closer look at the *Brentwood* case to get an idea of the Court's reasoning.

Brentwood Academy v. Tennessee Secondary School Athletic Association

531 U.S. 288 (2001)   FOCUS CASE

FACTS

In 1997, the Tennessee Secondary School Athletic Association (TSSAA) determined that Brentwood Academy, a private school member of the TSSAA, had violated a rule prohibiting certain types of recruiting practices. The recruiting rule in question prohibited member high schools from using "undue influence" in recruiting middle school student-athletes. The purpose of the rule was three-fold: one, to prevent the exploitation of children; two, to ensure that academics take precedence over athletics; and three, to promote fair competition among member schools.

Brentwood Academy's football coach had sent a letter inviting several eighth-grade boys to attend spring high school football practices. The recruiting letter contained statements indicating that football equipment would be distributed, and that "getting involved as soon as possible would definitely be to your advantage." It was also signed "Your Coach." The TSSAA believed this to be an example of "undue influence" in recruiting that violated its rule, and decided to sanction Brentwood Academy. During the TSSAA board's deliberations, it also heard additional evidence that an AAU coach had encouraged talented kids to attend Brentwood Academy- ex parte evidence to which Brentwood Academy did not have a chance to respond. The TSSAA then placed the athletic program on probation for four years, declared the boys' basketball and football team's ineligible to compete in the playoffs for two years, and imposed a fine of $3,000. At the time of the enforcement decision, all the voting members of TSSAA's board of control and the legislative council were administrators in the public schools. There was also evidence of animosity between the private and public-school members of the TSSAA.

Brentwood Academy responded to the sanctions by suing the TSSAA, claiming its enforcement action violated the First and Fourteenth Amendments. The district court found in favor of the school, holding that the TSSAA was a state actor that was thus bound by the Constitution. The Court of Appeals for the Sixth Circuit reversed, finding no state action, and Brentwood appealed to the Supreme Court.

HOLDING

The Supreme Court, in a 5–4 decision, reversed the Sixth Circuit, holding that the TSSAA was indeed a state actor, and remanded the case for further proceedings consistent with this holding.

RATIONALE

The Supreme Court found that 84 percent of the TSSAA's membership was composed of public schools and that public-school officials serving as member school representatives in the TSSAA overwhelmingly performed all but the most routine functions of the TSSAA – that, indeed, they "were" the TSSAA. Additionally, State Board of Education members were assigned as ex officio members of the TSSAA's board of control (enforcement arm) and legislative council. Also, the TSSAA's staff were treated as state employees, due to their eligibility to participate in the state retirement system.

According to the Court, these facts constituted an unmistakably high degree of entanglement of the TSSAA with the state sufficient to establish that the TSSAA acts as an arm of the state. The Court bolstered its holding with a statement that every circuit court to face the question of whether state high school athletic associations are state actors had found them to be so; therefore, its decision was in harmony with the majority of the circuit courts.

Upon remand, the district court concluded that the TSSAA had violated the Due Process Clause and enjoined it from enforcing the sanctions it had imposed on Brentwood Academy (*Brentwood Academy v. TSSAA*, 2003). The Court's reliance on a fact-specific inquiry in finding state action may have left open a judicial loophole for a school in another jurisdiction to challenge the state actor status of its state high school athletic association. However, for now, the majority position continues to be that state high school athletic associations are considered state actors. This means that administrators working for those organizations must be careful to provide procedural due process in any disciplinary action. Thus, state actor status imposes an important limit on the regulatory authority of state high school athletic associations – one that helps to ensure that governance decisions are fair to those governed by them.

As state actors, state high school athletic associations must be careful not to infringe on the civil liberties of athletes and other constituent groups granted to them by the U.S. Constitution, including rights protected by the First, Fourth, and Fourteenth Amendments. These three constitutional amendments provide for free speech and association, protections against unreasonable searches and seizures, and guarantees of due process and equal protection under the law. Due process and equal protection will be outlined next in this chapter, and then legal issues related to a variety of constitutional claims as well as other legal challenges impacting sport participation and access opportunities for athletes are explored further in Chapter 13.

Due Process Clause

One of the most frequent challenges asserted against a high school athletic associate questions whether the association has provided appropriate **due process** (that is, fairness in administrative procedures – see Exhibit 11.3) when enforcing their rules. A Due Process analysis can look at both "substantive" and "procedural" due process issues. Essentially, substantive due process asks the question – is the regulation or act itself within the proper authority of the state actor? And procedural due process asks the question – has the state actor followed appropriate procedures in exercising its

Exhibit 11.3 Definition of procedural due process and the *Mathews v. Eldridge* (1976) test for determining whether sufficient procedural due process was provided.

Under the Fourteenth Amendment's Due Process Clause, a state actor is obligated to provide procedural due process (that is, fundamental procedural fairness) when deciding whether to deprive someone of life, liberty, or property. Usually, notice of a hearing, a fair opportunity to present one's own case, and an opportunity to hear and confront the opposing evidence will suffice in cases of minimal deprivation. As the severity of the deprivation increases, so do the expectations for more stringently controlled fairness of procedure – for example, a trial with rules of evidence that must be followed. In *Mathews v. Eldridge* (1976), the Supreme Court established a balancing analysis to determine whether procedural safeguards should be required in a given case. It requires balancing three competing factors:

1 the private interest that will be affected by the official action;
2 the probable value, if any, of additional or substitute procedural safeguards;
3 the government's interest, including the fiscal and administrative burden that the additional or substitute procedural requirements would entail.

---

authority? For example, consider the following scenario: Jonathan is the quarterback on the football team, and while attending a school dance, drinks a glass of punch given to him by another student. Jonathan does not realize that the punch has been spiked with vodka. His coach walks up and sees that Jonathan has been drinking and notifies the principal who suspends Jonathan based on the school's alcohol no tolerance policy. Jonathan is not given an opportunity to explain that he did not realize the punch had alcohol in it and had not willingly violated the school's policy. In this situation, the principal's decision is consistent with his authority substantively in that suspending a student in violation of the policy would not violate the student's substantive due process rights, but by failing to provide Jonathan an opportunity to defend himself, Jonathan has been denied procedural due process. Most high school athletic associations and public schools will have appropriate authority to regulate in a wide range of areas – i.e., substantive due process, however, they will often experience legal challenges as to whether they have exercised that authority fairly and provided adequate procedural due process.

Due process is granted to us by the Due Process Clause of the Fifth and Fourteenth Amendments of the United States Constitution (see Exhibit 11.4). To establish a procedural due process violation, plaintiffs must show: (1) they have a life, liberty, or property interest in question; (2) defendants (who must be a state actor) deprived them of that interest; and (3) defendants did not afford them adequate procedural rights, or in other words, fairness of process in their decision-making (*Maki v. Minnesota State High School League*, 2016).

For a due process claim to be made, there must be an underlying deprivation of a constitutionally protected right of life, liberty, or property. Thus, a common question raised in challenges made by athletes is whether the right to participate in athletics is a protected liberty or property interest. The U.S. Supreme Court held in *Goss v. Lopez* that the right to public education was considered a property interest. As you read the following Case Opinion in *Goss*, considered how the right to education may or may not compare to the right to participate in athletics as part of the educational experience.

Exhibit 11.4 Amendment XIV of the U.S. Constitution.

Section 1

All persons born or naturalized in the United States, and subject to the jurisdiction thereof, are citizens of the United States and of the state wherein they reside. No state shall make or enforce any law which shall abridge the privileges or immunities of citizens of the United States; nor shall any state deprive any person of life, liberty, or property, without *due process of law*; nor deny to any person within its jurisdiction the *equal protection of the laws*.

Goss v. Lopez

FACTS

In Columbus, Ohio, nine public high school students were given a ten-day suspension from school for misconduct. Their suspension was awarded without a hearing, a meeting, or an opportunity for the students to disagree or dispute the suspension nor their involvement. Ohio state law did not require such a hearing by school officials. Lopez, among others, claimed he was not involved in the misconduct, rather simply a bystander, and that he was not given an opportunity to dispute or prove such. Consequently, the students brought suit against the school and its officials alleging that the Ohio state statute violated the Fourteenth Amendment's Due Process Clause. A federal court found in favor of the students, ruling that their rights had in fact been violated. The case was appealed all the way to the United States Supreme Court, who delivered the following opinion.

HOLDING

In a 5 to 4 decision, the Court affirmed the judgment of the federal court claiming students facing suspension do have a property interest to which they are entitled protection of the Fourteenth Amendment.

RATIONALE

The court reasoned that the misconduct charges, if sustained and recorded, could cause serious damage to the students' reputations, as well as their educational and employment opportunities later. The state statute was unilateral in its ability to determine a cause for suspension without process violated the purpose of the Fourteenth Amendment's Due Process Clause.

***

The very purpose of the Due Process Clause is to protect against arbitrary deprivations of life, liberty, and property interests by the state. Finding here that the students stood to be deprived of both property and liberty interests, due process is required. Protected interests in property are normally "not created by the Constitution. Rather, they are created and their dimensions are defined" by an independent source such as state statutes or rules (p. 573) entitling the citizen to certain benefits. *Board of Regents v. Roth*, 408 U.S. 564, 577 (1972).

Here, on the basis of state law, appellees plainly had legitimate claims of entitlement to a public education. Ohio Rev. Code Ann. §§ 3313.48 and 3313.64 (1972 and Supp. 1973) direct local authorities to provide a free education to all residents between five and 21 years of age, and a compulsory attendance law requires attendance for a school year of not less than 32 weeks. Ohio Rev. Code Ann. § 3321.04 (1972). Because Ohio chose to extend the right to an education to its citizens, a state school could not take away that right "on grounds of misconduct absent fundamentally fair procedures to determine whether misconduct has occurred."

It is true that § 3313.66 of the Code permits school principals to suspend students for up to ten days; but suspensions may not be imposed without any grounds whatsoever. All of the schools had their own rules specifying the (p. 574) grounds for expulsion or suspension. Having chosen to extend the right to an education to people of appellees' class generally, Ohio may not withdraw that right on grounds of misconduct, absent fundamentally fair procedures to determine whether the misconduct has occurred.

***

A short suspension is, of course, a far milder deprivation than expulsion. But, "education is perhaps the most important function of state and local governments," *Brown v. Board of Education*, 347 U.S. 483, 493 (1954), and the total exclusion from the educational process for more than a trivial period, [here, a 10-day suspension from school] is not *de minimis* and may not be imposed in complete disregard of the Due Process Clause (p. 566). Neither the property interest in educational benefits temporarily denied nor the liberty interest in reputation is so insubstantial that suspensions may constitutionally be imposed by any procedure the school chooses, no matter how arbitrary (pp. 575–577).

Due process requires, in connection with a suspension of ten days or less, that the student be given oral or written notice of the charges against him and, if he denies them, an explanation of the evidence the authorities have and an opportunity to present his version. Generally, notice and hearing should precede the student's removal from school, since the hearing may almost immediately follow the misconduct, but if prior notice and hearing are not feasible, as where the student's presence endangers persons or property or threatens disruption of the academic process, thus justifying immediate removal from school, the necessary notice and hearing should follow as soon as practicable (pp. 577–584).

QUESTIONS

1 What was the court's reasoning for finding the existence of a property interest?
2 Are there other examples of governmentally created "legitimate claims of entitlement" you can think of? State employment contract? Welfare?
3 In the opinion, the court discusses how principals do have the power to suspend, and punish misconduct, but what do you think is the importance of giving due process *prior* to such suspension or punishment?

As we have seen in the study of law, language matters. Do you think the court's word choice of "educational process" is intentionally more broad than simply the term "education"?

The *Goss* case, while not specific to sport, established that in the U.S., since students are required to attend school until a certain age, they therefore have a property interest in education. A property interest is a governmentally created expectation (*Goss*, 1975). Based on the Fifth and Fourteenth Amendments, if a person has a property interest, they are entitled to due process prior to it being taken away by a state actor. The following Focus Case considers whether the right to participate in athletics is a constitutionally protected property interest that cannot be denied without due process.

Taylor v. Enumclaw School District

133 P.3d 492 *(Wash. Ct. App. 2006)*   **FOCUS** CASE

FACTS

A suit filed by the parents of a minor student-athlete, Zachary Taylor, against his school district arose when the school received an anonymous phone call accusing certain student-athletes of underage drinking at a post-homecoming dance gathering. Additionally, Zachary was accused by his Head Football Coach of being under the influence of alcohol during a football game in the previous week. Taylor consented to a search of his car, in which security personnel and the principal found an alcohol container in his vehicle that was parked on school grounds. Taylor claims he "heard someone had put a beer box in his car that morning." Taylor received a ten-day academic and athletic suspension for violating the school drinking policy as a member of the football team at the prior game when it was alleged that he was under the influence. Taylor appealed his suspension. His suspension was upheld and consequently, Taylor brought suit alleging a constitutional violation of due process for taking away his ability to play his sport without first giving him a fair process, claiming he has a property and liberty interest in participating in interscholastic sports. Taylor alleged he was denied his right to due process for failing to give him an opportunity to confront his accusers, examine and cross-examine witnesses, and review the evidence against him in the athletic discipline hearings, as is guaranteed by the Due Process Clause of the Constitution prior to the deprivation of life, liberty and property interests.

HOLDING

The Court of Appeals of Washington upheld the summary judgment in favor of the school district.

RATIONALE

The student-athlete referenced the *Goss v. Lopez* Supreme Court ruling, establishing that a public school must provide minimal due process protection to students facing suspension from the "educational process" based on their protected property interest in their education.

Taylor argued that extracurricular activities, such as athletics, are in fact a part of his "educational process" and as such, give rise to a property interest. The school district argued that athletics were an extra privilege, and not part of the academic purposes for which the school functions. While a property interest in education indeed exists, the court reasoned that no such property or liberty interest exists in extracurricular activities, including athletics. Due to the nature of academics being a requirement, students have a governmentally created expectation to it. However, the court determined that athletics are not a part of the required curriculum, and therefore are not part of the overall educational process. Consequently, they are not entitled to due process protections when being taken away. The court found that more than enough process was given to Taylor in regard to his academic suspension when investigations were conducted prior to his suspension. Further, his appeal was heard and reviewed. In regard to the athletic suspension, because Taylor did not have a constitutional or statutory right to participate in interscholastic athletics, the granting of summary judgment in favor of the school district was upheld, as they were not legally required to provide him with any due process, so what was given was more than enough.

The outcome of the Taylor case in 2006 declined to recognize the existence of a property interest in interscholastic athletics and is consistent with the majority of cases similarly finding that the right to a public education does not include eligibility for interscholastic varsity athletic competition (see *Maki v. Minn. State H.S. League*, 2016). But it is worth noting there are more current trends that may help this argument hold more merit in the future. For example, at some high schools, interscholastic athletics are allowed to count for academic credit in terms of physical education courses. Additionally, as mentioned earlier, there is an all-time record high of athletic participation in high schools. Much of the literature on this topic also suggests that a large part of the motivation behind providing extracurricular activities to students, including athletics, is to help develop skills sets to be well-rounded and help them succeed (Swanson, 2002). There is also an emphasis on college applications and even some employment opportunities seeking applications to demonstrate their involvement in activities outside of the traditional classroom. As such, the argument for athletics being a part of the "educational process," as was coined by the Supreme Court in *Goss*, becomes more viable (Siegrist et al., 2016). There is also a trend in requiring student-athletes to pay a fee in order to participate in athletics.

Pay-To-Play Programs

More common in recent years, motivated by budgetary restraints, high schools are requiring student-athletes to pay fees in order to participate in athletic programs provided by the school (Cook, 2012). While some programs have nominal fees (i.e., $20 for processing and paperwork fees), others have hefty fees, such as $250 per sport, to play. It can therefore be argued that students who make the team and pay the fee now have more than a unilateral expectation of a "privilege" and may actually have a vested entitlement of implied continuance on the team, potentially giving rise to a protected property interest. While their eligibility may still be taken away through suspension or expulsion, the argument for a requirement of due process prior to that deprivation may be strengthened based on the language established in *Goss* (1975).

Equal Protection Clause

Equal Protection Rights, as our Due Process Rights, are included in the Fifth and Fourteenth Amendments to the U.S. Constitution (see Exhibit 11.4). The essence of equal protection is that similarly situated people must be treated similarly under the law unless there is a constitutionally permissible reason to do otherwise. If the government purposefully deprives someone of a fundamental right guaranteed to all citizens (such as the right to vote or the right to travel freely among the states), or purposefully singles out someone for differential treatment based on his or her status as a member of a prescribed group, the Equal Protection Clause provides a way to challenge the constitutionality of the rule or law through which the government or state actor has done this. However, a law that has an unintended discriminatory effect is not actionable under the Equal Protection Clause.

Most sport-related litigation under the Equal Protection Clause involves differential treatment on the basis of race or sex. Over time, the courts have established a hierarchy of three tests that are used to determine whether the Equal Protection Clause has been violated (see Exhibit 11.5). These three tests are based on the type of group classification found in the allegedly discriminatory rule or law. Strict scrutiny is the hardest test for a government rule to pass, and rational basis review is the easiest.

Strict Scrutiny

The strictest test, called strict scrutiny, is reserved for suspect classifications (including race, ethnicity, national origin, and alienage) and requires the court to scrutinize closely the law in question. It is

Exhibit 11.5 Equal protection clause tests.

Group Classification	Name of Test	Language of Test
Suspect class: race, ethnicity, alienage, national origin	Strict scrutiny: court will give rule a very hard look and almost always strike it down	Rule must be *necessary* to achieving a *compelling* government interest
Quasi-suspect class: gender, legitimacy of birth	Intermediate scrutiny: court will give rule a fairly hard look and usually strike it down	Rule must be *substantially related* to achieving an *important* government interest
Non-suspect class: all other groups singled out for differential treatment	Rational basis review: court will uphold rule if it seems reasonable	Rule must be *rationally/ reasonably related* to achieving a *legitimate* government interest

based on the premise that there is almost never a good reason for a law to differentiate on the basis of an immutable characteristic such as race or national origin. This test states that a law that incorporates a racial classification must be *necessary* to achieve a *compelling* government interest. The words necessary and compelling are key – they should be read as "absolutely necessary" and "extremely compelling."

A government rule passed strict scrutiny when a Japanese American sued the government for placing him (and many others like him) in a detention camp because of his race after Japan bombed Pearl Harbor in World War II. He claimed that he had been denied the equal protection of the laws based on his race. The U.S. Supreme Court ruled, however, that the government had a compelling interest in protecting national security and that detaining Japanese Americans was necessary to achieve that goal by ensuring they were not spying for Japan (*Korematsu v. United States*, 1944). This is one of the few cases in which a race-based classification has passed the difficult test of strict scrutiny. In almost every other conceivable kind of case where a racial classification is used (most situations are not as compelling as protecting national security), courts will rule that there is no compelling reason to use such a classification. To do so is almost always uncalled for, especially in situations involving athletic associations and athletes.

St. Augustine High School v. Louisiana High School Athletic Association (1967) provides an example of a high school athletic association rule that did not pass strict scrutiny. In this case, the Louisiana High School Athletic Association (LHSAA) added a new show-of-hands vote requirement to the existing criteria for attaining membership (and thus opportunity to participate in postseason tournaments) at the very meeting in which all-Black St. Augustine's membership application to the then all-White school LHSAA was being considered. Without using the actual "compelling government interest" code words, the court applied the first part of the strict scrutiny test in finding that the state could have no compelling reason (other than perpetuating racial segregation) to add the new membership vote requirement to existing criteria. The court thus did not need to determine whether the vote requirement was necessary to achieve a compelling government interest because there was no compelling reason for implementing such an arbitrary rule. So the court ordered the LHSAA to admit St. Augustine High School as a member, and enjoined it from refusing membership to any school that met the established written membership criteria solely on the basis of an arbitrary vote.

Intermediate Scrutiny

Down a notch in the hierarchy of Equal Protection Clause tests is the one used for gender-based classifications, or other quasi-suspect classifications, the intermediate scrutiny test. This test assumes that rarely, but occasionally, there may be an important reason for the government to rely on a law that differentiates on the basis of sex. The courts are required to scrutinize such a law closely, but not quite as critically as they would a race-based law. The intermediate scrutiny test states that the law in question must be *substantially related* to achieving an *important* government interest. Although the words *substantially related* sound a lot like *necessary*, and *important* sounds a lot like *compelling*, the courts intend the intermediate scrutiny test to be a little easier for governments to pass. Therefore, these words are not to be construed as synonymous and should be viewed as code words for the level of critical review a law will receive from the courts. Sex-based classifications may also be given heightened scrutiny, which requires the state actor show an exceedingly persuasive reason, which is a little higher standard.

Most of the time, gender-based classifications do not survive intermediate scrutiny because they often reflect archaic notions about women's capabilities, or they function to treat women differently without a good reason. The intermediate level of scrutiny was explained in a case filed by high school girls in Michigan, alleging that the Michigan High School Athletic Association (MHSAA) violated the Equal Protection Clause of the Fourteenth Amendment. The following Focus Case highlights the equal protection analysis the court used.

Communities for Equity v. Michigan High School Athletic Association

| 377 F.3d 504, 2004 U.S. App. LEXIS 15437 (6th Cir. 2004) | **FOCUS** CASE |

FACTS

The plaintiffs contended that MHSAA refused to sanction additional sports for high school girls, provided inferior practice and playing facilities for post-season tournaments held in certain girls' sports, and required girls to play certain sports in disadvantageous seasons, i.e., a season of the year different from when the sport is typically played, and that the nontraditional season is a disadvantageous time of the year to play the sport, causing inequities for girls. Defendant MHSAA argues that its placement of the girls' sports seasons at issue is advantageous for female athletes and thus not discriminatory. The MHSAA also asserts that legitimate reasons exist for scheduling some male and female teams of the same sports in different seasons, reasons which mostly encompass asserted logistical difficulties in putting more students in one season.

HOLDING

The court held that MHSAA is a state actor and concluded that MHSAA's scheduling practices violated the Equal Protection Clause.

RATIONALE

The court considered the following question: whether MHSAA's scheduling of only girls' sports in disadvantageous seasons violated the Equal Protection Clause. The Supreme Court has held that "[p]arties who seek to defend gender-based government action must demonstrate an 'exceedingly persuasive justification' for that action." *United States v. Virginia*, 518 U.S. 515, 531 (1996) (dealing with the admission of women to the Virginia Military Institute, hereafter referred to as *VMI*). In *VMI*, the court further explained the State's burden under the heightened standard for gender-based classifications. To summarize the court's current directions for cases of official classification based on gender: Focusing on the differential treatment or denial of opportunity for which relief is sought, the reviewing court must determine whether the proffered justification is "exceedingly persuasive."

The burden of justification is demanding and it rests entirely on the State. The State must show at least that the challenged classification serves *important* governmental objectives and that the discriminatory means employed are *substantially related* to the achievement of those objectives. The justification must be genuine, not hypothesized or invented post hoc in response to litigation. And it must not rely on overbroad generalizations about the different talents, capacities, or preferences of males and females.

On appeal, MHSAA reiterates its argument made below that the purpose of separate athletic seasons for boys and girls is to maximize opportunities for athletic participation. MHSAA asserts that statistics showing that Michigan has a higher number of female participants in high school athletics than most states satisfies the requirements of *VMI*. An "unavoidable consequence of separate teams," according to MHSAA, "was accommodation of twice the number of teams, games and participants." The evidence offered by MHSAA, however, does not establish that separate seasons for boys and girls-let alone scheduling that results in the girls bearing all of the burden of playing during disadvantageous seasons-maximizes opportunities for participation. MHSAA argues that bare participation statistics "are the link showing that separate seasons are substantially related to maximum participation." But a large gross participation number alone does not demonstrate that discriminatory scheduling of boys' and girls' athletic seasons is substantially related to the achievement of important government objectives.

MHSAA also contends that it cannot be liable under the Equal Protection Clause because there is no evidence that MHSAA acted with discriminatory intent. It points out that "[t]here is no evidence that MHSAA scheduled sports seasons because of 'sexual stereotypes' or as a result of any discriminatory purpose or intent." This argument appears to confuse intentional discrimination – that is, an intent to treat two groups differently – with an intent to harm. As stated above, Equal Protection analysis requires MHSAA to show that its disparate treatment of boys and girls "serves 'important governmental objectives and that the discriminatory means employed' are 'substantially related to the achievement of those objectives.'"

Disparate treatment based upon facially gender-based classifications evidences an intent to treat the two groups differently. *VMI* imposes no requirement upon CFE to show that an evil, discriminatory motive animated MHSAA's scheduling of different athletic seasons for boys and girls. In sum, we do not find that MHSAA's justification for its scheduling practices is "exceedingly persuasive" in meeting the heightened standard required by *VMI* for the gender-based classifications. We therefore affirm the district court's grant of relief to CFE on the Equal Protection claim.

Rational Basis Review

The easiest test to pass, and thus the lowest of the three in the hierarchy, is called rational basis review. This test is used for group classifications other than gender or suspect classifications. Under this test, the government must simply have a *rational* basis for adopting the questioned law to accomplish a *legitimate* goal. In other words, the law must reflect a *reasonable* means of achieving a *legitimate* government interest. Almost all laws to which this test is applied are upheld by the courts. All it takes is a reasonable justification supporting the rule.

For example, assume that a public university has a policy of refusing to hire student-athletes for certain jobs on campus. If an affected student-athlete were to challenge the policy on the grounds that student-athletes were being unfairly singled out from the rest of the student body, this claim would receive rational basis review. The group "student-athletes" is not a suspect class like race or a quasi-suspect class like sex. As long as the university could articulate a legitimate goal for the hiring policy – for example, that it would promote the educational welfare of athletes by protecting their available study time – and could show that the policy is a rational means of accomplishing that goal, the policy would withstand an equal protection challenge

The next Focus Case demonstrates the application of the **rational basis test** to an equal protection challenge to the Missouri State High School Activities Association (MSHSAA) rules restricting nonschool based participation by student-athletes.

Letendre v. Missouri State High School Activities Association

CASE OPINION   86 S.W.3d 63 (Mo. Ct. App. 2002)

FACTS

The plaintiff was a swimmer who had practiced and competed for her private swim club three hours a day for six days a week since the age of five. As a high school sophomore, she joined her school's swim team. The Missouri State High School Activities Association (MSHSAA), which governs interscholastic athletics in the state of Missouri, had a rule (Bylaw 235) prohibiting a student-athlete from practicing or competing in organized nonschool events in the same sport during the interscholastic sport season. Although aware that violating this rule would make her ineligible to participate in school swimming,

Letendre chose to practice with her swim club rather than her school team. When the MSHSAA proceeded to enforce Bylaw 235, Letendre sued for injunctive relief, claiming a violation of the Equal Protection Clause and the First Amendment freedom of association. The trial court denied her request for an injunction, and she appealed.

HOLDING

The court affirmed the judgment of the lower court denying the plaintiff's request for an injunction.

RATIONALE

The Fourteenth Amendment guarantees that no person shall be denied equal protection of the law. It assures all individuals fair treatment if fundamental rights are at stake. It also eliminates distinctions based on impermissible criteria such as race, age, religion, or gender. Where there is no suspect classification or impingement on a fundamental right explicitly or implicitly protected by the U.S. Constitution, Equal Protection claims are reviewed by this Court under the "rational relationship" standard. Claire's claim is not based upon a suspect classification, such as race, religion, national origin, or gender. Nor is it based upon a claim that her fundamental rights were violated, because she recognizes there is no fundamental right to play high school athletics. Accordingly, our inquiry is confined to whether there is a "rational relationship" between Bylaw 235 and any legitimate interest of the MSHSAA.

At trial, the Executive Director of the MSHSAA identified several reasons for the adoption of Bylaw 235, including: (1) preventing or reducing interference with a school's academic program; (2) preventing interference with athletic programs by organized nonschool athletics; (3) promoting and protecting competitive equity; (4) avoiding conflicts in coaching philosophy and scheduling; and (5) encouraging students not to overemphasize athletic competition. The director of the MSHSAA testified that the association's 76 years of experience allowed them to conclude that the potential for harm is not as great in activities such as music, speech, debate and academics as in extracurricular sports.

The issue for us, then, is not whether we agree with the Association, but whether the challenged rule bears a rational relationship to a reasonable goal of the MSHSAA. We conclude that there are reasonable grounds for Bylaw 235 because a reasonable person could believe that a legitimate goal of the Association is furthered by the rule. To determine reasonableness under Missouri law, the court must determine if the action is so willful and unreasoning, without consideration of the facts and circumstances, and in such disregard of them as to be arbitrary and capricious. Where there is room for two opinions on the matter, such action is not "arbitrary and capricious," even though it may be believed that an erroneous conclusion has been reached.

In 1975, the Association identified outside competition during the school year as one of the "principal areas of problems facing high schools and state associations." A reasonable person could conclude that it is not in the best interest of the majority of high school students to compete in the same sport at the same time on two different teams, with different coaches, different rules, different practice schedules, and different competition schedules. ... Here there is substantial evidence to conclude that Bylaw 235 is rationally related to the legitimate goal of protecting that interest. Claire's Equal Protection argument must fail.

While we might personally believe that a better rule could be drafted, one that would allow a student-athlete who is getting good grades, such as Claire, to compete simultaneously on both her school and nonschool swim teams, the law does not permit us to interject our personal beliefs in the name of the Constitution. Claire's constitutional challenges must fail because Bylaw 235 is rationally related to the MSHSAA's purpose of drafting rules that protect the welfare of the greatest number of high school athletes possible. The judgment of the trial court is, therefore, affirmed.

Exhibit 11.6 Law of private associations and judicial review.

1   whether there are inconsistencies between the association's charter and bylaws and any action taken in respect to them (arbitrary & capricious);

2   whether the member has been treated unfairly, i.e., denied notice, hearing, or an opportunity to defend;

3   whether the association undertakings were prompted by malice, fraud or collusion; and

4   whether the charter or bylaws contravene public policy or law.

"It is only upon the clearest showing that the rules have been violated by a decision of the association's tribunal that courts should intercede."

Judicial Deference to Educational Policy

In the *Letendre* case, the court seems to simply accept that the MSHSAA is a state actor, and proceeded to the constitutional analysis. But the court did acknowledge that absent state action "the power of a court to review the quasi-judicial actions of a voluntary association is limited" (*Letendre*, 2002). As indicated in *Letendre*, the limited judicial review is based on the court's deference to decisions of educational associations with regards to educational policy issues. Thus, in challenges involving decisions of amateur athletic associations (absent state action), the courts rely on the law of voluntary private associations. Exhibit 11.6 identifies the four criteria available under the law of private associations to challenge actions taken by a voluntary private association.

The limited judicial review referred to in the *Letendre* case is known as "judicial deference." The four criteria identified above are provided for under the laws applicable to private associations as the primary ways in which the decisions of a private association can be challenged. Courts are historically reticent to intervene in educational institution decision-making concerning academic issues, unless the procedures followed were arbitrary and capricious or the institution failed to follow its own policies. This judicial deference to educational institution policy-making is less noticeable when a constitutional right is at issue, but even then it plays a role. And if an association rule is broken or challenged, the association's investigation and enforcement mechanism usually must be used before the aggrieved party may seek redress in the courts. We will see in the next section involving governance of college athletics, that the notion of judicial deference plays a prominent role when the governing organizations are not state actors or governmental entities.

Governance and Regulatory Authority in College Athletics

This section focuses on the NCAA because it is the most visible and powerful, as well as the most litigated, of the national sport governing bodies. As we consider the scope of regulatory authority possessed by the NCAA, we will examine challenges to that authority in the areas of due process concerns, eligibility of athletes to participate, compensation of coaches, restrictions on athletics-based aid to students, restricted postseason play, and business affairs of nonmembers. Additionally, this section will discuss the NCAA certification process and the tax-exempt status of the NCAA. Finally, the reform roles of the Knight Foundation's Commission on Intercollegiate Athletics (Knight Commission) and the Equity in Athletics Disclosure Act are briefly addressed.

Intercollegiate athletics administrators, whether they work within a university athletics department, in a conference office, or for the NCAA, are well served by a working familiarity with the potential legal ramifications of governance decisions. Not only does such an understanding help in avoiding litigation, it can also assist administrators in keeping their organizational efforts running smoothly and effectively, and in maintaining a strong and positive public image. As part of the educational enterprise, interscholastic and intercollegiate athletics play an integral role in shaping young people's lives. Athletics administrators who abide by appropriate limits on their authority to regulate athletics will provide a more positive and edifying educational experience for the athletes who participate in their programs.

National Governance: The National Collegiate Athletic Association

Most of the principles of governance discussed in the section on interscholastic athletics also apply to the governance of intercollegiate athletics, with the notable exceptions of the lack of a state-granted authority to regulate and the related issue of whether the Constitution is available for the protection of individual rights.

The NCAA is considered by the courts to be a private, voluntary membership organization. That is, members are free to join or not, and there is no statutory or judicial grant of authority from any particular state that delegates the power to regulate athletics to the NCAA. This is one way in which the NCAA differs from state high school athletic associations. Another difference is that the heavy representation of public university officials in the NCAA governance structure and rule-making process is not considered by the Supreme Court to be pervasive entwinement or joint action sufficient to consider the NCAA to be a state actor. The Court's position on the state actor status of the NCAA was established in *NCAA v. Tarkanian* (1988).

State Action and the NCAA

Prior to the *Tarkanian* case, nearly all the lower courts that addressed the issue had ruled that the NCAA was a state actor for purposes of the Constitution. They based their decisions on prevailing Supreme Court precedent that required a finding of joint action between a private actor and the state. If the court found that the private actor performed a public function in such a way that it wielded the authority of the state, or that the state had delegated its authority to the private actor to act on its behalf, joint action could be said to exist. Or, if there was a sufficient nexus of entanglement between the state and the private actor, a court could find joint action. Under these tests, courts uniformly found that the NCAA was a state actor, asserting that public institutions had delegated their authority to govern intercollegiate athletics to the NCAA, that the NCAA performed the public function of governing intercollegiate athletics nationally, and that the high representation of public institutions as NCAA members (it was the members who actually enacted the rules) constituted a sufficient nexus of entanglement.

However, shortly before the *Tarkanian* case, the Supreme Court decided a trilogy of cases in which it narrowed the grounds for finding state action. The language now endorsed by the Court is that the action in question must be *fairly attributable to the state* for it to be considered joint, and therefore state, action. The *Tarkanian* case shows how the Court applied its new theory of state action to the NCAA.

NCAA v. Tarkanian

488 U.S. 179 (1988)   **FOCUS** CASE

FACTS

After the NCAA found the University of Nevada, Las Vegas (UNLV) guilty of 38 rules infractions, including ten involving its men's basketball coach Jerry Tarkanian, it placed the basketball team on probation for two years and ordered the university to show cause why it should not impose further penalties unless UNLV suspended Tarkanian for the same two-year period. At the NCAA's request, UNLV conducted an investigation of Tarkanian, which it completed with the assistance of the Attorney General of Nevada. After receiving the results of the university's investigation exonerating Tarkanian, the NCAA's Committee on Infractions conducted a four-day hearing at which counsel for both Tarkanian and UNLV presented their views and challenged the credibility of the NCAA investigators and informers. During the hearing on whether UNLV should impose the NCAA's recommended sanctions, the NCAA was not represented, so Tarkanian had no chance to confront his accusers in that hearing. The day before his suspension was to begin, Coach Tarkanian filed suit against UNLV in Nevada state court claiming he had been denied due process. He later added the NCAA as a defendant. The trial court ruled in favor of Tarkanian, finding that the NCAA was a state actor and that it had acted arbitrarily and capriciously in the disciplinary actions against him. It enjoyed UNLV from disciplining the coach and enjoined the NCAA from conducting any further proceedings against the university and from enforcing its "show cause" letter against UNLV. On appeal, the Nevada Supreme Court affirmed. The NCAA then appealed to the United States Supreme Court.

HOLDING

The Supreme Court, in a 5–4 decision, reversed, holding that the NCAA is not a state actor and therefore was under no constitutional obligation to provide due process to Tarkanian.

RATIONALE

According to the Court, the NCAA was in an adversarial relationship with UNLV regarding termination (because the university wanted to keep its winning coach) and thus could not be seen as engaged in joint action with UNLV. Furthermore, agreement by the collective NCAA membership to rule-making and to be subject to NCAA rules enforcement could not be fairly attributable to the State of Nevada. Also, the NCAA's principle of institutional control of athletics showed that member institutions had not delegated their authority to regulate athletics to the NCAA. Finally, the voluntary nature of membership meant that the NCAA did not have ultimate control over intercollegiate athletes, because institutions could simply choose not to be members. For all these reasons, the NCAA could not be considered as acting with the power of the state, and therefore it was not bound by the Constitution and did not have to afford due process to Tarkanian.

In 2007, the question of whether the NCAA could ever be deemed a state actor was raised in *Cohane v. NCAA*. In this case, the plaintiff, Cohane, was terminated from his position as head men's basketball coach at SUNY-Buffalo after the NCAA investigated him for major rules violations. He sued the NCAA under the Fourteenth Amendment, claiming he had been defamed and deprived of his liberty interest in working in his chosen profession without proper due process of law. Cohane alleged that, in order to placate the NCAA, the university had colluded with the NCAA in denying him a fair hearing. The district court granted the NCAA's motion to dismiss. On appeal, the Second Circuit reversed, stating that under facts like these it is conceivable that a plaintiff could prove that the state university willfully engaged in joint action with the NCAA to deprive him of his liberty interest. According to the court, Cohane might be able to prove that without the state's assistance and coercive power, the NCAA would not have been able to issue the defamatory report and impose sanctions on him. The court concluded that the district court had erred in holding categorically that the NCAA could never be a state actor when it conducts an investigation of a state school. The Second Circuit remanded the case and the district court granted summary judgment to the NCAA, determining that SUNY-Buffalo and the NCAA had not acted jointly. Cohane appealed a second time to the Second Circuit, and on the second appeal the court of appeals stated "To show that a private entity acted as a state actor through joint activity with the state, a plaintiff must show that the private entity and the state "share[d] some common goal to violate the plaintiff's rights," and that "the state was involved with the activity that caused the injury giving rise to the action," Cohane failed to raise a genuine dispute as to whether the NCAA, a private entity, and SUNY Buffalo, a state actor, shared a common goal to violate his rights, let alone that they shared such a goal with respect to the decision to impose the show-cause order or to place a record of Cohane's infractions in the NCAA's personnel files. Because there was no evidence of a material state-imposed burden or state-imposed alteration of Cohane's status or rights, the Second Circuit held that the District Court properly granted summary judgment in defendants' favor on Cohane's due process claims (*Cohane v. NCAA*, 2007).

While it is not beyond the realm of possibility that the NCAA could be so involved with a state university through joint activity that the NCAA would be considered a state actor, it is highly unlikely given the past judicial precedent of *Tarkanian*. As a result, ever since the *Tarkanian* case, the NCAA has enjoyed immunity from constitutional attacks on its policies and practices. Hence, most of the current sport-related litigation against the NCAA is based on a number of federal statutes, including Title VI, Title IX, the Americans with Disabilities Act, and the Sherman Anti-Trust Act. In addition, as discussed earlier, since the NCAA is not subject to constitutional scrutiny, courts will exercise judicial deference toward the NCAA when its rules are challenged on basic fairness grounds, or ones that exceed the scope of their authority. Thus, the three primary avenues to challenge the rules or regulations of the NCAA are (1) private association law, (2) federal anti-discrimination statutes, and (3) federal antitrust laws (see Exhibit 11.6 detailing private association law).

Before we explore the legal pathways to challenge NCAA rules and regulations, it is important to understand the basic NCAA organizational structures and the regulatory processes used by the NCAA to both adopt rules and to enforce those rules against member institutions, coaches, athletes, and other individuals or organizations.

NCAA Structure and the Regulatory Process

In 1997, the NCAA restructured and moved from a one institution–one vote rule-making process, to a structure that uses a representative form of governance. Interestingly, in 1985 the NAIA, seeking to add a more democratic dimension to decision-making, abandoned a representative governance system and adopted a one institution–one vote process instead. The current NCAA representative governance structure, including functions of the various boards, committees, and councils, is set forth in Exhibit 11.7. In 2014, the NCAA restructured again, passing the changes with an easy 16-2 vote (New, 2014).

Exhibit 11.7 NCAA governance structure.

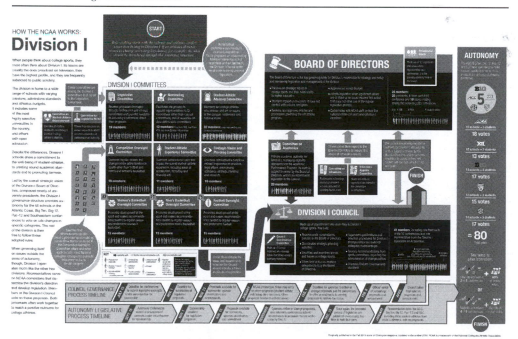

Source: 2019 NCAA Division I, Governance: How the NCAA Works, www.ncaa.org.

The NCAA Division I Manual (NCAA, 2019) includes the Constitution and By-laws, and documents the structure and functions of the organization's governance layers. Focusing on Division I, there exists a Board of Governors, a Board of Directors, a Division I Council, a Committee on Academics, and Committees/Cabinets as part of the substructure of the Council. The Board of Directors is comprised of 20 positions for presidents/chancellors (10 FBS, 5 FCS, F Division I) (NCAA Constitution, Article 4). The Board of Governors is comprised of institutional presidents and chancellors ensuring consistency in fundamental policies and general principles of the Association (NCAA Constitution, Article 4.01.1). The Board of Directors provides oversight and addresses strategic issues, while the Council handles more of the day-to-day policy and legislative responsibilities. The Council includes 40 members with representatives from all conferences and stewardship by athletic directors (NCAA Constitution, Article 4.3). The duties of Division I Board of Directors is provided in Exhibit 11.8.

Each NCAA division may adopt operating bylaws and regulations pertaining to the administration of college athletics by its member institutions, the administration of NCAA championships and enforcement procedures for NCAA rules, and adoption of rules of play (NCAA Constitution, Article 5.2.2). Changes to the Division I rules must be supported by a two-thirds majority vote of the Legislative Council. Any such changes will be considered adopted unless the Board of Directors amends or defeats them at their next meeting. If at least 75 member institutions or an athletic conference provides a written request to override a piece of legislation, a five-eighths majority vote of the full membership will

Exhibit 11.8 The duties of the Division I Board of Directors.

a Address future issues, challenges, opportunities and outcomes, focusing on strategic topics in intercollegiate athletics and its relationship to higher education.
b Review and set parameters that guide and determine present and future decisions, embracing general goals and acceptable procedures.
c Monitor legislation to ensure it does not conflict with basic policies and strategic goals.
d Ratify, amend or defeat academically related legislation adopted by the Council and, at its discretion, adopt academically related legislation otherwise addressed by the Council.
e Rescind or adopt other legislation addressed by the Council in order to prevent an extraordinary adverse impact on the Division I membership.
f Adopt legislation or grant relief from the application of legislation in circumstances in which significant values are at stake or the use of the regular legislative process is likely to cause significant harm or hardship to the Association or the Division I membership because of the delay in its effective date.
g Delegate to the Council responsibilities for specific matters it deems appropriate.
h Appoint members of the Committee on Infractions, Infractions Appeals Committee, the Independent Resolution Panel, Council and Committee on Academics.
i Review and approve policies and procedures governing the infractions program and revise the operating procedures of the independent accountability resolution structure in consultation with the Independent Accountability Oversight Committee.
j Determine whether legislation proposed as an area of autonomy is consistent with the scope and nature of the applicable area of autonomy as set for in NCAA Constitution 5.3.2.1.2.
k Ensure that there is gender and ethnic diversity among its membership and the membership of each of the other bodies in the administrative structure.
l Require bodies in the administrative structure to alter (but not expand) their membership to achieve diversity;
m Approve an annual budget.
n Approve regulations providing for the expenditure of funds and the distribution of income consistent with the provisions of NCAA Constitution 4.01.2.2.
o Collaborate with NCAA staff, as necessary, to determine how the national office can best to serve the Division I membership.
p Advise the Board of Governors concerning the employment of the NCAA president and concerning the oversight of his or her employment.
q Conduct biannual assessments to evaluate the operation of the governance structure and to monitor membership standards and criteria affecting Division I and sub-divisional membership.
r Elect institutions to active Division I membership (NCAA Constitution, Article 4.2.2).

result in the rescission of that piece of legislation (NCAA Constitution, Article 5.3). Otherwise, members are obligated to apply and enforce NCAA legislation or be subject to enforcement procedures (NCAA Constitution, Article 1.3.2).

The members of the five high-revenue conferences (referred to as the A5 or Autonomy 5) only make up 18 percent of all Division I colleges, however this new structure affords those same five conferences nearly 40 percent of the voting power (New, 2014). The NCAA's rationale for this change is that they "recognize the unique pressures and challenges faced by the ACC, the Big Ten, the Big 12, the Pac-12 and the SEC, in operating intercollegiate athletics programs that properly balance educational and athletics' interests of student-athletes and institutions in the 21st Century" (NCAA, 2014, p. 10). It is not uncommon to hear concern and criticism of the new autonomy given to those five high-revenue conferences. Some other Division I institutional presidents are concerned that it allows those five conferences to have free reign and causes a major divide and disadvantage to the other Division I institutions. While the autonomy only applies to certain areas, these changes in governance will certainly impact the nature and handling of many public and legal pressures that the NCAA and its major conferences are under, including concussion lawsuits, compensation over the use of image and likeness, and even student-athletes' attempts to unionize (New, 2014). In 2020, the world faced a national pandemic as a result of the Covid-19 virus. Widespread impacts were seen even in the sports world, including the cancelation of the 2020 NCAA Basketball Tournament and spring sports seasons. Consequently, the NCAA created an NCAA Eligibility Center COVID Response, addressing flexibility in eligibility standards for student-athletes to try to best manage implications in a timely manner. The scrutiny of the NCAA is high as the media and world watch closely in their governance of these revolutionary issues.

NCAA Rules Enforcement Mechanism

The purpose of the enforcement program is to investigate rules infractions and enforce the rules by imposing appropriate penalties. Under Bylaw 19.01.3, all representatives of member institutions are obligated to cooperate fully with the NCAA in these processes. Full cooperation includes full and complete disclosure of relevant information requested by NCAA investigation and enforcement personnel. The NCAA Committee on Infractions (COI) is charged with investigating allegations of rules violations and with determining disciplinary actions, with the exception of suspension or termination of membership (Bylaw 19.01.2). Before imposing any penalties, the COI must provide the member institution with notice of the charges that will be brought against it, as well as an opportunity for a hearing before the committee (Bylaw 19.7.1). In newly adopted procedures, institutions must demonstrate a Show-Cause Order, meaning the member institution must demonstrate to the satisfaction of the COI (or Independent Resolution Panel) why it should not be subject to a penalty or additional penalty for not taking appropriate disciplinary or corrective action in regards to the issue or personnel in question for a violation of an NCAA bylaw (NCAA Constitution, Article 19.02.3). The cases of alleged violations with a Level I or II severity are reviewed by the COI, but a 2019 change to this process allows for a more independent approach to investigating alleged rule violations with the creation of independent resolution panels who have no affiliation to NCAA entities or its members, reviewing the findings, overseeing hearings and administering punishments (Lederman, 2019; NCAA Constitution, Article 19.02.4). The process for a typical infraction investigation is shown in Exhibit 11.9.

Scope of NCAA Regulatory Authority

The NCAA regulates nearly every aspect of the conduct of intercollegiate athletics, from the conduct of university personnel to the conduct of athletes. Article 1.2 of the NCAA Constitution stipulates that one of the purposes of the NCAA is to legislate in any area of athletics administration that is of general concern to the membership (NCAA, 2019a). A review of the contents of its operating bylaws reveals that the NCAA regulates in the areas shown in Exhibit 11.10.

Exhibit 11.9 Process for a typical NCAA infraction investigation.

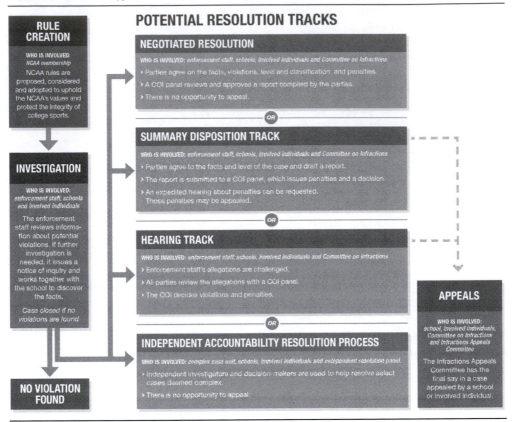

Source: 2019 NCAA Division I, Infractions, www.ncaa.org.

NCAA regulation of these aspects of intercollegiate athletics is generally accepted as legitimate by the member institutions that choose to join and thereby consent to the scope of these regulations. However, there are limits to the scope of the NCAA's regulatory authority, including internally and externally imposed constraints. As mentioned earlier, court challenges to the NCAA's authority to regulate athletics usually arise under three areas of the law: (1) the law of private associations (see Exhibit 11.6); (2) federal

Exhibit 11.10 Aspects of intercollegiate athletics regulated by the NCAA.

- Ethical conduct
- Conduct and employment of athletics personnel
- Amateurism
- Recruiting
- Academic eligibility
- Financial aid
- Athletes' benefits and expenses
- Playing and practice seasons
- Championship events
- Enforcement policy
- Division membership
- Athletics certification
- Academic performance program (penalizes programs that do not demonstrate satisfactory academic progress of their student-athletes)

antidiscrimination statutes; and (3) federal antitrust laws. In this next section, NCAA rules and regulations related to amateurism and athlete eligibility are used to illustrate the application of private association law and federal antidiscrimination statutes to NCAA decisions. Then, the NCAA's decisions impacting compensation, financial aid, and business operations of the NCAA are used to illustrate the application of federal antitrust laws to the NCAA. The line between NCAA rules and regulations associated with amateurism and restraints related to advancing NCAA business activities continues to become less distinct as we will see in some of the following cases. Chapter 12 will explore how individual universities and colleges are impacted by federal nondiscrimination laws and other federal statutes.

Athlete Eligibility and Private Association Law

The following two Focus Cases, *Oliver v. NCAA* and *Bloom v. NCAA*, examine student-athlete challenges to NCAA bylaws prohibiting athletes from seeking the advice of an attorney when exploring professional contract opportunities and receiving endorsement income.

Oliver v. NCAA

920 N.E.2d 203 (2009)	**FOCUS** CASE

FACTS

In 2006, professional baseball teams began to approach high school baseball star pitcher, Andy Oliver, to discuss the possibility of being signed straight out of high school. Due to the magnitude of this decision, Oliver and his father sought the advice of a local attorney and agent, Tim Baratta. The Minnesota Twins met with Oliver and his father at their home to negotiate a contract for $390,000. Baratta was in attendance of this meeting as counsel to Oliver. Ultimately, Oliver decided not to accept the deal and instead accepted a full scholarship to Oklahoma State University. Baratta was not pleased with Oliver's decision and sent invoices to him for his services, and also informed OSU and the NCAA of the meeting with the Twins. Subsequently, Oliver's amateur status was investigated and called into question by the NCAA in 2008. While a student-athlete may seek advice from an attorney according to NCAA Bylaw 12.3.2, NCAA Bylaw 12.3.2.1 prohibits a lawyer's presence at contract discussions or negotiations between an athlete and a professional organization.

HOLDING

The plaintiff's requests for permanent injunction and declaratory relief were granted.

RATIONALE

The court in *Oliver* (2009) determined NCAA Bylaw 12.3.2 should be void, as it overreaches and is against public policy because it creates potential for young athletes to be taken advantage of by professional teams and/or to make poor decisions about their future. The common pleas court determined that Oliver would have suffered irreparable harm if injunctive relief was not granted, and that because the NCAA Bylaw was arbitrarily being applied, such enforcement of the rule would have been an exploitation of the student-athlete. Further, the court also reasoned that the Bylaw attempts to regulate attorneys, which is not within the NCAA's scope of authority. The court stated the NCAA cannot and should not tell attorneys when and how to provide legal counsel to clients. The rule poses attorneys with a choice between providing a client proper representation and risking a client's potential eligibility with the NCAA, an authority that does not belong to the NCAA, but rather to the state bar association of which the attorney is a member.

Although the eventual settlement of this case vacated this court order in regard to the NCAA Bylaw being null and void, the *Oliver* case is a good example of our earlier discussion on judicial deference. The court in *Oliver* was not constrained by the principle of judicial deference to the NCAA's decision-making and rules enforcement because those rules ran counter to public policy. Recall that courts will intervene in the affairs of a private association when the charter or bylaws contravene public policy or law, as the NCAA's Bylaw 12.3.2 did in *Oliver*. By prohibiting a student-athlete from seeking expert legal and professional advice for a potentially life-changing decision that he is not qualified to make on his own, the NCAA was overreaching and going beyond the acceptable authoritative boundaries of their voluntary organization (Siegrist & Blosio, 2015).

The next Focus case, *Bloom v. NCAA*, illustrates the application of the law of private associations, in which the court shows substantial deference to the decision-making of those entities unless they have acted in an arbitrary and capricious manner or failed to abide by their own policies.

Bloom v. NCAA

93 P.3d 621 (Colo. Ct. App. 2004)	**FOCUS** CASE

FACTS

The NCAA prohibited Jeremy Bloom, a U.S. Olympic team skier, from earning endorsement and modeling money to finance his ski training if he wished to remain eligible to play football at the University of Colorado. The NCAA's decision was based on its bylaws prohibiting student-athletes from accepting payment for endorsing products. These bylaws were enacted to further its goal of preserving the distinction between amateur and professional athletics. When the university sought a waiver of these rules on Bloom's behalf, it was denied by the NCAA. Bloom filed suit, claiming that denying him a waiver of these rules was arbitrary and capricious. He sought an injunction against NCAA enforcement of its rules pertaining to his endorsement and paid media opportunities. The trial court found that he was not likely to succeed on the merits of his claims and refused to enter the requested injunction. Bloom appealed.

HOLDING

The Colorado appellate court affirmed the denial of Bloom's request for a preliminary injunction, finding that the NCAA had not been arbitrary or capricious in enforcing its rules and denying a waiver of those rules for Bloom.

RATIONALE

According to the court, Bloom failed to provide adequate evidence that the NCAA's enforcement of its rules was arbitrary and capricious. The court found that Bloom's reliance on NCAA Bylaw 12.1.2, which states that "[a] professional athlete in one sport may represent a member institution in a different sport," was misplaced. Bloom had argued that, because a professional is one who "gets paid" for a sport, a student-athlete is entitled to earn whatever income is customary for his professional sport, which, in the case of professional skiers, primarily comes from endorsements and paid media opportunities.

In the court's view, other NCAA bylaws written to protect the amateurism principle express a clear and unambiguous intent to prohibit student-athletes from engaging in endorsements and paid media appearances, without regard to: (1) when the opportunity for such activities originated; (2) whether the opportunity arose or exists for reasons unrelated to participation in an amateur sport; and (3) whether income derived from the opportunity is customary for any particular professional sport. The court felt it could not disregard the clear meaning of the bylaws simply because they might disproportionately affect those who participate in individual professional sports. The court concluded that although student-athletes have the right to be professional athletes, they do not have the right to engage in endorsement or paid media activity and simultaneously maintain their eligibility to participate in amateur competition. Furthermore, the court found ample evidence that this interpretation was consistent with both the NCAA's and its member institutions' construction of the bylaws.

Finally, the court found that the bylaws bore a rational relationship to the NCAA's legitimate goal of preserving the distinction between amateur and professional sport. Additionally, it ruled that the NCAA had not applied its waiver review process unreasonably in Bloom's case. The court concluded that the NCAA had not acted in an arbitrary and capricious manner and affirmed the decision of the trial court.

An interesting comparison here is the standard of review the court used even when deferring to the NCAA's rule-making authority. Note that the court found the bylaws were rationally related to a legitimate goal of preserving amateurism – thus, the arbitrary and capricious standard under private association law is a similar standard a court would use when evaluating an equal protection claim or due process claim under the U.S. Constitution using the lowest level of scrutiny – rationale relationship test. For the most part, so long as the NCAA acts consistently and within its authority as provided in the NCAA Constitution and Bylaws and does not take actions that violate public policy or the law, their authority will be upheld if challenged by a member institution, coach, or student-athlete.

However, the NCAA is a representative organization and has also established internal constraints which further define the scope of its authority to govern the member institutions and the member institutions responsibilities to adhere to the NCAA rules and regulations. The NCAA also continues to address growing concerns about student-athlete representation and due process in the rule-making and enforcement functions of the NCAA.

Institutional Control of Athletics

An internally imposed constraint is found in Article 2.1 of the NCAA Constitution. This provision establishes the NCAA's position that member institutions must maintain control of and responsibility for their own intercollegiate athletics programs, although such control must be in conformity with NCAA regulations. Article 6.01.1 adds the idea that athletic conferences also have responsibility for controlling the conduct of their member universities' athletics programs (NCAA, 2019). Universities are expected to self-monitor for compliance with eligibility requirements, Title IX, and other applicable laws and NCAA regulations.

Occasionally, the NCAA brings an action against a member institution for failure to control its athletics program if it appears that university officials failed to take corrective action once aware of questionable practices. The authority to do so appears to place ultimate control of intercollegiate athletics in the hands of the NCAA, which seems contrary to the principle of institutional control. However, an institution that disagrees with a rule or a sanction against it could choose to withdraw its membership and thus retain institutional autonomy with regard to athletics governance. As you will recall, the Supreme Court in *NCAA v. Tarkanian* (1988) used a member institution's option to withdraw from NCAA membership to support its view that the NCAA does not have the coercive power of a state actor. It would be rare indeed, though, to find a university willing to withdraw its membership from the NCAA, thus giving up, for example, the opportunity to participate in NCAA championship postseason play.

NCAA Provision of Due Process

The threat of external constraints has at times pushed the NCAA to adopt rules of its own accord that further limit its regulatory authority. The Supreme Court held in *Tarkanian* that the NCAA was not a state actor and so was not required to provide due process when it investigated and sought to enforce rules violations against UNLV and its men's basketball coach. In response, several states, including Nevada, introduced legislation that would have required any national collegiate athletics association to provide fair procedures in its enforcement process when conducted within the state. Many of the procedures required by the Nevada statute were not included in the NCAA enforcement program. For example, the NCAA did "not provide the accused with the right to confront all witnesses, the right to have all written statements signed under oath and notarized, the right to have an official record kept of all proceedings, or the right to judicial review of a Committee decision" (*NCAA v. Miller*, 1993).

The Nevada statute further provided that a state district court could enjoin any NCAA proceeding that violated the statutory provisions. Furthermore, an institution that successfully challenged the NCAA would have been entitled to costs, attorneys' fees, and compensatory damages. Finally, the NCAA would have been prohibited from impairing the rights or privileges of membership of any institution on the basis of rights conferred by the statute. Thus, the NCAA would not have been able to avoid compliance simply by expelling its Nevada members (*NCAA v. Miller*, 1993).

In *NCAA v. Miller* (1993), the NCAA successfully challenged the Nevada law as a violation of the Commerce Clause of the U.S. Constitution. The Supreme Court's Commerce Clause analysis prohibits states from passing laws that cannot be enforced equitably across different states. According to the court, laws like the Nevada statute could result in several states having differing due process requirements that would force inconsistent obligations on the NCAA, which would in turn lead to the inequitable application of its enforcement mechanism across different states – results that the Commerce Clause prohibits. Despite this decision in its favor, the NCAA subsequently revised its bylaws to strengthen due process protections in its enforcement scheme. Among the changes was the creation in 1993 of the Infractions Appeals Committee, as well as revised notice, evidentiary, and conduct of hearings procedures.

Arguably, and practically speaking, the NCAA's current procedures likely meet the requirements for due process regardless of their status as a private actor who therefore need not provide it, if and only if they follow their procedures and hearings set out in their constitution, which has not always historically been the case. As such, the point may be moot in regard to the process owed and the precedent set forth by *Tarkanian*. Nonetheless, student-athletes, member institutions, state legislatures, and even the federal government persist. Congress has proposed bills to directly counteract the outcome of *Tarkanian* and rein in the NCAA's lack of required due process, however, they have yet to have success getting them out of their House or Senate subcommittees (Despain, 2015). Some potential remains with the Department of Education's (DOE) role. Their responsibility to improve and ensure fair American education certainly could include student-athlete's rights in relation to due process protections (Despain, 2015).

Despite the due process the NCAA does or does not afford, the existence of their Restitution Rule is a potential mechanism for deterring student-athletes from pursuing any sort of litigation. Essentially the Restitution Rule lays out the following: "if any college athlete ruled ineligible by the NCAA is allowed to participate thanks to a court order, and said order is later vacated, stayed, or reversed, then the association can force the athlete's school to forfeit victories, surrender television revenue, pay fines, and endure postseason ban" (Silver, 2016). This rule, coupled with the student-athletes lack of a right to counsel in a dispute of an alleged violation, effectively allows the NCAA to reign supreme (Silver, 2016).

Athlete Eligibility and Federal Anti-Discrimination Statutes

Another set of cases deals with eligibility regulations that might implicate federal antidiscrimination statutes. One such case was a Title VI challenge alleging that the NCAA intentionally discriminated on the basis of race by raising the initial eligibility requirements when it adopted Proposition 16 (*Pryor v. NCAA*, 2002). (See Chapter 12 for an in-depth discussion of the race discrimination issue raised in *Pryor*.) Another was a Title IX challenge alleging that the NCAA granted more waivers of eligibility restrictions to male athletes than to females (*Smith v. NCAA*, 2001), and yet another was a Rehabilitation Act § 504 challenge to the NCAA's core course requirement as applied to a student with a learning disability (*Bowers v. NCAA*, 2000). More recently, cases surrounding student-athletes taking a knee during the National Anthem as a matter of protest for racial divide in our country (Nwadike, Baker, Brackebusch, & Hawkins, 2016) and a challenge of the NCAA's Proposition 16, claimed to be aimed at increasing African American graduation rates, but potentially having a disparate impact on African American student-athlete eligibility (Munczinski, 2003) have added fuel to the fire on these discussions of alleged institutional racism within the organization.

These cases are grouped together here because the federal statutes mentioned apply only to recipients of federal funds. Thus, the ability to restrict the NCAA's authority to regulate in ways that might infringe on student-athletes' rights to be free from discrimination on the basis of race, gender, and disability depends in part upon the answer to the question of whether the NCAA is a recipient of federal funds. The courts in all three cases addressed this question but never resolved it because, for various reasons, none has proceeded to a full trial on the merits of the statutory issues.

In *NCAA v. Smith* (1999), the Supreme Court ruled that dues payments to the NCAA by member institutions that have received federal funds do not suffice to make the NCAA qualify as a recipient of federal funds, because that was not a sufficiently direct recipient relationship. However, the Court left open the issue of the applicability of these federal statutes if it were proven that the NCAA receives federal funds for its National Youth Sports Program (NYSP). Two federal courts concluded that the NCAA was a recipient of federal funds because of the extensive control it exercised over the NYSP and its National Youth Sports Program Fund (which received grant monies from the U.S. Department of Health and Human Services; see *Bowers v. NCAA*, 2000, for a list of the ways in which the NCAA controlled the NYSP; also see *Cureton v. NCAA*, 1999).

In sum, existing case law suggests that the courts thought there might have been sufficient evidence to support a finding that the NCAA was a recipient of federal funds due to its relationship with the NYSP and NYSP Fund. The NCAA, however, ended its sponsorship of the NYSP in 2005 (National Youth Sports Program, n.d.), which eliminated any support for federal funding recipient status for the NCAA. Moreover, all the cases mentioned are unlikely to be pursued further, either because the plaintiffs have died or graduated (and were unable to certify a class action that would enable the claim to survive a ruling of mootness caused by graduation), or because the NCAA took subsequent actions to eliminate the basis for a claim.

For example, following the ruling in *Pryor*, the NCAA revised its initial eligibility standards once again, eliminating the elevated Proposition 16 minimum standardized test score by implementing a sliding scale in which a lower test score is allowable so long as it is balanced with a higher high school grade point average. Now that the offending portion of the eligibility standard has been removed, a plaintiff would find it very difficult to establish proof of the alleged intentional discrimination on the part of the NCAA.

Other federal statutes are not limited to federal funding recipients. For example, when athletes with learning disabilities have challenged the NCAA's eligibility requirements as applied to them, the courts have generally agreed that Title III of the Americans with Disabilities Act (ADA) applies. The NCAA, due to its control of athletic events at university facilities, has been ruled to be a place of public accommodation for purposes of the ADA (see, e.g., *Bowers v. NCAA*, 2000; *Ganden v. NCAA*, 1996; *Matthews v. NCAA*, 2001; *Tatum v. NCAA*, 1998). Thus, the ADA has successfully been used to place limits on the NCAA's ability to regulate eligibility of athletes with learning disabilities.

NCAA Business Practices and Federal Anti-Trust Statutes

Another example of a federal statute that does not require federal funding recipient status is the Sherman Act antitrust law; however, it has been held to have limited application to the NCAA's activities. Several U.S. District Court decisions concluded that the antitrust laws generally apply to the NCAA's business or commercial activities, but not to its promulgation of eligibility requirements (*College Athletic Placement Service, Inc. v. NCAA*, 1974; *Gaines v. NCAA*, 1990; *Jones v. NCAA*, 1975). Next we explore several of these cases to illustrate how the courts have treated NCAA regulations related to its business or commercial activities differently than those regulations related to amateurism and eligibility. We will also see that courts do not always agree as to where the line between the NCAA's business or commercial activities and regulatory activities related to amateurism should be drawn. First let's look at *NCAA v. Board of Regents of the University of Oklahoma* to see how the Supreme Court applied antitrust law in this situation.

NCAA v. Board of Regents of the University of Oklahoma

468 U.S. 85 (1984)	FOCUS CASE

FACTS

In 1981, the NCAA entered into exclusive multiyear contracts with the ABC and CBS television networks — contracts that were designed to limit the number of college football games that were televised. The NCAA's stated purpose was to prevent televised football from adversely affecting live spectator attendance at games. The College Football Association (CFA), a separate organization composed of major football powers within the NCAA, then negotiated its own contract with NBC in order to get more of its members' games televised. In response, the NCAA threatened disciplinary action against any CFA member university that honored the CFA's contracts with NBC. Two CFA members, the University of Oklahoma and the University of Georgia, sued the NCAA under § 1 of the Sherman Act, arguing that the NCAA's plan caused an unreasonable restraint of trade on teams that could otherwise obtain more television exposure. The district court found that the NCAA's television plan was illegal horizontal price-fixing and output limitation. The NCAA appealed, the Tenth Circuit affirmed, and the NCAA appealed again.

HOLDING

The Supreme Court affirmed, holding that the NCAA's plan violated § 1 of the Sherman Act.

RATIONALE

The Court found that the NCAA had provided no convincing evidence that its television plan promoted competitive balance among member institutions any more effectively than would restrictions on alumni donations or any other revenue-producing activity. It also would not protect live attendance because it allowed games to be broadcast at all hours during which the games were played. Applying the rule of reason analysis, the Court concluded that any procompetitive effects were outweighed by the anticompetitive effects — most particularly that fewer games would be telecast under the plan than in a free market, significantly suppressing consumption by television-viewing fans.

The *Board of Regents* decision was the first ruling by the U.S. Supreme Court to address NCAA business practices which restrained market competition and to distinguish those from NCAA restraints related to maintaining amateurism. The next few cases will highlight the many businesses and individuals impacted by NCAA regulations and business practices resulting in numerous antitrust lawsuits.

Rules Limiting the Number and Size of Logos on Athlete Uniforms

In *Adidas America, Inc. v. NCAA* (1999), Adidas sued under the Sherman Act alleging that the NCAA's Bylaw 12.5.5, which limited the number and size of manufacturers' trademarked logos on athletes' uniforms, was an unreasonable restraint on the market for promotional rights. This time, the Kansas federal district court held in favor of the NCAA. It found that the logo restriction rule did not provide the NCAA with any commercial advantage that could be construed as restraining trade. It further found that Bylaw 12.5.5 had a threefold purpose: (1) to support the NCAA's amateurism principle by protecting student-athletes from commercial exploitation; (2) to preserve the integrity of intercollegiate sports by preventing universities from turning their student-athletes into billboards in the pursuit of advertising revenues; and (3) to avoid excessive advertising that could interfere with the immediate identification of the athlete's number and team to teammates and to game officials. The court concluded that, similar to the NCAA's eligibility rules, the purpose and effect of Bylaw 12.5.5 was noncommercial in nature. Following the majority position that antitrust law is meant to apply only to commercial activity, the court held that the antitrust laws were inapplicable and denied Adidas' request for an injunction against NCAA enforcement of its rule.

Rules Restricting Earnings of Coaches

When the NCAA attempted to limit the number of coaches and restrict the earnings of coaches, these restrictions attracted challenges as illegal price fixing in violation of federal antitrust laws. Some universities have the wherewithal to hire the maximum allowable number of assistant coaches, but some do not. In 1992, in an attempt to cut escalating hiring costs in such a way as to maintain competitive balance among competing universities, the NCAA implemented a restricted earnings coach position for Division I sports (excluding football). A restricted earnings coach was limited by NCAA rules to a total annual compensation amount of $16,000. The following academic year, men's basketball assistant coaches affected by the new rule filed a class action suit alleging that the rule constituted an unreasonable restraint of trade under the Sherman Act (*Law v. NCAA*, 1998). The Tenth Circuit Court of Appeals held that the restricted earnings rule was **horizontal price fixing** (i.e., an agreement between parties to eliminate competitive pricing), which would normally be an automatic antitrust violation. The *Law* court followed the *NCAA v. Board of Regents* precedent and applied the rule of reason analysis normally reserved for anticompetitive business practices that have counterbalancing procompetitive effects. (See Chapter 10 for a more detailed discussion of rule of reason analysis.) The Tenth Circuit found that the anticompetitive effect of preventing experienced coaches from earning market value salaries outweighed any procompetitive effects identified by the NCAA, such as holding down rising athletic program costs and retaining entry-level coaching positions. In fact, the court found no evidence that these salary restrictions helped to hold down overall spending or that the restricted earnings coach positions were typically filled by entry-level applicants. Thus, the Tenth Circuit held that the restricted earnings salary cap violated antitrust law and affirmed the lower court's granting of the coaches' motion for summary judgment. In a court-approved settlement, the NCAA agreed to pay $54.5 million to be apportioned among the plaintiff coaches (*Law v. NCAA*, 2000).

Restraints on Post Season Tournaments Play

The antitrust laws have also been used to challenge the NCAA's efforts to regulate member institution participation in postseason tournament play. The NCAA had a long-standing rule that required colleges invited to its NCAA Championship Men's Basketball Tournament to accept that invitation over invitations to any others. The National Invitational Tournament (NIT) is a competing postseason tournament that is a year older than the NCAA Championship Tournament and that used to be a bigger event. In 1962, the NIT agreed to let the NCAA invite its teams first (Neumeister, 2005). Since then, the NCAA tournament has steadily increased in popularity. In 2001, the NIT sued under the antitrust laws, alleging that the NCAA was attempting to establish a monopoly and put it out of business. In 2005, the parties settled, with the NCAA agreeing to pay $56.5 million for the rights to both the preseason and postseason NIT tournaments (O'Connell, 2005). As part of the settlement agreement, the NCAA's invitation acceptance rule was retained, according to its lawyer, in order to prevent someone from luring the top teams to abandon the tournament for a more lucrative made-for-TV event (Neumeister, 2005).

Rules Limiting Approved Equipment Designs

In 2008, the NCAA changed its rule governing the dimensions of lacrosse stick heads in order to address player safety concerns arising from new stick head designs then in increasing use. The rule change rendered all 15 of Warrior Sports' stock of stick heads illegal, so they sued, asserting that the rule was an unreasonable restraint of trade. The Sixth Circuit found that the new rule applied equally to all stick manufacturers and, by the company's own admission, would "neutralize Warrior's … market position … opening the door and paving the way for new entrants." Stating that the Sherman Act protects competition, not competitors, the court concluded that the new rule had no adverse effect on competition. Because the rule of reason analysis requires evidence of anti-competitive effects, Warrior Sports had failed to state a claim upon which relief could be granted (*Warrior Sports, Inc. v. NCAA*, 2010).

Rules Restricting Postgraduate Eligibility

In *Smith v. NCAA* (1998), the plaintiff alleged that the NCAA rule restricting postbaccalaureate eligibility to the same school at which the athlete earned her undergraduate degree constituted an unreasonable restraint of trade under the Sherman Act. The district court had dismissed the claim holding that "the actions of the NCAA in refusing to waive the Postbaccalaureate bylaw and allow the plaintiff to participate in intercollegiate athletics is not the type of action to which the Sherman Act was meant to be applied" (*Smith v. NCAA*, 1997). On appeal, Smith argued that the district court erred in limiting the application of the Sherman Act to the NCAA's commercial and business activities. The Third Circuit disagreed with Smith and stated that the purpose of the antitrust laws is to prevent unreasonable restraints in business and commercial transactions. The court of appeals also acknowledged that at the time of this lawsuit, no court of appeals had expressly addressed the issue whether antitrust laws apply to the NCAA promulgation of eligibility rules. Ultimately, the court of appeals concluded that eligibility rules are not related to the NCAA's commercial or business activities because, unlike the commercial activities which are intended to provide the NCAA with a commercial advantage, eligibility rules primary seek to ensure fair competition in intercollegiate athletics.

Rules Restricting Athletics Based Financial Aid

In 2008, the U.S. District Court in Los Angeles approved a settlement of the *White v. NCAA* class action suit, which claimed that the NCAA's limiting of athletics-based aid to tuition, books, housing, and meals was an unreasonable restraint of trade in violation of antitrust law. Per the settlement agreement, the NCAA had to create a $10 million fund to which former athletes may apply to get assistance in covering educational expenses. The settlement also facilitated greater flexibility for athletes in accessing the NCAA's existing Student Assistance and Academic Enhancement funds (Elfman, 2008). In 2017–2018, distributions from the Student Assistance Fund and the Academic Enhancement Fund were $82.2 million and $46.7 million, respectively (NCAA, 2019).

As noted in *Smith* and revealed in the previous cases, while the NCAA has defended multiple antitrust challenges that involved rules imposing restrictions on athletes, only one court of appeals decision focused on the precise issue as to whether eligibility rules were subject to antitrust law. The NCAA has settled multiple cases challenging rules restraining athletes over the years rather than see those cases resolved in court. However, our next Focus Case may signal a significant shift in how NCAA rules imposing restrictions on athletes' financial opportunities will be evaluated when challenged in court under antitrust law.

O'Bannon v. NCAA

802 F.3d 1049 (9th Cir. 2015)   **FOCUS** CASE

FACTS

Ed O'Bannon was an NCAA men's basketball player at UCLA, where he was named MVP of the 1995 championship winning team. In 2008, he was visiting a friend's house when informed that his likeness was depicted in the NCAA Basketball game produced by EA. Thereafter, O'Bannon saw himself virtually represented in the game – the avatar looked like O'Bannon, played for UCLA and wore his jersey number. O'Bannon never consented to his likeness appearing in the video game and was not paid by EA, the NCAA or its licensing company, CLC, for the appearance. The NCAA is the governing body of intercollegiate sports for over 1,000 universities across the United States. Each of its Divisions – Division I, Division II, and Division III – has a set of bylaws that member institutions are required to follow to maintain good standing. Included in the NCAA's bylaws is an amateurism standard, which largely prohibits NCAA athletes from receiving compensation beyond a scholarship and does not allow them to profit off of the use of their name, image and likeness. O'Bannon sued the NCAA and CLC asserting that the prohibition of NCAA athletes profiting off of their names, images and likenesses under the NCAA amateurism rules violated § 1 of the Sherman Act. In a bench trial in U.S. district court, a federal judge applied the Rule of Reason and ruled for O'Bannon finding that prohibiting NCAA athletes from profiting off of their names, images and likenesses violates § 1 of the Sherman Act. The order permanently enjoined the NCAA from prohibiting its member schools from (1) compensating FBS football and Division I men's basketball players for the use of their NILs by awarding them grants-in-aid up to the full cost of attendance at their respective schools, or (2) paying up to $5,000 per year in deferred compensation to FBS football and Division I men's basketball players for the use of their NILs, through trust funds distributable after they leave school. The NCAA appealed the district court's decision to the Ninth Circuit Court of Appeals.

HOLDING

The NCAA's bylaws are subject to antitrust scrutiny. Applying the Rule of Reason test the Court of Appeals held NCAA bylaws violated federal antitrust law.

RATIONALE

The Ninth Circuit found that the Supreme Court's decision in *NCAA v. Board of Regents of the University of Oklahoma* (468 U.S. 85, 1984) did not hold that the NCAA's bylaws are valid under the Sherman Act, but rather, the Rule of Reason must be applied to determine their legality under the Sherman Act. Further, the Ninth Circuit found that the NCAA's bylaws prohibiting NCAA athletes from profiting off of their names, images, and likenesses are rules that regulate commercial activity and thus, subject to Sherman Act scrutiny. Additionally, the Ninth Circuit argued that the plaintiffs were injured in fact, because they were deprived of name, image and likeness compensation they would otherwise receive.

Applying the Rule of Reason, the Ninth Circuit found that the Sherman Act was violated by the NCAA's rules prohibiting NCAA athletes from profiting off of their names, images and likenesses. The NCAA's amateurism rule prohibiting NCAA athletes from profiting off of their names, images and likenesses was more restrictive than necessary to maintain amateurism and, thus, violated the Sherman Act. While the Ninth Circuit largely affirmed the district court's ruling, it found no evidence to rationalize the award of $5,000 per year in deferred compensation and thus, vacated that part of the order. The Ninth Circuit upheld the district court's order enjoining the NCAA from preventing member institutions from granting full cost of attendance scholarships.

Although appealed to the Supreme Court, the Court declined to hear it, thus leaving the topic of amateurism still somewhat unclear for the time being (McCann, 2016). A similar victory for student-athletes came in 2013 when Electronic Arts (EA Sports) settled for $40 million with plaintiffs alleging the uncompensated use of their name, image, and likeness in the company's college video games. While the Supreme Court's denial to hear the O'Bannon appeal is not entirely surprising, it leaves us with some unanswered questions. However, the court of appeals ruling does provide some good precedent and legal argument moving forward in other antitrust and amateur aspects circling the NCAA and its restraints on athletes (McCann, 2016).

The Knight Foundation's Commission on Intercollegiate Athletics

The Knight Commission, established in 1989 and composed of a group of university administrators concerned about the integrity of intercollegiate athletics, serves as a constraint on NCAA governance by being an influential advocate for reform. The Commission is composed of current and former university presidents and chancellors, trustees, and former student-athletes. Through the prompting of The Knight Commission, the NCAA now calculates an Academic Progress Rate (APR) for each member institution's athletics program that takes into account eligibility, graduation, and retention data. Failure to meet the NCAA's cut-off score can result in a team's loss of practice time, reduction in competition opportunities, loss of athletics scholarships, coaching suspensions, or restricted NCAA membership, as well as ability to compete in postseason championships (NCAA, 2019).

Considering the recent college basketball scandals surrounding the corruption and fraud charges against coaches and other athletic personnel for alleged bribery, laundering, and wire fraud involving sports apparel companies and sponsors, the Knight Commission is urging the NCAA to clean up the sport (To Speed Reform, 2019). The NCAA has adopted recommendations from the Commission in the past to give more freedom and flexibility to college basketball players in their professional pursuits, financial support for degree completion, harsher penalties for broken rules by school officials and administrators, and more independent membership to the NCAA Board of Governors (To Speed Reform, 2019). The recent motivations of the committee in light of the scandal is to seek transparency and ensure financial integrity in apparel and sponsorship deals (To Speed Reform, 2019). The NCAA recently took an important step by adopting a Knight Commission recommendation to reinstate annual, internal reporting of all athletically-related income received by athletics personnel from outside sources, including shoe and apparel companies, to their school. But the Knight Commission believes these disclosures must be made public.

Equity in Athletics Disclosure Act – 20 U.S.C. §§ 1092(e) and (g)

In 1994, Congress enacted the Equity in Athletics Disclosure Act, a statute that affects the governance of intercollegiate athletics by requiring university athletics programs to prepare, make available to the public, and submit to the U.S. Department of Education an annual report. This report is to contain information about such things as graduation rates, athletic scholarships, participation opportunities, revenues and expenditures, and coaches' gender and salaries. Because of this law, the public as well as the NCAA can better monitor member schools' progress toward improving the graduation rates of athletes and achieving gender equity.

"Regional" Governance: Intercollegiate Athletics Conferences

Athletics conferences comprise another significant layer in the governance of intercollegiate athletics. These conferences are organized to provide regular competition among relatively similar universities within loosely defined geographic regions. The member institutions pay a fee to join the athletics

Exhibit 11.11 Areas of athletics typically regulated by intercollegiate athletic conferences.

- Governance policies and procedures
- Conference membership requirements
- Rules compliance and enforcement procedures
- General athletics regulations

  o Eligibility
  o Financial aid
  o Recruiting
  o Sportsmanship
  o Control of relationships with the broadcast media
  o Scheduling of competitions
  o Procedures for hosting conference championships
  o Crowd control policies
  o Ticket distribution policies

conference, as well as regular membership dues, and they agree to abide by the conference constitution and regulations. The athletics conferences composed of NCAA member institutions are themselves members of the NCAA, so these conferences require their member institutions' athletics programs to abide by NCAA regulations unless the conference rules are more stringent. Each intercollegiate athletics conference has its own set of athletics regulations, which may cover the areas listed in Exhibit 11.11 (see, e.g., Pacific-12 Conference, 2019). Since athletics conferences are voluntary and private membership organizations (like the NCAA), the courts consider them nonstate actors and would probably grant a level of judicial deference in ruling on challenges to the application of conference regulations, similar to the deference that they accord the NCAA and would be unlikely to subject an athletic conference to any level of constitutional scrutiny.

For the most part, the relationships between the athletic conferences and the member institutions is a harmonious relationship. However, a cycle of conference realignment between 2010 and 2012 also led to some litigation related to exit fees and revenue distribution. An athletics conference's constitution is considered a contract between the member universities of the conference. (See Chapter 3 for more information on contracts.) This principle was highlighted in *Trustees of Boston College v. The Big East Conference* (2004). When several universities chose to defect from the Big East Conference to join the Atlantic Coast Conference (ACC), the Big East attempted to prevent their departure by amending its constitution to quintuple the penalty for withdrawal from $1 million to $5 million. The court applied contract law principles in holding that the Big East's constitutional amendment had not been adopted in accordance with its own constitutional procedures. Therefore, it ruled that Boston College was entitled to withdraw from the conference upon payment of the $1 million withdrawal fee found in the original contractual agreement (the constitution). The court further ruled that, until the effective date of its withdrawal, Boston College was entitled to retain the same rights and benefits provided to all other members of the Big East conference, with the exception of voting rights.

When an institution leaves a conference, the separation can become problematic as well. In 2012, Rutgers sued the Big East conference over their attempt to enforce the multi-million dollar exit fee or waiting period before leaving (Heyboer & Luicci, 2019). Rutgers argued the Big East was arbitrarily enforcing the rules against them when they had allowed Syracuse, West Virginia University, the University of Pittsburgh, and TCU to leave without such penalty (Heyboer & Luicci, 2019). In the alternative, we also see conferences bring claims against institutions, such as when the ACC sued Maryland for the $50 million exit fee when they left for the Big Ten (The Associated Press, 2012). As is evident, the contractual agreements and relationships between conferences and member institutions can become convoluted, particularly when multi-millions of dollars are on the line.

Competitive Advantage Strategies

Governance and Regulatory Authority in College Athletics

- If you work in an intercollegiate athletics setting, be sure you are familiar with your national collegiate athletic association's rules and regulations, in particular its waiver procedures and infractions investigation and rules enforcement processes. If you are a high-level administrator, take steps to ensure that your staff is also familiar with its state high school association's processes in these matters.
- If you work in management for a company like Adidas and your business is negatively affected by a sport organization's rules, you may consider seeking a remedy under the antitrust laws. If you do so, work closely with your lawyer to arrive at an appropriate interpretation of whether the sport organization's rule regulates commercial activity so that you can make the best decision about whether you have a likelihood of success in court. With a justifiable argument that the rule has a commercial purpose and effect, the court will be less likely to reject your claim before it even begins to apply the rule of reason analysis.
- To avoid lawsuits, school administrators should follow a standard process before suspending or expelling student-athletes at both the high school and collegiate level
- Utilizing consistent procedures to establish consistent punishments across offense and sport will more fairly govern each individual case

Conclusion

Sports governing bodies have asserted broad authority to regulate interscholastic and intercollegiate athletics. The NCAA's status as a nonstate actor has insulated it from legal attack in many areas. Nevertheless, public visibility keeps the pressure on the NCAA to enact reform measures that minimize image problems resulting from the public perception of injustice. In contrast, state high school athletic associations (the majority position is that they are state actors) operate under greater restrictions because constitutional protections of rights and civil liberties apply to them. Additionally, federal and state statutory laws (including antidiscrimination laws, antitrust laws, and tax laws) function to limit the regulatory authority of the NCAA, athletic conferences, and state high school athletic associations. Other factors influencing the governance of college athletics include the Knight Commission and the Equity in Athletics Disclosure Act, both of which serve as agents of reform. Additionally, even without precedent that establishes a property interest in sport participation, the changing tides athletics and the ever-evolving governance of such means sport managers need to be thinking ahead (Saturday et al., 2018).

In the final analysis, governing bodies in interscholastic and intercollegiate athletics are frequently granted judicial deference to their rule-making and enforcement decisions and thus are able to exercise broad regulatory authority.

Discussion Questions

1. What interest do you think high school athletic associations have in governing high school athletics?
2. How do you feel about pay-to-play programs and their relationship to the creation of a property interest? Did your high school require students to pay a fee to participate in extracurricular activities such as athletics?
3. After the *Tarkanian* decision, public universities can, by acting collectively through the NCAA, regulate areas that they might not be able to regulate on their own. For example, the NCAA can conduct drug testing of student-athletes without having to face scrutiny under the Fourth Amendment prohibition

of unreasonable searches. But if a public university implemented its own drug testing program, the Fourth Amendment would apply (see Chapter 12 for a fuller explication of this issue). Can you make a rational argument for why this is just? How about for why it is unjust?

4 In Sherman Act antitrust cases, the commercial activities of sport organizations are treated differently from those of other types of businesses. Why is this so?

5 Does the *Tarkanian* case provide another example of a situation where some sport organizations are different from other types of business organizations? That is, should courts consider the special nature of sport organizations and carve out an exception to the state action doctrine for collective membership organizations like the NCAA? Or should constitutional issues be treated differently than antitrust issues?

6 Why do you think the Knight Commission pushed for a regularly recurring external objective review of university athletics programs?

7 Why do you think courts are reluctant to become involved with the activities and membership governance of private, voluntary associations?

8 What are some examples of when a court should interfere with the activities of a private association? Why do you think this is important to the sport industry?

9 As a result of the 2020 Covid-19 national pandemic, many NCAA student athletes had their seasons canceled. What implications on eligibility does such an incident have? With such a large amount of athletes having an extra year of eligibility, what impacts might be seen by incoming recruits and scholarships?

Learning Activity

1 Research some of the extracurricular eligibility rules from your former high school and try to determine the purpose behind the rule. Is there an eligibility restriction if a student-athlete is over the age of 19? Why would a school want to prevent someone over the age of 19 from participating in interscholastic athletics? Fairness? Safety? What else?

2 Using an online database such as NEXIS UNI or Westlaw, locate the *McNatt* (1995) and *Davis* (1995) decisions about whether home-schooled students should be allowed to participate in interscholastic athletics. From those cases, distill the arguments for and against allowing such students to participate.

3 Go to the website for the Knight Commission (www.knightcommission.org) and write a two-page summary of one of the commission's most recent white papers related reform and governance issues in college athletics.

4 Locate a copy of the complete opinion from *O'Bannon v. NCAA* (2015). Read it with the following question in mind: Should student-athletes be paid for the use of their name, image, and likeness, or does the institution have a valid argument to claim their use as a part of their well-established programs? Write a two-page rationale for why you would or would not support the court's reasoning in this case.

Case Study

In coordination with a review of the *Oliver v. NCAA* case discussed earlier in this chapter, read the following Vice Sports article: How a Little-Known NCAA Rule Shuts Athletes Out of the Legal System by Steve Silver from https://www.vice.com/en_us/article/8qy533/how-a-little-known-ncaa-rule-shuts-athletes-out-of-the-legal-system. The article points out whether the Restitution Rule makes it even worth the risk of pursuing litigation against the NCAA when a student-athlete has a complaint. After reviewing the case and reading the article, write a position paper articulating a rationale for whether or not the NCAA's Restitution Rule is against public policy.

References

Cases

Adidas America, Inc. v. NCAA, 40 F. Supp. 2d 1275 (D. Kan. 1999).

Bloom v. NCAA, 93 P.3d 621 (Colo. Ct. App. 2004).

Bowers v. NCAA, 118 F. Supp. 2d 494 (D.N.J. 2000).

Brentwood Academy v. Tennessee Secondary Sch. Athletic Ass'n, 531 U.S. 288 (2001), *remanded* to 304 F. Supp. 2d 981 (M.D. Tenn. 2003).

Brentwood Academy v. Tennessee Secondary Sch. Athletic Ass'n, 2008 U.S. Dist. LEXIS 55312 (M.D. Tenn. 2008).

Cohane v. NCAA, 2007 U.S. App. LEXIS 1841 (2d Cir. 2007), *cert. denied*, 2007 U.S. LEXIS 12179 (2007).

College Athletic Placement Serv., Inc. v. NCAA, 1974 U.S. Dist. LEXIS 7050 (D.N.J. 1974).

Communities for Equity v. Michigan High Sch. Athletic Ass'n, 377 F.3d 504 (2004)Cureton v. NCAA, 37 F. Supp. 2d 687 (E.D. Pa. 1999), *rev'd*, 198 F.3d 107 (3d Cir. 1999).

Davis v. Massachusetts Interscholastic Athletic Ass'n, 1995 Mass. Super. LEXIS 791 (Mass. Super. 1995).

Gaines v. NCAA, 746 F. Supp. 738 (M.D. Tenn. 1990).

Ganden v. NCAA, 1996 U.S. Dist. LEXIS 17368 (N.D. Ill. 1996).

Goss v. Lopez, 419 U.S. 565 (1975).

Jones v. NCAA, 392 F. Supp. 295 (D. Mass. 1975).

Korematsu v. United States, 323 U.S. 214 (1944).

Law v. NCAA, 134 F.3d 1010 (10th Cir. 1998).

Law v. NCAA, 108 F. Supp. 2d 1193 (D. Kan. 2000).

Letendre v. Missouri State High Sch. Activities Ass'n, 86 S.W.3d 63 (Mo. Ct. App. 2002).

Ludtke v. Kuhn, 461 F. Supp. 86 (S.D.N.Y. 1978).

Maki v. Minn. State High Sch. League, Case No. 16-cv-4148 (D. Minn. 2016).

Mathews v. Eldridge, 424 U.S. 319 (1976).

Matthews v. NCAA, 179 F. Supp. 2d 1209 (E.D. Wash. 2001).

McCormack v. NCAA, 845 F.2d 1338 (5th Cir. 1988).

McGowan v. Maryland, 366 U.S. 420 (1961).

McNatt v. Frazier Sch. Dist., 1995 U.S. Dist. LEXIS 21971 (W.D. Pa. 1995).

NCAA v. Board of Regents of the Univ. of Okla., 468 U.S. 85 (1984).

NCAA v. Miller, 10 F.3d 633 (9th Cir. 1993), *cert. denied*, U.S. LEXIS 2914 (1994).

NCAA v. Smith, 525 U.S. 459 (1999).

NCAA v. Tarkanian, 488 U.S. 179 (1988).

O'Bannon v. NCAA, 802 F.3d 1049 (9th Cir. 2015).

Oliver v. NCAA, Case No. 2008-CV-0762, Ct. of Common Pleas, Erie County, OH (2009).

Pryor v. NCAA, 153 F. Supp. 2d 710 (E.D. Pa. 2001), *aff'd in part, rev'd in part, and remanded*, 288 F.3d 548 (3d Cir. 2002).

Rostker v. Goldberg, 453 U.S. 57 (1981).

Smith v. NCAA, 978 F. Supp. 213 (W.D. Pa. 1997).

Smith v. NCAA, 139 F.3d 180 (3d Cir. 1998).

Smith v. NCAA, 266 F.3d 152 (3d Cir. 2001).

St. Augustine High School v. Louisiana High School Athletic Ass'n, 270 F. Supp. 767 (E.D. La. 1967), *aff'd*, 396 F.2d 224 (5th Cir. 1968).

Swanson, C. B. (2002). Spending time or investing time? Involvement in high school curricular and extracurricular activities as strategic action. *Rationality & Society*, 14(4), 431–471. Retrieved March 01, 2017, from cswanson@ ui.urban.org

Tatum v. NCAA, 992 F. Supp. 1114 (E.D. Mo. 1998).

Taylor v. Enumclaw School District, 132 Wn. App. 688 (2006).

Tennessee Secondary Sch. Athletic Ass'n v. Brentwood Academy, 551 U.S. 291 (2007).

Trustees of Boston College v. The Big East Conference, 2004 Mass. Super. LEXIS 298 (Mass. Super. 2004).

Warrior Sports, Inc. v. NCAA, 2010 U.S. App. LEXIS 17650 (6th Cir. 2010).

Statutes

Equity in Athletics Disclosure Act of 1994, 20 U.S.C. §§ 1092(e) and (g).

Sherman Act, 15 U.S.C. §§ 1–3.

Other Sources

Batista, P. J., & Hatfield, L. C. (2005). Learn at home, play at school: A state-by-state examination of legislation, litigation and athletic association rules governing public school athletic participation by homeschool students. *Journal of Legal Aspects of Sport*, 15, 213–255.

Cook, B. (2012, August 20). Will "pay to play" become a permanent part of school sports? *Forbes*. Retrieved from http://www.forbes.com/sites/bobcook/2012/08/22/will-pay-to-play-become-a-permanent-part-of-school-sports/#79f2897e57c9.

Despain, J. J. (2015). From off the bench: The potential role of the U.S. Department of Education in reforming due process in the National Collegiate Athletic Association. *SSRN Electronic Journal*. doi: 10.2139/ssrn.2490113.

Elfman, L. (2008, August 8). NCAA to provide former student-athletes with benefits. *Diverse Online*. Retrieved from www.diverseeducation.com/artman/publish/printer_11535.shtml.

Farris, M. P., & Smith, J. M. (2019, July 26). State laws concerning participation of homeschool students in public school activities. *Home School Legal Defense Association*. Retrieved from https://hslda.org/content/docs/nche/Issues/E/Equal_Access.pdf.

Heyboer, K., & Luicci, T. (2012, December 6). Messy divorce: Rutgers sues Big East for breach of contract over $10M exit fee. Retrieved from https://www.nj.com/rutgersfootball/2012/12/rutgers_suit_against_big_east.html.

Knight Commission. (2019, May 24). To speed reform, Knight Commission calls for more transparency in college basketball. *Knight Commission on Intercollegiate Athletics*. Retrieved from https://www.knightcommission.org/2019/05/to-speed-reform-knight-commission-calls-for-more-transparency-in-college-basketball/.

Lederman, D. (2019, August 2). NCAA unveils details of new rules-enforcement process. *Inside Higher Ed*. Retrieved from https://www.insidehighered.com/quicktakes/2019/08/02/ncaa-unveils-details-new-rules-enforcement-process.

McCann, M. (2016, October 3). Supreme Court decision leaves NCAA amateurism in limbo. *Sports Illustrated*. Retrieved from https://www.si.com/college/2016/10/03/ed-obannon-ncaa-lawsuit-supreme-court.

Munczinski, A. (2003). Interception – The courts get another pass at the NCAA and the intentional discrimination of proposition 16 in Pryor v. NCAA.*Villanova Sports and Entertainment Law Journal*, 10(2), 389–414.

National Youth Sports Program (n.d.). Retrieved from www.utoledo.edu/eduhshs/clinics/nysp/nationalyouth.html.

NCAA (2014, May 1) Division I Governance Model Review. *NCAA*. Retrieved from www.ncaa.org.

NCAA (2019). *2019–2020 NCAA Division I Manual*. Indianapolis, IN: NCAA Publications.

Neumeister, L. (2005, August 16). Tentative settlement announced in NIT vs. NCAA case. *Associated Press State and Local Wire*. Retrieved from LEXIS-NEXIS.

New, J. (2014, August 8). NCAA adopts structure giving autonomy to richest Division I leagues, votes to college athletes. Retrieved from https://www.insidehighered.com/news/2014/08/08/ncaa-adopts-structure-giving-autonomy-richest-division-i-leagues-votes-college.

NFHS. (2018). High school sports participation increases for 29th consecutive year. Retrieved from www.nfhs.org.

Nwadike, A. C., Baker, A. R., Brackebusch, V. B., & Hawkins, B. J. (2016). Institutional racism in the NCAA and the racial implications of the "2.3 or Take a knee" legislation. *Marquette Sports Law Review*, 26(2), 523–543.

O'Connell, J. (2005, August 18). NCAA purchases NIT for $56.5 million to end legal fight. *Associated Press State and Local Wire*. Retrieved from LEXIS-NEXIS.

Otto, K. A., & Stippich, K. S. (2008). Revisiting Tarkanian : The entwinement and interdependence of the NCAA and state universities and colleges 20 years later. *Journal of Legal Aspects of Sport*, 18, 243–308.

Pacific-12 Conference (2012). *2012–13 Pac-12 Handbook*. Retrieved from http://compliance.pac-12.org.

Potuto, J. R. (2012). NCAA as state actor controversy: Much ado about nothing. *Marquette Sports Law Review*, 23, 1–44.

Saturday, D., Siegrist, A., & Czekanski, W. A. (2018). Get off the courts: Using ADR principles to resolve high school sport disputes. *Marquette Sports Law Review*, 28(2), 359–378.

Should home-schoolers take the field? (2013, February 12). *Washington Post* (editorial board opinion), p. A16. Retrieved from LEXIS-NEXIS.

Siegrist, A., & Blosio, N. (2015). An examination of the language governing athlete agents. *The Legal Blitz*. Retrieved from http://thelegalblitz.com/blog/2015/08/18/an-examination-of-the-language-governing-athlete-agents/.

Siegrist, A., Czekanski, W. A., & Silver, S. (2016). Interscholastic athletics and due process protection: Student-athletes continue to knock on the door of due process. *Mississippi Sports Law Review*, 6(1), 1–22.

Silver, S. (2016, December 20). How a little-known NCAA rule shuts athletes out of the legal system. *VICE*. Retrieved from https://www.vice.com/en_us/article/8qy533/how-a-little-known-ncaa-rule-shuts-athletes-out-of-the-legal-system.

Smith, S. H., & Dempsey, C. W. (1997, October 20). Editorial – Newspaper failed to tell whole story. Comment in *The NCAA News*. Retrieved from www.ncaa.org/news/1997/19971020/comment.html.

Spears, V. H. (2017, December 15). Can Kentucky charter schools have basketball teams? (And other burning questions). *Lexington Herald Leader*. Retrieved from https://www.kentucky.com/news/local/education/article189942499.html.

Sports and Charter Schools (2019, May 20). *American Preparatory Schools*. Retrieved from https://www.americanprep.org/sports-and-charter-schools/.

Swanson, R. A., & Spears, B. (1995). *History of sport and physical education in the United States* (4th ed.). Dubuque, IA: W. C. Brown.

The Associated Press (2012, November 27). ACC files lawsuit against Maryland. Retrieved October 20, 2019, from https://www.nj.com/collegefootball/2012/11/acc_files_lawsuit_against_mary.html.

UHSAA Handbook (2019).Utah High School Activities Association: Handbook 2019–2020. Retrieved from https://www.uhsaa.org/handbook/.

Web Resources

www.ncaa.org ■ The NCAA is the largest governing body in college sports. At this website you can find news, information on the NCAA's governance structure, NCAA rules, and a lot of other information related to intercollegiate athletics.

www.osaa.org ■ Here the Oregon State High School Activities Association (OSAA) has a page for Support & Equity on their webpage with resources in anti-discrimination, anti-hazing and more. In addition, note that each state high school association provides its own website with resources.

www.nfhs.org ■This is the website for the National Federation of State High School Associations, the governing body that oversees interscholastic athletics for more than seven million high schools. Under the "Athletic Activities" tab, the organization provides rules, regulations, resources, and more for each recognized high school sport.

www.theacc.com ■ At websites of intercollegiate athletics conferences like this one, you will find news, conference rules, and information about the conference governance structure, among other things. Many of them include annual reports discussing the mission statement, vision statement, core values, and administrative structures.

www.thedrakegroup.org ■This website provides a resource for Academic Integrity in Collegiate Sport. It offers updates and discussion on NCAA Reform centered around the current hot topics in academic integrity, antitrust, athlete compensation, enforcement and due process, and more.

www.ncpanow.org ■ The National College Players Association website aims to provide information, resources and garner support for ensuring the protection of future, current and former college athletes.

www.sc.edu/study/colleges_schools/hrsm/research/centers/college_sport_research_institute/index.php/ ■ Here is a resource to the College Sport Research Institute which comes out of the University of South Carolina. It disseminates information and college-sport research results to academics, college-sport practitioners and the general public.

12 Regulation of Participation and Athlete Rights in High School and College Athletics

Erica J. Zonder

Introduction

As we saw in Chapter 11, the U.S. Constitution guarantees certain rights through several Amendments. In Chapter 11, Equal Protection and Due Process rights contained in the Fifth and Fourteenth Amendments were presented and we will further examine those rights as they relate to participation of athletes in high school and college. Additionally, the First and Fourth Amendments have applicability to participant rights, as do Title IX, Title VI, and § 504/ADA. Each of these constitutional provisions and federal anti-discrimination statutes that apply to participant rights are the focus on this chapter. Therefore, this chapter focuses on legal issues concerning regulation of high school and college athletic participants in the areas of eligibility/discipline issues, transfer rules, drug testing, religious discrimination, freedom of expression in national anthem protests and social media, dress and grooming codes, gender equity, race, and disability discrimination. Exhibit 12.1 outlines the management contexts, legal issues, and relevant law discussed in this chapter.

Constitutional Challenges for Schools and Universities

Eligibility, Discipline, and Transfer Rules

Eligibility and Discipline

In eligibility cases, an issue has often been whether a student has a right to participate in athletics that cannot be taken away without appropriate due process (usually fair notice and a hearing as we discussed in Chapter 11; see Exhibit 11.3). Some courts have found a protected property interest in an athletic scholarship or a liberty interest in one's reputation as a star athlete, but that is not the majority position.

As we also discussed in Chapter 11, most courts have held that athletic participation is a privilege, not a right that is protected by the Due Process Clause. In *Palmer v. Merluzzi* (1988), a high school football player was suspended from the team for 60 days, in addition to receiving a ten-day suspension from school, for consuming marijuana and beer on campus. The football suspension was challenged under the Due Process Clause because the athlete had had no notice that this penalty existed, nor had he received a hearing before he was suspended from the team. The district court followed the majority of states in ruling that there is no due process liberty or property interest that generates a right to participate in school athletics; instead, participation is a privilege, and therefore the student had no right to receive due process.

Sometimes, however, an unduly lengthy suspension from athletics will trigger a court to find that a student-athlete was entitled to due process. In *Pegram v. Nelson* (1979), a high school student received a ten-day suspension from school and a four-month suspension from extracurricular activities. The court ruled that although the opportunity to participate was not in itself a property right, "total exclusion from participation ... for a lengthy period of time could ... be sufficient deprivation to implicate due process." This decision appears to be based on the idea that such a lengthy suspension deprived the student of too large

Exhibit 12.1 Management contexts and legal issues pertaining to regulation of amateur participation in interscholastic and intercollegiate athletics, with relevant laws and cases.

Management Context	Major Legal Issues	Relevant Law	Illustrative Cases
High School & College Athletics	Eligibility and Discipline issues	Due Process Clause; Equal Protection Clause	Bunger, Palmer, Pegram, Long
	Transfer rules	Due Process Clause, Arbitrary and capricious standard	Yeo, Wideman, DeLaTorre
	Drug testing	Fourth Amendment	Derdeyn, Vernonia, Earls
	Dress/grooming codes	First Amendment; Equal Protection Clause	Stephenson, Stotts, Dunham, Menora, Moody
	Pregame prayer	First Amendment	Santa Fe, Chandler, Kountze
	National Anthem	First Amendment	V.A.
	Social Media	First Amendment	T.V.
	Gender Equity	Title IX and regulations	Cohen, Mercer, EMU, Adrian, Biedeger
	Pregnancy	Title IX	Brady
	Sexual harassment	Title IX	Morrison, Jennings, Simpson
	Transgender	Title IX	Boyertown
	Race discrimination	Title VI	Elliott, Pryor
	Disability discrimination	§ 504; ADA	Knapp, Dennin, Matthews

a portion of the overall education process – a process that is partly comprised of extracurricular activities. As we discussed in Chapter 11, in *Maki v. Minn. State H.S. League* (2016) even though the court held Maki did not have a protected property right in varsity athletic competition, in reaching that conclusion, the court did recognize that Maki's deprivation was only limited to varsity athletic competition in a single sport and that numerous other activities were still available for Maki. This would seem to reinforce the notion that short-term deprivation of participation rights or deprivation of only one type of activity would not rise to the level of a total exclusion sufficient to trigger any due process rights.

In a very few cases, some students have successfully identified a recognizable property interest related to athletics participation when that participation could be connected to something tangible such as a scholarship opportunity, based on the notion that such participation could lead to a valuable college athletic scholarship without which a student might be unable to attend (*Boyd v. Board of Directors*, 1985; *Duffley v. New Hampshire Interscholastic Athletic Association*, 1982). The courts justified these decisions partly on the basis of the high skill level of the athletes. However, the Texas Supreme Court held that an athlete's high level of skill and earnings potential did not overcome the speculative nature of her interest in future financial opportunities based on her reputation in her sport and refused to recognize a protected property or liberty interest in her reputation (*NCAA v. Yeo*, 2005). The *Yeo* case is discussed later in the chapter in conjunction with transfer rules.

While not dealing with discipline, a recent case reaffirmed that participating in sports is a privilege. In 2018, a student at Ladue Horton Watkins High School in Missouri alleged that a "policy" banning male students-athletes with junior standing from playing on the JV team if they didn't make varsity was a violation of several laws, including Title IX, and sought an injunction. At a hearing, the varsity coach testified that because freshman and sophomores have more remaining years of eligibility, they had more opportunity to improve and their development was prioritized (*Doe v. Ladue Horton Watkins High School*, 2018, p. 4). The school argued that "Doe will suffer no harm because he has no legal right to participate in high school sports" (p. 5) and the court agreed, stating that courts have "long held" that participation in interscholastic athletics was not a property right but a privilege (p. 6).

Disciplinary rules have also been challenged under the Equal Protection Clause. (To refresh your memory on the strict scrutiny, intermediate scrutiny, and rational basis review tests used in Equal Protection Clause analysis, refer back to Exhibit 11.5 and the accompanying text.) In *Palmer v. Merluzzi* (1988), the court was also asked to decide whether the school's good conduct rule unfairly singled out athletes as its focus by subjecting them, and not other students, to punishment if they had not "demonstrated good citizenship and responsibility." Because the category "athletes" is not a suspect classification, the court applied the easiest test – rational basis review – and upheld the use of suspensions as a reasonable means of achieving the school's legitimate goal of enforcing compliance with its drug and alcohol policy.

Transfer Rules

Both high school athletic associations and college athletic associations have rules in place regulating the circumstances under which athletes may transfer to other schools or colleges. The intent of transfer rules on the high school level is to regulate the behavior of school districts that might attempt to entice a star athlete to move from one school district to another. Transfers should be based on reasons other than athletic competition. For example, in the case of *Indiana High School Athletic Association v. Wideman* (1997), the Indiana High School Athletic Association (IHSAA) had decided that a student who transferred to another school district should be ineligible for a year of competition in her sport. The IHSAA Transfer Rule 19-4 penalized students who transferred "primarily for athletic reasons" and finding them ineligible to participate in interschool athletics at the new school for a period not to exceed 365 days. Rule 19.5 allowed students who transferred to a new school immediate eligibility provided the change of residence was bona fide. Therefore, the motivation behind the student's move was a factual issue. The court found that there was substantial evidence that the move in this case was for legitimate family, health, and employment concerns rather than athletic reasons, and the initial ruling by the IHSAA was "arbitrary and capricious," or without reasonable grounds or adequate consideration of the circumstances (see "Judicial deference to educational policy" and *Letendre* in Chapter 11). The Wideman family had several reasons for moving, including an elderly grandfather who could not live independently, a long work commute, and that commute's effect on the father's multiple sclerosis. As the IHSAA is a quasi-public institution, there is an overriding public interest that it does not act arbitrarily in dealing with student-athletes, and further that the public interest would not be disserved by granting the plaintiff injunctive relief.

In 2016, a high school soccer player ruled ineligible brought a lawsuit alleging a violation of his right to due process under the Fourteenth Amendment. The student, who lived with his mother and stepfather and attended ninth grade at Cretin-Derham Hall High School (CDH) in Minnesota, moved to Mexico to live with his father for tenth grade. He returned to CDH for his junior year and wanted to play varsity soccer. The Minnesota State High School League (MSHSL) ruled him ineligible for his junior year as he had two transfers and must sit out one year. And further, the MSHSL had a divorce waiver that could be used once that the plaintiff did not use, but even if he had, it would apply to the first transfer to Mexico (*DeLaTorre v. Minnesota State High School League*, 2016). According to the court, in order to make out a procedural due process claim, the plaintiff had the burden of showing that he was deprived of a life, liberty, or property interest protected by the Due Process Clause and was not afforded adequate procedural rights prior to that deprivation. The court ruled that while the plaintiff's legitimate entitlement to a public education is a property interest that is protected by the Due Process Clause, eligibility for interscholastic varsity athletic competition is not included. The property right protected by the Due Process Clause is the entire educational process and not the right to participate in each individual component (see *Goss*). The plaintiff had notice of the MSHSL's eligibility bylaws, he was given meaningful opportunity to be heard (there were several emails, conversations, and a hearing), and ultimately had his eligibility restored by February of that school year. He "received sufficient process that satisfied whatever requirements the Due Process Clause might impose" (p. 24). The court also dismissed the student's claim that the ineligibility determination was arbitrary.

On the college level, transfer rules are an attempt to ensure competitive balance. A student who transfers from one four-year college to another is prohibited by NCAA rules from participating in athletic competition for a year, but this restriction may be waived under certain circumstances. The standard for a waiver was "mitigating circumstances" in 2018, and "extenuating, extraordinary and mitigating circumstances" in 2019 (Rosenberg, 2019). The following Focus Case deals with a transfer rule.

NCAA v. Yeo

FACTS

Joscelin Yeo from Singapore was a world-class swimmer when she was recruited to swim at the University of California at Berkeley. She was an All-American swimmer while at Berkeley and was a member of a world record-setting relay team in 1999.

Yeo's coach at Berkeley left for employment at the University of Texas (UT), and Yeo then transferred to UT. The NCAA transfer rule prohibited her from swimming at UT for a full academic year unless Berkeley agreed to waive this restriction. Berkeley would not waive it, so Yeo was ineligible for an academic year.

Yeo did not enroll in classes in that fall semester so that she could compete in the 2000 Olympics. She enrolled in classes in the spring but did not compete. UT mistakenly believed that the fall 2000 semester counted toward the time Yeo had to sit out, and so she was allowed to compete in the fall of 2001. Berkeley complained about this, and the NCAA determined that the fall 2000 semester did not count toward satisfying the transfer rule because of the way in which they interpreted another rule related to her having competed in the Olympics that semester.

Therefore, the NCAA ruled that Yeo had to sit out more events in the Spring 2002 semester to complete her inactive year. The end result was that Yeo would not have been able to participate in the Spring 2002 NCAA national swimming and diving championship. More than once during this string of rules interpretations pertaining to Yeo's eligibility, UT made adverse eligibility decisions without telling her in time for her to present her side of the story. Because of this, Yeo sought an injunction against UT, claiming a due process violation. She won, and she was permitted to compete in the championship event. After a trial, the lower court decided that UT had denied her procedural due process by depriving her, without fair process, of a protected liberty interest in her reputation and a property interest in her endorsement offers. The state court of appeals affirmed, and the NCAA and UT appealed.

HOLDING

The Texas Supreme Court reversed, holding that Yeo was not entitled to due process because she had no protected interest in college athletics participation.

RATIONALE

The court noted that the overwhelming majority of jurisdictions hold that students do not possess a constitutionally protected interest in their participation in extracurricular activities. Thus, participation alone does not rise to the level of a protectable property or liberty interest.

In this case, Yeo had argued that her case should be treated differently because of her unique reputation as a world-class swimmer, especially in her native land of Singapore and because of her earning potential in the sport of swimming. Yeo contended that it is the *degree* of her interests, and not merely the *character* of those interests, that should bring them within constitutional protection.

The court disagreed, however, and stated that whether an interest is protected by due process depends upon the nature of the interest, not its weight. The nature of one's interest in a good reputation is the same no matter how good the reputation is. Furthermore, Yeo's claimed interest in future financial opportunities was too speculative to deserve due process protection. Thus, Yeo had no constitutionally protected interests.

Exhibit 12.2 Fourth Amendment, United States Constitution.

"The right of the people to be secure in their persons, houses, papers, and effects, against unreasonable searches and seizures, shall not be violated, and no warrants shall issue, but upon probable cause, supported by oath or affirmation, and particularly describing the place to be searched and the persons or things to be seized."

Drug Testing

As we know, when a state high school athletic association or public high school adopts drug-testing programs, those requirements are subject to constitutional scrutiny. Specifically, drug-testing programs can be challenged under the Fourth Amendment which restrains the government from conducting unreasonable searches and seizures (see Exhibit 12.2). Of course, not all searches are forbidden under the Fourth Amendment, only unreasonable searches are prohibited. Additionally, an initial question arises as to whether a drug test is a search or seizure. Courts have uniformly agreed that a mandatory urine, blood, or breath test constitutes a search under the Fourth Amendment. Thus, the focus of the courts then turns to the "reasonableness" of that search in the context of a mandatory drug-testing program. The primary legal analysis in drug-testing cases involves application of a balancing test to evaluate the reasonableness of the search under the Fourth Amendment (see Exhibit 12.3). Essentially, the individual's privacy interest is weighed against the government's interest in conducting the search (i.e., drug test). This analysis considers both the manner in which the drug test is conducted and the purposes served by the drug test.

Student-athletes in both high school and college settings are routinely subjected to mandatory drug testing. These drug-testing programs can be conducted in a variety of ways. For example, a urine test can be collected by permitting a student to urinate privately while someone listens for the sounds of urination (auditory observation). It may also be collected under direct observation of urination (visual observation). Tests can be conducted randomly or as a result of personal behavior or appearance that may indicate drug use. A drug test can be required in order to be permitted to participate at the beginning of a sports season or conducted at the conclusion of a tournament or season. Positive tests can lead to retesting, warnings, voluntary or mandatory counseling, and even dismissal or disqualification of eligibility.

In 2017, the NCAA surveyed approximately 23,000 student-athletes and found that 77 percent reported having used alcohol and 24 percent had used marijuana that year, while only 1.5 percent had used amphetamines, and 0.4 percent reported use of anabolic steroids (NCAA, 2018c). Nevertheless, there

Exhibit 12.3 Legal analysis of a drug-testing search under the Fourth Amendment.

In general, the issues in a student-athlete drug testing case proceed as follows:

1 Was there state action? If yes,
2 Does the complained-of activity constitute a search and/or seizure? If yes,
3 Was the search reasonable?

   a Was it justified at its inception? (by probable cause, reasonable suspicion, exigent circumstances, or random searches based on other special governmental needs, e.g., airport searches)
   b Was it reasonable in scope?

4 If the search was reasonable, the Fourth Amendment was not violated.

(1) Individual's reasonable expectation of privacy	*balanced against*	(1) Government's interest in conducting the search
(2) Nature and degree of the intrusion		(2) Efficacy of the search in meeting the government's goal

is a perception of a drug problem in school sports. A 2017 National Institute on Drug Abuse (NIDA) survey of teens showed that 0.6 percent of 8th graders, 0.8 percent of 10th graders, and 1.1 percent of high school seniors have used steroids (NIDA, 2018). Numerous studies have also questioned the effectiveness of school drug testing programs especially given their cost (Ingraham, 2015), yet, the CDC reports that the percentage of high schools who have adopted student drug-testing programs has gone from 25.5 percent in 2006 to 37.5 percent in 2016 (CDC, 2016). The most common reasons that schools, universities, and sport governing bodies give when justifying their drug-testing programs is that they are necessary to protect the health and safety of student-athletes, to maintain a level playing field for athletes, and preserve the integrity of athletic contests. Arguments commonly raised by athletes against drug-testing programs include that it is an embarrassing invasion of their privacy, it is unfair to single out student-athletes, and it is unfair to condition participation in extra-curricular activities and sports on submitting to a drug test.

To determine whether the drug-testing program is legal, courts apply the balancing test for reasonableness depicted in Exhibit 12.3. What is considered reasonable will vary depending upon whether the drug-testing program is at the secondary or post-secondary levels due to a diminished expectation of privacy for middle and high school students. In middle school and high school settings, athletes are minors, which reduces their constitutional protection somewhat. The doctrine of *in loco parentis* gives the school extra authority to regulate students because the school is responsible for the well-being of those students in the absence of the parents. Additionally, student-athletes in general are considered to have a somewhat diminished expectation of privacy in both the interscholastic and intercollegiate settings due to such factors as sharing physical spaces in locker rooms, submission to medical exams, and agreement to abide by team and association rules.

Two significant cases have examined the constitutionality of drug testing programs in both the secondary school and collegiate athletic environment and are presented in our next two focus cases. *Derdeyn* (1993) involves a college drug-testing program and *Vernonia* (1995), involves a middle school drug-testing program. A comparison of the two cases illustrates that courts applying the balancing test can reach widely divergent conclusions about the reasonableness of essentially the same drug-testing policy. In this section, we compare the courts' application of the balancing test in *Derdeyn* and *Vernonia*.

University of Colorado v. Derdeyn

863 P.2d 929 (Colo. 1993)	**FOCUS** CASE

FACTS

The NCAA requires a mandatory random drug test that is visually monitored in order to ensure "ownership" of an untampered-with urine sample. In this case, the University of Colorado (CU) had implemented a drug policy nearly identical to that used by the NCAA. CU then amended the policy to require that testing be based on reasonable suspicion rather than random selection of athletes and to make it less intrusive by requiring only aural, and not visual, monitoring of the sample collection. However, the consent form continued to indicate that athletes were required to consent to random suspicion-less testing. The trial court issued a permanent injunction prohibiting CU from enforcing its drug-testing policy, and finding a lack of genuine consent on the part of student-athletes. CU appealed.

HOLDING

The Colorado Supreme Court held that the testing procedure was an unreasonable search under the Fourth Amendment.

RATIONALE

After acknowledging that random searches in the school context could be justified by **special needs** (i.e., to combat widespread drug use by students), the court conducted the balancing test for reasonableness, weighing the intrusiveness of the search against the university's need to conduct it.

Intrusiveness and Reasonable Expectation of Privacy

First, the court examined whether the athletes had a reasonable expectation of privacy. The university argued that the athletes had a diminished expectation of privacy because:

1 They routinely provide urine samples as part of their annual pre-participation physical examinations.
2 They submit to extensive regulation of their behavior, including diet, conditioning, academic performance, and so forth.
3 They are already subject to the NCAA's drug-testing protocol.
4 The consequence of refusing to provide a urine sample is not severe because they only lose their opportunity to participate in athletics (in contrast to losing one's job, for example).
5 Positive test results are kept confidential and are not provided to criminal law enforcement authorities.

The court responded to these arguments as follows:

1 Athletic department personnel were involved in the sample collection process, rendering it less private than if it had been conducted by "strangers" in a medical setting.
2 None of the other behavioral regulations imposed on the athletes entailed an extensive invasion of their privacy.
3 Although submission to the NCAA's drug-testing program might seem to render submission to CU's program less intrusive, the athletes testified that CU's policy was more intrusive because it transformed otherwise trusting relationships between athletic trainers and athletes into untrusting and confrontational interactions.
4 Although most college athletes will never turn pro, many athletes who could not otherwise afford to attend college do so by means of their athletic scholarship, thus increasing their future earning potential – so it is not just the chance to have fun playing that is lost by those who refuse to be tested.
5 While there is no risk of criminal penalties, there is also no warrant or probable cause impediment to these mandatory searches that would provide the same protection against abuse to athletes that is provided to criminal suspects.

Overall, the court felt that CU's arguments did not successfully establish a strongly reduced expectation of privacy on the part of student-athletes.

In assessing the intrusiveness of the search procedure itself, the court found that while aural monitoring is indeed less intrusive than visual monitoring, the university had admitted that under certain circumstances it might return to a policy of visual monitoring. This lack of assurance of less intrusiveness combined with a finding that the athletes had a reasonable expectation of privacy led the court to conclude that CU's policy permitting random, suspicion-less drug testing was significantly intrusive. This high level of intrusiveness then had to be balanced against the university's interests in conducting the drug-testing program.

Government (University) Interests in Conducting the Search

According to CU, they needed to test in order to: (1) prepare their athletes for undergoing NCAA drug testing during postseason play; (2) promote the integrity of their intercollegiate athletics program; (3) deter drug use by other students who view athletes as their role models; (4) ensure fair competition; and (5) protect the health and safety of the athletes. In the court's view, all of these interests were commendable, but the only one that rose to the level of an important governmental concern was the need to protect the health and safety of the athletes. The court assessed the governmental need to search by comparing the current case to the large body of non-athletics related case law, in which a majority of courts have required the government to have truly compelling interests to justify having a testing policy, such as preventing public transportation safety disasters or protecting national security.

In this case, concluded the *Derdeyn* court, the university's interests simply were not comparable to those established precedents. Thus, CU's need to search athletes did not outweigh the significant intrusiveness of its drug-testing program; therefore, the drug-testing procedure constituted an unreasonable search.

Voluntary Consent to Justify the Search

Finally, the university argued that even if its policy was determined to be unreasonable under the Fourth Amendment, it should not be considered to violate the Constitution because the student-athletes gave their voluntary consent to be tested. The court acknowledged that a warrantless search is generally considered reasonable if an individual has consented to it. However, the court went on to quote from a U.S. Supreme Court decision in which consent was defined as "a consent intelligently and freely given, without any duress, coercion or subtle promises or threats calculated to flaw the free and unconstrained nature of the decision" (*Schneckloth v. Bustamonte*, 1973). Applying this definition, the *Derdeyn* court concluded that in this case the athletes' "consent" was clearly coerced because they could not participate without a signed consent form.

Now, let's contrast the *Derdeyn* case with *Vernonia*.

Vernonia School District 47J v. Acton

115 S. Ct. 2386 (1995)   **FOCUS** CASE

FACTS

The school district's athlete drug testing policy was challenged by a seventh-grade football player. The only relevant factual differences between *Derdeyn* and *Vernonia* are that in this (the latter) case: (1) the athletes were minors; (2) the sample collection was monitored aurally, except that the boys were sometimes watched from behind; and (3) the Vernonia school district claimed the existence of a large-scale drug abuse crisis led by athletes.

HOLDING

The U.S. Supreme Court decided 6 - 3 to uphold the school district's athlete drug-testing policy.

RATIONALE

The Court applied the usual balancing test to determine the reasonableness of the search. In contrast to the Colorado court's analysis in *Derdeyn*, the Court found that the athletes did indeed have a *diminished expectation of privacy* for four reasons: (1) in choosing to participate, they submitted themselves to a higher degree of regulation than other students and thus, should expect intrusions on normal rights and privileges; (2) they regularly engage in a state of "communal undress" in the locker room; (3) they routinely undergo pre-participation physical examinations; and (4) they are minors, so schools standing in the shoes of the parents (*in loco parentis*) while children are in their care possess a degree of control that exceeds what could be exercised over adults. The Court considered the *in loco parentis* factor as central to its analysis of the students' expected level of privacy.

Having concluded that the student-athletes did have a diminished expectation of privacy, the Court went on to characterize the *intrusiveness of the search as minimal*. Because it was aurally monitored, because the test assessed only the presence of banned drugs and not other medical conditions, and because disclosure of the results was limited and not used for criminal law enforcement, the Court concluded that the invasion of student privacy was insignificant.

Conversely, the *government's interest in conducting the drug-testing program was found to be strong*, based on the school district's evidence of student-athlete involvement in a disciplinary rebellion of "epidemic proportion" that was fueled by drug and alcohol abuse. Additionally, the Court asserted the importance of deterring drug use by the nation's schoolchildren, and particularly among students for whom drug use would pose immediate risks of harm, such as athletes. In rejecting the argument that suspicion-based testing would accomplish the deterrence objective just as efficaciously as random testing but less invasively, the Court asserted that parents would be less likely to accept it due to its potential for appearing accusatory, which might "transform … the process into a badge of shame."

Additionally, the Court thought that teachers and coaches might abuse a nonrandom testing process by imposing testing arbitrarily on troublemakers who were not necessarily likely drug users. Finally, the Court said that suspicion-based testing would, because of its accusatory nature, require that more due process be provided, and would place teachers and coaches in the role of being drug abuse spotters – a role for which they are not well-prepared. Thus, concluded the Court, the school district's interests in continuing to conduct random drug testing of athletes outweighed the minimal intrusion on student privacy that it created.

As you can see, the *Vernonia* Court reached the opposite conclusion from the *Derdeyn* court on the reasonableness of nearly identical drug-testing policies. Once again, while this difference may be partially explained by the age difference in the populations tested and the "special needs" that exist in the secondary school context, a comparison of the courts' analyses of the reasonableness factors highlights the inherent subjectivity of the inquiry. Subsequently, the Supreme Court extended the constitutionality of drug testing in secondary schools from student-athletes to all students who participate in extracurricular activities, including cheerleaders, the band, the choir, the academic team, and the Future Farmers of America (*Board of Education of Independent School District No. 92 of Pottawatomie County v. Earls*, 2002). In a 5–4 decision, the Supreme Court dismissed the idea that individualized suspicion should be required to justify a search, saying that "special needs" are inherent in the public school setting. The Court similarly found that the aural monitoring procedures were less intrusive, and deferred to the school district's concerns about drugs, deciding that the school did not have to wait for a crisis to develop before implementing deterrence procedures. The efficacy requirement did not require a close nexus between the groups tested and those most likely to use drugs.

The importance of the *Earls* case is that, in its analysis, the Court ignored the facts that nonathletic extracurricular activities differ in significant ways from athletics. Compared to sport activities, the non-sport activities lack the same type of safety concerns, do not all involve pre-participation physical exams and "communal undress," and do not have the concern as to fairness or integrity of competition. These factors were an important part of the Court's justification for the result it reached in the *Vernonia* case. The Court's willingness to ignore this is a cause for concern. Bereft of mooring in the special context of athletics, the *Earls* decision allows the Court to drift toward the possibility that the next step will be to allow drug testing of *all* secondary school students – not just participants in extracurricular activities. Legal commentary has recognized the ease with which courts have permitted the government interests to outweigh the individual privacy interests in the context of combatting drug use. One legal scholar commented some 30 years ago "in our well-intended desire to stop the flow of drugs into the country and reduce drug abuse, we are rapidly becoming a nation of suspects. Perfectly law abiding citizens who are under no suspicion of drug use are increasing being called upon to prove their innocence" (Glantz, 1989, p. 1431).

Competitive Advantage Strategies

Drug Testing of Athletes

- Consider whether the monetary costs and the costs to individual privacy are outweighed by the deterrent value of implementing a drug-testing program. Steroid-and-stimulant screening can cost up to $50 per test (Shipley, 2003). As of November 2008, only 7 percent of U.S. high schools and middle schools had implemented random drug testing. After two years of testing, the New Jersey State interscholastic Athletic Association had tested 1,000 student-athletes and only two had tested positive (both for steroids). A study of 900 schools by the University of Michigan found no evidence that testing decreased student drug use (Winerip, 2008).
- Minimize the intrusiveness of the search by only requiring aural monitoring by a same-sex monitor from outside a closed bathroom stall.
- Limit consequences of positive test results to restrictions on participation opportunities and requiring the student to undergo treatment or rehabilitation. Avoid involvement of criminal law enforcement.
- Maximize anonymity and accuracy in the sample collection and testing processes, as well as confidentiality in the reporting and data storage processes.
- Provide opportunities for retesting samples to verify positive results.
- Arrange for sample collection to be performed by non-athletic department personnel.

A final point that needs to be made is this: the NCAA's drug-testing program is beyond the reach of the Constitution, but public universities that choose to supplement the NCAA's program with their own drug-testing procedures are subject to constitutional restraints. This has created an interesting twist for drug-testing law, because it means that virtually identical drug-testing procedures could be held unconstitutional if administered by a public university but be untouchable if administered by the NCAA. This scenario is, in fact, close to the reality of current law, as you can see by comparing the NCAA's drug-testing situation with the situation at the University of Colorado following the *Derdeyn* decision.

Thus, sport managers working in school environments will have wide latitude to implement drug-testing programs without running afoul of the constitution. But it is important to note that the average annual cost of a drug-testing program can be around $100,000 for a school district. That cost coupled with inconsistent results from many studies of the effectiveness of these programs to actually deter drug use or to identify those who are most likely to abuse drugs continues make this a challenging management decision for school administrators.

One final important point to note is that school drug testing programs are also subject to state constitutional scrutiny. Sometimes state constitutions protect civil liberties more rigorously than does the U.S. Constitution (see *Hill v. NCAA*, 1994). A few states have relied on their state constitutions in deciding drug testing cases. Testing upheld: *Hill v. NCAA*, 1994; *Hageman v. Goshen County Sch. Dist. No. 1*, 2011; *Brennan v. Bd. of Trustees for University of Louisiana Systems*, 1997; *Weber v. Oakridge Sch. 76*, 2002; and *Joye v. Hunterdon Central Regional High Sch. Bd. of Educ.*, 2003. Testing struck down: *York v. Wahkiakum Sch. Dist. No. 200*, 2008; *Theodore v. Delaware Valley Sch. Dist.*, 2000; and *Brown v. Shasta Union High Sch. Dist.*, 2010.

Religious Speech and Activities

High school athletic associations as well as individual schools and universities may have personal conduct or participation codes that have the potential to limit or restrict the First Amendment rights of student athletes. In the next few sections we will explore how these rules impact religious speech, protest speech, and personal expression under the First Amendment (see Exhibit 12.4). The First Amendment protects

Exhibit 12.4 First Amendment to the U.S. Constitution.

Congress shall make no law respecting an establishment of religion, or prohibiting the free exercise thereof; or abridging the freedom of speech, or of the press; or the right of the people peaceably to assemble, and to petition the Government for a redress of grievances.

individuals' right to engage in religious speech as well as political speech and other valued types of speech. The general rule is that the government may not impose content-based restrictions on speech unless it has a compelling reason and the restriction can pass a strict scrutiny test. If the restriction on speech is content-neutral, the government may impose reasonable time, place, and manner restrictions on the speech activity as long as the content of the message is not thereby suppressed. We begin with religious speech and activities including dress and grooming codes and school prayer policies.

Freedom of Religion and Dress Codes

A dress code violation prompted a freedom of religion lawsuit in *Menora v. Illinois High School Association* (1982). A Jewish basketball player wanted to wear his yarmulke while playing in order to honor his religious beliefs. But the athletic association enforced its "no headgear rule," asserting that loose headgear could create a safety hazard on the basketball court. The court ruled in favor of the athletic association, holding that this rule was a neutral rule with a legitimate purpose and was not an attempt to target Judaism for suppression. The court did, however, suggest that the athletic association modify its rule to allow secure headgear to be worn in order to accomplish their safety objective without unnecessarily burdening students with similar religious practices.

In *Moody v. Cronin* (1980), the court ruled in favor of two Pentecostal plaintiffs who were suspended for refusing to attend coeducational physical education classes in which they would have been required to wear shorts in violation of their religion's stance on appropriate public modesty. They sued under the First Amendment, claiming their right to freely exercise their religion was being infringed upon.

Legal issues surrounding Muslim dress are becoming more prevalent. While not a First Amendment case, in 2015 the U.S. Supreme Court found Title VII religious discrimination where a clothing retailer's "look policy," which barred the wearing of caps or black clothing, resulted in the non-hiring of a Muslim woman who wore a head scarf (*EEOC v. Abercrombie & Fitch*, 2015). According to a 2017 survey, 22 percent of Americans polled did not know if Muslims in the United States had First Amendment rights (Annenberg, 2017; Smith, 2017) and 42 percent of Muslims with children in K-12 schools report bullying associated with their hijab or clothing (Drake, 2017; ISPU, 2017). During the 2012 Olympics, the women's soccer team from Iran was disqualified for wearing headscarves (a ban that was subsequently lifted), as FIFA claimed safety and dress code issues (Aljabri, 2016). A Muslim-American weightlifter waited nearly a year for the International Weightlifting Federation (IWF) to decide to allow her to wear clothes covering her body. The IWF claimed that long sleeves prevented them from seeing if arms or legs were locked (Aljabri, 2016).

School Prayer

The issue of pregame prayer impacts students' freedom of religion and speech rights as both spectators and participants. As seen in Exhibit 12.4, the First Amendment restricts government from making laws "respecting an establishment of religion, or prohibiting the free exercise thereof." These two clauses are generally referred to as the Establishment Clause and the Free Exercise Clause. The Establishment Clause prohibits the government from establishing a preferred, government-endorsed religious faith or practice, while the Free Exercise Clause prohibits the government from impermissibly targeting a religious faith or practice for suppression. Taken together, these two clauses are meant to protect religious liberty. Constitutional challenges related to school prayer issues arise most often in one of two ways: a team prayer in the locker room or on the field/court prior to the game in which a coach participates, or a prayer included in the pre-game public announcements or activities as part of the pre-game schedule of sponsored events. Both of these situations raise the question as to whether the school, and therefore the government, has violated the Establishment Clause of the First Amendment.

The Supreme Court has used three different tests to identify violations of the Establishment Clause – the **endorsement test**, the **coercion test**, and the **Lemon test** (Borden v. Sch. Dist. of the Township of East Brunswick, 2008). The **endorsement test** asks whether a reasonable observer would perceive the practice in question to be a government endorsement of religion. The **coercion test** looks at whether the government's action might have the effect of coercing anyone to support or participate in religion, and Lemon v. Kurtzman (1971) established a three-pronged test, the **Lemon test**, examining whether the government's conduct (1) lacks a secular purpose, (2) has the primary effect of advancing or inhibiting religion, or (3) fosters an excessive government entanglement with religion.

Our next Focus Cases explore how the federal courts navigated school prayer cases prior to the U.S. Supreme Court deciding its first school prayer case in the context of prayer at sporting events in Santa Fe v. Doe. These cases help to better understand the nuanced interplay and balancing between the Establishment Clause and the Free Exercise Clause.

Chandler v. James (Chandler I)

180 F.3d 1254 (11th Cir. 1999)	FOCUS CASE

FACTS

In 1993, Alabama enacted a statute that explicitly permitted nonsectarian, non-proselytizing student-initiated prayer during school-related events, including sports events. In 1996, Chandler sued, challenging the statute and its application as unconstitutional. The district court ruled the statute unconstitutional as a violation of the Establishment Clause and issued a permanent injunction against its enforcement. In addition to prohibiting the schools from organizing or officially sanctioning prayer and other religious activities, the permanent injunction prohibited the schools from permitting all vocal prayer that might have occurred at school events and required school officials to forbid students from praying aloud while at school-related events.

HOLDING

The Eleventh Circuit vacated the district court's permanent injunction and remanded the case back to the district court, holding that the lower court could not constitutionally enjoin the school system from permitting student-initiated religious speech in its schools.

RATIONALE

The court reviewed a number of school prayer cases and concluded that what rendered the relevant prayer policies unconstitutional was not that they had permitted religious speech but that they had required that the speech be religious. The court went to great length to explain that the principle of government neutrality toward religion has been misunderstood and often misapplied by the courts, and elaborated on the necessity for striking the appropriate balance between the prevention of an impermissible establishment of religion and the protection of the free exercise of religion. In support of this position, the court quoted from the Supreme Court in the case of School District of Abington Township v. Schempp (1963) as follows:

> untutored devotion to the concept of neutrality can lead to invocation or approval of results which partake not simply of that noninterference and noninvolvement with the religious which the Constitution commands, but of a brooding and pervasive dedication to the secular and a passive, or even active, hostility to the religious. Such results are not only not compelled by the Constitution, but … are prohibited by it. (p. 306)

According to the Eleventh Circuit, a person who does not agree with a speaker's religious belief is free not to listen or participate. The court observes that,

> accommodation of religious beliefs we do not share is … a part of everyday life in this country… . Respect for the rights of others to express their beliefs, both political and religious, is the price the Constitution extracts for our own liberty. This is a price we freely pay. It is not coerced. Only when the speech is commanded by the State does it unconstitutionally coerce the listener. (p. 1263)

The court further stated that, while a school must not participate in or actively supervise otherwise genuinely student-initiated speech, the mere presence of a teacher or coach is not, in the court's view, unconstitutional coercion. Additionally, a school may impose reasonable time, place, or manner restrictions on religious student speech only to the same extent it would for nonreligious student speech. To treat religious speech differently would be to engage in viewpoint discrimination, which is the most egregious form of a freedom of speech violation because it is censorship.

In 2000, the Supreme Court decided its first school prayer case directly implicating pregame prayer practices of public schools in *Santa Fe Independent School District v. Doe* decision. Compare the Supreme Court's analysis in the following Focus Case with that of the Eleventh Circuit Court of Appeals in *Chandler*.

Santa Fe Independent School District v. Doe

120 S. Ct. 2266 (2000)	**FOCUS** CASE

FACTS

The Santa Fe School District had student-led prayers at their high school varsity football games. The Does filed a suit against the prayer for violation of their First Amendment rights. Prior to 1995, an elected student council chaplain regularly delivered a prayer over the public address system before each home football game. Then, in response to the initiation of litigation in this case, the school district adopted a new policy that permitted, but did not require, student-initiated prayer at football games. The policy authorized a student election to determine whether an "invocation and/or message" should be delivered and a second election to determine which student would deliver it. The stated purpose of the invocation or message was to promote sportsmanship and safety, to establish the appropriate social environment for the competition, and to solemnize the event. In the school district's view, this policy permitted private student speech that could be religious or nonreligious in content. Hence it did not promote government speech endorsing religion but instead promoted speech protected by the freedom of speech and free exercise of religion clauses of the First Amendment. The school district also considered the policy to be neutral because it did not endorse or favor any particular religion and had a secular purpose of promoting good sportsmanship.

HOLDING

The Supreme Court held that a pregame prayer before each home football game was an unconstitutional establishment of religion.

RATIONALE

The key question for the Court was whether the student prayer was protected private speech or a state-sponsored religious endorsement. Justice John Paul Stevens, writing for the 6-3 majority, opined that the student-led prayer was government speech. The Supreme Court found that the words *solemnize* and *invocation* conveyed the idea that religious messages were encouraged and that this idea matched the students' actual understanding of the policy. The Court also found relevant that the pregame prayers were delivered over the public address system, as part of a larger pregame ceremony clothed in the indicia of school-sponsored sports events (e.g., school colors and insignia, uniforms, and involvement of the band and cheerleaders) and structured as part of a school-sponsored event held on school property. It concluded that, instead of private speech, the pregame prayer was a public expression of the view of the majority of students that was delivered with the approval of the school administration. In the Court's view, therefore, this policy represented an improper state endorsement of religion.

The Court also was persuaded that the election policy structured by the school district was designed to permit the majority preference for pregame prayers to continue to prevail. Because the policy required that only those messages considered appropriate under the policy (solemnization, sportsmanship, etc.) were delivered, the majoritarian election process ensured that the views of the minority would not have a chance to be voiced. Thus, the election process was so dictated by the school district that it did not remove entanglement of the government with religious activity. In fact, the Court implied that the policy was a sham instituted to preserve the practice of pregame prayer. While the choice of the speaker was the students', the decision to hold the elections and the structure and mandated purpose of the "invocation and/or message" was a choice attributable to the state.

The Court also stated its view that while spectator attendance at the football games was voluntary, certain people (e.g., band members, cheerleaders, athletes) were required to be there, making them a captive audience. Justice Stevens applied the coercion test announced in Lee. Under that test, students should not be faced with the choice of not attending or attending and hearing a personally offensive religious ritual. Furthermore, the Court felt that the delivery of a pregame prayer over the public address system impermissibly coerced all those present to participate in an act of religious worship – which some might find offensive – and thus the policy would not pass the coercion test.

In addition to the endorsement and coercion tests, the Court applied the Lemon test for analyzing Establishment Clause violations (Lemon v. Kurtzman, 1971). It concluded that the policy's affirmative sponsorship of prayer violated the Establishment Clause because of its religious purpose, as well as the school district's continuing entanglement with structuring religious activity.

Chief Justice Rehnquist dissented and argued that the policy gave students a choice about the nature of the message to be delivered; therefore, the policy had a plausibly secular purpose and potentially secular effect. Justice Rehnquist noted that Establishment Clause jurisprudence does not mandate complete neutrality of content, so a policy may tolerate religion without endorsing it. Finally, the dissent also argued that the election process succeeded in disentangling the school district from religion by permitting the students to engage in private, as opposed to state-orchestrated, religious speech.

As you recall, our first Focus Case, Chandler v. James (Chandler I) (1999), reached a different conclusion about a pregame prayer policy than the Supreme Court did in Santa Fe. Thus, the Supreme Court also vacated the judgment in Chandler I and remanded it back to the Eleventh Circuit for reconsideration in light of the holding in Santa Fe. Upon review, the Eleventh Circuit concluded that its earlier decision did not conflict with Santa Fe and reinstated it (Chandler v. Siegelman (Chandler II) (2000)). According to the court, "Santa Fe condemns school sponsorship of student prayer. Chandler condemns school censorship of student prayer … the cases are complementary rather than inconsistent" (p. 1315). The court reiterated its view that "It is not the public context that makes some speech the State's. It is the entanglement with the State … . Remove the sponsorship, and the prayer is private" (p. 1316). Furthermore, "A policy which tolerates religion does not improperly endorse it" (p. 1317).

Using reasoning apparently in line with the *Chandler* court's perspective, a Texas state district court judge ruled that members of a high school cheerleading squad were not prohibited by the Establishment Clause from displaying religious messages (e.g., "I can do all things through Christ which strengthens me. Phil. 4:13") on football team pre-game run-through banners (Popke, 2013b). This decision was affirmed in *Kountze Independent School District v. Matthews* (2017), where the court analyzed three recognized categories of school-speech: government speech, school-sponsored speech, and private speech. The school district asserted that the banners were prepared by the cheerleaders, who are part of an official school-sponsored and supervised organization, to use at a school-sponsored event on school property. Therefore, the school district employee supervisors have a right to review and control content. The cheerleaders contended that since the school district allows them to select the message, regardless of school supervision or review, the messages must be categorized as pure private speech. According to the court, this is not government speech because the banners aren't required or always used, the banners are temporary and destroyed after the players run through it, and the idea behind school approval was to root out obscene language. It is not school-sponsored speech because cheerleading is a non-curriculum activity and is not designed to impart particular knowledge or skills. Generally, students are free to express their views unless it substantially disrupts or materially interferes with the education process (*Tinker v. Des Moines*, 1969). The school district here did not offer any evidence of such disruption or interference. The Texas Supreme Court denied Kountze ISD's petition for review in 2018 (Lawrence, 2018).

As we can see from *Chandler* and *Santa Fe*, the role of the students in initiating the religious speech in question can be a significant factor in determining whether the speech is protected. Thus, a question that often arises is whether the prayer is actually student-initiated and what role, if any, the coach plays in initiating prayer or other religious speech. In 2019, the U.S. Supreme Court declined to review *Kennedy v. Bremerton School District* (2017). Kennedy was a high school football coach who prayed at midfield after the games (and apparently in the locker room). The school district policy stated that school staff "shall neither encourage or discourage a student from engaging in non-disruptive oral or silent prayer or any form of devotional activity" (p. 7). The coach was not rehired as he failed to follow district policy, and he filed a lawsuit claiming that his First Amendment rights were violated. The court concluded he spoke as a public employee, not a private citizen (refer back to Chapter 5 regarding free speech rights of public employees). The coach was: (1) at school or a school function (the game); (2) in the general presence of students – he kneeled and prayed while in view of students and parents, refusing an accommodation that would allow him to pray after the stadium emptied – suggesting that the speech is directed, at least in part, to the students; and (3) in a capacity one might reasonably view as official – he "spoke" at a school event, on school property, wearing school logoed attire, while acting as a coach/supervisor in a prominent location on the field where he knew students (and others) would observe his behavior.

Also, in *Borden v. Sch. Dist. of the Township of East Brunswick* (2008) a court ruled that a high school football coach who led his team in prayer for 23 years would still be considered to be endorsing religion when bowing his head or taking a knee for student-led prayer. Thus, when coaches at public schools and universities play an active role in directing athletes in team prayers or other religious activities, the coach is likely to be considered a representative of the school in that capacity and this can often create Establishment Clause challenges, as well as undermine the Free Exercise rights of the student-athletes. Notwithstanding these concerns, though, it is relatively common for coaches to be highly visible and vocal about their faith, which continues to raise questions concerning the appropriate role that faith and religion have in the management and operation of a high school and collegiate sports programs. For example, a coach may gain a competitive advantage in recruiting based upon his religious proclamations, actually using faith to sway kids and parents as to the benefits of attending a particular school and as a tool to bridge race and socio-economic differences between young recruits (Baumgaertner, 2019). This has been a recurring observation related to coach Dabo Swinney at Clemson which has only intensified as Clemson's dominance in collegiate football has grown.

Protest Speech and Activities

High Schools and Middle Schools

In *Tinker v. Des Moines* (1969), the Supreme Court found that the First Amendment applied to public schools and students are free to express their views unless it substantially disrupts or materially interferes with the education process. Tinker cemented students' free speech rights in public schools. Mary Beth Tinker and a group of junior high school students wore black armbands to school to protest the war in Vietnam. When she refused to remove the armband, she was suspended. In its historic ruling, the Court stated that students do not "shed their constitutional rights to freedom of speech or expression at the schoolhouse gate."

The *Tinker* standard asks whether school officials can reasonably forecast whether the student expression will cause a substantial disruption or material interference with school activities. If the speech is not a substantial disruption or material inference with school operations, the speech cannot be censured. Since *Tinker*, the Court has recognized some exceptions that permit school restraints including restricting speech that is lewd, vulgar, or indecent (*Bethel v. School District v. Fraser*, 1986), reasonable restrictions on school sponsored publications such as a school newspaper (*Hazelwood School District v. Kuhlmeier*, 1988), and restrictions on student speech at a school sanctioned event that is reasonably viewed as promoting illegal drug use (*Morse v. Frederick*, 2007). Essentially, this trilogy of exceptions suggests a school may prohibit lewd, vulgar, or profane language on school property or at school sanctioned events, may regulate school-sponsored speech if there is a legitimate pedagogical concern, and may regulate speech that poses a direct threat to the safety of students. Presumably, speech outside of these exceptions could not be regulated absent substantial disruption with school operations. Thus, *Tinker* cleared the way for students to engage in social and political expression across a range of issues including apartheid in South Africa, Black Lives Matter, and gun violence in schools.

Similarly, sports have long been a platform for political expression (think Muhammed Ali and the Vietnam war, Tommie Smith and John Carlos at the 1968 Mexico City Olympics, and NBA star Mahmoud Abdul-Rauf's refusal to stand for the national anthem in 1996). NFL Quarterback Colin Kaepernick's kneeling before the national anthem at an NFL game in 2016 has been the subject of much controversy and heightened awareness of the role of athlete activism. Soon after Kaepernick first knelt during the playing of the national anthem, high school and college students, staff, and faculty across the country similarly joined in Kaepernick's efforts to raise awareness about social justice and later to even protest Kaepernick's treatment by the NFL. Athletic administrators responded with a variety of polices ranging from expressly requiring athletes to stand or prohibiting them from kneeling during the national anthem, to remaining in the locker room during the playing of the national anthem, to strong statements of support for any athletes that choose to express themselves (Roll, 2017). Obviously, for those schools who restricted or prohibited student expression, such policies and practices raised questions as to whether those rules violated the free speech rights of the student-athletes guaranteed in the First Amendment.

In *V.A. v. San Pasqual Valley Unified School District* (2017), the plaintiff was a football player who kneeled before the anthem. The second time he did it, at an away game, students from the other school (Mayer High School) threatened the plaintiff as well as other San Pasqual students. In reaction, the San Pasqual Valley school district sent a memorandum as follows:

> Students and coaches shall stand and remove hats/helmets and remain standing during the playing or singing of the National Anthem. Kneeling, sitting, or similar forms of political protest are not permitted during athletic events at any home or away games. Violations may result in removal from the team and subsequent teams during the school year. (p. 3)

Plaintiff filed first for a temporary restraining order and then a preliminary injunction, claiming the anthem policy violated his First Amendment rights. The court found that plaintiff's kneeling during the anthem is speech and that it is closely linked to Kaepernick and as protest to racial injustice in our country.

As plaintiff's actions were "easily interpreted and distinguished as his own expression, and not that bearing the school's imprimatur" (p. 7), the court applied the *Tinker* standard – the school can regulate speech if that speech could cause substantial disruption or material interference with school activities. Here, the court ruled that plaintiff's silent kneeling is not likely to cause either, and further that the incident after the second game did not affect the playing of the game or lead to any physical violence, and the school removed Mayer High School from its future schedule. The court enjoined the school district from using the policy.

Colleges and Universities

Not surprisingly, college sports have also seen a number of student-athlete protests (National Coalition Against Censorship (NCAC), 2019). Beginning in 2016, numerous athletes and band members either participated in or planned protests similar to Kaepernick's (NCAC, 2019). In 2019, eight University of Mississippi basketball players kneeled to protest two pro-Confederate marches on campus that were going on during the game (Jacobo, 2019). The NCAA and college sport leaders expressly supported athlete protests and activism (New, 2017) and according to the NCAA, "Participants should be allowed to express their opinions (e.g., kneeling during the national anthem) as long as the action does not delay or disrupt competition" (NCAA, 2018b).

The Supreme Court has not explicitly stated whether the *Tinker* standard applies in a post-secondary speech context but it has often acknowledged the differences between the public-school environment and a college campus environment and the differences between the students and their schools relationship to them (*Board of Regents v. Southworth*, 2000). Colleges and universities are entirely voluntary pursuits and most college students are legal adults. Additionally, the college experience is designed to promote freedom of thought and to expose students to diverse viewpoints. Thus, a more deferential view of college-student speech is typically recognized at public universities and college students are afforded a greater degree of free speech protections than high school or junior high school students.

Dress, Grooming, and Personal Expression

Expression and Social Media

In 2010, a student-athlete from University of North Carolina (UNC) posted a tweet that contained language from a rap song, alluding to possible bylaw infractions. The NCAA noticed and began an investigation which ultimately led to uncovering an academic scandal at the school (Richardson, 2017). For the tweet itself, the NCAA reprimanded UNC for failing to monitor its athlete's social media accounts. This led to other schools adopting social media policies, and in some cases, restrictions and bans. It is worth considering whether the First Amendment will prevent athletics departments from enforcing their social networking policies with suspension or expulsion for student-athletes who post prohibited content on social media platforms (Orland, 2009; Wilson, 2009). Bans on student-athlete use of social media might run afoul of the First Amendment's protection of the freedom of speech, particularly if such a ban extends beyond the duration of the playing season for their sport. An example might be the year-long ban imposed by Old Dominion coach Bobby Wilder, which could be construed as an impermissible prior restraint on speech (Steinbach, 2012). In 2018, former University of Central Florida backup kicker Donald De La Haye alleged that the school violated his First Amendment free speech right to "communicate on social media platforms" by punishing him with a loss of his scholarship (Greenberg, 2018). The school claimed that De La Haye's social media activity ran afoul of the NCAA's amateurism rules because he was receiving advertising revenue, and further that he was profiting off of his athletic ability. He argued that his large following was acquired before he joined the football team and his YouTube videos are related to his pursuit of a social media and film career. A federal district court denied UCF's motion to dismiss, and the case was ultimately settled (Henneke & Riches, 2018).

By 2013, roughly 20 percent of high schools had included a social media policy in their codes of conduct for student-athletes (Popke, 2013a). In Maine, Brunswick High School has a social media agreement built into its athletic code that requires athletes to be positive and refrain from online attacks (Bonifant, 2018). Some student codes of conduct are being used to suspend student-athletes from sports or from school. When those athletes have challenged their suspensions on First Amendment grounds, the courts have applied the *Tinker* (1969) standard, which allows schools to restrict student speech only if it is substantially disruptive to the learning environment. Two Circuit Courts of Appeals have found that no substantial disruption was caused by the student use of social media in their schools, and both held that the students' free speech rights had thus been violated by their suspensions (Popke, 2013a).

In *T.V. v. Smith-Green Community Sch. Corp.* (2011), two high school volleyball players had posted some lewd photos of themselves on their MySpace and Facebook sites. Pursuant to the school district's extracurricular activity code of conduct, the girls were ultimately suspended from 25 percent of their fall extracurricular activities, including a handful of volleyball games and a choir performance. The District Court found that the *Fraser* standard enabling schools to regulate lewd on-campus speech did not apply because these postings were off-campus speech. The court went on to apply the *Tinker* standard and found that the volleyball players' social media speech did not create the level of substantial disruption required to render the speech-restrictive suspensions constitutional.

Several states, including Arkansas, California, Delaware, Michigan, New Mexico, and Oregon, have enacted or proposed legislation aimed at protecting student speech in social media. Typically, these laws prohibit public secondary and post-secondary schools from requiring or requesting students to disclose their passwords and usernames, add employees of the school to their list of contacts, or access their accounts in the presence of an agent of the school. Schools are also prohibited from taking or threatening disciplinary action or prohibiting participation in curricular or extracurricular activities for exercising their rights as students under these laws (Arkansas Code Annotated, 2013; Deering's California Codes Annotated, 2013; Delaware Code Annotated, 2013; Michigan Compiled Laws Service, 2013; New Mexico Statutes Annotated, 2013; Oregon Senate Bill 344, 2013; Oregon House Bill 2426, 2013). Such laws, however, do not typically prevent an institution from accessing information posted by students that is publicly available online.

Expression in Dress and Grooming

As we noted previously, dress codes and grooming requirements can run afoul of the Free Exercise clause in the First Amendment protecting religious speech. In addition, dress and grooming codes can be challenged under both the Free Expression clause of the First Amendment and the Equal Protection clause in the Fourteenth Amendment. In 1969, the federal courts began to recognize freedoms to determine one's own hair-style and otherwise govern one's personal appearance. One judge wrote that this right clearly exists "whether this right is designated as within the penumbras of the first amendment freedom of speech" … or encompassed within additional fundamental rights applicable to the states through the due process clause of the fourteenth amendment (*Breen v. Kahl*, 1969).

For the free expression claims it might be unclear whether the clothing is conveying a specific message that might implicate the First Amendment, or simply a fashion statement which would likely not be protected under the First Amendment. Some courts apply the *Tinker* standard to determine if school officials can regulate student clothing. This standard asks whether school officials can reasonably forecast whether the student expression will cause a substantial disruption or material interference with school activities. For instance, a three-judge panel of the Fourth U.S. Circuit Court of Appeals struck down a portion of a school's dress code in *Newsom v. Albemarle County School Board* (2003) that prohibited clothing depicting weapons. The controversy arose after school officials forced a student to quit wearing his National Rifle Association T-shirt, which depicted three silhouettes of men holding guns and bore the message "NRA Sports Shooting Camp." The school policy prohibited "messages on clothing, jewelry, and personal belongings that relate to ... weapons." The Fourth Circuit determined that the policy was too broad and was not necessary to prevent disruptions at school. The court explained that the language of the school dress code would prohibit clothing bearing the state seal of Virginia, which depicts a woman holding a spear, or clothing bearing the athletic mascot of the University of Virginia, which contains two crossed sabers.

Other courts have applied a threshold test established by the Supreme Court in a flag burning case to determine whether the speech was protected expressive speech. Applying this two-part test to students asks: (1) whether the student intended to convey a particular message, and (2) whether reasonable observers would understand this message. A federal district court in New Mexico used this test to hold that a public school student did not have a First Amendment right to wear sagging jeans since sagging is not associated with a single racial or cultural group, was merely a fashion trend, and reasonable observers would not understand any message from wearing sagging pants (*Bivens v. Albuquerque Public Schools*, 1995).

However, the federal courts are split on the issue of whether dress and grooming codes violate the First Amendment right to freedom of expression. Some courts have upheld such codes, ruling that grooming (e.g., hairstyle, makeup) and dress choices (e.g., jewelry, clothing styles) are simply a type of individual self-expression that does not rise to the type of valuable speech that the First Amendment was designed to protect (see, e.g., *Zeller v. Donegal School District*, 1975; *Davenport v. Randolph County Board of Education*, 1984). Other courts have struck down such codes as unconstitutional, ruling that First Amendment protection does extend to such low-value expression (see, e.g., *Dunham v. Pulsifer*, 1970; *Long v. Zopp*, 1973).

Students have had greater success when challenging dress or grooming codes based on Equal Protection grounds. In *Dunham v. Pulsifer* (1970), the federal court recognized a fundamental right in one's appearance and hairstyle. A high school tennis player used the Equal Protection Clause successfully to challenge a grooming code that specified acceptable hair length for athletes. Since the court found that choice of hairstyle was a fundamental right, the school's regulation had to pass strict scrutiny. In finding a fundamental right to determine one's appearance, the court relied on precedent that had been fairly unanimous in finding such a right. Additionally, the court stated the following:

> Whether hairstyles be regarded as evidence of conformity or of individuality, they are one of the most visible examples of personality ... Furthermore, the cut of one's hair style is more fundamental to personal appearance than the type of clothing he wears. Garments can be changed at will whereas hair, once it is cut, has to remain constant for substantial periods of time. In addition to manifesting basic personality traits, hair style has been shadowed with political, philosophical and ideological overtones and as such has to be afforded a measure of the protection given these underlying beliefs. (p. 419)

Although agreeing that maintaining team discipline was a compelling interest, the court ruled that there was no evidence of a reasonable relationship between requiring compliance with a grooming code and any performance objective. Thus, the code violated the Equal Protection Clause.

Additionally, if dress or grooming codes are different as they are applied to boys vs. girls, those regulations would be subject to intermediate scrutiny. In 2014, The Seventh Circuit ruled that an Indiana high school policy requiring boys to wear their hair cut above their ears violated the Equal Protection Clause of the Fourteenth Amendment (and Title IX) (Davis, 2014; see the *Hayden v. Greensburg* Focus Case below). One important point to note is that using gender as a differential in these policies requires a higher level of scrutiny. It is likely that applying the same policy uniformly to both boys and girls would withstand constitutional scrutiny under the equal protection clause since being a student-athlete is not a suspect or protected classification.

Hayden v. Greensburg Community School Corporation

No. 13-1757 (7th Cir. 2014)   **FOCUS** CASE

FACTS

On behalf of their son, A.H., Patrick and Melissa Hayden challenge a policy which requires boys playing inter-scholastic basketball at the public high school in Greensburg, Indiana, to keep their hair cut short. The Haydens make two principal arguments: (1) the hair-length policy arbitrarily intrudes upon their son's liberty interest in choosing his own hair length, and thus violates his right to substantive due process; and (2) because the policy applies only to boys and not girls wishing to play basketball, the policy constitutes sex discrimination. The district court rejected both claims and granted judgment to the defendants. *Hayden ex rel. A.H. v. Greensburg Cmty. Sch. Corp.*, 2013 WL 1001947 (S.D. Ind. Mar. 13, 2013).

A.H.'s home is in Greensburg, Indiana, a city of approximately 11,500 people in the south-central region of the state. The Greensburg Community School Corporation comprises an elementary school, a junior high school, and a senior high school, which combined have an enrollment of 2,290 students.

The board of trustees that establishes policy for the school district has adopted a provision – Policy 5511, entitled "Dress and Grooming" – which in relevant part directs the district superintendent to "establish such grooming guidelines as are necessary to promote discipline, maintain order, secure the safety of students, and provide a healthy environment conducive to academic purposes" (R. 81 at 3 ¶12); these guidelines are to include dress standards for members of school athletic teams. The district guidelines implementing this directive leave it to the individual principal of each school, in consultation with staff, parents, and/or students, to develop and enforce appropriate dress and groom-ing policies.

HOLDING

We reverse in part. Because the hair-length policy on its face treats boys and girls differently, and because the record tells us nothing about any comparable grooming standards applied to girls playing basketball, the evidence entitles the Haydens to judgment on their sex discrimination claims.

RATIONALE

What we have before us is a policy that draws an explicit distinction between male and female athletes and imposes a burden on male athletes alone, and a limited record that does not supply a legally suf-ficient justification for the sex-based classification. We know that there is a rule prohibiting both male and female athletes at the junior high school from wearing hairstyles that might in some way interfere with their vision or pose some other type of problem; we have assumed that the same rule applies to high school athletes of both sexes. But there is no suggestion that A.H. wishes to wear his hair in an extreme fashion, let alone that hair worn over a boy's ears or collar or eyebrows is invariably problematic. The record also tells us that Coach Meyer offered two reasons for the policy: promoting team unity, by having team members wear their hair in a uniform length, and projecting a "clean-cut" image. We may assume that the hair-length rule is consistent with these reasons and that both reasons are legitimate grounds for grooming standards that apply to interscholastic athletes. What is noteworthy, for purposes of the Haydens' equal protection claim, is that the interests in team unity and projecting a favorable im-age are not unique to male interscholastic teams, and yet, so far as the record reveals, those interests are articulated and pursued solely with respect to members of the boys basketball team (and baseball team, assuming that the hair- length rule is applied to that team for the same reasons). If there is an argument that the goals of team unity and a "clean cut" image are served through comparable, albeit different, grooming standards for female athletes, it has neither been advanced nor supported in this case. And the fact that other boys teams are not subject to a hair-length policy casts doubt on whether such an argu-ment could be made.

The parties consented to the entry of final judgment on the record as it stands, and that record entitles the Haydens to judgment on the equal protection claim. The policy imposes a burden on only male athletes. There has been no showing that it does so pursuant to grooming standards for both male and female athletes that, although not identical, are comparable. Finally, no rational, let alone exceedingly persuasive justification has been articulated for restricting the hair length of male athletes alone.

Expression and Tattoos

In a non-sport related tattoo case, a high school threatened to suspend a student if she did not remove a tattoo of a cross that administrators said violated a rule forbidding the display of gang symbols. The court found that her tattoo was merely a form of self-expression that did not rise to the level of important communication the First Amendment was designed to protect. However, it also found that there is a liberty interest in determining one's personal appearance and that the rule in question was too vague about defining what constituted a symbol of gang activity to have provided the student with clear notice of what was prohibited (*Stephenson v. Davenport Community School District*, 1997). However, the U.S. District Court for the Central District of Illinois upheld a high school basketball team's grooming rule. Plaintiff Jeff Stotts was

---

Competitive Advantage Strategies

Athletic Policies that do not Infringe on the Bill of Rights

- Coaches and school authorities who wish to impose dress or grooming codes for their athletics teams will probably be fine. To be on the safe side, dress or grooming choices of student-athletes that involve important communication of the sort the First Amendment was designed to protect should probably be avoided. Having a sport-performance-related objective for a dress code would aid in its justification.
- According to McCaw, Jones, & Brown (2012), in order to avoid an NCAA finding of failure to adequately monitor student-athlete use of social media, university athletics departments would be wise to take the following steps:

  1 Identify the COI's guiding principles and develop monitoring protocols consistent with those principles. A monitoring protocol should, at a minimum, identify which social media sites will be monitored, the frequency and duration of the monitoring, the personnel tasked with monitoring, whether the student-athletes will be requested or required to provide greater access than what is publicly available on the site, and what words and phrases will be flagged.
  2 Consider any relevant state social media laws in developing the contours of the policy.
  3 Consider First Amendment freedom of speech limitations on a school's ability to restrict or sanction student speech activity.
  4 Have students read "Blog: 9 Social Media Dos and Don'ts for Student-Athletes" (www.athleticbusiness.com/corporate/blog-9-social-media-dos-and-don-ts-for-student-athletes.html).

- School administrators should avoid creating and implementing pregame prayer policies. if a pregame solemnizing message is desired, the policy should be carefully worded to avoid the appearance of any religious intent, and it should ensure that the selection of messages and speakers is administered by the students. If the students still choose to include religious content in their speech, it might be wise not to censor it because a court may consider this protected freedom of speech.

suspended from the team for getting a tattoo of a dragon on his back in violation of the rule, and he sued under the First Amendment and the Equal Protection Clause. The district court denied his request for an injunction prohibiting the school district from enforcing the rule, finding that Stotts had little likelihood of succeeding on the merits of his claim. On appeal, the Seventh Circuit dismissed the claim as moot because Stotts had by then graduated, and a decision by the court could have no practical impact (*Stotts v. Community Unit School District No. 1*, 2000).

Gender Discrimination Issues in Schools and Universities

Gender inequities in interscholastic and intercollegiate athletics have coexisted for many years with sex discrimination in other educational contexts, such as admissions policies. In 1972, Congress passed Title IX as a remedial statute intended to address sex discrimination throughout the whole spectrum of educational offerings, not just athletics. As a result, many educational opportunities have been created for women in diverse areas such as in law and medical schools, as well as in competitive athletics. Between 1972 and 2016, there had been a 990 percent increase in the percentage of girls playing high school sport and a 545 percent increase in women playing college sport (Brooke-Marcinak & de Varona, 2016). By 2017–2018, the number of girls participating in high school athletics was over 3.4 million in 2017/2018 (NFHS, 2018), and the number of women playing college sport was 216,378 (NCAA, 2018d).

Nevertheless, inequities continue. Women constituted approximately 56 percent of the overall undergraduate student body nationwide as of 2017 (Marcus, 2017), while only making up 43.7 percent of athletes competing in NCAA Championship sports (NCAA, 2018d). In light of the great value Title IX has proven to be for females who want to compete, as well as the great expense to an institution of being found in violation of Title IX, prudent athletics administrators should make every effort to act in good faith with respect to *all* their student-athletes and aggressively move toward Title IX compliance if they have not yet done so.

Regulatory and Compliance Framework for Title IX

Under Title IX, individual athletes who have experienced sex discrimination may bring suit for monetary damages and injunctive relief. Additionally, individuals and organizations (such as the Women's Sports Foundation or the National Women's Law Center) may file claims with the U. S. Department of Education's Office for Civil Rights (OCR), which then must investigate. Finally, the OCR itself may initiate investigations into Title IX compliance. In addition to court orders to improve opportunities for women and monetary damages awards to successful plaintiffs, punitive damages may be awarded when the discrimination is found to have been intentional. Another very threatening remedy, which to date has never been used, is that a school could be punished with a complete loss of its federal funding, which would mean losses in the millions of dollars for some universities that receive research dollars from large federal grants.

Title IX Regulations – The Three Compliance Areas

Generally speaking, there are three primary areas of Title IX compliance in athletics – **Participation** (the Three-Prong Test or Three-Part Test), Equal **Treatment** (in other program benefits & opportunities), and **Financial Assistance** (scholarships).

Area One – Participation Opportunities

The first area of Title IX compliance examines comparative opportunities to participate in athletics between males and females. Much of the athletics-related Title IX litigation so far has centered on the issue of participation opportunities. Title IX regulations require institutions to "effectively accommodate the interest and abilities" of male and female athletes. In effectively accommodating the interests and

Exhibit 12.5 Three-part test for compliance regarding equity in participation opportunities: The 1979 OCR Policy Interpretation.

---

a   Compliance will be assessed in any one of the following ways:

1   Whether intercollegiate level participation opportunities for male and female students are provided in numbers substantially proportionate to their respective enrollments; or
2   Where the members of one sex have been and are underrepresented among intercollegiate athletes, whether the institution can show a history and continuing practice of program expansion which is demonstrably responsive to the developing interest and abilities of the members of that sex; or
3   Where the members of one sex are underrepresented among intercollegiate athletes, and the institution cannot show a continuing practice of program expansion such as that cited above, whether it can be demonstrated that the interests and abilities of the members of that sex have been fully and effectively accommodated by the present program.

Source: U.S. Dept. of Education, 1979.

abilities of male and female athletes, institutions must provide both the opportunity for individuals of each sex to participate in intercollegiate competition, and for athletes of each sex to have competitive team schedules which equally reflect their abilities. The regulations further provide for three ways in which an institution can demonstrate compliance in this area (see Exhibit 12.5 OCR three-part test for compliance). In 1996, the first federal appellate court adopted and applied the OCR three-part test and since that time, the three-part test has been the accepted standard for testing compliance in Area One – participation opportunities. Let's examine the decision in *Cohen v. Brown University* (1996) to see how the First Circuit Court of Appeals applied the three-part test. Each of the issues raised in *Cohen* and addressed by the First Circuit are instrumental to understanding the full breadth of this area of compliance and how sport managers need to assess their strategies for providing equivalent athletic participation opportunities for females.

Cohen v. Brown University

101 F.3d 155 (1st Cir. 1996)   **FOCUS** CASE

FACTS

In 1993–1994, Brown University offered 32 varsity sports, 16 of which were women's teams. Although women comprised 51 percent of the undergraduate student body, only 38 percent of the athletes were female. In response to a university-wide order to cut the budget, the athletic department decided to demote two men's sports (water polo and golf) and two women's sports (volleyball and gymnastics) to club sport status. As a result, the demoted teams received lower priority in scheduling practice times and in access to athletic training services, and they lost admissions preferences in recruiting freshmen. Additionally, the coaches of the demoted women's teams lost their office space, long-distance telephone access, and clerical support (*Cohen v. Brown University*, 1992). Members of the demoted women's gymnastics and volleyball teams brought suit under Title IX, claiming that Brown's action exacerbated the university's existing failure to provide women with equitable opportunities to participate in varsity-level intercollegiate athletics. The district court applied the three-part test it found in the 1979 Policy Interpretation issued by the OCR and held that Brown University was not providing equitable participation opportunities in violation of Title IX. The university appealed.

HOLDING

The U.S. Court of Appeals for the First Circuit affirmed the decision of the district court, holding that an institution violates Title IX if it ineffectively accommodates its students' interests and abilities in athletics, regardless of its performance relative to the other areas of concern listed in the athletics regulations (the "laundry list"). The First Circuit ruled that under this analysis Brown University had violated Title IX and thus would have to adhere to a court-ordered compliance plan, which included reinstating the demoted women's teams to varsity status. As part of its decision, the court explicitly adopted the three-part compliance test enumerated in the OCR's 1979 Policy Interpretation. The Following issues were discussed by the court:

1 The validity of the Policy Interpretation's three-part test
2 The validity of Brown's quota argument
3 The meaning of full accommodation of interest and ability
4 The validity of Brown's relative interest argument

RATIONALE

Issue #1: Affirmation of the Validity of the Policy Interpretation's Three-Part Test

Brown University challenged the appropriateness of the district court's adoption of the three-part test for equity in participation opportunities that OCR had introduced in its 1979 Policy Interpretation. In affirming the district court's adoption of that test, the First Circuit stated that it is well-settled law that when Congress has expressly delegated authority to an administrative agency to promulgate regulations to implement a statute, the courts should grant substantial judicial deference and accord those regulations controlling weight unless they are arbitrary, capricious, or clearly contrary to the statute. Here, the court found that the Policy Interpretation reflected OCR's interpretation of Title IX and its implementing regulations regarding athletics, and thus the policy supported the intent of the statute.

Issue #2: Rejection of Brown University's Quota Argument

Brown University argued that the compliance test establishes a quota of participation slots that must be provided for women – a quota that disregards what they referred to as women's lesser interest in sport compared to men – and therefore gives preferential treatment to women when there are many more male students who would be interested in participating if there were more opportunities for them. Section 1681(b) of the statute does state that the law does not

> require any educational institution to grant preferential or disparate treatment to the members of one sex on account of an imbalance which may exist with respect to the total number or percentage of persons of that sex participating ... in comparison with the total number or percentage of persons of that sex in any community, State, section or other area.

That portion of the law provides, however, that subsection (b) "shall not be construed to prevent the consideration in any ... proceeding under this chapter of statistical evidence tending to show that such an imbalance exists." Therefore, using statistical evidence to measure compliance with the law is permitted by the statute.

What is not permitted is granting *preferential treatment* to the underrepresented sex on the sole basis of a statistical imbalance in participation numbers. In the words of the court:

> ... the three-part test is, on its face, entirely consistent with § 1681(b) because the test does not require preferential or disparate treatment for either gender. [It does not mandate] statistical balancing; rather, the policy interpretation merely creates a presumption that a school is in compliance ... when it achieves such a statistical balance. (*Kelley v. Board of Trustees*, 35 F.3d 265, 7th Cir. 1994)

If a school is unable to satisfy the first prong of the test to create such a presumption, it can still use the second or third prong to demonstrate compliance with the law. Thus, the test does not depend solely on statistical balancing. In dismissing Brown's argument that Title IX is a quota system, the First Circuit court stated,

Brown's approach fails to recognize that, because gender-segregated teams are the norm in intercollegiate athletics programs, athletics differs from admissions and employment [situations] in analytically material ways. In providing for gender-segregated teams, intercollegiate athletics programs necessarily allocate opportunities separately for male and female students, and, thus, any inquiry into a claim of gender discrimination must compare the athletics participation opportunity provided for men with those provided for women

... Rather than create a quota or preference, this unavoidably gender-conscious comparison merely provides for the allocation of athletics resources and participation opportunities between the sexes in a non-discriminatory manner ... In contrast to the employment and admissions contexts, in the athletics context, gender is not an irrelevant characteristic. Courts and institutions must have some way of determining whether an institution complies with the mandate of Title IX ... and some way of fashioning a remedy.

Additionally, the court stated that OCR could have required that the women's programs have exactly the same teams as the men's, including women's football, for example, which would have made it easy to assess compliance in the provision of participation opportunities. Instead, OCR opted to allow schools flexibility in offering differing sports to men and women, which means that compliance must be measured by other criteria, such as percentages of participation slots and differences in dollar amounts allocated. The OCR has provided additional guidance on acceptable disparities between numerical goals and reality in the recognition that the student body gender ratios and athlete gender ratios will fluctuate slightly from year to year at any given school.

The OCR's 1996 Policy Interpretation states:

As another example, over the past five years an institution has had a consistent enrollment rate for women of 50 percent. During this time period, it has been expanding its program for women in order to reach proportionality. In the year that the institution reaches its goal – i.e., 50 percent of the participants in its athletic program are female – its enrollment rate for women increases to 52 percent. Under these circumstances, the institution would satisfy part one. (U.S. Department of Education, 1996).

In sum, prong one of the compliance test does universities a favor by providing them with a clear and measurable way of knowing they are safely in compliance with the law; they do not have to guess whether a court would find that they had satisfied the other prongs of the test, which are inherently less objective ways to measure compliance. Quoting *Kelley* again, the court stated that:

"... if compliance with Title IX is to be measured through this sort of analysis, it is only practical that schools be given some clear way to establish that they have satisfied the requirements of the statute. The substantial proportionality contained in Benchmark 1 merely establishes such a safe harbor." (Kelley, 35 F.3d at 271).

Issue #3: Defining the Meaning of Full (and Effective) Accommodation of Interest and Ability

The First Circuit court determined that prong three "demands not merely some accommodation, but full and effective accommodation. If there is sufficient interest and ability among members of the statistically underrepresented gender, not slaked by existing programs, an institution necessarily fails this prong of the test." Where, as in this case, a university has demoted or eliminated viable women's teams, clearly existing interest and ability are no longer being fully accommodated.

In a case where there has been no such demotion or elimination, but female athletes have requested a new varsity team or elevation of a club team to varsity status, the court stated that

the mere fact that there are some female students interested in a sport does not ipso facto require the school to provide a varsity team to comply with the third benchmark. Rather, [the third prong would require granting such a request] ... when, and to the extent that, there is "sufficient interest and ability among the members of the excluded sex to sustain a viable team and a reasonable expectation of intercollegiate competition for that team." (*Cohen II* at 898)

Issue #4: Rejection of Brown University's relative interest argument

In disputing its failure on prong three, Brown University argued that the third prong should be interpreted to require allocating participation opportunities on the basis of the ratio of interested and able females versus interested and able male students. For example, if Brown surveyed its student body and found that 80 percent of its male students would participate in athletics if the opportunity existed versus only 40 percent of the females, then twice as many participation opportunities should be given to males because twice as many males were interested. Given women's lesser interest in participating in sports, Brown argued, affording them fewer opportunities based on the relative interests of the two sexes would still effectively accommodate existing interest and ability under prong three.

Brown's relative interest argument was resoundingly rejected by the court, which stated that such an approach "reads the 'full' out of the duty to accommodate 'fully and effectively.'" Indeed, measuring effective accommodation of interest using the relative interest method would cause the law itself to limit program expansion for women to the status quo level of interest. The court recognized that women's lower participation rate reflects an historical lack of opportunities and encouragement to participate in athletics. In the court's words, "Interest and ability rarely develop in a vacuum; they evolve as a function of opportunity and experience." The court concluded that "even if it can be empirically demonstrated that, at a particular time, women have less interest in sports than do men, such evidence, standing alone, cannot justify providing fewer athletics opportunities for women than for men."

Brown University's approach would have contravened the whole purpose of Title IX because it does not permit a "court to remedy a gender-based disparity in athletics participation opportunities. Instead, this approach freezes that disparity by law.... Had Congress intended to entrench, rather than change, the status quo – with its historical emphasis on men's participation opportunities to the detriment of women's opportunities – it need not have gone to all the trouble of enacting Title IX." The court found that the explosive growth in women's participation in sport since the enactment of Title IX was evidence that interest is closely related to opportunity.

Evidence of "Interest" after Cohen v. Brown

In March 2005, the OCR issued another policy clarification, focused on the third prong of the three-part test. The OCR endorsed the use of interest surveys of enrolled students to assess interest and ability. In support of this endorsement, the policy clarification was accompanied by a "User's Guide to Developing Student Interest Surveys Under Title IX," which permitted a lack of student response to an interest survey to be interpreted by an institution as a lack of interest in athletics participation. Under any circumstances, attempting to extract substantive meaning from a failure to respond is a highly problematic approach to survey research. It was especially troubling here, given that the OCR found that in the past most of the institutions it investigated had reported their response rates as low or failed to report them at all (U.S. Department of Education, 2005). In fact, the OCR reported that "few if any institutions made an effort to obtain high response rates" (U.S. Department of Education, 2005, p. 6). In 2010, the OCR issued a policy clarification that withdrew the 2005 policy clarification and all related documents pertaining to interest surveys. The 2010 clarification explicitly states that interest surveys, standing alone, cannot justify eliminating an existing sport. It also specifies that multiple methods are to be used in assessing whether prong three has been met and discusses in detail how interest surveys should be developed, administered, and interpreted as one optional part of that prong three analysis. This clarification also provides guidance for athletics departments as to how to determine compliance with prong three. The three central questions to be asked are:

1 Is there unmet interest in a particular sport?
2 Is there sufficient ability to sustain a team in that sport?
3 Is there a reasonable expectation of competition for that team?

If the answer to all three is yes, then OCR will find a prong three violation and conclude that the institution is not in compliance with the law (U.S. Department of Education, 2010).

Elimination of Opportunities for Women

In 2018, a federal court found that Eastern Michigan University (EMU) violated Title IX. EMU had previously eliminated Women's Tennis and Softball, as well as Men's Wrestling and Men's Swimming. A lawsuit was brought by a tennis student-athlete and a softball student-athlete, alleging that EMU failed to comply with each prong of the three-part test and further sought an injunction to prevent the two women's programs from being eliminated. The court considered each prong and found that, (1) women comprised 59.5 percent of EMU's undergraduate enrollment while only 44.3 percent of its athletes; (2) the school failed to provide evidence that its 2014 roster management plan was achieved and the lack of concrete numbers are not useful in determining whether the school had a history of program expansion, the school made no showing regarding a policy for requesting new sports, and the participation disparity has lingered for at least 15 years with no serious effort to address it; and finally (3) as plaintiffs are members of eliminated teams, interests and abilities are obviously not accommodated by the present program (*Mayerova v. Eastern Michigan University*, 2018). The court required that EMU reinstate Women's Tennis and Softball. After reinstating Women's tennis, EMU moved to stay the order to create a new Softball team, preferring to explore adding Women's Lacrosse instead. The 6th Circuit, in granting that stay, stated that it is "the reality of Title IX requires equality between men's and women's teams, not that certain teams be reinstated rather than other sports teams be created ..." (*Mayerova v. Eastern Michigan University*, 2019, p. 2). This case was ultimately settled in early 2020, with a schedule created for adding Women's Lacrosse and a cash payout for the two female athletes, as well as meeting other compliance thresholds, including the university putting more money into women's sports, and adding a Title IX consultant (Associated Press, 2020). For sport managers and administrators, this case illustrates the dangers of eliminating women's teams. And further, as we saw here and below, the use of roster management is not necessarily an effective tool in satisfying any one prong of the three-prong test.

Roster Management and Manipulation

Finally, some universities have attempted to meet their Title IX participation opportunity obligations by manipulating roster sizes and counting competitive cheerleading as a varsity sport. In *Biedeger v. Quinnipiac University* (2012), the university triple-counted cross-country athletes by requiring them to also be members of the indoor and outdoor track teams, thus counting the 18 cross country slots as 54 female participation opportunities. While the Department of Education's 1996 policy clarification does state that athletes who participate in more than one sport should be counted as filling two participation slots, the District Court in this case found that 11 of the spots on the indoor and outdoor track teams rosters were held by cross-country athletes who were either injured or red-shirted, and thus these slots were not genuine participation opportunities. On appeal, the Second Circuit Court upheld this ruling. Quinnipiac had also counted competitive cheerleading as a varsity sport with 30 participation slots for women. The Second Circuit also affirmed the District Court's determination that the competitive cheerleading program at Quinnipiac and the competitions in which the team participated were decidedly not yet sufficiently similar to other varsity sports to constitute a true varsity sport experience for the participants. Thus, the 30 women's participation slots could not be counted for purposes of Title IX compliance. In particular, the court noted that the university conducted no off-campus recruitment for cheerleading competitors, nor was there a uniform set of competition rules that applied across the season and postseason events, and the team might even have competed against high-school age opponents. In the words of the court, "application of a uniform set of rules for competition and the restriction of competition to contests against other varsity opponents are the 'touchstones' of a varsity sports program. Those features ensure that play is fair in each game, that teams' performances can be compared across a season, and that teams can be distinguished in terms of quality" (*Biedeger*, 2010, p. 99–100). The court acknowledged that someday competitive cheerleading might evolve so as to become a legitimate varsity sport, but asserted that that day has not yet arrived. In 2019, the NCAA recommended that Acrobatics & Tumbling be added to the Emerging Sports for Women program in 2020. This sport was developed "to provide fair and safe opportunities for young women to compete at the varsity intercollegiate level in skill sets primarily developed through youth participation in all disciplines of gymnastics and cheerleading" (NCATA, 2019, para. 9).

Area Two – Equal Treatment in Other Program Benefits and Opportunities

Under the general non-discrimination provisions in Title IX regulations, covered institutions must also demonstrate that they are providing equal opportunities for members of both sexes across a number of factors. The DOE regulations include a list of at least ten factors to be considered when evaluating whether an institution is providing equal opportunities (see Exhibit 12.6). When the OCR investigates a school for not complying with regards to the second area of Title IX-equal treatment, benefits and opportunities in other program areas it evaluates the program as a whole. We will explore how each of these factors are evaluated using the Adrian College example below.

The OCR would not typically rule a university noncompliant if, for example, the university fails to provide adequate resources for one item in the list of athletics benefits and opportunities, such as publicity, as long as the overall negative effect – program-wide – is negligible. The federal courts, however, have been willing to find Title IX violations in cases focused on inequitable facilities and inequitable scheduling of competitive seasons when the inequity was deemed substantial enough to deny equal opportunity to the participants. With regard to equitable provision of facilities, where a high school had failed to provide

---

Exhibit 12.6 Title IX athletics regulations.

34 C.F.R. § 106.41 Athletics

a   *General*. No person shall, on the basis of sex, be excluded from participation in, be denied the benefits of, be treated differently from another person or otherwise be discriminated against in any interscholastic, intercollegiate, club or intramural athletics offered by a recipient, and no recipient shall provide any such athletics separately on such basis.

b   See Exhibit 12.8 (*Separate Teams* subsection).

c   *Equal opportunity*. A recipient which operates or sponsors interscholastic, intercollegiate, club or intramural athletics shall provide equal athletic opportunity for members of both sexes. In determining whether equal opportunities are available the Director will consider, among other **factors**:

   1   Whether the selection of sports and levels of competition effectively accommodate the interests and abilities of members of both sexes;
   2   The provision of equipment and supplies;
   3   Scheduling of games and practice time;
   4   Travel and per diem allowance;
   5   Opportunity to receive coaching and academic tutoring;
   6   Assignment and compensation of coaches and tutors;
   7   Provision of locker rooms, practice and competitive facilities;
   8   Provision of medical and training facilities and services;
   9   Provision of housing and dining facilities and services;
   10   Publicity.

Unequal aggregate expenditures for members of each sex or unequal expenditures for male and female teams if a recipient operates or sponsors separate teams will not constitute noncompliance with this section, but the Assistant Secretary may consider the failure to provide necessary funds for teams for one sex in assessing equality of opportunity for members of each sex.

a girls' softball facility of comparable quality to the boys' baseball complex with regard to scoreboard, batting cages, bleachers, signage, restrooms, concessions stand, field maintenance, and lighting, the District Court found a Title IX violation (*Daniels v. School Board of Brevard County, Florida*, 1997). There were similar inequities between baseball and softball in the Huntsville, Alabama school district – resulting in two separate settlements. In 2019, the Huntsville Board of Education settled a lawsuit at Lee High school over disparities in pitching machines, infield tarps, locker rooms, dugouts and more, with additional issues across all sports, including weight room access and publicity (Conner, 2019; *Tyler v. Huntsville City Schools Board*, 2019). In 2017, The Huntsville Board settled similar issues, including pitching machines, dugouts, and lighting, at Huntsville High School ("Huntsville City," 2017).

In *Communities for Equity v. Michigan High School Athletic Association* (2001), discussed previously in Chapter 11, you might recall that the Michigan High School Athletic Association lost a lawsuit on the issue of inequities in sport season schedules for girls versus boys. Certain girls' sports had been scheduled as fall or spring sports, when the more appropriate season would have been the other one given the college recruiting seasons for those sports. The boys' teams, however, were scheduled in seasons appropriate for their sports. Thus, the girls' sports had been treated unfairly so that the boys' teams could have the facilities in the season most advantageous to them. In addition to the equal protection violations, the district court also found that the inequitable scheduling system violated Title IX. Since the Sixth Circuit later affirmed with regard to the equal protection claim it did not find it necessary to reach a decision on the Title IX claim. On similar facts, the Second Circuit found a Title IX violation (*McCormick v. School District of Mamaroneck*, 2004).

The Office of Civil Rights often uses what are known as Resolution Agreements upon completion of an investigation to identify the remedial steps the university needs to take in order to address an area of non-compliance.

In 2011, The OCR concluded that Adrian College, a Division III school in Michigan, was not "providing equal athletic opportunity to its male and female student-athletes in a number of areas covered by Title IX" (U.S. Department of Education, Office of Civil Rights, 2011, p. 1). The investigation stemmed from a complaint that Adrian discriminated against the women's softball team by constructing a new men's baseball facility while neglecting the existing softball field, as well as providing fewer and lower quality locker rooms to female athletes. As one can see from Exhibit 12.6 – locker rooms and facilities are covered in factor number (7) in § 106.41(c). The OCR and Adrian College entered into a Resolution Agreement containing a detailed description of the remedies required of OCR in order for Adrian College to correct its Title IX violations. This is a good example of how the OCR looks at the whole program in terms of benefits and opportunities during an Area Two investigation – all of the areas in § 106.41(c) are reviewed, not just the single area of facilities and locker rooms that were the subject of the complaint. Using the DOE factors and a program wide assessment, the OCR found the following program components were deficient (refer to Exhibit 12.6 to review the factors):

Provision of equipment and supplies (factor 2). Adrian College provided more uniforms (competition, warm-ups) to the men's program, specifically seven men's teams received warms-up: football, baseball, soccer, tennis, cross-country, indoor track, and outdoor track. Only four women's teams received warm-ups: tennis, cross-country, indoor track, and outdoor track). The College also provided Softball with deficient sport-specific equipment and Volleyball with inadequate storage space.

Scheduling of games and practice times (factor 3). For this category, the OCR considered four areas: the number of competitive events per sport, time of day the competitive events are scheduled, the number and length of practice opportunities, and time of day practices are scheduled, and opportunities to engage in pre-season and post-season competition. The OCR found that four women's teams had fewer competitive events than their male counterparts, the time of day for competitive events was equivalent, most sports had equivalent practice opportunities except for 6 a.m. Softball practices, and all sports had equal opportunity for pre- and post-season competition.

Assignment and compensation of coaches (factor 6). The OCR's investigation revealed that Adrian College hired coaches with more experience for men's teams, it paid the head coaches of men's teams more than the head coaches of women's teams, and exceptions to standard rates of pay were only made when hiring coaches for men's teams (four assistant coaches hired for men's teams were paid beyond the standard rate). According to the OCR, "these practices taken together constitute a compliance concern in this program component" (p. 20).

Provision of locker rooms, practice, and competitive facilities (factor 7). The OCR found that there were "significant differences" (p. 24) between the quality of the softball and baseball facility, as well as the football and volleyball venues. There were also "significant disparities" (p. 24) in favor of the men in the provision of locker rooms – every men's team had superior locker room facilities to every women's teams in availability, quality (with the exception of ice hockey), and for some, exclusivity of use.

Quality and availability of training staff (factor 8). The Head Trainer, who had more experience than the Assistant Trainer, was more frequently assigned to men's practices and competitions. Therefore, the female athletes did not have equivalent access to experienced training staff.

Housing (factor 9). While male and female athletes received equivalent housing and dining, some male athletes received benefits that were not offered to female athletes. Specifically, male hockey players were allowed to live off campus, and baseball players were allowed to live in a "theme house" together.

Publicity (factor 10). The Sports Information Director spent 50 percent of his time with football, the football media guide was double the size of any media guides for women's teams, and the football team received more radio time and maintenance of statistics than the women's program.

Office Space (program-wide). Two assistant football coaches had offices in the main office area, no other assistant coaches had offices.

Recruitment (program-wide). The number for personnel and recruitment trips conducted by the football team resulted in a significant disparity in favor of the men in terms of opportunity to recruit. And, the heavy emphasis on football resulted in more campus visits for male athletes.

Ultimately, the OCR determined that Adrian College only provided equivalent opportunities in tutoring and travel and per diem (factors 4 & 5). "While some of these disparities result in the denial of equal opportunity on their own (e.g., participation, practice and competitive facilities), others when taken together, constitute a denial of equal athletic opportunity to female students" (p. 35). The Resolution Agreement required, among other things, that the school complete construction on a new locker room in the stadium for exclusive use by the women by the end of the 2012–2013 academic year. The locker room was to have "34 lockers similar to the metal wood grain finish lockers in the varsity stadium locker room, a television, a stereo area, and a small lounge" (U.S. Department of Education, Office of Civils Rights, n.d., p. 5).

Area Three – Financial Assistance (Athletics Scholarships)

The third area of Title IX compliance, scholarships, requires that the scholarship dollars be spent proportional to athletic participation (see Exhibit 12.7). The regulations provide that when a college or university awards athletic scholarships, these scholarships must be granted to members of each sex in proportion to the number of students of each sex participating in intercollegiate athletics (34 C.F.R. 106.37(c). Because of football and its 85 scholarships, it is difficult for most schools to achieve proportional scholarship spending. For example, let's assume a large Midwestern University awards 56 percent of athletically related student aid to men, and 44 percent to women. Additionally, this university has 910 student athletes of which 471 (51.7%) are male and 439 (48.3%) are female. Since 48.3 percent of the students participating are female, 48.3 percent of the athletic scholarships should be awarded to female athletes. However, in this situation, only 44 percent of the athletic scholarships are awarded to female athletes. Thus, this distribution would be a violation of Area Three (see Dear Colleague Letter, 1998). If a disparity can be explained based on legitimate nondiscriminatory factors, a university may be found to be in compliance, but generally, a disparity greater than 1 percent creates a strong presumption of a violation.

Exhibit 12.7 34 C.F.R. § 106.37(c) Financial assistance

(c) *Athletic scholarships*. (1) To the extent that a recipient awards athletic scholarships or grants-in-aid, it must provide reasonable opportunities for such awards for members of each sex in proportion to the number of students of each sex participating in interscholastic or intercollegiate athletics.

(2) Separate athletic scholarships or grants-in-aid for members of each sex may be provided as part of separate athletic teams for members of each sex to the extent consistent with this paragraph and § 106.41.

Competitive Advantage Strategies

Gender Equity in High School and College Athletics

- Strongly consider adding a women's sport or elevating it to varsity status if the requesting female athletes can show evidence of interest and ability to compete and a reasonable expectation of competitive opportunities for the team.
- In keeping with the spirit of the law, try to consider alternatives to dropping men's sports when attempting to move toward Title IX compliance. However, recognize that Title IX does not mandate that schools create more opportunities or spend more money on women's sports; instead, it leaves the choice of method for achieving compliance up to the individual school – until it is successfully sued.
- Know that when boosters or alums give money in support of a sex-specific program, the Title IX regulations require that the school balance what is purchased with something comparable in quality for the other gender's programs. A good way to handle this is to make clear in fund-raising campaigns and literature that the law requires you to do this type of balancing, so that a large gift could actually hurt the overall athletics program unless it is not restricted by sex.
- Remember that Title IX applies to club sports and intramurals as well as to varsity sports, so be sure to evaluate the compliance status of those types of programs too.
- Be sure to consider the "laundry list" of athletics benefits found in the Title IX regulations whenever making decisions about the items listed there, such as, expenditures on publicity, hiring coaches, creating or upgrading facilities, and scheduling practices.
- Conduct training seminars for coaches and players that provide guidance on avoiding behavior and comments that could be construed as sex discrimination.
- Be wary of inviting a negligence lawsuit by taking shortcuts to Title IX compliance that would increase the numbers of female athletes but do so in an unsafe manner or increase the risk of injury by not ensuring adequate facilities and coaching supervision.
- Invite Title IX consultants to campus to assist with program evaluation and development of compliance strategies.
- Reallocate resources in a more equitable fashion by identifying ways to reduce unnecessary or extravagant costs.
- Plan fundraising efforts to increase resources available for sports for females, including corporate sponsorships.
- Do not become reliant on soft money as part of your regular athletics budget, but put donated money into interest-bearing accounts that will continue to generate income in perpetuity.
- Conduct a self-evaluation of your program by utilizing checklists available on the website of the National Women's Law Center: www.nwlc.org.

Additional Issues Covered Under Title IX's Non-Discrimination Umbrella

In addition to understanding the regulatory framework under Title IX, sport managers also need to be aware of several continuing or recurring issues that arise in athletics which are subject to the reach of Title IX's broad non-discrimination mandate. A few of these issues will be presented in the next section and include claims of reverse discrimination made by male athletes, the applicability of the separate teams and contact sport exemption for women seeking to compete alongside men, the applicability of Title IX to pregnant student-athletes, the inclusion of sexual harassment and sexual violence as a form of gender discrimination, and protections for transgender athletes. Each of these will be explored in greater detail next.

Reverse Discrimination

In several cases male athletes alleged discrimination under Title IX when male sports teams were eliminated. The courts have made it clear that Title IX and its application do not constitute reverse discrimination against male athletes. For example, in *Kelley v. Board of Trustees, University of Illinois* (1994), the Seventh Circuit held that when the University of Illinois terminated its men's swimming program but retained its women's swimming program, it did not violate Title IX because even after doing so, the percentage of athletes who were male exceeded the percentage of males in the undergraduate student body. See also *Miami University Wrestling Club v. Miami University* (2002). In both *Kelley* and *Miami University Wrestling Club*, the courts also ruled that the elimination of men's teams did not violate the Equal Protection Clause, because those actions are permissible measures to remedy past discrimination.

Separate Teams and Contact Sport Exemption

The *separate teams* provision under Title IX essentially relies on the notion that separate can be equal. Schools are not required to offer the same sports for each sex, nor do they have to offer the equal number of sports for each sex. The separate teams provision expressly allows a school to sponsor separate teams based on sex where selection for those teams is based on competitive skills or the sport is a contact sport. However, the Title IX regulations further require that where a particular sport is offered to one sex but not the other, persons of the excluded sex must be allowed to try out for the existing team. So, for example, if there is a boy's tennis team but no girls' team, a girl who wants to play high school tennis must be allowed to try out for the boy's team. This rule is less clear at the college level, as the NCAA and other governing bodies have specific rules regarding gender and participation. However, at all levels, an exemption to this try-out requirement is provided if the sport is a contact sport (see Exhibit 12.8; 34 C.F.R. § 106.41(b)).

With regard to the contact sport exemption, an important case is *Mercer v. Duke University* (1999). Here, Heather Sue Mercer was a placekicker who had made the Duke football team. When she was subsequently treated in a discriminatory fashion based on her sex, she sued. Duke argued that the contact sport exemption means that Title IX is simply inapplicable to contact sports, and thus the football coach's actions (dropping her from the team because of her sex and making gender-biased remarks to her) did not violate Title IX. The court saw things differently and held that Mercer's claim was valid because the contact sport

---

Exhibit 12.8 34 C.F.R. § 106.41 Athletics.

(b) **Separate teams**. Notwithstanding the requirements of paragraph (a) of this section, a recipient may operate or sponsor separate teams for members of each sex where selection for such teams is based upon competitive skill or the activity involved is a contact sport. **However, where a recipient operates or sponsors a team in a particular sport for members of one sex but operates or sponsors no such team for members of the other sex, and athletic opportunities for members of that sex have previously been limited, members of the excluded sex must be allowed to try-out for the team offered unless the sport involved is a contact sport.** For the purposes of this part, contact sports include boxing, wrestling, rugby, ice hockey, football, basketball and other sports the purpose or major activity of which involves bodily contact.

exemption merely means that a school need not allow a female to try out for a contact sport. If and when they do, however, the general antidiscrimination provisions still apply, and the athlete must be treated in a gender equitable manner. The trial court awarded Mercer one dollar in compensatory damages (connoting a moral victory) and $2 million in punitive damages, finding that the university had engaged in intentional discrimination. The Fourth Circuit later vacated the punitive damages award, holding that punitive damages are not available as a remedy in private Title IX actions. Mercer was awarded $349,243 in attorneys' fees (Mercer, 2004).

Pregnancy

Individuals may use Title IX to seek a remedy for discrimination suffered due to pregnancy. Pregnancy-based discrimination falls under Title IX because it is considered a form of gender-based discrimination, because only women get pregnant, and, historically, becoming pregnant has led to unfavorable treatment with regard to holding jobs and participating in sport. Myths about health risks associated with continuing to play sports, loss of focus, and scandals or distraction had led athletic departments to discriminate against pregnant student-athletes in the past. In the case of *Brady v. Sacred Heart University*, which was settled out of court in 2003 (Chronicle of Higher Education, 2003). Tara Brady was the starting center on Sacred Heart University's basketball team during her sophomore year. In June of that year, she discovered she was pregnant and notified her coach. When her athletic scholarship for the following year was rescinded, Brady sued the university under Title IX, alleging that her coach had discriminated against her based on her pregnancy in telling her she would be a "distraction" and "an insurance risk," and by deciding that Brady would be dismissed from the team and lose her scholarship for the following year.

According to Brady, she repeatedly sought a hardship waiver that is commonly given to allow athletes a medical redshirt year so they can retain their scholarship and not lose eligibility. These requests were denied until her parents complained to an NCAA compliance officer. Finally, Sacred Heart reinstated Brady's scholarship and told her she would be reinstated to the basketball team; however, she alleged that her coach made it clear that he still did not want her to play on the team. Brady then withdrew from Sacred Heart and transferred to West Chester University, where she played out her senior year.

Ultimately the NCAA introduced the NCAA Model Pregnancy and Parenting Policy with the goal of helping institutions effectively meet the needs of student-athletes dealing with pregnancy (NCAA, n.d.). The policy is gender neutral and covers both women and men. It addresses policies that provide for punishment for pre-marital sex – citing a potential Title IX violation if only punishing pregnant women. The policy also addresses physical health, physiologic concerns, emotional health, and privacy. At the high school level, the National Federation of State High School Associations recommends following the OCR's 2013 Dear Colleague Letter in terms separate programs for pregnant student-athletes (only if voluntary), prohibition on exclusion in extracurricular activities, school's must excuse pregnancy-related absences (regardless of individual teacher policies), and make the same reasonable accommodations that they would to students with other medical conditions (Green, 2017).

Sexual Harassment and Sexual Violence

Sexual Harassment

We first discussed sexual harassment in the context of employment under Title VII in Chapter 6. As an employer an educational institution would naturally be subject to Title VII. However, educational institutions can also be liable for sexual harassment occurring in their educational programs or activities (including their athletics programs) under Title IX. In 1979, the Supreme Court recognized the implied right of victims of discrimination to file private lawsuits against educational institutions (see *Cannon v. University of Chicago*, 1979). Sexual harassment is considered a form of sex discrimination under Title IX (*Alexander v. Yale University*, 1980). The Supreme Court has also upheld the use of monetary damages under Title IX as a remedy for sexual harassment in cases of intentional discrimination (*Franklin v. Gwinnett County Public Schools*, 1992). To establish a Title IX sexual harassment claim, a plaintiff must show the following:

1 Plaintiff was a student at an educational institution receiving federal funds.
2 Plaintiff was subjected to harassment based on sex.
3 The harassment was sufficiently severe or pervasive to create a hostile (or abusive) environment in an educational program or activity.
4 Grounds existed for imputing liability to the institution.

Particularly with regard to the grounds for imputing liability to educational institutions for sexual harassment, Title IX differs significantly from Title VII. First, Title VII differentiates between quid pro quo sexual harassment and hostile environment harassment. For quid pro quo harassment, an employer is strictly liable, which means the employer has no affirmative defenses and if the harassment occurs and is proven, liability is automatic. Title IX does not utilize the quid pro quo/hostile environment paradigm in sexual harassment claims. Instead, to impose liability on an educational institution and recover money damages, a plaintiff must also show that the institution had *actual knowledge* of the harassment and acted with *deliberate indifference* to eliminate the discrimination (*Davis v. Monroe County Board of Education*, 1999). Whereas employers may be strictly liable for sexual harassment under Title VII whether or not they knew the harassment was occurring, a successful private claim for damages under Title IX requires that school officials with authority to intervene have known that harassment was occurring and through deliberate indifference failed to stop it.

It is important to note though, that for purposes of OCR enforcement of Title IX, or for court cases in which plaintiffs simply seek injunctive relief, actual knowledge and deliberate indifference of harassment is not required. Although the regulations have undergone revisions, generally in such cases, a school must take corrective action if it knows or should know that student-on-student harassment is creating a hostile learning environment (U.S. Department of Education, 2011). Thus, while anyone may report harassment,

Competitive Advantage Strategies

Avoiding Sexual Harassment Claims

- An athletic department should endorse a sexual harassment policy that includes a reporting process and appeals procedure and include this information in its student-athlete handbook. Refer to Chapter 6 for information on essential elements of a sexual harassment policy and guidance on where to find a sample policy.
- Publicize and review your existing sexual harassment policy with student-athletes, coaches, and athletics department staff and administrators.
- Sensitize all constituents to the fact that sexual harassment is not just an issue of men harassing women – males can also be victims and females can also be harassers.
- Ensure that the hostile environment type of harassment is understood, because it is often perpetrated unintentionally by those who are insensitive to the issue. Thus, it is often preventable if those individuals are educated about the problem.
- Establish and disseminate a reporting procedure that encourages nonvictims who observe sexual harassment to report it.
- Investigate allegations of harassment promptly so you do not appear to be indifferent to the problem, and take immediate corrective action if you find it has indeed occurred.
- Hold orientation sessions for teams planning to compete internationally that inform athletes and coaches about the university's drinking and sexual harassment policies.
- Require these individuals to sign a statement acknowledging that all policies that govern on-campus behavior also apply while they are abroad.

a student-athlete who is being sexually harassed by a peer or a coach should report the problem to the appropriate school officials in order to ensure that the university has been put on notice, thereby maximizing the potential for judicial relief.

One example of a Title IX sexual harassment lawsuit is found in *Morrison v. Northern Essex Community College* (2002). In *Morrison*, two female athletes sued Northern Essex Community College on the grounds that the college had noticed that its women's basketball coach was sexually harassing his players but allowed him to continue to coach for seven years and then for three more years following a four-year suspension for misbehavior. These two basketball players claimed that the coach had asked for massages, grabbed their breasts, made jokes about their breasts, and benched them for rejecting his advances. Both players reported the problem to university officials, including the associate dean and the sexual harassment counselor of the college, and both eventually withdrew from the college.

The college argued that it had allowed the coach to resume coaching after his four-year suspension because it had received no further complaints of harassment. Therefore, argued the college, it had not acted with deliberate indifference to the current plaintiffs. The court ruled that knowledge of harassment of the current plaintiffs was not necessarily required since the college already had notice of previous harassment of other student-athletes. Thus, the court felt there was a reasonable question of fact as to whether the college knowingly failed to respond to sex discrimination in its athletics program. The court vacated the lower court's grant of summary judgment for the defendant and remanded the case back to the trial court for reconsideration (*Morrison v. Northern Essex Community College*, 2002). For similar cases, see *Brodeur v. Claremont School District* (2009); and *Bloomer v. Becker College* (2010).

In another case, two female soccer players filed a $12 million lawsuit against their coach, Anson Dorrance, and the University of North Carolina at Chapel Hill (UNC), alleging that he sexually harassed them by creating a hostile environment. Additionally, one of the athletes claimed that Dorrance retaliated against her for filing this lawsuit by intentionally interfering with her attempt to be selected for the 1999 U.S. National Soccer Team, resulting in a loss of income and recognition when that team won the World Cup.

UNC's defense was that Dorrance's conduct was simply the teasing that typically occurs in a college athletics environment and did not rise to the level of inappropriate conduct that would constitute sexual harassment. The university moved to dismiss the Title IX claim, but the court ruled that the plaintiffs had alleged sufficient facts to allow the claim to go forward (*Jennings v. University of North Carolina*, 2002). Subsequently, UNC settled out of court with one of the plaintiffs, while the other plaintiff continued to pursue the lawsuit, and, in 2004, a federal judge dismissed the case, finding that the coach's behavior was not severe and pervasive enough to constitute hostile environment sexual harassment ("Judge throws out," 2004). Eventually, the Fourth Circuit, sitting en banc, decided this controversy as described in the Focus Case below.

Jennings v. University of North Carolina

482 F.3d 686 (4th Cir. 2007)   **FOCUS** CASE

FACTS

Anson Dorrance, arguably the most acclaimed collegiate women's soccer coach in the country, repeatedly asked prying personal questions about his players' sex lives, using vulgar and sexually explicit language. He also made inappropriate gestures and advances, made comments about his players' bodies that objectified them as sex objects, discussed his sexual fantasies about players with other players – and did all this on a regular basis. While Jennings was only directly targeted two or three times because she made every effort to "fly beneath the coach's radar" and avoid his abuse, she claimed she was further traumatized by watching it happen repeatedly to her teammates. In addition to Jennings, several teammates testified as to how uncomfortable and "dirty" his conduct made them feel and also testified that they put up with it so that he would continue to let them play.

When Jennings was cut from the team after her sophomore year, she sued under Title IX, claiming that Coach Dorrance had created a hostile, sexually harassing environment. She also sued UNC's legal counsel, Susan Ehringhaus, using a theory of supervisor liability under § 1983 because, when she had reported the coach's misconduct to Ehringhaus, Ehringhaus took no action and advised Jennings to "work it out" with Dorrance.

HOLDING

The Fourth Circuit vacated the summary judgment that the district court had awarded to the defendants on both the Title IX claim and the § 1983 claim, and remanded the case back to the district court.

RATIONALE

The court identified four elements necessary for a plaintiff to establish a Title IX sexual harassment claim:

1. Plaintiff was a student at an educational institution receiving federal funds.
2. Plaintiff was subjected to harassment based on sex.
3. The harassment was sufficiently severe or pervasive to create a hostile (or abusive) environment in an educational program or activity.
4. Grounds existed for imputing liability to the institution.

Clearly, Jennings satisfied the first element of proof. As to the second, the court found that Dorrance's sexually charged comments went far beyond ordinary teasing – even of the nature that often occurs in a sport environment – and were persistently degrading and humiliating to his players as women, thus constituting sex-based harassment. Third, the court found that a jury could objectively conclude that the two incidents (which occurred over a two-year period) of direct harassment of Jennings were more abusive due to the general pattern of sexual abuse that instilled "fear and dread" in many of the players. Thus, the incidents of abuse were not considered trivial and isolated but instead were severe and pervasive events. The evidence that several other players experienced similar discomfort and humiliation supported the court's conclusion that Jennings was objectively reasonable in perceiving the environment to be hostile and abusive.

The court relied on an earlier Supreme Court Title IX harassment decision in *Davis v. Monroe County Board of Education* (1999), which stipulated that a plaintiff must prove she had been effectively denied equal access to educational benefits or opportunities, or that the harassment had had "a concrete, negative effect on her ability to participate." Here, the court concluded that the humiliation and anxiety caused by the coach's sexual harassment concretely and negatively affected Jennings' academic performance and ability to participate on the soccer team. With respect to institutional liability, the court concluded that the university's legal counsel acted with deliberate indifference (the required Title IX standard for institutional liability) when Ehringhaus took no action on Jennings' complaint.

Ultimately, this case was settled, the coach issued a formal apology, and Melissa Jennings was awarded $385,000, mostly in attorney's fees. Dorrance remains employed as the head coach of women's soccer at UNC (Wolverton, 2008).

Sexual Violence

In response to what were considered alarming statistics, the U.S. Department of Education issued a "Dear Colleague" letter in 2011. According to the letter, research showed that 1 in 5 women were victims of completed or attempted sexual assault while in college (Krebs et al., 2007), and in 2009, Clery Act reporting showed 3300 forcible sex offenses on college campuses (U.S. Department of Education, 2007–2009). The Letter clarified that it considers sexual violence to be a form of sexual harassment covered under

Title IX and further defined sexual violence as "physical sexual acts perpetrated against a person's will or where a person is incapable of giving consent due to the victim's use of drugs or alcohol. An individual also may be unable to give consent due to an intellectual or other disability" and further states that "a number of different acts fall into the category of sexual violence, including rape, sexual assault, sexual battery, and sexual coercion" (U.S. Department of Education, 2011). As forms of sexual harassment, these acts obligate school employees such as coaches and athletics administrators to report allegations of sexual violence to appropriate school officials, meaning those who have the authority to address the allegations and take corrective measures (U.S. Department of Education, 2011). The 2011 Letter was rescinded in 2017, leaving Department of Education policy and guidance in this area in flux (U.S. Department of Education, 2017). New regulations were promulgated by the DOE in 2020 which have narrowed the group of appropriate school officials for purposes of mandatory reporting (along with other grievance processes and investigative procedural changes). However, universities do have the flexibility to continue to operate with a broad mandatory reporting structure to enable them to better respond to reports of sexual violence (U.S. Department of Education, 2020).

Concerns across college campuses regarding the prevalence of sexual violence are of particular importance to sport managers working in college athletic administration. While the basketball and soccer student-athletes in the prior cases were victims of sexual harassment, there have been other cases where the student-athlete is the perpetrator. In 2001, two female students at the University of Colorado were sexually assaulted by football players and football recruits. There had been numerous past incidents of sexual assault by players and recruits at the school, and perhaps a culture of recruits being offered sex – the school had female "ambassadors" who were there to show the recruits a good time. After the incident was reported, several players were charged criminally, but the school continued to recruit one of the assailants and none of the current players lost eligibility (Avery-Washington, n.d.). The Plaintiffs brought suit under Title IX and on appeal of a summary judgment ruling for the school, the court focused on whether the university "sanctioned, supported, even funded, a program that, without proper control, would encourage young men to engage in opprobrious acts" (*Simpson v. University of Colorado*, 2007, para. 1177). The then-current head coach showed an attitude that was inconsistent with having made any effort to instruct players not to commit sexual harassment or assault, he retaliated against or threatened others who made complaints, including a female kicker on the football team and a female trainer. The court found that the risk of sexual assault during recruiting trips was obvious, which meant that a jury could reasonably find that the coach was deliberately indifferent to Title IX discrimination. The case was remanded and a settlement was ultimately reached, with Lisa Simpson receiving $2.5 million, and the other plaintiff, Anne Gilmore, receiving $350,000 (Pankratz, 2007).

There have been other high-profile college sexual assault cases which have led to settlements. Florida State University paid $950,000 to a former student who sued the school under Title XI for which she believed to be an indifferent response to her rape accusation against QB Jameis Winston (Kirschner, 2016). She later settled a civil suit with Winston. In 2018, Baylor University settled a Title XI lawsuit with a former volleyball player who she claimed was gang-raped by up to eight football players in 2012. A Baylor equestrian athlete filed suit in 2019, claiming that the university took an unreasonably long time to investigate her sexual assault by two football players (who also made a video of the assault) and further she was treated in a "shaming, embarrassing, and hostile manner," during the investigation (Erickson, 2019, para. 6). These cases are just two examples of several lawsuits against Baylor in connection with its "sexual assault scandal" that led to the firings of University President Ken Starr and Head Coach Art Briles, along with the resignation of Athletic Director Ian McGaw.

In 2018, Michigan State University (MSU) agreed to a $500 million settlement with 332 women and girls who were sexually assaulted by USA gymnastics and MSU team doctor Larry Nassar. A 2017 federal lawsuit (one of several in this case) alleging sexual assault, battery, molestation, and harassment between 1996 and 2016 also revealed that athletes raised concerns periodically during that time and MSU failed to act (Mencarini, 2017). According to a Department of Education report, MSU violated the Clery Act for years, including 11 examples dating back to 1997 in which Nassar victims reported his abuse to campus staff who failed to follow proper protocol (Rock, 2019). MSU's Title IX office investigated, and cleared, Nassar in 2014. Nassar was sentenced to 40 to 175 years in prison after pleading guilty to seven counts of criminal sexual conduct in a Michigan state court, and was also given 60 years for federal convictions, including child pornography (Levenson, 2018). Many MSU officials resigned in the wake of Nassar scandal, including then-President Lou Anna Simon and Athletic Director Mark Hollis. One victim claims that Simon's successor offered her money to forgo a formal settlement proceeding, and another claimed that a former Athletic Director tried to conceal a rape by Nassar in 1992 (Kitchener & Wong, 2018).

Third Party and Peer-to-Peer Harassment

Title IX protects any "person" from sex discrimination; accordingly both male and female students are protected from sexual harassment engaged in by other students or third parties. For example, if members of a visiting athletic team created a sexually hostile environment for a student at the home team university, it would be conduct prohibited under Title IX. Also, Title IX prohibits sexual harassment regardless of the sex of the harasser, that is, even if the harasser and the person being harassed are members of the same sex. For example, Title IX has been used successfully to challenge same-sex peer sexual harassment. The rationale used by these courts is that harassment based on sexual orientation violates Title IX because Title IX prohibits harassment based on gender nonconformity (*Theno v. Tonganoxie Unified Sch. Dist.*, 2005; *Montgomery v. Indep. Sch. Dist. No. 709*, 2000; *Schroeder v. Maumee Bd. of Educ*, 2003; *Ray v. Antioch Unified Sch. Dist.*, 2000). See also *Snelling v. Fall Mountain Regional School District* (2001); *Doe v. Southeastern Greene School District* (2006); *Riccio v. New Haven Board of Education* (2006). In addition, DOE issued a new Guidance in January 2020 clarifying that if harassment is based on conduct of a sexual nature, it may be sexual harassment prohibited by Title IX even if the harasser and the harassed are the same sex or the victim of harassment is gay or lesbian.

Title IX's protections also apply to students when traveling abroad such as when college athletics teams travel to other countries for preseason play. Often, the drinking age in other countries is 18, and the likelihood of inappropriate sexual conduct increases with excessive alcohol consumption. In a lawsuit against Eastern Michigan University (EMU; since settled out of court), a U.S. District Court judge ruled in a pretrial motion that Title IX applies when students who are U.S. citizens are harassed in foreign countries while participating in study abroad programs. One of the alleged harassers was an associate professor who was an assistant to the trip leader. EMU had argued that Title IX applies only to students in the United States (Young, 2002). The following hypothetical case considers a similar situation in the context of sport.

Considering … Sexual Harassment Occurring Abroad

An assistant coach of the Middle America University women's basketball team sexually harasses a student-athlete on multiple occasions during a 10-day team trip to Europe where they are playing four games against European teams. When the team returns to Kansas, the athlete reports the harassment to the athletic director. The director tells the player that, if it happens again on U.S. soil, the player should report it and she will take action. She will not, however, take further action on this first complaint because it did not happen in the United States.

Questions

- If the judge in the EMU study abroad case was correct, did the athletic director handle the problem correctly?
- If not, how should she have dealt with the player's complaint?

Note how you would answer the questions and then check your responses using the Analysis & Discussion at the end of this chapter.

Finally, a student who has been sexually assaulted by an athlete on campus should not give in to pressure from coaches or athletic department personnel to refrain from reporting the incident to the police. After a female basketball player at La Salle University was allegedly raped by a member of the men's basketball team, news reports claimed that the coaches persuaded her not to report it to the authorities. A cover-up of this sort would be a violation of the Clery Act, which requires college officials to report such incidents (Byrne, 2004). Pennsylvania State University was subjected to investigation by the U.S. Department of Education for violating the Clery Act in its cover-up of boys who were sexually assaulted by former assistant football coach Jerry Sandusky (Snyder, 2013).

Transgender Athletes

Another issue facing sport managers today is how schools should handle athletics participation for transgendered athletes. Which locker room should a transgendered athlete use? What pronouns should be used to refer to him or her? Should he or she play on the men's team or the women's team? Such questions prompted the Women's Sports Foundation to co-sponsor a report that explains what transgender is and discusses policy recommendations and best practices for implementing inclusive policies (Griffin & Carroll, 2010). Relying in part on this report, in 2011 the NCAA developed and approved a policy with the dual goals of allowing transgendered athletes to participate in line with their gender identity while maintaining competitive equity among teams. Under the NCAA's policy, a female athlete adding testosterone to transition to male is prohibited from competing on a women's team, and a male transitioning to female using testosterone suppression drugs may not compete on a women's team until one year of treatment has been completed (Lawrence, 2011). At the high school level, 44 states had some sort of transgender athlete policy by 2019, however there are large discrepancies among them. Nine states, including Texas, have what could be considered "discriminatory" policies, requiring transgender athletes to either compete per their birth certificate or requiring surgery and hormones (Transathlete, 2019). A transgender wrestler in Texas won two state championships competing against girls, even though the athlete was transitioning from female to male and was taking a low dose of testosterone. The athlete had asked to wrestle in the boy's division (Associated Press, 2018). Seventeen states have policies that need modification or decisions are made on a case-by-case basis, and 18 states have inclusive policies that do not require surgery or hormones (Transathlete, 2019).

In 2018, the Third Circuit upheld a Pennsylvania District Court verdict refusing to enjoin a school district policy allowing transgender students to use the bathrooms and locker rooms that are consistent with their gender identities. The Boyertown Area School District (BASD) was sued by four cisgender students claiming the policy violated both their constitutional right to bodily privacy and Title IX (a tort law claim is not examined here). According to the court, the constitutional right of privacy is not absolute and must be weighed against important competing governmental interests. "… The constitution forbids governmental infringement on certain fundamental interests unless that infringement is sufficiently tailored to serve a compelling state interest" (*Doe v. Boyertown*, 2018, p. 528). As transgender students face extraordinary social, psychological, and medical risks, and because transgender individuals face discrimination, harassment, and violence, shielding these students from discrimination becomes a matter of life and death, therefore BASD had a compelling state interest in protecting these students. And then, assuming the policy it subject to strict scrutiny, achieving that compelling interest must be narrowly framed. Because BASD also had single-user bathrooms (not required for use by any group of students), any students with privacy concerns can use these bathrooms instead of communal ones. The policy does not force any cisgender student to disrobe in front of any other student, regardless of whether they are cisgender or transgender. "School locker rooms and restrooms are places where it is not only common to encounter others in various stages of undress, it is expected" (p. 531). Regarding the Title IX claim, BASD's policy treated all students equally and therefore did not discriminate on the basis of sex as well not meeting the elements of a hostile environment harassment claim. And further, the appellants did not provide any authority to suggest that a sex-neutral policy can give rise to Title IX claim. There is no disparate treatment based on

Exhibit 12.9 Title VI of the Civil Rights Act of 1964, 42 U.S.C. § 2000d.

No person in the United States shall, on the ground of race, color, or national origin, be excluded from participation in, be denied the benefits of, or be subjected to discrimination under any program or activity receiving federal financial assistance.

sex when all students are allowed to use the bathroom and locker room that aligns with their gender identity. And, the presence of transgender students in bathrooms and locker rooms does not give rise to sexual harassment that is so severe, pervasive, or objectively offensive that it undermines and detracts from a student's educational experience, effectively denying that student equal access to the school's resources and opportunities. In 2019, the Supreme Court declined to hear an appeal to this case, allowing BASD's transgender-friendly policies to continue (ACLU, 2019).

Race Discrimination and Title VI

Title VI, like Title IX, prevents discrimination by educational institutions that receive federal funds, but Title VI protects against discrimination based on race (see Exhibit 12.9). Although for decades sport sociologists have trained their floodlights on race discrimination in sport, there has been very little litigation brought by student-athletes over this issue. Why haven't there been court battles over ethnicity equity as there have been over gender equity? The best answer is probably that when racism affects sport participation, it is much more subtle and less overt than gender discrimination. Discrimination based on race is often more difficult to detect and even more difficult to prove because we do not purposefully operate separate Black teams from White teams, as we do female teams from male teams. Thus, as we learned regarding gender discrimination, we are able to compare and contrast the treatment of male athletes and female athletes using a variety of tests and factors. Since teams are not separate based on race, these comparisons are unavailable to detect potential discrimination. Our first Focus Case, Elliott v. Delaware State University (2012), explores one of the few cases in which a student-athlete brought a race discrimination claim against a university. Then we will examine a number of legal challenges alleging racial bias brought against NCAA and its initial eligibility standards.

Elliott v. Delaware State University

879 F. Supp. 2d 438 (D. Del. 2012)	FOCUS CASE

FACTS

The plaintiff Sara Elliott, who is White, lived in a freshman dorm with a Black non-athlete named Kristen Williams who, together with some Black friends, twice engaged in racially abusive and threatening verbal attacks on Elliott. After Elliott complained to Christopher Hall (the residence hall director), he criticized her for "pulling the race card," and warned her not to pursue it any further because "that would be throwing me under the bus and it will come back." In September 2009, Elliot submitted a formal complaint anyway, and Hall's supervisor requested that he file a formal incident report, which he then did. At that time, Hall told Elliott she would be transferred to a different dorm. After Elliott's mother protested that Sara should not be the one who had to move, Hall required Williams to relocate instead, and eventually charged her with a Student Conduct Code violation for the racially hostile verbal abuse. Williams was acquitted due to lack of evidence, in part because Elliott did not wish to testify at the hearing, citing a desire not to miss class.

Meanwhile, Elliott's mother had informed her daughter's volleyball coach, Renee Arnold, that she and her daughter believed Sara was experiencing retaliation for reporting the racial hostility. According to

Sara, Arnold became angry in October 2009 that Sara had first taken her complaint to other university officials. In October, Coach Arnold allegedly began to retaliate against Elliott. According to Elliott, Arnold stopped speaking to her, did not allow her to play in any volleyball games, and told her and a Black player that their scholarships would not be renewed due to budget cuts (when in fact the budget had not actually been cut).

On April 22, 2010, Sara's mother complained to the athletics director that Coach Arnold was discriminating and retaliating against her daughter. The athletics director then reinstated Sara's scholarship, but told the coach about the mother's complaint, adding that Sara thought Arnold was a racist and that she was suing the university. Soon thereafter, Arnold told the rest of the team that the only reason Elliott was still on the team was because of the accusation of racism and the related lawsuit.

In June Arnold removed Elliott's profile from the team's website, excluded her from team text messages, issued punishments in practices that were disproportionate to those received by other players, told her she could not travel with the team, required Elliott and a Black player to submit to a drug test based on information received from a recruit (the test turned out to be positive), forced Elliott to practice with shin splints unless she provided medical documentation advising to the contrary (such documentation was not required of other players complaining of injuries), and gave her only a few minutes of playing time during the entire 39-game season. In March of the following year, Elliott was so dissatisfied that she left Delaware State University (DSU).

Elliott then sued DSU under Title VI for race discrimination, hostile environment, racial harassment, and retaliation against her for complaining of racial discrimination. The university then moved for summary judgment on all three claims.

HOLDING

The district court granted summary judgment to DSU on the race discrimination and racially hostile environment claims, but denied summary judgment on the claim of retaliation with respect to Coach Arnold's behavior.

RATIONALE

In deciding this case, the court was careful to distinguish between the actions of the residence hall director and the coach. To prevail on her Title VI race discrimination claim, Elliott had to prove that she (1) was a member of a protected class; (2) was qualified to continue to pursue her education; (3) was treated differently from similarly situated students who were not members of that protected class; and (4) suffered an adverse action. The court found that while the first two elements were satisfied, the latter two were not. It concluded that while Hall might have been racially biased, he ultimately took no adverse action against Elliott. Also, while Arnold treated her harshly, there was no evidence that she was treated differently on the basis of her race. The court stated that just because a coach treats a player of a different race unfairly, that does not necessarily mean she did so because of her race. Here there was evidence that she subjected Black players to similarly harsh treatment (drug testing and scholarship non-renewal). Thus, the court found insufficient evidence to infer race discrimination under the third element of the race discrimination claim.

As to the racially hostile environment claim, Elliott had to prove that: (1) there was racial harassment that "was so severe, pervasive, and objectively offensive that it deprived her of access to education opportunities"; and (2) that DSU officials acted with deliberate indifference in failing to correct it. The court found that the two incidents of verbal abuse were too few and not severe enough to qualify as harassment, particularly because Elliott was only in the uncomfortable living situation for 22 days before Williams was removed. Also, although Hall's reluctance to pursue a complaint was problematic, DSU officials did respond to Elliott's formal complaint by removing Williams from the dorm room and filing a conduct charge against her. With respect to the coach, the court reiterated that there was no evidence of racial animus in her treatment of Elliott.

Elliott also claimed a violation of Title VI on the grounds that Hall and Arnold were retaliating against her because she filed a formal race discrimination complaint. To prevail, she had to prove: (1) that she engaged in a protected activity; (2) the university subjected her to an adverse action at that time or thereafter; and (3) a causal link existed between the protected activity and that adverse action. The court found no retaliation on the part of Hall, although he had threatened to retaliate if Elliott filed a formal complaint, he did not ultimately cause her to suffer an adverse action because she was allowed to remain in her dorm room.

However, the retaliation claim against the coach survived DSU's motion for summary judgment because Elliott's evidence of harsh treatment, combined with Arnold's statement to the team, established sufficient support that the coach was retaliating in reaction to being told that Elliott thought she was a racist and was suing. The court stated that the harsh treatment occurring after the date of the formal complaint could constitute a constructive discharge type of adverse action if those actions were so intolerable as to make continued participation in an education program or activity impossible. While the threatened non-renewal of Elliott's scholarship preceded her formal complaint and thus would not count as a retaliatory act, all the actions taken by Arnold after April 22 would. In the court's words, "Arnold went to considerable lengths to make Elliott's life as a volleyball player miserable. It is hard to imagine that a student-athlete would be expected to endure such openly hostile treatment by her own coach." The court concluded that because these conditions could be viewed as objectively intolerable, and because they appeared to be causally linked to Elliott's allegations of racism against Arnold, the retaliation claim against the coach was retained.

NCAA Initial Eligibility Criteria

In two race discrimination cases involving disputes over eligibility criteria, African American student-athletes brought suit against the NCAA, alleging that the initial eligibility standards unfairly discriminated against them on the basis of race (Cureton v. NCAA, 1999; Pryor v. NCAA, 2002). Both cases centered on Proposition 16. Proposition 16 is the name of the standard for determining initial eligibility that was implemented in 1992 in an effort by the NCAA to improve the graduation rates of student-athletes. It placed the student's high school grade point average (GPA) and admission test scores (SAT or ACT) on a sliding scale that allowed a student to qualify with a lower standardized test score if she had a higher GPA, and vice versa. It replaced Proposition 48, which had required a minimum high school GPA of 2.0 and a minimum SAT score of 700. Proposition 16 placed greater emphasis on the standardized test score than its predecessor by setting the minimum test score at 820 for students with a 2.5 GPA and requiring a 1010 for students with a 2.0 GPA.

When the NCAA was in the process of evaluating whether Proposition 16 would achieve its goal of improving graduation rates, it considered three other standards and determined that, of the four, Proposition 16 would promote the largest increase. As part of this analysis, the NCAA obtained data on the effect that the four proposed standards would have on initial eligibility of Black student-athletes. The projections found that Proposition 16 would raise the graduation rates of all athletes and would raise the graduation rates of African Americans the most. However, it would also have the effect of excluding a greater number of Black athletes at the outset than would the other three proposed standards. Knowing this, the NCAA membership went ahead and voted to adopt Proposition 16 anyway.

In Cureton v. NCAA (1999), the plaintiffs brought suit under Title VI alleging that Proposition 16 had a discriminatory disparate impact on African Americans (see Chapter 5 for a detailed discussion of the difference between a disparate impact claim, which alleges that a neutral rule has an unfair effect on a protected group of people, and a disparate treatment claim, which alleges intentional discrimination). The Cureton case was never fully heard, having been voided by a later Supreme Court case in which the Court ruled that there is no private right to bring a disparate impact claim under Title VI (Alexander v. Sandoval, 2001).

> ## Competitive Advantage Strategies
>
> *Race Discrimination in High School and College Athletics*
>
> - Persons with influence on rule-making should avoid establishing eligibility standards that place a lot of weight on data that may be racially biased (such as standardized test scores).
> - Policy-makers should be aware of the distinction between a policy that has a negative effect on members of an ethnic minority group *because* of their ethnicity and one that does so *in spite* of their ethnicity. Evidence that the policy-makers had prior knowledge that a rule or policy would probably have a disproportionately negative effect on an ethnic minority group will be scrutinized closely by a court to determine whether it was implemented *because* of the likelihood of that negative effect.

In contrast, the plaintiffs in *Pryor v. NCAA* (2002) claimed that the NCAA engaged in intentional race discrimination when it adopted Proposition 16, thus violating Title VI. The Third Circuit found that because the NCAA had researched the likely effects of Proposition 16 and thus knew the rule would disproportionately impact the initial eligibility of Black student-athletes, the plaintiff had alleged sufficient facts to support a claim of intentional discrimination.

In the aftermath of the decision in *Pryor* to let the plaintiffs' claims proceed, the NCAA revised the initial eligibility standards to de-emphasize the standardized test score. The rule change took the wind out of the sails of the *Pryor* case. Effective in 2003, the revised standard requires only a minimum SAT score of 400, as long as the student has a high enough GPA (3.55) to balance that out on the sliding scale. Although a higher incoming GPA is required, instead of placing so much weight on initial eligibility, these new rules have tightened up the requirements for continuing eligibility. Student-athletes must accrue 24 semester hours before entering their second academic year and must maintain a minimum load of 18 hours each academic year and six hours per semester. Additionally, under rule 14.4.3.2 student-athletes in four-year programs must complete 40 percent of their credits by the end of their second year and 60 percent by the end of year three, and students entering their fifth year of college enrollment must have completed 80 percent of their credits by the end of their fourth year (NCAA, 2012).

Disability Discrimination and Section 504/ADA

The U.S. has a patchwork of legal protections for students with disabilities covering public and private secondary schools and post-secondary educational institutions (see Exhibit 12.10). Chapter 5 discussed disability discrimination in the context of employment under Title I of the Americans with Disabilities Act (ADA) and Chapter 17 provides a more detailed discussion of the law of disability discrimination at it applies to places of public accommodation such as stadiums, arenas, and venue operations under Title III of the ADA. In this chapter we primarily explore § 504 of the Rehabilitation Act of 1973 (Section 504)

Exhibit 12.10 Federal disability rights and discrimination laws.

Individuals with Disabilities Education Act (IDEA) (2004) an act to provide federal financial assistance to state and local education agencies to guarantee special education and related services to eligible children with disabilities.

Section 504 of the Rehabilitation Act of 1973 (504 or Section 504) (2015) a civil rights law prohibiting discrimination on the basis of disability in programs and activities, public and private, that receive federal financial assistance.

Americans with Disabilities Act (ADA) (2008) a civil rights law prohibiting discrimination solely on the basis of disability in employment (Title I), public services (Title II), and public accommodations (Title III).

and Title II of the ADA and the impact of these federal laws on athletic participation opportunities for students with disabilities in our public schools and universities. However, we will also briefly discuss the applicability of the ADA to the NCAA or other private sport governing bodies.

Section 504 prohibits discrimination on the basis of disability in programs or activities that receive Federal financial assistance from the U.S. Department of Education. Title II of the ADA prohibits discrimination on the basis of disability by state and local governments which includes public schools and universities. Just as we learned in the gender discrimination section, OCR is responsible for the enforcement of Section 504 and Title II of the ADA. Thus, eligibility and competition rules that exclude students with disabilities from athletics participation will be evaluated under both § 504 and ADA to ensure the students are not being excluded unlawfully. In the context of high school and college athletics, sport managers must understand these laws to both protect students with disabilities from discrimination, but to also ensure that persons with disabilities had an equal opportunity to participate in sport, recreation, physical activity, and physical education. In this chapter, we examine eligibility requirements of high school athletic associations and the NCAA that may tend to exclude or disproportionately impact students with disabilities in accessing sport opportunities. We also explore what participation opportunities must be provide by schools and universities for students with disabilities under the mandate of § 504 and Title II.

The legal analysis under Title II of the ADA is the same as that under § 504 and that will be our focus in this chapter (see Exhibit 12.11). Section 504 states: "No otherwise qualified individual with a disability … shall solely by reason of her or his disability, be excluded from participation in, be denied the benefits of, or be subjected to discrimination under any program or activity receiving federal financial assistance." (29 U.S.C. § 794(a); 34 C.F.R. § 104.4(a)). If a plaintiff can establish that she is a qualified person with a disability and is excluded from participation or access to programs or serviced because of her disability, § 504 and ADA require the school or organization to (1) make reasonable modifications in policies, practices, or procedures when modifications are necessary to avoid discrimination on the basis of disability; and (2) furnish appropriate auxiliary aids and services where necessary to afford the individual an equal opportunity to participate in and enjoy the benefits of the service, program, or activity. These adjustments are required unless the school or organization can show that the modifications would fundamentally alter the nature of the service, program or activity or that making the modifications or providing the auxiliary aids would impose an undue burden upon the school or organization. (For a more detailed discussion of "fundamental alteration" in sports programs, see Chapter 17.)

As previously mentioned, sport related claims brought under § 504 and ADA generally involve athletic eligibility requirements imposed by high school or collegiate athletic associations. Typically, these requirements most often challenged include (1) age requirements that prevent athletes from participating who turn 19 years old before the beginning of the school year; (2) eight semester rules

---

Exhibit 12.11 Legal analysis under § 504 and Title II of the ADA.

The plaintiff must prove that she or he is:

1   Disabled
2   Otherwise qualified
3   Excluded solely on the basis of disability

To prove she or he is disabled, the plaintiff must prove that she or he has a:

1   Physical or mental impairment
2   Which substantially limits
3   One or more major life activities

which prohibit athletes from participating beyond eight semesters in high school; and (3) minimum academic requirements that might preclude certain classes from GPA or other qualifying academic credits. Athletes denied the opportunity to participate would request that the eligibility requirements be modified or waived triggering the reasonable modification provisions of Section 504. In addition to requests for reasonable modifications, we are seeing an increasing number of claims filed by athletes who have requested auxiliary aids and services from schools or associations. For example, in 2015, a deaf high school wrestler filed a lawsuit alleging violations of Title II of the ADA and § 504 (among other claims) because the Michigan High School Athletic Association (MHSAA) would not allow his interpreter to move around the mat to stay in his sight line. The MHSAA policy allowed for an interpreter, but that interpreter must sit with the coaches, which according to the plaintiff, negated the effectiveness of the interpreter and cut off communication with the coaches (*Kempf v. MHSAA*, 2015; Greenwood, 2015; Wenzel, 2015). The lawsuit was settled quickly, with MHSAA modifying their policy to allow "360 degree access around the 28-foot circle" but that the interpreter shall make "reasonable efforts not to interfere" with participants, coaches, etc. including blocking views (*Kempf v. MHSAA*, 2015, p. 3). Several lawsuits have been filed against schools by athletes alleging discrimination on the basis of having either a physical or a learning disability. We will explore a few of these in our next Focus Cases.

Lawsuits Against Public Entities – § 504 and Title II of the ADA

Physical Disabilities

A case of a student who wanted to play basketball at the college level, despite a heart abnormality, illustrates the application of § 504 to an athletics situation. The court in *Knapp v. Northwestern University* (1996) considers the issue of whether the plaintiff's disability substantially limited a major life activity.

Knapp v. Northwestern University

101 F.3d 473 (7th Cir. 1996)   **FOCUS** CASE

FACTS

The plaintiff Knapp had been recruited to play basketball on an athletics grant-in-aid for Northwestern University (NU). However, once the school found out that Knapp had a heart abnormality that had triggered cardiac death and required him to have a defibrillator implanted in his heart, they refused to allow him to play. The NU team doctors ruled Knapp medically ineligible because the implanted defibrillator had never been tested under the intense conditions of elite college basketball, and thus Knapp would be exposed to what they determined was an unacceptable level of risk. These doctors based their decision on published guidelines from medical conferences as well as consultations with other doctors.

NU admitted that Knapp had been excluded solely on the basis of his heart problem. Knapp sued the university, claiming he had been discriminated against on the basis of disability in violation of § 504 of the Rehabilitation Act. The district court found the university in violation of § 504 and entered a permanent injunction barring the university from excluding Knapp from the team for any reason related to his heart condition. NU appealed.

HOLDING

The Seventh Circuit reversed and entered summary judgment for Northwestern University, holding that Knapp was not disabled under the law.

RATIONALE

The central issue for the court was whether Knapp's physical impairment substantially limited a major life activity. The court ruled that playing basketball is itself not basic enough to constitute a major life activity (as compared to standing, breathing, or hearing). Nevertheless, they considered whether playing intercollegiate basketball implicated learning, which is generally considered to be a major life activity for purposes of this law. According to the *Knapp* court, although playing an intercollegiate sport may be part of the learning experience at a university, not being able to play does not render a person unable to get a satisfactory education. Therefore, the court held that Knapp was not disabled under the law, because his impairment did not substantially limit the major life activity of learning.

Moreover, according to the court, NU had not excluded Knapp based on stereotypes about people with disabilities, but rather had acted reasonably in relying on competent, case-specific medical evidence. The court further ruled that even if Knapp were considered to have met the criteria for being disabled, he was not otherwise qualified to participate. This is because there was a significant health risk, and significant risk can disqualify a person when that risk cannot be reduced by a reasonable accommodation – which in this case it could not. The court concluded that NU's decision was not illegal under § 504.

The decision in *Knapp* appears to have redefined sport participation as not being a major life activity. It also seems to stand for the proposition that doctors should be allowed to determine what are acceptable versus unacceptable risks for potential participants with disabling conditions. Instead of blithely allowing any athlete with a disability to take any and all risks associated with participation in her preferred sport, such a stance probably comports well with the case-by-case, fact-specific approach of disability law. It would also seem to provide schools with protection from negligence liability as long as they act reasonably in relying on the advice of appropriate medical personnel.

Learning Disabilities

Learning disabilities have posed an even more difficult challenge for the courts. Athletes with learning disabilities may run afoul of several eligibility rules, such as the age-limit rule for high school participation, the longevity rules in high school participation that limit the number of semesters of eligibility, or academic standards and progress rules in college.

Many high school athletic associations have a rule limiting interscholastic athletics participation to students age 18 and under. The federal courts have been divided on the issue of whether such an age limit violates the disabilities laws when applied to students whose educational progress has been delayed (thus making them over the age of 18 by the time they graduate) due to a learning disability. This same type of analysis is pertinent to the alleged violation of longevity rules, since they also are concerned with keeping the playing field fair so that older and more mature students do not gain an unfair advantage in participation.

The Sixth and Eighth Circuit Courts have ruled that to grant a waiver of the age-limit eligibility rule to a student over the age of 18 who is learning disabled would constitute an undue administrative burden by requiring too much case-by-case analysis on the part of the school and would constitute a fundamental alteration of the interscholastic sports program by allowing older students to participate (creating an unlevel playing field and an unsafe one because of severe mismatches in size, weight, and strength) (*Sandison*, 1995; *Pottgen*, 1994).

However, several U.S. district courts have ruled to the contrary, holding that a case-by-case analysis is exactly what Congress intended when it passed § 504 and the ADA. They contend that such an analysis is not an undue burden and is necessary to enable a court to determine whether a waiver in the individual case would work a fundamental alteration in the competitive sports program. The *Dennin* case provides an example.

Dennin v. Connecticut Interscholastic Athletic Conference

913 F. Supp. 663 (D. Conn. 1996)   **FOCUS** CASE

FACTS

The plaintiff Dennin was a 19-year-old with Down syndrome who was a member of the swim team. He had been held back a year in middle school due to his educational needs, with the result that he was 19 years old during his senior year in high school. He was thus denied eligibility for his senior year under the Connecticut Interscholastic Athletic Conference (CIAC) age-limit rule. His request for a waiver of the rule was denied, but because his participation on the team was written into his individualized education plan, the CIAC said they would allow him to continue to participate as a nonscoring exhibition swimmer on his relay team. This meant that his relay team could not earn any points for the overall team. Dennin sued under § 504 and the ADA.

HOLDING

The court found in favor of Dennin, holding that it would be a reasonable accommodation for the CIAC to grant a waiver in his case.

RATIONALE

According to the court, allowing Dennin to participate only as an exhibition swimmer would be to treat him differently on the basis of his disability, thus potentially damaging his self-esteem and his willingness to attempt to function in the larger community. This, said the court, would violate the goal of the disabilities laws to enable the full and equal participation of persons with disabilities. In contrast, granting Dennin a waiver of the age-limit rule would not impose an undue burden on the CIAC because they already conduct similar individualized assessments for a waiver process for transfer students. The occasional difficulties caused by doing these assessments did not rise to the level of an undue burden.

   Furthermore, in the eyes of the court, granting such a waiver did not create a fundamental altera-tion in the conduct of interscholastic athletics. The court found there were five purposes behind the age-limit rule:

   1 To prevent a competitive advantage for older, stronger athletes
   2 To protect younger, less mature athletes from injury
   3 To discourage athletes from delaying the completion of their education for athletics purposes
   4 To prevent coaches from redshirting athletes to gain a competitive advantage
   5 To avoid having younger athletes lose out on participation opportunities due to the greater physical prowess of older athletes

Because Dennin was always the slowest swimmer in the pool, the court found that none of the competitive advantage purposes of the age-limit rule would be undermined by granting him a waiver, and Dennin's older age would not pose an injury risk to others because swimming is not a contact sport. The court concluded, therefore, that granting a waiver would not fundamentally alter the nature of the interscho-lastic swimming program.

In *Dennin*, the CIAC also argued that their age-limit rule was a neutral rule neutrally applied, and thus Dennin was not excluded from participation solely because of his disability. Instead, he was excluded because the passage of time simply made him too old to participate during his senior year. The court found that this argument ignored the reality that he was too old solely due to his disability.

Other courts have disagreed with the *Dennin* rationale. These courts have held that age-limit rules are neutral rules, and have taken the position that the fact plaintiffs like Dennin were allowed to participate during their first three years is evidence that they had not been discriminated against solely because of their disability. Instead, they were excluded simply because they became too old during their senior year (see, e.g., *Sandison*, 1995).

Lawsuits Against Places of Public Accommodation – Title III of the ADA

Athletes may sue the NCAA or other collegiate governing body under Title III of the ADA, which allows litigation against private entities that own, lease, or operate places of public accommodation. Title III litigation has primarily been used in lawsuits against the NCAA, which has been deemed a private entity by the courts since the 1988 Supreme Court decision in *NCAA v. Tarkanian*. Initially, the federal courts were divided on whether Title III applied to suits against the NCAA, because the statute and its regulations seem to suggest that a place of public accommodation refers to a place with an actual physical location, and of course the NCAA does not conduct events within any facility of its own.

However, in *PGA Tour, Inc. v. Martin* (2001), the Supreme Court ruled that the PGA Tour operates places of public accommodation when it conducts its professional golf tournaments at various golf courses around the country. In that case, the Court held that a place of public accommodation is not limited to the spectator areas during the golf tournaments, but also extends to the opportunity to compete in the golf competition. It is true that the PGA Tour actually leases and operates each golf course during a given professional tournament, whereas the NCAA rarely does such a thing. Nevertheless, in accord with the *Martin* decision, most federal courts have ruled that, for purposes of ADA Title III litigation, the NCAA is a private entity operating a place of public accommodation. In drawing that conclusion, they reason that a strong enough nexus exists between the university's athletics program and the NCAA by virtue of the control the NCAA exerts over access to participation through its eligibility requirements and requirements of compliance with its other rules (*Matthews v. NCAA*, 2001; *Ganden v. NCAA*, 1996; *Tatum v. NCAA*, 1998; *Bowers v. NCAA*, 1998). The *Matthews* case provides an example of how Title III of the ADA applies to the NCAA.

Matthews v. NCAA

179 F. Supp. 2d 1209 (E.D. Wash. 2001)   FOCUS CASE

FACTS

The plaintiff Matthews was a football player at Washington State University who suffered from severe learning disabilities with respect to reading comprehension (he had scores in the 6th to 10th percentile) and written expression, and whose IQ was in the 13th percentile. In his first year, he had been granted a waiver of the NCAA's full-time student credit hour rule and the 75/25 rule that prohibited student-athletes from completing more than 25 percent of their yearly credit hour requirement in summer school. The NCAA denied Matthews' request for a second waiver of the 75/25 rule the following year, declaring him academically ineligible and asserting that his failure to meet the 75/25 rule was due to his lack of effort and poor class attendance (offering evidence that he had attended only half of the lectures in his criminal justice class) rather than to his learning disability. Matthews sued the NCAA under Title III of the ADA.

HOLDING

The district court held that: (1) the plaintiff's learning disability was a covered disability, citing the federal regulations promulgated under the ADA that state that mental impairments include "any mental or psychological disorder such as mental retardation, organic brain syndrome, emotional or mental illness, and specific learning disabilities," 28 C.F.R. § 36.104 (2005); (2) Matthews' learning disability substantially limited his ability to learn (learning is included in the regulations' list of covered major life activities); and (3) Matthews was discriminated against by the NCAA's denial of his request for a second year's waiver of the 75/25 rule.

RATIONALE

The NCAA argued that the ADA should not protect Matthews because playing football is not a major life activity (this is similar to the argument successfully used in the *Knapp* case, discussed earlier). However, the court decided that playing football was not the major life activity in question – instead, learning was. According to the court, the NCAA's action against Matthews resulted from an impairment affecting his ability to learn – not from a physical impairment affecting his physical capability of playing football. Thus, the ADA protected Matthews from discrimination based on eligibility requirements that discriminated against him based on his learning disability.

The court also felt that the requested waiver was a reasonable accommodation of his learning disability, especially given the fact that the NCAA had granted him a similar waiver the year before. Thus, granting this waiver could not be construed as modifying an essential part of the NCAA's policies and so would not constitute a fundamental alteration of the NCAA's purpose of promoting student-athlete development. According to the court, the NCAA has plenty of other rules to ensure a focus on academics.

Furthermore, the court asserted (without explanation) that granting this waiver would not give Matthews an unfair advantage over other student-athletes. Therefore, the court would have granted in part Matthews' motion for summary judgment. However, the court also recognized the potential validity of the NCAA's argument that Matthews' failure to meet the 75/25 rule was due to lack of effort, not disability, and found a sufficient question of fact to deny in part Matthews' motion for summary judgment. The case as a whole was rendered moot and dismissed because Matthews had since transferred to Eastern Washington University and played out his eligibility, and the court was thus left with no remedy to grant him, since under Title III money damages are not available to plaintiffs – the only remedy is injunctive relief.

Separate Teams for Athletes with Disabilities

Another issue for consideration is whether high schools and universities are legally obligated to provide separate interscholastic, intercollegiate, or intramural teams for athletes with physical disabilities. Occasionally, such athletes have competed on varsity teams, including Aimee Mullins, a female sprinter with artificial legs on the track team at Georgetown University, and Casey Martin, who rode a cart in varsity golf play for Stanford University (Suggs, 2004). As another example, in 2006, a court issued a temporary injunction ordering a Maryland school district to allow Tatyana McFadden, a two-time Paralympic Games medalist in 2004, to compete in interscholastic middle-distance races in a wheelchair alongside able-bodied competitors ("Wheelchair athlete disqualified," 2006). McFadden has since won seven gold medals at the Paralympic Games, and has won the wheelchair division of the Boston Marathon, Chicago Marathon, London Marathon, and New York City Marathon multiple times (Price, 2018).

Some universities provide athletic opportunities for athletes with disabilities. The University of Illinois, for instance, offers a men's and a women's wheelchair basketball team, as well as a wheelchair track team. Illinois has a 2,100 square foot dedicated track facility that is designated as a U.S. Paralympic training site for wheelchair racing (Kuzma, 2016). And athletes get scholarships (NCAA, 2013). As of the 2018–2019 season, ten schools offered participation opportunities on wheelchair basketball teams (some teams had mixed male/female rosters), and five schools had women's teams (NWBA, 2019). These teams are sanctioned by the National Wheelchair Basketball Association.

Competitive Advantage Strategies

Avoiding Disability Discrimination Claims

- Consider offering separate teams, such as wheelchair basketball or sledge ice hockey, for people with disabilities.
- Always make an individualized assessment of each request for accommodation. The individualized inquiry should include informing potential participants of their rights and assuring them a prompt and fair review if questions arise concerning eligibility or safety issues (Grady & Andrew, 2003).
- Establish an internal complaint procedure for resolving ADA and § 504 disputes that includes the following:

  o   Procedures for filing written complaints
  o   A timeline for resolution of complaints
  o   Procedures for tracking complaints
  o   Resolutions
  o   Accommodations offered and implemented
  o   Policies regarding the retention of dispute files (Grady & Andrew, 2003)

In 2008, Maryland became the first state to enact legislation requiring its public schools to provide students with disabilities with equal opportunities to participate in physical education and athletics programs (Mullins, 2008). Also, in 2013 the U.S. Department of Education issued a "Dear Colleague" letter to provide policy guidance, making it explicit that public schools and universities must offer equal opportunities for students with disabilities to participate in interscholastic, intercollegiate, club, and intramural athletics (U.S. Department of Education, 2013). This policy guidance states that when the interests and abilities of student-athletes with disabilities cannot be met by the existing athletics program, the school should offer separate participation opportunities for those students with disabilities and support them on an equal footing as its other athletics activities. It remains to be seen how these guidelines will be implemented and enforced, especially at the post-secondary level.

Conclusion

After reading this chapter, you should understand that regulating high school and college sport participation involves a myriad of issues, from various forms of constitutionally protected interests, to discrimination, to application of eligibility and athlete conduct rules, to drug testing, and to religious expression, among others. A good manager will be able to use this knowledge to recognize a potential legal problem ahead of time and take steps to prevent it from blossoming – before finding herself on the defensive because someone has filed a complaint or a lawsuit.

Discussion Questions

1   If someone sues a university under § 504 or the ADA for its failure to provide equal participation opportunities to individuals with disabilities, the decision will probably turn on whether the athlete with a disability is considered a "qualified" person with a disability. Does qualified mean qualified to compete with and against able-bodied athletes? Or could it also mean qualified to compete as a wheelchair-bound athlete on a team for wheelchair athletes?

2 The court in *Cohen v. Brown* explicitly addressed the argument that the first prong of the three-part test for compliance in participation opportunities constitutes an impermissible quota. In your own words, what were the court's reasons for rejecting that argument? Was the court's reasoning on this issue persuasive to you? If so, why? If not, why not?

3 After *Earls*, we are now in the strange position of having the Colorado Supreme Court and the U.S. Supreme Court in virtual agreement that there is little difference between the privacy expectations of athletes and other types of students – but one court uses that argument to strike down drug testing, and the other uses it to allow drug testing of even wider groups of students. Is there an argument that the *Derdeyn* and *Earls* cases can be logically reconciled?

4 Can you draw a meaningful distinction between the free exercise of religion cases, *Moody* and *Menora?*

5 Consider a hypothetical case of an intercollegiate basketball player who turns her back to the flag during the pregame playing of the national anthem in order to protest racial injustice or police brutality. Would a court be more likely to decide that the First Amendment protected this student than the student with the tattoo in *Stephenson* or in *Stotts?*

6 In 2007, Iowa State University stirred up controversy by considering appointing a "life skills assistant" to serve as a spiritual advisor to its football team. As proposed, the advisor would report to the athletic director; serve those athletes who sought out spiritual counsel; not "pressure, coerce or proselytize" athletes; and have access to practices and games. Any prayer during mandatory team functions would be student-initiated and student-led (Mytelka, 2007). Based on *Santa Fe* and *Chandler II*, as well as the *Borden* case, do you think this policy would be considered constitutional?

Learning Activities

1 Engage in role-reversal. If men's athletics were to receive only what the women have, would the men be satisfied? If not, there is still a problem. Identify the changes you think the athletic program at your university needs to make in order to make you happy according to this standard. Online, visit the site of the National Women's Law Center (www.nwlc.org) or the Women's Sports Foundation (www.womenssportsfoundation.org) and discover what kinds of Title IX educational aids are available there.

2 Online, visit the site of the Women's Sports Foundation (www.womenssportsfoundation.org) and evaluate its position statement on athletics competition for individuals with disabilities.

3 Visit the NCAA's website (www.ncaa.org) and evaluate the guidelines pertaining to pregnant student-athletes.

4 Find out what the policy is at your institution for monitoring student-athletes' uses of social media and determine whether it would violate a typical state statute on monitoring social media. Also, examine its specific provisions and requirements, and discuss whether a court might find it, or parts of it, unconstitutional under the First Amendment.

Case Study

The American Civil Liberties Union (ACLU) filed an internal grievance at New World State University (NWSU; a public university in Colorado) alleging that the NWSU football coach engaged in religious discrimination against a Muslim student-athlete. The grievance claims that Coach Al West violated the First Amendment by repeatedly questioning his running back Mohammed Ahman about Islam and its ties to al-Qaeda and by requiring the team to recite the Lord's Prayer after each practice.

Additionally, some evidence suggests that religious discrimination played a role in Ahman's release from the team after six games. Ahman had begun the season at the top of the depth chart. He started the first game and rushed for 21 yards in seven carries. He did not start the next game, however, and was not even included on the roster for the next four games prior to his release. The coach claims that Ahman's release was performance-related because his replacement was one of the leading rushers in the SMAC Conference. Ahman claims he learned of his release via a message left on his cell phone by an assistant coach. He also claims that his requests to meet with the coaching staff to discuss it have been denied. Two other Muslim players were also released from the team under similar circumstances.

In response to the grievance, NWSU hired a law firm to investigate the allegations, and it reported finding no evidence of religious discrimination. The ACLU has questioned the impartiality of the investigation. Ahman's father has stated that the family intends to pursue the complaint in federal court. Meanwhile, Ahman has petitioned the NCAA for a hardship waiver to allow him to transfer to Coastal California State University without having to lose a year of eligibility.

1   Could Ahman bring a religious discrimination claim under the First Amendment Free Exercise Clause? Refer to Chapter 6 for detailed information on the religion clauses in the First Amendment to help you describe what Ahman's freedom of religion argument would be under the First Amendment.
2   Could Ahman bring an Equal Protection Clause claim? If so, on what grounds? What level of review would a court give such a claim?
3   Could Ahman bring a Title VI claim for race discrimination? If so, what would his arguments be? If not, why not?
4   Could Ahman bring a Due Process Clause claim? If so, on what grounds?

Analysis & Discussion

Considering … Sexual Harassment Occurring Abroad

The athletic director erred. She should have investigated the complaint because she was put on notice that sexual harassment had occurred. If the athlete were to be harassed again back in the United States, a court could find that the university knew that harassment had occurred previously but was deliberately indifferent in failing to act to prevent it from happening again. In that case, the student could be awarded monetary damages.

References

Cases

Alexander v. Sandoval, 121 S. Ct. 1511 (2001).
Alexander v. Yale University 631 F.2d 178 (2d Cir. 1980).
Bercovitch v. Baldwin Sch., Inc., 133 F.3d 141 (1st Cir. 1998).
Bethel v. School District v. Fraser 478 U.S. 675 (1986).
Biedeger v. Quinnipiac University, 728 F. Supp. 2d 62 (D. Conn. 2010), 691 F.3d 85 (2d Cir. 2012).
Bivens v. Albuquerque Public School, 899 F. Supp. 556 (D.N.M. 1995).
Bloomer v. Becker College, 2010 U.S. Dist. LEXIS 82997 (D. Mass. 2010).
Board of Educ. of Indep. Sch. Dist. No. 92 of Pottawatomie County v. Earls, 122 S. Ct. 2559 (2002).
Board of Regents v. Southworth, 529 U.S. 217 (2000) (Souter, J., concurring).
Borden v. Sch. Dist. of the Township of East Brunswick, 2008 U.S. App. LEXIS 8011 (3d Cir. 2008).
Bowers v. NCAA, 9 F. Supp. 2d 460 (D.N.J. 1998).
Boyd v. Board of Dirs., 612 F. Supp. 86 (E.D. Ark. 1985).
Breen v. Kahl, 419 F.2d 1034 (7th Cir. 1969).
Brennan v. Bd. of Trustees for University of Louisiana Systems, 691 So. 2d 324 (La. App. 1997).
Brodeur v. Claremont Sch. Dist., 626 F. Supp. 2d 195 (D.N.H. 2009).
Brown v. Shasta Union High Sch. Dist., 2010 Cal. App. Unpub. LEXIS 7051 (Cal. App. 2010).

Bunger v. Iowa High Sch. Athletic Ass'n, 197 N.W.2d 555 (Iowa 1972).

Cannon v. University of Chicago, 441 U.S. 677 (1979).

Chandler v. James, 180 F.3d 1254 (11th Cir. 1999) (Chandler I).

Chandler v. Siegelman, 230 F.3d 1313 (11th Cir. 2000) (Chandler II).

Cohen v. Brown Univ. (Cohen I), 809 F. Supp. 978 (D.R.I. 1992), aff'd, (Cohen II) 991 F.2d 888 (1st Cir. 1993), on remand, (Cohen III), 879 F. Supp. 185 (D.R.I. 1995), aff'd, (Cohen IV) 101 F.3d 155 (1st Cir. 1996), cert. denied, 117 S. Ct. 1469 (1997).

Communities for Equity v. Michigan High Sch. Athletic Ass'n, 178 F. Supp. 2d 805 (W.D. Mich. 2001), aff'd, 377 F.3d 504 (6th Cir. 2004).

Cook v. Colgate Univ., 992 F.2d 17 (2d Cir. 1993).

Cureton v. NCAA, 198 F.3d 107 (3d Cir. 1999).

Daniels v. Sch. Bd. of Brevard Cty, Florida, 985 F. Supp. 1458 and 995 F. Supp. 1394 (M.D. Fla. 1997).

Davenport v. Randolph County Bd. of Educ., 730 F.2d 1395 (11th Cir. 1984).

Davis v. Monroe County Bd. of Educ., 119 S. Ct. 1661 (1999).

DeLaTorre v. Minnesota State High School League, Case 0:16-cv-00235-JNE-KMM. (D. Minnesota, 2016).

Dennin v. Connecticut Interscholastic Athletic Conference, 913 F. Supp. 663 (D. Conn. 1996).

Doe v. Boyertown, 897 F.3d 518 (3d Cir. 2018).

Doe v. Ladue Horton Watkins High School. Case: 4:18-cv-01637-JAR (E.D. Missouri, 2018).

Doe v. Southeastern Greene Sch. Dist., 2006 U.S. Dist. LEXIS 12790 (W.D. Pa. 2006).

Duffley v. New Hampshire Interscholastic Athletic Ass'n, 446 A.2d 462 (N.H. 1982).

Dunham v. Pulsifer, 312 F. Supp. 411 (D.Vt. 1970).

EEOC v. Abercrombie & Fitch, 135 S. Ct. 2028 (2015).

Elliott v. Delaware State University, 879 F. Supp. 2d 438 (D. Del. 2012).

Eng v Cooley, 552 F.3d 1062 (9th Cir. 2009).

Florida High Sch. Athletic Ass'n v. Bryant, 313 So.2d 57 (Fla. Dist. Ct. App. 1975).

Franklin v. Gwinnett County Pub. Sch., 112 S. Ct. 1028 (1992).

Ganden v. NCAA, 1996 U.S. Dist. LEXIS 17368 (N.D. Ill. 1996).

Hageman v. Goshen Cty. Sch. Dist. No. 1, 256 P.3d 487 (Wyo. 2011).

Hazelwood School District v. Kuhlmeier, 484 U.S. 260 (1988).

Hayden v. Greensburg Cmty. Sch. Corp., No. 13-1757 (7th Cir. 2014).

Hill v. NCAA, 865 P.2d 633 (Cal. 1994).

Hoot by Hoot v. Milan Area Sch., 853 F. Supp. 243 (E.D. Mich. 1994).

Indiana High Sch. Athletic Ass'n, Inc. v. Wideman, 688 N.E.2d 413 (Ind. Ct. App. 1997).

Jennings v. University of N.C., 240 F. Supp. 2d 492 (M.D.N.C. 2002) 482 F.3d 686 (4th Cir. 2007, en banc), cert. denied, 128 S. Ct. 247 (2007).

Joye v. Hunterdon Central Regional High Sch. Bd. of Educ., 826 A.2d 624 (N.J. 2003).

Kelley v. Board of Trustees, Univ. of Illinois, 35 F.3d 265 (7th Cir. 1994).

Kempf v. The Michigan High School Athletic Assoc., 2:15-cv-14227. (E.D. Mich, 2015)

Kennedy v. Bremerton School District, Case No. 16-35901 (9th Cir. 2017).

Kountze Independent School District v. Matthews, No. 09-13-00251-CV (Tex. App.-Beaumont 2017).

Knapp v. Northwestern Univ., 101 F.3d 473 (7th Cir. 1996).

Lee v. Weisman, 112 S. Ct. 2649 (1992).

Lemon v. Kurtzman, 91 S. Ct. 2105 (1971).

Long v. Board of Educ. Dist. 128, 167 F. Supp. 2d 988 (N.D. Ill. 2001).

Long v. Zopp, 476 F.2d 180 (4th Cir. 1973).

Maki v. Minn. State H.S. League, Case No. 16-cv-4148 (D. Minn. 2016).

Matthews v. NCAA, 179 F. Supp. 2d 1209 (E.D. Wash. 2001).

Mayerova v. Eastern Michigan University, Case 2:18-cv-11909-GCS-RSW (E.D. Michigan 2018); Mayerova v. Eastern Michigan University, Case 19-1177 (6th Cir. 2019).

McCormick v. School Dist. of Mamaroneck, 370 F.3d 275 (2d Cir. 2004).

Menora v. Illinois High Sch. Ass'n, 683 F.2d 1030 (7th Cir. 1982).

Mercer v. Duke Univ., 190 F.3d 643 (4th Cir. 1999) on remand, 301 F. Supp. 2d 454 (M.D.N.C. 2004).

Miami Univ. Wrestling Club v. Miami Univ., 302 F.3d 608 (6th Cir. 2002).

Montgomery v. Indep. Sch. Dist. No. 709, 109 F. Supp. 2d 1081 (D. Minn. 2000).

Moody v. Cronin, 484 F. Supp. 270 (C.D. Ill. 1980).

Morrison v. Northern Essex Cmty. Coll., 780 N.E.2d 132 (Mass. App. Ct. 2002).

Morse v. Frederick 551 U.S. 393 (2007).

NCAA v. Tarkanian, 488 U.S. 179 (1988).

NCAA v. Yeo, 171 S.W.3d 863 (Tex. 2005).

Palmer v. Merluzzi, 689 F. Supp. 400 (D.N.J. 1988).

Pegram v. Nelson, 469 F. Supp. 1134 (M.D.N.C. 1979).

Personnel Adm'r of Mass. v. Feeney, 99 S.Ct. 2282 (1979).

Pickering v. Board of Education of Township High School District, 391 U. S. 563 (1968).

PGA Tour, Inc. v. Martin, 532 U.S. 661 (2001).

Poole v. South Plainfield Bd. of Educ., 490 F. Supp. 948 (D.N.J. 1980).

Pottgen v. Missouri State High Sch. Athletic Ass'n, 40 F.3d 926 (8th Cir. 1994).

Pryor v. NCAA, 288 F.3d 548 (3d Cir. 2002).

Ray v. Antioch Unified Sch. Dist., 107 F. Supp. 2d 1165 (N.D. Cal. 2000).

Riccio v. New Haven Bd. of Educ., 467 F. Supp. 2d 219 (D. Conn. 2006).

Sandison v. Michigan High Sch. Athletic Ass'n, 64 F.3d 1026 (6th Cir. 1995).

Santa Fe Indep. Sch. Dist. v. Doe, 120 S.Ct. 2266 (2000).

Sch. Dist. of Abington Township v. Schempp, 374 U.S. 203 (1963), Harlan, J., concurring.

Schneckloth v. Bustamonte, 93 S.Ct. 2041 (1973).

Schroeder v. Maumee Bd. of Educ., 296 F. Supp. 2d 869 (N.D. Ohio 2003).

Simpson v. University of Colorado Boulder, 500 F.3d 1170 (10th Cir. 2007).

Snelling v. Fall Mountain Regional Sch. Dist., 2001 U.S. Dist. LEXIS 3591 (D.N.H. 2001).

Stephenson v. Davenport Cmty. Sch. Dist., 110 F.3d 1303 (8th Cir. 1997).

Stotts v. Community Unit Sch. Dist. No. 1, 230 F.3d 989 (7th Cir. 2000).

Tatum v. NCAA, 992 F. Supp. 1114 (E.D. Mo. 1998).

Theno v. Tonganoxie Unified Sch. Dist., 377 F. Supp. 3d 952 (D. Kansas 2005).

Theodore v. The Delaware Valley Sch. Dist., 836 A.2d 76 (Pa. 2003).

Tinker v. Des Moines Indep. Cmty. Sch. Dist., 89 S.Ct. 733 (1969).

T.V. v. Smith-Green Cmty. Sch. Corp., 807 F. Supp. 2d 767 (N.D. Ind. 2011).

Tyler v. Huntsville City Schools Board, Case No. 5:18-cv-00958-MHH (D. Alabama 2019).

University of Colo. v. Derdeyn, 863 P.2d 929 (Colo. 1993).

V.A. v. San Pasqual Valley Unified School District, Case No. 17-cv-02471-BAS-AGS (S.D. California 2017).

Vernonia Sch. Dist. 47J v. Acton, 115 S.Ct. 2386 (1995).

Walker v. Texas Division, Sons of Confederate Veterans, 135 S. Ct. 2239 (2015).

Wanders v. Bear Hill Golf Club, Inc., 1998 Mass. Super. LEXIS 650 (Mass. Super. 1998).

Weber v. Oakridge Sch. Dist. 76, 56 P.3d 504 (Ore. App. 2002).

Williams v. Wakefield Basketball Ass'n, CA-01-10434-DPW (unreported decision) (D. Mass. 2003).

York v. Wahkiakum Sch. Dist. No. 200, 178 P.3d 995 (Wash. 2008).

Zeller v. Donegal Sch. Dist., 517 F.2d 600 (3d Cir. 1975).

Constitution

U.S. CONST. amend. I.

U.S. CONST. amend. IV.

U.S. CONST. amend. XIV.

Statutes and Regulations

Americans with Disabilities Act of 1990, 42 U.S.C. § 12101 et seq.

Americans with Disabilities Act Regulations, 28 C.F.R. § 36.104 (2005).

Arkansas Code Annotated, § 6-60-104 (2013) (social media accounts of current and prospective students and employees).

Civil Rights Act of 1964, 42 U.S.C. § 1981.

Civil Rights Act of 1964, 42 U.S.C. § 1983.

Education Privacy Act, Delaware Code Annotated, §§ 8102–8103 (2013).

House Bill 2426, Oregon Advance Legislative Service, chapter 98, 77th Legislative Assembly, 2013 (relating to use of technology in schools).

Individuals with Disabilities Education Act, 20 U.S.C. § 1400 et seq.

Internet Privacy Protection Act of 2012, Michigan Compiled Laws Service, §§ 37.274-37.277 (2013).

Jeanne Clery Disclosure of Campus Security Policy and Campus Crime Statistics Act of 1990, 20 U.S.C. § 1092(f).

Rehabilitation Act of 1973 (§ 504), 29 U.S.C. § 701 et seq.

Request for access to social networking account prohibited, New Mexico Statutes Annotated, § 21-1-46 (2013).

Senate Bill 344, Oregon Advance Legislative Service, chapter 408, 77th Legislative Assembly, 2013 (relating to online information).

"Social media," Deering's California Codes Annotated, Cal. Ed. Code § 99120 (2013).

Title II of the Civil Rights Act of 1964, 42 U.S.C. § 2000a.

Title VI of the Civil Rights Act of 1964, 42 U.S.C. § 2000d.

Title IX of the Education Amendments of 1972, 20 U.S.C. §§ 1681(a).

Title IX Athletics Regulations, 34 C.F.R. § 106.41 Athletics.

Title IX Athletics Regulations, 34 C.F.R. § 106.37(c) Financial Assistance.

Other Sources

ACLU (2019, July 1). *Doe v. Boyertown Area School District*. Retrieved from https://www.aclu.org/cases/doe-v-boyertown-area-school-district.

Aljabri, Z. (2016, August 5). Why some faith-based sports uniforms get banned. *Refinery 29*. Retrieved from https://www.refinery29.com/en-us/2016/08/119200/olympics-modest-dress-women-of-faith-uniforms.

Annenberg Public Policy Center (2017, September 12). Americans are poorly informed about basic constitutional provisions. *Annenberg Public Policy Center*. Retrieved from https://www.annenbergpublicpolicycenter.org/americans-are-poorly-informed-about-basic-constitutional-provisions/.

Associated Press (2018, February 25). Transgender Texas wrestler wins second high school girls title. *NBC News*. Retrieved from https://www.nbcnews.com/feature/nbc-out/transgender-texas-wrestler-wins-second-high-school-girls-title-n851106.

Associated Press (2020, January 22). Eastern Michigan pays $125,000 to settle Title IX lawsuit. *Apnews.com*. Retrieved from https://apnews.com/939aff803930dcfd9a4de3941666fc37.

Avery-Washington, E. (n.d.). Court Case: Lisa Simpson, et al. v. University of Colorado. *AAUW*. Retrieved from https://www.aauw.org/resource/lisa-simpson-et-al-v-university-of-colorado/.

Baumgaertner, G. (2019, September 18). Baptisms at practice: How college football became a Christian Empire. *The Guardian*. Retrieved from https://www.theguardian.com/sport/2019/sep/18/dabo-swinney-christianity-clemson-football-recruiting.

Bonifant, D. (2018, February 15). The good and bad of social media use among student-athletes. *Central Maine News*. Retrieved from https://www.centralmaine.com/2018/02/15/social-media-use-among-student-athletes-prompting-policy-discussions/.

Brooke-Marcinak, B.A., & de Varona, D. (2016, August 25). Amazing things happen when you give female athletes the same funding as men. *World Economic Forum*. Retrieved from https://www.weforum.org/agenda/2016/08/sustaining-the-olympic-legacy-women-sports-and-public-policy/.

Byrne, R. (2004, August 6). 2 La Salle U. coaches quit amid allegations of rapes by players. *Chronicle of Higher Education*, p. A34. *Chronicle of Higher Education*. Retrieved from https://www.chronicle.com/article/2-La-Salle-U-Coaches-Quit/26616.

CDC (2016). SHPPS: School Health Policies and Practices Study. *Center for Disease Control*. Retrieved from https://www.cdc.gov/healthyyouth/data/shpps/pdf/2016factsheets/Trends-SHPPS2016.pdf.

Conner, K. (2019, July 25). Huntsville City Schools settles Lee High School Title IX Lawsuit. *WHNT.com*. Retrieved from https://whnt.com/2019/07/25/huntsville-city-schools-settles-lee-high-school-title-ix-lawsuit/.

Davis, L. (2014, March 12). 7th Circuit rules that hair grooming codes applied only to male students athletes violate Equal Protection Clause and Title IX. *Education Law Proof Blog*. Retrieved from https://lawprofessors.typepad.com/education_law/2014/03/7th-circuit-rules-that-hair-grooming-codes-applied-only-to-male-student-athletes-violate-equal-prote.html.

Deadspin. (2013, May 24). Here are the best states to be a transgender high school athlete. *Deadspin*. Retrieved from LEXIS-NEXIS.

Drake, A (2017, October 23). PE dress codes leave many Muslim students on the bench. *National Education Association Today*. Retrieved from http://neatoday.org/2017/10/23/muslim-students/.

Erickson, P. (2019, March 29). New Title IX lawsuit accuse Baylor of botching rape case involving football players. *Waco Tribune-Herald*. Retrieved from https://www.wacotrib.com/news/courts_and_trials/new-title-ix-lawsuit-accuses-baylor-of-botching-rape-case/article_5a4df2fa-6877-5aef-a658-4fe11adf1672.html.

Furman, B. J. (2007). Gender equality in high school sports: Why there is a contact sport exemption to Title IX, eliminating it, and a proposal for the future. *Fordham Intellectual Property, Media and Entertainment Law Journal*, 17, 1169–1195.

Glantz, L. H. (1989). A nation of suspects: Drug testing and the Fourth Amendment. *American Journal of Public Health*, 79(10), 1427–1431.

Gose, B. (2003, November 7). Sacred Heart U settles pregnancy suit. *Chronicle of Higher Education*. Retrieved from https://www.chronicle.com/article/Sacred-Heart-U-Settles/516.

Grady, J., & Andrew, D. (2003). Legal implications of the Americans with Disabilities Act on recreation services: Changing guidelines, structures, and attitudes in accommodating guests with disabilities. *Journal of Legal Aspects of Sport*, 13(3), 231–252.

Green, L. (2017, March 17). Legal obligations of schools to pregnant and parenting student-athletes. *NFHS*. Retrieved from https://www.nfhs.org/articles/legal-obligations-of-schools-to-pregnant-and-parenting-student-athletes/.

Greenberg, Z. (2018, February 7). Former student-athlete sues UCF to vindicate First Amendment Rights. *thefire.org*. Retrieved from https://www.thefire.org/former-student-athlete-sues-ucf-to-vindicate-first-amendment-rights/.

Greenwood, T. (2015, December 14). Deaf wrestler, MHSAA agree to wider use of interpreters. *The Detroit News*. Retrieved from https://www.detroitnews.com/story/sports/high-school/2015/12/14/deaf-wrestler-mhsaa-settle-interpreter-matches/77301050/.

Griffin, P., & Carroll, H. J. (2010). On the team: Equal opportunity for transgender athletes. *Women's Sports Foundation*. Retrieved from http://www.womenssportsfoundation.org/en/home/research/articles-and-reports/lgbt-issues/transgender-student-athlete-report.

Harrer, K. M. (2004). Baylor rowers seek better opportunities – for everyone. *Women's Sports Foundation Newsletter*, 14.

Henneke, R., & Riches, J. (2018, November 16). Attorneys: UCF's De la Haye settles for a bright future off the field. *Orlando Sentinel*. Retrieved from https://www.orlandosentinel.com/opinion/os-op-ucf-kicker-de-la-haye-success-story-20181116-story.html.

Huntsville City Schools board votes to settle Title IX lawsuit. (2017, July 28). *WHNT.com*. Retrieved from https://whnt.com/2017/07/28/huntsville-city-schools-expected-to-settle-title-ix-lawsuit/.

Iacobelli, P. (2007, August 3). Awareness key issue for pregnant athletes. *South Florida Sun Sentinel*. Retrieved from www.sun-sentinel.com/sports/.

Ingraham, C. (2015, April 15). School drug tests: Costly, ineffective, and more common than you think. *The Washington Post*. Retrieved from https://www.washingtonpost.com/news/wonk/wp/2015/04/27/schools-drug-tests-costly-ineffective-and-more-common-than-you-think/.

Institute for Social Policy and Understanding (2017). American Muslim Poll 2017. *Ispu*. Retrieved from https://www.ispu.org/public-policy/american-muslim-poll-2017/.

Jacobo, J. (2019, February 24). Ole Miss basketball players kneel during national anthem to protest pro-confederate rally. *ABC News*. Retrieved from https://abcnews.go.com/US/ole-miss-basketball-players-kneel-national-anthem-protest/story?id=61274475.

Jenkins, S. (2002, June 24). Title IX opponents a bunch of sad sacks. *Washington Post*, p. D01.

Judge throws out sexual harassment suit against UNC coach. (2004, October 28). *Associated Press, Sports News*. Retrieved from LEXIS-NEXIS.

Keys, P. (2008, July 28). UIL to expand steroid testing. *Beaumont Enterprise*. Retrieved from www.beaumontenterprise.com.

Kirschner, A. (2016, January 25). Florida State settles Title IX lawsuit with Jameis Winston accuser for $950,000. *SB Nation*. Retrieved from https://www.sbnation.com/college-football/2016/1/25/10827774/fsu-title-9-lawsuit-settlement-jameis-winston-erica-kinsman.

Kitchener, C., & Wong, A. (2018, September 12). The moral catastrophe at Michigan State. *The Atlantic*. Retrieved from https://www.theatlantic.com/education/archive/2018/09/the-moral-catastrophe-at-michigan-state/569776/.

Krebs, C. P., Lindquist, C. H., Warner, T. D., Fisher, B. S., & Martin, S. L. (2007, December). The campus sexual assault (CSA) study. *U.S. Department of Justice*. Retrieved from https://www.ncjrs.gov/pdffiles1/nij/grants/221153.pdf.

Kuzma, C. (2016, September 6). Why the fastest women in the world wheel through Illinois cornfields. *ESPN*. Retrieved from http://www.espn.com/espnw/sports/article/17474397/why-fastest-women-world-wheel-illinois-cornfields.

Lawrence, M. (2011, September 13). Transgender policy approved. *NCAA*. Retrieved from www.ncaa.org.

Lawrence, S. (2018, August 31). KFDM/Fox 4 learns Kountze cheerleaders win religious banners case. *KFDM.com*. Retrieved from https://kfdm.com/news/local/kountze-cheerleaders-win-religious-banners-case.

Levenson, E. (2018, January 24). Larry Nassar sentenced to up to 175 years in prison for decades of sexual abuse. *CNN*. Retrieved from https://www.cnn.com/2018/01/24/us/larry-nassar-sentencing/index.html.

Marcus, J. (2017, August 8). Why Men Are the New College Minority. *The Atlantic*. Retrieved from https://www.theatlantic.com/education/archive/2017/08/why-men-are-the-new-college-minority/536103/.

McCaw, C., Jones, M., & Brown, S. (2012, May 1). North Carolina infractions case establishes social media monitoring principles. *Ice Miller Legal Council*. Retrieved from www.icemiller.com/publication_detail/id/1892/index.aspx.

Mencarini, M. (2017, January 10). 18 more alleged victims sue MSU, Nassar. *Lansing State Journal*. Retrieved from https://www.lansingstatejournal.com/story/news/local/2017/01/10/larry-nassar-michigan-state-lawsuit/96246098/.

Mullins, A. (2008, July 24). Advocates back athletes with disabilities. *Women's Sports Foundation* .Retrieved from https://www.womenssportsfoundation.org/articles_and_report/advocates-back-athletes-disabilities/.

Mytelka, M. (2007, July 13). Iowa State U allows chaplain for athletes. *Chronicle of Higher Education*, 53(45), 25.

National Coalition Against Censorship (n.d.). Student protests during national anthem: A resource and timeline. *NCAC.org*. Retrieved from https://ncac.org/students-protesting-during-anthem-pledge-a-resource-timeline.

NCAA (2012). *2012–2013 NCAA Division I Manual*. Indianapolis, IN: NCAA Publications.

NCAA (2018a, January 25). *Boundless Determination: Wheelchair sports advocates are steadily toppling barriers*. Retrieved from http://www.ncaa.org/champion/boundless-determination.

NCAA (2018b, September 21). Frequently asked questions on uniforms and contests. *NCAA.org*. Retrieved from http://www.ncaa.org/sites/default/files/2018MFB_FAQ_Uniforms_Contest_Delays_20180921.pdf.

NCAA (2018c). *NCAA National Study on Substance Use Habits of NCAA College Student-Athletes*. *NCAA.org*. Retrieved from http://www.ncaa.org/sites/default/files/2018RES_Substance_Use_Final_Report_FINAL_20180611.pdf.

NCAA (2018d). Student-athlete participation: 1981-82– 2017-18, NCAA Sports Sponsorship and Participation Rates Report. *NCAA Publications*. Retrieved from https://ncaaorg.s3.amazonaws.com/research/sportpart/Oct2018RES_2017-18SportsSponsorshipParticipationRatesReport.pdf.

NCAA (n.d.). Pregnancy and parenting student athletes: Resources and model policies. *NCAA.org*. Retrieved from http://www.ncaa.org/sites/default/files/PregnancyToolkit.pdf.

New, J. (2017, February 3). Athletes and activism. *Inside Higher Ed*. Retrieved from https://www.insidehighered.com/news/2017/02/03/ncaa-meeting-college-sports-leaders-recommend-supporting-athlete-protests.

NFHS (2018a). *2017–82 High School Athletics Participation Survey*. Retrieved from http://www.nfhs.org/ParticipationStatistics/PDF/2017-18%20High%20School%20Athletics%20Participation%20Survey.pdf.

NFHS (2018b, September 11). High school sports participation increases for 29th consecutive year. *NFHS.org*. Retrieved from https://www.nfhs.org/articles/high-school-sports-participation-increases-for-29th-consecutive-year/.

NIDA (2018, February). *Steroids and Other Appearance and Performance Enhancing Drugs (APEDs)*. Retrieved from https://www.drugabuse.gov/node/pdf/815/steroids-and-other-appearance-and-performance-enhancing-drugs-apeds.

NWBA (2019). *Standings*. Retrieved from https://www.nwba.org/page/show/4319339-intercollegiate-men?subseason=527217.

Orland, R. (2009, July 10). Socially unacceptable; NCAA tries to stay a step ahead of networking sites. *The Washington Times*, p. C01.

Pankratz, H. (2007, December 5). $2.8 million deal in CU rape case. *The Denver Post*. Retrieved from https://www.denverpost.com/2007/12/05/2-8-million-deal-in-cu-rape-case/.

Popke, M. (2013a, April). Social media complicating efforts to oversee student-athlete behavior. *Athletic Business*. Retrieved from https://www.athleticbusiness.com/social-media-complicating-efforts-to-oversee-student-athlete-behavior.html.

Popke, M. (2013b, May). Judge: HS cheerleaders can display biblical banners. *Athletic Business*. Retrieved from https://www.athleticbusiness.com/civil-actions/judge-hs-cheerleaders-can-display-biblical-banners.html.

Price, K. (2018, April 16). *Tatyana McFadden wins Fifth Boston Marathon. Team USA*. Retrieved from https://www.teamusa.org/News/2018/April/16/Tatyana-McFadden-Wins-Fifth-Boston-Marathon.

Richardson, B. (2017, October). Colleges educate student-athletes on social media use. *AthleticBusiness*. Retrieved from https://www.athleticbusiness.com/web-social/colleges-education-student-athletes-on-social-media-use.html.

Rock, A. (2019, February 1). Michigan State violated Clery Act for years: Department of Education finds. *Campus Safety Magazine*. Retrieved from https://www.campussafetymagazine.com/clery/michigan-state-clery-act/.

Roll, N. (2017, September 27). Taking a knee on campus. *InsideHigherEd.com*. Retrieved from https://www.insidehighered.com/news/2017/09/27/inspired-kaepernick-and-nfl-professors-and-students-protest-field.

Rosenberg, M. (2019, August 16). Harbaugh-Fickell drama lays bare the real problem with the NCAA's waiver rule. *SI.com*. Retrieved from https://www.si.com/college-football/2019/08/16/ncaa-waiver-rule-transfer-portal-recruiting-coaches.

Rubenstein, L. (2013, January 3). Belly aches predicted. Globe and Mail (Canada), p. S1. Retrieved from LEXIS-NEXIS.

Sabo, D., & Snyder, M. (2013). Progress and Promise: Title IX at 40, A White Paper. *Women's Sport Foundation*. Retrieved from https://www.womenssportsfoundation.org/articles_and_report/progress-promise-title-ix-40/.

Samuels, J., & Galles, K. (2003). In defense of Title IX: Why current policies are required to ensure equality of opportunity. *Marquette Sports Law Review*, 14, 11–47.

Shipley, A. (2003, May 30). NCAA initiates EPO testing, extends existing drug protocols. *Washington Post*, D03.

Smith, L. (2017, September 19). Tens of millions of American do not believe Muslims and Atheists have First Amendment Rights, study finds. *The Independent*. Retrieved from https://www.independent.co.uk/news/world/americas/us-politics/muslims-atheists-free-speech-first-amendment-rights-polls-americans-dont-believe-a7955586.html.

Snyder, S. (2013, January 22). Pennsylvania State University now a leader in Clery compliance. *Philadelphia Inquirer*, p. A01. Retrieved from LEXIS-NEXIS.

Solari, C. (2018, August 30). NCAA clears MSU in investigation related to Larry Nassar, basketball and football programs. *Lansing State Journal*. Retrieved from https://www.lansingstatejournal.com/story/sports/college/msu/2018/08/30/michigan-state-football-basketball-ncaa-investigation/1143565002/.

Steinbach, P. (2012, November). Schools attempting to control athletes' use of social media. *Athletic Business*. Retrieved from https://www.athleticbusiness.com/web-social/schools-attempting-to-control-athletes-use-of-social-media.html.

Suggs, W. (2004, February 13). "Varsity" with an asterisk. *Chronicle of Higher Education*, A35.

Transathlete (2019). *K-12 Policies*. Retrieved from https://www.transathlete.com/k-12.

Ulrich, L. (May 2007). Probing pregnancy participation policies. *Training-Conditioning*. Retrieved from www.training-conditioning.com/2007/05.

U.S. Department of Education (1979, December 11). *The three-part test for compliance regarding equity in participation opportunities* (1979 OCR Policy Interpretation). Fed. Reg., vol. 44, No. 239.

U.S. Department of Education (1996, January 16). *Dear Colleague Letter: Clarification of intercollegiate athletics policy guidance: The three-part test* (1996 OCR Policy Clarification).

U.S. Department of Education (1998, July 23). *Dear Colleague Letter: Bowling Green State University*.

U.S. Department of Education (2005, March 17). *Dear Colleague Letter: Additional clarification of intercollegiate athletics policy: Three-part test – part three* (2005 OCR Policy Clarification).

U.S. Department of Education (2007–2009). Summary Crime Statistics. Retrieved from https://www2.ed.gov/admins/lead/safety/criminal2007-09.pdf.

U.S. Department of Education (2010, April 20). Dear Colleague Letter: Intercollegiate athletics policy clarification: The three-part test – part three (2010 OCR Policy Clarification).

U.S. Department of Education (2011, April 4). Dear Colleague Letter: Sexual violence.

U.S. Department of Education (2013, January 25). Dear Colleague Letter: Students with disabilities in extracurricular athletics.

U.S. Department of Education (2020, May 6). Nondiscrimination on the Basis of Sex in Education Programs or Activities Receiving Federal Financial Assistance: Final Rule. Retrieved from https://www2.ed.gov/about/offices/list/ocr/docs/titleix-regs-unofficial.pdf.

U.S. Department of Education, Office of Civil Rights (2011, September 2). Findings: Adrian College (OCR Case No. 15-07-2103).

U.S. Department of Education, Office of Civil Rights (n.d). Resolution Agreement: Adrian College (OCR Case No. 15-07-2103).

Wenzel, M. (2015, December 3). Deaf high school wrestler sues MHSAA over use of interpreter. *MLive.com*. Retrieved from http://highschoolsports.mlive.com/news/article/-7581473389629030751/deaf-high-school-wrestler-sues-mhsaa-over-use-of-interpreter/.

Wheelchair athlete disqualified at state meet (2006, May 28). WTOP News. Retrieved from www.wtopnews.com.

Will, G. (1988, October 2). Why the chemistry has to be right. *Newsday*, 9.

Wilson, C. (2009, October 30). School sued for punishing teens over MySpace pix. *Brattleboro Reformer* (Vermont). Retrieved from LEXIS-NEXIS.

Winerip, M. (2008, November 23). Drawing the line on drug testing. *The New York Times*, p. 4. Retrieved from LEXIS-NEXIS.

Wolverton, B. (2008, January 15). U of North Carolina settles sex-harassment suit against coach. *Chronicle of Higher Education*. Retrieved from https://www.chronicle.com/article/U-of-North-Carolina-Settles/400.

Young, J. R. (2002, October 4). When trips go bad: A recent ruling extends sex-discrimination protections beyond U.S. borders. *Chronicle of Higher Education*, A49–50.

Web Resources

www.athleticbusiness.com/corporate/blog-9-social-media-dos-and-don-ts-for-student-athletes.html ■ This *Athletic Business* article discusses social media dos and don'ts for student-athletes and the importance of educating student-athletes on appropriate uses.

www.beachdistrictva.org/images/files/b7_file27_30208.pdf ■ A sample social media policy for student-athletes.

www.ncaa.org ■ The NCAA's drug testing program was created to protect the health and safety of student-athletes and to ensure that no one participant might have an artificially induced advantage or be pressured to use chemical substances. Click on the link to Sport Science Institute and then the NCAA Health and Safety Page to find information about the NCAA's drug testing policy and research on student-athlete substance use.

www.ncaapublications.com ■ To access the NCAA publication *Pregnant and Parenting Student-Athletes – Resources and Model Policies*, on this site search on the keywords "pregnant and parenting."

www.ncaa.org/titleix ■ The NCAA website includes an educational and interactive page titled Sporting Chance: The Lasting Legacy of Title IX. It includes perspectives shared by noteworthy athletes, athletics administrators, and government officials.

www.nfhs.org ■ On this National Federation of State High School Associations site, click on Publications to locate information such as the NFHS High School Athletics Participation Survey History, the *National High School Sports Record Book*, *A Guide for College-Bound Student-Athletes and Their Parents – Updated*, and Steroids Awareness Information.

www.nwlc.org ■ The mission of the National Women's Law Center is "to expand, protect, and promote opportunity and advancement for women and girls at every stage of their lives – from education to employment to retirement security, and everything in between." The site offers tools to help readers discover if schools are providing equal opportunities to girls. Students can conduct a self-evaluation of their university's program by using checklists available on the site.

www.womenssportsfoundation.org ■ The Women's Sport Foundation aims to "advance the lives of girls and women through sports" in many different ways. Go to the Research section and then click on the link to Articles and Reports to see reports on Title IX, sexual harassment, media issues, health and fitness, and more.

13 Governance Issues and Participant Rights in Olympic Sport

Introduction

The Olympic Movement is based on the concept of Olympism, which states "The goal of Olympism is to place sport at the service of the harmonious development of humankind, with a view to promoting a peaceful society concerned with the preservation of human dignity" (IOC, 2017a, p. 11). The Olympic Movement is also a moneymaker, and during the 2013–2016 quadrennium it generated $5.7 billion from broadcast rights, ticket sales, official sponsorships, and other marketing and licensing efforts (IOC, 2019a). During this same timeframe, broadcast revenue alone totaled $4.25 billion, and The Olympic Partner (TOP) Programme generated sponsorship revenue of $1 billion (IOC, 2019a). Governance of such a large and continuous international undertaking is understandably complex. This chapter will examine the legal structures and relationships of the various governing bodies that participate in the Olympic Movement. It will also discuss the impact of the Amateur Sports Act of 1978 (ASA) and the Ted Stevens Olympic and Amateur Sports Act of 1998 (OASA) on Olympic governance within the United States and the functioning of the United States Olympic and Paralympic Committee (USOPC). Finally, the authority of Olympic governing bodies to regulate events and participants will be examined. Exhibit 13.1 presents the management contexts, legal issues, and relevant law discussed in this chapter.

Organizational Relationships & Governing Bodies in Olympic Sport

The governing bodies and legal relationships among organizations operating in the Olympic sport realm are decidedly complex. In Chapters 7 and 10, we learned how with professional sports, dispute resolution systems were established as a result of a collective bargaining process between the leagues (management) and the players associations (unions). Similarly, disputes in Olympic sport are also often resolved through a system of internal grievance procedures and arbitration. In Olympic sport, these systems are the result of carefully crafted contractual agreements among governing bodies at both the international and national levels rather than a collective bargaining process. These contractual agreements between governing bodies, such as the International Olympic Committee (IOC) and a National Olympic Committee (NOC), set forth the rights, duties, and expectations between those two organizations. In addition, each governing body at each level within the Olympic Movement (e.g., IOC, USOPC, Federation Internationale de Hockey, and USA Field Hockey) has contractual agreements (governing documents) such as a Constitution, Bylaws, or Handbooks. These documents codify the authority of the governing body as well as its rights and responsibilities toward individuals, organizations, or groups eligible for membership under its authority. Similar to what we discovered about high school and collegiate amateur sport associations in Chapters 11 and 12, the courts

Exhibit 13.1 Management contexts in which governance and regulation issues may arise, with relevant laws and cases.

Management Context	Major Legal Issues	Relevant Law	Illustrative Cases
Authority of governing bodies	Private right of action	Amateur Sports Act	*Sternberg*
	Judicial/arbitral review	Law of private associations	*Harding*
Regulation of events	Events included in program	Olympic Charter, federal antidiscrimination laws	*Martin*
	Team/nation participation	U.S. Constitution: Amateur Sports Act	*Spindulys, DeFrantz*
	Selection of host cities	IOC procedures	
	Sponsorship/advertising: use of Olympic trademarks	Olympic Charter, Amateur Sports Act, Lanham Act	*San Francisco Arts & Athletics, Intelicense*
	Security measures	4th Amendment	
Regulation of participants	Disputed competition outcomes	IOC rules	*Yang Tae-Young*
	Amateurism	Olympic Charter	
	Drug testing	WADA Code/IF rules	*C. v. FINA, Cilic, Medvedev, Sharapova*
	Sex tests	IOC Medical Commission policy, sex discrimination laws	*Semenya*
	General competition rules	IOC rules	*Pistorius, Walton-Floyd*
	Disciplinary action	Law of private associations	*Samoa NOC, Harding,*
	Duty of care/Special Relationship	Tort/Negligence	*Pliuskaitis* *Brown*

extend a great deal of deference to the decision-making authority of Olympic sport organizations. This is primarily due to the voluntary and contractual nature of the relationships between organizations in this industry segment. Thus, before we explore the dispute resolutions systems and legal issues in the Olympic Movement, we need to first review some basics of the governance structures involved.

The governance of Olympic sport is hierarchical and involves several layers of national and international governing bodies as well as multiple governing bodies within each governance layer. The major governance layers are overseen by the following **governing bodies**: the International Olympic Committee (IOC), the International Paralympic Committee (IPC), the national Olympic and Paralympic committees (NOCs), the international sports federations (IFs), the national governing bodies (NGBs), and the organizing committees for the Olympic Games (OCOGs). A basic illustration of the hierarchical relationships is presented in Exhibit 13.2. These relationships are contractual in nature. Olympic sport also has relationships with independent organizations working within the Olympic Movement which regulate and enforce rules and regulations. These relationships are established based on a complex and detailed set of governing documents and national laws or regulations. In addition, each governing body has its own set of governing documents. These governing documents define the rights and responsibilities of all individuals associated with the governing body. For example, USOPC applicable laws and governing documents include the Ted Stevens Olympic and Amateur Sports Act, the USOPC Bylaws, and the USOPC Code of Conduct. In addition, specific rules and agreements cover a variety of areas from doping, to protests and demonstrations, to commercial licensing rights (USOPC, 2020). Thus, understanding the complex nature of these organizations and the importance of their governing documents is central to managers working in Olympic sport. Next we will explore the key Olympic governing bodies and Olympic partners responsible for assisting with the enforcement and review of Olympic rules and regulations. Additional information regarding the organizational structure of the Olympic Movement can be accessed at the IOC's website (see Web Resources).

Exhibit 13.2 Basic hierarchical structure of the Olympic movement

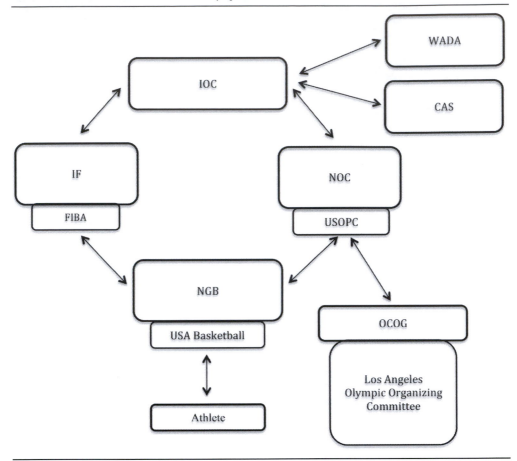

International Olympic and Paralympic Committees

The Olympic and Paralympic Movements are governed internally by the International Olympic Committee and the International Paralympic Committee (IPC), respectively. Both organizations are private, non-governmental, non-profit international organizations. The Olympic and Paralympic Movements are composed of organizations and individuals who agree to abide by the IOC's Olympic Charter and the IPC's Handbook, which codifies the by-laws and regulations of the respective organizations. The IOC consists of a maximum of 105 members elected from a list of nominees generated by the IOC Executive Board. The members are elected for renewable eight-year terms. The Session, which is the general assembly of IOC members, meets annually (meetings have been open to the media only since reforms were enacted in 1999) and has the ultimate responsibility for amending and interpreting the Olympic Charter. A 15-member Executive Board oversees the administrative affairs of the IOC. The IOC President is elected by secret ballot of the IOC members for an eight-year term of office, which may be extended once for an additional four years (IOC, 2017b). The IOC has exclusive ownership of all rights pertaining to the organization, marketing, reproduction, and broadcasting of the Olympic Games, and it may seek gifts and other resources needed to fulfill its mission. The IOC's regulatory decisions are final; however, the IOC has agreed to submit disputed decisions for final arbitration to the Court of Arbitration for Sport (CAS) – an international arbitral court originally created by the IOC in 1984.

The IOC relies primarily on arbitral courts and the NOCs to enforce its decisions. The International Paralympic Committee (IPC) was founded as an international non-profit organization in Düsseldorf, Germany to act as the global governing body of the Paralympic Movement. The IPC organization is composed of an elected Governing Board, a management team, and various Standing Committees and Councils. Since 1999 it has been headquartered in Bonn, Germany.

International Federations and National Olympic Committees

International Federations (IFs) are independent, nongovernmental, international organizations responsible for governing a particular Olympic sport or set of sports worldwide such as the International Handball Federation (IHF) and the International Wheelchair Basketball Association (IWBA). Their regulatory activities must conform to the Olympic or Paralympic Charter and also include establishing and enforcing competition rules and participant eligibility criteria for their sports, as well as providing internal dispute resolution procedures.

National Olympic Committees (NOCs) are the officially recognized governing bodies within a single nation responsible for representing that nation with the IOC in all matters involving Olympic sports. As of 2020, 206 NOCs and 40 IFs govern sports in the Summer and Winter Games. Two examples are the United States Olympic and Paralympic Committee (USOPC) and the Canadian Olympic Committee (COC). The NOCs are charged with guiding the Olympic Movement within their respective countries. They are also independent, non-governmental agencies and must comply with the Olympic Charter and the governing authority of the IOC, as well as being subject to the laws of their country. The NOCs select the athletes who will represent their countries at the Games, usually based on the recommendations of the NGBs. The NOCs are also responsible for recognizing the NGBs for amateur sports within that country. Each NOC governs a wide array of NGBs. For example, the USOPC oversees 50 NGBs. The NOCs are also responsible for preventing violence, discrimination, and participant use of substances banned by the IFs. When disputes occur, they are usually resolved using arbitration and the American Arbitration Association (AAA). The AAA provides publicly available information on its website concerning arbitration of Olympic athlete disputes in the US. Most countries have one NOC for Olympic participation and a separate entity for Paralympic participation. However, the United States has made a significant strides for inclusion for all athletes. In 2019, the USOC was renamed to the USOPC (United States Olympic and Paralympic Committee) and the USOPC is revising and updating its governance structures in fully integrate the Paralympic sports into the Olympic Movement (Pavitt, 2019). Expanding inclusivity for Paralympic athletes first started with the amendments to the Amateur Sports Act, the Ted Stevens Olympic and Amateur Sports Act of 1998 (OASA), which made a number of changes, one of which was to locate responsibility within the USOPC for governing U.S. activities related to both the Paralympic and Pan-American Games. The Paralympic Movement at the international level, though, is not governed by the IOC instead, they are governed by the IPC. See the web resources at the end of the chapters for links for the NGBs under the USOPC umbrella.

National Governing Bodies and Organizing Committees for the Olympic Games

The NGBs are the governing authorities for particular sports within each country such as USA Softball. In addition to being subject to the laws of their respective countries, NGBs must comply with the Olympic Charter, the regulatory authority of their NOC, and the rules of the IF relevant to their sport(s). For example, USA Climbing (an NGB) would be subject to rules and regulations from both the USOPC (a NOC) and the International Federation of Sport Climbing (IFSC) (an IF). Lastly, anytime a country is interested in hosting the Olympic Games, the country would establish an Organizing Committee for the Olympic and Paralympic Games (OCOG) which would develop and present the bid proposal, and if selected, be responsible for the administration of the Games in that county. An OCOG, such as the Paris 2024 Organising Committee for the Olympic and Paralympic Games, is formed by the NOC of the host city's country (France) and is charged with organizing and carrying out the hosting of the Games. Many OCOG's now adopt a more marketing friendly moniker to identify their organizing committees such as Milano Cortina 2026 and LA2028 for the 2026 winter games in Milan and Cortina, Italy and the 2028 summer games in Los Angeles, California, USA, respectively. The OCOG must comply with the Olympic Charter, the IOC Executive Board's instructions, and its contractual agreements with the IOC, the NOC, and the host city. Among the OCOG's responsibilities are constructing the facilities necessary for holding the Games, ensuring adherence to the competition rules of the IFs, limiting disruptive political demonstrations, providing adequate security, and establishing procedures for dealing with legal disputes occurring during the Games. Additionally, as many as four OCOGs may be operating simultaneously, some in the planning stages, some in the operational phase, and some wrapping up the affairs of past Games. All of the previous examples of organizations are part of the official organizational structure of the Olympic Movement.

Independent of these governing bodies, but still part of the Olympic regulatory and oversight structure are two additional groups which are important with respect to legal aspects of governance – the World Anti-Doping Agency (WADA) and the Court of Arbitration for Sport (CAS).

World Anti-Doping Agency

WADA is an independent agency established in 1999 following the doping scandal in cycling in the summer of 1998. A World Conference on Doping in Sport was held in February of 1999 and recommended the creation of an independent international anti-doping agency to be operational for the 2000 Sydney Olympic Games. Funded equally by Olympic sport organizations and governments around the world, WADA is charged with implementing a universal anti-doping policy (WADA, 2020a). Its activities include scientific research, education, monitoring the World Anti-Doping Code that defines banned substances, drug-testing procedures, and penalties for doping in sport. The World Anti-Doping Code is intended to harmonize the doping policies for all sports and in all countries. The WADA Foundation Board is composed of representatives from the IOC, NOCs, and IFs, as well as Olympic and Paralympic athletes and government representatives.

Court of Arbitration for Sport

CAS was established by the IOC in 1984 and is based in Lausanne, Switzerland. Its purpose is to resolve legal disputes in international sport quickly through arbitration or mediation, using procedures adapted specifically to the needs of the international sport context. The intent is for CAS to provide a single adjudicating body that can bring consistency, and thus fairness, in applying the rules of the many international sport governing bodies. The IOC and all the Olympic IFs have agreed to be subject to the jurisdiction of CAS, and the IFs also require their NGBs and individual athletes to submit all disputes with the IF to CAS.

The International Council of Arbitration and Sport (ICAS) was established in 1994 to govern the operations of CAS, manage its funds, and appoint its members, thereby removing these functions from the IOC. The Code of Sports-Related Arbitration was promulgated to codify the operations and procedures of CAS and ICAS. This code provides for four different dispute resolution processes available under the auspices of CAS:

1 To resolve disputes referred to them through ordinary arbitration, such as a sponsorship contract dispute.
2 To resolve appeals from final decisions of the federations, associations, or other sports-related bodies where provided in their governing document such as an IF determining an athlete ineligible to compete.
3 To resolve anti-doping related matters (WADA has a right of appeal to CAS for doping cases).
4 To resolve disputes referred to them through mediation.

Competitive Advantage Strategies

Relationships of Governing Bodies

If you work for an Olympic sport governing body, be sure you investigate and understand the interrelationships among the various governing bodies and their regulations applicable to your sport and your nation. This will help prevent you from inadvertently running afoul of important regulations that may apply to you simply by virtue of your organization's relationship with another governing body.

Parties must enter a written agreement to submit their dispute to CAS for final resolution, and courts will generally enforce that agreement as final and therefore not subject to judicial review (see, e.g., *Raguz v. Sullivan*, 2000). Third parties, such as athletes whose interests may be affected by an arbitration ruling, are allowed to intervene in CAS proceedings. (The CAS website at www.tas-cas.org is a good source for information about topics covered in this section and included in the web resources at the end of the chapter.)

Parties in ordinary arbitration or appeals arbitration proceedings exchange written statements of the case and have an oral hearing before CAS arbitration. In all CAS proceedings, the parties may be represented by legal counsel and may choose who will hear their case from a pool of around 275 CAS arbitrators. Additionally, the parties may choose to agree on the rules of law to be applied by CAS in their case or the choice of law may be stipulated in the IF's governing documents. If none are so chosen or stipulated, the proceedings are governed by Swiss law. CAS arbitration is final and binding, and it may be judicially enforced by courts in countries that have signed the New York Convention on the Uniform Enforcement of Foreign Arbitral Awards (see *Slaney v. IAAF*, 2001). CAS decisions may lead to awards for money damages and legal costs. Finally, CAS provides a panel of arbitrators at each Olympic Games to enable resolution within 24 hours of disputes that arise onsite during the Games.

Significant recent decisions of CAS are posted on its website at www.tas-cas.org (see Web Resources). Archived cases are available for decisions rendered since 1986. Additionally, the website provides statistics for each year since CAS was created documenting the numbers of filed arbitration requests, awards granted, and advisory opinions rendered. It also provides the annual numbers for ordinary arbitration and appeals arbitration cases filed compared to numbers decided. The numbers are always higher during the actual years the Games are held, but they jumped from 76 cases filed in the year 2000 to 599 in 2016. Of those 599 cases, 142 resulted in a formal substantive CAS award decisions or advisory opinions. The remaining cases were procedural decisions (CAS, 2016). With such a robust dispute resolution system, most disputes involving individuals or organizations within the Olympic Movement are resolved in arbitration and subject to CAS final review. However, both in the United States and internationally a number of disputes have been resolved outside the dispute resolution system described above. In the next section we will briefly examine the rationale for deferring to the dispute resolution mechanisms and also explore the most frequent areas in which legal challenges arise involving Olympic and Paralympic organizations and how those disputes have been resolved either by CAS or in those limited circumstances where the federal courts have reviewed decisions of Olympic organizations. A detailed description of the organizational relationships and governance responsibilities of Olympic organizations are illustrated in Exhibit 13.3.

Exhibit 13.3 Primary areas of responsibilities for Olympic governing bodies.

	Responsible to	Responsibility	Example
Court of Arbitration for Sport (CAS)	International council of arbitration & sport	Review legal disputes in international sport	
Work Anti-Doping Agency (WADA)	Independent	Administers universal antidoping policy/testing	
International Olympic Committee (IOC)	Olympic charter, CAS review	Overarching control of all Olympic sport; controls all rights pertaining to Games, program of events	
International Paralympic Committee (IPC)	IPC Constitution	Control of Paralympic sport	
International Federation (IF)	Olympic Charter, CAS review	Governing worldwide competition, rules/eligibility, dispute resolution within NGB's	International Judo Federation (IJF)
National Olympic Committee (NOC)	IOC, Olympic Charter, laws of country, arbitration reviews	Guiding Olympic movement in country, selecting athletes for national teams, resolving disputes for NGBs/athletes, preventing violence/discrimination/substance abuse, controlling use of Olympic trademark in country	United States Olympic and Paralympic Committee (USOPC)
Organizing Committee for the Olympic Games (OCOG)	IOC executive board, Olympic charter, contracts w/IOC, home country NOC, host city	Organizing and hosting games, constructing venues & providing security for games, preventing political disruptions of games, ensuring adherence to competition rules	Los Angeles Committee for the Olympic Games (LA2028)
National Governing Body (NGB)	Olympic charter, NOC, IF competition and eligibility rules, home country laws	Governing sport within home country, recommending athletes to NOC for selection to national team	USA Judo

Regulatory Authority of Olympic Organizations in the United States

As described in the previous section, Olympic organizations have complex and detailed rules and regulations defining the rights and responsibilities of the different governing bodies and participants in Olympic sport. As we have seen with other amateur sport governing bodies, Olympic amateur sport organizations also regulate a wide range of areas including athlete eligibility, event selection, competition rules, marketing and sponsorship rights, drug testing, and disciplinary conduct. Ideally, the governing bodies would perform their functions consistent with those rules and regulations, and those rules and regulations would be clear and universally understood by all those subject to them. Realistically, though, disputes will arise which must be settled through some internal or external dispute resolution, or a judicial review process. In order to understand how to resolve these disputes, we first have to understand how and why Olympic governing bodies have the authority to govern themselves. Thus, first we will explore the source of authority for Olympic governing bodies in the United States, and then we will explore examples of the legal challenges involving Olympic organizations.

Statutory Authority and Federal Charter of USOC

The Amateur Sports Act of 1978 (ASA) was enacted by Congress to revise the federal charter it originally granted to the then USOC in 1950. The ASA was also intended to position the USOC (now USOPC) to create and manage a highly successful Olympic program. The catalyst for the ASA was the overall decline of U.S. achievement in the Olympic Movement due in part to the disputes and disorganization among the various organizations controlling sport in the United States. The ASA vested the USOC with exclusive jurisdiction over participation and representation of the United States in the Olympic Games. The USOC was also granted the authority to recognize each NGB in the United States and grant them the exclusive right to determine athlete eligibility to participate in Olympic competition for their sports. Section 374 of the Amateur Sports Act grants authority to the USOC to resolve disputes involving the NGBs, amateur athletes, and amateur sports organizations, with the purpose of protecting the opportunities of athletes, coaches, and other relevant individuals to participate in amateur athletics. The ASA was amended by the Ted Stevens Olympic and Amateur Sports Act of 1998 (OASA) to update the ASA and reflect changes in the Olympic Movement including allowing professional athletes to compete in some Olympic sports, such as basketball. The OASA also noted that the Paralympic Movement had grown in size and prestige, adding language to extend complete recognition of the US Paralympic Movement. Under the OASA, the USOC was tasked with the same duties for the Paralympic Games as it had with the Olympic Games including selecting athletes for teams and providing financial support for athletes with disabilities. OASA also provided for the creation of an Athlete's Advisory Council and additional protections for athletes. Section 220506 of the OASA grants exclusive rights to the USOC to control the commercial use of Olympic trademarks within the United States, which may conflict with the IOC's ultimate right to its trademarks (see discussion of *USOC v. Intelicense Corp.*, 1984, later in this chapter). Further, section 220509 requires the USOC to establish regulations for resolving eligibility disputes and to employ an ombudsman who will provide cost-free advice to athletes and their attorneys in such disputes.

U.S. Olympic Governing Bodies and State Action

As mentioned previously, even though the USOPC and NGBs in the United States represent and govern the United States participation in Olympic sport, they are independent, non-governmental entities. Congress made it clear that it did not want the federal government running amateur athletics, thus, the USOC was granted a federal charter as a non-profit patriotic corporation, and not a federal government entity. This is an importance distinction. As you recall we introduced the importance of state actor status when evaluating the regulatory authority of high school and collegiate athletic associations in Chapter 11. A state actor is a government entity or an entity that may be said to act with the authority of the government due to joint action or entwinement with government. State action is a prerequisite to establishing that constitutional protections apply to alleged violations of individual rights. Being deemed a state actor added another significant layer of legal oversight and review for public high schools and colleges. However, the Supreme Court has ruled that the USOPC is not a state actor because its corporate charter even though granted by Congress was insufficient to transform it into a **state actor**. Thus, constitutional protections of individual rights, such as freedom of expression or prohibitions against unreasonable searches and seizures, are not applicable to the USOPC (*San Francisco Arts & Athletics, Inc. v. USOC*, 1987; see also *DeFrantz v. USOC*, 1980). Nor are NGBs considered state actors (*Behagen v. Amateur Basketball Association of the United States*, 1989; see also *Harding v. United States Figure Skating Association*, 1994). Our first Focus Case, *DeFrantz v. USOC*, illustrates the scope of the USOPC's authority.

DeFrantz v. USOC

492 F. Supp. 1181 (D.D.C. 1980)   **FOCUS** CASE

FACTS

In 1980, under considerable pressure from President Carter, the USOC voted to boycott the 1980 Moscow Olympic Games because the U.S. government felt that by sending a team to compete it would be communicating a message that it condoned the Soviet invasion of Afghanistan. The USOC's decision was challenged by the plaintiffs, who claimed that this decision exceeded the USOC's statutory authority and violated their constitutional rights to liberty, to self-expression, to travel, and to pursue their chosen occupation of athletics.

HOLDING

The U.S. District Court upheld the USOC's decision to boycott the Games as a legitimate exercise of its statutory authority.

RATIONALE

First, the court found that the USOC was not a state actor; hence, there was no violation of the Constitution. Next, it found that the Olympic Charter granted the right to the NOCs to determine their nation's participation and that the language of the Amateur Sports Act of 1978 defining the USOC's authority did not contradict the Charter. The plaintiffs had pointed to language in § 374 of the act that directed the USOC to provide for speedy resolution of disputes between amateur sports organizations and to protect the participation opportunities of any amateur athlete. They argued that this duty to protect participation opportunities would be breached by the elimination of opportunities inherent in a decision to boycott. The court looked to the legislative history of the act and construed § 374 to mean only that participation opportunities were protected against the effects of interorganizational conflicts between amateur sports governing bodies. Hence, the USOC's authority to decide whether to send a team was not threatened by this provision of the Amateur Sports Act, and its decision to boycott was upheld.

Consistent with the holding in *DeFrantz*, the IOC's policy is that Olympic governing bodies are to be separate entities from the government. The IOC contends that government actors in the Olympic Movement will ruin the pureness of the Games. Nevertheless, governments have started to take an interest in their respective Olympic governing bodies. For example, Italy's Milano Cortina 2026 bid faced several hurdles to secure sufficient governmental financial support from both the national and regional governments (Dampf, 2018). However, following the successful bid, the IOC sent a warning letter to the Italian National Olympic Committee (CONI) in response to the Italian Parliament's approval of a new law which would establish a separate government controlled organization to distribute funds to NGBs, presumably reducing CONI's role to only handling preparation for the Olympic Games (O'Kane, 2019). Preservation of CONI''s autonomy, which is a basic foundation of the Olympic Charter, was a key issue in the IOC's warning.

Similar actions have been considered in the US where Congress has introduced bills to give more power to the US government in controlling the USOPC (Schrotenboer, 2019). Most of these proposals in the US were in response to numerous scandals and claims by athletes alleging rampant sexual or physical abuse and the corresponding lack of oversight on the part of the NGBs and the USOPC. These claims began with Larry Nassar, the USA Gymnastics team doctor who was convicted for sexual assault of more than 150 girls occurring over a 20-year period. USA Volleyball and USA Taekwondo have faced similar sexual misconduct claims. Yet another case involved USA Badminton's financial struggles and a sexual assault case involving long time coach and Olympic champion Bob Malaythong (Reid, 2018, 2019). Many in Congress support additional restraints and oversight of the USOPC (see discussion later in this Chapter related to the Safe Sport Act of 2018). This call for additional oversight by Congress echoes views from Koller (2008) who has criticized previous court rulings holding the Olympic organizations as non-state actors. Koller has argued that those decisions are frozen in time and have allowed the organizations to exploit and endanger amateur athletes. The argument is seeded in the belief that, currently, the government has large influence on the USOPC and that this power is unchecked by the courts. Despite these concerns, since the USOPC and the various NGBs are not considered state actors and their decisions are not subject to constitutional challenge, most disputes will be resolved through administrative procedures laid out in the organizations' governing documents. In the next section, we explore the dispute resolutions systems and processes used in U.S. Olympic sports contexts.

Dispute Resolution Processes of U.S. Olympic Organizations

The ASA requires the USOPC and the NGBs to establish uniform eligibility standards and a comprehensive mechanism for the prompt resolution of disputes outside the judicial process. To illustrate the dispute resolution process within the Olympic Movement, let's consider one of the core functions and duties of Olympic organizations which is to determine eligibility to participate and selection of athletes for Olympic sports. These decisions are specifically covered in the dispute resolution procedures established in the ASA. If an athlete is unhappy with the NGB's or USOPC's selection process or internal dispute resolution, the act provides that the dispute may be submitted to the American Arbitration Association (AAA) for binding arbitration (§ 220529). Exhibit 13.4 illustrates the typical dispute resolution process for claims involving U.S. Olympic organizations and athletes.

This dispute resolution process is rarely subject to external judicial review, especially when the Olympic organization's actions are directly related to their responsibility to administer the Games and enforce the rules. U.S. courts have generally ruled that the OASA preempts judicial review pursued in state court when athletes attempt to use state law to challenge USOPC or NGB regulation of athlete eligibility (see *Slaney v. IAAF*, 2001; *Walton-Floyd v. USOC*, 1998). Courts also generally find that there is no **private right of action** under the statute, which means that individuals cannot use it to sue the USOPC or NGBs for **injunctive relief** (i.e., a court order to rectify an injury) or **damages** (i.e., a monetary award to compensate them for an injury) (*DeFrantz v. USOC*, 1980; *Martinez v. USOC*, 1986). (Also see *Michels v. USOC*, 1984 – no private right of action to challenge suspension for positive drug test; *Walton-Floyd v. USOC*, 1998 – no private cause of action for breaching duty of care in connection with drug testing hotline; *Dolan v. U.S. Equestrian Team, Inc*, 1992 – no private right of action for challenge to nonselection for U.S. equestrian team). The federal district court in *Lee v. U.S. Taekwondo Union* (2004) stated it as follows: "The USOC may be sued only with respect to matters not arising under the ASA, such as, for example with respect to a dispute over a lease that the USOC may have signed with the landlord of its offices" (*Lee*, p. 1257).

Thus, claims against the USOC or NGBs asserting state based contract and tort claims that are in response to a USOC or NGB decision under the ASA, are generally pre-empted and dismissed if asserted in federal court.

Federal Discrimination Claims

In a few cases, courts have held claims of race, sex, and disability discrimination in violation of federal law are not pre-empted by the ASA. In *Lee v. United States Taekwondo Union* (USTU) (2004) the district court held that while Lee's state law claims challenging the NGB's eligibility requirements were pre-empted by ASA, the ASA does not supersede or nullify federal anti-discrimination laws. Thus, Lee was permitted to pursue his federal race discrimination claim against USTU. Additionally, in *Shepherd v. USOC* (2006) the district court rejected the USOC's argument that ASA preempted Shepherd's claims under the Rehabilitation Act and the Americans with Disabilities Act. (For a case to the contrary, see *Sternberg v. USA National Karate-Do Federation, Inc.*, 2000.) Another example of federal court's jurisdiction over disputes involving national governing bodies is the lawsuit brought in 2019 by the USA Women's National Team against USA Soccer alleging violations of the federal Equal Pay Act and Title IX.

Exhibit 13.4 Dispute resolution process for athlete disputes with U.S. Olympic Organizations.

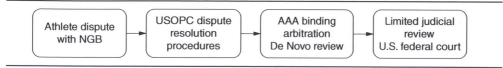

Due Process and Fairness Claims

In rare instances, courts are willing to review cases providing an athlete has first exhausted all administrative remedies (i.e., they have pursued all internal and external grievance procedures mandated by the organization; see *Barnes v. IAAF*, 1993). These cases are rare because the dispute resolution procedures incorporate several aspects of due process including the right to counsel and the right to an appeal. Similar to the scope of review we discussed in Chapter 11 regarding reviewing decisions of the NCAA related to amateurism and eligibility, U.S. courts will apply the law of private associations (see Chapter 11 and Exhibit 11.6) and will only rule on the issues of whether the USOPC or an NGB met three conditions:

- followed its own rules
- provided appropriate due process
- was not arbitrary and capricious in applying its rules

(See *Lindemann v. American Horse Shows Association*, 1994; *Schulz v. United States Boxing Association*, 1997.) For example, in *Harding v. U.S. Figure Skating Association* (1994), a federal court found that Tonya Harding's disciplinary hearing conducted by the U.S. Figure Skating Association, for her alleged misconduct in the incident that injured fellow Olympic skater Nancy Kerrigan, was unfairly scheduled in contravention of the skating association's own bylaws. The court found that this procedural injustice justified judicial review. However, in *Pliuskaitis v. USA Swimming* (2017), Pliuskaitis tried to sue for damages based on the arbitrator's decision that Pliuskaitis had been treated arbitrarily and capriciously by USA Swimming when it banned him from coaching based on allegations of sexual misconduct. The arbitrator held that USA Swimming's hearing process was in violation of their rules and reinstated Pliuskaitis as a coach member. However, Pliuskaitis also sought money damages which the arbitrator refused to award. The federal district court dismissed his suit holding that all of his claims challenging the hearing process rest on allegations related to USA Swimming's determination of his eligibility as a coach member of USA Swimming, thus all of his claims were resolved in final binding arbitration. The court held that he had a full and fair opportunity to resolve his claims in arbitration, he simply disagreed with the arbitrator's decision not to award him damages. For almost all disputes involving Olympic organizations, the dispute resolution systems established in the governing documents will control and the decisions resulting from those systems will be final.

Legal Issues in the Olympic Movement

Now that we have a solid understanding of the nature and source of authority for Olympic governing bodies, we are going to examine several areas related to the regulation of Olympic events and participants. It is helpful to understand these areas and how these disputes are resolved within the framework of the Olympic Movement. This section explores legal issues related to Olympic organizations' administration of the Olympic Movement in areas such as the program of sports and events offered; team/nation participation; determination of host cities; protection of intellectual property, sponsorship, and advertising; and security measures. Next, this section explores legal issues related to regulation of participant rights and challenges to Olympic organizations enforcement of restraints on athletes in areas such as eligibility, drug testing, sex testing, protests and demonstrations, and marketing activities. Finally, this section explores the duty of Olympic organizations to protect athletes.

Administration of the Games

Sports and Events Program for the Games

Under the Olympic Charter, the IOC Executive Board retains the authority to decide which sports and specific events are included on the menu of events for the Summer and Winter Olympic Games. The Board reviews the program of events after each Games to determine whether changes should be made. For example, in July 2005 the IOC voted to eliminate baseball and softball from the Olympic program after the 2008 Summer Games in Beijing (Wilson, 2005). In making these decisions, the IOC typically considers such issues as number of potential competitors, spectator interest, and potential for revenue generation in deciding whether to drop an existing sport or support a new sport. So, in 2013, International Federations for baseball and softball merged to create the World Baseball Softball Confederation (WBSC) which led to the IOC accepting them as a sanctioned sport for the 2020 Olympic Games in Japan. The support for this move was partly due to the popularity of baseball and softball in Japan (IOC, 2018). As another example, golf and rugby were both added to the programme for the 2016 Summer Olympic Games in Rio de Janeiro due to the heightened excitement and fandom of the sports on the national level ("Golf and Rugby," 2016). In addition to determining the program for the Games, the IOC also controls scheduling of the Games including the difficult decision to postpone the 2020 Tokyo Olympics due to the Covid-19 global pandemic (Keh, Rich, & Panja, 2020). The IOC's postponement triggered a domino effect among governing bodies to cancel and reschedule championship qualifying events around the world. The Olympic Games have been canceled during wartime in the past, but never postponed, so the impact of this decision could be unprecedented.

The IOC's authority to determine inclusion of events has rarely faced a legal challenge. In *Martin v. IOC* (1984), the Ninth Circuit Court of Appeals refused to interfere in the IOC's decision not to include 5,000 and 10,000 meter track events for women in the 1984 Olympic Games program. The court of appeals upheld the district court's denial of injunctive relief agreeing that the plaintiffs did not have a strong likelihood of success in prevailing on their gender discrimination claims under state law. Additionally, the court asserted that U.S. courts should be wary of applying state law to alter the content of an event conducted under an international agreement like the Olympic Charter. In April 2009, the Supreme Court of British Columbia heard a lawsuit brought by women ski jumpers against the Vancouver Olympic Organizing Committee (VANOC), challenging the IOC's decision to exclude women's ski jumping from the 2010 Winter Games. The complaint alleged that VANOC's unwillingness to include the event (ostensibly due to budget constraints) influenced the IOC's decision, and that the exclusion violated the Canadian Charter of Rights and Freedoms by treating women differently from men (CBC Sports, 2008). The IOC's position was that there were insufficient competitors to support adding women's ski jumping to the Olympic menu. VANOC argued that the power to determine what events can be held resides solely with the IOC. The Supreme Court of British Columbia agreed that the exclusion discriminated against the women in violation of the Canadian Charter but ruled that the IOC was beyond its reach (Fong, 2009). The British Columbia Court of Appeals later agreed that neither VANOC nor the Canadian government had any authority to challenge the IOC policy, explaining that the gender equity section of the Charter was inapplicable because there was no law or government contract related to the Olympic Games that transferred control over the selection of events from the IOC to anyone in Canada (Keller, 2009).

Team/Nation Participation

A nation's NOC has the authority to determine whether that country sends a competitor or team to the Olympic Games. However, the IOC has the authority to exclude or suspend a country or team. For example, the IOC suspended the Russian Olympic Committee and banned Russia from the 2018 Winter Olympic Games due to Russia's system of state-supported cheating by athletes using performance-enhancing drugs. Russian athletes were still permitted to compete in the 2018 Games but could not wear their country's uniform, had to compete under the Olympic flag, and were designated as "Olympic Athlete from Russia" (Chappell, 2017). The OCOGs are also charged with preventing political demonstrations at the Games. In *Spindulys v. Los Angeles Olympic Organizing Committee* (1985), certain groups from the countries of Estonia, Latvia, and Lithuania wished to participate in the opening ceremonies of the 1984 Los Angeles Olympic Games by performing dances in native folk costumes. At the time, these countries were part of the Union of Soviet Socialist Republics (USSR), which was the governmental entity recognized by the IOC. The plaintiffs wished to participate as recognized representatives of their own three countries to protest what they claimed was the Soviet Union's illegal annexation of their homelands. The Los Angeles Olympic Organizing Committee denied them the opportunity to participate, and they sued claiming discrimination on the basis of ancestry, national origin, and political beliefs under the state of California's Unruh Civil Rights Act. The court ruled that the issue presented by the plaintiffs was a political issue for governments to handle and not a legal issue that the courts should decide. The New York courts made a similar decision when a Taiwanese athlete accused the Lake Placid Olympic Organizing Committee of discriminating against him by refusing to allow him to carry the flag of Taiwan in the opening ceremonies because Taiwan was not formally recognized by the U.S. government at that time (*Ren-Guey v. Lake Placid 1980 Olympic Games*, 1980). IOC rules prohibiting player protests will be discussed further in the next section focusing on participant regulations.

Selection of Host Cities

The IOC selects the host cities for each Olympic and Paralympic Games. The NOCs are responsible for conducting a selection process in their own countries for cities that wish to bid to host the Games. The selection process takes place in two stages: An *Invitation Phase* which is not a formal commitment to submit a bid, and a *Candidature Process* which is a formal commitment to bid. The IOC presents the Invitation Phase as a one-year non-committal dialogue stage, bringing the NOCs and IOC together to discuss benefits and requirements of the Games. The IOC will provide the host city local interactive working sessions, on-site expert support, attendance to the next upcoming Olympic Games, and attend the debriefing of that event. At the end of the Invitation Phase, NOCs and cities are invited to commit to the Candidature Process. Once the NOC commits to the Candidature Process, the city becomes an official Candidate City for an Olympic Games and enter the official Olympic Candidature Process (IOC, 2019b). This Candidature Process spans a period of two years culminating in the Host City Election by the IOC session. The Candidate Cities submit a candidature file to an Evaluation Commission composed of representatives from IFs and NOCs, IOC members, representatives of the IOC Athletes' Commission, the International Paralympic Committee, and other experts. The Evaluation Commission submits a final report to the membership, and then the Executive Board compiles a final slate of candidates for an election held during the appropriate IOC Session. The cities will present their final version to the IOC and IOC members, followed by a vote to elect the host city (IOC, 2019b). The host city election is typically held seven years prior to the Games, although the IOC did not follow this protocol with the 2017 selection of Los Angeles to host the 2028 Summer Games. The LA2028 bid was the last bid under the old selection system.

   The IOC's unanimous decision to change the protocol for accepting host city bids was intended to create sustainability for the upcoming Olympic Games (Long, 2019). The two-step selection process is focused on transparency among the IOC, NOCs, city representatives, and stakeholders. The new Candidature Process is a condensed version of the past candidature stage and includes the proposal from the host cities. The IOC's Olympic Agenda 2020 further provided a new strategic roadmap for the future of the Olympic Movement. The document addresses key changes to the candidature procedures to invite bids that fit the planning needs of the candidate cities, to reduce costs for bidding, and to move from a sport-based to an event-based programme (IOC, 2020).

Protection of Intellectual Property

Rule 7 of the Olympic Charter provides that the IOC has exclusive ownership of all rights to the symbols of the Olympic Games, although it permits the NOCs to use and license Olympic trademarks for nonprofit Olympic fundraising and related activities. The NOCs are also charged with

Exhibit 13.5   36 U.S.C. § 380. Use of Olympic symbols, emblems, trademarks and names.

---

a   **Unauthorized use; civil action**

Without the consent of the Corporation, any person who uses for the purpose of trade, to induce the sale of any goods or services, or to promote any theatrical exhibition, athletic performance, or competition —

1   the symbol of the International Olympic Committee, consisting of 5 interlocking rings;
2   the emblem of the Corporation, consisting of an escutcheon having a blue chief and vertically extending red and white bars on the base with 5 interlocking rings displayed on the chief;
3   any trademark, trade name, sign, symbol, or insignia falsely representing association with, or authorization by, the International Olympic Committee or the Corporation; or
4   the words "Olympic," "Olympiad," "Citius Altius Fortius," or any combination or simulation thereof tending to cause confusion, to cause mistake, to deceive, or to falsely suggest a connection with the Corporation or any Olympic activity;

---

protecting against the unauthorized use of Olympic trademarks. In several instances, U.S. courts have upheld the right of the USOPC to protect against unauthorized use of the name "Olympics." For example, in *San Francisco Arts & Athletics, Inc. v. USOC* (1987), the Supreme Court upheld the USOPC's right to prevent a nonprofit organization from using the title "The Gay Olympic Games" to host its own athletic competition. The Court also ruled that the Amateur Sports Act incorporated the civil liability remedies of the Lanham Act, but not its defenses, so the USOPC is not required to show that unauthorized use is likely to cause consumer confusion as to the source of the goods or services. This has made it easier for the USOPC to bring successful claims of trademark infringement against unauthorized users of the Olympic marks. (Trademark infringement actions are discussed more fully in Chapter 18.)

Although the Olympic Charter reserves exclusive ownership of the Olympic symbols to the IOC, § 220506 of the OASA grants to the USOPC the exclusive right to control the commercial use and licensing of the Olympic trademarks in the United States. Section 380 further authorizes the USOPC to pursue a civil action against any person who uses the protected marks and symbols without consent (see Exhibit 13.5).

In the *Intelicense* case below, the court had to address a perceived conflict in the rights to control the use of the Olympic symbols.

USOC v. Intelicense Corporation

CASE OPINION   737 F.2d 263 (2d Cir. 1984), cert. den., 469 U.S. 982 (1984)

FACTS

In 1979, Intelicense Corp. entered into two agreements with the IOC under which Intelicense was granted the exclusive worldwide rights to be the marketing agent for the official pictograms of the IOC. These pictograms are designs of athletes in various sports portrayed against a background that includes the Olympic symbol of the five interlocking rings. Under the agreements, Intelicense was to receive 60 percent of the licensing revenues, and the IOC would get the remaining 40 percent. Finally, the agreements provided that Intelicense was required to obtain the approval of each NOC prior to any commercial use of the symbol in the respective countries.

During the next year, Intelicense sought permission from the USOPC to use the mark in the United States. The USOPC refused to grant permission, asserting that the Intelicense proposal to market the pictograms would diminish the USOPC's ability to obtain corporate sponsorships critical to the support of the U.S. Olympic Movement. Intelicense proceeded to license the use of the pictograms on products marketed in the United States without USOPC permission. The USOPC then filed suit, requesting an injunction forbidding Intelicense to contact corporate sponsors in the United States. The U.S. District Court entered a permanent injunction under § 380 of the Amateur Sports Act requiring Intelicense to stop its commercial use of the Olympic symbol in the United States without the consent of the USOPC.

HOLDING

The Second Circuit affirmed the permanent injunction entered by the district court.

RATIONALE

An understanding of this case is predicated largely upon a complete appreciation of the language and purpose of The Amateur Sports Act of 1978. This statute, enacted in 1978, empowers the USOC (now USOPC) to exercise exclusive jurisdiction over all matters pertaining to the participation of the United States in the Olympic Games. The Act further vests the USOC with the responsibility of financing the participation of the United States in the Olympic Movement. Because the USOC is the only NOC that does not receive formal financial assistance from the Government, financing the United States Olympic team poses unique obstacles.

Consequently, the marketing of the Olympic symbol in the United States assumes great importance. Indeed, during the period of 1980–1982, the USOPC received 45 percent of its income from its 44 corporate sponsors. Under the USOPC's corporate sponsorship program, each participant is authorized to use the USA Olympic emblem which contains the Olympic rings in exchange for a minimum guaranteed monetary contribution to the USOPC. As the trial court concluded, if the USOPC could not grant exclusive rights to market the Olympic symbol, the number of corporate participants would greatly be reduced and the USOPC would find itself unable to raise the funds required for participation in the Olympic Movement. Protecting the value of the Olympic symbol was, therefore, a significant factor that led to passage of the Act. It is clear that the Congressional intent in enacting § 380 was to promote the United States Olympic effort by entrusting the USOC with unfettered control over the commercial use of Olympic-related designations. This would facilitate the USOC's ability to raise those financial resources from the private sector that are needed to fund the United States Olympic Movement.

* * *

Intelicense claims, however, that because it is not falsely associated with the IOC, its conduct falls outside the proscriptive ambit of subsection (a)(3) and, therefore, cannot be reached by § 380. But, such a construction constitutes a patent misreading of the statute and would render § 380(a)(1) superfluous. The view urged is contrary to this Circuit's established rules of statutory construction (a statute should be construed to give force and effect to each of its provisions rather than render some of them meaningless). Accordingly, a violation of § 380 can properly be grounded upon a violation of subsection (a)(1) alone, notwithstanding Intelicense's exhortations to the contrary.

When viewed against the factual landscape present in the instant case coupled with Congress's intent in enacting § 380 and the plain statutory language of subsection (a)(1), we cannot imagine a more blatant violation of the Act. Indeed, it is uncontroverted that Intelicense made commercial use of the Olympic symbol to induce the sale of goods in the United States, without having secured the consent of the USOC. This is all that subsection (a)(1) requires.

* * *

Congress expressly chose to safeguard the United States Olympic Movement by enacting § 380. We hold that Intelicense has violated both the letter and spirit of § 380 by commercially marketing the pictograms in the United States without the consent of the USOPC. Accordingly, we affirm the district court's permanent injunction.

QUESTIONS

1 Why did the USOC refuse to grant permission to Intelicense to market the Olympic symbol within the United States?

2 What canon of statutory interpretation did the court use to rule that the Amateur Sports Act did in fact grant unequivocal authority to the USOC to control the use of Olympic symbols in the United States?

3 Besides the statutory interpretation analysis, what other argument did the court make for why the Amateur Sports Act should outweigh any potentially conflicting "right to control" provided to the IOC by the Olympic Charter?

Disputed Competition Outcomes

The Olympic Charter grants the IFs the authority to regulate the competitions of their sport(s) worldwide, including regulating the fairness of those competitions. Olympic judges and officials are approved by the IFs, and the IFs have the authority to suspend them for violating rules or ethical codes of conduct. For example, during the 2002 Winter Olympic Games in Salt Lake City, the French judge for the pairs figure skating event accused the French skating federation president of pressuring her to vote for the Russian pairs team (Berezhnaya and Sikharulidze) which had made some technical errors, over the Canadian skaters (Sale and Pelletier), who had performed without a mistake. As a result, the Russian team won the gold medal by a 5–4 judges' vote. The IF (International Skating Union) suspended both the judge and the French skating federation president for three years including the 2006 Winter Games in Torino (Shipley, 2002). Similarly, in the men's all-around gymnastics event in the 2004 Athens Olympic Games, the judges incorrectly scored Korean gymnast Yang Tae-Young's performance, causing US gymnast Paul Hamm to be erroneously awarded the gold medal. As a result, the International Gymnastics Federation (FIG) suspended the three judges responsible for the error (Gardner, 2004).

Despite suspensions of judges that acknowledge flawed competition results, the affected athletes do not always get the relief they seek. Because of the improprieties involved in the pairs skating judging, the Russian skaters were allowed to keep their gold medals, and Sale and Pelletier were awarded duplicate gold medals. However, in the gymnastics situation above, the IOC refused to issue gold medals to both Hamm and Yang Tae-Young, indicating that it would reallocate the medals upon the request of the FIG. The FIG, however, declined to make such a request because of a procedural technicality – the Korean Olympic Committee (KOC) had not filed a timely protest to the appropriate referee on its gymnast's behalf. Instead, the FIG requested that Hamm voluntarily relinquish his gold medal, but the USOPC rejected that request. Yang Tae-Young and the KOC then petitioned the CAS to correct the judging error and reallocate the gold medal (Gardner, 2004).

The CAS typically does not overrule competition judges' decisions, unless they were made as a result of corruption, fraud, arbitrariness, or were in violation of the law. In *Yang Tae-Young v. International Gymnastics Federation* (2004), the CAS refused to correct an error in scoring identified in hindsight, stating that the error might or might not have cost the Korean the gold medal. According to CAS, he had one more apparatus on which to perform after the scoring error, and it is anyone's guess as to whether he would have risen to the occasion or crumbled under pressure if he had been the leader at that point instead of being (albeit mistakenly) in third place (*Yang Tae-Young v. International Gymnastics Federation*, 2004).

Furthermore, according to the CAS panel, certain issues are not the proper province of the law. The court's refusal to second-guess competition results would

> contribute to finality. It would uphold, critically, the authority of the umpire, judge, or referee, whose power to control competition, already eroded by the growing use of technology such as video replays, would be fatally undermined if every decision taken could be judicially reviewed. Each sport may have within it a mechanism for utilizing modern technology to ensure a correct decision is made in the first place … or for immediately subjecting a controversial decision to a process of review … but the solution for error, either way, lies within the framework of the sport's own rules; it does not license judicial or arbitral interference thereafter.

The CAS panel also said it is an inevitable fact of life all sports participants must accept that sometimes referees make mistakes, as do players. Therefore, it refused to reallocate the medals, and Hamm retained the gold.

Security Measures

The NOCs create the OCOGs, which are responsible for the nuts-and-bolts preparations for and conduct of the Games, including security procedures. The IOC evaluates the overall emergency response and security plans to ensure that acceptable standards have been met. The NOC and OCOG determine the specific security procedures regarding access to venues, security of the Olympic Village, searches for weapons and other unauthorized possessions, and so forth.

Video surveillance by unmanned aerial vehicles, commonly known as drones, has reportedly been used at international sports mega-events as early as the 2012 Olympic Games in London (McCann, 2012) and the 2014 Winter Olympic Games in Sochi (Ayed, 2014). However, during the Sochi 2014 Games, security measures took another step forward. To ensure that the Games went on without any security breaches, the plans included drone surveillance, video face recognition, and Deep Packet Inspection (DPI) in the WiFi. This DPI software allowed organizers to trace all calls, texts, emails, and social media messages occurring in Sochi (Schultz, 2014). Arguably, drone surveillance is more invasive than surveillance by fixed cameras, because drones might be used from a height at which spectators are unaware they are under surveillance. The surveillance procedures now being established are the most extensive ever seen for an Olympic Games, especially due to the spectators being unaware of the surveillance measures being used in and around the venues. Tokyo 2020 planned even more extensive security measures including advanced AI technologies on an unprecedented scale for improving security efficiency, solving staff shortages, and providing intelligent early warnings ("One Year Countdown," 2019).

It is arguable that combining highly invasive surveillance technology with information-gathering functions to search sports spectators on a mass, suspicionless basis is an illegal search under the Fourth Amendment (Claussen, 2006). Thus, conceivably, a spectator attending a future Games hosted on U.S. soil (e.g., LA2028) might challenge invasive search procedures as a violation of his Fourth Amendment right to be free from unreasonable searches. The involvement of the police, military, city, and governmental officials might serve to establish the OCOG as a state actor in its function of providing security measures. The question would then be whether a U.S. court faced with a Fourth Amendment unreasonable search claim would insist on applying the Constitution or would it follow the pattern of judicial deference to the decision-making of Olympic governing bodies we have seen in other contexts. Chapter 15 discusses the constitutionality of searches and seizures at sport venues in greater detail.

Competitive Advantage Strategies

Contracts with Olympics-Related Governing Bodies

- If you work for an organization like Intelicense that has a contract with an NOC or an NGB, find out how the OASA and other laws, as well as the inter-relationships among Olympic-related governing bodies, may affect your business decisions.
- If you work in the social media/marketing area, be aware that USOPC aggressively prohibits unauthorized use of Olympic marks and the name "Olympics," and the IOC does not allow the posting of photos or videos of the Olympic Games to social media.

Regulation of Participants

In addition to administering the Games' events and competitions, Olympic sport governing bodies possess the authority to regulate the behavior of participants, including athletes, coaches, and officials. This section discusses legal issues arising in the context of regulating participants in six areas: amateurism, disciplinary actions for rules violations, eligibility and competition rules, drug testing, sex testing, conduct and protests, and endorsements and personal sponsors.

Amateurism

The principle of amateurism has been embedded in the Olympic Movement since the beginning, but as sport modernized in the twentieth century, the line separating true amateurism from professionalism became increasingly blurred. In response, the IOC voted in 1974 to delete the word "amateurism" from the Olympic Charter. However, the change was not implemented until 1986, when the 91st IOC Session decided to permit professional ice hockey players to participate in the Winter Games, subject to the approval of the relevant IF, the International Ice Hockey Federation (IIHF). Subsequently, professional tennis players were allowed to play beginning with the Seoul Summer Games in 1988, and in 1992 professional basketball players first participated in the Summer Games in Barcelona.

The IOC completely abandoned the amateurism principle when former President Juan Samaranch opened participation in the Games to professional athletes, stipulating only that they cannot receive any money during the Games for their participation. Most Olympic and Paralympic athletes do not earn any compensation for Olympic competition. Many countries provide travel and training expenses, but most direct income for Olympic and Paralympic athletes comes from personal sponsorships. Athletes can also earn medal bonuses for each medal won. The bonus amount will vary by sport and by country ranging from as much as $1 million for a gold medal for an Olympic athlete from Singapore to $8,000 for a bronze medal for an athlete from Canada (Weliver, 2019). In 2018, Olympic gold medals earned U.S. athletes $37,500, silver medals $22,500, and bronze medals $15,000 (Elkins, 2018). Beginning in 2020, U.S. Paralympic medalists will earn the same bonus amounts of their Olympic counterparts (Allentuck, 2019). The importance of sponsorship monies for Olympic and Paralympic athletes is further discussed later in this chapter when we explore the impact of Rule 40 of the Olympic Charter which prohibits participants (including athletes, coaches, and trainers) from allowing their "person, name, picture, or sports performance to be used for advertising purposes during the Games" (IOC, 2019a). Even though the concept of amateurism is no longer strictly adhered to, the IOC still exercises significant control over the conduct of participants during the Games to regulate economically motivated conduct.

Disciplinary Actions for Rules Violations

NGBs typically have the authority to impose disciplinary sanctions when international federation rules have been violated. The CAS has demonstrated a willingness to overturn NGB and IF sanctions if they appear arbitrary or if an organization fails to follow its own rules. In one case, a Samoan Olympic weight-lifter was accused of statutory rape and suspended for one year by his NGB, which would have prevented him from competing in the Sydney 2000 Games. This penalty was then endorsed by the International Weightlifting Federation (IWF), even though no criminal charges had been brought and no arrest made. As an NGB, the Samoan Weightlifting Federation (SWF) was subject to Samoan law, and the Samoa Supreme Court overturned the SWF's suspension. The IWF, however, refused to lift its endorsement of the suspension to Sydney officials.

The CAS ruled that once the Samoa Supreme Court invalidated the SWF's suspension based on a presumption of innocence until proven guilty, the IWF could no longer sustain its decision because it was now considered to be based on an invalid prior decision by the Samoan NGB. Therefore, the CAS set aside the IWF's arbitrary suspension and allowed the weightlifter to compete (*Samoa NOC and Sports Federation, Inc. v. International Weightlifting Federation*, 2000).

In *Harding v. United States Figure Skating Association* (1994), the U.S. District Court found that the NGB violated its own due process rule requiring that upon receipt of the athlete's reply to the disciplinary charges against her, it must set a time and place for a disciplinary hearing that is reasonably convenient for both parties. The U.S. Figure Skating Association (USFSA) had set Tonya Harding's hearing date before it received her reply to the charges, and set it for only three days after her reply was filed. The court found this unreasonable because she would not have had enough time in those three days to prepare an adequate defense to the charges against her. Thus, because the NGB had not followed its own rules, the court would have upheld an earlier injunction delaying the disciplinary hearing for three and a half months, had it not dismissed the case for other reasons.

Although the court in *Harding* would have upheld an injunction delaying the hearing out of concern for the plaintiff, in other situations quick resolution of a dispute is what the plaintiff needs so that they can meet approaching deadlines for qualifying events or to compete in scheduled events at the Games themselves. However, § 220509(a) of the OASA prohibits any court from granting relief to an athlete regarding an eligibility dispute with the USOPC that occurs within 21 days of the beginning of the Games, as long as the USOPC has provided a written statement saying it cannot resolve the dispute in time. The purpose of this provision is to prevent courts from infringing on the regulatory authority of the USOPC when it does not have time to fully implement its dispute resolution procedures.

Eligibility and Competition Rules

Per the Olympic Charter, the IFs determine the general rules of competition for its particular sport(s) worldwide. These rules would include, for example, rules defining how the sport is to be played, scoring methods to be used, criteria for eligibility and disqualification, and specifications for legal equipment. Oscar Pistorius, an elite South African sprinter who competed in the Paralympic Games with the aid of prostheses on both legs, sought to compete in international track events against able-bodied competitors to qualify for the Olympic Games.

The case that follows illustrates how the CAS analyzed the eligibility rules of the International Association of Athletics Federations (IAAF). IAAF renamed itself to World Athletics in 2019 (Mackay, 2019).

Pistorius v. Int'l Ass'n of Athletics Federations (IAAF)

CASE OPINION   CAS 2008/A/1480 *Pistorius v. IAAF*

FACTS

World-class sprinter Oscar Pistorius had both legs amputated below the knee when he was 11 months old. He wears a prosthetic device, known as the Cheetah Flex-Foot, on both legs when he runs. Pistorius held the Paralympic world record in the 100-, 200-, and 400-meter races, and his time in the 400-meter event was only 1.01 seconds slower than the Olympic qualifying standard. He wished to continue to compete in IAAF-sanctioned track meets, which would allow him the chance to qualify to compete in the 2008 Olympic Games against able-bodied competitors. Pistorius had been allowed to compete in qualifying events in 2004 and 2007, but in March 2007 the IAAF (World Athletics) adopted Rule 144.2(e) that carried a new prohibition:

> Use of any technical device that incorporates springs, wheels or any other element that provides the user with an advantage over another athlete not using such a device [is prohibited].

In June 2007, the IAAF president stated in a press conference that Pistorius would not be excluded from IAAF track events unless the IAAF received scientific evidence that demonstrated his prostheses gave him an advantage over able-bodied athletes. One month later, the IAAF arranged for an Italian sports laboratory to videotape a race run by Pistorius for the purpose of analyzing whether his stride length and time of ground contact differed significantly from other runners, and they did not. The tape also showed that while Pistorius ran his fastest 100-meter splits on the straightaways, the able-bodied runners' fastest splits were in the first and second 100 meters. Pistorius was slower than the other runners off the starting blocks, during the first 50-meter acceleration phase, and around the first curve.

The IAAF later requested that the Institute of Biomechanics and Orthopaedics at the German Sport University in Cologne conduct tests designed to determine whether the Cheetah Flex-Foot prosthesis gave Pistorius any biomechanical or metabolic advantages over other athletes, and Pistorius agreed to be tested. The German scientists reported that Pistorius received significant biomechanical advantages and benefited from a lower metabolic cost due to the use of the prostheses. Based on these findings, in January 2008 the IAAF determined that Pistorius's use of the Flex-Foot contravened Rule 144.2(e) and declared him immediately ineligible to compete in IAAF-sanctioned events. Pistorius appealed the IAAF Council's decision to CAS. The three issues ruled upon *de novo* by CAS were:

1 Was the IAAF's decision-making process procedurally unsound?
2 Did the IAAF's decision constitute unlawful discrimination on the basis of disability?
3 Was the IAAF wrong in determining that Pistorius' use of the Cheetah Flex-Foot contravenes Rule 144.2(e)?

HOLDING

CAS overturned the decision of the IAAF Council, clearing Pistorius to compete.

RATIONALE

CAS found it likely that the new rule was introduced with Pistorius in mind. It also found that the testing protocol commissioned by the IAAF instructed the Cologne lab only to test Pistorius while he was running in a straight line after the acceleration phase (it was known by then that this was the stage of a race when he would usually run his fastest). In the court's view, these instructions created a distorted view of his advantages and disadvantages by failing to consider the effect of the device on his performance over all stages of the race. CAS concluded that this distortion rendered dubious the validity and relevance of the Cologne lab's test results.

CAS further found that the scientist nominated by Pistorius to participate in the Cologne tests declined because he was going to be allowed to do so only as an observer, with no input on the testing protocol or data analysis. Additionally, IAAF officials failed to provide the IAAF Council with any scientific data other than their own summary of the Cologne analysis, which was later criticized by the Cologne scientists as inaccurate. In addition to other procedural problems associated with unfairness in the voting process, IAAF officials announced to the press prior to the Council's vote that Pistorius would be banned from IAAF-sanctioned events. CAS concluded that there was sufficient procedural unsoundness which gave rise to the impression that the IAAF had predetermined that they would try to prevent Pistorius from competing in international IAAF-sanctioned events, regardless of the outcomes of scientific testing. However, CAS stated that its finding of procedural unsoundness made little difference to the outcome of Pistorius' appeal since its panel was considering the appeal *de novo*.

CAS found that Monaco (the home of the IAAF) had neither signed nor ratified the United Nations Convention on the Rights of Persons with Disabilities. Even if it had, the Convention only encourages signatory states to promote the participation of people with disabilities in sports on an equal basis with able-bodied participants. Therefore, according to CAS, the Convention did not help Pistorius in this appeal because whether he was competing on an equal basis with other athletes was precisely what this appeal sought to determine. In other words, if he had no artificial advantage, then the IAAF would have allowed him to compete, but if the prostheses did give him an advantage, then the Convention would not apply. CAS thus rejected Pistorius's claim of disability discrimination.

CAS also rejected the IAAF's view that Rule 144.2(e) prohibited use of a technical device that provided an athlete with *any* advantage over others, however small, regardless of any compensating disadvantages. The court found that proper interpretation of the rule required proof that the device provided the user with an *overall net advantage* over nonusers. According to CAS, "If the use of the device provides more disadvantages than advantages, then it cannot reasonably be said to provide an advantage over other athletes, because the user is actually at a competitive disadvantage." CAS concluded that the testing protocol followed by the Cologne lab was thus inadequate because it assessed only the advantages of using the device.

Pistorius presented his own scientific evidence from tests conducted by a lab in Houston that showed the Flex-Foot provided him no metabolic advantage over nonusers. CAS requested that the two scientific teams cooperate in producing for the court a list of scientific findings summarizing points on which they agreed and disagreed. Upon review of this list, CAS found that the experts agreed that neither group had quantified all the possible advantages and disadvantages of Pistorius' use of the device in a 400-meter race, thus the IAAF did not prove an overall net advantage. The court also found that the scientists acknowledged that current knowledge in the field of biomechanics was inadequate on the issue of whether Pistorius' flatter running gait was an advantage or disadvantage, as well as on the issue of whether energy spared by a prosthetic ankle could be effectively transferred to other parts of the body. Thus, based on current scientific knowledge, the experts were unable to say whether the Flex-Foot prosthesis provided more of a spring effect than a human ankle and lower leg. Moreover, the experts agreed that a mechanical advantage provided by a prosthetic device would be expected to create a concomitant metabolic advantage, and neither lab had been able to find one. Finally, the court took notice of the fact that the same device had been in use by other runners for ten years, and no one except Pistorius had run fast enough to compete effectively against able-bodied runners.

On these grounds, CAS concluded that the IAAF failed to carry its burden of proof (on the balance of probability) that Pistorius' use of the Cheetah Flex-Foot violated Rule 144.2(e). In closing, CAS clarified that its decision on this appeal was specific to the facts of this case and would have no application to any other athlete, any other version of the same device, or any other type of prosthetic limb. Further, this decision would not exclude the possibility that other advances in scientific knowledge and a more relevant testing protocol that assesses overall net advantage might lead to the IAAF's future ability to prove this device provides an unfair advantage after all.

QUESTIONS

1 Do the actions taken by the IAAF appear to you to have been aimed at reaching an objective and fair decision about whether to allow Pistorius to compete in sanctioned track events? What fears or concerns might have been behind some of the actions taken by IAAF officials?

2 How did CAS determine that Pistorius had not suffered discrimination on the basis of his disability?

3 Do you think CAS reached the right decision in this case and for the right reasons? If so, why? If not, why not?

4 What are the practical implications of the *Pistorius* decision for future decisions regarding the use of new technology by athletes with disabilities in order to compete with able-bodied athletes?

The *Pistorious* case illustrates several important aspects of legal challenges asserted against IFs by athletes. First, the burden of proof was on IAAF (World Athletics) to demonstrate that Pistorious' prosthetic devices gave him an advantage. Thus, his eligibility hinged on whether IAAF could prove he had a demonstrable competitive advantage, not simply because he used a prosthetic device in order to compete. Second, even though these organizations are not state actors and are not required to provide fundamental due process prior to depriving an athlete of the opportunity to compete, some basic procedural fairness is required and the IAAF's failure to provide that basic fairness was inconsistent with the bylaws of that organization. However, the IAAF (World Athletics) is also an excellent case study in the authority of governing bodies to amend and modify eligibility requirements. Following the outcome in *Pistorius*, World Athletics amended its rules to shift the burden of proof to the athlete to prove that he does not have a competitive advantage when using a prosthetic device. Thus, in 2020, when double amputee Blake Leeper sought approval to compete in World Athletics-sanctioned events, including the Olympic Games while using his prosthetics, Leeper's application included expert reports that his prosthetics did not give him a competitive advantage. World Athletics denied his application, finding he had not met his burden of proof that he would not have a competitive advantage over other competitors. Leeper appealed to CAS, challenging the requirement that he bear the burden of proof as unlawful since the burden was on World Athletics up until 2015 ("Double-Amputee," 2020). On October 26, 2020, the CAS panel determined that the WA Technical Rule was unlawful to the extent it placed the burden of proof upon Leeper to establish that his prosthetic device did not give him a competitive advantage (CAS, 2020). The CAS ruling regarding Leeper has important implications for governing bodies related to who bears the burden to prove that an athlete does not meet eligibility requirements.

Drug Testing

In general, the IFs have the authority to promulgate antidoping and drug-testing rules, which are then investigated and enforced by the respective NGBs. In practice, this led to inconsistency in antidoping efforts. Thus, as mentioned in the previous section, WADA was formed with the purpose of promoting a uniform and equitable drug-testing policy for international sport athletes, one that would include common standards for doping control (WADA, 2020a). The World Anti-Doping Code (Code) provides the framework for sport organizations and governments to adopt uniform anti-doping polices, rule, and regulations (WADA, 2020b). However, because some countries are not permitted to be legally bound by a non-governmental document such as the Code, UNESCO unanimously adopted the International

Convention against Doping in Sport (Anti-Doping Convention) in October 2005. The Anti-Doping Convention enables governments which cannot be legally bound to the Code to ratify the Convention in accordance with their respective constitutional constraints. Almost all sport organizations have approved the Code and 189 countries have agreed to abide by the Anti-Doping Convention (UNESCO, 2020). The United States ratified the Anti-Doping Convention on August 25, 2008. The Code was revised in 2015 and is available on WADA's website included in the Web Resources at the end of the chapter.

U.S. professional athletes who are subject to collective bargaining agreements are not bound by the Code unless they give their express consent to be so bound. College athletes who are also Olympic or Paralympic athletes are bound by the Code based on their participation with the NGB of their sport and its affiliation with the respective IF for that sport. College athletes also agree to participate in University drug testing programs and adhere to NCAA and Conference drug regulations, but any collegiate drug testing programs operated by a public university would also be subject to scrutiny under the Fourth Amendment to the Constitution. We discuss the Fourth Amendment and unconstitutional searches and seizures in Chapter 17.

The United States Anti-Doping Agency (USADA), formed in 2000, serves as the drug-testing agency for Olympic and Paralympic sports in the United States. It is not subject to the control of the USOPC, but independently conducts drug-testing, investigation, and adjudication functions. If the USADA finds evidence of a doping violation, it proposes sanctions in accordance with the relevant IF's disciplinary rules. The athlete may accept those sanctions or request an arbitration hearing before a panel of the American Arbitration Association consisting of individuals who are also members of the North American CAS pool of arbitrators. Either party, the athlete or the IF, may appeal the AAA decision to the CAS, whose decision will be considered final and binding on the parties. Information about USADA can be found on its website at www.usantidoping.org.

Strict Liability Standard

CAS generally applies a principle of strict liability (see Chapter 14) when it finds a valid positive test for banned substances. In this context, strict liability means that even if an athlete can prove he did not

---

Competitive Advantage Strategies

Regulation of Participants

- Familiarize yourself with the decision-making standards of the Court of Arbitration for Sport. This knowledge will stand you in good stead if the Olympic sport governing body for which you work becomes a party in a CAS arbitration, by giving you a framework for determining the best approach to preparing your case.
- From the perspective of a sport manager at an NGB or IF, it would seem important to communicate to coaches the message that their athletes can and will be punished for doping – even for accidental consumption. Coaches, strength coaches, and athletic trainers would then be on notice that they need to be careful when providing food and beverages to their athletes, because the CAS nearly always rules that even accidental consumption will result in disqualification from an upcoming event, and it may also result in suspensions depending upon the severity of the offense. The coaching staff should also be instructed to educate their athletes about the CAS strict liability approach so that the athletes themselves can be cautious about what they ingest.
- If you work for a recognized Olympic Movement organization, advise any staff you may supervise, such as coaches and trainers, about which governing bodies may have the authority to regulate their conduct, as well as that of participating athletes, and in what areas of conduct.

purposefully take a banned substance, he will be automatically disqualified from competition. The CAS believes such a policy is best, even though it seems unfair to the disqualified athlete, because it would be unfair to all the other athletes in the event to allow the (albeit inadvertently) performance-enhanced athlete to compete with a drug-induced advantage.

As part of its strict liability framework for deciding drug-testing appeals, the CAS insists that (a) IOC and IF antidoping policies provide clear notice of the rules to athletes; (b) the testing procedures be designed to be reliable; and (c) the procedures be followed. Thus, in a case for example where the rules of the IOC and the International Ski Federation (FIS) did not clearly ban marijuana, the CAS overturned the IOC's decision to strip the gold medalist in the giant slalom event at Nagano of his medal after he tested positive for that drug (*R. v. International Olympic Committee*, 1998). In addition to disqualification, the World Anti-Doping Code authorizes the IOC to impose sanctions for doping violations that include:

- Issuing a warning to the athlete.
- Imposing a ban on competition.
- Imposing a fine.
- Imposing a suspension from participation.

The hypothetical case below helps to illustrate how the CAS applies strict liability in the case of inadvertent consumption of a banned substance.

Considering ... Strict Liability

B. K. Stroker, an Olympic swimmer, tested positive for a stimulant on the list of prohibited substances. Federation Internationale de Natation (FINA) (the IF for international swimming competition) investigated and decided to expel Stroker from her event later that day and suspend her from international competition for two years. She appealed within the IF, but her appeal was denied, so she is now appealing to the CAS for a final decision. Stroker has evidence that she did not knowingly ingest the stimulant. She indicates that 30 minutes before every race she relinquishes control over her food and drink choices to her coach. Her coach admitted that in this instance he inadvertently gave Stroker a capsule of the stimulant when providing her with food and drink before her race. Stroker has a reputation for unimpeachable moral integrity and generally exemplary conduct.

Questions

- Will the CAS apply a strict liability approach to Stroker's case, or will it decide in her favor and overturn her suspension?
- If the CAS finds Stroker to bear very little of the blame, will it reduce the severity of the penalty imposed by FINA, or is proportion of blame irrelevant to CAS decisions?

Note how you would answer the questions and then check your responses using the Analysis & Discussion at the end of this chapter.

No Significant Fault Standard

The CAS has indicated that instead of the fixed penalty structure adopted by some IFs, it prefers to impose penalties based on the proportion of fault attributable to the athlete (*C. v. Federation Internationale de Natation Amateur*, 1996). To rebut the presumption of guilt on the part of one who has tested positive, the athlete would have to provide evidence establishing with near certainty that he was not at fault.

Although the athlete would still be disqualified to prevent competitive unfairness, proof of a lack of fault claim would mitigate additional penalties, such as suspension from future competition. WADA Code, Article 10.4 (*No Fault or Negligence*) applies in exceptional circumstances where an athlete can show that despite all due care and based on no significant fault (NSF) on the part of the athlete, they produced a positive test result. CAS determined in *Cilic v. ITF* (2013) that both a subjective and objective level of fault should be considered to decide if an athlete qualified for the no significant fault (NSF) exception. The objective level of fault looks to what standard of care could have been expected from a reasonable person in the athlete's situation. The subjective level of fault asks what could have been expected from that particular athlete in light of his particular capacities (*Cilic*, 2013). CAS rejected a cyclist's claim of NSF based on a substance administered by an emergency room physician for injuries suffered during a training ride (*Medvedev v. Russian Anti-Doping Agency*, 2017). However, CAS reduced the 24-month suspension imposed on Maria Sharapova by the International Tennis Federation (ITF) to 15 months after finding that Sharapova had continued taking meldonium with the good faith belief it was appropriate. She had been taking it over a long period of time and was not clearly informed that the anti-doping authorities had changed the rules to include the drug on the banned substance list (*Sharapova v. ITF*, 2016). The NSF exception is a high bar for an athlete to meet but helps to balance the rigid application of strict liability.

Sex Testing

Beginning in 1968 at the Grenoble Winter Games and the Mexico City Summer Games, the IOC mandated sex tests to ensure that competitors in Olympic women's events are in fact female. The purpose of these tests was to ensure that males were not entering women's events and thus automatically disadvantaging the female entrants, who were presumably less capable than males. Mandatory sex testing continued until 1998 when the IOC and IFs, such as the IAAF/World Athletics, implemented various types of "gender verification" policies regarding eligibility in female athletic competition (Cooky & Dworkin, 2013). Concerns about discrimination against transgender athletes have increasingly been voiced in opposition to these policies. Sex testing can apply to transgender athletes who have undergone sex reassignment, as well as transgender athletes based on self-identification. IOC regulations on female hyperandrogenism also fall under the general umbrella of sex testing in international sport competition.

The issue of eligibility impacted by female hyperandrogenism was highlighted in 2009 when South African runner Caster Semenya won the 800-meter race in the world championships held in Berlin. Her femaleness was questioned, ultimately leading to a determination that she has a condition known as female hyperandrogenism. That is, her naturally elevated levels of androgen production produce higher levels of testosterone and put her in the intersex category, somewhere in between the conventional categories of male and female. As a result, her eligibility to compete as a female was challenged. In April 2011, the IAAF (World Athletics) updated their regulations regarding female elite athletes with hyperandrogenism: Females whose testosterone levels crossed into the male range could not compete with other females unless it is shown that they are resistant to the effects of testosterone (IAAF, 2011). After much controversy, Semenya was cleared to compete internationally and ended up winning the silver medal in the 2012 London Olympic Games. The ongoing controversy caused the IOC to re-enter the arena of sex testing, and in 2012 it issued new regulations governing the eligibility to compete in women's events (Macur, 2012). These regulations expressly reject any attempt to determine an athlete's sex, focusing instead on determining eligibility based on whether the athlete's testosterone levels are within the normal male range and would confer a competitive advantage (IOC, 2012). Thus, both the IOC and World Athletics moved from a gender verification based policy framework to a hormone-based rule to define eligibility for women's sports (Buzuvis, 2016).

The IOC's 2013 Hyperandrogenism Rule excludes women from participation if suspicion based testing revealed endogenous or natural testosterone levels of 10 nanomoles per liter (nmol/L) of serum, a level typically within a normal "male range" (Buzuvis, 2016). A female athlete with natural testosterone levels higher than to 10 nmol/L may still compete if she undertakes medical treatment to suppress the effect of testosterone in her body, or if she proves that her body is insensitive to androgen.

In 2015, CAS suspended World Athletics' hyperandrogenism regulations in the case of Dutee Chand, an Indian athlete who has hyperandrogenism. CAS held that not enough scientific evidence indicated that higher levels of natural testosterone gave any athletic advantages to female athletes. This opened the door for Semenya to compete and win the 800 meters Olympic gold medal in 2016. However, Bermon and Garnier (2017) published an article in the *British Journal of Sports Medicine* that argued higher natural hormone levels for females provided a 1.8% "performance advantage" in longer distance races and specifically in the 800 meter race (Semenya's favorite event).

This information led World Athletics to introduce new regulations to take effect on November 1, 2018 requiring any athlete who has Difference of Sexual Development (DSD), defined as women athletes with testosterone levels 5 nmol/L or above and who are androgen-sensitive, to meet certain criteria in order to be eligible to compete in middle distance races ("IAAF Introduces," 2018). To meet eligibility criteria a DSD athlete must be recognized at law as either female or intersex and must reduce her blood testosterone level to below the 5 nmol/L for over six months before being cleared to participate and maintain that level continuously. To reduce the naturally occurring testosterone in the blood, the athlete would be required to take hormonal contraceptives. If athletes refused to take medicine to reduce their testosterone levels or unable to reduce their testosterone levels they would be banned from participation in any World Athletics sanctioned event. Semenya and Athletics South Africa (ASA) filed a challenge to the new regulation with CAS and requested arbitration to declare the DSD regulation invalid and void. Semenya and ASA argued that the DSD rules were discriminatory and unreliable (Jiwani, 2019; Palar, 2019). On May 1, 2019, CAS dismissed the request for arbitration finding that the regulations are discriminatory but based on the evidence submitted such discrimination is necessary, reasonable and a proportionate means of achieving the IAAF's aim of preserving the integrity of female athletics in restricted events ("Media Release," 2019). Even though CAS dismissed the request for arbitration, it also included several serious concerns it had with the DSD regulations as follows:

1 The difficulties of implementation of the DSD Regulations in the context of a maximum permitted level of testosterone. The Panel noted the strict liability aspect of the DSD Regulations and expressed its concern as to an athlete's potential inability to remain in compliance with the DSD Regulations in periods of full compliance with treatment protocols, and, more specifically, the resulting consequences of unintentional non-compliance.

2 The difficulty to rely on concrete evidence of actual (in contrast to theoretical) significant athletic advantage by a sufficient number of 46 XY DSD athletes in the 1,500 m and 1 mile events. The CAS Panel suggested that the IAAF consider deferring the application of the DSD Regulations to these events until more evidence is available.

3 The side effects of hormonal treatment, experienced by individual athletes could, with further evidence, demonstrate the practical impossibility of compliance which could, in turn, lead to a different conclusion as to the proportionality of the DSD Regulations ("Media Release," 2019).

Semenya appealed the CAS decision to the Federal Supreme Court of Switzerland which denied her appeal on September 8, 2020 (Associated Press, 2020). The Swiss federal tribunal said CAS had the right to uphold eligibility criteria for female athletes with the genetic variant "46 XY DSD" in order to guarantee fair competition for certain running disciplines in female athletics (Associated Press, 2020). Based on this ruling Semenya will be ineligible to defend her Olympic 800 meter title in future Olympic Games unless she agrees to lower her testosterone level through medication or surgery.

This challenging issue will continue to evolve for sport managers in the Olympic sport segment. CAS seemed to acknowledge as much in its decision noting that the DSD regulations are a "living document" which will continue to be informed with experience and further evidence of proportionality. Lastly, CAS's concerns about the strict liability standard of the DSD regulations may draw some comparisons to their position in drug testing cases to explore less rigid outcomes for athletes.

Expressive Activities and Marketing Activities

The IOC has established guidelines and rules regulating athletes' expressive activities and marketing activities during the Olympic Games. In this section we are going to focus on Rule 50 (protests and political demonstrations) and Rule 40 (athlete marketing). Rule 40 and Rule 50 are presented in Exhibit 13.6.

Rule 50

Rule 50 of the Olympic Charter provides a framework to protect the neutrality of sport and the Olympic Games. The IOC announced new guidelines in January 2020 that prohibit athletes from making political, religious, and ethnic demonstrations at the 2020 Tokyo Olympic Games ("Rule 50 Guidelines," 2020). The previous Rule 50 already prohibited athletes from protesting at the Games, but the 2020 guidelines specify what activities would qualify as a protest or demonstration (see Exhibit 13.6). Numerous athletes have been disciplined for violating the IOC's or their NOCs' rules prohibiting protests or political demonstrations during the Games. Two U.S. athletes who protested during the national anthem at the 2019 Pan Am Games in Peru were given 12 months' probation by the USOPC (Longman, 2019). Although the IOC advocates for political neutrality, the Olympic Games have been a stage for political protests for most of its history (Godin, 2020). See Exhibit 13.7 for a sample of political protests

Exhibit 13.6 IOC/USOC Rule 50 and Rule 40.

RULE 50: Demonstrations and Propaganda

"No kind of demonstration or political, religious or racial propaganda is permitted in any Olympic sites, venues or other areas." (Rule 50 Olympic Charter)

Here are some examples of what would constitute a protest, as opposed to expressing views (non-exhaustive list):

- Displaying any political messaging, including signs or armbands;
- Gestures of a political nature, like a hand gesture or kneeling;
- Refusal to follow the Ceremonies protocol.

RULE 40: Athlete Marketing for Olympic and Paralympic Games

2016 – "Except as permitted by the IOC Executive Board, no competitor, coach, trainer or official who participates in the Olympic Games may allow his person, name, picture or sports performances to be used for advertising purposes during the Olympic Games" (IOC, n.d).

2020 – "Competitors, team officials and other team personnel who participate in the Olympic Games may allow their person, name, picture or sports performances to be used for advertising purposes during the Olympic Games in accordance with the principles determined by the IOC Executive Board" (Bye-law 40.3 of the Olympic Charter-Rule 40, 2020).

Exhibit 13.7 Examples of political protests and platforms at the Olympic Games.

Games	Sport/Org	Protest Activity
1906 Athens	Track & Field	Scaled a 20-foot flagpole in the stadium waving a green flag protesting Irish athletes forced to compete under British flag.
1968 Mexico City	Track & Field	John Carolos and Tommie Smith famously raised their fists in Black Power salute on the medal podium.
1968 Mexico City	Gymnastics	Czechoslovakian gymnast turned her head away from Soviet flag in protest to Soviet invasion of Czechoslovakia.
1980 Moscow	USA, Canada, West Germany, and Japan	Boycott of Olympic Games after Soviet Union invaded Afghanistan in 1979.
2004 Athens	Judo	Iranian world champion refused to fight Israeli champion to sympathize with the suffering of the people in Palestine.

during the Olympic Games. During the summer of 2020 following the postponement of the 2020 Tokyo Olympic Games due to the Covid-19 pandemic, the IOC opened talks to consider relaxing the new rule it adopted in January 2020. The IOC's announcement followed the murder of George Floyd, a black man in Minneapolis, by a police officer which sparked global protests and demonstrations calling for racial justice and an end to police brutality toward black people (Burns, 2020; Morgan, 2020). John Carlos, a renowned protestor from the 1968 Summer Olympic Games in Mexico City initiated efforts during the Summer of 2020 to abolish Rule 50 prior to the rescheduled Tokyo Olympic Games in 2021 (Pells, 2020).

Rule 40

The IOC has established official guidelines regarding athlete marketing especially efforts by athletes to promote their personal sponsors during the Olympic Games. The purpose and policy reasons for Rule 40, as stated by the IOC, are: "[t]o preserve the unique nature of the Olympics by preventing over-commercialization," "to allow the focus to remain on athletes," and to protect the Olympic Games' source of funding, essentially the sponsorship revenues and Olympic sponsors (IOC, n.d.). Rule 40 helps to preserve the value of the Olympic brand and gives the IOC, NOCs and local organizing committees an additional Brand Protection tool in their ongoing fight against Olympic ambush marketing (IOC, n.d.). Presumably Rule 40 restricts ambush marketing practices of non-official sponsors. See Chapter 19 for a more detailed discussion of ambush marketing.

As discussed earlier in this Chapter, Olympic and Paralympic athletes are not paid to compete in the Games. Instead, they rely heavily on personal sponsors to fund their training and competitions. So naturally, if an athlete is successful at achieving an opportunity to compete in the Olympic or Paralympic Games they desire to acknowledge and reward their personal sponsors for their support. However, Rule 40 of the Olympic Charter restricts how competing Olympic athletes can be used in advertising when their personal sponsor is not also an official sponsor of the Games (IOC, n.d.). Since London 2012, the IOC has restricted athletes' marketing activities and Rule 40 has been amended for each successive Olympic Games. Exhibit 13.6 provides the 2016 and 2020 versions of Rule 40. In 2016, Rule 40 was proscriptive, prohibiting athletes from allowing their person, name, picture, or sports performances to be used for advertising purposes during the Olympic Games (Olympic Charter, 2016). By 2020, Rule 40 was drafted to appear more permissive – allowing athletes to engage in advertising and marketing activities in accordance to Olympic principles. The IOC then left it to each NOC to decide how to implement the more permissive or relaxed advertising restraints. The 2020 amended Rule 40 stemmed from a German Cartel Office ruling in 2019 that stated the restrictions were "too far-reaching" and in violation of German competition law (similar to U.S. anti-trust laws) (Sports Business, 2019). By delegating implementation to the NOCs, some athletes, such as the German athletes, will likely enjoy significantly more freedom to promote themselves and their persona sponsor relationships than the U.S. athletes (Race, 2019).

While generating significant controversy and backlash among athletes and advocates, Rule 40 has been generally effective, primarily in protecting official sponsors' exclusivity (IOC, 2012; Rovell, 2016) as the practice of ambush marketing (see Chapter 19) has shifted toward social media, referred to as "social ambush" (*Chavanat & Desbordes*, 2014).

Protection of Athletes

The growing concern over athlete safety was addressed by Congress in 2018 with the passage of the Protecting Young Victims from Sexual Abuse and Safe Sport Authorization Act of 2017 (Safe Sport Act) (36 U.S.C § 101 et seq., 2018; 36 U.S.C. §§ 220541 et seq., 2018). The Safe Sport Act designates the

U.S. Center for SafeSport as the independent organization charged with exercising jurisdiction over the USOPC and NGBs to safeguard amateur athletes against all forms of abuse. Prior to the passage of the Safe Sport Act, it was less clear whether NGBs had a specific duty to ensure the safety and protection of athletes. The governing documents generally discuss the overall welfare and safety of athletes, but did not necessarily impose a legal duty upon the NGB to protect athletes from foreseeable harm. However, the exposure of years of sexual abuse of young athletes at the hands of coaches and physicians produced dozens of lawsuits seeking to impose liability on the NGBs such as USA Gymnastics (Larry Nassar), USA Swimming (more than 150 coaches on banned list) (*Starr*, 2018), and as presented in the Focus Case below, USA Taekwondo.

Brown v. USA Taekwondo

40 Cal. App. 5th 1077 (Cal. App. 2019)   **FOCUS** CASE

FACTS

Plaintiffs Brianna Bordon, Yazmin Brown, and Kendra Gatt filed this action alleging causes of action for negligence, negligent hiring and retention, and negligent and intentional infliction of emotional distress against their taekwondo coach, Marc Gitelman, the United States Olympic Committee (USOC), USA Taekwondo (USAT), and others arising from Gitelman's sexual abuse of the then 15- and 16-year-old plaintiffs leading up to Gitelman's arrest and later felony convictions. Plaintiffs appeal from a judgment of dismissal in favor of USOC and USAT to plaintiffs' first amended complaint. On appeal, plaintiffs contend USOC and USAT are liable for negligence because the organizations failed to protect plaintiffs from Gitelman's sexual abuse.

HOLDING

Trial court's dismissal is reversed as to USAT and affirmed as to USOC.

RATIONALE

As the national governing body of taekwondo, "USAT is responsible for the conduct and administration of taekwondo in the United States." Further, USAT formulates the rules, implements the policies and procedures, and enforces the code of ethics for taekwondo in the United States. Gitelman was required to register with USAT to coach taekwondo at USAT-sponsored competitions, athletes could only compete in competitions with registered coaches. USAT could (and later did) implement policies and procedures to protect athletes from sexual abuse by their coaches, and USAT could (and later did) bar Gitelman from coaching athletes at taekwondo competitions for his violations of USAT's policies and procedures. USAT was in a special relationship with the plaintiffs and therefore in the "best position to protect against the risk of harm" and "meaningfully reduce the risk of the harm that actually occurred."

Our examination supports a finding on the alleged facts that USAT had a duty to implement and enforce policies and procedures to protect youth athletes from foreseeable sexual abuse by their coaches. In determining whether policy considerations under *Rowland v. Christian*, 443 P.2d 561 (Cal. 1968) ("Rowland factors") justify excusing or limiting a defendant's duty of care, we look to "the foreseeability of harm to the plaintiff, the degree of certainty that the plaintiff suffered injury, the closeness of the connection between the defendant's conduct and the injury suffered, the moral blame attached to the defendant's conduct, the policy of preventing future harm, the extent of the burden to the defendant and consequences to the community of imposing a duty to exercise care with resulting liability for breach, and the availability, cost, and prevalence of insurance for the risk involved."

Here, plaintiffs allege in 1992 the USAT national team coach was caught having sex with a young female Olympian, and sexual abuse of youth athletes by credentialed coaches "was so rampant that by 1999 defendant USOC required all [national governing bodies] to have specific insurance to cover coach sexual abuse." USAT purchased this insurance in 1999. In addition, plaintiffs allege "[b]y 2007 sexual abuse of minors by figures of authorities, like priests, coaches, and scout leaders was a widely known risk in American society." Based on these allegations, it was foreseeable youth athletes attending Olympic qualifying competitions with their coaches might be sexually molested by their coaches, regardless of whether USAT had knowledge of prior sexual misconduct.

Plaintiffs allege USAT was negligent in failing to adopt and enforce policies and procedures to protect athletes from sexual abuse by coaches. Specifically, they allege that, although USAT was aware as early as 1992 that coaches were sexually abusing taekwondo athletes, it did not adopt policies to prevent sexual abuse until the late summer of 2013 – after Gitelman sexually abused plaintiffs. USAT's failure to take any steps prior to 2013 to prevent taekwondo coaches from sexually abusing female athletes is closely connected to the injury Plaintiffs suffered because action by USAT could have reduced the risk of plaintiffs being abused by limiting inappropriate contact between coaches and youth athletes. Here, the societal goal of safeguarding youth athletes from sexual abuse weighs in favor of imposing a duty on USAT to implement and enforce policies and procedures to protect the athletes. Incentivizing USAT to adopt policies that adequately protect youth athletes and to ensure the policies are followed would not impose a substantial burden on USAT. We conclude USAT, which is the national governing body for the Olympic sport of taekwondo, had a special relationship with Gitelman.

This is a significant decision in an area of liability for national governing bodies that is continuing to evolve as more instances of sexual and physical abuse by coaches has come to light. However, it is important to note that the court also held that the USOC did not owe a duty of care to protect the plaintiffs because it did not have a special relationship with Gitelman or plaintiffs. Although USOC had the ability to control USAT, including requiring it to adopt policies to protect youth athletes, it did not have direct control over the conduct of coaches.

This section explored a wide range of legal issues related to the administration of the Olympic and Paralympic Games, the regulation of participant rights and discipline of participants, and also examined the duty of Olympic organizations to protect athletes from harm at the hands of coaches, medical personnel, or others entrusted with their care.

Conclusion

The governance and regulation of Olympic sport are relatively complex due to the multilayered governance structures with many participating governing bodies, as well as the international scope of the enterprise. Jurisdictional conflicts between Olympic sports governing bodies are common, although efforts to create shared standards, such as those espoused by the WADA and the CAS, are showing some success. With improved governance, the regulation of events and participant conduct will become more effective and, ideally, more responsive to the needs of those whose interests have been harmed.

Discussion Questions

1 Do you think the CAS perspective on strict liability for doping violations is fair? Why or why not?
2 Is it always in athletes' best interest to have a governance and regulatory scheme that requires them to exhaust all administrative remedies before seeking review from the judicial system? Why do you think such a requirement exists? Is this consistent with the IOC's statement that one of its major purposes is to promote the well-being of athletes?
3 Can you think of any negative aspects related to an international arbitration body, such as the CAS, being the final avenue of appeal on athlete participation eligibility and disciplinary issues?
4 Who benefits from the Olympic and Amateur Sports Act prohibition of judicial review for eligibility disputes against the USOPC that occur within 21 days of the Games? Does it help or hinder most athletes who might have a dispute? Why or why not?
5 Respond to the following question regarding Stroker's hypothetical situation on drug testing: If you were a sport management professional working for FINA, what might you learn from such rulings as Stroker's? What would you communicate to elite swimming coaches?

Learning Activities

1 Explore the International Olympic Committee website. Follow the links to find out about the specialized IOC commissions that are part of the organizational structure of the IOC. In particular, examine the information on the IOC Athletes' Commission and its role to expand rights of athletes.
2 Access the Olympic Charter on the IOC's webpage and locate the provisions relating to the criteria for inclusion of a sport or event in the Olympic program.
3 Choose an NGB or IF that is of particular interest to you and visit its website to examine its regulations governing disciplinary procedures applicable to participants who violate rules.
4 Visit the websites of the IOC and the OCOG for the upcoming Summer or Winter Olympic Games and try to discover what kinds of security measures they are planning to implement.
5 Visit the website of the Court of Arbitration for Sport and read one of the cases featured in the case law section. If it is a doping case, analyze whether the CAS followed a strict liability approach in reaching its decision.

Case Study

Personal Sponsors Recognition of Athletes / Performance

According to USOPC 2020 Domestic Rule 40 Guidance, during the Rule 40 period, personal sponsors with Rule 40 permission may create and post one message congratulating or recognizing sponsored athletes on their performance, or providing other well wishes. This message can only be posted on the personal sponsor's social media or corporate website targeted to a U.S. audience and in accordance with the following requirements.

With the exception of Team USA sponsors, any other media beyond social, including traditional media (e.g., print, TV, out of home), may not be used to recognize athletes during the Rule 40 period. The athlete recognition message may not mention or promote the personal sponsor's products or services; may not use any still or moving images of the athlete at the Games, or any Olympic or Paralympic IP, including but not limited to the Olympic or Paralympic symbol, the Games emblems, the Games may not imply a relationship between a personal sponsor and Team USA, the Olympic or Paralympic movements, an NGB or the Games. These posts cannot be supported by paid advertising. Any visual imagery of the message cannot contain third-party marks.

Based upon your understanding of USOPC 2020 Domestic Rule 40 Guidance, create three or more Congratulatory and Well-wishing examples which would be permitted for a track and field athlete who wins a gold medal in the 100 and 200 meter races during the Summer Olympics. Now, compare those permitted messages to messages permitted by the German Olympic Committee for a German athlete.

Considering … Analysis & Discussion

Strict Liability

First, yes, the CAS will approach this case energetically wielding the club of strict liability. Although Stroker took the stimulant accidentally and unbeknownst to her, to allow Stroker to compete later in the day with a performance-enhancing substance in her system would be to impose a purposeful unfairness on all the rest of the competitors while trying to remedy an accidental unfairness to one. Therefore, under strict liability the CAS will exclude her from competing in her upcoming event and will probably uphold at least part of the suspension. Second, if the CAS finds Stroker's case credible and thus that she bears little blame for her positive drug test, it will reduce the severity of the penalty imposed by FINA to a length of suspension that it believes is just.

References

Cases

Barnes v. International Amateur Athletic Federation, 862 F. Supp. 1537 (S.D. W.Va. 1993).

Behagen v. Amateur Basketball Association, 884 F.2d 524 (10th Cir. 1989).

C. v. Federation Internationale de Natation Amateur, Arbitration CAS 95/141 (1996).

Chanavat, N., & Desbordes, M. (2014). Towards the regulation and restriction of ambush marketing? The first truly social and digital mega sport event: Olympic Games, London 2012. *International Journal of Sports Marketing & Sponsorship*, 15(3), 151–160.

Cilic v. ITF, CAS 2013, Case No. A-3335 (2013).

DeFrantz v. United States Olympic Committee, 492 F. Supp. 1181 (D.D.C. 1980).

Dolan v. U.S. Equestrian Team, Inc., 608 A.2d 434 (App.Div.1992).

Harding v. United States Figure Skating Association, 851 F. Supp. 1476 (D. Or. 1994), *vacated on other grounds*, 879 F. Supp. 1053 (D. Or. 1995).

Lee v. United States Taekwondo Union, 331 F. Supp. 2d 1252 (D. Haw. 2004).

Lindemann v. American Horse Shows Association, 624 N.Y.S.2d 723 (N.Y. Sup. Ct. 1994).

Martin v. IOC, 740 F.2d 670 (9th Cir. 1984).

Martinez v. USOC, 802 F.2d 1275 (10th Cir. 1986).

Medvedev v. Russian Anti-Doping Agency, CAS 2017, Case No. A-5317 (2017).

Michels v. USOC, 741 F2d 155 (7th Cir. 1984).

Pistorius v. International Association of Athletics Federations (IAAF), CAS 2008/A/1480 Pistorius v. IAAF (2008).

Pliuskaitis v. USA Swimming, Inc., 243 F. Supp. 3d 1217 (D. Utah 2017), aff'd, 720 Fed. Appx. 481 (10th Cir. 2018).

R. v. International Olympic Committee, Arbitration CAS ad hoc Division (O.G. Nagano 1998) 002, in Digest of CAS awards 1986–1998 at 419. (Reeb, ed. 1998).

Race, R. (2019, March 1). Olympic Charter Rule 40 relaxed big-time for German Olympic athletes. *Swim Swam*. Retrieved from https://swimswam.com/olympic-charter-rule-40-relaxed-big-time-for-german-olympic-athletes/.

Raguz v. Sullivan, 2000 NSW LEXIS 265 (Sup. Ct. NSW, Ct. of Appeal 2000).

Ren-Guey v. Lake Placid 1980 Olympic Games, 1980 N.Y. App. Div. LEXIS 9699 (N.Y. App. Div. 1980), *aff'd*, 403 N.E.2d 178 (N.Y. 1980).

Samoa NOC v. International Weightlifting Federation, Arbitration CAS ad hoc Division (O.G. Sydney 2000) 042 (2000).

San Francisco Arts & Athletics, Inc. v. United States Olympic Committee, 483 U.S. 522 (1987).

Schulz v. United States Boxing Association, 105 F.3d 127 (3d Cir. 1997).

Sharapova v International Tennis Federation, CAS 2016, Case No. A-4643 (2016).

Shepherd v. United States Olympic Committee, 464 F. Supp. 2d 1072 (D. Colo. 2006).

Slaney v. International Association of Athletics Federations (IAAF), 244 F.3d 580 (7th Cir. 2001).

Spindulys v. Los Angeles Olympic Organizing Committee, 1985 Cal. App. LEXIS 2824 (Cal. Ct. App. 1985).

Starr, A. (2020, March 11). USA Swimming to settle sex abuse lawsuit filed by former Olympian. *NPR.org*. Retrieved from https://www.npr.org/2020/03/11/814377679/usa-swimming-to-settle-sex-abuse-lawsuit-filed-by-former-olympian.

Sternberg v. USA National Karate-Do Federation, Inc., 123 F. Supp. 2d 659 (E.D.N.Y. 2000).

United States Olympic Committee v. Intelicense Corp., 737 F.2d 263 (2d Cir. 1984), *cert. denied*, 469 U.S. 982 (1984).

Walton-Floyd v. United States Olympic Committee, 965. S.W.2d 35 (Tex. App. 1998).

Yang Tae-Young v. International Gymnastics Federation, Arbitration CAS 2004/A/704 (2004).

Statutes

Amateur Sports Act of 1978, 36 U.S.C. §§ 371 *et seq.*

Protecting Young Victims from Sexual Abuse and Safe Sport Authorization Act of 2017, 36 U.S.C § 101 et seq., 2018 and 36 U.S.C. §§ 220541 et seq., 2018 (Public Law 115-126, February 14, 2018).

Ted Stevens Olympic and Amateur Sports Act of 1998, 36 U.S.C. §§ 220501 *et seq.*

Other Sources

Allentuck, D. (2019). Paralympians see big welcome in small title change. Retrieved from https://www.nytimes.com/2019/06/29/sports/olympics/usoc-paralympians-.html#:~:text=Prize%20money%20for%20Paralympians%20is,only%20%247%2C500%2C%20%245%2C250%20and%20%243%2C750.

Associated Press (2020, September 8). Caster Semenya loses Swiss Supreme Court appeal over World Athletics' testosterone regulations. *Sports Illustrated*. Retrieved from https://www.si.com/olympics/2020/09/08/caster-semenya-loses-appeal-swiss-court-testosterone-regulations-tokyo-olympics.

Ayed, N. (2014, January 13). Russia's Olympic security to set new surveillance standard at Sochi. *CBC News (World)*. Retrieved from www.cbc.ca/news/world.

Bermon, S., & Garnier, P. Y. (2017). Serum androgen levels and their relation to performance in track and field: Mass spectrometry results from 2127 observations in male and female elite athletes. *British Journal of Sports Medicine*, 51, 1309–1314.

Burns, K. (2020, January 9). Why you might not see any athletes protest at this summer's Olympic Games. *Vox*. Retrieved from https://www.vox.com/2020/1/9/21058912/summer-olympics-tokyo-ban-athlete-protests.

Buzuvis, E. (2016). Hormone check: Critique of Olympic rules on sex and gender. *Wisconsin Journal of Law, Gender & Society*, 31, 29–55.

Cooky, C., & Dworkin, S. L. (2013). Policing the boundaries of sex: A critical examination of gender verification and the Caster Semenya controversy. *Journal of Sex Research*, 50(2), 103–111.

Court of Arbitration for Sport (2016). *Statistics*. Retrieved from https://www.tas-cas.org/fileadmin/user_upload/CAS_statistics_2016_.pdf.

CBC Sports (2008, November 18). Frustrated ski jumpers to have case heard in April. Retrieved from www.cbc.ca/Canada/british-columbia/story/2008/11/18/ski-jumpers-court.html?ref=rss.

Court of Arbitration for Sport (2020, October 26). Media Release: Athletics: The Court of Arbitration for Sport (CAS) partially upholds the appeal of Blake Leeper. Retrieved from https://www.tas-cas.org/fileadmin/user_upload/CAS_Media_Release_6807.pdf

Chappell, B. (2017, December 5). Russia is banned from 2018 Olympics; Athletes told to compete under Olympic flag. *NPR*. Retrieved from https://www.npr.org/sections/thetorch/2017/12/05/568585759/russia-is-banned-from-2018-olympics-athletes-told-to-compete-under-olympic-flag.

Claussen, C. L. (2006). The constitutionality of mass searches of sports spectators. *Journal of Legal Aspects of Sport*, 16, 153–175.

Dampf, A. (2018, November 8). Italy's 2026 Olympic bid moves forward with no funding from federal government. *CBC*. Retrieved from https://www.cbc.ca/sports/olympics/italy-2026-olympic-bid-1.4896964.

Double-amputee Blake Leeper appeals World Athletic's denial of application to compete against able-bodied athletes, including in the 2020 Olympic Games (2020, February 27). *PRNewsWire*. Retrieved from https://www.prnewswire.com/news-releases/double-amputee-blake-leeper-appeals-world-athletics-denial-of-application-to-compete-against-able-bodied-athletes-including-in-the-2020-olympic-games-301012912.html.

Elkins, K. (2018). Here's how much Olympic athletes earn in 2 different countries. CNBC. Retrieved from https://www. cnbc.com/2018/02/23/heres-how-much-olympic-athletes-earn-in-12-differentcountries.html#:~:text=The%20 International%20Olympic%20Committee%20doesn,member%20splits%20the%20pot%20evenly.

Fong, P. (2009, November 14). Female ski-jumpers lose Olympic bid; won't be competing after B.C. court dismisses their appeal. *The Toronto Star*, p. A02.

Gardner, C. F. (2004, October 22). Winner and still champion: Court rules that Hamm should keep his gold medal. *Milwaukee Journal Sentinel*, p. C1.

Golf and rugby – New kids on the block. (2016, March 17). *Olympic.org*. Retrieved from https://www.olympic.org/ news/golf-and-rugby-new-kids-on-the-block.

Godin, M. (2020, January 14). Athletes will be banned from protesting at the 2020 Tokyo Olympics. But the Games has a long history of political demonstrations. *Time*. Retrieved from https://time.com/5764614/political-protests-olympics-ioc-ban/.

International Association of Athletics Federations (2011). IAAF regulations governing eligibility of females with hyper-androgenism to compete in women's competitions. Retrieved from www.iaaf.org.

IAAF introduces new eligibility regulations for female classification. (2018, April 26). *World Athletics*. Retrieved from https://www.worldathletics.org/news/press-release/eligibility-regulations-for-female-classifica.

International Olympic Committee (n.d.). Use of a participant's image for advertising purposes during the Rio 2016 Olympic Games. Retrieved from https://stillmed.olympic.org/Documents/Athletes_Information/Rule_40-Rio_ 2016-QA_for_Athletes.pdf.

International Olympic Committee (IOC) (2004). IOC approves consensus with regard to athletes who have changed sex. Retrieved from www.olympic.org/uk/organisation/commissions/medic.

International Olympic Committee (IOC) (2012). IOC regulations on female hyperandrogenism. Retrieved from www. olympic.org/Documents/Commissions_PDFfiles/Medical_commissions/2012-06-22-IOC-Regulations-on-Female-Hyperandrogenism-eng.pdf.

International Olympic Committee (IOC) (2017a). Olympic charter. Retrieved from https://stillmed.olympic.org/ media/Document%20Library/OlympicOrg/Olympic-Studies-Centre/List-of-Resources/Official-Publications/ Olympic-Charters/EN-2017-Olympic-Charter.pdf#_ga=2.21742075.1521518976.1592165830-65331301. 1591117105.

International Olympic Committee (IOC) (2017b). Elections of Presidents of the International Olympic Committee. The Olympic Studies Center. Retrieved from https://stillmed.olympic.org/media/Document%20Library/ OlympicOrg/Factsheets-Reference-Documents/Olympic-Movement/IOC-Presidents/Reference-document-Elections-of-the-IOC-Presidents.pdf.

International Olympic Committee (IOC) (2018). Baseball and softball on the road to Tokyo 2020. Retrieved from https://www.olympic.org/news/baseball-and-softball-on-the-road-to-tokyo-2020.

International Olympic Committee (IOC) (2019a). IOC funding. Retrieved from https://www.olympic.org/funding.

International Olympic Committee (IOC) (2019b). Olympic Charter. Retrieved from www.olympic.org.

International Olympic Committee (IOC) (2020). Olympic Agenda 2020. Retrieved from https://www.olympic.org/ olympic-agenda-2020.

International Olympic Committee Medical Commission (2003). Explanatory note to the recommendation on sex reas-signment and sports. Retrieved from www.olympic.org.

Jiwani, R. (2019, June 13). Swiss Supreme Court upholds ruling in favour of Caster Semenya. *Olympic Channel*. Retrieved from https://www.olympicchannel.com/en/stories/news/detail/caster-semenya-cleared-run-swiss-supreme-court/.

Keh, A., Rich, M., & Panja, T. (2020, March 25). Deciding to postpone the Olympics was tough. Actually moving them may be tougher. *The New York Times*. Retrieved from https://www.nytimes.com/2020/03/25/sports/olympics/ coronavirus-olympics-postponement.html.

Keller, J. (2009, November 21). Court explains why women ski jumpers excluded; says IOC is only body that can decide which events are at Olympics. *The Toronto Star*, p. A25.

Koller, D. (2008). Frozen in time: The state action doctrine's application to amateur sports. *St. Johns Law Review*, 82, 183–233.

Long, M. (2019, June 27). Olympic bidding process overhauled as IOC approves major reforms. *Sports Pro Media*. Retrieved from https://www.sportspromedia.com/news/olympic-games-bidding-ioc-session.

Longman, J. (2019, August 21). Pan Am Games protestors get probation. Olympians get a warning. *The New York Times*. Retrieved from https://www.nytimes.com/2019/08/21/sports/olympics/pan-am-olympic-punishment.html.

Mackay, D. (2019, November 15). IAAF officially changes name to World Athletics. *Inside the Games*. Retrieved from https://www.insidethegames.biz/articles/1087059/world-athletics-officially-changes-name.

Macur, J. (2012, June 24). IOC adopts policy for deciding whether an athlete can compete as a woman. *The New York Times*. Retrieved from https://www.nytimes.com/2012/06/24/sports/olympics/ioc-adopts-policy-for-deciding-whether-athletes-can-compete-as-women.html.

McCann, E. (2012, July 13). UK Olympics are the deadliest Games in town. *Belfast Telegraph Online*. Retrieved from LEXIS-NEXIS.

Media release: Athletics, CAS Arbitration: Caster Semenya, Athletics South Africa. (2019, May 1). *Court of Arbitration for Sport*. Retrieved from https://www.tas-cas.org/fileadmin/user_upload/Media_Release_Semenya_ASA_IAAF_decision.pdf.

Morgan, L. (2020, June). IOC miss primary opportunity to relax rules on athlete protests at Olympic Games. *Inside the Games*. Retrieved from https://www.insidetheGames.biz/articles/1095200/ioc-miss-opportunity-athlete-protests#.XuYQ5tQLBw8.twitter.

O'Kane, P. (2019, August 7). IOC issues stern warning to CONI over potential Olympic Charter breaches. *Inside The Games*. Retrieved from https://www.insidethegames.biz/articles/1083142/ioc-warning-for-coni.

One year countdown: Readying AI security for the Tokyo 2020 Olympics. *Synced Review*. Retrieved from https://syncedreview.com/2019/07/20/one-year-countdown-readying-ai-security-for-the-tokyo-2020-olympics/.

Palar, S. (2019, May 29). Caster Semenya files appeal against CAS ruling – "The IAAF will not drug me or stop me from being who I am." *Olympic Channel*. Retrieved from https://www.olympicchannel.com/en/stories/news/detail/caster-semenya-appeal-cas-ruling-/.

Pavitt. M. (2019, June 21). USOPC announces name change to United States Olympic and Paralympic Committee. *Inside the Games*. Retrieved from https://www.insidetheGames.biz/articles/1080967/usoc-announces-name-change-to-united-states-olympic-and-paralympic-committee.

Pells, E. (2020, June 27). Carlos, United States athletes take stand to end Olympic protest rule against protests. Star Tribune. Retrieved from https://www.startribune.com/carlos-us-athletes-take-stand-to-end-olympic-protest-rule/571521352/.

Reid, S. M. (2018, October 29). USOC Audit finds USA Badminton at "high risk" for failing to comply with Safe Sport requirements. *The Orange County Register*. Retrieved from https://www.ocregister.com/2018/10/29/usoc-audit-finds-usa-badminton-at-high-risk-for-failing-to-comply-with-safe-sport-requirements/.

Reid, S. M. (2019, December 3). USA Badminton hires fraud investigator to examine its finances. *The Orange County Register*. Retrieved from https://www.ocregister.com/2019/12/03/usa-badminton-hires-fraud-investigator-to-examine-its-finances/.

Rovell, D. (2016, July 21). USOC sends letter warning non-Olympic sponsor companies. *ESPN.com*. Retrieved from https://www.espn.com/olympics/story/_/id/17120510/united-states-olympic-committee-battle-athletes-companies-sponsor-not-olympic.

Rule 50 guidelines developed by the IOC athletes' commission (2020, January). IOC. Retrieved from https://www.olympic.org/-/media/Document%20Library/OlympicOrg/News/2020/01/Rule-50-Guidelines-Tokyo-2020.pdf.

Schrotenboer, B. (2019, July 30). Senators introduce bill to hold U.S. Olympic sports accountable after sex scandals. *USA Today*. Retrieved from https://www.usatoday.com/story/sports/olympics/2019/07/30/olympic-scandal-bipartisan-bill-would-overhaul-oversight-after-nassar/1864097001/.

Schultz, C. (2014, January 17). The Sochi Olympics are turning into the security Olympics: Russian authorities have far-reaching plans to spy on guests. *Smithsonian.com*. Retrieved from https://www.smithsonianmag.com/smart-news/sochi-olympics-more-security-olympics-180949388/.

Shipley, A. (2002, May 1). 2 French skating officials banned: Olympic scandal prompts decision. *The Washington Post*, p. A01.

Sports Business (2019, June 27). IOC relaxes Rule 40 ahead of Tokyo 2020. Retrieved from https://www.sportbusiness.com/news/ioc-relaxes-rule-40-ahead-of-tokyo-2020/.

United Nations Educational, Scientific, and Cultural Organization (UNESCO) (2020). International convention against doping in sport: Paris, 19 October 2005. Retrieved from http://www.unesco.org/eri/la/convention.asp?KO=31037&language=E.

United States Olympic Paralympic Committee (USOPC) (2020). Legal.TeamUSA.org. Retrieved from https://www.teamusa.org/Footer/Legal.

World Anti-Doping Agency (WADA) (2020a). Who we are. Retrieved from https://www.wada-ama.org/en/who-we-are.

World Anti-Doping Agency (WADA) (2020b). World Anti-Doping Code. Retrieved from https://www.wada-ama.org/en/questions-answers/world-anti-doping-code.

Weliver, D. (2019, March 19). How much do Olympic (both summer and winter) athletes earn? *MoneyUnder30*. Retrieved from https://www.moneyunder30.com/how-much-do-olympic-athletes-earn.

Wilson, S. (2005, October 26). IOC to review process for determining sports program. Associated Press, Sports News section. Retrieved from LEXIS-NEXIS.

Web Resources

www.tas-cas.org ■ Visit this site to access current and archived decisions of the Court of Arbitration for Sport (CAS) since 1986.

www.olympic.org ■ Visit this site to get the most current information on the financing and governance structure of the IOC, as well as links to NOCs, IFs, and other affiliated organizations.

www.isu.org ■ Visit IF sites like this one for the International Skating Union to access rules, history, and news pertinent to the sport(s) regulated by the IF.

www.usantidoping.org ■ At this site for the U.S. Anti-doping Agency you will find the list of prohibited substances, as well as news and other resources, such as FAQs on doping in sport.

www.wada-ama.org ■ Here you will find the World Anti-doping Agency's anti-doping code, news, and information about anti-doping educational programs.

Part IV

Operating Venues and Event Management

Introduction to the Law in Operations Management

Your sport and recreation programs and your facilities are the cornerstones of your organization. Providing safe and beneficial participation opportunities is a critical facet of sport and recreation. Enhancing the viewing experience of spectators is also critical. Ensuring that your facility operates within the parameters of the law is crucial to successful and competitive sport/recreation operations.

If you perform any of the diverse responsibilities related to the operations of your facilities or programs, you will encounter a number of legal issues. You and your organization can be much more successful with a fundamental understanding of some of the legal areas implicated in the operations management function of a sport organization.

Legal Principles and the Operations Management Function

Many legal areas are implicated in operations management. In this section we explore the various interactions and relationships associated with operating sports and recreation venues and programs. Chapter 14 focuses on negligence law as related to the participants in the programs you develop and oversee, as well as participant liability for violent acts. Chapter 15 focuses on our relationships with our guests, fans, and spectators in terms of premise liability relating to operating a sport/recreation facility and managing sporting events. Chapter 16 revisits contractual agreements with an emphasis on those agreements necessary to the operation of venues and events including exculpatory agreements such as waivers. Finally, Chapter 17 highlights the increasingly important and complex role of financing and constructing venues as well as the continuing emphasis on accessibility for our patrons with disabilities.

The operational issues described in these chapters will require you to be knowledgeable in a variety of legal theories so that you can develop effective policies to protect and enhance the welfare of participants in your programs and guests/spectators at your events.

14 Liability Issues and Sports Participants

Kristi L. Schoepfer

Introduction

A solid understanding of the law related to torts and the prevalent liability issues in your sport organization is critical in gaining a competitive advantage in the marketplace. This chapter discusses the law of torts as it applies to those who are athletes or participants in the activities or sports you offer in your organization. The law of torts generally covers any wrongful acts or interferences with rights (other than under contract law) which lead to civil liability. Torts are often referred to as "civil wrongs." Tort liability exists on a spectrum where culpability and liability are imposed to some degree based upon the wrongful actor's state of mind. Additionally, liability sometimes is imposed regardless of intent, which is called strict liability discussed in this chapter relating to products liability. Your participants are important stakeholders in your organization, and your organization's success is directly tied to making the participant experience enriching. Understanding the liability concerns related to participants can help you reframe potential liabilities as opportunities to make your programs safer and less prone to litigation.

This chapter first introduces you to the concept of negligence, discussing its elements as a legal cause of action and the applicable defenses. Much of the chapter is devoted to discussing those areas that are most likely to lead to participant liability concerns: lack of supervision, improper instruction or training, equipment concerns, medical care, and transportation. Further, the remainder of the chapter discusses legal issues related to participant violence and claims based on recklessness and intentional torts of assault and battery. See Exhibit 14.1 for an overview of the managerial contexts, major legal issues, relevant laws, and illustrative cases pertinent to this chapter.

General Principles of Negligence Liability

Negligence is a claim for relief based in tort law. Negligence is defined as conduct that "falls below the standard established by law for the protection of others against unreasonable risk of harm" (Restatement [Second] of Torts § 282) (1965). As an unintentional tort, negligence appears at the opposite end of the intent spectrum from torts such as battery and assault (discussed later in this chapter). The defendant in a negligence action has allegedly acted in an unreasonable fashion but did not intend to commit the act or to cause the harm. Therefore, because the law recognizes that the defendant in a negligence action simply failed to act reasonably, no punitive damages may be awarded. In most cases of negligence, the defendant acted in a careless or inadvertent fashion; this conduct is far removed from the type of conduct in which a defendant intends to commit an act and to cause harm and which may lead to an award of punitive damages.

Exhibit 14.1 Management contexts in which participant liability issues may arise, with relevant laws and cases.

Management Context	Major Legal Issues	Relevant Law	Illustrative Cases
Oversight of sport/recreation program	Pleading a case in negligence	Elements of negligence Duty	Davidson, Cope, Kennedy
		Causation	Bellinger
	Defenses in negligence case	Negligence defenses	Stevens
		Government immunity	Stahr
		Charitable immunity	
Oversight of land opened for recreational use	Defining recreational use	Recreational use statutes	Marcus
Oversight of outdoor activities	Assume risks of activity outlined in statutes	Shared responsibility statute/ sport safety acts	Smith
Supervision of activities/ programs	Lack of supervision	Negligence law	Garman, Trupia
Administration of sport/ recreation program			
Coaches, instructors	Improper instruction/training	Negligence law	Scott
Coaches, equipment managers, administrators	Provision of safe equipment	Negligence law	Elledge, Bello
Athletic trainers, team physicians, coaches, administrators	Medical care	Negligence law	Krueger
		Fraudulent concealment	
Administration of organized sport program	Liability for transportation	Negligence law	Fenrich v. Blake School
Game management	Violence by sport Participants	Criminal law	
Coaching	Assault		
League administration	Battery		
		Reckless misconduct	Nabozny, Karas
Provision of sports equipment	Liability for defective equipment	Products liability law	DeRienzo

Elements of Negligence

A person acts negligently if the person does not exercise reasonable care under the circumstances. Primary factors to consider in ascertaining whether the person's conduct lacks reasonable care are the foreseeable likelihood that the person's conduct will result in harm, the foreseeable severity of any harm that may ensue, and the burden of precautions to eliminate or reduce the risk of harm. See Restatement [Third] of Torts: Liability for Physical Harm § 3 (Part III, Chapter 5(A), PFD, 2010).

Although the Restatement [Third] of Torts (2010) has modernized the concept of duty as it relates to negligence liability in general, the cases and concepts provided in this chapter will discuss the concept of duty as it has been used in a sport context and evolved over time. Thus, this chapter will utilize the traditional elements of negligence contained in most cases involving sport and recreation situations currently. The cause of action of negligence has four elements that must all coexist to enable the plaintiff to prevail. These elements are: (1) duty; (2) breach of duty; (3) causation; and (4) damages. These elements are discussed below.

Duty

The first element in a negligence case is **duty**, which means that the defendant must have some obligation, imposed by law, to protect the plaintiff from unreasonable risk. As noted, the need to act upon a duty is based on the foreseeable likelihood that the person's conduct will result in harm and the foreseeable severity of any harm that may ensue. Duty is a question of law for the court to ascertain and is a foundational issue. The legal concept of duty is based on policy considerations that lead courts to say that a particular plaintiff is entitled to protection from a particular defendant. Absent duty, there is no cause of action in negligence. For example, let's assume that two strangers pass each other on a trail in a national park. One of the strangers steps on the edge of the trail and begins to slide down a steep slope. Will the law impose a duty of care on the second stranger to help this person who is in peril? No: there is no legal duty to help; the parties have no relationship such that one party is legally obligated to help the other. Of course, morality would dictate otherwise, and presumably on this basis the second stranger would help.

Determining whether a "duty" exists as a matter of law is an important and sometimes complex analysis. In the context of higher education, for example, courts need to find some policy justification for imposing a duty of care for the student-athlete, since the student is an adult. In contrast, it is relatively simple to find that a duty of care exists between the K–12 teacher and student; or coach and athlete during the school day, team practice or game. The courts use the theory of *in loco parentis* (standing in the place of a parent) and acknowledge that the custodial relationship of a teacher or coach with a minor student or athlete should lead to a duty of care. A California case discussed the duty of care owed to a minor student who participated in a voluntary after-school playground program. In the case of *Agbeti v. Los Angeles Unified School District* (2010), a California appellate court held that the defendant school district and its employees who supervised the program did owe a duty of care to the plaintiff, a minor who was physically and sexually assaulted by some of the co-participants at the program. The trial court had ruled that there was no duty of care related to voluntary after-school programs. However, the appellate court held that the defendants had the duty to use ordinary care in supervising the students in this program, even though it was not a program during the school day.

In a few cases, courts have found a duty of care to exist for the college student-athlete on the basis of a special relationship. The following case addresses this issue.

Davidson v. University of North Carolina

543 S.E.2d 920 (N.C. Ct. App. 2001)	FOCUS CASE

FACTS

The plaintiff was a junior varsity cheerleader at the defendant university. While warming up before a basketball game, the plaintiff fell from the top of a two-one-chair pyramid, approximately 13 feet to the wood floor. The spotters were unable to prevent the plaintiff from hitting the floor, and she suffered permanent brain damage as a result of the fall.

The cheerleading squad did not have a coach, and they taught themselves how to perform stunts. The squad members made their own decisions about what stunts to perform, and they were not given any training to evaluate when they were ready to perform them. Although the varsity cheerleaders were sent to a summer camp where they learned techniques and safety information, the junior varsity squad was not provided that opportunity. The university did provide the squad with uniforms, transportation to away games, and access to university facilities and equipment. The squad cheered at junior varsity basketball games, women's basketball games, and wrestling events, and represented the university at a trade show.

The plaintiff filed a claim against the university under the state tort claims act alleging negligence for failing to provide supervision and training for the cheerleaders. The North Carolina Industrial Commission's deputy commission heard the claim and ruled for the plaintiff. However, the full commission reversed, as it found that the university owed no duty to the plaintiff.

HOLDING

The North Carolina appellate court reversed and remanded the case for further consideration of the evidence.

RATIONALE

The primary issue before the court in this case was whether the university owed a duty of care to a student-athlete who is a member of a school-sponsored intercollegiate team. In this situation, one which is based on allegations that the school failed to provide necessary supervision and training, a special relationship must be found in order to establish a duty of care.

The court noted that the relationship between a student-athlete and the university is different from the university's relationship with the general student body. With an athlete, there is a situation of mutual dependence – the university received benefits from the cheerleaders' appearances and the cheerleaders were provided uniforms, transportation, and equipment. Second, the court commented on the degree of significant control exerted by the university over the participation of the cheerleaders. Third, the court found the precedent of *Kleinknecht v. Gettysburg College* (1993) persuasive, as it held that there was a special relationship between the college and the members of the lacrosse team who were recruited by the college to play in intercollegiate competition.

Based on the above policy factors and legal precedent, the court held that there was a **special relationship** in this situation in which the plaintiff was injured while practicing as part of a school-sponsored intercollegiate team. The court specifically noted that this finding of a special relationship cannot be extended to a university's students generally or even to other members of student groups, clubs, intramural teams, or organizations. In this situation, however, the university did owe the plaintiff a duty of care.

Contrast the previous cases with *Kennedy v. Robert Morris University* (2016). Kennedy, an incoming freshman student at Robert Morris University (RMU) in 2010, was selected as a member of the University's cheerleading squad. Prior to school, she attended a pre-camp for RMU cheerleaders at the University of Scranton, conducted by Universal Cheerleader Association (UCA). Kennedy was severely injured while practicing a new stunt at the camp; she filed a negligence claim against RMU. Kennedy alleged that there was a special relationship between herself and RMU due to her participation in the University's cheerleading, which arranged her attendance at a mandatory UCA camp. However, RMU concedes that, although it owed a duty to Kennedy to use due care in the selection of a cheerleading camp, Kennedy did not allege negligence in the selection of the UCA camp or that UCA's instructors were unqualified. RMU contended that it had no duty with respect to UCA's instruction generally or its instruction of the stunt at issue. The court found that Kennedy was following the instructions of UCA, *not* RMU, at the time of her injury. It based that finding on Kennedy's own testimony that the camp was operated entirely by UCA and that she did not expect supervision by her own coach. This case helps clarify that, although a university may have a special relationship with a student-athlete, that relationship does not provide a blanket duty of care in all circumstances.

In the following hypothetical case, a university assumes a duty of care and is therefore bound to act reasonably.

Considering ... Duty of Care

As a part of her course of study for a degree in sport management, Jill Lefour, age 22, must complete a university-mandated internship program at a site specifically approved and suggested by the university. Lefour was assigned to complete her internship at a fitness club about 15 minutes from the university. One evening after her internship duties were completed, Lefour was abducted from the fitness club's parking lot and assaulted.

The fitness club was located in a dangerous part of town. The university personnel who assigned Lefour to this location were aware of other criminal incidents that had occurred in the fitness club's parking lot.

> **Question**
>
> •   If Lefour attempts to sue her university, does she have any arguments that the university has a duty of care to her in this circumstance?
>
> *Note how you would answer the question and then check your response using the Analysis & Discussion at the end of this chapter.*

The foregoing hypothetical case is based on the case of *Nova Southeastern University v. Gross* (2000), in which the Florida Supreme Court held that a university may be liable in tort when it assigns a student to an internship site that it knows to be unreasonably dangerous but gives no warning to the student and the student is injured during the internship. Although the student is an adult, the university assumed the duty to assign the student to a reasonably safe location.

In most of the cases we will study, however, the duty of care is evident, and the courts do not focus on this aspect of the case. As stated earlier, there is a duty of care between teacher or coach and student or athlete on the K–12 level and between facility owner and spectator. Schools have custodial and tutelary responsibilities for the minors in their care.

In the cases that we discuss in this chapter, the courts have ascertained that a duty exists. For our purposes, therefore, we will pay more attention to the second element, whether there was a breach of the duty of care.

Breach of Duty

There is a **breach of duty** if the defendant has failed to meet the standard of care required. The **standard of care** is ascertained by asking what a reasonably prudent person would have been expected to do in the same or similar circumstances. You can see from this that the law of negligence is closely tied to the factual circumstances. There can be no breach of duty in the abstract; whether a breach of duty exists is always relative to the particular circumstances.

To assist in ascertaining whether a breach of duty has occurred, the courts have developed an objective standard, the **reasonably prudent person**. This legal fiction is used as the standard against which an actual defendant is held. If the defendant acts in a way consistent with the actions of the fictional reasonable prudent person, then the defendant has not breached the duty of care; thus, element number two of the cause of action is not met. However, if the actions of the defendant fall below what would have been expected of the reasonable prudent person, then the defendant has breached the duty of care. The reasonably prudent person serves as a basis of comparison between how the defendant acted and how the defendant *should have* acted in a given circumstance. For example, if an athletic trainer is sued by an athlete because the athlete feels a treatment resulted in further injury, the conduct of the athletic trainer will be compared to the "reasonable athletic trainer."

Further, if the defendant possesses knowledge that is superior to the ordinary person, then the defendant is accountable for the care that is reasonable in light of the person's special skills, knowledge, or training. Thus, a coach with a master's degree in physical education who has coached for ten years and who has special certifications pertinent to coaching will be held to a standard of care based on that special skill and knowledge.

How does a jury decide what the reasonably prudent person should have been expected to do in a particular context? Juries do not have the expertise to ascertain the standard of care on their own. The parties to a lawsuit use expert witnesses to attempt to convince the jury what standard of care is applicable in a particular circumstance. Standards or recommendations or best practices usually arise from an organizational mandate or "suggestion." These organizations range from independent bodies such as the Consumer Product Safety Commission (CPSC) to sports or fitness organizations such as the

American College of Sports Medicine (ACSM) and the National Federation of State High School Associations (NFHS) (Cohen, 2008). Expert witnesses are familiar with these standards and will present them to the jury as evidence of the standard of care that is applicable. In many cases, the expert witnesses called by the plaintiff may disagree with the expert witnesses called by the defendant. It is up to the jury to decide which experts to believe since this is a question of fact.

In some circumstances expert testimony may not be needed to establish that the standard of care was breached. If, for example, the defendant fails to meet a statutory requirement that was established for the safety of participants, that failure is considered to be a breach of the standard of care. This is called **negligence per se**. The breach of the statutory standard is itself indicative of the breach of the standard of care, and the plaintiff has only to establish causation and damages to prevail in such a case.

To illustrate this concept, let's look at a tragic occurrence that happened in the fall of 2010. Declan Sullivan, a student who worked as a videographer for the Notre Dame football team, was killed when the scissor lift on which he stood was toppled by extremely high winds ("Investigation into Notre Dame," 2010). In the wake of this tragedy, the Indiana Department of Labor concluded that Notre Dame had violated six aspects of the Indiana workplace safety laws in allowing Sullivan to use the lift in adverse weather conditions. Notre Dame eventually paid $42,000 in fines to the Indiana Department of Labor (Coyne, 2011). If the Sullivan family had sued Notre Dame for wrongful death, the fact that Notre Dame had violated state safety laws that led to Sullivan's death would have been a negligence per se case.

The following hypothetical case also demonstrates this concept.

Considering ... Negligence Per Se

You are the aquatics manager for a health and fitness club in Maricopa County, Arizona. In 2012, the federal Consumer Product Safety Commission adopted the Virginia Graeme Baker Pool and Spa Safety Act (2019) requiring unblockable drains, known as antivortex drain covers, to be installed in all pools to prevent suction entrapment in pool drains; this federal regulation was updated in 2018 to incorporate new pool safety standards.

Your club has just built a new pool, but the owners of the club chose not to adhere to the law's requirements due to cost. One of your patrons lost a limb after becoming entangled in the pool drain. This result would not have occurred if the new pool met the law's requirements.

Question

- If the patron sues your club, does the plaintiff have a negligence per se case? Why or why not?

Note how you would answer the question and then check your response using the Analysis & Discussion at the end of this chapter.

Causation

The third necessary element of a negligence cause of action is **causation**, a causal connection between the breach of duty and the resulting injury. When an act or failure to act directly produces an event, and the event would not have occurred otherwise, this is known as **proximate causation** (or legal cause). Causation addresses the essential question of whether a party should be held accountable for the consequences of an action. It encompasses both the notion of causation in fact and the policy question of whether a court should hold someone accountable for an injury based on the notion of foreseeability (57A Am. Jur. 2d Negligence § 412).

Causation in fact depends on whether a particular outcome would have taken place even if the breach of duty had not occurred. The concept here is that if something would have occurred anyway, then the breach of duty cannot be said to have caused the outcome, and hence the requisite element of causation is lacking. The following Focus Case illustrates this point.

Bellinger v. Ballston Spa Central School District

FACTS

A fifth grader was playing one-hand touch football at recess when she collided with a teammate as both players ran toward the opponent. The teammate's head hit the girl in the mouth and she lost three teeth. The girl's mother sued the school district on her behalf and alleged that there was negligent supervision. The trial court denied the defendant's motion for summary judgment.

HOLDING

The New York appellate court reversed.

RATIONALE

The court noted that even if the plaintiff could show that there was inadequate playground supervision, the negligent supervision must be shown to be the cause of the injuries. In this case, there was a spontaneous and accidental collision between players. There was no history of bad behavior or rough play. In this case, no amount of supervision could have prevented the collision. Therefore, there is no causation.

In addressing causation, courts also look to another aspect of proximate causation that speaks to the issue of whether the defendant should be legally responsible for the injury, even if there was causation in fact. This issue is primarily a question of law for a court to address, and it often relates to the question of foreseeability. This means that courts often decide that the scope of liability should extend only to those risks that are foreseeable.

Damages

The final element of negligence is **damages**. Damages can be shown when some actual loss or damage has been sustained as a result of the breach of duty. Damages can be actual or compensatory. Actual damages reflect harms that can be specifically proven or itemized, such as medical bills and lost wages. Compensatory damages are awarded to compensate for harms that cannot be itemized, such as emotional distress, and pain and suffering. The threat of future harm is not sufficient damage, as this type of damage is speculative.

Defenses Against Negligence

Once the elements of the cause of action are established, the question becomes whether the defendant, in whole or in part, can avoid liability. The defendant's first recourse is always to argue that one or more of the elements of the cause of action have not been established; a plaintiff's failure to prove negligence is an absolute defense against liability. However, if all the elements do exist, the defendant must raise defenses. The most common defenses are the statute of limitations, act of God, contributory and comparative negligence, assumption of risk, and immunity.

Statute of Limitations

A cause of action must be filed in a timely fashion; this is known as the **statute of limitations**. If a plaintiff fails to file a case within the statute of limitations, the defendant will use this as a defense. This defense is a procedural one, not a substantive one. This means that, regardless of the merits of the plaintiff's case, the cause of action may be dismissed if the complaint has not been filed in a timely manner. Each state has legislation that specifies the time period for bringing a certain cause of action. Generally, if the action is not brought within that designated time period, the action may be dismissed. For example, many states provide that an action in negligence must be brought within two years from the time the tort occurred.

Act of God

An **act of God** defense rests on the idea that a person has no liability if an unforeseeable natural disaster resulting in injury to the plaintiff; the defendant's negligence, therefore, did not cause the injury. There are two aspects to this defense that must coexist:

1 There must truly be an act of God – some natural disaster such as a storm, lightning, earthquake, flood, or hurricane that caused the injury.
2 This act of God must have been unforeseeable. If it was foreseeable, the defendant may still have liability since the defendant did not act reasonably in protecting the plaintiff from the disaster.

The following hypothetical case illustrates this defense.

Considering ... The Act of God Defense

The baseball coach at High River Academy is running the last practice before the playoffs. He is determined to have all the players get their turns at bat. Storm clouds appear in the sky above, and there is lightning nearby. Practice continues. The third baseman is hit by lightning and killed.

Question

•   Does the coach have a viable act of God defense? Why or why not?

Note how you would answer the question and then check your response using the Analysis & Discussion at the end of this chapter.

Contributory and Comparative Negligence

Contributory and comparative negligence are also defenses against negligence. In discussing the elements of negligence, we have used the legal fiction of the reasonably prudent person to set the standard for whether the defendant breached the duty of care. With **contributory negligence**, we ask whether the plaintiff acted as a reasonably prudent plaintiff. With a child plaintiff, we ask whether the child exercised the level of care that should be expected of a child of like age, knowledge, judgment, and experience (*Clay City Consolidated School District Corp. v. Timberman*, 2008). We use the legal fiction of the **reasonably prudent plaintiff** to determine what the plaintiff should have done in a particular circumstance to protect his or her own safety. If the plaintiff's conduct falls below the standard of care, then the plaintiff is said to be contributorily negligent. If a court uses the contributory negligence theory, any conduct that is unreasonable by the plaintiff results in no recovery for the plaintiff.

The rule of contributory negligence is rather harsh; any negligence by the plaintiff completely bars recovery. Therefore, almost all states have adopted a rule of **comparative negligence**, where any negligence by the plaintiff is compared to the degree of negligence by the defendant. There are two primary approaches to comparative negligence:

1 Under **pure comparative negligence**, a plaintiff's damages are reduced in proportion to the plaintiff's fault, so that even if the plaintiff's proportion of negligence is greater than the defendant's proportion, the plaintiff will still recover something. Thus, a plaintiff with damages of $100,000 who is 25 percent at fault would be able to recover $75,000, and even if 99 percent at fault would still be able to recover $1,000.

2   Under **modified comparative negligence**, a plaintiff's negligence will bar recovery completely if it is a specified proportion of the total fault. Typically the separation point is around the 50 percent mark for recovery. Some states would permit recovery so long as the plaintiff's fault is less than or equal to (<=50 percent) of the defendant's fault; other states would only permit recovery if the plaintiff is less than 50 percent at fault, so a finding of 50 percent or higher would preclude the plaintiff from recovery.

The legislatures of each state decide which form of comparative negligence will be used in that state. The following hypothetical situation illustrates variations of the two forms of this defense.

Considering ... Comparative Negligence

Bob Bright has brought a negligence action against Rock On, a company that offers indoor rock-climbing instruction. Bright suffered a fractured leg while he was climbing the wall. Bright failed to follow some of the safety rules that were explained to him prior to his climb. The jury heard all the evidence and decided that Bright failed to act as a reasonably prudent plaintiff in violating safety rules and that his behavior, in part, contributed to his injury. The jury also decided that Rock On was also negligent. The jury heard evidence relating to damages as well and ascertained that the damages should be $100,000.

Question

● If we are in a modified comparative negligence state and the jury ascertains that Bright was 60 percent responsible for his own injury, what amount of damages will he receive? How would the recovery be different in a pure comparative negligence state?

Note how you would answer the question and then check your response using the Analysis & Discussion at the end of this chapter.

Assumption of Risk

Assumption of risk is the defense that is most prevalently discussed in contexts of physical activity, sport, and recreation. Assumption of risk is frequently discussed as being either primary or secondary. Primary assumption of the risk frees the defendant from the duty to protect plaintiffs from a sport's inherent risks because the plaintiff consents to those risks. The defendant does still owe duty not to increase the inherent risks. Secondary assumption of the risk applies when a defendant has a duty of care and has failed to meet his duty of care, but the plaintiff acts unreasonably in voluntarily choosing to encounter the risks anyway. These distinctions are important and discussed in greater detail below.

Primary. A **primary assumption of risk** means that a plaintiff understands and voluntarily agrees to accept the inherent risks of an activity. The inherent risks of an activity are those risks that are obvious and necessary to the conduct of the activity. With primary assumption of risk, the defendant has no duty of care toward the plaintiff to protect the plaintiff from the particular risk of harm that caused injury, since the plaintiff agreed to encounter the risks that are common to that activity.

For example, in *M.F., Etc., Et Al. v. Jericho Union Free School District* (2019), the primary assumption of risk defense barred the minor plaintiff from recovering damages for injuries he sustained at junior varsity football practice when a five-person blocking sled that was being used during a drill ran over his left foot. The plaintiff had attended ten practices with the junior varsity team in the weeks before the incident and had participated in the same drill with the blocking sled. However, on the day the plaintiff was injured, the plaintiff was not physically participating in practice because he did not feel well, but had asked the coach to be allowed to stay. The plaintiff was directed to stand parallel to the sideline to watch practice, an area that was "maybe 10 yards away" from where team members were performing a drill pushing the blocking sled. At the time of the accident, the plaintiff was three to five yards away from the sled when the five players started to push it, but he was not paying attention to the drill. When he looked back from where he was standing, he saw that the sled had veered toward him. The sled was less than five yards away from the plaintiff when a coach began yelling at him to get out of the way. The sled ran over the plaintiff's left foot, causing injury to his ankle. The court held that since the plaintiff had observed and participated in drills involving the blocking sled, the plaintiff fully comprehended the risks inherent in the drill. Specifically, that court found the risk that a blocking sled could veer to the left or the right while it was being used in a drill is inherent to football, and thus assumed by the plaintiff.

The plaintiff does not agree, however, to accept risks that are beyond those inherent in the activity; the plaintiff does not assume the risk of the negligence of the coach, instructor or operator increasing or enhancing the inherent risks of an activity. The California Supreme Court, in the case of *Nalwa v. Cedar Fair, L.P.* (2012), held that the primary assumption of risk doctrine applies to recreational activities, not just sports. In this case, the plaintiff injured her wrist in a collision while riding on the bumper cars at an amusement park and argued the operator was negligent in configuring or operating the bumper cars so as not to prevent her injury. The court held that the duty not to unreasonably increase the risks of riding on the bumper cars did not extend to preventing head-on collisions. This concept also arises in the following hypothetical situation.

Considering … Assumption of Risk

A skydiver breaks his ankle upon landing in a field. This is an inherent risk of skydiving, because some impact with the ground is both obvious and necessary for the activity. There is no way to make the landing without risk; sometimes the force of landing may cause a broken or sprained ankle. Likewise, perhaps the wind comes up suddenly after the jump and the skydiver is injured because he cannot avoid a tree. This is a risk inherent in the very nature of skydiving, and it would therefore be an assumed risk.

Questions

- If a skydiver is killed because neither of his parachutes opened, is the failure of the parachutes an inherent risk?
- Is the failure of the parachutes an obvious and necessary risk of the activity?

Note how you would answer the questions and then check your responses using the Analysis & Discussion at the end of this chapter.

Secondary. A **secondary assumption of risk** means that a plaintiff deliberately chooses to encounter a known risk created by the defendant's negligence and in doing so acts unreasonably. For example, if a skier notices that a ski operator has failed to properly mark the difficulty of the slopes on a newly opened section of the resort and deliberately chooses to ski the improperly marked slopes, the skier has himself acted unreasonably or contributed to his own injury. In many jurisdictions, this concept of secondary assumption of risk has been subsumed by the concept of comparative negligence, discussed above. The underlying notion of secondary assumption of risk is the same as comparative negligence; that is, the plaintiff acted unreasonably in behaving as he or she did.

Recklessness as a Defense

As we have seen, in the context of participating in an athletic event or physical activity a number of risks are considered inherent to participation. The physical and unpredictable nature of these activities and acts of the participants themselves are in some cases inherent risks. For example, in *Cann v. Stefanec* (2013), where a university swimmer was injured during a team workout when a teammate dropped a weight on her, California appellate court held that this was an inherent risk of weightlifting as sometimes weights are dropped. Similarly, in *Maida v. St. Bonaventure University* (2019), a New York State appellate court held that a member of the men's swim team assumed the risk when he was injured during an ultimate Frisbee game that took place during practice under direction of the coach. The student athlete asserted that the doctrine of primary assumption of risk should not apply because he was compelled to participate in the ultimate Frisbee game by his coach and he did not have the opportunity to assess the risks of playing. The court ultimately dismissed the student's claims as untimely but did not determine whether the compulsion argument could defeat the defendant's assumption of the risk defense.

Thus, if a plaintiff is coerced into attempting an activity, there may be no assumption of risk. For example, in the case of *Calouri v. County of Suffolk* (2007), a 40-year-old student was injured in a community college backpacking class while attempting to do an agility drill. The court held that, as a neophyte, she was in the position of following the directions of the gym instructor, her superior, whose direction she was obliged to follow. The court concluded that the jury should decide whether her participation was voluntary under the circumstances. In addition to the potential assumption of the risk defenses discussed above, in several states co-participants cannot recover for the ordinary negligence of another participant that occurs during the athletic event. In almost all recent cases to decide the appropriate standard of care for determining liability involving co-participants in an athletic event, the courts have adopted the recklessness or deliberate misconduct standard, and not one of ordinary negligence.

Additionally, in California, an interesting line of precedent has been decided indicating that, in some circumstances, even a coach is not liable for his or her own negligence. In the case of *Kahn v. East Side Union High School* (2003), the California Supreme Court held that a high school swimming coach would not be liable unless his or her actions were reckless. Using the higher reckless misconduct standard was based on the notion that coaches needed some leeway to challenge and push athletes beyond their comfort level. One court summarized the rationale as follows:

> As for coaches, "[t]o the extent a duty is alleged against a coach for 'pushing' and/or 'challenging' a student to improve and advance, the plaintiff must show that the coach intended to cause the student's injury or engaged in reckless conduct – that is, conduct totally outside the range of the ordinary activity involved in teaching or coaching the sport. Furthermore, a coach has a duty of ordinary care not to increase the risk of injury to a student by encouraging or allowing the student to participate in the sport when he or she is physically unfit to participate or by allowing the student to use unsafe equipment or instruments. These principles are in line with the underlying policy of not creating a 'chilling effect on the activity itself, nor … interfering with the ability of the instructor to teach the student new or better skills.'" (*Eriksson*, 191 Cal.App.4th at p. 845)

Essentially, this means that in those states that have chosen to adopt the higher reckless misconduct standard, an athlete assumes the risk of negligence by a coach or instructor so long as the coaches conduct is not totally outside the range of ordinary activities involved in the sport. The following Focus Case followed the *Kahn* reasoning. The reckless misconduct standard is also further explored later in the chapter related to co-participant liability for injuries occurring during a sport contest.

Stevens v. Azusa Pacific University

Cal. App. Unpub. No. B286355 (Cal. Ct. App. May 29, 2019)	**FOCUS** CASE

FACTS

The plaintiff was a member of the Azusa Pacific University (APU), cheerleading team. She suffered two head injuries during practices, which led her to consult with two physicians, including a doctor at the APU student health center. Both doctors diagnosed a concussion. The doctor at the APU student health center advised the plaintiff not to attend cheer practice until she was symptom free for a number of days.

The plaintiff followed that advice, and sat out for what amounted to approximately one month. When she rejoined the team, plaintiff practiced for two additional months without incident. She was then struck again on the head, this time with what she alleges are continuing neurological consequences. The plaintiff filed a negligence lawsuit against APU and its cheerleading coach. The trial court granted summary judgment in favor of defendants, finding the claims barred by the doctrine of primary assumption of the risk. The plaintiff appealed from that order.

HOLDING

The California appellate court affirmed the trial court's decision.

RATIONALE

The court noted that sponsoring organizations and instructors/coaches are not insurers of student safety. A sponsor of athletic activity "posing inherent risks of injury ha[s] no duty to reduce or eliminate those risks, but do[es] owe participants the duty not to unreasonably increase the risks of injury beyond those inherent in the activity." (*Nalwa v. Cedar Fair, L.P.* (2012) at p. 1162.) As for coaches, the court held that to the extent a duty is alleged against a coach for "pushing" and/or "challenging" a student to improve and advance, the plaintiff must show that the coach intended to cause the student's injury or engaged in reckless conduct – that is, conduct totally outside the range of the ordinary activity involved in teaching or coaching the sport. The court held that the plaintiff could not present a triable question of fact as to whether the cheerleading coach unreasonably increased the risks of injury beyond those inherent in the sport.

In this case, there is no claim that the coach intentionally injured the student. The injury occurred as the coach was supervising cheerleading practice and thus was within the ordinary activities in teaching a sport. There is no basis for finding that the coach acted recklessly. Therefore, the doctrine of primary assumption of risk applies and the plaintiff's action was properly dismissed.

However, contrary to *Stevens*, the court in the following Focus Case declined to use the *Kahn* precedent in a case decided under South Dakota law against a high school gymnastics coach.

Wilson v. O'Gorman High School

2008 U.S. Dist. LEXIS 49489 (S.D.D.C., June 26, 2008)   **FOCUS** CASE

FACTS

The plaintiff, an elite gymnast, became a paraplegic after a serious fall during her high school gymnastics practice. She was attempting a very difficult maneuver on the uneven bars and her coach made her practice it repeatedly. According to the plaintiff's allegations, she was injured after approximately 30 previous attempts. She further alleged that her injury resulted from the negligence of her coach, who did not have the expertise to teach this particular advanced technique. The defendant sought a dismissal of the lawsuit on the basis that allegations of mere negligence should not be sufficient to state a cause of action against the coach, i.e., a "reckless disregard" standard should be adopted in South Dakota.

HOLDING

The federal district court in South Dakota denied summary judgment for the defendant.

RATIONALE

The court declined to use the *Kahn* reckless duty of care standard from California, which was urged by the defendant. Instead, the court deemed it appropriate to use the prudent person duty of care standard (negligence) in accordance with the law of South Dakota. The court noted that the South Dakota legislature could have altered the negligence standard applicable to the coach–athlete relationship if it had so desired and had not done so, even though it had altered the negligence standard in other circumstances. Furthermore, there was no case law precedent that would support the defendant's position that South Dakota had adopted, or should adopt, the reckless disregard standard.

Immunity

Defenses related to immunity are different from the defenses discussed above in that if a defendant is held to have **immunity**, this precludes the defendant from being found liable in a negligence lawsuit. The notion is that even if a defendant has engaged in tortious behavior, the status of the defendant is of such social importance that the defendant may escape liability for that behavior.

Governmental Immunity

Historically, the concept of governmental immunity is rooted in the idea that "the king can do no wrong." Of course, that idea is erroneous; kings can do wrong, and in our system of government the states and the federal government also may do wrong. However, the notion of granting governmental entities freedom from suit grew out of this notion of the sovereign as deserving of immunity.

Today the federal government has allowed itself to be sued for certain tort claims arising under the Federal Tort Claims Act (FTCA; 28 U.S.C. §§ 1346 *et seq.*). This statute gives a general consent to be sued in tort, although there are several restrictions placed upon the lawsuit. One important aspect of this act provides for an exception to the waiver of immunity in cases involving discretionary functions. The gist of this concept is that there are certain governmental activities that should not be subject to suit because the government is acting in ways that involve policy judgments pertinent to the government's legislative or executive functions. When the government is acting in ways to further those functions, tort liability should not be imposed.

More common are the use of state statutes that provide immunity when a governmental entity, such as a school district, engages in activities that are considered to be in furtherance of its governmental mission as opposed to engaging in activities that are proprietary in nature. The following Focus Case illustrates this concept.

Stahr v. Lincoln Sudbury Regional High School District

93 Mass. App. Ct. 243, 102 N.E.3d 995 (2018)   **FOCUS** CASE

FACTS

Plaintiff participated in field hockey practice as a member of the defendant's varsity field hockey team. Defendant is a public school. Practice drills were introduced by a volunteer assistant coach and the head coach was also present at practice. During the drill, the plaintiff was struck in the face by a teammate's field hockey stick after the teammate chose to pass the ball via a "hard-drive" as opposed to a "push-pass." The blow knocked out two of Alexandra's teeth and caused her to lose consciousness. The volunteer coach did not provide plaintiff with assistance after she was injured. The head coach left the field to find first aid supplies and did not immediately assist the plaintiff or assess her injuries.

Further, when the plaintiff's father arrived, he was not informed that the plaintiff may have suffered a concussion. Plaintiff was subsequently diagnosed with a concussion. The symptoms of her concussion caused her academic performance to suffer over a prolonged period of time. Plaintiff filed a negligence lawsuit which the trial court dismissed in its entirety after finding that state immunity statues insulated the defendant from liability. Plaintiff appealed.

HOLDING

The Massachusetts appellate court held that the school district was entitled to governmental immunity and granted summary judgment for the defendant.

RATIONALE

The plaintiff alleged that the coaches' lack of supervision and inadequate instruction prior to allowing the players to engage in the drill – both omissions – caused plaintiff's injuries. The plaintiffs' claim in this respect amounts to an attempt to hold the defendant liable for failing to ensure plaintiff's safety during field hockey practice. However, the state immunity laws confer significant protection from tort liability to public employers by barring "any claim based on an act or failure to act to prevent or diminish the harmful consequences of a condition or situation, including the violent or tortious conduct of a third person, which is not originally caused by the public employer or any other person acting on behalf of the public employer." The Court did not find that the lack of supervision or instruction was the original cause of the plaintiff's injury' thus, the immunity statutes were properly applied in this case, serving as a bar to the claim.

Charitable Immunity

Historically, U.S. courts established a doctrine that charitable entities were immune from tort liability. However, most contemporary courts have repudiated the idea of complete immunity for charities. A few states retain a limited version of charitable immunity, and this can be ascertained by checking state statutes related to immunity.

Good Samaritan Statutes

You will recall from the discussion of duty, the law does not impose a duty upon a stranger to act to help another stranger in distress. Under common law, if a person assumes the duty of aiding another, that person is liable for a failure to act reasonably in assisting the injured person. However, as a matter of social policy we would like to encourage individuals to come to the aid of others who are in distress, even absent a legal duty to do so. Therefore, all states have adopted some version of the **Good Samaritan statutes**, which generally provide that persons who act in good faith to help others in distress by providing emergency medical aid may not be sued for ordinary negligence based on their efforts to assist. This type of legislation furthers the social policy of encouraging people to assist others by immunizing them from liability for negligence should they make an error in providing medical aid to another. Some jurisdictions extend immunity to all persons administering emergency care; other states limit immunity to specified medical personnel or to physicians (57A Am. Jur. 2d Negligence § 193).

Recreational Use Statutes

All states have adopted some type of **recreational use statute** that provides a level of immunity for landowners who open their property to recreational use by the public with no fees charged. This type of legislation represents an attempt to encourage landowners to give property access to the public so that more land will be available for recreational purposes. Recreational use statutes are discussed in greater detail in Chapter 15.

Volunteer Immunity Statutes

Unfortunately, we live in a litigious climate where people may sometimes sue others at the slightest provocation. Many of our sport-related activities for youth could not exist without the generous participation of volunteers to serve as coaches, instructors, supervisors, and so forth. To encourage people to volunteer in these capacities certain legislation, federal and state, has been passed. The U.S. Congress passed the Volunteer Protection Act of 1997 (42 U.S.C. §§ 14501 *et seq.*) to encourage volunteers to offer their services to nonprofit entities, including youth sport organizations. The legislation essentially provides that no volunteer of a nonprofit organization or a governmental entity shall be liable for harm caused by the volunteer due to negligence, providing that the volunteer was "properly licensed, certified or authorized by the appropriate authorities for the activities" (§ 14503). This legislation preempts state laws on this matter, unless the state law provides more protection for the volunteer. This act provides protection only for the volunteer, not for the organization or governmental entity.

Some states have adopted statutes providing similar protection for volunteers. Some of the statutes are broad ones, protecting volunteers in any type of nonprofit setting. Other statutes are more specific and provide protection specifically for those who volunteer in sport and recreation settings. The case of *Weiss v. Pratt* (2011) dealt with Florida's volunteer team physician immunity statute. In this situation, an orthopedic surgeon, who served as a volunteer team physician for a high school, allegedly treated an athlete with a neck injury improperly by failing to use a backboard to take the athlete from the field. This statute provides a volunteer physician with immunity if the service is "rendered as a reasonably prudent person similarly licensed to practice medicine would have acted under the same or similar circumstances." It requires a plaintiff to prove that the volunteer physician failed to act "as a reasonably prudent person similarly licensed to practice medicine" to prevail in an action. A jury awarded Pratt $750,000, and the appellate court upheld the verdict as it noted that the statute, while purporting to immunize a volunteer physician, provides no real protection because the immunity standard is essentially the same standard used under basic tort law.

Sport and Recreation Safety Acts

In many states, a variety of outdoor activities are important to the state's economy, primarily in terms of tourism dollars. These activities may include, for example, skiing, equine activities, whitewater rafting, hunting/fishing, hiking, and golf. See Exhibit 14.2 for the Wyoming Recreational Safety Act covered activities. You can see that the State of Wyoming in addition to protecting numerous general recreational

---

Exhibit 14.2 Wyoming Recreational Safety Act, Wyo. Stat. Ann. §§ 1-1-121 to 1-1-123 (2014).

(iii) "Sport or recreational opportunity" means commonly understood sporting activities including baseball, softball, football, soccer, basketball, swimming, hockey, dude ranching, Nordic or alpine skiing, mountain climbing, river floating, hunting, fishing, backcountry trips, horseback riding and any other equine activity, snowmobiling and similar recreational opportunities;

(iv) "Equine activity" means:

A Equine shows, fairs, competitions, performances or parades that involve any or all breeds of equines;
B Any of the equine disciplines;
C Equine training or teaching activities, or both;
D Boarding equines;
E Riding, inspecting or evaluating an equine belonging to another, whether or not the owner has received some monetary consideration or other thing of value for the use of the equine or is permitting a prospective purchaser of the equine to ride, inspect or evaluate the equine;
F Rides, trips, hunts or other equine activities of any type however informal or impromptu;
G Day use rental riding, riding associated with a dude ranch or riding associated with outfitted pack trips; and
H Placing or replacing horseshoes on an equine.

Competitive Advantage Strategies

Supervision

- Make sure that all employees who have supervisory responsibilities are competent to identify unsafe behaviors within the activity or sport they are supervising.
- The Nonprofit Risk Management Center has a free app which provides state by state laws applicable to volunteer liability. This and similar apps are a good way for sport managers running events in multiple states to gain a quick check for immunity protections. They also should consult with attorneys licensed in those states for the most accurate information.
- Develop supervisory plans that have an appropriate ratio of supervisors to participants, considering such factors as

    o   the nature of the activity,
    o   the age and maturity of participants,
    o   the skill level of participants, and
    o   any limitations posed by the type of activity area or facility.

- Develop supervisory plans that designate certain areas of the activity area for each supervisor. You may have a reasonable number of supervisors, but if they all congregate together, you will not have proper coverage.
- Ensure that all supervisors are trained to identify and stop rowdy behavior.

activities has also included very detailed protections for equine activity which are an integral part of that state's economic activities valued at close to $300 million (American Horse Council Foundation, 2005). Many state legislatures have chosen to protect a specific sector of the economy by passing some version of a recreation safety act or **shared responsibility statute**. The essence of this type of statute is to stipulate in the statute that participants in the specified activities assume the risk of hazards inherent in these activities (the inherent hazards are sometimes listed in the statute). These hazards are those that a participant should expect to confront in that activity. If the participant, or in some cases, the spectator, choosing to take part in the activities, the activity provider does not owe a duty of care to the participant relative to those risks, under the concept of primary assumption of risk. Under these acts, the provider cannot be sued based in negligence for injuries resulting from the inherent risks of the sport or recreational activity. A provider could still be sued for gross negligence or recklessness.

Common Liability Issues Regarding Safety of Participants

There are many ways in which a plaintiff may allege that a defendant sport or recreation program provider may be negligent. This section discusses a number of frequently occurring allegations, including: (1) a lack of supervision; (2) improper instruction or training; (3) the unsafe use of equipment; (4) improper medical care; and (5) negligence in transportation.

Lack of Supervision

Many liability concerns relating to participant injuries occur because of a failure of supervision. Proper supervision of participants means that the person(s) entrusted with this responsibility are competent to oversee the participants (quality of supervision) and that there are sufficient supervisors to fulfill the duty of care (quantity of supervision). The obligation to supervise does not mean that there is a duty of instruction, but it does mean that supervisors must be able to recognize dangerous behaviors and stop them.

Quality of Supervision

The issue of quality of supervision involves the competence of the supervisor. Even if there is a one-to-one ratio of supervisors to participants, the supervision may be inadequate if a supervisor does not have the competence to identify dangerous behavior and, therefore, to intervene and stop the behavior. For example, supervision was allegedly improper in the case of *Lujan v. Chowan University* (2019). The plaintiff, a collegiate soccer player, suffered a near fatal heat stroke during a soccer conditioning drill. The plaintiff was evaluated prior to participation and supervised during participation by an unlicensed athletic trainer. Although the temperature was 105 degrees on the day of the conditioning drill, the university allowed an unlicensed trainer to supervise the soccer team's practice. While this case ultimately settled, it demonstrates that simply having a person onsite is not the equivalent of competent supervision; a supervisor must know enough about the activity in question to identify danger and respond in such situations.

Quantity of Supervision

The question of quantity of supervision is whether the number of competent supervisors is sufficient relative to the number of participants; i.e., whether the ratio of supervisors to participants is reasonable. In a case from the New York Court of Appeals, *MP v. Mineola Union Free School District* (2018), the court held that a nine-year-old student (injured while playing a game of touch football on a field during recess at his school) did not assume the risk of being unsupervised. Specifically, the student was injured while playing "outside the boundaries" set by the recess monitor for group play. Although the plaintiff and his friends routinely played beyond the boundary, school personnel did not have adequate supervision in place to prevent the impermissible play. Whether the ratio is proper is a question that cannot be answered in the abstract. *There is no magic number that is proper for all occasions.* The type of activity must be factored in; obviously, an activity such as gymnastics, with more risk than table tennis, would suggest that the ratio of gymnasts to supervisors must be lower than it is for table tennis players. The age and maturity of the participants must also be considered. Generally, youthful participants require more supervisors than adults. If a particular group has shown a propensity for rowdy behavior, then this must be taken into consideration when assigning the number of supervisors. If the participants have any physical or mental disability that makes them more prone to injury, more supervisors will be necessary. There may also be concerns related to the facility or area in which an activity is taking place. For example, more supervisors are necessary if the participants are spread out over a large area or if a supervisor cannot make visual contact with all participants because of the way the area is configured.

A manager should consider all of the above factors when making decisions about the number of supervisors to assign. All of these issues bear on the essential question: What number of competent supervisors is reasonable in this setting, at this time? Furthermore, supervisory plans should delineate not just the number of supervisors but also the specific areas of supervision. Designating specific areas of supervision is necessary because supervisors may tend to cluster together, thereby leaving certain areas without supervisory coverage.

Improper Instruction or Training

The question of proper instruction or training in the context of physical activity and sport has more severe liability implications than it has in other educational contexts. Of course, we would hope that an English teacher would properly instruct students that the author of *The Inferno* is Dante and not Shakespeare, but the student will not suffer physical injury as a result of such an error. However, if a physical educator, coach, or activity instructor fails to act reasonably in the way she teaches a physical skill, serious consequences may ensue, including severe physical injury or death. The following discussion focuses on a number of critical issues related to competent instruction.

Competitive Advantage Strategies

Instruction and Training

- Develop criteria to assess whether a person is competent to serve as an instructor or coach for an activity.
- Have all instructors attend risk management workshops that cover the principles of safe instruction.
- As part of the introduction to any activity, make sure that specific risk information is shared with participants.
- Emphasize that the proper progression of activities or skills must be followed.
- Discuss the dangers of mismatch based on size, maturity, or skill.

Selection and Supervision of Properly Qualified Instructors

The first issue related to instruction is whether the instructor has the appropriate competence to provide instruction. In some cases, administrators who are selecting instructors or coaches may be able to rely upon a teaching certificate or other accepted credential to ensure that the person has the level of competence necessary for the activity. In cases where there is no credentialing process, the employer must be more actively engaged in ascertaining what the proper competence for a position entails and whether the applicant possesses those credentials. If the person doing the hiring does not act as a reasonably prudent person in choosing someone who is competent for the position, then there may be liability for negligent hiring, as discussed in Chapter 4.

In the fitness industry, those who hire personal trainers should be aware of the controversy surrounding certification programs. There are numerous "certification" programs for personal trainers and no nationwide standard for competency, so some states have introduced legislation to license or otherwise regulate personal trainers (Butland, 2015). For example, in 2015, the Massachusetts legislature considered a bill that was designed to encourage well qualified practitioners in the field of personal training. Specifically, *Mass.* H.B. 185 (2015) required that in order for a person to hold himself or herself out as a personal trainer, he/she be (a) be certified as a personal trainer or its equivalent by national independent organization whose certification procedures for personal trainers have been approved by the National Commission for Certifying Agencies (NCCA); or (b) possess a credential or certification in either the field of personal training, exercise science, or similarly related field, from an educational institution accredited by an accrediting body recognized by either the Council for Higher Education Accreditation or by the United States Department of Education. However, experts in the fitness industry believe that the answer is not licensing but rather a good formal education in exercise science or exercise physiology. Furthermore, some professionals believe that the language in many state bills is not helpful in meeting the stated goals of consumer protection (Butland, 2015; Goldman, 2009; Herbert, 2008). Fitness professionals should stay current with the discussion relating to the certification of personal trainers.

The responsibility to supervise instructors in a reasonable fashion remains, regardless of the instructors' qualifications. What is considered reasonable supervision will vary depending upon an instructor's experience levels. Regardless of the instructor's expertise, a complete abdication of supervisory responsibility is unacceptable and may lead to liability for negligent supervision, as discussed in Chapter 4.

Adequacy of Instruction

Instruction must be suitable for the intended audience. The language used must be understandable by the participants based on their age and familiarity with the activity. Also, since verbal instruction of physical skills is often accompanied by physical demonstration, the language used must be congruent with the demonstration. There cannot be an incongruence between what is conveyed to the participant verbally and what is shown to the participant. Whether instruction is adequate is often considered by courts. For example, in *Clark County School Dist. v. Payo* (2017), the Nevada Supreme Court considered whether verbal instructions prohibiting "high-sticking" in a middle school field hockey class was sufficient instruction, or whether the physical education teacher had a legal responsibility to demonstrate the proper technique. While ultimately the Court found that the lack of instruction was not the proximate cause of the injury (previously discussed in this chapter), the case reaffirms that adequacy of instruction matters. Further, demonstration of an activity must be done safely. In *Murphy v. Polytechnic University* (2009), a softball coach hit a player in the face while he was demonstrating a batting technique to her. The coach swung the bat while the player stood close enough to be hit with the bat. This was determined to be negligent behavior.

If participants are relatively young and immature, important instructional concepts will need to be repeated more frequently than with an older audience. Also, younger groups tend to be very literal as they listen to instruction, so certain departures from instruction may be foreseeable. For example, in the case of *Glankler v. Rapides Parish School Board* (1992), a group of kindergarten children was taken on a field trip to a very large park with many types of playground equipment. This park had 47 adult swings, which were heavy and potentially dangerous for small children. The children were told that they were not allowed to push the swings. However, they were not forbidden to climb up on the swings, which led to dangerous behavior because the children's feet could not touch the ground as they sat in the swings. It is foreseeable that children will take action to get the swing to move. Expert testimony established that the children should have been told not to play on the swings at all.

Instructors and coaches should always follow the practices that have been widely accepted by experts in the activity. This is true because courts will give great deference to the standards that have been developed by those persons or organizations that have expert knowledge about the activity. Therefore, instructors should exercise great caution in developing drills or methods that vary from widely accepted practices. Even if a certain method seems to make sense, it is advisable to explore the issue and choose a method that is endorsed widely in the sport or activity. Coaches and instructors should attend workshops and seminars to ensure that the most current practices are being used.

Proper Progression of Skill

A culminating activity should not be attempted unless the proper lead-up activities are presented and practiced. Physical skills are often taught in a sequential manner, and no shortcuts can be taken if the participant is to be properly prepared for engaging in the final outcome. In *Scott v. Rapides*, the court defined proper preparation to include:

1 An explanation of basic rules and procedures
2 Suggestions for proper performance
3 Identification of risks

Teachers and coaches should include these three elements in their instruction for culminating physical activities. Let's look more closely at this case.

Scott v. Rapides Parish School Board

732 So.2d 749 (La. Ct. App. 1999)   **FOCUS** CASE

FACTS

The plaintiff, Zwireck Scott, was a high school student who injured his knee during a physical education class as he attempted a long jump and landed improperly. On the day he was injured, Scott was attempting to do the long jump for the first time while running full speed. He hoped to try out for the track team, and the team's coach was the class instructor.

Scott had been jumping in the sand pit for several days, but he had never before run full speed and attempted a jump while going "all out." The teacher/coach gave him no instruction. He had not spoken to Scott about proper landing or control in the air, nor did he discuss any risks involved in the long jump.

The trial court found liability for improper instruction and awarded damages in the amount of $207,000.

HOLDING

The Louisiana appellate court affirmed the judgment.

RATIONALE

The appellate court noted that "when an activity is potentially dangerous a student should not be required to attempt such activity without first receiving proper instruction and preparation, including an explanation of basic rules and procedures, suggestions for proper performance, and identification of risks" (p. 753). In this case, the court held that the coach had a duty to provide Scott, who was unfamiliar with the long jump, instruction that would permit him to complete the long jump successfully and safely under the maximum-effort conditions. Long jumping is a skilled sport, and there must be a reasonable amount of preparatory instruction before students are permitted to attempt a maximum-effort jump.

Dissemination of Safety Rules and Warnings

An important component of learning any activity is knowing what aspects could be dangerous to oneself or others. Safety rules and procedures should be discussed and reinforced on a frequent basis. The reason for the safety rules should also be shared with participants. Every practice session should have some time devoted to safety, and the safety rules and warnings pertinent to each activity should be given proper attention. Instructors should warn participants about the specific risks of each activity and discuss the possible adverse consequences if safety rules are not followed.

Participants are entitled to rely upon the safety procedures that have been identified and shared with them. For example, in the case of *Rosania v. Carmona* (1998), a karate student was injured during a proficiency test match when he was kicked in the face by the instructor. The student alleged that the safety rules of the dojo identified the head as an illegal target area. These no-contact karate rules were mandatory, and the student relied upon these rules when he chose to study at this dojo. Therefore, the violation of these rules was negligence, since the inherent risks of the sport, as practiced at that dojo, prohibited the type of contact encountered in this situation.

The safety rules pertinent to an activity must be both shared and enforced. Dangerous behaviors must be penalized, and coaches must be consistent in trying to stop them by penalizing players every time they engage in them – even if the unsafe behavior resulted in a good consequence for the team.

Mismatch of Opponents

Competitive situations will almost always pit opponents who are not exactly equal in size, strength, or competency. In some cases, it is not reasonably prudent to allow competition between those who are so different in size, strength, or competency that those disparities may result in injury beyond what is accepted as inherent in the activity itself. Often, there may be formal guidelines established by a league or governing body to address this. For example, the age and weight restrictions for youth football represent an attempt to level the playing field.

In some cases, participants may be equal in terms of size but so different in skill level that it is imprudent for them to be matched up. An example of this is presented in the case of *Gurule v. Board of Education of The Los Lunas Public School District* (2019), a 12-year-old student who had never before participated in any school-sponsored sports program joined the school wrestling team. On the first day of practice, he was paired with an older, stronger boy, who had at least one year of wrestling experience. The boys engaged in practice matches; in the second match, the plaintiff was taken down on his neck forcefully enough to cause some injury. The parents filed multiple negligence claims, including an allegation that the coaches were not paying appropriate attention to the students on the day of the injury and thus allowed a dangerous mismatch between the skill and experience levels of the plaintiff and the other student. In denying the defendant's motion for summary judgment, the court allowed the claim against the coaches and the school district to continue.

Unsafe Use or Supervision of Equipment

Part of instructional and coaching responsibilities is to provide necessary equipment that is proper and safe for an activity and to make sure the equipment is used safely. If necessary protective equipment cannot be provided, the activity should be discontinued – the courts do not view lack of funds as a legal defense. In *Powers v. Greenville Central School District* (2019), the court considered whether eye goggles were necessary in a physical education lacrosse game; the school argued that the students were playing "soft lacrosse," which is a modified version of the game that uses modified equipment. The parents of the minor plaintiff who was injured (struck in the eye) argued that the game more closely resembled classic lacrosse and that protective eye goggles should have been provided to the students. Understanding what equipment is necessary is critical to this legal responsibility.

Further, necessary equipment means equipment that is essential to do the activity; it does not mean state-of-the-art equipment. It must simply reasonably meet the participants' needs. Protective equipment must be in good condition. For example, in the case of *Fithian v. Sag Harbor Union Free School District* (2008) a student alleged that the school district was negligent in providing him with a cracked batter's helmet. The equipment must also fit properly. A football helmet that is in good shape, for example, but falls over the eyes of the wearer does not meet the criterion of acceptable equipment. Players should be taught how to fit equipment properly and how to inspect the equipment prior to each use.

The equipment provided must meet the standards mandated for that type of equipment. For example, pertinent standards for pole vaulting equipment have been promulgated by the NFHS as well as by the NCAA. Football helmet standards are set by the National Operating Committee on Standards for Athletic Equipment (NOCSAE). Playground equipment standards are found in Consumer Product Safety Commission (CPSC) guidelines and in the American Society for Testing and Materials (ASTM) standards.

Considering ... Safety and Use of Equipment

Taylor is told to use the new weight machine the school recently purchased to work on her shoulder strength for wrestling. The new weight machine is designed for professional athletes and there was an extensive training manual on how to safely use the machine. Taylor is not provided any instructions on how to use the new weight machine but only told to look at the illustrations on the machine. The coach has not reviewed the training manual and does not observe her at any time while she is using the machine. Taylor injures her rotator cuff because she attempted too much weight while using the unfamiliar machine.

Question

- If Taylor's parents sue the coach/school, alleging negligent training and instruction, will they win? Why or why not?

Note how you would answer the question and then check your response using the Analysis & Discussion at the end of this chapter.

Competitive Advantage Strategies

Equipment Use

- Provide equipment that is in good condition and maintain the equipment properly.
- Teach participants how to check for equipment problems prior to each use.
- Make sure equipment meets all pertinent specifications.
- Make sure instruction is given on the proper use of all equipment.

Improper Medical Care

Medical care issues related to participants in sport and recreation programs are important to address. In some cases, you may have an obligation to screen for health problems or monitor the well-being of athletes. In all cases, you have an obligation to develop a protocol for and provide emergency medical care. Issues related to medical malpractice and fraudulent concealment are also important to understand.

Preventive Health Concerns

In organized sport settings, there is usually a screening mechanism to ensure that players are healthy enough to compete in activities. On the high school level, most states have a standardized medical history form for student-athletes provided by or overseen by the state high school athletic federation. These forms are filled out by the student, parents, and family doctors. Collecting this information aids schools in becoming aware of a variety of health issues including increased risks for cardiac death, eating disorders, nutritional deficiencies, and others.

At the NATA Annual Meeting and Clinical Symposia in 2013, leading health care professionals pre-released inter-association task force recommendations titled, "Preventing Sudden Death in Secondary School Athletics Programs: Best Practices Recommendations." The statement is believed to be the first ever scientific/medical document that focuses on the serious conditions that can affect the high school athlete. A copy of the complete statement is available online; see the Web Resources at the end of this chapter. The task force's recommendations are designed to provide secondary school administrators, physicians, athletic trainers, coaches, athletes, and others with best practices for preventing sudden deaths, establishing emergency action plans, and providing appropriate medical care.

Concussions

Concerns related to concussions have always been a part of many sports. However, now the concerns have reached epidemic proportions, resulting in the passage of many preventive measures at all levels of competition. For example, Pop Warner football has banned all head-to-head hits. Recently passed rules at the high school and college levels require football players who lose their helmets during play to sit out a subsequent play (Popke, 2012a). The Ivy League passed rules limiting the number of full-contact practices its football teams can have ("League limits practices," 2011). USA Hockey banned body checking in boys' hockey until players are age 13 to 14 years, eliminating body checking for players 12 and under (Yang & Baugh, 2016). In 2015, US Soccer (made up collectively of US Soccer Federation, US Youth Soccer Association, American Youth Soccer Organization, US Club Soccer, and California's Youth Soccer Associations) announced a comprehensive campaign for safety in youth soccer. The initiative eliminated heading soccer balls for youth players younger than ten years and limited the practice of heading for children ages 11 to 13 years (Yang & Baugh, 2016). The initiative was the result of *Mehr v. Féderation Intern. De Football Ass'n* (2015), in which seven youth soccer players filed a class action lawsuit aimed at forcing soccer governing bodies to implement safety standards related to concussion prevention.

As of 2019, all 50 states have passed concussion laws to protect youth athletes. Most of these statutes provide that parties such as coaches, parents, youth league administrators, and sometimes game officials, receive education pertaining to the symptoms of concussions. The statutes also provide that a possibly concussed athlete must be taken out of practice or competition and then remain out of the activity until cleared to return by a medical professional (Jones, 2013). Amberg (2012) has a good discussion of these statutes and enforcement issues with the laws. Similarly, the Centers for Disease Control and prevention (CDC) has created a "Heads Up" database containing multiple resources related head injury prevention; this database can be found online; see the Web Resources at the end of this chapter. Similarly, the National Center for Injury Prevention and Control (NCIPC) conducted a case study evaluation on the Return to Play protocol implementation efforts in two states: Washington and Massachusetts; the evaluation was designed to assess implementation efforts, including related challenges and successes in implementation.

Emergency Medical Care

Two major issues are associated with the provision of emergency medical care to participants: (1) making sure that qualified personnel are available to render emergency first aid and CPR; and (2) ensuring that there is a protocol to get outside medical personnel to the site as quickly as possible.

Availability of Qualified Personnel to Render Emergency Medical Care

Whether you are dealing with a team situation or with participants at a fitness club, for example, you have a duty to provide emergency medical care to participants. This also applies to other recreational facilities (see *Spotlite Skating Rink, Inc. v. Barnes*, 2008; this case dealt with a failure to render emergency medical care at a roller skating rink). In a team situation, if you do not have the luxury of a qualified athletic trainer at all your practices, your coaches should be certified in CPR and first aid. You cannot rely upon calling the training room for a first responder if an emergency arises. Time is of the essence, particularly in a cardiac or respiratory emergency. First responders should only respond in accordance with their training; they should not attempt to diagnose or treat an injury as if they were physicians. Discussions related to the provision and use of Automated External Defibrillators (AEDs) are found in Chapter 15.

In a fitness club, each shift should be staffed with multiple individuals who are trained to respond to medical emergencies. It is not prudent to have just one person per shift who is trained in emergency first aid and CPR. When that person leaves the building for lunch or calls in sick, the club is left in a precarious position.

Competitive Advantage Strategies

Medical Care

- Make sure that one or more persons with first aid and CPR training are always readily available to deal with emergency medical conditions.
- Develop a protocol to contact outside emergency medical assistance quickly. Make sure all employees understand this protocol.
- Try to eliminate any conflict of interest issues in medical treatment by giving the team physician the final authority as to whether a player is medically able to play. The coach should not have the prerogative to override competent medical opinion.
- Always provide full disclosure to players regarding their injuries.

Clear Protocol for Outside Emergency Personnel

All employees should go through an orientation on their first day at work that familiarizes them with how emergency help is summoned. In one particularly unfortunate situation, a death occurred at a city recreation swimming pool because the employees did not realize that they had to dial 9 for an outside line before dialing 911. By the time the employees realized the problem, the delay in getting the EMTs to the location resulted in the death of the swimmer (*Carter v. City of Cleveland*, 1998). In another case, the delay in getting medical assistance to a student who had suffered a head injury allowed a blood clot to enlarge from the size of a walnut to the size of an orange. A $2.5 million judgment was rendered against the school district (*Barth v. Board of Education*, 1986). The Learning Activities for this chapter include an activity for developing an emergency action plan (EAP) for medical emergencies in your organization.

With experience, sport and recreation organizations have become better at dealing with medical emergencies. However, the matter of heat-related injuries, especially related to summer football conditioning, continues to be problematic. In an early case (*Mogabgab v. Orleans Parish School Board*, 1970), a high school football player suffered heat stroke and the coaching staff simply allowed his condition to worsen by putting him in the locker room, where he did not have access to medical assistance for over two hours. This is egregious conduct, but similar scenarios are repeated across the country every year. Since 1995, three football players a year on average have died of heat stroke, most of them high schoolers, according to the National Center for Catastrophic Sport Injury Research (NCCSIR) (*Bruggers*, 2018). In the decade spanning 2007–2017, the NCCSIR reported 120 deaths indirectly related to football; death from heat stroke is one cited indirect cause. While heat stroke can occur in all areas of the country, researchers studying student athletes (especially football players during summer workouts) "see more of it in the East, and particularly the Southeast, where sweltering temperatures, high humidity and intense sunshine make for a trifecta of deadly risk, and where high school football is very popular. These weather conditions are only getting worse as the climate changes, bringing more heat and humidity" (*Bruggers*, 2018, para. 8). One recent case that is particularly alarming is the death of Jordan McNair, a football player at the University of Maryland. McNair died two weeks after suffering a heat related illness; initial injury evaluation did not include an assessment or documentation of vital signs, including his core temperature (Ellis, 2018). An investigation after his death revealed that emergency care was inadequate because no one identified escalating symptoms linked to a heat illness. Had emergency care been appropriate, McNair would have received adequate cooling promptly, lessening the likelihood of a fatal outcome.

Heat stroke injuries are avoidable, for the most part, if proper practice planning is implemented, such as scheduling water breaks, implementing shorter practice sessions, or moving the practice to cooler times of the day. However, often coaches become so focused on using the heat as a test of players' prowess that precautions relating to the prevention of heat stroke are ignored. In an effort to address this critical safety issue, the NFHS issued a position statement encouraging all state associations to adhere to new guidelines and to use a new online course (Popke, 2012b). In 2013, Michigan and Pennsylvania proposed new model policies related to acclimatization periods, heat index restrictions, frequency of water breaks, scheduling of practices, and other factors (Popke, 2013). Further, as of 2018, 12 states require either cooling tubs, heat stress monitors, or a combination of both to be present at football practices (*Bruggers*, 2018).

The following four cases also raise the specter of the "no pain, no gain" mentality. At the University of Missouri a freshman football player, who had sickle cell symptoms, died during a summer workout in 2005. The University settled the lawsuit for $2 million after several problems came to light, including the sports medicine director's refusal to examine the player even after he had blurry vision and collapsed. The department personnel also were unfamiliar with exercise-induced complications arising from the sickle cell trait (Scherzagier, 2009). At the University of Central Florida, football player

Ereck Plancher died in March 2008, during offseason conditioning drills, and a lawsuit was filed in March 2009. Plancher also had the sickle cell trait, which exacerbated the likelihood of distress during fatigue. In this case, the trainers and coaches allegedly ignored Plancher's exhaustion, dizziness, shortness of breath, and collapse (Fainaru-Wade, 2009). A jury verdict of $10 million was awarded in June 2011 ("Judge deals blow," 2011). In 2010, a football player at the University of Mississippi collapsed on the first day of spring practice. He died as a result of complications from sickle cell trait. The wrongful death lawsuit alleged that the University failed to follow the NCAA guidelines relating to spring practices, especially for those players with sickle cell trait. The lawsuit also named the NCAA as a defendant, alleging that it had failed to implement adequate guidelines for off-season practices and was settled in 2013. The family received $50,000 from the Ole Miss Foundation and $275,000 under an NCAA insurance policy ("Family settles," 2013). Most recently, in *Mt Ex Rel. Eison v. Peterman* (2019), a first time football player with sickle cell nearly died when coaches failed to implement a hydration plan, failed to monitor the player for heat stroke symptoms, and failed to provide emergency care when the player became incoherent at practice. The NCAA's guidelines relating to sickle cell trait may be found in the 2014–2015 *NCAA Sports Medicine Handbook* (see the Web Resources).

Finally, in a well-publicized high school case, a Kentucky high school football player died after running sprints in the summer of 2008 in 94-degree weather. This situation resulted in reckless homicide charges being brought against the football coach (Popke, 2009). One commentator has argued that criminal prosecutions against coaches in these types of circumstances may have a greater deterrent effect than civil liability (Marck, 2011). These tragedies are preventable with good risk management protocols. There is no acceptable reason for these types of injuries and fatalities to occur.

Negligence in Transportation

The transportation of athletic participants is a critical function, and when an organization assumes the duty to provide transportation, it must be provided in a reasonably safe manner. There are four primary issues related to transportation:

1 The selection of competent drivers.
2 The selection of a safe mode of travel.
3 The proper maintenance of vehicles.
4 The proper training of drivers.

Selection of Competent Drivers

In many cases, an organization may choose to contract with an outside agency for the provision of transportation services. As we discussed in Chapter 4 this contract would, most likely, be structured as an independent contractor relationship to allow the organization to avoid vicarious liability for the negligent acts of drivers. However, due care must be taken with the selection of the independent contractor. The credentials of the transportation agency must be scrutinized to ensure that the agency and its drivers can provide reasonably safe transportation. If the organization selects a transportation agency without reviewing the fitness of the agency to provide these services and the agency, if scrutinized, would not have been chosen because of its safety record, a possible cause of action against the employing organization may arise under the principles of negligent selection (see Chapter 4).

If the organization chooses to have its own employees serve as drivers, care must be taken to ensure that the drivers possess the necessary credentials for this purpose. If vans or buses are to be driven, the state usually mandates that the driver possess a type of chauffeur's license. The organization should implement a policy to ensure that drivers have proper, current credentials.

Selection of a Safe Mode of Travel

Many athletic programs use passenger vans to transport athletes. In 2005, the National Highway Traffic Safety Administration issued a consumer advisory stating that 15-passenger vans are three times more likely to roll over when they are used to carry ten or more passengers ("NHTSA restates rollover warning," 2005). In view of this disclosure, many schools have invested substantially in other types of vehicles, particularly school buses and motor coaches.

Although buses or motor coaches would seem to be a better choice, accidents are unpreventable. For example, in 2018, one student athlete died and 40 were injured in a bus crash in Tennessee (Conway, 2018); also in 2018, dozens of band students were injured when their bus fell down a 50-foot ravine on a return trip from Disneyland (Ketterer, 2018). Lastly, in 2019, over 20 high school volleyball players were treated for injury after a rollover crash in Montana (Cooper, 2019). In these examples, schools may have been using charter bus companies that did not meet federal safety standards or were not hiring competent drivers. ESPN disclosed that at least 35 of 85 Division I universities during 2007 and 2008 used charter bus companies with conditional ratings which means they have a serious record of infractions and that the universities had little knowledge of the violations, even though DOT provides detailed safety records for charter companies (Holtzman, 2009; Lavigne, 2009). This emphasizes the need to research bus companies and to choose those with proven safety records that meet federal safety standards.

One of the usual legal benefits of using a charter bus company is that the company, as an independent contractor (see Chapter 4), would be liable for any travel-related accidents. Therefore, the insurance company for the charter bus company would be responsible for any claims, rather than the University. However, the Ohio Supreme Court, in the case of *Federal Insurance Co. v. Executive Coach Luxury Travel, Inc.* (2010), came to a different conclusion. In this case, five Bluffton University baseball players were killed and others injured in a bus crash in 2007. The university had contracted with a charter bus company for transportation for the baseball team on a road trip. Although the victims of the crash had received compensation from the bus company, the issue before the Ohio Supreme Court was whether under the omnibus clause of the University's insurance policy further compensation could be given to the victims. The court, in a rather strained interpretation of the definition of *insured*, held that the driver of the charter bus could be considered to be an "insured" under the university's policy. Two justices dissented, claiming that this decision unreasonably extended coverage to a third party (Lederman, 2011).

After the Bluffton University crash, initiatives were taken to require seatbelts on motor coaches. The National Highway Transportation Safety Administration passed this requirement in July 2012, and as of June 2013, the U.S. Department of Transportation's National Highway Traffic Safety Administration (NHTSA) issued its final rule requiring three-point seat belts for each passenger and driver seat on new motor coaches and other large buses. This rule was intended to enhance the safety of these vehicles by significantly reducing the risk of fatalities and serious injuries in frontal crashes and the risk of occupant ejection in rollovers.

With regard to air travel, in November 2011 two coaches of the women's basketball team at Oklahoma State University (OSU) were killed in a single-engine plane crash. In January 2001, eight people associated with the men's basketball program at OSU were killed in a small plane crash. This latest tragedy has resulted in another policy for OSU employees who travel by air. As a part of the policy OSU will hire an aviation consultant who will clear all employee air travel requests (Steinbach, 2013). The National Transportation Safety Board ruled out mechanical failure as a cause of the November 2011 crash but could not ascertain why the pilot lost control of the plane (Smith, 2013).

Organizations must also be aware of potential liability issues that arise when athletes are permitted to provide their own transportation to sponsored athletic events. The following **Focus Case** illustrates this issue.

Fenrich v. Blake School

| 920 N.W.2d 195 (Minn. 2018) | FOCUS CASE |

FACTS

A 16-year-old high-school student caused a fatal accident while driving his cross-country teammates and a volunteer coach to an extracurricular athletic competition in Sioux Falls, South Dakota; the student athlete did not receive any driving instructions from the coaching staff and was permitted to drive his teammates, even though an adult parent had offered to drive the students. Gary Fenrich was killed and his wife, appellant JeanAnn Fenrich, was severely injured. She brought a negligence action against respondent Blake School. The district court granted the school's motion for summary judgment, concluding that, as a matter of law, the school did not owe a duty of care to members of the general public. The court of appeals affirmed, but on a different ground, holding that the school's conduct did not create a foreseeable risk of injury to a foreseeable plaintiff.

HOLDING

The Minnesota Supreme Court reversed the court of appeals finding summary judgment was not proper in the circumstances of this case.

RATIONALE

The Minnesota Supreme Court considered whether a school owed a duty of care to members of the general public. In considering the defendants motion for summary judgment, the court noted that as a general rule, an organization does not owe a duty of care to another if the harm is caused by a third party's conduct. However, there are two exceptions to this rule: "(1) when there is a special relationship between a plaintiff and a defendant and the harm to the plaintiff is foreseeable or (2) when the defendant's own conduct creates a foreseeable risk of injury to a foreseeable plaintiff" (p. 202). If either the "special relationship" or the "own conduct" exception applies, a negligent defendant may be held liable to a plaintiff for harm caused by a third party (p. 202). The Court determined that the Blake School did not have a special relationship with the plaintiff; however, using the second exception, the court found that the school's own conduct created a foreseeable risk by assuming supervision and control over its athletic team's trip to the cross-country competition. Specifically, the court found that the assistant coach took active responsibility for coordinating transportation to, and lodging at, the cross-country competition. The coach approved the plan to have a student drive team members and the volunteer coach more than 200 miles, and did not give the volunteer coach any safety instructions (such as to sit in the front seat, to pay attention to the driver [rather than be distracted by electronic devices]).

Proper Maintenance of Vehicles

Many lawsuits in the area of vehicle maintenance have arisen because vehicles were neither inspected nor properly maintained prior to use. Maintenance personnel must have experience dealing with the types of vehicles used and must know the proper air pressure for tires, ensure that headlights and wiper blades are in good shape, and check all fluids for proper levels. Underinflated tires may result in blowouts, which can be dangerous on the open road. An inspection checklist should be filled out each time a vehicle is checked out for use.

Competitive Advantage Strategies

Transportation

- As a part of your risk management plan, appoint a transportation coordinator to develop and oversee this critical aspect of your program.
- Ensure that all drivers are properly credentialed.
- Drivers should obtain a certification from an emergency Vehicle Operator's Course in the type of vehicle they will be operating.
- A qualified, paid driver should be used if participants are traveling farther than 350 miles one way or if the trip is expected to extend later than 2:00 a.m. or overnight.
- Twelve-passenger vans should be loaded with no more than eight passengers and equipment. Fifteen-passenger vans should be loaded with no more than ten passengers and equipment (NTSB, 2003).

Proper Training of Drivers

Not only must an organization use properly credentialed drivers, it must have and enforce safety policies for all drivers. Drivers should have the knowledge to conduct a vehicle inspection and know the specifications for each type of vehicle. They should also undergo a safety orientation and learn how to react to emergency situations, such as icy roads or a tire blowout. Finally, it is critical that drivers have proper rest before beginning a lengthy drive and that they take rest stops at reasonable intervals.

Injuries Due to Defective Products

Malfunctioning or defective sports equipment can cause injury without any negligent action on the part of an instructor or participant. When this occurs as a result of some defect in the equipment, the injured party may sue under products liability law. Products liability law blends elements of tort law and contract law. Aspects of tort law concepts of negligence and strict liability apply to products liability, and aspects of contract law apply to issues related to warranties such as the implied warranty of fitness for an intended purpose. In this section, we will briefly examine examples of claims based on the law of products liability and explore ways in which sport managers can avoid or minimize these claims.

Potential Causes of Action Using Products Liability Law

A person injured by a defective product has three potential causes of action under products liability law:

1 Negligence.
2 Strict liability.
3 Breach of warranty.

Negligence Claims

A manufacturer, seller, or supplier may be sued for negligence in design, manufacturing, or distribution of a defective product, or for negligent failure to warn about an unobvious (and therefore unreasonable) risk presented by the product.

Negligent design. Design defects are defects that are inherent in the design of a product. A negligent design claim asserts that a duty was breached in the design phase of the product, causing an unsafe product to be distributed. In *Dudley Sports Co. v. Schmitt* (1972), a baseball-pitching machine injured a custodian when he

Exhibit 14.3   Product warning label in baseball-pitching machine case (*Dudley Sports Co. v. Schmitt*, 1972).

WARNING! SAFETY FIRST.

READ INSTRUCTIONS BEFORE ROTATING MACHINE EITHER ELECTRICALLY OR MANUALLY.

STAY CLEAR OF THROWING ARM AT ALL TIMES.

DON'T REMOVE THIS PACKING BLOCK UNTIL YOU FULLY UNDERSTAND THE OPERATION OF THE THROWING ARM AND THE DANGER INVOLVED.

---

bumped the unplugged machine and the throwing arm was triggered unexpectedly. The court held that the pitching machine was defective because it had been designed without a protective guard around the throwing arm. This case is an example of a case in which a court found the manufacturer liable for negligently designing a product that proved unsafe because it lacked a safety feature that would have protected against an unobvious danger.

Negligent failure to warn. In *Dudley Sports Co. v. Schmitt* (1972), the court also found that the manufacturer had been negligent in failing to provide an adequate warning about the danger of a baseball pitching machine. The only warning provided with the machine was a label that read as indicated in Exhibit 14.3. The court ruled that the manufacturer should have provided a more specific warning about the propensity of the throwing arm to snap forward even when the machine was not plugged in. Additionally, some courts have held that failure to warn about the inherent risks of using sports equipment may establish product liability even when there is no underlying manufacturing or design defect. In *Prince v. Parachutes, Inc.* (1984), the court ruled that the plaintiff, who became a quadriplegic as a result of a skydiving collision, had a legitimate claim for failure to warn. He admitted that there was nothing wrong with his parachute, claiming instead that the cause of the collision was his inability to control the chute, which was too advanced for his skill level. The court agreed that he would not have used such an advanced piece of equipment if a warning about such a risk had been sewn into the parachute itself, instead of only being provided in a detailed user's manual that came with the chute, and thus found the warning inadequate. Courts have also held that manufacturers have a duty to warn consumers, not just about dangers inherent in a product's normal use, but also about dangers associated with foreseeable misuses (Van der Smissen, 1990). Finally, failure to warn claims can also be brought by persons who are not actual consumers or users of the products; thus, bystanders who are passively enjoying the benefit of the product can also assert product liability claims against manufacturers. A consumer does not have to be the purchaser of product, they may be a family member, employee, guest, or mere donee from the purchaser (*Patch v. Hillerich & Bradsby*, 2011).

Defenses to negligent product claims. Defenses to a negligence products liability claim include:

- The defect or failure to warn was not the proximate cause of the injury.
- The plaintiff was contributorily negligent.
- The plaintiff assumed any increased risk created by the defect that was beyond the inherent risk of the activity itself.
- The danger was open and obvious.
- The product was not in fact defective.
- An adequate warning was provided.

Strict Liability Claims

Most claims based in tort are concerned with fault or intent. Strict liability is an exception to this approach and holds a manufacturer or seller liable for an injury caused by a defective product even if it was reasonably careful in designing and manufacturing the product and regardless whether the manufacturer's conduct contributed to the injury directly. Strict liability for defective products is based on a public policy rationale that responsibility for unreasonably dangerous products ought to be placed where it will most

Exhibit 14.4 Factors in the risk-utility balancing test (Restatement [Third] of Torts, 2010).

Magnitude of the danger
Likelihood of injury
Obviousness of the danger
Cost and technological feasibility of a safer design
Adequacy of warnings
Desirability and usefulness of the product as designed   Level of consumer awareness of the risk

Social utility   Consumer risk

effectively reduce the risks to consumers. Defects in products can be either *manufacturing defects* (does not conform to design specifications or performance standards) or *design defects* (the design itself is what makes it unreasonably dangerous) (Stearns, 2001). Because products often pose dangers beyond the contemplation of ordinary consumers but foreseeable to the manufacturer or seller, responsibility is placed on them through the strict liability cause of action, thus relieving the consumer of the difficult challenge of having to track down hard-to-find evidence of corporate negligence. Policymakers also reason that manufacturers and merchants are in the best position to spread the costs of consumer safety and litigation by building them into the prices of their products. Additionally, exposure to strict liability is thought to motivate businesses to take consumer safety seriously (Garrett, 1972; Nader, 1972; Plant, 1957).

Prevailing in a strict liability claim. To prevail in a strict liability claim, a plaintiff must establish that the product was indeed defective by proving that the defect was present at the time the product left the manufacturer's control, and that it was unreasonably dangerous to consumers. Traditionally, a product would be considered unreasonably dangerous if the ordinary consumer would be unaware of the nature and extent of the danger, or if an economically feasible safer design existed. Several jurisdictions, however, have begun to adopt the position recommended in the Restatement (Third) of Torts (2010) that courts should use a risk–utility balancing test to determine the unreasonableness of the danger. If, on balance, the social utility of the product outweighs the risk to the consumer, then it will not be considered unreasonably dangerous. The factors to be weighed include those presented in Exhibit 14.4.

Wallach v. American Home Products Corp. (2001) illustrates the application of risk–utility balancing in a case where the plaintiff, who was an experienced treadmill jogger, was injured when he fell off the back of a treadmill. He sued the manufacturer in strict liability, claiming that the treadmill's design was unreasonably dangerous because it had no side handrails and because the front motor cover forced him too far back to be able to reach the front handrail when he lost his balance. The court found that, while there is always a risk of falling off, this product's risk was minimal because it provided the user with complete control of grade, speed, and stride. Additionally, the court disagreed that a safer design was feasible, because it found no evidence that side rails were safer than front rails; indeed, there was evidence that normal human reaction time would not have enabled the plaintiff to grab a side rail before he was thrown off after suddenly losing his balance. Thus, the lack of side rails, while not decreasing the likelihood of injury, did not increase it either. Finally, the court concluded that the danger of falling off the treadmill was open and obvious, particularly to an experienced user like Wallach, who thus could be held to have assumed the risk. Balancing these risk factors against the social utility of the treadmill, which allows users to get cardiovascular exercise without undue exposure to bad weather, traffic, or unsafe surfaces, the court held that the utility of the treadmill outweighed the risks to the consumer, and thus the product was not unreasonably dangerous. Therefore, Wallach's strict liability claim was rejected.

Defenses to a strict liability claim. Defenses available to the manufacturer or seller include:

- Unforeseeable misuse by the consumer.
- Alteration of the product after it left the manufacturer's control.
- Predictable deterioration of an aging product.

- Provision of an adequate warning.
- Secondary assumption of the risk by the consumer.
- Social utility that outweighs the consumer risk so that the product is not unreasonably dangerous.

It should be noted that in those jurisdictions that have adopted risk–utility balancing, provision of a warning is only one factor in determining the reasonableness of the risk and will not serve as a complete defense sufficient in itself to defeat a strict liability claim (Samborn, 1998).

The predictable deterioration defense would be used when a product malfunctions due to its age. Because all products eventually wear out, it would be unfair to hold the manufacturer responsible for an injury caused by predictable deterioration. The defense of unforeseeable misuse by the consumer might be used by a golf club manufacturer who has been sued by a plaintiff who was injured by breaking her club when she smashed it against a tree in frustration over her poor play. If golf clubs had to be designed to withstand such forces, they would not be well suited for hitting a golf ball with appropriate distance and accuracy. In another example of the unforeseeable misuse defense, a court found for the defendant in holding that the plaintiff's consumption of 125 ephedrine tablets per day was an unforeseeable misuse of that nutritional supplement (*Green v. BDI Pharmaceuticals*, 2001).

Breach of Warranty Claims

A **warranty** is an assertion of fact or promise made by a manufacturer or seller that is relied upon as part of the consumer transaction. Several warranties may be involved in the sale of sports equipment. When such warranties are found to be false, a breach of warranty claim may be brought. Breach of warranty claims are contract-based actions, so **privity of contract** (a direct contractual relationship between user and provider) may be required in some states; however, many states do not require privity for breach of warranty claims in personal injury actions. There are two types of warranty: express and implied. An **express warranty** is one that is explicitly made by a manufacturer or seller, either orally or in writing, or as a visual image (e.g., in a catalog or advertisement). This type of warranty is intended to induce a purchase by making an assertion of fact or a promise regarding the quality of the goods. An implied warranty can take two forms: implied warranty of merchantability and implied warranty of fitness. The **implied warranty of merchantability** is an implied promise that the product is fit for its ordinary intended use and thus is merchantable (or saleable). It accompanies any sale of goods by a merchant in the regular course of their business. Such a warranty accompanying a purchase of catcher's masks would imply that those masks would protect a face as well as any ordinary catcher's mask on the market. The **implied warranty of fitness** accompanies a sale when the seller has reason to know the particular purpose of a purchase and the buyer relies on the seller's expertise in providing a product appropriate for that purpose.

Defenses to breach of warranty claims. Defenses to breach of warranty claims include:

- Lack of privity between user and provider (depending on state law).
- Provision of an adequate disclaimer (such as a statement indicating that the item is "For Sale – As Is").
- Unforeseeable misuse by the consumer.

In addition to understanding the law related to torts and the prevalent liability issues in your sport organization, you must also understand legal issues related to participant violence and claims based on recklessness and intentional torts of assault and battery. The following sections examine these areas.

Liability Issues Regarding Participant Violence in Sport

Imagine you are taking a stroll around your campus on a beautiful spring day. As you meander down the sidewalk, you come upon a large individual who is blocking your way. You do not feel that it is appropriate that you should have to step off the sidewalk to accommodate this person, so you yell, "Excuse me, clear the way!" He does not respond to your demand. Incensed by his refusal to move, you push him and begin pummeling him with an umbrella you are carrying. In this scenario, you are clearly violating norms of social behavior in your conduct. Even if you were miffed by this intrusion upon your right of way, society would not tolerate your behavior. We do not condone physical violence as a reaction to discourtesy. If we did, we would have a very uncivil society indeed. This incident could very easily result in both criminal and civil sanctions against you.

However, if you take these same individuals engaging in the same behavior at an ice rink during a hockey game, society might not just condone the same behaviors, but actually reward or encourage it. In fact, pushing one's opponent with great force and sometimes using an implement (a hockey stick) to further intimidate the opposition is not uncommon. Thus, in many sports, and especially contact sports, we allow a degree of violent behavior that, if found in a nonsporting context, would subject the perpetrator of violence to criminal and/or civil sanctions.

In our roles as event and game managers, coaches, league administrators, program directors, or athletic directors, we need to find solutions to stem the increase in violence on the playing fields. Developing strategies to make athletic contests displays of sportsmanship and prevent unnecessary displays of violence makes sense legally, and it makes our sport organizations more socially responsible and competitively sound. To respond to the issues related to violence during competition, it is necessary to explore the legal frameworks that are used in dealing with issues of player-to-player violence in sport participation.

Participant Violence – Criminal Violations vs. Civil Claims

As the example above illustrated, certain types of conduct can result both in violations of criminal law, such as an assault or battery, as well as expose one to civil liability. While the underlying conduct is the same, criminal charges and civil claims differ in several important ways. One difference relates to who actually files the lawsuit. Criminal law concerns itself with societal harms based upon what the legislature decides is reprehensible or unacceptable conduct by society's members. If someone allegedly violates a criminal statute, the government, not the injured party, is responsible to enforce those statutes and bring a criminal complaint against the offender. In addition, the victim may also file a civil case against the alleged offender. In the civil case, the plaintiff/victim is seeking money damages for the injury. In the criminal case, the state is seeking retribution for the state in the form of a fine or incarceration. Additionally, keep in mind that criminal statutes have their own elements that must be proven; the elements of a crime are not synonymous with the elements of a civil action for assault or battery.

In sport, violent acts that could lead to potential criminal or civil liability typically include violence between participants during a sports contest and violence against sport officials.

Although violent behavior is a common occurrence in sport, relatively few criminal cases have arisen. There are a number of reasons for this infrequency, including the reluctance of prosecutors to bring criminal actions based on conduct in a sporting contest. Prosecutors often have demanding workloads dealing with "real" crime, such as rape, homicide, and burglary. Therefore, prosecutors may believe that it is a waste of taxpayer money to file criminal complaints based on sport violence; they need to use their resources to bring to justice those who commit more egregious crimes. They may also believe that the sport leagues are in the best position to control violence through internal regulation and punishment, should they desire to do so.

Even if a criminal action is brought to trial, juries often have difficulty seeing "criminal" behavior by athletes. In a very rare case, prosecutors in Kentucky brought criminal homicide charges against a coach for his actions toward a player who collapsed due to a heat stroke, but the jury only deliberated for 90 minutes to reach its "not guilty" verdict (English, 2009). Even though this example alleged reckless rather than violent behavior, it still illustrates the difficulty in pursuing criminal charges in a sport context. We also know that coaches and teams often reward athletes for violent behavior. Some league administrators appear to condone violence, and they sometimes use violence as a marketing strategy. Why should members of society be offended by this behavior if the behavior is not reprehensible to those within the sport?

Another case that illustrates the difficulty of attaining any real deterrence through criminal law for violent behavior occurring during a sporting contest, Todd Bertuzzi of the NHL Vancouver Canucks broke the neck of Steve Moore of the Colorado Avalanche in a game on March 8, 2004. Bertuzzi "sucker-punched" Moore in the head and then drove him to the ice, causing multiple fractures in Moore's neck and a concussion. Despite this senseless and egregious violence, Bertuzzi, after being charged with assault causing bodily harm, accepted a plea bargain with the Vancouver prosecutor for a one-year probation with 80 hours of community service and no criminal record (Samson, 2005). Due to the difficulties inherent in the current U.S. criminal system as mentioned above, violent acts of sport participants have primarily been addressed through several civil tort remedies.

Tort Law and Participant Violence

This section will focus on two primary areas in which civil claims based in tort law most often occurs – participant violence toward other participants and violence toward sports officials. As you will recall, tort law is concerned with individual civil wrongs. The state is not involved in civil cases; individual parties bring damage claims against each other. We mentioned at the beginning of this chapter that the spectrum of tort claims range from ordinary negligence to intentional torts. The distinctions made between types of torts are justifiable since there is a great difference between negligent behavior in which a plaintiff fails to act reasonably but does not intend to commit any harm and a situation in which a person intentionally acts in a way that is very likely to cause harm to someone.

These latter actions, which are characterized as intentional torts, carry different consequences. For example, in negligence actions a plaintiff receives compensatory damages, which means that the defendant pays damages in an effort to "make good" or replace the loss or injury sustained. If the plaintiff has suffered personal injury, then compensatory damages will pay for medical bills, lost wages, and pain and suffering. In this way, the plaintiff receives compensation, but there is no attempt to punish the defendant since the defendant's behavior was unintentional.

However, if the defendant commits an intentional tort, there may be punitive damages which may be awarded in addition to the compensatory damages. Punitive damages are awarded to punish the defendant and to deter that type of conduct from occurring again. Intentional torts are reprehensible to society, so juries and courts are given the latitude in this situation to award damages that have the sole purpose of sending a message to the defendant not to repeat that type of behavior.

In the middle of this spectrum of tort law lie actions based on **reckless misconduct or gross negligence** in which someone intends to commit an act, but not to cause harm. Exhibit 14.5 presents the spectrum of tort law actions. First, we will examine the legal requirements related to two intentional torts that arise in sport/recreation settings: assault and battery. Then we will discuss the elements of reckless misconduct. Lastly, we will explore these concepts in the context of violent behavior between co-participants and violent behavior toward sports officials.

Exhibit 14.5 The torts spectrum.

Negligent Behavior	Reckless Misconduct/Gross/Negligence/ Willful Wanton Misconduct	Intentional Torts
No intent to harm	No intent to harm but conscious indifference to risk	Intent to harm
Compensatory damages	Compensatory damages (generally)	Compensatory damages and punitive damages

Assault

Assault is an intentional tort that often arises in the context of sport violence. The focus of this tort is on some type of menacing or threatening behavior (Restatement [Second] of Torts § 21 (1965)). There is no contact involved in this tort; battery deals with contact. Three elements must be established by a plaintiff to plead a successful cause of action based on assault. They are:

1 Intent to cause immediate harm, which is menacing or threatening behavior.
2 Apprehension of immediate harm by the plaintiff.
3 Lack of consent.

Intent to Cause Immediate Harm

In regard to the first element, how do courts ascertain what is really intended by a defendant? If we look only at subjective intent, as evidenced by a defendant's motivation, it would be difficult ever to prove intent. For example, if we asked a person who had just hit someone with a baseball bat whether he meant to harm the person, most likely that defendant would disclaim any intent to hurt the person in an effort to avoid the legal consequences. He would say that he didn't really "mean" any harm or that he was not "motivated" by any intent to injure the person.

Because of this difficulty, the law provides its own definition of intent, one that allows courts to look objectively at the circumstances to determine what was intended. In the baseball bat example, the courts would look at what was actually done and from that determine intent based on what was "substantially certain" to happen from that act. In this case, hitting a person with a baseball bat is "substantially certain" to result in injury. Courts use the test of whether the consequences of an act are "substantially certain" to occur (Restatement [Second] of Torts § 8A, 1965) in order to fashion a more objective measure of intent.

Apprehension by the Plaintiff

In regard to the second element, three aspects must be considered. First, the plaintiff, in order to be apprehensive, must be *aware* of the threatening or menacing behavior. For example, if I raise my hand as if I were ready to strike A but I do so behind A's back and she cannot see my gesture, there is no apprehension and therefore no assault. Similarly, you cannot assault someone who is comatose or asleep. Apprehension is commonly analogous to fear or worry; however, as an element of civil assault, apprehension means awareness.

Second, according to the view taken by the Restatement (Second) of Torts, apprehension is gauged through the eyes of the victim (plaintiff). If I threaten X with a water pistol, yet X believes it to be a real pistol and is therefore apprehensive, the second element is met. What is at issue is not the actual ability to carry out the threat; it is the apparent ability to do so as gauged by the plaintiff.

Third, there must be an immediate threat. If I threaten to punch someone next week, this does not meet the elements of assault. There is no immediacy to my threat.

Lack of Consent

The last element, lack of consent, becomes the crucial issue within the context of sport. The issue of lack of consent has been included in the elements of the tort to emphasize its importance. We could also look at consent as a defense to the tort.

The issue of consent is the crux of most discussions of sport violence. **Consent** may be defined as "the willingness that an act or invasion of an interest shall take place" (Restatement [Second] of Torts § 892 (1979)). Consent need not be communicated overtly; it may also be customarily understood.

In assault, we may have threatening behavior, and the plaintiff may be apprehensive, but there is no cause of action if we can find that the menacing behavior was somehow permitted within the sport context – that is, if we find consent.

How do we ascertain what is consented to within a sport setting? Consider the following hypothetical case.

Considering … Consent

A Major League Baseball player intentionally throws a fastball at the batter's torso to "encourage" the batter not to crowd the plate. The ball zips past the batter, but the batter becomes upset at this affront and charges the pitcher's mound with bat in hand. The batter throws the bat at the pitcher and misses by a few inches.

Questions

- In the above scenario how many assaults, if any, do we have?
- Was either of these threatening situations consented to, thus negating the assault?

Note how you would answer the questions and then check your responses using the Analysis & Discussion at the end of this chapter.

As this hypothetical case shows, the issue of consent depends upon an understanding of the nature of the sport. From the starting point of the rules of the sport, we then analyze what continues to be acceptable behavior. We look at the culture of the sport and see what the sport has done to identify the parameters of permissible conduct.

Sport and recreation administrators are in control of the issue of consent and, by extension, the degree of permissible aggression and violence within sport. The courts do not decide in a vacuum what level of violence and intimidation is acceptable. Coaches, officials, rule-makers, and administrators of leagues decide what the landscape of aggression and violence will look like in various sports. We define for the courts what behaviors are permissible within various sports and the different competitive levels of those sports. If we believe that levels of aggression are unacceptable, it is our responsibility to set those parameters, which will then be adopted by courts as they deal with civil cases of assault or battery.

Battery

In many cases, violence in sport occurs as actual physical contact, some of which may be well outside the rules or the acceptable levels of contact permitted within the sport. The intentional tort of battery differs from assault in that battery involves actual physical contact, not merely menacing or threatening behavior.

Elements of Battery

The intentional tort of **battery** is offensive contact resulting from one's acts intending to cause a harmful or offensive contact with another person or the imminent apprehension of such contact. (See Restatement [Second] of Torts §§ 18 and 19 (1965).) To prevail in a claim for battery, the plaintiff must show the following elements:

1 Intent to cause harmful or offensive touching.
2 Harmful or offensive touching.
3 Lack of consent.

Regarding the first element, remember that, like assault, battery is an intentional tort. As with assault, intent is defined in an objective manner; the question of motivation is irrelevant.

Also, note the word *touching* in the first element. Although the contact that becomes battery in sport often has a violent context, it is not technically necessary to have touching that causes bodily harm. The gist of this tort is unconsented touching; the contact need not be violent. For example, let's assume that a sport manager touched his assistant on the shoulder every morning when he stopped by the assistant's desk. Even though the assistant shies away from the contact (a clear message that this touching lacks consent), the manager continues to engage in this behavior. Technically, this is battery, since it meets the elements of the tort, regardless of the lack of physical injury.

In regard to the second element, the plaintiff does not have to be aware of the touching for a battery to occur. This is different from assault, where the plaintiff has to have been "apprehensive," denoting awareness. Battery can occur even if the plaintiff was sleeping or otherwise lacking in the ability to feel the contact. For example, if a surgeon performing a leg amputation removed the incorrect appendage, this is technically battery, even though (hopefully) the patient was unaware of the mistake as it occurred. The actual touching may also occur through an instrumentality over which the defendant has control. If I hit you with a baseball bat or with a ball that I threw at you, that meets the requirement of touching, even though I have not made direct physical contact with you. The touching must be harmful or offensive. Bodily contact is "offensive if it offends a reasonable sense of personal dignity" (Restatement [Second] of Torts § 19 (1965)).

As with assault, the critical element in most sport violence battery cases is consent. We must look to the culture and norms of a sport to ascertain what is acceptable contact (and therefore consented to) within that sport.

The following hypothetical case addresses the important aspect of intent.

Considering ... Intent

During an adult recreational softball league game, a runner is on first base. When a ground ball is hit to the shortstop, the runner begins to run toward second base. The shortstop quickly fields the ground ball and tosses it to the second baseman, who tags second base and throws the ball to first to complete the double play. The second baseman, after throwing the ball to first, steps well away from second base toward the pitcher's mound. Although the double play has been completed, the runner from first veers out of the base path, continues to run at the second baseman, and hits the second baseman with great force. The runner did not slow down, and he also brought his arm up into the second baseman's chin, at the point of contact. The runner is a much larger man than the second baseman, outweighing him by at least 40 pounds. The second baseman suffers severe injury to his jaw.

Questions

- Is this battery?
- What if the runner testifies at trial that he did not mean to hurt the second baseman?
- What if the runner alleges that he was not motivated by any desire to hurt a member of the opposing team?
- What are the natural and probable consequences of running at full speed and hitting a person in such a manner, considering the size disparity between the two men?
- What consequences were "substantially certain" to result from the runner making contact with the second baseman in this way?

Note how you would answer the questions and then check your responses using the Analysis & Discussion at the end of this chapter.

Exhibit 14.6 Factors for ascertaining the reasonableness of the use of force with children (Restatement [Second] of Torts §§ 147, 150, 151, and 155).

1 The age, sex, and condition of the child.
2 The nature of the offensive conduct.
3 Whether force was reasonably necessary to compel obedience to a proper command.
4 Whether the force was disproportionate to the offense or likely to cause serious injury.

Privilege as a Defense to Battery

Two aspects of privilege are relevant as defenses to battery (Restatement [Second] of Torts § 10). The first pertains to a concept commonly known as **self-defense**, that is, a person may be entitled to use reasonable force to defend himself or herself from attack. To use self-defense, however, a person cannot be the initiator of contact.

The second aspect of privilege, which is relevant for those who teach or coach in an educational environment, is the privilege to use **reasonable force** to control, train, or educate a child (6 Am. Jur. 2d *Assault & Battery* § 104). To ascertain the reasonableness of a use of force, we look at a variety of factors, including those presented in Exhibit 14.6.

If the force used is excessive, then the privilege is defeated, and there is battery. The following hypothetical case addresses this aspect of privilege.

Considering ... Reasonable Force

At a junior high school football practice, the adult coach is displeased with a player's tackling technique. The coach yells loudly at the child, age 12, and then grabs the facemask on the child's helmet, twists it, and throws the child to the ground. The child suffers a severe neck injury.

Question

*   When the coach is sued for battery, can he use the defense of privilege to argue that this contact was necessary to train and discipline the young football player?

Note how you would answer the question and then check your response using the Analysis & Discussion at the end of this chapter.

Reckless Misconduct

In many circumstances involving player violence, courts do not find that an intentional tort has occurred. However, a cause of action may nonetheless exist so that an injured player may receive compensation. **Reckless misconduct**, which is usually synonymous with *gross negligence* or *willful and wanton misconduct*, is defined as follows:

A person acts with recklessness in engaging in conduct if:

a. the person knows of the risk of harm created by the conduct or knows facts that make that risk obvious to anyone in the person's situation, and
b. the precaution that would eliminate or reduce that risk involves burdens that are so slight relative to the magnitude of the risk as to render the person's failure to adopt the precaution a demonstration of the person's indifference to the risk. (Restatement [Third] of Torts § 2 (2010)).

Unlike the theory of negligence discussed previously, which is well established, the use of reckless misconduct in cases involving athletic participants has slowly emerged as a legal theory. In the past 26 years, numerous states have adopted or applied the theory of reckless misconduct in sport cases: Illinois: *Nabozny v. Barnhill* (1975); Missouri: *Ross v. Clouser* (1982); New Mexico: *Kabella v. Bouschelle* (1983); Massachusetts:

Gauvin v. Clark (1989); Nebraska: *Dotzler v. Tuttle* (1990); Louisiana: *Picou v. Hartford Insurance Co.* (1990); Ohio: *Marchetti v. Kalish* (1990); Texas: *Connell v. Payne* (1991); California: *Knight v. Jewett* (1992); New Jersey: *Crawn v. Camp* (1994); and Kentucky: *Hoke v. Cullinan* (1995).

Violent Actions Between Co-Participants in a Sport/Recreation Contest

There is clearly growing acceptance by courts of the reckless-misconduct standard to impose co-participant liability. This standard is becoming so well established that it is difficult to believe that any state presented with the issue for the first time would not follow the lead of *Nabozny*. Thus, we need to examine the court's reasoning in *Nabozny* in the following Case Opinion.

Nabozny v. Barnhill

CASE OPINION   334 N.E.2d 258 (Ill. App. Ct. 1975)

FACTS

A soccer match was held between two amateur teams at Duke Child's Field in Winnetka, Illinois. Plaintiff played the position of goalkeeper for the Hansa team. Members of both teams were of high school age. Approximately 20 minutes after play had begun, a Winnetka player kicked the ball over the midfield line. Two players chased the ball, and a Hansa player passed the ball to the plaintiff. The plaintiff went down on one knee to receive the pass and pulled the ball to his chest. The defendant player from Winnetka continued to run in the direction of the plaintiff and kicked the left side of the plaintiff's head, causing severe injuries.

Witnesses agreed that the defendant had time to avoid contact with plaintiff and that the plaintiff was in the "penalty area," an area in which the rules prohibit contact with the goalkeeper when he is in possession of the ball. Experts agreed that the contact in question should not have occurred.

In the action to recover damages for personal injuries, trial was before a jury. However, the trial court directed a verdict in favor of the defendant on the basis that, as a matter of law, the plaintiff had no cause of action against the defendant. The trial court found that no duty of care existed to benefit the plaintiff. The plaintiff appealed this ruling.

HOLDING

The appellate court reversed and remanded.

RATIONALE

The appellate court found a "dearth of case law involving organized athletic competition wherein one of the participants is charged with negligence."

* * *

This court believes that the law should not place unreasonable burdens on the free and vigorous participation in sports by our youth. However, we believe that organized athletic competition does not exist in a vacuum. Rather, some of the restraints of civilization must accompany every athlete on to the playing field. One of the educational benefits of organized athletic competition to our youth is the development of discipline and self-control.

* * *

For these reasons, this court believes that when athletes are engaged in an athletic competition; all teams are trained and coached by knowledgeable personnel; a recognized set of rules governs the conduct of the competition; and a safety rule is contained therein which is primarily designed to protect players from serious injury, a player is then charged with a duty to every other player on the field to refrain from conduct proscribed by a safety rule. A reckless disregard for the safety of other players cannot be excused. To engage in such conduct is to create an intolerable and unreasonable risk of serious injury to other participants.

* * *

It is our opinion that a player is liable for injury in a tort action if his conduct is such that it is either deliberate, willful or with a reckless disregard for the safety of the other player so as to cause injury to that player.

QUESTIONS

1 Based on this decision, is mere negligence actionable in player-to-player violence cases in contact sports? Cite language from the decision that supports your view.

2 Why would this court decline to set the standard of care at mere negligence? What effect would a negligence standard have upon "free and vigorous participation in sports"?

3 Why did the court decide that it was necessary to intervene at all in situations of player violence? Discuss what the notion that the "restraints of civilization must accompany every athlete on to the playing field" means in this context.

Nabozny is the seminal case in the realm of player-to-player violence. Most jurisdictions continue to follow the reckless disregard standard today. As one exception, Wisconsin courts adopted a negligence standard for player-to-player contact (*Lestina v. West Bend Mutual Insurance Co.*, 1993). In that state, however, the legislature acted in response to the courts' adoption of the negligence standard by passing a statute (Wisconsin Stat. §895.525 (4 m) (a)) that provides immunity from negligence actions for participants in a recreational activity that involves physical contact between persons in an amateur sport. In an application of that statute, the Wisconsin Supreme Court held that cheerleading participants were immune from a negligence action as it held that cheerleading was a "contact sport" for the purposes of this statute (*Noffke v. Bakke*, 2009).

Another example of the "contact sports" exception is found in the case of *Feld v. Borkowski* (2010). In that case, the Iowa Supreme Court held that softball was a "contact sport" and therefore, a participant cannot recover damages against another participant unless the offending behavior was reckless misconduct. In this situation, the plaintiff was playing first base during a team batting practice. The defendant was batting and as he made contact with the ball, which went to left field, the bat left his hands and hit the plaintiff in the head. The plaintiff sued for negligence, but that suit was dismissed because there is no liability in this situation unless the defendant's conduct was reckless. Although the Iowa Supreme Court agreed that the reckless conduct standard applied to softball, the case was remanded to the lower court to ascertain whether the defendant's behavior was reckless. The plaintiff had provided expert testimony that the bat's flight was aberrant, and this was sufficient to support an inference of recklessness by the defendant as he released the bat after contact with the ball.

In a case decided in 2012, in the state of Michigan, the court extended the reckless misconduct standard to co-participants in the recreational activity of tobogganing. The defendant, who was in the front of the sled, was not a competent driver and the toboggan crashed. The plaintiff rider on the toboggan sued the defendant, but the court affirmed summary judgment for the defendant as it held that the proper standard was reckless misconduct in this situation, not negligence.

In sport where any contact between participants is part of the game, the majority of courts hold that the recklessness standard is required. And, even in some sports that typically do not involve participant contact, if contact with other objects such as golf balls or golf carts in inherent, the standard will be still be recklessness. For example, although golf is not a contact sport, some courts have used the recklessness standard for golfers. In *Bertin v. Mann* (2018), the court considered whether being hit by a golf cart during a round of golf is an inherent risk of the sport. If so, a plaintiff would need to demonstrate that the defendant acted recklessly to succeed with a claim. An interesting law review article by Dexter (2012) argues that the negligence standard is the appropriate one for the sport of golf. An article by Wilson (2011) suggests that the negligence standard be adopted for mixed martial arts competitions.

There are essentially two policy reasons for adhering to the reckless disregard standard:

1   The promotion of vigorous participation in athletic activities.
2   To avoid a flood of litigation that would ensue if the negligence standard were employed.

The following 2008 case has modified the *Nabonzy* standard for cases in Illinois involving full contact sports such as ice hockey and football.

Karas v. Strevell

884 N.E.2d 122 (Ill. 2008)	**FOCUS** CASE

FACTS

On January 25, 2004, Benjamin Karas, a member of his high school's junior varsity ice hockey team, was injured when two members of the opposing team body checked Karas from behind, causing neck and head injuries. The hockey league's rules prohibited body checking from behind, and every player's jersey had the word *STOP* on the back to remind players not to hit others from behind.

Karas's father filed suit on his son's behalf, alleging that the two players who hit his son should be liable for their willful and wanton conduct. He also alleged that the hockey associations should be liable for their negligence and willful and wanton conduct in failing to enforce the body-checking prohibition and for failing to instruct players properly regarding this rule. The trial court dismissed all claims. The appellate court affirmed dismissal of only the willful and wanton claim against the hockey associations.

HOLDING

The Illinois Supreme Court affirmed in part and reversed in part the appellate court judgment. The court affirmed the trial court judgment. The court remanded the matter to the trial court to permit the plaintiff to amend the complaint to plead facts to conform to the decision, if the plaintiff were able to do so.

RATIONALE

The case of *Pfister v. Shusta*, 657 N.E.2d 1013 (Ill. 1995), is the controlling precedent in Illinois, which adopted the exception to the standard of ordinary care for participants engaged in contact sports. Under *Pfister* a participant in a contact sport may not be held liable for negligent conduct that injures a co-participant. Instead, liability must be predicated upon behavior that is intentional or willful or wanton (essentially the *Nabozny* standard).

One the one hand, in the context of hockey, football, and other sports involving violent contact, some rules violations are inherent and anticipated in a sport, and not all rules violations in themselves are sufficient to impose liability. On the other hand, as the *Nabozny* court stated, "Some of the restraints of civilization must accompany every athlete on to the playing field" (p. 134).

In this case, however, the *Pfister* standard is unworkable in the context of ice hockey or football, because body checking or tackling evinces a "conscious disregard for the safety of the person being struck" (p. 132). Physical contact in these "full-contact sports" is a fundamental part of the way the game is played, so it is problematic to adopt a standard that holds participants liable for consciously disregarding the safety of co-participants. The traditional willful and wanton standard is not workable and is contrary to the *Pfister* rationale, which was developed in order to avoid a chilling effect upon the participants who are simply engaging in the inherent risks of an activity. As currently pled in the complaint, the conduct by the two opposing players would not rise to the standard set forth by the court. Although the body check was a rules violation, there were no allegations that it was deliberate or occurred after play had been stopped. Therefore, in sports such as ice hockey or football, a participant breaches a duty of care to a co-participant only if the participant intentionally injures the co-participant or engages in conduct "totally outside the range of the ordinary activity involved in the sport" (p. 134).

The *Karas* court recognized that rules and anticipated violent conduct during competition can vary based on the nature of the sport. In the context of hockey, football, and other sports involving violent contact, some rules violations are inherent and anticipated in a sport, therefore the mere rules violations in themselves may be sufficient to impose liability. On the other hand, the court also noted that, as the *Nabozny* court stated, "Some of the restraints of civilization must accompany every athlete on to the playing field" (p. 134).

Violent Actions Toward Sports Officials

Unfortunately, largely due to the increasing violence in youth sport, 19 states have adopted specific statutes providing for criminal penalties for those who assault sports officials, while two other states have civil statutes ("Sports officials' legislative scorecard," 2019); legislation is also under consideration in additional states. Further, some states with existing legislation are seeking to reclassify violence against referees as a felony (as opposed to a misdemeanor). Bipartisan legislation in the Ohio General Assembly seeks to ensure that umpires and referees in the state remain safe by raising the penalty for assaulting a sports official while on the job from a misdemeanor to a fifth-degree felony, punishable by up to a year in prison and a $2,500 fine (Pelzer, 2019). In one particularly egregious scenario, after a referee issued a yellow card during a recreational soccer game, a 17-year-old player punched the referee in the head. After a week in a coma, the referee, Ricardo Portillo, died (Whiteside, 2013). Much of the violence toward sports officials is perpetrated by unhappy parents. Whether "sports rage" is perpetrated by players, parents, coaches, or fans, game officials are increasingly becoming the target of this excessive violence.

Conclusion

Understanding negligence liability is critical for managers in sport organizations. This chapter addressed the legal theory of negligence and applicable defenses. This chapter also discussed the most prevalent liability claims against sport organizations relating to participants, as well as liability issues pertaining to violent acts committed by participants. Lastly, the chapter considered liability for defective sport products. Increased knowledge of liability issues should translate into better preventive efforts to enhance participants' experiences by making them safer and more enriching. Satisfied participants lead to better competitive success in the sport marketplace.

Discussion Questions

1 What are the elements of negligence? Define and discuss each.

2 Explain the concept of negligence per se.

3 Explain the act of God defense. What two elements must exist to use this defense?

4 What is the core concept for both contributory and comparative negligence? What is the difference between the two?

5 Based on your understanding of an inherent risk being one that is "obvious and necessary," list a number of activities or sports and then identify some inherent risks for each activity or sport. Do you think that inherent risks may change as technology and rules change in sport? Explain.

6 What is the difference between primary assumption of risk and secondary assumption of risk?

7 Discuss a number of aspects of competent instruction or training. Give examples of poor instruction in a sport or physical activity of your choice.

8 What are the key items to consider when arranging transportation for an athletic team?

9 Discuss whether or not having a cause of action in strict liability for defective products makes good sense. Why is it fair to hold manufacturers strictly liable for defective products without regard to how careful they were in designing and manufacturing those products? What is the benefit to consumers of having the option to pursue a strict liability claim?

10 An adult player in a recreational softball game strikes out. He becomes angry and throws his bat at the catcher, hitting the catcher and fracturing his nose. Do you think that a prosecutor would believe that this is criminal behavior and file charges against the batter? Why or why not? Regardless of the criminal aspect, what civil cause of action would the catcher have against the batter? Explain the elements of the cause of action.

11 How do you determine whether a certain contact was consented to within a game? Give examples of contact that might be consented to within professional football versus youth level football.

Learning Activities

1 Find five agencies or companies via an online search that offer certification for personal trainers. Compare and contrast the rigor of each certification. What are the criteria for becoming certified? What type of education is required? Assess whether any of these certifications ensure that a personal trainer you might hire is sufficiently qualified for the position.

2 Do an Internet search to locate a sample emergency action plan for a sport or recreation program of your choice. For example, the NCAA has developed criteria for an EAP in intercollegiate sport in its *NCAA Sports Medicine Handbook, Guideline 1c Emergency Care and Coverage*, found at www.ncaapublications.com/productdownloads/MD12.pdf.

3 Conduct an online search to find your state concussions law for youth sport. What are the specific provisions of the law? Is there an enforcement aspect of the law? Discuss the positive and negative aspects of the law.

4 As a youth league administrator, you are concerned with the lack of sportsmanlike behavior shown by many parents who attend your games. Often, they make very rude comments to the game officials, and, on a couple of occasions, one of your supervisors has had to intervene before a parent physically attacked a referee. Research whether your state has a statute making the assault of a sports official a criminal offense. Then, prepare a memorandum to the parents identifying their possible liability for their interactions with game officials. If your state does not have such a specific statute, make your recommendations for parental conduct based on your state's definition of criminal assault generally.

5 Do an Internet search regarding the player violence that occurred on March 8, 2004, in an NHL game between Steve Moore of the Colorado Avalanche and Vancouver Canucks player Todd Bertuzzi. Ascertain what happened in this case, both as to the criminal charges that were filed against Bertuzzi in British Columbia and as to the civil case that was filed by Moore against Bertuzzi. Was the handling of this incident of violence consistent with what you learned in this chapter?

Case Study

In the case of *Rostai v. Neste Enterprises*, 138 Cal. App. 4th 326 (2006), a client alleged that he suffered a heart attack in his first training workout because of the negligence of the personal trainer in failing to investigate the cardiac risk factors of the client. The appellate court stated that the trainer's function is to challenge a participant, and "inherent in that process is the risk that the trainer will not accurately assess the participant's ability and the participant will be injured as a result." The court, therefore, held that the client had assumed the risk of this erroneous advice and assessment.

1 What are the consequences of using the "reckless disregard" standard in cases involving a teacher, coach, or personal trainer?
2 As a matter of policy, discuss whether it makes sense to essentially "immunize" a coach, teacher, or personal trainer from the consequences of their failure to act as a reasonably prudent professional.

Considering ... Analysis and Discussion

Duty of Care

Yes, Lefour will argue that the university assumed a duty of care in this case. When the university assumed the obligation of assigning students to internship sites, it assumed the duty to act with reasonable care in choosing sites that did not create a foreseeable zone of risk for the students.

Negligence Per Se

Yes, this plaintiff could win this case based on negligence per se. The plaintiff would not have to call a swimming pool design expert to testify that this pool was unsafe. The pool was not constructed in accordance with the pool law, and the provisions of that law were there specifically to prevent the type of entrapment incident that occurred here. Thus, the violation of the law establishes a breach of the standard of care, and all the plaintiff has to show is causation, established by the fact that this incident would not have happened if the pool law had been followed.

The Act of God Defense

Although lightning is "an act of God," it was foreseeable. The storm was imminent and lightning was close. The coach continued to practice and ignored the danger. In this case, the coach could not use the act of God defense successfully because the natural disaster was foreseeable.

Comparative Negligence

If a pure comparative negligence model is applicable, then Bright would receive $40,000 in damages, since his award of $100,000 would be reduced by the percentage of fault attributable to his behavior (60 percent), even though the percentage of fault attributable to his behavior exceeds the percentage of fault attributable to the defendant's conduct. Under pure comparative negligence Bright would recover damages even if he were found 99 percent negligent, in the amount of $1,000 ($100,000 minus $99,000).

In a jurisdiction that uses a modified comparative negligence rule of "50/50 not greater than," Bright would receive nothing, since the percentage of fault attributable to his behavior exceeds 50 percent. If the jury had found, for example, that Bright was 49 percent responsible for his own behavior, under this model, Bright would receive $51,000 ($100,000 minus $49,000).

Assumption of Risk

The answer to both questions is no, because the failure of the parachutes to open was caused by the negligence of the person who packed the chute or by the malfunction of the chute itself. In either case, these were not risks assumed by the skydiver; they are risks beyond what the skydiver anticipated when he began the jump. In this latter scenario, there is no primary assumption of risk.

Enforcement of Safety Rules

Most likely, they can prevail. Although Roche taught the proper sliding techniques at practice, she ignored Winn's previous dangerous behavior when she ran over the catcher the first time. Ignoring dangerous behavior can lead to a repetition of that behavior, since players will often repeat behaviors that have been successful and have not been punished by their coach. Roche, in allowing the dangerous behavior to continue, failed to act as a reasonable, prudent coach.

Consent

As we analyze the first two elements of assault, it seems clear that both elements are present. First, we do have menacing or threatening behavior in both the actions of the pitcher and the retaliatory behavior by the batter. Further, the batter would be apprehensive of a fastball thrown very close to his body. Likewise, the pitcher would be apprehensive of the behavior of the batter.

Therefore, we must address the issue of consent. To ascertain consent, we first look at the rules of the sport to see what behaviors are prohibited. Rules prohibit the intentional throwing of pitches at batters. It is up to the umpire's judgment, of course, to determine the intent of the pitcher – but if an umpire does decide that a pitcher is throwing intentionally at the batter, there are consequences. There are also, of course, prohibitions against the type of behavior engaged in by the batter. If the rules of the sport were the only consideration in analyzing consent, then we would have two assaults in this scenario. Consent, however, cannot be restricted to simply an analysis of the rules. We must look beyond the rules at the culture and context of the sport (Restatement [Second] of Torts § 50, comment b). In baseball, we know that players are taught from very early ages that pitchers must move batters away from the plate. When batters crowd the plate, they know that it is very likely that the pitcher will send a message by throwing a pitch at them. This behavior, even though it technically violates a rule of the sport, is consistent with the accepted norms of baseball. On the one hand, any coach, player, or umpire would attest to the fact that throwing at batters is an accepted custom in baseball, one that is intrinsic to the nature of that sport. The pitcher's actions are consented to, based on the nature of the sport, and there is no assault by the pitcher. On the other hand, even though we know of incidents in which the batter has "gone after" the pitcher, this rules violation is not treated as a custom or as part of the culture in the sport. Batters who engage in this retaliatory behavior are severely penalized by umpires and league sanctions; therefore, we can see that this type of behavior is not consented to within baseball. The behavior by the batter would be considered an assault.

Intent

Regardless of what the runner says about intent, there is intent to cause a harmful contact. Intent to touch is evident as we look at what actually transpired, rather than what the runner tells us about his motivation. As to the second element, we certainly have actual harmful contact. Finally, there is a lack of consent because this type of contact is forbidden by the rules and goes beyond what is acceptable within the custom of the sport. It is common for a runner to slide into a second baseman while the baseman is on or near the base, in an attempt to disrupt the double play. However, it is not permissible, after the play is over, to go well outside of the base path to make contact with an opposing player. This fact pattern reveals battery, and the jury may award compensatory and punitive damages.

Reasonable Force

The question is whether the force used here can be considered reasonable. In this scenario, the coach will likely lose in his assertion that the contact (battery) was privileged. The child was young, and the size difference between the adult coach and the player was considerable. The player was not being disruptive or unruly at practice; he simply was not tackling well. The force used was disproportionate to the offense, and serious injury ensued. This is a case in which the force used to discipline the player exceeded privilege. The coach is liable for battery.

References

Cases

Agbeti v. Los Angeles Unified Sch. Dist., 107 Cal. Rptr. 3d 182 (Cal. Ct. App. 2010).
Barth v. Board of Educ., 490 N.E.2d 77 (Ill. App. Ct. 1986).
Bellinger v. Ballston Spa Cent. Sch. Dist, 871 N.Y.S.2d 432 (App. Div. 2008).
Bertin v. Mann, 918 NW 2d 707 (Mich. Sup. Ct 2018).
Calouri v. County of Suffolk, 841 N.Y.S.2d 598 (App. Div. 2007).
Cann v. Stefanec, 2013 Cal. App. LEXIS 497 (June 24, 2013).
Carter v. City of Cleveland, 83 Ohio St. 3d (1998).
Clay City Consol. Sch. Dist. Corp. v. Timberman, 896 N.E.2d 1229 (Ind. Ct. App. 2008).
Clark County School Dist. v. Payo, 403 P. 3d 1270 (2017).
Connell v. Payne, 814 S.W.2d 486 (Tex. Ct. App. 1991).
Cope v. Utah Valley State College, 290 P.3d 314 (Utah Ct. App. 2012).
Crawn v. Camp, 643 A.2d 600 (N. J. 1994).
Davidson v. University of No. Carolina, 543 S.E.2d 920 (N.C. Ct. App. 2001).
DeRienzo v. Trek Bicycle Corp., 376 F. Supp. 2d 537 (S.D.N.Y. 2005).
Dotzler v. Tuttle, 449 N.W.2d 774 (Neb. 1990).
Dudley Sports Co. v. Schmitt, 279 N.E.2d 266 (Ind. Ct. App. 1972).
Federal Ins. Co. v. Executive Coach Luxury Travel, Inc., 944 N.E.2d 215 (Ohio 2010).
Feld v. Borkowski, 790 N.W.2d 72 (Iowa 2010).
Fenrich v. Blake School, 920 NW 2d 195 (Minn. Sup. Ct 2018).
Fithian v. Sag Harbor Union Free Sch. Dist., 864 N.Y.S.2d 456 (App. Div. 2008).
Gauvin v. Clark, 537 N.E.2d 94 (1989).
Glankler v. Rapides Parish Sch. Bd., 610 So.2d 1020 (La. Ct. App. 1992).
Green v. BDI Pharmaceuticals, 2001 La. App. LEXIS 2390 (2001).
Gurule v. Bd. of Educ. Los Lunas Public School District, No. No. A-1-CA-35146, 2019 N.M App. Unpub. LEXIS 348 (2019).
Hoke v. Cullinan, 914 S.W.2d 335 (Ky. 1995).
Kabella v. Bouschelle, 672 P.2d 290 (N. M. Ct. App. 1983).
Kahn v. East Side Union High Sch., 75 P.3d 30 (Cal. 2003).
Karas v. Strevell, 884 N.E.2d 122 (Ill. 2008).
Kennedy v. Robert Morris University, 133 A. 3d 38 (2016).
Kleinknecht v. Gettysburg College, 989 F.2d 1360 (3d Cir. 1993).
Knight v. Jewett, 834 P.2d 696 (1992).
Lestina v. West Bend Mutual Ins. Co., 501 N.W.2d 28 (Wis. 1993).
Lujan v. Chowan University, Dist. Court, North Carolina (2019).
MF v. Jericho Union Free Sch. Dist., NY Slip Op 3781 (2019).

MP v. Mineola Union Free School District, 166 AD 3d 953 (2018).

Maida v. St. Bonaventure Univ., NY Slip Op 6389 – Appellate Div., 2nd Dept. (2019).

Marchetti v. Kalish, 559 N.E.2d 699 (Ohio 1990).

Mehr v. Féderation Intern. De Football Ass'n, 115 F. Supp. 3d 1035 (2015).

Mogabgab v. Orleans Parish Sch. Bd., 239 So.2d 456 (La. Ct. App. 1970).

Murphy v. Polytechnic Univ., 872 N.Y.S. 2d 505 (App. Div., 2009).

Nabozny v. Barnhill, 334 N.E.2d 258 (Ill. App. Ct. 1975).

Nalwa v. Cedar Fair, L.P., 55 Cal. 4th 1148 (2012).

Noffke v. Bakke, 760 N.W.2d 156 (Wisc. 2009).

Nova Southeastern Univ. v. Gross, 758 So.2d 86 (Fla. 2000).

Patch v. Hillerich & Bradsby Co., 257 P.3d 383 (Mont. 2011).

Picou v. Hartford Insurance Co., 558 So.2d 787 (La. Ct. App. 1990).

Powers v. Greenville Central School District, 169 AD 3d 1324 (2019).

Prince v. Parachutes, Inc., 685 P.2d 83 (Alaska 1984).

Rosania v. Carmona, 706 A.2d 191 (N.J. Ct. App. 1998).

Ross v. Clouser, 637 S.W.2d 11 (Mo. 1982).

Scott v. Rapides Parish Sch. Bd., 732 So.2d 749 (La. Ct. App. 1999).

Smith v. J. H. West Elementary Sch., 861 N.Y.S. 2d 690 (App. Div. 2008).

Spotlite Skating Rink, Inc. v. Barnes, 988 So.2d 364 (Miss. 2008).

Stahr v. Lincoln Sudbury Regional High School District, 93 Mass. App. Ct. 243 (2018).

Stevens v. Azusa Pacific University, Cal: Court of Appeal, 2nd Appellate Dist., 1st Div. (2019).

Wallach v. American Home Products Corp., Case Index #25642-97 (S. Ct., Nassau Cty, 2001), aff'd, 2002 N.Y. App. Div. LEXIS 12729 (N.Y. App. Div. 2002).

Weiss v. Pratt, 53 So.3d 395 (Fla. Ct. App. 2011).

Wilson v. O'Gorman High School, 2008 U.S. Dist. LEXIS 49489 (S.D.D.C., June 26, 2008).

Statutes

6Am. Jur. 2d, Assault & Battery § 104.

57A Am. Jur. 2d Negligence § 193, § 412.

Federal Tort Claims Act, 28 U.S.C. §§ 1346 et seq.

Immunity, Wisc. Stat. § 895.525 (4m) (a).

Restatement (Second) of Agency.

Restatement [Second] of Torts §§ 2, 8A, 10, 18, 19, 21, 50, 147, 150, 151 & 155 (1965).

Restatement [Second] of Torts § 282 (1979).

Restatement [Third] of Torts § 2 & 3 and related comments (2010).

Virginia Graeme Baker Pool and Spa Safety Act, 84 Fed. Reg. 24021-24027 (May 24, 2019). (Effective Date November 24, 2020), to appear at 16 CFR § 1450.

Volunteer Protection Act of 1997, 42 U.S.C. §§ 14501 et seq. (PL 105-19).

Other Sources

Amberg, P. A. (2012, Fall). Protecting kids' melons: Potential liability and enforcement issues with youth concussion laws. Marquette Sports Law Review, 23, 171–190.

American Horse Council. (2005, June 28). Most comprehensive horse study ever reveals a nearly $40 billion impact on the U.S. economy. AmericanEquestrian.com. Retrieved from http://www.americanequestrian.com/pdf/American_Horse_Council_2005_Report.pdf.

Bruggers, J. (2018, July 20). "This was preventable": Football heat deaths and the rising temperature. Inside Climate News. Retrieved from https://insideclimatenews.org/news/20072018/high-school-football-practice-heat-stroke-exhaustion-deaths-state-rankings-health-safety

Butland, B. (2015, August 20). Government licensure for personal trainers: A solution in search of a problem. Starting strength. Retrieved from https://startingstrength.com/article/government_licensure_for_personal_trainers_a_solution_in_search_of_a_proble.

Cohen, A. (2008, April). Objection! Athletic Business, pp. 60–66.

Conway, T. (2018, December 3). 1 Killed, 40 Injured in Tennessee youth football team bus crash. Bleacher Report. Retrieved from https://bleacherreport.com/articles/2808988-1-killed-40-injured-in-tennessee-youth-football-team-bus-crash.

Cooper, R. (2019, September 7). Rollover bus crash carrying junior high volleyball team. KXnet.com. Retrieved from https://www.kxnet.com/news/local-news/junior-high-volleyball-team-in-the-hospital-after-morning-bus-crash/.

Coyne, T. (2011, July 1). Notre Dame and Indiana reach settlement in Declan Sullivan's death. *Huffington Post*. Retrieved from www.huffingtonpost.com/2011/07/01/declan-sullivan-death-set_n_888645.html.

Dexter, G. M. (2012, Fall). Tort liability for golf shots: Time to reject the recklessness standard and respect the rule of golf. *DePaul Journal of Sports Law and Contemporary Problems, 9*, 1–58.

Ellis, L. (2018, September 21). Emergency care was delayed for Maryland football player who died, consultant says. *Chronicle of Higher Education*. Retrieved from https://www.chronicle.com/article/Emergency-Care-Was-Delayed-for/244605.

English, L. (2009, September 17). Former PRP football coach found not guilty on all charges. *Wave3 News*. Retrieved from https://www.wave3.com/story/11150646/former-prp-football-coach-found-not-guilty-on-all-charges/.

Fainaru-Wade, M. (2009, March). Plancher's parents sue Central Florida. *ESPN*. Retrieved from http://sports.espn.go.com/ncf/news/story?id=3973607.

Family settles wrongful death lawsuit against Ole Miss, NCAA. (2013, July 9). *PRNewswire*. Retrieved from https://www.prnewswire.com/news-releases/family-settles-wrongful-death-lawsuit-against-ole-miss-ncaa-214795331.html.

Garrett, M. C. (1972). Allowance of punitive damages in products liability claims. *Georgia Law Review, 6*(3), 613–630.

Goldman, S. (2009, May). License to train. *Fitness Business*, pp. 35–38.

Herbert, D. L. (2008, December). Certification for personal trainers. *Fitness Management*, p. 50.

Holtzman, B. (2009, March 31). Bus safety an issue for colleges. *ESPN*. Retrieved from http://sports.espn.go.com/espn/otl/news/story?id=3997988.

Investigation into Notre Dame fatality will focus on workplace safety issues. (2010, October 30). *The Coloradoan*, p. D5.

Jones, T. (2013, April 26). Ohio latest state to enact concussion law, but questions remain. *Columbus Dispatch*, p. 1A.

Ketterer, S. (2018, April 16). Lawsuit filed in fatal crash that injured Channelview ISD band students. *Houston Chronicle*. Retrieved from https://www.chron.com/news/houston-texas/houston/article/Bus-company-sued-in-Alabama-crash-that-killed-12835705.php.

Lavigne, P. (2009, March 19). Bus safety an issue for colleges. *ESPN*. Retrieved from https://www.espn.com/espn/otl/news/story?id=3997988.

Lederman, D. (2011, January 3). Expanded view of travel liability. *Inside Higher Ed*. Retrieved from www.insidehighered.com/layout/set/print/news/2011/01/03/court_holds_university_liable.

Marck, D. (2011). Necessary roughness?: An argument for the assignment of criminal liability in cases of student-athlete sustained heat-related deaths. *Seton Hall Journal of Sports and Entertainment Law, 21*, 177–202.

Nader, R. (1972). *Unsafe at any speed: The designed in dangers of the American automobile*. New York, NY: Grossman.

National Transportation Safety Board (2003, January 21). Safety recommendation. Retrieved from www.ntsb.gov/recs/letters/2003/a03%5F01.pdf.

NHTSA restates rollover warning for users of 15-passenger vans. (2005). Retrieved from https://one.nhtsa.gov/About-NHTSA/Press-Releases/2005/ci.NHTSA-Restates-Rollover-Warning-For-Users-of-15%E2%80%93Passenger-Vans.print.

Plant, M. L. (1957). Strict liability of manufacturers for injuries caused by defects in products: An opposing view. *Tennessee Law Review, 24*(7), 938–951.

Popke, M. (2009, June). Emergency response. *Athletic Business*, 15–17.

Popke, M. (2012a, September). Making headlines. *Athletic Business, 21*, 22, 24, 26.

Popke, M. (2012b, July). Cooling trend. *Athletic Business*, 62–64.

Popke, M. (2013, May). Handle on heat. *Athletic Business*, 10, 12.

Samson, C. (2005, Fall). Comment: No time like the present: Why recent events should spur Congress to enact a sports violence act. *Arizona State Law Journal, 37*, 949–972.

Samborn, H. V. (1998, October). Manufacturer beware: A warning on a product may not bar liability, two courts hold in decisions citing the new Restatement. *ABA Journal*, 30–31.

Scherzagier, A. (2009, April 14). Documents show Missouri missteps in O'Neal death. *The San Diego Union Tribune*. Retrieved from https://www.sandiegouniontribune.com/sdut-fbc-missouri-player-collapse-041409-2009apr14-story.html.

Smith, K. (2013, February 28). Airplane crash that killed Oklahoma State women's basketball coach Kurt Budke was not caused by mechanical failure: NTSB. *New York Daily News*. Retrieved from http://www.nydailynews.com/sports/college/mechanical-failure-budke-plane-crash-ntsb-article-1.1276083#ixzz2YK5HMBXP.

State legislation aimed at protecting sports officials from assaults (2019). National Association of Sports Officials. Retrieved from http://www.naso.org/Resources/Legislation/StateLegislation.aspx.

Steinbach, P. (2013, January). Flying coaches. *Athletic Business*, 46–47.

Van der Smissen, B. (1990). *Legal liability and risk management for public and private entities*. Cincinnati, OH: Anderson Publishing.

Whiteside, K. (2013, May 7). Death puts treatment of referees at forefront; Sports officials work in increasingly violent field. *USA Today*, p. 8C.

Wilson, U. S. (2011). Comment: The standard of care between coparticipants in mixed martial arts: Why the recklessness standard should "submit" to the ordinary negligence standard. *Widener Law Journal, 20*, 375–420.

Yang, Y. T., & Baugh, C. M. (2016). US youth soccer concussion policy: Heading in the right direction. *JAMA pediatrics, 170*(5), 413–414.

Web Resources

www.aacca.org ■ This is the website for the American Association of Cheerleading Coaches and Administrators, an educational association for cheerleading coaches in the United States. There is a link to its safety course.

www.nata.org/sites/default/files/preventing-sudden-death.pdf ■ This is the National Athletic Trainers' Association website presenting the 2013 report "Preventing Sudden Death in Secondary School Athletics Programs: Best Practices Recommendations."

www.ncaa.org/health-and-safety ■ This is the NCAA's link for student-athlete well-being.

www.ncaa.org/sport-science-institute/athletics-health-care-administrator-resource-center ■ NCAA Athletics health care administrator resource center.

www.ncaa.org/sport-science-institute ■ NCAA Sport Science Institute.

www.unc.edu/depts/nccsi ■ The National Center for Catastrophic Sport Injury Research provides annual reports about injuries in football in particular and more inclusive annual reports about other catastrophic sport injuries.

www.ncaapublications.com/productdownloads/MD12.pdf ■ This link brings up the *NCAA Sports Medicine Handbook*, which covers numerous issues, including sickle cell trait and concussions.

http://nonprofitrisk.org/library/state-liability.shtml ■ A free PDF listing of state liability laws for charitable organizations and their volunteers is available here. Since many sport-related activities function thanks to the help of volunteers, it is important to know how to minimize risk and harm due to negligence.

www.naso.org ■ This is the website for the National Association of Sports Officials. Currently 23 states have specific legislation relating to assaults upon sports officials and here you can find information on these state statutes. The site also includes model legislation and an archive of articles relating to attacks upon sports officials.

15 Liability Issues and Venue/Event Operations

Kristi L. Schoepfer

Introduction

This chapter focuses on the legal responsibilities of owners of land and facilities to those who use the land and facilities. We will address the general principles of premises liability law holding property owners and possessors of property liable for injuries occuring on the property. Premise liability law also includes specific legal duties land owner/operators must be aware of, as well as many defenses to liability.

Facility operation, maintenance, and policies and procedures are often the foundation of a sport or recreation enterprise. In many cases, the only contact someone will have with an organization is by visiting its facility. To be competitive in the sport business, therefore, familiarity with the legal principles applicable to this area is crucial. You may have many opportunities to develop policies and procedures for your facility to minimize exposure to liability relative to the concerns addressed in this chapter. See Exhibit 15.1 for an overview of the managerial contexts, major legal issues, relevant laws, and illustrative cases pertinent to this chapter.

General Principles of Premises Liability

When we refer to *premises liability*, we are discussing your legal responsibilities to those who use your land and facilities. We discussed the general principles of negligence in Chapter 14. Premises liability is predicated upon negligence principles; however, in most jurisdictions, your duty of care depends upon how the courts characterize those who are injured. Thus, the legal status of the injured person is critical to this type of lawsuit.

Status of the Person upon the Premises

In most jurisdictions, the duty owed by a facility owner or operator is dependent upon the status of the person who is on the premises. That is, the scope of the duty owed varies depending upon whether the person is on the property with permission or without permission. The duty also varies depending upon whether a person who is there with permission brings an economic benefit to the property owner. These three general "types" of persons on our premises are invitees, licensees, and trespassers. Generally speaking, our duty of care owed to an invitee will be greater than that owed to a licensee, and the duty of care owed to a licensee will be greater than that owed to a trespasser. A minority of jurisdictions has abolished these status distinctions, in whole or in part, so the law of the state in which an incident occurred must be consulted. You should discuss these laws with your attorney.

Exhibit 15.1 Management contexts in which issues related to premises liability and sport facilities and events may arise, with relevant laws and cases.

Management Context	Major Legal Issues	Relevant Law	Illustrative Cases
Maintenance of sport/ recreation facility	Determining duty owed to person on property	Negligence law	
		Open and obvious danger	Krzenski
	Defenses in premises liability case	Distraction doctrine	Lowe, Harting
Owner of unimproved land	Recreational use statute	State statutes	Lee
Sport/recreation facility planning	Duties to invitees to design facility safely	Negligence law	
Facility maintenance/ operation	Duty to warn	Negligence law	
	Duty to inspect		
	Duty to repair dangers		
Facility operation	Duty to provide emergency medical assistance	Negligence law	
		AED statutes	Limones, Miglino
Game/event management	Spectator injuries/crowd control	Foreseeability	Bearman
		Prior similar incidents rule	Stow
	Spectators injured by players	Negligence law	
	Spectator hit by projectile	Limited duty rule	Coomer, Reed-Jennings, Southshore Baseball, Rountree
		Assumption of risk	

Invitee

A person whose status is that of **invitee** – a person on the property with the permission of the landowner – is owed a duty of reasonable care by the premises owner. A **business invitee** is on the premises with the permission of the landowner and brings some economic benefit to the landowner. For example, if we pay an admission charge to attend a sporting event, or pay a registration fee to play in a summer basketball league, or run a 5k race, we would be considered business invitees. If you are a university student, you would be considered a business invitee when you use the university's recreation facility. Even if you do not pay a fee on a per-use basis, you have paid for this amenity in your student fees. **Public invitees** are persons who are legally on public land for a purpose for which the land is available to the public. For example, when you attend a community event at a local public park or go hiking or cycling in a public recreation area you are a public invitee.

Invitees are owed a duty of *reasonable care*. You should be familiar with this concept from the discussion of negligence and its elements in Chapter 14. In general terms of premises liability, the duty of reasonable care means that the facility owner must exercise ordinary care to keep and maintain the premises in reasonably safe condition. How a facility owner satisfies this duty of reasonable care is discussed in depth later in this chapter. In most instances, the status of the injured person will not be disputed, but occasionally a premise operator may attempt to argue that an invitee is a licensee in order to lessen its duty of care. For example, in the case of *Griffin v. Grenada Youth League* (2017), a woman, attending a charity baseball tournament held at public fields owned and maintained by the Grenada Youth League (GYL), fell and suffered a broken ankle as she walked down a grassy hill from the parking lot to the ballfields. Griffin sued GYL on a premises liability theory alleging that she fell because she stepped into a one-inch-deep "hole" that was obscured by grass that was three or four inches high. GYL argued that Griffin was a mere licensee thus they owed her a lower duty of care. The circuit court ultimately assumed that the plaintiff was a public invitee, who was invited to enter or remain on land as a member of the public for a purpose for which the land is held open to the public, concluding that as either an invitee or a licensee, the hole was not a dangerous condition that GYL had a duty to correct or warn about.

Licensee

Unlike an invitee, a **licensee** is a person who is on the premises with the consent of the owner but who *does not bring any economic benefit to the property owner.* A person who is invited to your house for a party, for example, is considered a licensee. As seen in the *Griffin* case above, at times the distinction between an invitee and licensee can be subtle and is said to lie in the difference between an invitation vs mere permission. According to Restatement (Second) of Torts § 342, the scope of duty owed to a licensee is considerably less than that owed to an invitee. There is no duty of inspection due to the licensee, and the landowner is liable for harm due to defects or dangers on the property only if the owner has knowledge of the danger and the licensee does not.

In the case of *Combs v. Georgetown College* (2011), the plaintiff was injured when she tripped on a lip at the edge of the platform in a high school gymnasium. The plaintiff was in the gym watching her grandson play basketball during a basketball camp. There were no entrance fees for spectators, the event had not been advertised to the public, and the only available seating consisted of folding chairs. The plaintiff filed a premises liability action against the defendant alleging that the platform lip was an unsafe condition. The defendant argued that the plaintiff was a licensee; thus, no breach of duty had occurred. The lower court granted summary judgment to the defendant, as it held that the plaintiff was a licensee, and the Kentucky appellate court affirmed. The appellate court noted that the plaintiff was in the gym only with permission, not by invitation. Therefore, the defendant only owed the plaintiff the duty to refrain from willfully causing her injury. One area in which we will find variation between states relates to employees of our vendors and contract personnel. Many sport and recreation facilities utilize a wide variety of vendors and contract personnel whose employees are on our premises both by invitation and with our consent. Since the distinction between invitee and licensee often looks at the underlying purpose of the entry on the premises, the venue owner or operator is deriving a benefit from the presence of the vendor's employees; however, the vendor's employees are also present for their own benefit, so it is not always clear whether contract service personnel will be treated as invitees or licensees. (See, *McMillion v. Selman*, 1995.)

Trespasser

A **trespasser** is one who is on the premises without permission. In this situation, the landowner's scope of duty is diminished even further. His or her only duty is to refrain from wantonly inflicting injury upon that person (Restatement [Second] of Torts § 333). For example, you cannot protect your racing yacht from trespassers' intrusions by setting up a trapdoor that sends the intruders to the depths of the ocean should they step into the cabin.

This general rule relating to the duty owed to trespassers, however, is altered when the trespasser is a child. If the **attractive nuisance doctrine** is applicable, a duty of ordinary care is created when normally there would be none. This doctrine provides that there is an affirmative duty on landowners to use reasonable care to protect child trespassers who may be attracted to the property because of some man-made or artificial feature of the land that poses some serious danger to a child (e.g., a swimming pool).

Defenses Available in a Premises Liability Case

As with any claim based on negligence, there are defenses to consider. Two prevalent defenses are the **open and obvious defense** and statutory **recreational use defense**.

Open and Obvious Defense

In a premises liability case, the plaintiff will not be able to recover if the danger complained of is **open and obvious**. According to the Restatement (Second) of Torts § 343A,

> A possessor of land is not liable to invitees for physical harm caused to them by any activity or condition on the land whose danger is known or obvious to them, unless the possessor should anticipate the harm despite such knowledge or obviousness.

If the danger is one that a plaintiff should be or actually is aware of, then the plaintiff has assumed the risk of that danger or defect. Additionally, "the determination of whether the condition is open and obvious depends not on plaintiff's subjective knowledge but, rather, on the objective knowledge of a reasonable person confronted with the same condition" (*Racky v. Belfor*, 2017, p. 466). When the open and obvious defense is successfully used, the defendant will have no liability. The following Focus Case illustrates this point.

Krzenski v. Southampton Union Free School District, NY

173 A.D.3d 725, 102 N.Y.S.3d 693 (2019)	**FOCUS** CASE

FACTS

The plaintiff was injured while playing floor hockey during an after-school event in Southampton High School's gymnasium, which is owned by the defendant. Two sets of fully extended bleachers were being used as the sideline boundaries for the floor hockey playing area. The plaintiff alleged that an opposing team member hit her in the back, causing her to hit her head and shoulder on the unpadded metal railing of the bleacher stairs. The plaintiff commenced this action to recover damages for personal injuries, alleging theories of recovery based on premises liability and negligent supervision. The defendant moved for summary judgment dismissing the complaint, arguing, among other things, that the action was barred by the open and obvious risk defense.

HOLDING

The Appellate Division of the Supreme Court of New York, Second Department affirmed summary judgment for the defendant.

RATIONALE

The plaintiff, who was in eleventh grade at the time of the accident, testified that she volunteered to play floor hockey at the "class night" event during which she was injured, and that she had previously played floor hockey in the school's gymnasium during physical education classes. In addition, she had played floor hockey during similar class night events in her freshman and sophomore years. Additionally, a physical education teacher at the school, who witnessed the accident, testified at his deposition that the bleachers were used as boundaries in physical education classes. Consequently, the proximity of the bleachers to the playing area was *open and obvious*, and the risk of collision with the bleachers was an inherent risk in playing indoor floor hockey in the subject gymnasium. The plaintiff failed to raise a triable issue of fact as to whether the failure to pad the metal railings on the bleacher stairs or to use a buffer zone between the bleachers and the playing area created a risk beyond the risk inherent in the sport of indoor floor hockey. Accordingly, we agree with the determination to grant summary judgment.

One exception to the "open and obvious danger" defense is known as the "deliberate encounter exception." Under Restatement (Second) Torts § 343A, cmt. f (1965), the deliberate encounter exception applies when "a possessor of land has reason to anticipate, or expect that the invitee will proceed to encounter an open and obvious danger, because to a reasonable person in their position the advantages of doing so would outweigh the apparent risk." This exception is analyzed in the case of *Morrissey v. Arlington Park Racecourse* (2010). In *Morrissey*, a horse and jockey fell while exiting a training track at the defendant's racecourse. The horse slipped on standing soapy water that accumulated on the asphalt next to the track exit. The defendants argued that the plaintiff encountered an "open and obvious danger" and therefore was precluded from recovery. However, according to the *Morrissey* court:

> in the present case, for the reasons already fully articulated above, it is impossible to conclude, as a matter of law, that the defendant, which was clearly aware that on a daily basis riders used the east exit because of its proximity to the training track, so as to exercise all of their horses within a span of only five hours, could not have anticipated that the plaintiff would elect to choose the east exit, despite the dangerous condition there. (p. 659)

Therefore, summary judgment for the defendant was not appropriate in *Morrissey* since the deliberate encounter exception could be applicable to the risks associated with a puddle of soapy water.

Another exception to the **open and obvious defense** is known as the **distraction doctrine**. This doctrine provides that, in some cases, even though a condition appears to be open and obvious, the plaintiff may somehow be distracted from appreciating the danger. This doctrine is often considered in spectator situations. For example, if a mascot is distracting fans during play and as a result a spectator fails to get out of the way of a ball, the fan has been distracted by the mascot, and the open and obvious nature of the foul ball may be secondary to the distraction. The following two Focus Cases provide examples of the distraction doctrine as applied to spectators at baseball games. While the distraction doctrine has been used successfully by plaintiffs to eliminate their assumption of risk, comparing the two cases below will demonstrate that is not always the court's decision.

Lowe v. California League of Professional Baseball

56 Cal. App. 4th 112 (App. Ct. 1997)   **FOCUS** CASE

FACTS

John Lowe was seriously injured when struck on the left side of his face by a foul ball while attending a professional baseball game. The game was being played at the Epicenter, the home field of the Rancho Cucamonga Quakes, a Class A minor league baseball team. The Quakes, at their home games, feature a mascot called Tremor. He is a caricature of a dinosaur, standing seven feet tall with a tail that protrudes from the costume. Tremor was performing his antics in the stands along the left field foul line. Tremor was behind plaintiff and had been touching him with his (Tremor's) tail. Lowe was distracted and turned toward Tremor. In the next moment, just as Lowe returned his attention to the playing field, he was struck by a foul ball before he could react to it. Very serious injuries resulted from the impact. As a result, the underlying action was commenced against the California League of Professional Baseball and Valley Baseball Club, Inc., which does business as the Quakes. The case was resolved in the trial court by summary judgment entered in favor of defendants.

HOLDING

The court of appeals reversed.

RATIONALE

The Quakes were able to persuade the trial court, under the doctrine of primary assumption of the risk (*Knight v. Jewett*, Cal. 1992), that defendants owed no duty to the plaintiff, as a spectator, to protect him from foul balls. Such rationalization was faulty. Under *Knight*, defendants had a duty *not to increase* the inherent risks to which spectators at professional baseball games are regularly exposed and which they assume. As a result, a triable issue of fact remained, namely whether the Quakes' mascot cavorting in the stands and distracting plaintiff's attention, while the game was in progress, constituted a breach of that duty – that is, whether it constituted negligence in the form of increasing the inherent risk to plaintiff of being struck by a foul ball. The California Supreme Court has stated (in the context of injuries to participants) that a defendant generally has no duty to eliminate or protect a plaintiff from risks inherent to the sport itself, but has only a duty not to increase those risks. A mascot is not integral to the sport of baseball.

In other words, the key inquiry in *Lowe* was whether the risk that led to plaintiff's injury involved some feature or aspect of the game that is inevitable or unavoidable in the actual playing of the game. In the first instance, foul balls hit into the spectators' area clearly create a risk of injury. If such foul balls were to be eliminated, it would be impossible to play the game. Thus, foul balls represent an inherent risk to spectators attending baseball games. Under *Knight*, such risk is assumed. Can the same thing be said about the antics of the mascot? The court decided no. Our next Focus Case reaches a different conclusion.

Harting v. Dayton Dragons Professional Baseball Club

171 Ohio App. 3d 319 (2007)	FOCUS CASE

FACTS

Harting attended a baseball game between the Dragons and the Wisconsin Timber Rattlers at Fifth Third Field in downtown Dayton, Ohio. For this particular game, the Dragons contracted for the services of the Chicken to entertain the crowd throughout the course of the game. Harting was seated along the third base line directly behind the dugout in the front row. During the bottom of the sixth inning, a player for the Dragons hit a line drive foul ball into the stands along the third-base line. Harting was struck in the head and knocked unconscious by the foul ball when it entered the stands. Harting was transported by ambulance to Miami Valley Hospital. Harting filed a complaint against the Dragons and the Chicken, alleging personal injuries sustained as a result of her attendance at the baseball game. Harting argued that the Chicken hired to entertain the crowd during the baseball game constituted an intervening cause outside the normal course of the game, which distracted her and negated her duty of assumed risk in regard to accepted dangers associated with the game. The trial court granted summary judgment for the baseball club and dismissed her case. She appealed to the Ohio Court of Appeals.

HOLDING

The Ohio Court of Appeals affirmed the trial court's judgment for the baseball club.

RATIONALE

Primary assumption of risk generally applies when there is no duty owed by the defendant to the plaintiff, and in such cases it is a complete bar to recovery. The consensus of opinion is that it is common knowledge in baseball games balls are thrown and batted with great swiftness and are thrown or batted outside lines of the diamond and that spectators in positions which may be reached by such balls assume the risk thereof. Harting clearly understood the inherent dangers associated with being a spectator at a baseball game and understood that one must pay attention to the game to avoid being stuck by a foul ball or piece of broken bat.

Harting's distraction argument ignores the fact that team mascots and their antics are common phenomena and the mascots are normally present during the entire course of the game. In many cases, the team mascots are more popular than the team itself. The fact that the Chicken appeared while the game was being played does not absolve Harting from the duty to protect herself from the ordinary risks inherent in the sport. Harting does not claim the Chicken obscured her view of home plate or the flight path of the ball. Had Harting been paying attention, she would have had a clear view of the action, but instead she was watching the Chicken. Harting understood the risks associated with being a spectator at a baseball game, and management for the Dragons made numerous announcements designed to warn patrons of the possible dangers inherent in the sport. Thus, no genuine issue exists with respect to Harting's claim, and the trial court did not err when it sustained appellees' motions for summary judgment.

Statutory Recreational Use Defense

All states have passed a type of **recreational use statute** that confers immunity upon a landowner in certain situations (see Exhibit 15.2). As discussed in Chapter 14, these statutes are designed to encourage landowners to open portions of their unimproved land to the general public to use for recreational purposes, free of charge. In most states, the definition of a landowner has been extended to include government entities, such as public parks and recreation areas, and public school sport and recreation

Exhibit 15.2 Sample Recreational Use Statute.

An owner of land who either directly or indirectly invites or permits without charge any person to use that property for recreational purposes does not thereby: (1) Extend any assurance that the premises are safe for any purpose; (2) Confer upon that person the legal status of an invitee or licensee to whom a duty of care is owed; nor (3) Assume responsibility for or incur liability for any injury to any person or property caused by an act of omission of that person . . .

Nothing in this chapter limits in any way any liability which, but for this chapter otherwise exists: (1) For the willful or malicious failure to guard or warn against a dangerous condition, use, structure or activity after discovering the user's peril; or (2) For any injury suffered in any case where the owner of land charges the person or persons who enter or go on the land for the recreational use thereof.

areas (Kozlowski, 2016). Although this is the common intent of the statutes, they vary widely in interpretation from state to state. The following is a representative case from California.

Lee v. Department of Parks and Recreation

38 Cal. App. 5th 206 (Cal. App. 1st, 2019)   **FOCUS CASE**

FACTS

Plaintiff Michele Lee injured herself on a stairway in the Bootjack Campground within Mt. Tamalpais State Park and sued respondent California State Department of Parks and Recreation ("State Parks") for premises liability. Bootjack Campground is owned and controlled by State Parks. From the nearest parking lot, there are two ways to access Bootjack Campground: a stone stairway built into a hill and a longer ADA-compliant path. Lee fell and suffered an injury while descending the stone stairway. After camping overnight at Bootjack Campground with her boyfriend, Lee started to descend the stairway from the campground to the parking lot. She slipped on an "uneven portion" of the stairs, fell, and broke her ankle in three places. Both Lee and her boyfriend asserted that the stairway contained uneven and protruding stones and depressions. They also claimed that leaves from a nearby tree shaded and concealed those protrusions and depressions. In response to Lee's claim, State Parks raised an affirmative defense under Government Code section 831.4, asserting that it is immune from liability for injuries caused by any trail or unpaved road that provides access to recreational or scenic areas. The trial court granted summary judgment in favor of State Parks. On the finding that the stairway to Bootjack Campground is a trail, or at least an integral part of a trail, that provides access to recreational areas, the trial court concluded State Parks is "absolutely immune" from liability pursuant to the statutory recreational trail immunity provided by Government Code section 831.4, subdivision (b).

HOLDING

The Court of Appeals of California affirmed the finding of recreational use immunity.

RATIONALE

The court initially recognized that whether a property is considered a trail turns on accepted definitions of the property, the purpose for which the property was designed and used, and the purpose of the immunity statute. The court further noted previous decisions suggesting that even if a property is not "in and of itself" a trail, it might nonetheless be immune because it is integrated into and essential to the trail. The court rejected Lee's argument that the stairway was not essential to the trail due to the existence of the alternate ADA route finding such argument to be illogical to lose immunity by offering an alternative ADA route for members of the public who cannot climb stairs. Essential does not mean absolutely necessary. It is sufficient that the stairway is essential for campers to ascend and descend the steep hillside more safely, easily, and quickly.

The court further reasoned that treating the stairway as a trail fulfills the purpose of the immunity statute … the statute's paramount purpose is keeping recreational areas open to the public by preventing burdens and costs on public entities. Further, the court noted that denying immunity would impose on State Parks the burden of inspecting and repairing every path in every park in the State of California that contains steps and defending itself in litigation. Facing such liability, the State might well decline to build stairs into steep paths – a result that would ensure the State's immunity but would make our parks and public spaces less safe. The court declined to adopt a rule that would discourage, rather than encourage, such safety measures.

Duties Owed to Invitees

A facility owner or operator has the duty of reasonable care for the safety of invitees. This section discusses a number of these obligations, including the duty to design a safe facility, the duty to warn of dangers, the duty to inspect for defects, the duty to repair dangers promptly, and the duty to provide emergency medical assistance.

Duty to Design the Facility Safely

There is a duty to design a facility safely for its intended uses. This, of course, should be done in conjunction with an architectural firm that has expertise in the type of facility being constructed. It is a fact of life that construction budgets are often overrun and initial plans are often modified. Care must be taken, however, to ensure that cost-saving modifications do not affect safety issues.

If mandatory safety standards are in force, you must ensure that these standards are adhered to. Failure to do so may result in negligence per se (discussed in Chapter 14). Even if a standard is only a recommendation or a suggestion, experts use these to set the standard of care, and courts give great deference to national association standards even if they are voluntary in nature.

Playgrounds and pools offer special challenges in this regard (Brown, 2008). Stadium escalators and bleachers also pose design issues (*Dibartolomeo v. New Jersey Sports and Exposition Authority*, 2011; *Davis v. Cumberland County Bd. of Education*, 2011; "Off the rails," 2012). Similarly, there have also been issues at ballparks related to individuals falling over front row railings, which may not have been built high enough to be safe and challenges for spectators to navigate increasingly steeper arena bowls (Odum, 2018; Rossetti, 2018). For example, when Levi's Stadium in Santa Clara, California opened in July 2014, the facility was criticized for using steel-capped glass panels as railings; the glass panels were only slightly more than 30 inches tall and the cap had no sufficient gripping surface. As noted in a complaint published in the local press, the 2013 California Building Code Standards (BCS) sets forth safety criteria for balconies and open areas. Specifically, "BCS Section 1013.2 and 1013.3 require that guards be installed along open walking surfaces no less than 42 inches in height, including when glass surfaces are used as guards" (BCS 1013.2.1; Dolan, 2014). "These height limits are in place to prevent a person's center of mass being above the edge of the guard as it is well recognized that lower rails can lead to serious, fatal falls" (Dolan, 2014). Additionally, CBC Section 1012.3 provides standards for graspability, requiring that the handrails have a grasping surface where the opposable thumb can affect a meaningful grip (round or mushroom-shaped). The rectangular nature of the panel at Levi's Stadium fails to provide the proper grasping surface (Dolan, 2014). While there have not been any serious injuries or fatal falls at Levi's Stadium to date, this example highlights the importance of adhering to safety standards.

There are many other examples that highlight the importance of adhering to safety standards inside sport stadia. Watkins and Mungin (2013) shares multiple examples of fatal, or near fatal incidents at sport stadia. Specifically, in 2013 alone, a woman fell 40–50 feet at Oakland County Coliseum during a Raiders game, a 48-year-old man suffered severe head injuries after falling down steps at M&T Bank Stadium during a Baltimore Ravens game, a Buffalo Bills fan injured himself and another patron as he tried to slide down the rail of the upper deck of Ralph Wilson Stadium during a Buffalo Bills game, a woman fell about 20 feet from the stands at Floyd Stadium at a game at Middle Tennessee State University, and a man fell about 85 feet from the upper level of Atlanta's Turner Field (this death was ruled a suicide). All of these incidents occurred within a three-month span. Further, this is just one snapshot from one year; these types of incidents are not declining (Gorman & Weeks, 2015). All of these examples reinforce the need for sport stadiums to comply with set safety standards.

Duty to Warn

The courts have held that there is a duty to warn invitees about hidden dangers – those dangers that would not be obvious to an average user. Hidden dangers are ones that the user is not able to discover with a casual inspection.

Competitive Advantage Strategies

Duty to Inspect

- Develop an inspection protocol for all land and facilities. Develop inspection checklists for a facility, incorporating safety standards as necessary. Use inspection checklists to make sure that the inspection is thoroughly completed.
- Ensure that the persons who do facility inspections are properly trained to identify dangerous conditions.
- Make sure that inspections are done as often as necessary based on the type of facility and the use of the facility.

For example, say you own a private beach, and you charge admission for users to sunbathe and swim there. From the beach, the water looks calm and inviting. An average user of the area would not realize that there is a severe undertow in the water not far from shore. You have an obligation to post a warning sign concerning this danger because it is not obvious to the average swimmer using your beach.

Duty to Inspect

The facility possessor has the duty of reasonable inspection to discover dangers. What reasonable inspection is depends upon the frequency and type of use of the area. For example, an infrequently used area may reasonably be inspected less often than a high-use area in a facility; determining a reasonable and appropriate inspection interval for a facility, or multiple parts of a facility, is an important consideration.

Landowners are responsible for correcting defects of which they, as reasonably prudent landowners, should have been aware, as well as defects of which they are actually aware. Thus it is imperative to have a regular protocol for inspection. **Actual notice** implies that the landowner knows of a danger through inspection by employees. **Constructive notice** means that a court will hold a landowner responsible for dangers that the landowner should know about if reasonable inspections were undertaken. (See the *Bearman* case, discussed later, regarding the concepts of actual and constructive notice.)

The principle of constructive notice is evident in *Beglin v. Hartwick College* (2009). In this case, a student who was working out at the school's fitness center was injured when metal weight plates weighing about 140 pounds fell on the student's hand. The plates had become jammed and fell on the plaintiff's hand, which was resting on the machine as he tried to figure out why the plates were stuck. The defendant sought summary judgment as it contended, through two of its employees, that they had no knowledge of any problem with the machine. In contrast, the plaintiff's witness, a fitness center custodian, testified that the jamming of the plates on this machine was a recurring problem requiring repair on a number of occasions. Based on this testimony, the court declined to grant summary judgment for the defendant since there was a genuine issue of fact for the jury. This case points out the necessity of having regular inspections of equipment and of taking appropriate and prompt remedial action when a danger is ascertained.

Duty to Repair Dangers

After a property owner has notice of a danger, the danger must be repaired or remedied within a reasonable period of time. As with all issues of reasonableness, this becomes a question of fact for a jury to decide. In some cases, reasonable behavior may mean that a danger cannot be repaired quickly but that users are kept away from the dangerous area (by roping it off, using cones to warn of the danger, etc.). The following hypothetical case illustrates this concept.

Considering ... Duty to Repair Dangers

Mary King is the athletic director at New River High School and is responsible for overseeing all school athletic events. One evening at a home volleyball match a spectator spills a soda as she climbs the bleachers. The person who is walking immediately behind her slips and falls because of the spill.

Question

- Is the school liable? Why or why not?

Note how you would answer the question and then check your response using the Analysis & Discussion at the end of this chapter.

Competitive Advantage Strategies

Duty to Repair Dangers

- Develop a system for reporting dangerous conditions so that all employees know how to report a facility problem promptly. Make sure that the reports are conveyed promptly to the persons who can actually remedy them.
- Make sure that warning signs are placed in plain view and that they remain intact and legible.

Duty to Provide Emergency Medical Assistance

Under Restatement (Second) of Torts § 314A at 118 (1965), "a possessor of land who holds it open to the public is under a similar duty to members of the public who enter in response to his invitation." The "similar duty" is to "give them first aid after the landowner knows or has reason to know that they are ill or injured, and to care for them until they can be cared for by others." This duty owed to the business invitee generally means that there is an obligation to provide emergency first aid and to have a protocol to get further medical assistance in a timely manner (see Chapter 14). All states have some law or regulation in force requiring the availability of automated external defibrillators (AEDs) in a number of types of public buildings, including apartment buildings, public schools, transportation centers, office complexes, health clubs, and other facilities in which sudden cardiac arrest may occur. The statutes usually mandate the availability of AEDs, require training for those who will use the AEDs, and provide some type of Good Samaritan immunity for those who use the AEDs in good faith.

This is an area in which the standard of care is evolving, and owners must exercise vigilance to ensure that their organizations are in compliance with state statutes (Connaughton, Spengler, & Zhang, 2007; Fortington, West, Morgan, & Finch, 2019). (The status of state legislation is available online; see the Web Resources at the end of this chapter.) As mentioned in Chapter 14, the National Athletic Trainers' Association (NATA) issued the statement "Preventing Sudden Death in Secondary School Athletics Programs: Best Practices Recommendations," which focuses on the serious medical conditions that can affect the high school athlete (see Web Resources for information on accessing this statement online). The task force's recommendations are designed to provide the best practices for preventing sudden deaths, establishing emergency action plans, and providing appropriate medical care, including the use of AEDs.

Furthermore, in regard to the use of AEDs in a school setting, on July 21, 2011, the National Association for Sport and Physical Education (NASPE) strongly supported the position that AEDs should be present in all schools and at all school-sanctioned athletic events/activities and venues in its statement

"Availability and Access to Automated External Defibrillators in Schools during Participation in Physical Activity" (see Web Resources).

With 75 percent of all sudden cardiac arrest cases in schools occurring in relation to a sporting event or practice, studies have found coaches, athletic trainers, and nurses are most likely to act as first responders. NASPE's "National Standards for Sport Coaches" (NASPE, n.d.) addresses this responsibility directly, stating that coaches should "recognize injuries and provide immediate and appropriate care." Early and immediate use of cardiopulmonary resuscitation (CPR) and AEDs can save the lives of children and young athletes (NASPE's full position statement on the use and placement of AEDs in a school setting is available online; see Web Resources).

The following Focus Case deals with whether an AED must actually be used if one is available on the premises.

Limones v. School Dist. of Lee County

161 So.3d 384 (2015)	FOCUS CASE

FACTS

A high school soccer player in Florida collapsed on the field and stopped breathing. A nurse bystander and the coach performed CPR and 911 was called. An AED was available on a golf cart stationed near the field's end zone but no one retrieved it, even though the coach testified that he had requested someone to get it. When the EMS personnel arrived 23 minutes after the 911 call, they used their own AED to resuscitate the player. During that time the player suffered severe, irreversible brain damage. The player's parents sued the school board, alleging that it was negligent in failing to make the AED available for use and for failing to use it. The lower court granted summary judgment for the defendant.

HOLDING

The appellate court affirmed summary judgment for the school board stating that the duty of care did not include a duty to use the AED; however, the supreme court of Florida reversed, finding the duty to use the AED did exist.

RATIONALE

In the original case, as well as in each level of appellate review, the plaintiff had argued that the Florida statute requiring an operational AED on school grounds also required that the AED actually be used in an emergency. While the appellate court disagreed noting that "section 1006.165 does not require the School Board to do anything more than have an operational AED on school grounds, register its location, and provide appropriate training." The Florida Supreme Court found that the respondent owed a common law duty to supervise Abel, and that once injured, respondent owed a duty to take reasonable measures and come to his aid to prevent aggravation of his injury, including the use of an AED. The case was remanded for a jury to determine whether school board breached the duty and resulted in the damage Limones suffered.

Another case, *Miglino v. Bally Total Fitness* (2013), also dealt with whether the statutory duty for fitness facilities to provide an AED mandated the facility to actually use the device. In this situation, a racquetball player collapsed at the defendant's club. Although the AED was brought over to the injured person, it was not used. An employee who had been trained to use the AED testified that it was not appropriate, in his opinion, to use the AED since the stricken individual was still breathing. When the EMS personnel arrived about eight minutes later the plaintiff was unresponsive. He was pronounced dead at the hospital. The

Competitive Advantage Strategies

Duty to Provide Emergency Medical Assistance

- Prior to purchasing an AED, make sure you have a comprehensive system to manage the program and a quality assurance program to make sure that you keep proper records, maintain the devices, and review your program as necessary.
- Make sure that you know all relevant state laws pertaining to the use of AEDs in your facility.
- Make sure that your AED program is developed with the assistance of qualified medical personnel.
- Ensure that your employees are trained properly in the use of the AED through recognized programs (such as the American Heart Association).
- Integrate the use of the AED into your overall emergency medical protocol.

New York Court of Appeals (New York's highest court) was faced with the issue of whether the statute mandating the presence of an AED at fitness clubs should also be interpreted as a requirement to use the device. The court declined to add a duty to use the device into the clear statutory language to provide the AED. The court further noted that "there is nothing meaningless or purposeless about a statute that seeks to insure the availability of AEDs and individuals trained in their use at locations – that is, health clubs – where there is a population at higher risk of sudden cardiac arrest. Obviously, though, AEDs are not meant to be employed mindlessly. For example, the implied duty would cause a dilemma for the lay health club employee whenever a volunteer medical professional is furnishing aid at the scene. A law that mandates the presence of AEDs and trained individuals at health clubs is easy to obey and enforce. An implied duty is neither; such a duty would engender a whole new field of tort litigation, saddling health clubs with new costs and generating uncertainty. The Legislature is unlikely to have imposed such a new duty absent an express statement.

In comparing the *Limones* case to the *Miglino* case, it is easier to see the court's reasoning in *Miglino*. In the *Miglino* situation, an employee trained regarding the use of the AED did make an informed judgment not to use the device. However, in *Limones*, there was no apparent reason for not bringing over the AED that was at the venue. Surely, it makes sense to require its use, or at least the informed decision not to use it. Otherwise, a statute mandating that an AED be present has no real meaning.

There is also a duty to have emergency response plans in place to deal with states of emergency in a facility, whether the emergency arises from medical disasters, fire, bomb threats, power loss, or weather-related circumstances. Evacuation plans should be developed, and an emergency response team should be formed to deal with all types of emergency situations within a facility (see Web Resources for specific information on developing appropriate emergency response plans).

Spectator Injuries

Generally, spectators at a facility or event are invitees, and the owner has a duty of reasonable care for their safety. This section discusses a number of issues relating to spectator injuries: crowd control, injuries related to alcohol consumption, injuries caused by projectiles from the playing area, and other spectator injuries.

Crowd Control

In tort law, there is generally no duty to protect others from the actions of a third party. However, a landowner has the duty to keep a facility reasonably safe for spectators. As a part of this duty, "a landowner who opens his property to the public for business purposes has a duty to exercise *reasonable care* to protect the public from physical harm caused by the accidental, negligent, or intentionally harmful acts of third persons" (Restatement [Second] of Torts § 344). Reasonable care is predicated on the question of what is foreseeable. The following is a seminal case regarding this proposition.

Bearman v. University of Notre Dame

453 N.E.2d 1196 (Ind. Ct. App. 1983)   **FOCUS** CASE

FACTS

Christenna Bearman attended a Notre Dame football game in 1979. She left the game before it ended and walked through a parking lot toward her car. She saw two men who appeared to be drunk and fighting and did not walk toward the altercation. The two men walked away from each other, and then one of the men pushed the other, falling into Bearman from behind, breaking her leg. There were no security personnel from Notre Dame in the area when the injury occurred.

Bearman sued, alleging that she, as a business invitee, should have been protected by Notre Dame from the act of this third party. Notre Dame argued that it had no liability absent any actual notice of a particular danger to a patron. The trial court granted Notre Dame's motion for summary judgment.

HOLDING

The Indiana Court of Appeals reversed and remanded.

RATIONALE

In this case Notre Dame argued that it had no duty of care regarding the third-party actions because it had no actual knowledge of a particular disturbance in the parking lot. However, the court noted that actual knowledge is not the only concern here; a facility owner may also have liability if it had constructive knowledge of a danger. If Notre Dame should reasonably anticipate careless or criminal conduct by third parties, it may be under a duty to take precautions against this conduct.

The court then built a logical chain of foreseeability from the fact that the university was fully aware of the tailgating that occurred before and during games in university parking lots. The university was fully cognizant that tailgating often includes the consumption of alcoholic beverages, which results in some patrons becoming intoxicated. Those inebriates then pose a general threat to the safety of other patrons. The court concluded, therefore, that Notre Dame had a duty to take reasonable precautions to protect those who attend its football games from injury caused by the acts of third parties.

Competitive Advantage Strategies

Crowd Control

- Develop crowd control plans based on factors specific to a contest, such as whether there is a rivalry, whether there has been prior violence, whether alcohol will be served, and what the demographics of a contest are likely to be. Use all information available to determine what crowd behaviors may be foreseeable.
- At football games, consider whether you will attempt to keep fans off the field or simply control their access to goalposts. Consider using goalposts that can be lowered quickly, either mechanically or manually, to avoid fan injury during postgame celebrations.
- For youth sports, consider having parents sign an agreement to cheer only in ways that are positive and that support the goal of good sportsmanship.

The *Bearman* case is important because it emphasizes that a facility owner is responsible to deal not only with dangers of which the owner has *actual knowledge* – for example, when facility employees know that a brawl is occurring – but that the owner has a duty to exercise care regarding dangers of which the owner should, as a reasonably prudent facility owner, be aware – that is, *constructive knowledge*. This point is crucial because it puts a duty of inspection and/or awareness upon a facility owner. Whether the danger is one of sagging bleachers or rowdy fans, courts expect facility owners to act reasonably in ascertaining whether a danger may exist. If the danger is reasonably foreseeable, there is a duty to exercise care in taking precautions against that danger.

Unfortunately, fighting and the use of weapons at sporting events are becoming more prevalent. Many high schools have developed plans to deal with violence and unsportsmanlike conduct, often instituting a zero-tolerance policy for any bad behavior (Niehoff, 2019). Further, in 2014, the NFL developed a code of conduct regarding fan behavior in an effort to reduce violence and disruptive behavior at games and in parking lots. Fans can not only be ejected for violating the code of conduct, but are also subject to a temporary ban from the stadium (Van Milligen, 2015) Despite these efforts, fan violence continues to be a serious concern and arrests during sporting events continues an upward trend in the United States (Babb & Rich, 2016).

Stow v. Los Angeles Dodgers

No. BC462127 (Cal. Super. Ct. May 24, 2011)	**FOCUS** CASE

FACTS

Bryan Stow, a San Francisco Giants fan, attended opening day at Dodger Stadium in Los Angeles to cheer on the Giants. After the game, he was brutally attacked in the parking lot of the stadium by two rival Dodgers fans. Stow suffered extensive and traumatic brain damage from which he will never fully recover. Stow subsequently sued Los Angeles Dodgers, LLC and Frank McCourt, the owner of the Dodgers at the time of the altercation in 2011. The matter proceeded to trial against Los Angeles Dodgers, LLC and Frank McCourt on the claims of negligence and premises liability.

The civil case brought by Stow against the Dodgers organization alleged that the defendant was negligent in its failure to provide enough security and in its failure to light the parking lot properly, among other allegations. Stow argued that the individuals responsible for the attack were being unruly during the second inning of the game, when they were yelling obscenities and throwing food at another couple wearing Giants clothing. Neither of the individuals were ejected from the stadium, nor were they approached by security personnel. Stow further asserted that this allowed the men to continue drinking and initiate other altercations before the altercation with Stow in the parking lot after the game. The defendants argued that it is impossible to prevent every incident that occurs at a sports stadium with a capacity of 56,000 people. Further, the defendants asserted that there was an unprecedented level of security for the Opening Day game, including more than 100 uniformed, on-duty Los Angeles Police Department officers that were deployed in the parking lots. Defendants also denied having any knowledge of the attacker's prior behavior while in the stadium. Defendants ultimately argued that the attackers were solely at fault for the tragic and unfortunate incident, and that Stow was comparatively at fault since he had a blood alcohol level of between 0.16 and 0.20 at the time of the incident.

HOLDING

The jury issued a multi-million dollar verdict in favor of Stow, finding that the Dodgers did not provide adequate security and were partly to blame for the attack; Frank McCourt was found not liable.

RATIONALE

Testimony throughout the trial revealed that parking lot security concerns had been raised within the Dodgers organization prior to the attack on Stow, thus triggering the issue of foreseeability. According to the **prior similar incidents rule**, courts will ascertain whether a certain incident was foreseeable by looking at what has occurred previously at that location that was sufficiently similar in character to make it foreseeable that another occurrence of the kind could happen. It is not enough, under this rule, to simply point out that, for example, fights and other altercations occur frequently at sporting events. The prior similar incidents rule demands that prior incidents be very similar in kind and location in order to imply foreseeability.

Another consideration related to fan violence are Safe Place statutes, such as the law adopted in Wisconsin (Wis. Stat. §101.11(1) (2009–2010)). Swenson (2012) urges more states to adopt a Safe Place statute because the statutes makes it easier for a victim of fan violence to prevail. Safe Place statutes impose a more stringent standard of care than that found in common law negligence. As such, a standard of actual or constructive notice would be used instead of the foreseeability standard, discussed above, which would be more favorable to plaintiffs who are victims of fan violence.

In addition to fan violence, the specter of injury or death due to terrorist acts continues to be a liability concern for venue owners/operators. Multiple recent examples include the 2017 targeting of Dortmund's team bus during the Champions League quarter-finals, the 2015 bombing outside the Stade de France in Paris during a soccer game, and the bombing at the 2013 Boston Marathon (Conn, 2017). Each of these attacks was a wake-up call for those who operate events at large scale venues, or at events that are not confined to one location. Although much effort has gone into securing traditional sporting event locations, these tragedies made event managers think more carefully about the measures necessary to secure events (Steinbach, 2013). One report conducted shortly after the Boston Marathon bombing concluded that many of the security efforts with sporting events and venues are essentially flawed, due in large part to hiring private security personnel who are often poorly trained. (Schrotenboer, 2013)

Injuries Due to Alcohol Consumption

Alcohol consumption is tied to the spectator experience in sport. For example, at Louisiana State University (LSU), the football stadium holds 91,600 people, but approximately 100,000 people routinely show up, leaving nearly 10,000 individuals to engage in tailgating with no hope of entering the stadium. The LSU athletic department has characterized the experience as follows:

> Tailgating has become a part of college football all across the country, but at LSU, for Tiger fans it is an art form. Over two-thirds of Tiger fans tailgate for five or more hours before every game, and many begin celebrating the great Tiger football experience more than 24 hours before kickoff. LSU encourages its fans to come to campus early and enjoy the great tradition of tailgating. LSU also encourages its fans to tailgate in a responsible manner, respectful of the campus and of other Tiger fans and fans from visiting schools. (LSUSports.net, 2013)

The prevalence of tailgating and the ever-present possibility of the overconsumption of alcohol make it foreseeable to a facility owner that some misbehavior due to alcohol will occur. The *Bearman* case showed the importance of foreseeability in crowd control liability. Thus, in order to act reasonably a facility owner or operator must have sufficient personnel to deal with the prospect of rowdy, inebriated fans.

Competitive Advantage Strategies

Injuries due to Alcohol Consumption

- Develop alcohol management policies regarding tailgating and, if applicable, serving alcohol.
- Do not allow patrons to return to the parking lot during the game or after the end of the game to continue their tailgating.

  o Enforce all alcohol management policies consistently and fairly.
  o Educate patrons regarding what constitutes responsible drinking.
  o Give incentives to "designated drivers" to encourage this practice.

- If you use an independent contractor as your liquor concessionaire, select a concessionaire that has a strong safety record and that uses recognized training techniques, such as TIPS and TEAM.

There is another liability issue associated with alcohol. **Dram shop acts** provide for liability against commercial establishments that serve alcohol to minors or to persons who are visibly intoxicated when the inebriate subsequently injures a third party. At least 30 states have statutes allowing licensed businesses, including sports venues, to be held liable for selling or serving alcohol to individuals who cause injury or death as a result of their intoxication (Morton, 2013). Under these statutes, when a person who has overconsumed alcohol drives drunk and injures or kills another motorist, the person (and entity) who served the alcohol may be liable. In 2007, the beer refreshment vendor at Giants Stadium agreed to pay $25 million to settle the case of a girl paralyzed in a crash with a drunken football fan. Antonia Verni was injured in an October 24, 1999 crash caused by drunken fan, Daniel Lanzaro, a few hours after a game. Verni spent one year in the hospital after the accident, and was rendered a quadriplegic who needs a breathing tube. During the original trial, Lanzaro testified that vendors at Giants Stadium had served him while intoxicated; the case cast nationwide attention on the problem of binge drinking at American sports events (Gottlieb, 2008).

There may also be liability for someone who serves as a host in a social setting and allows the overconsumption of alcohol by a partygoer who then causes injury to a third party. See the law review by Diamantopoulos (2008), which discusses the dram shop acts and social host liability. In addition to all the professional sports venues that serve alcohol, many universities have also decided to serve alcohol at sporting events. In 2008, "fewer than a dozen big-time football universities permitted beer sales in their stadiums. Today more than 50 (about a third of all Division I FBS schools) sell beer at their football venues, and a growing list of smaller schools are also bellying up to stadium bars" (Nietzel, 2018). More recent evidence of this trend continuing is the vote by the Southeastern Conference (SEC) in May 2019 allowing universities to sell alcohol at sporting events. Additionally, "several universities are going a step further, allowing brewers to place university brands and logos on their products. At the University of Texas, Longhorn fans have a new slogan – "Horns Up, Limes In" – the result of UT's partnership with Corona" (Nietzel, 2018). Further, in-venue alcohol sales are now permitted at most postseason football bowl games, and the NCAA no longer bans alcohol sales at its championship events. Although this may often add to the experience for a number of fans (Smith, 2018), at least one commentator has discussed the dram shop liability ramifications for these universities (McGregor, 2012). A review of best practices for stadium alcohol management is necessary given the prevalence of alcohol at sporting events (Filce, Hall, & Phillips, 2016).

Considering … Alcohol Management

ABC University has recently decided to sell alcohol at baseball games and soccer games held on campus. The event management staff at the university does not believe it needs to specifically consider crowd management related to alcohol sales for these venues, because collegiate baseball and soccer are not sports where alcohol is commonly part of the spectator experience. The decision was made as an attempt to entice more spectators to attend games, but the athletics staff does not consider the decision as impactful as serving alcohol at football games.

Question

- Is ABC properly considering crowd management and alcohol related liability? Why or why not?

Note how you would answer the question and then check your response using the Analysis & Discussion at the end of this chapter.

Injuries Caused by Projectiles from the Playing Area

Spectators at baseball or hockey games are frequently hit by batted balls, broken bats, or hockey pucks; since 2018, no fewer than four patrons have been seriously injured at Major League Baseball (MLB) games, including one fatality (Bergman & Axelrod, 2019). It is part of the excitement for spectators at such events to be as close to the action as possible with an unimpeded view; stadium owner operators also desire the higher priced seats to have an unobstructed sightline to the field of play. However, such closeness to the action carries certain risks, since balls, bats, and pucks do find their way into the stands and can be dangerous projectiles.

The alarming number of recent injuries, particularly at baseball stadiums, has resulted in a call by MLB players and the Major League Baseball Players Association (MLBPA) to call for protective netting from foul pole to foul pole, modeled after the approach in Japanese baseball stadiums (Bergman & Axelrod, 2019). While all 30 MLB teams have extended their stadium netting around home plate (since 2018), there is mixed opinion as to whether the pole-to-pole approach is viable. MLB Commissioner Rob Manfred has said that "while fan safety is important, it would be difficult to adopt uniform standards" (Bergman & Axelrod, 2019). By the summer of 2019, the only MLB team to commit to pole-to-pole netting was the Chicago White Sox, although the Nationals and Pirates also committed to extending protective netting at their stadiums, but not pole-to-pole (Acquavella & Axisa, 2019).

The majority of baseball stadium owner operators' reluctance to provide additional protective screening due is most likely due in part to the legal protections available to them derived from what is known as the **limited duty rule**. The **limited duty rule** provides that a facility owner "is not liable for injuries to spectators that result from projectiles leaving the field during play if (1) safety screening had been provided … and (2) there are a sufficient number of protected seats to meet ordinary demand"

Competitive Advantage Strategies

Injuries by Projectiles from the Playing Area

- At baseball or hockey games, make sure that patrons who wish to be seated in protected areas are given the opportunity to do so.
- Make sure that mascots do not distract patrons from the field of play while the game is ongoing.
- At baseball games, make sure that spectators are protected from foul balls while they are purchasing food or beverages from mobile concessions areas.

(*Benejam v. Detroit Tigers, Inc.*, 2001, p. 219). The limited duty rule has been applied and interpreted by many courts in recent years; courts have consistently applied the rule when spectators are injured during the nine innings of a baseball game. For example, in *Southshore Baseball v. DeJesus* (2013) a plaintiff injured by a foul ball at a minor league baseball game could not recover in Indiana because the limited duty rule precluded recovery so long as the baseball club had provided protective screening in the most dangerous areas and provided an adequate number of seats in protected areas. However, application of the limited duty rule to injuries occurring during pre-game or post-game activities or that occur in more congested areas of the stadiums have led to less consistent application of the rule. Let's look at a series of cases that illustrate this principle.

Jennings v. Baseball Club of Seattle

351 P.3d 887 (2015)	**FOCUS** CASE

FACTS

The plaintiff was seriously injured during batting practice before a Seattle Mariners baseball game, when a batter hit a foul ball into the stands along the right field foul line. The plaintiff and her husband sat along the right field foul line, two rows up from the field. The plaintiff saw a foul ball land near her seat during batting practice. Shortly after, a batter hit a ball into center field, and the plaintiff attempted to track the ball's flight. Before that ball was caught, the plaintiff heard another ball being hit. When she turned her head, the second ball hit her in the face. The plaintiff sustained serious injuries to her left eye. Plaintiffs' ticket included a warning that explained the dangers of balls and bats entering the stands; additionally, several support posts for the lower level warned spectators about bats and balls leaving the playing field. Further, the back of each seat warned spectators about "bats and balls leaving the field." The plaintiff maintained that she did not see any of these warnings but "knew that balls could come into the stands" during batting practice.

HOLDING

The Washington Court of Appeals affirmed the trial court's dismissal of the negligence claim.

RATIONALE

For many decades throughout the United States, the majority of jurisdictions have applied the limited duty rule to define the duty a baseball stadium operator owes to its patrons injured from foul balls before or during a game. The limited duty rule requires baseball stadium operators "to screen some seats ... to provide protection to spectators who choose it." The rule imposes two requirements on baseball stadium operators. First, baseball stadium operators must provide a sufficient number of protected seating for those spectators "who may be reasonably anticipated to desire protected seats on an ordinary occasion." Second, baseball stadium operators must "provide protection for all spectators located in the most dangerous parts of the stadium, that is, those areas that pose an unduly high risk of injury from foul balls (such as directly behind home plate)."

The plaintiffs argued that the Mariners breached its duty of care because a heightened risk was posed by multiple batted balls being simultaneously in play during batting practice. The plaintiff contends that because she was distracted by a previously hit ball, she "could not be reasonably expected to avoid such an injury." However, batting practice typically involves pitchers throwing balls in quick succession with the chance that multiple balls could be simultaneously in play. Similar to throwing balls pregame, batting practice is a normal part of pregame warmups. A reasonable person in the plaintiff's shoes would know and consider that by choosing to sit in an unscreened area, there is a possibility that a ball could enter the stands and injure her. Even if this particular circumstance of multiple batted balls simultaneously in play could be considered "somewhat bizarre," the Mariners clearly satisfied its limited duty to screen a reasonable number of seats, as well as the most dangerous areas of the ballpark.

Rountree v. Boise Baseball LLC

296 P.3d 373 (Idaho 2013)	FOCUS CASE

FACTS

The plaintiff had been a season ticket holder at this minor league professional baseball franchise for over 20 years. His tickets were in the "Viper" section, which was protected by netting. Sometime during the game on August 13, 2008, the plaintiff and his family went to the Executive Club, the only area in the stadium not covered by vertical netting. While conversing with someone there, the plaintiff stopped paying attention to the game. As he heard crowd noise the plaintiff turned and was hit in the eye by a foul ball. As a result, the plaintiff lost his eye.

The plaintiff brought an action against the baseball club alleging negligence. The defendant baseball club moved for summary judgment, alleging that the baseball rule (limited duty rule) should be adopted by the court. Since the club complied with this rule, summary judgment for the ball club should be granted. The trial court did not adopt the limited duty rule and denied summary judgment. The defendant was given permission to appeal this issue to the Idaho Supreme Court.

HOLDING

The Idaho Supreme Court affirmed the trial court's order.

RATIONALE

First, the court reviewed the case law from various jurisdictions, acknowledging that some version of the limited duty rule was the majority position. However, the court noted that it did not believe that there was any public policy reason to adopt the limited duty rule in this jurisdiction. The court stated that the defendant did not show any statistical evidence that there was a high prevalence of foul ball injuries to spectators nor did the defendant address any design issues to prevent the occurrence of foul ball injuries. Furthermore, the court stated that "[w]ithout this information, drawing lines as to where a stadium owner's duty begins, where netting should be placed, and so on, becomes guesswork." The court then concluded that if the baseball rule was to be adopted in Idaho, it should be the legislature's prerogative to do so. The court, therefore, declined to adopt the baseball rule in Idaho.

Although the limited duty rule is often referred to as the baseball rule, this same principle does apply in other sport contexts, such as hockey, auto racing, and golf. There have been multiple cases where fans have been injured by projectiles leaving the "field of play" and injuring a patron or spectator (Read, et al., 2019). Additionally, courts have been asked to consider whether projectiles other than baseballs are covered by the limited-duty rule or assumption of risk doctrine. This issue was considered in a unique case that went all the way to the Missouri Supreme Court.

Coomer v. Kansas City Royals Baseball Corporation

437 S.W.3d 184 (2014)	FOCUS CASE

FACTS

John Coomer claimed he was injured when he was hit in the eye with a hotdog thrown by Sluggerrr, the Kansas City Royals mascot. The game in question was poorly attended, so Coomer left his assigned seats early in the game and moved to empty seats six rows behind the visitor's dugout. Shortly after Coomer changed seats, Sluggerrr mounted the visitor's dugout to begin the "Hotdog Launch," a feature of every

Royals home game since 2000. The launch occurs between innings, when Sluggerrr uses an air gun to shoot hotdogs from the roof of the visitor's dugout to fans seated beyond hand-tossing range. When his assistants are reloading the air gun, Sluggerrr tosses hotdogs by hand to the fans seated nearby. Sluggerrr generally tossed the hotdogs underhand while facing the fans but sometimes throws overhand, behind his back, and side-armed. Coomer was seated approximately 15 to 20 feet from Sluggerrr, directly in his view. After employing his hotdog-shaped air gun to send hotdogs to distant fans, Sluggerrr began to toss hotdogs by hand to fans seated near Coomer. Coomer testified that he saw Sluggerrr turn away from the crowd as if to prepare for a behind-the-back throw, but, because Coomer chose that moment to turn and look at the scoreboard, he admits he never saw Sluggerrr throw the hotdog that he claims injured him. Coomer testified only that a "split second later … something hit me in the face," and he described the blow as "pretty forceful." Two days later, Coomer felt he was "seeing differently" and something "wasn't right" with his left eye. The problem progressed until, approximately eight days after the incident, Coomer saw a doctor and was diagnosed with a detached retina. Coomer underwent surgeries to repair the retina and to remove a "traumatic cataract" in the same eye. Coomer sued the Kansas City Royals Baseball Corporation, claiming the team is responsible for Sluggerrr's negligence and the damages it caused. The Royals argued that under the baseball rule, Coomer was responsible for paying attention to everything going on around him, whether that be foul balls flying into the stands or a hot dog tossed by the mascot. A jury found in favor of the Royals, and Coomer appealed.

HOLDING

The Supreme Court of Missouri vacated the trial court's judgement and remanded the case, holding that the risk of being injured by a hotdog toss is not one of the inherent risks of watching a baseball game.

RATIONALE

An overwhelming majority of courts have recognized that spectators at sporting events are exposed to certain risks that are inherent to watching the contest. Thus, under the theory of implied primary assumption of the risk, the spectator has assumed the risks of being injured by a ball or bat flying into the stands. However, the rationale for this rule extends only to those risks that the home team is powerless to alleviate without fundamentally altering the game or the spectator's enjoyment of it. In addition, the home team also owes a duty of reasonable care to not alter or increase the inherent risks. The court determined that "the risk of injury from Sluggerrr's hotdog toss is not one of the risks inherent in watching the Royals play baseball that Coomer assumed merely by attending a game at Kauffman Stadium." This risk can be increased, decreased or eliminated altogether with no impact on the game or the spectators' enjoyment of it. As a result, Sluggerrr (and, therefore, the Royals) owe the fans a duty to use reasonable care in conducting the Hotdog Launch and can be held liable for damages caused by a breach of that duty. Sluggerrr's tosses may – or may not – be negligent; that is a question of fact for the jury to decide. But the Royals owe the same duty of reasonable care when distributing hotdogs or other promotional materials that it owes to their 1.7 million fans in all other circumstances, excepting only those risks of injury that are an inherent part of watching a baseball game in person.

Courts have recognized a number of exceptions to the limited duty rule when fans are injured when the game is not underway or where fans might not be expected to be on the lookout for balls or bats leaving the field (see Exhibit 15.3). In the 2015 retrial of the *Coomer* case, the jury found that neither party was at fault for Coomer's injury, leaving open the question of whether the limited duty rule only applies to bats and balls, or applies to projectiles that leave the field of play during a between innings promotion.

Exhibit 15.3 Limited duty rule cases.

Case	Decision
Maisonave v. Newark Bears Prof'l Baseball Club, Inc. (NJ. 2005)	Deciding as a matter of law that, "in areas outside of the stands, including concourses and mezzanines such as the one in this appeal, a commercial sports facility is no different than any other commercial establishment, and we do not hesitate to apply general negligence principles
Jones v. Three Rivers Mgmt. Corp. (Pa. 1978)	Deciding as a matter of law that "one who attends a baseball game as a spectator [cannot] properly be charged with anticipating as inherent to baseball the risk of being struck by a baseball while properly using an interior walkway
Turner v. Mandalay Sports Entm't, LLC. (Nev. 2008)	Barring claim as a matter of law because spectator was injured while eating in concession area because "primary implied assumption of risk doctrine merely goes to the initial determination of whether the defendant's legal duty encompasses the risk encountered by the plaintiff," which is a question for the court
Loughran v. The Phillies (Pa. 2005)	Holding as a matter of law that, even though risk of being injured by a ball tossed into the stands during a break in the game was not part of the sport of baseball, such risks were inherent in watching professional baseball games because such "activities [by players] have become inextricably intertwined with a fan's baseball experience
Sparks v. Sterling Doubleday Enterprises (N.Y. 2002)	Holding as a matter of law that team owed no duty beyond screening seats behind home plate and was not liable to member of high school band hit during batting practice while waiting to participate in pre-game ceremonies on opening day

Conclusion

This chapter applied numerous legal principles in the context of operating sport and recreational facilities and events. Specifically, we examined the basic principles of premise liability and common defenses available to venue and event operators. We also learned the scope of the duty of care owed by the stadium owner or operator to the spectator and the range of risks occurring during event and venue operations that can cause injuries to our spectators. A solid understanding of the varied legal issues presented in this chapter will enable you to operate your events and facilities more safely and effectively.

Discussion Questions

1 Define the terms *invitee*, *licensee*, and *trespasser*. What difference do these classifications make in the scope of duty owed by a facility owner or operator?
2 When does a plaintiff assume the risk of a dangerous condition on the property? Discuss the open and obvious doctrine and give an example. What is the distraction doctrine? Give an example.
3 What is the purpose of the recreational use statutes?
4 Compare and contrast the concepts of actual notice and constructive notice. Give an example of each.
5 Consider the duty to inspect; is it realistic that all facilities will be fully inspected prior to each use? How do you balance feasibility with best practice recommendations?

6   What is a reasonable interval for facilities to be inspected? Does the type of facility matter?
7   Explain dram shop laws. Why is it important for sport facility mangers to understand these laws?
8   Explain the prior similar instances rule.
9   Explain the limited duty rule applied to spectators who are hit by foul balls at baseball games.
10 Do you think the limited duty rule should apply to projectiles thrown or launched into the stands during promotional activities? Why or why not?

Learning Activities

Conduct an online search for your state statutes that mandate emergency medical protocols at sport facilities. For example, is there legislation mandating automated external defibrillators at fitness centers? Is there legislation providing that an ambulance must be present at sporting events where the seating capacity of the facility exceeds a certain number?

Case Study

The Daytona Deacons are a minor league, single A baseball team in Florida. As is common in minor league baseball, the marketing and promotions staff routinely try to implement unique promotional concepts to drive attendance to the games. A reality in minor league baseball is that many fans attend games for the atmosphere and the giveaways, not the baseball. A new promotion titled "Orange ya Glad You Came" night was developed for the upcoming season and would include the following: fans encouraged to wear orange colored clothing; special orange flavored concessions; coupons for free creamsicles from a local ice cream shop distributed to fans; a raffle drawing for two free tickets to the upcoming Orange Bowl (an NCAA D1 bowl game held in Florida); and, an orange toss during the 7th inning stretch, where members of the promotional staff throw oranges into the crowd from atop the dugout. Certain oranges will be marked with codes redeemable for prizes and team merchandise, including cash and free game tickets.

Assume you have been asked to review this promotion for any legal and/or risk management concerns. What would you recommend? What is the basis of your recommendation?

Considering ... Analysis & Discussion

Duty to Repair Dangers

In this case, the answer is most likely no. Since virtually no time passed between the time of the spill and the time of the fall, it was reasonable for the school personnel to fail to react to the spill and clean it up. If we change the facts to suggest that the spill had been there since a game held the week prior, that period of time is clearly unreasonable. (See Scott v. Herschend Family Entm't, 2020 U.S. Dist. LEXIS 73154 (M.D. Ga 2020) discussing how long a candy apply remained on the floor during a concert.)

Injuries Due to Alcohol Consumption

In this case, ABC University is not meeting its duty to properly consider crowd control related to alcohol service and consumption. While the number of spectators is certainly lower at a collegiate baseball or soccer game, and the environment may not be a charged, anytime alcohol is consumed or served, the facility operator has a responsibility to manage risk in a proactive manner.

References

Cases

Bearman v. University of Notre Dame, 453 N.E.2d 1196 (Ind. Ct. App. 1983).

Beglin v. Hartwick College, 888 N.Y.S.2d 320 (App. Div. 2009).

Benejam v. Detroit Tigers, Inc., 635 N.W.2d 219 (Mich. Ct. App. 2001).

Bourgeois v. Peters, 387 F.3d 1303 (11th Cir. 2004).

Brannum v. Overton County School Board, 516 F.3d 489 (6th Cir. 2008).

Coomer v Kansas City Royals Baseball Club, 437 S.W.3d 184 (2014).

Combs v. Georgetown College, 2011 Ky. App. LEXIS 629 (August 26, 2011).

Davis v. Cumberland County Bd. of Educ., 720 S.E.2d 418 (N.C. Ct. App. 2011).

Dibartolomeo v. New Jersey Sports and Exposition Auth., 2011 N.J. Super. Unpub. LEXIS 345 (February 16, 2011).

Griffin v. Grenada Youth League, 230 So. 3d 1083 (Miss: Court of Appeals 2017).

Johnston v. Tampa Sports Authority, 442 F. Supp. 2d 1257 (M.D. Fla. 2006).

Johnston v. Tampa Sports Authority, 530 F.3d 1320 (11th Cir. 2008).

Johnston v. Tampa Sports Authority, 555 U.S. 1138 (2009).

Jones v. Three Rivers Mgmt. Corp., 394 A.2d 546, 551 (Pa. 1978).

Harting v. Dayton Dragons Professional Baseball, 171 Ohio App. 3d 319 (Ohio Ct. App. 2007).

Katz v. United States, 389 U.S. 347 (1967).

Knight v. Jewett, 3 Cal. 4th 296 (1992).

Krzenski v. Southampton Union Free Sch. Dist., 173 A.D.3d 725, 102 N.Y.S.3d 693 (2019).

Lee v. Department of Parks & Recreation, 38 Cal. App. 5th 206 (Ct. App. 2019).

Limones v. School Dist. of Lee County, 161 So.3d 384 (2015).

Loughran v. The Phillies, 888 A.2d 872 (Pa. Sup. Ct. 2005).

Lowe v. California League of Prof'l Baseball, 56 Cal. App. 4th 112 (App. Ct. 1997).

Maisonave v. Newark Bears Prof'l Baseball Club, Inc., 881 A.2d 700, 709 (N.J. 2005).

McMillion v. Selman, 456 S.E.2d 28 (W. Va. 1995).

Miglino v. Bally Total Fitness of Greater N.Y., Inc., 20 N.Y.3d 342 (2013).

Morrissey v. Arlington Park Racecourse, 935 N.E.2d 644 (Ill. App. Ct. 2010).

Racky v. Belfor USA Group, Inc., 83 NE 3d 440 (Ill. App. Ct. 2017).

Reed-Jennings v. Baseball Club of Seattle, 351 P.3d 887 (2015).

Rountree v. Boise Baseball LLC, 296 P.3d 373 (Idaho 2013).

Southshore Baseball v. DeJesus, 982 N.E.2d 1076 (Ind. Ct. App. 2013).

Sparks v. Sterling Doubleday Enterprises, I.P., 752 N.Y.S.2d 79, 80 (2002).

Stow v. Los Angeles Dodgers, No. BC462127 (Cal. Super. Ct. May 24, 2011).

Turner v. Mandalay Sports Entm't, LLC, 180 P.3d 1172, 1177 (Nev. 2008).

Statutes

Building Standards Code, Title 24 California Code of Regulations (2013).

Restatement (Second) of Torts (1965).

United States Constitution, Fourth Amendment.

Wisconsin Statutes §101.11(1) (2009–2010).

Other Sources

Acquavella, K., & Axisa, M. (2019, June 27). White Sox, Nationals, Pirates become first MLB teams to further extend protective netting at stadiums. Retrieved from https://www.cbssports.com/mlb/news/white-sox-nationals-pirates-become-first-mlb-teams-to-further-extend-protective-netting-at-stadiums/.

Babb, K., & Rich, S. (2016, October 28). A quietly escalating issue for NFL: Fan violence and how to contain it. *Chicago Tribune*. Retrieved from https://www.chicagotribune.com/sports/ct-nfl-fan-violence-stadium-20161028-story.html

Bergman, M., & Axelrod, J. (2019, July 13). After numerous foul ball fan injuries, Baseball reconsiders protective netting. NPR. Retrieved from https://www.npr.org/2019/07/13/739967250/after-numerous-foul-ball-fan-injuries-baseball-reconsiders-protective-netting.

Bryant, K. B. (2017). Sport: A well manicured battlefield. *Journal of Sport Safety and Security*, 2(1), 1–13.

Conn, D. (2017, April 12). Dortmund bombs highlight challenge of combating modern terrorism acts. Retrieved at https://www.theguardian.com/football/2017/apr/12/dortmund-bombs-highlight-challenge-combating-modern-terrorism-acts.

Connaughton, D., Spengler, J. O., & Zhang, J. J. (2007). Symposium: Risk management issues in sports: An analysis of automated external defibrillator implementation and related risk management practices in health/fitness clubs. *Journal of Legal Aspects of Sport, 17*, 81–101.

Dolan, C. (2014, August 21). Beautiful Levi's Stadium has dangerous characteristics. *San Francisco Examiner*. Retrieved from https://www.sfexaminer.com/features/beautiful-levis-stadium-has-dangerous-characteristics/.

Diamantopoulos, G. P. (2008). Note and comment: A look at social host and dram shop liability from pre-game tailgating to post-game barhopping. *DePaul Journal of Sports Law and Contemporary Problems, 4*, 201–227.

Filce, R., Hall, S. A., & Phillips, D. (2016). Stadium alcohol management: A best practices approach. *International Journal of Sport Management, Recreation and Tourism, 21*, 48–65.

Fortington, L. V., West, L., Morgan, D., & Finch, C. F. (2019). Implementing automated external defibrillators into community sports clubs/facilities: A cross-sectional survey of community club member preparedness for medical emergencies. *BMJ Open Sport & Exercise Medicine, 5*(1), 1–8.

Gorman, R., & Weeks, D. (2015). *Death at the Ballpark: More than 2,000 game-related fatalities of players, other personnel and spectators in amateur and professional baseball, 1862–2014*. Jefferson, NC. McFarland Publishing.

Gottlieb, H. (2008, December 5). Stadium beer vendor liability suit settled for $25 Million. *Law.com*. Retrieved from https://www.law.com/almID/1202426492772/.

Kozlowski, J. (2016) Recreational use statutes in state Supreme Courts. *National Recreation and Park Association*. Retrieved from https://www.nrpa.org/parks-recreation-magazine/2016/july/recreational-use-statutes-in-state-supreme-courts/.

LSUSports.net (2013, June 28). Tiger Stadium Tailgating Policies. Retrieved from http://www.lsusports.net/ViewArticle.dbml?DB_OEM_ID=5200&ATCLID=205418795.

McGregor, E. M. (2012). Comment: Hooray beer!?: How the reemergence of alcohol sales at campus stadiums will affect Universities. *Marquette Sports Law Review, 23*(1), 211–230.

Morton, H. (2013, June 14). Dram Shop Liability State Statutes. Retrieved from https://www.ncsl.org/research/financial-services-and-commerce/dram-shop-liability-state-statutes.aspx.

NASPE. (n.d.). *National standards for sport coaches* (2nd ed.). Retrieved from http://www.aahperd.org/naspe/standards/nationalStandards/SportCoaches.cfm.

Niehoff, K. (2019, December 4). Wake-up call for increased security at high school sports events. *Auburn Reporter*. Retrieved from https://www.auburn-reporter.com/sports/wake-up-call-for-increased-security-at-high-school-sports-events/.

Nietzel, M. (2018, December 1). Sobering thoughts about alcohol sales at college stadiums. *Forbes*. Retrieved from https://www.forbes.com/sites/michaeltnietzel/2018/12/01/second-sobering-thoughts-about-alcohol-sales-at-college-stadiums/#5f4b04086259.

Odum, C. (2018, October 22). Lawsuit over fan death at Atlanta Braves stadium claims team, MLB ignored safety. *Insurance Journal*. Retrieved from https://www.insurancejournal.com/news/southeast/2018/10/22/505191.htm.

Read, C., Beaumont, C., Isbell, J., Dombrowsky, A., Brabston, E., Ponce, B., Hale, H., Mccollough, K., Estes, R., & Momaya, A. (2019). Spectator injuries in sports. *The Journal of Sports Medicine and Physical Fitness, 59*(3), 520–523.

Rossetti, M. (2018, April). Can spectator seating be both steep and safe. *Athletic Business*. Retrieved from https://www.athleticbusiness.com/stadium-arena/can-spectator-seating-be-both-steep-and-safe.html.

Schrotenboer, B. (2013, May 2). Holes in stadium security. *USA Today*. Retrieved from https://www.usatoday.com/story/sports/2013/05/02/stadium-security-boston-marathon-kentucky-derby/2130875/.

Smith, E. (2018, April 18). Alcohol sales at NCAA championships approved by Division I council. *USA Today*. Retrieved from https://www.usatoday.com/story/sports/college/2018/04/18/alcohol-sales-ncaa-championships-approved-division-council/530028002/.

Steinbach, P. (2013, July). Rethinking security post-Boston. *Athletic Business*, 10–14.

Swenson, S. J. (2012). Unsportsmanlike conduct: The duty placed on stadium owners to protect against fan violence. *Marquette Sports Law Review, 23*(1), 135–153.

Van Milligen, D. (2015, February). How to prevent fan violence at sporting events. *Athletic Business*, 15–17.

Watkins, T., & Mungin, L. (2013) Stadium deaths: What's behind fatal falls? CNN. Retrieved from https://www.cnn.com/2013/11/26/us/stadium-falls/index.html.

Web Resources

www.aahperd.org/naspe/standards/upload/Availability-Access-to-AEDs-Final-5-5-11.pdf ∎ This is NASPE's position statement on the placement and use of AEDs in school settings.

www.nata.org/sites/default/files/preventing-sudden-death.pdf ∎ This site provides the complete statement by the National Athletic Trainers Association (released June, 2013) titled "Preventing Sudden Death in Secondary School Athletics Programs: Best Practices Recommendations." This report encompasses a variety of recommendations, including information on the use of AEDS.

www.ncaapublications.com/productdownloads/MD12.pdf ■ Link to the 2012–13 *Sports Medicine Handbook* to find Guideline 1D, "Lightning Safety," for a statement that planned access to early defibrillation should be a part of any emergency plan.

http://www.ncsl.org/research/health/laws-on-cardiac-arrest-and-defibrillators-aeds.aspx ■ This link from the National Conference of State Legislatures provides information on the state laws pertaining to the use of AEDS.

www.ncs4.com ■ This is the website for the National Center for Spectator Sports Safety & Security housed at the University of Southern Mississippi. The Center conducts workshops to train sport venue personnel in professional and college sports on issues related to risk management and security for sports venues.

http://www.ncsl.org/research/financial-services-and-commerce/dram-shop-liability-state-statutes.aspx ■ The site for National Conference on State Legislatures includes the status of state legislation regarding Dram Shop Laws.

www.ncsl.org/issues-research/health/laws-on-cardiac-arrest-and-defibrillators-aeds ■ The site for National Conference on State Legislatures includes the status of state legislation regarding AEDs.

https://www.ready.gov/business/implementation/emergency ■ A website from the Department of Homeland Security, serves as a resource for developing emergency action plans.

16 Contract Issues and Venue/Event Operations

Amanda M. Siegrist

Introduction

The ways in which you communicate with sport and recreation participants, lessees, business partners, and guests will affect many aspects of how well you manage legal issues associated with operating sport venues and events. This communication occurs across a variety of interactions including operating agreements, promotional materials, online ticketing and registration systems, and onsite. As in any relationship, business or personal, what you say to people and how you say it become a cornerstone of the relationship. Use your communication mechanisms to convey and reinforce the message that you are concerned about the welfare of participants and that you are sharing information with them to make their participation experiences better and safer, as this should be the primary goal. The notion of using agreements to avoid or minimize liability, such as the exculpatory clause, is only a secondary aspect but an important operational detail. Using the law to attain a competitive advantage in the business of sport has particular application in the context of information exchange, since you and your organization have complete control over the messages you send to your participants and guests. This philosophy should sound familiar to you – it represents the essence of the preventive law process as discussed in Chapter 1.

This chapter focuses on the types of information exchanges you may have with outside parties first from the view of a variety of standard contractual agreements related to operating venues and events, and second from the perspective of managing potential liability for injuries to participants and guests. We discuss the legal concerns relevant to each of these as well as the managerial implications of each for your business. See Exhibit 16.1 for an overview of this chapter's managerial contexts, major legal issues, relevant laws, and illustrative cases.

Facility and Event Operations and Contractual Agreements

Agreements associated with the operation of sport venues and events raises additional questions for sport managers. This section examines the importance of common contractual agreements used in venue and event operations, including lease agreements, promotional materials and sponsorship agreements, as well as ticketing and game agreements.

Operating stadiums and arena often involve agreements with a primary tenant, usually a professional or collegiate team. These teams depend on many revenue streams such as luxury suites, personal seat licenses (PSLs), naming rights, concessions, broadcasting, licensing, and sponsorships. Stadiums and arenas also allow the use of the facility for a variety of other events (e.g., concerts, high school sporting events, e-sports, community events, etc.) in order to serve the public and generate revenue. Thus, a basic understanding of contract law is essential for facility owners and operators. Persons working for sport facilities must navigate a myriad of agreements and issues. Each of these components creates unique challenges for sport managers. Below we examine some of these issues in greater detail. But first, an important

Exhibit 16.1 Management contexts in which issues related to event and operating agreements, with relevant laws and cases.

Management Context	Major Legal Issues	Relevant Law	Illustrative Cases
Oversight of any activity	Setting standard of care	Negligence	
Development of marketing materials	Accuracy of promotional materials	Breach of contract	Nicklaus
Oversight of youth sport programs	Validity of waivers signed by minors or parents	Contract law	Boom, Hamill
Supervision of K–12 athletics			
Athletic directors of school sports or university sports	School sports as essential services	Contract law	Wagenblast, Kyriazis
Ski resort managers	Skiing as essential service	Contract law	Gregorie
Providers of commercial outfitters	Violation of statutory duty and waivers	Contract law	Murphy
		Statute setting standard of care	
Oversight of any sport/ recreational activity	Public policy and waivers	Contract law	Walker
	Waiver language clarity	Contract law	Geczi
	Conduct within scope of activities	Contract law	Semeniken, Lewis
	Conduct beyond negligence	Contract law	McGregor
	Agreements to participate	Assumption of risk Comparative negligence Failure to warn	

underlying piece of all contract law is a legal concept commonly referred to as the Covenant of Good Faith and Fair Dealing.

Covenant of Good Faith and Fair Dealing

The Covenant of Good Faith and Fair Dealing clause is key to the foundation of contract law. When dealing with another party through a contractual agreement, it is not only understood, but also legally required, that you deal with each other with honesty and fairness. If this is not followed, a court could rule the contract, or breach, as void. Each and every word of a contract is critical. For example, there is a big difference from saying a party "shall" pay a certain amount versus a party "can" pay a certain amount. Just because one "can" pay it, does not mean they "have" to. As such, your contract should clearly state that they "shall" or "must" in order to create a covenant. It is in the best interest of your organization to avoid ambiguous language or use clichés in agreements. For example, if A contracts with B to perform when the clock "strikes noon," the implied covenant of good faith would impose liability if A destroyed the clock to avoid having to meet the precise terms of the contracts. In other words, a technicality done in bad faith (i.e. with ill will or poor intentions) will not be upheld in court. This is seen in some insurance cases where an insurance company's bad faith refusal to pay the insured can exist and the insurance company has the leverage on the claimant who suffered a loss (Diamond, Levine, & Madden, 2007).

Lease Agreements

Lease agreements are important both to the facility owner and operator (**lessor**) and the person or entity that rents or leases the facility (**lessee**). As with any contract, the **lease agreement** defines the rights and responsibilities of the parties and typically addresses such issues as how much rent must be paid, when access will be provided, what physical areas may be used, what services are provided by the facility owners (such as utilities, promotional assistance, ticket sales, security, and concessions), how to handle radio or television broadcasts, and a host of other issues that may arise.

To examine some of the key components of a lease agreement, let's consider a typical scenario in the sport industry. The local sports commission, Charleston Sports Council, has helped to attract a major event to the city, and the event will need a facility to use. Thus, the event promoter, ABX Sports, Inc., wants to enter into a lease agreement with the local stadium authority, Charleston Sports Property Management (CSPM), to lease the 25,000-seat arena owned by the City of Charleston and operated by CSPM. A standard lease agreement would include the following key elements.

Right to Use and Occupy

The lease will grant ABX Sports the right to use the facility and occupy certain spaces. Such spaces must be clearly and specifically defined, such as field and court area, all seating areas, press box, ticket booths, and parking lots. The duration of the right to use and occupy must also be clearly and specifically defined. For example, the lease may provide that the lessee is entitled to use and occupy the premises from 8:00 a.m. on the 10th day of July until 4:00 p.m. on the 14th day of July.

Specifying the exact time access is permitted is important so that the event organizers have ample time to set up and prepare for the event. A lease may also contain a clause that permits access (as opposed to occupancy) for a certain number of hours before and a certain number of hours after the lease term begins or ends for setup, deliveries, and teardown.

Rental Fees

The rental fees represent the consideration for the contract, and they should be clearly expressed. A facility may demand a flat rental fee plus a percentage of gross ticket sales. A golden rule in facility management is "always take a percentage." Most facility operators will want a percentage of the gate or ticket sales. Of course, the amount of that percentage is negotiable, and it may be structured to apply only when ticket sales reach a certain point or to vary as ticket sales meet or exceed certain targets. Fees may also be based on the duration of occupancy, such as daily or hourly rental fees. A portion of the fee may be required in advance as a non-refundable fee or deposit. Agreements will also address when and how the payment is due. This could be in multiple payments or in one lump sum. Often, a down payment is required and then an invoice is provided immediately following the conclusion of the event, with a deadline for payment. As mentioned throughout this section, some fees may vary and thus, final numbers will not be known until the conclusion and wrap-up of the event.

Fee for Additional Services

The facility may provide a number of additional services that the lessee will have to agree to pay for, such as event security, merchandise sales, ushers, parking attendants, ticket takers, labor for setup and teardown, audio, maintenance, and administrative assistance. The lease may stipulate a fixed amount for these services, or a schedule of available services and their corresponding costs could be attached as an addendum to the lease agreement. Thus, the lessee may not be required to use the facility's services, but if it does, it agrees to pay the stated fees.

However, some facilities may require that a lessee use only approved vendors for some services or use the facility's in-house services such as catering services. For example, an event organizer may have several local restaurants as sponsors who are willing to donate meals or other catering services to the event, but unless the event organizer has carefully negotiated with the facility to be able to use the sponsors' catering services and bring outside food and beverages onto the premises, the value of that sponsorship may not be realized.

Revenue Sharing

The lease will provide whether or not the various revenues that will be generated from the event from concessions, merchandise sales, and parking are to be shared between the parties. Facility operators may either take or give a percentage of those revenue streams depending on how the lease agreement is structured. Most large multipurpose sports facilities retain all these revenue streams for themselves, but they may be willing to share a small percentage of net sales with the lessee. In a smaller facility, the operator may be more willing to negotiate those revenues.

Renter's Facility Requirements

Particularly for varying levels of sporting events, different court or field set-ups will be necessary. Many facility lease agreements for events, particularly sporting events, include an area for the renter to specify these details (such as the number of seats to be open for viewers, dimensions of courts, number of fields or courts to be used or set-up, height of nets, or distance between bases).

Rental Usage Terms and Conditions

The agreement will also specify the "do's and don'ts" of the facility. Lease agreements should address the rules, requirements and prohibited behavior of the facility that must be followed by the renter's and its guests. For example, if the city that the venue is located within has city ordinances preventing smoking, the lease should inform and require the renter to abide by such ordinances. If the venue does not allow pets, they should include a clause such as "Pets, except for service animals pursuant to the Americans with Disabilities Act, will not be allowed inside the venue." This clause establishes that by accepting this agreement, the renter accepts responsibility for its employees and guests to abide by the city ordinances and venue rules and regulations.

Kitchen Sink Provisions

The lease will include a number of provisions that, while they are generic or common to most contracts, are also very important in defining the potential liability of the parties. These provisions include the following:

- A *non-assignment clause* preventing the lessee from assigning its rights to another person or organization.
- A *choice of law clause* designating that the lease will be governed by the law of a particular state.
- A *hold harmless clause* stating that one party, usually the lessor, will be held harmless by the second party, usually the lessee, for any tort liability of the lessor that arises out of the business activity referenced in the contract. In essence, the lessee is simply agreeing in advance that it will assume responsibility (legal liability) for any negligent acts, errors, or omissions of the lessor.
- An *indemnification clause* protecting the lessor in the event the lessee causes an injury to a guest that results in a lawsuit against the lessor. To try to shift potential liability to the lessee, most lessors will require that the lessee promise to "indemnify" the lessor. Under such an agreement, the lessor cannot recover until it has actually suffered a loss. The scope of the indemnification should be spelled out and normally includes compensatory damages, punitive damages, and litigation costs and attorneys' fees (Van der Smissen, 1990, § 25.21).
- An *insurance clause* requiring the lessee to buy insurance and provide proof of insurance before it will be permitted to occupy the facility.
- A *force majeure* (literally meaning "greater force") *clause* excusing or relieving a party from having to perform under the lease agreement due to natural disasters or other "acts of God," war, or the failure of third parties – such as suppliers and subcontractors – to perform their obligations to the contracting party. Force majeure clauses excuse a party only if the failure to perform could not be avoided by the exercise of due care by that party. (An example being the 2020 Covid-19 crisis where events and facilities were closed by law.)
- A *damage clause* holding the lessee financially responsible for any damage it may cause to the building, premises, furnishings, or equipment.

This list includes only the main areas for negotiation that must be included in a facility lease agreement. The sophistication and complexity of the agreement will vary considerably from one event to the next depending upon the event and the amenities and services available at the facility. If a facility has convention or meeting space, restaurants, or luxury suites, those items may be part of the lease transaction.

The following hypothetical case demonstrates the importance of clearly identifying when access to the facility is granted.

Considering ... Facility Lease Agreements

Imagine your Myrtle Beach-based sport management company is hosting a basketball camp with current and former NBA players as guest coaches. You hire a marketing group to help promote the event in and around the Myrtle Beach area. Some of the guest coaches take it upon themselves to post about the event through their own social media accounts and websites, really boosting the awareness for your event. With over 100 sign-ups a month prior to your event, your company begins to order t-shirts for campers and arrange flight and hotel accommodations for the out of town coaches.

Severe weather is not uncommon in the Carolinas, especially during hurricane season. When a major hurricane hits the area two weeks prior to your camp, the venue you intended to use is flooded. The venue does not inform you that they are flooded; rather, they intend to get the damage fixed in time for your camp. After another week passes and the venue has had a clean-up crew at their facility, they realize the damage was more extensive than originally thought. The venue informs you that you will be unable to use their facility.

Your company is able to find another venue; however, it is more expensive and further away, requiring you to provide transportation for the majority of your already-signed-up campers.

Questions

- Does the implied covenant of Good Faith and Fair Dealings apply in this situation? If so, how and where?
- What type of clause in the lease agreement would be triggered by these circumstances? Will the venue be held liable for breaching the contract?
- What additional provisions could have been made in the lease agreement to provide some protection for your company, if any?
- What strategies would you implement to solve this dilemma?

Note how you would answer the questions and then check your responses using the Analysis & Discussion at the end of this chapter.

Ticket Agreements

Ticket sales raise some interesting legal issues for sport managers. First, as with any contract, issues will arise as to what rights or benefits a fan has obtained when he or she purchases a ticket. Ticket agreements can involve sales of single game tickets, group tickets, or season tickets, renewable season ticket agreements, and personal seat licenses. The majority of courts have consistently held that a ticket constitutes a revocable license. A **license** is defined as a privilege to go on the premises for a certain purpose, but it does not operate to confer on the licensee any title or interest in the property (Garner et al., 2004). Thus, a **revocable license** is a license that may be revoked, withdrawn, or canceled. Typically, when a fan purchases a ticket to a sporting event, that ticket represents a privilege to access the premises according to the terms and conditions of the license. The majority view is that individual, group, and season ticket sales and renewal agreements are not property, but are rather revocable licenses.

In addition to language included in a ticket purchase agreement, the ticket itself generally contains a number of restrictions and conditions. For example, on the back of the ticket the following may appear:

> This ticket is a revocable license. Failure of the ticket holder to comply with any of the following conditions will automatically terminate this license. Coolers, kegs, bottles, cans, alcoholic beverages, food, fireworks, illegal substances, weapons, umbrellas, horns, or other noisemakers may not be brought into the stadium. Smoking is prohibited. Consuming alcohol in Sections 111 and 211 is prohibited. Throwing objects onto the playing field is strictly forbidden. Unless specifically authorized in advance by the licensor, this ticket may not be offered in a commercial promotion or as a prize in a sweepstakes or contest.

If the ticket holder violates any of these conditions, the license may be revoked. Many sport organizations impose further restrictions on season ticket holders, such that if the ticket holder violates any rules of the stadium or conditions of the ticket, he forfeits the right to buy tickets in the future. For example, the Appeals Court of Massachusetts affirmed the dismissal of a 20-year New England Patriots season ticket holder's action against the team. The holder's privileges were terminated after an incident at Gillette Stadium in which a business associate of the holder was ejected. The court rejected the plaintiff's argument that a contractual right to renew its season tickets annually existed based on the 20-year relationship with the team, citing the general rule that the purchase of a ticket to a sports event creates nothing more than a revocable license (*Yarde Metals v. New England Patriots*, 2005).

More recently, ticketing lawsuits are arising as a result of secondary market ticket brokers and digital ticket sales. In 2019, four ticket brokers filed a joint lawsuit against the Los Angeles Dodgers organization, alleging the team breached an oral contract to use secondary market brokers as a reliable source for ticket sales (Solis, 2018). For the 2017 World Series, the lowest ticket price sold by the team was $166 but on the morning of Game 7, the same ticket was being sold by brokers for more than $1,000 (Shaikin, 2019). The Dodgers, and other similar organizations, are quickly realizing that millions of dollars are being made by second-party brokers. As such, teams, as well we venues for concerts and other events, are singing a different tune. Teams are saying they cannot guarantee a ticket unless it is sold directly by them (Shaikin, 2019). Further, in the age of technology, we can now access tickets via smart phones, email, and through applications, through which not only tickets can be sold but also advanced concessions, merchandise, future tickets, and more.

Another example of the digital ticket age dilemma is with the Minnesota Timberwolves. A class action lawsuit from ticket buyers was filed against the Timberwolves in March of 2016. Season-ticket holders claimed they were not adequately notified of the changes in the ticketing policy, which is now all digital and included a 75 percent resale price minimum. Ticketholders claim it is too hard for fans to exchange tickets, sell them on secondary markets, or even give them away by adding fees and resale price minimums (Frederick, 2017; Greder, 2016). The lawsuit was settled with the Timberwolves more prominently disclosing the 75 percent resale value minimum. A few other settlement terms came with some perks for the lead-plaintiffs, including free upper-bowl tickets for a certain amount of games for the 17–18 season, as well as a complimentary tour of the arena (Frederick, 2017).

While it is clear that game tickets and season ticket renewal agreements are treated as revocable licenses, the legal treatment of other ticket agreements, such as PSLs, is not as clear. Organizations tend to have the upper hand, as they may arguably have a right to; however, just because tickets are licenses does not mean the holder has no rights (Hamill & Poulos, 2017).

Therefore, sport managers working in sales and ticket operations must pay close attention to season ticket holder agreements, personal seat license agreements, and back of ticket language to address those situations where the sport organization may properly revoke the ticket privilege or restrict the transferability of the ticket purchaser's rights.

Promotional Materials

Language is not only a problem in terms of setting or raising the standard of care; an organization may also incur liability for breach of contract, fraud, misrepresentation, or a violation of a consumer protection statute if the language is inaccurate. As seen throughout this text, it is vital to take a holistic approach to every aspect of the organization. Therefore, when you are developing brochures, videos, and promotional materials for your programs, you should involve not only the marketing and advertising employees but also your attorney. The attorney can advise you regarding the legal impact of certain words or phrases that you wish to use. The following Focus Case provides an example of this issue.

Donner v. Nicklaus

778 F.3d 857 (10th Cir. 2015)	**FOCUS** CASE

FACTS

Legendary golfer Jack Nicklaus was named as a charter member in marketing materials for a development project in Utah of a luxury ski and golf resort. Investors, Mr. and Ms. Donner, claim they would not have chosen to invest their $1.5 million if it were not for Nicklaus' attributed involvement. The investors, Mr. and Ms. Donner, filed suit against Mr. Nicklaus and Nicklaus Golf Club, LLC (Nicklaus Defendants) on the grounds of intentional misrepresentation. The plaintiffs allege that via press releases and marketing materials, Jack Nicklaus made multiple statements supporting his involvement of this grandiose development such as "When I walked to Mt. Holly Club, I was so captured by its potential, I thought through all 18 holes. In fact, I have been so impressed with the club and its management team that I became a founding charter member" (*Donner v. Nicklaus*, 2015, p. 863). The Donners also alleged that Nicklaus Defendants falsely represented that Nicklaus as a charter member had paid the $1.5 million purchase price, when, in actuality, Nicklaus was merely an "honorary" Founding Member and invested no money in the development. The development of the golf and ski resort never came to fruition. The plaintiffs allege the Nicklaus and the developers mischaracterized his membership role in an effort to convince investors to join the multi-million-dollar project that eventually failed, going bankrupt before it could open. The district court dismissed the Donners' claims for intentional misrepresentation.

HOLDING

The U.S. 10th Circuit Court of Appeals reversed the district court and remanded the case to the district court for further proceedings on the intentional misrepresentation claim.

RATIONALE

The court concluded that the Donners had adequately alleged intentional misrepresentation of Mr. Nicklaus' membership status. A review of the marketing materials involved – a press release and a brochure – provided sufficient grounds for the Donners to proceed with their claim. In the context of these marketing materials, the Donners had adequately alleged that Mr. Nicklaus held himself out as a charter member and that a fact-finder could reasonably infer that Mr. Nicklaus was implying that he had paid the $1.5 million purchase price. A failure to distinguish between an honorary member and one who had paid the $1.5 million entry fee was enough to satisfy the required element of representing a material fact that was false in order to induce another party to act, and that party did in fact act in reliance.

The *Nicklaus* case illustrates the role our promotional materials can play in creating legal obligations toward our consumers. Information contained in promotional materials must be accurate, complete and truthful (Moorman, 2015). While it is a goal of marketing to sell your products and services in an appealing manner, sport managers want to avoid claims of intentional or fraudulent misrepresentation. In a world where media tends to be dominated by celebrity and star power, the *Nicklaus* case, and other non-sport event examples such as the Fyre Festival (a failed destination-concert promoted by celebrities and musicians in 2017) (Garcia-Navarro, 2019), should serve as a cautionary tale for celebrity endorsement and advertising that

Competitive Advantage Strategies

Brochures, Videos, and Promotional Materials

- Information exchange with your participants is a crucial aspect of your preventive law plan. Incorporate the preparation of all documents into this process.
- Draft all documents to support your corporate culture and your goal of fostering the well-being of your participants.
- Never promise "perfection" in your brochures or other advertising materials. Perfection is unattainable, and your promise may serve to set an unrealistic standard of care for your program.
- Never promise that an activity is "perfectly safe"; that is inaccurate because there are always inherent risks in any physical activity.
- Consult an attorney when developing your advertising and marketing materials to avoid using language that may be detrimental to your legal position.

is not truthful, honest or well-informed, as it may well invite litigation. In Chapter 19 you will study the concept of false advertising and misrepresentation in greater detail.

Codes of Conduct and Stadium Policies

In the operation of an event, your risk management plan will identify certain risks that could arise. All of the documents, instructions and signage you use must contain accurate information about the nature of the activity and the actual risks that participants may encounter.

Organizations can and should also post Codes of Conducts for rules and expected behavior of participants. This type of language allows you to have the authority to remove or reprimand a participant who does not follow it. See Exhibit 16.2 for an example of the NBA Fan Code of Conduct.

Fan codes of conduct typically encourage guests to report inappropriate behavior to the nearest usher, security guard or guest services staff member. These codes empower the facility operator to eject noncompliant fans and even revoke tickets from season ticket holders. Language can be one of the most powerful tools to facilitate a safe environment and clarify expectations and liability, but as sport managers, you must ensure it is stated properly and as accurately as possible.

Exhibit 16.2 NBA fan code of conduct.

The National Basketball Association and team arenas are committed to creating a safe, comfortable, and enjoyable sports & entertainment experience. NBA fans have a right to expect an environment where:

- Players will respect and appreciate each and every fan.
- Guests will be treated in a consistent, professional and courteous manner by all arena and team personnel.
- Guests will enjoy the basketball experience free from disruptive behavior, including foul or abusive language or obscene gestures.
- Guests will consume alcoholic beverages in a responsible manner. Intervention with an impaired, intoxicated or underage guest will be handled in a prompt and safe manner.
- Guests will sit only in their ticketed seats and show their tickets when requested.
- Guests will not engage in fighting, throwing objects or attempting to enter the court, and those who engage in any of these actions will immediately be ejected from the game.
- Guests will smoke in designated smoking areas only.
- There will not be any obscene or indecent messages on signs or clothing.
- Guests will comply with requests from arena staff regarding arena operations and emergency response procedures.

The NBA and team arenas thank you for adhering to the provisions of the NBA Fan Code of Conduct (NBA Media Ventures, LLC, 2019).

Sponsorship and Event Vendor Agreements

Sponsorships are a key aspect of successful facilities and events. A sponsorship is deemed successful if they solve an existing problem for a business, such as a need for more exposure or to drive sales. Regardless of the reason, once you have a sponsorship secured, whether large or small, it is critical to have it in writing. An agreement for smaller or in-kind sponsorships (i.e., goods or resources rather than cash) should not be overwhelming or intimidating. Larger, cash sponsorships do, however, require a thorough agreement. These agreements should cover details such as the money or goods/resources to be exchanged, dates of delivery and payment, which party is responsible for delivery, what happens in the event of a cancelation, and more. Exhibit 16.3 is an example of a fairly straight-forward or common event vendor agreement to demonstrate the logistics of what these contracts may contain.

Exhibit 16.3 Sample event vendor contract.

Event Vendor Contract

This is an agreement between _____ (hereafter referred to as "Host") and _____ (hereafter referred to as "Vendor").

The Host will be hosting the following Event _____ to take place at _____ location on ____/____/____, starting at ____:____ AM / PM, and has the legal ability to issue permission for vending during the above mentioned Event, and

Vendor desires to vend _____ at and during the above mentioned Event, and has issued the Host a sum of $_____ for permission to vend at the Event,

The Host and Vendor parties both agree to the following terms:

1 Vendor will be given access to the place that is agreed upon by both parties no less than _____ hours before the Event starts to set up the Vendor's station, goods to be sold, and anything else that is needed and customary to vend at that specific location.
2 The Vendor will not vend any items or services that are not disclosed here at the Event without prior written consent from the Host.
3 Items that will be sold:

   _____

   _____

   _____

4 Vendor's station shall be no bigger than _____ × _____ feet or taller than _____ feet; and shall be clean and orderly; and shall follow all applicable laws and regulations of the County and State of said Event.
5 Vendor will supply own tables, tent, chairs, and extension cords if needed.
6 Vendor's staff may exhibit that goods are for sale only while the staff is within the area of the vendor's specified location.
7 Vendor's staff will be properly dressed and their appearance will be clean and neat and they shall conduct themselves in an orderly fashion.
8 There is to be no loud distracting music, noise, and or sound amplification devices used by Vendor's staff at the above mentioned Event.
9 Vendor will have access to the location for up to _____ hours following the Event has concluded at ____:____ AM / PM to dismantle and remove all items brought to the Event by Vendor. Vendor shall leave the location free from trash and in similar condition that it was in before the Vendor was there.
10 Vendor agrees to hold the Host free from any damages or claims that may develop in connection with participating in the above mentioned Event.

In agreement to the above mentioned terms a representative of the Event and Vendor sign below:

This contract shall be governed by the laws of the State of _____ in _____ County and any applicable Federal Law.

_____ Date_____

Signature of Event Representative

_____ Date_____

Signature of Vendor Representative

Game Contracts

Many large public facilities do not host their own events (events that they create and operate). Instead, they are primarily in the business of renting or leasing space, providing support services, and serving the public interest by attracting visitors to the community, producing a positive economic impact for the community, and enhancing the image of the community. Other sport facilities are owned or operated by actual users of the facility, such as collegiate athletic teams, professional sports teams, high schools, and private training facilities. In these facilities, the owner is often also a user of the facility. For example, a college basketball team will host another college in a contest and use its home arena to play the game. In these circumstances, the visiting team is not going to enter into a lease agreement to use the arena. Of course, the host team does not need a lease to use its own facility. Instead, the two colleges will enter into a game contract, which will identify the particular rights and responsibilities related to the contest. Consider the following situation involving a game contract. You will notice that some provisions are similar to those involved in a lease agreement.

You are the athletic director for Victory University (Victory), and you want to play a non-conference powerhouse, University of Pigskin (Pigskin), in football in the upcoming season as a home game. You know that you can fill your 60,000-seat stadium if Pigskin agrees to the game. You are also confident that ESPN will also want to broadcast the game. Let's explore some of the key components that must appear in this game contract.

Location, Date, and Time of the Event

The location, date, and time of the game must be clearly stated. You may have to make the exact time of the game dependent upon your contract with a broadcasting partner, such as ESPN.

Financial Arrangements

The financial arrangements must be delineated. How much will you pay Pigskin for playing you at home? You may pay Pigskin a guarantee (a set amount), a percentage of the net revenue for the game,

---

Competitive Advantage Strategies

Facility Operations and Agreements Issues

- Facility managers should carefully examine all contractual agreements to determine if they are both clear and comprehensive. Agreements should be readily understandable and address all questions that are likely to arise between the parties.
- While it is important to maximize revenue from ticket sales, it is equally important to avoid costly litigation or disenfranchising ticket holders and fans. Ticket policies and purchase agreements must be clear, and special attention should be paid to resolving customer complaints. Nowhere is customer service as important as in ticket sales and facility operations.
- Ticket sales managers must review back-of-ticket language and season ticket renewal agreements for clear statements related to the revocability of the privilege associated with the ticket and actions that may subject the tickets to revocation, such as unauthorized resale, misconduct, or other violations of the ticket agreement. Similarly, PSL agreements should clearly outline any transfer limitations on the right to purchase seats.
- If your organization is experiencing a high number of ticket holder complaints, it may be time to contact the sport management or marketing department at a local university to conduct customer service quality studies for your organization.

or a combination of the two. If you choose to share the revenue, you must define exactly what constitutes net revenue. For example, does revenue include only ticket sales, or are other revenue items included as well, such as concessions, parking, and broadcasting fees? You must also set a date on which you will disburse the payment to Pigskin. It is to your advantage to delay this date until the very end of the season so that you can have use of the money until then. Pigskin, however, will try to negotiate to have the compensation disbursed as soon after the game as possible. Pigskin may also negotiate an audit provision in the contract so that if Pigskin disagrees with your calculations about how much money you owe, an independent third party can have access to your financial records for this game to settle the dispute.

Eligibility and Game Rules

Since this is a non-conference game, a provision must set forth which conference's eligibility and game rules will apply. A provision will also define which party chooses the officials and from what conference(s) the officials will be chosen.

Termination Provisions

Since this event has the potential to generate a great deal of revenue, it is very important to negotiate a termination provision that protects Victory's interest. Sometimes schools do breach a game contract because a better opportunity comes along. Therefore, as part of your worst-case scenario mentality, you would want to incorporate a liquidated damages clause. We discussed the worst-case concept in Chapter 3 in the context of a coaching contract. You will also recall from Chapter 3 that this type of clause provides that the breaching party must pay an amount to the non-breaching party that is a reasonable estimate of the damages to be sustained. In this case, assume that Victory could sustain approximately $500,000 in damages if Pigskin breached the agreement. Although we cannot state an exact number, since attendance cannot be predicted with absolute certainty, we can be close in our approximation. Therefore, Victory would try to negotiate a clause providing that Pigskin would pay $500,000 in liquidated damages if it breached the agreement.

Force Majeure

The contract should include a force majeure clause, as in a facility lease. This clause provides that neither party is in breach of the contract if the game cannot be played due to an act of God, such as a hurricane, an earthquake, or some unforeseen event beyond the control of the parties. For example, in 2017 when Hurricanes Harvey and Irma devastated parts of Texas, Louisiana, and Florida, hitting parts of Georgia and Tennessee as well, any number of high schools, colleges, and professional sport teams found themselves without facilities and resources (Wong, 2017). A force majeure clause would have excused these organizations' non-performance without making them liable for breach of contract. When negotiating a force majeure clause, make sure that the clause applies equally to all parties to the agreement. It is helpful if the clause sets forth some specific examples of acts that would excuse performance under the clause, such as wars, natural disasters, and other major events that are clearly outside a party's control, such as the Covid-19 pandemic, as previously mentioned. Inclusion of examples will help clarify that the clause is not intended to apply to failures to perform for reasons within the control of the parties.

Broadcast Rights Provisions

The contract should include a provision that discusses broadcast rights. Television and radio rights generally belong to the home team, unless a conference agreement takes precedence. However, as an inducement to Pigskin, Victory may offer to split the broadcast revenues, or at least share a percentage of the broadcast revenues with Pigskin. Broadcasting agreements are discussed in more detail in Chapter 19.

Insurance and Indemnification Provisions

The contract should include insurance and indemnification provisions, as discussed in the previous section on leases.

Complimentary Tickets and Credentials

The contract should include a provision dealing with the number of complimentary tickets allocated to Pigskin. It is very common for a university to provide complimentary tickets for VIPs and donors who may travel with the team. Additionally, issues relating to sideline passes and admission of the visiting team's staff, band, and cheerleaders must also be addressed. These individuals will need access to secured areas of the facility; thus proper credentials will be needed.

Promotional Rights

The game contract should acknowledge that the colleges are bound by exclusive sponsorship agreements that must be considered and incorporated into the game contract. For example, Victory may have an exclusive sponsorship agreement with Gatorade, while Pigskin has an exclusive sponsorship agreement with Powerade. Victory would want to assure its sponsor that no Powerade logos will be affixed or displayed in any areas within the facility. Thus, if Pigskin brought its own water coolers and sport drink coolers and those coolers bore the logos of Powerade, Victory may want the right to cover those logos or require Pigskin to use coolers provided by the facility so that competing logos would not be visible to the live or television audience.

Considering ... Force Majeure Clauses and Game Cancellations

A severe thunderstorm forced the cancelation of Nebraska University's 2018 football season opener against the University of Akron (McKowen, 2018a). The guaranteed game contract between the two institutions had a force majeure clause identifying certain weather related force majeure events. The clause detailed that the agreement would be voided if canceled due to reasons, "including ... hurricane, tropical storm, flood, or earthquake" (Abraham, 2018). The force majeure clause did not contain language specific to thunderstorms or lightning. Nebraska proposed the teams play in a Sunday make-up game. Staying would have required Akron to spend the night in Omaha, an hour away from Lincoln where the game would have occurred, only to wake up Sunday morning and drive an hour back to play the make-up game. The other option was to have the team stay in Lincoln for the night and wake up and play on Sunday. Using the Lincoln option, the nearly 75-player roster would have been split up in separate dormitories across campus; a liability Akron's head coach was not willing to take on. As such, Akron returned without making up the canceled game, for which they were entitled to receive around $1.17 million dollars as part of the game contract guarantee. Nebraska argued the cancelation of the game was out of their control and they had attempted a make-up game solution for the following day. After a few months of negotiation, the two universities came to an agreement for Nebraska to pay $650,000.00 to cover the University of Akron's lost expenses and an agreement to play each other in the 2025 season, for which Akron will then receive $1.45 million dollars as a game contract guarantee (McKowen, 2018b).

Questions

- Do you think Akron should have stayed to play the make-up game? Why or why not? What potential liability, if any, would Akron have incurred by staying in Omaha for the night?
- Do you think the contractual language of a "tropical storm" versus a "thunderstorm" is a valid contractual distinction for a force majeure clause? Why or why not?
- How would you revise the force majeure clause to better cover weather related disruptive events on behalf of Nebraska?

It is obvious and accepted that issues preventing the completion of a contract can and will arise. Knowing this, it is important to use foresight (predicting what may occur in the future) in the drafting of an agreement. If parties can think of anything and everything that could possibly go wrong ahead of time, it will be much easier to resolve if and when a problem occurs. Both the timeliness and use of resources, financial and otherwise, will be benefitted by a clear agreement which uses foresight on potential problems. Think of a contract as a road map guiding and directing the relationship between the parties. Another example of this concept is utilized through exculpatory agreements. Exculpatory agreements use language to predict when one party's behavior may give rise to liability for another party, but they wish to be held harmless.

Exculpatory Agreements

An **exculpatory agreement**, by definition, is a contract in which a person or entity that is legally "at fault" tries to excuse itself from fault. An **exculpatory clause** is defined as a "contractual provision relieving a party from any liability resulting from a negligent or wrongful act" (*Black's Law Dictionary*, 2009, p. 647). Often, in sport/recreation situations, the agreement is in the form of a waiver, or a pre-injury release. The party signing the waiver or release agrees to give up his or her right to sue the party at fault. There are technical differences between a waiver and a release, but either may be used in situations in which someone gives up his or her right to sue someone prior to participating in a sport or an activity.

This area of the law becomes complex because courts are involved in a difficult balancing act between two pillars of the law – tort law and contract law. Under the principles of tort law, defendants are held accountable for tortious acts that injure others. The plaintiffs have the right to seek damages against defendants who have injured them in situations in which the courts give a remedy. In contrast, contract law gives adults the right to engage in various undertakings, including giving up certain rights.

A **waiver or a release** is a type of contract in which one party gives up his or her right to sue the other party, thus altering the outcome that would transpire under the usual tort law principles. An **agreement to participate** is an agreement acknowledging and consenting to risks associated with participating in a particular activity. An agreement to participate is a form of informed consent that can be coupled with an exculpatory clause to attempt to avoid tort liability if the participant is injured during the activity. If a court upholds one of these agreements, it is making a choice to give precedence to contract law instead of tort law. The Colorado Supreme Court summarized this conflict when it stated that a release exists "at the crossroads of two competing principles: freedom of contract and responsibility for damages caused by one's own negligent acts" (*Heil Valley Ranch v. Simkin*, 1989, p. 784).

Often people remark that "waivers are not worth the paper they are written on." This remark is fallacious, particularly as it pertains to physical activities and sport, because waivers are often upheld, unless they are poorly written or violate public policy. However, in today's digital environment, many waivers are embedded on the back of tickets, included as part of packaging or advertising materials, or even included in the form of "click wrap" agreements that you agree to as you click through an online purchase or registration system.

In 2000, the Electronic Signatures in Global and National Commerce Act (ESIGN Act) defined and legalized the use of electronic signatures, e-signing, for electronic and online waivers. This may not even need be in the actual form of a signature, but rather clicking a box or accepting terms before proceeding to the next page is considered an effective approval (Cotten, 2017). For example, in 2013, in *Berenson v. USA Hockey*, a waiver was enforced in the state of Colorado without the "signed" waiver ever being presented in court, based on an affidavit that established the participant could not have even registered for the event without going through the waiver process online (Cotten, 2017). As with the changes in the tides of ticket sales, the digital age of technology requires we conduct new procedures carefully and with an eye on precedent being established around us. Even though they take many forms today and may be met with skepticism, waivers and releases are often enforceable so long as they satisfy two criteria:

1   They are used in the right circumstances (*context*).
2   They are written properly (*content*).

Context – Circumstances in Which Waivers May be Appropriate

Because of the competing considerations between tort and contract law, courts will not uphold waivers in all circumstances. Giving up one's right to sue is an important decision, and courts must be satisfied that the context is appropriate for doing so. There are two primary aspects to consider when looking at the context issues:

1   Whether the person giving up the right to sue is a minor
2   Public policy considerations

Minors and Exculpatory Agreements

Because a waiver is a contract, the usual rules of contract law apply. As we discussed in Chapter 3, if a minor signs a contract, the minor might later disavow that contract. This is because the law considers minors to be under a legal disability in entering into contracts (Restatement [Second] of Contracts §§ 7 and 12, 1981). Therefore, the usual rule today is that contracts entered into by minors are voidable (42 Am. Jur. 2d *Infants* § 82, 2013).

Generally speaking, parents cannot give up their children's rights to sue, either. Read the following Focus Cases and consider which approach to this issue makes more sense to you. The first case is representative of the majority of courts that have addressed the parental release issue, and the second case is representative of the minority position.

E.M. v. House of Boom, LLC (In re Miller)

575 S.W.3d 656 (Ky. 2019)	FOCUS CASE

FACTS

A parent of a minor signed an injury waiver for a trampoline park in Louisville, Kentucky. The parent's 11-year-old daughter broke her ankle while at the park in 2015. The mother sued the park alleging their failure to adequately supervise customers and failure to follow safety procedures. The trampoline park sought to seek dismissal of the suit on the grounds of the signed waiver.

HOLDING

The Supreme Court of Kentucky ruled that a parent's pre-injury waiver of a minor child's claim against a for-profit business is unenforceable.

RATIONALE

The question before the court was whether a parent has the authority to sign a pre-injury exculpatory agreement on behalf of her child, thus terminating the child's potential right to compensation for an injury occurring while participating in activities sponsored by a for-profit company. The court recognized that 11 of 12 jurisdictions addressing this issue previously had followed the common law and held such waivers unenforceable. The court reasoned that pre-injury waivers are not per se invalid but are generally disfavored in the Commonwealth and strictly construed against the parties relying on them. The general common law in Kentucky is that parents have no right to compromise or settle the child's cause of action as that right exists in the child alone; and parents have no right to enter into contracts on behalf of their children absent special circumstances. The court rejected that there were sufficient public policy grounds to support a change in the common law. The court expressly questioned in terms of public policy "whether a parent has the authority to enter into an exculpatory agreement on their child's behalf, negating any opportunity for a tort claim – a child's property right – if House of Boom's negligence causes injury to the child." The court also refused to extend the policy justifications for granting limited immunity to school districts to a for-profit business. A commercial entity has the ability to purchase insurance and spread the cost between its customers. It also has the ability to train its employees and inspect the premises for unsafe conditions. Thus, it is the commercial business, not the minor child, who has a duty to protect against the negligence of others and from unsafe conditions within the commercial establishment. If pre-injury waivers were permitted, the incentive to take reasonable safety precautions would be removed.

Hamill v. Cheley Colorado Camps, Inc.

262 P.3d 945 (Colo. Ct. App. 2011)	**FOCUS** CASE

FACTS

In July 2004, a 15-year-old attendee at a horse camp fell off one of the defendant's horses and broke her arm. The plaintiff sued for negligence and gross negligence, arguing that one of the defendant's wranglers had inappropriately saddled the horse she rode. Before she attended the camp, the plaintiff's parents had signed a waiver. The district court granted the defendant's motion for summary judgment on the two negligence claims, ruling that, although the plaintiff was a minor, the waiver barred her claims and that there was no gross negligence as a matter of law.

HOLDING

The Colorado appellate court affirmed the lower court and upheld the waiver.

RATIONALE

The primary issue before the court was whether parents can bind their child to a waiver of liability. In 2002, the Colorado Supreme Court held that it was against public policy for parents to prospectively waive liability on behalf of minor children. The following year, the General Assembly superseded that case by enacting Section 13-22-107(3), C.R.S. 2010, which allows parents to "release or waive the child's prospective claim for negligence." The statute declares "that parents have a fundamental right to make decisions on behalf of their children, including deciding whether the children should participate in risky activities." The statute states that "[s]o long as the [parent's] decision is voluntary and informed, the decision should be given the same dignity as decisions regarding schooling, medical treatment, and religious education" (§ 13-22-107(1)(a)(V)).

Relying on the "informed" language of the statute, the plaintiff asserted that the defendant's failure to identify the possibility that she might fall from a horse in the manner she did invalidates her mother's consent. The court noted, however, that the fact that the plaintiff's mother may have contemplated the precise mechanics of her daughter's fall does not invalidate the release and does not create a genuine issue of material fact. She knew her daughter would be riding horses and she was advised that there were risks, known and unknown, associated with the activity. The court emphasized that the plaintiff's mother acknowledged in her deposition testimony that when horseback riding, there is "a risk of a child being thrown or falling off a horse." The plaintiff's argument that her mother did not give informed consent, despite her signature on the agreement and the language in the agreement indicating the contrary, is not persuasive and does not create a genuine issue of material fact. As a matter of law, the agreement sufficiently informed the plaintiff's mother about the risks involved in horseback riding.

As the *House of Boom* and *Hamill* cases show, courts are divided about the nature of the parent–child relationship and how much discretion should be vested in a parent to give up a child's right to sue. The *House of Boom* case reflects the position of most courts and some commentators that public policy should protect minor children against possibly unwise decisions by parents (Bittakis, 2012). The *Hamill* case, representing the minority position and using the Colorado statute, presumes that parents will act in the best interests of their children, even in this type of situation.

Public Policy and Exculpatory Agreements

As discussed in the previous section, protecting the interest of minors was an important public policy interest for most states. Some states adopt similar public policy approaches toward exculpatory agreements in general. The concept of public policy can be rather nebulous. Courts address a number of considerations when ascertaining whether a waiver may be used and will not violate the public interest. The following concerns are often addressed in discussing public policy.

First, some jurisdictions either **disallow or disfavor waivers** holding that no waivers will be upheld, or making it very difficult for waivers to be upheld. Some jurisdictions allow the use of waivers in certain limited circumstances. In some circumstances, federal law supersedes and no waivers are permissible.

Second, many courts address the public policy aspect by determining whether the situation concerns a provision of **essential services**.

Third, the **principle of unfair dominance** provides that a waiver will not be upheld if the party getting the benefit of the waiver has so much power in the transaction that it is not a "fair deal." A contract law principle referred to as "unconscionability" is a defense which can be raised against the enforcement of a contract that is unfair or left the disadvantaged party with an absence of meaningful choice. In such instances, a court may find reason to refuse its enforcement (Legal Information Institute, 2015). Beware of presenting contracts that feel as if they are "take it or leave it" to consumers or participants.

Finally, on some occasions it is inappropriate to use a waiver because to do so would allow a provider of recreational services to **violate a statutory duty of care** imposed upon it. Below we discuss these concepts at greater length.

Waivers Disallowed or Disfavored

A few states have resolved the conflict between principles of freedom to contract and responsibility for one's negligent acts by stating that no waivers will be allowed, regardless of the context. For example, in a Virginia case, the plaintiff became a quadriplegic after sustaining an injury in a recreational triathlon. The plaintiff, Hiett, struck his head on an underwater object in a lake during the swimming event. He had signed a release form prior to the event, but the Virginia Supreme Court held that, according to long-standing precedent, "the pre-injury release provision signed by Hiett is prohibited by public policy and, thus, it is void" (*Hiett v. Lake Barcroft Community Association, Inc.*, 1992, p. 897). One critic argued that this decision, which used broad and sweeping language, was wrongly decided in view of the trend across the country to uphold exculpatory contracts in athletic events (Espaldon, 1994). Two other jurisdictions, Montana and Louisiana, have also adopted this blanket prohibition against enforcing waivers (Kufahl, 2012), but most jurisdictions allow waivers (see Matthiesen, Wickert, & Lehrer, 2019). The following Focus Case from New York deals with the question of whether a release signed for activities at a summer camp should be upheld.

Walker v. Young Life Saranac Village

2012 U.S. Dist. LEXIS 166057 (N.D.N.Y. Nov. 21, 2012)	**FOCUS** CASE

FACTS

The plaintiff, who was 17 at the time of her injury, attended a summer camp operated by a national religious non-profit organization. While at the camp, the plaintiff sustained a fractured ankle as she exited a water slide and hit bottom. She had been directed by a camp leader to negotiate this slide in the dark without sufficient instruction. The defendant camp sought summary judgment because a waiver had been signed by the plaintiff's parents. The plaintiff argued that the waiver was void as against public policy since there is a New York statute (N.Y. Gen. Oblig. Law § 5-326) that voids releases that are used in "places of amusement or recreation."

HOLDING

The New York federal district court held that the waiver was not void according to New York statutory law.

RATIONALE

The district court assessed whether the defendant camp was instructional or recreational. To do so, the court found that the camp's purpose was to introduce students to the gospel through fun and adventurous activities. The court also noted that in defendant's certificate of incorporation, there is an explicit mention of "ministry," which can be construed as instructional in nature. Therefore, the court concluded that the defendant was engaged in instructional activities, not recreational, for the purpose of the statute in question.

A provider of recreational services that operates on federal land may not use an exculpatory agreement. Federal policies require the provider to use a "visitor's acknowledgment of risks" form, if a form is used at all (Hansen-Stamp, 2003). Exhibit 16.4 provides an example.

Exhibit 16.4 Sample acknowledgment of risk form for the National Park Service (U.S. Dept. of the Interior, 2019).

In consideration of the services of _____ their officers, agents, employees, and stockholders, and all other persons or entities associated with those businesses (hereafter collectively referred to as "_____") I agree as follows: Although _____ has taken reasonable steps to provide me with appropriate equipment and skilled guides so I can enjoy an activity for which I may not be skilled, _____ has informed me this activity is not without risk. Certain risks are inherent in each activity and cannot be eliminated without destroying the unique character of the activity. These inherent risks are some of the same elements that contribute to the unique character of this activity and can be the cause of loss or damage to my equipment, or accidental injury, illness, or in extreme cases, permanent trauma or death. _____ does not want to frighten me or reduce my enthusiasm for this activity, but believes it is important for me to know in advance what to expect and to be informed of the inherent risks. The following describes some, but not all, of those risks. [enter description of risks] I am aware that _____ entails risks of injury or death to any participant. I understand the description of these inherent risks is not complete and that other unknown or unanticipated inherent risks may result in injury or death. I agree to assume and accept full responsibility for the inherent risks identified herein and those inherent risks not specifically identified. My participation in this activity is purely voluntary; no one is forcing me to participate, and I elect to participate in spite of and with full knowledge of the inherent risks. I acknowledge that engaging in this activity may require a degree of skill and knowledge different from other activities and that I have responsibilities as a participant. I acknowledge that the staff of _____ has been available to more fully explain to me the nature and physical demands of this activity and the inherent risks, hazards, and dangers associated with this activity. I certify that I am fully capable of participating in this activity. Therefore, I assume and accept full responsibility for myself, including all minor children in my care, custody, and control, for bodily injury, death, or loss of personal property and expenses as a result of those inherent risks and dangers identified herein and those inherent risks and dangers not specifically identified, and as a result of my negligence in participating in this activity. I have carefully read, clearly understood, and accepted the terms and conditions stated herein and acknowledge that this agreement shall be effective and binding upon me, my heirs, assigns, personal representative, and estate and for all members of my family, including minor children.

_____

Signature Date

Signature of Parent of Guardian, if participant is under 18 years of age

_____ _____

Signature Date

Exhibit 16.5 The Tunkl factors used in developing public policy analysis, *Tunkl v. Regents of the University of California* (1963).

1   The agreement concerns an endeavor of a type generally thought suitable for public regulation.
2   The party seeking exculpation is engaged in performing a service of great importance to the public, which is often a matter of practical necessity for some members of the public.
3   Such party holds itself out as willing to perform this service for any member of the public who seeks it, or at least for any member coming within certain established standards.
4   Because of the essential nature of the service, in the economic setting of the transaction, the party invoking exculpation possesses a decisive advantage of bargaining strength against any member of the public who seeks the services.
5   In exercising a superior bargaining power, the party confronts the public with a standardized adhesion contract of exculpation, and makes no provision whereby a purchaser may pay additional reasonable fees and obtain protection against negligence.
6   The person or property of members of the public seeking such services must be placed under the control of the furnisher of the services, subject to the risk of carelessness on the part of the furnisher, its employees, or agents.

Essential Services

Some organizations owe a duty to serve the public, and the courts deem it inappropriate for that type of organization to gain the benefit of a waiver. You will never, therefore, see a waiver upheld in a health care setting. A patient may be asked to sign a document advising her of the inherent risks of surgery or other medical procedure, but a waiver will not be upheld. Hospitals and medical personnel are expected to serve the public, so it would violate public policy to allow a patient to give up the right to sue if a hospital or physician acts negligently. The seminal case of *Tunkl v. Regents of the University of California* (1963) provides courts with a number of factors to use in developing the public policy analysis. These factors were used in the case of *Wagenblast v. Odessa School District* (1988) (see Exhibit 16.5 and the excerpted case below).

Interscholastic or intercollegiate sport as essential service. Some courts have held that waivers or releases may be inappropriate in the context of interscholastic or collegiate sport since the extracurricular participation in sport flows from the educational mission of the school and education is an essential service. Since the school owes a duty to its students in offering education, it may not take away any of the participants' rights or avoid its duty of care by using waivers. The excerpted case below explores how one court addressed this.

Wagenblast v. Odessa School District No. 105-157-166J

CASE OPINION   *758 P.2d 968 (Wash. 1988)*

FACTS

The plaintiffs were students in the Odessa School District who wished to participate in interscholastic athletics. As a condition of participation, the defendant school district required students and parents to sign a release of liability form. It released the school district from "liability resulting from any ordinary negligence that may arise in connection with the school district's interscholastic activities programs" (p. 969). The Seattle School District had a similar requirement and a similar form.

Students and parents in both districts objected to this practice on the basis that the release form violated public policy. The lower court in the Odessa case enjoined the school district from using the releases as it agreed with the plaintiffs that the release should be void as against public policy. The lower court in the Seattle case came to a contrary decision. These cases were consolidated upon appeal and heard by the Washington Supreme Court.

HOLDING

The Washington Supreme Court held that the release requirements violated public policy, thereby affirming the lower court in the Odessa case and reversing the judgment in the Seattle case.

RATIONALE

Conclusion. We hold that the exculpatory releases from any future school district negligence are invalid because they violate public policy. The courts have generally recognized that, subject to certain exceptions, parties may contract that one shall not be liable for his or her own negligence to another.

In accordance with the foregoing general rule, appellate decisions in this state have upheld exculpatory agreements where the subject was a toboggan slide, a scuba diving class, mountain climbing instruction, an automobile demolition derby, and ski jumping.

As Prosser and Keeton [legal commentators] further observe, however, there are instances where public policy reasons for preserving an obligation of care owed by one person to another outweigh our traditional regard for the freedom to contract. Courts in this century are generally agreed on several such categories of cases. Courts, for example, are usually reluctant to allow those charged with a public duty, which includes the obligation to use reasonable care, to rid themselves of that obligation by contract.

Probably the best exposition of the test to be applied in determining whether exculpatory agreements violate public policy is that stated by the California Supreme Court. In writing for a unanimous court, the late Justice Tobriner outlined the factors in *Tunkl v. Regents of Univ. of Cal.* [citation omitted]: [The court then set forth the Tunkl factors; see Exhibit 16.5]. Obviously, the more of the foregoing six characteristics that appear in a given exculpatory agreement case, the more likely the agreement is to be declared invalid on public policy grounds. In the consolidated cases before us, all of the characteristics are present in each case. We separately, then, examine, each of these six characteristics as applied to the cases before us.

1 The agreement concerns an endeavor of a type generally thought suitable for public regulation.

Regulation of governmental entities usually means self-regulation. Thus, the Legislature has by statute granted to each school board the authority to control, supervise, and regulate the conduct of interscholastic athletics. In some situations, a school board is permitted, in turn, to delegate this authority to the Washington Interscholastic Activities Association (WIAA). ... In the cases before us, both school boards look to the WIAA for regulation of interscholastic sports. The WIAA handbook contains an extensive constitution with rules for such athletic endeavors. Clearly then, interscholastic sports in Washington are extensively regulated, and are a fit subject for such regulation.

2 The party seeking exculpation is engaged in performing a service of great importance to the public, which is often a matter of practical necessity for some members of the public.

This court has held that public school students have no fundamental right to participate in interscholastic athletics. Nonetheless, the court also has observed that the justification advanced for interscholastic athletics is their educational and cultural value. ... [I]nterscholastic athletics is part and parcel of the overall educational scheme in Washington. ... In sum, under any rational view of the subject, interscholastic sports in public school are a matter of public importance in this jurisdiction.

3 Such party holds itself out as willing to perform this service for any member of the public who seeks it, or at least for any member coming within certain established standards.

Implicit in the nature of interscholastic sports is the notion that such programs are open to all students who meet certain skill and eligibility standards. ...

4 Because of the essential nature of the service, in the economic setting of the transaction, the party invoking exculpation possesses a decisive advantage of bargaining strength against any member of the public who seeks the services.

Not only have interscholastic sports become of considerable importance to students and the general public alike, but in most instances there exists no alternative program of organized competition.... While outside alternatives exist for some activities, they possess little of the inherent allure of interscholastic competition. ... In this regard, school districts have near-monopoly power. And, because such programs have become important to student participants, school districts possess a clear and disparate bargaining strength when they insist that students and their parents sign these releases.

5   In exercising a superior bargaining power, the party confronts the public with a standardized adhesion contract of exculpation, and makes no provision whereby a purchaser may pay additional reasonable fees and obtain protection against negligence.

Both school districts admit to an unwavering policy regarding these releases; no student-athlete will be allowed to participate in any program without first signing the release form as written by the school district. In both of these cases, students and their parents unsuccessfully attempted to modify the forms by deleting the release language. In both cases, the school district rejected the attempted modifications. Student-athletes and their parents or guardians have no alternative but to sign the standard release forms provided to them or have the student barred from the program.

6   The person or property of members of the public seeking such services must be placed under the control of the furnisher of the services, subject to the risk of carelessness on the part of the furnisher, its employees or agents.

A school district owes a duty to its students to employ ordinary care and to anticipate reasonably foreseeable dangers so as to take precautions for protecting the children in its custody from such dangers. This duty extends to students engaged in interscholastic sports. As a natural incident to the relationship of a student-athlete and his or her coach, the student-athlete is usually placed under the coach's considerable degree of control. The student is thus subject to the risk that the school district or its agent will breach this duty of care.

In sum, the attempted releases in the cases before us exhibit all six of the characteristics denominated in *Tunkl v. Regents of Univ. of Cal.* [citation omitted]. Because of this, and for the aforesaid reasons, we hold that the releases in these consolidated cases are invalid as against public policy.

QUESTIONS

1   The *Wagenblast* court did a very thorough job of applying all six factors from the *Tunkl* decision. Comment specifically upon the court's view of interscholastic athletics as being a part of a service of great importance to the public. Do you agree with this view? Why or why not? Would this reasoning extend to intercollegiate athletics?

2   The court also noted that school districts possess a decisive bargaining advantage in this type of situation. Discuss the court's analysis that school districts possess a "near-monopoly power." This decision was written in 1988. Do you think that school districts today have more or less monopoly power?

3   Could the *Wagenblast* court have ended the controversy simply by using the principle that minors (all the high school students here) can disavow any contract they sign, including waivers? Why do you believe the court chose to address the public policy issue?

Many jurisdictions have yet to address the public policy issue of whether waivers should be upheld in the context of interscholastic sports. One commentator has suggested that the use of waivers in school settings may actually promote public policy, since without releases some schools could not afford to offer sports because of the financial risk that a large verdict or settlement could bring (Murr, 2002).

Similarly, only a few cases on the intercollegiate level have directly addressed the question of whether the provision of sport should be considered an essential service. The next Focus Case provides one court's view.

Kyriazis v. West Virginia University

450 S.E.2d 649 (W.Va. 1994)	**FOCUS** CASE

FACTS

As a condition of participating in the university's rugby club, participants had to sign a release. Jeffrey Kyriazis, a novice rugby player, signed the release and was injured playing in his first club match. Kyriazis left the game in the second half after he became dizzy and lost his balance. Later, medical tests ascertained that he had suffered a basilar-artery thrombosis. He sued the university for negligence, and the university contended that the release barred suit. The lower court granted the university's motion to dismiss.

HOLDING

The highest court in West Virginia, the West Virginia Supreme Court of Appeals, held that the release violated public policy, reversing and remanding the lower court's decision.

RATIONALE

The court primarily focused on whether participation in the rugby club was an essential or public service. To do so, the court reviewed the *Tunkl* criteria and found that "When a state university provides recreational activities to its students, it fulfills its educational mission, and performs a public service" (p. 655). Furthermore, "athletics are integral and important elements of the education mission at West Virginia University" (p. 655). The court also noted that the release was signed with a decisive bargaining advantage by the university. University counsel prepared the release, whereas Kyriazis had no legal representation. Students had no choice but to sign the release if they wished to play. Based on these two factors, the court held that the release was void as a matter of public policy.

A 2006 case, *Zides v. Quinnipiac University*, also noted that college-age students should not necessarily be characterized as "educated adults," because many of them are not experienced in the risks presented to them in daily life. The court also mentioned the *Wagenblast* decision (see the earlier Case Opinion) as indicative of the public policy concerns that may arise in the context of school waivers.

Non-school sport and recreation as essential service. Most courts agree that, outside of the context of an educational institution, sport, recreation, fitness, and adventure activities are not essential services provided to the public. Therefore, the use of waivers or releases in those situations does not generally violate public policy. The following Focus Case is indicative of the reasoning used in these cases.

Gregorie v. Alpine Meadows Ski Corp.

2009 U.S. Dist. LEXIS 69237 (E.D. Cal. August 6, 2009)   **FOCUS** CASE

FACTS

A 24-year-old experienced snowboarder was killed at the defendant's ski resort when she slid over a cliff. The decedent had purchased a season ski pass for this resort and had signed a waiver as a part of this transaction. Her parents brought a wrongful death action against the defendant alleging negligence in various aspects, including a failure to warn of terrain dangers. The defendant sought summary judgment on the basis that the waiver precluded the action against the resort. The plaintiffs argued that the waiver should be unenforceable as violative of public policy.

HOLDING

The federal district court in California granted summary judgment for the defendant ski resort.

RATIONALE

The district court noted that California law consistently holds that a release of liability in a recreational context, like a ski resort, does not violate public policy. Applying this principle, the court stated that "[e]xculpatory agreements in the recreational sports context do not implicate the public interest." The court further noted that "California courts have consistently declined to apply *Tunkl* and invalidate exculpatory agreements in the recreational sports context." Additionally, the court concluded that skiing is not an essential activity, even if it is beneficial.

Another case of note exemplifies the minority position, as one court held that health clubs do provide essential services. In *Schneeloch v. Glastonbury Fitness & Wellness, Inc.* (2009), a plaintiff was injured in an exercise class conducted at a health club. The court declined to uphold the waiver of liability provision because it opined that an exculpatory agreement that would excuse the potential negligence of a health club was in conflict with the public policy of encouraging participation in athletics and other recreational activities.

Principle of Unfair Dominance

In some circumstances, notions of fairness may be offended if the enforcement of a waiver is allowed. This is the case when there is a huge disparity in bargaining power or the person signing the waiver has no real choice about whether to participate in the activity – situations that may be found to involve coercion or a contract of adhesion, concepts addressed in Chapter 3.

For example, in the case of *Bagley v. Mt. Bachelor, Inc.* (2014), the Oregon Supreme Court held a ski resort's anticipatory exculpatory release to be unconscionable and against public policy due to its one-sided nature and the circumstances upon which it was entered. As a matter of whether or not the ski resort is a "public service" and therefore poses a "take it or leave it" option to a participant, the court reasoned that because the resort is open to the public, and is therefore a place of public accommodation, it is providing a public service (*Bagley*, 2014).

Another case involved a release signed by a student who wished to participate in a college-sponsored study abroad trip to Peru. In *Fay v. Thiel College* (2001), the plaintiff student had a medical emergency in Peru.

The group supervisors left her at a clinic, and she underwent an unnecessary appendectomy. The surgeon and anesthesiologist also sexually assaulted her. The college asserted that the release should be upheld in regard to the college supervisors' alleged negligence. The court refused to uphold the release on the basis that it was a contract of adhesion, that is, the student had no bargaining power. If the student had refused to sign the release, she would not have been permitted to go on the trip. In this "take it or leave it" situation, the court refused to uphold the release. Although not a sport-specific case, one can draw potential parallels to similar situations in the sport industry involving travel, student-athletes, or players with medical or otherwise pressing emergencies.

However, some case law provides that if a student could choose another class to fulfill a curricular requirement, then the release may be upheld since it does not violate the adhesion contract prohibition. For example, in *Thompson v. Otterbein College* (1996), a college student signed a release prior to taking an equestrian course. She was injured when her horse was spooked. The court upheld that release as it stated that the equestrian course was not a required course. Although this course could be used to fulfill the physical education requirement, there were a variety of other courses available for that purpose that did not require a release to be signed. The plaintiff was not in an unequal bargaining position; hence, the release was enforceable.

Outside of the realm of education, the principle of unfair dominance does not mean that those who want to engage in commercial health, recreation, or fitness endeavors must have an opportunity to negotiate the content of the release. Although prospective participants should be given enough time to read the document before engaging in the activity, courts have consistently held that objections to the document do not have to be accommodated since participants are not taking part in an essential activity. Participants are free to choose not to go on the rafting trip or to use that health club. For example, in the case of *Schlobohm v. Spa Petite, Inc.* (1982), the court upheld an exculpatory clause in a membership contract for a health spa. The court stated that it was not a contract of adhesion because the services of the spa were not a public necessity and were available elsewhere. A decision in New Jersey, *Stelluti v. Casapenn Enterprises* (2009), in which the plaintiff was injured when the handlebars of a stationary bike detached, echoed this point and added that giving health clubs waiver protection actually benefitted the public by insulating clubs from liability for injuries on their premises, thus keeping them viable in the marketplace and keeping membership fees under control.

It is essential, however, that the document be available to participants for prior review if they are traveling to a location specifically for an activity. Release documents should be provided to participants as soon as they register for the event or activity. Also, there may be a problem if the release document specifies that arbitration is mandatory for any dispute. For example, a California appellate court has found unconscionability within the context of a mandatory arbitration clause. In *Lhotka v. Geographic Expeditions, Inc.* (2010), a client died of an altitude-related illness while on the defendant's expedition to climb Mount Kilimanjaro. The decedent signed a release of liability form that included a clause providing that any dispute be submitted to mediation and then to binding arbitration. The appellate court found that this clause was unconscionable because it was so one-sided and onerous. The clause guaranteed that any plaintiffs could not receive full compensation for any injury suffered since recovery was limited to the cost of the trip.

Use of Waiver Would Violate Statutory Duty

In some cases, a provider of commercial recreation activities may be mandated by a state statute to meet a certain standard of care in providing the activities. In such a case, a court may find that it would be incongruent and unfair to allow a release to be upheld. The following Focus Case provides an example.

Murphy v. North American River Runners, Inc.

| 412 S.E.2d 504 (W.Va. 1991) | FOCUS CASE |

FACTS

The plaintiff was injured while whitewater rafting as a paying passenger in the defendant's raft. The plaintiff's guide attempted a rescue operation of another raft. When the plaintiff's raft bumped the other raft, she was thrown forcefully in her raft, injuring her knee and ankle. The plaintiff had signed a release prior to participating in the trip. The lower court upheld the release.

HOLDING

The Supreme Court of Appeals of West Virginia (the state's highest court) reversed and remanded.

RATIONALE

Under a provision of a West Virginia statute (W. Va. Code 20-3B-3 [b]), commercial whitewater guides must "conform to the standard of care expected of members of their profession" (p. 512). This statute, therefore, establishes a statutory safety standard for the protection of those who choose to go on whitewater rafting expeditions. The court stated that a release clause is unenforceable if its purpose is to exempt a party from tort liability based on a statutory standard of care. In this case, the release was unenforceable since it violated this principle.

A case decided by the New Mexico Supreme Court, *Berlangieri v. Running Elk Corp.* (2003), dealt with the effect of that state's Equine Liability Act on the effectiveness of a release. The plaintiff was injured during a trail ride. The court noted that most of the act explains the types of activities for which equine operators may be liable. The court held that the intent of the statute was to express a public policy that operators should be held accountable for their own negligence. Based on this interpretation of the statute and a review of the *Tunkl* factors, the court found that this release violated public policy and was not enforceable.

Also, in the case of *Capri v. L.A. Fitness International* (2006) a California court determined that a waiver signed by a health club patron was void because it pertained to a claim based on negligence per se (see Chapter 15). The plaintiff had slipped and fallen due to an accumulation of algae around the drain on the pool deck. These algae were indicative of a violation of the state health and safety code. The court declined to uphold the waiver because that would contravene Section 1688 of the California Civil Code that stated it was against public policy to exempt a party from liability if the party had violated the law, in this case the health code.

Content – Drafting Enforceable Exculpatory Agreements

Most cases dealing with waivers in the recreation and commercial sport context pass scrutiny on the above factors, and the question then becomes whether the document is written properly. The focus shifts to the document itself and whether the document has the necessary language and format to be upheld. Understand that each state varies regarding language that is absolutely necessary for a valid waiver. There are general principles, to be sure, but you should consult with an attorney who knows your state's specific requirements when you wish to implement a waiver in your setting. The three most common requirements are the (1) terms must be conspicuous; (2) language used must be clear, unambiguous, and explicit; and (3) language cannot exonerate conduct beyond negligence. Each of these requirements is explored below together with several cases applying these requirements.

Terms Must Be Conspicuous

Something is conspicuous if it stands out like the proverbial sore thumb. Therefore, language in a document is conspicuous if it is called to the reader's attention. We can accomplish this by using a larger typeface, by putting the words in boldface, or by putting the information in a location in a document that the reader will easily see. For example, if you have a multipage document, you would not hide the exculpatory clause at the end of the document in very small type. The courts recognize that the right to sue someone is a very important right; therefore, if individuals do give up this right, they must be cognizant of the fact they are doing so. The requirement of conspicuousness ensures that the signer cannot miss this important information.

Note, however, that it is not necessary for an exculpatory agreement to use express language or list every possible way a plaintiff could be injured (*Sanislo v. Give Kids the World*, 2015). Further, it is not even necessary that the word "negligent" is used in the language of the exculpatory clause; although it is best

---

Competitive Advantage Strategies

Exculpatory Agreements Best Practices

- If you choose to use exculpatory agreements, consult with an attorney to understand your state's requirements for a valid waiver or release. A waiver of a certain standard of care that is set by state law will not be enforceable.
- Even if you cannot or do not use an exculpatory agreement, you should always use an agreement to participate. This is important in sharing risk information with participants to avoid a failure to warn allegation.
- Having participants agree to follow the rules of conduct to make the experience enjoyable and safe for all also enables a comparative negligence defense, should the participant endanger himself or herself by violating the rules of the activity.
- Remember that in most jurisdictions, a minor may disavow a waiver. Also, in most jurisdictions, a parent cannot give up a minor's right to sue.
- Do not use an exculpatory clause, if you know that it is not valid, in an effort to persuade people not to sue.
- Exculpatory clauses should be placed conspicuously within your documents. The typeface for this clause should be large and bold. If you have a multipage document such as a membership agreement, put the exculpatory clause on a separate page. *Draw attention to the exculpatory language.*
- The language of the exculpatory clause must be clear, unambiguous, and explicit. In some jurisdictions, you must specifically use the word *negligence* in the waiver. Consult with your attorney on this point.
- Instruct your employees to give participants adequate time to read the waiver before signing. If participants are traveling to your location to participate, send the waiver document to them ahead of time for their review.
- Do not use a group release form. Have a separate agreement for each participant, even if group members are engaging in the activity at the same time.
- Instruct your employees never to say that the waiver is "meaningless" or that it is "just policy." participants are giving up their right to sue your organization, and that is a valuable right.
- The exculpatory agreement is not there just to avoid liability. It is there to share valuable information about the nature of the activity and the risk (Connell & Savage, 2003), as is a participation agreement, all which help support a negligence defense of assumption of risk by the participant regardless of the enforceability of the waivers or agreements.

practice to do so. An exculpatory agreement should be dated, signed, witnessed and have the actual language that is exculpatory in nature be clearly visible in conspicuous print.

In the case of *Atkins v. Swimwest Family Fitness Center* (2005), the Wisconsin Supreme Court found that a waiver contained in a guest registration card was not "distinguishable" enough to be conspicuous (i.e., obvious and noticeable for the reader). The court noted that the form was printed on one card with the same size print, font, and color as the other information. Nothing set apart the critical waiver language from the rest of the document.

Language must be Clear, Unambiguous, and Explicit

Two aspects frequently arise when courts address whether the language of an exculpatory agreement is sufficiently clear, unambiguous, and explicit to be upheld. First, courts address whether it is evident from the language that the signer of the document is giving up his or her right to sue when the party getting the benefit of the agreement is engaging in "negligent" behavior. The following Focus Case illustrates this concept.

Geczi v. Lifetime Fitness

973 N.E.2d 801 (Ohio Ct. App. 2012)	FOCUS CASE

FACTS

The plaintiff, a member of the defendant's health club, sustained injury when a treadmill malfunctioned. As the plaintiff increased the speed of the treadmill on which she was running, the incline function engaged and the machine began to jerk severely. The plaintiff sustained a serious injury to her arm as she attempted to gain her balance. The complaint against the defendant club alleged negligence in maintaining the treadmill. The defendant argued that the exculpatory provision in the membership application precluded her claims, and the club sought summary judgment. However, the plaintiff argued that the waiver should not be upheld as it was ambiguous. The lower court granted summary judgment for the defendant.

HOLDING

The Ohio appellate court affirmed the lower court's grant of summary judgment for the defendant health club.

RATIONALE

The court held that the waiver language was not ambiguous. After reviewing the precedent, this court adopted as its touchstone for ambiguity the following test: "whether it is clear from the general terms of the entire contract, considered in light of what an ordinary prudent and knowledgeable party of the same class would understand, that the proprietor is to be relieved from liability for its own negligence."

The court did not state that the term *negligence* always had to appear, but in this case the exculpatory provision in Lifetime's membership agreement was clearly specified as a release and the word *negligence* was used. The provision stated that Lifetime "will not be liable for *any injury*, including and without limitation, personal, bodily or mental injury, economic loss or any damage to the undersigned, the undersigned's spouse, guest or relatives *resulting from the negligence.* ..." Furthermore, the court noted that injuries resulting from the use of the exercise equipment were included within the risks specified.

In another health club case (*Kotcherquina v. Fitness Premier Management*, 2012), the court upheld a waiver relating to the alleged negligence of a personal trainer. In that situation, a federal district court in Arkansas dealt with a plaintiff who was a resident alien for whom English was a second language. However, the court noted that the plaintiff had been living in the United States since 1999, and her testimony clearly reflected that she understood English and was aware of the consequences of her actions in signing the waiver documents.

Another aspect to consider is whether the scope of the release covers the activity that led to the injury in question. Essentially, the court looks at the language of the release and determines whether it is written in a way that would allow the signer to understand just what kinds of injuries might be related to the purpose of the release. Compare the following two Focus Cases on this aspect.

Semeniken v. Town Sports International, Inc.

2010 N.J. Super. Unpub. LEXIS 2681 (Oct. 29, 2010)   **FOCUS** CASE

FACTS

In this case, a health club patron was seriously injured. The plaintiff found an unmarked spray bottle that contained eucalyptus oil and sprayed it in the sauna. The oil was flammable and the plaintiff was seriously burned. The plaintiff alleged that the defendant club was negligent for failing to put a warning about the oil's flammability on the bottle. The defendant sought summary judgment because the plaintiff had signed a membership agreement containing a waiver clause.

HOLDING

The New Jersey Superior Court held that the waiver clause was unenforceable and denied defendant's motion for summary judgment.

RATIONALE

The primary issue before the court was whether the type of injuries sustained here were within the scope of the injuries contemplated in the waiver. In this regard, the court noted that the risks and injuries involved in this case are clearly distinguishable from the risks and injuries involved in *Stelluti* (referenced earlier in the chapter). In that case, the plaintiff faced the risk of injury resulting from strenuous physical activity and the use of exercise equipment, a foreseeable, inherent risk of health club membership. Here, in contrast, the court stated that the plaintiff faced the risk of injury from the improper use of a flammable material, a risk that most would not consider inherent to exercise and the use of exercise equipment. The court concluded its analysis by stating: "Whereas club members assume the risk of exercise related injuries, they cannot be said to assume the risk of being engulfed in flames when using eucalyptus oil in a club sauna."

Lewis v. Mammoth Mountain Ski Area

2009 U.S. Dist. LEXIS 13050 (E.D. Cal. Feb. 19, 2009)   **FOCUS** CASE

FACTS

The plaintiff was injured while participating in a guided snowmobile tour at the defendant's resort. The plaintiff, riding as a passenger on a snowmobile driven by her husband, sustained injury when the snowmobile encountered a variation in terrain while the group was off-trail.

The snowmobile became airborne and the plaintiff sustained injury when the snowmobile came down with great force. The defendant sought summary judgment based on the waiver signed by the plaintiff before the tour began. The plaintiff argued that the injuries sustained were not ones covered by the waiver.

HOLDING

The federal district court in California granted summary judgment for the defendant on the negligence claim.

RATIONALE

The issue in this case was whether the waiver covered the risk of becoming airborne while riding the snowmobile. The court noted that the participant agreement containing the waiver language was extremely broad as to time and place for any activities arising out of snowmobiling. Specifically, the document provided that "snowmobiling entails known and unanticipated risks which could result in physical or emotional injury, paralysis, death, or damage to myself, property, or to third parties." The agreement provided specific examples of risks inherent in snowmobiling: "riding on uneven snow covered terrain, changing snow conditions and variations in elevations; lost participants; tree, rocks and other man-made or natural obstacles; exposure to the elements, extreme temperatures, inclement weather and encounters with animals and wildlife; mechanical and/or equipment problems; and unavailability of immediate medical attention in case of injury."

The court further noted that although the risk of becoming airborne is not specified in the release, the risk of variations in terrain is explicitly identified. A variation in elevation involves a change in the height of ground level. According to the court, common sense dictates that when a snowmobile, running on the surface of the ground, encounters an abrupt change in elevation, the vehicle is likely to leave the ground surface as it travels from higher to lower ground levels. A wind-ridge two to six feet higher than the adjacent ground level is a variation in terrain, which caused the plaintiff's snowmobile to become airborne. The specific consequences of becoming airborne were not articulated among the inherent risks; however, the risk of injury caused by a variation in terrain was disclosed. Coming into contact with a variation in elevation is a risk inherent in snowmobiling. The court concluded that in a case where a participant in an activity has expressly released the defendant from responsibility for the consequences of any act of negligence, "the law imposes no requirement that [the participant] have had a specific knowledge of the particular risk which resulted in [the injury]."

As these cases show, courts use contract interpretation guidelines to determine whether a reasonable person, trying to interpret the language in a release, would fully understand just what the purpose of the release was and what rights were being given up in signing the document. Any ambiguity in interpretation will be resolved against the drafter of the document, since the choice of language is within the control of the one who writes the document.

The case of *Huverserian v. Catalina Scuba Luv, Inc.* (2010) decided by a California appellate court illustrates this concept. This wrongful death suit was precipitated by the death of a person who rented scuba gear for a day dive only to have the air supply run out beneath 60 feet of water. The decedent suffered cardiac arrest and then died. The decedent had signed a rental form for the scuba gear, which contained an exculpatory clause. However, the caption for the form stated that it was an "[e]quipment rental agreement, liability release and assumption of risk of scuba and snorkel gear for boat dives or multiple day rentals." The appellate court refused to uphold the exculpatory clause because it was applicable only for boat dives or multiple-day rentals, neither of which applied to the decedent's situation. Therefore, the only interpretation possible, according to the court, was that the exculpatory provisions of this agreement did not apply to the one-day rental by the decedent. This case further illustrates the necessity of having legal advice when developing a waiver form for a business.

Language Cannot Exonerate for Conduct Beyond Negligence

Generally speaking, courts will not uphold releases that attempt to exonerate a party for behavior that is something beyond negligence, such as gross negligence, reckless behavior, or intentional torts. The following Focus Case illustrates this issue.

McGregor v. Daytona International Speedway, LLC

263 So.3d 151 (Fla. 2018)	**FOCUS** CASE

FACTS

The plaintiff was standing in a restricted area of the Daytona International Speedway when a tow-truck driver was instructed by two other employees of the raceway to back the truck into that area. The plaintiff was ran over and killed by the tow-truck. Prior to the incident, in order to enter the non-spectator restricted area, the plaintiff signed a release and waiver of liability and assumption of risk agreement to "release, waive and discharge" the defendant for "all acts of negligence" in the context of closed-course motorsport facilities resulting in injury or death. The plaintiff's husband filed a wrongful death case again Daytona International Speedway arguing gross negligence (i.e. conduct beyond ordinary negligence demonstrating reckless disregard for the safety or lives of others) on behalf of the raceway and its employees. Defendant alleges the waiver signed by the plaintiff releases liability and asked for the case to be dismissed. The trial court dismissed the plaintiff's claim due to the signed waiver and release of liability. The plaintiff appealed.

HOLDING

The court reversed and remanded the trial court's decision holding the waiver does not excuse potential liability for gross negligence.

RATIONALE

The issue on appeal was whether an agreement attempting to release liability for "all acts of negligence" may be upheld. The appellate court ruled the waiver does not in fact release liability for grossly negligent acts based on state law. Because state statute explicitly excludes gross negligence from the definition of negligence for injuries occurring in the non-spectator areas of facilities, the release cannot be enforced against acts potentially arising to the level of gross negligence. Because the plaintiff is alleging, and the court agreed she has grounds to do so, gross negligence on behalf of the defendant, the waiver cannot excuse potential liability.

While exculpatory agreements more explicitly seek for a party to be held harmless, another type of agreement that can be used as a tool to evade liability is an agreement to participate. Agreements to participate take more of an approach to put the onus on the participant in an explicit way, establishing his or her willingness to voluntarily partake in the activity or service provided which we explore in the next section.

Agreements to Participate

Another version of an agreement that can be used either in conjunction with or in lieu of an exculpatory agreement is an agreement to participate. See Exhibit 16.6 for a sample agreement to participate. Regardless of the use of or effectiveness of an exculpatory agreement for your particular situation and location, you must still disclose information, including the risks of the activity, to the participant. You may also want to inform the participant of his or her obligations in the undertaking. You can provide this information in an agreement to participate. Van der Smissen (1990) identified three essential components of all agreements to participate:

1 The nature of the activity
2 The expectations of the participant
3 The condition of the participant

Exhibit 16.6 Sample agreement to participate.

University of Oklarado, School of Sport and Exercise Science

Agreement to Participate in PE 124 Paddle Sports

Participation in all sports and physical activities involves certain inherent risks and, regardless of the care taken, it is impossible to ensure the absolute safety of the participant. *Paddle sports is an activity requiring moderate coordination and cardiovascular fitness. It involves deep and moving water and may require repetitive movement over long periods of time (i.e., paddling long or difficult river sections).* Moreover, undue joint and muscle stress may occur, causing temporary pain or discomfort in the affected body regions. While it is a reasonably safe sport as long as safety guidelines are followed, some elements of risk cannot be eliminated from the activity.

A variety of injuries may occur to a *paddle sports* participant. Some examples of those injuries are:

1 Minor injuries such as *scrapes, bruises, strains, and sprains; sunburn, dehydration, burns, and cold weather injuries;*
2 More serious injuries such as *broken bones, cuts, concussions, and eye injuries (including loss of vision);*
3 Catastrophic injuries such as *heart attacks, near drowning, and death.*

These, and other injuries, sometimes occur in *paddle sports* as a result of hazards or accidents such as capsizing, oncoming obstacles (e.g., rocks, strainers, holes, low head dams, debris, the boat), foot entrapment, being struck by lightning, encountering water-borne/insect-borne illnesses, or excessive stress placed on the cardiovascular and muscular systems.

To help reduce the likelihood of injury to yourself and to other participants, participants are expected to follow the following rules:

- All participants are expected to wear proper footwear.
- All participants are expected to wear proper clothing, including PFDs and helmets when required.
- All participants are expected to be "aware" of their environment (changing weather, etc.).
- All participants are expected to follow all posted safety rules as well as those associated with the rules of paddle sports.
- All participants are expected to maintain a positive attitude and to avoid injurious behavior.

I agree to follow the preceding safety rules, all posted safety rules, and all rules common to the sport/activity of *paddle sports*. Further, I agree to report any unsafe practices, conditions, or equipment to the instructor.

I certify that (1) I possess a sufficient degree of physical fitness to participate safely in *paddle sports*, (2) I understand that I am to discontinue activity at any time I feel undue discomfort or stress, and (3) I will inform the instructor in writing of any health-related conditions that might affect my ability to participate in *paddle sports* and I will verbally inform the instructor immediately.

I have read the preceding information and it has been explained to me. I know, understand, and appreciate the risks associated with participation in *paddle sports*, and I am voluntarily participating in the activity. In doing so, I am assuming all of the inherent risks of the sport/activity. I further understand that in the event of a medical emergency, the instructor will call DPS to render assistance and that I will be financially responsible for any expenses involved.

Name of Participant (Print) Date Signature

You may add an exculpatory clause to the agreement to participate, if the circumstances are appropriate. In regard to the nature of the activity, you should describe the demands of the activity and the risks inherent in the activity. This serves three purposes:

1 It lets the participant know that you are doing whatever you can to communicate necessary and important information about a program or activity.
2 The dissemination of risk information serves to ensure that the participant cannot bring a successful action against you for failure to warn, as discussed in Chapter 15.
3 This disclosure strengthens your ability to use the affirmative defense of primary assumption of risk, as discussed in Chapters 14 & 15, since the participant is voluntarily encountering the inherent risks of the activity with knowledge and understanding of those risks.

The next component of the agreement to participate is sharing your expectations for the participant's behavior. In every activity, participants must follow certain rules and regulations to try to minimize hazards to themselves and co-participants. The statement of what is expected behavior and the participant's assent to behave in that way are at the core of this component. If the participant is injured because he or she violates these behavioral expectations, you have the defense of comparative negligence (discussed in Chapter 14). Because the participant knew what reasonable behavior is and deviated from that, the participant failed to act as a reasonably prudent participant.

The final component of the agreement to participate is the section in which you ask the participant to state that he or she has the appropriate skill level to participate and that he or she is in proper medical condition to engage in the activity. If the participant misrepresents this information, this may be viewed as unreasonable behavior leading to the participant's own injury – another way in which the defense of comparative negligence may be used.

Conclusion

Information exchange with participants, sponsors, partners, competition and facilities are all a critical aspect of any sport or recreation program. You communicate with those parties through many avenues, but the most legally relevant avenues are our contractual agreements and written communications. As such, it is crucial to have clearly written language across the board – from brochures, signage, waivers, and instructions, to facility lease agreements and game day contracts. To understand that the use of language through agreements is binding, you can position yourself to work to your competitive advantage.

Discussion Questions

1 A school district seeks your advice regarding its waiver form. All of the student-athletes are minors. Based on your knowledge of the law regarding minors and waivers, would you recommend that a waiver form be used? Of what use is a parental signature – can parents release their minors' claims in most jurisdictions? Regardless of the minority issue, what are the public policy issues that may arise when an educational institution attempts to use a waiver form? Use the *Wagenblast* decision as a guide in answering this last point.
2 After reviewing the *House of Boom* and *Hamill* decisions, think about how you would answer the following questions to reinforce your understanding of parents' versus minors' rights: how far should parental rights extend regarding decision-making for one's children? Is there a need to protect minors even from the actions of parents? Or should we empower parents to make this type of decision for children, just as we allow parents to make many other decisions for their children?
3 In regard to the *Kyriazis* v. West Virginia University decision, do you agree with the court's view that the provision of recreational activities to students is a part of a university's mission? That case dealt with "club" sport. How would you extend the rationale to intramural sport? In which case does the argument of an extension of "educational mission" make more sense?

4   What is your opinion on giving up your right to sue before you actually have it? Until you have sustained injury or received a wrongdoing, your right to call "foul" is not yet present; as such, do you feel it is legally acceptable to give up that right prior to having it and/or fully understanding the nature or extent of foregoing those rights? How does this relate to the issue with the enforceability of waivers?

5   Discuss the concept of conspicuousness. What does this mean when you are developing your waiver form?

Learning Activities

1   Visit the websites of sport or recreation providers in your area or locate their brochures or other promotional materials. Look at the language and identify words or phrases that might convey inaccurate information about the activity. Identify whether the language in any way promises a "perfect" "perfectly safe" experience. Suggest changes to the language where necessary.

2   Find out whether agreements to participate are being used in activity classes at your university. If so, review them in class. Do they have the necessary three components?

Case Study

You are thinking of operating a summer camp for high school soccer players, you want to use whatever documents will be helpful in dealing with liability issues. First, review the law of the state in which you plan to operate and ascertain whether waivers will be upheld if signed by your camp participants, who minors. Will the waiver be upheld if signed by a minor's parent or guardian? Second, develop an agreement to participate that has the necessary components and may be used with the players at your camp.

Considering ... Analysis & Discussion

Facility Lease Agreements

In this instance, the Good Faith and Fair Dealings Clause may apply; however, there did not seem to be intentional deceit by that of the facility. If, for argument's sake, the facility lied and said they were not flooded, with the intention of having it cleaned up in time, then they would be in violation of this clause. But if they truly believed there was no need to inform you of the situation, confident it would be resolved, then they acted in good faith. This clause calls for analyzing the subjective intent of a contracting party, which can be difficult to ascertain. As such, we must look at the objective facts to help deduce if we believe they were acting in good faith. If, based on the objective facts, it was unreasonable of the facility to think it would be cleaned up in time, then perhaps there would be an argument for a violation of this clause.

It is important to note that the hurricane may be considered an "act of God" which triggers the *force majeure* clause of a contract. Force majeure clauses excuse a party only if the failure to perform could not be avoided by the exercise of due care by that party. Regardless of the precautions taken by the facility, a hurricane causing flooding was likely unavoidable and out of their control. As such, they may not be held responsible for their non-performance of the contract.

Here, though, the situation has another layer. Because the facility failed to inform the company of the situation, time was lost in finding a new venue. The company may be able to claim what are called reliance damages, in so far as they relied on the expectation that they were going to be using the facility even after the hurricane hit. If the company can show that the pricing and/or availability of choosing a new facility negatively affected them in the week the facility failed to inform them of their situation, then the facility will likely be liable for the difference in cost and added transportation expenses.

Had the lease agreement included a clause setting out expectations of timely communication, the facility would have had guidelines to follow in their handling of the situation. An option is to add a clause to the Kitchen Sink provisions stating something such as: "Parties are obligated to inform one another, in writing, of any changes in their situation which may substantially affect their performance of the contract in a timely manner." Or to be even more specific, the clause could set a deadline such as "within two business days of their discovery of the change." Perhaps an amended agreement between the two parties could be reached. For example, rather than working through timely and costly litigation, perhaps it could be negotiated that the facility helps cover the added transportation costs but need not pay the difference in rental price if they honor the agreement and same (or better) pricing of the event for the following year.

Remember, a contract serves as a roadmap to the relationship between the contracting parties. And we can contract to anything (as long as it is legal). Which means, the more foresight and risk management you can work into the language of your contract, the better.

References

Cases

Atkins v. Swimwest Family Fitness Center, 691 N.W.2d 334 (Wis. 2005).

Bagley v. Mt. Bachelor, Inc., 340 P.3d 27 (Or. 2014).

Berlangieri v. Running Elk Corp., 76 P.3d 1098 (N.M. 2003).

Capri v. L.A. Fitness Internat'l, 136 Cal. App. 4th 1078 (2006).

Donner v. Nicklaus, 778 F.3d 857 (10th Cir. 2017).

Fay v. Thiel College, 55 Pa. D. & C. 4th 353 (Pa. Com. Pleas Ct. 2001).

Geczi v. Lifetime Fitness, 973 N.E.2d 801 (Ohio Ct. App. 2012).

Gregorie v. Alpine Meadows Ski Corp., 2009 U.S. Dist. LEXIS 69237 (E.D. Cal. August 6, 2009), aff'd 2010 U.S App. LEXIS 26328 (9th Cir. Dec. 7, 2010).

Hamill v. Cheley Colorado Camps, Inc., 262 P.3d 945 (Colo. Ct. App. 2011).

Heil Valley Ranch v. Simkin, 784 P.2d 781 (Colo. 1989).

Hiett v. Lake Barcroft Community Association, Inc., 418 S.E.2d 894 (Va. 1992).

Huverserian v. Catalina Scuba Luv, Inc., 184 Cal. App. 4th 1462 (2010).

Kotcherquina v. Fitness Premier Mgmt., 2012 U.S. Dist. LEXIS 27675 (E.D. Ark. March 2, 2012).

Kyriazis v. West Virginia University, 450 S.E.2d 649 (W. Va. 1994).

Lewis v. Mammoth Mountain Ski Area, 2009 U.S. Dist. LEXIS 13050 (E.D. Cal. Feb. 19, 2009).

Lhotka v. Geographic Expeditions, Inc., 181 Cal. App.4th 816 (2010).

McGregor v. Daytona International Speedway, LLC., 263 So.3d 151 (2018).

Murphy v. North American River Runners, Inc., 412 S.E.2d 504 (W. Va. 1991).

Sanislo v. Give Kids the World, Inc., 157 So. 3d 256 (Fla. 2015).

Schlobohm v. Spa Petite, Inc., 326 N.W.2d 920 (Minn. 1982).

Schneeloch v. Glastonbury Fitness & Wellness, Inc., 2009 Conn. Super. LEXIS 191 (Feb. 2, 2009).

Semeniken v. Town Sports Internat'l, Inc., 2010 N.J. Super. Unpub. LEXIS 2681 (Oct. 29, 2010).

Stelluti v. Casapenn Enterprises, 975 A.2d 494 (N.J. Super. Ct., 2009).

Thompson v. Otterbein College, Ohio App. LEXIS 389 (Ohio Ct. App. 1996).

Tunkl v. Regents of University of California, 60 Cal. 2d 92 (Cal. 1963).

Wagenblast v. Odessa School District No. 105-157-166J, 758 P.2d 968 (Wash. 1988).

Walker v. Young Life Saranac Village, 2012 U.S. Dist. LEXIS 166057 (N.D.N.Y. Nov. 21, 2012).

Woodman v. Kera LLC, 785 N.W.2d 1 (Mich. 2010).

Yarde Metals v. New Eng. Pat., No. 03-3832-E (Mass. Cmmw. Sep. 26, 2003). Zides v. Quinnipiac University, 2006 Conn. Super. LEXIS 473 (Feb. 7, 2006).

Statues

42 Am. Jur. 2d, *Infants* § 82 (2013).

New York General Obligation Law § 5-326 (2011).

Restatement (Second) of Contracts (1981).

Restatement (Second) of Torts (1965).

Other Sources

Abraham, A. (2018, September 4). Cancellation of Akron's football opener against Nebraska puts possible large payout in jeopardy. *WKYC Studios*. Retrieved from https://www.wkyc.com/article/sports/high-school/football/cancellation-of-akrons-football-opener-against-nebraska-puts-possible-large-payout-in-jeopardy/95-590860960.

Bittakis, M. (2012). Walking away from Omelas: Why parental preinjury releases for children engaging in commercial activities should be unenforceable. *Kansas Journal of Law & Public Policy*, 21, 254–279.

Black's Law Dictionary (9th ed., 2009). St. Paul, MN: West Publishing.

Connell, M. J., & Savage, F. G. (2003). Releases: Is there still a place for their use by colleges and universities? *Journal of College and University Law*, 29(3), 579–617.

Cotten, D. (2017, February 4). Electronic or Online Waivers: How Good Are They? *Sports Waiver: Sport Risk Consulting*. Retrieved from https://www.sportwaiver.com/electronic-or-online-waivers-how-good-are-they/.

Diamond, J. L., Levine, L. C., & Madden, M. S. (2007). *Understanding torts* (3rd ed.). Albany, New York, NY: Lexis Publishing.

Espaldon, K. M. (1994). Virginia's rule of non-waiver of liability for negligent acts: *Hiett v. Lake Barcroft Community Association, Incorporation*. *George Mason Law Review*, 2, 27–52.

Frederick, J. (2017, July 25). Timberwolves reach settlement with season-ticket holders in Flash Seats lawsuit. *Twin Cities Pioneer Press*. Retrieved from https://www.twincities.com/2017/07/24/timberwolves-reach-settlement-with-season-ticket-holders-in-flash-seats-lawsuit/.

Garcia-Navarro, L. (2019, January 13). Fyre Festival. NPR. Retrieved from https://www.npr.org/tags/526073306/fyre-festival.

Garner, B. A., et al. (2004). *Black's law dictionary* (8th ed.). St. Paul, MN: Thompson.

Greder, A. (2016, March 4). Timberwolves sued over digital ticket soles. *Twin Cities Pioneer Press*. Retrieved from https://www.twincities.com/2016/03/03/timberwolves-sued-digital-tickets-flash-seats/.

Hamill, J. J., & Poulos, A. (2017, May 15). Ticketing lawsuits point to further turmoil. *Sports Business Daily*. Retrieved from https://www.sportsbusinessdaily.com/Journal/Issues/2017/2017/05/15/Opinion/Shearman.aspx.

Hansen-Stamp, C. (2003). Risk management: A different perspective. *Recreation and Adventure Program Law and Liability* (pp. B-12–19). Vail, CO: CLE International.

Kufahl, P. (2012). Well-written release and waiver forms are vital for protecting fitness facilities in case of litigation. *Club Industry*, pp. 14–16. Retrieved from https://www.clubindustry.com/profits/well-written-release-and-waiver-forms-are-vital-protecting-fitness-facilities-case-litigation.

Legal Information Institute (2015, June 13). Unconscionability. Cornell Law School. Retrieved from https://www.law.cornell.edu/wex/unconscionability.

Matthiesen, B. W., Wickert, G. L., & Lehrer, D. W. (2019). Exculpatory agreements and liability waivers in all 50 states. *MWL Attorneys at Law*. Retrieved from https://www.mwl-law.com/wp-content/uploads/2018/05/EXCULPATORY-AGREEMENTS-AND-LIABILITY-WAIVERS-CHART-00214377x9EBBF.pdf.

McKowen, S. (2018a). Nebraska-Akron cancellation voids game contract. *Athletic Business*. Retrieved from https://www.athleticbusiness.com/contract-law/nebraska-akron-cancellation-voids-game-contract.html.

McKewon, S. (2018b, December 17). Nebraska agrees to pay Akron $650,000 for canceled game, and teams will play in 2025. *Omaha World-Herald*. Retrieved from https://www.omaha.com/huskers/football/nebraska-agrees-to-pay-akron-for-canceled-game-and-teams/article_099b7f0f-9f1c-5b1f-bc49-e1106a3ff6d0.html.

Moorman, A. M. (2015). Marketing materials and intentional misrepresentation: A word of warning for marketers and celebrity athlete promoters. *Sport Marketing Quarterly*, 24(3), 198–201.

Murr, A. (2002). Chalk talk: Sports waivers: An exercise in futility? *Journal of Law & Education*, 31, 114–120.

NBA Media Ventures, LLC. (2019, October 30). NBA Fan Code of Conduct. Retrieved from https://www.nba.com/nba-fan-code-of-conduct.

Shaikin, B. (2019, May 10). Dodgers hope to bolster bottom line by cutting out ticket brokers. *LA Times*. Retrieved from https://www.latimes.com/sports/dodgers/la-sp-dodgers-tickets-brokers-lawsuit-fans-secondary-market-20190509-story.html.

Solis, N. (2018, March 30). Dodgers face lawsuit from ticket sellers over consolidation deal. *Courthouse News Service*. Retrieved from https://www.courthousenews.com/dodgers-face-lawsuit-from-ticket-sellers-over-consolidation-deal/#targetText=Thebrokers who filedthe,inflateticketpricesforfans.&targetText=PlaintiffsnamedtheLosAngeles, and othercausesofaction.

U.S. Department of Interior (2019). Commercial use authorization application. *National Park Service*. Retrieved from https://www.nps.gov/isro/learn/management/upload/ISRO_Web_Accessible_Acknowledge-Risk-CUA_Applicant_2017.pdf.

Van der Smissen, B. (1990). *Legal liability and risk management for public and private entities*. Cincinnati, OH: Anderson Publishing.

Wong, G. (2017, December 5). Event cancellation: What is a game worth to your institution? *Athletic DirectorU*. Retrieved from https://athleticdirectoru.com/articles/event-cancellation-what-is-one-game-worth-to-your-institution/.

Web Resources

www.nirsa.info/know/2007/07/risk001.html ■ This article discusses the use of electronic waivers in campus recreation. It provides a checklist to use when preparing an electronic waiver.

https://www.elkhartindiana.org/egov/documents/1387127863_682037.pdf ■ This webpage contains a waiver from the Elkhart Parks & Recreation Office for a rental agreement for the local Riverview Softball Park.

http://recsports.osu.edu/posts/documents/oac-waiver.pdf ■ This website contains the waiver used by the Ohio State University for those who wish to use the climbing wall. It is a good model for a waiver used in that situation.

17 Planning and Accessibility Issues in Venue/Event Operations

Introduction

This chapter focuses on the variety of legal issues pertinent to constructing, financing, and operating facilities and events. First, we address legal issues relevant to the financing and construction of sport facilities. Next, we discuss legal issues related to several operational functions of a facility or an event. These operational functions include regulatory aspects such as compliance with the Americans with Disabilities Act (ADA) and privacy concerns related to spectator searches and surveillance activities.

Facility operation, maintenance, and policies and procedures are often the foundation of a sport or recreation enterprise. In many cases, the only contact someone will have with a sport or recreation organization is by visiting its facility. To be competitive, therefore, familiarity with the legal principles applicable to this area is crucial. You may have many opportunities to develop policies and procedures for your facility that will minimize exposure to liability relative to the concerns addressed in this chapter. See Exhibit 17.1 for an overview of the managerial contexts, major legal issues, relevant laws, and illustrative cases pertinent to this chapter.

Facility Financing and Planning Issues

This section explores legal issues related to facility financing proposals, team relocation, and property acquisition for new stadiums and arenas. We have witnessed significant changes in facility financing and planning since the mid-20th century. Stadiums of the past tended to be utilitarian structures built to accommodate multiple uses. Sightlines and seating configurations could not truly accommodate any single sport very well. In addition, most sport venues in the Unites States, prior to the 1960s were funded primarily or entirely by teams and their owners such as Chicago's Wrigley Field and Boston's Fenway Park. The funding shift began after World War II, giving way to public rather than private financing for most or all of a sports facility development. State and local governments viewed the stadiums and arenas as a benefit to the larger communities where the facilities were located. However, as more revenue came into professional sports, teams and owners realized they could generate more revenue with sport specific venues and enhanced amenities. These amenities include everything from stadium style seating, luxury suites, loge boxes, family and standing room only sections, sponsored party decks, club areas, enhanced technology, interactive fan zones, food service, player/locker room lounges, and full-blown entertainment districts surrounding the actual stadium or arena footprint (Steinbach, 2017). Of course with all these amenities comes a hefty price tag and decisions as to who is going to pay for the rising costs of stadiums and arenas. In the 1990s, the average public cost for a new sports facility was estimated around $142 million, but by 2010, that figure climbed to $240–260 million: an increase of 70 percent (Gordon, 2013). Now the average cost of professional sports venues is in the billions of dollars which requires teams and cities to decide who is going to bear the cost of constructing a new sports facility. Many stadium development plans have also started to include proposals to expand entertainment districts

Exhibit 17.1 Management contexts in which issues related to pro sport facilities and events may arise, with relevant laws and cases.

Management Context	Major Legal Issues	Relevant Law	Illustrative Cases
Financing proposals	Use of public funds for new sport facilities	State statutes and constitutions Open and obvious danger	Rowe, Minnesota Vikings, Atlanta Braves Kelly, King County
Team relocation	Long-term tenant agreements with professional teams	Contract law	St. Louis Rams, Oakland Raiders
Property acquisition	Government condemnation of private lands for stadium projects	Fifth Amendment	Berman, City of Orlando, Boise State, DC United
Access for people with disabilities	Avoiding discrimination against patrons with disabilities	Americans with Disabilities Act	PGA Tour, Inc., Miller, Feldman, Charlebois, Celano, Clark, Orioles, Cubs, Seattle Mainers, Salsccia, California Parks and Recreation, Landis
Spectator searches	Searching spectators prior to entry to facility and surveillance during events	Fourth Amendment	Katz, Johnston
		Privacy	Brannum

surrounding the stadium. These entertainment districts seek to boost the local economy by attracting more commercial activity to the area including concerts, events, extreme sporting events, and events of other sport leagues. With the taxpayers still bearing the bulk of the cost, it has become fairly common for new stadium proposals involving public financing to face legal challenges. Exhibit 17.2 provides

Exhibit 17.2 Examples of legal challenges to new professional sport stadiums & arenas.

Venues	Location/Team	Legal Issue	Nature of the Legal Challenge
• Miami Freedom Park • Qualcomm Stadium • AT&T Stadium • U.S. Bank Stadium	• Inter Miami IC • San Diego Chargers • Texas Rangers • Minnesota Vikings	Public Referendum required for Public Subsidy Violation of State Constitution	Whether voting referendum is necessary Whether city, county, or state is authorized to issue bonds and qualify for tax exemption
• Howard Terminal Ballpark • Belmont Arena	• Oakland A's • New York Islanders	Compliance with State Environmental Review Guidelines and Urban Renewal Statutes	Whether the project poses environmental concerns
• Angel Stadium of Anaheim	• Anaheim Angels, California	State Transparency Laws	Whether city officials have a conflict of interest or lack of transparency in approving financing proposals
• Petco Park • Golden 1 Centre • Nationals Stadium • Global Life Park • AT&T Stadium • Kansas City Speedway • Barclays Center • Exploria Stadium • Top Golf • Nissan Stadium	• San Diego Padres • Sacramento Kings • Washington Nationals • Texas Rangers • Dallas Cowboys • Kansas City, Kansas • Brooklyn Nets • Orlando City Soccer Club, MLS • Louisville, Kentucky • Nashville Soccer Club, MLS	Eminent Domain and Condemnation	Whether public land should be taken via eminent domain for private enterprise Whether nearby businesses or landowners will be harmed by the development

List compiled from: Custodio (2020); Greenberg (2004); Kallergis (2018); London (2019); Mosier (2017); Muret (2016); Sandefer (2015); Spedden (2020); Winzelberg (2019).

examples of legal challenges associated with new professional sport stadium and arena construction and development projects. The legal issues raised often include:

- whether a voting referendum is necessary (i.e., must the public be allowed to approve or reject the financing proposal at the polls) (Kallergis, 2018; Muret, 2016).
- whether a city, county, or state is authorized to issue bonds to finance the construction (e.g., may a city increase its debt to or beyond certain levels) ("Lawsuit delays," 2014).
- whether the project poses environment concerns (Spedden, 2020; Winzelberg, 2019)
- whether city officials have a conflict of interest or lack transparency in approving bid proposals (Custodio, 2020; London, 2019).
- whether neighboring properties and businesses will be harmed or benefited from the development, especially for the entertainment district plans (Aulbach, 2019).
- whether the taking the property of adjoining landowners for the project is legally permissible (Sandefer, 2015; Somin, 2014).

In the next section, we explore legal issues associated with stadium financing proposals relying on public funding.

Financing Plans and Proposals

Beginning in the mid-1980s, taxpayers began to push back on public financing, particularly as teams and owners demanded new facilities to replace seemingly suitable ones already in existence. Beginning in the 1990s, sport economists also began questioning the financial return on public investments in professional sport stadiums (BER Staff, 2019; Noll & Zimbalist, 1997). In 2010, the average cost of a major league arena was around $260 million with an average public subsidy of 70 percent, or $182 million per venue. By 2018, the average cost of a major league arena was $430 million, and the average public subsidy had declined to 56 percent, or about $207 million (Gerretsen, 2018). The share of public funding had decreased slightly, however, the overall amount of funding had increased, due to the high expense rate of stadium construction. Despite the questionable customer and financial impact, more than 100 sports facilities were built from 1990 to 2010, a 90 percent replacement rate (Gordon, 2013; Long 2013). Furthermore, in the time span between 2015 and 2017, nearly $17 billion was spent on stadium construction or renovations (Broughton, 2018). Spending continues to rise, with the Atlanta Falcons receiving $700 million in public funds and the Raiders move to Las Vegas saw $750 million in public funds (DeMause, 2017; Velotta, 2018). Only a few recent stadiums have received zero public funding. One is the Chase Center in California, the new home of the Golden State Warriors with total costs are upward of $1.2 billion (Keeling, 2019). Similarly, in the summer of 2020, the new home of the Rams and Chargers opened in Los Angeles. It is the most expensive sporting facility in US history, totaling upward of $5 billion, without using any public funding (Shaikin, 2019).

Lawsuits filed by stadium opponents raise complex constitutional and statutory issues that are beyond the scope of this text, but the underlying policy arguments will certainly impact sport managers who are involved in the planning, financing, and construction of new sport facilities. The basic argument a stadium manager will encounter is whether the use of taxpayer money to construct private sport facilities with no guarantee of financial repayment is an appropriate or permitted use of public funds, especially in difficult economic times (Greenberg & Hughes, 2011). For example, in *Rowe v. Pinellas Sports Authority* (1984), opponents challenged the building of a new dome in St. Petersburg, Florida, on statutory and constitutional grounds, but the Florida Supreme Court held that state sunshine laws and the Florida Constitution were not violated. Similarly, in *Kelly v. Marylanders for Sports Sanity, Inc.* (1987), opponents sued to force a referendum for the financing plan for Oriole Park at Camden Yards in Baltimore, but the Maryland Court of Appeals held that the appropriation was proper. In *King County v. Taxpayers* (1997), opponents of the Seattle

Mariners financing plan argued that the plan was an unconstitutional gift of public money and that legislative authority had been unconstitutionally delegated to the public facilities district, but the Washington Supreme Court upheld the financing plan and said the stadium project served a valid public purpose. Also, in 2013, public dissent surrounding the Minnesota Vikings stadium prompted numerous legal challenges ranging from statutory spending limits to encroaching on jurisdiction of the Minnesota Park Board over adjacent park land included in the project (Nelson, 2013). In January 2014, the Minnesota Supreme Court dismissed all lawsuits finally clearing the way for the financing and building of the new stadium (Nelson, 2014). Lastly, the new SunTrust Park built for the Atlanta Braves opened for the 2017 MLB season with $392 million in public funding on the line. The Cobb County representatives expressed frustration over delays in receiving receipts and reports for over $148 million in stadium costs creating high tension between local government officials and the team representatives (Lutz, 2018).

While a detailed discussion of the legal arguments raised in these disputes is beyond the scope of this text, sport managers need to be prepared for opposition to public funding proposals for new sport facilities. Delays associated with resolving these disputes need to be anticipated and sport managers should build alliances early in the planning process to minimize opposition. Even though the opponents of public financing of sports stadiums have not been particularly successful in their opposition, the legal challenges can pose a threat to new stadium financing proposals in terms of the litigation costs and delays in the projects themselves.

Team Relocation

Legal challenges can also arise when a team threatens to leave for another city. Certainly in circumstances where the public has made a substantial investment in building a new sport venue or provided tax or other financial incentives for the team, the departure by the team threatens the ability of the community to recover on their investment. There are a limited number of professional sports franchises, so when a franchise departs one city for another, often the abandoned city is left without a professional sports franchise which can have many negative economic and cultural consequences.

Cities trying to attract a professional sports franchise often use the lure of a new stadium, even though the sport franchise is already committed to a long-term lease agreement in its home city. Since the Baltimore Colts loaded their moving vans under cover of darkness on a cold, snowy morning on March 28, 1984, to relocate to Indianapolis, cities have struggled with how to ensure that their coveted professional sport franchises remain loyal to their city. Even though it has been more than 25 years since the Colts left Baltimore and Baltimore has since acquired a new NFL franchise with the Ravens, Baltimore fans still harbor resentment toward the NFL team located in Indianapolis, Indiana (Hybl, 2010).

Typically, in a new sports stadium with a major league sports team, the team is the primary tenant and is responsible for the stadium's operation. These lease agreements are usually very advantageous to the team in that the team pays little if any rent and retains a large share of revenue streams from concessions, advertising, luxury suites, club seats, naming rights, and ticket sales. However, cities also recognize that the benefits bestowed upon the team represent a significant investment of public funds and trust such that the team's commitment to stay in the city is critical for the city to reap the economic rewards of its investment. A few cities have exercised their contractual rights under the stadium or arena lease agreements to either prevent the team from leaving or at least slow its departure. For example, as the NBA Seattle SuperSonics notified the City of Seattle that they were planning to part ways, the City sued to enforce the Sonics' Key Arena lease and sought a court order forcing the team to play out the final two years on its lease at Key Arena through September 2010. Typically, courts are reluctant to force parties to fulfill contract obligations against their will. Instead, they require monetary damages to make the injured party whole. But the Sonics lease specifically states that either side can force the other to fulfill its obligations. The City argued that a cash settlement from the NBA franchise to leave early would not be an adequate remedy. The Sonics tried to force the dispute to arbitration. However, the lease expressly said that disputes between the city and the team over the "term" or length of the lease were not subject to arbitration and the federal court found the dispute was excluded from arbitration (Greenberg, 2008). The case was settled just before the federal district judge in Oklahoma City was scheduled to render a verdict in the case. The settlement paved the way for the franchise to move from Seattle to Oklahoma City. Sonics owner Clay Bennett agreed to pay the City of Seattle $45 million, plus another $30 million in five years if the NBA had not agreed to place another franchise in Seattle (Greenberg, 2008). The City of Seattle also retained the Sonics name and the team's green and gold colors (Alberg, 2008). The ability of the City to potentially force the team to honor its lease agreement and require the team to remain at Key Arena through the 2010 season helped to apply pressure on the owner to resolve the dispute.

The latest example of teams relocating to a new city is in Los Angeles, when the city secured financing for a new $5 billion NFL stadium, attracting both the San Diego Chargers and the St. Louis Rams. Four separate multi-million dollar lawsuits were brought against the Rams. Two of the suits were filed by disgruntled fans including season ticket holders, personal seat licenses, team merchandise customers (Allred, 2019; Currier, 2019). The first two lawsuits were known as the "Personal Seat License" lawsuit and the "Ticket/Merchandise" lawsuit. The fans and ticketholders alleged the Rams' owner and team made misleading statements about their plans to move to another city therefore deceiving them into purchasing tickets and merchandise. The Rams entered into multiple class action settlements in 2020 to resolve these two lawsuits. The Rams agreed to pay $25 million in refunds to Missouri football fans for tickets and merchandise and another $24 million to Rams ticketholders who purchased seat licenses at the St. Louis stadium ("St. Louis Rams," 2020). The Rams, however, prevailed in an arbitration hearing over the city's Regional Convention and Sports Complex Authority. The arbitration award permitted the Rams to exercise an option in their lease agreement to purchase the Earth City practice facility valued at $12.7 million for $1 in 2024 at the end of the lease (Brennan, 2019). The final lawsuit filed by the City of St. Louis and the Regional Convention and Sports Complex Authority against the Rams and the NFL (NFL suit) alleges the Rams violated the NFL's relocation rules. The NFL tried to have this suit settled in arbitration, but the Missouri Supreme Court denied that request. The U.S. Supreme Court denied the NFL's petition for certiorari in April 2020 leaving the fall 2021 trial date in place (Rubbelke, 2020).

In the past, despite the pain of losing a team to another city, cities and fans usually had few legal remedies to prevent a team from relocating and abandoning the city. The Rams lawsuits may signal a new trend in relocation litigation when fans can document misleading and false statements made by teams and owners about their intentions. Both the Sonics and Rams examples also highlight the importance of how we draft our lease agreements (Chapter 16) to protect our long-term interests and financial investments in the lease and the team.

Competitive Advantage Strategies

Facility Financing and Construction

- Stadium financing is a highly specialized area. Whether representing teams and leagues, state and local governments, or citizen interest groups, sport managers need legal counsel to prepare contracts with public partners and to anticipate potential lawsuits, as well as to advise the parties on important tax and property law issues.
- Anticipating legal challenges or public criticism of a project in advance enables the parties to resolve disputes more quickly and perhaps less publicly.
- Potential delays due to legal challenges should be taken into consideration in setting financing and construction timelines.

Stadium Location and Property Acquisition

The next common legal issue associated with new stadiums and arenas relates to securing a desirable location. Some stadium or arena projects simply involve tearing down or imploding the old stadium or arena and building the new one. However, more frequently, stadium and arena projects involve much more than just the sport facilities. These construction projects now commonly include hotels, restaurants, shopping malls, and other related commercial developments. In these types of projects, more land is needed; thus, both commercial and residential properties surrounding these stadium projects are vulnerable to what is known as a *taking* by the city or county so that the land can be used for the stadium project.

Eminent Domain and Condemnation

When a government agency seizes or *takes* private land for public use such as a Metro Planning Commission approving a new stadium development project in an under-developed part of the city, it exercises authority that is referred to as its eminent domain and condemnation powers to take or condemn land while providing its previous owners with fair market value (Trimble, 2019). Government taking of privately owned commercial and residential properties is controversial and subject to legal challenges under the Fifth Amendment to the U.S. Constitution, along with most state constitutions. The Fifth Amendment limits the power of the government to interfere with private property rights and expressly states that private property shall not "*be taken for public use, without just compensation.*" Historically, the government used eminent domain powers only for projects such as the construction of new roads, bridges, dams, or utilities that were considered a public use of the private land taken. However, beginning in the 1950s the Supreme Court expanded the concept of *public use* to include a *public purpose.* The Supreme Court unanimously ruled that private property could be condemned and resold to another private party because the redevelopment plan served a public purpose to improve a blighted neighborhood even though some of the land being taken was being used productively by the property owners and was not blighted (*Berman v. Parker,* 1954). Use of eminent domain or condemnation powers for an overall public purpose also permits economic development as a rationale for taking property of one private citizen and selling it to another private citizen to redevelop for the benefit of the public. Some critics suggest the *Berman* decision "forged an unholy alliance between cities strapped for cash and entrepreneurs promising economic bounty" (Greenberg, 2005; Greenberg & Hughes, 2011). The Institute for Justice documented over 10,000 eminent domain cases from 1998 to 2002 in which local governments attempted to condemn real estate for private redevelopment (Greenberg, 2005; Greenberg & Hughes, 2011).

In a landmark case in 2000, the City of New London, Connecticut, implemented a redevelopment project to increase tax revenues and improve the economic conditions within its municipality. Although the 115 residential and commercial lots within the 90 acres to be acquired and redeveloped were not blighted, the city eventually utilized its eminent domain power to acquire 15 parcels owned by citizens who refused to sell to the redevelopment corporation (*Kelo v. City of New London,* 2005). Kelo and other owners argued that seizing one party's private property in order to transfer ownership to another private entity – strictly for the economic benefit of the community – did not qualify as proper public use or purpose (*Kelo v. City of New London,* 2005). On June 23, 2005, the Supreme Court (5–4) held for the city of New London. The Court reasoned that, under Connecticut state law, public benefits, such as the economic growth and increased taxes likely to result from the city's redevelopment plans, qualified as a permissible "public use" under the Fifth Amendment's Takings Clause.

Sport organizations, particularly those operating in large facilities, are no strangers to the use of eminent domain and condemnation for construction of new sport stadiums. Acquiring adequate contiguous acreage from disparate parcels to build a new stadium can be difficult and potentially expensive, especially when accessing land in a large metropolitan area. This urban environment reality resulted in eminent domain–related discussions in nearly half of all new major professional sport construction projects in the 1990s (McGraw, 2005). Eminent domain has often assisted a team's new stadium construction.

Notable eminent domain controversies involved the Dallas Cowboys (Joyner, 2005; Mosier, 2008), the Florida Marlins ("SB 4 and Eminent Domain News," 2005), the Washington Nationals (Natarajan & O'Connell, 2007), Oklahoma State University ("Oklahoma State wins," 2009), Atlantic Yards project in Brooklyn (Bagli, 2009), DC United (Sernovitz, 2018), and Boise State University (Associated Press, 2018). However, in the aftermath of the *Kelo v. City of London* decision, 44 states reformed their eminent domain laws restricting the use of eminent domain to take private property for nonpublic uses and allowing for more clear guidelines on just compensation (Institute for Justice, 2019).

Florida is one of the states enacting strong eminent domain reforms. Florida state laws are beneficial to the private property owners, stating that land cannot be taken for private use, even if the city owns the property and is leasing the facility (Somin, 2014). These reforms were evident when the City of Orlando approved the use of eminent domain and condemnation proceedings to take private property from land-owners to build an MLS stadium in 2014. Two of these landowners did not contest the city's claim that the land was being taken for a public use (Somin, 2014). However, a Church on the proposed land refused to sell to the City of Orlando, subsequently, leading to the stadium to abandon its eminent domain fight and move the project a block over from where originally proposed on property acquired by the city (Damron, 2014). In the District of Columbia, when DC United used eminent domain to start construction on commercial land. A jury valued the land at roughly $32 million to be paid to the previous owner of the land (Sernovitz, 2018). Overall, most eminent domain cases do not end well for the private property owners, with most states ruling that the process is for the greater good of the state even when the compensation offered to the property owners is less than they believe they should receive (Huang, 2019; Sandefer, 2015; Trimble, 2019).

Zoning Challenges

Even when eminent domain or condemnation is not being used, developers can still experience push back from residential and commercial landowners in and around a new stadium development project. Depending on where your land is, your town or state will have different building and zoning regulations. It is imperative to understand these regulations and ensure your plan is in accordance with them before you dig the first hole. Normally for a new sports venue, you must present your plans to your local municipality for approval. Typically, you'll have to specifically meet with their zoning department. Only after these plans are approved can you move forward, so zoning approvals are done early in the process. Most zoning proposals will also be subject to public review and comment at which stage they can attract opposition. For example, in 2018 Topgolf planned to move into a former Sears store in an urban shopping mall in Louisville, Kentucky. Surrounding residents opposed the move claiming the Topgolf facility would interfere with and damage their properties from excessive lighting and noise. The Louisville Metro Planning Commission approved the project in 2019 and the residents appealed to the Jefferson County Circuit Court asserting the TopGolf application was not accurate and complete as required by Kentucky Zoning statutes. The Circuit Judge held for TopGolf and the residents again appealed, this time to the Kentucky Court of Appeals. While the latest appeal has yet to be resolved, this case illustrates the importance of public support for the project, obtaining early zoning approvals, and the myriad of legal issues that can surround a sport facility project in urban and densely populated areas (Aulbach, 2019; Vogt, 2020).

The government is an important partner with most stadium or arena projects; thus, sport managers need to be well versed in working in this public environment and have an understanding of the legal issues surrounding acquiring new property for stadium expansion or construction projects. This section has illustrated how securing and financing new sport facilities or trying to relocate a team from one city to another can involve a complex array of potential problems, including: financing and lease agreements, ticketing agreements, voter approval, and political red tape. The complexity of these activities will naturally create a number of legal issues, as discussed above, surrounding the financing, construction, or location of a stadium or arena. However, sport facility managers face additional legal issues associated with how well we manage the spectator experiences at our facilities which we will explore in the next section.

Spectator Accessibility and the Americans with Disabilities Act

In this section we discuss federal statutes regulating accessibility for spectators and guests at sports venues and events. We explore the application of the ADA to sports facilities, which includes large public access stadiums and arenas, as well as private sport-related businesses such as sporting goods retail stores. As discussed in Chapters 5 and 12, the ADA (42 U.S.C. § 12101 *et seq.*) is a comprehensive civil rights law that prohibits discrimination on the basis of disability. The ADA ensures that people with disabilities will be able to gain equal access to employment (Title I, discussed in Chapter 5), state and local government facilities (Title II), and places of public accommodation (Title III) discussed in Chapter 12. For purposes of this chapter, we focus again on Title III of the ADA, dealing with places of public accommodation, specifically sports venues and events.

Overview of the ADA's Broad Mandate

The ADA was enacted in 1990 and was intended "to provide clear, strong, consistent, enforceable standards addressing discrimination against individuals with disabilities" (42 U.S.C. § 12101(b)(2)). Title III addresses "public accommodations and services operated by private entities" and provides that

> [n]o individual shall be discriminated against on the basis of disability in the full and equal enjoyment of the goods, services, facilities, privileges, advantages, or accommodations of any place of public accommodation by any person who owns, leases (or leases to), or operates a place of public accommodation (42 U.S.C. § 12182).

The ADA has a broad mandate and has been interpreted broadly by the courts in its application to sport facilities. For example, in the only ADA case decided by the Supreme Court in the context of professional sport, *PGA Tour, Inc. v. Martin* (2001), the Court had to determine whether the PGA Tour competition was a *place of public accommodation* under the ADA. The PGA Tour openly admitted the ADA applied to all golf courses at which it held events in terms of spectator access but drew a line between physical access to the golf course and participation as part of the tour competition. The PGA Tour instead argued that the "opportunity to compete in its event" was not a "place" as that term is used under the ADA. The Court disagreed as follows:

> Petitioner's golf tours and their qualifying rounds fit comfortably within the coverage of Title III. The events occur on "golf courses," a type of place specifically identified by the Act as a public accommodation. In addition, at all relevant times, petitioner "leases" and "operates" golf courses to conduct its Q-School and tours. As a lessor and operator of golf courses, then, petitioner must not discriminate against any "individual" in the "full and equal enjoyment of the goods, services, facilities, privileges, advantages, or accommodations" of those courses. Certainly, among the "privileges" offered by petitioner on the courses are those of competing in the Q-School and playing in the tours; indeed, the former is a privilege for which thousands of individuals from the general public pay, and the latter is one for which they vie. Martin, of course, is one of those individuals. (*PGA Tour, Inc. v. Martin*, 2001, p. 677).

Thus, the Supreme Court made it clear that the reach of the ADA is not limited only to physical spaces and facility access issues. Instead, the best practice for sport managers is to understand that the ADA applies to the entire facility, and all programs and services offered within that facility or by the organization.

Tools and Resources for ADA Compliance

Sport managers have a number of tools and resources available to them to aid in complying with the ADA. When the ADA was enacted, the Department of Justice (DOJ) was instructed to establish and promulgate regulations and standards to guide businesses, service providers, employers, and governmental entities in complying with Title III of the statute. See 42 U.S.C. § 12134(a) & 12186(b). Congress further required that these implementing regulations must be consistent with the minimum guidelines issued by the Architectural and Transportation Barriers Compliance Board, now known as the United States Access Board ("Access Board"). The Access Board is an independent federal agency charged with issuing guidelines to ensure that public accommodations are accessible to individuals with disabilities. The DOJ uses the Access Board guidelines to develop formal ADA standards and the ADA standards issued by the DOJ are legally enforceable standards. As we will explore later in the chapter, the courts must extend substantial deference to the DOJ's interpretation of the ADA regulations and guidelines when resolving ADA lawsuits.

Six months after the enactment of the ADA, the Access Board published its first proposed ADA Accessibility Guidelines ("ADA Guides"), which were finalized in July 1991. The ADA Guides are readily available for designers and operators to ensure that a sport facility is accessible and compliant with the ADA requirements (U.S. Access Board, 2019). In addition, the Access Board has published ADA accessibility guidelines for several specific types of recreation facilities such as golf facilities, boating facilities, fishing piers, and swimming pools (see the Web Resources at the end of this chapter). The DOJ also publishes technical assistance manuals (TAMs) which are meant to guide entities in some of the more technical elements of complying with the regulations (DOJ, 1993). In 1994, the DOJ supplemented the 1993 TAM (DOJ, 1994). In addition to the Guides and the TAMs, the DOJ also publishes more informal guidelines regarding its interpretations of the ADA, the Guides, and its own regulations. For example, in 1996 it published *Accessible Stadiums* in order to "highlight" key accessibility requirements of the ADA that apply to stadiums built after the ADA's effective date (DOJ, 1996).

In 2004, the Access Board completed a comprehensive update of the 1991 Guides, which the DOJ adopted on September 15, 2010. Under the 2010 Guide, any stadiums or arenas constructed after March 2012, must be in compliance with the 2010 standards. The 2010 Standards included several new standards specifically applicable to sport facilities which will be discussed in more detail later in the chapter.

An initial question often arises as to whether a sport facility has to comply with the 1991 or the 2010 ADA standards. Generally, the 1991 standards apply to construction built prior to September 2010 (28 C.F.R. § 36.406(a)(1)), while the 2010 standards apply to construction after March 2012 (28 C.F.R. § 36.406(a)(3)). But, if a stadium was supposed to be constructed according to the 1991 standards, and fails to meet that original standard, it must now "be made accessible in accordance with the 2010 standards" (28 C.F.R. § 36.405(a)(5)(ii)).

Discrimination under the ADA

Even though a number of resources are available to sport managers to aid in ADA compliance, one may not always be able to avoid litigation. Thus, it is important to understand the basic elements of an ADA discrimination claim under Title III and explore critical issues related to such claims arising in the sport context.

Private Enforcement of the ADA

The ADA creates a private right of action for individuals who are being discrimination against. It provides:

> "Any person who is being subjected to discrimination on the basis of disability in violation of the Act or this part or who has reasonable grounds for believing that such person is about to be subjected to discrimination in violation of section 303 of the Act or subpart D of this part may institute a civil action for preventive relief, including an application for a permanent or temporary injunction, restraining order, or other order" (28 C.F.R. § 36.501, 2010).

Typically, a private lawsuit requests injunctive relief (i.e., an order requiring the place of public accommodation to come into compliance with the ADA). However, the ADA also authorizes the DOJ to seek monetary penalties for noncompliance. Private individuals will not normally be awarded money damages

Exhibit 17.3 The elements of an ADA discrimination claim.

An individual alleging discrimination under Title III must show that:

1 he is disabled as that term is defined by the ADA;
2 the defendant is a private entity that owns, leases, or operates a place of public accommodation;
3 the defendant employed a discriminatory policy or practice; and
4 the defendant discriminated against the plaintiff based upon the plaintiff's disability by

    a failing to make a requested reasonable modification that was
    b necessary to accommodate the plaintiff's disability.

for violations unless the DOJ requests the award of money damages. Even though money damages are typically not available in private lawsuits, a plaintiff who sues for injunctive relief is entitled to recover her attorneys' fees if she is the prevailing party in the lawsuit. The ability to recovery attorneys' fees is an important feature of the enforcement scheme of the ADA. The recovery of attorneys' fees helps to ensure that entities will not ignore the ADA mandate under the belief that a plaintiff would not be able to afford to go to court.

Exhibit 17.3 identifies the essential elements of an ADA discrimination claim, i.e. what a plaintiff must prove to establish discrimination under the ADA. If the plaintiff makes such a showing, the defendant must make the requested modification unless it proves that doing so would alter the fundamental nature of its business. This exception has become known as the *fundamental alteration* exception or defense. The basic idea is while the requested modification is necessary (Element 4b in Exhibit 17.3), it is not reasonable (Element 4a in Exhibit 17.3) to require a modification that would fundamentally alter the nature of the provider's business. This defense is often raised when it is undisputed that the plaintiff is a person with a disability and the defendant is operating a place of public accommodation. Therefore, the main issue remaining is whether the plaintiff is being discriminated against on the basis of his disability and being denied a reasonable accommodation.

As mentioned earlier, the U.S. Supreme Court first considered a case involving an ADA claim in the sport industry in *PGA Tour, Inc. v. Martin* (2001). The PGA Tour argued that Casey Martin's requested modification would fundamentally alter the nature of the PGA Tour competition and therefore was not a reasonable modification. The "walking rule" required all PGA Tour elite golfers to walk the course during competition. Read the following Focus Case to see how the court evaluated the *fundamental alteration* defense asserted by the PGA Tour.

PGA Tour, Inc. v. Martin

532 U.S. 661 (2001)   **FOCUS** CASE

FACTS

Casey Martin was a participant in a professional golf event operated by the PGA. The PGA Tour hosted its events at public and private golf courses throughout the United States. Both the events and the competition were open to the general public. The PGA Tour, when it was hosting tour events, was a place of public accommodation. Martin is an individual with a disability. Martin has a degenerative bone disease that causes atrophy in one leg. He is very limited in his ability to walk and to bear weight on the affected leg. As a college athlete he requested and received a reasonable accommodation from the NCAA and the PAC-10 Conference that permitted him to use a golf cart during competition to transport him from one shot location to another. When Martin earned a place on the PGA Tour, he requested a similar accommodation and was denied. The PGA Tour contended that permitting Martin to ride in a golf cart would be a fundamental alteration of its event, which is an elite professional golf contest. Martin sued claiming his request to use a cart was a reasonable modification of the PGA Tour rules, and the PGA's denied of his request was a violation of the ADA. The district court found that, assuming the purpose of the walking rule was to inject fatigue into the competition, such purpose was not being fundamentally altered by permitting Martin to participate with the aid of a cart due to his individual circumstances and the severity of his disability. The PGA Tour appealed.

HOLDING

Martin's requested modification was not a fundamental alteration of the tour competition.

RATIONALE

Section 12182(b)(2)(A)(ii) identifies the elements and evidentiary burdens for a discrimination claim. Martin was required to and offered competent evidence that he was an individual with a disability, that a modification was requested, and that the modification requested was reasonable. The burden then shifted to the PGA to demonstrate that the requested modification would fundamentally alter the nature of the PGA Tour event. The PGA argued that walking was a fundamental aspect of the game of golf and that the purpose of its rule requiring competitors to walk at all times during the competition was to inject the element of fatigue into the competition. When evaluating accommodation requests under Title III, the court must conduct an **individualized inquiry**, a fact-specific inquiry relative to the stated purpose of a rule and a person's individual disability and circumstances, to determine whether a requested modification of the rule is reasonable. The PGA argued that only the nature of the public accommodation or its programs should be examined to determine whether a modification of a rule or policy would result in a fundamental alteration, and that substantive rules of a competition could not be waived without fundamentally altering the nature of the competition. Thus, in essence the PGA's argument was that once a rule is designated as a substantive rule, any modification would result in a fundamental alteration. However, § 12182 provides that "reasonable modification in policies, practices, or procedures" must be made. The statute does not say that only policies, practices, or procedures that are not substantive are subject to modification. To determine whether a modification of a substantive rule of competition would result in a fundamental alteration of the competition involves two questions. First, the requested modification must not fundamentally alter the essence of the sport. Second, the requested modification must not give the disabled athlete a competitive advantage. Walking is not a fundamental part of the sport of golf – golf tests one's shot-making skills, not walking skills. Next, given Martin's individual circumstances, affording him the use of a cart would not give him a competitive advantage. The requested modification is reasonable and necessary; and is not a fundamental alteration of the PGA Tour competition.

After the *Martin* decision was released, some critics speculated that it would open a floodgate of modifications requests. However, it has not had that effect. Few requests to modify competition rules would satisfy the Court's two-part inquiry. An example of a rule modification that would satisfy the two-part inquiry is using a blinking light instead of a starting gun to signal the start of a race for a hearing-impaired swimmer. Clearly, the essential nature of the competition, which is swimming, has not been altered, nor has the hearing-impaired athlete been given a competitive advantage. The more important effect of the *Martin* decision is that it reinforced (1) the broad mandate and reach of the ADA beyond physical structural accessibility, and (2) the requirement of an individualized inquiry to determine if the requested modifications of rules, policies, and procedures would fundamentally alter the program or services.

Since the ADA's mandate does not stop at the physical structure, nor is it limited only to spectators at stadiums and arenas, facility managers and operators of sport competitions must review their eligibility policies, competition rules, and other operating practices to determine if those policies or practices are

Exhibit 17.4 Definition of a "public accommodation" under the ADA, with sport- and recreation-related examples.

A public accommodation is defined as the following private entities if the operations of such entities affect commerce –

A an inn, hotel, motel, or other place of lodging, except for an establishment located within a building that contains not more than five rooms for rent or hire and that is actually occupied by the proprietor of such establishment as the residence of such proprietor;

B a restaurant, bar, or other establishment serving food or drink;

C a motion picture house, theater, concert hall, stadium, or other place of exhibition or entertainment;

D an auditorium, convention center, lecture hall, or other place of public gathering;

E a bakery, grocery store, clothing store, hardware store, shopping center, or other sales or rental establishment; …

I a park, zoo, amusement park, or other place of recreation;

J a nursery, elementary, secondary, undergraduate, or postgraduate private school, or other place of education; …

L a gymnasium, health spa, bowling alley, golf course, or other place of exercise or recreation (42 U.S.C. § 12181(7)(2013)).

having the effect of denying equal access to people with disabilities. Now that we know all sport facilities will need to comply with Title III of the ADA, let's consider how to understand ADA requirements with regard to the physical structure or property itself, and then we will look at how the ADA impacts operating policies. Common questions raised in ADA litigation relates to what is a place of public accommodation? Who is responsible for ensuring ADA compliance? What services and amenities must be made available for persons with disabilities? When are reasonable modifications required to the facility? We are going to explore all these questions as they arise in the context of sports venues and events.

Defining Places of Public Accommodation

Essentially, any facility, event, or activity that is a place of exhibition, entertainment, exercise, or recreation is covered by the ADA. *Places of public accommodation* include several specific types of sport facilities, including gymnasiums, health clubs, bowling alleys, golf courses, and stadiums (see Exhibit 17.4). More importantly, the general categories of places that are deemed places of public accommodation under the ADA encompass virtually all sport facilities. Thus, the following are common examples: parks, fitness clubs, sports museums, arenas, stadiums, training centers, recreation centers, a community 5K, a marathon, a Spartan race, and so on are all places of public accommodation. In addition, within a single facility, separate elements or areas are also places of public accommodation, such as restaurants, museums, galleries, day care centers, bars, concessions areas, convention meeting halls, and auditoriums; these are also subject to the ADA.

Owners and Operators of Public Accommodations

Another issue frequently raised in ADA cases relates to who has the responsibility for compliance with the ADA. As mentioned previously, the congressional mandate of the ADA is very broad, not only as to the types of places considered a public accommodation, but also the scope of persons responsible for ADA compliance. Any owner, operator, lessor, or lessee has a responsibility to ensure ADA compliance and can be sued under Title III for noncompliance. For example, in *Clark v. Simms* (2009), patrons of a hunting store sued the owners of the building, as opposed to the operators of the Hunt 'N' Shack business, alleging that architectural barriers prevented them from accessing the premises. The building lacked handicap accessible parking spaces and an accessible route to the store. The owners had leased the store to the hunting store operators, the Hunt 'N' Shack. The court held that the plain terms of the ADA applies to those who own, lease, or lease to others a place of public accommodation. In no way does the language of the statute suggest that a person must both own and operate a place of public accommodation to be held liable. As the owners and the lessors of the property on which the Hunt 'N' Shack is located, the Simms's could be held liable under the ADA. Furthermore, the owners may not assign their responsibilities for compliance with the ADA to the tenants who operate the Hunt 'N' Shack because "a landlord has an independent obligation to comply with the ADA that may not be eliminated by contract" (*Clark v. Simms*, 2009, p. 6). The following Focus case explores the owner and operator issue in a more complex contractual relationship – a professional sport stadium context.

Bailey v. Board of Commissioners

427 F. Supp. 3d 806 (E.D. La. 2019)   **FOCUS** CASE

FACTS

On June 14, 2018, Plaintiff filed a Complaint naming as defendants SMG as the operator of the Superdome, the Board of Commissioners of the Louisiana Stadium and Exposition District (the "Board") as the owner of the Superdome, and Kyle France ("France") in his official capacity as chairman of the Board (collectively, "Defendants"). Plaintiff brings claims against the Board and France for declaratory and injunctive relief pursuant to Title II of the Americans With Disabilities Act ("ADA"), 42 U.S.C. § 12101, *et seq.*, and the Rehabilitation Act, 29 U.S.C. §794, *et seq.* Plaintiff has a disability and relies on an electric wheelchair for mobility. Plaintiff alleges that he has been a Saints season ticket holder for over 30 years. Plaintiff alleges that prior to 2011, his seat was located on a wheelchair accessible raised platform in the 100-level section of the Superdome. Plaintiff alleges that in 2011, Defendants began extensive renovations on the Superdome and reconfigured the accessible seating section for patrons with disabilities. Plaintiff alleges that as a result of the renovations, the wheelchair accessible seating at the Superdome was moved to other positions where the views are obstructed by barriers and other patrons or players standing during the game, or the seating is not fully accessible by wheelchair. As a result, Plaintiff alleges that Defendants have failed to comply with various parts of the ADA and Rehabilitation Act. SMG filed its Motion for Summary Judgment arguing that it cannot be held liable as an operator of a place of public accommodation because it is not in charge of ticketing or programming for Saints games.

HOLDING

Motion for Summary Judgment is denied, SMG could be held liable as an operator of a place of public accommodation.

RATIONALE

Plaintiff contends that SMG can be held liable as an operator of the Superdome. Plaintiff asserts that Title III of the ADA applies to "any person who owns, leases (or leases to), or operates a place of public accommodation." Plaintiff argues that the Fifth Circuit has stated to "operate," in the context of a business operation, means "to put or keep in operation," "to control or direct the functioning of," or "to conduct the affairs of; manage." Plaintiff argues that SMG manages the Superdome as evidenced by its contract with the Saints, which refers to SMG as "the Manager" and states that it "shall provide all services to manage and operate the Superdome in a first-class, businesslike and efficient manner substantially consistent with the operation and management of other NFL stadiums."

   Title III of the ADA applies to "any person who owns, leases (or leases to), or operates a place of public accommodation." In an action under Title III of the ADA the Fifth Circuit explained that "[b]ecause the ADA does not define the term 'operates,' we 'construe it in accord with its ordinary and natural meaning.'" The Fifth Circuit found that the term "operate" means "to put or keep in operation," "[t]o control or direct the functioning of," or "[t]o conduct the affairs of; manage." The Fifth Circuit has held that the relevant question is whether the defendant controls the modification of the public accommodation such that the defendant could cause the accommodation to comply with the ADA.

The Stadium Agreement states that SMG "shall provide all services to manage and operate the Superdome in a first-class, businesslike and efficient manner substantially consistent with the operation and management of other NFL stadiums." Further, SMG is obligated to "maintain the physical structure of the Superdome and all features, fixtures, equipment and improvements therein, including but not limited to … spectator and other seating. …" Additionally, SMG is responsible for "caus[ing] the seating arrangement of the Superdome to be placed in the standard football configuration." The Stadium Agreement also states that SMG "hereby grants the [Saints] the exclusive use of the Superdome … on all Game Days," and that "[d]istribution and sale of tickets for admission to Home Games shall be under the sole direction and control of the [Saints]." Although SMG does not appear to have control over ticketing for Saints games, SMG is obligated to maintain the physical structure of the Superdome including spectator and other seating. Accepting as true the allegations in the Complaint, SMG could be held liable as an operator of the Superdome because SMG controls modification of the Superdome and could cause the Superdome to comply with the ADA.

These cases help illustrate not only the scope of the ADA, but also the relationships between owners, lessees and lessors, and operators of places of public accommodation. The *Clark* case reminds us that the ADA is applicable to many places related to the sport industry other than just stadiums and arenas. *Bailey* reinforces that owners and operators with any control or management of the functioning of the facility fall under the broad umbrella of the ADA compliance framework.

When evaluating how the ADA applies to the physical structure of sport facilities, we examine two separate issues: (1) structural accessibility including alterations and renovations; and (2) substantially equal access to the services and amenities offered by the facility, which looks at the spectators' overall enjoyment and ability to access all of the benefits and services offered to patrons without disabilities.

Structural Accessibility and Equal Enjoyment of Services

Undoubtedly, the ADA requires owners and operators of places of public accommodation to ensure that persons with disabilities can gain entry to their physical structures and move freely within those structures. A few common examples of this type of accessibility are wheelchair ramps, automatic doors, elevators, and directional signage posted in Braille. All places of public accommodation must comply with the ADA in some fashion, regardless of the age of the building. The ADA accessibility standards distinguish between (1) newly constructed or renovated facilities and (2) facilities built prior to 1992.

Structural Accessibility and Renovations

The ADA requires that newly constructed and renovated places of public accommodation be readily accessible to and usable by individuals with disabilities. All new construction (and to the *maximum extent feasible*, all alterations) must be designed and constructed to be accessible to and usable by people with disabilities. This covers buildings and facilities covered by Title II (state and local governments) and Title III (places of public accommodation and commercial facilities). The ADA also requires places of public accommodation to remove "architectural barriers … in existing facilities built prior to 1992 … where such removal is **readily achievable**." Removal is "readily achievable" when it is "*easily accomplishable and able to be carried out without much difficulty or expense.*" Examples include: the simple ramping of a few steps, the installation of grab bars where only routine reinforcement of the wall is required, the lowering of telephones, and similar modest adjustments.

Alterations to Facilities built after January 26, 1992

Alterations to a place of public accommodation covered by Title III of the ADA that are undertaken *after January 26, 1992*, are required to ensure that, to the *maximum extent feasible*, the altered portions of the facility comply with the ADA Accessibility Guidelines (ADAAG) adopted by the DOJ as current federal ADA standards. These ADA standards set forth the minimum requirements for accessibility in alterations. Each element or space that is altered must meet the technical criteria for new construction where feasible. Where an entire room or space is altered, the room or space must be made fully accessible. Comprehensive renovations will trigger a greater number of ADA standards than limited small-scale projects, however, the ADA standards still apply to all building repairs that are considered alterations. An **alteration** is defined as a change that affects usability. Certain improvements, such as re-roofing, painting, or changes to mechanical and electrical systems, are excluded (unless they affect the usability of the facility).

If the alteration affects an area of primary function – a principal use area – of the building, it may be necessary to include other improvements. If alterations are made to an area containing a primary function, an accessible "path of travel" is required, which means a continuous route connecting the altered area to an entrance. Phones, restrooms, and drinking fountains that, where provided, serve the altered area are also required to be accessible. Since this may involve modifications outside the intended alteration, compliance is required to the extent it is not "disproportionate" to the cost of alterations to the primary function area. "Disproportionality" is defined by the DOJ as costing more than 20 percent of the costs of the alteration to the primary function area.

Alterations to Facilities Built Prior to 1992

For a facility *built prior to* 1992, the ADA distinguishes between two situations, "alterations" and "repairs" and requires a different standard of compliance. If the project involves an **"alteration"** of an existing facility, the areas being altered must be made accessible to the *maximum extent feasible* as described above. If the project is merely a **repair**, the space should be made accessible if *"readily achievable."*

For example, if a YMCA swimming pool built in the 1970s was scheduled to have its filters and drainage systems replaced, the project would likely fit under the definition of a repair. Assuming the pool deck is elevated and accessible only through the locker rooms and involves several narrow walkways and a series of concrete steps, the YMCA may not be required to modify the space to make the pool area wheelchair accessible, since the widening of the walkways, removal of the concrete steps, and installation of wheelchair access ramps may not be readily achievable. However, if the YMCA began a project to upgrade its entire pool facility, including those same repairs mentioned earlier to the pool area, it is likely the project would be considered an alteration, which would require the YMCA to make the space accessible to the maximum extent feasible. This was the situation Chicago's famous Wrigley Field faced when it completed its $1 billion makeover only to be subject to a lawsuit alleging the renovations did not comply with the 2010 ADA standards (Kozlarz, 2019). The complaint alleged that the stadium does not contain sufficient wheelchair accessible seats and the seats provided were not properly distributed through the venue. Wrigley Field had been exempt from the more recent ADA standards but the scope of its renovation brought it under the 2010 standards requiring substantially equivalent choice in seating locations and viewing angles (Kozlarz, 2019). The 2010 standards will be discussed more fully later in the chapter.

Equal Enjoyment of Services and Amenities

Managers should ensure that individuals with disabilities are generally able to access a sports facility and have access to the various amenities and services offered within the facility. For example, in a large stadium, in addition to having access to the venue, a person with a disability would also need to be able to access parking, concession areas, restrooms, shopping areas, restaurants, and so on. In a recreation facility such as a YMCA or a fitness club, managers need to make sure all areas within the facility are accessible, including parking spaces, exit routes, doors, assembly sections, and toilet and bathing facilities. Section 12182(a) of the ADA provides a general prohibition against discrimination against an individual with a disability in the full and equal enjoyment of goods, services, facilities, and privileges of any place of public accommodation. Several issues arise in assuring full and equal enjoyment of patrons with disabilities. For example, the San Francisco 49ers were sued based on the allegation that the 49ers had failed to comply with ADA requirements. The suit alleged more specifically, that the 49er's violated state and federal disability access laws by failing to make Levi's Stadium, the parking lots, pedestrian right of way, and shuttles that serve it, as well as the ticketing and other services readily accessible to individuals with mobility disabilities and their nondisabled companions. The plaintiffs further contended that "individuals with mobility disabilities (specifically those individuals who use wheelchairs, scooters, or other mobility aids for mobility) and their nondisabled companions have been discriminated against because they have been denied full and equal access to Levi's Stadium and related facilities, services, amenities, and privileges (Florio, 2020). The 49ers initially argued that any accessibility issues have been addressed and that they are in full compliance under the ADA (Chapoteau, 2019). However, after a class action was certified, the 49ers settled the case for $24 million (Florio, 2020). The next Focus Case illustrates how the ADA applies to all amenities and services offered at a golf resort.

Celano v. Marriott International, Inc.

U.S. Dist. LEXIS 6172 (N.D. Cal. 2008)	FOCUS CASE

FACTS

The plaintiffs filed suit under the ADA, alleging that the defendant failed to provide accessible or single-rider golf carts in violation of the ADA. The plaintiffs sought a declaration that Marriott's policies were unlawful and an injunction requiring the defendant to provide single-rider carts at each of its golf facilities. Due to varied mobility disabilities, the plaintiffs all required a single-rider cart to play golf. A single-rider cart is a specially designed golf cart that allows individuals with mobility impairments to hit the golf ball while seated in the cart on a rotating swivel seat. The carts also contain hand brakes and accelerators to allow mobility-impaired users to drive them. Marriott owns and operates 26 golf courses throughout the United States. The plaintiffs contacted several Marriott golf resorts expressing an interest in playing at the resort's golf courses and requesting a single-rider golf cart. Each plaintiff was told that Marriott does not maintain single-rider carts at its courses and that it was not required by current ADA rules to do so. Marriott informed the plaintiffs that they could bring their own single-rider carts to its courses.

HOLDING

The court found that Marriott's policy of not providing single-rider carts was a violation of the ADA.

RATIONALE

The plaintiffs' ADA claim rested on Title III of the ADA, which prohibits discrimination against disabled individuals in any place of public accommodation. The determination as to whether a particular modification is "reasonable" and "necessary" involves a fact-specific, case-by-case inquiry that considers, among other factors, the effectiveness of the modification in light of the nature of the disability in question and the cost to the organization that would implement it. The plaintiffs argued that this modification was reasonable because it would enable each of the plaintiffs to play at Marriott courses that they were otherwise unable to play. Financially, the modification was reasonable given Marriott's operational budget. Marriott contended that it does not discriminate against golfers who are disabled because it allows them to bring their own accessible carts.

Title III of the ADA outlaws not just intentional discrimination but also certain practices that have a disparate impact upon persons with disabilities even in the absence of any conscious intent to discriminate. Thus, a public accommodation may not utilize standards or criteria or methods of administration that have the effect of discriminating on the basis of disability. The ADA requires more than merely refraining from active discrimination. … As a general rule, the objective of Title III is to provide persons with disabilities who utilize public accommodations with an experience that is functionally equivalent to that of other patrons, to the extent feasible given the limitations imposed by that person's disability.

Marriott's policy did not provide the plaintiffs with an experience equivalent to that of other patrons. The court held that providing accessible golf carts at Marriott's courses was both reasonable and necessary to accommodate the plaintiffs' disabilities.

The *Marriott* case discussed the requirement that a person with a disability have access to an experience that is functionally equivalent to that of other patrons. This standard impacts several operational aspects specific to sport facilities including the number and disbursement of accessible seats, sightlines for patrons using wheelchairs, the availability of assistive listening devices, and service animals. Our next section will explore these requirements.

Impact of ADA Guidelines on Sport and Recreation Facilities

As we discussed previously in this chapter, sport facilities are continuing to be upgraded or built across the sport industry and especially in the professional sport industry. These renovations and new construction projects raise several ADA challenges (Zagger, 2019). In this next section, we are going to explore the legal issues facility owners and operators have faced in these areas and their efforts to comply with ADA requirements.

Number and Placement of Wheelchair Accessible Seating

For stadiums built or renovated after January 26, 1992, the ADA requires that 1 percent of the total available seats be *wheelchair accessible* and those seats must be *dispersed* throughout the stadium. As mentioned in the previous section, for a facility built prior to 1992, the ADA distinguishes between repairs and alterations and requires a different standard of compliance under these circumstances. If the project involves an alteration of an existing facility built prior to 1992, the areas being altered are subject to the 1 percent accessible seating requirement.

The University of Michigan encountered this issue when it began a $226 million renovation of its football stadium (Wolverton, 2007). A group for veterans with disabilities sued, claiming people who used wheelchairs were being denied equal access to the stadium and that the University of Michigan was avoiding compliance with the ADA requirements, regarding the number and location of wheelchair seating in stadium. The renovation would add luxury suites, 3,200 club seats, and widen seating and aisles in the 107,501-seat stadium. Before the renovation, the stadium had 90 wheelchair accessible seats divided equally within each end zone of the stadium. The disabled-veterans group claimed that the University of Michigan tried to label its renovation as a "repair" instead of an "alteration" to avoid compliance with the ADA, which would require 1 percent, or around 1,000 wheelchair accessible seats. Based on the university renovation plan, the stadium would increase its wheelchair accessible seats to 282, dispersed equally throughout the stadium, including the outdoor and indoor club seat areas, and one wheelchair accessible seat would be located inside each new luxury suite, while they also included the offering of companion tickets for some seats as well. This case illustrated that when major upgrades and renovations are undertaken, it is likely that the facility will be required to bring the entire venue into compliance with the 2010 standards (Associated Press, 2007). In addition to the negative publicity surrounding the University of

Michigan's renovation plan, the Department of Education also investigated the university for violations of disability laws ("U of Michigan to Increase," 2007; Wolverton, 2007). Ultimately, the University of Michigan signed a consent agreement with the U.S. DOJ and the disabled-veterans group to resolve the lawsuit. By 2010, the stadium had a total wheelchair seating of 329, including companion seats and seats in multiple locations throughout the stadium (Gershman, 2008). In 2015, the University of Michigan was making more renovations to keep up compliance with the ADA requirements. Michigan Stadium removed 2,300 seats, to include wider walkways and hand railings around the bowl of the stadium (Shea, 2015). The lawsuit mentioned previously involving Wrigley Field also challenged the number of seats available for fans with disabilities as well as the disbursement of those seats (Hanna, 2019). The DOJ launched an official review and the Cubs promised to drastically improve the number and diversity of seats by the 2020 season (Eadens, 2019; Kozlarz, 2019).

Comparable Lines of Sight

In late 2004, the Architectural and Transportation Barriers Compliance Board (the "Access Board") released a suggested amendment to Title III of the ADA that requires people who use wheelchairs be provided a choice of seating locations and viewing angles that are substantially equivalent to, or better than, those available to all other spectators. The U.S. Department of Justice (DOJ) revised its regulations and guidance documents for Title III of the ADA, effective January 2005, to include the Access Board's suggested amendment. This amendment only applies to new construction and altered facilities. In its letter to then MLB Commissioner, Bud Selig in 1996, the DOJ stated:

> "Without question the single most prevalent issue that arises in new stadium projects involves the lines of sight afforded to patrons who use wheelchairs and sit in the stadium's wheelchair seating locations. The ADA's Standards for Accessible Design – the architectural requirements applicable to new stadiums – require that wheelchair seating areas provide people with disabilities with lines of sight comparable to those for members of the general public. Thus, we believe that facilities like sports stadiums, where spectators can be expected to stand during the event, must provide wheelchair locations with lines of sight over those standing spectators." (Deval, 1996)

Sight lines for patrons in wheelchairs is a central question under the DOJ Guides. In 2008, Robert Miller, a NASCAR fan who is a quadriplegic and uses a wheelchair, attended three to six events a year at the California Speedway in Fontana. Miller's view of the track and the cars from his viewing area in the grandstand was regularly blocked by fans standing immediately in front of him. Unable to fully enjoy his spectator experience, Miller filed suit, claiming that the Speedway had violated Title III of the ADA. The district court dismissed Miller's case finding that the DOJ guidelines requiring lines of sight over standing spectators was perhaps a good recommendation, but was not entitled to judicial deference as part of the regulatory scheme for the ADA (*Miller v. California Speedway Corp.*, 2006). The Ninth Circuit reversed the district court and held that it is perfectly reasonable to interpret the term "lines of sight comparable to those for members of the general public" as requiring lines of sight that are comparable in the actual conditions under which a facility operates. If spectators are widely expected to stand during the key moments of an event – from the singing of the national anthem to the fourth quarter – it does not take a fertile legal imagination to understand that relatively immobile patrons will not have a comparable line of sight. The court finally stated that "the regulatory scheme at issue in this case is complex, but our conclusion is simple: The DOJ's interpretation of its own regulation is reasonable and therefore entitled to substantial deference" (*Miller v. California Speedway Corp.*, 2008).

Despite the Ninth Circuit's decision in *Miller*, courts are divided over whether the ADA standards require lines of sight over standing spectators (Wolohan, 2009). The Oregon federal district court (*Independent Living Resources v. Oregon Arena Corp.*, 1997) and the Third Circuit (*Caruso v. Blockbuster-Sony Music Entertainment Centre at the Waterfront*, 1999), concluded that the DOJ regulations do not require lines of sight over standing spectators. However, the D.C. Circuit (*Paralyzed Veterans of America v. D.C. Arena L.P.*, 1997), the Minnesota federal district court (*United States v. Ellerbe Becket Inc.*, 1997) held that 100 percent of accessible seating did not need sight lines over standing spectators, instead substantial compliance was sufficient. The next Focus Case may help to resolve some of the questions about line of sight regulations.

Landis v. Wash. State Maj. Baseball Stadium Pub. Facilities Dist. Baseball of Seattle, Inc.

U.S. Dist. LEXIS 215159 (W.D. Wash. 2019)   **FOCUS** CASE

FACTS

Plaintiffs are lifelong baseball fans who, because of mobility disabilities, use wheelchairs. Defendants are the collective owners and operators of T-Mobile Park, home of Major League Baseball's Seattle Mariners (collectively, "Defendants"). The current action involves Plaintiffs' attempt to procure better wheelchair seating through enforcement of (1) the Americans with Disabilities Act ("ADA"), 42 U.S.C. § 12101 *et seq.* and its subsequent regulations and guidelines

HOLDING

Sightlines from accessible seats are comparable to the sightlines from nonaccessible seats and, therefore, T-Mobile Park complies with Section 4.33.3 of the 1991 ADAAG.

RATIONALE

The Court finds that since T-Mobile Park was being constructed contemporaneously with the *Accessible Stadiums* guideline, the Court finds that the applicable standard is: "[a] comparable line of sight ... allows a person using a wheelchair to see the playing surface *between the heads and over the shoulders* of the persons standing in the row immediately in front and over the heads of the persons standing two rows in front." See *Accessible Stadiums* at 2.

Since *Accessible Stadiums* is the DOJ's most contemporaneous interpretation of Section 4.33.3, the standard set forth therein should be afforded deference. The Court, therefore, finds that *Accessible Stadiums*' interpretation of Section 4.33.3 as requiring sightlines "between the heads and over the shoulders" of standing spectators is the correct standard to apply and the court further finds that the standard is neither plainly erroneous nor inconsistent with the regulation. See *Miller*, 536 F.3d at 1029. Therefore, this Court concludes that to comply with the 1991 Guide, and Section 4.33.3 therein, sightlines at T-Mobile Park must provide wheelchair users views of "the playing surface between the heads and over the shoulders of the persons standing in the row immediately in front and over the heads of the persons standing two rows in front." See *Accessible Stadiums* at 2.

When the Court reviews the illustrations considering what can be seen over the line representing the standing spectator's shoulders, that is, "over the shoulders and between the heads," more of the field is visible from the accessible seat, making the views comparable. For example, when considering the shoulder line in Mr. Terry's illustrations, several of the locations have 100 percent visibility of the field. For the others, the percentage of field viewable is close to 100 percent. Thus, the Court concludes that when taking into account what percentage of the field that can be seen utilizing the standard set by the *Accessible Stadiums* guideline, the sightlines are comparable.

Miller and *Landis*, when taken together should confirm that the DOJ Guides are entitled to substantial deference by the courts in ADA cases, and the Guides approach to sight lines over standing spectators is reasonable and appropriate to ensure that fans in accessible seating locations are able to have comparable views to other spectators. Moving forward, facility managers at new or altered stadiums should investigate the possibility of improving lines of sight for patrons who use wheelchairs. Spectators standing in front of the designated accessible seating areas may block sightlines for patrons with disabilities. If this is the case, the facility should make necessary modifications to provide unobstructed views for its wheelchair patrons.

Assistive Devices for the Hearing and Visually Impaired

The DOJ's guidelines for accessible stadiums also address assistive listening devices. The guidelines provide that when audible communications are integral to the use of a stadium, assistive listening systems are required for people who are hearing and visually impaired (Department of Justice, n.d.). Additional changes as part of the 2010 *ADA Standards for Accessible Design* went into effect in 2012. These include such changes as ensuring a venue has accessible routes from the seating area to the performance area, as well as reducing the quantity and type of assisted listening devices required, and signage related to such devices.

Assisted listening devices amplify and deliver sound to a special receiver that is worn by the spectator, or to the spectator's hearing aid, depending on the type of system that is used. The stadium must provide receivers for the assistive listening system. The number of available receivers must equal 4 percent of the total number of seats. Further, signs must be provided to notify spectators of the availability of receivers for the assistive listening system. Given that new stadiums are frequently multipurpose facilities that also host concerts, conventions, and other events, stadium managers must be aware that the ADA standards require any facility to have a permanently installed assistive listening system.

Closed-captioning demonstrates how facilities can further assist hearing-impaired patrons to more fully enjoy the services and experiences of attending a sporting event. Closed-captioning can be made available on video boards and concourse televisions. In 2006, patron Shane Feldman sued the Washington Redskins at FedEx Field for not providing captioning at their football games. Prior to the 2006 football season, FedEx Field did not caption any announcements made over its public address system. The Redskins had always offered listening devices to fans who requested one; however, Feldman did not benefit from an assistive listening device. In September 2008, the Maryland federal district court ruled that the ADA requires facility operators to provide deaf or hearing-impaired fans equal access to the aural information broadcast over the stadium public address system (*Feldman v. Pro Football, Inc.*, 2008). This information includes music with lyrics, game commentary, advertisements, referee calls, and safety and emergency information.

To help accommodate individuals with visual disabilities, teams and stadiums alike must allow for their websites and team apps to be "screen reader" friendly. A screen reader allows visually impaired individuals to use websites and apps by reading the subsequent banners and headings to help assist navigation. An example of this type of case was seen with the San Jose Sharks and their new mobile app, *San Jose Sharks + SAP Center mobile application*, which was introduced to improve fan engagement and experiences. However, this mobile app was not screen reader friendly and when the problem was addressed by concerned visually impaired patrons, nothing was done by the Sharks. The suit filed against the Sharks in 2019, called for equal access to the digital fan experience via websites and mobile apps (*Salsiccia v. Sharks Sports & Entertainment LLC*, 2019). Similarly, a California man has filed suit against a computer software corporation for their lack of access for people with visual impairments in a recent addition of the California State Parks and Recreation campground reservation website. The recent update of the reservation website was not screen reader friendly, therefore, discriminatory to people with visually impairments (Egelko, 2019). Related lawsuits regarding website accessibility have seen a dramatic increase over the past few years. In 2018 alone, there were 2,285 ADA website lawsuits, up 181 percent from 2017 (Behnken, 2019). The digital fan experience is becoming increasingly important for sport venues and event operators, therefore, they need to ensure that their websites and mobile apps meet ADA accessibility guidelines.

Ticketing Policies and Accessibility

The 2010 Guide established new and specific ticketing guidelines governing accessibility for persons with disabilities. In the past, some public and private venues, ticket sellers, and distributors have not provided the same opportunity to purchase tickets for wheelchair-accessible seats and nonaccessible seats (Department of Justice, 2010). Up until 2010, direct ticket purchase options available to the general public had simply not been available to many individuals with disabilities because transactions frequently could not be completed. Patrons seeking accessible seating had to comply with a myriad of different ticket request policies and practices resulting in either not being able to successfully purchase tickets or having to endure a particularly burdensome process. Beginning on March 15, 2011, venues that sell tickets for assigned seats must implement policies to comply with the ADA ticketing requirements. These requirements impact a variety of different policies and practices for sports venues including those shown in Exhibit 17.5. The International Association for Venue Managers has identified these new requirements as the most significant aspect of the new ADA regulations (Simons, 2011). Even though many venues may already meet these guidelines, it is still important to become familiar with the details so that nothing is missed.

The DOJ also observed that a critical and often overlooked component of ensuring successful ADA compliance is comprehensive and ongoing ticket sales staff training. Regardless of how good or accurate your policies are, if the sales staff is not aware of the policies or does not know how to implement them, problems may arise and legal claims could result. For example, the MLB Angels settled a suit where a patron using a wheelchair sought access to the stadium's club level and was told the two available accessible seats on that level were occupied, indicating that the entire club level, a level likely desirable to individuals using wheelchairs because of its in-seat food and beverage services, only contained two

Exhibit 17.5 The ADA ticketing requirements.

Ticket sales: Venues are required to sell tickets for accessible seats in the same manner and under the same conditions as all other ticket sales. Tickets for accessible seats must be sold during the same hours; through the same methods of purchase (by telephone, on site, through a website, or through third-party vendors); and during the same stages of sales (pre-sales, promotions, general sales, wait lists, or lotteries) as non-accessible seats.

Ticket prices: Venues cannot charge higher prices for accessible seats than for nonaccessible seats in the same seating section. This concept also applies to service charges added to the cost of a ticket, whether charged by the venue or a third-party seller. Venues must offer accessible seats in all price categories available to the public.

Identification of available accessible seating: Venues and third-party sellers must provide the same information about accessible seats as provided about nonaccessible seats, using the same text and visual representations.

Purchasing multiple tickets and group sales: People purchasing a ticket for an accessible seat may purchase up to *three additional seats* for their companions in the same row and these seats must be contiguous with the accessible seat. Many venues offer a group sales rate for groups of a pre-determined size. If a group includes one or more individuals who need accessible seating, the entire group should be seated together in an area that includes accessible seating.

Hold and release of tickets for accessible seating: Generally, tickets for accessible seats may not be sold to members of the general public who do not need the specific features of accessible seats. However, in three specific circumstances – typically involving sold out sections, sold out price categories, or sold out events – unsold accessible seats may be released and sold to members of the general public but venues are not required to release unsold accessible seats.

Ticket transfers and secondary ticket market: If venues permit patrons to give or sell their tickets to others, the same right must be extended to patrons with disabilities who hold tickets for accessible seats and to persons with disabilities who intend to buy or receive tickets on the secondary ticket market.

Prevention of fraud: Venues cannot require proof of disability as a condition for purchasing tickets for accessible seats. Venues may ask purchasers to state that they require, or are purchasing tickets for someone who requires, the features of an accessible seat.

Source: adapted from http://www.ada.gov/ticketing_2010.htm.

accessible seats – well below the 1 percent required under the ADA. As part of the settlement, the Angels began selling tickets for accessible seats on the club level for $50 that typically sell for $150 and increased the number of available seats on the club level to 14 (Carpenter, 2013). The Angels case also reinforces the risks faced by stadium operators who fail to comply with the ticketing guidelines, because even though the Angels entered into a settlement agreement with the plaintiffs, the plaintiffs were still able to recover attorneys' fees of almost $750,000 (*Charlebois v. Angels Baseball, L.P.*, 2012). The new ticketing regulations provided by the DOJ deal with exactly this type of dispute and now provide clear guidance on how to provide patrons with disabilities equal access to tickets. Proper training should be provided to all employees including venue managers, box office staff, customer service representatives, and all other staff involved in ticket sales about the ADA's requirements.

These few examples illustrate the importance of being a proactive facility manager to ensure compliance with the ADA. Many components of any facility can serve as barriers to people with disabilities. Simply considering the availability and placement of seating, sightlines, and closed-captioning may serve to address many, if not most, requests made by patrons with disabilities. Continuous staff training on how to accommodate patrons with disabilities can also avoid many legal claims as well as dissatisfied customers.

Service Animals

The ADA permits people with disabilities to bring their service animals into a sports facility in whatever areas customers are generally allowed. The ADA defines a service animal as any guide dog, signal dog, or other animal individually trained to provide assistance to an individual with a disability. Prior to the 2010 Guide, "other animal" was not defined, but based on the 2010 updated standards, the only recognized service animal other than a dog, is a miniature horse.

The ADA does not require licensure or certification to meet the definition of a service animal. Instead, service animals must perform functions and tasks that the individual with a disability cannot perform for him or herself. Guide dogs are a common example of service animal, used by some individuals who are blind. This is the type of service animal we are perhaps the most familiar, but there are service animals that assist persons with other kinds of disabilities in their day-to-day activities as well. Some examples include: alerting persons with hearing impairments to sounds; pulling wheelchairs or carrying and picking up things for persons with mobility impairments; and assisting persons with mobility impairments with balance.

A service animal is not a pet and the ADA definition of a service animal excludes emotional support animals. A venue operator may also exclude a service animal, from the facility when that animal's behavior poses a direct threat to the health or safety of others. For example, any service animal that displays vicious behavior toward other guests or customers may be excluded. However, our staff may not make assumptions about how a particular animal is likely to behave based on past experience with other animals. For example, a guest may have a German shepherd dog as a service animal, and we cannot assume that her service animal will be aggressive based on our general knowledge about that particular breed of dog or past experience with an aggressive German shepherd. Each situation must be considered individually.

The service animal must be permitted to accompany the individual with a disability to all areas of the facility where customers are normally allowed to go. Although a public accommodation may exclude any service animal that is out of control, it should give the individual with a disability who uses the service animal the option of continuing to enjoy its goods and services without having the service animal on the premises.

Staff should be trained properly on how to manage situations when customers seek entry with a service animal. In situations where it is not obvious that the dog is a service animal, staff may ask only two specific questions: (1) is the dog a service animal required because of a disability? and (2) what work or task has the dog been trained to perform? Staff are not allowed to request any documentation for the dog, require that the dog demonstrate its task, or inquire about the nature of the person's disability so this can be challenging. In the following situation faced by the Tulsa Drillers minor league baseball club, consider whether the entry staff handled the situation properly.

Considering ... Service Animals

You are an entry staff person at a Tulsa Drillers minor league baseball game and a woman is seeking entry to the game accompanied by her small dog. You followed the protocol provided by your management team, asked appropriate questions, and determined that the dog was not an ADA service animal but was instead an emotional support animal, therefore you refused to allow the fan to enter with the dog. The women posted a video of the exchange on social media which led to additional media coverage of the incident (Jackson, 2018). Was this situation handled correctly, and how should you handle the negative publicity.

Questions

1   What two questions are you permitted to ask the patron seeking entry with her dog?
2   Assuming those answers revealed that the dog was an emotional support animal instead of a service animal, was your refusal of entry legally permitted under the ADA? Why?
3   What should your media relations staff do in response to media inquiries about the incident?

Note how you would answer the question and then check your response using the Analysis & Discussion at the end of this chapter.

This section focused on the application of the ADA to the operation of sport facilities. We highlighted that all sport facilities are subject to the ADA in some fashion, further, that the ADA's mandate extends to accessing the building and its amenities as well as the programs and services offered by the owner or operator of the facility. We also discovered that both the owner and an operator of a facility have responsibility for ADA compliance. In the next section, we examine sport facility operations related to spectator privacy rights and searches or surveillance during sporting events.

Competitive Advantage Strategies

ADA Compliance

- Facility management staff must understand the ADA requires that patrons with disabilities be able to access all public areas of the sport facility and that reasonable requests to modify rules, practices, and policies be granted.
- Facility management staff should regularly investigate sight lines and accessible seating locations and numbers to improve customer access and experiences within the facility and to ensure the required minimum number of seats are available for patrons with disabilities.
- Ticket sales staff should be provided comprehensive and ongoing training on ADA policies and customer service training in responding to inquiries and requests from patrons with disabilities.
- Gate entry staff should be trained on ADA requirements regarding service animals and provided clear instructions on how to interact and communicate with fans seeking entry with animals.

Spectator Privacy Rights

This section examines venue and event operating policies that directly affect guests and spectators such as spectator search policies and spectator surveillance. Sport facilities engage in a number of practices that have the potential to interfere with spectator privacy rights. For example, a bag search or passing through a metal detector upon entry to an arena, or using video recorders to monitor entrances and exits to the facility or to locker rooms within the facility, or using advanced GPS tracking technology or facial recognition technology to monitor spectator movement in and around the facility. All of these practices involve some level of intrusion into a person's private information, physical biometrics, or name and likeness. Publicity rights are presented in Chapter 18 and privacy rights are presented in greater detail in Chapter 19. When we refer to privacy rights in this chapter it will be useful to refer to Exhibit 19.8, which identifies the four types of common law privacy rights to supplement our discussion here of new legislation related to data privacy rights. In this section, we are going to focus our attention on spectator searches and surveillance techniques commonly used at large sporting events and the potential legal issues associated with those practices.

Spectator Searches

In Chapter 12, the limitations imposed on the government by the Fourth Amendment to the Constitution were discussed in the context of drug-testing programs in state schools and universities. The issue there was whether a drug test represented a search and whether such a search was reasonable under the Fourth Amendment. Issues related to searches and seizures also arise in the context of facility and event management. The policies or procedures used by a stadium or arena to screen or limit access to the facility can implicate the Fourth Amendment also. A Fourth Amendment analysis generally asks three questions:

1 Is there state action? If so,
2 Does the challenged activity constitute a search and/or seizure? If so,
3 Was the search reasonable, i.e., does the state have probable cause and a warrant, or some other acceptable justification for the search without a warrant?

The Supreme Court has consistently held that under the Fourth Amendment "a search conducted without a warrant issued upon probable cause is 'per se unreasonable … subject only to a few specifically established and well-delineated exceptions'" (*Katz v. United States*, 1967). A few exceptions to the probable cause and warrant requirements have been recognized by the courts. For example, in the school drug-testing

---

Competitive Advantage Strategies

Spectator Search & Surveillance Issues

- Facility operators must carefully balance the need for conducting spectator searches with the potential intrusion imposed upon their customers. Any search should be effective at addressing a specific need for protection or safety, and should be as nonintrusive as possible to achieve those objectives.
- If pat-down or bag search or screening is going to occur, the venue operator should provide advance notice to patrons and spectators through media communications, website notices, back-of-ticket disclosures, and season ticket sales/renewals correspondence.
- Facility and event operators need to be familiar with emerging restrictions on the use of facial recognition technology and GPS data tracking to make sure they are in compliance with any notice and consent requirements.

Exhibit 17.6 Three factors for determining reasonableness under the Fourth Amendment.

1   *Need.* The analysis of need examines the nature of the threat, whether the threat is real or perceived, and whether the threat is particularized. Also considered is the significance of the harm in terms of its scope and size and whether those likely to be injured are unsuspecting.

2   *Efficacy.* For a proposed search to meet the standard of being efficacious, the courts examine whether the search will likely avert the harm identified as part of the need.

3   *Nature of the intrusion.* Examining the nature and degree of intrusion involves both a subjective and objective component. The subjective component looks at the amount of stigma associated with the search, whether the search is a mass or individualized search, and whether the procedures that are being used could frighten or humiliate or merely annoy. The objective component compares the search techniques to assess the scope of the intrusion.

situation, the "special needs" of the public schools substitute for probable cause, and relieved the public school of the requirement to obtain a warrant before conducting a drug test. However, in the context of public venues, the court has only recognized a few exceptions for airports and courthouse to a probable cause and warrant requirement. Prior to the terrorist attacks on September 11, 2001, the courts had considered only a few cases involving screening and spectator searches at stadiums, arenas, and theaters. In these cases, the courts focused on the overall reasonableness of the search.

Reasonableness of the Search

The analysis for determining reasonableness in the context of spectator searches at public venues requires that courts look at the "totality of the circumstances." Typically, the analysis hinges on three factors presented in Exhibit 17.6.

In applying these factors and evaluating the nature of the intrusion, we also consider whether the search is being conducted by uniformed officers who may tend to frighten or inject a level of authority that plainclothes searchers do not. For example, a typical stadium security contractor who provides personnel to assist with access points would be much less likely to create fear or inject a high level of authority for fans as they pass through scanners and checkpoints. In addition, visual inspections are less intrusive than physical touching. You may have been asked to permit visual inspection of your bag upon entry. Typically, the screener would conduct a visual inspection and perhaps use a small baton to examine the contents of the bag. Additionally, delaying a spectator for a few seconds to inspect a purse or bag is less intrusive than detaining them for a full pat-down search or handheld scope.

The constitutionality under the Fourth Amendment of a pat-down search at stadiums was first tested in relation to the pat-down policy implemented by the NFL in 2005. The NFL required the teams in its league to initiate and conduct pat-down searches at all NFL games. The policy was immediately challenged in several courts. A Tampa Bay Buccaneer season ticket holder sued the Tampa Sports Authority and challenged the pat-down searches implemented in response to the NFL policy. The following discussion will help explain how the district court analyzed this issue and how stadium and arena managers are responding as well. Next, the court of appeals decision is provided as a Case Opinion for you to contrast with the district court's decision.

In August 2005, the NFL declared that all persons attending league games must be physically searched before entering any of the venues where games are played, aiming to prevent terrorist attacks in the stadiums. The Buccaneers implemented this directive at Raymond James Stadium. Gordon Johnston had been a Buccaneers season ticket holder for several years and had renewed his season tickets for the 2005 season at a cost of $869.20 plus $250.00 for stadium parking. At that time Johnston was not given notice that he would have to submit to a pat-down search before entering the stadium. When Johnston learned of this new policy, he contacted the Buccaneers to complain, but he was told that the Buccaneers would not refund his payment for the season tickets. Moreover, even if Johnston were permitted to return his

2005 tickets for a refund, he would lose the remainder of his seat deposit and be put at the bottom of a 100,000-person waiting list if he desired to purchase season tickets in the future.

In *Johnston v. Tampa Sports Authority* (2006), Johnston sued the Tampa Sports Authority (TSA), seeking to enjoin them from conducting pat-down searches of every person who attended a Tampa Bay Buccaneers home football game. A primary issue before the district court was whether Johnston had consented to the searches. Initially the district court found that the TSA was a state actor and subject to the Fourth Amendment to the U.S. Constitution. The Fourth Amendment restraint generally bars government officials from undertaking a search or seizure without individualized suspicion. The district court acknowledged that the sanctity of one's person is the starting point for a Fourth Amendment analysis. The TSA contended that Johnston consented to the search by repeatedly attending NFL games – knowing in advance that he would be either subjected to a pat-down search or denied entry to the stadium. The essence of this argument is that Johnston was not compelled to submit to the search but rather that he consented to it when he chose to attend the Buccaneers' games. The district court held that where the government conditions the receipt of a benefit (i.e., attending the event) on the wavier of a constitutional right (i.e., to be free from unreasonable search without cause), the implied consent is invalid as an unconstitutional condition. The doctrine of unconstitutional conditions prohibits terminating benefits if the termination is based on motivations that are unconstitutional. Johnston's interest in his season tickets and his right to attend games and assemble with other Bucs fans constitute a benefit or privilege that cannot be conditioned on relinquishment of his Fourth Amendment rights.

The district court also held that, even without the unconstitutional conditions, Johnston's conduct did not constitute implied consent because it was not voluntarily given. The district court found that Johnston was not notified of the pat-down policy prior to purchasing his season tickets; once notified, he was informed he could not receive a refund; and even if a refund were available, he would have lost his ticket priority. Johnston verbally objected each time he was asked to submit to the pat-down search. Thus, the district court concluded that Johnston's consent was not voluntarily given. The TSA appealed to the Eleventh Circuit Court of Appeals; whose decision is provided in the following Case Opinion.

Johnston v. Tampa Sports Authority

CASE OPINION   530 F.3d 1320 (11th Cir. 2008)

FACTS

Under a franchise agreement, the public sports authority adopted a professional football league's policy of patting down patrons entering the authority's stadium to attend league games. The sole purpose of the pat-downs was to protect patrons from terrorism in the form of improvised explosive devices. The ticket holder allowed himself to be patted down over objection three times. The district court found that the pat-downs violated both the Florida and U.S. Constitutions.

HOLDING

We conclude that Appellee Gordon Johnston consented to the searches.

RATIONALE

The United States Supreme Court has consistently held that "a search conducted without a warrant issued upon probable cause is 'per se unreasonable … subject only to a few specifically established and well-delineated exceptions.'" "It is equally well settled that one of the specifically established exceptions to the requirements of both a warrant and probable cause is a search that is conducted pursuant to consent."

Consensual Searches

Whether consent is voluntary is a question determined according to the totality of the circumstances and determined on a case-by-case basis. Both the federal and Florida courts have enumerated non-exhaustive lists of factors to be considered in performing the analysis. We have previously identified the following non-exhaustive factors to consider in determining voluntariness: (1) whether the person is in custody; (2) the existence of coercion; (3) the person's awareness of his right to refuse consent; (4) the person's education and intelligence; and (5) whether the person believes incriminating evidence will be found.

Florida courts look for the existence of express or implied consent and consider the following implied consent factors: (1) whether the defendant was aware his conduct would subject him to search; (2) whether the search was supported by a "vital interest"; (3) whether the searching officer had apparent authority to search and arrest; (4) whether the defendant was advised of his right to refuse; and (5) whether refusal would result in a deprivation of a benefit or right. Consent is not voluntary if the government conditions receipt of a right or a benefit on the relinquishment of a constitutional right (*Bourgeois v. Peters*, 2004). Johnston knew well in advance that he would be subjected to a pat-down search by the Authority if he presented himself at an entrance to the Stadium to be admitted to a Buccaneers game. The factors above demonstrate the voluntariness of Johnston's consent. Johnston was not in custody at the time of the search, rather, he presented himself willingly at the search point. The screeners did not coerce Johnston; they merely performed the search to which Johnston submitted. Johnston was well aware of his right to refuse to submit to the pat-down search and did in fact express his objection to the searches to specific screeners and over the telephone to the Buccaneers before the searches were implemented. At the search point, Johnston pulled his shirt up (apparently to show that he was not wearing an IED) and asked not to be patted down. When screeners insisted on the pat-down before permitting Johnston to enter, Johnston elected to be patted down and thereby gain entrance to the Stadium. Johnston appears from the record to be a man of heightened intelligence and well-educated. The record shows he did not believe that the search would disclose incriminating evidence, as shown by his attempt to show screeners he was not carrying any suspicious devices under his shirt.

Johnston also impliedly consented to the search under the factors for implied consent developed by Florida courts. Johnston was well-aware his insistence in entering the Stadium would cause him to be subject to a search. The record also reflects that Johnston was aware of his ability to refuse to be searched and leave the Stadium. There is no evidence that the Authority would have detained Johnston if he refused, or that Johnston otherwise believed the searches to be compulsory.

Doctrine of Unconstitutional Conditions

The district court found that the consent exception did not apply in this case, in part, because of the "unconstitutional condition" doctrine developed by federal and Florida courts. "The doctrine of unconstitutional conditions prohibits terminating benefits, though not classified as entitlements, if the termination is based on motivations that other constitutional provisions proscribe." ("This is a classic 'unconstitutional conditions,' in which the government conditions receipt of a benefit or privilege on the relinquishment of a constitutional right.") The district court erred in its application of the unconstitutional conditions doctrine because in this case the condition for entry was imposed by the NFL and the Buccaneers, both private entities, and not the government.

As we noted, Johnston did not have any right or entitlement to enter the Stadium. His purchase of a ticket granted him at most a revocable license to a seat. As is typical of sporting events, the NFL and the Buccaneers explicitly retained the right to exclude him from the Stadium for any reason. The NFL chose to impose a pat-down as a condition for entry. Although the Authority acquiesced to the NFL's requests by hiring screeners to conduct pat-downs, the conclusion that this policy was the NFL's – and not the Authority's – condition for entry is reinforced by the Authority's security measures at other non-NFL events at the Stadium, including collegiate football games, where the Authority does not conduct pat-downs. In other cases where we have used the unconstitutional conditions doctrine to invalidate consent, we found that it was the government imposing the condition and performing the search.

In this case, the government had no role in formulating or mandating the pat-down policy. The policy exists solely because of the NFL's mandate. Because the condition for entry was imposed by a private party, Johnston was not forced by the government to choose between assertion of his constitutional rights and obtaining a benefit to which he was entitled. The NFL's condition does not invalidate Johnston's voluntary consent to the pat-downs. Considering the totality of the circumstances, the Court concludes that Johnston voluntarily consented to pat-down searches each time he presented himself at a Stadium entrance to attend a game.

QUESTIONS

The Supreme Court denied Johnston's petition for certiorari on January 21, 2009 (*Johnston v. Tampa Sports Authority*, 2009). The Johnston case presents an excellent opportunity to review Fourth Amendment issues in the context of stadium operations. It is important to note, however, that the Eleventh Circuit Court of Appeals reversed the district court, focusing almost exclusively on the issue of implied consent. Consider the following discussion questions to compare and contrast the two decisions.

1 How do the factors for determining voluntariness and those used to evaluate implied consent differ?
2 Based on the district court's decision, how did the principle of unconstitutional conditions apply to Johnston as a season ticket holder seeking to gain entry to the event? How did the court of appeals address this issue?

Numerous types of spectator searches are now commonly used by stadium and event operators as part of their security policies and practices from local high schools to professional sports teams. For example, pat down searches, metal detector screenings, bag searches, and clear bag policies are all used in some combination at many large public access sporting events across the Unites States (Speier, 2020). Most of these heightened security measures were implemented following the 9-11 attacks at the World Trade Center and were further expanded following the Boston Marathon bombing in 2013 (Bryant, 2017). The holding in *Tampa Bay v. Johnston* lends additional support to stadiums and arenas to implement these types of searches without fear of facing a Fourth Amendment challenge. Also, following the Covid-19 pandemic, sport facilities implemented access screening procedures for purpose of public health that included taking the patrons' temperature upon entry and also required the use of face masks while on the premises as well as social distancing (Yip, 2020).

Surveillance Activities

Surveillance activities associated with the operation of sporting events and venues has also become much more common and legal issues associated with the use of surveillance technologies are quickly emerging. Venue and event operators around the world use enhanced surveillance technology to monitor fan activity and to make facilities more secure. These technologies include a variety of activities that raise important questions about consumer privacy as well as Fourth Amendment concerns regarding search and seizure. Common law privacy rights are explained in greater detail in Chapter 19, but in the following section, we will identify the primary surveillance activities available to and employed by sport facility and event operators and legislative efforts to protect privacy in a digital age. As we will see in the next section, two recurring questions as to the permissibility of surveillance activities relate to notice and consent. Has the stadium provided the spectator clear and effective notice of surveillance activity, and has the spectator expressed his consent to the activity?

Biometric Attributes

Biometric attributes are physical or behavioral human characteristics that can be used digitally to identify a person such as fingerprints, facial patterns, and voice patterns. Use of facial patterns and facial recognition systems are used by sport organizations to improve the fan experience or to improve security at the facility or during events. In 2018, it was reported that the New York Knicks and Madison Square Garden were using facial recognition systems, to screen for potential problem attendees. However, most major sport leagues keep their security tactics close to the vest, so little is known about everyday security measures at stadiums across the country (Draper, 2018). West (2019) identified five ways stadiums were using facial recognition technology including (1) prevent stadium violence, (2) speed up staff screening; (3) secure locker rooms and facilities; (4) tailor advertising to fan demographics; and (5) recognize VIPs. However, identifying and tracking people by their unique biometric attributes has produced legal challenges (Brand & Pulliam, 2020). Consumers argue that facial recognition technology used by social media and photo-sharing platforms invades users' privacy (Starr, 2019). The ACLU conducted an experiment with photos of professional athletes from Massachusetts professional sports leagues. The facial recognition software erroneously matched the official headshots of 27 Boston athletes to mugshots in a law enforcement database. The athletes were from the New England Patriots, the Boston Bruins, the Red Sox and the Celtics (Vaughn, 2019). With the news reports creating buzz over facial recognition software (and sometimes misuse), lawmakers at all levels – federal, state, and local – actively drafted bills in 2019 to begin regulating in this area.

Information Privacy Acts

There are no current federal regulations covering biometric information tracking but state legislatures are beginning to enact privacy protections for consumers (Statt, 2020). In 2008, Illinois enacted the Biometric Information Privacy Act (BIPA). Illinois was the first state to enact biometric privacy protections and is still the only state law that includes a private right of action for individuals to sue for damages. Washington, California, and Texas have similar legislation, but without a private right of action. In *Rosenbach v. Six Flags Entertainment Corp.* (2019), a mother sued the far north suburban Gurnee theme park for violating the BIPA after her son was fingerprinted without his written consent to access a season pass she had purchased for him. The theme park also failed to disclose what it does with the biometric data it collects, in violation of the law (Starr, 2019). *Rosenbach* is significant because it concluded that a plaintiff does not need to claim actual harm to bring a suit under BIPA.

Four states, Illinois, California, Texas, and Washington, all require notice before collecting biometric data. And in both Illinois and Texas, the notice must also be accompanied by consent. If the company is going to disclose information for commercial purposes, the consent must specifically address commercial use of the data. In states with these laws, sports venues will need to consider how their data collection processes meet these requirements if they plan to collect and use biometric information. In order to bolster claims that spectators have consented to the collecting of biometric data, some sports leagues and associations post signs at sponsored events putting attendees on notice about the possibility that their image, voice or likeness could be recorded and used (Masters & Rose, 2020). The legality of these notices has not been tested. It may be that, consistent with the court of appeals decision in *Johnston*, the ticket purchasing process could include notice and consent to data collection in this manner. However, this type of notice would likely only be effective for direct team to consumer sales, and may not cover tickets given away as prizes or procured on the secondary market. Signage (i.e., notice) can also be helpful to counter a right of publicity claims because publicity rights claims would restrict the use of images for commercial purposes regardless of whether the biometric laws posed a problem. (Publicity rights are discussed in detail in Chapter 18). For these areas, the notice and consent required above is still recommended even for the use of images of crowds in public spaces. And if an individual is identifiable or particularly focused upon, a specific release would be the best practice to avoid publicity rights claims.

If a sports venue collects, stores, or sells this information for any purpose, but especially for commercial purposes, it may fall under this new and emerging legislation. Facial recognition initiatives by sports organizations in the United States and abroad are just getting started and will likely increase as stadiums, teams and leagues find compelling – and potentially lucrative – uses for this technology for security and beyond. Each venue will need to look to both federal and state laws and regulations in crafting programs that consider individual rights, safety, and security, and each venue needs to have legal advice and support from a legal team with experience in dealing with such programs.

Video and Camera Surveillance

Dozens of firms offer specialized video surveillance services in cooperation with law enforcement at major sporting events. As part of an enhanced security plan developed after the Boston Marathon bombings in April 2013, the New York Police Department deployed helicopters, police boats, scuba divers, bomb-sniffing dogs, and hundreds of cameras, as well as hundreds of officers for the New York City Marathon later that year (Steinbach, 2013). Similarly, Corporate Security Services deployed more than 130 megapixel cameras throughout MetLife Stadium located around the bowl of the stadium to provide a view of every seat in every section; 180° coverage of entrances and common areas; and in the stadium's security entrance areas. The cameras are controlled using a unified video management system (VMS) which is monitored by a centralized security command center within the stadium. MetLife Stadium's policy is to initiate real-time recording 24 hours prior to game day to allow security staff to easily search and play back detailed video of any incidents (Ritchey, 2014). To date, video surveillance at sporting events as part of the spectator security plan has not been challenged as a violation of the Fourth Amendment. However, one example of surveillance camera litigation was seen in *Brannum v. Overton County Sch. Bd.* (2008). A surveillance camera placed in a middle-school locker room was held to be a violation of the students' Fourth Amendment rights because the students had a significant privacy interest in their unclothed bodies in the locker room area. Unlike players in a locker room, spectators at a sporting event would likely not have a significant privacy interest in an open, public venue, so whether a fan could successfully challenge video surveillance under the Fourth Amendment is unclear. This is another area, where venue and event operators could use signage to inform spectators that video and camera surveillance was occurring. Signage could be posted at all the entrances, and notices could also be included during the ticket purchase process through online notifications.

Drones and Unmanned Aerial Vehicles

In addition to traditional surveillance, as we briefly discussed in Chapter 13 related to security measures used by the Olympic Host cities, sport facility operators may also begin to employ the use of drones or unmanned aerial vehicles (UAVs) for surveillance or to provide aerial views in and around a venue or event. The American Civil Liberties Union (ACLU) has issued a position statement with recommendations for government use of drone aircraft and several state legislatures are also considering placing limitations on government use of drones (ACLU, 2020a; Stanley & Crump, 2011). The ACLU states, "drones have many beneficial uses, including in search-and-rescue missions, scientific research, mapping, and more. But deployed without proper regulation, drones equipped with facial recognition software, infrared technology, and speakers capable of monitoring personal conversations would cause unprecedented invasions of our privacy rights" (ACLU, 2020b). Further, "an effort to grant states and local governments additional authority to regulate drone operations is ongoing in both chambers of Congress. In the House, Representative John Lewis (R-Minn.) introduced the Drone Innovation Act while in the Senate, Senator Dianne Feinstein (D-Calif.) introduced the Drone Federalism Act. While not companion bills, both aim to provide statutory authority to states and local governments to issue reasonable, time, manner, and place restrictions on drone operations" (NSCL, 2018). Neither bill has received a vote, but they are likely to be included in future debate.

The Supreme Court has not taken a position on whether the Fourth Amendment places limits on use of UAV surveillance at sporting events. The appropriate and legal parameters of advanced surveillance techniques, including UAV's, are a rapidly emerging and evolving area of sport facility management for which sport managers will want to seek continued guidance and training. Several sports venues have used drones to display real time images during an event to enhance the spectator experience. This real-time use of the drone, similar to video surveillance may be less problematic if the team or facility does not also record or stores images. If these images are used for commercial purposes and an individual is identifiable, some of the same concerns discussed regarding biometric data and publicity rights would be equally applicable in this circumstance.

GPS Tracking Technology

Over the past several years there has also been a growing demand for big data in sport organizations, with all of the major professional sport franchises putting *analytics* to use (ESPN, 2019). Large and small data technology firms are using Internet Protocol (IP) addresses and geographic location-based targeting to increase the marketing efforts for sport organizations seeking to attract larger populations of individuals and consumers. This type of location-based targeting or marketing (Geotracking) is the use of a consumer's geographic location to plan and execute relevant marketing campaigns (Miller, 2019). The ability for technology firms to catalogue a personal device's ID, store the data and then sell the personal home information to target consumers with banner and video advertisements creates explicit digital privacy rights concerns.

From a marketing perspective, the benefits of geotracking is to identify and/or retain season ticket holders, streamline stadium or arena attendance, and to incentivize live attendance. One example in 2019 was the decision by the University of Alabama to have students who attend football games install a version of the app FanMaker, which tracks their locations while inside the stadium. If they leave the game early, the app knows and will not award them loyalty points needed for perks like College Football Playoff tickets. According to Campisi (2019), FanMaker runs similar programs for 40 universities – including Clemson University, the University of Southern California and Louisiana State University – that incentivize students through prizes such as T-shirts. Yet, the use of personal data and using latitude and longitude data to target consumers down to the square meter as part of a marketing strategy without an option to consent (opt-in) raises critical questions concerning data privacy (Venue Replay, 2019).

There is no single data protection law in the United States, but several laws at the Federal and State level designed to protect U.S. residents and their data (Chabinsky & Pittman, 2020. There are U.S. data privacy laws which prohibit companies from matching IP addresses to a user's Personal Identifiable Information (PII), but the PII data protection only protects information about an individual that is maintained by specific agencies such as motor vehicle records, addresses and collection of personal medical information (Chabinsky & Pittman, 2020; McCallister, Grance, & Scarfone, 2010). The Federal Trade Commission (FTC) offers broad federal data protection legislation with the FTC Act over unfair and deceptive practices, but the FTC identifies that mobile devices do have the ability to reveal a user's location and "build detailed profiles of consumers movements over time in ways that may not be anticipated by consumers" (Dreifach, 2015, para. 12; Federal Trade Commission, 2018).

At the state level, California is currently a leader in personal data privacy protection laws with the passage of the California Consumer Privacy Act (CCPA). This law, which took effect in January 2020, requires companies to disclose what personal data is collected on consumers, the purpose for collecting the data, and with whom the data will be shared (Chabinsky & Pittman, 2020; Davies, 2019). The CCPA is closely modeled after the data privacy legislation enacted in the European Union in 2018 referred to as the General Data Protection Regulation (GDPR). The GDPR's purpose is to ensure protection and privacy for all individuals within the EU by imposing rules on controlling and processing PII. One of its more notable features is the requirement for individuals to specifically and knowingly 'opt-in' to any data collection and tracking initiative of personal information (Location-Based Marketing, 2019). Within the regulation, it is explicitly stated that "the protection of natural persons in relation to the processing of personal data is a fundamental right" and that "everyone has the right to the protection of personal data concerning him or her" (Regulation EU, 2016, Article 4).

As new technologies emerge, and sport organizations continue to use these technologies to obtain data about patrons and spectators, questions regarding privacy rights will continue to be important considerations for sport managers to balance against the commercial objectives of the facility or event. At a minimum sport managers need to develop sound policies and practices centered on notice and consent requirements in many of these statutes.

Conclusion

This chapter applied numerous legal principles in the context of sport facility financing and location. We also examined the application of the ADA to places of public accommodation, specifically to stadiums and arenas. Lastly, we explored the constitutional law issues that arise when operators of public stadiums seek to conduct searches of spectators who are without suspicion and the use of advanced technology in security and marketing activities. A solid understanding of the varied legal issues presented in this chapter will enable you to be a more effective facility owner or operator.

Discussion Questions

1 Explain how the lease agreement between the Seattle Sonics and the City of Seattle benefitted the City of Seattle when the Sonics tried to leave for OKC, and how the lease agreement for the Rams practice facility in St. Louis worked to the advantage of the Rams.
2 Explain whether modern stadium development projects would best fit the definition of a public use or a public purpose/benefit when a government entity attempts to use eminent domain to take property from private landowners in the planned development.
3 What is the purpose and mandate of the ADA?
4 What is a place of public accommodation under the ADA and how do you know whether sports facilities are covered by the ADA?
5 How is an "alteration" defined under the ADA and how are alterations and repairs different under the ADA, and why is that distinction important for facility operators contemplating a renovation or upgrade to their facilities.
6 Explain the DOJ's basis for requiring facilities to provide people with disabilities comparable lines of sight.
7 Identify the seven new requirements related to accessibility and ticket sales under the ADA and explain the DOJ's rationale for developing these new requirements.

8   Apply the three factors used to determine the reasonableness of a search under the Fourth Amendment, and explain why spectators attending sporting events may be legally subject to pat-down searches before they are permitted to enter the stadium or arena.

9   What are biometric attributes and what are some of the ways in which stadiums use facial recognition technology before, during, and after events.

10   What at the two most important privacy requirements stadium operators should consider when determining if they are permitted to use surveillance technology to capture biometric or geotracking information of spectators and customers.

Learning Activities

1   Locate online the ADA technical assistance guide for accessible stadiums provided by the DOJ's Office of Civil Rights. What are two key features of accessible stadiums? What other accessible features are covered in the guidelines? What percentage of drinking fountains should be wheelchair accessible? Take the guidelines to a recreational facility in your area and evaluate how well the facility meets the accessibility criteria.

Case Study

DOJ's guidelines in *Accessible Stadiums*, states that "[w]heel chair seating must be dispersed throughout all seating areas and provide a choice of admission **prices and views** comparable to those for the general public." In *Landis*, the question was whether the wheelchair seating was dispersed sufficiently to provide **comparable views**. The Plaintiffs in Landis argued that that at least 50 percent of the total accessible seats in Level 100 should be located on the front row and the remaining 50 percent on the back row. The court in *Landis* determined that the 100 Level should have at least five accessible seats on the front row. To do this, the court used a proportionality formula. First, it calculated the total number of accessible seats required in Level 100 which has 18,573 seats using the ADA's 1 percent formula. (See 2010 ADAAG at § 221.2.1.1.) Next, it determined that of the 18,573 seats in Level 100, 2.4 percent of them were located on the front row. Finally it determined, of the total number of accessible seats (1 percent of 18,573), how many needed to be located in the front row if those seats were proportionality distributed to the total front row seats. Thus, 1 percent of 18,573 was 186 accessible seats required for Level 100. Of those 186 accessible seats, only 2.4 percent needed to be located on the front row to be in proportion to the total number of front row seats in Level 100.

Questions

1   Break down the court's formula and make sure you understand how the court reached the conclusion that T-Mobile Park only needed five accessible seats on the front row in Level 100.

2   In *Landis*, accessible seats were available in all sections and at all price points, but we would also need to use a proportionality formula to determine if we needed to offer tickets at different price points? For example, assume our venue has two seating sections (Floor and Balcony) with 3,000 total seats with accessible seats disbursed at the price points below. Using a proportional approach, what proportion of our total seating is not accessible? If we need to make a proportional number of our accessible seats, priced at the lower price point, how many of our twenty $100 Floor accessible seats need to be available for purchase at the Balcony price point of $50?

   a.   Floor 2,700 Seats @ $100 (has 20 accessible seats)
   b.   Balcony 300 Seats @ $50 (has no wheelchair or companion seats)

Considering ... Analysis & Discussion

Service Animals

The two questions permitted by your entry staff are: (1) is the dog a service animal required because of a disability? and (2) what work or task has the dog been trained to perform? Staff are not allowed to request any documentation for the dog, require that the dog demonstrate its task, or inquire about the nature of the person's disability. If those answers revealed that the dog was an emotional support animal, the ADA does not require the facility to modify its no-pets policy. Even though the Drillers probably made the correct conclusion about the animal, we do have to be prepared to navigate negative publicity or viral social media coverage and have a plans in place to respond to media or public inquires. The Drillers should issue a detailed statement addressing their protocols and providing additional information on their ADA website. This situation can be a particular challenge for minor league baseball clubs who often host "dog friendly" events to increase attendance at games. So it is particularly important that the teams provide clear information to fans, and enforce their policies consistently. See Jackson (2018) to see the video of this incident, how the entry staff handled the customer, and the Drillers official statement in response.

References

Cases

Berman v. Parker, 348 U.S. 26 (1954).
Bourgeois v. Peters, 387 F.3d 1303 (11th Cir. 2004).
Brannum v. Overton County School Board, 516 F.3d 489 (6th Cir. 2008).
Caruso v. Blockbuster-Sony Music Entertainment Centre at the Waterfront (3d Cir. 1999).
Celano v. Marriott International, Inc., U.S. Dist. LEXIS 6172 (N.D. Cal. 2008).
Charlebois v. Angels Baseball LP, 993 F. Supp. 2d 1109 (C.D. Cal. 2012).
Clark v. Simms, 2009 U.S. Dist. LEXIS 29027 (W.D. Va. 2009).
Feldman v. Pro Football, Inc, 579 F. Supp. 2d 697 (S.D. Md., 2008).
Independent Living Resources v. Oregon Arena Corp., 982 F. Supp. 698 (D. Ore. 1997).
Johnston v. Tampa Sports Authority, 442 F. Supp. 2d 1257 (M.D. Fla. 2006).
Johnston v. Tampa Sports Authority, 530 F.3d 1320 (11th Cir. 2008).
Johnston v. Tampa Sports Authority, 555 U.S. 1138 (2009).
Katz v. United States, 389 U.S. 347 (1967).
Kelly v. Marylanders for Sports Sanity, Inc., 530 A.2d 245 (Md. Ct. App. 1987).
Kelo v. City of New London, 545 U.S. 469 (2005).
King County v. Taxpayers, 949 P.2d 1260 (Wash. 1997).
Landis v. Wash. State Maj. Baseball Stadium Pub. Facilities Dist., Baseball of Seattle, Inc. 2019 U.S. Dist. LEXIS 215159 (W.D. Wash. 2019).
Miller v. California Speedway Corp., 453 F. Supp. 2d 1193 (2006).
Miller v. California Speedway Corp., 536 F.3d 1020 (9th Cir. 2008).
Paralyzed Veterans of America v. D.C. Arena, L.P., 117 F.3d 579 (D.C. Cir. 1997).
Salsiccia v. Sharks Sports & Entertainment LLC, 2019 U.S. Dist. LEXIS 163570 (N.D. Cal. 2019).
PGA Tour, Inc. v. Martin, 532 U.S. 661 (2001).
Rowe v. Pinellas Sports Auth., 461 So. 2d 72 (Fla. 1984).
United States of America v. Ellerbe Becket, Inc., 976 F. Supp. 1262 (D. Minn. 1997).

Statutes

1. 28 C.F.R. Pt. 36, 2010 *ADA Standards for Accessible Design* (2010). Retrieved from www.ada.gov/regs2010/2010ADAStandards/2010ADAStandards.pdf.
2. 28 C.F.R. § 36.406(a)(1) & § 36.406(a)(3) (2020).
Americans with Disabilities Act of 1990, 42 U.S.C. § 12101–12213 (1990), 28 C.F.R. § 36.104 (2011).
Americans with Disabilities Act. (2002). Accessibility Guidelines for Buildings and Facilities; Recreation Facilities, 36 C.F.R. Part 1191.

Americans with Disabilities Act, 42 U.S.C. § 12101 *et seq.* (2010).

Americans with Disabilities Act, 42 U.S.C. § 12101(b)(2); 12182; 12134(a); 12186(b) and 12181(7) (2020).

Regulation EU (2016). *General provision of the European Parliament and the council.* EUR-Lex. Retrieved from https://eur-lex. europa.eu/legal-content/EN/ALL/?uri=CELEX:02016R0679-20160504.

Restatement (Second) of Torts (1965).

United States Constitution, Fifth Amendment.

United States Constitution, Fourth Amendment.

Other Sources

American Civil Liberties Union (ACLU) (2020a, March 2). Comments of the American Civil Liberties Union ("ACLU"). Before the Federal Aviation Administration. Retrieved from https://www.aclu.org/letter/aclu-comments-federal-aviation-administration-drone-remote-id-nprm.

American Civil Liberties Union (ACLU) (2020b). Domestic drones. Retrieved from https://www.aclu.org/issues/privacy-technology/surveillance-technologies/domestic-drones.

Alberg, A. (2008, July 2). *USA Today.* Retrieved from www.usatoday.com/sports/basketball/nba/sonics/2008-07-02-seattle-trial_N.htm.

Allred, A. (2019, November 17). Getting bucks from the Rams: 3 lawsuits getting millions from the Rams. *KSDK.* Retrieved from https://www.ksdk.com/article/news/local/big-3-lawsuits-against-rams/63-83eebae5-1303-4749-9486-9f247a86b71e.

Associated Press (2007, April 17). Disabled vets challenging Michigan stadium upgrades. *Sports Illustrated.* Retrieved from http://www.callsam.com/bernstein-media-center/richard-bernstein-news-fighting-for-justice/fighting-for-disabled-veterans-rights/disabled-vets-challenging-michigan-stadium-upgrades.

Associated Press (2018, August 17). Boise State gets ok to use eminent domain for stadium. *The Seattle Times.* Retrieved from https://www.seattletimes.com/nation-world/bsu-approved-to-use-eminent-domain-for-stadium-plans/.

Aulbach, L. (2019). TopGolf fight to continue as Hurstbourne neighbors plan to appeal. *Louisville Courier Journal.* Retrieved from https://www.courier-journal.com/story/news/local/2019/07/22/topgolf-louisville-appeal-filed-attorney-says/1795770001/.

Bagli, C. V. (2009, November 24). Ruling lets Atlantic Yards seize land. *The New York Times.* Retrieved February 16, 2010, from http://www.nytimes.com/2009/11/25/nyregion/25yards.html?_r=1.

BER Staff. (2019, April 4). The economics of sports stadiums: Does public financing of sports stadiums create local economic growth, or just help billionaires improve their profit margin? *Berkley Economic Review.* Retrieved from https://econreview.berkeley.edu/the-economics-of-sports-stadiums-does-public-financing-of-sports-stadiums-create-local-economic-growth-or-just-help-billionaires-improve-their-profit-margin/.

Behnken, S. (2019, February 6). Businesses "sitting ducks" for lawsuits because websites aren't ADA complaint. *New Channel 8.* Retrieved from https://www.wfla.com/8-on-your-side/better-call-behnken/businesses-sitting-ducks-for-lawsuits-because-websites-arent-ada-compliant/.

Brand, R. L., & Pulliam, E. (2020, April 28). Faces in the crowd: Legal consideration for use of facial recognition technology at sports arenas. *LawInSport.* Retrieved from https://www.lawinsport.com/topics/sports/boxing/item/faces-in-the-crowd-legal-considerations-for-use-of-facial-recognition-technology-at-sports-arenas?category_id=163.

Brennan, V. (2019, April 18). Rams will arbitration case over Earth City practice facility. *St Louis Business Journal.* Retrieved from https://www.bizjournals.com/stlouis/news/2019/04/18/rams-win-arbitration-case-over-earth-city-practice.html.

Broughton, D. (2018, January 12). Sport venue construction spending to take off again in 2019. *New York Business Journal.* Retrieved from https://www.bizjournals.com/newyork/news/2018/01/12/sports-venue-construction-spending-to-take-off.html.

Carpenter, E. (2013, August 21). Angels settle lawsuit over wheelchair access. *Orange County Register.* Retrieved from http://www.ocregister.com/articles/angels-349543-level-wheelchair.html.

Chabinsky, S., & Pittman, P. F. (2020, June 7). USA: Data protection laws and regulations 2020. *ICLG.com* Retrieved from https://iclg.com/practice-areas/data-protection-laws-and-regulations/usa.

Chapoteau, R. C. (2019, July 15). Sport venues and the Americans with Disabilities Act. *The National Law Review.* Retrieved from https://www.natlawreview.com/article/sports-venues-and-americans-disabilities-act.

Currier, J. (2019, September 6). Kroenke, Rams, NFL to appeal relocation lawsuit to U.S. Supreme Court. *St. Louis Post Dispatch.* Retrieved from https://www.stltoday.com/news/local/crime-and-courts/kroenke-rams-nfl-to-appeal-relocation-lawsuit-to-u-s/article_5ba8739f-1552-5824-9dda-6183dfc0e9d2.html#2.

Custodio, S. (2020, January 21). Lawsuit likely against Anaheim over secretive stadium negotiations. *Voice of OC.* Retrieved from https://voiceofoc.org/2020/01/lawsuit-likely-against-anaheim-over-secretive-stadium-negotiations/.

Damron, D. (2014, August 4). Orlando drops eminent domain action against church, moves soccer stadium farther west. *Orlando Sentinel.* Retrieved from https://www.orlandosentinel.com/news/breaking-news/os-orlando-soccer-stadium-church-eminent-domain-20140804-story.html.

Davies, D. (July 31, 2019). How tech companies track your every move and put your data up for sale. *NPR Fresh Air.* Retrieved from https://www.npr.org/2019/07/31/746878763/how-tech-companies-track-your-every-move-and-put-your-data-up-for-sale.

DeMause, N. (2017, September 29). Why are Georgia taxpayers paying for a new NFL stadium? *The Guardian.* Retrieved from https://www.theguardian.com/sport/2017/sep/29/why-are-georgia-taxpayers-paying-700m-for-a-new-nfl-stadium.

Department of Justice (DOJ) (n.d.). Accessible stadiums. Retrieved from http://www.ada.gov/stadium.txt.

Department of Justice (DOJ) (2010). ADA 2010 revised requirements: Ticket sales. Retrieved from http://www.ada.gov/ticketing_2010.htm.

Department of Justice (DOJ), *ADA Title III Technical Assistance Manual Covering Public Accommodations and Commercial Facilities* (1993), https://www.ada.gov/taman3.html ("1993 TAM").

Department of Justice (DOJ) (2010, September 15). 2010 ADA Standards for Accessible Design. Department of Justice. Retrieved from https://www.ada.gov/regs2010/2010ADAStandards/2010ADAStandards.pdf.

Department of Justice (DOJ), *Accessible Stadiums* (1996), https://www.ada.gov/stadium.pdf ("Accessible Stadiums").

Department of Justice (DOJ). *Title III Technical Assistance Manual 1994 Supplement* (1994), https://www.ada.gov/taman3up.html ("1994 Supplement to the TAM").

Deval, P. L. (1996, October 22). Letter to Commissioner Bud Selig, Major League Baseball. Department of Justice, Civil Rights Division.

Draper, K. (2018, March 13). Madison Square Garden has used face-scanning technology on customers. *The New York Times.* Retrieved from https://www.nytimes.com/2018/03/13/sports/facial-recognition-madison-square-garden.html.

Dreifach, K. (August 12, 2015). Don't get lost finding your customers: New rules for mobile geo-targeting. *ZWillGenBlog.* Retrieved from https://blog.zwillgen.com/2015/08/12/dont-get-lost-finding-your-customers-new-rules-for-mobile-geo-targeting/.

Eadens, S. (2019, April 1). After lawsuit, Wrigley includes more wheelchair seating in latest renovations. *Chicago Sun Times.* Retrieved from https://chicago.suntimes.com/2019/4/1/18482506/after-lawsuit-wrigley-includes-more-wheelchair-seating-in-latest-renovations.

Egelko, B. (2019, May 24). Lawsuit filed over California recreation reservation website unusable by the blind. *San Francisco Chronicle.* Retrieved from https://www.sfchronicle.com/news/article/Lawsuit-filed-over-Calif-recreation-reservation-13892789.php?psid=nylhO#photo-17375669.

Federal Trade Commission (2018). *Privacy & data security.* Retrieved from https://www.ftc.gov/system/files/documents/reports/privacy-data-security-update-2018/2018-privacy-data-security-report-508.pdf.

Florio, M. (2020, March 26). 49ers agree to settle mobility disability case for $24 million. *Pro Football Talk.* Retrieved from https://profootballtalk.nbcsports.com/2020/03/26/49ers-agree-to-settle-mobility-disability-case-for-24-million/.

Gerretsen, S. F. (2018). Sport-led urban development strategies: An analysis of changes in built area, land use patterns, and assessed values around 15 major league arenas. [Unpublished doctoral dissertation]. University of Michigan.

Gershman, D. (2008, October 29). Disabled fans cheer new handicapped seating at Michigan Stadium. *Ann Arbor News.* Retrieved from http://www.mlive.com/news/ann-arbor/index.ssf/2008/10/disabled_fans_cheer_new_handic.html.

Gordon, A. (2013, July 17). America has a stadium problem. *Pacific Standard.* Retrieved from http://www.psmag.com/business-economics/america-has-a-stadium-problem-62665/.

Greenberg, G. (2005, January/February). The condemned. *Mother Jones.* Retrieved from http://www.motherjones.com/news/feature/2005/01/01_407.html.

Greenberg, M. (2008, July/September). Sleeping in Seattle – Good-bye NBA. *For the Record.* Retrieved from https://law.marquette.edu/assets/sports-law/pdf/for-the-record/v19i3.pdf.

Greenberg, M. J. (2004). Sports facilities financing and development trends in the United States. *Marquette Sports Law Review,* 15(1), 93–174.

Greenberg, M. J., & Hughes, D. (2011). It takes a village to build a sports facility. *Marquette Sports Law Review,* 22(1), 91–186.

Hanna, J. (2019, September 17). Cubs ADA lawsuit narrowed but can continue, judge rules. *Sport and Entertainment Law Insider.* Retrieved from https://sportslawinsider.com/cubs-ada-lawsuit-narrowed-but-can-continue-judge-rules/.

Huang, R. (2019–2020). Eminent domain and stadium construction: Why "Just Cause" compensation is insufficient. *McGeorge Law Review,* 51, 79–99.

Hybl, D. (2010, January 15). Is it time for Baltimore's ultimate revenge on the Colts? *Baltimore Sports Then and Now.* Retrieved from http://baltimore.sportsthenandnow.com/2010/01/is-it-time-for-baltimore%e2%80%99s-ultimate-revenge-on-the-colts/.

Institute for Justice (IOJ) (2019). Eminent domain. Retrieved from https://ij.org/issues/private-property/eminent-domain/.

Jackson, K. (2018, August 27). Woman says service dog denied entrance to baseball game. *KTUL News.* Retrieved from https://ktul.com/news/local/woman-says-service-dog-denied-entrance-to-baseball-game.

Joyner, J. (2005, June 25). Eminent domain ruling affects Dallas Cowboys stadium. *Outside the Beltway*. Retrieved from http://www.outsidethebeltway.com/archives/eminent_domain_ruling_affects_dallas_cowboys_stadium/.

Kallergis, K. (2018, November 6). Miami election: Voters approve Beckham's MLS stadium, convention center hotel. *The Real Deal*. Retrieved from https://therealdeal.com/miami/2018/11/06/miami-election-beckham-stadium-convention-center-hotel/.

Keeling, B. (2019, August 27). Chase Center has landed. *Curbed San Francisco*. Retrieved from https://sf.curbed.com/2019/8/27/20835188/chase-center-photos-open-date-warriors-san-francisco.

Kozlarz, J. (2019, December 10). Wrigley Field renovations under federal scrutiny for potential accessibility violations. *Chicago Curbed*. Retrieved from https://chicago.curbed.com/2019/12/10/21003390/wrigley-field-renovation-wheelchair-accessible-review-lawsuit.

Lawsuit delays bond sale for new NFL stadium in Minneapolis (2014, January 13). *Grand Forks Herald*. Retrieved from https://www.grandforksherald.com/sports/2206569-lawsuit-delays-bond-sale-new-nfl-stadium-minneapolis.

Location-Based Marketing (October 8, 2019). *Interactive Advertising Bureau*. Retrieved from https://www.iab.com/insights/location-based-marketing-glossary/.

London, D. (2019, September 12). Lawsuit alleges conflict of interest in MLS stadium contracts. *WSMV News*. Retrieved from https://www.wsmv.com/news/davidson_county/lawsuit-alleges-conflict-of-interest-in-mls-stadium-contracts/article_3cb5ba42-d59b-11e9-b4bb-2be7d71064d7.html.

Long, J. G. (2013). *Public/private partnerships for major league sports franchises*. New York, NY: Routledge/Taylor & Francis.

Lutz, M. (2018, November 19). As another season passes, Cobb in dark about final Braves stadium costs. *The Atlanta Journal-Constitution*. Retrieved from https://www.ajc.com/news/local-govt–politics/another-season-passes-cobb-dark-about-final-braves-stadium-cost/ph2p4MVl1FqNbrh1rzkLbN/#.

Masters, D. N., & Rose, S. A. (2020, February 18). Facial recognition cameras bring mixed results to sports. *Chicago Daily Law Bulletin*. Retrieved from https://www.chicagolawbulletin.com/masters-rose-facial-recognition-cameras-bring-mixed-results-to-sports-20200218.

McCallister, E., Grance, T., & Scarfone, K. (2010, April). *Guide to protecting the confidentiality of personally identifiable information*. U.S. Department of Commerce, NIST Special Publication. Retrieved from https://tsapps.nist.gov/publication/get_pdf.cfm?pub_id=904990.

McGraw, D. (2005, May). Demolishing sports welfare. *Reason Online*. Retrieved from http://www.reason.com/0505/fe.dm.demolishing.shtm.

Miller, D. (2019, September 30). What is location-based marketing? And why small business should care about it. *The Balance Small Business*. Retrieved from https://www.thebalancesmb.com/what-is-location-based-marketing-4172454.

Mosier, J. (2008, September 10). Court case challenges eminent domain for Dallas Cowboys stadium. *The Dallas Morning News*. Retrieved from www.dallas-news.com/sharedcontent/dws/news/localnews/cowboys-stadium/stories/091108dnmetstadium.616aec1e.html.

Mosier, J. (2017). Rangers secure $600 million loan for new ballpark; Arlington refinances Cowboys bonds. *The Dallas Morning News*. Retrieved from https://www.dallasnews.com/business/real-estate/2017/09/13/rangers-secure-600-million-loan-for-new-ballpark-arlington-refinances-cowboys-bonds/.

Muret, D. (2016, October 31). San Diego, Arlington prepare for stadium votes. *Street & Smith's Sports Business Journal*. Retrieved from https://www.sportsbusinessdaily.com/Journal/Issues/2016/10/31/Facilities/Referendums.aspx.

Natarajan, P., & O'Connell, J. (2007, October 5). Fight for land near Nats' stadium goes to extra innings. *Washington Business Journal*. Retrieved from http://washington.bizjournals.com/washington/stories/2007/10/08/story2.html.

National Conference of State Legislatures (NCSL). (2018, January 17). 2017 unmanned aircraft systems (UAS) state legislation update. *NCSL.org*. Retrieved from https://www.ncsl.org/research/transportation/2017-unmanned-air-craft-systems-uas-state-legislation-update.aspx.

Nelson, T. (2013, August 20). Lawsuits look to ask voter approval for Vikings stadium financing deal. *Minnesota Public Radio News*. Retrieved from http://blogs.mprnews.org/stadium-watch/2013/08/20/lawsuits-look-to-ask-voter-approval-for-vikings-stadium-funding-deal/.

Nelson, T. (2014, January 22). Lawsuit dismissed, Vikings stadium builders must close financial gap. *Minnesota Public Radio*. Retrieved from https://blogs.mprnews.org/stadium-watch/2014/01/22/lawsuit-dismissed-vikings-stadium-builders-must-close-finance-gap/.

Noll, R., & Zimbalist, A. (1997, Summer). Sports, jobs, & taxes: Are new stadiums worth the cost? *The Brookings Institution*. Retrieved from http://www.brookings.edu/research/articles/1997/06/summer-taxes-noll.

OHSAA says mistake was made in benching legless player (2005, October 7). *Sports Litigation Alerts*, 2(16), 17.

Oklahoma State wins eminent domain case (2009, December 10). *Inside Higher Ed*. Retrieved from http://www.inside-highered.com/quicktakes/2009/12/10/oklahoma-state-wins-eminent-domain-case.

Ritchey, D. (2014, July 1). Balancing security and the fan experience in sports security. *Security Magazine*. Retrieved from https://www.securitymagazine.com/articles/85610-balancing-security-and-the-fan-experience-in-sports-security.

Rubbelke, N. (2020, April 20). U.S. Supreme Court deals another blow to Rams in relocation lawsuit. *St. Louis Business Journal*. Retrieved from https://www.bizjournals.com/stlouis/news/2020/04/20/u-s-supreme-court-deals-another-blow-to-rams-in.html.

Sandefer, D. (2015, September 18). Foul ball: Ten cities that used eminent domain for sports stadiums. *Institute for Justice*. Retrieved from https://ij.org/action-post/foul-ball-ten-cities-that-used-eminent-domain-for-sports-stadiums/.

SB 4 and eminent domain news. (2005, June 23). Retrieved from http://newballpark.blogspot.com/2005/06/sb-4-and-eminentdomain-news.html.

Sernovitz, D. (2018, June 29). D.C. appeals $32 million verdict in Buzzard Point eminent domain case. *Washington Business Journal*. Retrieved from https://www.bizjournals.com/washington/news/2018/06/29/d-c-appeals-32-verdict-in-buzzard-point-eminent.html.

Shaikin, B. (2019, June 24). L.A. doesn't pay to build sport stadiums, but billions are generated from them anyway. *Los Angeles Times*. Retrieved from https://www.latimes.com/sports/la-sp-los-angeles-economic-impact-sports-20190624-story.html.

Shea, B. (2015). Michigan to reduce Big House capacity by 2,300 seats. *Crain's Detroit Business*. Retrieved from https://www.crainsdetroit.com/article/20150810/NEWS/150819995/michigan-to-reduce-big-house-capacity-by-2300-seats.

Simons, R. (2011). Revised ADA guidelines: An operator's perspective. *Facility Manager*. Retrieved from http://www.iavm.org/Facility_manager/pages/2011Apr_May/feauture_3.

Spedden, Z. (2020, March 18). Lawsuit filed to block fast-tracking of Howard Terminal ballpark. *Ballpark Digest*. Retrieved from https://ballparkdigest.com/2020/03/18/lawsuit-filed-to-block-fast-tracking-of-howard-terminal-ballpark/.

Speier, A. (2020, April 17). What will the sports fan experience look like after coronavirus. *Boston Globe*. Retrieved from https://www.bostonglobe.com/2020/04/17/sports/what-will-sports-fans-experience-look-like-after-coronavirus/.

Somin, I. (2014, February 7). Orlando condemns private property in order to a Major League Soccer stadium. *The Washington Post*. Retrieved from https://www.washingtonpost.com/news/volokh-conspiracy/wp/2014/02/07/orlando-condemns-private-property-in-order-to-build-a-major-league-soccer-stadium/.

St. Louis Rams tickets and merchandise class action settlements (2020, January 6). Top Class Actions. Retrieved from https://topclassactions.com/lawsuit-settlements/sports-teams/st-louis-rams-tickets-merchandise-class-action-settlement/.

Stadium eminent domain (2008, February 11). *Settlements and Verdicts*. Retrieved from http://www.lawyersandsettlements.com/case/football-stadium-eminentdomain.html.

Stanley, J., & Crump, C. (2011, December). Protecting privacy from aerial surveillance: Recommendations for government use of drone aircraft. *American Civil Liberties Union*. Retrieved from http://www.aclu.org/files/assets/protectingprivacyfromaerialsurveillance.

Starr, K. (2019). Facial recognition tech: No longer science fiction, but a threat to privacy. *Daily Utah Chronicle*. Retrieved from https://dailyutahchronicle.com/2019/10/16/print-10-14-starr-facial-recognition-software-is-a-step-too-far-for-utah/.

Statt, N. (2020, May 28). ACLU sues facial recognition firm Clearview AI, calling it a "nightmare scenario" for privacy. *The Verge*. Retrieved from https://www.theverge.com/2020/5/28/21273388/aclu-clearview-ai-lawsuit-facial-recognition-database-illinois-biometric-laws.

Steinbach, P. (2013, July). Rethinking security post-Boston. *Athletic Business*, 10–14.

Steinbach, P. (2017, April). Stadium design evolution in the AB era. *Athletic Business*. Retrieved from https://www.athleticbusiness.com/stadium-arena/stadium-design-evolution-from-1977-to-2017.html.

Trimble, L. (2019). Eminent domain a decade after *Kelo*: Are takings to build professional and college sport stadiums in Texas a valid public use. *Texas A&M Journal of Property Law*, 5, 1101–1120.

U of Michigan to increase wheelchair-accessible seating in stadium (2007, November 19). *Chronicle of Higher Education*. Retrieved from http://chronicle.com/news/article/3458/u-of-michigan-to-increase-wheelchair-accessible-seating-at-stadium.

United States Access Board. (2019). What are the requirements for accessible routes? Retrieved from https://www.access-board.gov/guidelines-and-standards/recreation-facilities/guides/play-areas/accessible-routes.

Vaughn, A. (2019, October 21). Here are the 27 Boston athletes facial recognition technology mistakenly matched to mugshots. *Boston Magazine*. Retrieved from https://www.bostonmagazine.com/news/2019/10/21/facial-recognition-boston-athletes-misidentified/.

Velotta, R. N. (2018, March 21). 65,000-set Las Vegas Raiders stadium will cost $1.5B to build. *Las Vegas Review-Journal*. Retrieved from https://www.reviewjournal.com/business/stadium/65000-seat-las-vegas-raiders-stadium-will-cost-1-8b-to-build/.

Venue Replay (2019, October 11). *el toro*. Retrieved from https://www.eltoro.com/venue-replay-geoframing/.

Vogt, D. (2020, February 26). Louisville Topgolf trial moving forward by the Kentucky Court of Appeals. *WAVE3 News*. Retrieved from https://www.wave3.com/2020/02/26/louisville-topgolf-trial-moving-forward-by-kentucky-court-appeals/.

West, J. D. (2019, July 25). Five ways facial recognition is being used in sports today. *FaceFirst*. Retrieved from https://www.facefirst.com/blog/ways-facial-recognition-is-being-used-in-sports-today/.

Winzelberg, D. (2019, September 22). Second lawsuit filed against Belmont arena project. *Long Island Business News*. Retrieved from https://libn.com/2019/09/22/second-lawsuit-filed-against-belmont-arena-project/.

Wolohan, J. T. (2009, September). An unobstructed view. *Athletic Business*. Retrieved from http://www.athleticbusiness.com/articles/article.aspx?articleid=2573&zoneid=31.

Wolverton, B. (2007, October 31). Education Department accuses U. of Michigan of broad violations of disabilities law in stadium changes. *Chronicle of Higher Education*. Retrieved from http://chronicle.com/daily/2007/10/557n.htm.

Yip, S. (2020, April 28). Doctors on return of sports: "Fans may not be in stadiums until well into 2021." *The Guardian*. Retrieved from https://www.theguardian.com/sport/2020/apr/28/when-will-sports-return-coronavirus-covid-19-medical-experts.

Zagger, Z. (2019, July 3). Parks face costly fixes as ADA suits target sightlines. *Law 360*. Retrieved from https://www.law360.com/articles/1174869.

Web Resources

www.ada.gov/ticketing_2010.htm ■ This site provides the full document relating to the ADA's ticketing requirements governing ticket sales accessibility for persons with disabilities.

www.aahperd.org/naspe/standards/upload/Availability-Access-to-AEDs-Final-5-5-11.pdf ■ This is NASPE's position statement on the placement and use of AEDs in school settings.

www.access-board.gov/guidelines-and-standards/recreation-facilities/guides ■ An overview of accessibility guidelines for recreation facilities such as amusement rides, golf courses, and swimming pools put together by the United States Access Board. The organization is dedicated to accessible design, and this section of their site provides an overview of the legislation that affects different recreational areas, sample accessible routes, and descriptions of possible devices that can help accessibility.

www.accessgolf.org ■ The National Alliance for Accessible Golf focuses on promoting golf for persons with disabilities and on increasing accessibility at golf facilities. The site offers studies and statistics as well as tool kits for golfers and golf course owners. The organization's GAIN program is offered for organizations wishing to implement an inclusive golf program.

www.usga.org/rules/disabilities/Rules-for-golfers-with-disabilities ■ The United States Golf Association has compiled information for golfers with disabilities, creating the Rules for Golfers with Disabilities. USGA provides a list of permissible modifications of the official rules of golf for players with disabilities.

www.ncaonline.org ■ The Department of Recreation, Park and Tourism Studies at Indiana University houses the National Center on Accessibility. They provide real-world case studies of organizations and places that worked to become more accessible, in addition to research, recommendations, and news. The Resources tab provides listings of resources to assist with making a variety of recreational and outdoor areas accessible.

www.ncpad.org ■ The site for the National Center on Health, Physical Activity, and Disability provides a wealth of resources. A large database of videos contains clips of exercise programs, recreational instruction, and stretches. The site also provides resources regarding accessibility and disabilities, including links to journals, magazines, books, and news reports.

Part V

Marketing Management

582   *Stephanie A. Tryce*

Introduction to the Law in Marketing Environments

Sport marketing professionals perform a wide range of functions that vary depending upon the type of sport organization. For example, the responsibilities of a marketing director for a major league sports franchise and those of a marketing director for a local YMCA or a state university athletics program will be quite different in nature and scope. Sport marketing can encompass a wide range of activities such as ticket sales, corporate sponsor sales, premium suites sales, product placement, publicity, and so forth. Retail and manufacturing sport organizations employ marketing professionals in product design and development as well as sales. Marketing directors are also often responsible for creating advertising campaigns, conducting special promotions or game day promotions, developing digital marketing activities, managing social media, and monitoring intellectual property rights.

In the performance of these diverse responsibilities, a marketing professional will encounter a number of legal issues. The next two chapters will explore marketing functions, including topics such as product development and design, promotions and sales, public relations, and pricing. The marketing of products and services, and the primary laws that have an impact on the various aspects of marketing in the sport industry will also be examined.

Legal Principles and the Marketing Function

There are many legal implications in marketing management. The most constant and recurring legal area is contract law. All sport marketing activities require the negotiation, creation, drafting, modifying, execution, and performance of contractual obligations. Whether it is a corporate sponsor renewal, a group ticket package, a mascot appearance at a game promotion, displaying brand signage in a venue, producing a weekly podcast, or a licensing agreement with a local retailer for merchandise, each activity requires a contractual agreement between the parties. Chapter 3 covered the basic contract principles you will need to use on a daily basis to perform your duties effectively.

In addition to the general application of contract law (Chapter 3) to many functions of sport marketing, several other legal areas are involved in marketing. Chapter 18 discusses the importance of protecting intellectual property to product development and branding. Specifically, Chapter 18 involves a discussion of trademark law, copyright law, patent law, and publicity rights. Chapter 19 addresses the legal issues faced by sport managers as they begin to operationalize marketing initiatives through advertising, sales, promotions, ticket pricing, broadcasting agreements, sponsorship agreements, and public relations. Chapter 19 revisits constitutional law issues arising from First Amendment protections of commercial speech, and contract law issues related to sponsorship agreements, broadcasting agreements, and sales agreements. Product liability and warranty issues discussed in Chapter 14, are also is an important element of the marketing mix.

18 Development and Protection of Intellectual Property

Stephanie A. Tryce

Introduction

Intellectual property or "IP" rights are the cornerstone for any sport organization to establish effective branding strategies and to begin implementing effective marketing strategies. The term *intellectual property* is commonly used to refer to rights associated with patents, copyrights, trademarks, trade secrets, and trade dress. One goal of intellectual property law is to create and maintain an open and competitive marketplace. The various intellectual property laws both complement and challenge each other. For example, creators of original materials need to be rewarded for their creation and permitted to profit from their creativity. Creators of original works are granted an exclusive right to use and control their works; however, a robust marketplace also needs vibrant competition and access to creative ideas. Thus, the duration or scope of the right is limited so that at some point the marketplace can gain free and continuing access to the invention, image, idea, or word. Intellectual property law is intended to provide a compromise between these competing goals so that a delicate balance is maintained.

Different areas of intellectual property law have overlapping protections and distinct purposes. For example, patent law and copyright law are intended primarily to protect inventions and creative works, while trademark law and unfair competition law are intended to protect consumers from confusing, deceptive, and misleading advertising and marketing practices. A single product could receive intellectual property protection for its design (patent), label (copyright), packaging (trade dress), and slogan (trademark), and for preventing false claims of competitors (unfair competition). The creation and protection of intellectual property (IP) rights is also one of the fastest-growing concerns for sport organizations. Often, many IP functions are performed by the marketing department staff. This chapter explores the law relating to trademarks, copyrights, patents, and publicity rights. Exhibit 18.1 provides an overview of the management contexts, major legal issues, and relevant laws and cases discussed in this chapter.

To begin our discussion, consider the following scenario. You are the marketing director for a minor league basketball team, the Baton Rouge Gators. Some of your many functions are developing promotional ideas, creating and implementing marketing strategies, reviewing and approving advertisements, managing social media, coordinating new merchandise designs, and communicating with the licensees and vendors who sell your team's merchandise. You will be better prepared to perform these functions effectively if you understand how to develop and protect the team's intellectual property. Let's begin with a new advertising campaign that you have created for the team to increase ticket sales and engagement of Millennials and Gen Z: "Geauxing Gator." This theme will emphasize to the local community that nothing is quite as enjoyable as going to the arena and watching the Gators. It will also allow you to emphasize the team's winning record. Your marketing mix will include digital and social media, content marketing, augmented and virtual reality, email, and the team's website. You plan to develop a new logo with the team mascot, Godfrey the Gator, leaning back in his arena seat wearing sunglasses and holding a red stick in one hand and a beverage in the other hand with your exclusive soft drink partner's logo on the cup.

Exhibit 18.1 Management contexts in which issues of intellectual property may arise, with relevant laws and cases.

Management Context	Major Legal Issue	Relevant Law	Illustrative Cases
Creating promotions and advertising campaigns/ slogans, brand management	Creating a protectable property interest	Lanham Act	Elliott v. Google Inc, Converse, Inc. v. International Trade Commission, Board of Supervisors of LSU v Smack Apparel, In re Seats, Pro-Football, Inc. v. Harjo, Blackhorse v. Pro-Football, Matal v. Tam, Inacu v. Brunetti
	Registration of trademark/copyrights	Copyright Act of 1976	In re Seats, Inc, NBA v. Motorola, Anti-Monopoly, Inc. v. General Mills Fun Group, Padres, Affiliated Hosp. Prods., Inc. v. Merdel Game Mfg. Co., Hoopla Sports Entertainment, Inc. v. Nike, Inc., Feist Publications, Inc. v. Rural Telephone Service Co., Fourth Estate Public Benefit Corp. v. Wall-Street.com
	Protection of trademark/copyrights through policing and infringement actions		March Madness Athletic Association v. Netfire, SportFuel, Inc. v. PepsiCo Inc. (The Gatorade Company), Atlanta National League Baseball Club, LLC v. Braves Taxi, UGAA v. Laite, Polaroid Corp. v. Polaroid
Using artwork and advertising messages from outside sources	Works made for hire versus copyright ownership	Copyright Act of 1976	Leonard v. Nike Inc., Fleurimond v. NYU, Phillies v Harrison/Erickson Inc., NASCAR v. Scharle
Merchandise sales and licensing	Permitted uses of protected trademarks and copyrights	First amendment, Free Speech, Parody, and Fair Use	Boston Athletic Association v. Velocity, Nitro, TRG Motorsports v. The Media Barons, North Face, TrafFix, Talking Rain, Smack Apparel, Maker's Mark, Campbell v. Acuff-Rose Music, Inc.
	Limitations on uses	Functionality	Talking Rain Beverage Co. v. South Beach Beverage Co, Robert M. Lyden v. Adidas America, Inc.
	Response to infringing activities or non compliant licensees	Copyright Act of 1976	USOC v. San Francisco Arts & Athletics, Inc., Solid Oak Sketches, LLC v. Visual Concepts, Bouchat v. Baltimore Ravens, Inc.
	Excessive licensing and potential abandonment of protected marks	Lanham Act	Indianapolis Colts. v. Metropolitan Baltimore Football Club Ltd. Partnership, Sed Olet
Monitoring competitors' advertising and promotional activities; and media activities	Media and artist use of protected marks and copyrights	Visual Rights Act of 1990	NASCAR v. Scharle
	Permitted uses of protected marks/ copyrights	First Amendment, free speech	Campbell v. Acuff-Rose Music
	Trademark dilution	Trademark Dilution Act	Moseley v. V Secret Catalogue, LeCharles Bentley et al. v. NBC Universal, Anheuser-Busch, Inc. v. Andy's Sportswear, Board of Regents, The University of Texas System v. KST Electric, adidas-America v. Payless Shoesource, Daubert v. Merrell Dow Pharmaceuticals, Nike v. Nikepal International, University of Kansas v. Sinks
Use of an athlete's likeness	Rights to Publicity	State Law	Haelan Laboratories, Inc. v. Topps Chewing Gum, Inc., Comedy III Productions v. Saderup, White v. Samsung Electronics, Keller v. Electronic Arts, Hart v. Electronic Arts
	Defenses to Rights to Publicity claims	First Amendment	Zacchini v. Scripps-Howard Broadcasting Co., Winter v. DC Comics, ETW Corp. v. Jireh Publishing Co., Rogers v. Grimaldi, Davis v. Electronic Arts Inc.

Implementing this marketing strategy will create a number of legal issues for you to consider. For example, can or should the slogan "Geauxing Gator" be trademarked? If you are going to seek trademark registration, should it be state or federal registration? The same questions must be asked with regard to the new logo design featuring Godfrey the Gator in his stadium seat. Is the new logo sufficiently creative to warrant copyright protection as well as trademark protection? If one of your summer interns or another employee actually creates the new logo design, does he or she have any copyright interests to be considered? Does your sponsorship agreement include licensing provisions with your soft drink sponsor that permit or require the use of their marks and logos in your promotional activities? Below, we discuss the legal principles that will help you answer these questions and make sound management decisions.

The Law of Trademarks

A **trademark** is defined as "a word, name, symbol, or device or any combination thereof adopted and used by a manufacturer or merchant to identify his goods and distinguish them from those manufactured or sold by others" (15 U.S.C. § 1127). Many highly recognizable marks serve this purpose extremely well, such as those for Coca-Cola, Walt Disney, McDonald's, FedEx, and ESPN, just to name a few. A mark may consist of words, numbers, abstract designs, drawings, slogans, sounds, distinctive packaging, and virtually anything that can be used to identify the source or origin of a product or service. Logos and slogans are common examples of trademarks. However, distinctive colors, sounds, and scents can be trademarks as well. For example,

- The color, Pantone 159, is the protected school color for the University of Texas-Austin.
- The Nike "swoosh" is a symbol used as a trademark for sports gear.
- The famous ESPN intro sound is used as a trademark for television broadcast services.
- "Know Your Why" is a slogan trademarked by Robert Griffin III
- Distinctive shoe design is registered trade dress for a number of manufacturers including Converse Chuck Taylor shoes, the adidas Stan Smith shoe, and ASICS distinctive shoe design.

If the word, name, or symbol relates to a good or product (e.g., Coca-Cola, adidas, Samsung, Nike), it is called a **trademark**. If the word, name, or symbol relates to a service (e.g., Ticketmaster, IMG, YMCA), then it is called a **service mark**. In addition, marks that are used to indicate membership within an organization, such as a professional players association, are called **collective marks** (e.g., National Football League Players Association, Sports Lawyers Association). Another type of trademark is a **certification mark**, which indicates that a product meets certain certification standards, such as those maintained by Underwriters Laboratory, Inc. Here, we focus on federal trademark laws, and the term *trademark* or *mark* will be used to refer to any of the types of marks identified above. Exhibit 18.2 below summarizes important definitions related to the various types of trademarks.

Purpose of Trademarks

A trademark can serve several functions or purposes. Following are five common purposes served by trademarks:

1 **To identify the source or origin of a product or service and to distinguish it from others**. For example, when a consumer purchases a T-shirt bearing the logo of adidas or Nike, the logo indicates the shirt comes from a single, identifiable source. For a trademark to function effectively, it should not be confused with the competitor's products or services (Roberts, 2019). Thus, distinguishing products from their competitors is an important function of a trademark. It is not required that the consumer know the company that owns the mark in order for the mark to perform this function.

Exhibit 18.2 Summary of trademark types.

Type of Mark	Description	Examples
Trademark	Applied to commercial goods	Nike's Swoosh, Olympic "Rings"
Sound mark	Applied to a unique sound which identifies of the origins of products or services	ESPN's "DaDaDa DaDaDa" and Harlem Globetrotters's "Sweet Georgia Brown"
Color mark	Assigned to a color or combination of colors in a specific market sector where the public strongly associates the color or colors with a certain product or service.	University of Texas's "Burnt Orange," and University of North Carolina's "Carolina Blue"
Olfactory (Smell) mark	Applied to a smell is recognized as a unique identifier for a product or service. The smell must be distinct from the product (nonfunctional). Additionally, the trademark applicant must be able to visually represent the product's scent, which can be accomplished via oscillogram, spectrum, spectrogram and sonogram.	Smell of freshly cut grass as a trademark for tennis balls by Vennootschap onder Firma Senta Aromatic Marketing of Holland
Service mark	Applied to commercial services	NCAA, CoachUp, IMG
Collective mark	Applied to indicated membership in a group	National Football League Players Association
Certification mark	Given to goods or services meeting certain qualifications	Athletic Trainer Credential "ATC"
Trade dress	Refers to the overall impression of a package or product produced by the shape, size, color, and packaging	Hershey's Kiss
Trade name	The mark given to a business	Under Armour

2   **To protect consumers from confusion and deception**. The historical and primary purpose of the Trademark Act of 1946 (also known as the Lanham Act) is to serve as a consumer protection law. Thus, a critical function of a trademark relates to protecting consumers from being confused or deceived in the marketplace. Although businesses often perceive trademark law as protection for their marks and logos, protecting the trademark owner's rights is actually a secondary goal of federal trademark law. Interestingly, although consumer protection is the primary function of federal trademark law, consumers who are misled or confused cannot sue under the Lanham Act, nor is any government agency charged with enforcement of the Lanham Act. Rather, the Lanham Act is enforced by the trademark owners. Trademark owners have an affirmative duty to police their marks and to sue to enforce their rights against any misuse or unauthorized use.

3   **To designate a consistent level of quality of a product or service**. For example, the purchaser of a Mercedes automobile has a clear impression of a standard of quality associated with this automobile. However, the standard of quality does not have to be expensive or lavish for the trademark to function very effectively at creating a clear impression in the mind of the purchaser regarding the source of the product. For example, the Walmart brand also connotes a clear standard of quality, albeit an affordable, no-frills standard. The function of the Walmart trademark is no less effective than the Mercedes mark. In fact, Walmart's brand is consistently identified among the 20 most valuable brands in the world (Guttmann, 2020).

4   **To represent the goodwill of the owner or the owner's products and services**. **Goodwill** is "the primary intangible asset of a company, generally comprised of reputation, contact networks, intellectual property, and branding" (The Law Dictionary, 2019). An established trademark or service mark can be a symbol of goodwill, generating that "warm, fuzzy feeling" you get when you see a certain trademark that almost compels you to purchase that particular brand. For example, enormous amounts of goodwill are associated with the marks and images of Winnie the Pooh, such that Disney can put the Pooh family of marks on almost anything and make children and adults alike want to buy

it. The same can be said of the marks of many professional sports clubs or other well-known brands, such as those of the Green Bay Packers, the New York Yankees or Notre Dame. Goodwill is a key ingredient in a successful merchandising and licensing program for any sport organization.

5 **To signify a substantial advertising investment and business asset**. The functions identified here are not easily or automatically performed by a trademark. It may take a company many years and thousands, even millions, of dollars to create effective and meaningful trademarks. The law recognizes this investment and treats trademarks as property connected with the goodwill of the company, capable of being sold, assigned, divided, licensed, or destroyed as the owner of the property chooses. The owner of the mark has the exclusive rights to the mark. The value associated with goodwill derived from trademark properties adds to the value of a company for purposes of taxation, licensing, estate valuation, and damage awards (McCarthy, 2017). If a company were to be purchased by another company, the intangible trademark property rights would be just as valuable as tangible property rights such as inventory, buildings, and furniture.

Creation of Trademarks

Marketing managers must understand that not all trademarks are created equal. The United States Patent and Trademark Office (USPTO) gives more importance to the *distinctiveness* of a mark over *use* as a mark when evaluating protectability. It is fair to say that the marks and logos of Nike are stronger than those of Q4 Sports. Similarly, the marks and logos of ESPN (Entertainment and Sports Programming Network) are stronger and more distinctive than those of NESN (New England Sports Network). The value and effectiveness (*strength*) of a trademark or service mark relate to the *distinctiveness* of the mark and determine the level of protection that will be afforded the mark under the federal trademark laws. Marks are classified into various levels based upon their distinctiveness. The more distinctive the mark, the stronger it is considered for protection under the federal trademark laws.

Protection for Trademarks

Trademarks can either be inherently distinctive or possess acquired distinctiveness. A mark has high levels of inherent distinctiveness if the mark itself it unrelated to the goods or services such as Reebok for sports footwear. However, if a mark simply describes the nature or quality of the goods or services such as The Bowling Alley for a bowling center, it is not distinctive and less likely to function as a strong trademark, if registrable at all.

Inherently Distinctive Marks

Inherently distinctive marks are further classified as *fanciful*, *arbitrary*, or *suggestive*. We will explore each of these classifications of inherently distinctive marks.

Fanciful Marks

These marks are the most distinctive trademarks and are defined as coined words that have been invented for the sole purpose of functioning as a trademark. For example, Reebok, Pepsi, eBay, Kodak, and iPod are all fanciful marks because these words or names were created solely for the purpose of serving as a trademark. Fanciful marks are considered strong marks and are given a broad scope of protection (Linford, 2017; McCarthy, 2017).

Arbitrary Marks

These marks are also inherently distinctive. Arbitrary marks are defined as words, names, symbols, or devices that are in common linguistic use, but when used with the goods or services, neither suggest nor describe any ingredient, quality, or characteristic of the goods or services. These marks would not ordinarily be associated with the product or service but for the advertising and marketing efforts of the owner. For example, Fathead, Maker's Mark, Hershey's, Domino's and Polo are actual words or names in the English language, but they do not describe or suggest characteristics of giant sports posters, bourbon, chocolate, pizza, or a clothing line. Many acronyms may belong in this category as well, such as ESPN, MLB, and The Y (YMCA), even though the full names, Entertainment and Sports Programming Network, Major League Baseball, and Young Men's/Women's Christian Association, are generic or descriptive. Acronyms or initials which stem from a generic phrase can be protected under trademark law, if the acronym gained a meaning distinct, from the underlying phrase. The critical question is, "Can the acronym serve to identify a unique source, even if the underlying generic phrase does not?" (See Rocchi, 2018; and the discussion of descriptive marks below.)

Suggestive Marks

This is the last category of inherently distinctive marks. A **suggestive mark** subtly connotes something about the service or product but does not actually describe any specific ingredient, quality, or characteristic of the good or service. The mark uses terms that relate to some characteristic of the product or its use, but does not actually describe the product or its use. Thus, the consumer must use imagination to draw the association between the suggestive mark and the product or service. The more consumer imagination that is required to make the association between the mark and the actual product or service, the stronger the suggestive mark. For example, Nike, Puma, Trek, and Louisville Slugger could be considered suggestive of some ingredient, quality, or characteristic of the goods or services sold. Nike, a Greek goddess, was the personification of victory in many arenas, not the least of which was athletics. "Nike" as a trademark for an athletic shoe clearly benefits from the suggested connection between athletic victory and wearing Nike shoes. Similarly, a puma is the largest of the small cat species and is known for its agility and jumping ability, much like athletes. "Trek" suggests a long journey but does not directly say that journey must occur on a bicycle. "Louisville Slugger" does not actually describe a baseball bat, but with a little imagination a consumer can appreciate the connection between a person considered a strong hitter (a slugger) and, of course, the place where the item was made, Louisville. Other suggestive marks may include PlayStation, Jaguar, LIDS, Netflix, Gatorade, and Coppertone. Although a suggestive mark is not as distinctive or as strong as a fanciful or arbitrary mark, it is still inherently distinctive and may be registered as a trademark or service mark. The distinction between suggestive marks and the descriptive marks discussed next is not always clear. For example, Wet Ones was held to be suggestive when used in the context of a moist towelette, even though it describes an attribute of the product. But a Work-n-Play van to be used as a mobile office and recreational vehicle was held to be descriptive (Heath & Tanski, 2010). While the line may not always be clear, it is important since a suggestive mark is considered inherently distinctive and therefore subject to immediate protection, unlike the nondistinctive descriptive and generic marks discussed next.

Non-Distinctive Marks

Trademarks that are not inherently distinctive may either be able to possess or acquire the required distinctiveness and therefore obtain registration, or be deemed generic and not eligible for registration as a protected trademark. These classifications are descriptive and generic marks.

Descriptive Marks

These marks are defined as those marks that describe the intended purpose, function, or use of the goods; the size of the goods; the class of users of the goods; a desirable characteristic of the goods; or the end

Exhibit 18.3 Seven-factor test for establishing secondary meaning for trademarks.

1   Length and manner of the use of the mark or trade dress.
2   Volume of sales.
3   Amount and manner of advertising.
4   Nature of use of the mark or trade dress in newspapers and magazines.
5   Consumer survey evidence.
6   Direct consumer testimony.
7   The defendant's intent in copying the trade dress.

effect upon the user. Since descriptive marks are not inherently distinctive, they are not afforded any immediate protection under the federal trademark laws. Descriptive marks may eventually possess the required distinctiveness for trademark protection if they have acquired **secondary meaning**. This is called *acquired distinctiveness*.

Secondary meaning requires the mark to become associated in the mind of the public with a particular source or origin and is a way for descriptive marks to obtain protection that otherwise they would not be entitled to receive. To satisfy the secondary meaning requirement, the mark must denote to the consumer a single thing coming from a single source. Courts use a seven-factor test as shown in Exhibit 18.3 for establishing secondary meaning. Examples include Dick's Sporting Goods, *Sports Illustrated*, Pizza Hut, Gold's Gym, Hunting World, and National Football League. All of these particular marks describe a characteristic of the goods or the intended purpose of the goods. As such they are not very distinctive. However, since these marks have a clear designation of origin recognizable to the consumer, they have acquired secondary meaning and are able to receive full protection under federal trademark laws.

As mentioned earlier, abbreviations such as acronyms or initials (i.e., MLB, ESPN, or YMCA) may be protected under trademark law if the abbreviation serves to identify a unique source of goods or services. Abbreviations are generally thought to be a poor choice for a trademark because they lack distinctiveness. If, the party seeking trademark protection; however, can provide evidence the abbreviation has a meaning in the mind of the public that is distinct from the underlying generic words for which it stands, it can garner protection under trademark law. A word of caution, even if great care is given to establish, in an abbreviation, a meaning that is distinct from the underlying generic term, courts will not likely find the abbreviation to be protectable if it is widely used and recognized in a specific industry. In this circumstance, courts have reasoned the abbreviation, itself, is a generic term, incapable of acquiring true distinctiveness through secondary meaning (Thomas, 2009; see Gioconda, 2018, discussing university nicknames and trademarks).

Establishing secondary meaning can be expensive, requiring consumer surveys and expert testimony. Other types of descriptive marks that must acquire secondary meaning to gain trademark protection include geographic descriptions, colors, and personal names. See the *Board of Supervisors* Focus Case later in the chapter for an example of whether sport teams' color schemes and designs have acquired secondary meaning. Managers should carefully weigh these issues before making an investment into a descriptive mark that could later be determined to be too non-distinctive for trademark protection.

The issue of distinctiveness will typically come up either during the registration process or during an infringement action. In 2019, Tom Brady's TEB Capital Management Inc. ("TEB") filed intent-to-use trademark applications for "Tom Terrific" with respect to two classes of goods, T-shirts, shirts, and collectible trading cards, sports trading cards, posters, and printed photographs. On August 22, 2019, the USPTO refused the registration of "Tom Terrific" under Section 2(a) recognizing that the nickname is that of Tom Seaver. Because the record before the USPTO did not contained evidence of consent from Mr. Seaver to register the nickname or evidence of a connection between Tom Brady and Tom Seaver, the registration was refused. Further, the USPTO cited § 2(c) of the Trademark Act as an additional basis for refusing the registration request by Mr. Brady, as the mark consists of a name identifying a particular living person whose written consent was absent from the record. The USPTO, citing a Letter of Protest to the registration stating

Hall of Fame baseball player Tom Seaver is publicly known by the nickname "Tom Terrific," reasoned that the general public would reasonably assume a connection between Tom Seaver and the class of goods listed in the trademark application.

Generic Marks

The final class of non-distinctive marks, **generic marks**, are the common names of products or services and are considered part of the public domain. For example, words such as *gymnasium* and *arena* are common names for certain types of venues. Can you imagine Yankee Stadium trying to prevent every other stadium owner or operator from using the term *stadium* to identify their venue? Think of how many soccer teams refer to themselves as a "football club" or "FC." A basic principle of trademark law is, "no matter how much money and effort the user of a generic term has poured into promoting the sale of its merchandise and what success it has achieved in securing public identification, it cannot deprive competing manufacturers of the product of the right to call an article by its name" (*Abercrombie & Fitch Co. v. Hunting World, Inc.*, 1976). For example, an Internet company could not trademark *the web* and prohibit others from using that term. The Denver Broncos could not trademark the term *football team*, and so on. In contrast, the District Court for the Northern District of Texas rejected the defense of an Internet domain owner who operated www.marchmadness.com and asserted that the term *March Madness* was generic and incapable of trademark protection. The court ruled instead that the term was descriptive and had acquired secondary meaning (*March Madness Athletic Association, LLC v. Netfire, Inc.*, 2003). However, prior to summer 2020, the USPTO consistently held that a generic term combined with .com, is also generic and not eligible for trademark registration. The Supreme Court addressed this issue in *USPTO v. Booking.com* (2020) and rejected the USPTO's automatic designation of a generic.com term as generic. The Court held that whether a given "generic.com" term is generic for purposes of trademark registration depends on whether consumers in fact perceive the term as the name of a class of products (i.e., generic), or instead as a term capable of distinguishing the source among members of a class (i.e., distinctive). Booking.com therefore was permitted to register their .com name as a trademark.

The following Focus Case, *In re Seats, Inc.* (1985), presents the issue of distinctiveness raised during the trademark registration process.

In re Seats, Inc.

757 F.2d 274 (Fed. Cir. 1985)   **FOCUS CASE**

FACTS

Seats, Inc. appealed a decision of the Trademark Trial and Appeal Board (TTAB) in the USPTO refusing to register SEATS as a service mark for a computerized ticket reservation and issuing service. The TTAB rejected the registration application based on the grounds that the requested mark was descriptive. Seats, Inc. argued that the mark was suggestive and, even if descriptive, had acquired the necessary secondary meaning. The hearing examiner viewed the term *SEATS* as referring to a generic name of the end product of the applicant's services and ruled that it could never become distinctive with regard to those services. Seats, Inc. had customers statements asserting that the name did indicate the origin of the services. Nevertheless, the TTAB concluded that SEATS was so descriptive as to render it incapable of designating origin.

HOLDING

The Federal District Court reversed, concluding that the TTAB never discussed whether SEATS was so descriptive *of the services themselves* as to be incapable of ever becoming distinctive.

RATIONALE

The district court observed that the TTAB did not find that SEATS was generic, nor could it have so found. The term *seats* may be generic in relation to chairs, couches, or bleachers, but it clearly is not generic with regard to ticket reservation services. Seats, Inc. is not selling seats, but is a reservation service. It is equally clear that SEATS is not the common descriptive name of reservation services. Moreover, the issuance of registration would not deprive competitors from using such advertising phrases as "seats are available," "balcony seats – $12," and "reserve your seats through us." The court ruled that SEATS had acquired the necessary distinctiveness to be registered.

The previous case focused on whether the term SEATS was being used generically to describe chairs or bleachers which may have prevented it from being sufficiently distinctive to be registered as a trademark. The concept of genericness also arises related to well-recognized trademarks that may become generic over time. For example, many once-protected trademarks have become so identified with a particular product or service that all distinctiveness has been lost. Aspirin, Nylon, YoYo, Cornflakes, Escalator, Raisin Bran, Dry Ice, and Trampoline were all protected trademarks at one time and have since lost that protection to "**genericide**" (In, 2002).

In the case deeming ASPIRIN generic in the United States, the late Judge Learned Hand set forth a standard for determining whether a mark has become generic:

> The single question, as I view it, in all these cases, is merely one of fact: What do the buyers under-stand by the word for whose use the parties are contending? If they understand by it only the kind of goods sold, them [sic], I take it, it makes no difference whatever what efforts the plaintiff has made to get them to understand more. He has failed, and he cannot say that, when the defendant uses the word, he is taking away customers who wanted to deal with him, however closely disguised he may be allowed to keep his identity. (Bayer Co. v. United Drug Co., 1921)

Today, the courts use a two-part inquiry to determine if a term is generic:

- First, what is the genus of the goods or services at issues?
- Second, is the term sought to be registered understood by the relevant public primarily to refer to that genus of goods or services (Fechter & Slavin, 2011).

If the answer to the second inquiry is yes, the marks are likely to be considered generic and deemed to have lost any inherent or acquired distinctiveness.

Some companies have work diligently to police and protect their marks's distinctiveness to avoid gene-ricide. For example, when Band-Aid was faced with potential genercide, it struck back with a nationwide media blitz, "I am stuck on Band-Aids brands cause Band-Aid's stuck on me," to protect its brand. You can probably think of many more, such as Frisbee, Hi-Liter, ChapStick, Ping Pong, Xerox (Fechter & Slavin, 2011; Tobak, 2010). Google is another notable trademark that is used widely used in private and public communication, and therefore at the risk of falling into the generic category. A decision by the U.S. Court of Appeals for the Ninth Circuit in *Elliott v. Google, Inc.* provides some relief for those trademarks subjected to genericide. In *Elliott*, the plaintiff sought the cancelation of the GOOGLE trademark under the Lanham Act by arguing: (1) it is primarily understood and used as a verb to mean the act of searching the internet; and (2) verb use of the trademark constitutes generic use as a matter of law. In rejecting Elliott's two argu-ments, the court ruled: "if the relevant public primarily understands a mark as describing 'who' a particu-lar good or service is, or where it comes from, then the mark is still valid." The court further ruled that verb usage (as opposed to noun usage) does not automatically constitute generic use of the trademark. (See *Elliott v. Google Inc.*, 2017.) This decision strengthens a company's defense to an assertion of genericism by requiring the claim to establish the chief importance of the trademark to the relevant public is as the name for a particular type of good or service notwithstanding its source (Hughes, 2018).

Considering … Generic Marks

The Zamboni ice resurfacing machine has been identified by many as also facing genericide. Musicians have recorded songs about the Zamboni, and Zamboni races during intermission at hockey games are common. Such things have led to the Zamboni name becoming more of an identifier of the class of ice resurfacing machines, even though several other manufacturers of the machines are in the market, including Resurface and Ice Master. The Frank J. Zamboni Company, producers of the resurfacers, prominently displays its marks on its website and reminds visitors that Zamboni is a protected trademark. The website contains the following statement:

> The ZAMBONI brand name is a valuable trademark which we must diligently protect. Like Coke, Kleenex, and Jeep, it has close identity in the public mind with a particular type of commodity – but the public doesn't always remember that it is a particular brand. … A trademark is always an adjective. Never a noun. So when referring to ZAMBONI, please use it in the correct context. The machine is not "a Zamboni," it is a ZAMBONI ice resurfacing machine. (Zamboni, 2006)

Let's explore this issue with the following discussion questions.

Questions

- If a local minor league hockey team hosted a "let's zamboni tonight" promotional night, which gave miniature generic ice resurfacing machines away to the first 1,000 guests. Would Zamboni be able to establish a protected property interest for purposes of a trademark infringement action?
- What if any significance would relate to the team using zamboni as a verb, meaning "clear the ice" or "attend tonight's ice hockey match." How is the argument of genercide impacted if Zamboni is being use as a verb? Once you have reviewed the elements of trademark infringement, also consider whether this promotion would infringe on Zamboni's trademark.

Note how you would answer the questions and then check your responses using the Analysis & Discussion at the end of this chapter.

Protection of Trade Dress

The term **trade dress** is legally defined as the "total image and overall appearance" of a product, or the totality of the elements, and "may include features such as size, shape, color or color combinations, texture, graphics." *Two Pesos, Inc. v. Taco Cabana, Inc.*, (1992). Trade dress can include product packaging or product configurations that have sufficient distinctiveness to function as a trademark with federal trademark protection. Trade dress disputes occur frequently in the sport industry. In 2017, Puma filed a lawsuit against Forever 21 claiming trade dress infringement, among other claims. The suit alleges that Forever 21 offered for sale footwear whose design and shape are confusingly similar to Rihanna's Fenty line for Puma (The Fashion Law, 2018). Puma settled its trade dress infringement action against Forever 21, only to find itself as a defendant in a trade dress infringement suit brought by In-N-Out Burgers. In the complaint, In-N-Out Burgers alleged Puma launched its Cali-0 Drive Thru and California Drive Thru shoes using In-N-Out Burgers's federally registered palm tree mark, confusingly similar red and yellow design elements and insoles which bears an illustration of a burger (*In-N-Out Burgers v. Puma*, 2019).

Product packaging, as a form of trade dress, refers to the box, bottle or container holding or displaying the product. For example, the Coca-Cola bottle's contoured shape is protected trade dress. For trade dress to be sufficiently distinctive to acquire trademark protection it must: (1) create a separate commercial impression; and (2) and its use must be primarily to identify or distinguish the product or service.

Essentially, the trade dress or product packaging creates a visual impression that performs like a trademark. It essentially identifies a business's total image and overall appearance. Unique product packaging is inherently distinctive and can be entitle to immediate trademark protection.

Product configurations, as a form of trade dress, refers to the design or appearance of the product itself. The design or appearance of the product may entice consumer interest or appeal, but it is generally not inherently distinctive, thus for this type of trade dress to qualify for protection is must have acquired distinctiveness through *secondary meaning* (treated similarly to descriptive trademarks discussed earlier). For example, the product designs such as WEBER barbeque grills and LIFE SAVERS candies are protected trademarks and possess secondary meaning in the marketplace based on their unique and identifiable product configuration. The products themselves, rather than their packaging, are distinctive. But, compare to Buffalo Trace distillery's unsuccessful attempt to establish inherent distinctiveness in its trade dress for its packaging using a pair of buffalo together with white and gold lettering and the Buffalo Trace word mark on its label. The court held that, although a buffalo has no readily apparent connection to bourbon, that disconnect alone does not result in inherent distinctiveness, and thus Buffalo Trace had to prove secondary meaning. The court further held that Buffalo Trace could not prove acquired distinctiveness through secondary meaning either due to low brand recognition and comprises only one half of a percent of the whiskey market (*Sazerac Co. v. Fetzer Vineyards, Inc.*, 2017, aff'd, No. 17-16916 (9th Circ. 2019).

Our next Focus Case explores the required elements of a trade dress infringement claims and the factors used to establish secondary meaning for trade dress protection.

adidas America, Inc. v. Skechers USA, Inc.

890 F.3d 747 (9th Cir. 2018)	FOCUS CASE

FACTS

Adidas is a leading manufacturer of athletic apparel and footwear. Skechers is a footwear company that competes with adidas in the active footwear and apparel market. Skechers has grown to become the second largest footwear company in the United States, ahead of adidas and behind only Nike. The Stan Smith has become one of adidas's most successful shoes in terms of sales and influence since its release in the 1970s. The Stan Smith has received extensive media coverage and been featured in such print and online publications as *Time*, *Elle*, *InStyle*, and *Vogue*. adidas filed the present lawsuit against Skechers on September 14, 2015, alleging, among other things, that Skechers's Onix shoe infringes on and dilutes the unregistered trade dress of adidas's Stan Smith shoe. Adidas sought a preliminary injunction to prohibit the sale of Skechers's Onix shoe and the district court granted the injection. Sketchers appealed.

HOLDING

The district court did not abuse its discretion in granting the injunction and adidas was likely to succeed on the merits of the trade dress claim.

RATIONALE

"Trade dress protection applies to 'a combination of any elements in which a product is presented to a buyer,' including the shape and design of a product." *Art Attacks Ink, LLC v. MGA Entm't Inc.*, 581 F.3d 1138, 1145 (9th Cir. 2009) (quoting 1 J. Thomas McCarthy, *McCarthy on Trademarks and Unfair Competition* § 8:1 (4th ed. 2008)). To prove infringement of an unregistered trade dress, "a plaintiff must demonstrate that (1) the trade dress is nonfunctional, (2) the trade dress has acquired secondary meaning, and (3) there is a substantial likelihood of confusion between the plaintiff's and defendant's products." *Id.*

A trade dress has acquired secondary meaning when consumers associate the design features with a particular producer. "Secondary meaning and likelihood of buyer confusion are separate but related determinations … ." *Levi Strauss & Co. v. Blue Bell* (1980). Some of the relevant factors for determining secondary meaning include the exclusivity, manner, and length of use of the trade dress, the amount and manner of advertising, the amount of sales, and proof of intentional copying by the defendant.

The district court's finding that the Stan Smith has likely acquired secondary meaning is supported by ample evidence in the record. The evidence showed that adidas has used the Stan Smith trade dress exclusively since the early 1970s, expended considerable capital and human resources to promote the shoe, and reaped significant but difficult-to-quantify value from placing the Stan Smith with celebrities, musicians, athletes, and other "influencers" to drive consumer hype and recognition of the trade dress – which, in 2014, became adidas's top selling shoe of all time with the 40 millionth pair sold. Also indicative of secondary meaning is the considerable amount of unsolicited media coverage praising the Stan Smith's influence and iconic status as one of the most famous sneakers of all time.

Skechers's own conduct also supports the district court's finding. "[P]roof of copying strongly supports an inference of secondary meaning" (*Vision Sports, Inc. v. Melville Corp.*, 1989). Skechers placed metadata tags on its website that directed consumers who searched for "adidas Stan Smith" to the page for the Onix shoe. "Using another's trademark in one's metatags is much like posting a sign with another's trademark in front of one's store." We agree with the district court that "the only reason 'adidas Stan Smith' is a useful search term is that consumers associate the term with a distinctive and recognizable shoe made by adidas." Therefore, the district court did not err by finding the Stan Smith had acquired secondary meaning.

Functionality and Trade Dress

Functionality is a common defense in trademark infringement cases and is discussed in greater detail later in this chapter. With regard to trade dress, to establish that a product design feature is not functional, it may be shown that the design feature is merely ornamental, incidental, or an arbitrary aspect of the device, called *aesthetic functionality*. Maker's Mark won a lawsuit to prevent Jose Cuervo from including a dripping red wax seal on its tequila bottles. The U.S. Court of Appeals for the Sixth Circuit held that the red wax on each bottle of Maker's Mark bourbon was a valid trademark and rejected Cuervo's argument that the wax was merely aesthetically functional (*Maker's Mark Distillery, Inc. v. Diageo N. Am.*, 2012). The court held that when a feature such as color serves a significant function the question is whether exclusive use would interfere with legitimate competition. Because there is more than one way to seal a bottle with wax to make it appealing and red wax is not the only pleasing color of wax, Maker's Mark's exclusive use of red wax would not interfere with a competitive marketplace.

Protection of Color as a Trademark

The U.S. Supreme Court has held that color can also serve as a trademark (*Qualitex Co. v. Jacobson Products*, 1995; see also *NFL Properties, Inc. v. Wichita Falls Sportswear, Inc.*, 1982), so long as it possesses the basic legal requirements of a trademark: distinctiveness, source identification, and nonfunctionality. Generally, for color to be eligible for trademark protection it must have acquired secondary meaning, the same requirement discussed earlier for descriptive trademarks. In *Qualitex*, the Supreme Court confirmed that the scope of things that can be protected as trademarks is relatively broad, including letters, numbers, two-dimensional designs, sounds, scents, and colors. The following Focus Case further explores whether sport teams's color schemes and designs have acquired secondary meaning.

Board of Supervisors of LSU v. Smack Apparel Company

FACTS

Louisiana State University (LSU), the University of Oklahoma (OU), the Ohio State University (OSU), and the University of Southern California (USC) (i.e., "university plaintiffs"), along with their licensing agent, Collegiate Licensing Company (CLC), sued Smack Apparel Company for trademark infringement under the Lanham Act. The university plaintiffs owned trademark registrations for their names and commonly used initials; however, they did not have registered trademarks in the color schemes. Additionally, more than a century ago, each university adopted a particular color combination as its school colors (LSU, purple and gold; OU, crimson and cream; OSU, scarlet and gray; USC, cardinal red and gold); since then, they have spent millions of dollars in marketing and promoting items bearing their initials and school colors.

The university plaintiffs alleged each of their color combinations functions a source-identifier, particularly when used with additional indicia and that Smack infringed upon their trademarks by selling T-shirts bearing the distinctive colors used by the respective universities, along with other symbols that identify the universities, such as:

- OU: "Bourbon Street or Bust" (with the ou in Bourbon in a different font); these shirts refer to the 2004 Sugar Bowl contest in New Orleans between OU and LSU.
- LSU: "Beat Oklahoma and Bring It Back to the Bayou!" (front), and "2003 College Football National Championship" (back); these shirts also refer to the 2004 Sugar Bowl contest in New Orleans.
- OSU: "Got Seven?" (front), "We do! 7 Time National Champs," with a depiction of the state of Ohio and a marker noting Columbus (back).
- USC: "Got Eight?" (front), "We Do! Home of the 8 Time National Champions!" and depiction of the state of California with a star marked "SoCal" (back).

HOLDING

The court of appeals upheld the district court's granting of summary judgment for the universities finding the universities had established secondary meaning in their particular color schemes, logos, and designs on shirts referencing the universities or their accomplishments.

RATIONALE

The plaintiffs must demonstrate, ownership in a legally protectable mark among other things to prevail in an infringement case. The Lanham Act states that a trademark may be "any word, name, symbol, or device, or any combination thereof" used or intended to be used "to identify and distinguish" one's goods from another's goods and to indicate the source of the goods. The unregistered marks at issue are described by plaintiffs as "color schemes in the context of merchandise that makes reference to the Plaintiff Universities or their accomplishments and is directed to their fans and other interested consumers." Whether or not an unregistered mark will be protected will depend upon the same approach to make a mark eligible for registration under the Lanham Act. Are the marks classified as generic, descriptive, suggestive, arbitrary or fanciful? The plaintiffs and the district court view the marks as descriptive and, therefore, require secondary meaning to be protected under the Lanham Act.

The court of appeals applied the seven-factor test for establishing secondary meaning (shown in Exhibit 18.3). In doing so, the circuit court found that the universities had used their color schemes for a long period of time (since the late 1800s), and they had marketed scores of items bearing their color schemes, logos, and designs, resulting in sales exceeding tens of millions of dollars. The universities also advertised items with the school colors in almost every conceivable manner and even used the colors to refer to themselves. The defendant admitted it had used the plaintiffs's color schemes on its shirts to reference plaintiff universities in the minds of the consumer. Thus, balancing the factors for establishing secondary meaning the circuit court held that the university plaintiffs's color schemes, logos, and designs and other identifying indicia on college-sport themed merchandise have achieved secondary meaning.

Protection of Trade Names

A **trade name** is "any name used by a person to identify his or her business or vocation" (15 U.S.C. § 1127). Normally, a trade name does not identify a specific product or service but rather the underlying business entity, while a trademark is the logo or other indicia that appears on the product or on its packaging and a service mark appears on advertising for the services. A trade name will not be considered a trademark or service mark unless it is actually used on the products or used to identify the service. If a business uses its trade name to identify the source of specific products or services produced by the business, then the name can be considered a trademark or service mark. For example, Lululemon Athletica Canada, Inc. uses the trade name LULULEMON as a trademark on its athletic apparel. The trademark, LULULEMON, must be registered separate from the trade name.

It is important to note that many states require the registration of a trade name for purposes of doing business in that state. The registered trade name will be used to identify those doing business in the state, the products or services offered, and for tax purposes. Typically, registering your trade name does not protect you from others using the same or similar name in their business. Thus, sport managers should consult their state's laws for the trade name registration rules, and trade names should be registered as trade names even if they are not intended to be trademarked. Remember, trade name and trademarks serve different functions, and registration of the former is at the state level and registration of the latter, though not required, occurs at the federal level.

Registration of Marks

Once an individual or business has created a mark and is preparing to use the mark in commerce, it must decide whether to seek federal trademark registration or to rely on common law and state law protections. The law governing trademark registration at the federal level is found in the Trademark Act of 1946 (Lanham Act), 15 U.S.C. §§ 1051–1127. The USPTO is responsible for processing registration applications. The USPTO governs requests to register trademarks, service marks, collective marks, trade dress, and trade names.

Registration with the USPTO (federal registration) provides substantial benefits and protections and the most far-reaching benefits since it would provide protection throughout the nation and internationally for the mark. The USPTO makes an initial determination as to the registrability of a mark (often based on the criteria discussed above regarding the distinctiveness of the mark). For example, on August 8, 2019, The Ohio State University filed a trademark application with the USPTO for the word mark, "THE" to be used in connection with clothing, specifically T-shirts, baseball cap, and hats (Wolly, 2019). The USPTO issued an initial denial of OSU's application stating the mark was merely a decorative or ornamental feature of applicant's clothing and did not function as a trademark to indicate the source of the clothing or distinguish it from others. However, this finding by the USPTO does not indicate that OSU could never gain protection for the word, only that its planned use does not qualify. Thus, THE would need to become part of the marketing of OSU merchandise and must be on the tag or label of the merchandise to potentially be registrable. OSU can reapply in the future if it feels it can meet these criteria (Daniels, 2019).

In addition to granting registration, the USPTO resolves disputes related to registration. For example, if a mark is refused registration or if registration is challenged by another trademark holder, the TTAB (the part of the USPTO that receives and decides disputes) will hear the dispute. For example, the Denver Broncos filed for trademark registration for the phrase "ORANGE CRUSH" in 2015 in reference to the moniker often associated with the team's defense. This application was opposed by Dr. Pepper Snapple Group which owns the Crush orange soda brand (Rovell, 2016). Denver ultimately abandoned their trademark registration on August 8, 2016. The University of South Carolina also attempted to register an USC trademark, but was denied registration when the University of Southern California opposed the registration (Kobi, 2010). University of South Carolina finally gave up trying to use the USC or SC abbreviations and redesigned a new acronym, UofSC, in 2019 (Daprile, 2019).

Applications for federal registration are typically one of two types: a *use application*, where the mark is already being used in commerce, or an *intent to use application*, used when the applicant is not yet using the mark in commerce but has a bona fide intention to use it. Normally, if one is making a significant investment in a company name and logos, it is worthwhile to seek federal trademark registration. Registration can be done without the assistance of counsel; however, it can also be a complicated and technical process. An IP attorney can be very useful in searching for potentially conflicting marks and navigating the USPTO registration procedures. Searching for conflicting marks prior to applying for registration is not required, but it is highly advisable since the initial application fee of $225–$400 per class of goods is nonrefundable. If a conflicting mark exists, the registration fee will not be refunded and the application will likely be denied. The USPTO does not conduct searches for the public, but it does provide a public library of marks and a searchable electronic database (USPTO, 2019). If a federal trademark is obtained, the designation ® should always accompany the use of the mark. If federal trademark registration is either not sought or not yet obtained, then the designations ™ and ℠ should be used to provide notice that you are claiming the mark as a trademark and are asserting a property interest in it.

Competitive Advantage Strategies

Brand Protection Through Trademark Law

Register your trademarks. Registration gives you exclusive rights to use your logo. Federal registration provides the most extensive protections. You should not delay in registration either — as soon as you have identified your brand marks or logos, you should register them.

- Avoid becoming generic. Never use your brand as a noun or verb. The brand name and protected trademarks should always be an adjective identifying the products or services related to them.
- Actively enforce and protect your marks. Be cognizant of counterfeit products or other companies using similar marks or logos and notify any non-consensual users that they are infringing on your protected marks.
- Build goodwill. Understanding consumer expectations and building brand recognition is essential for a business success and creating goodwill. Be prepared to make mistakes and be able to respond quickly to preserve positive brand recognition.
- Use your marks consistently. A registered trademark must be used exactly as it has been represented to the USPTO. When you affix it or reproduce it you should avoid changing any aspect of its appearance, size, shape. If it is placed on your products it should be placed consistently in the same place, size, and shape.

Trademark Infringement

The unauthorized use of another's mark is called *infringement*. **Trademark infringement** occurs when a person uses in commerce any *"reproduction, counterfeit, copy, or colorable imitation of a registered mark* in connection with the sale, offering for sale, distribution, or advertising of any goods or services on or in connection with which such use is *likely to cause confusion*, or to cause mistake, or to deceive" without consent of the registrant (15 U.S.C. § 1114(1)(a)). The key elements of a trademark infringement claim are summarized in Exhibit 18.4.

As mentioned earlier, the federal trademark laws are enforced by the trademark owners. The Lanham Act provides for both injunctions and damages as remedies for infringement. In a typical infringement action, the trademark owner is trying to prevent the defendant (usually a direct competitor) from using identical or similar marks that would cause consumers to purchase the defendant's good or services instead of those of the actual trademark owner. For example, on November 1, 2018, the Atlanta Braves, sued Braves Taxi for trademark infringement, alleging that "Defendants are intentionally freeriding on the success and popularity of the Atlanta Braves by brazenly copying the Atlanta Braves' trademarks in an effort to dupe unwitting fans or other Atlantans into believing the taxi company is owned by, associated or affiliated with or sponsored or endorsed by the Atlanta Braves." The complaint further avers that "Defendants are using identical and confusingly similar iterations of the Atlanta Braves' community outreach vehicles," including the Atlanta Braves logo with a tomahawk. Defendant Braves Taxi filed an appeal in this case in April 2019. (See *Atlanta National League Baseball Club, LLC v. Braves Taxi, LLC*, 2018.)

Proving Trademark Infringement

The owner of a mark has the burden to prove that the mark is being infringed upon. Federal registration helps prove the first two elements of a claim (see Exhibit 18.4). If a mark is registered, then the owner can demonstrate that he or she is the only authorized user, and a valid registration is evidence of a protectable property interest. At this point, the owner need only prove that the unauthorized use is likely to confuse consumers. The courts have identified a series of factors to consider in determining **likelihood of confusion**. No one factor is more important than the others and not every factor must be shown to establish likelihood of confusion (*UGAA v. Laite*, 1985). These factors, first developed in the case of *Polaroid Corp. v. Polaroid, Inc.* (1963), have become known as the Polaroid test. Other courts have added to or modified the factors over the years, and most courts today use the eight factors presented in Exhibit 18.5, or some combination of the factors, to determine whether likelihood of confusion has been proven.

Meta tags Infringement

Information Technology (IT), involves the storing, retrieving and sending of information across telecommunications platforms, including mobile and computers. IT is driving the expansion of the service sector into the goods sector, deepening customer relationships, as marketing becomes more "individual customer centered and relationship driven" (Rust & Huang, 2014, p. 207). As brands seek every advantage in engaging with the consumer in a fragmented marketplace, some companies have turned to using a competitor's trademark as a meta tags on their website. A meta tag is a word or short phrase embedded in the source code of a website, invisible on the actual webpage. Search engines, like Google and Bing,

---

Exhibit 18.4 Key elements of a trademark infringement claim.

1   Protectable property right in trademark (registered mark)
2   Plaintiff owns the trademark and
3   Defendant used trademark without consent in a manner which is *likely to cause confusion*, mistake or deceive ordinary consumers.

Exhibit 18.5 Likelihood of confusion factors.

Factor	Description
1 Strength/weakness of the mark	How distinctive is it (fanciful, arbitrary, suggestive, descriptive with secondary meaning or generic)?
2 Similarity between the marks	Appearance, size, shape, impression, sound and meaning of the mark.
3 Similarity of the products or service	Are the class of goods related or similar, such as T-shirts and golf shirts, or seemingly dissimilar, such as bicycles and race cars?
4 Marketing/distribution channels	Is the defendant in the same marketing or distribution channel? If not, is it likely that the defendant will enter the market that the plaintiff is in or may enter in the near future.
5 Defendant's intention in adopting the mark	To what extent is the defendant trying to capitalize on consumer recognition of the plaintiff's marks?
6 Evidence of actual consumer confusion	To what extent are consumers actually confused by the defendant's use of the similar marks? This is often shown with consumer surveys and market research.
7 Sophistication of the consumer	To what extent can buyers protect themselves from being confused by the defendant's marks? More sophisticated buyers are presumed to be less likely to be misled, and children are often considered unsophisticated and unlikely to distinguish between similar marks.
8 Quality of Defendant's product	The lesser the quality of the defendant's product, the more harm is likely from consumer confusion.

use meta tags, as a way to locating webpages relevant to the search request. If a Company X uses the trademark of a competitor in its meta tags, it diverts searches intended for the competitor's website to Company X's website. The court in Brookfield Communications v. West Coast Entertainment (1999) described this practice as tantamount to one shop owner placing a sign with the trademark of a competitor in front if its shop. Is this meta tag practice a form of trademark infringement?

A plaintiff typically alleges meta tag infringement under the initial interest confusion doctrine. Initial interest confusion occurs when the customer is lead to a product or service, notwithstanding the fact that the customer becomes fully aware of the actual source of the products or services before the purchase transaction is finalized. Initial interest confusion alone may not be enough to demonstrate the likelihood of confusion requirement in trademark infringement claims. The Ninth Circuit in Brookfield Communication v. West Coast Entertainment (1999) found actual consumer confusion; however, did not find the defendant committed trademark infringement on the initial interest confusion doctrine alone. The court in the Southern District of New York explained that a pure bait-and-switch scam, is actionable under the initial interest confusion doctrine; however, if the use of the competitor's trademark is for comparison purposes only, it does not constitute trademark infringement under the Lanham Act (Alzheimer's Disease & Related Disorders Ass'n, Inc. v. Alzheimer's Found. of Am., Inc., 2018). Even if the trademark of a competitor is used in the meta tags of another company's website, without other actions which likely cause consumer confusion, the claim will not be actionable.

Besides giving rise to infringement cases, meta tags have been used by courts as evidence of intent to cause consumer confusion. Recall our previous Focus Case, adidas v. Skechers (2018), where the court viewed Skechers use of "adidas Stan Smith" meta tag on their website as "evidence [which] supports an inference that Skechers intended [emphasis added] to confuse consumers; it not only created a nearly identical shoe [Onix] to the Stan Smith, but then used meta data tags to direct consumers who searched for "'adidas stan smith' to the Onix web page" belonging to Sketchers. Whether meta tag infringement is a viable claim or evidence of intent to cause consumer confusion is an unsettled area of the law.

Defenses to Trademark Infringement

In response to a trademark infringement claim, the defendant may raise a number of defenses. These defenses include fair use, parody, abandonment, and functionality.

Fair Use

Trademark law generally is used to stop others from using a protected trademark, however, in some circumstances one is permitted to use a protected mark and not infringe upon those trademark rights based on the concept of "**fair use**." In general, there are two types of fair use: descriptive fair use and nominative fair use.

Descriptive fair use permits use of another's trademark to describe the user's products or services, rather than as a trademark to indicate the source of the products or services. This usually is appropriate where the trademark concerned has a descriptive meaning in addition to its secondary meaning as a trademark such as when a protected trademark includes ordinary words or phrases.

Nominative fair use permits use of another's trademark to refer to the trademark owner's actual goods and services associated with the mark. Nominative fair use generally applies to comparative advertising, parody, and noncommercial use of trademarks in academic articles, and media reports. Nominative fair use generally is permissible as long as (1) the product or service in question is not readily identifiable without use of the trademark, (2) only so much of the mark as is reasonably necessary to identify the product or service is used and (3) use of the mark does not suggest sponsorship or endorsement by the trademark owner. For example, one could refer to "the professional football team from Baltimore," but it is simpler and more understandable to say the Baltimore Ravens. Nominative fair use is illustrated in a case involving the Boston Marathon. The Boston Athletic Association (BAA) first organized the Boston Marathon in 1897, and had spent an enormous amount money over the years promoting the event. The BAA registered the words "Boston Marathon" as a trademark in connection with the event and licenses the mark for a fee. A local television station, who did not pay a licensing fee to air the event, broadcasted the words "Boston Marathon" in connection with the event. By doing so, BAA alleges that the television station violated federal trademark law. The First Circuit court of appeals held that television stations could use the term "Boston Marathon" to describe the event, whether or not they paid a licensing fee and do so does not constitute trademark infringement. This decision paved the way for the Ninth Circuit's articulation of the nominative fair use doctrine. It should be noted that there is a split among circuit courts regarding the nominal use analysis. See *Boston Athletic Association v. Velocity LLC*, (2015). Our next Focus Case below will explore the descriptive fair use defense.

SportFuel, Inc. v. PepsiCo, Inc. (The Gatorade Company)

932 F.3 589 (7th Cir. 2019)   **FOCUS** CASE

FACTS

SportFuel, a Chicago-based sports nutrition and wellness consulting firm who count professional athletes and amateur athletes as their clients. In addition to personalized nutrition consulting, SportFuel sells SportFuel-branded dietary supplements. The business holds two registered trademarks for "SportFuel, one for "food nutrition consultation, nutrition counseling, and providing information about dietary supplements and nutrition," which after several years of use became incontestable. In 2015, SportFuel also registered a trademark for "goods and services related to dietary supplements and sport drinks enhanced with vitamins." Gatorade, created in 1965, is a well-known sports drink, and is the official sports drink of the NBA, PGA, MLB, MLS, and many other professional and collegiate organizations. In 2016, Gatorade made efforts to rebrand itself. That effort included registering the trademark "Gatorade The Sports Fuel Company." Notwithstanding the fact that Gatorade filed its registration after the Patent and Trademark Office (PTO) advised Gatorade that the phrase was merely descriptive of its products, SportFuel filed suit in August of 2016. SportFuel alleged trademark infringement. Gatorade raised a fair use defense, stating that it used the words "Sports Fuel" in a descriptive manner.

HOLDING

The court of appeals found that Gatorade's slogan was a fair use protected by the Lanham Act.

RATIONALE

The fair use defense is an affirmative defense, which can be used against incontestable trademarks like SportFuel's trademark. This defense permits entities to use otherwise trademarked language in a descriptive manner if the defendant can show that: (1) it did not use "Sports Fuel" as a trademark; (2) the use is descriptive of its goods; and (3) it used the mark fairly and in good faith. As to the first prong of the fair use defense, the court of appeals found that Gatorade did not use "Sport Fuel" as a trademark, because it "primarily features the slogan on in-store displays and other advertisements -appearing almost as subtitle to the house mark." The court of appeals also recognized that during the application process for its slogan, the PTO advised Gatorade that it viewed "Sports Fuel" as descriptive and not appropriate for trademark use. The panel determined that notwithstanding Gatorade's use of the "TM" symbol with their slogan, Gatorade never employed the term "Sports Fuel" as a trademark in its slogan. As to the second prong of the fair use defense, the circuit court concluded from the evidence that the term "Sports Fuel" in the slogan "clearly describes the category of goods that Gatorade produces." Therefore, the panel concluded Gatorade's slogan used "Sports Fuel" in a descriptive sense. Finally, in judging whether the defendant used the "plaintiff's mark fairly and in good faith" the panel looked at whether Gatorade's purpose in using their slogan was subjective. The court of appeals determined that Gatorade produced sufficient evidence to show that it descriptively used the term "Sports Fuel" in its slogan fairly and in good faith and further found that SportFuel failed to provide sufficient evidence of Gatorade's bad faith.

Parody

Well-known companies can expect to be the object of parody and ridicule. Oftentimes, highly recognizable marks and logos are an attractive target. When this happens, it is not uncommon for identical or substantially similar elements of the protected intellectual property to be used or incorporated into a third party's merchandise or advertising materials. It may be undisputed that the third party is using protected marks, but the third party will argue that such use is permitted under the fair use doctrine and/or commercial speech protections of the First Amendment. Fake Twitter and Facebook accounts or parody news broadcasts are commonplace among athletes, teams, and owners. Many organizations may threaten to file lawsuits for parodies and are sometimes criticized for being a trademark bully (Grinvald, 2015; Manta, 2012), but most are better advised to recognize that ridicule and satire are often associated with high-profile companies and celebrities. The Washington Redskins suggested they would pursue legal action in response to a series of weekly parodies on a Washington sports talk radio station featuring a mock play-by-play of a game and ridicule over parking delays and high ticket costs. Despite the team spokesman's statements that the routines were malicious enough to justify legal action, it is unlikely such an action would succeed and it often simply prolongs the negative attention (Farhi, 2013; McGeveran, 2015). The nature of the use (i.e., the parody) is considered as each likelihood of confusion factor is analyzed by the court. If one employs a successful parody, the customer is not confused, but amused. The keystone of parody is imitation, but it must convey two simultaneous — and contradictory — messages: that it is the original, yet also that it is not the original but a parody instead. To the extent that it does only the former but not the latter, it is not only a poor parody but also vulnerable as trademark infringement, since the customer will be confused.

Abandonment

Another defense to trademark infringement is abandonment. Abandonment occurs when an owner of a mark discontinues its use and does not intend to resume use within a reasonable amount of time. Typically, nonuse of a mark for three consecutive years is considered evidence of abandonment. For sport organizations, another significant form of abandonment is excessive licensing and lack of supervision. If a sport organization fails to develop adequate safeguards in its licensing programs to supervise the use of its marks and to challenge unauthorized uses of its marks, the defendant could argue that the owner abandoned the mark and lost its trademark protection.

Two seminal cases reaching conflicting results are *Major League Baseball Properties, Inc. v. Sed Olet Denarius, Ltd., d/b/a, The Brooklyn Dodger Sports Bar & Restaurant* (1993) and *Indianapolis Colts, Inc. v. Metropolitan Baltimore Football Club Ltd. Partnership* (1994). In the *Brooklyn Dodger* case, a district court in New York held that MLB had abandoned its trademark rights in the Brooklyn Dodgers by its nonuse for more than 20 years. The district court noted that in order for a trademark to remain active, it must actually be used. And because there was no likelihood that the Brooklyn Dodger restaurant would be confused with the Los Angeles Dodgers baseball club, the trademark was canceled. The opposite result was reached in *Indianapolis Colt v. Metropolitan Baltimore Football Club* (1994), where the Court of Appeals enjoined a Canadian Football League franchise in Baltimore from using the name Baltimore CFL Colts, even though the NFL Baltimore Colts had left town nine years earlier. The court held use of the name Colts would likely mislead consumers into believing the Baltimore CFL team was in some way associated with the Indianapolis franchise of the NFL. The mere fact that the new Baltimore team is likely to conjure associations with the old Baltimore Colts was enough to justify the Seventh Circuit's decision.

Functionality

Functionality is a defense to trademark infringement claims. We first presented the functionality concept related to whether trade dress and color could be protected trademarks. The functionality defense prevents product designs or features that have a useful purpose from being monopolized under trademark law (LaLonde, 2011). The Supreme Court has recognized two types of functionality: utilitarian functionality and aesthetic functionality (*TrafFix Devices v. Marketing Displays*, 2001). *Utilitarian functionality* relates to whether a product feature is essential to the product's purpose or use, or affects the cost or quality of the product. For example, AstroTurf is usually green because it replaces and is supposed to look like grass; therefore, green AstroTurf would be functional and not protectable as a trademark (Knaug, 2010). Similarly, the Ninth Circuit found in *Talking Rain Beverage Co. v. South Beach Beverage Co.* (2003) that a water bottle meant for use by cyclists was functional because its shape was designed to fit well in bicycle water holders and to be easy to hold while cycling; therefore, it was not protectable under trademark law.

Aesthetic functionality applies to those features that make a product visually appealing but are not source identifying. Recall the *Smack Apparel* case. In that case, Smack Apparel asserted that university color schemes were aesthetically functional and therefore not protectable as trademarks. The Fifth Circuit found that the university color schemes were not aesthetically functional because their sole purpose was to signify the universities and their reputations, thus properly serving as source identifier (*Board of Supervisors v. Smack Apparel*, 2008). Aesthetic functionality also would apply to features without which another company cannot fairly compete — in such cases the question becomes: If a company were given a monopoly on this feature, would other companies be able to fairly and effectively compete for consumers? This was the question raised in *Maker's Mark Distillery v. Diageo N. Am.* (2010). The Kentucky federal district court ruled that competitors were not disadvantaged by recognizing Maker's Mark's distinctive red wax design on bourbon bottles as a trademark because there are other ways to signify reputation and to make a bottle look artisanal other than red dripping wax. In contrast, though, the Eleventh Circuit held that Dippin' Dots colored ice cream dots were functional because the color indicated the different flavors of ice cream (*Dippin' Dots, Inc. v. Frosty Bits Distribution*, 2004). Imagine if an ice cream company could prevent its competitors from making brown chocolate ice cream or pink strawberry ice cream. The functionality defense helps to provide the balance between what trademark law protects and those product design and artistic features that are better protected by patent or copyright laws (Rudensky, 2013). Our next Focus Case explore utilitarian functionality claims in a trademark registration case.

Robert M. Lyden v. adidas America, Inc. et al.

184 F. Supp. 3d 962 (2016)   **FOCUS** CASE

FACTS

Plaintiff Robert Lyden ("Lyden") was granted Trademark Registration No. 3,629,011 for footwear with "a spring element in the rearfoot area of the footwear" and Trademark Registration No. 3,633,365 for "a heel counter and spring element in the rearfoot area of the footwear," hereinafter collectively referred to as "Springshoe Marks." Lyden avers he sold and promoted footwear under these trademarks for more than ten years. Over the course of the ten-year period, Lyden also offered to license or sell the Springshoe Marks to companies in the footwear industry, including adidas, and as recently as 2014. Lyden alleges that adidas was familiar with the Springshoe Marks and "intentionally adopted and used confusingly similar imitations of the Springshoe Marks." Defendants adidas America, Inc et al ("adidas") argue that Lyden's trademarks are functional and thus incapable of being protected by trademark law.

HOLDING

The court found that Lyden's trademarks to be functional and cannot be protected by trademark law.

RATIONALE

The court recognized that "[t]he physical details and design of a product may be protected under the trademark laws only if they are nonfunctional[.]" Functionality is a question of fact and it is the plaintiff who bears the burden of proof in an infringement claim. The court used four factors to determine if the features of the Springshoe Marks were functional: (1) whether the design yields a utilitarian advantage; (2) whether alternative designs are available; (3) whether advertising touts the utilitarian advantages of the design; and (4) whether the particular design results from a comparatively simple or inexpensive method of manufacture.

In applying the factors to determine functionality, the court reasoned that Lyden's "spring and heel counter are the subject of both his marks and his patents," which provide strong evidence of functionality. Further, the language Lyden used in the patent registrations related to the Springshoe Marks, further support the finding of functionality, that is, "the article of footwear includes a spring element *which can provide improved cushioning, stability, running economy, and a long service life*" and "selectively removable and replaceable" parts of the heel indicate a utilitarian benefit. The court reasoned that the existence of alterative designs would not be dispositive in this case, since there was strong evidence of functionality provided by Lyden's own language in the patent registrations related to the Springshoe Marks. As to the third factor, the court concluded that Lyden's interviews regarding the Springshoe Marks wherein he describes the spring as serving as a heel and shock absorber, demonstrates functionality. The method of production is the final factor for the court to consider and weigh. Lyden offered little evidence that the Springshoe Mark "design achieves economies in manufacture or use." The court concluded that Lyden failed to meet his burden of proof on the element of functionality.

Cancelation of Marks

The USPTO has the authority to cancel a trademark. Section 2(a) of the Lanham Act, enacted in 1946, "enumerates two distinct clauses: (1) the immoral, deceptive, or scandalous clause; and (2) the disparagement clause" (Davis, 2015, p. 3). In 1992, a nearly 30-year controversy began when a group of Native Americans requested cancelation of the Washington Redskins trademarks. Suzan Harjo, on behalf of herself and six other Native Americans, sued the owners of the Washington Redskins football team, Pro-Football, Inc., contending that the Redskins's name and marks were disparaging to Native Americans and bring Native Americans into contempt or disrepute. The Trademark Trial and Appeal Board found that the marks were disparaging to Native Americans and recommended cancelation. Pro-Football, Inc. appealed to the U.S. District Court. The district court judge reversed the TTAB finding and ruled that the finding of disparagement was not supported by the evidence and applying to standard for latches determine the Plaintiffs waited too long to seek cancelation of the mark.

The district judge specifically stated that "this opinion should not be read as making any statement on the appropriateness of Native American imagery for team names" (*Pro-Football, Inc. v. Harjo*, 2003, p. 144). Following unsuccessful subsequent appeals by the Harjo plaintiffs, the Washington Redskins were ultimately able to retain the trademark. However, in 2013 a new group of plaintiffs in *Blackhorse v. Pro-Football* (2014) brought a challenge to the Trademark Trial and Appeal Board based on the Redskins's mark. The TTAB canceled the Pro-Football's trademarks. Pro-football appealed to the U.S. District Court for the Eastern District of Virginia, where Judge Gerald Bruce Lee 2015 decision found the team name to be disparaging. Pro-Football appealed this decision to the Fourth Circuit in Richmond, Virginia, where the case was stayed pending the outcome of *Matal v. Tam*.

In *Matal v. Tam* (2017), an Asian-American band sought a federal trademark for the band name, THE SLANTS. The USPTO found the band name to be disparaging to a substantial composite of Asian Americans. The band, asserting their first amendment rights, appealed the decision and the case rose to the Supreme Court of the United States. In June of 2017, the Supreme Court, in a unanimous decision, struck down the disparagement provision of the Lanham Act as an unconstitutional viewpoint-based restraint under the First Amendment. Following the decision in the *Matal v. Tam* case, the U.S. Court of Appeal for the Fourth Circuit vacated the decision, which canceled Pro-Football's federal trademark registrations, ending a 27-year legal battle over its name and moniker (Brady, 2018; Conrad, 2018). Similarly, in June of 2019, following the holding in *Matal v. Tam*, the Supreme Court also struck down the immoral, deceptive, and scandalous provisions of the Lanham Act in *Inacu v. Brunetti* (2019), reversing the USPTO's refusal to register the word "FUCT" for a clothing brand. The Court concluded the immoral or scandalous restraints were also viewpoint-based and therefore violated the First Amendment.

Trademark Dilution and Famous Marks

The **trademark dilution** is similar to trademark infringement, but it occurs when the defendant is not a direct competitor and when the defendant's use of a similar mark either tarnishes the reputation of the plaintiff's mark or blurs the ability of the plaintiff's mark to distinguish the plaintiff's goods and services from those of the defendant. The Lanham Act prohibits trademark dilution. On January 16, 1996, the Federal Trademark Dilution Act of 1995 (Trademark Dilution Act; FTDA) became effective (Federal Trademark Dilution Act, 1996). Dilution was not previously recognized as a federal cause of action even though many states provided a state law dilution cause of action. The underlying purpose of establishing a claim for dilution was to protect the value of the trademark to the trademark holder (Oswald, 1999).

The essence of a dilution claim is not that consumers are confused between the two marks, but rather that the defendant's use *taints, damages, lessens, or weakens the exclusive association that the plaintiff has created between its mark and its products or services*. Thus, the value of the mark is diminished or diluted.

The Trademark Dilution Act defines dilution as "the *lessening of the capacity of a famous mark* to identify and distinguish goods or services, *regardless of* the presence or absence of (1) *competition* between the owner of the

Exhibit 18.6 Factors used by courts to determine whether a trademark is famous.

1 The duration, extent, and geographic reach of advertising and publicity of the mark, whether advertised or publicized by the owner or third parties.
2 The amount, volume, and geographic extent of sales of goods or services offered under the mark.
3 The extent of actual recognition of the mark.
4 Whether the mark is registered.

famous mark and other parties; or (2) the *likelihood of confusion*, mistake or deception" (Trademark Dilution Act of 1995, 15 U.S.C. § 1125(c)).

The scope of protection available under FTDA was somewhat limited when the U.S. Supreme Court held in *Moseley v. V Secret Catalogue* (2003) that a plaintiff must prove **actual dilution or actual economic loss** in order to prevail on a trademark dilution claim. In *Moseley*, the owners of the Victoria's Secret retail chain and the Victoria's Secret trademark sought to compel a husband and wife, Victor and Cathy Moseley, to stop using the name "Victor's Little Secret" for their adult entertainment retail store in Kentucky. Victoria's Secret claimed trademark infringement, trademark dilution, and unfair competition under the Lanham Act. The U.S. Supreme Court held that relief under the FTDA requires objective proof of actual injury to the economic value of a famous mark, since the text of the FTDA unambiguously requires "actual dilution" rather than a likelihood of dilution (*Moseley v. V Secret Catalogue*, 2003). This was quite different from the burden of proof in a trademark infringement case, where the plaintiff need only prove a **likelihood** of confusion to prevail.

In response to the *Moseley* decision, Congress amended the FTDA in 2006 (Trademark Dilution Revision Act [TDRA]) and replaced the actual dilution requirement with a "**likelihood of dilution**" requirement. Due to these amendments, now in order to recover monetary damages for trademark dilution, a trademark holder is only required to show a likelihood of dilution if the allegedly unlawful conduct began after October 6, 2006. However, money damages can only be recovered if the dilution is intentional; otherwise, the sole remedy is injunctive relief (15 U.S.C. § 1125(c)).

Famous Marks

Only famous marks are protected under the Trademark Dilution Act (TDA). An essential ingredient of a famous mark is its value or selling power or strength. Thus, newly registered marks or weak marks with little or no instant recognition cannot be diluted. To determine whether a mark is famous under the Trademark Dilution Act, courts may consider the factors shown in Exhibit 18.6. Our next Focus Case discusses the test for establishing a famous mark under the TDA and the concept of niche fame.

LeCharles Bentley v. NBC Universal, LLC

2016 U.S. Dist. LEXIS 191368 (C.D. Cal., September 28, 2016)   FOCUS CASE

FACTS

LeCharles Bentley, a former NFL player, and O-Line Academy LLC ("O-Line") (collectively, "Plaintiffs"), developed a mark using the letters LB. The LB mark was first used in January, 2013 to identify Plaintiffs's business, which sell sports and fitness training services, nutritional services, dietary programs, equipment, and apparel. Plaintiffs began using the LB mark in commerce in April, 2013. In January, 2016 Plaintiffs filed a trademark dilution action against Defendants NBC, BL4 Productions, Inc., and Universal Television, LLC (collectively "NBC"), when NBC began using a logo similar to the Plaintiffs's LB mark for the reality show, *The Biggest Loser*. NBC moved to dismiss for Plaintiffs's failure to state a claim.

HOLDING

The district court granted summary judgment for NBC Universal concluding the Plaintiffs failed to prove their marks were famous under TDA.

RATIONALE

The court explained that because the Plaintiffs's marks are comprised of initials, they are merely descriptive, not distinctive. As a result, the LB marks must acquire secondary meaning to be protectable under trademark law. The Plaintiffs offered evidence that the LB marks were used in commerce for a couple of years and that "individuals interested in sports performance associate the LB marks with O-Lines and Bentley's business." Although, the court accepted Plaintiffs evidence, finding the LB marks acquired distinctiveness via secondary meaning, the court went on to explain a claim of trademark dilution requires a showing that the marks are famous, meaning they are household names.

In determining whether a mark meets the fame requirement, the court considers the factors identified in Exhibit 18.6. According to the court, the Plaintiffs failed to provide sufficient evidence their marks were famous, that is "widely recognized by the general consuming public of the United States," as required by the trademark dilution statute. Instead, the Plaintiffs alleged their LB marks are recognized by those interested in "football, sports performance, and fitness training," a small fraction of the general consuming population. The court, relying on the 2006 Congressional revision to the Trademark Dilution Statute, which "specifically exclude[s] dilution protection for marks whose fame extended only to niche markets," concluded that the LB marks were not famous.

The University of Texas also encountered the niche fame issue when it sued KST Electric (KST) for a number of state and federal trademark claims, including federal trademark dilution, alleging that several logos developed and used by KST infringed on UT's registered trademark, which depicts its mascot, a longhorn steer, in silhouette (referred to by UT as its "longhorn silhouette logo," or LSL). KST argued that it should be granted summary judgment on UT's federal dilution claim because UT has not provided any evidence that the longhorn silhouette logo is famous for purposes of the TDRA. The central problem for UT was that it was not at all clear that someone who wasn't a college football fan (or, to a much lesser extent, college baseball or basketball fan) would recognize the LSL as being associated with UT. The court was well aware that National Collegiate Athletic Association (NCAA) college football is a popular sport, but this hardly equals a presence with the general public of the United States. Simply because UT athletics had achieved a level of national prominence does not necessarily mean that the longhorn logo is so ubiquitous and well-known as to belong in the same category as KODAK. Because UT's evidence failed to demonstrate the extremely high level of recognition necessary to show fame under the TDRA, summary judgment was granted to KST (*Board of Regents v. KST Electric*, 2008). Even though the KST court held UT's longhorn silhouette had only acquired niche fame, which is not protected under the TDRA, in another case involving collegiate sport marks, the court held that similar evidence of use and sales created a genuine issue of material fact as to whether the University of Kansas's marks were famous (*University of Kansas v. Sinks*, 2008).

In most cases, it is obvious whether a mark is famous, and many courts have held marks to be famous based primarily on the first two factors under the FTDA: the extent and amount of use of and sales under the mark. For example, in several cases, marks, such as NIKE, PEPSI, STARBUCKS, TIFFANY, HOT WHEELS, and the adidas three-stripe design were held famous based primarily on evidence of large advertising expenditures and extensive sales (Llewellyn, 2008). Thus, proof of sales and advertising use often will suffice to show that obviously well-known marks are famous, while owners of less well-known marks also add survey evidence on the issue of fame. Survey evidence is admissible in trademark litigation and is commonly used to demonstrate consumer recognition and association (*Daubert v. Merrell Dow Pharmaceuticals*, 1993). For example, Nike complemented their evidence of sales and advertising with consumer surveys showing actual association between Nike's marks and those of Nikepal, Inc. (*Nike v. Nikepal International*, 2007) and adidas used consumer survey evidence to prove likelihood of confusion and blurring (*adidas America v. Payless Shoesource*, 2008). Sport and recreation organizations may conduct this research in house using their own research staff, outsource it to a consumer research firm, or partner with a local university's sport administration program or business school. It is important for sport managers to understand the role consumer research plays in protecting its intellectual property. As mentioned earlier, dilution typically takes one of two forms, either tarnishment or blurring.

Tarnishment

For **tarnishment** to occur, a similar mark must be used in such a way as to disparage or harm the reputation of a famous mark. Most cases involving tarnishment claims involve a similar mark being used in connection with shoddy products or sexual, obscene, or socially unacceptable activities. For example, the "Detroit Right Wings," a white nationalist group who participated in the Unite the Right rally in Charlottesville, Virginia in August of 2017, which turned violent and where one person was killed. In addition to the similarities in names between the white nationalist group the "Detroit Right Wings" and the NHL hockey team, "The Detroit Red Wings," the white nationalist group adopted a logo, used on signs and on their social media accounts, which looked almost identical to that of the National Hockey League (NHL) hockey team, a winged motorcycle wheel logo, where the spokes of the wheel were changed to lightning bolts, similar to symbols used by the Nazis. The NHL and the hockey team issued statements repudiating any association with the white nationalist group and denouncing the misuse of the team's logo. The NHL and the Detroit Red Wings vowed to investigate all of their legal options to protect their intellectual property. Dilution by tarnishment may be a viable legal claim for the Detroit Red Wings (Greene, 2017; Masters & Rose, 2017).

Blurring

Blurring, the more traditional form of dilution, occurs when a mark that is similar to a famous mark is used by a *noncompetitor* in such a way that over time will diminish the famous mark's value by detracting from the exclusiveness of the famous mark. Blurring theory focuses on the diminishment of a trademark's ability to function as a unique identifier of the source or origin of goods and services. Remember, source identification is an essential purpose of a trademark. If one is permitted to use a mark similar to a famous mark, even though consumers may not be confused between the two marks or uses, eventually consumers will no longer *exclusively* associate the famous mark with the goods and services of the owner of the mark (Oswald, 1999). Dilution protection dates back to 1927 and has been justified as follows: "If you allow Rolls Royce restaurants, and Rolls Royce cafeterias, and Rolls Royce pants, and Rolls Royce candy, in 10 years you will not have the Rolls Royce mark any more" (Schechter, 1927). Nike's opposition to the registration of the trademark, "JUST JESU IT" in connection with athletic apparel and other clothing was sustained by the TTAB. In analyzing the factors for a dilution by blurring claim, the TTAB determined that Nike's mark was famous and became famous prior to Maher's registration filing date. Nike's "mark is inherently distinct and the degree of public recognition is extremely high. [Nike] engaged in substantially exclusive use of its mark, policing unauthorized use … and refusing permission to use it to all who ask." It is important to note that the marks need not be "identical or very or substantially similar to the plaintiff's marks, as required prior to the passage of the TDRA. Under the TDRA, the question is "whether the two marks are sufficiently similar to trigger consumers to conjure up a famous mark when confronted with the second mark" (*Nike v. Maher*, 2011).

Trademark Law and the Olympics

Not surprisingly, the United States Olympic & Paralympic Committee owns several valuable trademarks. Unlike a typical business or sport organization, the USOPC did not need federal registration under the Lanham Act in order to avail itself of the Lanham protections. Instead, the USOPC's trademark ownership rights flow from the Amateur Sports Act of 1978 (ASA) and amendments to the ASA codified in the Ted Stevens Olympic and Amateur Sports Act of 1998 (OASA).

The ASA empowered the USOC (now the USOPC) to finance American athletes' participation in the Olympic Movement. The United States is one of the few countries that does not provide any direct governmental funding to its Olympic programs. Thus, the exclusive protections provided in the OASA allow the USOPC to defend against ambush marketing activities as well as protect the value of a significant revenue stream through sponsorships, broadcasting, and licensing (Park, 2019). Several provisions grant the USOPC exclusive rights within the United States to the words *United States Olympic Committee*; the symbols of the International Olympic Committee, including the five interlocking rings; and the words *Olympic* and *Olympiad*, *Citius Altius Fortius*, *Paralympic*, *Paralympiad*, *Pan-American*, and *America Espirito Sport Fraternite*, and any combination of those words. The USOPC possesses the exclusive right to license the use of these marks. The OASA further provides that the USOPC may pursue any remedies traditionally available for trademark infringement (e.g., under the Lanham Act) if any person uses the protected symbols "for the purpose of trade, to induce the sale of any goods or services, or to promote any ... athletic performance, or competition."

Thus, the OASA extends to the USOPC the same protections that the Lanham Act provides to traditional trademark owners. However, the elements of a trademark infringement action as identified in the Lanham Act have been modified by the courts for the USOPC. In *USOC v. San Francisco Arts & Athletics, Inc.* (1987), the U.S. Supreme Court held that the USOPC need not prove that the contested use of its marks is likely to cause confusion. Being relieved of this evidentiary burden has provided the USOPC with broader protection than that available to ordinary trademark owners. An unauthorized user of USOPC protected marks and symbols is often hit with a cease and desist order easily obtained by the USOPC without any showing of consumer confusion. Essentially, to prevail in an infringement action under the OASA, the USOPC need only show that the unauthorized user's marks are similar to the USOPC's protected marks.

The IOC depends on international intellectual property treaties to protect the Olympic properties, which is at the center of being able to offer corporate sponsor exclusivity in their association with the Olympic Games. Securing these partnerships, insures the IOC ability to fund the Olympic Movements. The IOC relies heavily on Nairobi Treaty of 1981, which requires member countries to protect the Olympic symbol (the five interlocking rings) from commercial use with the authorization of the IOC.

The USOPC as well as local organizing committees in other countries have been criticized for their heavy-handed policing of Olympic marks and logos. Consider the London committee's handling of dozens of local businesses during the 2012 Summer Games. A café in London was ordered to remove five bagels hanging in its window or face legal action. And a butcher who fashioned links of sausages into a facsimile of the Olympic logo was also rebuked. A florist was told to stop arranging flowers with the colors of the Olympic rings (Worthington, 2012). During the 2018 Olympics in PyeongChang, SK Telecom produced three advertisements using two South Korean Olympic athletes with the phrases, "See you in PyeongChang" and "See you in 5G Korea." Although there was no direct association between SK Telecom and the Olympic Games, the Korean Intellectual Property Office determined that SK Telecom's campaign violated the rights of the official sponsor, KT Corporation. The IOC brand protection policies also apply to social media. Instagram personality, Bob Menery received a cease and desist letter after he posted the team figure skating event with his satirical voiceover.

Competitive Advantage Strategies

Managing Brands and IP

- Have a coordinated plan to inventory all intellectual property and maintain up-to-date records of how such property is being used.
- Carefully develop a licensing program to provide a mechanism for monitoring the use of protected marks, as well as to build and enhance goodwill associated with the marks.
- Before beginning any new marketing activities, take the steps necessary to (a) identify whether any new IP rights are or will be created; (b) determine what level of protection should be pursued to protect your investment in the IP; and (c) seek and obtain the necessary protections before launching the campaign.
- Once a trademark has been registered, it must be used continuously; thus, its use must be monitored and documented in the event an abandonment claim is asserted.
- Develop an aggressive strategy to counter unauthorized use of your protected marks. Even if an infringement claim cannot be sustained, the threat of litigation may deter offending uses of your protected marks and logos.
- An active licensing program is a good way to strengthen trademark rights. A licensing program should assure that any licensees are producing goods of a quality that reflects positively on your organization. Thus, it is important to create and implement a trademark quality control program to monitor the permissive uses of your marks and logos.
- Before selecting a mark, conduct a thorough search to include, but not be limited to, federal registered or applied trademarks, international uses, and common law uses.
- Other recommended search areas include the following: the United States Patent and trademark Office, United States pending trademark applications, state registrations, market directories, domain names, and trade name listings. A simple Internet search may reveal existing or competing uses of your proposed mark.

In the period leading up to the hosting of the Olympics, may countries adopt permanent national legislation to safeguard the Olympic intellectual properties, and Brazil was no different (Castro, 2018). Marianne Wüthrich (2016), Trademark Senior Legal Counsel for the International Olympic Committee, writing for the World Intellectual Property Organization, noted the following laws were relied upon to protect Olympic intellectual properties in Brazil: Industrial Property Law, Pele Law, Brazilian Copyright Law, Brazilian Copyright Act, and Brazilian Olympic Act.

See Exhibit 18.7 below summarizing laws in place to protect Olympic IP and marketing rights for the PyeongChang, Tokyo, Beijing, and Paris Olympics.

Due in part to the heightened trademark protection and in part to the expense of litigating against an organization with such significant financial resources, the USOPC's tactics are generally successful. Due to the reach of social media, however, such tactics are much quicker to be exposed and criticized. For example, the USOPC sent a cease and desist letter to an online knitting community who was planning the "Ravelympics" during the Olympic broadcast, where their members would participate in such activities as an afghan marathon and scarf hockey. The letter stated:

> We believe using the name "Ravelympics" for a competition that involves an afghan marathon, scarf hockey and sweater triathlon, among others, tends to denigrate the true nature of the Olympic Games. In a sense, it is disrespectful to our country's finest athletes and fails to recognize or appreciate their hard work. (See Chen, 2012a.)

Exhibit 18.7 Olympic IP protection legislation for PyeongChang, Tokyo, Beijing, and Paris.

PeyongChang 2018	
Copyright Act	"to protect the rights of authors and the rights neighboring on them and to promote fair use of works in order to contribute to the improvement and development of culture and related industries."
Trademark Act	"to contribute to industrial development and to protect the interests of consumers by ensuring the maintenance of the business reputation of persons using trademarks through the protection of trademarks."
Special Act on Support for the PyeongChang 2018 Olympic and Paralympic Winter Games	"to contribute to the national development by promoting national sports and strengthening the Olympic heritage by supporting the successful hosting of the 23rd Winter Olympics and the 12th Winter Paralympics held in 2018."
Tokyo 2020*	
Trademark Act	"Prevention of the infringement of trademarks"
Unfair Competition Prevention Act	"Prohibition of commercial use of a mark of an international organization."
Copyright Act	"Prevention of acts that infringe copyrights"
Beijing 2022*	
Regulation on Protection of Olympic Symbols (Amended)	"Incorporates the most recent 'legislative achievements and law enforcement experience,' 'strengthens the protection of the Olympic symbols,' adjusting Olympic symbols and licensing procedures, and further clarifies what constitutes Ambush Marketing."
Paris 2024*	
Law no. 2018-202	Restrictive ad hoc legislation, often exempt from common law, in place to enable the preparation of the event.
French Intellectual Property Code	Protects intellectual and industrial property
The Act on the Organization of the Olympic and Paralympic Games	"addresses an overall commitment on the part of the State to plan this landmark event in the best possible manner, by setting up all of the architecture for the Games' governance within six months of their award to France."

*Dialogue regarding additional legislation are ongoing.

In response, the knitters's social media posts went viral with such posts as "Oh no they didn't: @USOlympic just suggested that knitting 'denigrates' Olympic brand. The 1 in 3 Americans who knit just got really angry." The backlash was so immediate the USOPC issued an apology the very next day admitting their language was too harsh (Chen, 2012b). The USOPC's trademark protection strategies will be discussed in the context of ambush marketing practices in Chapter 19.

The Olympics are not the only agencies that get heightened trademark rights under federal law. Some 200 entities benefit from some degree of "super" trademark protection, mostly government agencies or government-related entities, nonprofit groups such as veterans's associations, and charitable or public service entities like the American Red Cross. Conservation symbols Smokey Bear and Woodsy Owl are among the trademarks controlled by the U.S. government with their own statutory protection.

This section on trademark law has revealed important legal issues associated with trademarks. You should have a better understanding of the value of trademarks as part of a business's intellectual property portfolio, the requirements for registration of trademarks, and the protections afforded trademark owners. Next, we continue to explore intellectual property as we examine copyright law and its impact on sport marketing managers.

The Law of Copyrights

> The Congress shall have Power ... To promote the Progress of Science and useful Arts, by securing for limited Times to Authors and Inventors the exclusive Right to their respective Writings and Discoveries. (U.S. Constitution, Article I, § 8, cl. 8)

If you are a sport enthusiast, you encounter copyrights in your daily life in a variety of ways – for example, through purchasing *Sports Illustrated* magazine or *Street & Smith's SportsBusiness Journal*, installing a new app on your mobile device, downloading video files, streaming or recording an ESPN broadcast, or playing an EA Sports video game. All of these are creative, original works that are protected by U.S. copyright laws. Copyright law is a compromise forged many years ago between the interests of authors of creative works and the public's interest in having access to those works. Copyright is a type of protection provided to authors of "original works," which includes writing, music, art, performances, and other creative pursuits. Copyright law gives the holder a limited monopoly over a creative work to prevent others from using the work without the owner's permission.

You will recall that a trademark's main function is to serve as a source identifier for products and services, and it only represents a property interest to the extent that it is attached to a product or service. In contrast, a copyright represents a property interest from the moment a creative work is created and put into a tangible form. In the sport industry, copyright applies in numerous situations, such as product labels, website content and design, merchandise logo design, broadcasts and live streaming of sporting events, sport novels, sport figure biographies, halftime performances by musical groups, the music played throughout an event, paintings of sport celebrities and events, and even the famous Vince Lombardi Trophy awarded to the victor of the NFL Super Bowl. Certainly, trademarks tend to appear more prominently in the sport industry due to the emphasis placed on branding. Copyright, however, also has an important role and pervades many sport organizational decisions.

Purpose of Copyrights

The purpose of copyright law is to encourage creativity by extending protection to works of art, literature, and music, and other works of authorship. However, the goal of encouraging creativity competes with other laws seeking to foster a competitive marketplace and with First Amendment guarantees of free speech. Copyright law attempts to balance these competing goals in a variety of ways. To maintain this balance, the interests of the creator, the owner, and the public or users of the work must be considered (see Exhibit 18.8).

On one hand, copyright law grants exclusive rights to the creator of an original work of authorship, but on the other hand, the law limits the duration of those rights and protects only the specific method used by the author to express his or her idea. Additionally, the law allows for *fair use* of copyrighted materials. Fair use practices together with time limits on copyright protections attempt to ensure a free and robust public domain for the expression of ideas, thereby balancing competing interests between authors or owners and the public domain or users. Similarly, laws relating to works for hire and protecting the moral rights of authors help to balance the competing interests of authors and owners.

The law does not protect an idea itself, but only an author's or artist's *fixed expression* of the idea. To illustrate, suppose you have an idea for a movie about an aging minor league baseball player and his relationship with a promising but erratic rookie pitcher. Both players become romantically involved with the same woman. This may sound like an idea for a great story, so you tell your friend about it. However, your

Exhibit 18.8 Balancing competing interests in copyright law.

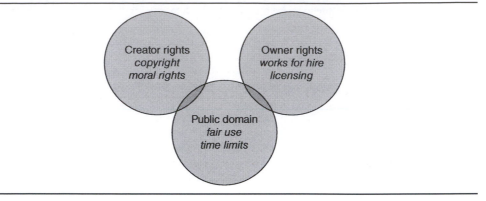

Note: This figure represents the intersection and balance between competing interests related to copyrights. Although the image may also bear a resemblance to a famous and well-known copyrighted character, Mickey Mouse, such similarities are purely for educational and informational purposes. If Congress had not recently passed the Sonny Bono Copyright Term Extension Act, many images of Mickey Mouse would have passed into the public domain in 2003. Instead, the public will not have free and open access to these artistic creations until the year 2028.

idea is not protected by copyright law unless and until you take your idea and write it down or otherwise put it into a tangible "fixed" form. A word is fixed in a tangible form "when its embodiment in a copy or phonorecord . . . is sufficiently permanent or stable to permit it to be perceived, reproduced, or otherwise communicated for a period of more than transitory duration" (Copyright Act, 1976, § 101). If you actually write a script telling the above story, at that point you have a copyright to the creative work. If your screenplay carries the name *Bull Durham*, the film version of your story would also be a separate creative work subject to copyright protection. The sheet music for a song is a different form of expression from an audio recording of a song. The public performance of a song that has not been written down or recorded represents the basic idea, not an expression of that idea. Thus, a performance cannot be copyrighted unless and until it is expressed in a copyrightable form. The same is true for an idea for a sport event. The idea is not copyrightable, nor is the live event. Instead, only the taped or recorded expression of the idea or event will ultimately be copyrightable.

Source of Copyrights

Copyright law is primarily provided for under the Copyright Act of 1976, as amended. In addition, the Digital Millennium Copyright Act (1998, 2010) provides copyright laws regarding digital creations and the Internet, and the Sonny Bono Copyright Term Extension Act (1998) extends the duration of previous limits on copyrights. Exhibit 18.9 identifies the duration of copyright protection for protected, creative works.

Exhibit 18.9 Duration of copyrights and moral rights.

Author/ Artist Work Created	Duration of Copyrights
Prior to January 1, 1978	Copyright protection lasts for 95 years from date of creation
After to January 1, 1978	Life of author + 70 years
	Works for hire: 95 years after first publication or 100 years after creation, whichever is earlier
Author's Moral Rights in Fine Art	*Duration of Moral Rights*
Created after June 1, 1991	Life of the author

Exhibit 18.10 Materials and subject matter protected by the Copyright Act of 1976 (17 U.S.C. § 102).

Literary Works	Pictorial, graphic, and sculptural works
Musical Works	Motion pictures and audiovisual works
Dramatic Works	Sound recordings
Pantomimes and Choreographic Works	Architectural works

Creation of Copyrights

Many types of materials and subject matter may receive copyright protection. The Copyright Act specifically includes the items shown in Exhibit 18.10. Essentially, to qualify for copyright protection the material must meet two requirements: *originality* and *fixation*.

Originality Requirement

Originality requires a work to be created by the author himself or herself and to contain some *minimal amount of creativity*. Words, short phrases, and familiar symbols or designs do not meet this requirement and may not be copyrighted. In the context of copyright, originality doesn't necessarily mean "novel." Instead, it requires that the expression be original to the author (i.e., it cannot be copied from someone else), and it must possess at least a *minimal* amount of creativity. Collections of data or facts do not meet the originality requirement and may not be copyrighted. For a collection of data or facts to be protected, it must possess some minimal amount of creativity or uniqueness. For example, the U.S. Supreme Court held that a listing of phone numbers in a phone book did not meet the originality requirement but was instead just a collection of data or facts (*Feist Publications, Inc. v. Rural Telephone Service Co.*, 1991). The Court noted that only minimal originality is required, but it must exist. The collection of phone numbers represented significant effort, but copyright does not reward effort. It rewards originality, which was lacking in an alphabetical listing of names, addresses, and phone numbers.

Originality also was raised in *NBA v. Motorola, Inc.* (1997), when the court held that live sporting events are not original works of authorship. Congress specifically amended the Copyright Act of 1976 to extend copyright protection to broadcasts of live sporting events, but the underlying events and concepts for a game or event are not copyrightable. See *Anti-Monopoly, Inc. v. General Mills Fun Group, Inc.* (1979), which ruled that a game concept cannot be copyrighted, and *Affiliated Hosp. Prods., Inc. v. Merdel Game Mfg. Co.* (1975), which ruled that games that are in the public domain and the rules to those games are not copyrightable. Thus, the methods or rules of playing sports and games are not generally copyrightable. See *Nimmer on Copyright* § 2.18[H][3]: "no copyright may be obtained in the system or manner of playing a game or engaging in any other sporting or like activity."

One unique copyright issue often impacting famous athletes, relates to the copyrightability of and copyright ownership of tattoos. The threshold question in determining if a particular tattoo is protected by copyright is whether the tattoo is sufficiently original. The original creation and fixing of the tattoo on a person's skin would appear to meet the requirement of originality. The opinion of the Copyright Office seems to be that tattoos are indeed worthy of copyright protection – on April 19, 2011, the tattoo artist responsible for Mike Tyson's distinctive facial tattoo received a registration for it as artwork on a 3D object. However, the issue becomes more complicated in the context of video game depictions of tattoos. In 2012, Christopher Escobedo, a tattoo artist based in Arizona, sued THQ, Inc., the makers of the video game UFC Undisputed 2010, for its depiction of a tattoo that Escobedo designed and tattooed on the torso of Carlos Condit – who was at the time the "interim Ultimate Fighting Championship ("UFC") Welterweight Champion." The case was ultimately settled out of court. In 2016, tattoo company Solid Oak Sketches sued Take-Two Interactive for copyright infringement based on the company's depiction of Lebron James's tattoos in the game and cover art for the game. The district court dismissed Solid Oak's complaint holding that it had granted the NBA players an implied license to use the tattoos as part of their likeness, and the defendants had obtained licenses to use the players' likenesses in the video game. (See *Solid Oak Sketches, LLC v. 2K Games, Inc.* 2020.)

In this context, the copyrightability of the tattoo is not always the critical issue, but rather whether the use of the copyrighted tattoo in the video game or other artwork infringes on the tattoo copyright. We will explore copyright infringement and defenses to those claims later in the chapter. To date, there is no published opinion to provide guidance, as all previous suits were settled. Scholars continue to explore the right balance between the rights of the copyright owner and an athlete's right to control the commercial use of their bodies (Baker & Brison, 2016; Boozer, 2018). In addition to originality, a work must be "fixed" in order to be protected by copyright law, as discussed next.

Fixation Requirement

Fixation requires that the work be put into a tangible form – written down or recorded. This may involve paper, fabrics, compact discs, digital files, portable or hard drives, and DVDs. Consider the example of a Division I men's basketball game. The game itself is not tangible; it exists only in the moment. However, if the game is recorded, broadcast, or otherwise put into a tangible form, the fixed form of the game becomes copyrightable. Just writing down an idea for an event or game is not fixation of the expression of the idea or concept for purposes of copyright. For example, the court held in *Hoopla Sports & Entertainment, Inc. v. Nike, Inc.* (1996) that Hoopla had not complied with the necessary requisites to copyright its idea. Hoopla developed an idea for a United States versus the world basketball game featuring high school boys, called "Father Liberty Game" or "FLG." Even if a basketball game were copyrightable, Hoopla did not record or otherwise fix in any tangible medium of expression its idea for FLG. Thus, it did not possess a copyright in the FLG itself under the Copyright Act. It is a requirement of the Copyright Act that the expression must be fixed in a tangible medium before it can be copyrighted. Fixation is not merely a statutory requirement of the Copyright Act, but is required by the text of the Constitution itself, which protects only writings; that is, tangible forms of expression. See *Nimmer on Copyright* § 2.03[B].

Notice that the *Hoopla* court did not determine whether a game or a sports contest was a copyrightable event, because that issue was previously addressed in *NBA v. Motorola* (1997).

National Basketball Association v. Motorola, Inc.

CASE OPINION   105 F.3d 841 (2d Cir. 1997)

FACTS

The facts are largely undisputed. Motorola manufactures and markets the SportsTrax paging device while STATS supplies the game information that is transmitted to the pagers. The product became available to the public in January 1996, at a retail price of about $200. SportsTrax's pager has an inch-and-a-half by inch-and-a-half screen and operates in four basic modes: "current," "statistics," "final scores," and "demonstration." It is the "current" mode that gives rise to the present dispute. In that mode, SportsTrax displays the following information on NBA games in progress: (1) the teams playing; (2) score changes; (3) the team in possession of the ball; (4) whether the team is in the free-throw bonus; (5) the quarter of the game; and (6) time remaining in the quarter. The information is updated every two to three minutes, with more frequent updates near the end of the first half and the end of the game. There is a lag of approximately two or three minutes between events in the game itself and when the information appears on the pager screen.

SportsTrax's operation relies on a data feed supplied by STATS reporters who watch the games on television or listen to them on the radio. The reporters key into a personal computer changes in the score and other information, such as successful and missed shots, fouls, and clock updates. The information is relayed by modem to STATS's host computer, which compiles, analyzes, and formats the data for retransmission. The information is then sent to a common carrier, which then sends it via satellite to various local FM radio networks that in turn emit the signal received by the individual SportsTrax pagers.

HOLDING

The court ruled that the SportsTrax device and AOL reproduced only factual information and did not infringe on the NBA broadcast copyright.

RATIONALE

The NBA asserted copyright infringement claims with regard both to the underlying games and to their broadcasts. ... In our view, the underlying basketball games do not fall within the subject matter of federal copyright protection because they do not constitute "original works of authorship" under 17 U.S.C. § 102(a). Section 102(a) lists eight categories of "works of authorship" covered by the act, including such categories as "literary works," "musical works," and "dramatic works." ... The list does not include athletic events, and, although the list is concededly non-exclusive, such events are neither similar nor analogous to any of the listed categories.

Sports events are not "authored" in any common sense of the word. There is, of course, at least at the professional level, considerable preparation for a game. However, the preparation is as much an expression of hope or faith as a determination of what will actually happen. Unlike movies, plays, television programs, or operas, athletic events are competitive and have no underlying script. Preparation may even cause mistakes to succeed, like the broken play in football that gains yardage because the opposition could not expect it.

What "authorship" there is in a sports event, moreover, must be open to copying by competitors if fans are to be attracted. If the inventor of the T-formation in football had been able to copyright it, the sport might have come to an end instead of prospering. Even where athletic preparation most resembles authorship – figure skating, gymnastics, and, some would uncharitably say, professional wrestling – a performer who conceives and executes a particularly graceful and difficult – or, in the case of wrestling, seemingly painful – acrobatic feat cannot copyright it without impairing the underlying competition in the future. A claim of being the only athlete to perform a feat doesn't mean much if no one else is allowed to try.

For many of these reasons, *Nimmer on Copyright* concludes that the "far more reasonable" position is that athletic events are not copyrightable. ...

We believe that the lack of case law is attributable to a general understanding that athletic events were, and are, uncopyrightable. Indeed, prior to 1976, there was even doubt that broadcasts describing or depicting such events, which have a far stronger case for copyrightability than the events themselves, were entitled to copyright protection. ... Congress found it necessary to extend such protection to recorded broadcasts of live events. The fact that Congress did not extend such protection to the events themselves confirms our view that the district court correctly held that appellants were not infringing a copyright in the NBA games. ...

QUESTIONS

1 What characteristics of athletic events are used by the court to support its conclusion that sport events are not "authored" for purposes of copyright protection?

2 How does Congress's decision to entitle live broadcasts of sporting events to copyright protection hinder the NBA's arguments for protection of the games themselves?

Registration of Copyrights

Registration is not required for a copyright to exist. The copyright comes into existence as soon as the work is created and put into a tangible form. However, similar to trademark registration, registration of a copyright carries with it procedural benefits in the event of an unauthorized use in that (1) registration is required to bring an infringement claim, and (2) failure to register can reduce damages recoverable for infringement. It is a wise business practice to submit creative works promptly for registration with the U.S. Copyright Office and always to include the claim of copyright on all creative works. In March of 2019, the Supreme Court of the United States issued a unanimous opinion settling a longstanding split in the circuit courts regarding when a copyrighted work is considered "registered" for the purpose of filing a lawsuit for copyright infringement. Registration is "not when an application for registration is filed, but when the Register has registered a copyright after examining a properly filed application. The Supreme Court also held that a copyright infringement lawsuit can only be filed after the U.S. Copyright Office issues a registration certificate for the work. (See *Fourth Estate Public Benefit Corp. v. Wall-Street.com, LLC*, 2019.)

The U.S. Copyright Office regulates registration and deposit of copyrighted materials and has three basic functions. It registers copyrights, issues certificates of registration, and regulates and stores copyrighted material. If an author's work meets the originality and fixation requirements, then the author may register and deposit the work with the U.S. Copyright Office simply by paying a small online registration fee ($35–$55, 2019). The Copyright Office provides resources for authors and online registration at its website, www.copyright.gov.

The proper designation of a copyright contains three basic elements: the copyright symbol or word, the date, and the name of the author or copyright holder. Two examples include, © 2021, Jane Doe and Copyright 2021, Jane Doe. While the law no longer requires this designation on copyrighted works, it is still a good practice to include it on original works. The notification will provide additional evidence of a claim of copyright in the event of unauthorized use.

Determining Ownership of Copyrights

When a single author creates an original work composed solely of new materials, determining ownership is fairly simple. Once the work is created in a fixed form, the single author immediately becomes the owner of the work *and* the copyright, unless he or she has entered into an agreement to the contrary. Determining ownership is more difficult when a work has joint authors, when a work is included within another work as part of a collection of works (collective works), and when a work is a work for hire. A controversy following the 2019 NBA Championships arose regarding a dispute over copyright ownership involving Kawhi Leonard and Nike. One month after winning the 2019 NBA Championship with the Toronto Raptors, Kawhi Leonard filed suit against his former sponsor, Nike. Leonard maintained that he was the creator and owner of the stylized claw logo that incorporates Leonard's initials and jersey number. Nike had registered a Kawhi Leonard logo in May of 2017, claiming authorship of the logo. Leonard asserted he conceptualized the logo in college and refined it in December 2011. Leonard sought a legal declaration that

> (i) Leonard is the sole author of the Leonard Logo; (ii) Leonard's use of the Leonard Logo does not infringe any rights of Nike, including without limitation any rights Nike may claim to possess with respect to the Leonard Logo; and (iii) Defendant [Nike] committed fraud on the Copyright Office in registering the Leonard Logo. (*Leonard v. Nike Inc.*, 2019)

In April of 2020, the U.S. District Court for the District of Oregon, dismissed Leonard's claims with prejudice (McCann, 2020). This dispute illustrates the importance of clearly identifying ownership interests in creative works and registering those works even if they were created prior to an athlete obtaining prominent recognition during his or her professional career.

Joint Authors and Collective Works

The authors of a **joint work** are co-owners of the copyright in the work unless they have entered into an agreement to the contrary. In addition, each separate contribution to a periodical or **collective work** represents a distinct copyright from the collective work as a whole. The copyright for each separate part of a periodical rests with the author of that part, while the copyright for the collective work rests with another. For example, a typical issue of *The Business Insider* may contain a dozen articles written by different authors. Each individual article represents a separate copyright owned by the author of that article. The entire magazine or collective work, represents another copyright work owned by Insider, Inc. In addition, each photograph, video, and the web design also represent separate copyrights, owned by the photographer, videographer, or Insider, Inc.

Works for Hire

A **work for hire** can result in two ways, during employment or based on a contractual agreement. First, in an employment relationship a work made for hire is a work prepared by an employee within the scope of his employment. For example, marketing assistant in the Ohio State Athletic Department may create a new media guide for women's basketball. This work would be considered a work for hire, as a work prepared by an employee within the scope of her employment. Both the work and the copyright would be owned by Ohio State. For an employee to protect a creative work as his own, an express agreement must exist reserving those rights to the employee. Otherwise, employee creations are presumed to belong to the employer.

Outside of the employment relationship, a work made for hire may be created pursuant to a contract. A *contracted work* is defined as a work specially ordered or commissioned for use as a contribution to a collective work, a part of a motion picture or other audiovisual work, a translation, a supplementary work, a compilation, an instructional text, a test, answer material for a test, or an atlas. For a contracted work to qualify as a work for hire, the parties must expressly agree in a written instrument signed by them that the work shall be considered a work made for hire. Without a written agreement to the contrary, the author or creator of the work is presumed to own the copyright. This issue came up when a student assistant at New York University Athletics created a new mascot design for the athletic department. While her original job was as an equipment manager assistant, she was also paid extra to perform certain graphic design services for the athletic department due to her artistic skills. Her new mascot design was ultimately adopted by the university, and she alleged that the work she did in creating and drawing the new mascot was outside the scope of her employment. Thus, it was not a work for hire. The court disagreed and held that since graphic design was part of her duties, her mascot drawings and designs were the property of NYU Athletics, and they owned the copyright to them (*Fleurimond v. NYU*, 2012). Sport organizations should be careful when conducting logo or mascot design competitions to clearly establish ownership rights for any submitted designs or drawings from either the general public or employees. (See *Bouchat v. Baltimore Ravens* in the next section describing a lengthy copyright dispute for unsolicited designs and drawings.)

Rights Granted with Copyright

The rights granted with a copyright can be categorized as either property rights or moral rights. Property rights are the primary rights associated with copyright protections and are derived expressly from the Copyright Act of 1976. Moral rights are more limited and protected, based on a combination of federal and state protections.

Property Rights

A property right provides the creator or owner of a copyright the exclusive economic and property interests to the work. Property rights recognized under current copyright law grant to the owner of copyright the exclusive rights to do and to authorize any of the following:

1 Reproduce the copyrighted work in copies or phonorecords.
2 Prepare derivative works based upon the copyrighted work.
3 Distribute copies or phonorecords of the copyrighted work to the public by sale or other transfer of ownership, or by rental, lease, or lending.
4 Perform the copyrighted work publicly (in the case of literary, musical, dramatic, and choreographic works, pantomimes, and motion pictures and other audiovisual works).
5 Display the copyrighted work publicly (in the case of literary, musical, dramatic, and choreographic works, pantomimes, and pictorial, graphic, or sculptural works, including the individual images of a motion picture or other audiovisual work).
6 Perform the copyrighted work publicly by means of a digital audio transmission (in the case of sound recordings) (17 U.S.C. § 106, 2013).

It is possible for the creator of a work and the owner of the work to be two different people or entities. The creator may sell, assign, transfer, or license her rights to another, who becomes the owner of the copyright and the rights included with the copyright. Or the author may retain the copyright but transfer the exclusive distribution rights to another. For example, an artist may create an original painting depicting the winner of the Kentucky Derby, sell the painting to a collector, and license another company to create prints for mass distribution. The purchaser of the original is the owner of the painting but not the copyright. Similarly, the distribution company owns exclusive licensing and distribution rights but not the copyright itself, which is still owned by the artist.

Interesting issues regarding copyright ownership were raised in an August 2, 2019, federal lawsuit filed by the Philadelphia Phillies against Harrison/Erickson ("H/E"), Inc. The complaint alleged that then Phillies Executive Vice President Bill Giles decided to develop a new mascot. Mr. Giles wanted the mascot to be named the Phillie Phanatic and be highly active, family friendly, green, fat, loveable with a big nose. Beginning in March of 1978, the Phillies entered into a series of agreements, the first of which required H/E to design and construct a costume based on Giles's specifications, with the Phillies granted the right to use the costume on TV, in commercials, and in personal appearances. The second agreement related to H/E's development of Phanatic-themed promotional items. The third agreement settled a copyright infringement claim brought by H/E and settled in November 1979, resulting in an agreement where the Phillies received exclusive rights to exploit the Phanatic costume and make certain reproductions, and H/E received a lump sum payment followed by annual payments, which increased each year.

In the fall of 1984, the Phillies and H/E renegotiated another agreement which terminated the 1979 agreement and was the conveyance of rights "forever" to the Phillies. On June 1, 2018, H/E's attorneys sent a letter to then Phillies Chairman, David Montgomery, claiming authorship of the copyrighted character, the Phanatic, as he had a right to terminate the Phillies's right in the Phanatic as of June 15, 2020 pursuant to 17 U.S.C. §203 of the Copyright Act, which allows authors to terminate a grant of a transfer or license of a copyright. The purpose of this section is to protect authors with no bargaining power from transferring their rights for little to no money prior to the market value of the work having been established. It does not grant authors with multiple opportunities to renegotiate grants or transfers of copyrights after the author has full knowledge of the market value of the work. The key question in this case is under what circumstances can an assignment or license of a copyright be considered permanent or forever such that it is outside the scope of § 203. This could be an important case to watch going forward. (See *Phillies v Harrison/Erickson Inc.*, 2019.)

Competitive Advantage Strategies

Copyright

- Engage the services of an intellectual property attorney or other expert for sophisticated and complicated tasks such as trademark searches, copyright renewals, and digital rights management.

- Establish procedures for responding to instances of possible trademark or copyright infringement. Often, an innocent infringement can be curtailed by a simple letter notifying the infringer of your superior rights to a mark or copyright.

- To avoid finding itself in the position of the Baltimore Ravens and having to defend a copyright infringement case, a sport organization should have a firm policy prohibiting any employee from accepting creative works from outside sources. An internal policy to refuse to accept sample artwork, drawings, or other creative works from anyone who is not an employee of the organization will strengthen your defense to a copyright infringement case by making it more difficult for the plaintiff to prove "access."

- Include the copyright symbol, ©, on all sponsorship proposals or promotional ideas that you present to other businesses. This should serve to notify them that the promotional idea is your property and cause them to think before implementing your promotion without your permission.

- Live streaming of sporting events is growing in popularity and may provide many college athletic departments with a much-needed revenue stream; thus, television broadcasting agreements should clearly reserve the webcasting rights to the university. It is, of course, likely that the broadcaster will prohibit live streaming for high-profile events for fear of reducing the value of their broadcast rights or that the broadcaster itself will want to live stream the event free over the Internet or using a pay-for-view platform.

Moral Rights

Regardless of how an author chooses to dispose of her copyright, she will retain certain moral rights to a visual work even if the original copyright or work has been sold or transferred. The United States has recognized moral rights only since the Visual Arts Rights Act of 1990 (VARA, 1990, 2013) and has recently proposed amendments to VARA to provide stronger protections for moral rights (Copyright Office, 2019). Moral rights attach to a copyright because authorship is an extension of an author's personality. Moral rights generally fall into two categories: right of attribution and right of integrity. The **right of attribution** prevents others from claiming authorship or attributing authorship falsely to an individual. The **right of integrity** prevents others from distorting, mutilating, or misrepresenting the author's work. See Exhibit 18.11.

VARA protects the rights of attribution and integrity of the author of a "work of visual art" (17 U.S.C. § 106A). Passed by Congress in 1990 to bring this country more in line with others in protecting certain "moral" rights of artists, VARA, among other things, allows artists to claim authorship of certain works of art. Congress, however, recognized the problems inherent in expanding VARA protection too broadly, so it therefore went to extreme lengths to narrowly define the works of art to be covered by the act. As such, Congress decided that VARA would protect only "works of visual art," as defined by the Copyright Act.

The meaning of "works of visual art" was addressed in a case involving a dispute over attribution to the design of the trophy for the NASCAR Nextel Cup in *NASCAR v. Scharle* (2006). Scharle worked as an independent contractor for the Franklin Mint and was asked to help design a new trophy to replace the

Exhibit 18.11 The Visual Artist Rights Act of 1990.

Visual Artists Rights Act of 1990, 17 U.S.C. § 106A. Rights of certain authors to attribution and integrity

a Rights of attribution and integrity. Subject to section 107 [17 USCS § 107] and independent of the exclusive rights provided in section 106 [17 USCS § 106], the author of a work of visual art —

   1 shall have the right —

      A to claim authorship of that work, and

      B to prevent the use of his or her name as the author of any work of visual art which he or she did not create;

   2 shall have the right to prevent the use of his or her name as the author of the work of visual art in the event of a distortion, mutilation, or other modification of the work which would be prejudicial to his or her honor or reputation; and

   3 subject to the limitations set forth in section 113(d) [17 USCS § 113(d)], shall have the right —

      A to prevent any intentional distortion, mutilation, or other modification of that work which would be prejudicial to his or her honor or reputation, and any intentional distortion, mutilation, or modification of that work is a violation of that right, and

      B to prevent any destruction of a work of recognized stature, and any intentional or grossly negligent destruction of that work is a violation of that right.

Winston Cup. Scharle created numerous computer images for the trophy design and presented them to the Franklin Mint. When the new trophy was unveiled, the new trophy design was credited to the Franklin Mint, not Scharle. Scharle wanted attribution under VARA. The *Scharle* court carefully examined the definition of a "work of visual art" in the statute in reaching its decision. Among other things, a work of visual art does not include any "technical drawing, diagram, model, ... merchandising item[,] or advertising [or] promotional ... material." The court concluded that Scharle's works (computer images) did not exist in a single copy or a limited quantity of signed and numbered copies but instead as multiple attempts to arrive at the optimal design for the trophy. Because Scharle's drawings are not "works of visual art" as defined by the Copyright Act, they were not protected by VARA.

Very few cases have been decided on the merits under VARA, but in 2018 an important case awarded significant damages to 21 street artists for the destruction of their work. For years, Jerry Wolkoff, the owner of a warehouse complex in Long Island City known as 5Pointz, permitted and encouraged a group of artists to paint the exterior of the buildings. The 5Pointz paintings were a lively and memorable landmark on the daily commute for residents and a regular destination for tourists and school groups (Tortorelli, 2018). When Wolkoff decided to demolish the buildings and replace them with condominiums, the artists sought legal action to protect their artworks. The artists sought a preliminary injunction to prevent the destruction of their work. The district court denied the request for injunctive relief, stating in its order that it would issue a final written decision soon. Rather than wait for the court's final decision (which was issued eight days later), Wolkoff whitewashed the artworks and destroyed almost all of the paintings on the buildings. The court awarded $6.7 million in damages to be distributed to the 21 affected artists (*Cohen v. G&M Realty, LP*, 2018).

Considering ... Works of Visual Arts

Recall Kyle Busch's destruction of the guitar trophy awarded to the winner of the Nationwide Series Federated Auto Parts 300 at a racetrack in Nashville. The Gibson guitar has become the symbol of Nashville Superspeedway. The one Busch smashed in celebration of his victory was the 30th designed by Bass, who said the trophy has come to be "a very revered piece of history ... and revered by the fans here in Tennessee" (Woody, 2009). Bass estimated that he and Gibson put "hundreds and hundreds of hours" of work into the guitar, which is so unique that "you can't just buy this thing right off the shelf."

Questions

1 Would any action against Busch by longtime NASCAR artist Sam Bass, who painted the Gibson guitar, be covered by VARA?

2 Since this was a spontaneous destruction rather than the planned demolition involved in the 5Pointz case, what remedies are available for Bass?

Copyright Infringement

Copyright infringement occurs when someone makes an unauthorized use of a copyrighted work. To prove copyright infringement, the copyright owner must (1) prove ownership of a valid copyright and (2) prove copying of constituent elements of the work that are original. Even accidental or inadvertent copying constitutes infringement. Courts have adopted a substantial similarity test to satisfy the copying element of direct infringement. The test has two parts:

1 The defendant had access to the copyrighted work.
2 The allegedly infringing work is substantially similar to the copyrighted work.

The United States Court of Appeals affirmed the dismissal of a copyright infringement action filed by writers against HBO, alleging the series "Ballers" infringes on their copyright for a proposed series called "Off-Season." The general standards for establishing copyright infringement of this nature requires that once the plaintiff has demonstrated "ownership in a valid copyright" and "copying of constituent elements of [the copyrighted] work are original," the plaintiff must also demonstrate the defendant had "access to the copyrighted work of the plaintiff" and the "works at issue are substantially similar in their protected elements." To determine if the works are substantially similar, the court uses a two-part intrinsic and extrinsic test articulated in *Kouf v. Walt Disney Pictures & Television* (1994). "The intrinsic test is a subjective comparison that focuses on 'whether the ordinary, reasonable audience' would find the works substantially similar in the 'total concept and feel of the works.'" Because of its subjective nature, the intrinsic test is an assessment to be determined by a jury.

Next, the court applies the objective extrinsic test, comparing "specific expressive elements which seek to find 'articulable similarities between the plot, themes, dialogue, mood, setting, pace, characters, and sequence of events in two works'" (*Kouf*, p. 1045). After applying the "extrinsic test," the court concluded that there were "surface similarities" and the similarities indicated by the Appellants "fall under the category of general plot ideas, familiar stock scenes, or scenes-a-faire, which are not protectable." The court did not find substantial similarity between "Off-Season" and "Ballers" (MetNews, 2018; see *Silas v. Home Box Office, Inc.*, 2018).

In the case that follows, copyright infringement was raised by Frederick Bouchat against the Baltimore Ravens for the alleged copying of a logo design he created after it was announced that the former NFL Cleveland Browns were moving to Baltimore.

Bouchat v. Baltimore Ravens, Inc.

241 F.3d 350 (4th Cir. 2000)   **FOCUS** CASE

FACTS

The plaintiff, Frederick Bouchat, filed an action in federal district court seeking $10,000,000 in damages. He alleged that the Baltimore Ravens and NFL Properties had infringed his copyright rights in a "shield logo." Bouchat is an amateur artist who works full-time as a security guard at the State of Maryland Office building in Baltimore. As public knowledge of the new team spread in 1995, Bouchat, on his own, created drawings and designs for his favorite possible team name – the Ravens. Bouchat put his design on a miniature football helmet and gave the helmet to Eugene Conti, a state official who worked in the state office building in late 1995. Thereafter, Conti set up a meeting between Bouchat and John Moag, the chair of the Maryland Stadium Authority.

In March 1996, Bouchat met Moag at Moag's law office. The office suite that held Moag's office also held the temporary offices of the Ravens and the team owner, David Modell. After learning of Bouchat's work, Moag urged Bouchat to send his drawings to him (Moag), and Moag stated that he would give them to the Ravens for consideration. On April 1 or 2, 1996, Bouchat faxed his drawings as requested. On April 2, 1996, Modell met with the NFL Properties design director to discuss the development of a team logo. In June of 1996, the Ravens unveiled their new logo, which Bouchat immediately recognized as his work. Bouchat copyrighted the drawing in August 1996 and later filed a copyright infringement suit against the Ravens and NFL Properties. A jury returned a verdict for Bouchat and the Ravens appealed.

HOLDING

The court of appeals ruled in favor of Bouchat.

RATIONALE

To prove copyright infringement, a plaintiff has to prove that the defendant copied protected elements of the work. The plaintiff may prove by circumstantial evidence that the alleged infringer had access to the work and that the supposed copy is substantially similar to the author's original work. In this case, to prove access, the plaintiff successfully showed that the NFL designers, the alleged infringers, had an opportunity to view Bouchat's drawings because Bouchat had evidence that he faxed the drawing to Moag, who shared an office with Modell. By proving that the drawings were sent to Moag and that Modell shared office space with Moag, the plaintiff proved that Modell had access to the drawing. Bouchat was not required to prove that Modell actually saw the drawings, merely that Modell had access to the drawings.

The court had to determine how the doctrine of striking similarity would be applied in this case. The court had two interpretations of the strikingly similar doctrine from which to choose. The Fifth Circuit has held that access need not be proven if there is a striking similarity. However, the Second and Seventh Circuits have held that striking similarity is only circumstantial evidence of copying that supports the inference of access. The Fourth Circuit adopted the rationale of the Second and Seventh Circuits and held that the striking similarity of the works was a proper factor for the jury to consider, with all other evidence, to determine whether the plaintiff had proven copying.

Bouchat's case is one of the most litigated sport copyright infringement cases as of 2014, as evident by the U.S. Court of Appeals considering Bouchat's fourth appeal in 2010. In that appeal Bouchat's copyright infringement case against the Baltimore Ravens football organization and the NFL related to their unauthorized copying of a Ravens team logo drawn by Bouchat that was used for three seasons as the team's official symbol (*Bouchat v. Baltimore Ravens Ltd. Pshp*, 2010). Bouchat filed an action to enjoin defendants' depictions of the copyrighted logo in season highlight films. The district court found that defendants's depictions of the logo were a fair use and entered judgment against Bouchat. The court of appeals addresses the fair use defense in the Case Opinion in the next section.

A district court in Minnesota also considered the substantial similarity requirement in a copyright infringement case filed between the NFL and Titlecraft, Inc. Titlecraft manufactured fantasy football league trophies which were similar to the NFL's Vince Lombardy Trophy (Lombardy Trophy). The Lombardi Trophy was created by Tiffany & Co for the NFL is made of sterling silver and consists of a replica football sitting at an angle on top of a three sided based with concave sides. The NFL's copyright for the trophy was not disputed nor was Titlecraft's access to the trophy. Titlecraft asserted that the two items were not substantially similar since their trophies were made from wood and the sides on the base were not concave. The court began its decision stating that it is often confronted with difficult cases but that this was not one of them. The court easily concluded that Titlecraft had infringed on the NFL's copyright. The court did however discuss that substantial similarity requires the works to be similar in both *idea* and *expression*. The idea is evaluated extrinsically, focusing on objective similarities in the details of the works including the type of artwork, materials used, subject matter and setting for the subject. To determine the similarity of the expression, the court evaluates intrinsically based on how an ordinary and reasonable person would respond to the form of expression. Expression similarities are mindful of the total concept and feel of the work. It does not require exact duplication. The court concluded that both the idea and expression of Titlecraft's trophies were substantially similar to the Lombardy Trophy (*Titlecraft, Inc. v. National Football League*, 2010).

Defenses to Copyright Infringement

The Copyright Act provides for several exceptions to the exclusive rights granted a copyright owner. The defense most often used in the entertainment and sport industries is **fair use** discussed previously in the context of trademark law. The fair use defense as it relates to copyrights was originally created by the courts as an equitable rule of reason that permitted courts to avoid rigid application of a copyright statute if such application would stifle the very creativity that the law is designed to foster. This defense is now expressly included in the Copyright Act as presented in Exhibit 18.12.

The line between infringement and fair use is not clearly drawn. A finding of a commercial purpose will not automatically defeat a fair use claim, and there is no magic portion or percentage calculation to use to determine substantiality. Cases raising fair use defenses are decided on a case-by-case basis. In general, if the new work substantially transforms the original one through comment, criticism, or additional materials, it is likely deserving of fair use protection and represents creative work on the part of its author. A parody is recognized as a fair use, as was reaffirmed by the Supreme Court in *Campbell v. Acuff-Rose Music, Inc.* (1994), where rap group 2 Live Crew released a song containing musical and lyrical elements very similar to the classic Roy Orbison song "Pretty Woman."

Exhibit 18.12 Fair use as defined in the Copyright Act.

[T]he fair use of a copyrighted work . . . for purposes such as criticism, comment, news reporting, teaching (including multiple copies for classroom use), scholarship, or research, is not an infringement of copyright. In determining whether the use made of a work in any particular case is a fair use the factors to be considered shall include –

- the purpose and character of the use, including whether such use is of a commercial nature or is for nonprofit educational purposes;
- the nature of the copyrighted work;
- the amount and substantiality of the portion used in relation to the copyrighted work as a whole; and
- the effect of the use upon the potential market for or value of the copyrighted work (17 U.S.C. § 107 (2013)).

Now let's consider how fair use applies to protected copyrighted works in the following Case Opinion in which the saga between Frederick Bouchat and the Baltimore Ravens continues.

Bouchat v. Baltimore Ravens Limited Partnership

CASE OPINION   619 F.3d 301 (4th Cir. 2010)

FACTS

Bouchat owns the copyright in a drawing he created in 1995 and proposed for use as the Ravens team logo (the Shield logo). The Ravens used a strikingly similar logo design during the team's first three seasons, 1996, 1997, and 1998 (the Flying B logo). The Flying B logo was displayed on the side of the Ravens football helmet, painted on the Ravens field, and printed on flags, hats, tickets, and other assorted objects. This appeal arises from an action brought by Bouchat for an injunction prohibiting all current uses of the Flying B logo and requiring the destruction of all items exhibiting the Flying B logo.

The Ravens and the NFL currently display and sell Ravens highlight films of the 1996, 1997, and 1998 seasons for $50 each. The highlight films contain actual game footage, edited with slow motion effects, musical scores, and a narration. The Flying B logo is displayed in the films just as it was during each game: the logo appears primarily on the helmets of the Ravens players. Absent a valid defense of fair use, defendants's current depictions of the Flying B logo would violate Bouchat's copyright in the Shield logo. The district court issued a decision determining that all of defendants's depictions of Bouchat's copyright constituted fair use. Bouchat appeals this final order, challenging the fair use determination.

HOLDING

The depiction of the Flying B logo in the season highlight films sold by the NFL and the highlight film played during the Ravens home football games is an infringement of Bouchat's copyright.

RATIONALE

Section 106 of the Copyright Act grants "a bundle of exclusive rights to the owner of the copyright," including the rights "to publish, copy, and distribute the author's work." These rights, however, are "subject to a list of statutory exceptions, including the exception for fair use provided in 17 U.S.C. § 107." Fair use is a complete defense to infringement. In other words, "the fair use of a copyrighted work ... is not an infringement of copyright."

The fair use inquiry is "not to be simplified with bright-line rules, for the statute, like the doctrine it recognizes, calls for case-by-case analysis." See *Campbell v. Acuff-Rose Music, Inc.*, 510 U.S. 569, 576, 114 S. Ct. 1164, 127 L.Ed.2d 500 (1994). Nevertheless, it is appropriate to use the four statutory factors listed in § 107.

Factor One: Purpose and Character of the Use

Under § 107's first factor we consider "the purpose and character of [defendants'] use [of the Flying B logo], including whether such use is of a commercial nature or is for nonprofit educational purposes" 17 U.S.C. § 107(1). This inquiry "may be guided by the [fair use] examples given in the preamble to § 107, *Campbell*, 510 U.S. at 578, specifically, "criticism, comment, news reporting, teaching ... scholarship, or research." The 1996 highlight film played by the Ravens during home football games is part of an entertainment package included in the price of tickets to the games. The longer season highlight films for 1996, 1997, and 1998 are also objects of entertainment, marketed and sold to the public on the NFL's website for $50. The core commercial purpose of the highlight films does not align with the preamble's protected purposes of comment, news reporting, research, and the like.

We also ask whether and to what extent the new work is transformative." "A 'transformative' use is one that 'employ[s] the [copyrighted work] in a different manner or for a different purpose from the original,' thus transforming it." A logo is an identifying symbol. The Flying B logo was designed and used as a symbol identifying whatever or whomever it adorned with the Baltimore Ravens football organization. There is no transformative purpose behind the depiction of the Flying B logo in the highlight films. The use of the logo in the films serves the same purpose that it did when defendants first infringed Bouchat's copyrighted Shield logo design: the Flying B logo identifies the football player wearing it with the Baltimore Ravens. The simple act of filming the game in which the copyrighted work was displayed did not "add something new" to the logo. It did not "alter the [logo] with new expression, meaning or message."

We disagree with the district court's conclusion that the purpose behind the use of the Flying B logo in the highlight films was "primarily historical." While the films no doubt add to the historical record of Ravens play, the use of the logo in those films simply fulfilled its purpose of identifying the team. The logo continues to fulfill that purpose whenever a highlight film is shown. Simply filming football games that include the copyrighted logo does not transform the purpose behind the logo's use into a historical one. Merely labeling a use as historical does not create a presumption of fair use. Here, there is nothing transformative in the use of the Flying B logo in the season highlight films.

Consideration of the purpose and character of the use also includes an examination of "whether [the] use is of a commercial nature or is for nonprofit educational purpose" 17 U.S.C. § 107(1). Here, the commercial purpose behind the season highlight films "tends to weigh against a finding' that the challenged use is a 'fair use." It is customary for NFL teams to license their copyrighted logos for use in any number of commercial products (see *Bouchat III*, 506 F.3d at 325). Of course, Bouchat did not receive the customary price for the use of his copyrighted logo in the highlight films. Because defendants' use of Bouchat's logo is non-transformative, we have no hesitation in concluding that the commercial nature of the use weighs against a finding of fair use. In sum, the purpose and the character of the use of the Flying B logo weighs against a finding of fair use in the depiction of the logo in the highlight films.

Second Factor: Nature of the Copyrighted Work

The second statutory factor directs us to consider "the nature of the copyrighted work" 17 U.S.C. § 107(2). The copyrighted work here is a creative drawing, and "[c]reative works ... are closer to the core of works protected by the Copyright Act." We agree with the district court that the creative nature of Bouchat's work "would ... tend to indicate that making a copy would not be fair use." This factor weighs against a finding of fair use of the Flying B logo in the highlight films.

Third Factor: Amount and Substantiality of the Copyrighted Work

The third factor directs us to consider "the amount and substantiality of the portion used in relation to the copyrighted work as a whole" 17 U.S.C. § 107(3). "Copying an entire work weighs against finding a fair use." Bouchat's entire work is reproduced in the highlight films. The "ordinary effect" of "the fact that the entire work is reproduced ... militat[es] against a finding of fair use." Unless the use is transformative, the use of a copyrighted work in its entirety will normally weigh against a finding of fair use. The district court weighed the third factor in favor of finding a fair use because "the Flying B logo, although depicted in its entirety, is not a major component of the entire work in which it is used." This conclusion was error because "a taking may not be excused merely because it is insubstantial with respect to the infringing work," for "no plagiarist can excuse the wrong by showing how much of his work he did not pirate." What matters is the amount of the copyrighted work used. Here, Bouchat's entire work was copied. We consequently weigh the third factor against a finding of fair use.

Fourth Factor: Effect of the Use on the Market for the Copyrighted Work

The fourth factor directs us to consider "the effect of the use upon the potential market for or value of the copyrighted work." "This last factor is undoubtedly the single most important element of fair use." We "consider not only the extent of market harm caused by the particular actions of the alleged infringer, but also whether unrestricted and widespread conduct of the sort engaged in by the defendant would result in a substantially adverse impact on the potential market for the original."

The Ravens and the NFL did not submit any evidence to the district court about potential markets. Despite their lack of evidence about potential markets, defendants argue that the fourth factor (market effect) weighs in favor of fair use because "[a] jury has already determined … that none of Defendants' profits from their active use of the Flying B logo in merchandise was attributable to Bouchat's work." However, a finding that none of defendants' profits derived from the Flying B logo has no bearing on "the potential market for or value of the copyrighted work" 17 U.S.C. § 107(4). In fact, we know that there was a market for Bouchat's copyrighted logo when the Ravens used the Flying B logo for the 1996, 1997, and 1998 seasons. In 1996, the NFL granted "licenses and other forms of permission" allowing the Flying B logo to be "used by hundreds of manufacturers, distributors, sponsors, etc. in connection with their respective business operations" *Bouchat v. Champion Products, Inc.*, 327 F.Supp.2d 537, 540 (D. Md. 2003). In light of the market in licensing historic logos, defendants' unrestricted use of the infringing Flying B logo "would result in a substantially adverse impact on the potential market for [Bouchat's] original" logo. These findings, and defendants' failure to show the lack of a market, require us to weigh the fourth factor against a finding of fair use.

CONCLUSION

We have considered each of the four statutory factors separately and found that each one goes against a finding of fair use.

QUESTIONS

1 What is the purpose of the fair use doctrine?
2 What factors do the courts consider when determining whether the use of a copyrighted work qualifies as a "fair use"?
3 Which of the above factors carried the most weight in this case and why?
4 What makes the use of a copyright sufficiently transformative to meet the fair use requirements?

Read the full text of the case, *Bouchat v. Baltimore Ravens Limited Partnership*, 619 F.3d 301 (4th Cir. 2010) and compare the court's analysis regarding the use of the Shield logo in highlight films versus its depiction in the Ravens's corporate lobby.

Bouchat carefully applies the traditional fair use factors to a common copyright infringement claim. However, in a digital world, where broadcasts are live streamed and instantaneously captured on video, Tweeted, or turned into GIF's and circulated via social media, traditional application of fair use principles is particularly confounding. Therefore, an understanding of the legal protections provided to internet service providers is necessary.

Digital Millennium Copyright Act

The Digital Millennium Copyright Act (DMCA), amending Copyright Act of 1976 by implementing the World Intellectual Property Organization (WIPO) Copyright Treaty and the WIPO Performances and Phonograms Treaty. The DMCA is divided into five titles: Title I, WIPO Copyright and Performances and Phonograms Treaties Implementation Act of 1998, Title II, Online Copyright Infringement Liability Limitations Act, Title III Computer Maintenance Competition Assurance Act, Title IV contains provision regarding exceptions for libraries, distance education, webcasting, and application under collective bargaining agree and Title V, Vessel Hull Design Protection.

Title II, Online Copyright Infringement Liability Limitations Act, of the DMCA is of particular importance in understanding infringement activity on the internet and a service provider's responsibility under the DMCA. Title II amends the Copyright Act by creating a safe harbor for online service providers and special rules regarding the manner in which these limitations are applied to nonprofit educations institutions. A service providers liability for copyright infringing conduct are limited in the following ways: (a) Transitory communications where the service provider role is that of one who simply routs or connects information through systems; (b) System caching, "intermediate and temporary storage of material on a system or network" (i.e., an operating system which reads data from a disk and writes it to the application buffer); (c) Storage of information on systems or networks at direction of users; and d. Information location tools, "linking users to and online location containing infringing material or infringing activity" (DMCA, 1998).

If a content owner notices that their property it is being used on the web without their authorization, he can file a DMCA takedown request. The content owner must first determine the geographic location of the host website (not search engines like Google, which merely discovers content hosted by websites). Once the host's locations has been determined, the content owner can prepare the take down request. Pursuant to the DMCA, the take down request must include (a) personal contact information, (b) the name (or title) and address (i.e., URL of the webpage) of the content being appropriated, (c) a statement indicating the use of the content was not authorized, (d) a statement that identifying the content owner as the authorized copyright owner, and (e) a signature. After the correspondence has been sent to the appropriate address, the internet service provider is obligated to act "expeditiously to remove or disable access to the infringing material" (DMCA, 1998), from their servers within a reasonable time period. If the accused infringing party submits a counter-notice contending the content should not have been removed, the internet service provider is legally required to replace the content. At this point the content owner must file a lawsuit for any redress.

The DMCA was passed in 1998 and last amended in 2010. In a digital world where content is captured and reposted instantly and where technological advancements occur at blistering rates, critics of the DMCA urgently call for the modernization of the act to "more adequately address the intensifying struggle between protecting creativity and preserving free speech" (Valdez, 2016).

The Law of Patents

The law of patents is a highly specialized area, so we don't cover it in detail in this text; but a brief overview will help sport managers understand how patents impact the sport industry and how they differ from copyrights and trademarks. Remember that the law of trademarks relates to protections for brand names, logos, and slogans, and copyright law protects artistic works. Patents protect inventions. A patent is an intellectual property right granted by the federal government to an inventor "to exclude others from making, using, offering for sale, or selling the invention" throughout the United States in exchange for public disclosure of the invention when the patent is granted (35 U.S.C. § 154(a)(1)). Generally, the grant of a new patent lasts for 20 years from the date on which the application was filed (35 U.S.C. § 154(a)(2)).

Types of Patents

Two types of patents are relevant to the sports industry: utility patents and design patents. *Utility patents* may be granted to anyone who invents or discovers any new and useful process, machine, article of manufacture, or composition of matter, or any new and useful improvement thereof (USPTO, 2015). For example, the invention of a competition swimsuit used to enhance a swimmer's performance in the water or a football helmet designed to limit concussions would be registered as a utility patent. The unique performance-enhancing features of the swimsuit and the protective material used in the helmet are useful innovations to their respective sports, and thus the process and development of the physical products would be patentable. *Design patents* may be granted to anyone who invents a new, original, and ornamental design for an article of manufacture (USPTO, 2015). The design of a tennis racket or soccer cleat would qualify as a design patent. Newly developed sports products and equipment are often filed as both utility and design patents by an applicant.

Patent Litigation

In the world of sport, major sporting goods and equipment manufacturers such as Nike, Spalding, and Under Armour seek patent protection by submitting product designs and inventions to the USPTO. Among sports in the United States, patents for sports equipment and products make up the vast majority of applications and patents for everything from golf clubs and balls, baseball bats, high-tech bicycles, football cover fabrics, and running shoes. In recent years, there has been much interest in "non-practicing entities" (NPEs), which are organizations that do not produce any product based on an invention protected by a patent. Instead, NPEs purpose is to obtain patents for the purpose of monetizing the patents via licensing the patent or vigorous patent infringement litigation against practicing entities (Choudhary & Rastogi, 2012). Recent narratives see NPEs as "brokers" or "clearinghouses" boosting the secondary markets for intellectual property, by turning patents and patent litigation into a commodity, which are bought and sold on the open market. For others, NPEs are often referred to as "patent trolls" (Leiponen & Delcamp, 2019). While patent litigation has steadily declined between 2015 and 2018, as did NPE lawsuit filings, NPE filing remains high when compared to companies which derive most of their revenues from the sales of good and services. Most stunningly, by September 2018, NPE patent litigation against small- and medium-sized enterprises (SMEs) accounted for 40 percent of new patent claim filings (80 percent against SMEs in the high-tech industry) (Patent Dispute Report, 2018). Companies like adidas, Fitbit, and New Balance Athletes are some of the sports equipment practicing enterprises who were named defendants in litigation brought by an NPE.

There are two strategies defendants can employ against patent trolls. First, requesting an Inter Partes Review (IPR). An example of how the Inter Partes Review functions is illustrated in litigation brought by Sportsbrain Holdings LLC. Between 2013 and 2018, Sportsbrain Holdings LLC, an NPE, filed a single patent lawsuit against more than 100 defendants, including Apple Inc., New Balance Athletics (Brachmann, 2017). The patent lawsuit related to personal data collection technology integrated into smartwatches. One of the defendants requested an IPR. The IPR allows the defendants to challenge the validity of a patent. A court in one of the Sportsbrain cases, issues a stay pending the outcome of the IPR. The Patent Trial and Appeal Board (PTAB) performed the review and found Sportsbrain's patent invalid (Parker, Mullen, & Karas, 2018).

A second strategy is to unite defendants into a joint defense group (Parker et al., 2018). Because NPEs often sue multiple companies, forming a joint defense group would allow them to coordinate their defense, and benefit from "common interest privilege" so they are able to share information across defendants represented by different counsel without waiving attorney–client privilege.

Publicity Rights and Intellectual Property

Using the name or image of professional or collegiate athletes implicates rights known as publicity rights, and use of a person's name or image without their consent in advertising is prohibited in most states. Publicity rights are created either by common law or statute and are a matter of state law, in other words, there is no federal right of publicity (McCarthy & Schechter, 2020, although some lawyers have advocated for Congress to enact a federal right of publicity statute (Roesler & Hutchinson, 2020; Vick & Jassy, 2011). Around 40 states have some form of protection for the right of publicity either based upon common law or state statute (Digital Media Law Project, 2020).

The right of publicity was first recognized in 1953 in *Haelan Laboratories, Inc. v. Topps Chewing Gum, Inc.* Haelan claimed that a competing chewing gum company, Topps, induced professional baseball players to breach their baseball card contracts with Haelan. Topps argued that any contract between Haelan and the baseball players was merely a release that protected Haelan from liability for violating the players' right of privacy. However, the court acknowledged the commercial value present in a famous person's persona. The court stated,

> For it is common knowledge that many prominent persons (especially actors and ball-players), far from having their feelings bruised through public exposure of their likenesses, would feel sorely deprived if they no longer received money for authorizing advertisements, popularizing their countenances, displayed in newspapers, magazines, busses, trains and subways. This right of publicity would usually yield them no money unless it could be made the subject of an exclusive grant which barred any other advertiser from using their pictures. (Haelan, 1954, p. 868)

Elements for Right of Publicity Claims

The following elements have been developed in the Restatement (Third) of Unfair Competition, § 46 for a right of publicity claim:

1 *Use of a person's identity*: Identity typically can include a name, image, or likeness that is identifiable as a specific person. For celebrities, protectable aspects of identity may also include photographs, use of look-alikes, voice, sound-alikes, catchphrases, and roles synonymous with the celebrity. For example, a literal depiction such as that found in the Three Stooges case (*Comedy III Productions v. Saderup*, 2001) clearly established this element when a charcoal drawing of the Three Stooges was put on a T-shirt and sold. Another example satisfying this element includes, a robot dressed to look and act like game show presenter, Vanna White (*White v. Samsung Electronics*, 1992). The Hart Focus Case that follows relates to whether digital avatars of college students that can be manipulated and altered by gamers would constitute the identity of the athlete in question.

2 *Without consent*: This element was also raised in the Hart Focus Case in which the NCAA relied on consent forms signed by NCAA athletes, including one stating, "You authorize the NCAA [or a third party acting on behalf of the NCAA (e.g., host institution, conference, local organizing committee)] to use your name or picture to generally promote NCAA championships or other NCAA events, activities or programs" (NCAA, 2013). Whether this general consent is sufficient to actually authorize the NCAA to license student likeness to gaming or other companies and whether this consent lasts indefinitely was a critical issue in the consolidated student-athlete cases (*Hart, Keller,* and *O'Bannon*) discussed below.

3 *To gain a commercial advantage*: Note that the harm must be a commercial loss. The original misappropriation claim, on the one hand, did not contain the commercial element – the nonconsensual use of a person's name just had to be done for an advantage to the person making the unauthorized use, and the plaintiff could recover for monetary losses and emotional harm (Banta, 2016). The right of publicity claim, on the other hand, requires that the advantage gained be a commercial advantage, and the plaintiff can recover only for commercial losses. **Commercial advantage** is defined narrowly; typically, it includes uses in advertising or the promotion or sale of a product or service.

In essence, a right of publicity is the right of a famous individual, such as a professional athlete or sport celebrity, to control the commercial value and use of their name, likeness, or image. This right is protected based upon principles related to invasion of privacy claims. The common law tort of invasion of privacy recognizes that misappropriation of a person's identity, image, name, or likeness interferes with their personal right to privacy. Modern right of publicity claims have evolved beyond the original misappropriation and personal invasion of privacy notions and are now intended to protect the commercial interest a person has in the exclusive use of their identity. This is particularly relevant in the sport industry, because athletes, coaches, sports reporters, and many others who are highly visible find a significant part of their success connected to their ability to market their name, image, and likeness. For instance, despite playing nine NFL seasons, when he retired from the league, Rob Gronkowski had not spent a dime of his NFL playing salary, relying instead on income generated from the use of his name, image and likeness in endorsement deals (Elkins, 2017). The importance of publicity rights to athletes is further demonstrated by the fact that Forbes' top-100 earning athletes in 2019 generated close to $1 billion in income from endorsements (Badenhausen, 2019).

Survival of Publicity Rights on Death

Another issue related to publicity rights is whether they survive the death of the athlete or sport celebrity. The law is divided on this and varies from state to state. Some states hold that rights of publicity cease at death, while as of 2016, 23 states recognized a postmortem right of publicity via statute or common law. Typically, these states view the right as an economic interest that the heirs of an athlete or sport celebrity may protect. A sport celebrity's domicile at death can be significant in determining whether his or her image retains protection enforceable by their estates or heirs, or whether it can be used freely in the public domain. Further, the length of time an estate may exploit the dead celebrity or athlete's right of publicity varies by state. Thus, it is critical that athlete estate advisors properly advise clients on where to domicile to best protect their estate's interests (Kahn & Lee, 2016).

Defenses to Right of Publicity Claims

On the one hand, the use of a person's identity in news, entertainment, and creative works for the purpose of communicating information or expressive ideas about that person is a form of protected expressive speech. On the other hand, the use of a person's identity for purely commercial purposes, such as advertising goods or services or placing the person's name or likeness on merchandise, is not expressive speech but is instead commercial speech, and afforded less protection than expressive speech as discussed earlier in the chapter. This limitation of the right of publicity is intended to maintain a balance between First Amendment protections for a free press and free speech and the individual privacy interests involved. A First Amendment defense to a right of publicity claim was first raised in 1977. In *Zacchini v. Scripps-Howard Broadcasting Co* the U.S. Supreme Court acknowledged the right of publicity and held that the defendant violated the common law rights of Hugo Zacchini, known professionally as the "Human Cannonball," by secretly taping his performance and broadcasting it on the evening news. The Court acknowledged, that the right of publicity does not always override the right of free speech. Explaining the competing rights, the Court observed that "the rationale for protecting the right of publicity is the straightforward one of preventing unjust enrichment by the theft of goodwill. No social purpose is served by having the defendant get free some aspect of the plaintiff that would have market value and for which he would normally pay" (*Zacchini*, 1977, p. 576).

Since *Haelan* and *Zacchini*, several right of publicity cases have been decided involving athletes and First Amendment issues. Right of publicity cases often focus on the threshold legal question of whether the use of a person's name and identity is "**expressive**," in which case it is fully protected under the First Amendment and will probably override a right of publicity claim, or "**commercial**," in which case it is less protected and a right of publicity claim will likely prevail.

Balancing Publicity Rights with the First Amendment

The courts have struggled with how to balance the right of publicity with First Amendment protections for expressive speech. At least three different tests have been used by the courts:

Rogers Relatedness Test

Several states follow the Restatement (Third) of Unfair Competition and use a relatedness test that protects the use of another person's name or identity in a work that is "related to" that person. The *Rogers* or relatedness test was developed in the case of *Rogers v. Grimaldi* (1989) and examines the relationship between the likeness and the work as a whole to determine whether the use of the person's identity is wholly unrelated to the product being sold. Related uses include:

> the use of a person's name or likeness in news reporting, whether in newspapers, magazines, or broadcast news[;] ... use in entertainment and other creative works, including both fiction and nonfiction[;] ... use as part of an article published in a fan magazine or in a feature story broadcast on an entertainment program[;] ... dissemination of an unauthorized print or broadcast biography; [and use] of another's identity in a novel, play, or motion picture. ... [However,] if the name or likeness is used solely to attract attention to a work that is *not related* to the identified person, the user may be subject to liability for a use of the other's identity in advertising (§ 47).

Under the Restatement's relatedness test, any person who soley uses another person's name, likeness, or other indicia of identity without their consent in connection with the sale of goods, or in connection with the offering or providing of services, is subject to liability.

Transformative Use Test

California courts use a different approach, called the transformative use test, that was invoked in *Winter v. DC Comics* (2003). Johnny and Edgar Winter, well-known musicians with albino complexions and long white hair, brought a right of publicity action against defendant DC Comics for its publication of a comic book featuring the characters "Johnny and Edgar Autumn," half-worm, half-human creatures with pale faces and long white hair. The California Supreme Court considered whether the action was barred by the First Amendment. The court adopted "a balancing test between the First Amendment and the right of publicity based on whether the work in question adds significant creative elements so as to be transformed into something more than a mere celebrity likeness or imitation" (*Winters*, 2003, p. 475; citing *Comedy III Productions, Inc. v. Gary Saderup, Inc.*, 2001). Finding that the comic book characters Johnny and Edgar Autumn "are not just conventional depictions of plaintiffs but contain significant expressive content other than plaintiffs' mere likenesses," the court held that the characters were sufficiently transformed so as to entitle the comic book to full First Amendment protection.

In another case involving famous sports artist Rich Rush's creation and sale of lithographs featuring a collage of images of Tiger Woods following his first victory at The Masters, the court again applied the transformative use test and concluded that Rush's artwork was more than a literal depiction of Woods. This is because the artist "added a significant creative component of his own to Woods' identity," making the lithographs protected speech (*ETW Corp. v. Jireh Publishing Co.*, 2003). The U.S. Courts of Appeals for the Ninth and Third Circuits also applied the transformative use test in the *Keller* and *Hart* (Focus Cases, below).

Predominant Purpose Test

In a well-publicized case, *Twist v. TCI Cablevision* (2003), the Missouri Supreme Court created its own balancing test called a predominant purpose test. Twist was a former pro hockey player. He found that a comic book titled "Spawn" contained a villain called Twist, who was shown as possessing several of the same features that characterized his hockey career. He sued TCI, on the ground that the creators, publishers and marketers of the comic book were responsible to pay for the market value of using his name and also to pay damages for the injury to the value others would be willing to pay to use his name in their product endorsements. The Missouri Supreme Court stated that its predominant purpose test would better address cases where speech is both expressive and commercial. If a product is sold that predominantly exploits the commercial value of an individual's identity, that product should be held to violate the right of publicity and not protected by the First Amendment. It is a violation even if there is some "expressive" content in it that might qualify as "speech" in other circumstances. However, if the predominant purpose of the product is to make an expressive comment on or about a celebrity, the expressive values could be given greater weight. Finding the expressive elements in the comic book were "purely subservient" to the commercial use of Twist's name to promote the book, the court rejected TCI's First Amendment defense.

Generally, publicity rights disputes in sport have involved professional athletes and famous celebrities; however, beginning in 2009, several former college athletes challenged the NCAA's continued use of the students' names and images in the NCAA College Football video game licensed through the Collegiate Licensing Company (CLC) and produced by Electronic Arts (EA). This series of cases not only raised critical legal questions regarding the NCAA's control of student-athlete publicity rights, but also highlighted the challenges faced by courts when balancing the intellectual property rights of college athletes with the right to make creative works, including video games, which are protected by the First Amendment. Creative works such as video games are a form of expressive speech, and just like commercial speech are entitled to some level of First Amendment protection. Our next two focus cases examine the different approaches courts use to balance these competing interests.

Keller v. Electronic Arts, Inc.

724 F.3d 1268 (9th Cir. 2013)	**FOCUS** CASE

FACTS

Samuel Keller was a quarterback at Arizona State University and the University of Nebraska. EA made a video game, NCAA Football, in which users could "control avatars representing college football players as those avatars participate in simulated games." Realism was a central tenet of EA's NCAA Football game, with the video game maker sending detailed questionnaires to NCAA teams to gain information about football players' behaviors and the company worked to depict "realistic virtual versions of actual stadiums" in the game.

Keller's likeness was depicted as an avatar in the 2005 and 2008 versions of the game, in that the games included avatars that were shown wearing Keller's teams' jerseys and bearing his number and personally identifying characteristics, such as weight, height and hair color. Keller sued EA in California federal court asserting "that EA violated his right of publicity under California Civil Code § 3344." EA defended the case on First Amendment grounds.

HOLDING

The Ninth Circuit affirmed the district court's ruling that EA did not have a First Amendment defense against Keller's right of publicity claims.

RATIONALE

California's "transformative use" defense did not apply in this instance, as EA's NCAA Football videogame depicted Keller "in the very setting in which he has achieved renown." The Ninth Circuit applied four defenses raised by EA "derived from the First Amendment: the 'transformative use' test, the *Rogers* test, the 'public interest' test, and the 'public affairs' exemption."

As for the "transformative use" test, the court applied the standard developed in *Comedy III Productions, Inc. v. Gary Saderup, Inc.*, which requires a balancing between the First Amendment and right of publicity to determine if a work "adds significant creative elements so as to be transformed into something more than a mere celebrity likeness or imitation." In this balancing test, five factors were considered (see Exhibit 18.13).

Applying precedent and the *Comedy III* "transformative use" test, the court found for Keller, arguing "EA's use of Keller's likeness does not contain significant transformative elements," because it replicated his physical characteristics, users were allowed to manipulate Keller in the video game in the same performance type he engaged in in reality (football) and the video game depicted venues similar to those Keller actually played in.

The court also evaluated a defense under the *Rogers* relatedness test, which arose from *Rogers v. Grimaldi*, wherein the Second Circuit balanced "First Amendment rights against claims under the Lanham Act," holding that titles of works can include celebrities' names as long as the title has "artistic relevance to the underlying work" and does not "explicitly mislead as to the source or the content of the work." In this case, the Ninth Circuit refused to apply the *Rogers* test to right of publicity claims, finding that it is only applicable to Lanham Act claims.

Next, let's compare the Ninth Circuit's decision in *Keller* to the Third Circuit's decision in *Hart*, which also involves the right of publicity but also examines how consumer interactivity with video game usage may impact the First Amendment analysis.

Exhibit 18.13 The five-factor transformative use test (*Comedy III*, 2001).

1   Whether the celebrity likeness is one of the materials of a work or the sum and substance of the work.
2   Whether the work is primarily the defendant's expression of something other than the likeness of the celebrity.
3   Whether the work is predominated by literal and imitative or creative elements.
4   Whether the marketability of the work is driven by the subject's fame.
5   Whether the artist's skill and talent was mostly used for the purpose of creating a conventional portrait of a celebrity to exploit their fame.

Hart v. Electronic Arts, Inc.

717 F.3d 141 (3d Cir. 2013)   **FOCUS** CASE

FACTS

Plaintiff Ryan Hart played quarterback for Rutgers University from 2002 to 2005. In accordance with NCAA by-laws as an amateur student-athlete, Hart was unable to realize commercial opportunities while at Rutgers. Hart had a very successful college football career, setting school records for career passing attempts and completions. Hart's participation in college football also ensured his inclusion in defendant Electronic Arts, Inc.'s (EA) highly successful *NCAA Football* video game franchise. EA's success with the *NCAA Football* franchise can be largely attributed to the game's focus on realism and detail. Users could access over 100 virtual teams in the game, all populated by digital avatars resembling their real-life counterparts, and share their vital and biographical information. In EA's *NCAA Football 2006*, for example, users can play as the Rutgers quarterback, player number 13, an *avatar* resembling Hart at 6'2" tall and 197 pounds. The default game version of the Rutgers quarterback also wore a visor and armband on his left wrist, as Hart typically did during games as a college player. While users are able to change the digital avatar's appearance and most of the vital statistics (height, weight, throwing distance, etc.), certain details remain immutable: the player's home state, hometown, team, and class year.

Hart filed suit against EA alleging a claim pursuant to the right of publicity based on EA's purported misappropriation of his identity and likeness to enhance the commercial value of *NCAA Football*. The district court granted EA's summary judgment motion, holding that *NCAA Football* was entitled to protection under the First Amendment, and dismissed Hart's claim. Hart appealed.

HOLDING

The U.S. Court of Appeals for the Third Circuit reversed the district court's grant of summary judgment to EA and remanded the case for further proceedings.

RATIONALE

The Third Circuit sought to "balance the interests underlying the right to free expression against the interests in protecting the right of publicity." The court addressed the question by analyzing the three established balancing tests used to resolve conflicts between the right of publicity and the First Amendment: the predominant use test, the *Rogers* relatedness test, and the transformative use test.

The court ultimately opted to conduct its analysis of the case using the transformative use test, finding it to be "the most consistent with other courts' ad hoc approaches to right of publicity cases." In applying the transformative use test to the case, the court sought to determine whether Hart's identity is "sufficiently transformed" in the *NCAA Football* game. The court focused on three elements in its analysis: (1) Hart's avatar as a digital recreation of his identity; (2) the context within which the avatar exists in the game; and (3) the user's ability to alter the avatar's appearance. Considering Hart's avatar in *NCAA Football* is a clear match in terms of appearance, hair color, hair style, skin tone, and other features, in addition to the avatar's identical accessories worn by Hart during his time as quarterback at Rutgers and his vital and biographical details, the court could not find a transformative element in the game's digital recreation. In regard to context, looking at how Hart's identity is incorporated into and transformed by *NCAA Football*, the court was again unable to find any transformative element. "The digital Ryan Hart does what the actual Ryan Hart did while at Rutgers: he plays college football, in digital recreations of college football stadiums, filled with all the trappings of a college football game. This is not transformative; the various digitized sights and sounds in the video game do not alter or transform the Appellant's identity in a significant way."

Finding no transformative elements in the game's digital representation of Hart and the context of his avatar in the game, the Third Circuit analyzed the user's ability to alter the avatar's appearance. The court noted at the outset that the mere presence of the feature, without more, cannot satisfy the test. "If the mere presence of the feature were enough, video game companies could commit the most blatant acts of misappropriation only to absolve themselves by including a feature that allows users to modify the digital likenesses." Citing the realism of the game and its appeal to fan bases, the Third Circuit held that the interactivity of the game is insufficient to transform student-athletes' likeness into EA's own protected expression. Because the realistic depictions of college football players, like Hart, is central to the gaming experience, the court declined to hold that the users' ability to alter the digital avatars in *NCAA Football* was sufficient to satisfy the transformative use test.

Both *Keller* and *Hart* saw the video game creator, Electronic Arts, unsuccessfully asserting a First Amendment defense to right of publicity claims based primarily on the use of the Transformative Use test. In addition to right of publicity claims, NCAA athletes have challenged their appearance in video games using antitrust law. How athletes have utilized antitrust challenges to restraints imposed on their ability to profit from their collective rights of publicity is more fully presented in Chapter 11.

The next Focus Case reviews the elements of a right of publicity claim and examines the predominant use test applicable to a First Amendment free speech defense.

C.B.C. Distribution and Marketing, Inc. v. Major League Baseball Advanced Media, L.P.

505 F.3d 818 (8th Cir. 2007)   **FOCUS CASE**

FACTS

C.B.C. Distribution and Marketing, Inc. (CBC) sells fantasy sports products. Its fantasy baseball products incorporate the names, along with performance and biographical data, of actual MLB players. Before the commencement of the MLB season each spring, participants form their fantasy baseball teams by "drafting" players from various MLB teams. Participants compete against other fantasy baseball "owners" who have also drafted their own teams. A participant's success, and their team's success depends on the actual performance of the fantasy team's players on their respective actual teams during the course of the MLB season. Participants in CBC's fantasy baseball games pay fees to play and additional fees to trade players during the course of the season.

From 1995 through the end of 2004, the MLB Players Association licensed to CBC "the names, nicknames, likenesses, signatures, pictures, playing records, and/or biographical data of each player" to be used in association with CBC's fantasy baseball products. In 2005, however, the Players Association agreed to license to Advanced Media the exclusive right to use baseball players' names and performance information "for exploitation via all interactive media." Advanced Media began providing fantasy baseball games on its website and MLB.com, the official website of Major League Baseball. Advanced Media offered CBC, in exchange for a commission, a license to promote the MLB.com fantasy baseball games on the CBC website but did not offer CBC a license to continue to offer its own fantasy baseball products.

CBC sued to establish its right to use, without license, the names of and information about MLB players in connection with its fantasy baseball products. The district court held that CBC was not infringing any state law rights of publicity that belonged to MLB players.

HOLDING

CBC's First Amendment rights in offering its fantasy baseball products supersede the players' rights of publicity; therefore, summary judgment is affirmed.

RATIONALE

The right of publicity claim. An action based on the right of publicity is a state law claim. See *Zacchini v. Scripps-Howard Broad. Co.* (1977). In Missouri, "the elements of a right of publicity action include: (1) That defendant used plaintiff's name as a symbol of his identity (2) without consent (3) and with the intent to obtain a commercial advantage." The parties all agree that CBC's continued use of the players' names and playing information after the expiration of the 2002 agreement was without consent. The district court concluded, however, that the evidence was insufficient to make out the other two elements of the right of publicity claim and addressed each of these in turn.

Symbol of identity. With respect to the symbol of identity element, the Missouri Supreme Court observed that "the name used by the defendant must be understood by the audience as referring to the plaintiff." The state court further held that "[i]n resolving this issue, the fact-finder may consider evidence including 'the nature and extent of the identifying characteristics used by the defendant, the defendant's intent, the fame of the plaintiff, evidence of actual identification made by third persons, and surveys or other evidence indicating the perceptions of the audience.'" The district court explained that "identity," rather than "mere use of a name," "is a critical element of the right of publicity."

Commercial advantage. It is true, that with respect to the "commercial advantage" element of a cause of action for violating publicity rights, CBC's use does not fit neatly into the more traditional categories of commercial advantage, namely, using individuals' names for advertising and merchandising purposes in a way that states or intimates that the individuals are endorsing a product. But a name can be used for commercial advantage when it is used "in connection with services rendered by the user." The plaintiff need not show that "prospective purchasers are likely to believe" that the plaintiff endorsed the product or service. The court determined that the players' identities were being used for commercial advantage, thus the players successfully established all the elements of the primary right of publicity claim.

First Amendment defense. CBC argued that the First Amendment nonetheless overrides the right of publicity action under Missouri law. The Supreme Court has affirmed that state law rights of publicity must be balanced against First Amendment considerations. The CBC court concluded that state law must give way to the Constitution. First, the information used in CBC's fantasy baseball games is all readily available in the public domain, and it would be a strange law that denied a person the First Amendment right to use information available to everyone.

While it is true that CBC's use of the information is meant to provide entertainment, "[s]peech that entertains, like speech that informs, is protected by the First Amendment because '[t]he line between the informing and the entertaining is too elusive for the protection of that basic right.'" The court also found no merit in the argument that CBC's use of players's names and information in its fantasy baseball games is not speech at all. On the contrary, "the pictures, graphic design, concept art, sounds, music, stories, and narrative present in video games" is speech entitled to First Amendment protection. Similarly, here CBC uses the "names, nicknames, likenesses, signatures, pictures, playing records, and/or biographical data of each player" in an interactive form in connection with its fantasy baseball products.

It is important to note that even though the Missouri Supreme Court found the players' publicity rights were infringed upon, in applying the predominant purpose test, the court concluded CBC's First Amendment interests *outweighed* the unauthorized use as constitutionally protected speech in the context of a video game. Conversely, the decision in *Hart* and *Keller*, used the transformative use test and decided in favor of the plaintiffs' publicity rights. It is also important to recognize the range of commercial products involved in this type of right of publicity litigation, containing some type of protected expressive speech such as: video games, comic books, T-shirts, and art prints, to name a few.

Additionally, there is split among courts as to which of these tests is appropriate to use to resolved right of publicity claims. At a very basic level, the transformative use test is rooted in Copyright Law fair use principles, while, the predominant purpose test is rooted in trademark law principles. Some commentators feel strongly that trademark law is a better fit for analyzing these cases because it focuses on commercial intent of using a person's identity and the impact on consumers (McSherry, 2013). Nevertheless, until the Supreme Court weighs in on the matter, sport managers need to have a general understanding of all the tests and whether a particular test has been adopted in their state or jurisdiction.

The *Hart* and *Keller* publicity rights cases raised legal questions about how courts should balance the intellectual property rights of college athletes with the right to make creative works, including video games, which are protected by the First Amendment. On September 26, 2013, EA and the Collegiate Licensing Company settled all the claims brought against them by the current and former athletes in the *NCAA Student-Athlete Name & Likeness Licensing Litigation*. The NCAA was the only remaining defendant in the cases. The cases moved forward on antitrust grounds (discussed in Chapters 10 & 11), alleging that NCAA conspired with its member schools and conferences, using the rules for amateurism to misappropriate college athletes' names and likeness for commercial gain. The district court found in favor of the plaintiffs. On appeal, the Ninth Circuit affirmed the district court's determination that the NCAA violated the athletes' rights to publicity but, reversed the District Court's less restrictive alternatives to the NCAA's practices and policies related to athletes' rights to publicity.

The controversy over college athletes' rights to publicity did not end with this decision (Gerrie, 2018). On September 12, 2019, the California state legislature pass Senate Bill 206, known as the "Fair Pay to Play Act." This bill, signed by Governor Newsom on October 9, 2019, will take effect in 2023 and would entitle college athletes in California's 58 NCAA schools an unrestricted ability to earn money on their name, image, and likeness (NIL) (Gutierrez & Fenno, 2019). Several other states followed California's lead and proposed new NIL legislation for college athletes. The Florida NIL statute included an effective date of July 2021 (Furones, 2020). The NCAA has proposed a new framework for college athletes to profit off their publicity rights, but is also intensively lobbying Congress to override the state NIL legislation with federal legislation (Colin, 2020).

The following Focus Case reviews the elements of a right of publicity claim and examines the First Amendment as incidental speech defense as applied to former professional football players featured in EA's video games.

Davis v. Electronic Arts, Inc.

| 775 F.3d 1171(2015), cert. denied, 137 S. Ct. 277 (2016) | **FOCUS** CASE |

FACTS

Electronic Arts Inc., ("EA") is a video game company, which develops and publishes video games, including *Madden NFL*. Madden NFL replicates the physical characteristics of players, allowing the user to player virtual football games between NFL teams by controlling the movements of the players' avatar. Each annual edition of Madden NFL using all 32 NFL teams, team logos, colors and uniforms, including accurate player names. EA paid a licensing fee to the National Football Players Inc., which is the licensing entity of the National Football League Players Association. From the years 2001 through 2009,

Madden NFL included successful or popular "historic teams;" however, did not secure a license to use the likenesses of the former players from these historic teams. The avatars on the historic teams had identical characteristics as the Plaintiff, as well as approximately 6,000 other former NFL players.

HOLDING

EA's use of the likenesses of former football players is not incidental because it is essential to EA's chief purpose of creating realistic virtual simulations of football games using current and former NFL teams.

RATIONALE

The cases and treaties relied on by the parties define the factors for determining *incidental use defense* as "(1) whether the use has a unique quality or value that would result in commercial profit to the defendant; (2) whether the use contributes something of significance; (3) the relationship between the reference to the plaintiff and the purpose and subject of the work; and (4) the duration, prominence or repetition of the name or likeness relative to the rest of the publication." See *Aligo v. Time-Life Books, Inc.* (1994).

As to the first and second factors, EA went to great lengths to depict accurate likenesses of the players in *Madden NFL*, which included paying millions of dollars in licensing fees for the ability to use the likeness of current NFL players. EA, itself, recognized that its Madden NFL video are successful, in part, because users can simulate play using each of the 32 NFL teams and NFL players. This acknowledgment does not comport with EA's argument that because there are several thousand player avatars, any individual player's likeness has "only de minimis commercial value." If there was no value in having an avatar closely portray individual players, EA would not go to great lengths it does to attain the desired realism.

As to the third and fourth factors, the main purpose and subject of Madden NFL is "to create an accurate virtual simulation of an NFL game. The likenesses of the former players is essential to this end. Citing EA's public statement regarding its dedication to "creating the most true-to-life NFL simulation experience as possible … We want to accurately deliver an amazing NFL experience in our game." The accurate likeness of the players is central to creating the true-to-life simulation.

Conclusion

For sport organizations, effectively managing intellectual property is certainly becoming more complex. It requires the ability and knowledge to navigate technical statutory requirements for registering trademarks and copyrights, as well as the ability to understand and interpret court decisions explaining the scope of the rights and protections available. A successful sport manager must be able to integrate knowledge of these legal concepts with his or her daily decision-making strategies.

Discussion Questions

1 What are the five functions of a trademark?
2 Explain how fanciful, arbitrary, and suggestive marks differ and why they all are considered distinctive trademarks.
3 When is secondary meaning required to establish distinctiveness, and what is the seven-factor test for secondary meaning?
4 What are the elements of a trademark infringement claim? What is the most effective way to prove the first two elements?

5 Explain the parody defense to trademark infringement.

6 Explain the difference between trademark infringement and trademark dilution.

7 Explain the concepts of tarnishment and blurring.

8 According to *KST Electric & LeCharles Bently*, when is a mark a famous mark? And what is niche fame?

9 What is the purpose of copyright law?

10 Explain the concept of originality and fixation as it relates to copyrights.

11 Explain the extrinsic and intrinsic tests for determining substantial similarity under copyright law.

12 Explain the concept of fair use and identify the four factors used when determining fair use as it relates to copyright.

13 Assume a city hosts an annual 10K run that originates at a local park, which contains a statue of a man, woman, and child. For purposes of decoration and promotion, the event organizers decide to fit each statue with an event T-shirt so when people walk or drive by they will be reminded of the upcoming event. Would this decoration violate the sculptor's moral rights (right of integrity) such that he or she could prevent the distortion of the artwork under VARA?

14 What is patent law intended to protect and how long does patent protection last?

Learning Activities

1 Visit the website for the United States Patent and Trademark Office, www.uspto.gov, and search for trademarks of a popular sport organization or sport product, such as the New York Yankees, Dallas Cowboys, National Football League, or Reebok. See if you can find the following information about the marks: owner, date of first use, date of registration, registration number, description of the mark, and type of mark.

2 The rapid growth of Internet fantasy sports has raised the question of whether use the name and likeness of former NCAA athletes in a Daily Fantasy Sports (DFS) company's marketing materials, including website and apps, fall under the newsworthy and public interest exceptions? Base your arguments on the decision in *Daniels v. FanDuel, Inc.*, 2017 U.S. Dist. LEXIS 162563.

Case Study

Andreas Papantoniou, owner of Greek restaurant in Philadelphia operated for 30 years under the name "Olympic Gyro" before receiving a cease and desist order from the USOPC, demanding the name and logo of the restaurant be changed (Geigner, 2012). The Amateur Sports Act gives the USOPC property rights to identifiers including but not limited to "Olympic Games" and "Games of the Olympiad."

Andreas cannot decide if he should comply with the cease and desist order or take on the IOC. If he decides to, it will cost him more than $6,000 to change the name, logo, signs, employee uniforms, menus, and marketing materials.

1 What factors will a court consider in deciding whether Papantoniou's mark infringes on USOPC intellectual property?

2 What business factors will Papantoniou need to take into consideration in deciding how to proceed?

3 What should Papantoniou have done when he selected the name?

4 Create four potential new names for Papantoniou's business, including: (a) a fanciful name; (b) an arbitrary name; (c) a suggestive name; and (d) a descriptive name.

5 Using the USPTO's database, conduct a preliminary search for one of your potential names to see if it is available.

Considering ... Analysis & Discussion

Generic Marks

The first element of a trademark infringement claim requires a protected property interest. Zamboni is a federally registered trademark and would be considered an arbitrary trademark that is inherently distinctive. However, the team may argue that Zamboni's mark has lost its distinctiveness and has become generic, thus no longer entitled to trademark protection. In order to prove its property interest, Zamboni would need to establish that the mark's registration is still active, that it is currently and actively being used in the advertising, marketing, and sale of its products, and that Zamboni actively monitors unauthorized uses of the mark. Based on Zamboni's website information, it would appear as though Zamboni does actively use the mark and also actively monitors its use by others in reminding consumers that it is a protected trademark. Thus, Zamboni would be able to establish a protected property interest. Zamboni should send a cease and desist letter to the team requesting that they remove the reference to Zamboni in their promotion. Zamboni may also invite the team to discuss licensing or other sponsorship options in the future.

As long as the relevant public primarily understands that Zamboni describes a particular ice resurfacing machine or that it belongs to the Zamboni Company, the mark is still valid. The use of Zamboni as a verb does not automatically constitute generic use of the mark.

Works of Visual Arts

Whether NASCAR artist Sam Bass would have any action against Busch who smashed the guitar painted by Bass turns on the question of whether the painted guitar falls under the definition of "works of visual are" under VARA. VARA was created to protect original "works of visual art," that is a painting, drawing, or sculpture existing in a single copy or limited edition. Applied art, where ornamentation or decoration is applied to an ordinary object is excluded from the definition of "works of visual art" under VARA. The test to determine if art falls in the category of "works of visual art" and therefore, protected under VARA or "applied art" and not protected under VARA turns on whether the object originally and continues to be utilitarian in nature. In this circumstance, a painted guitar originally had a utilitarian function as a musical instrument and continues to that that function, and therefore is "applied art" and does not fall under the protection of VARA.

VARA gives artists the right to prevent the destruction of art; however, when the destruction has occurred and injunctive relief is not possible, the courts allow for money damages.

References

Cases

Abercrombie & Fitch Co. v. Hunting World, Inc., 537 F.2d 4 (2d Cir. 1976).
Adidas-America, Inc. v. Payless Shoesource, Inc., 546 F.Supp.2d 1029 (D. Ore. 2008).
Adidas-America, Inc. v. Skechers USA, Inc., 890 F.3d 747 (9th Cir. 2018).
Affiliated Hosp. Prods., Inc. v. Merdel Game Mfg. Co., 513 F.2d 1183 (2d Cir. 1975).
Anheuser-Busch, Inc. v. Andy's Sportswear, Inc., 1996 U.S. Dist. LEXIS 15583 (N.D. Cal. 1996).
Anti-Monopoly, Inc. v. General Mills Fun Group, Inc., 611 F.2d 296 (9th Cir. 1979).
Atlanta National League Baseball Club, LLC, et al., v. Braves Taxi, LLC et al., No 1:18-cv-05051 (N.D. Georgia, filed November 1, 2018).
Bayer Co. v. United Drug Co., 272 F. 505 (S.D.N.Y. 1921).
Bentley et al., v. NBC Universal, LLC, et al., No 16-03693 (C.D. Cali, Western Division, September 28, 2016).
Board of Regents, The University of Texas System v. KST Electric, 550 F.Supp.2d 657 (W.D. Tex. 2008).
Board of Supervisors v. Smack Apparel Co., 550 F.3d 465 (5th Cir. 2008).
Bouchat v. Baltimore Ravens, Inc., 241 F.3d 350 (4th Cir. 2000).

Bouchat v. Baltimore Ravens Limited Partnership, 619 F.3d 301 (4th Cir. 2010).

Brookfield Communications v. West Coast Entertainment, 174 F.3d 1036 (9th Cir. 1999).

Campbell v. Acuff-Rose Music, Inc., 510 U.S. 569 (1994).

Cohen v. G&M Realty L.P., 988 F.Supp.2d 212 (2018).

Daniels v. FanDuel, Inc., 2017 U.S. Dist. LEXIS 162563 (2017).

Daubert v. Merrell Dow Pharmaceuticals, Inc., 509 U.S. 573 (1993).

Davis v. Electronic Arts Inc., 775 F.3d 1172 (2015), cert. denied, 137 S. Ct. 277 (2016).

Dippin' Dots, Inc. v. Frosty Bits Distribution, LLC, 369 F.3d 1197 (11th Cir. 2004).

Elliott v. Google, Inc. 860 F.3d 1151 (2017).

Feist Publ'ns, Inc. v. Rural Tel. Serv. Co., 499 U.S. 340 (1991).

Fleurimond v. New York University, 2012 U.S. Dist. LEXIS 95379 (E.D.N.Y. 2012).

Fourth Estate Public Benefit Corp. v. Wall-Street.Com, LLC, et al., 139 S. Ct. 881 (2019).

Hoopla Sports & Entertainment, Inc. v. Nike, Inc., 947 F.Supp. 347 (N.D. Ill. 1996).

Iancu, Under Secretary of Commerce for Intellectual Property et al., v. Brunetti, 139 S. Ct. 2294 (2019).

In-N-Out Burgers v. Puma North America Inc., et al., No. 8:19-cv-00413 (C.D. Cali filed March 1, 2019).

In re NCAA Student-Athlete Name & Likeness Licensing Litigation, 724 F.3d 1268 (9th Cir. 2013).

In re Seats, Inc., 757 F.2d 274 (Fed. Cir. 1985).

Indianapolis Colts, Inc. v. Metropolitan Baltimore Football Club, Ltd., 34 F.3d 410 (7th Cir. 1994).

Kouf v. Walt Disney Pictures & Television, 16 F.3d (9th Cir. 1990).

Leonard v. Nike, Inc., No. 3:19-cv-01035 (S.D. Cal. filed June 3, 2019).

Lyden v. adidas America, Inc., 184 F.Supp.3d 962 (2016).

Major League Baseball Props., Inc. v. Sed Olet Denarius, Ltd., 817 F.Supp. 1103 (S.D.N.Y. 1993).

Maker's Mark Distillery, Inc. v. Diageo N. Am., 679 F.3d 410 (6th Cir. 2012).

March Madness Athletic Ass'n, LLC v. Netfire, Inc., 2003 U.S. Dist. LEXIS 14941 (N.D. Tex. 2003).

Matal v. Tam, 137 S. Ct. 1744 (2017).

Moseley v. V Secret Catalogue, Inc., 123 S. Ct. 1115 (2003).

NASCAR v. Scharle, 184 Fed. Appx. 270, U.S. App. LEXIS 15254 (3d Cir. 2006).

National Football League Props., Inc. v. Wichita Falls Sportswear, Inc., 532 F.Supp. 651 (W.D. Wash. 1982).

NBA v. Motorola, Inc., 105 F.3d 841 (2d Cir. 1997).

Nike Inc. v. Maher, 100 U.S.P.Q.2d 1018 (T.T.A.B. 2011).

Nike, Inc. v Nikepal International, Inc., 2007 U.S. Dist. LEXIS 66686 (E.D. Cal. 2007).

North Face Apparel Corp. v. Williams Pharmacy. (2012, October 16). Consent Judgment of Contempt. United States District Court, Case No. 4:09-cv-02029-RWS (ED Mo., 2012).

Padres L.P. v. South Dakota Board of Regents, Ref. No. 21307.022. Consolidated Notice of Opposition (USPTO, 2013).

Phillies v. Harrison/Erickson Inc. et al., No. 19-07239 (S.D. N.Y filed August 2, 2019).

Polaroid Corp. v. Polaroid, Inc., 319 F.2d 830 (7th Cir. 1963).

Pro-Football, Inc. v. Harjo, 284 F. Supp. 2d 96 (D.D.C. 2003).

Rogers v. Grimaldi, 875 F.2d 994 (2d. Cir. 1989).

Qualitex Co. v. Jacobson Prods. Co., Inc., 514 U.S. 159, 115 S. Ct. 1300, 131 L.Ed.2d 248 (1995).

Sazerac Company Inc., et al v. Fetzer Vineyards, Inc., 265 F.Supp.3d 1013 (2017).

Sazerac Company Inc., et al v. Fetzer Vineyards, Inc., No. 17-16916 (9th Cir. 2019)

Silas v. Home Box Office, Inc., No. 16-56215 (9th Cir. filed Feb. 22, 2018).

Solid Oak Sketches, LLC v. 2K Games, Inc., 449 F. Supp. 3d 333 (S.D.N.Y. 2020).

SportsFuel, Inc. v. PepsiCo, Inc. and The Gatorade Company, No. 18-3010 (7th Cir. filed August 2, 2019).

Talking Rain Beverage Co. v. South Beach Beverage Co., 349 F.3d 601 (9th Cir. 2003).

Titlecraft, Inc. v. National Football League, 2010 U.S. Dist. LEXIS 134367 (2010).

TrafFix Devices, Inc. v. Marketing Displays, Inc., 532 U.S. 23 (2001).

TRG Motorsports, LLC. v. The Media Barons, Case No. B244937, (Cal. App., 2d District, 2013).

University of Ga. Athletic Ass'n v. Laite, 756 F.2d 1535 (11th Cir. 1985).

University of Kansas v. Sinks, 644 F. Supp. 2d 1287 (D. Kan. 2009).

USOC v. San Francisco Arts & Athletics, Inc., 483 U.S. 522; 107 S. Ct. 2971 (1987).

USPTO v. Booking.com, 591 U.S.; 140 S. Ct. 2298 (2020).

White v. Samsung Electronics, 971 F.2d 1396 (9th Cir. 1992).

Zacchini v. Scripps-Howard Broadcasting Co., 433 U.S. 562; 97 S. Ct. 2849 (1977).

Statutes

Amateur Sports Act of 1978, 36 U.S.C. §§ 220501 et seq. (1978).

Copyright Act of 1976, 17 U.S.C. §§ 101–1332 (2013).

Digital Millennium Copyright Act, 17 U.S.C. 1201– 1205 (2010).

Digital Millennium Copyright Act of 1998, 17 U.S.C. § 1201 *et seq.* (1998).

Federal Trademark Dilution Act of 1995, 15 U.S.C. § 1125(c) (Supp. II 1996).

Patents, 35 U.S.C. § 154(a) (2013).

Sonny Bono Copyright Term Extension Act of 1998, 17 U.S.C. § 301–304 (1998).

Ted Stevens Olympic and Amateur Sports Act of 1998, 36 U.S.C. §§ 220501, 220506(a), and 220506(c)(3) (2000).

Trademark Act of 1946, 15 U.S.C. §§ 1051, 1114, 1127 *et seq.* (2003).

U.S. CONST. art. I, § 8, cl. 8.

Visual Artists Rights Act of 1990, 17 U.S.C. § 106A (2013).

Other Sources

Amended Regulations on Olympic Symbols to Ensure Rights of Beijing 2022 Marketing Partners. (2018, September 13). Retrieved from https://www.beijing2022.cn/a/20180913/0602.htm.

Baker, III, T. A., & Brison, N. T. (2016). Boiler plate inked: Copyright actions brought by tattooists threaten athlete endorser publicity rights. *Sports Marketing Quarterly*, 25, 128–130.

Black's Law Dictionary. (2004). St. Paul, MN: West Publishing Co.

Boozer, C. (2018). When the ink dries, whose tatt is it anyway? The copyrightability of tattoos. *Jeffrey S. Moorad Sports Law Journal*, 2(25) 275–313.

Brachmann, S. (2017, February 11). Sportsbrain files smartwatch fitness tracker patent suits against Apple, HP, Michael Kors and New Balance. *IP Watchdog*. Retrieved from https://www.ipwatchdog.com/2017/02/11/sportbrain-smart-watch-fitness-tracker-patent-suits-apple-hp-michael-kors-new-balance/id=78162/.

Brady, E. (2018). Appeals court vacates decisions that canceled Redskins trademark registrations. *USA Today Sports*. Retrieved from https://www.usatoday.com/story/sports/nfl/2018/01/18/appeals-court-vacates-decisions-canceled-redskins-trademark-registrations/1046758001/.

Castro, C. (2018, February 6). A fresh look at the Olympic properties. *World Intellectual Property Organization*. Retrieved from https://www.wipo.int/portal/en/news/2018/article_0002.html.

Chen, A. (2012a, June 20). Knitters outraged after U.S. Olympic Committee squashes knitting Olympics – and disses knitters. *Gawker.com*. Retrieved from http://gawker.com/5920036/us-olympics-committee-is-mad-at-knitting-olympics-for-denigrating-real-athletes.

Chen, A. (2012b, June 21). U.S. Olympic Committee apologizes to knitters, but knitters will not be appeased. *Gawker. com*. Retrieved from http://gawker.com/5920315/us-olympic-committee-apologizes-to-knitters-but-knitters-will-not-be-appeased.

Choudhary, K., & Rastogi, P. (2012, September 29). Non-practicing entities (NPEs) and their impacts. Retrieved from: https://www.lexology.com/library/detail.aspx?g=2bc351e0-c393-4637-9c38-306ff7713557.

Colin, P. (2020, May 21). What's in a name? The battle over name, image & likeness rights for NCAA student-athletes continue. *Legal Current*. Retrieved from http://www.legalcurrent.com/whats-in-a-name-the-battle-over-name-image-likeness-rights-for-ncaa-student-athletes-continues/.

Conrad, M. (2018). Matal v. Tam – A victory for the slants, a touchdown for the Redskins, but an ambiguous journey for the First Amendment and Trademark Law. *Cardozo Arts & Entertainment Law Journal*, 36, 83.

Copyright Office (2019). Authors, attribution, and integrity: Examining Moral Rights in the United States. Retrieved from https://www.copyright.gov/policy/moralrights/.

Daniels, T. (2019). Ohio State's bid to trademark the word "The" denied by US Patent Office. *Bleacher Report*. Retrieved from https://bleacherreport.com/articles/2853354-ohio-states-bid-to-trademark-the-word-the-denied-by-us-patent-office.

Daprile, L. (2019). Tired of competing for "USC," South Carolina pushes a new abbreviation. *The State*. Retrieved from https://www.thestate.com/news/local/education/article224224035.html.

Davis, A. (2015). Disparaging trademarks: An analysis of Section 2(A)'s disparagement standard and the standard's application from Harjo to Blackhorse. *Oklahoma City University Law Review*, 40, 385–448.

Dean, J. (2018, February 17). Pyeongchang update: The hypervigilance of Olympic trademark protection. *University of Buffalo Sports and Entertainment Forum*. Retrieved from https://ublawsportsforum.com/2018/02/17/pyeongchang-update-the-hypervigilance-of-olympic-trademark-protection/.

Digital Media Law Project. (2020, September 10). State law: Right of Publicity. *DMLP.org*. Retrieved from https://www.dmlp.org/legal-guide/state-law-right-publicity.

D. Greene, (2017, September 5). Can the Detroit Red Wings sue the Detroit Right Wings? *The Hockey Blawg*. Retrieved from: https://www.thehockeyblawg.com/single-post/2017/09/05/Can-the-Detroit-Red-Wings-sue-the-Detroit-Right-Wings.

Farhi, P. (2013, December 3). Redskins allegedly view WJFK's parodies as a personal foul. *Washington Post*. Retrieved from http://www.washingtonpost.com/lifestyle/style/redskins-allegedly-view-wjfks-parodies-as-a-personal-foul/2013/12/03/77686ac8-5c6a-11e3-be07006c776266ed_story.html.

Fechter, G. H., & Slavin, E. (2011, November 15). Practical tips on avoiding genericize. *The Voice of the International Trademark Association*, 66(20).

Recent cases: First Amendment – right of publicity – Ninth Circuit rejects First Amendment defense to right-of-publicity claim. *In re NCAA student-athlete same & likeness licensing litigation*, 724 F.3d 1268 (9th Cir. 2013). (2014). *Harvard Law Review*, 127(4), 1212–1219.

Furones, D. (2020, June 12). Florida Gov. Ron DeSantis signs bill that allows college athletes to earn endorsements. *Sun-Sentinel*. Retrieved from https://www.sun-sentinel.com/sports/miami-hurricanes/fl-sp-desantis-ncaa-name-image-likeness-20200612-sklikkmwnvaujhjo2767q3v3ym-story.html.

Geigner, T. (2012). US Olympic Committee forces 30-year-old Philadelphia gyro restaurant to change its name. *TechDirt*. Retrieved from https://www.techdirt.com/articles/20120713/06513919689/us-olympic-committee-forces-30-year-old-philidelphia-gyro-restaraunt-to-change-its-name.shtml.

Gerrie, W. (2018). More than just the game: How Colleges and the NCAA are violating their student-athletes' rights of publicity. *Texas Review of Entertainment and Sports Law*, 18(2), 111–130.

Gioconda, J. C. (2018, Fall). School nicknames and acronyms as trademarks: Kicking the band off the bandwagon. *Arizona State Sports & Entertainment Law Journal*, 8, 1–25.

Grinvald, L.C., (2015). Policing the cease-and-desist letter, *University of San Francisco Law Review*, 49, 411–468.

Gutierrez, M., & Fenno, N. (2019). California would allow college athletes to profit from endorsements under bill sent to Newson. *Los Angeles Times*. Retrieved from latimes.com/california/story/2019-09-11/california-college-athletes-endorsement-bill.

Guttmann, A. (2020). Brand value of the 25 most valuable brands in 2020. *Statista*. Retrieved from https://www.statista.com/statistics/264875/brand-value-of-the-25-most-valuable-brands/.

Heath, E. J., & Tanski, J. M. (2010, Fall). Drawing the line between descriptive and suggestive trademarks. *ABA Commercial & Business Litigation Newsletter*, 12(1).

Hughes, E. (2018). A search by any other name: Google, genericism, and primary significance. *American University Business Law Review*, 7, 269–295.

In, S. (2002). Death of a trademark: Genericide in the digital age. *Review of Litigation*, 21, 159–189.

International Olympic Committee (2019). *Olympic charter*. Lausanne, Switzerland.

Kahn, E. W., & Lee, P. (2016). "Delebs" and postmortem right of publicity. *Landslide*, 8(3), 11–15.

Knaug, K. E. (2010). Shades of gray: The functionality doctrine and why trademark protection should not be extended to university color schemes. *Marquette Sports Law Review*, 21, 361–379.

Kobi, A. (2010, October 11). Supreme Court denies cert: USC triumphs over USC in trademark dispute. *Intellectual Property Brief*. Retrieved from http://www.ipbrief.net/2010/10/11/supreme-court-denies-cert-usc-triumphs-over-usc-in-trademark-dispute/.

LaLonde, A. G. (2011, March 28–30). Like what you see? A half-century of the controversial, confusing doctrine of aesthetic functionality. Paper presented at the *27th Annual ABA Intellectual Property Law Conference*. Retrieved from http://apps.americanbar.org/intelprop/spring2012/coursematerials/docs/TheRiseandFallandRiseofAestheticFunctionality/LikeWhatYouSee.pdf.

Leiponen, A., & Delcamp, H. (2019). The anatomy of a troll? Patent licensing business models in the light of patent reassignment data. *Research Policy*, 48, 298–311.

Linford, J. (2017). Are trademarks ever fanciful? *Georgetown Law Journal*, 105, 731–766.

Llewellyn, P. C. (2008, September 5). Trademark dilution revisions: Proof of fame, dilution. *New York Law Journal*, 240 (47). Retrieved from http://udel.edu/~pollack/Acct350/Handouts/trademake%20Dilution%202006.pdf.

Manta, I. D. (2012). Bearing Down on Trademark Bullies. *Fordham Intellectual Property Media & Entertainment Law Journal*, 22, 853–872.

Masters, D. N., & Rose, S. A. (2017, September 12). Misused sports logo raises legal questions over marks. *Chicago Daily Law Bulletin*, 163, 177.

McCann, M. (2020). Kawhi Leonard loses copyright lawsuit against Nike over logo. *Sports Illustrated*. Retrieved from https://www.si.com/nba/2020/04/23/kawhi-leonard-loses-lawsuit-against-nike.

McCarthy, J. T. (2017). *McCarthy on Trademarks and Unfair Competition* (5th ed.). Deerfield, IL: Clark Boardman Callaghan.

McCarthy, J. T., & Schechter, R. E. (2020). *The Rights of Publicity & Privacy* (2nd ed.). Deerfield, IL: Thomas Reuters/West.

McGeveran, W. (2015). The imaginary trademark parody crisis (and the real one). *Washington Law Review*, 90, 713–753.

MetNews (2018). HBO's "Ballers" is not an infringement. *Metropolitan News-Enterprize*. Retrieved from http://www.metnews.com/articles/2018/ballers022318.htm.

NCAA (2018–2019). *Division I Manual*. National Collegiate Athletic Association: Indianapolis, Indiana.

Nimmer, M. B., & Nimmer, D. (2004). *Nimmer on Copyright*. New York, NY: M Bender, 1978.

Organisation of the 2024 Olympic and Paralympic Games. Retrieved from: https://www.gouvernement.fr/en/organisation-of-the-2024-olympic-and-paralympic-games.

Oswald, L. J. (1999). "Tarnishment" and "blurring" under the Federal Trademark Dilution Act of 1995. *American Business Law Journal*, 36, 255–300.

Park, K. (2019, April). Ambush marketing: when sponsors cry "foul." *World Intellectual Property Organization*. Retrieved from https://www.wipo.int/wipo_magazine/en/2019/02/article_0004.html.

Parker, A. L., Mullen, J. N., & Karas, M. M. (2018, July 27). How sports tech companies can fight back against patent trolls. *SportTechie*. Retrieved from https://www.sporttechie.com/how-sports-tech-companies-can-fight-back-against-patent-trolls-legal-law/.

Patent Dispute Report (2018, September 28). Retrieved from: https://www.unifiedpatents.com/insights/2018/9/28/q3-2018-patent-dispute-report.

Protecting trademarks during the Olympic Games: The major issues and challenges (2019, August 5). Retrieved from https://dreyfus.fr/en/2019/08/05/protecting-trademarks-during-the-olympic-games-the-major-issues-and-challenges/.

Roberts, A. J. (2019). Trademarks failure to function. *Iowa Law Review*, 104, 1977–2054.

Rocchi, E. (2018, November 19). Fashion brands, acronyms, and trademark protection. *AMD Law Group*. Retrieved from https://amdlawgroup.com/fashion-brands-acronyms-and-trademark-protection/.

Roesler, M., & Hutchinson, G. (2020, September 16). What's in a name, likeness, and image? The case for a federal right of publicity law. *American Bar Association, Section of Intellectual Property Law*. Retrieved from https://www.americanbar.org/groups/intellectual_property_law/publications/landslide/2020-21/september-october/what-s-in-a-name-likeness-image-case-for-federal-right-of-publicity-law/.

Rovell, D. (2016). Company opposes Broncos' bid to trademark "Orange Crush." *ESPN*. Retrieved from https://www.espn.com/nfl/story/_/id/16003079/denver-broncos-attempt-trademark-orange-crush-slowed.

Rudensky, R. (2013, April 1). Aesthetic functionality after *Louboutin*. *INTA Bulletin*. Retrieved from http://www.inta.org/INTABulletin/Pages/AestheticFunctionalityAfterLouboutin.aps.

Rust, R. T., & Huang, M. (2014). The service revolution and the transformation of marketing science. *Marketing Science*, 33(2), 206–221.

Schechter, F. I. (1927). The rational basis of trademark protection. *Harvard Law Review*, 40, 813–833.

The Fashion Law. (2016). Adidas claims victories in lawsuit against former Nike inventor. *The Fashion Law*. Retrieved from http://www.thefashionlaw.com/home/adidas-claims-victories-in-lawsuit-against-former-nike-inventor.

The Fashion Law. (2018). Forever 21, Puma Settle Lawsuit Over Copied Fenty Footwear. *The Fashion Law*. Retrieved from http://www.thefashionlaw.com/home/forever-21-puma-settle-lawsuit-over-copied-fenty-footwear.

The Law Dictionary. (2013). What is goodwill. Retrieved from http://thelawdictionary.org/goodwill.

Thomas, L. M. (2009). Protecting acronyms under U.S. trademark law. *The Voice of the International Trademark Association*, 64(1).

Tobak, S. (2010, September 15). 20 brand names you don't realize are brand names. *CBSNews.com*. Retrieved from http://www.cbsnews.com/news/20-brand-names-you-dont-realize-are-brand-names/.

Tortorelli, M. (2018). Considering the 5pointz decision and the Visual Artist Rights Act. Retrieved from https://joan-mitchellfoundation.org/blog/considering-the-5pointz-decision-and-the-visual-artist-rights-act.

United States Copyright Office (2019). *Authors, attribution, and integrity: Examining moral rights in the United States*. Retrieved from https://www.copyright.gov/policy/moralrights/.

USPTO. (2012, April 11). *General information concerning patents*. Retrieved from http://www.uspto.gov/patents/resources/general_info_concerning_patents.jsp.

USPTO. (2015). Trademark electronic application system. Retrieved from http://www.uspto.gov/trademarks/fees-payment-information/overview-trademark-fees.

U.S. Trademark Application Serial No. 88446266, filed May 24, 2019.

Valdez, G. (2016, August 31). The need to update DMCA. *Columbia Undergraduate Law Review*. Retrieved from http://blogs.cuit.columbia.edu/culr/2016/08/31/the-need-to-update-dmca-2/.

Vick, K. L., & Jassy, J. (2011). Why a federal right of publicity statute is necessary. *Communication Lawyer*, 28(2), 1–21. Retrieved from https://www.americanbar.org/content/dam/aba/publications/communications_lawyer/august2011/why_federal_right_publicity_statute_is_necessary_comm_law_28_2.authcheckdam.pdf.

Wolly, B. (2019). The Ohio State University seeks to trademark "The". Retrieved from https://www.smithsonianmag.com/smart-news/ohio-state-university-seeks-trademark-180972925/.

Woody, L. (2009, June 8). Busch guitar-smashing backlash grows. *The City Paper*. Retrieved from http://nashvillecitypaper.com/content/sports/busch-guitar-smashing-backlash-grows.

Worthington, P. (2012, July 28). Using the Olympic symbols sans permission? Off with your head. *The Huffington Post*. Retrieved from http://www.huffingtonpost.ca/peter-worthington/2012-summer-olympics-canada_b_1707459.html.

Wüthrich, M. (2016). Protecting the Olympic properties, *WIPO Magazine*. Retrieved from wipo.int/sipo-magazine/en/2016/04/article_0004.html.

Zamboni, Inc. (2006). Proper use of Zamboni trademarks. Retrieved from http://www.zamboni.com/wp-content/uploads/2013/11/Trademark-Letter_2013.pdf.

Web Resources

www.copyright.gov ■ The site for the U.S. Copyright Office provides resources for authors and for online copyright registration.

www.law.harvard.edu/faculty/martin/art_law/esworthy.htm ■ View a handy guide to the Visual Artists Rights Act at the Harvard Law School website. This act prevents others from falsely claiming authorship of a work or from distorting or misrepresenting a visual work.

www.uspto.gov ■ The USPTO maintains a searchable database of registered trademarks and patents. This database should be used to search for similar marks when a new trademark is being developed.

www.theglobalipcenter.com/ ■ This website for Global Intellectual Property offers resources on patents, trademarks, design, domain names, and copyright.

19 Promotional and Operational Issues in Marketing

Alicia Jessop

Introduction

In the previous chapter, we discussed the legal issues associated with developing and protecting intellectual property (IP) rights associated with marketing products and services. This chapter focuses on how legal issues arise throughout the process of implementing marketing strategies to sell, promote, and distribute products and services. The chapter is divided into four sections relating to marketing implementation, which closely parallels several elements of a traditional marketing mix: promotion, pricing, and public relations. The first section examines legal issues arising when sport organizations promote their products and services through advertising. It includes such topics as: false advertising; athlete endorsements and rights of publicity; and special offers, such as bait, bargain, and comparative advertising. The next section examines legal issues arising when sport organizations engage in marketing promotions and sales. This section covers topics including: regulation of unfair business practices, sweepstakes and contests, fantasy sports and gambling, and ambush marketing. The third section covers legal issues involved in pricing, ticket sales, and strategic partner interactions. The final section examines public relations, including media relations, broadcasting agreements, and privacy rights. Exhibit 19.1 outlines the managerial contexts, legal issues, and relevant laws and cases covered in this chapter. But first, a brief overview of consumer protection laws impacting marketing, regulatory authority of the Federal Trade Commission (FTC), and commercial speech will help readers understand the regulatory landscape for marketing practices.

Overview of Consumer Protection and the Federal Trade Commission

A **consumer** is any individual who purchases goods or services for personal or household consumption. Consumer protection laws arose as a response to the perceived inequities of the common law following the United States' transformation into a consumer society. The common law as it relates to consumers and consumer transactions was developed in times when merchants and customers engaged in face-to-face transactions and all parties were required to protect their own interests. This was known as the doctrine of **caveat emptor** – let the buyer beware. Under the common law doctrine of caveat emptor, the duty fell on buyers to examine products for defects and imperfections prior to purchase. There was no responsibility for sellers to actively inform buyers of possible product defects or imperfections. Consumers could rely only on themselves when entering into business transactions (Hamilton, 1931). However, the modern consumer protection movement began in the 1960s with the creation and expansion of consumer rights and consumer advocacy emphasizing greater government oversight in response to unsafe products and deceptive trade practices (Waller et al., 2011). As a result, U.S. consumers enjoy a wide range of state and federal legal protections related to unsafe products, fraud, deceptive advertising, and unfair business practices.

Exhibit 19.1 Management contexts in which issues related to marketing promotion and operations may arise, with relevant laws and cases.

Management Context	Major Legal Issues	Relevant Law	Illustrative Cases
Advertising development and placement	Deceptive trade practices regulations	FTCA, State DTPA	
	Other regulations or limitations of commercial speech or advertising activities	First Amendment free speech	Central Hudson, Albarado, Nike
	False advertising	False or deceptive advertising	Stokely-Van Camp, Baden Sports, MillerCoors LLC
Celebrity endorsements	Scope of the right of publicity	Unfair competition law and Tort of Invasion of Privacy	Haelan, Zacchini, Hart, Keller, O'Bannon, C.B.C.
	Liability of celebrity endorsers for false product claims	FTCA, 16 CFR § 255.0	FTC v. Garvey
Competitors' business practices	Ambush marketing and misappropriation of goodwill	Common law misappropriation	NHL v. Pepsi, NFL v. Delaware
		Lanham Act – trademark infringement	NCAA v. Coors
Sales, ticket sales	Consumer contract rights	Uniform Commercial Code FTC and state sales regulations	Oshinsky
Developing partnerships and business relationships	Negotiating and drafting effective contracts	Contract and agency law	
	Exclusivity in contracts	Price fixing	American Needle, Dang
Interacting with and through the media	Broadcasting agreements Liability for disclosure of private information	Digital Millennium Copyright Act FERPA; Tort of Invasion of Privacy	Andrews
	Defamation	Tort of Defamation	Woy, Montefusco, Fine, McGraw, Knievel, Curtis Publishing

The Federal Trade Commission Act (FTCA) is the basic consumer protection statute of U.S. federal law and the U.S. FTC works together with a number of other federal agencies to administer consumer protection laws. In general, the FTCA regulates business practices that are either deceptive or unfair (15 U.S.C. § 45(a)(1)). Recognizing that the FTC could not fully protect consumers, state legislatures enacted consumer protection laws to protect the public. Each of the 50 states have adopted consumer protection laws related to false or deceptive advertising (Carter, 2018). All states have also passed Unfair and Deceptive Trade Practices Acts (UDAPs), approved to prohibit deceptive acts or practices in the conduct of trade or commerce, along with a laundry list of deceptive trade practices relating to unfair competition. UDAPs were also enacted in response to the consumer empowerment movement of the 1960s and are patterned after the FTCA. Most of these statutes provide for enforcement either by the state attorney general's office or an administrative agency in charge of consumer protection.

However, the specific scope of the consumer protection laws varies from state to state, because each state may adopt various forms of model acts or create its own unique consumer protection laws and enforcement schemes (Carter, 2018). For example, the growing legalization of sport gambling by states has led individual states to enact consumer protection laws specifically governing sport gambling (Jessop, 2018). In 2019, New Jersey enforced its consumer protection law by fining a daily fantasy sport operator $30,000 for not properly registering for a license to operate within the state and failing to provide consumers with notice that the information it collected from them would be shared with third parties (Reitmeyer, 2019). The emergence of new technology has also prompted consumer protection claims. In 2017, California's attorney general sued Gatorade under the state's consumer protection laws arguing that a mobile videogame application the company hosted was misleading, because it portrayed Gatorade as making athletes run faster and water causing them to slow down. Ultimately, the case was settled for $300,000, with $120,000 going to fund children's water consumption initiatives (Evangelista, 2017). Consumer protection laws are easily found on state and federal government websites. State regulations usually fall under the office of the attorney general. Sport marketers must become informed about the specific consumer protection laws applicable in the states in which they work as well as the federal regulations impacting marketing and consumer practices.

Authority of the Federal Trade Commission

At the federal level, the FTC is empowered to enforce prohibitions against "unfair or deceptive acts or practices in or affecting commerce," including prohibiting false or deceptive advertising (15 U.S.C. § 45(a)(1)) occurring anywhere in the United States. An individual consumer may not bring a private action under the FTCA. Instead, alleged violations of the Act are investigated by the FTC. The FTC periodically publishes guides intended to inform the public and businesses about how to comply with the law in their advertising and marketing practices. These guides cover a wide range of issues, including but not limited to: digital advertising, advertising to children, endorsements, health claims, and telemarketing (FTC, 2019). The guides are a basis for voluntary compliance; they are not binding law. In any law enforcement action, the FTC has the burden of proving that the challenged conduct violates the FTCA.

As you might recall from our previous chapters related to amateur athletic associations as state actors, the FTC is also a state actor, since it is a government agency. Thus, its authority and enforcement powers cannot infringe on constitutionally protected rights. Since advertising is a form of speech, FTC regulatory activities may raise First Amendment (free speech) questions. For example, if the FTC were to issue an order compelling a company to pull an advertisement or edit language in an advertisement, the action would be a government restraint on speech. Thus, the FTC's actions must be consistent with the First Amendment and not be an impermissible restraint on speech. Legal challenges to government restraints on speech have produced the **commercial speech doctrine**, which outlines the limits of the government's authority to regulate private businesses' commercial speech, such as advertising and other commercial messages. Thus, understanding the commercial speech doctrine and how it has impacted sport organizations' advertising activities helps to better conceptualize what restrictions on marketing activities are permissible by both state and federal agencies. This chapter also discusses several specific advertising practices in the sport industry that are regulated by the FTC.

Commercial Speech Doctrine Limits on FTC Authority

The First Amendment to the U.S. Constitution describes the limitations imposed upon the government if and when it attempts to inhibit expressive activities such as prayer, speech, assembly, and the press. Two key questions arise in a commercial context: (1) whether speech by a commercial enterprise, such as Nike or the NFL, is entitled to any protection under the free speech provisions of the First Amendment; and (2) if this speech is protected, how much protection must be provided. The amount of protection, if any, will determine whether the FTC can regulate that speech without violating the Constitution.

Not all speech is protected under the First Amendment, and some speech receives more protection than other types of speech. For example, obscene speech or speech intended to incite violence receives no First Amendment protection, while political speech receives the highest level of protection. The Supreme Court has held that the First Amendment embodies the principle that free expression is both vital in its own right and essential to the representative government. Political speech, even if erroneous or false, has been protected from government interference. The Supreme Court in *New York Times v. Sullivan* (1964) observed that "erroneous statement is inevitable in free debate, and it must be protected if the freedoms of expression are to have the 'breathing space' that they need to survive" (pp. 271–272). In between these two forms of speech is the right to not speak, such as: refusing to salute the flag, engaging in symbolic speech like kneeling during the national anthem, and even contributing money to a political campaign.

Exhibit 19.2 The four-factor test to determine whether a state's restrictions on commercial speech are constitutional (*Central Hudson*, 1980).

1 The commercial speech must concern a lawful activity and not be misleading.
2 The state must have a substantial interest in the restriction of the speech.
3 The regulation must directly advance the state's interest.
4 The regulation must be no more extensive than necessary to meet the state's interest.

Advertising commercial products and professional services also falls along this spectrum of protected speech and is generally referred to as commercial speech (U.S. Courts, 2019).

Commercial speech has been defined as speech that does no more than propose a commercial transaction. Advertising is the most notable example of commercial speech. Prior to 1975, it appeared clear that commercial advertising simply was not "speech" for the purposes of the First Amendment (Piety, 2005). However, in 1975, the Supreme Court in *Bigelow v. Virginia* suggested it should not be assumed that advertising is not entitled to First Amendment protection. In 1976, the Supreme Court affirmed in *Virginia State Board of Pharmacy v. Virginia Citizens Consumer Council* that speech does not lose its First Amendment protection "because money is spent to project it" (p. 761). The protection for commercial speech flows more from the consumer's right to hear about the information, than the advertiser's right to speak (Piety, 2005).

Since it is clear commercial speech is entitled to some protection under the First Amendment, the next step is determining *how much* protection it has and when the government may regulate or restrict it. As presented in Chapter 11, when the government attempts to regulate or restrict a constitutionally protected right, those regulations are subject to some level of scrutiny or review to determine if they are constitutionally permissible. As mentioned above, restrictions on political speech are subject to strict or exacting scrutiny, similar to that used for suspect classifications under the Equal Protection Clause. However, government restrictions on commercial speech must only meet an *intermediate level of constitutional scrutiny*.

The intermediate level of scrutiny requires the governmental purpose or objective in regulating the commercial speech to be *sufficiently important* to warrant the intrusion on the First Amendment and that the proposed restrictions are *directly connected* to achieving those objectives. In other words, there must be a *direct connection* between the *important goals* or *objectives* of the regulation and the actual accomplishment of those goals or objectives. The Supreme Court developed a four-factor test in *Central Hudson* (1980) to determine whether a state's restrictions on commercial speech satisfy intermediate scrutiny (see Exhibit 19.2).

The following Focus Case presents an example of how the *Central Hudson* factors, along with the intermediate level of scrutiny, are applied when a state imposes restraints on commercial speech.

Albarado v. Kentucky Racing Commission

496 F. Supp. 2d 795 (W.D. Ky. 2004)   **FOCUS** CASE

FACTS

The Kentucky Racing Commission (now known as the Kentucky Horse Racing Authority, KHRA) imposed rules prohibiting jockeys from wearing advertising on their clothing during a race. This rule first came under scrutiny soon after the 129th Kentucky Derby in 2003, when a group of jockeys (the plaintiffs) were denied permission to wear commercial endorsement patches during the 2003 Spring Meet at Keeneland Racetrack in Lexington, Kentucky. Thoroughbred horse racing is subject to extensive state regulation and control in states with a horse racing industry. Kentucky, like other states with horse racing, has expressly designated horse racing as an important and vital industry to the state and has vested a horse racing commission with broad authority and responsibility to regulate, control, and maintain the industry. As the

130th Kentucky Derby approached, many jockeys desired to pursue sponsorship opportunities; thus the plaintiffs filed suit to enjoin enforcement of the advertising ban on commercial sponsorships during the 2004 Kentucky Derby.

HOLDING

The district court ruled in favor of the jockeys holding the Commonwealth's regulations were not sufficiently connected to the stated interest of protecting the integrity of horse racing.

RATIONALE

It was undisputed that the jockeys' desire to wear corporate logos was expressing commercial speech (essentially an advertisement); thus, the four-factor test established in *Central Hudson* (1980) must be used to determine whether the state's restrictions on commercial speech were unconstitutional (see Exhibit 19.2). It was undisputed that the plaintiffs' commercial speech was neither unlawful nor misleading and that the state has a substantial interest in regulating the sport of horse racing. However, the state needed to demonstrate how this *specific regulation was directly connected* to the accomplishment of its stated goal or objective (emphasis added).

The KHRA is authorized to promulgate administrative regulations prescribing conditions under which all horse racing is conducted and establishing requirements for jockeys and apprentice jockeys (810 KAR 1:1009). These regulations cover such areas as license qualifications, amateur status, weight allowances for apprentices, jockey fees, and the contested regulation – jockey attire. Section 14 of the Kentucky regulations states that "Advertising, promotional, or cartoon symbols or wording which in the opinion of the commission are not in keeping with the traditions of the turf shall be prohibited" (810 KAR 1:009, Section 14(3)).

Thus, on its face, the objective of the regulation is to ensure that jockey attire and appearance are in keeping with the "traditions of the turf." However, KHRA produced no evidence of what specific "traditions" would warrant restricting advertising or other symbols on jockeys' attire. It was arguable that traditions of the turf related to preserving the genteel, pristine appearance and atmosphere at the racetracks. Permitting logos on jockeys' attire could create the commercialized appearance that is often associated with other professional sports but would not be in keeping with the traditions of the turf. However, despite these obvious arguments, the KHRA instead argued that the state interest at stake was protecting the integrity of horse racing and that the restriction on sponsor logos and advertising would (1) ensure an unobstructed view of the jockey if misconduct is alleged and (2) foster confidence in the betting public by avoiding collusion among jockeys sponsored by the same advertiser. The court did not question that Kentucky's interest in avoiding collusion connected with horse racing was a "laudable objective." However, "to intrude on one's First Amendment rights… requires more justification than simply establishing a substantial state interest. Logically enough, "*the regulation that limits speech must itself bear some direct and material relationship to that interest*" (p. 15). The express purpose of the regulation related entirely to a jockey's appearance as that appearance reflects on maintaining the traditions of the turf. The regulation at issue and as applied appears to have nothing to do with assessing foul play or avoiding collusion.

Interestingly, the federal district court did not question that the Commonwealth of Kentucky had an *important* interest or objective in regulating the sport of horse racing, including the attire and manner of dress of the jockeys. However, in order to restrict speech (even commercial speech) the government must do more than just have an important objective. There must be a "reasonable fit" between the regulation and the objective. If the regulation and the objective are not sufficiently related or connected, the regulation is likely to be found unconstitutional. Also, in the *Kentucky Racing Commission* case it was undisputed that the speech involved was commercial speech, but this is not always so clear. Determining whether particular speech is properly categorized as commercial or noncommercial speech requires

Exhibit 19.3 Elements used by courts to categorize speech as commercial (*Nike, Inc. v. Kasky*, 2002).

The speaker: Someone engaged in commerce. Generally involved in the production, distribution, or sale of goods or services, or acting on behalf of a person so engaged.

The intended audience: Actual or potential buyers or customers of the speaker's goods or services, or persons acting for actual or potential buyers or customers, or persons (such as reporters or reviewers) likely to repeat the message to or otherwise influence actual or potential buyers or customers.

The factual content of the message: Message is commercial in character. In the context of regulation of false or misleading advertising, this typically means that the speech consists of representations of fact about the business operations, products, or services of the company made for the purpose of promoting sales or other commercial transactions.

---

consideration of three elements: **the speaker**, **the intended audience**, and **the factual content of the message** (see Exhibit 19.3). In the next Focus Case, the California Supreme Court looks at these three elements to determine whether statements made by Nike as part of a public relations campaign following allegations that it utilized sweatshop labor to produce its products in Asia would be considered commercial or noncommercial speech. The distinction is important since the California deceptive trade practices act applies only to commercial speech. Thus, if Nike's statements were determined to be noncommercial speech, it would not be subject to the state law.

Nike, Inc. v. Kasky

45 P.3d 24, 119 Cal. Rptr. 2d 296 (2002)	**FOCUS** CASE

FACTS

Plaintiff Marc Kasky sued Nike on behalf of the general public of the State of California under Business and Professions Code §§ 17204 and 17535. Nike manufactures and sells athletic shoes and apparel. Most of Nike's products are manufactured by subcontractors in China, Vietnam, and Indonesia. Beginning at least in October 1996 with a report on the television news program *48 Hours*, and continuing at least through December 1997 with the publication of articles in the *Financial Times*, the *New York Times*, the *San Francisco Chronicle*, the *Buffalo News*, the *Oregonian*, the *Kansas City Star*, and the *Sporting News*, it was alleged that in the factories where Nike products are made, workers were not paid required minimum wage or overtime wages and were also subject to unsafe working conditions.

In response to this adverse publicity, Nike made statements to the California consuming public. Kasky alleged that Nike's statements regarding working conditions were false and misleading. Nike made these statements in press releases, in letters to newspapers, and in a letter to university presidents and athletic directors. Nike also bought full-page advertisements in leading newspapers to publicize a report that GoodWorks International, LLC, had prepared under a contract with Nike.

HOLDING

The California Supreme Court concluded that Nike's allegedly false and misleading statements were properly characterized as commercial speech.

RATIONALE

The issue was whether the defendant corporation's false statements are commercial or noncommercial speech. The Supreme Court has stated that the category of commercial speech consists at its core of "speech proposing a commercial transaction." The high court also cautioned that statements may properly be categorized as commercial "notwithstanding the fact that they contain discussions of important public issues" and that "advertising which 'links a product to a current public debate' is not thereby entitled to the constitutional protection afforded noncommercial speech." The Court further explained that "[a]dvertisers should not be permitted to immunize false or misleading product information from government regulation simply by including references to public issues." (See Exhibit 19.3 for the elements of commercial speech test.)

In the above case, the first element – a commercial speaker – is satisfied because the speakers, Nike and its officers and directors, are engaged in commerce. Specifically, they manufacture, import, distribute, and sell consumer goods in the form of athletic shoes and apparel.

The second element – an intended commercial audience – is also satisfied. Nike's letters to university presidents and directors of athletic departments were addressed directly to actual and potential purchasers of Nike's products, because college and university athletic departments are major purchasers of athletic shoes and apparel.

The third element – representations of fact of a commercial nature – is also present. In describing its own labor policies, practices and working conditions in factories where its products are made, Nike was making factual representations about its own business operations. Nike was in a position to verify the truth of any factual assertions it made on these topics. To the extent that application of these laws may make Nike more cautious and cause it to make greater efforts to verify the truth of its statements, these laws will serve the purpose of commercial speech protection by "insuring that the stream of commercial information flow[s] cleanly as well as freely" (*Va. Pharmacy Bd. v. Va. Consumer Council*, 1976, p. 772).

Applying the reasoning of the California Supreme Court in *Nike v. Kasky*, consider whether statements made during an interview by an organization's representative, such as a league's commissioner, could be deemed commercial speech if the commissioner had commercial motives. Furthermore, a number of sport executives have testified before Congress on issues such as steroid use in professional sports, sport gambling, labor exemptions in Major League Baseball, and compensation of NCAA athletes, all of which are clearly issues of significant interest to the public. When sport executives speak in that setting, is their speech considered private speech relevant to a public debate? If their motive in speaking is in part to influence consumers' perception of their league or company, is the speech more correctly classified as commercial speech? These questions relate to the critical distinguishing characteristic between political or private speech and commercial speech and draw specific attention to the leeway afforded false speech when made in a political or public debate versus the potential penalties imposed for false speech when made in the commercial marketplace. The Supreme Court held in *Central Hudson Gas & Electric Co. v. Public Service Commission of New York* (1980) that the First Amendment only protects commercial speech that is truthful and not misleading. Thus, governmental restrictions on false, untrue, or deceptive advertising have been deemed constitutionally permissible restraints on speech. Thus, the FTC authority to regulate these types of activities is constitutional under the *Central Hudson* test if the statements are considered commercial speech.

To help understand the scope of the FTC's authority to regulate deceptive or unfair advertising and business practices, we will now explore some specific regulations related to advertising in sport and recreation.

Advertising and Promotions

Sport marketers naturally want to communicate with their customers and clients about a sport organization's goods and services. This communication is usually accomplished through some method of advertising or promotional communication. The sport marketer confronts a number of state and federal regulations on advertising. At the federal level, two primary sources of law govern advertising claims: **The Lanham Act** and the **FTCA**. As discussed in regard to trademark infringement in Chapter 18, the Lanham Act permits individual and corporate consumers to enforce various protections under the act. However, the restrictions imposed in the FTCA are designed to protect consumers as a whole and ensure advertisers are truthful in their advertising to consumers. However, consumers generally are not permitted to sue directly for false advertising claims under federal law. Instead, the regulatory scheme empowers the FTC to challenge these practices if they violate federal law and state attorneys general if they violate state consumer protection laws. For example, in 2015, daily fantasy sports operators, DraftKings and FanDuel, were sued by the Attorney General for the State of New York for conspiracy to commit negligence, fraud, and deception under New York state law. The lawsuit arose after a then DraftKings employee used private company information to allegedly gain an advantage in a FanDuel game and win $350,000. The state argued that DraftKings and FanDuel advertisements were misleading, because they highlighted the relative ease of winning competitions and did not note that some competitors had inside information (McCann, 2015). Ultimately, DraftKings and FanDuel settled the case for $6 million each and were required to highlight information on their websites indicating the likelihood of success in their contests and percentages of winnings by top players (Slefo, 2016). The remedies provided in the Lanham Act for false advertising enable individuals and companies to protect their own interests in their intellectual property. The intended benefit is to avoid confusing consumers about the source or origin of products and services. The FTCA, Lanham Act, and state laws work cooperatively to limit false advertising in the marketplace. We will first explore remedies available under the Lanham Act for individuals and businesses for false advertising or unfair business practices, and then shift focus to the role of the FTC in regulating a variety of marketing activities including advertising and other promotional activities.

Advertising and the Lanham Act

Complaints under the Lanham Act typically challenge a company's false or misleading statements either about their own products or a competitor's product in some type of television, radio, or print media advertising campaign. There is generally no question that these forms of traditional advertising fall squarely within the scope of the Lanham Act. What is not as clear is when false statements appear in less traditional forms such as social media posts, surveys, letters sent to consumers, and oral statements made during sales pitches.

Defining Commercial Advertising and Promotion

Section 43(a) of the Lanham Act prohibits statements in commercial advertising or promotion that contain misrepresentations, but it does not define "commercial advertising or promotion." Some courts have noted that the touchstone of whether something is commercial advertising or a promotion is whether the advertising is part of an organized campaign to penetrate the relevant market. A majority of federal courts considering the question whether a statement qualifies as commercial advertising or promotion have applied four requirements: (1) commercial speech (see *Nike v. Kasky*, above); (2) by a defendant who is in commercial competition with the plaintiff; (3) for the purpose of influencing consumers to buy defendant's goods or services; and (4) the representation whether part of a classic advertising campaign or less formal promotion must be sufficiently disseminated to the relevant purchasing public (Weinberger, Wagner, & Simon, 2003). The Sixth Circuit recently recognized that an organized advertising campaign in 2015 would look very different than in years past as producers use data to track consumption habits and send out personalized promotional material directly to consumers, such as internet browser history based advertising, Facebook targeted ads, and ads for retail family and friends sales. While these focused messages may not be widely disseminated, they are clearly advertisements and promotions. Thus, the Sixth Circuit explained, to be "sufficiently disseminated" for purposes of being treated as commercial advertising, the campaign need only target communications to a substantial portion of the plaintiff's or defendant's existing customer or client base (*Grubbs v. Sheakley*, 2015). Based on *Grubbs*, while there is still not a statutory definition of commercial advertising and promotion, sport marketers should carefully craft all consumer messaging toward an expectation that it would likely fall within the scope of Lanham Act requirements.

Additionally, advertisements containing implied claims that are false or exaggerated may also meet the legal definition of deception (Sheldon & Carter, 2004, pp. 165–166). Actions such as puffing, incomplete comparisons, and implied superiority claims operate in a gray area within the limits of the law (Lord,

Kim, & Putrevu, 1997; Tushnet, 2011). The distinction between actual deception and sales puffing is not clear, but general expressions of opinion not made as factual representations are considered sales puffing. Sales puffing or puffery means sales talk or harmless exaggeration. Puffing statements are statements that no reasonable person would rely upon or believe represent the literal truth regarding the product or service. Puffery can be both in the form of exaggerating your own product's characteristics or those of your competitors' products. For example, an advertising campaign used by the University of Louisville referring to the City of Louisville as the "Best College Sports Town in America" would be a clear example of puffing. An exaggeration is merely expression of opinion, not actual product facts about the University of Louisville's sport programs or the city itself. Thus, a seller has some latitude in the use of sales puffing, but may not factually misrepresent the benefits or virtues of its products or services. However, in what has been referred to as the "yogurt wars" between Chobani and General Mills, a federal district court held that Chobani's claim in a television advertisement that the potassium sorbate used as a preservative in Yoplait Greek 100 was "used to kill bugs" was literally false, rather than allowable puffery. Chobani's media campaign implied the preservative in Yoplait was "bad stuff" and included a hashtag #NOBADSTUFF when featuring its Chobani 100 Greek yogurt. The court warned that an advertiser who uses exaggeration or overstatement treads a thin line when it directly attacks a competitor rather than lauding its own product. A message conveyed in advertising may be literally false if its clear meaning considered in context is false. Since the implication was that the preservative somehow made Yoplait yogurt unsafe to eat, the statement was held to be literally false (*General Mills, Inc. v. Chobani, LLC*, 2016).

False Advertising Claims Under the Lanham Act

Section 43(a) of the act permits an individual or company to sue another individual or company (its competitor) for false or misleading representations of facts, including **false advertising**. The statute states:

> (1) Any person who, on or in connection with any goods or services, or any container for goods, uses in commerce any word, term, name, symbol, or device, or any combination thereof, or any false designation of origin, false or misleading description of fact, or false or misleading representation of fact, which —
>
> > (B) In *commercial advertising or promotion, misrepresents the nature, characteristics, qualities, or geographic origin of his or her or another person's goods, services, or commercial activities*, shall be liable in a civil action by any person who believes that he or she is or is likely to be damaged by such act.

The courts have identified five factors to use to evaluate whether a claim or statement is considered false advertising under Section 43(a). (See Exhibit 19.4 for the elements of a false advertising claim under the Lanham Act.)

For example, Pepsi sued Coca-Cola, accusing Coca-Cola of false advertising and other unfair competition in connection with a two-week advertising campaign for Coca-Cola's Powerade ION4 sports drink (Berlik, 2009). In the advertising campaign, Powerade, which is marketed as "the complete sports drink," claimed to be superior to Pepsi's Gatorade due to Powerade's inclusion of trace amounts of two electrolytes, calcium and magnesium. According to the lawsuit, no evidence exists to suggest that the addition of

Exhibit 19.4 Elements of false advertising claims under the Lanham Act **Section 43(a)**.

1 A false statement of fact by the defendant in a commercial advertisement about its own or another's product;
2 The statement actually deceived or has the tendency to deceive a substantial segment of its audience;
3 The deception is material, in that it is likely to influence purchasing decision;
4 The defendant caused its false statement to enter interstate commerce; and
5 The plaintiff has been or is likely to be injured as a result of the false statement, either by direct diversion of sales or a lessening of goodwill associated with its products.

these two minerals – especially in such tiny quantities – provides any nutritional or physiological benefits. Pepsi argued Coca-Cola was misleading consumers when it displayed a photo of a Gatorade bottle cut in half alongside the slogan, "Don't settle for an incomplete sports drink." Pepsi sought an injunction halting Coca-Cola's advertising. The key issues were whether the statements in Coca-Cola's advertising were actually false and whether labeling Gatorade an "incomplete sports drink" tends to deceive consumers and/ or influence purchasing decisions. The federal district court denied the injunction based on Pepsi's own aggressive advertising claims related to the benefits of calcium and magnesium in sports drinks (*Stokely-Van Camp v. The Coca Cola Company*, 2009).

In addition to the content of the advertising message, product labeling must also be truthful and not misleading. POM Wonderful pomegranate juice is a good example of the overlapping regulatory landscape for product labeling and advertising. In 2014, POM Wonderful prevailed in a suit under Section 43(a) against Coca-Cola. POM Wonderful asserted that Coca-Cola's product labeling was false and misleading. Coca-Cola labeled its product "POMEGRANATE BLUEBERRY" with "100% JUICE" strategically placed in large font next to the name. Much smaller print disclosed that the product was a blend of five different juices. In fact, Coca-Cola's juice product contained three drops of pomegranate juice and even less blueberry juice, and was primarily a blend of apple and white grape juice. Coca-Cola argued that its label met FDA requirements and thus was exempt from claims under Section 43(a). The Supreme Court held that businesses could sue under the Lanham Act even when those labels did not violate FDA guidelines (*POM Wonderful, LLC v. The Coca-Cola Company*, 2014).

While the Lanham Act affords companies the right to sue for false advertising, the posturing of the company bringing the lawsuit can have unanticipated consequences similar to what Sketchers encountered when it filed suit against Adidas alleging that Adidas' illegal and secret bribes to top NCAA athletes prevented Sketchers from effectively competing for players' footwear endorsements while they were amateurs or professionals. Sketchers dismissed their complaint just 20 days after filing following a social media backlash demeaning Sketchers' actual likelihood of signing top basketball players (Sayers, 2018).

As the Pepsi/Coca-Cola example illustrates, businesses can pursue direct false advertising claims against competitors based on alleged false or deceptive advertising activities under the Lanham Act. On the other hand, the FTCA empowers the FTC to regulate advertisements to protect consumers. Next, we will focus attention on marketing activities in sport that are commonly within the scope of FTC regulatory oversight under the FTCA. The FTC regulates and monitors a variety of marketing activities involving some form of advertising including: false advertising, comparative advertising, use of athletes for endorsements, special offers (e.g., bait, bargain offers), and providing guidance to businesses concerning federal advertising standards (FTC, 2019). According to the FTCA (14 U.S.C. §§ 41-58), advertising (1) must be truthful and nondeceptive; (2) must have evidence to back up claims; and (3) cannot be unfair (FTC, 2019). The FTC has broad authority to investigate alleged deceptive or unfair advertising practices and to issue cease and desist orders prohibiting certain advertising. Several advertising and promotional activities regulated by the FTC are discussed in the next section as they relate to marketing of sports products, services, and properties.

False or Deceptive Advertising under the FTCA

The FTC has issued a Deception Policy Statement defining a **deceptive advertisement** as one containing a statement or omission, which is misleading in a material respect (FTC, 1983). Generally, the deceptive advertisement would be misleading in a material respect if it is likely to mislead a reasonable consumer and is important to the consumer's decision to buy or use the product (Federal Trade Commission Regulations, 2019). Deception can result from insinuation, not just an outright false statement. In addition, deceptive advertising may cause consumers to make inferences that go beyond what is claimed in the ad (Burke, DeSarbo, Oliver, & Robertson, 1988; Demaine, 2012; Gaeth & Heath, 1987). Exhibit 19.5 identifies the factors the FTC considers when it investigates false advertising claims.

Exhibit 19.5 Factors considered by the FTC in evaluating false advertising claims.

- A representation, omission or practice that is likely to mislead the consumer,
- the perspective of a consumer acting reasonably in the circumstances, and
- the representation, omission, or practice must be a material one.

When a sport organization develops an advertising message containing specific factual claims about its products, those advertising claims must be truthful or have a reasonable basis. If advertisements contain false or deceptive information, the FTC can conduct an investigation and impose fines and penalties against the advertiser. A case involving apparel company, Reebok, highlights this issue. In ads for its Easy Tone shoes, Reebok asserted that sole technology placed in the shoes "creates 'micro instability' that tones and strengthens muscles as you walk or run." The advertisements claimed that the Reebok shoes strengthened and toned leg and buttock muscles at a greater rate than other shoes. This claim was found to be untrue. Ultimately, the FTC and Reebok settled the deceptive advertising case for $25 million and the FTC encouraged consumers to closely examine the claims made in sport apparel advertisements (FTC, 2011).

The FTC also has primary responsibility for monitoring health-related claims in advertisements and aggressively pursues false or misleading advertising involving health-related claims. For example, in 2012 the FTC announced that Skechers USA, Inc. would pay $40 million to settle charges that the company deceived consumers by making unfounded claims that its shoe products would help people lose weight, and strengthen and tone their buttocks, legs, and abdominal muscles (FTC, 2012). The FTC complaint challenged several Skechers advertisements related to the company's Shape-ups line, arguing Skechers violated federal law by making deceptive advertising claims, including falsely representing that clinical studies backed up the claims. The FTC settlement barred Skechers from making claims about physical health or fitness-related benefits for its toning shoes unless the claims were truly backed by scientific evidence (FTC, 2012). New Balance also settled a false advertising case for $2.3 million for its false claims that its toning shoes, TrueBalance and Rock&Tone, would activate lower body muscles and help burn more calories (Hines, 2012).

Health-related claims are also monitored by the Food & Drug Administration (FDA). The FDA requires manufacturers to obtain pre-approval for health claims on product labels. So, the FDA regulates statements on the *product labels* and the FTC regulates statements contained in *product advertising*. One of the most significant decisions from the FTC came in response to POM Wonderful's unsubstantiated claims in advertising that drinking POM pomegranate juices would treat, prevent, or reduce the risk of heart disease or prostate cancer. The FTC issued an order barring POM from making disease prevention claims on any products, unless supported by at least two randomized controlled research trials (FTC, 2013).

The following hypothetical case illustrates how statements contained in advertising and public statements (as discussed earlier) may create a situation where a claim of false or deceptive advertising could be raised.

Considering ... Deceptive Advertising

The following statement is made by a manager of a local health food store during an interview with a local newspaper: "Sport supplements do not pose any health risks for athletes." The newspaper is writing a story regarding sports supplements. The headline of the story reads: "Local Health Food Store Says Supplements Are Safe." The article is lengthy and ultimately concludes that many sports supplements are shipped in from foreign countries with little or no product testing. The manager of the store cuts out the first page of the article with the headline, makes a number of copies, and posts them throughout the store for customers to read while they shop. But the entire article, including the portion discussing the risks associated with sports supplements, is not included on the copied page.

Question

- Can either the manager's statements to the newspaper or the posting of the article be considered false or deceptive advertising?

Note how you would answer the question and then check your response using the Analysis & Discussion at the end of this chapter.

Private Regulation of Advertising Activities

Private organizations also monitor and investigate truth and accuracy in advertising, such as the National Advertising Division ("NAD"), a program of the Better Business Bureau ("National Advertising Division (NAD)," n.d.). One such investigation involved claims by BodyArmor Sports Drink that its beverage was "better" and "more natural" than Gatorade. In its analysis of BodyArmor's claims, NAD found that its statement that it was a "more natural sports drink" was not mere puffery, because it provided an "objective, measurable attribute" in its advertising statement, albeit one that was not substantiated. Based on NAD's findings, it encouraged BodyArmor to end the respective ad campaign. BodyArmor rejected this suggestion and the case was referred to the FTC for review (Seligman, 2018).

These cases demonstrate how closely advertising claims must be monitored, both from the perspective of the company making the claims and that of its competitors. Seeking a legal remedy alone may not be an adequate response for marketers. Sport managers involved in developing or approving advertisements should take care to substantiate their claims, because industry watchdog groups and consumers often alert the FTC to advertisements appearing to be false or deceptive.

Special Offers: Bait, Bargain, and Comparative Advertising

The FTC also provides guides for a variety of deceptive or potentially deceptive advertising practices that occur in the sport industry, including special offers such as: bait advertising; "buy one, get one free" bargain advertising; and comparative advertising. Each of these practices is the subject of specific guidance from the FTC on permitted uses and deceptive and false practices. The FTC guides are easy to understand and thorough. Any sport manager working in sales or advertising should familiarize themselves with these basic rules.

Bait Advertising

Bait advertising is a practice whereby a seller makes "… an alluring offer to sell a product or service"… that the seller really does not want to sell to the consumer (16 e-CFR § 238.0, 2019). The purpose is to "bait" consumers to attract them and then either (1) refuse to show the advertised product; (2) disparage the merchandise being offered in favor of another product that is priced higher or will generate more profit for the seller; (3) require the consumer to select a higher-priced alternative item due to having insufficient quantities of the advertised product in stock or refuse to take orders for the advertised goods to be delivered within a reasonable time; (4) use defective, unusable or impractical products to demonstrate the product implied in the advertisement to sway consumers from purchasing it; or (5) impose a sales method which penalizes or discourages the company's salespeople from selling the advertised product (16 e-C.F.R. § 238.3, 2019). The law is violated if a statement or illustration is made in an advertisement creating "… a false impression" of the characteristics of the product such that upon disclosure of the true product, the purchaser is sold on a different product (16 e-C.F.R. § 238.2, 2019).

Bargain Offers

Bargain offers are advertisements offering additional merchandise on the condition that the customer purchase a particular item at the regular price. Common examples include advertisements promoting buy-one-get-one-free, 2-for-1, or half-price sales. Anytime the word *free* is used in an advertisement, care must be taken not to mislead the customer, because most bargains require some type of purchase to acquire the free item. The following tactics would likely be misleading and violate the FTC guides: increasing the price of the regular item to offset the cost of the free item; increasing the price of the regular item to only sell it at a "discount;" and claiming an item is reduced to a lower price from its regular price. Normally, unless the regularly priced item has in fact been sold for a reasonably substantial period of time on a regular basis at the price advertised, these offers may be misleading.

The growing trend of subscription services purchased online led to a recent FTC case. In 2017, the FTC ordered that online marketing companies promoting "free" cooking and golfing products pay a $2.5 million settlement after the FTC found that the companies did not inform customers that upon receiving the "free" products, their credit card would be charged for a monthly subscription fee for additional products unless they canceled the subscription. This case highlights the need for companies to clearly inform consumers of charges they will incur in exchange for offers advertised (FTC, 2017a).

Comparative Advertising

Comparative advertising refers to advertisements featuring references, images, or other characterizations of a competitor's products or services made in comparison to the seller's products or services. The FTC guides permit comparative advertising that attacks, discredits, or criticizes another product so long as the advertisements are truthful and not deceptive (FTC, 1979). The Lanham Act also permits comparative advertising so long as there is no misrepresentation of the nature, characteristics, qualities, or geographic origin of another person's goods, services, or commercial activities (Lanham Act, § 43(a)).

Following the 2019 Super Bowl, two beverage giants found themselves tangled in a false advertising lawsuit due to comparative advertising. During the Super Bowl, Budweiser ran an advertisement seen by 100 million viewers asserting its Bud Light beer has "100 percent less corn syrup than Coors Light." Budweiser subsequently ran an advertisement campaign featuring this message across TV, print, and billboards. According to MillerCoors, corn syrup is not present in the finished product of Coors Light, but only used in the fermentation process. MillerCoors asserted that the advertisement amounted to "fearmongering" over consumers' growing distaste for corn syrup and caused deliberate deception. Budweiser defended that its claim was true as Bud Light is not brewed with corn syrup (Reiley, 2019). MillerCoors sought an injunction preventing Budweiser from continuing the advertisement campaign and for a jury trial to award damages and attorney's fees (*MillerCoors LLC v. Anheuser-Busch Companies, LLC,* 2019). Early in the case, a federal court judge ordered the injunction, temporarily prohibiting Budweiser from using "corn syrup" in ads lacking relevant context, but allowed the television commercials to continue (Zhang, 2019).

Often companies will immediately counter what is believed to be a false or misleading advertisement with their own advertising campaign to correct the allegedly false claims. MillerCoors did this following the 2019 Super Bowl by running a full-page advertisement in the *New York Times* informing consumers of how corn syrup is used in beer brewing and distinguishing it from high-fructose corn syrup (Schultz, 2019).

Companies can take several actions in response to potentially impermissible comparative advertising, including: (1) sending a cease and desist letter; (2) submitting a take-down request to media outlets running the advertisement; (3) alerting regulators, such as the FTC, about the advertisement; (4) bringing the issue before the National Advertising Division of the Council of Better Business Bureaus; or (5) litigating under the Lanham Act (Villafranco, 2010).

Use of Athletes in Advertising

Studies show that 60 percent of celebrity endorsed advertisements feature an athlete (Desmarais, 2016; Peetz & Lough (2016).). These product endorsements can earn a professional athlete substantial sums of money, while some professional athletes earn more from endorsements than their salaries. For example, Roger Federer ($93+ million) and Serena Williams ($29+ million) are regularly reported among the highest paid male and female athletes and earn more than four times as much from endorsements than they do from tournament prize money (Ellenport, 2019). The FTC advertising regulations prohibiting false or deceptive advertising also apply to athlete endorsements; 16 C.F.R. § 255.0 *et seq.* addresses endorsements. Not surprisingly, the use of an athlete's name or image in advertising without his or her consent can interfere with the rights known as publicity rights. The right of publicity as it relates to professional and collegiate athletes was discussed in Chapter 18.

Athlete Endorsements

For a celebrity endorsement not to be deceptive, it must meet the following criteria:

1 The endorsement must reflect the honest opinion, findings, beliefs, or experience of the celebrity.
2 The advertiser must substantiate the accuracy of the celebrity's claims.
3 Efficacy claims must be substantiated, if capable of substantiation, if such claims are made by the advertiser.
4 If the advertisement claims the celebrity uses the product or service, the celebrity must in fact be a bona fide user.
5 The advertiser can use the endorsement only so long as it has a good faith belief that the celebrity continues to hold the views expressed in the advertisement.

As the regulation states, an endorsement would be considered deceptive if the athlete does not in fact use or prefer the product or service. Further, an advertiser may not continue to use the endorsement if the athlete stops using the product or service. Despite these specific regulations on celebrity endorsements, enforcement is difficult for the FTC. For example, unless a professional athlete who is a celebrity endorser admits that he or she no longer uses a product or did not in fact ever use the product, it is difficult to prove a violation.

Normally, the FTC will choose to pursue the advertiser instead of the endorser regarding claims of substantiation. But on occasion, the FTC has pursued the endorser for false or deceptive advertising. For example, the FTC attempted to impose endorser liability on former Los Angeles Dodgers player, Steve Garvey, in FTC v. *Garvey* (2004). The FTC sued Garvey based on statements that Garvey made during an infomercial and television interviews endorsing the Enforma System's Fat Trapper, Fat Trapper Plus, and Exercise in a Bottle. The court held that Garvey's statements that Enforma was "all natural," "safe," and "it works" were sufficiently substantiated by some scientific materials Enforma provided him. The court observed that to find Garvey liable would require a showing that he was recklessly indifferent to the truth of his statements. In addition, his representations about his and his wife's personal weight loss experiences reflected his honest opinion or beliefs about the product. Finally, the court acknowledged there is no settled standard for the level of inquiry to which a celebrity spokesperson should be held when hired to participate in an advertisement. Although the court did not find Garvey liable, this case reveals the potential for liability of celebrity endorsers who make false or unsubstantiated claims about a product or misrepresent actual use of the product. Further, some scholars assert that the FTC v. *Garvey* case may have been decided differently under the 2009 FTC Guidelines, discussed below (Brison, Baker, & Byon, 2012).

Remember that states also have consumer protection laws that can impact endorsers. Former NBA players Shaquille O'Neal and Lamar Odom were named defendants in a lawsuit filed against Power Balance for alleged violations of the California Unfair Competition Law based on their statements in advertisements claiming the Power Balance bands improved their performance ("False advertising lawsuit," 2011).

In 2009, the FTC updated its guidelines for endorsers to include examples of statements in social media falling under the FTC regulations. Celebrity endorsers, such as professional athletes, are expressly addressed in the revised guides. Under the 2009 guides, unlike the 1980 guides, endorsers as well as advertisers could be liable under the FTCA for statements they make in an endorsement on Twitter, Facebook, Instagram, and other social media channels. The revised guides clearly state that both advertisers and endorsers may be liable for false or unsubstantiated claims made in an endorsement – or for failure to disclose material connections between the advertiser and endorsers.

The revised guides also make it clear that athlete endorsers have a duty to disclose their relationships with advertisers when making endorsements outside the context of traditional ads, such as in social media. Notably, this does not apply if an athlete endorser is discussing a product bought on their own, but only if the endorsement is part of a sponsored campaign (FTC, 2017b). For endorsements that are part of sponsored campaigns, athlete endorsers should disclose any material connections with the sponsors by using hashtags such as #sponsored or #ad. Some athletes have included disclaimers on their social media profiles. For instance, NFL player Drew Brees' Twitter profile read, "Please note that Drew Brees is an endorser for several companies and promotes them through his social media" (Bercovici, 2010). Further, endorsers should be wary of endorsement methods not allowing them to disclose a relationship with a brand, such as hitting "like" buttons on Facebook and Instagram, as the FTC could take action against this if it finds the endorser's "likes" were material in patrons' decisions to buy products (FTC, 2017b).

Along with requiring disclosures of an endorsement relationship, the FTC's guidelines have expanded to specify when and where endorsers must disclose information. For instance, if an athlete is being paid to endorse a product on Instagram, a disclosure must be made within the first two lines of the post's description, since descriptions are truncated on smartphones, making them not immediately viewable by users. Further, endorsements made on YouTube must include disclosures within the video itself, as the FTC asserts many viewers watch YouTube videos without reading their descriptions (FTC, 2017b).

It is important that individuals and companies managing athlete endorsements are aware of and ensure compliance with the FTC's guidelines regarding disclosure of endorsement relationships on social media, as the FTC has a history of taking action against high-profile celebrities. In 2017, the FTC sent letters to 90 entertainers, athletes, influencers and brands warning them of the requirement to clearly disclose endorsement relationships (FTC, 2017c). The proliferation of social media channels and use has led to nontraditional endorsers with niche followings, known as influencers, securing paid opportunities to promote products (Comenos, 2018). That these influencers were amongst the group of 90 individuals who received warning letters signals that despite influencers being a new marketing mode, the FTC will enforce its guidelines against them. This breadth of how the FTC will enforce its guidelines was further demonstrated in 2019 when it and the FDA sent letters to companies who sell e-liquids used in vaping, informing them that social media posts made by influencers promoting the products must not only include the requisite disclaimer that the posts are sponsored, but the necessary FDA-required warnings (Fair, 2019). Thus, those advising endorsers and influencers must be aware of the range of laws that can be implicated based on their promotion of a particular product.

In addition to the FTC guides, most professional sports leagues, as well as the IOC, have created rules and policies regarding the use of social media by athletes, highlighted in more detail in Chapter 13 (Cady, 2018; USOPC, 2019).

Next, we explore legal issues associated with conducting promotions and sales activities.

Conducting Sales Promotions

In addition to advertising, managers working in marketing, ticket sales, or event management will likely be involved with a variety of promotional and sales activities. For example, sweepstakes or contests; giveaways; sales promotions; or other consumer activities are subject to FTC regulations and various state consumer protection or gaming laws. This section discusses FTC regulations on unfair business practices, illegal gambling activities in the context of contests and fantasy sports, and ambush marketing.

FTC Regulations on Unfair Business Practices

The FTC's Policy Statement on Unfairness (1980) identifies three factors used to determine whether a business practice is unfair:

1   Whether the practice injures a consumer.
2   Whether the practice violates public policy.
3   Whether the practice is unethical or unscrupulous.

With regard to the consumer injury factor, three additional criteria must be met:

a.   The injury is substantial (trivial or speculative harms are not sufficient).
b.   The injury could not reasonably have been avoided.
c.   The injury is not outweighed by any countervailing benefits to consumers or competition (FTC, 1980).

The evaluation of unfairness can consider whether the practice offends public policy, is immoral, or is unethically oppressive or unscrupulous. Generally, the FTC expects the marketplace to be self-regulating and relies on consumer choice to govern it. However, sellers may adopt business practices that interfere with or hinder consumer choice and free market decisions. For example, withholding or failing to provide critical price or performance data may leave buyers with insufficient information to make informed comparisons. Some sellers may engage in overt coercion, such as dismantling a treadmill or other sport equipment for "inspection" and then refuse to reassemble it unless a service contract is signed. Others may exercise undue influence over a highly susceptible class of purchasers, such as promoting a weight loss product as a cure for obesity.

With regard to violations of public policy, the policy must be clear and well-established in sources such as statutes, judicial decisions, or the Constitution. For example, a cigarette manufacturer's distribution of cigarette samples at a NASCAR race in such a way that they could come into the hands of children would likely violate the public interest and public policies in place to prevent underage smoking (FTC, 1980). Regarding benefits outweighing the injury, the FTC recognizes that many sales practices involve a tradeoff between consumer and competitive interests. Several specific promotions and sales practices requiring balancing of consumer and competitive interests when implemented are presented below.

Sweepstakes and Contests

The FTC provides guidelines for conducting sweepstakes and contests. Additionally, each state regulates sweepstakes and contests, so it is vital that sport marketers understand these laws if they plan to conduct such an event. These are popular promotional strategies for sport organizations, and particularly corporate sponsors, who often include sporting events among their prize packages.

The growing popularity of and reliance on social media has led sport managers to utilize social media platforms for sweepstakes and contests. Such sweepstakes or contests may require consumers to create media, vote in elections or polls, utilize the platforms to nominate or promote a candidate for winning and more. Before hosting a sweepstakes or promotion on social media, sport managers must be aware not only of the relevant FTC guidelines, but the respective social media platform's rules related to sweepstakes and contests. Traditionally, social media platforms have differed in how they regulate sweepstakes and contests. Thus, sport managers must take the time to read and fully understand a respective social media platform's policy before hosting a sweepstakes or contest (Larkin & McKelvey, 2015).

Another issue related to conducting contests and giveaways is whether the contest represents some form of illegal gambling. Courts generally distinguish between bona fide entry fees and bets or wagers. Generally, entry fees do not constitute bets or wagers when they are paid unconditionally for the privilege of participating in a contest and the prize is for a specified amount that is guaranteed to be won by one of the contestants (but not the entity offering the prize). When the entry fees and prizes are unconditional and guaranteed, the element of risk necessary to constitute betting or wagering is missing. The best practice for a direct promotional giveaway is permitting consumers to obtain at least one entry into the contest without a purchase or entry fee and to obtain any additional entries through the purchase of products or services.

Along with the laws and policies specifically governing sweepstakes and contests, sport managers must also be aware of the potential tax implications that arise from such practices. Federal income tax liability may be imposed on fans, depending on the value of the prize awarded (Hawkins, 2011). Further, some state courts have ruled on whether the promotional value of giveaways provided by teams to fans can be taxed to teams (*Cincinnati Reds, LLC v. Testa*, 2018). This means sport managers should consider informing contestants and sweepstakes participants of the value of prizes and potential tax liability. Further, teams should be aware of the tax implications of giveaways in the state in which they conduct business.

Ambush Marketing

Ambush marketing has been defined as an intentional effort to weaken or "ambush" a competitor's official association with a sport organization, which is secured through payment of sponsorship fees (McKelvey, 1992, 1994). Another definition is a marketing practice with the "ability to reasonably confuse" the consumer regarding the ambushing company's status as an official sponsor (McAuley & Sutton, 1999). Ambush marketing takes on various forms, but a recent definition explains it as "a practice of entities who are not sponsors of a major sporting event using proximity and subtle references to imply a relationship and boost sales (Chahardovali, Ternes, & Holden, 2019).

Many companies view ambush marketing as an effective marketing strategy since studies show that fans associate the ambushing company with the ambushed event (Hill, 2016; Hutter & Schwarz, 2012; Moorman & Greenwell, 2005; Scassa, 2011; Séguin & O'Reilly, 2008). Over the years, ambushing styles and strategies have emerged and shifted, as depicted in Exhibit 19.6. Presently, companies utilize both direct and indirect ambushes. Direct ambushes are those in which the actual trademarks of the event organizer are used to create the false impression that they are associated with an event (Park, 2019). An example of a direct ambush would be a corporation that has not paid to be an official NFL sponsor placing NFL logos and insignia on its merchandise to attract NFL fans to purchase its products. Indirect ambushing is less obvious and involves corporations who are not official sponsors of an event using words, imagery, locations and other insignia to evoke in the minds of consumers an association between the brand and event (Park, 2019). For example, Subway is not an official IOC TOP partner. However, during the 2014 Winter Olympic Games, Subway aired commercials with Olympic-like imagery that featured a variety of

Exhibit 19.6 Evolution of prominent ambush marketing campaigns.

1984 Los Angeles Olympics: Kodak film company sponsors TV broadcasts of the Games as well as the U.S. track team, despite the fact that Fuji film company is an official sponsor. Fuji returns the favor during the Seoul 1988 Games when Kodak is the official sponsor.

1992 Barcelona Olympics: Nike sponsors press conferences with the U.S. basketball team despite Reebok's being the official sponsor.

1996 Atlanta Olympics: Nike's Atlanta ambush is still seen as the ambush of all ambushes. Saving the $50 million cost of an official Olympic sponsorship, Nike plasters the city with billboards, hands out "swoosh" banners to wave during the competitions, and erects an enormous "Nike center" overlooking the stadium.

2000 Sydney Olympics: Qantas Airlines' slogan, "The Spirit of Australia," sounds strikingly similar to the Games' slogan, "Share the Spirit." Qantas claims it's just a coincidence, while official sponsor Ansett Air helplessly protests.

2002 Salt Lake City Winter Olympics: Anheuser-Busch pays more than $50 million to become an official Olympic sponsor. In accordance with its agreement, it has exclusive rights to use the word "Olympic" and the five-ring logo. Schirf Brewery, a small local company, rather ingeniously (and apparently legally) marks its delivery trucks with "Wasatch Beers. The Unofficial Beer. 2002 Winter Games." In accordance with copyright and trademark laws, Schirf has used neither the word "Olympics" nor the five-ring logo (Sauer, 2002).

2007 U.S. Open: The Arizona Beverage Company hands out free samples of their sports drink to fans around the event facility. Andy Roddick is an endorser of the Arizona Beverage product; however, Gatorade is the official sports drink sponsor of the event (Kaplan, 2007).

Euro 2008: Heineken passes out large green hats to fans buying their beer prior to a Dutch soccer match ("Playing the game," 2008).

2010 FIFA World Cup: Bavaria Beer attempted to ambush the official sponsor Budweiser by sending in 36 blonde models clad in orange mini-dresses to capture the attention of the TV viewing audience during the Denmark/Netherlands match (Daly, 2010).

2012 London Olympics: Beats Electronics' staff "bumped" into Olympic athletes and gave them free headphones, which were seen prominently on many athletes prior to and during competition (Grady & McKelvey, 2012).

2012 London Olympics: Nike's "Find Your Greatness" campaign filmed athletes running, jumping, and diving alongside the word "London" in towns located in the United States, Norway, Jamaica, and Nigeria (Grady & McKelvey, 2012).

2014 FIFA World Cup: Following Brazil's match versus Cameroon, famed Brazilian striker, Neymar, was photographed shirtless with his boxer shorts showing. The photograph was widely shared. The boxer shorts were made by and featured the logo of Brazilian company, Blue Man, which is not a FIFA sponsor (Willens, 2016).

2016 Rio Olympics: Apple, which has historically avoided sport sponsorships, engaged in ambush marketing when it sold country-specific bands for iWatches ahead of the Games and Michael Phelps was seen wearing Beats headphones before races (Baker, 2018; Gaines, 2016).

2018 NBA All-Star Game: After not renewing its NBA sponsorship and Nike stepping into its place, adidas engaged in ambush marketing during the league's marquee event, when it rented an entire square block in Los Angeles and hosted concerts featuring top performers, fashion shows, pop up shops, a museum, and more (Ehrlich, 2018).

Olympic athletes, which could provoke the idea of a partnership between it and the IOC in a consumer's mind (Boudway, 2014).

Exhibit 19.6 provides a few examples of prominent ambushes. The Focus Case below, *NHL v. Pepsi-Cola Canada*, confirmed what many sport managers suspected since the early 1990s: that most common law and statutory remedies simply do not encompass common ambush marketing practices. Thus, sport properties have developed a variety of strategies to minimize or restrict ambush marketing, which are explored in this section.

The first significant legal challenge to ambush marketing was *NHL v. Pepsi-Cola Canada Ltd.* (1992), presented in the following Focus Case.

NHL v. Pepsi-Cola Canada Ltd.

70 B.C.L.R.2d 27 (BCSC 1992)   **FOCUS** CASE

FACTS

Pepsi-Cola Canada (Pepsi) utilized numerous ambush marketing techniques to associate itself with the 1990 Stanley Cup hockey playoffs. Pepsi conducted a nationwide promotional campaign in Canada in which consumers were eligible for up to $10,000 if they matched certain information on bottle caps and specially marked cups with the outcome of the Stanley Cup playoffs. The Pepsi campaign worked like this: Assume that the Edmonton Oilers won the Stanley Cup in the fifth game of the series in 1990, and a lucky consumer had acquired a Pepsi bottle cap reading "If Edmonton wins in 5 games you win $10,000." That consumer would be eligible to win the $10,000 prize upon submitting the contest entry form and winning game piece and successfully completing a skills test included on the entry form. Several other prizes, such as free Pepsi products and merchandise and small cash awards, were also available.

Pepsi ran extensive television advertising during the television broadcasts of the NHL playoffs to promote its prize contest. The NHL sued Pepsi in an effort to protect the rights it sold to Coca-Cola as the official sponsor of the NHL. Unfortunately, in 1989, when the NHL entered into its sponsorship agreement with Coca-Cola, television broadcast advertising rights were not among the rights included in the agreement. The broadcast advertising rights had been licensed to Molson Breweries, who in turn granted Pepsi the right to be the exclusive advertiser of soft drinks during the broadcast of all NHL postseason and playoff games.

HOLDING

The Canadian court rejected each of the NHL's claims and dismissed the action.

RATIONALE

The NHL alleged four theories of recovery: common law tort of passing off, statutory passing off, trademark infringement, and interference with economic relations and future business relations. The passing off claims were rejected since the NHL's consumer survey evidence was not adequate to demonstrate that Pepsi's promotional activities created a false impression that the product or activity was authorized, approved, or endorsed by the NHL. Even if the survey evidence was acceptable to the court, the court cited *NFL v. Delaware* (1977) arguing Pepsi's disclaimers would have been sufficient to dispel any impressions of sponsorship or approval. The trademark infringement claims were easily dismissed since none of the NHL's actual registered marks were used by Pepsi. Finally, the court dismissed the interference with economic relations claims since the NHL could not base its claim on the rights of another (i.e., Coca-Cola), and none of Coca-Cola's rights under its sponsorship agreement with the NHL were disrupted. The court noted that Coca-Cola's sponsorship agreement did not include any advertising rights with respect to television broadcasts.

Probably the most outright and unapologetic brand to embrace ambush marketing is Nike (Klara, 2016; Sauer, 2002). Examples of Nike ambush campaign "victims" include: Converse in Los Angeles in 1984; Reebok in Atlanta in 1996; and Adidas on just about every continent (Sauer, 2002). Nike's tactics, like those that began at the 1996 Olympics and continued through the 2012 London Olympics, are criticized as seriously eroding the IOC's credibility and forcing sport organizations to adopt more assertive and aggressive anti-ambushing strategies. However, in most ambush marketing situations, the marketers do not make any false claims about their products or services, and the athletes do in fact endorse the products or services. Thus, false and deceptive advertising laws are not very effective in combating ambush marketing. Similarly, companies employing ambush marketing techniques rarely use the actual marks or logos of the event or their competitors; thus, trademark and copyright laws are of little help (McKelvey & Grady, 2004; Nakamura, 2018).

Ambush marketing takes many forms today. The most common and effective of these strategies are:

1   Purchasing advertising time during an event broadcast.
2   Conducting sweepstakes or contests using event tickets as prizes.
3   Creating premium offers thematically tied to the event.
4   Using notable athletes affiliated with the sport or event to endorse the products or be featured in advertising (Lefton, 2003).
5   Hiring fans to hold up signs bearing logos during a televised event.
6   Utilizing social media to drive conversation away from an official sponsor and to an ambushing brand (Smith, 2017).

Other strategies include: flyover blimp or airplane advertising, stadium advertising, individual team or player sponsorships, and even forehead tattoos (Epstein, 2014; Jensen, 1996; Liberman, 2003; Nakamura, 2018; Pahwa, 2019).

Sport organizations continue to identify or even create new business and legal strategies to combat ambush marketing practices. For example, a few sport organizations have sued ambush marketers under common law principles of unfair competition. This remedy allows recovery for the misappropriation of goodwill and reputation of a sport organization. In such cases, the sport organization must show the following:

1   It is the owner of the event or right in question.
2   The ambusher has participated in unauthorized activity.
3   Its goodwill or reputation has been appropriated or damaged through the use of false representations in relation to products or services (McKelvey, 1992; Sheridan, 2010).

Sport organizations have not had much success with misappropriation claims to date because of the difficulty of proving actual damage to goodwill or reputation. Also, for a misappropriation claim to succeed, the objectionable activity must include false representations. To counter this, many ambush marketers simply use a disclaimer indicating "truthfully" that their promotional activity is in no way endorsed or associated with the sport organization or event in question. For example, the Delaware federal district court rejected the NFL's misappropriation of goodwill claims against the Delaware State Lottery for a lottery game based on NFL games. The ruling rested on the fact that the Delaware State Lottery used a disclaimer indicating the NFL had not endorsed the lottery game (*NFL v. Delaware*, 1977).

The *NFL v. Delaware* case has been most often cited for its holding permitting ambush marketers to avoid trademark infringement and all unfair competition claims by using disclaimers in their advertising. The NFL presented survey evidence that between 19 percent and 21 percent of those surveyed were confused as to the NFL's sponsorship or endorsement of the state lottery game. The court agreed that this was sufficient evidence to demonstrate consumer confusion and stated that "one may not . . . advertise one's services in a manner which creates an impression in the mind of the relevant segment of the public that a connection exists between the services offered and the holder of the registered mark when no such connection exists" (*NFL v. Delaware*, 1977, p. 1380). However, the district court determined that an adequate remedy for this transgression was for the state lottery to include a clear and conspicuous statement that the game was not associated with or authorized by the NFL (p. 1381). The impact of the *NFL v. Delaware* decision has made it very difficult for sport organizations to challenge ambush marketing practices using unfair competition theories.

In *NCAA v. Coors Brewing Company* (2002), the NCAA sued Coors Brewing Company to thwart the beer company's use of tickets to the NCAA Men's Basketball Championship Tournament in an advertising promotion. This was the first lawsuit to challenge the use of sports tickets in an unauthorized sweepstakes promotion as unfair competition (McKelvey, 2003). Since the case was settled before trial, it is unknown how the court would have ruled on the NCAA misappropriation claims. However, Coors ceased its promotion.

What is proving to be more successful outside the United States has been ambush marketing-specific legislation protecting the marks and symbols associated with major sporting events, such as the Olympics or the World Cup. Such legislation creates a "zone" in and around an event within which a nonofficial sponsor may not conduct any type of advertising or promotional activities. For example, in anticipation for the 2012 Summer Olympics, the London Olympic Games and Paralympic Games Act 2006 and the London Olympic Games and Paralympic Games (Advertising and Trading) (England) Regulations 2011 were passed in the United Kingdom to restrict the use of representations that signify a link or association with the London Games and to control certain types of advertising activity in the vicinity of the events.

Issues in Pricing, Ticket Sales, and Strategic Partner Interactions

The previous sections identified several instances when managers working in marketing may encounter legal issues as they advertise and promote their products and services. This section focuses on legal issues that may be implicated in a manager's or firm's interactions with consumers in pricing strategies, ticket sales, and with interactions amongst strategic partners.

Pricing Activities

Many businesses may seek to eliminate competition by controlling the price, quantity, and quality of the goods they produce. If a business tries to eliminate competition through tactics such as fixing prices or assigning exclusive territories to different competitors within an industry, antitrust laws come into play. Antitrust laws, as first discussed in Chapter 10, seek to eliminate certain anticompetitive market behaviors and promote free and fair marketplace competition. The prevailing economic theory supporting antitrust laws in the United States is that the public is best served by free competition in trade and industry. 18th Century economist, Adam Smith, is widely credited with popularizing this concept in his book *The Wealth of Nations* (Krugman, 2019). When businesses fairly compete for the consumer's dollar, the quality of products and services increases while prices decrease. Federal antitrust laws attempt to prohibit anticompetitive practices and prevent unreasonable concentrations of economic power that disrupt competition, such as price fixing. An agreement to inhibit price competition by raising, depressing, fixing, or stabilizing prices is the most serious example of a per se violation of the Sherman Act (15 U.S.C. §§ 1 *et seq.*). Under the act, it is immaterial whether the fixed prices are set at a maximum price, a minimum price, the actual cost, or the fair market price. It is also immaterial under the law whether the fixed price is reasonable. Price fixing can carry both civil and criminal penalties. Sport companies have seen their fair share of price fixing allegations. For example, Electronic Arts (EA) was sued for illegal price fixing for the *Madden NFL* series. The suit alleged following the release of *ESPN NFL 2K5* at a budget price of just $20, EA charged just $30 for *Madden NFL 05* in order to stay competitive. But when EA gained the exclusive rights to the NFL brand, prices for the *Madden* games went back up to $60. The suit asserts that EA used its exclusive licensing deals with the NFL to force consumers to pay an artificially high price for certain sports titles (Westbrook, 2010). EA ultimately agreed to a $27 million settlement (Sarkar, 2012).

All horizontal and vertical price-fixing agreements are per se illegal, which means they have no pro-competitive benefits and only serve to disrupt the free marketplace. **Horizontal price-fixing agreements** include agreements among sellers to establish maximum or minimum prices on certain goods or services. This can also include competitors' changing their prices simultaneously in some circumstances. **Vertical price-fixing agreements** include situations where a wholesaler mandates the minimum or maximum price at which retailers may sell certain products. A number of sports brands or manufacturers have been involved in FTC investigations involving alleged price fixing. In 2019, the Northern District of California held that the NCAA engaged in horizontal price-fixing by limiting the compensation to college football and basketball players. In its decision, the court found that the NCAA could not limit grant-in-aid scholarships to less than the cost of attendance at a university nor could it limit education-related benefits paid to NCAA athletes (*In Re: NCAA Athlete Grant-In-Aid Cap Antitrust Litigation*, 2019). Related to vertical price-fixing,

New Balance was sued by the FTC for price fixing when it fixed the resale price of its shoes. New Balance required dealers to raise retail prices, maintain certain prices set by New Balance, or refrain from discounting New Balance products. New Balance surveilled retailers' prices and threatened to terminate or suspend shipments to any retailers who were discounting their products. New Balance entered into a consent agreement with the FTC in 1996, prohibiting them from fixing or controlling resale prices (FTC, 1996a). A manufacturer may suggest retail prices for products, but retailers must be free to determine for themselves the price at which they will advertise and sell their merchandise. The New Balance case was one of three cases the FTC filed in the 1990s against athletic shoe manufacturers; Keds and Reebok were also found to have engaged in anticompetitive behavior (FTC, 1996b).

Another exclusive sponsorship agreement raised price fixing and antitrust concerns. In 2001, the NFL granted Reebok an exclusive license to manufacture headwear featuring the logos and trademarks of every professional football team in the NFL. Due to this new exclusive agreement, American Needle (an apparel manufacturer) lost its 20-year license to manufacture NFL branded caps. American Needle quickly filed an antitrust lawsuit against the NFL, National Football League Properties (NFLP), the NFL teams, and Reebok, claiming that the exclusive headwear license violated Section 1 of the Sherman Act, 15 § U.S.C. 1, which outlaws any "contract, combination . . . or conspiracy, in restraint of trade." In response, the NFL, NFLP, and Reebok asserted that the member teams were united to produce a common product, namely professional football games, and thus were a single entity not subject to the regulations of the Sherman Act. The NFL is an unincorporated association of 32 separately owned professional football teams. Through NFLP, the NFL develops, licenses, and markets certain intellectual property owned by the NFL teams. The Supreme Court concluded that the members of the NFL (a collection of franchises owned by separate entities) that make up the NFLP are independent centers of business and economic decision-making and therefore not a single entity (*American Needle v. NFL*, 2010). The case was remanded to the district court, which heard arguments on a motion for summary judgment brought by American Needle alleging that the NFL's exclusive apparel agreement with Reebok unreasonably restrained trade in violation of the Sherman Act. The district court denied American Needle's motion for summary judgment, finding that the per se rule was inapplicable in this scenario and the Rule of Reason needed to be applied, because the NFL was able to show "numerous procompetitive effects" of its exclusive partnership with Reebok (*American Needle, Inc. v. New Orleans Saints*, 2014). In August 2013, a federal district court also refused to dismiss a case filed by a group of consumers, who also challenged the NFL's exclusive licensing agreement with Reebok (Adamson, 2013; *Dang v. San Francisco 49ers*, 2013).

Exclusive sponsorships and licensing agreements are commonplace in the sport industry, so sport managers need to carefully enter into these agreements and set the prices of their products or services so they do not run afoul of federal antitrust laws.

Contracts and Ticket Sales Activities

Chapter 16 presented issues related to ticket operations during events, while this section will examine the sales operations surrounding ticket sales and negotiations. Interactions with customers in the sale of products and services, such as tickets, raise several unique challenges for sport managers, especially since contract law is a matter of state law. (Contract law principles were presented in Chapter 3). If your organization is in one state and you want to sell products in another state, you must know which state's laws will apply to the transaction. The easiest way to handle this problem is to include what is known as a *choice of law clause* in contracts. A choice of law clause simply specifies that each party agrees that if a dispute arises regarding the agreement, the law of a specified state will be applied to resolve the dispute. Since contract law is a matter of state common law, before agreeing to be bound by the law of a particular state, a sport marketer or sport manager should become familiar with the specific consumer protection statute and contract law in that state and seek advice from legal counsel.

The economic downturn in the late 2000s coupled with rising ticket prices and increased pressure on teams to generate revenue caused some professional and college sports teams to experience strained relationships with their season ticket holders. For example, the Washington Redskins and New England Patriots were sharply criticized for suing several season ticket holders who were unable to pay for their season tickets and defaulted on their multi-year ticket agreements (Grimaldi, 2009). This practice has been widely criticized because it is unclear whether the teams have actually suffered any damage from the ticket holder's breach. As discussed earlier, a party to a contract has a general duty to mitigate its damages. In many cases, when a season ticket holder fails to pay for and forfeits the tickets, the team should be able to resell the tickets. The monies received from the resell should reduce the amount of damages owed from the ticket holder. However, the Redskins and Patriots ticket agreements included liquidated damages provisions that arguably gave them a right to payment for every year on the multiyear ticket agreements, regardless of whether or when they resold the tickets. We first explored liquidated damages provisions in the context of coaches' employment agreements in Chapter 3. In the following Focus Case, a liquidated damages provision in a multi-year personal seat license (PSL) agreement is discussed.

NPS, LLC v. Minihane

886 N.E. 2d 670 (Mass. 2008)	FOCUS CASE

FACTS

NPS is the developer of Gillette Stadium and entered into an agreement with Paul Minihane for the purchase of a ten-year license for two luxury seats at the stadium. The terms of the PSL provided that Minihane would pay $3,750 per seat per season from 2002 to 2011 for a total commitment of $75,000. The PSL agreement included a liquidated damages clause providing that in the event of a default, Minihane's payments would be accelerated (acceleration clause), requiring him to pay the entire balance remaining on the 10-year agreement. Minihane paid his initial deposit and one payment toward the license fee, but made no further payments after the 2002 season. The trial court held that the accelerated damages clause was unenforceable because the amount due was "grossly disproportionate to a reasonable estimate of actual damages made at the time of contract formation." NPS appealed to the Massachusetts Supreme Judicial Court.

HOLDING

The Massachusetts Supreme Court upheld the liquidated damages provisions in the PSL agreement.

RATIONALE

The appellate court utilized a two-pronged test to determine the legality of the disputed clause:

1 the actual damages flowing from a breach must have been difficult to ascertain at the time of contracting, and
2 the sum agreed upon in the liquidated damages clause must represent a "reasonable forecast of the damages expected to occur in the event of a breach."

The court agreed with the trial judge that the harm resulting from a possible breach was difficult to ascertain at the time of the contract since damages would vary depending on demand for the tickets at the time of the breach. The court determined that, although the Patriots won their first Super Bowl championship in 2002, the demand for luxury seats remains variable. Next, the court disagreed with the trial judge that the amount of damages was grossly disproportionate to the real damages. To be grossly disproportionate, damages must be "unconscionably excessive." While the court agreed the terms were harsh since the breach occurred early in the life of the agreement, they were not unreasonably and grossly disproportionate to the actual damages.

Thus, in this case, Minihane not only was ordered to pay the $65,500 owed on the PSL agreement, but he also lost his luxury seats (Saltzman & Finucane, 2008). Despite these examples, however, most teams elect not to sue defaulting ticket holders. A 2019 case involving PSLs and the NFL was brought following the Rams' decision to relocate from St. Louis to Los Angeles. This led to the filing of a breach of contract class action lawsuit by individuals who purchased PSLs when the team was in St. Louis. According to the plaintiffs, they purchased 30-year PSLs that did not come to term when the team relocated before their expiration, leaving portions of the purchased PSLs unused. In 2019, the Rams settled with the plaintiffs for $24 million, which equated to refunding 10,000 PSL holders for nine-years remaining on their contracts (Faust, 2019).

Ticket holders have also sued teams for a variety of reasons. A New York Jets season ticket holder sued the Patriots and head coach Bill Belichick for deceiving consumers under the New Jersey Consumer Fraud Act and the New Jersey Deceptive Business Practices Act, asserting that secret videotaping by the Patriots violated contractual expectations and rights of Jets ticket holders. Season ticket holders also sued the New York Giants and Jets, claiming that the Jets and Giants PSL agreements were illegal restraints of trade in violation of federal antitrust laws and a violation of the New Jersey Consumer Fraud Act (Larson, 2009). The suit alleged that 45,000 season ticket holders were forced to purchase a PSL for a one-time payment between $1,000 and $25,000 in order to renew or purchase season tickets in the new stadium (*Oshinsky v. New York Football Giants, Inc.*, 2009). The Jets again faced a lawsuit arising from PSLs in 2018. In that case, a fan who purchased two PSLs for Jets games at MetLife Stadium argued that the value of the PSLs he purchased for $4,000 was erased when the team began selling seats in the section he held PSLs for to the general public. In ruling for the Jets, the U.S. District Court judge relied on the language in the PSL agreement to find that the fan did not have an exclusive right to purchase seats in the respective section over nonPSL holders (*Gengo v. Jets Stadium Dev., LLC*, 2018).

In another example involving the 2011 Super Bowl, 400 ticket holders were denied entry because the temporary bleachers where their seats were located were deemed unsafe. The NFL offered a variety of replacement options, including tickets to the next Super Bowl, roundtrip airfare, and hotel accommodations. However, several fans claimed in their lawsuit against the NFL that those offers were not adequate and did not compensate them for the disappointment and frustration of missing watching their teams compete in the Super Bowl. The fans' fraud claims were dismissed but the breach of contract claim went to trial, with the jury finding for the plaintiffs and awarding $76,000 in damages (Young, 2015).

An Arena Football League team, the Orlando Predators, offered a performance guarantee to season ticket holders and offered discounts for season ticket renewals if the team failed to win ten games (Ward, 2013). One sport economist referred to the sales promotion as lunacy and predicted the team would be sold or out of business by the end of the season. The managing partner of the Predators insisted more fans would renew the tickets based on the promotion. The managing partner offered a similar promotion when he was managing partner of the AFL's Rattlers (*Sports Business Daily*, 2007). By the end of the season, the Predators had a new managing partner and wrote an open letter to season ticket holders seeking their continued support and offering refunds to departing season ticket holders, but with no mention of the performance guarantees (Pearsall, 2013; Seh, 2013).

Generally, a sport organization's relationship with its season ticket holders is a mutually agreeable, harmonious, and beneficial relationship. However, the above disputes remind us of the importance of understanding basic contract law while drafting and negotiating season ticket renewal and PSL agreements, and the importance of becoming familiar with a state's consumer protection laws while promoting and selling products and services.

Interactions with Strategic Partners

In today's competitive marketplace, especially in the sport industry, strategic alliances are more important than ever. Strategic alliances are seen in a variety of relationships in sport, such as corporate sponsorships, facility naming rights, co-branding, cross-promotion, and integration of social media. More than ever, teams and leagues are entering into additional strategic partnerships with marketing and digital media rights distribution companies to assist them in selling their broadcasting and digital streaming rights and securing marketing partnerships.

These alliances offer advantages to a company wanting to connect to a specific customer base, particularly the customer base of major sporting events and sport leagues and teams. These relationships allow companies to open doors to new markets that would otherwise take months to develop and penetrate. However, developing these strategic relationships involves a number of legal issues requiring research and extensive planning. To be successful in relationships with strategic partners, a sport manager often needs a solid knowledge of contract law and contract negotiation skills. In addition to having a good grasp of contract law, the sport manager should take a number of steps and precautions as these strategic alliances are formed to avoid costly litigation later. These include researching the potential partner, planning an exit strategy, and preserving intellectual property.

Researching a Potential Partner

Know as much as possible about potential partners before approaching them. Study not just their products and business structure, but also their management, corporate culture, third-party relationships, intellectual property rights, and financial condition before deciding whether they are the right partners for you. To appreciate the importance of research and advance planning, consider the number of corporate naming partners whose failing financial conditions created serious challenges for their sport organization partners. In 1999, Wayne Huizenga reworked the naming rights contract between the Miami Dolphins' home field (Pro Player Stadium) and Fruit of the Loom, owner of the Pro Player trademark and clothing line (Ratner, 2001). The new contract allowed Huizenga to cancel the agreement with only two months' notice. Shortly after the contract revision, in February 2000, Fruit of the Loom filed for Chapter 11 bankruptcy and began liquidating Pro Player. After a bankruptcy filing, the naming rights agreement becomes an asset of the bankrupt estate, which can create legal problems for the sport organization and stadium owner partner. Perry Ellis International purchased the Pro Player trademark from the bankrupt estate of Fruit of the Loom, but did not acquire the naming rights agreement. Thus, while Huizenga was shopping for a new naming rights partner, Perry Ellis was getting exposure for the Pro Player mark for free.

Questions may also arise if a major sport organization or sporting event is associated with a sponsor who engages in misleading advertising or other questionable business practices. For example, while nutrition related products may seem like a good fit for a sport or event sponsorship relationship, several studies have questioned whether advertising associated with sports drinks and nutritional supplements claiming essential health benefits may be misleading, since many of these claims are not supported by credible research. A sport organization may be lending unwarranted credibility to the products. Some commentators also suggest that if sport teams and properties distanced themselves from supplements and drinks, any financial gaps would be quickly filled as was seen when the sport industry distanced itself from tobacco sponsorships (Caba, 2014).

Managing Disputes with Partners

Sometimes, despite employing best practices, disputes arise between partners that lead to litigation. Thus, along with fully researching and examining partners, sport managers must also be prepared to manage disputes and execute crisis management strategies.

Competitive Advantage Strategies

Consumer Communications and Advertising Practices

- Managers must recognize that their communications with consumers about competitors may have legal consequences, especially if there are inaccuracies in the communications.

- Procedures should be in place to verify the accuracy of any statements or representations contained in advertising. If advertisements use health-related claims to promote sales, those claims need some scientific substantiation to guard against false advertising or deceptive trade practice claims.

- A sport organization must have the consent of any person whose likeness is being used in an advertisement or promotion. For example, if a collegiate or professional sport team wants to feature a student-athlete or professional athlete in its marketing efforts, the athlete must give consent or else a right of publicity claim could result.

- Professional athletes should be proactive when using social media to disclose sponsorship relationships when promoting, advertising or posting about a product or service for which they are an endorser.

- To combat ambush marketing, sport organizations and sponsors must build as many protections as possible into their sponsorship and broadcasting agreements. Sport organizations may be requested to assume the responsibility to pursue legal recourse against ambush marketing companies. This could involve significant legal expense, so exercise care during contract negotiations.

- A sport organization must actively monitor the advertising practices of its competitors and notify competitors promptly if it believes an advertising practice is illegal or unethical.

- When conducting any sales activities using discounts or other incentive advertising, sport managers need to understand the FTC regulations on how those advertisements must be worded and offers satisfied in order to avoid violating false advertising regulations.

- Conduct extensive research about potential partners before approaching them or entering into agreements. Research their products, business structure, management, corporate culture, third-party relationships, intellectual property rights, and financial conditions.

- Marketing partners and teams, leagues and athletes must clearly clarify what inventory, such as number of social media posts, photo shoots, and giveaways, is included in the partnership and plans must be developed to adequately utilize said inventory in marketing promotions.

This was demonstrated in 2017 when race car driver Danica Patrick's NASCAR team sued its former sponsor, Nature's Bakery. Initially, Patrick's racing team entered into a three-year partnership with Nature's Bakery, citing the fit between it and Patrick's personal brand, which focuses on healthy living. In its second year of the partnership, Nature's Bakery terminated its contract, alleging Patrick "was in breach of contract for promoting competing products" on social media. The allegations followed Nature's Bakery asking to revise its payment schedule for the sponsorship, which Patrick's team alleged was motivated by cash flow issues the brand was facing. Ultimately, Patrick's team sued Nature's Bakery for breach of contract and the lawsuit was settled later that year (Bianchi, 2017). In the case of Nature's Bakery and Patrick, it could be argued that both sides were not clear of the expectations nor capacities the other possessed to execute the term and requirements of the partnership.

Related to expectations, it is important to understand each side's short- and long-term goals when entering into partnerships. The Columbia Public School District was one of the first high school sport districts to enter into an intercollegiate-like marketing partnership when it signed a multi-year deal with Kelly Sports Properties. Kelly Sports Properties helped generate revenues for the school district, allowing it to make a number of upgrades to its sport facilities. However, the school district opted not to renew the contract, after which Kelly Sports Properties sued the school district for unpaid commissions. While the sides previously praised each other publicly, this case highlights how relationships can quickly change and the need for both sides to fully understand how their respective goals may shape the longevity of a partnership (Keller, 2018).

As more teams and leagues enter into partnerships with marketing and digital media distribution companies, it is important that each side fully understand and contractually agree to how payments will be made and when commissions are disbursed. The need for this is demonstrated by a 2019 lawsuit that arose between the University of Pittsburgh and IMG College. Pittsburgh contracted with IMG College to license its athletic radio broadcasts and sell its marketing, promotional and commercial rights. At the conclusion of its seven-year agreement, Pittsburgh opted to not renew the contract with IMG College. Thereafter, IMG College withheld $3.6 million in royalties owed to Pittsburgh, leading Pittsburgh to sue IMG College for breach of contract (Faust, 2019).

Another issue sport managers must be prepared to navigate is when a corporate partner's reputation becomes tainted or when partners are drawn into public controversy. For example, following racist remarks by LA Clippers owner Donald Sterling, many sponsors suspended ties with the Clippers (Hallman, 2014). Similarly, the NFL and University of Louisville encountered this issue in 2017 and 2018 with the league's then official pizza sponsor and the University of Louisville's then stadium naming rights partner, Papa John's. Beginning in 2016, a number of NFL players began kneeling during the playing of the National Anthem to protest police brutality and racism. During a 2017 shareholders call, Papa John's CEO and public face, John Schnatter, blamed the players' National Anthem protests for the pizza chain's declining sales (Meyer, 2017). Schnatter's statement was made public, leading to public scrutiny and player outcry against the brand. Ultimately, Papa John's and the NFL mutually agreed to end their sponsorship (Schad, 2018). The next year, Schnatter was recorded on a phone call with his marketing team using the N-word (Kirsch, 2018). When that incident was reported, the University of Louisville removed the brand's name from its football stadium and Schnatter resigned from his position on the university's board of trustees (Whitten, 2018).

Plan an Exit Strategy

Strategic alliances will not endure indefinitely, as at some point, one of the partners will seek to end the partnership. How one ends a strategic relationship can be more important than how one enters it. Properly planning the exit strategy and negotiating it into all agreements can prevent future litigation. At a minimum, address issues of who will retain the rights to any joint intellectual property and how the rights and responsibilities for ongoing operations will be divided. Again, be sure to consult with legal counsel in developing a strategy.

As indicated above, an economic crisis can affect sport partnerships. Sport organizations need to be aware that their corporate partners may seek to escape contractual commitments or forgo future sponsorships. During the 2008 recession, for example, General Motors began scaling back its sports sponsorships (Thomas, 2008), and at least two lawsuits were filed against sponsors who tried to pull out of a sponsorship. The Chicago Cubs sued Under Armour for their alleged breach of a five-year, $10.8 million sponsorship contract (Katz, 2009), and the PGA Tour sued Ginn Development after Ginn dropped its sponsorship of the Champion's Tour Ginn Championship and the LPGA's Ginn Open. Ginn still had three years remaining on its sponsorship contract (Associated Press, 2009). In 2019, the Cleveland Browns sued beverage sponsor Hard Beverages for allegedly not paying $525,000 owed in the first year of a five-year deal (Miller, 2019). Amidst the 2020 Covid-19 pandemic, which saw the shutdown of global sports, sponsors similarly sought to exit partnership agreements (Patel, 2020). Most notably, Under Armour canceled their apparel deal with UCLA allegedly due to the coronavirus pandemic, however, UCLA filed suit seeking recovery of around $280 million (Schlabach, 2020). These lawsuits illustrate the importance of addressing whether extreme financial distress will permit one party to terminate the sponsorship agreement and the need to plan for such an eventuality when agreements are drafted and executed.

Preserve Intellectual Property

Preserving IP is a crucial legal issue (see Chapter 18). Whether your organization owns the IP, the partner owns it, or it is co-owned, these issues must be addressed. This is especially important if you or your partner do not own the IP rights to a brand or a technology that is critical to the partnership.

Relations with Media and Broadcast Partners

Media relations is an umbrella term that includes managers who may also be called sport information directors, publicity directors, or media relations directors. The functions of these managers are diverse, and media relations personnel may be asked to participate in negotiating broadcasting agreements or working with broadcasters after an agreement has been executed. In addition, the duties of media relations personnel may include collecting and disseminating factual information about the organization through press kits, press releases, press conferences, media guides, stat sheets, fact sheets, public announcements, social media, and websites. In the process of collecting and disseminating this information, media relations personnel must be aware of federal and state privacy laws and state defamation laws that could be invoked in the event of a false and negligent release of information. Below we explore the key elements of a broadcasting agreement and privacy issues related to media relations.

Broadcasting Agreements

Sport marketers and sport administrators are often involved in negotiations with the media for the sale of broadcast and digital streaming rights to sport events. When entering into such an agreement, both the rights owner (sport organization) and the broadcaster must consider a number of issues as they negotiate.

Quantification of Coverage

It is important for the parties to quantify the exact broadcast coverage desired. For example, if the NFL is seeking to negotiate an agreement for broadcast rights for all games occurring in both the regular and post-season, the exact number of games to be broadcast must be established. Of course, the NFL has hundreds of potential games and team combinations and often negotiates with multiple broadcasters. However, the actual number of games to be broadcast on a particular network's station must be negotiated.

In a more confined scenario, consider an NCAA Division I-A college athletic department seeking to negotiate the broadcast of all of its home football games. The team has exactly seven home games, and exact dates of the games and identities of the opponents have been determined. However, the broadcaster may want to approve the timing and scheduling of the events. For example, a game originally scheduled for Saturday afternoon at 3:00 p.m. may be perfect for the teams, but the broadcaster may have already scheduled that particular time slot. In this situation, the broadcaster will likely request to move the game to another time or even another day. This change will require the home team to negotiate with its opponent or to include in its game contracts provisions for moving the game day or time to accommodate broadcasting needs.

Scope of Coverage and Revenues

Broadcast rights represent the largest portion of the total revenues for most sport organizations and therefore need to be addressed in broadcasting agreements. Methods of revenue generation to be covered in a broadcasting agreement include: whether the broadcast will be free to air or pay-per-view; live in full, delayed or archived; available for use in news and/or available through video on demand, digitally, streaming, or resale in highlight packages. Also, the agreement needs to address exclusive licensing if any, description of license territories, and license periods.

As consumers increasingly "cut the cable cord" and rely on digital streaming technology to view sport broadcasts, multiple streaming services have emerged. As of 2019, most exclusive rights for sport leagues' content are held by traditional cable broadcasting companies, like ABC, CBS and NBC. However, responding to consumers' media consumption patterns, sport entities are turning to streaming to distribute content. The four major leagues in the United States – MLB, NBA, NFL, and NHL – each have their own streaming platforms, with media companies like ESPN, Fox Sports, and Bleacher Report, also active in the space (Fischer & Baker, 2019). Perhaps the most fascinating aspect of the digital streaming space, though, is how technology companies, like Amazon, Facebook, and YouTube, are working to disrupt traditional broadcast networks by bidding for the exclusive rights to sport content (Spangler, n.d.).

With sport media rights expected to generate $23.8 billion in revenue by 2022, the total valuation and impact of digital streaming rights in sport is yet to be seen (Gallagher, 2018). However, sport managers must be aware of negotiation and risk management issues related to streaming as it becomes more prevalent. Related to negotiating streaming deals, parties to the contracts must determine what will drive the monetary value of the contract. Traditionally, a league's overnight program ratings have driven how much a network is willing to pay to purchase a league's exclusive broadcast rights. Overnight program ratings may not continue to be as important when viewership is shifted from a cable network to a consumer's streaming device. The role advertising plays in generating revenue, especially when consumers can skip through recorded advertisements when streaming content on-demand, is also likely to change in this new digital landscape (Edwards, 2016). Further, the technologies related to how consumers access and purchase streaming rights are also likely to expand and develop, creating both new ways to monetize sports media consumption and new challenges in navigating legal issues. Current models, such as on-demand, pay-per-view, and bundled options, will seek to carve a share of the marketplace (Bailey, 2019).

Related to risk management, streaming rights holders' intellectual property rights must be protected given that most fans possess the opportunity to live stream sport content by recording games on their smartphones and broadcasting them online (Rodrigues & Pahl, 2019). Live streaming rights are protected by copyright and should be expressly addressed in a broadcasting or licensing agreement. As with any new technology, the legal impact is uncertain, but the notice-and-takedown system provided under the Digital Millennium Copyright Act (DMCA) provides a great deal of protection to users, as well as copyright holders (Bailey, 2009). This system requires hosts, such as YouTube, Twitter, and other digital and social media platforms to remove or disable access to infringing material once notified of the infringing content. If the host does not take down the infringing content, it may become liable for the infringement. In the coming years, sport managers and media leaders must work together to develop standards of best practice and legal protocols for this emerging market.

Mode of Transmission and Medium of Distribution

The broadcasting agreement should establish the transmission and distribution modes, such as satellite or cable, and whether the broadcast will be free to the public or pay-per-view. The parties must also negotiate whether the event will be broadcast live and simultaneous with the event, tape delayed, or broadcast as highlights only. The medium of distribution can include network or cable TV, the Internet, mobile phone networks, and fixed media, such as DVDs and CDs. For example, pay-per-view event agreements for boxing matches frequently permit moving images (live or tape-delayed) to be broadcast only by a single provider. A secondary provider, including the media, would only be permitted to broadcast still photos of select moments during the fight. A broadcaster will want the highest priority for its broadcast coverage to maximize its usage, and often the broadcaster will seek designation as the exclusive broadcaster for an event. This exclusivity does not prevent the news media from using small amounts of footage for legitimate news reporting purposes. (See Chapter 18 regarding copyright protection and the scope of the media's fair use of copyrighted materials.)

Access to the Event

Access to the event is also a concern for the broadcaster. The broadcasting agreement should specify details, such as: the number and positioning of cameras; availability and construction of scaffolding and rigging; positioning of commentary teams; and parking, power, and electrical requirements. As digital technology continues expanding, advanced technological capabilities should be addressed in the broadcasting agreement. The broadcaster will likely also want access to event personnel and participants for interviews.

Cancelation of the Event

The parties to the broadcasting agreement will want adequate event cancelation insurance, and must determine who is responsible for securing and paying for the insurance. Event cancelation insurance protects parties from financial losses they may suffer should an event be canceled, which may include missed revenue, promotional expenses, and production expenses.

Protection Against Ambush Marketing During a Broadcast

As mentioned earlier, ambush marketing can seriously interfere with official sponsors' abilities to maximize their investments; thus, a sport organization may seek a commitment from the broadcaster to protect actively against ambush marketing. The sport organization should request that official sponsors be given a right of first refusal to purchase advertising time during the broadcast. The sponsors may even desire to negotiate with the broadcaster for exclusivity to prevent competitors from purchasing advertising time during the broadcast.

These are only a few of the issues that are important in a broadcasting agreement that sport marketers should consider when negotiating with media entities.

Defamation and Privacy Rights

In the sport industry, defamation and invasion of privacy claims are raised in a variety of settings, but are often associated with statements made or disclosed by the media. These may include: disclosure of personal information about a coach or athlete; statements made by an athletic director about reasons for terminating a coach; statements made by a coach about an assistant coach; statements made by an agent about a client; statements published by a media site about an athlete; and statements published on social media about an athlete, coach, or shareholder of a professional sport team.

Any of these examples could easily form the basis of a defamation or invasion of privacy action. Thus, we are going to explore the types of defamation claims that can be raised when false statements are published by the media. Then we will also discuss the concept of privacy and the tort of invasion of privacy and emerging challenges for sport managers in the acquisition and use of data in our sales and marketing operations.

Defamation

Defamation cases are common in the sport industry and are a significant concern for sport organizations in their interactions with media outlets, and for media outlets when reporting events. Exhibit 19.7 highlights just a few disputes and lawsuits arising from statements made by both sport organizations and the media related to an employee's termination, NCAA investigations, and inappropriate behavior by coaches and athletes.

Exhibit 19.7 Examples of defamation cases in the sports industry.

Case	Facts/Context	Resolution
McNair v. NCAA (2018) O'Connor v. Burningham, 2007 Utah LEXIS 139 (2007)	McNair sued NCAA alleging the NCAA Infractions Committee and appeal committee made false statements about him during an investigation for rules violations. Coach sued parents of students in a local high school based on their attempts to have him fired from his job which included accusing him a misusing school money	The jury returned a verdict in favor of the NCAA (9-3) in May, 2018 The Utah Supreme Court held a high school coach was not a public official or public figure so he did not need to prove actual malice to prevail. The case was sent back to the district court for trial
Mike Leach v. ESPN & Spaeth Communications (August 8, 2013)	Former Texas Tech football coach sued ESPN and PR firm for libel and slander in 2010 based on claims they published about mistreatment of the ESPN analyst Craig James.	Texas judge granted summary judgment for defendants in 2013, and Leach's appeal was denied in 2015.
Fine v. ESPN, Inc., U.S. District Court for the Northern District of New York. Case No. 5:13-CV-0652 (April 4, 2013)	In April 2013, former Syracuse University assistant men's basketball coach Bernie Fine filed an $11 million defamation lawsuit against ESPN, stemming from broadcasts in which ESPN reported claims by two former ball boys that Fine had molested them in the 1980s and 1990s. Fine was fired from Syracuse in November 2011, although he was never charged with a crime in connection with the case.	Fine dropped the lawsuit in July of 2013.
Price v. Time, Inc., Jefferson County Circuit Court, State of Alabama. Complaint, Civil Action: CV 03 3855 (June 20, 2003)	Former University of Alabama head football coach Mike Price sued Time, Inc. for defamation based on a Sports Illustrated article reporting his alleged misbehavior. Price sued for $20 million, claiming he was defamed and slandered by the story, which detailed his alleged actions the night he visited a topless bar in Pensacola, Florida, in April 2003, shortly after being hired as the new head coach at Alabama. He acknowledged being heavily intoxicated but denied allegations of having sex at his hotel. Alabama fired Price a few days before the article was published.	The parties ultimately settled for an undisclosed sum without any admission of wrongdoing on the part of Time, Inc.

Nature of the Claim

Defamation claims are intended to protect a person from false statements that are damaging to his or her reputation or that diminish the esteem, respect, goodwill, or confidence in which a person is held, or that cause adverse, derogatory, or unpleasant feelings or opinions against a person. Generally, a **defamatory act** is defined in the Restatement (Second) of Torts as follows:

1 A false statement (truth is an absolute defense to defamation).
2 Published to a third party.
3 Involving some degree of fault or negligence on the part of the publisher.
4 Causing actual damage.

The tort of defamation includes both **slander** (spoken) and **libel** (written). Libel is broader than slander in that any number of tangible communications would fall under the heading of written communication,

---

Competitive Advantage Strategies

Consumer Interactions and Marketing Practices

- Document any strategic alliances with a memorandum of understanding. It can be used to define the parameters of the partnership and the basic interests of the partners. It does not have to bind the parties to a deal, but it should allow them time to explore the possibility without other parties intruding.

- Do not hesitate to involve lawyers in drafting agreements, participating in negotiations, and researching business practices and intellectual property ownership. Lawyers can force the parties to ask hard questions and raise negative scenarios without pitting the parties against one another.

- Communicating with the media is a critical part of media relations, but it is also imperative that any personnel dealing with the media verify and confirm any information provided and avoid disclosures about personnel, employment issues, or employment status of coaches.

- If possible, allow a resigning coach to make the official announcement regarding his reasons for leaving, rather than the team or university. If the coach is terminated, the organization will have to issue the press release or announcement; however, the reasons for dismissal must be carefully worded to avoid damaging the coach's reputation.

- Media relations personnel working in college athletics should be aware of limitations on the type of information that can be disclosed about a student-athlete's academic performance and medical treatments or conditions.

---

such as written comments, photographs, cartoons, and publications. Now digital technology preserves most media statements in a tangible form indefinitely and most jurisdictions refer to slander and libel interchangeably as simply defamation. A statement is defamatory per se if its harm is obvious and apparent on the face of it (*Green v. Rogers*, 2009). Each state may define defamation slightly differently, but typically a verbal or spoken comment is per se defamatory if it falls into one of the following categories:

1 Imputes that a person has engaged in criminal conduct.
2 Imputes that a person has a loathsome disease.
3 Imputes that a person has engaged in adultery or fornication.
4 Imputes that a person has engaged in misconduct in public office.
5 Imputes that a person is incompetent or unfair in that person's profession, business, or trade.

If a statement falls into one of these categories, it is presumed as a matter of law that the reputation of the individual about whom the statement was made will be injured. For example, false comments accusing a coach of sexual misconduct with an athlete or illegal recruiting practices could be construed as slanderous *per se* because these comments will always be considered damaging to a coach's reputation. In other words, a reasonable person could not interpret such statements as a positive reflection upon a coach.

Public Officials, Public Figures, and Limited Purpose Public Figures

Notice that the third element from the Restatement involves some degree of fault or negligence. This is the element most often at issue in defamation cases. The degree of fault required to extend liability varies depending upon whether the person allegedly defamed is a public official, public figure, or limited purpose public figure.

Public official. The 1964 Supreme Court decision in *New York Times Co. v. Sullivan* (hereinafter "*New York Times*") revolutionized the way the judiciary interpreted and applied defamation law. As stated by

Pember (1990), "This is one of the most important First Amendment cases ever decided ..." (p. 129). In *New York Times*, the Supreme Court prohibited *public officials* from recovering damages for defamatory comments relating to official conduct unless the plaintiff could prove that the statement was made with *actual malice*. Communication made with **actual malice** was defined as communication made "with knowledge that it was false or with reckless disregard of whether it was false or not" (*New York Times*, 1964, p. 380). The Supreme Court believed that the public had a right to know and evaluate for themselves how leaders governed. Further, open debate, although at times caustic and unpleasant, assured the exchange of ideas necessary to bring about political and social change desired by the people (*New York Times*, 1964). Further, the freedom of the people to criticize freely and without actual malice better balances the absolute privilege enjoyed by the public official. In *Rosenblatt v. Baer* (1966) the Court questioned whether all individuals employed by the state are public officials or just those employed in "high-powered" positions. Since many coaches are employed by the state through their public school and university employers, this designation becomes increasingly important. However, the majority of jurisdictions to consider this issue have held that coaches are not public officials for purposes of defamation law (*Moss v. Stockard*, 1990; *Verity v. USA Today*, 2019; *Milkovich v. News Herald*, 1984; *O'Connor v. Burningham*, 2007).

Public figure. A public figure is one who either has gained notoriety from his achievements or seeks public attention through vigor and success. The U.S. Supreme Court reduced the "public-figure question to looking at the nature and extent of an individual's participation in the particular controversy giving rise to the defamation." That is, the Court looked at the following:

- The extent to which the individual's participation is voluntary.
- The extent to which the individual has access to the media to counteract the false statements.
- The prominence of the individual's role in the public controversy.

The Supreme Court held in *Curtis Publishing Co. v. Butts* (1967) that a **public figure** (in that case the athletic director of the University of Georgia, Wally Butts) was an individual who has, because of his or her activities, "commanded sufficient continuing public interest." Thus, in order for a public figure to recover for defamation, like the public official, she must prove that the defamatory statements were made with "actual malice." That is, the statements were made with knowledge that they were false or with reckless disregard for whether they were false or not. Unlike a public figure or public official, a private person does not have to prove actual malice; thus, a private person must only prove that a false and defamatory statement was published negligently (unreasonably) in order to recover damages.

The courts have often classified professional athletes and coaches as public figures. Requiring professional athletes or other high-profile sport celebrities to prove actual malice is appropriate because (1) they have voluntarily placed themselves in the public eye and, having done so, are exposed to greater public scrutiny; and (2) they have more ready access to the media and other public forums in which they can defend against public criticism. In *Dykstra v. St. Martin's Press, LLC* (2020) the Supreme Court of New York dismissed a lawsuit filed by Lenny Dykstra wherein he sued for defamation based on comments in Ronald Darling's 2019 book, "*108 Stitches.*" Darling's 2019 book recounted a story from the 1986 World Series in which Starling said that while Dennis Boyd of the Boston Red Sox was warming up, Dykstra was in the on-deck circle shouting unimaginable insults at Boyd including racist insults. Since Dykstra is a public figure, in addition to proving the statements were false, he must also prove they were published with actual malice and caused damage to his reputation. The court first held that Dykstra could not prove that the statements were published with actual malice because a failure to investigate is not sufficient to establish reckless disregard. With regard to proof of damages, the court relied upon a doctrine referred to as *Libel-Proof Plaintiff Doctrine* which holds that someone with an already soiled reputation could not recover anything other than nominal damages. The court concluded that Dykstra's criminal offenses and general bad reputation for fairness and decency were far worse than the alleged racially charged bench-jockeying statements (*Dykstra*, at 16).

Limited purpose public figure. Sometimes the line between a private figure and public figure is not clear, and an individual who would normally be considered a private figure can be thrust into a public controversy or debate. In these circumstances the individual may be treated as a limited purpose public figure if the individual has voluntarily injected himself or has been drawn into a particular public controversy. The limited-purpose public figure has instant *local* recognition and constant media coverage on a *local* level. A limited purpose public figure is a person who becomes a public figure for a specific range of issues by being drawn into or voluntarily injecting himself into a specific public controversy. For example, a student-athlete would normally not be considered a public figure. However, if the student-athlete thrust himself into the forefront of a public issue or controversy, he may be considered a limited purpose public figure for the duration of the controversy. A good example would be a number of student-athletes who became active in the Black Lives Matter protests during the summer of 2020 (Coaston, 2020; Diaz, 2020). These athletes might be consider limited purpose public figures with regard to statements made about them related to their involvement in the Black Lives Matter movement. The following Focus Case explores the issue of the limited purpose public figure and how defamation law applies in that context.

McGuire v. Bowlin

932 N.W.2d 819 (Minn. 2019)	FOCUS CASE

FACTS

From the fall of 2012 to the spring of 2014, McGuire was the head coach of the girls' basketball program for Woodbury High School (WHS). While McGuire was coaching at WHS, respondents, all of whom were parents of players on the team, expressed concerns about McGuire's conduct, most notably alleging that he swore at practices, touched players in inappropriate ways, and flirted with players. In January 2014, these concerns ultimately culminated in a meeting with the parents (and writing a letter to) school administrators to discuss McGuire's conduct. Two days after the parents met with the school administrators, McGuire was placed on administrative leave from his coaching duties. Two months later, in March 2014, the school district decided not to renew his coaching contract. Around the same time, two parents (Bowlin & Danielson) filed maltreatment-of-minor reports against McGuire with the Minnesota Department of Education. Following an investigation, the Department concluded that Bowlin's daughter had not been subjected to maltreatment. Even after McGuire was removed from his coaching position, Bowlin continued to make statements about him. In August 2014, she emailed another parent that, "Last I heard yesterday he was recently put in jail … I will find out the truth and call the [Department of Education] today and find out." In December she sent that same parent's spouse a photo of a newspaper article titled "Woodbury man sentenced to jail in stolen funds case," accompanied by a text that said "I know we don't talk anymore but this was part of the Woodbury stuff with [McGuire] that was going on. This guy too got busted." It is undisputed that the subject of the article was not McGuire. In December 2015, McGuire served and filed a complaint alleging respondents had engaged in defamation, and that Bowlin and Danielson had filed false maltreatment-of-minor reports. The defendants moved for summary judgment. They argued that because McGuire was a public figure McGuire was required to prove malice and there was no such proof here. The district court granted their motions.

HOLDING

McGuire is not a limited purpose public figure and the grant of summary judgment was erroneous.

RATIONALE

Respondents argued that McGuire is a limited-purpose public figure, a status that would require McGuire to prove actual malice. In 1974, the Court held in Gertz v. Robert Welch, Inc., that "public figures," like public officials, may recover for injury to reputation only upon a showing of actual malice. 418 U.S. 323, 342 (1974). The Court went on to define three types of public figures. First, involuntary public figures are people who become public figures "through no purposeful action of [their] own." Id. at 345. The Court noted that involuntary public figures are "exceedingly rare." Id. Indeed, no case from the Supreme Court, our court, or the Minnesota Court of Appeals has ever concluded that a plaintiff is an involuntary public figure. Second, all-purpose public figures are people who have attained their status having "assumed roles of especial prominence in the affairs of society … [with] such persuasive power and influence that they are deemed public figures for all purposes." Id. Finally, limited-purpose public figures are "those classed as public figures [who] have thrust themselves to the forefront of particular controversies in order to influence the resolution of the issues involved." Id. It is this last category that is at issue here.

Applying *Gertz*, we have held that three factors must be present for someone to be a limited-purpose public figure: "(1) whether a public controversy existed; (2) whether the plaintiff played a meaningful role in the controversy; and (3) whether the allegedly defamatory statement related to the controversy." In determining whether a public controversy existed, we do not look to any controversy created by the allegedly defamatory statements; instead, our inquiry is limited "to those controversies that are already the subject of debate in the public arena at the time of the alleged defamation." *Chafoulias*, 668 N.W.2d at 651.

We are unable to discern any public controversy here. Although controversy ensued after respondents made the allegedly defamatory statements about McGuire, that controversy cannot serve as a basis for concluding that McGuire is a limited-purpose public figure. As *Chafoulias* makes clear, a party cannot stir up controversy by making defamatory statements and then point to the resulting controversy as a basis for assigning the defamed party public-figure status. Hewitt seeks to avoid this conclusion by arguing that the controversy in question was "whether McGuire was effectively coaching the teams to win as many games as possible," but that is not persuasive. First, the record does not suggest that a controversy existed concerning this topic. Second, even if a controversy existed, respondents would nevertheless fail on the third public-figure factor – whether the allegedly defamatory statement related to the controversy. The statements at issue were unrelated to whether the team was being coached to win as many games as possible; instead, they related to allegedly inappropriate conduct toward players. Accordingly, we conclude that McGuire is not a limited-purpose public figure for the purpose of evaluating respondents' allegedly defamatory statements.

Where defamation claims seek to provide a redress for reputational damage, privacy based claims are focused on protecting the disclosure of confidential or harmful private information. Next we learn about the tort of invasion of privacy. We also examine how the use of private individual data of our customers, such as ticket purchasers, is becoming increasingly important for sport managers and raises concerns about protecting the individual privacy of our customers.

Privacy

Privacy is the expectation that confidential personal information disclosed in a private place will not be disclosed to third parties, when that disclosure would cause either embarrassment or emotional distress to a person of reasonable sensitivities. *Information* is a broad term that includes: facts; images such as photographs, videos, and audio recordings; and even disparaging opinions. Privacy rights exist both under the common law as expressed in the Restatement (Second) of Torts at §§ 652A–652I and also under a number of statutes prohibiting disclosure of certain kinds of information, such as the Family Educational Right to Privacy Act (FERPA), which protects the privacy of student records.

This section focuses on common law rights of privacy. The Restatement classifies four basic kinds of common law privacy rights. These are defined in Exhibit 19.8.

Exhibit 19.8 Four types of common law privacy rights.

1 Protection from unreasonable intrusion upon the seclusion of another – for example, physical invasion into a person's home (e.g., unwanted entry; looking into windows with binoculars or a camera; tapping the telephone); searching a person's wallet or purse; repeated and persistent telephone calls; or obtaining financial data (e.g., bank balance) without a person's consent.

2 Protection from appropriation of a person's name or likeness. This is similar to the concept of the right of publicity discussed previously.

3 Protection from publication of private facts – for example, income tax data; information about sexual relations; personal letters; family quarrels; medical treatment; or photographs of a person in their home.

4 Protection from publication that places a person in a false light. This is similar to defamation. A successful defamation action requires that the information be false. In a privacy action, the information is generally true, but the information creates a false impression about the plaintiff.

The first type of privacy right is most likely implicated by the release of private information about an individual, such as an athlete, coach, athletic staff member, or athletic director. Unreasonable intrusion upon seclusion applies only to secret or surreptitious invasions of privacy. For example, ESPN sports reporter Erin Andrews filed an invasion of privacy lawsuit seeking $10 million in damages against Marriott arising from an incident where a man filmed Andrews through her hotel room peephole (*Andrews v. Marriott International*, 2010). The hotel revealed Andrews's room location to the man, who then booked a room next door and altered the peephole to her room using a hacksaw. The man video recorded her in her undergarments and partially nude. The man then attempted to sell his recordings to TMZ and also posted the videos to the Internet himself. In a lawsuit for negligence against the owner and operator of the involved Marriott location and the man who video recorded her, Andrews was awarded $55 million by a jury in 2016 (Bieler, 2016).

The distinction between the right of publicity as discussed in Chapter 18 and the second type of privacy right is that a personal right to privacy protects against "injury to personal feelings," whereas the right of publicity protects against unauthorized commercial exploitation of a person's name or image. As a practical matter, a sport celebrity would generally sue under the right of publicity, and an ordinary citizen would sue under right to privacy.

An open and notorious invasion of privacy would be public, not private, and the victim could choose not to reveal private or confidential information. For example, recording telephone conversations is not wrong if both participants are notified before they speak that the conversation is, or may be, recorded, in states requiring such notice to be given. Furthermore, if two college athletes make extravagant purchases of sportswear at a local mall, those purchases have been made in a public place and the sales clerk and other customers do not owe the athletes any duty of confidentiality. Therefore, under current law, there is no expectation of privacy. The store clerk could report the amount that the athletes spent and the items they purchased, even if the disclosure may be harmful to the athletes (e.g., if the purchases were a violation of NCAA bylaws regarding benefits to student-athletes).

Businesses have no right of privacy (Am. Jur. 2d *Constitutional Law* § 606, 1979; *California Bankers Association v. Schultz*, 1974; Prosser, 1960; Restatement [Second] of Torts, § 652I, comment c, 1977; *U.S. v. Morton Salt Co.*, 1950). Privacy law is phrased only as an individual person's rights. However, businesses have rights analogous to the right of privacy. For example, corporate espionage might be prosecuted as an improper acquisition of a trade secret (Restatement [Third] of Unfair Competition § 43, 1995). Trade secrets, criminal proceedings, and patents are beyond the scope of this text, but many of those statutory protections are also grounded in privacy law. Further, trademark law, discussed in Chapter 18, permits a business to own a logo and prevent others from using the same mark or logo.

Sport Analytics and Data Privacy

From e-commerce to social media to athlete biometrics, data permeates across our sport business operations. Some sport businesses are intensely data driven, such as Formula One, while others may only be at the beginning stages of datafication of their sport and business operations, such as the London Irish rugby team (Marr, 2017). But as sport teams and leagues increasingly collect and rely on data to drive business and playing decisions, one of the biggest privacy issues the sport industry faces is how to securely protect that data. As we collect data from customers we must remember that the customers own their data and should have control over how that data is used. Data breaches can result from an external hack into systems by malicious third parties, or an erroneous or inadvertent release by the organization without the customers' consent. Some data breaches may result in lawsuits or federal investigations, but most certainly can erode customer confidence and loyalty. For example, the Ticketmaster data breach in 2019 affected thousands of customers whose confidential credit card information was compromised by a third-party hack (Taylor, 2019).

The United States does not have a universal data protection law, but several laws exist at the Federal and State levels designed to protect U.S. residents and their data (Chabinsky & Pittman, 2020). There are U.S. privacy laws prohibiting companies from matching IP addresses to a user's Personal Identifiable Information (PII), but the PII data protection only protects information about an individual that is maintained by specific agencies, such as motor vehicle records, addresses and collection of personal medical information (Chabinsky & Pittman, 2020; McCallister, Grance, & Scarfone, 2010). The FTC offers broad federal data protection legislation with the Federal Trade Commission Act over unfair and deceptive practices, but the FTC identifies that mobile devices do have the ability to reveal a user's location and "build detailed profiles of consumers movements over time in ways that may not be anticipated by consumers" (Federal Trade Commission, 2013b; Federal Trade Commission, 2018).

At the state level, California is currently a leader in personal data privacy protection laws with the passage of the California Consumer Privacy Act (CCPA). This law, which took effect in January 2020, requires companies to disclose what personal data is collected on consumers, the purpose for collecting the data, and with whom the data will be shared (Chabinsky & Pittman, 2020; Davis, 2020). The CCPA is closely modeled after the data privacy legislation enacted in the European Union in 2018. One of its more notable features is the requirement for individuals to specifically and knowingly "opt-in" to any data collection and tracking initiative of personal information (Location Based Marketing, 2019). This lack of consistent regulation means that businesses need to be proactive to ensure data privacy across a spectrum of issues, in addition to direct customer interactions.

>   **Wearable technology.** In addition to customer concerns, a number of sport teams and leagues collect athlete's biometric data using wearable technology devices. Data collected from players using wearable technology ranges from heart rate, speed and steps, to how long a player slept, the number of drinks they consumed or whether they had sex the night before. Given the depth of information procurable using wearable technology, athletes understandably have significant privacy concerns related to how the data is collected, used and stored. Further, improperly obtained and used data can have significant consequences to athletes, as teams and leagues have reportedly used said data to drive decisions ranging from playing time to signing free agents. Thus, players, players associations, leagues, and teams must work together to best promote their interests and secure the privacy of the data collected. This process must balance the interest in protecting players' privacy rights with teams' and leagues' interests in optimizing analytics to improve performance and revenue. At a minimum, players associations and leagues must negotiate the following: what wearable technology devices can be used in the league; whether use is mandatory; when a player's data can be collected using wearable technology; what data can be collected from the player; how the data is stored and secured; and how the data can be utilized (Jessop & Baker, 2019).

Misuse of data by opposing teams. While it is plausible an athlete's data could be misused by teams and leagues, teams also face the possibility that collected data could be misused by opposing teams. This issue is highlighted by a case that arose in 2014 when a former St. Louis Cardinals scouting director hacked into a Houston Astros' database and obtained access to the Astros' internal trade, draft and player evaluation notes. The hacking reportedly cost the Astros $1.7 million and led to an FBI investigation. Ultimately, the Cardinals employee pleaded guilty to five counts of unauthorized access of a protected computer and was sentenced to 46 months in prison and restitution. The Astros' data breach case highlights the possibility that passwords alone aren't enough to secure data and signifies that sport leaders must learn more about encryption and other protection software systems (Allen, 2016).

Sport gambling. Finally, with the growing legalization of sport gambling in individual U.S. states following the Supreme Court's decision in *Murphy v. NCAA* (2018) (see Chapter 10), the desire for access to data and issues surrounding ownership and protection will only intensify. Thus, sport managers must stay on the cutting edge of data security tools and practices to ensure the integrity of the games they oversee and protection of players' and employees' privacy rights (Sanders & Sharma, 2019).

Conclusion

This chapter covered legal issues that may arise as sport marketers and managers implement marketing strategies and interact with consumers, competitors, strategic partners and the media. Legal issues relevant when sport organizations communicate about their products and services with consumers through advertising, including such topics as false advertising, athlete endorsements and publicity rights and special offers, were examined. Legal issues relevant to a sport organization's interactions with consumers, the media, strategic partners, and competitors, including such topics as ambush marketing, commercial sales transactions, sponsorship and broadcasting agreements and privacy rights, were discussed.

Discussion Questions

1 What is the most common form of commercial speech?
2 What are the four criteria for determining whether a state's restriction on commercial speech is constitutional?
3 Which of these four criteria was not satisfied in the *Albarado v. Kentucky Racing Commission* case?
4 What are the five conditions that must be met to prove that an advertisement is false or deceptive?
5 For a celebrity endorsement to not be deceptive, what criteria must be met?
6 What is the recommended designation a celebrity endorser should include on any social media posts to disclose their relationship with a company whose products are being promoted?
7 When is comparative advertising permitted?
8 What is ambush marketing? Provide two or three examples of ambush marketing in sports.
9 What are at least five critical areas to be included in a broadcasting agreement?
10 What is the difference between horizontal price fixing and vertical price fixing?

Learning Activities

Locate your state attorney general's office website and search the links to the consumer protection division or consumer protection regulations. Does the website provide good and readily accessible information about consumer rights and regulations regarding deceptive trade practices? What special programs does your state operate to protect against consumer fraud or deceptive trade practices that may impact a sport organization in your area? Has your state adopted specific guidelines related to social media advertising and endorsements?

Case Study

1 Consider the popular Sprite advertisements featuring LeBron James. Sprite launches a new adver-
    tisement campaign featuring James. One commercial features James holding a bottle of Sprite and
    walking through various scenes announcing, "Let's be straight, I'd never tell you to drink Sprite" as
    it relates to each scene he encounters. However at the end, James looks into the camera and says,
    "Let's be straight, I'd never tell you to drink Sprite, I'd ask you, 'Do you want a Sprite?'" Would this
    be considered a celebrity endorsement?
2 What FTC regulations define celebrity endorsements?
3 Assume James does not actually drink Sprite. Can the FTC bring an action against Sprite or James?

Considering ... Analysis & Discussion

Deceptive Advertising

Since the Federal Drug Administration has determined that a number of sport supplements, particularly those containing the stimulant ephedra or metabolic steroids, have been connected to
athlete deaths and illnesses, we may assume that the manager's statement to the reporter is at best
deceptive and more likely false. However, if a false statement made by a sport manager as part of
a public debate (e.g., on the public health risks created by the use of sport supplements) is treated
as political speech, laws prohibiting false advertising, permitting private defamation actions, and
regulating deceptive business practices would likely not provide any remedy for that false statement. However, if that same statement were instead treated as commercial speech, because of either
the speaker's motive or the commercial context in which it was made, or simply because it was
made by a corporate representative, laws relating to false advertising, deceptive trade practices, and
defamation would likely prohibit the speech and provide a legal remedy for anyone injured by the
speech, including the general public.

The manager's posting of the article throughout the store would likely be a deceptive advertisement. Because the manager has omitted an important part of the article (namely, the risks of
using sports supplements), it is likely that a reasonable consumer could be misled into thinking the
article concurred with the manager's statements and verified them as truthful.

References

Cases

Albarado v. Kentucky Racing Commission, 496 F. Supp. 2d 795 (W.D. Ky. 2004).
American Needle v. New Orleans Saints, 2014 U.S. Dist. LEXIS 47527 (N.D. Ill. 2014).
American Needle v. National Football League, 560 U.S. 183 (2010).
Andrews v. Marriott International, Inc., Case No. 2010L 008186 [Complaint filed July 15, 2010] (Circuit Court of
    Cook County, Illinois).
Baden Sports, Inc. v. Kabushiki Kaisha Molten, 541 F. Supp. 2d 1151 (W.D. Wash. 2008).
Baden Sports Inc. v. Molten USA, Inc., 556 F.3d 1300 (Fed. Cir. 2009).
Bigelow v. Virginia, 421 U.S. 809 (1975).
California Bankers Association v. Schultz, 416 U.S. 21 (1974).
C.B.C. Distribution and Marketing, Inc. v. Major League Baseball Advanced Media, L.P., 505 F.3d 818 (8th Cir. 2007).
Central Hudson Gas & Elec. Co. v. Public Serv. Comm'n of N.Y., 447 U.S. 557 (1980).
Cincinnati Reds, L.L.C. v. Testa, 155 Ohio St. 3d 512 (2018).
Dang v. San Francisco 49ers, Ltd. et al., No. 5:12-CV-5481 (N.D.C.A. August 2, 2013).
Dykstra v. St. Martin's Press LLC, 2020 N.Y. Misc. LEXIS 2659 (Sup. Ct. N.Y. 2020).
Fine v. ESPN, Inc., U.S. District Court for the Northern District of New York. Case No. 5:13-CV-0652 (April 4, 2013).

FTC v. Garvey, 383 F.3d 891 (9th Cir. 2004).

General Mills, Inc., v. Chobani, LLC, 158 F. Supp. 3d. 106 (N.D.N.Y. 2016).

Gengo v. Jets Stadium Development, LLC, 2018 U.S. Dist. LEXIS 148056 (D. N.J. August 30, 2018).

Green v. Rogers, 234 Ill. 2d 478 (Ill. 2009).

Grubbs v. Sheakley Group, Inc., 807 F.3d 785 (6th Cir. 2015).

Haelan Laboratories, Inc. v. Topps Chewing Gum, Inc., 202 F.2d 866 (2d Cir. 1953).

Hart v. Electronic Arts, Inc., 717 F.3d 141 (3d Cir. 2013).

In Re NCAA Athlete Grant-In-Aid Cap Antitrust Litigation, 375 F. Supp. 3d 1058 (N.D. Cal, March 8, 2019).

Keller v. Electronic Arts Inc., 724 F.3d 1268 (9th Cir. 2013).

McGuire v. Bowlin, 932 N.W.2d 819 (Minn. 2019).

Milkovich v. News Herald, 473 N.E.2d 1191 (Ohio 1984).

MillerCoors LLC v. Anheuser-Busch Companies LLC, Case No. 19-cv-218 (W.D. Wis. 2019).

Moss v. Stockard, 580 A.2d 1011 (D.C. 1990).

Murphy v. NCAA, 138 S. Ct. 1461 (2018).

NCAA v. Coors Brewing Co., Case No. 49D01-Z207-PL-001290, Marion County, Indiana (2002).

New York Times v. Sullivan, 376 U.S. 254 (1964).

NFL v. Delaware, 435 F. Supp. 1372 (D. Del. 1977).

NHL v. Pepsi-Cola Canada Ltd., 70 B.C.L.R. 2d 27 (BCSC 1992).

Nike, Inc. v. Kasky, 27 Cal. 4th 939, 45 P.3d 24, 119 Cal. Rptr. 2d 296 (2002).

NPS, LLC v. Minihane, 886 N.E.2d 670, 451 Mass. 417 (Mass. 2008).

O'Connor v. Burningham, 165 P.3d 1214 (Utah 2007).

Oshinsky v. New York Football Giants, Inc., Class Action Complaint, Civil Action No. 09-cv. 1186 (PGS), United States District Court, District of New Jersey (March 16, 2009).

Stokely-Van Camp v. The Coca Cola Company, 646 F. Supp. 2d 510 (S.D. N.Y. 2009).

U.S. v. Morton Salt Company, 338 U.S. 632 (1950).

Verity v. USA Today, 436 P.3d 653 (Idaho 2019).

Virginia State Bd. of Pharmacy v. Virginia Citizens Consumer Council, 425 U.S. 748 (1976).

Statutes

American Jurisprudence, 2d. *Constitutional law* § 606 (1979).

Federal Trade Commission Act, 15 U.S.C. § 45 *et seq.*

Federal Trade Commission Regulations, 16 e-CFR § 238.0, Bait advertising defined (2019).

Federal Trade Commission Regulations, 16 e-C.F.R. §238.1, Bait advertisement. (2019).

Federal Trade Commission Regulations, 16 e-C.F.R. §238.2, Initial offer. (2019).

Federal Trade Commission Regulations, 16 e-C.F.R. §238.3, Discouragement of purchase of advertised merchandise. (2019).

Lanham Act, 15 U.S.C. § 1125 *et seq.*

Restatement (Second) of Torts, § 652A-I (1977).

Restatement (Third) of Unfair Competition, § 43, 46 (1995).

Other sources

Adamson, J. (2013, August 14). Consumers have standing to challenge NFL licensing agreements. *Weil.com*. Retrieved from http://antitrust.weil.com/articles/consumers-have-standing-to-challenge-nfl-licensing-agreements/.

Allen, S. (2016, July 18). Former Cardinals scout sentenced to 46 months in jail for hacking Astros. *The Washington Post*. Retrieved from https://www.washingtonpost.com/news/early-lead/wp/2016/07/18/former-cardinals-scout-sentenced-to-46-months-in-jail-for-hacking-astros/.

Associated Press (2009, January 30). PGA Tour sues Ginn for breach of contract after it drops event. *PGA.com*. Retrieved from www.pga.com/2009/news/industry/01/30/ginn.ap/index.html.

Bailey, G. (2019). Streaming is the name of the game: Why sports leagues should adapt to consumers and follow ad dollars toward live streaming. *Jeffrey S. Moorad Sports Law Journal*, 26, 323–363.

Bailey, J. (2009). Livestreaming and copyright issues. *The Blog Herald*. Retrieved from http://www.blogherald.com/2009/08/24/livestreaming-and-copyright-issues/.

Baker, L. B. (2018, February 20). The brand Olympics: getting attention without getting in trouble. *Reuters*. Retrieved from https://www.reuters.com/article/us-olympics-2018-guerillamarketing/the-brand-olympics-getting-attention-without-getting-in-trouble-idUSKCN1G412L.

Bercovici, J. (2010, December 23). Drew Brees toes FTC's line on Twitter endorsements. *Forbes.com*. Retrieved from http://www.forbes.com/sites/jeffbercovici/2010/12/23/drew-brees-toes-ftcs-line-on-twitter-endorsements/.

Berlik, L. E. (2009, April 14). Trademark litigation between Coke and Pepsi enters another round. *Virginia Business Litigation Lawyer Blog*. Retrieved from http://www.virginiabusinesslitigationlawyer.com/2009/04/trademark-litigation-between-c.html.

Bieler, D. (2016, March 7). Erin Andrews awarded $55 million in peephole lawsuit. *The Washington Post*. Retrieved from https://www.washingtonpost.com/news/early-lead/wp/2016/03/07/erin-andrews-awarded-55-million-in-peephole-case/?utm_term=.827a62eaaac8.

Bianchi, J. (2017, May 27). Stuart-Haas Racing settles lawsuit with Danica Patrick's former sponsor. *SB Nation*. Retrieved from https://www.sbnation.com/nascar/2017/5/27/15704460/stewart-haas-racing-settles-lawsuit-danica-patricks-former-sponsor-natures-bakery.

Boudway, I. (2014, February 3). Does a $5 footlong make you think of the Olympics? *Bloomberg*. Retrieved from https://www.bloomberg.com/news/articles/2014-02-03/subway-olympics-ambush-marketing-master.

Brison, N., Baker, T. A., & Byon, K. K. (2012). False advertising claims: Analysis of potential athlete endorser liability. *Arizona State Sports & Entertainment Law Journal*, 2, 163–176.

Burke, R. R., DeSarbo, W. S., Oliver, R. L., & Robertson, T. S. (1988). Deception by implication: An experimental investigation. *Journal of Consumer Research*, 14, 483–494.

Caba, J. (2014, September 22). Nutritional supplement and sports drink ads at major sporting events are misleading the public. *Medical Daily*. Retrieved from https://www.medicaldaily.com/nutritional-supplement-and-sports-drink-ads-major-sporting-events-are-misleading-public-304374.

Cady, D. (2018, March 14). Social media policies for employees: Lessons from the sports industry. *San Diego County Bar Association*. Retrieved from http://blawg401.com/social-media-policies-employees-lessons-sports-industry/.

Carter, C. (2018). Consumer protection in the states: A 50-state evaluation of unfair and deceptive practices and laws. *National Consumer Law Center*. Retrieved from https://www.nclc.org/images/pdf/udap/udap-report.pdf.

Chabinsky, S., & Pittman, F. P. (2020). USA Data protection laws and regulations 2020. *ICLG.com*. Retrieved from https://iclg.com/practice-areas/data-protection-laws-and-regulations/usa.

Chahardovali, T., Ternes, N. C., & Holden, J. (2019). Non-citizens, the First Amendment, and stadium speech. *Michigan State International Law Review*, 27, 283–304.

Coaston, J. (2020, June 17). College football players are taking a stand against racism – and taking a big risk. *Vox*. Retrieved from https://www.thenewsstar.com/story/sports/college/louisiana-tech/2020/06/14/local-black-college-athletes-talk-black-lives-matter-why-others-should-listen/5318911002/.

Comenos, J. (2018, May 21). How to determine if your brand should go with a celebrity endorser or influencer. *Ad Week*. Retrieved from https://www.adweek.com/brand-marketing/how-to-determine-if-your-brand-should-go-with-a-celebrity-endorser-or-influencer/.

Daly, J. (2010, June 17). Dutch brewery sends in blondes for World Cup ambush marketing stunt. *Huffington Post*. Retrieved from http://www.huffingtonpost.com/2010/06/17/world-cup-ambush-marketin_n_615872.html.

Davis, E. (2020). Protecting your business under new data privacy laws. Retrieved from https://www.elliottdavis.com/wp-content/uploads/2020/01/2218-California-Consumer-Privacy-Act-CCPA-v8.pdf.

Demaine, L. J. (2012). Seeing is deceiving: The tacit deregulation of deceptive advertising. *Arizona Law Review*, 54, 719–764.

Desmarais, F. (2016, December 7). Who is the athlete endorser? A cross-cultural exploration of advertising practitioners" views. *Journal of Global Marketing*, 30, 12–30.

Diaz, C. (2020, June 14). "Bigger than me": LA Tech, ULM Black student-athletes on Black Lives Matter, Why others need to listen. *News Star*. Retrieved from https://www.thenewsstar.com/story/sports/college/louisiana-tech/2020/06/14/local-black-college-athletes-talk-black-lives-matter-why-others-should-listen/5318911002/.

Edwards, M. (2016). Competitive advantage: The actions ESPN must take in order to maintain a leadership position in the wake of cable un-bundling. *Southwestern Law Review*, 46, 197–215.

Ehrlich, M. (2018, February 20). With 747 Warehouse St., adidas delivered an unprecedented basketball culture festival. *Front Office Sports*. Retrieved from https://frntofficesport.com/with-747-warehouse-street-adidas-delivered-an-unprecedented-basketball-culture-festival/.

Ellenport, C. (2019, June 12). Serena Williams, Roger Federer among five tennis players on Forbes' highest paid athletes list. *US Open*. Retrieved from https://www.usopen.org/en_US/news/articles/2019-06-12/fathers_day_gift_guide.html.

Epstein, A. (2014). The Olympics, ambush marketing and Sochi media. *Arizona State Sports & Entertainment Law Review*, 3(2), 110–131.

Evangelista, B. (2017, September 21). Gatorade settles with California over game that discouraged drinking water. *San Francisco Chronicle*. Retrieved from https://www.sfchronicle.com/business/article/Gatorade-settles-with-California-over-game-that-12218440.php.

Fair, L. (2019, June 7). FTC-FDA warning letters: Influential to influencers and marketers. *FTC*. Retrieved from https://www.ftc.gov/news-events/blogs/business-blog/2019/06/ftc-fda-warning-letters-influential-influencers-marketers.

False advertising lawsuit names celebrity endorsers as defendants (2011, April 27). *Winston & Strawn*. Retrieved from http://www.winston.com/en/thought-leadership/false-advertising-lawsuit-names-celebrity-endorsers-as-defendants.html.

Faust, J. (2019, July 18). Pitt suing sports marketing company for $3.6 million. *The Pitt News*. Retrieved from https://pittnews.com/article/149107/featured/pitt-suing-sports-marketing-company-for-3-6-million/.

Fischer, S., & Baker, K. (2019, August 13). The sports streaming landscape, mapped. *Axios*. Retrieved from https://www.axios.com/sports-streaming-networks-chart-tv-rights-6dd0a8bd-07ca-47bb-b3df-e21a7bd177c9.html.

FTC (1979). Statement of policy regarding comparative advertising. Retrieved from http://www.ftc.gov/statement-of-policy-regarding-comparative-advertising.

FTC (1980) FTC policy statement on unfairness. Retrieved from www.ftc.gov/bcp/policystmt/ad-unfair.htm.

FTC (1983, October 14). FTC policy statement on deception. Retrieved from https://www.ftc.gov/system/files/documents/public_statements/410531/831014deceptionstmt.pdf.

FTC (1996a, September 18). New Balance Athletic Shoe, Inc.; Proposed Consent Agreement with analysis to aid public comment. Retrieved from http://www.ftc.gov/policy/federal-register-notices/new-balance-athletic-shoe-inc-proposed-consent-agreement-analysis.

FTC (1996b, January 16). Vertical restraints enforcement at the FTC. Retrieved from http://www.ftc.gov/public-statements/1996/01/vertical-restraints-enforcement-ftc.

FTC (2009, October 5). FTC publishes final guides governing endorsements and testimonials. Retrieved from www.ftc.gov/opa/2009/10/endortest.shtm.

FTC (2011, September 28). Reebok to pay $25 million in customer refunds to settle FTC charges of deceptive advertising of EasyTone and RunTone shoes. Retrieved from http://www.ftc.gov/news-events/press-releases/2011/09/reebok-pay-25-million-customer-refunds-settle-ftc-charges.

FTC (2012, May 16). Skechers will pay $40 million to settle FTC charges that it deceived consumers with ads for "toning shoes." Retrieved from http://www.ftc.gov/news-events/press-releases/2012/05/skechers-will-pay-40-million-settle-ftc-charges-it-deceived.

FTC (2013, January 16). FTC commissioners uphold trial judge decision that POM Wonderful, LLC; Stewart and Lynda Resnick; others deceptively advertised pomegranate products by making unsupported health claims. Retrieved from http://www.ftc.gov/news-events/press-releases/2013/01/ftc-commissioners-uphold-trial-judge-decision-pom-wonderful-llc.

(FTC) (2013b, February). Mobile privacy disclosures: Building trust through transparency. Retrieved from https://www.ftc.gov/sites/default/files/documents/reports/mobile-privacy-disclosures-building-trust-through-transparency-federal-trade-commission-staff-report/130201mobileprivacyreport.pdf.

FTC (2017a, September 13). Online marketers banned from deceiving shoppers. Retrieved from https://www.ftc.gov/news-events/press-releases/2017/09/online-marketers-banned-deceiving-shoppers.

FTC (2017b, September). The FTC's endorsement guides: what people are asking. Retrieved from https://www.ftc.gov/tips-advice/business-center/guidance/ftcs-endorsement-guides-what-people-are-asking#SocialNetworkingSites.

FTC (2017c, April 19). FTC staff reminds influencers and brands to clearly disclose relationship. Retrieved from https://www.ftc.gov/news-events/press-releases/2017/04/ftc-staff-reminds-influencers-brands-clearly-disclose.

FTC (2018). Privacy & data security update: 2018. Retrieved from https://www.ftc.gov/system/files/documents/reports/privacy-data-security-update-2018/2018-privacy-data-security-report-508.pdf.

FTC (2019). Advertising FAQ's: A guide for small business. Retrieved from https://www.ftc.gov/tips-advice/business-center/guidance/advertising-faqs-guide-small-business.

Gaeth, G. J., & Heath, T. B. (1987). The cognitive processing of misleading advertising in young and old adults: Assessment and training. *Journal of Consumer Research*, 14, 43–54.

Gaines, C. (2016, August 7). Michael Phelps was forced to cover the logo of his Beats headphones and he did a lackluster job with the tape. *Business Insider*. Retrieved from https://www.businessinsider.com/michael-phelps-beats-olympics-headphones-2016-8.

Gallagher, K. (2018, November 28). Media rights will continue to propel sports revenue. *Business Insider*. Retrieved from https://www.businessinsider.com/media-rights-propel-sports-revenue-2018-11.

Grady, J., & McKelvey, S. (2012, October 22). Ambush marketing lessons from the Olympic Games. *Sports Business Journal*. Retrieved from http://www.sportsbusinessdaily.com/Journal/Issues/2012/10/22/Opinion/Grady-McKelvey.aspx.

Grimaldi, J. V. (2009, September 3). Washington Redskins react to fans' tough luck with tough love. *Washington Post*, https://www.washingtonpost.com/wp-dyn/content/article/2009/09/02/AR2009090203887.html.

Hallman, R. (2014). Carmax cuts off Clippers over racist remarks: Goochland-based car giant pulls support after remarks attributed to team's owner. *Richmond Times Dispatch*. Retrieved from https://www.richmond.com/business/carmax-cuts-off-clippers-over-racist-remarks/article_61b4c29f-5fcd-5145-95df-43a14abf4b31.html.

Hamilton, W. H. (1931). The ancient maxim caveat emptor. *Yale Law Journal*, 40(8).

Hawkins, S. (2011, May 10). Sweepstakes, contests and giveaway laws bloggers and brands need to know. *Sara F. Hawkins Attorney at Law*. Retrieved from https://sarafhawkins.com/blog-law-is-your-giveaway-legal/.

Hill, K. (2016). Ambush marketing: Is it deceitful or a probable strategic tactic in the Olympic Games? *Marquette Sports Law Review, 27*, 197–216.

Hines, A. (2012). New Balance pays fat settlement in toning shoe lawsuit to people it did not slim. *Huff Post*. Retrieved from https://www.huffpost.com/entry/new-balance-toning-shoe-settlement_n_1839537.

Hutter, K., & Schwarz, U. (2012). Image effect of ambush marketing: The case of FIFA Soccer World Cup 2010. Paper presented at the annual conference of the Australian & New Zealand Marketing Academy. Retrieved from http://anzmac.org/conference/2012/papers/080ANZMACFINAL.pdf.

Jensen, J. (1996). Flaunting the rings cheaply: Non-sponsors of Olympic games instead back teams. *Advertising Age, 67*(28), 4.

Jessop, A. (2018). 21st century stock market: A regulatory model for daily fantasy sports. *Journal of Legal Aspects of Sport, 28*, 39–62.

Jessop, A., & Baker, T. A. (2019). Big data bust: Evaluating the risks of tracking NCAA athletes' biometric data. *Texas Review of Entertainment and Sports Law, 20*, 81–112.

Kaplan, D. (2007, September 10). USTA blocks marketers looking to ambush Open. *Street & Smith's Sports Business Journal*. Retrieved from www.sportsbusinessjournal.com/article/56282.

Katz, J. (2009, January 27). Economy's toll on sports sponsorships evident in Cubs-Under Armour dispute. *FindingDulcinea* Retrieved from www.findingdulcinea.com/news/sports/2009/jan/Economy-s-Toll-on-Sports-Sponsorships-Evident-in-Cubs-Under-Armour-Dispute-.html.

Keller, R. (2018, February 20). Sports marketing company, CPS in legal battle. *Columbia Daily Tribune*. Retrieved from https://www.columbiatribune.com/news/20180220/sports-marketing-company-cps-in-legal-battle.

Kirsch, N. (2018, July 11). Papa John's founder used N-word on conference call. *Forbes*. Retrieved from https://www.forbes.com/sites/noahkirsch/2018/07/11/papa-johns-founder-john-schnatter-allegedly-used-n-word-on-conference-call/#18a53e7b4cfc.

Klara, R. (2016, August 10). How Nike brilliantly ruined Olympic marketing forever. *AdWeek*. Retrieved from https://www.adweek.com/brand-marketing/how-nike-brilliantly-ruined-olympic-marketing-forever-172899/.

Krugman, P. (2019). What is the invisible hand in economics? *MasterClass*. Retrieved from https://www.masterclass.com/articles/what-is-the-invisible-hand-in-economics#what-is-the-invisible-hand.

Larkin, B., & McKelvey, S. (2015). Of smart phones and Facebook: Social media's changing legal landscape provides cautionary tales of "Pinterest" for sport organizations. *Journal of Legal Aspects of Sport, 25*, 123–153.

Larson, E. (2009, March 18). Giants, Jets sued by fan over arena seat 'licenses.' *Bloomberg.com*. Retrieved from www.bloomberg.com/apps/news?pid=20601079&refer=amsports&sid=aRg_rO52oBWg.

Lefton, T. (2003). Ambush tactics evil, effective. *Sports Business Journal*, 9–10.

Liberman, N. (2003, April 28). Marathon ambush a real head-scratcher. *Street & Smith's SportsBusiness Journal*. Retrieved from https://www.sportsbusinessdaily.com/Journal/Issues/2003/04/28/This-Weeks-Issue.aspx.

Lord, K. R., Kim, C. K., & Putrevu, S. (1997). Communication strategies to counter deceptive advertising. *Review of Business, 18*(3), 24–29.

Marr, B. (2017). The big risk of big data in sport. *Forbes*. Retrieved from https://www.forbes.com/sites/bernardmarr/2017/04/28/the-big-risks-of-big-data-in-sports/#6a7c92b17c6f.

McAuley, A. C., & Sutton, W. A. (1999). In search of a new defender: The threat of ambush marketing in the global sport arena. *International Journal of Sports Marketing and Sponsorship, 1*, 64–86.

McCallister, E., Grance, T., & Scarfone, K. (2010). Guide to protecting the confidentiality of personally identifiable information (PII). *National Institute of Standards and Technology*. Retrieved from https://www.dla.mil/Portals/104/Documents/GeneralCounsel/FOIA/Privacy/NIST%20SP%20800-122%20Guide%20to%20Protecting%20Confidentiality%20of%20PII.pdf.

McCann, M. (2015, October 8). What impact will the lawsuit filed against DraftKings, FanDuel have? *Sports Illustrated*. Retrieved from https://www.si.com/nfl/2015/10/08/daily-fantasy-sports-lawsuit-draftkings-fanduel.

McKelvey, S. (1992). NHL v. Pepsi-Cola Canada, uh-huh! Legal parameters of sports ambush marketing. *Entertainment and Sports Lawyer, 10*, 5–18.

McKelvey, S. (1994). Atlanta '96: Olympic countdown to ambush Armageddon? *Seton Hall Journal of Sport Law, 4*, 397–445.

McKelvey, S. (2003). Unauthorized use of event tickets in promotional campaign may create new legal strategies to combat ambush marketing: *NCAA v. Coors. Sport Marketing Quarterly, 12*(2), 117–118.

McKelvey, S., & Grady, J. (2004, Summer). An analysis of the ongoing global efforts to combat ambush marketing: Will corporate marketers "take" the Gold in Greece? *Journal of Legal Aspects of Sport, 14*(2), 191–220.

Meyer, Z. (2017, November 1). Papa John's CEO blames NFL for declining sales due to mishandling of anthem protests. *USA Today*. Retrieved from https://www.usatoday.com/story/money/food/2017/11/01/papa-johns-ceo-blames-nfl-declining-sales-due-mishandling-anthem-protests/821368001/.

Miller, J. (2019, June 23). Browns suing Hard Beverages for not paying $525,000 sponsorship fee. *Crain's Cleveland Business*. Retrieved from https://www.crainscleveland.com/sports-business/browns-suing-hard-beverages-not-paying-525000-sponsorship-fee.

Moorman, A. M., & Greenwell, T. C. (2005). Consumer attitudes of deception and the legality of ambush marketing practices. *Journal of Legal Aspects of Sport*, 15(2), 183–211.

Nakamura, B. M. (2018). Is Olympic ambush marketing here to stay? Examining the issues surrounding ambush marketing as they relate to Olympic sponsors, athletes and other stakeholders. *Arizona Journal of International and Comparative Law*, 35, 499–531.

Patel, S. (2020). Live sports and entertainment are shut. Sponsorships are taking a hit. *The Wall Street Journal*. Retrieved from https://www.wsj.com/articles/live-sports-and-entertainment-are-shut-sponsorships-are-taking-a-hit-11587071253.

Pahwa, A. (2019, August 24). What is ambush marketing? How is it used in brand wars? *Fee Dough*. Retrieved from https://www.feedough.com/ambush-marketing/.

Park, K. (2019, April) Ambush marketing: When sponsors cry "foul." *WIPO Magazine*. Retrieved from https://www.wipo.int/wipo_magazine/en/2019/02/article_0004.html.

Pearsall, D. (2013, December 22). Letter to our 2014 season ticket holders and loyal fans. *OrlandoPredators.com*. Retrieved from http://orlandopredators.com/wordpress/wp-content/uploads/2013/12/A-Letter-to-Our-Season-Ticket-Holders-and-Loyal-Fans.pdf.

Peetz, T. B., & Lough, N. (2016). Celebrity athlete endorsers: A critical review. In S. Chadwick, N. Chanavat, & M. Desbordes (Eds.), *Routledge Handbook of Sport Marketing* (pp. 125–140). London and New York, NY: Routledge.

Piety, T. R. (2005). Grounding Nike: Exposing Nike's quest for a constitutional right to lie. *Temple Law Review*, 78, 151–200.

Prosser, W. (1960). Privacy. *California Law Review*, 48, 383–423.

Reiley, L. (2019, March 21). Miller Lite's maker is suing Anheuser-Busch over the Bud Light corn syrup Super Bowl commercials. *The Washington Post*. Retrieved from https://www.washingtonpost.com/business/2019/03/21/miller-coors-takes-gloves-off-over-corngate-files-suit-against-anheuser-busch-its-super-bowl-ad.

Reitmeyer, J. (2019, September 5). NJ fines online fantasy-sports site for breaking privacy and licensing rules. *NJ Spotlight*. Retrieved from https://www.njspotlight.com/2019/09/19-09-04-nj-fines-online-fantasy-sports-site-for-breaking-privacy-and-licensing-rules/.

Rodrigues, A. L., & Pahl, D. R. (2019, March 25). In-venue streaming and broadcasting of live sporting events – key legal issues for sports clubs and leagues. *DLA Piper Media, Sport and Entertainment Alert*. Retrieved from https://www.dlapiper.com/en/us/insights/publications/2019/03/in-venue-streaming-and-broadcasting-of-live-sporting-events/.

Saltzman, J., & Finucane, M. (2008, May 16). Patriots ticket buyer bound to contract. *Boston.com*. Retrieved from www.boston.com/news/local/articles/2008/05/16/court_patriots_ticket_buyer_bound_to_contract.

Sanders, E., & Sharma, A. (2019, March 12). Who's on first? The fight over official sports data after Murphy. *JD Supra*. Retrieved from https://www.jdsupra.com/legalnews/who-s-on-first-the-fight-over-official-81726/.

Sarkar, S. (2012, July 23). EA Sports agrees to $27 million settlement in football game monopoly lawsuit. *Polygon*. Retrieved from http://www.polygon.com/gaming/2012/7/23/3177295/ea-sports-monopoly-lawsuit-settlement.

Sauer, A. (2002, May 27). Ambush marketing steals the show. *Brandchannel.com*. Retrieved from http://www.brandchannel.com/features_effect.asp?pf_id=98.

Sayers, J. (2018, June 15). Skechers dismisses federal lawsuit against Adidas after just 20 days. *Courier Journal*. Retrieved from https://www.courier-journal.com/story/sports/college/louisville/2018/06/14/skechers-dismisses-lawsuit-against-adidas-fbi-scandal-investigation/699722002/.

Scassa, T. (2011). Ambush marketing and the right of association: Clamping down on references to the big event with all the athletes in a couple of years. *Journal of Sport Management*, 25, 354–370.

Schad, T. (2018, February 27). Papa John's, NFL make "mutual decision" to end sponsorship deal. *USA Today*. Retrieved from https://www.usatoday.com/story/sports/nfl/2018/02/27/papa-johns-nfl-end-sponsorship-protests-anthem/379169002/.

Schlabach, M. (2020, August 26). UCLA sues Under Armour for terminating $280 million sponsorship deal with school. *ESPN.com*. Retrieved from https://www.espn.com/college-sports/story/_/id/29749328/ucla-sues-armour-terminating-280-million-sponsorship-deal-school

Schultz, E. J. (2019, February 5). Miller Lite responds to Bud Light's corn syrup attack with full-page New York Times ad. *Ad Age*. Retrieved from https://adage.com/article/cmo-strategy/millerlite-responds-bud-light-s-corn-syrup-attack/316529.

Séguin, B., & O'Reilly, N. O. (2008). The Olympic brand, ambush marketing: Who gets the gold? *Journal of Sport Management and Marketing*, 4(1), 62–84.

Seh, J. (2013, July 18). Brett Bouchy, Orlando Predators managing partner steps down. *Click Orlando.com*. Retrieved from http://www.clickorlando.com/news/brett-bouchy-orlando-predators-managing-partner-steps-down/-/1637132/21041858/-/ipmvv3z/-/index.html.

Seligman, T. J. (2018, November 26). United States: Sports drink ads sent to FTC. *Mondaq*. Retrieved from http://www.mondaq.com/unitedstates/x/757910/advertising+marketing+branding/Sports+Drink+Ads+Sent+To+FTC.

Sheldon, J., & Carter, C. L. (2004). *Unfair and deceptive acts and practices* (6th ed.). Boston: National Consumer Law Center, Inc.

Sheridan, P. D. (2010). An Olympic solution to ambush marketing: How the London Olympics show the way to more effective trademark law. *Sports Law Journal*, 17, 27–47.

Slefo, G. P. (2016, October 26). FanDuel, DraftKings to pay $6 million each amid false advertising claims. *Ad Age*. Retrieved from https://adage.com/article/digital/fanduel-draftkings-agree-pay-6-million-amid-false-advertising-claims/306477.

Smith, D. (2017, July 13). #Sport: The digital battle between sponsors, rights holders and ambush marketers. *Law in Sport*. Retrieved from https://www.lawinsport.com/content/articles/item/sport-the-digital-battle-between-sponsors-rights-holders-and-ambush-marketers.

Spangler, T. (n.d.) Big media, Silicon Valley battle for multibillion-dollar sports TV rights. *Variety*. Retrieved from https://variety.com/2018/digital/features/olympics-rights-streaming-nbc-winter-games-1202680323/.

Sports Business Daily. (2007, October 31). AFL Rattlers will refund season-ticket costs if no playoffs in '08. *SBJSBD*. Retrieved   http://www.sportsbusinessdaily.com/Daily/Issues/2007/10/Issue-36/Franchises/AFL-Rattlers-Will-Refund-Season-Ticket-Costs-If-No-Playoffs-In-08.aspx?

Taylor, J. (2019, July 10). Ticketmaster data theft part of larger credit card scheme, security firm says. *NBC News*. Retrieved from https://www.nbcnews.com/business/business-news/ticketmaster-data-theft-part-larger-credit-card-scheme-security-firm-n890206.

Thomas, K. (2008, November 16). As GM begs for a bailout, sports sponsorship takes a hit. *The New York Times*. Retrieved from www.nytimes.com/2008/11/16/busi-ness/worldbusiness/16iht-16sponsor.17856078.html.

Tushnet, R. (2011). Running the gamut from A to B: Federal trademark and false advertising law. *University of Pennsylvania Law Review*, 159, 1305–1384.

United States Olympic and Paralympic Committee (2019). Athlete commercial guidelines. *TeamUSA.org*. Retrieved from https://www.teamusa.org/Team-USA-Athlete-Services/Athlete-Marketing/Athlete-Commercial-Guidelines.

U. S. Courts (2019). What does free speech mean? *United States Courts*. Retrieved from https://www.uscourts.gov/about-federal-courts/educational-resources/about-educational-outreach/activity-resources/what-does.

Villafranco, J. E. (2010). The law of comparative advertising in the United States. *IP Litigator*. Retrieved from http://www.kelleydrye.com/publications/articles/1335/_res/id=Files/index=0/Villafranco_Law%20of%20Comparative%20Advertising%20in%20the%20US_010210.pdf.

Waller, S. W., Brady, J. G., Acosta, R. J., Fair, J., & Morse, J. (2011). Consumer protection in the United States: An overview. *European Journal of Consumer Law*, 1–34.

Ward, A. (2013, June 22). Preds' managing partners confident in performance guarantee. *Orlando Sentinel*. Retrieved from http://articles.orlandosentinel.com/2013-06-22/sports/os-orlando-predators-money-back-guarantee-20130621_1_pittsburgh-power-preds-game-orlando-predators.

Weinberger, H. P., Wagner, J. M., & Simon, N. C. (2003, May 12). Defining commercial advertising or promotion. *New York Law Journal*. Retrieved from https://www.kramerlevin.com/images/content/1/5/v4/1558/Wagner.Lanham-Act.pdf.

Westbrook, L. (2010, December 24). Judge allows EA price fixing suit to proceed. *Escapist Magazine*. Retrieved from http://www.escapistmagazine.com/news/view/106421-Judge-Allows-EA-Price-Fixing-Suit-to-Proceed.

Whitten, S. (2018, July 13). University of Louisville removes Papa John's name from football stadium. CNBC. Retrieved from https://www.cnbc.com/2018/07/13/university-of-louisville-removes-papa-johns-name-from-stadium.html.

Wilking, C. (2012, May 8). Letter to FTC from the Public Health Advocacy Institute. *Public Health Advisory Institute Online*. Retrieved from http://www.phaionline.org/wp-content/uploads/2012/05/PHAIJordanAdLtr.pdf.

Willens, M. (2016, June 29). Ambush marketing is unstoppable in Rio. *Yahoo*. Retrieved from https://www.yahoo.com/news/ambush-marketing-unstoppable-rio-080313510.html.

Young, S. (2015, March 12). Plaintiffs in Dallas Super Bowl lawsuit set to split $75k. *Dallas Observer*. Retrieved from https://www.dallasobserver.com/news/after-a-four-year-fight-plaintiffs-in-dallas-super-bowl-lawsuit-set-to-split-76k-7146555.

Zhang, J. G. (2019, May 28). Bud Light must pull ads saying that Miller Lite and Coors Light use corn syrup, judge rules. *Eater*. Retrieved from https://www.eater.com/2019/5/28/18642560/bud-light-miller-lite-coors-light-anheuser-busch-lawsuit-corn-syrup.

Web Resources

www.law.cornell.edu/uniform/ucc.html ■ This site provides the text of all provisions of the Uniform Commercial Code as enacted in the various states.

www.business.ftc.gov/documents/bus35-advertising-faqs-guide-small-business ■ This site provides easy to understand answers for frequently asked questions related to the Federal Trade Commission's regulations of advertising practices.

www.eff.org/about ■ The Electronic Frontier Foundation is a nonprofit advocacy organization that tracks litigation on numerous issues involving digital rights, publicity rights, media rights, and consumer rights.

www.ftc.gov/ftc-policy-statement-on-deception ■ The Federal Trade Commission offers guides for advertising, including a deception policy statement that defines false advertising. Organizations that create promotional materials should be aware of laws against deceptive marketing practices.

www.ftc.gov/tips-advice/business-center/guidance/advertising-faqs-guide-small-business ■ The Federal Trade Commission provides insights into federal truth-in-advertising standards for businesses of any size.

www.legislature.idaho.gov/idstat/Title48/T48CH6.htm ■ Consumer protection laws are easily found on state government websites, like this one for Idaho. Usually they fall under the office of the attorney general.

www.uniformlaws.org ■ The National Conference of Commissioners on Uniform State Laws "provides states with non-partisan, well-conceived and well-drafted legislation that brings clarity and stability to critical areas of state statutory law." Its website offers a searchable listing of its acts, either by title or by state. The organization is responsible for sport-related laws such as the Uniform Athlete Agent Act and the Uniform Commercial Code.

Case Index

Subject Index